S0-BOC-385

T H E

HANDBOOK OF

MORTGAGE-BACKED SECURITIES

3rd
EDITION

FRANK J. FABOZZI

EDITOR

PROBUS PUBLISHING COMPANY
Chicago, Illinois
Cambridge, England

© 1992, Frank J. Fabozzi

ALL RIGHTS RESERVED. No part of this publication may be reproduced, stored in a retrieval system, or transmitted, in any form or by any means, electronic, mechanical, photocopying, recording, or otherwise, without the prior written permission of the publisher and the copyright holder.

This publication is designed to provide accurate and authoritative information in regard to the subject matter covered. It is sold with the understanding that the publisher is not engaged in rendering legal, accounting, or other professional service.

Authorization to photocopy items for internal or personal use, or the internal or personal use of specific clients, is granted by PROBUS PUBLISHING COMPANY, provided that the U.S. $7.00 per page fee is paid directly to Copyright Clearance Center, 27 Congress Street, Salem, MA 01970, USA. For those organizations that have been granted a photocopy license by CCC, a separate system of payment has been arranged. The fee code for users of the Transactional Reporting Service is 1-55738-257-3/92/$00.00 + $7.00.

ISBN 1-55738-257-3

Printed in the United States of America

BB

4 5 6 7 8 9 0

CONTENTS

PREFACE

The Handbook of Mortgage-Backed Securities, Third Edition, is designed to provide not only the fundamentals of these securities and the investment characteristics that make them attractive to a broad range of investors, but also extensive coverage on the state-of-the-art strategies for capitalizing on the opportunities in this market. The book is intended for both the individual investor and the professional money manager.

To be effective, a book of this nature should offer a broad perspective. The experience of a wide range of experts is more informative than that of a single expert, particularly because of the diversity of opinion on some issues. I have chosen some of the best known practitioners to contribute to this book. Most have been actively involved in the evolution of the mortgage-backed securities market.

DIFFERENCES BETWEEN THE SECOND AND THIRD EDITIONS

Money managers must justify their management and transaction costs to clients. Consequently, all money managers eventually must demonstrate to their clients how much *value* they've added to portfolio performance above and beyond what could have been achieved by employing a lower-cost buy-and-hold strategy. As the editor of *The Handbook of Mortgage-Backed Securities*, I am effectively the portfolio manager of the assets of this book"the chapters. The third edition must justify to my current clients (those who purchased the second edition of the *Handbook*) why they should *not* follow a buy-and-hold strategy of simply continuing to use the second edition and reduce advisory fees and transaction costs (i.e., the cost of this book). In short: What value has been added to the second edition?

Pages xii through xiv summarize the differences between the second and third editions. The number of chapters has been reduced from forty-nine to forty-one, plus an appendix. However, thiry-two of the chapters are new, and the others have been substantially revised. Consequently, this book can be characterized as a new book, reflecting the dynamic changes that have occurred in this market in terms of new product development and advances in technologies since the publication of the second edition in 1988. In the case of collateralized mortgage obligations, the second edition has four chapters devoted to this topic, while the third edition has twelve. There is much more detailed coverage of private-label pass-through securities, the option-adjusted spread technology, and prepayment modeling. The third edition also includes chapters on over-the-counter options on MBSs (two chapters) and new mortgage designs, topics not covered in the previous edition.

ACKNOWLEDGEMENTS

I would like to express my appreciation to the contributors and their organizations. The following individuals assisted in various ways: Scott Amero (Blackstone Financial Management), Charles Basner (TIPS), Paul Brown (MMAR Group), Carol Calhoun (Deloitte & Touche), David Canuel (Aetna Life and Casualty), John H. Carlson (Daiwa Securities), Peter Carrill (Daiwa Securities), Andrew S. Carron (First Boston), Glen Carter (U.S. Central Credit Union), Peter E. Christensen (PaineWebber), Gary Cole (Ernst & Young), Dessa Fabozzi (Merrill Lynch Capital Markets), Henry Gabbay (Blackstone Financial Management), Hal Hinkle (Goldman Sachs), Frank J. Jones (The Guardian), Dragomir Krgin (EJV Partners), Robert Kulason (Salomon Brothers), Martin Leibowitz (Salomon Brothers), Stewart Lucas (Bear, Stearns International Ltd.), Matt Mancuso (Bear, Stearns), Jan Mayle (TIPS), Franco Modigliani (MIT), Ed Murphy (Merchants Mutual Insurance Company), Scott Pinkus (Goldman Sachs), Mark Pitts (Lehman Brothers), Sharmin Mossavar-Rahmani (Fidelity Management Trust Company), Frank Ramirez (MMAR Group), Charles Richard III (Quantitative Risk Management), Ron Ryan (Ryan Financial Strategy Group), and David Yuen (Franklin Management Inc.).

Administrative assistance was provided by Ed Garlicki and Christine Palaia.

Frank J. Fabozzi

SUMMARY OF DIFFERENCES BETWEEN SECOND AND THIRD EDITIONS

The second edition has forty-nine chapters, divided into the following nine sections:

I.   Mortgages

II.   Pass-Through Securities

III.   Collateralized Mortgage Obligations

IV.   Stripped Mortgage-Backed Securities

V.   Prepayment Forecasting and Valuation Techniques

VI.   Hedging

VII.   Arbitrage, Swap and Portfolio Management Strategies

VIII.   Computer Technology, Taxation and Accounting

IX.   International Developments and Securitization of Other Assets

The third edition has forty-one chapters and an appendix, divided into the following seven sections:

I.   Mortgage Products

II.   Pass-Through Securities

III.   Prepayment Forecasting

IV.   Collateralized Mortgage Obligations and Stripped MBS

V.   Valuation Techniques

VI.   Portfolio Strategies

VII.   Accounting, Tax and Operational Considerations

The following thiry-two of the forty-one chapters in the third edition and the appendix are new:

CONTRIBUTING AUTHORS

William A. Barr
Associate Director
Mortgage Department
Bear, Stearns & Co., Inc.

Anand K. Bhattacharya, PhD
Vice President
Financial Strategies Group
Prudential Securities Inc.

Bella Borg
Associate Director
Financial Analytics & Structured
  Transactions Group
Bear, Stearns & Co., Inc.

Douglas T. Breeden, PhD
Research Professor of Finance
Fuqua School of Business
Duke University

Steven J. Carlson
Senior Vice President
Head of Whole Loan CMO Trading
Lehman Brothers Inc.

Howard W. Chin
Director
Financial Strategies Group
Prudential Securities Inc.

William J. Curtin
Senior Vice President
Lehman Brothers Inc.

Ed Daingerfield
Mortgage Trading
Smith Barney, Harris Upham & Co., Inc.

Andrew S. Davidson
Managing Director
Mortgage-Backed Securities Research
Merrill Lynch Capital Markets

Lynn M. Edens
Vice President
Mortgage Securities Research Department
Goldman, Sachs & Co.

Frank J. Fabozzi, PhD, CFA
Visiting Professor of Finance
Sloan School of Management
Massachusetts Institute of Technology

Sean C. Gallop
Vice President
J.P. Morgan Securities Inc.

Robert Gerber
Vice President
Fixed Income Research
The First Boston Corporation

Michael Giarla
Principal
Smith Breeden Associates, Inc.

Lakhbir S. Hayre, D.Phil
Director of Mortgage Research
Financial Strategies Group
Prudential Securities Inc.

J. Michael Henderson, CFA
Managing Director
Bear, Stearns & Co., Inc.

Michael D. Herskovitz
Director
Mortgage-Backed Securities Research
Merrill Lynch Capital Markets

David P. Jacob
Managing Director
J.P. Morgan Securities Inc.

Adrian Katz
Director
Prudential Securities Inc.

Brian Lancaster
Vice President
Financial Analytics & Structured
  Transactions Group
Bear, Stearns & Co., Inc.

Kenneth Lauterbach
Vice President
Financial Strategies Group
Prudential Securities Inc.

Andrew Lawrence
Vice President
Greenwich Capital Markets, Inc.

Nicholas C. Letica
Vice President
Bankers Trust Securities Corp.

Michael Levine
Vice President
Mortgage Trading
Bear, Stearns & Co., Inc.

Linda Lowell
Vice President, Head
Mortgage Investment Strategies
Smith Barney, Harris Upham & Co., Inc.

Bruce Mahood
Senior Portfolio Strategist
Merrill Lynch Capital Markets

Mary A. Maier, PhD
Research Associate
Gifford Fong Associates

David Martin
Associate
Financial Analytics & Structured
  Transactions Group
Bear, Stearns & Co., Inc.

Clark McGranery
Vice President
J.P. Morgan Securities Inc.

Cyrus Mohebbi, PhD
Vice President
Financial Strategies Group
Prudential Securities Inc.

Peter Muller
Manager
Model Research Group
BARRA

Errol Mustafa, PhD
Vice President
Financial Strategies Group
Prudential Securities Inc.

Michael Naughton
Managing Director
Financial Analytics & Structured
  Transactions Group
Bear, Stearns & Co., Inc.

David Z. Nirenberg
Associate
Cleary, Gottlieb, Steen & Hamilton

James T. Parks, CPA
Vice President for Financial Standards and
Corporate Taxes
Federal National Mortgage Association

Gregory J. Parseghian
Managing Director
The First Boston Corporation

James M. Peaslee
Partner
Cleary, Gottlieb, Steen & Hamilton

Vincent Pica
Managing Director
Prudential Securities Inc.

Chuck Ramsey
Partner
MMAR Group

Scott F. Richard, PhD
Vice President
Mortgage Securities Research Department
Goldman, Sachs & Co.

R. Blaine Roberts, PhD
Senior Managing Director
Financial Analytics & Structured
  Transactions Group
Bear, Stearns & Co., Inc.

Charles N. Schorin, PhD
Vice President
Kidder, Peabody & Co., Inc.

Dexter Senft
Director of Research
EJV Partners

Dan Spina
Associate Director
Financial Analytics & Structured
  Transactions Group
Bear, Stearns & Co., Inc.

David Sykes, PhD
Managing Director
Financial Analytics & Structured
  Transactions Group
Bear, Stearns & Co., Inc.

Jane Tang
Analyst
Financial Analytics & Structured
  Transactions Group
Bear, Stearns & Co., Inc.

John F. Tierney
Senior Vice President
Mortgage Strategies Group
Lehman Brothers Inc.

Lynn Tong
Vice President
J.P. Morgan Securities Inc.

Hendrik Van Schieveen
Associate Director
Financial Analytics & Structured
  Transactions Group
Bear, Stearns & Co., Inc.

Paul T. Van Valkenburg
Principal
Mortgage Industry Advisory Corp.

Rick Villaume
Vice President
Prudential Securities Inc.

Bruce E. Vollert
Vice President
Sungard Financial Systems

Michael L. Winchell
Senior Managing Director
Risk Management Group
Bear, Stearns & Co., Inc.

Sarah Wolf
Associate Director
Financial Analytics & Structured
  Transactions Group
Bear, Stearns & Co., Inc.

CHAPTER 1

OVERVIEW

Frank J. Fabozzi, PhD, CFA
Visiting Professor of Finance
Sloan School of Management
Massachusetts Institute of Technology
and
Editor, *Journal of Portfolio Management*

Innovation and growth have characterized the mortgage market in the past two decades. In the 1970s and early 1980s, the focus of innovations was in the design of new mortgage loans such as adjustable-rate mortgages, and the pooling of mortgage loans to create mortgage pass-through securities. New mortgage designs attempted to overcome the unappealing features of the traditional fixed-rate, level payment mortgage from the perspective of both borrowers and lenders/investors, thereby broadening the institutional base of potential investors.

The pooling of the traditional fixed-rate, level payment mortgages to create pass-through securities in February 1970 with the issuance of Ginnie Mae Pool #1 made investing in the mortgage market more palatable to an even greater institutional investor base, which had found the investment characteristics of owning individual mortgage loans unappealing. As issuers of pass-through securities became more comfortable with the securitization process, other types of mortgage designs were securitized.

Until 1977, all pass-through securities carried the full faith and credit of the U.S. government or a government-related organization. In 1977, the private-label or conventional pass-through security, was first publicly introduced by Bank of America. Since then, techniques for enhancing the credit quality of private-label pass-through securities have increased the appeal of these securities to investors willing to accept greater credit risk.

Aside from credit risk, the key characteristic that distinguishes Treasury securities, corporates, municipals, and mortgage pass-through securities from each other is the degree of uncertainty associated with the cash flow pattern. In the case of Treasuries, with the exception of some outstanding callable Treasury bonds, the amount and timing of the cash flow are known with certainty. Since most long-term corporates and municipals are callable by the issuer prior to maturity, the cash flow pattern of these securities is not known with certainty. Typically, however, the issue may not be called or refunded until a specified number of years after issuance. Generally, the bondholder can expect that the issuer will not "irrationally" exercise the call option; that is, the bondholder can expect that the issuer will not call the issue when the coupon rate is less than the current market interest rate.

Mortgage loans also have uncertainty with regard to the cash flow pattern, mainly because the investor has effectively granted the borrower/homeowner the option to prepay (call) part or all of the mortgage at any time. Any payment that is made in excess of the regularly scheduled principal payment is called a *prepayment*. Although the prevailing borrowing rate may be an important determinant affecting the homeowner's decision whether or not to exercise the option to prepay, other unique factors may dominate, resulting in unscheduled principal repayments when the prevailing mortgage rate is greater than the loan rate. These individual circumstances facing the borrower may affect the cash flow timing, making its uncertainty greater than that for callable corporates and municipals, which depend solely on the prevailing borrowing rate relative to the loan rate. Investors in mortgage-backed securities face this uncertainty about prepayments, referred to as *prepayment risk*, and wish to be compensated for accepting unscheduled payments.

An investor in a pass-through security is exposed to the total prepayment risk associated with the underlying pool of mortgage loans. The total prepayment risk can be divided into two components: *call* (or *contraction*) *risk* and *extension risk*. The former is the risk that prepayments will occur when interest rates have declined, forcing the investor to reinvest the cash flow at an interest rate lower than the coupon rate on the security. Extension risk results from the slow-down of prepayments when interest rates have increased, forcing the investor to realize less cash flow that can be reinvested at an interest rate greater than the coupon rate on the security.

In 1983, a new security structure was introduced by Freddie Mac called the *collateralized mortgage obligation* (CMO). In this structure, backed by mortgage pass-through securities and whole loans, the total prepayment risk was divided among classes of bonds (or tranches). Instead of distributing the monthly cash flow on a pro rata basis, as in the case of a pass-through security, the distribution of the principal (both scheduled and prepayments) was done on a prioritized basis, so as to redistribute prepayment risk among the various bond classes in the CMO structure.

In the first generation of CMOs, the priority was such that only one class of bonds would receive principal until it was completely paid off. Then, another class of bonds would begin receiving principal until it too was completely paid off. Such structures are known as *sequential pay* or *plain vanilla* CMOs. Then, to further reduce prepayment risk for some classes of bonds, tranches with a specified principal repayment schedule were introduced; the repayment schedule of such bonds is guaranteed if the actual speed of prepayments is within a designated range. These classes of bonds are known as *planned amortization class* bonds (PACs), and provide protection against both call and extension risks. They were particularly attractive to institutional investors who sought to reduce their exposure to the corporate bond sector as a result of an increase in event risk. PACs provided a structure similar to sinking fund corporate bonds.

Whereas some institutional investors want protection against both call and extension risks, some desire only protection from one of these risks. For example, there are instititutional investors who wish to be protected against call risk but are willing to accept extension risk. For them, a bond class known as a *targeted amortization class* (TAC) was created. The *reverse TAC* was created for institutional investors who are willing to accept call risk, but desire protection against extension risk.

The various types of CMO structures will be discussed throughout this book. The key to the success of the CMO innovation is that the principal distribution can be structured so as to satisfy the asset/liability needs of institutional investors. But, it must be clearly understood that the creation of a CMO does not eliminate the total prepayment risk associated with the underlying collateral; it can only redistribute it. Thus, the companion or support classes in a CMO structure must absorb the prepayment risk.

In July 1986, another type of derivative mortgage-backed security was introduced by Fannie Mae, the *stripped mortgage-backed security*. The principal and interest were divided unequally between two classes of bonds, not on a pro rata basis as with pass-through securities, and not on a prioritized basis as with CMOs. As a result of this unequal distribution, the two bond classes had different synthetic coupon rates and performed differently from the underlying collateral when interest rates changed. In the second generation of stripped mortgage-backed securities, all of the interest was distributed to one bond class (called the *interest-only* or *IO* class), and all of the principal was distributed to the other class (called the *principal-only* or *PO* class). The investment features of stripped mortgage-backed securities allowed institutional investors to create synthetic securities with risk/return characteristics previously unavailable in the market, and, more important, provided institutional investors with instruments that could be used more effectively to hedge a portfolio of pass-through securities or servicing rights than exchange-traded interest rate risk-control contracts could.

The growth of the market has brought with it techniques for valuing mortgage-backed securities and strategies for capitalizing on mispricing. The three basic approaches are the static cash flow yield approach, the option modeling approach, and the option-adjusted spread approach. All of these techniques can be incorporated into a total return framework suitable for use for asset/liability management.

Once past the pricing problem created by the uncertain cash flow pattern, the investor's next step is to measure the interest rate risk associated with a mortgage-backed security. The usual measure of interest rate risk used by investors is Macaulay (or modified) duration. This measure is, however, inappropriate for not only mortgage-backed securities, but also for current coupon and premium callable corporate and municipal bonds. In particular, as market yields decline, call risk increases. This results in price compression (popularly referred to as "negative convexity") because investors become unwilling to pay a premium far above the call price (par in the case of mortgage-backed securities) as the market rate falls below the coupon rate. Several approaches discussed in this book have been suggested for use in measuring the interest rate sensitivity of a mortgage-backed security.

ORGANIZATION OF THE BOOK

I have divided the book into seven sections. Section I describes the various mortgage products. Section II covers pass-through securities such as agency pass-throughs, private-label pass-throughs, and multifamily project securities, as well as adjustable-rate mortgages and adjustable-rate pass-throughs. Section III focuses on prepayment forecasting for both fixed-rate and adjustable-rate pass-throughs. (Preliminary information on prepayment behavior for recently introduced mortgage designs is also provided in

Chapter 3 of Section I.) The wide range of collateralized mortgage obligation products, including PACs, TACs, accrual (Z) bonds, floaters, inverse floaters, companion bonds, companions with schedules, POs, IOettes, residuals, and the various types of stripped mortgage-backed securities (IOs, POs, partial strips) are discussed in Section IV.

Valuation techniques are reviewed in Section V. Portfolio strategies, including hedging and the creation of synthetics, are discussed in Section VI. The final section covers financial accounting, federal income tax, and operational considerations for mortgage-backed securities.

The appendix to this book provides a review of mortgage mathematics.

SECTION I

MORTGAGE PRODUCTS

CHAPTER 2

INTRODUCTION TO MORTGAGES

Frank J. Fabozzi, PhD, CFA
Visiting Professor of Finance
Sloan School of Management
Massachusetts Institute of Technology
and
Editor, *Journal of Portfolio Management*

Dexter Senft
Director of Research
EJV Partners

A mortgage is a pledge of property to secure payment of a debt. Typically, property refers to real estate. The debt is a loan given to the buyer of the property by the lender. If the property buyer (the *mortgagor*) fails to pay the lender (the *mortgagee*), the lender has the right to foreclose the loan and seize the property in order to ensure that it is repaid.

Virtually all forms of real estate have been mortgaged, but these properties fall into several classes. First, property (and the mortgage on it) can be classified as either residential or nonresidential, depending on whether or not people use the property primarily for living. Residential properties include houses, apartments, condominiums, cooperatives, and mobile homes. These do not necessarily have to be someone's primary residence—for example, summer homes and skiing condominiums are classified as residential properties. Residential properties are subdivided into one- to four-family dwellings and multifamily dwellings. Nonresidential properties are subdivided into commercial properties and farm properties. The commercial category encompasses a wide variety of properties such as office buildings, shopping centers, hospitals, and industrial plants.

In order to understand and analyze mortgage-related securities, it is necessary to understand how mortgages operate. In this chapter, we examine several types of mortgage loans, their cash flow, and certain other aspects relevant to the analysis of mortgage-related securities. The next chapter focuses on new mortgage designs.

THE TRADITIONAL MORTGAGE

The form that a mortgage loan takes technically could be anything that the borrower and lender agree upon. Traditionally, however, most mortgage loans have been structured similarly: a fixed-rate, level payment, fully amortized mortgage. The basic idea behind this mortgage design, which we refer to as a traditional mortgage, is that the borrower pays interest and repays principal in equal installments over an agreed-upon period of time, called the maturity or term of the mortgage. Thus at the end of the term, the loan has been fully amortized.

The interest rate is generally above the risk-free interest rate, in particular the yield on a Treasury security of comparable maturity, with the spread reflecting the higher costs of collection, the costs associated with default that are not eliminated despite the collateral, poorer liquidity, and the uncertainty concerning the timing of the cash flow, which we explain later. The frequency of payment is typically monthly,[1]and the prevailing term of the mortgage is twenty to thirty years; however, in recent years an increasing number of fifteeen-year mortgages have been originated.

Each monthly mortgage payment for a level payment mortgage is due on the first of each month and consists of:

1. interest of 1/12th of the fixed annual interest rate times the amount of the outstanding mortgage balance at the beginning of the previous month, and

2. a repayment of a portion of the outstanding mortgage balance (principal).

The difference between the monthly mortgage payment and the portion of the payment that represents interest equals the amount that is applied to reduce the outstanding mortgage balance. The monthly mortgage payment is designed so that after the last scheduled monthly payment of the loan is made, the amount of the outstanding mortgage balance is zero (i.e., the mortgage is fully repaid).

To illustrate a level payment, fixed-rate mortgage, consider a thirty-year (360-month), $100,000 mortgage with a 10% mortgage rate. The monthly mortgage payment would be $877.57. The formula for calculating the monthly mortgage payment is given in the Appendix.

Exhibit 1 shows how each monthly mortgage payment is divided between interest and repayment of principal. (Ignore the last column, which will be explained later.) At the beginning of month 1, the mortgage balance is $100,000, the amount of the original loan. The mortgage payment for month 1 includes interest on the $100,000 borrowed for the month. Since the interest rate is 10%, the monthly interest rate is 0.0083333 (0.10 divided by 12). Interest for month 1 is therefore $833.33 ($100,000 times 0.0083333). The $44.24 difference between the monthly mortgage

---

[1] Recently there have been some mortgage loans with biweekly mortgage payments.

Exhibit 1 : Mortgage Amortization Schedule for a Traditional Mortgage

Mortgage loan: $100,000
Mortgage rate: 10.00%
Monthly payment: $877.57
Servicing fee: 0.50%

Month	Beginning mortgage balance	Interest for month	Principal repayment	Ending Mortgage balance	Servicing fee
1	$ 100,000.00	$ 833.33	$ 44.24	$ 99,955.76	$ 41.67
2	99,955.76	832.96	44.61	99,911.15	41.65
3	99,911.15	832.59	44.98	99,866.18	41.63
4	99,866.18	832.22	45.35	99,820.82	41.61
5	99,820.82	831.84	45.73	99,775.09	41.59
6	99,775.09	831.46	46.11	99,728.98	41.57
7	99,728.98	831.07	46.50	99,682.48	41.55
8	99,682.48	830.69	46.88	99,635.60	41.53
9	99,635.60	830.30	47.27	99,588.32	41.51
10	99,588.32	829.90	47.67	99,540.65	41.50
11	99,540.65	829.51	48.07	99,492.59	41.48
12	99,492.59	829.10	48.47	99,444.12	41.46
13	99,444.12	828.70	48.87	99,395.25	41.44
14	99,395.25	828.29	49.28	99,345.97	41.41
15	99,345.97	827.88	49.69	99,296.28	41.39
16	99,296.28	827.47	50.10	99,246.18	41.37
17	99,246.18	827.05	50.52	99,195.66	41.35
18	99,195.66	826.63	50.94	99,144.72	41.33
19	99,144.72	826.21	51.37	99,093.36	41.31
20	99,093.36	825.78	51.79	99,041.56	41.29
21	99,041.56	825.35	52.23	98,989.34	41.27
22	98,989.34	824.91	52.66	98,936.68	41.25
23	98,936.68	824.47	53.10	98,883.58	41.22
24	98,883.58	824.03	53.54	98,830.04	41.20
25	98,830.04	823.58	53.99	98,776.05	41.18
26	98,776.05	823.13	54.44	98,721.61	41.16
27	98,721.61	822.68	54.89	98,666.72	41.13
28	98,666.72	822.22	55.35	98,611.37	41.11
⋮	⋮	⋮	⋮	⋮	⋮
208	75,726.23	631.05	246.52	75,479.71	31.55
209	75,479.71	629.00	248.57	75,231.14	31.45
210	75,231.14	626.93	250.65	74,980.49	31.35
211	74,980.49	624.84	252.73	74,727.76	31.24
212	74,727.76	622.73	254.84	74,472.92	31.14
213	74,472.92	620.61	256.96	74,215.95	31.03
⋮	⋮	⋮	⋮	⋮	⋮
356	4,280.26	35.67	841.90	3,438.36	1.78
357	3,438.36	28.65	848.92	2,589.44	1.43
358	2,589.44	21.58	855.99	1,733.45	1.08
359	1,733.45	14.45	863.13	870.32	0.72
360	870.32	7.25	870.32	0.00	0.36

payment of $877.57 and the interest of $833.33 is the portion of the monthly mortgage payment which represents repayment of principal. This $44.24 in month 1 reduces the mortgage balance.

The mortgage balance at the end of month 1 (beginning of month 2) is then $99,955.76 ($100,000 minus $44.24). The interest for the second monthly mortgage payment is $832.96, the monthly interest rate (0.0083333) times the mortgage balance at the beginning of month 2 ($99,955.76). The difference between the $877.57 monthly mortgage payment and the $832.96 interest is $44.61, representing the amount of the mortgage balance paid off with that monthly mortgage payment. Notice that the last monthly mortgage payment is sufficient to pay off the remaining mortgage balance. When a loan repayment schedule is structured in this way, so that the payments made by the borrower will completely pay off the interest and principal, the loan is said to be *self-amortizing*. Exhibit 1 is then referred to as an *amortization schedule*.

As Exhibit 1 clearly shows, *the portion of the monthly mortgage payment applied to interest declines each month, and the portion applied to reducing the mortgage balance increases.* The reason for this is that as the mortgage balance is reduced with each monthly mortgage payment, the interest on the mortgage balance declines. Since the monthly mortgage payment is fixed, a larger part of the monthly payment is applied to reduce the principal in each subsequent month.

Prepayments and Cash Flow Uncertainty

In our illustration, we assumed that the homeowner would not pay any portion of the mortgage balance prior to the scheduled due date. But homeowners do pay off all or part of their mortgage balance prior to the maturity date. Payments made in excess of the scheduled principal repayments are called *prepayments*. Prepayments occur for many reasons; these are discussed in later chapters.

The effect of prepayments is that the cash flow from a mortgage is not known with certainty. This is true not only for level payment mortgages but for all the mortgages we discuss in this book.

QUALIFYING FOR A MORTGAGE

Borrowers who are interested in obtaining mortgage loans must meet certain standards set by the lender in order to be considered creditworthy. The first thing a lender checks is whether or not the borrower has any other loans or obligations outstanding; if so, these will diminish the borrower's ability to make mortgage payments. Next the lender determines the income and net worth of the borrower. Many mortgage lenders use these classical rules of thumb to determine whether or not a borrower's income is adequate for the mortgage:

1. The total mortgage payment (principal and interest) should not exceed 25% of the borrower's total income, less any payments owed for other obligations.

2. Total mortgage payments plus other housing expenses should not exceed 33% of the borrower's income, less payments for other obligations. Other housing expenses include such items as taxes, insurance, utilities, and normal maintenance costs.

Of course, these percentages may vary depending on the lender and the circumstances. In particular, borrowers with relatively high net worth and/or liquid assets will find lenders to be more flexible. Also, in times of high interest rates and tight money, lenders have been known to bend these rules in order to maintain a certain level of business.

The buyer is usually required to make a down payment on the property in order to qualify for the mortgage. The down payment might range anywhere from 5 to 25% of the purchase price. The reason for requiring a down payment is that in the event the lender is forced to foreclose the loan and sell the property, the mortgage balance will be more easily recovered. In other words, there is room for error if the property is sold—even if it cannot bring the original purchase price on the market, there can still be enough to cover the debt. Lenders use the term *loan-to-value ratio*, or LTV, to express the amount of protection on the mortgage. LTV is calculated as the ratio of the mortgage balance to the market value of the property, and is expressed as a percentage. The lower the LTV, the less the loan amount relative to the property value, and the greater the safety.

The LTV ratio tends to decrease over time. For example, if a buyer makes a 10% down payment on a property and mortgages the rest, the LTV is initially 90%. Over time, the mortgage balance declines from amortization and prepayments, while the property value may increase owing to inflation. Both of these changes serve to lower the LTV.

As with income requirements, down payment and LTV requirements depend on certain circumstances. These include not only the net worth of the borrower, but the condition and marketability of the property and the availability of credit. Higher LTV ratios are associated with newer, more marketable properties, and with easier credit and lower interest rates.

An important (if not obvious) conclusion about qualifying for a mortgage is that it becomes harder when interest rates rise. Because of the income and LTV requirements, smaller mortgage balances are affordable when rates rise, and yet this is also the time when inflation and therefore home purchase prices are rising. As a consequence, all but those buyers with large amounts of cash or equity are squeezed from the market.

MORTGAGE INSURANCE

There are two types of mortgage insurance that may be used when borrowers obtain mortgage financing. One type is originated by borrowers and the other by lenders. Although both have a beneficial effect on the creditworthiness of the borrowers, the latter is of greater importance from the lender's point of view.

The first type of mortgage insurance is taken out by the borrower, usually with a life insurance company. The policy provides for the continuing payment of the mortgage after the death of the insured person, thus enabling the survivors to continue living in the house. In the sense that the mortgage might just as well have been paid off with part of the proceeds of ordinary life insurance, this form of mortgage insurance is really only a special form of life insurance. It is cheaper than ordinary life insurance, however, because the death benefit, which is equal to the mortgage balance, declines over time.

The other type of mortgage insurance is taken out by the lender, although borrowers pay the insurance premiums. This policy covers some percentage of the loan amount and guarantees that in the event of a default by the borrower, the insurance company will pay the amount insured or pay off the loan in full.

An example of how this type of mortgage insurance works is shown in Exhibit 2. Suppose that a borrower finances $60,000 of property with a $5,000 down payment and a $55,000 mortgage. The initial LTV ratio is fairly high (91.7%), so mortgage insurance is obtained in the amount of $11,000 (20% of the loan). Suppose that the borrower defaults after five years (the mortgage balance having been paid down to $52,000 by then). Suppose further that the property has deteriorated in condition (or perhaps has been partially destroyed), and its market value falls to $50,000. The bank then turns to the insurance company.

Several options are open to the insurance company, perhaps the simplest of which is that it can assist the borrower financially so that the amount in arrears can be paid, and no foreclosure is necessary. Assuming that this fails, there are two other alternatives. First, the insurance company could pay the claim of $11,000 and let the bank foreclose. The bank, which gets $50,000 for the property and $11,000 insurance, actually makes a profit of $9,000 over the mortgage balance outstanding. A better alternative for the insurance company, however, is to pay off the mortgage balance

Exhibit 2: How Mortgage Insurance Works in the Event of a Default

Situation initially:

$$\text{LTV} = \frac{55,000}{60,000} = 91.7\%$$

$11,000 mortgage
insurance obtained

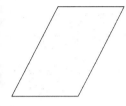

Mortgage: $55,000   Property value: $60,000
Down payment   5,000
Total $60,000

Situation after 5 years:
Borrower defaults
Property value falls

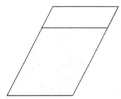

Mortgage balance: Property value: $50,000
$52,000

Option 1:   Insurance company pays claim
            Lender has $50,000   Property
                                     11,000   Insurance
                                    (52,000)   Bad debt
                                    $ 9,000   Net profit

            Insurance company has   ($11,000)   Loss

Option 2:   Insurance company takes title to property
            Lender has $52,000   From insurer
                                   ($52,000)   Bad debt
                                          0   Net profit

            Insurance company has $50,000   Property
                                   ($52,000)   Payment to lender
                                    ($2,000)   Net loss

($52,000), take title of the property, and sell it (for $50,000). The insurance company thereby loses only $2,000, instead of $11,000. Of course, the insurer could hold the property or even make improvements to it in hope of making a future gain, instead of selling it immediately.

The net effect of mortgage insurance from the lender's standpoint is to reduce its default risk. The exposure of a lender to loss equals the amount loaned less property value and mortgage insurance. In a sense, the insurance has an effect similar to that of having a higher down payment because both reduce the lender's exposure to loss. Mortgage insurance is advantageous to borrowers who do not have enough money for a large down payment but who can afford enough down payment and insurance to satisfy the lender.

The cost of the insurance can be passed on to the borrower in several ways. Traditionally, the cost was added to the mortgage rate as an extra 0.125% or 0.250%, depending on the amount of coverage. As mortgage rates escalated, however, increasing the rate further became less attractive. (In a sense, the insurance company would be increasing the chance of the default it was insuring against.) It has become increasingly common to pay for mortgage insurance in one lump sum at the time of mortgage origination.

It is not necessary to have mortgage insurance in effect for the entire term of a loan. Because the mortgage balance amortizes and the LTV tends to fall over time, the lender may deem mortgage insurance to be unnecessary when the mortgage balance has declined to some predetermined level. At that point, the policy is either cancelled or allowed to expire.

SERVICING

Among the jobs that mortgage lenders must perform in order to ensure that borrowers make timely and accurate payments are sending payment notices, reminding borrowers when payments are overdue, recording prepayments, keeping records of mortgage balances, administering escrow accounts for payment of property taxes or insurance, sending out tax information at year-end, and initiating foreclosure proceedings. These functions are collectively known as *servicing* the loans. Often the original lender is the one who services the loan, but this is not always the case. Sometimes the mortgage is sold to someone else, and the servicing of the loan may or may not go along with the mortgage.

In the event that one party owns a mortgage and another services it, the servicer receives a fee (the *servicing fee*) for the trouble. Servicing fees usually take the form of a fixed percentage of the mortgage balance outstanding. Although the percentage may vary from one servicer to the next, it is usually in the area of 0.25% to 0.50%. Small servicing fee percentages are usually associated with larger commercial property loans, and larger percentages with smaller residential loans. From the point of view of the owner of the mortgage, the servicing fee comes out of the interest portion of the mortgage payment. For example, if party A owns a 10% mortgage being serviced by party B for a three-eights of 1% fee, then A is really earning 9 5/8% (10% minus three-eighths of 1%) on the loan.

In addition to servicing fees, there are occasionally other fees that the servicer may keep. For example, some servicers are entitled to keep late-payment penalties paid by the borrower, foreclosure penalties, and certain other penalty fees. The specific types and amounts of fees that servicers are entitled to receive are set forth in a servicing agreement between the mortgage owner and the servicer.

Cash Flow with Servicing Fee

The monthly cash flow from the mortgage can therefore be decomposed into three parts:

1. the servicing fee;

2. the interest payment net of the servicing fee; and

3. the scheduled principal repayment.

Consider once again the thirty-year mortgage loan for $100,000 with a mortgage rate of 10%. Suppose the servicing fee is 0.5% per year. The last column of Exhibit 1 shows the cash flow for the mortgage with this servicing fee. The monthly mortgage payment is unchanged. The difference is that the interest received by the investor is reduced by the amount of the servicing fee. The servicing fee, just like the interest, declines each month because the mortgage balance declines.

MORTGAGE ORIGINATION

The original lender of mortgage money is called the *mortgage originator*. The major originators are commercial banks, thrifts (savings and loan associations, savings banks, and credit unions) and mortgage companies (or mortgage bankers). Commercial banks and thrifts may hold mortgages in their portfolio. In contrast, mortgage banks are rarely mortgage investors: the loans they originate are typically sold to other more permanent investors.

Overview of the Mortgage Origination Process

A potential home buyer who wants to borrow funds to purchase a home will apply for a loan from a mortgage originator. The process begins with the completion of an application form that provides financial information about the applicant and the payment of an application fee. The mortgage originator then performs a credit evaluation of the applicant. The two primary factors in determining whether or not the funds will be lent are the (1) payment-to-income (PTI) ratio, and (2) the loan-to-value (LTV) ratio, which were discussed earlier.

If the lender decides to loan the funds, a commitment letter will be sent to the applicant. This letter commits the lender to loan funds to the applicant. The length of time of the commitment varies between thirty and sixty days. At the time of the commitment letter, the lender will require that the applicant pay a commitment fee. The applicant loses the commitment fee if the applicant decides not to purchase the property, or if the applicant uses an alternative source of funds to purchase the property. Thus, the commitment letter states that for a fee the applicant has the right but not the obligation to require the lender to provide funds at a certain interest rate and with certain terms.

At the time the application is submitted for approval, the mortgage originator will give the applicant a choice of mortgage types and rates. The various types of mortgages are discussed later in this chapter. Usually, the choice is between a fixed-rate mortgage or an adjustable-rate mortgage. In the case of a fixed-rate mortgage, the lender typically gives the applicant a choice of when the interest rate on the mortgage will be determined. The choices may be (1) at the time the loan application is submitted, (2) at the time a commitment letter is issued to the borrower, or (3) at the closing date (i.e., the date that the property is purchased).

The mortgage rate that the originator will set on the loan will depend on the mortgage rate required by investors who purchase mortgages. There will usually be different mortgage rates for delivery at different times (thirty days, sixty days, or ninety days in the future).

Mortgage Securitization

Mortgage originators can either (1) hold a new mortgage in their portfolio, (2) sell the mortgage to an investor or conduit, or (3) use the mortgage as collateral for the issuance of a security. When a mortgage is included as part of a pool of mortgages that is the collateral for a security, the mortgage is said to be *securitized*.

When a mortgage originator intends to sell the mortgage, it will obtain a commitment from the potential buyer. Two federally sponsored credit agencies and several private companies buy mortgages. Since these agencies and private companies pool these mortgages and sell them to investors, they are called *conduits*.

The two agencies, the Federal Home Loan Mortgage Corporation (FHLMC, or "Freddie Mac") and the Federal National Mortgage Association (FNMA, or "Fannie Mae"), purchase only certain kinds of mortgages, known as *conforming* mortgages. A conforming mortgage is simply one that meets their underwriting standards. Three of the major underwriting standards established by these agencies for qualification as a conforming mortgage are (1) a maximum PTI ratio, (2) a maximum LTV ratio, and (3) a maximum loan amount. If an applicant does not satisfy these underwriting standards, the mortgage is called a *nonconforming* mortgage. Loans that exceed the maximum loan amount and therefore do not qualify as conforming mortgages are called *jumbo* loans. Private conduits typically will securitize both conforming and nonconforming mortgages.

NONTRADITIONAL MORTGAGES

There are dozens of different types of alternative mortgage designs, each with its own peculiar twist. We will review two types of fixed-rate mortgages in this chapter: graduated payment mortgages and growing equity mortgages. Adjustable-rate mortgages are discussed in Chapter YY. In the next chapter, several mortgage designs introduced in the late 1980s in the U.S. mortgage market are discussed: tiered payment mortgages, balloon mortgages, two-step mortgages, and fixed/adjustable-rate hybrid mortgages.

Graduated Payment Mortgages (GPMs)

The only essential differences between the GPM and the traditional mortgage is that the payments on a GPM are not all equal. Graduated payment refers to the fact that GPM payments start at a relatively low level and rise for some number of years. The actual number of years that the payments rise and the percentage

Exhibit 3: The Five Major GPM Plans

Plan	Term-to-Maturity (Years)	Years that Payments Rise	Percentage Increase per Year
I	30	5	2.5%
II	30	5	5.0
III	30	5	7.5
IV	30	10	2.0
V	30	10	3.0

increase per year depend on the exact type or plan of the GPM. The five major GPM plans work as illustrated in Exhibit 3. The first three GPM plans qualify for inclusion in certain types of mortgage pass-through securities.[2]

At the end of the graduation period, the monthly payment is held at its existing level for the remainder of the mortgage term. Exhibit 4 shows the payment schedule on a $100,000, 10%, Plan III GPM.

Exhibit 4: Mortgage Payment Schedule for a $100,000 Plan III GPM (30-Year Term, 10% Mortgage Rate)

(Years)	Monthly Payment
1	$667.04
2	717.06
3	770.84
4	828.66
5	890.80
6-30	957.62

Note: Plan III GPMs call for monthly payments that increase by 7.5% at the end of each of the first five years of the mortgage.

---

[2] The majority of the GPMs underlying certain types of pass-through securities are Plan III graduated payment mortgages because Plan III has the lowest initial monthly mortgage payment. Within a pool of mortgages that are collateral for a mortgage pass-through security, GPMs from all three plans may be found. However, analysts typically assume all GPMs are of the Plan III type.

The attraction of a GPM is the small payment in its early years. A first-time home buyer who might not be able to afford payments on a traditional mortgage might be able to afford the smaller payments of the GPM, even if both loans were for the same principal amount. Eventually, when the graduation period has ended, homeowners with GPMs make up the difference by paying larger monthly amounts than the traditional mortgages require. The originators of GPMs reason that most home buyers, particularly young, first-time home buyers, have incomes that will increase at least as rapidly as the mortgage payments increase. Thus, they should always be able to afford their monthly payments.

Because GPMs have smaller initial payments than do traditional mortgages, they do not pay down their mortgage balances as quickly. The interesting feature of GPMs is that in their early years they do not pay down any principal at all—in fact their mortgage balances actually *increase* for a short period of time. Technically, we say that they experience "negative amortization" at the outset. To see how this works, consider the first-month payment on the GPM in Exhibit 4.

Interest due for month 1 is 10% per year for one-twelfth year on $100,000 balance. The negative amortization can be calculated as follows:

$$\$100,000 \times 1/12 \times 10/100 = \$833.34$$
$$\text{Payment on GPM} = \$667.04$$
$$\text{Principal paid} = \$667.04 - \$833.34 = -\$166.30$$
$$\text{New mortgage balance} = \$100,000 - (166.30) = \$100,166.30$$

Of course, the mortgage balance must eventually be reduced to zero. The annual increases in the mortgage payment eventually catch up to and overtake the amount of interest due, and at that time the mortgage balance begins to decrease.

Origination of GPMs has declined dramatically in recent years.

Growing Equity Mortgages

A growing equity mortgage (GEM) is another fixed-rate mortgage whose monthly payments increase over time. However, unlike a GPM, there is no negative amortization. The initial monthly mortgage payment is the same as for a level payment, fixed-rate mortgage. By increasing the monthly mortgage payments, more of the mortgage payments are applied to paying off the principal. As a result, the principal amount of the GEM is repaid faster. For example, a $100,000 GEM loan at a rate of 10% might call for an initial monthly payment of $877.57 (the same as a traditional 10% thirty-year mortgage). However, the GEM payment would gradually increase, and the GEM might be fully paid in only fifteen years.

RISKS ASSOCIATED WITH INVESTING IN MORTGAGES

Investors are exposed to four main risks by investing in mortgage loans: (1) interest-rate risk, (2) prepayment risk, (3) credit risk, and (4) liquidity risk.

Interest-Rate Risk

Interest-rate risk is the risk of loss in the event that general market rates change. Since a mortgage is a debt instrument, its price will decline when interest rates rise, and vice versa. Since it is typically a long-term instrument, it exposes the investor to substantial interest-rate risk.

Prepayment Risk

As we explained earlier in this chapter, the borrower has the right to pay off all or part of the mortgage balance at any time. Effectively, someone who invests in a mortgage has granted the borrower an option to prepay the mortgage. The uncertainty associated with the cash flow as a result of this embedded option is called *prepayment risk*. In later chapters this risk is discussed in more detail. For now, it is sufficient to say that, by holding an individual mortgage, an investor is exposed to substantial prepayment risk.

Credit Risk

Credit risk is the risk of loss due to a homeowner/borrower default. For FHA-insured and VA-guaranteed mortgages, this risk is minimal because the credit of FHA and VA stand behind such loans. For privately insured mortgages, the risk can be gauged by the credit rating of the private insurance company that has insured the mortgage. For conventional mortgages without private insurance, the credit risk depends on the borrower. The risk exposure can be roughly gauged by the LTV ratio.

Liquidity Risk

Liquidity risk is the risk of loss in the event that the investment must be sold quickly. It is typically measured by the bid-ask spread in the marketplace for the investment. Most mortgage securities are highly liquid and therefore have minimal liquidity risk. While there is an active secondary market for mortgage loans, the fact is that bid-ask spreads are large compared to other debt instruments.

APPENDIX

MATHEMATICS OF TRADITIONAL MORTGAGES

Investors in mortgages must be able to calculate the scheduled cash flow associated with a particular mortgage, and servicers of mortgages must be able to calculate the scheduled servicing fee that will be earned. Moreover, when we explain pools of mortgage loans, it will be necessary to determine the cash flow from the pool. In this Appendix we present formulas for calculating the cash flow associated with traditional mortgages.

The Monthly Mortgage Payment

To compute the monthly mortgage payment for a level payment mortgage requires the application of the formula for the present value of an ordinary annuity, which gives:

$$MP = MB_0 \left[\frac{[i(1+i)^n]}{[(1+i)^n - 1]} \right]$$

where

    MP = monthly mortgage payment (\$);
    n   = number of months;
    MB_0 = original mortgage balance (\$);
    i   = simple monthly interest rate (annual interest rate/12).

The term in brackets is called the *payment factor*. It is the monthly payment for a \$1 mortgage loan with an interest rate of i and a term of n months.

To illustrate how the formula is applied, we'll use the \$100,000, thirty-year, 10% mortgage that we used in our illustrations in the chapter:

$n = 360;$

$MB_0 = \$100{,}000;$

$i = .0083333 \ (=.10/12).$

The monthly mortgage payment is then

$$MP = \$100{,}000 \left[\frac{[.0083333 \ (1.0083333)^{360}]}{[(1.0083333)^{360} - 1]} \right]$$

$$= \$877.57.$$

The Mortgage Balance and Interest for Each Month

It is not necessary to construct an amortization schedule such as Exhibit 1 in order to determine the remaining mortgage balance for any month. The following formula can be used:

$$MP_t = MB_0 \left[\frac{[(1+i)^n - (1+i)^t]}{[(1+i)^n - 1]} \right]$$

where

MP_t = mortgage balance after t months (\$);

n = original number of months of mortgage;

MB_0 = the original mortgage balance (\$);

i = simple monthly interest rate (annual interest rate/12).

For the mortgage in Exhibit 1, the mortgage balance at the end of the 210th month is:

$t = 210;$

$n = 360;$

$MB_0 = \$100{,}000;$

$i = .0083333.$

$$MB_{210} = \$100{,}000 \left[\frac{[(1.0083333)^{360} - (1.0083333)^{210}]}{[(1.0083333)^{360} - 1]} \right]$$

$$= \$74{,}980.59$$

The following formula can be used to determine the amount of the scheduled principal repayment in month t:

$$P_t = MB_0 \left[\frac{[i\,(1+i)^{t-1}]}{[(1+i)^n - 1]} \right]$$

where

P_t = scheduled principal repayment for month t.

The scheduled principal repayment for the 210th month for the mortgage in Exhibit 1 is

$$P_{250} = \$100,000 \left[\frac{[.0083333\,(1.0083333)^{210-1}]}{[(1.0083333)^{360} - 1]} \right]$$

$$= \$250.65$$

To compute the interest paid for month t, the following formula can be used:

$$I_t = MB_0 \left[\frac{i\,[(1+i)^n - (1+i)^{t-1}]}{[(1+i)^n - 1]} \right]$$

where

I_t = Interest for month t.

For the 210th month, the interest for the mortgage in Exhibit 1 is

$$I_{210} = \$100,000 \left[\frac{.0083333\,[(1.0083333)^{360} - (1.0083333)^{210-1}]}{[(1.008333)^{360} - 1]} \right]$$

$$= \$626.93$$

CHAPTER 3

NEW MORTGAGE DESIGNS: TIERED PAYMENT, BALLOON, TWO-STEP, AND FIXED/ADJUSTABLE-RATE HYBRID MORTGAGES

Lynn M. Edens
Vice President
Mortgage Securities Research Department
Goldman, Sachs & Co.

THE CHANGING PRIMARY MORTGAGE MARKET

In the previous chapter, the traditional fixed-rate, level payment mortgage and the graduated payment mortgage were reviewed. Since 1989, lenders have offered a number of new mortgage loan

The author would like to acknowledge the comments and assistance of her colleagues at Goldman Sachs, including Scott Pinkus, Mike Asay, Eric Bruskin, Scott Richard, Ashwin Belur, Kelly Ann LaRossa, and Adam Wizon. Special thanks are also due to Henry Cassidy and David Anrukonis at the Federal Home Loan Mortgage Corporation, Michael Sonnenfeld at Ryland Acceptance Corporation, and Larry Jackson at Citicorp Mortgage Inc. for their assistance in the section on tiered payment mortgages.

structures to single-family mortgage borrowers. Other structures, which are not new but were not previously popular, have also gained significant primary market share. These products include tiered payment mortgages, balloon mortgages, "two-step" mortgages, and fixed/adjustable mortgage hybrids. The innovation has occurred at a rapid rate last seen in the early 1980s, when extremely high mortgage rates forced lenders to create loan structures that offered lower initial payments. As we discuss shortly, current innovations are motivated by important, and probably enduring, changes in the market for mortgage originations.

Today, many of these new products are finding their way into the secondary market, where they present investors with both opportunities and challenges. The opportunities include the chance to invest in new securities that may provide a better portfolio fit than other mortgage products have to date. This opportunity is enhanced because unfamiliarity causes them to be priced cheaper than other mortgage securities. The challenges include the proper valuation of these new loan structures and an appropriate assessment of their long-term liquidity. Some of these loan types are likely to become permanent features of both the primary and the secondary mortgage market; others are likely to go the way of the dinosaur, the zeppelin, and the graduated payment mortgage.

The following sections of this chapter address several questions. First, what is motivating the development of these new mortgage loan structures? Our answer to this question will be a critical component of our view on the long-term viability of these products. Second, what are the features of the new mortgage structures, and what unique portfolio advantages, if any, do they offer? And finally, how should we value the new structures, and how attractively priced are those that currently trade actively?

Market Forces Motivating Innovation

The secondary mortgage market has historically provided originators with an incentive to produce mortgage loans that have short durations and are relatively insensitive to prepayments. In fact, it was the use of collateralized mortgage obligations to create mortgage securities with these characteristics that helped expand the breadth of the mortgage investor base so substantially over the past several years. Adjustable-rate mortgages (ARMs) were another response to this phenomenon. It has been the declining competitiveness of ARM teaser rates—which occurred both because of the flat or inverted yield curve in the late 1980s and early 1990s, and because of the decision by thrifts to price ARMs less aggressively—that has created room for new, short-duration mortgage products to flourish.

Other, more recent market developments also favor new mortgage products. Accompanying (and, in some cases, precipitating) the decline in the origination role of thrifts is a dramatic increase in the mortgage activity of banks, both as originators and portfolio lenders. Commercial banks have recently gained the greatest share of the mortgage origination market (for the first time since the advent of the modern secondary mortgage market). Risk-adjusted capital requirements for banks, which favor residential mortgages, particularly in securitized form, as well as a lack of appealing opportunities in their traditional lending sectors, will continue to drive the trend toward an origination market dominated by banks. Interest rate risk management concerns will focus the lending activity of banks on shorter-duration mortgage products, as we have seen already. Because many banks will experience a demand for mortgage securities beyond their origination capacity (if any), and because many other mortgage investors also prefer shorter-duration mortgage securities, these new mortgage loan structures can offer very competitive rates to borrowers. Other mortgage bankers are also actively marketing these loan types.

These new mortgage products are likely to continue to provide a lower rate to the borrower, and thus a marketing advantage to the originator, only if they enjoy a viable secondary market. A few of these new products are likely to become permanent and substantial elements of the securitized market. Others, with more complicated (and therefore harder to price) structures, or less obvious portfolio applications, may well fade from importance. In this chapter, we discuss the structure and portfolio applications of several of the predominant new mortgage loan types.

In our discussion, we will refer to mortgage-backed securities products, valuation technologies, and prepayment behavior. These topics are discussed in greater detail later chapters in this book. It is suggested that on first reading, the reader focus on the basic characteristics of these new mortgage designs.

FIXED-RATE TIERED PAYMENT MORTGAGES

Fixed-rate tiered payment mortgages (TPMs) are a successful new mortgage loan structure, incorporating a variety of features that give the mortgage appeal in both the primary and the secondary markets. Production of the fifteen-year TPM is currently estimated to be running at about $200 to $300 million per month, making TPMs one of the most successful new mortgage products since the adjustable-rate mortgage (ARM). Their acceptance in the secondary market has been illustrated by the over $1.3 billion in collateralized mortgage obligations (CMOs) issued since March 1989 that have been backed by TPMs. In fact, to date substantially all TPM pools issued by FHLMC have gone directly into CMOs. Trading in nonconforming TPMs is also increasing.

As with most new mortgage structures that have evolved over the past decade, TPMs were designed to provide originators with an advantage in the single most important competitive criterion: the ability to offer borrowers a low initial payment, which gives borrowers greater purchasing power than they would have under a standard thirty-year or fifteen-year fixed-rate mortgage lending program. This innovation trend was first stimulated by the high interest rates of the early 1980s, when buydown and graduated payment mortgage lending programs flourished. In more recent years, adjustable-rate mortgages originated with a teaser rate (a rate below the fully indexed rate on the ARM) have largely fulfilled the demand for low initial payments.

The contractual features designed to permit low initial payments on these types of mortgages have varied. *Buydown* origination programs carried market accrual rates and subsidized the payments in the early years with payments from a separate account typically established by the builder or owner of the property. *Graduated payment mortgages* (GPMs) also carried near-market accrual rates and allowed the mortgage to experience negative amortization in the early years of its life. On the other hand, most *adjustable-rate mortgages* relied on low initial accrual rates and subsequent limitations to interest rate increases to create low initial payment requirements; other adjustable-rate structures carried low initial rates, employed payment caps, and allowed the mortgage to negatively amortize to maintain a low payment schedule for some time into the future.

Tiered payment mortgages provide the payment advantage in a unique way. The mortgage carries a market accrual rate and a fifteen-year or, less commonly, thirty-year final maturity, but the payment is calculated based on an interest rate as much as 300 to 500 basis points lower than the actual interest rate on the loan (even lower for some thirty-year loans). The structure does not allow negative amortization. Therefore, it stipulates that if the payment is less than the amount required to pay the interest due on the loan based on the actual interest rate, then the difference between the borrower's payment and the amount required to pay the entire interest accrued must be made up from a subsidy account established by the borrower, seller, builder, or other party. The payments are adjusted annually and allowed to increase by a maximum of 7.5% per year until the payment fully amortizes the loan over its remaining term.[1]

---

[1] There are also six-month TPMs, which have semiannual payment adjustments. Payment increases are currently limited to between 5 and 7.5%, although other permutations are possible.

The primary way TPMs differ from GPMs is that TPMs do not experience negative amortization and typically carry a fifteen-year maturity. TPMs differ from buydowns because any initial subsidy to the borrower's payment (from the interest shortfall account) is typically much smaller than that required by a buydown loan, and is also frequently funded by the borrower. We describe more fully the cash flows from such a loan in the next section.

TPMs have unique comparative advantages to attract borrowers in the primary market. Unlike ARMs, TPMs have a certain payment schedule with relatively moderate annual payment increases. They also carry a fixed rate, and they typically offer a fifteen-year final maturity attractive to many borrowers. Unlike some ARMs and graduated payment mortgages, they do not experience negative amortization. The interest-only nature of the earliest total cash flows on the mortgage (including any necessary subsidies) also allows the payment to be set based on an extremely low accrual rate, much lower than can be profitably offered on most ARMs. Although ARMs will undoubtedly continue to be an important origination product in the future because of their short duration and attractive portfolio characteristics, we expect the TPM to be competitive with the ARM in the primary market, and an increasingly important secondary market opportunity for mortgage investors.

The Structure and Cash Flows of TPMs

As mentioned, TPMs feature a fixed accrual rate and can carry a fifteen- or thirty-year final maturity. Since most of the TPMs originated to date have carried a fifteen-year final maturity, our analysis will focus on that type of loan.

Because the TPM carries a fixed accrual rate, the exact payment schedule for the life of the loan is known at origination. Although the TPM borrower may make an initial payment *less* than the interest-only payment at the accrual rate on the loan, any shortfall between that initial payment and the payment required to meet the monthly interest payment at the loan's accrual rate is made up by a payment from a subsidy account (sometimes referred to as an "interest shortfall account") set aside at the loan's origination date. Therefore, the investor never receives a payment lower than the interest-only payment. However, unlike the investor in a typical buydown loan, the TPM investor does see a tiered payment schedule, with payment increases starting as early as year one and ending as late as years seven or eight. In contrast, the buydown investor receives level payments on the loan from its origination date—only the buydown borrower sees changing payments.

The total amount required (if any) in the TPM borrower's subsidy account is also known at origination; it is calculated as the total dollar shortfall that will occur over the loan's life less any interest earned on the account under the provisions of the loan's contract. No subsidy account is necessary if the scheduled initial payment is equal to or greater than the interest-only payment at the loan's accrual rate. Payments increase once annually and are limited to a maximum increase of 7.5%. The number of years it takes for the payment to reach the amount that will fully amortize the loan over its remaining term will vary according to how low the initial payment is set.

Exhibit 1 illustrates the cash flows on a hypothetical $100,000 fifteen-year TPM loan. The loan carries a 9.5% interest rate, but the initial payment is calculated based on an interest rate of 4.5%. This makes the borrower's initial payment $764.99. Since this is less than the $791.67 needed to cover the initial interest-only payment, a subsidy account is required to make up the $26.68 difference to the investor during each month of the first year. The payment that the borrower makes increases at a rate of 7.5% until it reaches the level of $1,188.36, which will fully amortize the loan over the remaining eight years of its life. The investor sees payments that increase from $791.67 to $1,188.36. Since a subsidy account is supplementing the borrower's payments during the first year (see the shaded area on the graph), the first-year payment increase the investor sees is slightly less than 7.5%.

Exhibit 1: Cash Flows on 9.5% 15-Year TPM Loan Versus Cash Flows on Level Pay 15- and 30-Year Loans

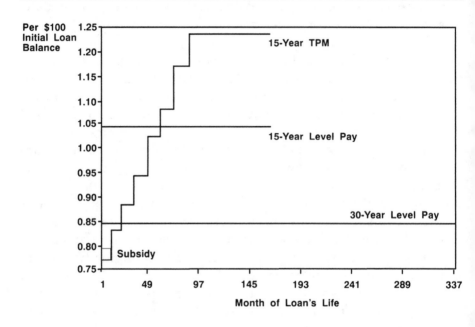

For comparison, we also show the cash flows of generic level pay 9.5% fifteen- and thirty-year mortgages. The timing difference of the cash flows is evident. It is interesting to note that although the origination market advantage of the TPM loan is its low initial payment, it actually has a lower payment than the thirty-year mortgage for only two years. Still, the $75.86 difference in the initial payment of the TPM versus the thirty-year level pay mortgage in that first year is enough for the borrower to qualify for nearly $10,000 of additional borrowing power at the margin (assuming the borrower is qualified on the first year's payment and before any relevant tax effects). For perspective, the average TPM mortgage loan size securitized in the FHLMC 73 Series securitization program among pools for which data are available is currently around $98,000. The initial payment is $279.23 less than that

Exhibit 2: Principal Balance of 9.5% TPM Versus 15- and 30-Year Level Pay Mortgages

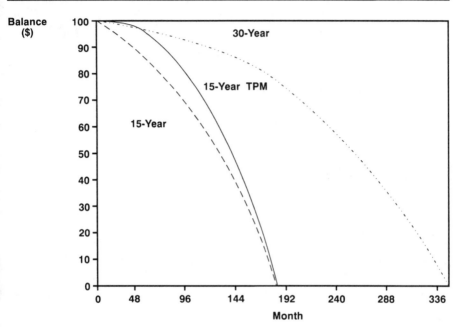

of the borrower who chose a generic fifteen-year mortgage at the same rate, which provides the borrower with an additional $35,000 in purchasing power versus a standard level pay fifteen-year loan.

The principal retirement schedules on these loans also vary. Exhibit 2 shows the remaining principal balances of the three loan types over time. For the first thirty-two months, the TPM loan has a higher remaining principal balance than either the fifteen-year or thirty-year generic mortgages. After month thirty-two, the rate of amortization of the TPM exceeds that of the thirty-year mortgage, but the TPM loan will always have a greater principal balance outstanding than the generic fifteen-year mortgage until the loans are entirely repaid. The TPM loan in this example has an average life of 10.5 years, versus 9.4 years for the generic fifteen-year loan. The thirty-year loan has an average life of 21.7 years.

In addition to the contractual differences that affect cash flow timing, we expect that TPMs will experience different prepayment rates from comparable coupon fifteen- and thirty-year level pay mortgages. More meaningful valuation of TPMs and an estimation of their comparative investment advantages and disadvantages versus generic mortgage securities require an estimation of, and some confidence in, their likely prepayment behavior.

BALLOON MORTGAGES

Most single-family balloon mortgages originated today carry a fixed rate and a thirty-year amortization schedule. They typically require a balloon repayment of the principal outstanding on the loan at the end of five or, more commonly, seven years. Other balloon dates are possible and may become common. Balloon mortgages are attractive to borrowers because they offer mortgage rates that are about 0.375 percentage points lower than generic thirty-year mortgages. In turn, the short final maturity of balloon mortgage pools offers investors substantial performance stability.

In Exhibit 3, the upper chart shows the remaining principal balance over time, using our current prepayment projections for three types of collateral, assuming an unchanged interest rate environment. It compares a seven-year balloon mortgage pool with a fifteen-year fixed-rate mortgage pool and a representative five-year average life planned amortization class (PAC) bond,[2] FHLMC 185 C.[3] The other charts show similar principal balances using our prepayment projections for plus and minus 300 basis points interest rate changes.

---

[2] PACs are discussed in Chapter 14.
[3] Since there is little evidence available on the prepayment behavior of balloon borrowers, our evaluation of these pools employs our prepayment model for thirty-year fixed-rate mortgages. Our reasoning is explained later in this section.

Exhibit 3: Remaining Principal Balances Over Time - *As of July 1990*

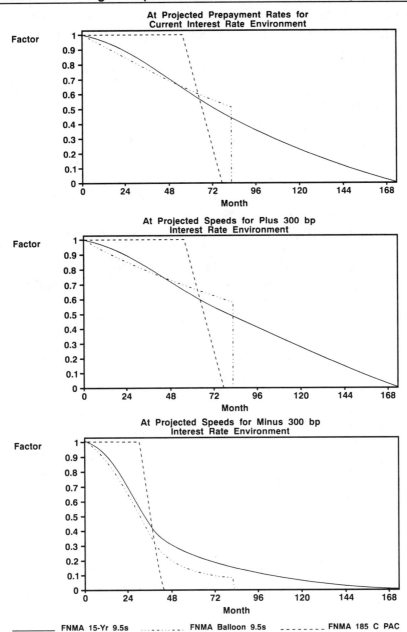

FNMA 15-Yr 9.5s   FNMA Balloon 9.5s   FNMA 185 C PAC

In all three prepayment environments shown, the principal balance of the balloon mortgage pool declines in a fashion similar to the principal balance of the fifteen-year mortgage pool until the final, balloon payment. In both the unchanged and the plus-300 basis points interest rate examples, the balloon mortgage pool has a final maturity only slightly later than that of the PAC. Only in the example where rates fall by 300 basis points does the PAC pay off fully much earlier than the balloon mortgage pool, although the outstanding principal balance of the PAC remains higher than that of the balloon pool for the first thirty-seven months of the securities' lives.

Today, many balloon mortgage contracts are actually hybrids that contain certain provisions allowing the borrower to take out a new mortgage from the current lender to finance the balloon repayment with minimal requalification requirements. In order for the new loan to qualify for a FNMA pool, for instance, the borrower receiving the new loan to finance a balloon payment must not have been delinquent on payments at any time during the preceding twelve months, must still be using the property as a primary residence, and must have incurred no new liens on the property. In addition, the interest rate on the new loan must be no more than 500 basis points greater than the rate on the balloon loan. If these conditions are met, FNMA requires no additional requalification of the borrower taking out a new mortgage to meet a balloon payment, and will accept the resulting mortgage in a generic FNMA pool.

Whether or not investors need concern themselves with the refinancing option offered to the borrower in conjunction with issuance of the balloon loan depends primarily on what form the balloon investment takes. Investors who own agency balloon mortgages can ignore the refinancing options offered to borrowers since, if the borrower fails to make the required balloon principal payment to the lender, the agency ultimately supports the balloon repayment to the investor. Investors in balloon mortgages with credit support provided in another manner should carefully assess the sufficiency of that support to meet borrower shortfalls at the balloon date, as the rating agencies do when assigning credit ratings to the bonds. It is possible, of course, that the nature of the refinancing option may influence borrower prepayment behavior before the balloon date, affecting both agency and non-agency balloon mortgage holdings; we discuss the implications of this shortly.[4]

Balloon mortgages have been a successful secondary market product. Exhibit 4 shows monthly issuance of FNMA and FHLMC seven-year balloon mortgages. Exhibit 5 illustrates current outstanding balances by coupon. The two charts emphasize the growing liquidity of the balloon product. Each agency also has a five-year balloon pool issuance program in its budding stage. In addition, an informal survey of originators suggests that more are offering balloon mortgages.

Who will find balloon mortgages an attractive investment option? Any investor that currently buys intermediate average life Planned Amortization Class (PAC) bonds will find that the average life stability offered by balloon mortgages is similar to that offered by PACs, but the balloons trade at wider yield spreads and offer the additional advantage of an increasingly liquid dollar roll market.[5] What's more, the short final maturities of the balloon mortgages mean that they will meet thrift liquidity requirements earlier than most comparable average life PAC bonds—in fact, the five-year balloon product will meet those requirements at origina-

---

[4] For investors who purchase the mortgages that were taken out to repay balloon mortgages, the credit-related aspects of valuation become somewhat more complicated. Most of the limited requalification options offered to borrowers are offered at a rate to be set at some positive spread to then current fixed-rate origination rates, allowing borrowers who are willing to undergo the full requalification process the opportunity to save money on a loan from a different lender. In cases where those savings are significant, this could lead to a selection bias in refinancing choices, where borrowers who are unable to meet the more stringent qualifications for a new loan from a different lender opt for what amounts to an extension option with the original lender, at a relatively high rate. These borrowers are likely to be poorer credit risks, which will have an effect on the value of the securities backed by these mortgages. Since it will be several more years before we have loans of this sort available in the secondary market, a discussion of their value would seem premature. However, loans that reset once prior to maturity may experience a similar selection bias, as we describe in the section on two-step loans.

[5] Dollar rolls are discussed in Chapter 38.

Exhibit 4: Seven-Year Balloon Pool Issuance by Month—*Since January 1990*

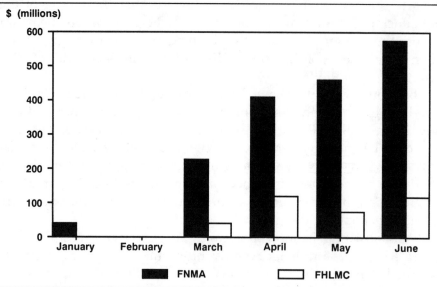

Exhibit 5: Outstanding Balance of 7-Year Balloon Pools—*As of July 1990*

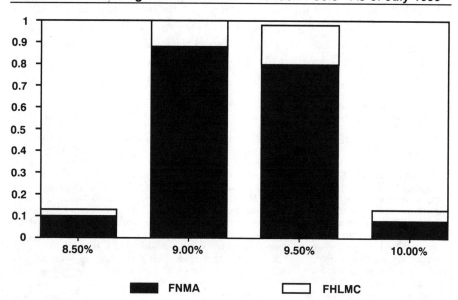

tion. Typically, bonds that qualify for thrift liquidity have traded at tighter yield spreads to Treasuries than similar bonds that do not meet the requirements.

Exhibit 6 shows an example of a comparison between an investment in a 9.5% FNMA balloon mortgage pool, fifteen-year FNMA 9.5s, and the FHLMC 185 C PAC illustrated earlier. The balloon mortgage has somewhat greater average life variability than the PAC—essentially call risk as opposed to extension risk, since the balloon cannot possibly extend beyond seven years even

Exhibit 6: Comparative Valuation Analysis - As of July 12, 1990

Yield/Average Life Analysis

				Average Life				
Bond	Price	Yield	Spd/Tsy	-200	-100	0	100	200
FH 185C	98-17	9.34	+84/5 yr	4.1	5.7	5.7	5.7	5.7
FNMA Balloon 9.5s	100-15	9.43	+93/5 yr	3.4	4.5	4.9	5.1	5.3
FNMA 15-Yr 9.5s	99-31	9.55	+94/7 yr	3.9	4.9	6.1	6.6	6.8

OAS Analysis*

Bond	Price	Option Adjusted Duration	Static Spread	OAS	Option Cost
FH 185C	98-17	3.86	71	63	8
FNMA Balloon 9.5s	100-15	3.62	81	65	16
FNMA 15-Yr 9.5s	99-31	3.74	91	67	24

*   The Static Spread evaluates cash flows by spreading them over the entire Treasury forward rate curve rather thanover a single Treasury issue. The OAS analysis assumes 12% short rate volatility. Prepayments for balloon pools are generated with our 30-year fixed rate prepayment model.

with absolutely no prepayments—but shows greater stability than the fifteen-year pass-through. On a yield spread basis, therefore, the balloon pool is priced wider than the PAC and slightly narrower than the fifteen-year pass-through. On an option-adjusted basis, which measures and adjusts for the differential option costs embedded in the mortgage structures, the balloon mortgage offers a wider option-adjusted spread (OAS)[6] than the PAC bond and a slightly narrower OAS than the fifteen-year mortgage, indicating that the market currently requires excessive yield compensation for the greater option cost associated with balloon and fifteen-year mortgages. In addition, the balloon pool will qualify for thrift liquidity in two years; the fifteen-year pool and PAC bond will not. Also, the valuation analysis for the fifteen-year pool is much more sensitive to the accuracy of the prepayment model used. This analysis suggests that even those willing to bear the greater prepayment risk of a fifteen-year security may still find balloon pools relatively attractive at these levels, while those who ordinarily buy PACs for stability and prepayment protection will also find some appealing opportunities in the balloon sector.

Ordinarily, any discussion of a new mortgage product would dwell extensively on the likely prepayment behavior of the underlying borrowers. With balloon pools, some complacency on this issue is justified, since, similar to an investment in PAC bonds, the value of an investment in balloon pools is relatively insensitive to the prepayment assumption used to value the pools. Much of the insensitivity derives from the security's short final maturity. Another determinant is the fact that most of the balloon pools currently trading are priced relatively close to par.

There are at least two schools of thought on the likely prepayment behavior of balloon borrowers. One theory suggests that conforming balloon borrowers have selected this type of mortgage because they believe they are likely to move before the balloon date, and thus pools backed by these mortgages will prepay faster than otherwise similar pools backed by generic fixed-rate loans. A

---

[6] OAS technology is described in Chapter 27.

second theory suggests that the lower rate offered to balloon borrowers will tend to attract a wide range of borrowers, including the marginal borrowers who are less able to afford their housing purchase. This theory suggests that the balloon pools would prepay similarly to or perhaps more slowly than generic thirty-year pools. At this point, there is little evidence to support or contradict either assumption.

We do know where current balloon borrowers live, however, as shown in Exhibit 7, which highlights the geographic concentrations of existing balloon pools. The high percentage of California loans in many existing pools suggests that in the short run, those balloon pools will probably prepay faster than our national thirty-year fixed-rate prepayment model would project without a correction for such geographic concentration. If the popularity of the balloon product continues to grow with lenders—as we expect—

Exhibit 7: Geographic Breakdown of FNMA 7-Year Balloon Pools - *As of July 1990*

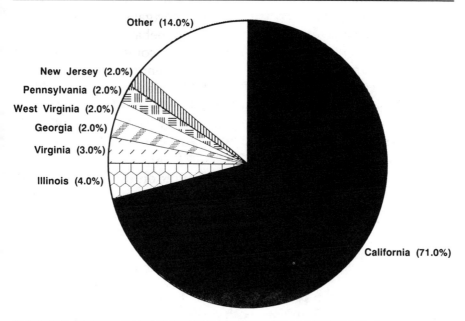

Exhibit 8: Balloon Prepayment Sensitivity

Change in OAS at Multiple of Prepayment Model

Security	Price	OAS	70%	80%	90%	100%	110%	120%	130%
BAL 8.5s	97-05	53	-2	-1	0	0	1	1	2
BAL 9s	99-01	55	2	1	1	0	0	0	0
BAL 9.5s	100-15	65	4	3	2	0	-1	-2	-3
BAL 10s	101-24	75	8	5	3	0	-2	-4	-6

Change in Price at Constant OAS

Security	70%	80%	90%	100%	110%	120%	130%
BAL 8.5s	($0.08)	($0.04)	($0.00)	$0.00	$0.04	$0.04	$0.08
BAL 9s	$0.08	$0.40	$0.04	$0.00	$0.00	$0.00	$0.00
BAL 9.5s	$0.16	$0.12	$0.08	$0.00	($0.04)	($0.08)	($0.12)
BAL 10s	$0.31	$0.20	$0.12	$0.00	($0.08)	($0.16)	($0.23)

the geographic diversification of the balloon market should increase over time. Similarly, we also know who the current servicers of balloon pools are; because of the relative newness of the product, this list is also fairly concentrated. Because some servicers are more efficient than others at soliciting refinancings, this might also shade our prepayment projections.

In any event, the current impact of varying our prepayment projections is relatively limited. Exhibit 8 shows the impact on the value of balloon mortgage pools of varying our prepayment projections from 70 to 130% of our current model for generic thirty-year fixed-rate loans, expressed in both OAS and price terms. The impact on value is not dramatic even for the premiums, allowing investors to invest comfortably in balloon pools even without a strong view on prepayments.

"TWO-STEP" MORTGAGE LOANS

Akin to the idea of a balloon loan with a refinancing option for the borrower is a fixed-rate loan with a single rate reset at some point prior to maturity. Unlike a refinancing option, this rate reset occurs without specific action on the part of the borrower.

One example of this structure is the so-called "two-step" loan structure, in which a loan carries a fixed rate for some period, usually seven years, and then resets once. The rate reset can be based on any rate; currently FNMA's two-step mortgage purchase program specifies that the new rate be calculated by adding 250 basis points to a weekly average of the ten-year constant maturity Treasury yield. FNMA also limits any increase in the mortgage rate to no more than 600 basis points over the initial mortgage rate; other cap levels may become popular as well. Unlike in balloon mortgages, the rate reset on the two-step does not consist of a repayment of the initial loan and the origination of a new one; thus, a pool backed by two-step loans has a thirty-year final maturity, rather than the shorter final maturity of a balloon pool. Essentially, then, the two-step mortgage is an adjustable-rate mortgage with a single reset. The borrower is compensated for assuming the rate reset risk by an initial mortgage rate that is about 0.375 percentage points lower than the generic thirty-year fixed rate.

To date, these mortgages have not been issued in securitized form by either FNMA or FHLMC, nor have they traded in securitized form with other means of credit enhancement.[7] It is likely that we will see this product in the secondary market some time in the near future. It presents an interesting valuation challenge.

In effect, the lender or investor who holds the two-step mortgage has extended an additional option to the borrower—the option to extend the loan when the available market rate at the reset date is more than 250 basis points above the ten-year Treasury rate. If the available mortgage rate from other lenders is less than 250 basis points above that of the ten-year Treasury, the borrower can prepay the two-step loan and achieve financing at a lower rate. In a rational world without transaction costs, this two-step

---

[7] However, convertible ARMs, which present some of the same challenges, have been securitized in both agency and double-A format.

loan would have to trade at wider levels than a balloon loan with a maturity equal to the reset date of the two-step loan, because the two-step is short one additional option that has some positive value.

However, because borrowers will not always prepay rationally and there are transaction costs associated with refinancing a loan, the reset may actually have some positive value to investors. For instance, it is likely that at the reset date there will be some borrowers in the pool who are unable to prepay their two-step loans, even if the new rate is higher than currently available fixed rates, because they are unable to qualify for the new loan. They may be unemployed, for instance, or the value of the property may have declined, requiring an additional down payment.[8] Also, the difference between the new rate on the two-step and the current mortgage rate may not be large enough to compensate borrowers for the costs of arranging a new loan.

For example, a two-step that reset at 250 basis points over the ten-year Treasury when generic mortgage rates were 200 basis points over the ten-year may not experience significant prepayments, but would offer enhanced value to investors. Because of the points typically charged for the origination of a mortgage, the borrowers' choice would also probably be a function of how long they expected to remain in their home. A borrower with a relatively short horizon over which to amortize the points on a new loan is more likely to accept the reset even if it means paying a relatively high mortgage rate versus the prevailing market.

The additional value offered by these types of borrower behavior may also be a function of the form of the investors' two-step mortgage holdings. Take, for instance, a nonagency pool where only the weakest borrower credits remained after a rate reset that was significantly above prevailing market rates. Such a pool could suffer an impairment in value as a result.

---

[8] This process of adverse selection also occurs in premium thirty-year mortgage pools, of course, and explains why some borrowers never prepay their high-rate mortgages.

Exhibit 9: Analysis of Two-Step Mortgage Pools

Security*	Price	Option-Adjusted Duration	Static Spread	OAS	Vs. Comparable Coupon FNMA Balloon		
					Option Cost	Balloon Duration	Balloon OAS
Two-Step 8.5s	97-05	4.36	88	66	22	4.10	53
Two-Step 9s	99-01	4.05	93	68	25	3.89	55
Two-Step 9.5s	100-15	3.70	104	76	28	3.62	65
Two-Step 10s	101-24	3.31	117	84	33	3.28	75

* Assumes 45-day delay, a gross WAC 75 basis points higher than the coupon, and a rate reset in seven years.

Exhibit 9 presents an analysis of the two-step mortgage and its current value if it traded at prices identical to balloon mortgages.[9] The analysis reflects the probable impact of transaction costs associated with refinancing a loan, because it employs our current prepayment model for thirty-year fixed-rate mortgages. This model considers the transaction costs historically incurred by borrowers, but does not assume an explicit relationship between the absolute level of interest rates and level of the mortgage/Treasury spread.[10] The exhibit suggests that the mortgagor's extension option actually has some value to the investor. If we ignore other market forces, this option makes the otherwise comparable two-step pool somewhat more valuable than a balloon pool at current levels of

[9] Although two-step mortgage pools are not actively traded in the secondary market at this time, it is reasonable to assume that they would trade at prices close to those of seven-year balloon pools of similar credit quality and coupon. In seven years, the balloon pool produces a bulk repayment of principal that must be reinvested at prevailing rates; the two-step contains an automatic coupon reset that is intended to place the new mortgage rate somewhere close to current rates. In the analysis that follows, we value the benefit (or cost) of the two-step mortgage's automatic reset at a fixed spread to the ten-year Treasury.

[10] In fact, when observations are taken from a period between January 1985 and May 1990, models of the mortgage/Treasury spread that include the level of rates, the shape of the curve (as measured by the yield spread between the two- and ten-year Treasuries), implied volatility, and the previous period's mortgage spread shows that the yield levels do not share a statistically significant relationship with the level of the mortgage/Treasury spread. Nor are changes in the level of yields particularly helpful in predicting changes in the level of the mortgage/Treasury spread.

Exhibit 10: Impact of Varying the Reset Margin on a 9.5% Two-Step Loan Pool

Reset Margin Over the 10-Year Treasury	Price Change Versus Base Case
50 bp	($1.28)
100	($0.88)
150	($0.52)
200	($0.23)
250 Base Case	$0.00
300	$0.16
350	$0.30

the mortgage/Treasury spread. The relative advantage declines as the coupon rises. However, the market will not necessarily trade them in this fashion, because many investors prefer a more certain final maturity.

Our conclusion that the extension option currently has slight positive value to the investor is also predicated on current levels of the mortgage/Treasury spread. However, the impact of the mortgage/Treasury spread assumption is indirectly reflected in Exhibit 10, which shows the incremental impact on value of varying the contractual margin over the ten-year Treasury from which the two-step mortgage rate resets at the end of seven years. Note that the value of the two-step pool declines as the margin declines (or the mortgage/Treasury spread increases). In fact, below a margin of roughly 150 basis points, the 9.5% two-step pool would be worth less than a comparable coupon balloon pool, because the reset option of successively lower margins has value to the mortgage borrowers.

FIXED/ADJUSTABLE-RATE MORTGAGE HYBRIDS

Another type of mortgage loan structure that has experienced growing popularity is the fixed/ARM mortgage hybrid. Typically, these mortgages are originated with fixed rates for their first five, seven, or ten years, after which the interest rate on the loan begins floating with contractual characteristics similar to those of current ARM structures. For instance, one popular hybrid structure carries a fixed rate for five years, and thereafter has a floating rate that resets every six months at a margin over the six-month CD index. Like many other ARMs, the coupon is subject to both periodic and lifetime limitations on the rate change. Other fixed/ARM hybrids turn into one-year Treasury ARMs, or monthly Eleventh District Cost of Funds Index (COFI) ARMs after their fixed period. In many cases, the first coupon reset is not subject to any periodic caps that may apply to later coupon resets, and instead is subject only to the lifetime cap.

Although this mortgage structure is a combination of two types of products with which the market is very familiar, the combination presents some unique valuation challenges. The first involves a choice of a prepayment model. Will the borrowers of this product prepay like fixed-rate borrowers or like ARM borrowers? Historically, these two borrower groups have responded differently to similar refinancing incentives. Exhibit 11 illustrates how those historical differences are reflected in our current prepayment models for both borrower types: it shows our projected prepayments for a new 10% conventional fixed-rate mortgage versus the projected prepayments for an ARM with 2% periodic caps and contractual features set so that its coupon, too, is always 10%. In addition to the differences in seasoning and absolute level illustrated here, our ARM prepayment model also embodies less interest rate sensitivity than our fixed-rate prepayment model.

A survey of demographic differences (other than regional location) between borrower types may provide some insight into a prepayment model choice. However, the fluidity of the origination market in recent years, when ARM originations rose to over 70% of total originations, only to drop back to less than 25%, will obfuscate comparisons. Also, the demographics of hybrid borrowers may not be readily available. As an alternative, investors may also speculate that aversion to a variable mortgage rate and payment schedule is what causes borrowers to prepay ARMs so quickly, in

Exhibit 11: Projected Prepayment Speeds for a Fixed 10% Coupon

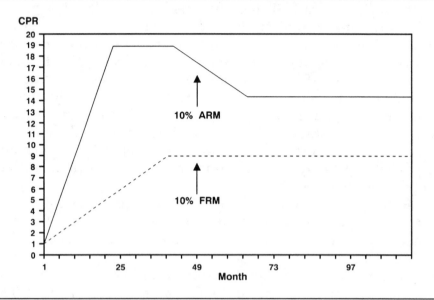

which case they might employ a fixed-rate prepayment model for the fixed period of a hybrid pool's life, and an ARM model thereafter.

In the absence of any prepayment history on the hybrid mortgages, we lean toward using a fixed-rate prepayment model with corrections for any geographic concentrations that exist in the hybrid pools, when they become available. Exhibit 12 shows the results of analysis of hypothetical hybrid pools, illustrating the contractual evolution from an ARM to a hybrid. It shows the structures' relative insensitivity to many of the ARM parameters that will be in force after the fixed-rate period. As the analysis suggests, the level of the lifetime cap on the hybrid structures has less of an impact on the value of the security at origination than do the lifetime caps on an ARM. Periodic caps are also more important to ARM value than to the value of the hybrid, because they take effect later in the securities' lives. This particular structure assumes that the periodic caps are not applied to the first

Exhibit 12: Hybrid FRM/ARM Sensitivity Analysis

Security Description		Base Case Price	Base Case OAS
Tsy ARM:	9.5% one-year Treasury ARM, 348 WAM, 200 bp margin, 2% periodic caps, 13% life cap, 12 MTR	101-27	100
5-yr Hybrid:	9.5% fixed for five years, then resets annually at 200 bp over the one-yr Treasury, 2% periodic caps after first adjustment, 13% life cap	100-19	100
7-yr Hybrid:	same as 5-year except first reset occurs in seven years	99-18	100

Impact of Periodic Caps
Change in Price From Base Case
For Various Life Caps

Security	12%	13%	14%	15%
Tsy ARM	($0.44)	$0.00	$0.28	$0.41
5-yr Hybrid	($0.40)	$0.00	$0.21	$0.32
7-yr Hybrid	($0.32)	$0.00	$0.18	$0.29

Impact of Periodic Caps
Change in Price From Base Case
For Various Periodic Caps

Security	1%	2%	3%	99%
Tsy ARM	($0.38)	$0.00	$0.09	$0.09
5-yr Hybrid	($0.13)	$0.00	$0.03	$0.04
7-yr Hybrid	($0.10)	$0.00	$0.03	$0.04

Impact of ARM Choice
Change in Price For
ARM Structure Choice

Security	Fixed/ COFI ARM*	Fixed/1 yr Tsy ARM	Fixed/5 yr Tsy ARM**
5-yr Hybrid	($1.08)	$0.00	($0.54)
7-yr Hybrid	($0.67)	$0.00	($0.40)

* Resets to monthly COFI ARM with 13% life cap.
** Resets to five-year Treasury ARM with other contractual features similar to the one-year Treasury ARM described above.

reset—a common structural innovation. Hybrid mortgages that applied the periodic caps to that first reset would show greater sensitivity to their level. The choice of index for the hybrid is of particular importance, as the analysis suggests. In fact, the index choice is also important to the marketability of the hybrid today; an esoteric index demands an additional liquidity premium.

CONCLUSION

With the exception of TPMs, the new products discussed here are really unique combinations of features with which the secondary market is already familiar: short final maturities, resettable rates, lifetime caps, and so on. As such, the primary challenge in valuing them is assessing the likely prepayment behavior of the borrowers who take out these loans. Although it will be some time before we have sufficient data to determine whether these borrowers will behave differently from those that take out traditional thirty-year fixed-rate loans, the valuation of these new loan types is, in general, less sensitive to the prepayment assumption than are otherwise similar generic thirty-year pass-throughs.

Investors are likely to see all of these structures—balloon mortgages, two-step mortgages, and fixed/ARM hybrids—grow in importance in the secondary market in the near term. Other permutations are also likely. Option-adjusted analysis of these structures will readily place them within a fundamental framework of value, but investors will still be left with the job of assessing the long-term viability of these products. As discussed in this chapter, many of these mortgage structures have obvious portfolio applications and offer values that compare favorably to existing products. Others will probably offer premiums to investors willing to do the additional homework to understand their structures. In either case, we believe that the cash flow characteristics and the potential returns available merit serious consideration from investors seeking high relative value opportunities in the intermediate maturity sector.

SECTION II

PASS-THROUGH SECURITIES

CHAPTER 4

MORTGAGE PASS-THROUGH SECURITIES

Linda Lowell
Vice President, Head
Mortgage Investment Strategies
Smith Barney, Harris Upham & Co., Inc.

Pass-throughs are the predominant form of mortgage-related security, so much so that the terms "mortgage-backed security," "MBS," and "pass-through" have become interchangeable in common usage. The scope of the MBS market extends, as well, to structured mortgage securities such as CMOs, REMICs, and Strips, for which pass-throughs are the most common form of collateral.

The pass-through market has achieved dramatic growth in the 1980s. Pass-throughs have fostered an extensive and stable secondary market for housing debt and, in recent years, spurred the securitization of other receivables such as automobile and credit card loans. By the end of the third quarter of 1990, there were approximately $1.0 trillion of agency pass-throughs outstanding; by comparison, the size of the high-grade corporate bond market was over $800 billion, and the marketable Treasury security market about $2.1 trillion.[1] Burgeoning investor interest has been a key factor spurring this tremendous growth. Pass-through securities are extensively held by every class of institutional investor, including commercial banks and savings institutions, insurance companies, mutual funds, and pension plans.

This growth has been fostered by the federal government's concern for the availability of housing and of mortgage credit. The involvement of three government-sponsored agencies has lent the market the stability, credit support, and standardization necessary to attract investors traditionally committed to the corporate and Treasury sectors of the debt market, as well as to encourage the participation of private guarantor/issuers.

The pass-through structure has proved to be an excellent vehicle for securitizing many different types of mortgage instruments available to home buyers. As a result, in addition to the standard level payment mortgage, large amounts of adjustable-rate mortgages and graduated payment mortgages have been securitized.

This chapter is intended to provide an overview of the variety of pass-through types and an introduction to the general structure and analysis of level payment pass-throughs, the largest and most frequently traded form of MBSs. The discussion then moves to the features of pass-throughs that distinguish them from noncallable corporate or Treasury debt instruments and that give them their market properties. The chapter concludes with a discussion of the economic or total rate of return performance of pass-throughs in various interest rate scenarios, and a relative value analysis of these securities. Methodologies for analyzing pass-through securities are discussed in greater detail in later chapters.

WHAT IS A MORTGAGE PASS-THROUGH SECURITY?

Pass-through securities are created when mortgages are pooled together, and undivided interests or participations in the pool are

---

[1] Taken from the *Federal Reserve Bulletin.*

sold. The originator (or another institution that purchases this right) continues to service the mortgages, collecting payments and "passing through" the principal and interest, less the servicing, guarantee, and other fees, to the security holders. The security holders receive pro rata shares of the resultant cash flows. A portion of the outstanding principal is paid each month according to the amortization schedules established for each individual mortgage. In addition, and this is a critical feature of mortgage pass-through securities, the principal on individual mortgages in the pool can be prepaid without penalty in whole or in part at any time before the stated maturity of the security. This characteristic has important implications for the price and yield of the security, as will be explored in detail later.

Mortgage originators (savings and loans, commercial banks, and mortgage bankers) actively pool mortgages and issue pass-throughs. In most cases, the originator obtains the guarantee of one of three federally sponsored agencies, GNMA (the Government National Mortgage Association, or "Ginnie Mae"), FNMA (the Federal National Mortgage Association, or "Fannie Mae") and FHLMC (the Federal Home Loan Mortgage Corporation, or "Freddie Mac"). A significant volume of mortgages is directly purchased, pooled, and securitized by the agencies as well. A smaller amount of mortgages is securitized directly by private issuers.

AGENCY PASS-THROUGH SECURITIES

The vast majority of regularly traded pass-throughs are issued and/or guaranteed by federally sponsored agencies. Differences between the agencies—the nature of their ties to the U.S. Government, their stated role in national housing policy, and so forth, affect the relative value and performance of their pass-throughs. In addition, considerable diversity exists within each agency's pass-through programs and differences exist between programs, which also influence the investment characteristics of the securities. For this reason, the agencies and their major programs are discussed in some detail.

The market generally classifies agency pass-throughs into two groups: those guaranteed by GNMA, and those guaranteed by FHLMC and FNMA. Since GNMA is part of the Department of Housing and Urban Development, it is an arm of the U.S. government. As such, a GNMA guarantee carries the full faith and credit of the U.S. government. FHLMC and FNMA are not government-related agencies; they are government-sponsored entities (GSEs). As such, their guarantee does not carry the full faith and credit of the U.S. government. In fact, at the time of this writing, the executive and legislative branches of the U.S. government are exploring the precise status of GSEs and the meaning of their guarantee.

The market perceives a difference in credit quality between GNMA and FHMLC/FNMA, and, as a consequence, demands a risk premium for the pass-throughs guaranteed by the latter. Typically, all other factors being equal, this would translate into a higher yield for the GSE-guaranteed issues. However, the vigorous participation of FNMA and FHLMC in the MBS derivative market as issuers of CMOs and Strips, has helped to bid up the price of these securities relative to GNMAs, largely obscuring the credit premium. In coupon classes that are unlikely to be used as CMO collateral or when market conditions temporarily halt CMO creation, perceived differences in credit quality result in wider price differentials.[2]

Conventional loans backing FHLMC and FNMA pass-throughs are due on sale, in contrast to FHA and VA loans, which can be assumed by the buyer. This is one of the features leading to notable differences in the prepayment characteristics of FHLMC and FNMA securities on the one hand, and GNMA securities on the

---

[2] Since 1984, the creation of derivative mortgage-backed securities has proceeded at such a brisk pace that the supply of many pass-through securities has been sharply reduced. As of the end of 1989, almost 50% of the outstanding principal amount of conventional pass-throughs with half or whole coupons (the more liquid of the tradable coupon classes) has been pledged to CMOs or Strips, and can no longer trade. By contrast only about 20% of the outstanding amount of frequently traded GNMA coupon classes has been pledged to structured products.

other, differences that affect the relative value of the securities. Other fundamental differences between conventional and FHA/VA mortgages include the fact that FHA and VA loans provide implicit housing subsidies to people with moderate incomes and to veterans, so that the rates tend to be below those for conventional mortgages. Similarly, the ceiling on VA and FHA loans is lower than that on the conventional loans pooled in FHLMCs.[3] In general, it is assumed that people with conventional mortgages are wealthier and more mobile than those with FHA and VA mortgages.

Government National Mortgage Association Pass-Through Securities

The largest and best-known group of pass-through securities is guaranteed by GNMA. The mortgage pools underlying GNMA pass-through securities are made up of FHA-insured or VA-guaranteed mortgage loans. GNMA pass-throughs are backed by the full faith and credit of the U.S. government.

Furthermore, the GNMA pass-through security is what is known as a *fully modified* pass-through security, which means that regardless of whether the mortgage payment is made, the holder of the security will receive full and timely payment of principal and interest. Among MBSs, GNMA is considered to be of the best credit quality, since it is backed directly by the U.S. government.

GNMA administers two primary pass-through programs, the original GNMA program (GNMA I), in existence since 1970, and GNMA II, established in 1983. The GNMA I and II programs are further divided into pool types depending on the type of mortgages and other characteristics of the pool. The most commonly held and traded of all pass-through types represents pools of thirty-year maturity, fixed-rate, level payment mortgages on single-family residential homes (SF). The GNMA SF pool type is cre-

---

[3] The current maximum VA loan amount is $144,000; the FHA maximum loan amount is $124,875. The maximum applies in high-cost areas such as new New York. The FNMA and FHLMC ceiling is $191,250; loan limits are higher in high-cost areas.

ated in both the GNMA I and GNMA II programs. Single-family mortgages with original maturities of fifteen years are part of the same SF pool type; the pools are called GNMA "Midgets" and differ from the thirty-year securities only in stated maturity.

GNMA pool types are based on other types of single-family mortgages as well, including graduated payment (GPM), growing equity (GEM), buydown (BD), and adjustable-rate (ARM) loans. Markets for these securities are smaller and less liquid than for the traditional GNMA SFs, and the differences between the underlying mortgages have important consequences for analysis of the securities' characteristics. Mobile home loans (MH) and project loans (PL) are also securitized. Project loan securities are normally backed by a single FHA-insured loan for multifamily housing, hospitals, and similar public benefit housing-related projects. Construction loans for projects are also securitized as CL pool types.

Among the various agency and private pass-through programs, GNMA pools are the most homogeneous. All mortgages in a pool must be of the same type and be less than twelve months old. Ninety percent of the pooled mortgages backing thirty-year pass-throughs must have original maturities of twenty or more years. The mortgage interest rates of GNMA I pools must all be the same and the mortgages must be issued by the same lender. The changes introduced with GNMA II include the ability to assemble multiple issuer pools, thereby allowing for larger and more geographically dispersed pools, as well as securitization of smaller portfolios. Also, a wider range of coupons is permitted in a GNMA II pool (the excess coupon income over the lowest rate is retained by the issuer or servicer as servicing income and is not passed through). Issuers are permitted to take greater servicing fees, ranging from 50 to 150 basis points. GNMA Is and IIs also differ in permitted payment delay; GNMA I payments are received with a fifteen-day delay, while GNMA IIs have an additional five-day delay passing through principal and interest payments because issuer payments are consolidated by a central paying agent. Finally, GNMA II requires a larger minimum pool size—$7 million principal value in contrast to the $1 million required for GNMA I pools.

Federal Home Loan Mortgage Corporation Participation Certificates

FHLMC was created in 1970 to promote an active national secondary market for conventional residential mortgages, and has been issuing mortgage-backed securities since 1971. At its creation, FHLMC was governed as an entity within the Federal Home Loan Bank System, with stock held by member thrift institutions. The 1989 Financial Institutions Reform, Recovery, and Enforcement Act (FIRREA) restructured FHLMC to give it a market-oriented corporate structure similar to that of FNMA under the regulatory control of the Department of Housing and Urban Development (HUD).

The agency pools a wide variety of fixed- and adjustable-rate mortgages under its Cash and Guarantor programs. The largest of these pass-through programs are the single-family, fixed-rate fifteen- and thirty-year Participation Certificates (PCs). Under the Cash program, FHLMC purchases conventional mortgage loans on owner occupied one-to-four family homes and participations from originators, pools them (minimum pool size is $50 million), and sells undivided interest in them as PCs. The Guarantor program was originally established to provide liquidity to the thrift industry by allowing originators to swap pooled mortgages (minimum pool size $1 million) for PCs in those same pools (hence these are sometimes called swap PCs). The certificates can be held, used as collateral for short- and long-term borrowings, or sold. This program quickly became popular with nonthrift mortgage originators as well, and now accounts for the bulk of FHLMC pass-through production.

In June 1990, FHLMC announced a major change in its pass-through programs. In particular, securities issued beginning in September 1990 have a stronger guarantee and a shorter payment delay. Historically, in its larger programs, FHLMC guaranteed the *timely* payment of interest and the *eventual* payment of principal. (Such securities are modified in contrast to GNMAs, which are "fully modified," as they guarantee the timely payment of both interest and principal.) A number of less liquid, smaller programs provided fully modified pass-throughs as well. The new Gold PCs are fully modified. Pass-throughs issued prior to September had seventy-five-day stated payment delays; under the new program the stated delay is shortened to forty-five days.

Mortgages underlying both the FHLMC regular and swap PCs are permitted to have original maturities of not less than fifteen or more than thirty years. Seasoned mortgages (mortgages outstanding for some time) are also permitted. Consequently, the actual life of the investment may differ significantly from the stated maturity of the security. Coupons also vary much more widely within a pool than with GNMA securities, but in this feature there are important differences between regular and swap PCs. Coupons of mortgages in swap pools must be above the pass-through rate, and may be as much as 250 basis points above the pass-through rate. In contrast, regular PC pools contain mortgages with rates up to 200 basis points above the pass-through rate, but the range between the highest and lowest mortgage rate may not exceed 100 basis points. Mortgages even may have interest rates below the coupon on the pool. This wide dispersion of mortgage rates can have a significant impact on the ability of investors to measure actual prepayments and to analyze the prepayment risk of the resulting security.

FHLMC regular and swap securities also are issued with fifteen-year maturities. (The shorter maturity regular PC is known as a "Gnome," the swap as a "non-Gnome.") These mortgages have original maturities of not less than ten years. In addition, FHLMC has both cash and guarantor FHA/VA programs, normally containing FHA/VA loans too seasoned for inclusion in GNMA pools. FHLMC also offers FHA/VA, ARM, and multifamily-backed securities, generally under both the cash and guarantor programs.

Federal National Mortgage Association Mortgage-Backed Securities

The Federal National Mortgage Association is the oldest of the three agencies, but the newest agency player in the pass-through market. FNMA was created in 1938 to provide liquidity to housing lenders. In 1968, the agency was split into GNMA and the private corporation FNMA, which was charged with the mission of promoting a secondary market for conventional mortgages on mid-priced housing and seasoned FHA/VA single and multifamily mortgages. The first FNMA MBSs were issued in 1981. FNMA is, in effect, a quasi-private corporation. While a number of federal constraints on its activities exist, it does not receive a government subsidy or appropriation, its stock is traded on the New York Stock Exchange, and it is taxed at the full corporate rate. In addition to holding loans purchased from originators in its portfolio, FNMA also may securitize and sell the mortgages. FNMA pools mortgages from its purchase programs and issues MBSs through a swap program similar to FHLMC's. Like GNMA, FNMA guarantees the timely payment of principal and interest for all securities it issues. Similarly, its securities are not rated by the rating agencies.

The thirty-year conventional security, FNMA CL, is based on level payment mortgages fully amortizing in sixteen to thirty years. FNMA also issues securities based on conventional mortgages amortizing in eight to fifteen years, FNMA CIs or Dwarfs. The agency also has played a significant role in issuing adjustable- and variable-rate mortgage pass-throughs. In addition, it administers programs to securitize FHA and VA thirty-year loans and FHA-insured project loans.

Pool size starts at $1 million and more than one originator may join together to form pools. FNMA pools may contain both new and aged mortgages, and coupons are permitted to vary in a range of 200 basis points, from 0.5% to 2.5% above the pass-through rate.

Private Pass-Through Securities

Mortgage pass-throughs are also issued by private entities such as commercial banks, thrifts, homebuilders, and private conduits. These issues are referred to as conventional pass-throughs, private label or "double-A" pass-throughs. The supply of these securities, roughly $5 to $6 billion a year, is very small in comparison to that of agency pass-throughs. These securities are not guaranteed or insured by any government agency. Instead, their credit is normally enhanced by pool insurance, letters of credit, guarantees, or subordinated interests. The great majority of private pass-throughs issued have received a rating of "AA" or better.

Private issuers provide a secondary market for conventional loans that do not qualify for FHLMC and FNMA programs. Normally, it is more profitable for originators of conforming loans (i.e., loans that do qualify for an agency security) to use the agency programs. There are a number of reasons why conventional mortgage loans may not qualify, but the chief one is that the principal balance exceeds the maximum allowed by the government (these are called "jumbo" loans in the market). Another significant difference from GSE pass-throughs is that there is no limitation by private issuers on the range of underlying mortgage rates above the pass-through coupon, or on servicing and guarantee fees. These features will influence the prepayment characteristics of private pass-throughs.

A more detailed discussion of private pass-throughs is provided in Chapters 6 and 7.

MORTGAGE AND PASS-THROUGH CASH FLOWS

The investment characteristics and performance of pass-throughs cannot be evaluated without a thorough understanding of what cash flows are received by the investor. Analysis of the cash flow pattern begins with the simplest case, the payment stream of a single mortgage, assuming a fixed mortgage rate, level payments, and no prepayment of principal. Following that, the effects of servicing fees (the amount retained by a servicer reduces the cash flow to pass-through holders) and prepayments on a pool of such mortgages are incorporated into the analysis.

Standard residential fixed-rate mortgages are repaid in equal monthly installments of principal and interest (hence, the term *level payment*). In the early years, most of the monthly installment consists of interest. Over time, the interest portion of each payment declines as the principal balance declines until, near maturity, almost all of each payment is principal.

Given the assumption that all of the mortgages have the same interest rates and maturities, the scheduled cash flow pattern from a mortgage pool is the same as that of an individual mortgage. Exhibit 1 shows the scheduled cash flow pattern for a $1 million pool of 10%, thirty-year mortgages without prepayments. Because there is a fixed rate of interest on the loan and no prepayments occur, the total mortgage cash flow is level over all periods. When the assumption that all the mortgages in the pool are identical is relaxed, the scheduled principal and interest payments cannot be

**Exhibit 1: Scheduled Mortgage Pool Cash Flows
($1 Million Pool of 10% 30-Year Mortgages)**

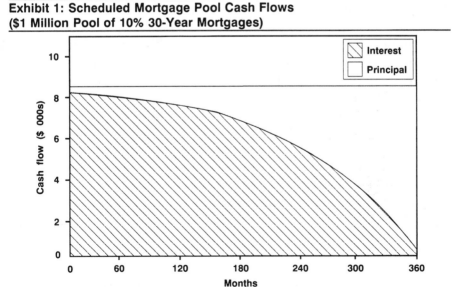

Note: Assumes no prepayments.

calculated with absolute accuracy unless they are determined for each individual mortgage and then aggregated. By treating the pool like a single mortgage and calculating principal and interest payments using the weighted average coupon (WAC) and maturity (WAM) for the pool,[4] it is possible to project the payments with reasonable accuracy when pools are fairly homogeneous, as GNMA pools are. (The discrepancy arises from the fact that amortization is not a "linear" function. Individual loans will be paying principal and interest at different rates depending on the age and term of the loan.) The accuracy of projected amortization schedules using WAC and WAM statistics is reduced somewhat when a wide range of coupons, maturities, and seasonings is permitted in a pool.

The cash flow from a pass-through certificate is similar but not identical to the cash flow from the underlying pool of mortgages. The differences arise from the deduction of servicing fees and a delay in the receipt of payments. While the scheduled total monthly cash flow from the mortgage pool is level, the cash flow from the corresponding pass-through is not. The servicing fee is defined as a percentage of the outstanding principal, and is subtracted from the interest paid on the underlying mortgages. The remaining interest income is passed through to the security holder as coupon income. (In other words, servicing is equal to the WAC less the coupon.) Thus the dollar amount of servicing fee decreases as principal declines. As a consequence, the total cash flows to pass-through owners increase slightly over the term. The cash flow from a pass-through certificate with a 9.5% coupon (the difference between the 10% WAC and a 0.5% servicing fee) is depicted in Exhibit 2. The graph shows that the decline in servicing fees leads to slightly increasing cash flow over time.

The delay does not alter the level of payments, but it does affect their timing. In effect, it pushes the stream of payments further out in time and effectively lowers the current value of the

---

[4] The WAC and WAM are computed using as weights the principal amount outstanding.

Exhibit 2: Scheduled Mortgage-Backed Security Cash Flows ($1 Million Pool of 10%, Thirty-Year Mortgages and a 9.5% Pass-Through Certificate).

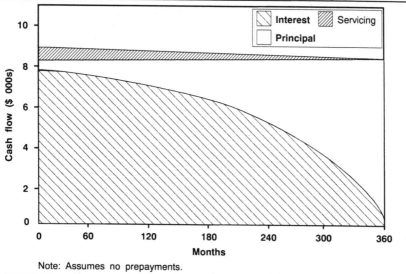

Note: Assumes no prepayments.

payment stream. There are two sources of payment delay in pass-throughs. Mortgage payments are made in arrears; that is, the first mortgage payment is due from the homeowner at the beginning of the second month after origination. Second, as a result of processing the payment, the holder of the corresponding pass-through does not receive this payment until later. An investor in a GNMA single-family pass-through, for example, does not receive payment until the fifteenth day of the second month. A GNMA trader will express that fifteen-day actual delay as a forty-five-day delay so as to include the normal mortgage delay of the preceding thirty-day month. FNMA securities have a stated delay of fifty-five days, which means the first payment takes place on the twenty-fifth day of the second month. Older FHLMC securities have a seventy-five-day delay, while newer Gold PCs have forty-five-day delays.

Delay decreases the current value of the stream of payments: the greater the delay, the lower the price for a given cash flow yield. Similarly, for a given yield and payment stream, yield declines as delay increases. Yield and cash flows held equal, GNMA

Exhibit 3: The Effect of Payment Delay on Pass-Through Yield and Price

Stated Delay	Yield	Change	Price	Change (%)
30	9.59		99 8/32	
45	9.54	-.05	98 27/32+	-0.39
50	9.53	-.06	98 23/32+	-0.52
55	9.51	-.08	98 19/32	-0.66
75	9.45	-.14	98 2/32	-1.20

Note: Assumes 9.5 coupon, $99 \frac{8}{32}$ price, 9.59 yield and no prepayments.

---

securities with lower delays will trade at higher prices than FNMAs or FHLMCs, and FNMAs will trade higher than FHLMCs. The effect of delay on the price and yield of a 10% coupon pass-through is indicated in Exhibit 3.

Analysis of the cash flows from pass-through securities would end here if individual loans in the pool never prepaid at any time prior to their stated maturities. The possibility of prepayments means that cash flows cannot be predicted with certainty. Assumptions concerning the likely prepayment pattern must be made in order to estimate the cash flows.

Exhibit 4 depicts the cash flow patterns for the pass-through when prepayments are introduced. The cash flow pattern shown in the diagram is based on the assumption that a constant fraction of the remaining principal is prepaid each month (in this case, at a constant prepayment rate of 0.5% per month). The cash flow is no longer level in each month over the period. Instead, it declines each month as both prepayments and scheduled principal payments reduce the remaining principal balance of the pool. The reader should note that prepayments lower the total amount of interest paid over the life of the pass-through.

The interest rate and age of a mortgage (or WAC and WAM of the underlying loans in a mortgage pool) determine the rate at which scheduled principal is paid to the investor. In general, for the same principal amount and term, the higher the mortgage rate is, the greater the interest payments, and, accordingly, the lower

**Exhibit 4: Scheduled and Unscheduled Mortgage-Backed Security Cash
Flows ($1 Million Pool of 10%, Thirty-Year Mortgages and a 9.5% Pass-
Through Certificate)**

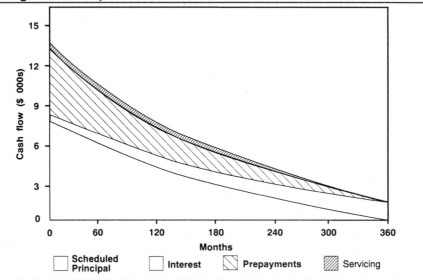

the principal payments in the early years of the mortgage are. A
look at any of the cash flow figures should make apparent the
effect of age on cash flows. All other things being equal, age affects the cash flow by establishing the amount of principal included in a given monthly payment and the number of payments
remaining. As the security ages, a greater proportion of the payments will be principal. For pass-throughs purchased at a given
discount price, older pass-throughs will have higher yields—more
principal is returned sooner at par. Age has the opposite impact
on premium securities; at the same price and coupon older pass-
throughs have lower yields, since less principal is outstanding for
shorter periods of time to earn high coupon income while principal is coming back to the investor at par. In either case, the further
the price of the security is from par, the greater the impact of seasoning on the yield. The yields for securities that are near par are
not significantly affected.

The issue date or stated maturity often does not give a complete idea of the seasoning of the underlying mortgages, particularly in the case of securities issued by FNMA and FHLMC, which can contain mortgages already seasoned at the time of issue. A weighted-average maturity statistic is available for many pass-through programs, but will not always be useful for determining the degree of seasoning in the pool, since original maturities may vary by as much as twenty years for thirty-year securities and five years for fifteen-year securities. Because of this ambiguity, it is possible significantly to misestimate a pool's scheduled principal payments. Moreover, when the historical scheduled principal payments are misstated, the calculation of experienced prepayments can also be in error.[5]

The cash flows from pass-throughs, particularly as they reflect monthly amortization, delays, and the likelihood of prepayments, give rise to the major differences between pass-throughs on the one hand and Treasury and corporate bonds on the other. The differences among these instruments are summarized in Exhibit 5.

DETERMINANTS OF PREPAYMENT RATES

The chief determinant of a pass-through's investment performance is the effect of prepayments on cash flows actually received. For this reason, MBS investors devote considerable attention to the underlying causes of prepayments and to projecting prepayments over the investment horizon. The causes of prepayments generally fall under two categories—refinancing and mobility. Homeowners tend to refinance when the current market mortgage rate is far enough below the rate on their existing mortgage to lower their monthly payment significantly. The difference in payments must

---

[5] Total principal payments are determined using the pool's factor, a statistic provided by the guarantor agency and indicating the fraction of original principal amount still outstanding for the pool. The drop between two consecutive factors measures the amount of total principal paid down over a single period. The amount of prepayments is estimated by subtracting estimated scheduled principal payments from total principal payments.

Exhibit 5: Features of Pass-Through, Government, and Corporate Securities Compared

	Pass-Throughs	Treasuries
Credit Risk	Generally high grade; range from government guaranteed to A (private pass-throughs)	Government guaranteed
Liquidity	Good for agency issued/guaranteed pass-through	Excellent
Range of Coupons (Discount to Premium)	Full range	Full range
Range of Maturities	Medium- and long-term (fast-paying and seasoned pools can provide shorter maturities than stated)	Full range
Call Protection	Complex prepayment pattern; investor can limit through selection variables such as coupon, seasoning, and program	Noncallable (except certain 30-year bonds)
Frequency of Payment	Monthly payments of principal and interest	Semiannual interest payment
Average Life	Lower than for bullets of comparable maturity; can only be estimated due to prepayment risk	Estimate only for small number of callable issues; otherwise, known with certainty
Duration/Interst-Rate Risk	Function of prepayment risk; can only be estimated; can be negative when prepayment risk is high	Unless callable, a simple function of yield, coupon, and maturity; is known with certainty
Basis for Yield Quotes	Cash-flow yield based on monthly payments and a constant CPR assumption	Based on semiannual coupon payments and 365-day year
Settlement	Once a month	Any business day

**Exhibit 5: Features of Pass-Through, Government, and
Corporate Securities Compared (continued)**

	Corporates	Stripped Treasuries
Credit Risk	High grade to speculative	Backed by government guarantees
Liquidity	Generally limited	Fair
Range of Coupons (Discount to Premium)	Full range for a few issuers	Zero coupon (discount securities)
Range of Maturities	Full range	Full range
Call Protection	Generally callable after initial limited period of five to ten years	Noncallable
Frequency of Payment	Semiannual interest (except Eurobonds, which pay interest annually)	No payments until maturity
Average Life	Minimum average life known, otherwise a function of call risk	Known with certainty
Duration/Interst-Rate Risk	Function of call risk; can be negative when call risk is high	Known with certainty; no interest-rate risk if held to maturity
Basis for Yield Quotes	Based on semiannual coupon payments and 360-day year of twelve 30-day months	Bond equivalent yield based on either 360- or 365-day year, depending on sponsor
Settlement	Any business day	Any business day

be at least great enough to permit the homeowner to recover the loan fees and other costs of refinancing over some reasonable horizon. A common rule of thumb puts this lower mortgage rate at 200 basis points below the existing mortgage's rate.[6] Because the

---

[6] The limitations of this rule are discussed in Chapter 10.

future level of interest rates is hard to predict, the resulting pre-payments are also difficult to predict. Refinancings are a negative event for pass-through investors since they are triggered by a fall in market rates and the principal returned must be reinvested at lower yields. Investors who purchase their high-coupon pass-throughs at a premium may experience additional losses, since the principal is repaid at par and must remain outstanding to earn interest.

Mobility refers to the fact that at any time, in any mortgage rate environment, homeowners sell their homes and move. (The due-on-sale clause, now enforceable by federal law, ensures this kind of prepayment. Notice that GNMA pools, made up of assumable mortgages, experience this form of prepayment at a lower rate.) The link between prepayments and interest rate levels also is important for loans with below-market coupons. In this case, high interest rates may work as a disincentive to homeowners who might otherwise move, while falling interest rates will be associated with increased prepayments. Related causes include terminations due to divorce, default, and disasters such as floods, fires, and the borrower's death. More affluent homeowners are generally thought to be more mobile. The fact that FHA/VA insurance in effect subsidizes less affluent homeowners is one of the reasons normally advanced to explain the slower prepayments of GNMA pass-throughs.

Pass-throughs with different coupons or, more to the point, with different WACs on the underlying loans, have different degrees of prepayment risk. The farther below current mortgage rates a pool's WAC is, the slower the pool is expected to prepay. Likewise, prepayments are faster for pools with above-market-rate WACs. Generally, pass-throughs with higher coupons prepay faster than pools with lower coupons; this fundamental characteristic of prepayment behavior has resulted in the grouping of pass-throughs within the various programs into different coupon classes with different trading characteristics depending on the market's perception of their prepayment risk.

It is important to remember that the pass-through coupon is less than the interest rate on the underlying mortgages by the amount of servicing (and guarantee fees) retained. The mortgage rates (WAC), not the coupon, determine whether or not it makes economic sense to refinance. In the case of GNMA I securities, the coupon precisely indicates the underlying mortgage rate, since every mortgage must have the same rate and the issuer strips off fifty basis points of servicing from that income stream. With other pass-throughs, there is considerable room for variation in underlying mortgage rates. For this reason, it is important to consider the weighted average coupon (WAC) of the underlying mortgages in any analysis of FNMA and FHLMC securities.

The age or seasoning of a pool is another key determinant of prepayment behavior. Normally, some months or years elapse after a mortgage is closed before the borrower is willing or able to go to the effort and expense of moving or refinancing. As a result, prepayment rates increase from a very low level during the early years of a pass-through's life to level off some time after twenty to sixty-five months (depending on program and coupon, among other factors). As a result, newly issued pass-throughs will demonstrate low prepayment rates, but high rates of increase from month to month. Likewise, the prepayment rates of fully seasoned securities will be relatively stable. ("Seasoned" means that the pass-through has been outstanding long enough for this process to have occurred, usually considered to be a period of two to three years, but typically longer for low-coupon securities and shorter for high-coupon securities.) For instance, more affluent homeowners are generally thought to be able to move or refinance sooner so that conventional pass-throughs season more quickly and level off at higher prepayment rates than GNMAs, which are backed by government-insured loans.

Considerable attention has been given to identifying the factors underlying prepayment activity in mortgage pass-throughs so that econometric models describing this activity can be formulated and used to predict prepayments. The spread between current mortgage rates and the underlying mortgage rates is typically modeled as the primary determinant of prepayment activity. The weighted average age of the pool is another important factor. Some models also attempt to capture the tendency for pools to become less sensitive to refinancing opportunities, or to "burnout," after sustaining very high prepayment rates for significant periods of time. Seasonality, that is, the tendency of homeowners to be more mobile in the spring and summer months, may also be modeled. These factors are discussed in greater detail in Chapter 10.

Measuring Prepayments

In order to facilitate trading and investment in mortgage-backed securities, the market has evolved a variety of conventions for quantifying prepayments. The oldest and simplest of these was the prepaid life assumption employed by secondary market traders of whole loan mortgages. At one time the twelve-year prepaid life assumption was the industry standard for quoting mortgage yields. Under this convention, the first twelve years of cash flows consist entirely of amortized principal and interest in each of the mortgages in the pool (based on a 360-month maturity). At the end of the twelfth year, the remaining principal balance is assumed to be paid in full. In other words, the entire pool is treated like a single mortgage prepaying in the twelfth year of its life. The yield-to-maturity (or internal rate of return) calculated for a given price and the cash flows derived from a twelve-year prepaid life assumption was termed the mortgage yield. (Mortgage yields were also calculated for other prepaid lives—for instance, seven-year prepaid life—but the twelve-year assumption was the standard.) During the 1970s and mid-1980s, however, increased volatility of interest rates led in turn to substantial increases in the level and volatility of prepayment rates. The prepaid life assumptions could not be adjusted for actual prepayment experience or the wide differences in coupon, maturity, seasoning, and other security characteristics prevalent in today's market.

Recognizing the problems with the prepaid life assumptions, traders and investors began using the termination experience[7] collected on FHA-insured mortgages issued since 1970 to model expected prepayments. This distribution of prepayments over the life of a pool is easily adapted to express faster or slower prepayment speeds by using a multiple of the base table. For instance, "0% of FHA" means no prepayments, "100% of FHA" refers to the average rate, and "200% of FHA" means twice the FHA rate. Another application of FHA experience was to fix the age and outstanding balance of a security and determine the multiple of FHA experience indicated by the pool's factor at that age. Assuming that the pool continues to prepay at the same percentage of FHA experience over its remaining life, a cash flow yield is calculated given the current market price.

Unfortunately, FHA experience is defined on a single parameter: age of the mortgage. By averaging individual mortgage data, it ignores the critical link between coupon (or WAC) and prepayments. Furthermore, the underlying data are from assumable FHA and VA mortgages and can be misleading when applied to conventional pass-throughs. Other disadvantages of using FHA experience to evaluate mortgage securities include the fact that it does not incorporate variables, such as the level of interest rates, known to influence prepayment activity. Finally, FHA experience did not provide a consistent standard because a new series is published each year or so, often based on different statistical manipulations of the underlying data.[8] For instance, in 1986, investors could conceivably be pricing MBSs based on 1981, 1983, 1984, or 1985 FHA statistics.

---

[7] These data are published periodically by HUD in the form of a table of thirty numbers indicating the probability of survival of a mortgage at any given year up to maturity. Prepayment rates are implicit in these survivorship rates.

[8] For instance, prior to FHA 83, all mortgages back to 1957 were included; subsequently all mortgages prior to 1970 were excluded. Extrapolation was used to a greater degree to derive experience for years not covered by actual data. Similarly, through 1981, each year's data were equally weighted; starting in 1982, mortgages issued in the 1980s were given additional weight.

Conditional Prepayment Rates. The FHA prepayment standard(s) gave way in the mid-1980s to the conditional prepayment rate (CPR), or single monthly mortality (SMM) rate, as it is alternatively termed. This measure has become the principal means traders and investors employ to quantify prepayment activity in pass-throughs. The convention assumes that a fraction of the remaining principal is prepaid each month, which implies that each individual mortgage in the pool is equally likely to prepay. The CPR measures prepayments based ("conditional") on the previous month's remaining balance (thus it can represent an average or compound rate over many periods, or a single-period rate). The resulting rate sometimes is expressed as an annualized percentage. (In recent years CPR has increasingly come to refer to an annualized prepayment rate, SMM to the monthly rate.) This simple quantification is intuitive and easy to incorporate into pricing and yield formulas. In calculating yields or prices, investors may employ a single CPR assumption across the term of the investment, or a series of varying CPR assumptions reflecting historical experience or prepayment expectations derived from formal prepayment forecast models. When an internal rate of return is calculated using realistic CPR assumptions over the life of the security, the result is termed "cash flow yield" (in contrast to the outmoded "mortgage yield" based on a prepaid life assumption).

The PSA Prepayment Standard Model. The Public Securities Association (PSA) introduced a Standard Prepayment Model to replace the FHA experience tables for the purpose of valuing collateralized mortgage obligation (CMO) issues. The PSA standard was intended to simplify the comparison and analysis of CMO yield tables, but is also occasionally used as a prepayment measure for pass-throughs. It is not really a model; more correctly, it is a measurement standard or yardstick, expressed as a monthly series of annual conditional prepayment rates. It begins at 0.2% per year in the first month and increases by 0.2% per year in each successive month until month 30, when the series levels out at 6% per year until maturity. Prepayments are measured as simple linear multiples of this schedule. For instance, 200% PSA is 0.4% per year in

Exhibit 6: PSA vs. FHA CPR Series

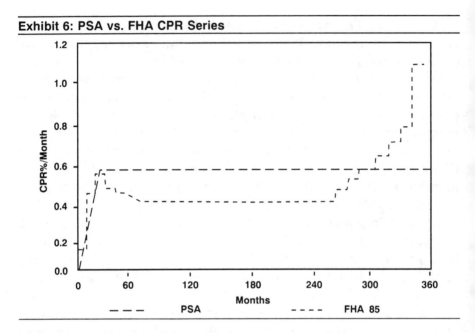

the first month, 0.8% per year in the second month, and 12% per year after month 30. This is unrealistic in the sense that prepayments in fast-paying pools do not increase proportionately in each month or year over the term of the pool. Exhibit 6 depicts both the PSA standard and the 1985 FHA series for comparison.

One advantage of the PSA CPR series is that it does reflect the increase in CPRs that occurs as the pool ages. This effect is also captured by the FHA series, but the PSA CPRs do not display the random fluctuation in prepayment rates found in the FHA tables. Finally, it should be noted that, beyond month 30, using the PSA is equivalent to applying a static CPR over the remaining life of the pool.

EVALUATING PASS-THROUGH SECURITIES YIELD, AVERAGE LIFE, AND DURATION

In order to make trading and investment decisions, participants in the pass-through market require some means of evaluating the risks and rewards in individual investment opportunities and of comparing a variety of possible investments. The price of a pass-through is the present value of the projected cash flows discounted at the current yield required by the market, given the specific risk and cash flow characteristics of the security in question. Agency pass-throughs trade on price. The yield-to-maturity on the projected cash flows (given a prepayment assumption) at a given market price is used by the investor as the basis for determining if the anticipated investment return is adequate, and for identifying relative value. Using yield as a prospective measure of performance, however, has the same disadvantages for pass-through evaluation as it has for other interest-paying obligations. With pass-throughs, yield measures have the added difficulty of being sensitive to the prepayment assumptions used to project the cash flows from which the yield is calculated.

Yield-to-maturity is a poor predictor of any bond's performance because it assumes that (1) all cash flows are reinvested at an interest rate equal to the yield, and (2) the security is held to maturity. Deviations from the first assumption are particularly significant for pass-throughs owing to their monthly coupon and principal payments, since interest on these payments compounds monthly in the yield calculation instead of semiannually on coupon payments only, as with Treasury and corporate bonds.[9] Exhibit 7 demonstrates how much the realized return or internal rate of return on the cash flows can vary when reinvestment rates different from the yield-to-maturity are used to project the total cash

---

[9] The difference in payment timing between pass-throughs and bonds also means their yields are not directly comparable in making relative value assessments. The greater frequency of payments increases the value of a pass-through of a given coupon compared to traditional corporate or government debt. Interest compounds monthly. This monthly compounding gives pass-through securities an advantage over other securities of the same coupon. Quoted cash flow yields, however, do not reflect the advantage. For instance, a 10.00% cash flow yield is equivalent to a 10.21% bond yield. In order to compare pass-through yields to yields on other securities, it is necessary to adjust the mortgage yield upward to its bond equivalent yield (BEY). Basically, the monthly coupons are treated as if they are collected and reinvested at the cash flow yield rate until the end of each semiannual or other period. The accumulated (compounded) amount is larger than the sum of the face amount of six monthly coupons.

Exhibit 7: Effect of Reinvestment Rate on Realized Yield from Monthly Payments on a 9.5% Pass-Through Priced at 99 8/32 to Yield 9.54%

Reinvestment Rate%	Realized Cash-Flow Yield(%)	Change from Expected Yield (%)
4	5.93	-37.84
6	7.16	-24.95
8	8.48	-11.11
10	9.87	3.46
12	11.33	18.76
14	12.84	34.59
16	14.41	51.05

Note: Assumes 0.50% service fee and no prepayments.

flows to be received from a pass-through. The second assumption is equally unrealistic for MBSs as for Treasury and corporate bonds. If an investment is not held to maturity, the realized yield will be affected by any capital gain or loss on the remaining cash flows, as market yields and prices are likely to have changed since the initial investment was made.

If the pass-through is priced at par, changes in prepayment speeds do not affect the yield calculation.[10] No matter when the principal is returned, the security will continue to yield its coupon rate on the remaining principal. The earlier receipt of principal offsets the loss of coupon income at faster speeds, and additional coupon income offsets the additional delay in return of principal at slower speeds. However, if the security is purchased at a premium, faster than expected prepayments will reduce the yield: prepayments shorten the amount of time principal remains outstanding to earn above-market coupon payments, thereby lowering the total cash flows. In a similar fashion, the yield of a discount security increases with faster prepayments as the time

---

[10] Actually, the yield does not change if the security was purchased at its *parity price* (slightly less than 100), which adjusts par for the payment delay. The delay lowers yield at a given price by moving the cash flows further out into the future.

Exhibit 8: Effect of Different Prepayment Rates on the Cash Flow Yield of Discount, Current and Premium Coupon Pass-Throughs*

CPR	Price		
(%/yr)	*89 20/32*	*99 28/32*	*105 4/32*
2	8.78	9.57	10.67
4	8.97	8.58	10.57
6	9.18	9.58	10.46
8	9.39	9.59	10.35
10	9.62	9.60	10.23
12	9.85	9.62	10.11
18	10.58	9.65	9.74
24	11.37	9.68	9.33

* 7.5%, 9.5%, and 11.5% coupons, respectively.

required to earn the discount is shortened. Principal purchased at, say, 90% of its value, is returned at 100%. The effect of prepayments on yield for securities purchased close to, above, or below par is shown in Exhibit 8.

A fundamental measure of the risk in any investment is its term, or longevity. Because the principal is returned throughout the pass-through's life, maturity is not a good measure of the longevity of this form of debt. The likelihood of prepayments amplifies this deficiency. For these reasons, a preferred measure for mortgage-backed securities, including pass-throughs, is the average elapsed time until the principal is fully returned. The commonly used measure, *average life*, is the weighted average time to principal repayment, with the amount of the principal paydowns (both scheduled and unscheduled) as the weights. Average life expresses the average number of years that each principal dollar will be outstanding. Clearly, the higher the prepayment rate, the sooner the principal is returned and hence the shorter the average life. It should also be apparent from the definition that average life declines as a security ages. Average life also is affected by coupon rate. For a given prepayment assumption, average life increases with coupon rates because, at higher interest rates, a larger proportion of the payment is interest in early years, in effect slightly delaying the repayment of principal. However, if prepayments are allowed to vary with interest rates so that they reflect increasing or decreasing incentives to refinance or move, they will swamp the coupon effect on average life in premium coupon securities.

In recent years, *duration* has become more important for the evaluation of pass-throughs than average life. Macaulay duration is the weighted average time to receipt of the present value of both principal and interest cash flows. Duration is appealing because it can be used to measure the price sensitivity of a bond. That is, "modified duration" expresses the amount the price (present value) will change given a small change in the yield used to discount the cash flows. Thus, duration has important applications as a measure of interest rate risk. As with yield and average life calculations, both Macaulay and modified duration are highly sensitive to the prepayment assumptions used to project the cash flows. As a result, duration can significantly misestimate the actual price change of pass-throughs when interest rates decline and the market changes its estimates of prepayment risk. More importantly, a pass-through's duration drifts as the expected prepayment rates used to calculate it change in response to changes in the general level of interest rates. Pass-through duration shortens in a bull market and lengthens in a bear market. As a result, a pass-through's price can decline more quickly for a small change in interest rates as the general level of interest rates rises. Similarly, pass-through prices increase more slowly for successive declines in the general level of interest rates. This characteristic of a pass-through's price behavior is generally referred to as "negative convexity."

Relative Value Analysis

A crucial ingredient in the analysis of mortgage-backed securities is the ability to compare these investments to other fixed-income securities. The variety of MBS programs and the broad range of coupons within programs give additional impetus to relative value analysis. Market participants have evolved various quantitative frameworks within which under- and overvalued securities can be identified and rational investment decisions made.

In simplest terms, relative value analysis seeks to compare securities of equivalent risk. Various attempts have been made to capture all aspects of pass-throughs' interest rate risk in a manner that allows comparison to Treasury securities.

Once the yield spread to an appropriate Treasury security is determined, that spread should be comparable to the spread provided by another fixed-income security of similar risk. The earliest attempts at relative value analysis matched maturities or average lives. This approach failed to account for the great difference between the cash-flow patterns of Treasuries and MBSs.

A sounder comparison is made using the duration calculated with a reasonable prepayment assumption. By matching durations, a point on the pass-through yield curve is compared to a point on the Treasury curve that should respond in a similar fashion to small changes in interest rates. The next step is to determine the required yield spread over the Treasury at which investors are willing to invest in mortgage-backed securities. This premium compensates investors for the prepayment risk as well as differences in credit quality, liquidity, and the additional reinvestment risk arising from monthly payments. Cheap securities would be those trading at a greater spread to the equivalent-risk Treasury than required; rich securities would be trading at a lower spread than required. Taking another approach, an investor can examine the entire pass-through yield curve in comparison to Treasuries in an attempt to identify those MBSs where the spread is widest and indicates the greatest value relative to other pass-throughs.

The success of relative value analysis depends on correctly identifying Treasury securities of equivalent interest rate risk. Unfortunately, as noted above, duration cannot correctly summarize the price sensitivity of pass-throughs, because it cannot account for the variation in prepayment experience as interest rates change. Actual price movements of pass-throughs in response to interest rate changes differ significantly from those predicted by their duration, both in magnitude and direction. That is, certain pass-throughs experience price declines during periods of falling interest rates (negative duration) because lower interest rates translate into higher prepayments, which in turn translate into capital losses and unrealized earnings. Consequently, the market demands a higher-risk premium for those coupons perceived to have increased prepayment risk.

Similarly, cash flow yield calculations do not reflect the likelihood that prepayment behavior can change from assumptions used at pricing. As a consequence, a new generation of analytic tools has been developed that treats the pass-through as a composite security consisting of a long position in mortgages and a short position in call options (each borrower's right to call a piece of the pool away from the investor). In brief, their objective is to evaluate explicitly the option to prepay given the current yield environment, a process for modeling likely changes in interest rates for realistic levels of interest rate volatility, and a prepayment model that links prepayment activity to interest rate levels. Different analytic techniques may be used to arrive at such models, but the basic outputs will include option-adjusted measures of yield and yield spread over Treasuries, as well as option-adjusted measures of price sensitivity or duration. (A larger discussion of the theory behind such models and how they are formulated is beyond the scope of this chapter.) Rich-cheap analysis is conducted using these measures in the same way as with older techniques"investments with similar risk characteristics are compared to identify superior value. The difference is that the investor has the advantage of being able to compare a theoretical value to the actual market spread to make a better-informed investment decision.

Total Return Analysis

Yield is not commonly used to describe the historical investment performance of a pass-through. Instead, the total rate of return is used. The actual or economic return received by an investor is the sum of interest and principal payments as well as any reinvestment income received over a holding or measurement period, plus any capital gain or loss if the bond is sold at the end of the period. If the bond is not sold, the total return calculation takes into account any appreciation or depreciation in market price as of the end of the period.

Total returns can also be projected to support trading and investment decisions. Such analysis, if performed with adequate care, overcomes many of the shortcomings of yield. For one thing, assumptions about interest rate and prepayment scenarios can be used to project principal and interest payments and reinvestment income over the period, as well as market prices at the end of the measurement horizon. Care is required, in particular, in determining terminal prices for pass-throughs, because the yield spreads investors require for securities reflect their perception of prepayment and other risks. Since interest rate shifts alter the magnitude of these risks as well as their impact on cash flows, it is not necessarily reasonable to assume that the required yield spread for a particular security would be the same at the end of the horizon as at the beginning. An approach that adjusts for this problem would be to use the yield spread earned by an otherwise similar pass-through that has the same average life at the outset as the security in question does at the end of the horizon. (Matching durations would involve an iterative search because average life is simply a function of principal paydowns and time, while duration is a function of yield as well). In other words, if a 9% GNMA single-family thirty-year pass-through shortens to a three-year average life in a down-100-basis-points scenario, its terminal price can be calculated from the yield found by adding the spread of the GNMA single-family thirty-year security that today has an average life closest to three years to the yield of the three-year Treasury less 100 basis points. Another approach prices the remaining cash flows at the same option-adjusted spread to Treasuries as demonstrated by the security at the beginning of the period. This ap-

Exhibit 9: One-Year Return (%)

Interest Rate Shift (Basis Points)	FNMA 8	FNMA 10	FNMA 12
-200	18.48	13.89	9.50
-150	16.39	13.19	9.73
-100	14.01	12.35	10.16
-50	11.68	11.52	10.24
0	9.89	10.04	9.76
50	7.62	8.32	8.79
100	5.41	6.34	7.64
150	3.28	4.39	6.70
200	1.21	2.88	5.39

proach has the advantage of incorporating a mathematical expectation rather than a point estimate of the required spread.

Projected returns for discount, current, and premium coupon FNMA securities are depicted in Exhibit 9. A constant spread to Treasuries is used to determine asset prices at the end of the horizon, and the Smith Barney Prepayment Model is used to project the cash flows and terminal values. Readers should note the differences in projected total return performance between pass-throughs from different coupon sectors of the market. The greatest variability is displayed by the FNMA 12. This pass-through displays significant negative convexity as rates decline, prepayments accelerate, and principal purchased at a high premium is returned at par. On the other hand, as interest rates rise and refinancing incentives disappear, prepayments rapidly slow down. As the security's duration lengthens, its performance dominates that of the discount and current coupon securities. This reflects the impact of high coupon income, as principal remains outstanding longer. The discount MBS, a FNMA 8, displays the opposite return pattern—as prepayments increase, more principal is returned at a gain, generating returns far in excess of those displayed by the current and premium pass-throughs. On the downside, as the duration of the discount pass-through extends, its market value drops more sharply, contributing to its low returns in the more bearish environments.

The security priced close to parity, the FNMA 10, displays a projected return pattern somewhere in the middle. More bullish scenarios induce rapid prepayments, which begin to erode performance beyond a 150-basis-point decline in yields. On the downside, prepayment rates slow down at a moderate pace, lengthening the time to receipt of principal and consequently increasing the security's price response to interest rate increases.

Total return projections may also be used in making relative value assessments. In this context, the investor would prefer the securities offering the greatest return advantage over comparable Treasuries.

SUMMARY

In this chapter, the investment characteristics of mortgage pass-through securities and the various types of securities are explained. In the next chapter, investing in specific mortgage pools is discussed. While the basic factors that influence prepayments are reviewed, a more detailed discussion of prepayment modeling is provided in Chapter 10. Cash flow yield and duration are parameters often used to describe the investment characteristics of these securities. Later chapters discuss the limitations of these measures in greater detail, and suggest better methodologies for valuing pass-throughs and estimating their price volatility.

CHAPTER 5

INVESTING IN SPECIFIED POOLS

Chuck Ramsey
Partner
MMAR Group

J. Michael Henderson, CFA
Managing Director
Bear, Stearns & Co., Inc.

At the most elementary level, a trade in a specified pool is merely a transaction in which the pool number is known. This contrasts with a typical TBA (to be announced) transaction, in which pool information is not known at the time of the trade. For example, an investor may purchase $1 million GNMA 8s on a TBA basis and receive up to three pools, the pool numbers of which will be announced shortly before settlement date. On the other hand, the investor might ask to know the pool number prior to purchase. In this latter case, the investor has specified a minor distinction from TBA delivery, and, in so doing, has entered into a specified trade at its most elementary level.

The degree of specification desired by the investor may also be more detailed. TBA offerings are generally for mortgage pools containing relatively recently issued mortgages maturing in approximately thirty years. Such an offering represents the norm, or generic type. Any departure from this norm, or TBA "good delivery," represents some degree of specificity. For example, the investor may request one pool per $1 million instead of the standard three pools per $1 million, or the investor may even request a single $10 million or a single $100 million pool. Perhaps the investor prefers a pool containing mortgages on which an average of ten years have elapsed and on which twenty years of time remain until the maturity of the pool. The investor may request a pool of mortgages that has experienced a particular rapidity of prepayments over an extended period of time. Because the speed of prepayments has a major effect on the yield and/or average life of the investment, the investor may attempt to employ such specificity in order to effect a greater degree of certainty concerning the yield and average life of the investment. Other examples of diversion from the TBA or generic norm will be discussed later in this chapter.

HISTORICAL EVOLUTION OF THE SPECIFIED POOL MARKET

The initial creation of GNMA pools occurred in the early 1970s. Within a few years, FHLMC and FNMA followed with their own pools issuance. In the early years, GNMA pools of a particular coupon traded interchangeably, and there were no marginal distinctions to render the pools greatly different from the norm. As noted above, however, investors did deviate from TBA "good delivery" by specifying different pool sizes than were represented by a TBA offering.

With the passage of time, enterprising investors began to realize that although many mortgage pools might have been created equally, there could be rather dramatic differences in prepayment speeds of different mortgage pools. Because the prepayment speed

Exhibit 1: FNMA Pool 64 Price/Yield Matrix

	8.00% CPP	14.09% CPP	0.00% CPP
Average Life	6.92	5.06	11.20
Price			
88-08	10.27	11.05	9.40

affected the yield and/or average life of a mortgage security investment, the astute investment manager attempted to understand the yield and average life ramifications caused by various speeds on a particular coupon at a particular dollar price.

Exhibit 1 is a price/yield table for FNMA pool 64 (coupon, 7.50; weighted average maturity, 7.05). At a dollar price of $88.25, assuming a constant prepayment percentage (CPP), or the interchangeably used constant prepayment rate (CPR), speed of 8%, the investor will earn a 10.27 bond equivalent yield and the average life will be about seven years. In actuality, prepayments during the last year have occurred at 14.09% CPP, and this speed results in a yield of 11.05 and an average life of about five years. If there were never a prepayment on FNMA 64, then the yield would be 9.40 and the average life would be about eleven years. Hence, varying prepayment speeds may cause some rather dramatic differences in yield and average life for a particular pool.

In 1981, FHLMC began issuing mortgage pools under the guarantor, or "swap" program. Among the results of this program was the creation of a vastly greater variety of mortgage paper. Whereas previously most issuance of pools was of current coupons with thirty-year maturities, the swap program provided investors with a wide array of coupons in new pools of older mortgages. Because the universe of coupons and average lives had been so greatly expanded, many investors who formerly were uninterested in mortgage securities (because these investors had limited or no particular need for ten- to twelve-year average life and/or current coupon paper with a final maturity of thirty years) now had reason to reexamine the possibilities available in the specified pool market. For example, deep-discount coupons of

---

Exhibit 2: FHLMC Pool 183161

Coupon:	5.00%			*Price/Yield Matrix*			
Servicing:	0.625%						
Issue date:	11/82		0.00%	8.00%	11.12%	13.11%	14.81%
Maturity:	1/96		CPP	CPP	CPP	CPP	CPP
		Avg. Life	3.29	2.82	2.66	2.56	2.48

Prepayment History:		Price					
3 month:	14.81 CPP						
6 month:	13.11 CPP						
1 year:	11.12 CPP						
Life:	7.58 CPP	89-24	8.64	9.22	9.47	9.64	9.79

---

four or five with weighted average maturities (WAMs) of five to ten years creating average lives of two to five years became available. An example of such a pool is presented in Exhibit 2.

As the variety of mortgage paper and the universe of potential investors increased, research staffs attempted to understand, quantify, and even predict what levels of prepayments might be appropriate for various combinations of coupons, WAMs, and weighted average coupons (WACs). Such analysis generally encompassed economic models. Analysts began to study the relationship between how rapidly mortgages prepaid and the geographic locations of the mortgages. For example, one may intuitively surmise that there are probably differences in prepayment speeds between pools with Los Angeles mortgages and pools with Houston mortgages. Investors began to try to quantify these relative differences in order to have a better understanding of prepayment speeds and, therefore, yields and average lives.

INVESTOR RATIONALE UNDERLYING THE PURCHASE OF SPECIFIED POOLS

Investors are drawn to mortgage securities because they are often able to pick up yield and/or quality versus many other investment vehicles. Because there are few free lunches to be had in the investment arena, there must be some trade-offs associated with these advantages. The trade-off is that the investor takes on uncertainty. If an investor purchases a seven-year Treasury, he or she is certain to receive fourteen equal interest payments on predetermined dates, and the principal back in seven years. The investor is also certain at the outset about the yield he or she has purchased, although the yield realized will depend on the rate and fashion in which he or she reinvests the interest payments.

With mortgage securities, however, the investor purchases an array of possibilities as to average life and yield. This variability is amply illustrated by FNMA 64, wherein there was approximately a 250-basis-point range between the yield earned at the three-month speed and the yield earned if there were never to be a prepayment on FNMA 64. Furthermore, the average lives under those two extreme circumstances varied from about four years to about eleven years. The variability of yield and average life is exacerbated by the fact that, whereas the investor in the seven-year Treasury note need only consider the effect of reinvestment rates on the stream of interest payments, the mortgage security investor must also consider the effect of that reinvestment rate on variable principal payments. The goal of the investor is to gather sufficient data concerning prepayment speeds so that he or she may quantify the range of possibilities and also predict the most likely range of average life and yield possibilities. If the investor is satisfied with a reasonable range of possible average lives and yields, and this range offers sufficient yield and quality inducement versus other investment vehicles, then the investment in mortgage securities is suitable for inclusion in the investment manager's portfolio. Therefore, the major challenge confronting the investment manager is to surmise a reasonable prepayment speed to assume for a particular mortgage pool.

SPECIFIED POOL ANALYSIS

Specified pool analysis begins with a look at the pool itself. Exhibit 3 presents a profile of FNMA pool 173.

FNMA 173 is an 8.50 coupon pool with a WAC of 9.301. The WAC is the average interest rate paid by the homeowner to the mortgage originator. The pool was issued in 1982, so the investor has the benefit of several years of prepayment history available in order to make a judgment concerning how well or how poorly the pool has prepaid. The pool has a WAM of 2-2007 and the longest mortgage in the pool has its final payment in 5-2011. Hence, FNMA 173 is an example of a pool that was issued about five years after the mortgages were created. The investor can readily see that the pool has experienced prepayments in excess of 8% CPP since issuance, and has experienced considerably more rapid prepayment speeds within the past year. If the investor were to

---

Exhibit 3: FNMA Pool 173-CL Conventional Thirty-Year Single Family, Midwest Federal Savings & Loan Association, Minneapolis, MN

			0.00% CPP	8.00% CPP	12.87% CPP	13.93% CPP	15.57% CPP
Coupon:	8.50%						
WAC:	0.625%	*Price/Yield Matrix*					
Pool size:	19,988,403.89						
Issue date:	3/82						
Maturity:	5/11						
WAM:	2/07	Avg. Life	12.58	7.34	5.64	5.34	4.92

Prepayment History:		Price					
1 month:	12.04 CPP						
3 month:	15.57 CPP	92	9.78	10.35	10.74	10.84	10.98
6 month:	13.93 CPP						
1 year:	12.87 CPP						
Life:	8.32 CPP						

pay $92 for the pool, he or she would earn a 10.35 yield, assuming that the pool will prepay at 8% CPP in the future.

The investor should note that the pool is from Minneapolis. One Wall Street firm tracks prepayment tendencies by state. An examination of Exhibit 4 reveals that mortgages from Minnesota should prepay slightly more slowly than national prepayment speed norms. The same firm has a sample of 124 pools containing $633 million of mortgages from Minneapolis with coupons ranging from 8% to 10%. In the past year, the weighted average CPP of this sample of pools has been 13.23%. FNMA 173 has experienced prepayments of 12.87% CPP within the last year, so it is very similar to the sample. However, since the range of coupons in the sample is from 8% to 10%, one might surmise that FNMA 8.50s, which

---

Exhibit 4: Regional Prepayment Index

Geographical Breakdown of FNMA CL 000173				
State	*Original Bal. Share*	*% Bal.*	*Loans*	*% Loans*
Minnesota	19,988,403.89	100.000	462	100.000

Attention

Regional Prepayment Index is calculated based on the *original* loan composition of the pool. The current loan composition is subject to change given unequal paydowns. This may be particularly true for seasoned pools where geography is widely dispersed.

RPI Index Rating: 95.163

RPI is based on a national average of 100. Values above 100 are expected to prepay faster than the national average while those below 100 are expected to be slower.

Assuming that unreported loans are generic, we project this pool will prepay 4.837% slower than generics.

State prepayment speeds are calculated from a large sample of pools.

Any specific pool can deviate from the average.

are in the lower part of the range, might have prepaid at somewhat less than the weighted average of 13.23% CPP, so FNMA 173 might actually be slightly faster than the average 8.50 coupon from Minneapolis.

Further specific geographic investigation may be undertaken through the appraisal of economic conditions and trends in the Minneapolis area. Exhibit 5 presents the work of a regional economist employed by one Wall Street firm. Such analysis provides further economic information that has bearing on mortgage termination rates in the Minneapolis-St. Paul Metropolitan Statistical Area (MSA).

The investor should also take into account the fact that within the past year FNMA 173 has prepaid at a somewhat more rapid rate than FNMA 8.50s. In the last six-month, three-month, and one-month comparison, FNMA 173 has prepaid at a considerably more rapid rate. (This increasing prepayment divergence between

---

Exhibit 5: FNMA Regional Analysis

MN-WI, Minneapolis-St. Paul

Conditions

Minneapolis-St. Paul's fortunes lie largely in high-tech and durable goods manufacturing and to a lesser extent agriculture. Due to its reliance on these areas, the MSA's economy, which also contains the state capital, is highly import sensitive and stagnated growth in its farming and goods-producing areas have recently slowed growth throughout much of the economy.

Manufacturing employment, 19.8% of the total (US = 18.7%), grew an average of 1.6% per year (1982-87, US = 0.3%) and rose by 0.9% in 1987 (US = 0.6%). Declining sectors include office and computing machinery, fabricated metals, pulp and paper products, and nonelectrical machinery. Growing sectors include commercial printing, chemical products, and transportation equipment.

Nonmanufacturing employment grew an average of 4.2% per year (1982-87, US = 3.2%) and gained 4.7% in 1987 (US = 2.9%). Every major sector continued to advance impressively in 1987 and with construction and services leading the way at 9.1% and 5.5% respectively.

Despite the growing local economy, evidenced by 4.0% employment growth in 1987 (US = 2.5%), and only slightly above average population increase the unemployment rate rose somewhat from 4.2% to 4.3% during the 1986-87 period (US = 6.2%).

FNMA 173 and all FNMA 8.50s will be examined and explained later in this chapter.)

Attention should also be turned to the payment consistency experienced by FNMA 173. Such consistency may be prized by the investor because returns are smoothed over shorter investment horizons. Part of the consistency may be explained by the fact that FNMA 173 is a fairly large pool of about $20 million original face amount. The likelihood of several mortgages terminating in any given month is greater than if the pool were, for example, $500,000. (In a $500,000 pool, if the mortgages average $30,000, there would be about seventeen mortgages in the pool. If the WAM were twenty years, then there would be an average of only one mortgage termination every fourteen months.) Hence, although the speed as measured by CPP might well be identical over an extended period of time, in the short run the less consistent pool might provide an extremely lesser or greater yield than the larger, more consistently prepaying pool.

Another area for analytical consideration is the prepayment speeds associated with various WAMs. One intuitively knows that homeowners typically do not move out of a house on which they have recently been granted a mortgage. The investor should attempt to include WAM evaluation in his or her overall analysis of a specific pool in an attempt to quantify the magnitude of differences of prepayment speeds among various WAMs. Exhibit 6 presents CPP speeds for one-year, six-month, three-month, and one-month time periods for all FNMA 8.50s sorted by WAM. This survey could be most helpful to the investor in his or her analysis of FNMA 173, a FNMA 8.50 with a WAM of 2007. The survey indicates that there was $15.2 billion original face of FNMA 8.50s outstanding on 9/14/87, of which 6.5%, or about $1 billion, was 8.50s with a 2007 WAM.

FNMA 8.50s with 2007 WAMS have prepaid at a CPP rate of 12.9% during the last year, 13.6% during the last six months and three months, and 11.1% in the latest month. Hence, FNMA 173 has prepaid at approximately the same speed in the last year and somewhat faster than 2007 8.50s in the other periods measured. As

Exhibit 6

	Coupon	WAM Mat	Avg WAC	Pools Report	Total Pools	Out $MM	Orig $MM	12 mo CPP	6 mo CPP	3 mo CPP	12 mo PSA	6 mo PSA	3 mo PSA	Aug CPP	1987 PSA
FNMA	8.500	1991	9.000	1	1	1	1	18.9	16.3	18.7	315	272	312	14.5	241
FNMA	8.500	1992	9.000	1	1	1	2	16.8	15.8	26.1	280	263	435	44.3	738
FNMA	8.500	1993	9.000	1	1	2	2	8.5	11.1	8.3	141	185	138	16.8	279
FNMA	8.500	1994	9.001	4	4	4	5	21.1	20.9	21.0	352	349	351	4.9	82
FNMA	8.500	1995	9.118	4	5	3	7	8.5	7.1	6.0	141	118	100	1.7	29
FNMA	8.500	1996	9.086	9	9	12	15	10.7	10.6	9.6	178	176	160	10.9	182
FNMA	8.500	1997	9.003	7	7	12	15	9.4	7.5	9.6	157	125	160	1.8	30
FNMA	8.500	1998	9.152	17	17	31	43	10.7	10.3	9.2	178	172	153	5.7	95
FNMA	8.500	1999	9.041	16	16	46	61	10.9	12.1	13.7	181	202	229	12.1	201
FNMA	8.500	2000	9.085	17	17	30	43	10.4	11.6	9.4	174	193	157	6.7	111
FNMA	8.500	2001	9.174	31	32	114	180	13.0	14.0	13.7	216	234	228	9.9	165
FNMA	8.500	2002	9.188	47	48	87	125	12.2	11.9	8.4	204	199	141	7.4	123
FNMA	8.500	2003	9.130	45	45	165	241	12.2	12.4	13.3	203	206	222	13.8	231
FNMA	8.500	2004	9.223	65	65	247	343	11.0	11.6	11.9	183	193	199	10.4	173
FNMA	8.500	2005	9.234	72	72	397	636	12.6	12.9	12.9	210	214	216	11.6	194
FNMA	8.500	2006	9.246	121	121	989	1505	12.9	13.6	14.4	214	227	239	12.6	211
FNMA	8.500	2007	9.424	115	115	989	1591	12.9	13.6	13.6	214	226	226	11.1	185
FNMA	8.500	2008	9.682	60	60	732	1178	15.1	16.5	16.1	251	275	269	14.9	248
FNMA	8.500	2009	9.426	12	12	50	58	29.7	24.1	12.8	494	401	213	8.8	147
FNMA	8.500	2010	9.767	7	7	10	11	21.4	24.6	10.6	356	409	176	1.3	22
FNMA	8.500	2011	9.205	10	10	16	17	N/A	10.4	2.7	N/A	174	46	0.6	11
FNMA	8.500	2012	9.275	13	13	15	19	6.3	6.1	5.6	105	102	93	5.4	90
FNMA	8.500	2013	9.246	24	24	45	46	2.9	1.4	2.7	49	23	46	5.1	86
FNMA	8.500	2014	9.339	60	60	109	112	2.7	4.6	5.2	44	76	87	4.9	82
FNMA	8.500	2015	9.456	213	213	503	524	5.0	6.8	7.0	102	137	140	6.5	131
FNMA	8.500	2016	9.451	1102	1102	3870	3971	5.4	5.1	4.5	165	185	174	4.1	162
FNMA	8.500	2017	9.132	1652	1652	6734	6786	N/A	2.0	2.0	N/A	130	159	202	189
FNMA	8.500	2013	9.300	3606	3729	14937	17129	11.5	9.6	6.5	208	214	203	5.5	188
Seasoned		2006	9.362	782	3729	4142	6288	13.0	13.6	13.5	216	227	225	11.7	195
						15215	17536								

FNMA CL 360 Prepayment Report

Source: Bear, Stearns & Co.

a discount coupon, the faster the prepayment speed, the higher the yield, since the collateral is prepaid at par. The reverse is true of premium coupon pools.

A further examination of Exhibit 6 exposes the fallacy of using averages of prepayment speeds by coupon when one is attempting to estimate prepayment speeds for a specific pool. Exhibit 6 shows that approximately 70%, or about $10.6 billion, of FNMA 8.50s was issued in 1986 and 1987 (WAMs of 2016 and 2017, respectively). This very large sample has prepaid at a much slower rate than the seasoned 2007 and similarly seasoned WAM paper. These different prepayment rates are what one would intuitively expect because, as was discussed above, homeowners with new mortgages are less likely to terminate their mortgages than homeowners who have had mortgages for several years. This intuitive observation has been captured in the sophisticated prepayment models that have been developed to project future speeds; it is referred to commonly as the pure aging effect.[1] Exhibit 3 indicates that FNMA 173 prepaid at a significantly more rapid rate than the average FNMA 8.50, but one may readily derive from Exhibit 6 the fact that average prepayment speeds are skewed dramatically downward because such a great portion of FNMA 8.50s is collateralized by new origination mortgages.

If the investor pays $92 for FNMA 173 and the pool prepays at 8% CPP in the future, he or she will earn a yield of 10.35. The 8% CPP assumption is nothing more than a benchmark, a point of comparison to other mortgage pools and other different sector investment vehicles. In this instance the investor is implicitly accepting 8% CPP as a reasonable and perhaps conservative estimate of how rapidly the mortgages will prepay. Such an acceptance appears to be perfectly rational, considering the volume and quality of facts brought to bear in the investment decision.

---

[1] See R. Blaine Roberts, "The Consequences of the Pure Aging Effect on the Yields of Mortgage-Backed Securities," in Frank J. Fabozzi (ed.), *Mortgage-Backed Securities: New Strategies, Applications and Research* (Chicago, IL: Probus Publishing, 1987).

In summary, FNMA 173 has had a long history of rapid and consistent prepayment. Prepayment speeds in Minneapolis are fairly rapid in relation to the universe of prepayments; these empirical data are bolstered by the qualitative and quantitative input of a regional economist concerning the economic health of the Minneapolis-St. Paul MSA. FNMA 173 has experienced prepayments perhaps slightly above the averages for the Minneapolis-St. Paul MSA. FNMA 173 has a WAM of 2007, and such WAMs have prepaid quite rapidly during the last year. Additionally, FNMA 173 compares quite favorably against the $1 billion sample of FNMA 8.50s with a 2007 WAM. This mass of data leaves the investor quite comfortable with the 8% CPP assumption.

If the Treasury yield curve is as follows:

5-year = 8.90

7-year = 9.15

10-year = 9.33

then the investor who pays $92 in order to earn a 10.35 yield at the 8% CPP assumption will earn 120 basis points over the seven-year Treasury note. If the pick-up of 120 basis points over the Treasury yield curve is acceptable and compares favorably with the yields available in other sectors of the bond market, then mortgage securities in general, and FNMA 173 specifically, warrant a place in the investor's portfolio. Furthermore, all of the data concerning FNMA 173 prepayment speeds, as they relate to the economic climate in the Minneapolis-St. Paul MSA, and prepayment speeds of FNMA 8.50s with a 2007 WAM, provide the investor with ample reason to anticipate that there might be prepayment speeds in excess of 8% CPP. For example, if FNMA 173 continued to prepay as it has within the past year, the investor would earn a 10.74 yield. This yield represents an absolute yield pick-up of another thirty-nine basis points over the yield earned at the 8% CPP assumption. The spread increment is even greater, since the faster speed shortens the average life to just over five years. The yield spread at the one-year speed over the five-year Treasury is 184 basis points. If there were never again a prepayment (such an occurrence would be historic) on FNMA 173, the yield would be 9.78, a forty-five basis point pick-up over the ten-year Treasury.

EXAMPLES OF OTHER TYPES OF SPECIFIED POOLS

Because of the large issuance of pools with older mortgages and because sufficient time has elapsed in order to view mortgage prepayment patterns over longer time periods, the specified pool market now offers a myriad of coupons, WAMs, WACs, and cash flows. Such a variety enables investment managers to find the cash flow they are seeking through careful analysis of specified pools.

Exhibit 7 presents a profile of FNMA pool 997. The most striking characteristic of FNMA pool 997 is that it has a WAC of 11.543 and a coupon of 9.50. This very high WAC, coupled with the fact that the mortgages have been outstanding for a long time, should result in a fairly short piece of paper. One Wall Street firm's prepayment model suggests that this pool, with its unique combination of coupon, WAM, and WAC, should prepay at a CPP speed of 11.18% when the prevailing mortgage rate is 10.75. The pool is

Exhibit 7: FNMA Pool 997

Coupon:	9.50%		*Price/Yield Matrix*			
Servicing:	2.043%					
Issue date:	12/82		11.18%	18.55%	33.93%	42.37%	37.06%
Maturity:	9/09		CPP	CPP	CPP	CPP	CPP
		Avg. Life	6.44	4.41	2.42	1.87	2.19

Prepayment History:		Price					
3 month:	37.06 CPP						
6 month:	42.37 CPP						
1 year:	33.93 CPP						
Life:	18.55 CPP	97	10.29	10.49	10.97	11.28	11.08

from a geographic area that has prepaid very rapidly during the past year (25.76% CPP). Armed with this information, investment managers who add FNMA 977 to their portfolios at $97 are implicitly making the judgment that, although they may not know exactly how long the average life of the investment will be, they will receive a very enticing spread over the Treasury curve regardless of the prepayment speed. If the Treasury curve is as follows:

2-year = 8.24

3-year = 8.54

4-year = 8.69

5-year = 8.90

7-year = 9.15

an investment manager would earn about 115 basis points over the seven-year at the prepayment model's estimated speed of 11.18% CPP, about 180 basis points over the four-year at the life speed of 18.55% CPP, and 250 basis points or more over the curve at the one-year, six-month, and three-month prepayment speeds. Such an investment would have a great appeal to many investment managers.

Just as FNMA 997 offers the investment manager unique characteristics for achieving a very unusual combination of yield and average life possibilities, FHLMC 183161, previously presented in Exhibit 2, offers an equally unique but greatly different array of yield and average life characteristics. FHLMC 183161 has a 5% coupon and a 1993 maturity. Such a short maturity dramatically reduces the average life variability. At $89.75, the investor would earn a yield of 9.22 at 8% CPP, or sixty-eight basis points above the three-year Treasury note shown above. At 8% CPP, the average life is 2.82 years. At the most rapid prepayment speed observed, the three-month speed of 14.81% CPP, the average life declines to only 2.48 years, and if there is never a prepayment the average life increases to only 3.29 years. Hence, as the WAM shortens, the average life variability declines, and the investment manager's degree of certainty about the average life and yield is greatly increased. Of course, in this example the prepayment speeds during the last year, six months, and three months will add an additional twenty-five, forty-two, and fifty-seven basis points, respectively, to the yield. Many investors might employ FHLMC 183161 as a surrogate for very short-term notes because there may be a yield pick-up without a particularly wide range of average life variability.

SUMMARY

Because mortgage securities have been issued for a number of years, and because of the large issuance in the last few years of older mortgages in new pools, the variety of combinations of coupon, WAM, and WAC is extensive. Mortgage securities no longer consist of only thirty-year generic prices, yields, and average lives. Because of a very diverse universe of pools and the resultant creation of large, sophisticated databases (containing information about specific pools and the different prepayment speeds associated with varying geography, WAMs, and WACs), the investment manager is now able to include specified pools for a wide variety of cash flow requirements. This wealth of research has enabled the investment manager to achieve the yield, average life, and issuer quality he or she desires, along with a greater degree of confidence concerning the yield or total return and average life outcomes the mortgages will experience.

CHAPTER 6

INTRODUCTION TO PRIVATE LABEL PASS-THROUGH SECURITIES

Robert Gerber
Vice President
Fixed Income Research
The First Boston Corporation

INTRODUCTION

Private label pass-throughs are securitized mortgage pools backed by fixed or adjustable-rate whole loans and issued by private institutions. Lack of conformity to government agency pooling requirements render these conventional mortgages ineligible for GNMA, FHLMC, or FNMA pass-through programs. Consequently, collateral quality and various credit enhancements, rather than agency guarantees, provide protection against investor loss; credit support (e.g., pool insurance or senior/subordinated structure) is typically sufficient to warrant a AA rating. Although currently much smaller than the agency-backed sectors of the market, these AA pass-throughs comprise a sizeable, expanding segment of the mortgage-backed securities market.[1]

Commercial banks and savings institutions have increasingly depended on asset securitization to raise funds, control interest rate risk, and improve their balance sheets. In this context, the existence of a large store of unsecuritized conventional mortgage debt, predominantly "jumbo" loans (those that exceed FNMA/FHLMC size limits), has fueled the rapid growth of the AA pass-through market.

Federal tax and regulatory policies can alter the incentives to securitize these loans and influence the form in which they are packaged. Tax changes, culminating with the 1986 REMIC legislation, reduced the effective cost of credit enhancement via the use of the senior/subordinated (A/B) pass-through structure. During the 1986-88 period, these developments encouraged further market expansion and a greater reliance on the A/B structure. More recently, new risk-based capital guidelines have been introduced for banks and thrifts. Regulatory changes may increase the effective cost of some credit supports, especially the A/B structure. As a consequence, issuer reliance on these credit enhancements, in their present form, may decline, and a moderation of market growth is possible. Nonetheless, the considerable economic incentives to securitize these loans should generate a substantial flow of new issuance when market conditions are favorable.

AA pass-through structures are likely to evolve further as new market conditions warrant. A variety of fundamental structural forms are now in use, however, and most modifications are expected to build on existing techniques. Moreover, pool insurance may again become a popular enhancement type in the new regulatory environment.

This chapter is an introduction to the AA pass-through market. The first and second sections describe the market's growth poten-

---

[1] Private label pass-throughs go by a variety of names. Originally called "Connie Macs," they are also known as non-agency and AA pass-throughs. Not all AA pass-throughs, however, are AA-rated.

tial and its historical development. The third section outlines the determinants of credit quality and Standard & Poor's rating criteria. The fourth section compares the currently used methods of credit enhancement, focusing on the senior/subordinated pass-through structure. The fifth and sixth sections briefly discuss prepayments and relative value.

GROWTH POTENTIAL

The amount of residential mortgage debt outstanding in the United State is approximately $2.5 trillion. Over the past 30 years the annual growth rate has averaged over 10%. The trend reflects growth rates of both new home production and housing values, with peaks and troughs corresponding to the level of business activity, interest rates, and seasonal variation. Unless there are improbable dramatic shifts in demographic patterns (e.g., birth, mortality, and family formation), continued long run growth is expected. Assuming the conservative growth rate estimate of 2.6% (which is less than one quarter of the historical average), residential mortgage debt would climb to $3 trillion before the end of the century.

New production of mortgage pass-throughs reflects both the outstanding quantity and new flow of unsecuritized mortgage debt. Since 1970, when GNMA first began securitizing mortgage pools, the market for agency pass-throughs has been expanding. The agency-backed sector is now a mature market. Currently over 80% of FHA/VA mortgages are either securitized or placed in government agency portfolios. The comparable securitized share for conforming conventional loans been estimated at 29%.

The AA pass-through sector is also maturing. With the conclusion of its infancy, the market is poised for further expansion. Loans may be ineligible for purchase or securitization by the federal agencies for a variety of reasons—loan size, limited documentation, lack of insurance, etc. Although all types of non-conforming mortgages are candidates to back these securities, jumbo fixed-rate whole loans currently comprise the single largest source, and most frequently used type, of collateral. Jumbo adjustable-rate mortgages also provide a substantial flow of additional collateral. In fact, ARM-backed securities dominated new issuance in the AA market for 1988 (approximately 66%). The size of the combined jumbo market can be used as an approximation of the AA pass-through market's growth potential.

In dollar terms, it has been estimated that approximately 25% (about $91 billion in 1988) of newly originated mortgages are jumbos. However, jumbos probably command a somewhat smaller percentage of mortgage debt outstanding. Periodic increases in FNMA/FHLMC loan ceilings, $187,600 for single-family homes in 1989, have allowed some seasoned jumbos to conform to the new agency standards. Nonetheless, the size of the jumbo market is substantial, estimated to be approximately $500 billion, only about $30 billion of which has been publicly securitized. The large store of existing jumbo whole loans, along with a steady flow of new production, suggests a market with substantial growth potential.

HISTORICAL DEVELOPMENT

The success of federal agency pass-through programs has encouraged private institutions to securitize conventional mortgage debt. In 1977 Bank of America launched the AA pass-through market. Since then private label pass-throughs have been issued by commercial banks, savings institutions and mortgage conduits. Five issuers have dominated the market with Citicorp, the market leader, commanding a 22% share (see Exhibit 1).

The market's evolution thus far can be divided into two phases. In the first stage, the 1977-1984 period, the market experienced erratic growth, with cumulative issuance reaching $3.75 billion. During the second period, beginning in 1985, issuance increased dramatically, climbing to $37 billion by March 1989 (see Exhibit 2). Cyclical interest rate movements and tax treatment effects have influenced growth patterns.

Exhibit 1: AA New Issuance by Issuer—1985 - March 1989 ($Billions)

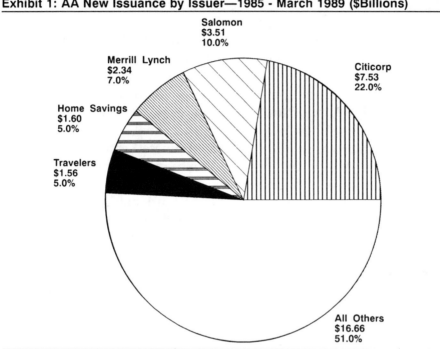

Salomon
$3.51
10.0%

Merrill Lynch
$2.34
7.0%

Citicorp
$7.53
22.0%

Home Savings
$1.60
5.0%

Travelers
$1.56
5.0%

All Others
$16.66
51.0%

AA pass-throughs may be collateralized by both new and seasoned loans. Interest rate levels affect the securitization of both types of loans. Many mortgage originators are hesitant to book a loss by selling underwater collateral. Thus, when interest rates rise, as occurred in 1980-82, 1987, and 1988-1989, the securitization of seasoned discount loans tends to decline. In addition, high interest rates tend to depress mortgage loan origination, which reduces the amount of new collateral available for mortgage pass-throughs.

Tax and accounting treatment have played a significant role in the market's development. The 1986 REMIC legislation permits use of various senior/subordinated (A/B) structures to enhance the credit quality of private label pass-throughs. This structural technique essentially divides the collateral pool into two classes, with the A (senior) class having priority over the B (subordinated) class; any losses are first absorbed by the B piece, which provides protection to the senior piece. One straightforward extension of this technique, often called the mezzanine structure, has been used to issue pass-throughs with more than two classes. Several credit tiers, rather than just two, can be used to create classes with credit qualities corresponding to their collateral cash flow priorities. Securities with this structure contain publicly offered classes that receive different ratings.

The market has increasingly relied on the senior/subordinated structure. In 1987, in the face of dramatic market disruptions and a moderation in new issuance, the production of A/B structures rose to almost $3 billion, 31% of total private-label production. During 1988, new issuance of A/B pass-throughs climbed to $11.6 billion, 82% of total new production (see Exhibit 2). Cost advantages provided the initial impetus for issuers to use this technique;

Exhibit 2: AA New Issuance by Structure

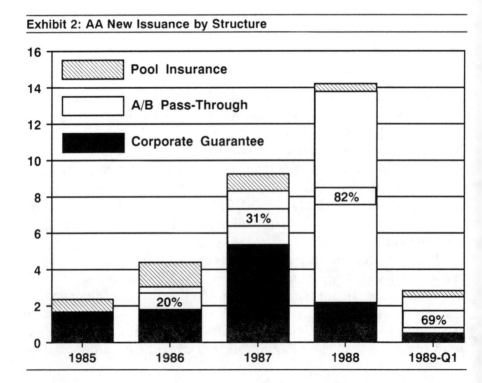

the need for expensive third-party credit enhancements, such as pool insurance, was eliminated. Investor interest, however, also contributed to its popularity; an attractive feature of this structure is the insulation it provides from the risk of an insurer or guarantor downgrading.

Market growth trends are normally expected to reflect interest rate cycles. The exact implementation and impact of the new risk-based capital guidelines for banks and thrifts, however, is much less certain.

In December 1988, the Federal Reserve Board published final risk-based capital guidelines for banks, and the Federal Home Loan Bank Board published proposed rules for thrifts. Although there are some differences, both require an increase in the amount of capital to be maintained against subordinated classes of A/B pass-throughs. Issuers usually retain the subordinated piece, so that increasing the capital requirement lowers the institution's leverage, thus potentially reducing the transaction's economic advantages. The new regulations also mandate that banks hold capital against letters of credit and third-party guarantees, thus potentially increasing the cost of providing these credit enhancements.

Not all institutions will be equally constrained under the new capital guidelines. Regulations for thrifts and banks may differ, with thrifts possibly required to hold a greater amount of capital against subordinated classes. In order to reflect the risk exposure of the subordinated class, proposed thrift guidelines require capital holdings against the entire collateral pool. At the present time, banks must only maintain capital against the subordinated class. A review of this approach, however, is currently underway and an application similar to the thrift guideline is under consideration.

Well capitalized institutions, those with capital in excess of the statutory minimum, will not necessarily be significantly constrained by the new guidelines. Unless a secondary market develops for subordinated pieces, A/B pass-through issuance may show significant declines.

CREDIT QUALITY AND RATING

Private label pass-through securities are typically evaluated by one or more of the rating agencies. Standard & Poor's and Moody's both evaluate these securities based upon collateral quality, quantity of credit support, originator/servicer performance, and legal soundness of the transaction. Ratings are based upon the security's ability to withstand stress. Stress level refers to the severity of loss experienced by the security's underlying collateral. It is equal to the product of mortgage default incidence and average loss per default.

Rating criteria are similar among the agencies. Differences in approach, however, do exist. Standard & Poor's primarily derives its requirements from a "worst case" scenario, the historical experience of the Great Depression of the 1930s. Moody's relies more upon an "expectations" approach. Statistical models are used to forecast expected loss severity, which depends upon loan characteristics and economic conditions. Loan loss severity is predicted under a variety of economic environments, including depression conditions. A weighted average, or expected, stress level is used to determine credit enhancement requirements. Support levels are adjusted to reflect the confidence Moody's has in model predictions, and the probability that actual losses will exceed the expectation.

The rating agencies continually monitor publicly rated pass-throughs for changes in credit quality. As pools age, credit support levels fluctuate with loan defaults, recoveries, and paydowns. An unexpectedly large default incidence may trigger a downgrading. To date, however, AA pass-throughs have been virtually immune from downgradings due to poor collateral performance. Adverse rating changes have been infrequent, and have typically been associated with the downgrading of either a corporate guarantor or a pool insurer. Recent experience, however, should not be viewed as a guarantee against future event risk. Nonetheless, investors can take comfort in a rigorous rating process and the market's historical performance.

Although the rating approaches vary slightly, general principles regarding homeowner defaults apply to both. A detailed discussion of the Standard & Poor's criteria, provided below, addresses these guidelines. Credit analysis begins by defining a standard of comparison, a "prime pool," according to a set of characteristics. When a security's characteristics are not up to "prime," mortgagor defaults are assumed to be more likely, and the ability to absorb larger losses via additional credit enhancement is necessary to obtain a high rating.

In practice, a pool is classified as "prime" if there is a very low probability of significant loss due to mortgagor defaults. Pool composition, as well as the quality of individual loans, is an important consideration. A prime pool is composed of a large number of fixed-rate mortgages (300 or more), none exceptionally large (exceeding $300,000), on properties from geographically diverse, economically secure areas. Thus, the health of the entire pool is not held captive by a small group of mortgages, or by an isolated housing market.

A "high quality" loan is soundly underwritten, has a first lien on a single family detached property, and does not exceed 80% of the property value. An 80% loan-to-value ratio (LTV) ensures that the owner-occupier has a substantial equity interest in the property and a strong incentive to avoid defaulting on the mortgage. Furthermore, in the event of a foreclosure, the homeowner's 20% equity interest provides a cushion limiting the mortgagee's loss. When the LTV is greater than 80% private mortgage insurance is often used as a replacement cushion in case of foreclosure, but not as an equivalent deterrent to default. For this reason the first 25% of the property value is typically covered by the combination of down payment and insurance if the LTV exceeds 80%.

Standard & Poor's bases its credit enhancement requirements not upon recent history, but upon their worst case scenario—the economic collapse witnessed during the Great Depression of the 1930s. For this period, Standard & Poor's has estimated the foreclosure rate on new, fully amortizing single family mortgages at 15.9%, and the average decline in price for these properties at 25%

to 30%. The desire for a timely sale tended to further depress the price of foreclosed properties, and foreclosure costs, which include accrued interest, brokerage fees, legal fees, and taxes, must be added to determine loss severity. Although fundamental economic and financial changes preclude an exact comparison, these numbers are used as conservative benchmarks in determining loss protection.

For a AAA rating the prime pool must withstand, without investor loss, a 15% foreclosure incidence, a 37% decline in property values, and foreclosure expenses approximating 25% of the loan balance. These conditions mandate a 7% loss coverage, the product of loss severity and foreclosure frequency. In order to attain a AA or A rating, the mortgage pool must be capable of withstanding slightly less severe economic stress, requiring 4% and 2.8% loss coverage, respectively. Seasoned mortgages default less frequently than new loans, primarily because their current LTVs are reduced by scheduled amortization and long run growth in real estate prices. Consequently, if the pool has performed adequately, loss coverage may decline over time as the mortgage ages. Exhibit 3 presents loss coverage requirements for investment grade ratings for a prime pool, and a detailed loss severity calculation for AA rating.

ARM collateral has a greater inherent default risk than fixed-rate loans. Mortgagor monthly payments periodically change (annually for most loans) in response to interest rate movements. When the mortgage coupon rises, some homeowners might experience a "payment shock," find themselves unable to meet the increased cash burden, and default on their mortgages. As a result, the rating agencies recognize that ARM securities require more loss protection than similar fixed-rate securities. ARMs are a recent financial innovation. Sufficient data to precisely quantify the additional default risk are not yet available. Nonetheless, the basic determinants of increased risk can be examined.

ARM features affect the likelihood and severity of payment shock. Although many ARM characteristics are important, the most significant are teaser rates and coupon caps. ARMs are often

---

Exhibit 3: Standard & Poor's Credit Support Requirements

Loss Coverage Criteria (Prime Pool)

Rating	Foreclosure Frequency	Loss Severity	Market Value Decline	Foreclosure Cost	Loss Coverage
AAA	15%	47%	37%	25%	7.0%
AA	10	40	32	25	4.0
A	8	35	28	25	2.8

	Loss Severity	Home Equity
Loss Severity Calculation—		
For AA rating of a prime pool		
1. Purchase price of home		$200,000
2. Loan balance (80% LTV)	($160,000)	
3. Market value decline (32% of purchase price)		(64,000)
4. Market value of foreclosure sale	136,000 ←	$136,000
5. Market loss	(24,000)	
6. Foreclosure costs (25% of loan balance)	(40,000)	
7. Total Loss	($64,000)	
8. Total loss ÷ loan balance = loss severity	40%	
($64,000 ÷ 160,000 = 0.40)		

Source: Standard & Poor's Corporation

---

originated with a teaser, a rate below the fully indexed level. Potential mortgagors are frequently qualified on the basis of this teaser rather than the fully indexed rate. As the mortgage rate rises to its fully indexed level, payment shock might result. The more attractive the teaser is to the borrower, the greater the potential payment shock.

Coupon caps, both periodic and lifetime, restrict movements in the mortgage rate. These limit the speed and extent to which mortgage payments can rise, thus moderating the degree of payment shock. Homeowners find caps especially valuable as loans exit the teaser period, often extending the transition time to the fully indexed rate. ARM index and coupon reset frequency also affect the speed to which mortgage rates respond to market interest rate movements. An ARM that infrequently resets to a lagging index is less likely to cause payment shock than one that frequently resets to a very sensitive index.

In two instances, monthly payments may not immediately rise with mortgage rates. First, payment caps can directly limit the periodic rise in payments. Second, the accrual rate can reset more often than the mortgagor's payments. In some cases, mortgage interest can exceed the monthly payment, and loans will experience "negative amortization," an increase in the outstanding mortgage balance. Homeowner equity thus declines, default becomes more likely, and, in the event of default, potential investor loss can increase. A limit on the amount of negative amortization is used in mortgage notes to mitigate this risk.

The rating agencies take into account these ARM features in determining their credit support requirements. For Standard & Poor's, credit support requirements have exceeded that of similar fixed-rate collateral by 20 to 100%. For most popular ARM programs, credit enhancement requirements are 50% higher than for fixed-rate programs. For example, a 6% requirement on fixed-rate mortgages might translate into a 9% level for similar ARM collateral.

Loss coverage has typically been provided by one of three enhancement types: a guarantee or letter of credit, pool insurance, or a senior/subordinated structure. The "quantity" of loss coverage for a particular rating does not depend upon the enhancement type. For example, 7% loss coverage is necessary for a prime pool to receive a AAA rating, whether it is in the form of a corporate guarantee, a private mortgage insurance policy, or a subordinated class. The rating does depend, however, upon the "quality" of the credit enhancement. In judging a structure by its weakest link, the desired rating on the pass-through cannot exceed that of the enhancement provider. When a guarantee or insurance policy provides loss coverage, the pass-through is exposed to an additional downgrading risk via the enhancement provider.

CREDIT ENHANCEMENT

Two types of enhancements—corporate guarantees and pool insurance—initially dominated the market. Corporate guarantees, provided by parents and third parties, are reimbursement obligations for mortgage delinquency and default. Pool insurance refers to an insurance policy written, typically by a private mortgage insurer, on the security's collateral.

Wide use of the senior/subordinated structure is a recent phenomenon, gathering momentum since the passage of the 1986 REMIC legislation. With the rapid market growth during 1988, the A/B structure now commands a 52% market share. Corporate guarantees currently account for approximately 35% of the market, while the market share for pool insurance has fallen to a mere 12%.

Although alternative credit enhancements must provide identical loss coverage for the security to attain a given rating, differences between enhancements do arise. Traditional enhancement types provide loss coverage through a source external to the security. The supply of AA-rated sources is limited and the cost of credit support, when provided by a third party, is high. With private mortgage insurance, policies often contain exclusions for fraud, mortgagor bankruptcy, and special hazard (e.g., earthquake), the latter of which imposes certain geographical restrictions on the mortgage collateral (e.g., parts of California). Supplemental credit support is sometimes necessary.

In addition, external sources are also exposed to event risk, a downgrading or insolvency, which could adversely alter the pass-through's credit quality. Market awareness of this type of risk has been heightened by the default of one private mortgage insurer (TMIC Mortgage Insurance) and the downgrading of another (Verex Assurance, Inc).

In a senior/subordinated structure the senior class is provided credit support by the subordinated class. Delinquencies and defaults are first drawn against the B class, the initial size of which is equal to the required loss coverage. Thus, credit enhancement depends only upon the quality of the mortgage collateral, not upon external pool insurance or guarantees. As such, the pool is not directly exposed to external event risk.

Unlike a traditional credit enhancement, the B class is not perfectly liquid; protection is in the form of a claim on all cash flows. In a given month, if principal and interest due the A class exceed total cash flows from the pool, a payment shortfall would result. In order to mitigate this possibility, a small reserve fund is often established for voluntary advances. If the shortfall exceeds this amount, it accrues interest, which is forwarded when, and if funds become available.

The amount of credit support by the subordinated class depends upon the quality of the pool of loans. Loss coverage requirements are based upon the initial characteristics of the mortgages. In a declining interest rate environment prepayments tend to rise, which may alter pool composition. Economically strained homeowners are often unable to refinance their mortgage. Therefore, as pool size contracts, these loans comprise a larger proportion of the premium pools.

Under these circumstances, the average quality of the collateral, and the protection offered by the subordinated class, may deteriorate. Two variants of the A/B structure have been used to avoid this weakness: the "reserve fund structure" (RF), and the "shifting interest structure" (SI). The quality of the credit support is maintained by either establishing a substantial liquid reserve fund (RF) or by disproportionately passing through prepayments to the A class (SI).

With the RF structure a reserve fund is created by an initial cash deposit. All B class cash flow are placed into the reserve fund until sufficient liquidity, the "Specified Reserve Fund Balance," is attained. Subsequently, class B receives its pro rata cash flows, subject to maintenance of the Specified Fund Balance and compensation of class A shortfalls. Over time, liquidity requirements can be reduced to reflect the higher credit quality of seasoned mortgages.

In the SI structure all prepayments are initially used to pay down the senior class, thus increasing the relative size of the subordinated piece. After a stated period of time, which depends upon the collateral type (e.g., 10 years for ARMs), a "step down" of loss protection is permitted to reflect loan seasoning. The B class begins to receive a greater prepayment percentage, which eventually rises to its pro rata share. Exhibits 4 and 5 diagram the cash flows of one SI structure.

Exhibit 4: Cash Flows from Shifting Interest Senior/Subordinated Pass-Through

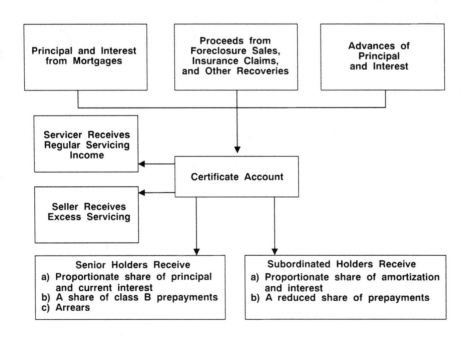

Exhibit 5: First Boston Mortgage Securities Corp.
Conduit Mortgage Pass-Through Certificates, Series 1989-2, Class A

Date: January 19, 1989

Original Balance: $79,830,397—represents 90.75% of mortgage pool

Coupon: Floats off 11th District Cost of Funds index—initially
                           set at 7.90%

Collateral: Primarily ARMs on 1-4 family California residences

LTVs: Almost all with LTV ≤ 80%

Shifting Interest: Certificate holders receive 100% of their pro rata share
                           of prepayments plus a proportion of Class B's
                           prepayments, based upon collateral performance and
                           upon the following schedule:

Year	Proportion
0-10	100%
11	70%
12	60%
13	40%
14	20%
15+	0%

Lead Manager: The First Boston Corporation

PREPAYMENTS

Many factors affect prepayments including interest rates, loan
type, property characteristics, and age. For agency pass-throughs
an established history and a plentiful supply of reliable data have
facilitated the analysis of this complex relationship. Unfortunately,
the private label pass-through market can make no such claim. It
is a young market with neither a long track record nor a central
source of data. To the extent that the loans backing a AA pass-

through are similar to agency collateral, however, the observed behavior of agency securities can be used as a benchmark.

The vast majority of agency issues are collateralized level payment mortgages on single family homes. In an individual pool, there is only one loan type (e.g., fixed rate, 30-year) and the loans are relatively homogeneous with respect to age and mortgage rate; statistical forecasts based upon these data are very reliable. In contrast, private label pass-throughs may contain different loan types and are not always homogeneous. These conditions reduce the precision of prepayment forecasts and require modification of prepayment projections.

There is some good news for projecting prepayments. For most AA pass-throughs, detailed information about geographic location of the properties, size, and LTV of the mortgages is available. Proper use of the data improves prepayment forecasts: prepayment speeds often differ by geographical location; the incentive to refinance a premium mortgage increases with its size; and loans with high LTVs default more frequently. As with agency issues, defaults and prepayments usually have equivalent cash flow consequences when credit enhancement is sufficient.

The diversity of collateral type, heterogeneity of mortgage pools, and increased geographic/financial data render prepayment analysis more complicated for AA pass-through securities. Nonetheless, the fundamentals of prepayment forecasting remain intact. Prepayments tend to increase as interest rates fall, and rise with the seasoning of the mortgages.

When available, the appropriate FNMA prepayment model is selected as a benchmark. For example, the FNMA 30-year, fixed-rate model is used as a starting point for fixed-rate jumbo loans with similar WACs and WAMs. The FNMA experience is applied because conventional mortgages back all AA pass-throughs and most FNMA pools, whereas FHA/VA loans secure GNMA pools. Prepayment patterns reflect collateral characteristics, rendering FNMA prepayments a more suitable benchmark than GNMA's.

Servicing fees for AA pass-throughs tend to be larger, and vary more, than those for FNMA securities. Therefore, the WAC on a

AA pass-through will usually exceed that on a comparable coupon FNMA security. Furthermore, the range of mortgage rates in a FNMA pool is typically much tighter than that in a AA pass-through. For a given WAC, mortgage rate heterogeneity increases prepayment rates.

RELATIVE VALUE ANALYSIS

In order to determine the relative value of an AA pass-through, three factors must be considered: credit and liquidity risk, payment rules, and the prepayment option. AA pass-throughs are currently less liquid and perceived to have greater credit risk than FNMA securities. In order to compensate investors for these risks, AA pass-throughs typically trade at higher yields than comparable coupon FNMAs. Growing investor acceptance and market liquidity, however, have contributed to yield spread stability. Over the last few years spreads have stayed in a 20 to 45 basis point range.

The credit and liquidity spread over FNMA issues can be expressed as the residual yield differential after other factors have been taken into account; it will vary over time with market conditions. Not all AA pass-throughs are alike. Collateral differences, such as location, LTVs, and credit enhancement type, will exist at issuance. As market conditions continue to evolve, relative credit quality within the AA pass-through market will respond. For most securities a rapid deterioration in credit quality is highly unlikely. Nonetheless, routine review of collateral characteristics and enhancement level is suggested.

The yield of a AA pass-through is determined, in part, by the security's payment practices. Although most AA pass-throughs, like FNMA securities, have a 55-day stated payment delay, interest on prepayments often receives different treatment. FNMAs pay interest on the outstanding balance as of the beginning of the month. A prepayment that occurs after the cutoff date does not affect the balance until the following month, and so a full month of interest is paid to the investor. Some AA pass-throughs, however, accrue interest only on each day's outstanding balance. For these securities, a full month's interest on prepayments is not paid, and yield is commensurately reduced.

A simple example will illustrate the importance of this point. Consider a FNMA security and a AA pass-through, both with a 12% coupon, prepaying at 2.0% SMM. Suppose prepayments are evenly distributed over the month. If the security does not pay interest on the 2% of the balance that prepays each month, it is equivalent to reducing its 12% coupon by 12 basis points, to 11.88%.

Structural elements can interact with collateral characteristics to affect relative value. For instance, the yield on shifting interest A/B structures is more sensitive to prepayments than is the collateral. The reason, of course, is that the senior class initially receives all prepayments. As would be expected, the further from par, and the larger the size of the B piece, the greater the yield impact. Moreover, as the collateral seasons, and the B piece draws more of its pro rata prepayments, this effect eventually vanishes.

A shifting interest structure does not always perform differently from other AA pass-throughs. However, if the security is priced far from par, and the B piece is of substantial size, yield differences can be significant. For example, consider a security backed by fixed-rate 30-year loans, two years seasoned, with an 8.75% weighted average coupon and 75 basis points of servicing. Similar FNMA collateral has recently been priced at 88 and is projected to prepay at approximately 120% PSA. Suppose AA security price and loan prepayments mirror those of similar FNMAs. Yield for the AA security, not packaged as a shifting interest structure, is 10.41%. If the collateral is pooled into a shifting interest structure, issued with a 10% B piece, prepayments directed toward the A class will initially equal 133 (120/.9)% PSA. Using this speed as a rough approximation for lifetime prepayments results in a yield of 10.51%, a differential of 10 basis points.

For ARM and fixed-rate collateral the amount of interest passed through to investors can differ by structure. ARMs with different reset dates are often pooled together. The average time to reset, or roll, can affect security price. In general, there is a small bias towards securities that reset frequently because they are slightly less exposed to temporary interest rate risk. More important, however, is the scheduled direction of the reset. For example, a short time to the roll is desirable if the ARM index has risen and loan coupons are scheduled to reset upwards. When the index is falling, a long time to the roll is usually preferred.

The weighted average pass-through, or WAPT, structure is a recent innovation used to package fixed-rate loans with a variety of coupons. The security's coupon is determined by subtracting a fixed servicing fee from each mortgage in the pool. As prepayments alter the composition of the pool, the pass-through rate moves in concert. Higher coupon loans tend to prepay more quickly than the lower coupon mortgages. If the underlying loans have widely dispersed coupons, the pass-through rate might tend to drift downward, thereby reducing security yield. In most instance, however, potential declines in the pass-through rate will be minor. For example, if the majority of the mortgage rates are within 50 basis points of the weighted average coupon, the effect on yield is less than 5 basis points.

SUMMARY

Private label pass-throughs comprise a new and rapidly expanding market. These securities, backed by whole loans, rely upon collateral quality and credit enhancements, rather than agency guarantees, to provide credit support. The satisfactory completion of a rigorous review is required in order to receive an investment grade rating. Nonetheless, changing market conditions suggest periodic review of the security's credit quality.

Credit support comes in the form of private mortgage insurance, corporate guarantees, or a subordinated class. Although private mortgage insurance has traditionally been the favored credit support, use of the senior/subordinated structure has gained popularity. In the A/B structure, the A class takes priority over the B class. All losses are first directed to the B class, thus providing the A class with protection. Advantages of this enhancement type are its cost effectiveness and the insulation it provides from the risk of an insurer or guarantor downgrading.

AA pass-throughs are typically priced off comparable coupon FNMA securities; a yield premium compensates for credit and liquidity risks. Prepayment forecasts are a major element in determining the relative value of a mortgage security. Scarcity of data in the AA market severely complicates this task.

CHAPTER 7

SELF-INSURING NON-CONFORMING MORTGAGES USING SENIOR-SUBORDINATED STRUCTURES

Anand K. Bhattacharya, PhD
Vice President
Financial Strategies Group
Prudential Securities Inc.

INTRODUCTION

One of the major financial innovations in the capital markets has been the securitization of assets. The process involves the transformation of whole loans into securities with appealing investment characteristics, such as credit worthiness, liquidity, and yields typically higher than comparable maturity Treasury securities.

Certain portions of this chapter are based upon Anand K. Bhattacharya and Peter J. Cannon, "Senior Subordinated Mortgage Pass-Throughs," in Frank J. Fabozzi, ed., *Advances and Innovations in the Bond and Mortgage Markets* (Chicago, IL: Probus Publishing, 1989), pp. 474-484.

131

While the wave of securitization has permeated to all sectors of asset markets, such as mortgages, credit cards, automobile and mobile home loans, computer leases, marine loans and home equity lines of credit, the manifestation of the securitization process is most visible in the mortgage market. Within the mortgage markets, the thrust of securitization has centered on loans which meet underwriting criteria (the "comforming" loans) specified by the various programs of the Government National Mortgage Association (GNMA), Federal National Mortgage Association (FNMA) and Federal Home Loan Mortgage Corporation (FHLMC). The development of the secondary market for GNMA, FNMA and FHLMC securities combined with the explicit and implicit federal guarantees associated with these securities, has made them attractive candidates for inclusion in portfolios of a variety of investors ranging from thrifts and banks to pension funds, money management firms, mutual funds and insurance companies.

However, mortgage loans which do not meet the underwriting criteria of the federal agencies, the so-called "non-conforming" loans, are not as easily amenable to the securitization process as are conforming loans. The main reason for this lies in the fact that non-conforming loans cannot be securitized under the aegis of the various programs of either FNMA or FHLMC. In the absence of the credit guarantees of such government-sponsored enterprises, the securitization of such loans relies heavily upon the availability of external credit support. While this credit risk can be mitigated by a variety of devices such as pool insurance, letters of credit and corporate guarantees, such devices are heavily dependent upon the credit quality of the provider of such insurance. On the other hand, self-insurance created by subordinating a portion of the mortgage pool cash flows to mimic the same level of credit support provided by external devices, allows originators of non-conforming loans to tap the capital markets without being dependent upon the long-term credit worthiness of a third-party credit enhancement institution.

CREDIT ENHANCEMENT OF NON-CONFORMING LOANS

Mortgage pass-through securities are created when the lender pools mortgages and sells ownership interests in the pool. As payments from homeowners are received, the servicing institution passes "through" to security holders the interest portion as well as scheduled and any unscheduled principal cash flows. The pass-through securities may further serve as collateral for a multi-class structure, such as a collateralized mortgage obligation (CMO). In such multi-class structures, the securitized pass-throughs serve as collateral for bonds of various maturity and cash flow characteristics designed to appeal to the risk-return preferences of a spectrum of investors.

Originators of comforming loans can choose from several alternatives in executing the securitization of mortgages. Loans which are insured either by the Federal Housing Administration (FHA) or guaranteed by the Veterans Administration (VA) are eligible for pooling under the various programs of GNMA. In addition to FHA or VA fixed-rate mortgages, graduated payment loans, growing equity mortgages, mobile home loans, as well as certain types of FHA/VA adjustable-rate mortgage quality for pooling under the GNMA guarantee programs. Since GNMA guarantees the full and timely payment of principal and interest, irrespective of the payment history of the underlying loans, the resultant securities are obligations of the U.S. government and hence of appeal to credit quality conscious investors. Conventional loans which do not qualify for inclusion under GNMA programs can be securitized under the various programs of FNMA and FHLMC. While these entities are not U.S. government agencies, securities issued by both FNMA and FHLMC are perceived as negligible credit risks, mainly due to the presumed government guarantees associated with the obligations of these agencies.

However, for originators of "non-conforming" loans, choices for accessing capital markets are limited. At first blush, the nomenclature, "non-conforming" may indicate negative connotations associated with the credit quality of the loan. This is not the case, as often mortgage loans may not conform to agency underwriting criteria because the original principal balance exceeds the government's prescribed limit as is the case with "jumbo" loans. Additionally, mortgages may not qualify for inclusion in various GNMA, FNMA and FHLMC programs due to non-standard documentation or the nature of the underlying collateral. In such cases, the securitization of such loans rests heavily upon obtaining external credit support to enhance the credit worthiness of the underlying loans.

At this juncture, it is useful to detail the various types of risks inherent in non-conforming mortgages that require insurance prior to the securitization process. In conforming mortgages, such risks are covered by the blanket guarantee provided by GNMA, FNMA and FHLMC. With respect to non-conforming mortgages, the cash flow stream of a pool of such mortgages could be restricted under a combination of the following circumstances:

- credit losses due to delinquencies and defaults by mortgagors in the mortgage pool.

- special hazard losses caused by "acts of God" such as earthquakes, floods and other losses due to fraud and negligence in the orgination process.

- losses due to fraud and negligence in the origination process.

- losses due to re-organization of the terms of the mortgagors' debt in the event of bankruptcy.

In view of the existence of such risks in a pool of non-conforming mortgages, the type and quality of the external devices used to enhance the credit quality of the pool will heavily influence investor interest in such structured securities.

TYPES OF CREDIT ENHANCEMENT

As a general rule, in order for the structure to be rated by major rating agencies, such as Standard and Poor's (S&P) and Moody's Investor Services (MIS), the credit quality of the pool is assessed. This requires an assessment of the underwriting guidelines and procedures of the originator, the quality of the operations of the servicer and the relative credit risk of the particular pool under consideration. This overall evaluation of the relative credit quality of the mortgage pool dictates the type and level of external credit enhancement required in order to upgrade the preceived credit of the pool to that implied by the assigned rating. In order to minimize any interruptions in the cash flow promised to investors, the overriding concern in this evaluation is to assess the level of loss protection required for the pool of mortgages to be assigned an investment grade rating. Once the level of credit protection has been decided, the mortgage pool may be structured as a single class pass-through security or as a multi-class structure, with securities of various maturities and cash flow profiles designed to appeal to varying risk preferences of investors.

As a general rule, mortgage lenders require certain types of insurance coverage on the loans in order to protect their perfected interest in the loans. Such coverage usually includes *primary mortgage insurance (PMI)*, for loans which involve lower down payments and higher loan-to-value (LTV) ratios. This type of insurance typically insures the loan up to such time as the loan balance is reduced to an LTV ratio of under 80%. Alternatively, the mortgagor can also self-insure the mortgage by paying a higher contractual rate, which is typically 0.25% higher. In geographical areas where the incidence of natural disasters such as earthquakes has been determined to be higher than usual, the lender may also require additional hazard insurance coverage which covers such "acts of God." Similarly, in areas determined to be in a federally designated flood zone, the mortgagor may also be required to obtain additional flood insurance. The default risk of the pool can be mitigated by a variety of external credit support mechanisms. The overall loss protection of the mortgage pool can be enhanced by a combination of corporate guarantees, pool insurance, letter of credit or self insurance by subordinating a certain segment of cash flows. In any case, the claims paying capability of the PMI insurer is an important factor in determining the level of required loss protection. Ideally, this should be at least as high as the desired rating. In cases, where the claims paying ability of the insurer is lower than the desired rating, the required external loss protection will be higher in order to compensate for the lower credit of the primary mortgage insurer. Similarly, in the event high LTV loans in the pool do not have PMI or if loans in hazard zones do not have either flood or special disaster insurance, the absolute level of the external credit protection can be enhanced to cover such contingencies.

Pool Insurance Policies

Pool insurance policies, underwritten by highly rated private insurance companies can be used to obtain external credit support for pools of non-conforming mortgage loans. Such policies are designed to cover credit losses up to a certain percentage of the principal balance of the mortgage pool. In any case, the credit rating of the structured securities cannot be higher than the rating of the insurer. In addition to the rating of the structure being dependent upon the ongoing credit of the insurer, pool insurance policies may have to be supplemented by special hazard coverage. In the event property damage occurs due to events such as natural disasters which are not covered by standard hazard insurance, special coverage against such events may also be required. Typically, special hazard coverage is determined as 1% of the aggregate unpaid balance of the loans in the pool. However, if the mortgage pool includes loans with large principal balances or includes properties in high risk zones, disaster coverage may have been increased to reflect the higher risk. Such increases are determined as the greater of either twice the principal balance of the largest loan or the aggregate principal balance of the loans included in the high risk geographical area.

In addition to issues such as special hazard coverage, the timing mechanism of the pool insurance policy is also of importance. In instances of temporary delinquency, when the mortgagor fails to make the monthly mortgage payment, the cash flows available for distribution to the holders of the structured securities are likely to be hampered. Despite the fact that such temporary shortfalls are likely to be cured in a short period of time, most pool insurance policies are designed to include an "advance claims endorsement." This feature of the policy allows the servicers to file claims against the pool insurer after a reasonable period of time has elapsed. In the event that this feature is not part of the pool insurance coverage, additional funds to cover such liquidity shortfalls may have to be posted by the issuer of the securities. Such supplemental liquidity may be provided in the form of a cash performance bond from a surety provider with a claims paying ability rated at least equal to the assigned credit rating of the pool. Alternatively, the liquidity facility may be in the form of a reserve fund or letter of credit.

Mortgagor Bankruptcy Insurance: In the event, certain mortgagors in the pool of non-conforming loans were to file for bankruptcy, it is possible that as part of the bankruptcy proceedings, the terms of the mortgage can be modified by either a mandated change of the mortgage rate or a reduction of the principal balance. In order to insure such risk, the issuer of the non-conforming securitized structure is required to post non-restorable coverage. Depending upon the type of mortgages, the amount may either be an absolute amount or determined as a function of the characteristics of the mortgage pool in order to reflect its relative riskiness. For instance, S&P requires coverage up to $100,000 for a pool of first mortgages on primary single-family homes. However, if the pool includes properties which are either multi-family dwelling, owned by investors or second homes, the non-restorable coverage $100,000 is increased by the greater of either 1% of the unpaid principal balance of all non-primary residence loans or the amount of the largest such loan. As a general rule, mortgages on dwellings which do not serve as the main residence of the mortgagor are considered more risky than primary single-family mortgages.

Fraud Insurance: In order to cover mortgage pool losses occurring due to fraud and misrepresentation in the origination process, rating agencies will require additional insurance coverage in order to cover such incidences. For instance, S&P assumes that the risk of such loss is the highest in the early years of origination and becomes significantly lower as the loans becomes seasoned. Additionally, the absolute level of such fraud coverage is linked to the overall level of external credit enhancement required under the doctrine of relative risk assessment. This is due to the thesis that a higher level of overall credit support indicates higher relative riskiness and hence, a greater incidence of potential losses due to fraud.

Corporate Guarantees, Letter of Credit and Bond Insurance

As an alternative to pool insurance, where the rating of the structure is a function of the rating of an external insurance agency, issuers can also rely on corporate guarantees provided by the parent company as a means of credit enhancement. The corporate guarantee provides the same level of coverage as would be provided by a pool insurance company. As with the case of pool insurance, the credit rating of the structure can be no higher than the credit rating of the parent guarantor. Similarly, the credit assignment of the structure is also susceptible to any downgrades in the credit rating of the parent corporation. Despite such similarities between pool insurance and corporate guarantees, subsidiaries of a large corporation may find it economical to use parent guarantees as such guarantees usually do not require supplemental credit insurance due to the unconditional nature of the guarantee.

Alternatively, issuers may obtain bond insurance from financial guarantee firms, such as Financial Guarantee Insurance Corporation (FGIC), Financial Security Assurance (FSA) and Capital Markets Assurance Corporation (CAPMAC) which underwrite policies to assure the timely payment of principal and interest on pass-through securities. Such guarantees are usually unconditional in that all losses ranging the gamut from default risk to special hazard risk are covered, obviating the need for any supplemental credit support. Issuers have also partially relied upon an external version of a corporate guarantee in the form of a letter of credit, which either covers all loans up to a certain percentage of the outstanding principal balance or covers only a portion ("top loss") of each loan. The main disadvantage in using a letter of credit from external sources is that such guarantees are usually not indefinite and may have to be renewed at the end of term. It is for this reason that letters of credit are most commonly used as supplemental rather than primary sources of credit enhancement.

Subordination of Cash Flows

While pool insurance and corporate guarantees as methods of credit enhancement depend upon the credit worthiness of the providing institution, such as an insurance company, bank or industrial corporation, the subordination of cash flows is the closest form of self insurance that can be structured in a mortgage pool. In such structures, labeled as "senior-subordinated" structures, the subordinated class supplies the credit enhancement for the senior class. In any credit enhanced transaction collateralized by mortgages, the overriding objective is to ensure that cash flows to the holders of the structurd securities are not interrupted by externalties such as default, delinquencies, natural disasters and bankruptcy. In a senior-subordinated structure, two primary classes of certificates are created—a senior class and a subordinated class. The subordinated class functions as the credit enhancement for the senior class because, should any delinquencies or defaults on the underlying mortgages occur, payments that would otherwise be made to the subordinated class are diverted to the senior class to the extent required to make the scheduled interest and principal payments. Accordingly, the majority of the credit risk is concentrated in the subordinated class since with any disruption in cash flows, payments to the subordinated class are made only if there is sufficient cash flow to make all senior pass-through payments.

While private label issuers had employed senior-subordinated participations as a means of credit enhancement for non-conforming loans, the tax status of trusts which issued such investments was jeopardized in 1984 when the Internal Revenue Service (IRS) proposed taxation of trusts which actively managed investments. However, in 1986, the IRS clarified that senior-subordinated participations issued via a grantor trust would not be subject to double taxation. Additionally, The Real Estate Mortgage Investment Conduit (REMIC) provision of the Tax Reform Act of 1986 added a further dimension of flexibility to senior subordinated structures by permitting the subordinated interest to be sold instead of being retained by the issuer as a means of self insurance, as well as permitting greater flexibility in the issuance of multi-class transactions. The REMIC provision in the tax law also allows the issuing entity to be elected as a REMIC for tax purposes without sacrificing the tax advantages available to a grantor trust.

From the issuer's perspective, the issuance of the senior-subordinated structure could be recorded as a sale of assets for the senior class of securities by following the tenants specified in Statement of Financial Accounting Standards 77, *Transfer of Receivables with Recourse*. According to SFAS 77, an issuer may report the transaction as a sale if the following conditions are met.

- The issuer surrenders control of future economic benefits. Control of future economic benefits is considered not to have been transferred if the issuer has an option to repurchase the receivables at a later date.

- The remaining obligations of the issuer to the buyer under recourse provisions can be reasonably estimated. The sale can be violated if the amount collectible, costs of collection and repossesion are not subject to reasonable estimation.

- The issuer cannot be required to repurchase receivables from the buyer except in accordance with the provisions of the recourse agreement. Additionally, the amount of such receivables to be repurchased pursuant to such provisions must be minimal. Minor "clean-up" calls or "redemptions" by the servicer (usually the seller) to keep the cost of servicing the receivables are permitted and do not jeopardize the sale treatment of assets.

By following the guidelines in SFAS 77, assuming that the subordinated class is retained, the creation of senior-subordinated transactions allows issuers to obtain sales treatment for the amount of the senior certificates. In the event any excess servicing associated with the loans is part of the sale, the present value of the excess servicing stream, calculated at a realistic discount rate and prepayment expectation, is added to the sale price for the purposes of determining the total price on the sale of assets. In order to meet sales treatment under SFAS 77, the issuer must surrender control of the future economic benefits embodied in the mortgage loans transferred and can not have an option to repurchase the loans at a later date. Additionally, the retention by the issuer of the right to service the loans and to receive excess servicing fees does not usually preclude sale accounting. In the event the transaction requires the retention of the subordinate class by the issuer, the recourse obligation can be reasonably estimated from historical data of the mortgage loans sold or loans with similar characteristics. Generally, this requires the issuer to have reasonable records on the historical foreclosure and loss experience of the mortgage loans (or similar loans) to be able to obtain a reasonable estimate of the recourse obligation. With respect to the recourse obligations, minor "clean-up" calls and "redemptions" do not violate the sales treatment of the senior assets. However, the assets cannot be recorded as a sale if the issuer has the option to call the receivables or the purchasers have the option to put the assets back to the seller at a specified future date. The subordinate interests are classified as retained assets which bear the default risk of the senior class of the structure.

THE SENIOR-SUBORDINATED STRUCTURE

The subordinated class in a senior-subordinated class is designed to function like an insurance policy against defaults and delinquencies on the underlying mortgages. However, in contrast to an insurance policy, which is liquid up to the coverage ceiling, the subordinated certificate holders can be required to forgo only the cash flows that currently are due to them or that previously have been accumulated in a reserve fund to cover shortfalls in the cash flows due to the senior class. Senior-subordinated mortgage pass-throughs are designed to ensure that cash flow deficiencies will not result to the senior class. While the senior class can be further structured as a multi-structure in a multitude of ways to appeal to the risk-return profiles of various investors (e.g., PAC-companion structure; current pay structure; floater-inverse floater structure), the following discussion focuses exclusively on the determination of the subordinated amount.

Determination of the Subordinated Amount

Since the subordinated class serves as credit enhancement for the senior class, the factors involved in determining the size of the subordinated piece are no different than determining the credit support required in a traditional pass-through structure utilizing an alternative credit enhancement vehicle, such as pool insurance. The credit support for a senior-subordinated structure is determined by adjusting pre-established credit support guidelines for a representative sample of prime loans, labeled as benchmark pools for the attributes of the specific pools under consideration in order to account for the relative risk of the asset being rated.

While the specifics of each case may vary, in general, the process may be outlined as follows.[1] According to MIS, the credit risk of a pool of non-conforming mortgages is assessed by comparing the characteristics of the pool under consideration to that of a standard pool. MIS defines a standard or "benchmark" pool as a pool of 30-year geographically diverse, fixed-rate, owner occupied, fully documented, newly originated, purchase-money mortgages on single family, average value properties. The credit support for each benchmark pool is a function of the forecasted *foreclosure frequency* and the expected *severity of loss* percentage. The foreclosure frequency refers to the probability of default of the mortgages in the pool. As a general rule, the prime determinant of default for a mortgagor is the amount of equity accumulated in the property. The greater the amount of price appreciation, the faster the rate of loan amortization and principal repayment, the greater the rate of equity accumulation and lower the incidence of default. In view of this consideration, benchmark pools for various LTV ratios are used in the assessment of credit risk for pools of non-conforming mortgages. The severity of loss measures the extent of the loss in the event of default as a function of factors such as specific loan attributes such as age, coupon rate, seasoning, LTV, adequacy of PMI and costs associated with delinquency and foreclosure.

Deviations in the characteristics of the pool under consideration from the attributes of a prime pool are expressed in terms of "risk weights" or multiples of prime pool credit support. For an individual mortgage with multiple deviations from the characteristics of the benchmark pool, the aggregate risk is determined as the product of the various risk weights and then averaged across individual mortgages to obtain a credit support level for the overall pool. On the micro level, contractual features of the mort-

---

[1] This description relies heavily on the criteria used by Moody's Investor Services in rating mortgaged-backed securities collateralized by whole loans. The interested reader is referred to *Moody's Approach to Rating Residential Mortgage Pass-Throughs'* Moody's Investor Services, April 1990.

gage along with the characteristics of the properly are considered in assessing the relative riskiness of the pool. This micro assessment of the mortgage loans is combined with a macro evaluation of features such as diversification of the pool, geographical concentration and structural features of securities in the determination of the overall credit support level.

Attributes of the Mortgage Loans: With respect to the attributes of the individual mortgage, an evaluation of the loans is conducted along the following dimensions.

1. **Mortgage type:** In order to accommodate the various types of mortgages in circulation, the contractual features of the type of mortgage loan under consideration are compared with the characteristics of the mortgages comprising the benchmark pool for the stated LTV level. With respect to adjustable-rate mortgages, an evaluation of features such as annual and lifetime caps, the existence of teaser rates, the potential for negative amortization and volatility of the underlying index are used to assess the extent of "payment shock" in the event interest rates increase. As a general rule, ARMs are considered more risky than fixed-rate mortgages due to a higher potential for credit losses due to the possibility of negative amortization and higher monthly payments. Additionally, certain ARMs with more market sensitive underlying indices (LIBOR as opposed to the Eleventh District cost of funds index) are more risky than other ARMs, especially in rising rate scenarios. Other fixed-rate loans, such as seller financed fixed-rate loans or buy down loans, graduated payment mortgages and growing equity mortgages are also considered more risky than fixed-rate level pay mortgages as such loans usually have some type of acceleration of monthly payments and borrowers are often qualified at lower rates.

2. **Mortgage amortization and coupon:** Since the amortization schedule of a mortgage affects the build-up of equity and hence the LTV of a loan, mortgages with a term shorter than 30 years are considered less risky. Conversely, longer term mortgages are assigned a higher risk weight in this category than a benchmark pool. Similarly, higher coupon mortgages lead to a faster build up of equity than lower coupon mortgages. However, this feature has to be tempered with the rate environment in which the mortgage was originated in order to assess whether the higher rate is indicative of the poor credit quality of the mortgagor on account of higher risk premia charged by the lender.

3. **Documentation standards:** Any mortgage loan not originally underwritten according to FNMA and FHLMC standards falls into the general category of "limited" or "partial" documentation loans. In full documentation loans, the lender conducts verification of income (VOI), verification of down payments (VOD), and verification of employment (VOE), as well as independent appraisals of the property and assesment of the credit reports. However, with non-conforming loans, several of these verifications may not have been conducted on a comprehensive basis. In such cases, the relative riskiness of a partial documentation loan is likely to be higher than full documentation loans. Hence, an evaluation of the deviation of the underwriting standards for the loans under consideration is necessary in order to assign qualitative risk weightings.

4. **Loan purpose:** The credit support for the benchmark pool assumes that the mortgage was taken out for the explicit purpose for the purchase of the property securing the mortgage. In the event the borrower uses a portion of the funds from the loans, as in the case of equity take-out refinancing, the loan is considered more risky than the loans comprising the benchmark pool and, therefore, is assigned a higher risk weight.

5. **Seasoning of the mortgage:** Loans which have been out-standing for a period of time can be more (less) risky than the benchmark pool mortgages. In areas where property values have appreciated (depreciated), the equity of the mortgagor would have increased (decreased) and hence the loan would be assigned a lower (higher) risk weight. Also for alternative mortgage instruments, such as ARMs and non-traditional fixed-rate mortgages, such as GPMs and GEMs, data on the payment history, especially during esca-lating rate periods may provide an assessment of the resil-iency of the borrower of payment shock.

6. **Credit quality of originator and private mortgage insurer:** Loan underwriting is an important consideration in analyz-ing the credit quality of the securities collateralized by non-conforming mortgages as the underwriting standards and quality of the originator are a direct reflection of the relative riskiness of the mortgage pool. Additionally, since most originators of such mortgages also perform the servicing function, the quality of the servicing operation is also of di-rect importance for the transaction, especially for senior-subordinated transactions since the timing of the cash flows to the senior class is heavily dependent upon the efficiency of the servicing operation. Similarly, the claims paying ca-pabilities of the private mortgages insurer will determine the extent to which potential delinquencies can be cured in the senior-subordinated transaction. Using the weak link approach, the assigned credit rating of the pool cannot be higher than the rated claims paying ability of the PMI provider.

Attributes of the Properties Securing the Loans: In addition to the attributes of the mortgage loan, the following characteristics of the properties securing the mortgage are also used to assess the relative risk weightings of the mortgage pool.

1. **Type of property and occupany status:** As a general rule, loans on single family homes tend to have lower default rates than mortgages secured by multifamily dwellings, condominiums, planned unit developments (PUDs) and townhouses. Additionally, in the event of default, it is easier to initiate foreclosure proceedings and eventually liquidate single-family homes. In periods of property appreciation, single-family residences tend to appreciate at a higher rate than condominium homes. Conversely, in periods of depreciating prices, single-family detached homes tend to maintain value better than attached planned dwellings. With condominium and PUDs, which involve common charges, the marketability of the property in the event of default is also reduced due to the additional cost of ownership. At the same time, such properties also require higher maintenance costs. With respect to occupany, the default rate on non-owner occupied properties is likely to be higher resulting in such mortgages being assigned higher risk weightings. Similarly, during periods of economic adversity, the default rate on second homes and vacation properties is likely to be higher due to the linkage between the costs of maintaining such properties and discretionary income. At the same time, in the event of default, the severity of losses associated with such mortgages is likely to be higher due to location (vacation homes) and the carrying costs of these properties.

2. **Geographic location:** The properties comprising the benchmark pools in each LTV category are considered as "average value" dwellings. Loans on properties whose appraised values are substantially higher than median values in the particular area are assigned a higher risk weight mainly due to the fact that such properties involve higher carrying costs in the event of default and are difficult to liquidate, especially during periods of slow activity in real estate mar-

kets. In addition to the actual location of the property, an assessment is also made of the economic conditions of the region in which the dwelling is located. Properties located in geographical locations, where the economy is diversified and not dependent upon the vagaries of conditions in a particular industry are more likely to withstand downturns in economic activity. In view of this reasoning, properties located in states with a less diversified economic base are assigned a higher risk weighting.

Attributes of the Mortgage Pool: In addition to assessing the relative riskiness of the contractual features of the mortgage loans and the characteristics of the properties securing the loans, an analysis of the attributes of the features of the mortgage pool is also required prior to assigning the final risk weighting. In general, the lower the number of mortgages in a pool, the greater the variability of losses and the higher the incidence that cash flows to certificate holders will be interrupted. In view of this consideration, pools with a higher number of mortgages are assigned a lower risk weighting. Both S&P and MIS consider a pool with less than 300 mortgages as a small pool. At the same time, a concentration of properties in certain geographical areas indicates a higher potential of loss during an economic downturn. In order to protect the investors of the structured securities against such contingencies, mortgage pools with a substantial concentration of properties in a particular region or a higher number of mortgage loans secured by properties located in the same condominium complex or PUD are assigned a higher risk weight.

In the final analysis, the subordinated amount is determined as the relative deviation of the mortgage pool from the credit loss coverage for a benchmark pool within a particular LTV class. In senior-subordinated structures, the credit support for losses or the loss coverage remains fixed at the initial level for a certain period of time, generally five years for fixed-rate mortgages and ten years for ARMs. Following this initial period, a "step-down" period occurs in which the required loss coverage declines according to a formula if the loss and delinquency experience have been favorable. After this step-down period, the loss coverage declines as a percentage of the declining mortgage pool balance. This step down in the level of loss coverage recognizes the fact that the greatest incidence of default generally is during the first five years of the life of a fixed-rate mortgage loan and the first ten years of an ARM. Furthermore, prepayments during this initial period generally do not reduce the level of credit risk commensurate with the reduction in the outstanding principal balance under the assumption that "good" loans are more likely to prepay than "bad" loans. However, if the loss and delinquency experience during the initial period is favorable, foreclosure losses over the remaining life of the mortgage pool can be expected to be less frequent and less severe than originally anticipated. Nonetheless, the credit support requirement for short-term delinquencies remains fixed over the life of the mortgage pool. Since this delinquency coverage is designed to maintain timely payments to investors in the face of temporary shortfalls, the level of such coverage is not subject to step-down provisions. In senior-subordinated structures, while delinquency coverage is usually considered separate from loss coverage, both sources of coverage draw upon the subordinated amount of the cash flows for overall credit support.

Liquidity Safeguards in Senior-Subordinated Structures

While the credit protection provided by the subordinated piece may be considered sufficiently adequate, it is not a perfect substitute for other credit enhancement devices such as pool insurance or a letter of credit. In the event of mortgagor delinquency and default, other credit enhancement alternatives provide immediate coverage up to the limit protection. However, the ability of the subordinated cash flows to meet shortfalls in the senior class flow is limited by the balance in any fund created specifically for the purposes of such contingencies and any current cash flow due to the subordinated holders. In order to guard against such occurrences, liquidity safeguards in the form of either a *reserve fund* or a *shifting interest* mechanism are used in senior-subordinated structures.

In a reserve fund structure, cash flows from principal payments that otherwise would be distributed to the subordinated certificate holders are maintained in a reserve fund. The combination of the reserve fund and the subordinated class principal allocation provide the credit support for the senior class. In such cases, while a cash performance bond or guarantor could be used to provide delinquency coverage, in most instances, such coverage is provided in the form of an initial deposit by the issuer up to the reserve fund under the aegis of self insurance. The issuer may retain the right to recover the initial deposit and subrogate the rights of the subordinated holders to receive cash flows over these funds.

In a shifting interest structure, a reserve fund is not established to provide the required loss coverage. Instead, the prepayments attributable to the subordinated class are diverted to the senior class, thereby increasing the subordination level of the junior class. The relative ownership interests in the underlying pool of mortgages shifts from the senior class to the subordinated class as prepayments are diverted to the senior class and the paydown of these certificates effectively accelerated. As a result, the senior class will experience an effective prepayment rate that is greater than the actual pool experience. Additionally, with the acceleration of the paydown of the senior class, the effective level of subordination for the senior class will be an increasing function of the rate at which the senior class is retired. During the initial period of the investment during which step-down of coverage cannot occur, the entire share of the principal attributable to the subordinated class is diverted to the senior class. After the conclusion of this initial period, this diversion of principal is stepped down so that by the tenth year (fifteenth for ARMs), subordinated shareholders receive the entire amount of the principal allocated to the junior class.

INNOVATION IN SENIOR-SUBORDINATED STRUCTURES

In the early stages of the development of the senior-subordinated market, prior to the advent of risk-based capital guidelines for thrift institutions, public issuance was dominated mainly by savings and loan institutions. The execution choice was usually in the form of senior-subordinated AA pass-through securities with the subordinated portion retain by the issuer. However, as part of the risk-based capital guidelines contemplated for Federal Deposit Insurance Corporation (FDIC) insured bank and thrift institutions, sales treatment for a pool of assets may be violated if there is recourse or retention of any subordinated interests. While the final rulings have not been mandated, it is expected that FDIC-insured institutions which issue senior-subordinated structures will have to reserve capital against the entire structure. Additionally, if the recourse retained by the institution is greater than the amount of probable loss that the institution has reasonably estimated that will occur, the transaction has to be treated as a financing rather than a sale. Since, as a practical matter, the recourse represented by subordinated securities almost always represents an amount greater than the amount of probable loss, all senior-subordinated transactions for FDIC-insured institutions are likely to be classified as financings rather than sale and hence require the institutions to reserve capital against the entire amount rather than just the subordinated interest.

With the possibility of such onerous capital requirements for senior-subordinated transactions, thrifts and banks have not been major participants in the market as issuers of securities. However, other originators of non-conforming mortgages, such as private conduits have extensively used the senior-subordinated structure as a viable disposition alternative for tapping the capital markets for securitized transactions. Additionally, the senior-subordinated structure has also been used for a host of non-mortgage transactions for the securitization of assets such as credit cards, home equity loans, manufactured housing loans, automobile loans and the like.

Along with the expansion of the senior-subordinated structure as the execution vehicle of choice for non-mortgage assets, there has also been a simultaneous development in the growth of multi-class senior-subordinated structures with varying levels of subordination. Multi-class subordinated structures have either been structured as those with classes where the losses are absorbed sequentially or structures with sequential pay classes where the loss allocation is distributed over all outstanding classes. For instance, an example of the first type of multi-class security, may be a three class structure with a senior class (investment grade rating), a rated subordinated class (speculative grade rating) and an unrated subordinated class which is essentially "carved" out of the total subordinate class. This simple structure can also be used as a template for structures with more than three classes with each class subordinated to the class below it, creating a class of super-senior, semi-senior, super-subordinate and subordinate classes. As a general rule, assuming the level of subordination is constant, the larger the size of the class, the smaller the severity of loss and consequently the higher the rating. Additionally, in such structures, the loss positions for each class are inversely related to the seniority of the class in the structure. For instance, in a four class subordinated mezzanine class structure, the super-senior bonds will have the fourth loss position in the structure and hence the credit risk for such bonds would be minimal. With respect to the other type of structures which use a scheme of sequential allocation of principal cash flows combined with a proportional allocation of credit losses, the losses can be determined either as a function of original or current balance of the bond classes. The use of current balance penalizes the longer dated classes in a sequential pay structure while the use of original balance appears more equitable. However, this method cannot equitably account for the allocation of losses which occur after a particular class has been paid off.

Along with the development of multi-class senior-subordinated structures, there have also been parallel developments in cultivating investor interest in subordinated classes. With the slowdown in the development of the high-yield market, traditional junk bond investors have been forced to pursue other higher yielding alternatives. Since prudent investments in high-yield investments involve extensive credit analysis as well as an understanding of the fundamental factors affecting the economy, subordinated classes can be considered a viable alternative for such investors mainly due to several commonalities in the evaluation process. However, by creating structuring alternatives which enhance investor comfort in obtaining cash flows from subordinated interests, the investor base for such classes could be expanded. One such option is to create a reserve fund for trapping excess servicing in a pool of non-conforming mortgage loans to provide additional liquidity to ensure timely payments of principal and interest. Another option is to carve out such excess servicing and elevate the loss position of this class over that of the subordinated class. In addition to "forcing" the servicer to maximize proceeds and exercise due diligence in collecting loan proceeds, this alternative also puts equity at risk before any losses accrue to the subordinate class.

A final word—there was a time when the demise of the senior-subordinated structure was imminent mainly due to the non-participation in this market by the largest set of originators of non-conforming loans—the savings and loan associations. This lack of participation stemmed from the fact that onerous capital requirements suggested that thrifts would have to reserve capital against the entire amount of the senior-subordinated class due to the contention that full recourse was implied by the retention of the subordinated class by the issuer. However, other originators have used this execution alternative successfully and have either retained the subordinated class or sold it in the capital markets. Recent developments in the capital markets, such as the downgrades of issues due to the downgrade of the parent gurantor's debt rating, the paucity of providers of unconditional long-term letters of credit, and high costs of pool and hazard insurance have highlighted the self insurance features of senior-subordinated structures. At the same time, with parallel developments in the market geared towards creating securities with varying cash flow characteristics and credit profiles, methods designed to raise the comfort level of investors of subordinated classes and non-traditional investors evaluating such structures, the final nail on the coffin is far from being nailed in.

CHAPTER 8

ADJUSTABLE-RATE MORTGAGES: PRODUCTS, MARKETS AND VALUATION

Robert Gerber
Vice President
Fixed Income Research
The First Boston Corporation

INTRODUCTION

Adjustable-rate mortgages (ARMs) are based on a simple modification of the familiar fixed-rate mortgage that has been the mainstay of the U.S. housing finance system. Contractual interest rates are not set for the life of the loan, but periodically change with movements in market yield levels. Lenders benefit from a reduction in interest rate risk. In turn, ARM coupons typically reset at levels below rates on new fixed-rate mortgages. Moreover, homeowners are offered initial below market ARM rates and are protected from extreme interest rate increases by coupon caps. It is no

The author acknowledges the research assistance of Alexander Crawford.

Exhibit 1: Effect of Interest Rates on ARM Originations

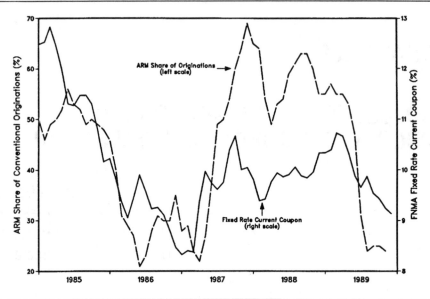

surprise that these loans have become popular with both lenders and homeowners. As illustrated in Exhibit 1, ARM popularity rises when interest rates are high and fixed-rate mortgages are costly. Yield curve shape, by altering the relative cost of fixed- and adjustable- rate mortgages, also affects ARM popularity.

After a few years of experimentation, lenders have fine-tuned the basic ARM instrument. Two ARM types with the greatest appeal to homeowners, lenders, and investors have emerged as industry standards—CMT and COFI ARMs. These ARM types differ according to how coupon rates reflect market interest rates—a set relationship, or an indirect correspondence via thrift industry cost of funds, respectively. The many variations on each theme, though minor in spirit, lead to analytical complexity and significant differences in mortgage valuation.

Features that have made ARMs attractive to borrowers—teasers, caps, margins, reset frequencies—complicate analysis for secondary market investors. Mortgage originators—thrifts and

Exhibit 2: ARM Security New Issuance ($ Billions)

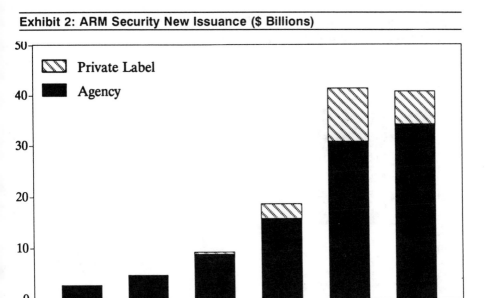

domestic banks—traditionally have been the major investors in ARM securities (both the individual mortgages and the securities are referred to as ARMs). A secondary market explosion bears witness to the asset value found by these groups. As shown in Exhibit 2, new issuance rose from $2.5 billion in 1984 to $40.9 billion in 1989, a phenomenal 75% annually compounded growth rate.

Money managers, insurance companies, and foreign banks are now investing in an increasingly liquid ARM market. For two reasons, investor participation will continue to expand. First, ARMs are short duration mortgage assets with attractive performance profiles. Exhibit 3 illustrates that investors interested in assets with these characteristics have few alternatives. Markets for similar assets—floating-rate collateralized mortgage obligations (FRCMOs) and high coupon agency pass-throughs—have been contracting. Mortgages backing these instruments have been paying down and new issuance has almost vanished. Second, the development and

**Exhibit 3: Short Duration Mortgage Products
(Net Change in Total Outstanding for 1989)**

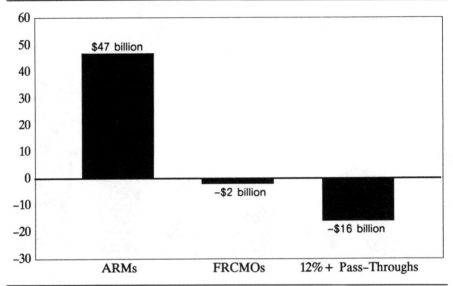

use of ARM analytical tools have increased investor awareness and understanding of these securities.

This chapter provides a guide to ARM valuation. The chapter is divided into five sections in order to accommodate readers' variety of interests and market familiarity; each section is self contained and can thus be read separately. The first section provides a brief review of ARM structural elements and an overview of the market. The second section contains a theoretical analysis of the impact of ARM features on security performance. The third and fourth sections provide detailed descriptions of First Boston's ARM analytical models. The fifth section discusses relative value analysis.

THE BASICS

Adjustable-rate mortgages are a hybrid of floating-rate notes (FRNs), interest rate options, and fixed-rate mortgages. ARMs, like

FRNs, have coupon rates that reset off a selected index at specified intervals. Unlike FRNs, ARMs generally have embedded interest rate options—periodic and life-of-loan caps that place restrictions on the level of the mortgage rate when it resets. Thus, while FRNs will maintain a constant spread to the underlying index on reset dates, the restrictions placed on the movement of the mortgage rate in an ARM may cause the spread between the mortgage rate and the index to vary.

Periodic caps denote the maximum change in mortgage rate at each reset date. Life-of-loan caps limit the mortgage rate to a certain range above its level at origination. These caps, therefore, can result in interest rate risk to the investor by making the floating-rate mortgage act more like a fixed-rate mortgage. Also, like fixed-rate mortgages, ARMs are amortizing assets, usually with 30-year final maturities, and are subject to prepayments. To value an ARM, therefore, it is imperative to understand both its floating- and fixed-rate characteristics, and which attributes are likely to dominate.

Indexes

The underlying index of an ARM represents the base or reference point for calculating the mortgage rate of an ARM loan. There are two main categories of indices—those based on Treasury securities and those derived from a thrift cost of funds index. To date, relatively few U.S. mortgages have been indexed to LIBOR, which is the standard for the FRN and FRCMO markets. As shown in Exhibit 4, about 90% of all securitized ARMs float off one of two indices—COFI and the one-year Constant Maturity Treasury (CMT).

The index most familiar to non-thrift investors is the one-year CMT—the average yield of a range of Treasury securities adjusted to a constant maturity of one year. It moves closely, but not precisely, in line with the one-year Treasury bill yield. The weekly auction rate on six-month Treasury bills is also used as an ARM index. Some lenders use a monthly or six-month average of the

---

Exhibit 4: Agency ARM Securities Outstanding as of December 31, 1989 ($ Billions)

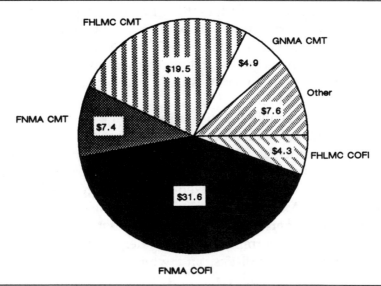

weekly rates to decrease the volatility of the index. For instance, CAML ARMs, an acronym for First Nationwide's Certainly Affordable Mortgage Loans, are indexed to the six-month average of the weekly six-month Treasury bill index.

Treasury bill indices for ARMs may use yields quoted on either a discount or bond equivalent basis. Indices expressed on a bond equivalent basis are significantly higher than those quoted on a discount basis. The higher the yield and the longer the maturity of the bill index, the greater the differential between the two measures. For example, if the discount yield of a Treasury bill with maturity of six months is 6.00%, then the bond equivalent yield would be 6.27%. For a discount yield of 9.00%, the bond equivalent yield is 9.55%.

The most commonly used ARM index is the 11th District Federal Home Loan Bank Cost of Funds index (COFI). It measures the average cost of funds for savings institutions in Arizona, California, and Nevada. The index is calculated as interest expense for the month, divided by average funds, multiplied by 12. A similar, though much less common, index is the Monthly Median National Cost of Funds Index. It is a national figure calculated from data contained in financial reports submitted by all thrift institutions.

Most thrift liabilities either have maturities longer than one month or are relatively insensitive to market interest rates. As shown in Exhibit 5, COFI, unlike the one-year CMT, changes slowly in response to interest rate movements. The lagging, muted nature of COFI versus money market rates acts to the investor's disadvantage when interest rates are rising, since investors do not immediately participate in the full rate increases. When interest rates fall, however, the lagging characteristics of the index work to the investor's advantage because investors continue to receive interest at higher rates. Other lagging indices such as six-month averages of Treasury yields, follow similar patterns.

Other rates, not currently commonplace, may become popular indices in the future. LIBOR, the prime rate and CD rates are all attractive indices to lenders and/or investors. Each is related to

Exhibit 5: ARM Index Levels

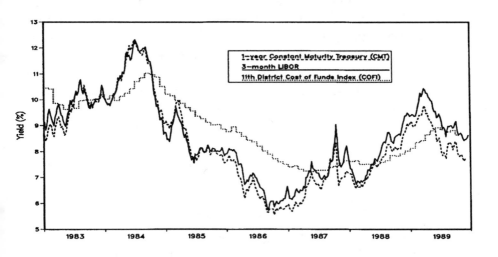

lender costs; LIBOR, in particular, serves as a key funding rate for many investors. These will succeed as ARM indices if loan features are made attractive to homeowners. Due to the appeal of LIBOR to the ARM investor base, and the fact that LIBOR is a market rate much like the one-year CMT, this index may soon grow in popularity.

ARM Mechanics

Index value alone does not determine ARM coupon level—several loan features have important roles to play. Some of these characteristics, such as lifetime caps, are common to most ARMs. Other features vary by ARM type.

Most ARMs contain a life-of-loan rate cap—a maximum interest rate for the life of the loan. Caps shift some interest rate risk from borrowers to lenders. If interest rates rise and the caps become binding, the lender protects the borrower from "payment shock" by providing funds at the capped rate, rather than the market rate. Many ARMs also have lifetime floors, which limit downward adjustments in the mortgage rate.

A common lifetime cap is 5% above the initial rate, but the initial rate is not necessarily equal to the market rate for comparable existing loans at the time. For example, an ARM with an initial rate of 8% and a life-of-loan cap of 5% implies that the ARM loan rate cannot exceed 13%. The market rate, however, may be 9%. If the initial rate is set significantly below the market rate, the lifetime cap may impose a relatively low maximum rate on the investor. As shown in Exhibit 6, lifetime caps for most outstanding ARMs are in the 12% to 14% range.

ARMs are usually originated at below market, or "teaser," rates to attract and/or qualify home buyers. As the teaser period ends, the ARM coupon will adjust towards its fully-indexed rate, which is equal to the index value plus a spread, or net margin. Gross margin refers to the spread of the ARM loan above its index. Security, or net, margin is the spread over the index received

Exhibit 6: Lifetime Cap Levels on ARM Securities (December 31, 1989)

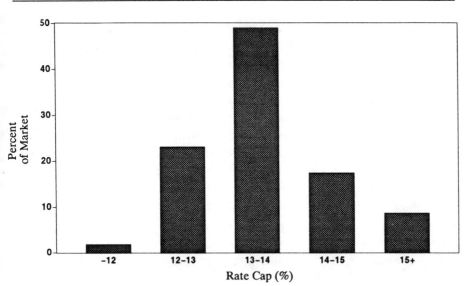

by investors—it is equal to gross margin less servicing fees and securitization expenses. Gross and security margins can span a wide range—100 to 400, and 25 to 300 basis points, respectively.

ARM coupon arithmetic can be illustrated with a simple example. Suppose the initial ARM coupon is 9%, the index is 8%, the gross margin is 2.5% and servicing fees amount to 50 basis points. The fully-indexed ARM coupon is 10% (8% + 2.5% - 0.5%). The teaser rate, at 2% below its fully-indexed level, is scheduled to increase to 10% on the first reset date if the index remains unchanged.

On the first reset date, the ARM coupon usually increases from its below market teaser rate. A downward coupon adjustment, however, is possible in a rapidly falling interest rate environment. After the teaser period, the coupon will periodically reset. ARMs with short reset intervals frequently adjust towards their fully-indexed rate and thus behave more like FRNs than those with infrequent resets. COFI ARMs most often have monthly resets while an annual reset frequency is most common for one-year CMT ARMs.

ARM coupons, even on reset dates, usually differ from the fully-indexed rate. A coupon adjustment lag is introduced because homeowners are given notification of mortgage rate changes prior to the reset date. Consequently, ARM coupon movements look back—typically one to three months—towards a previously stated index value. Index fluctuations subsequent to the look back date are not reflected in the next coupon change, but the one following. Exhibit 7 illustrates the combined affects of reset frequency and look back on a one-year CMT ARM.

ARM coupons can deviate from the fully-indexed rate as of the look back date. Loan contracts often limit the maximum amount by which the loan rate may change per reset. The most common periodic interest rate cap on conventional one-year CMT ARMs is 2% per annum; that is, the mortgage rate can be adjusted up or

Exhibit 7: 1-Year Treasury-Indexed ARM Coupon Rates (45-Day Lookback)

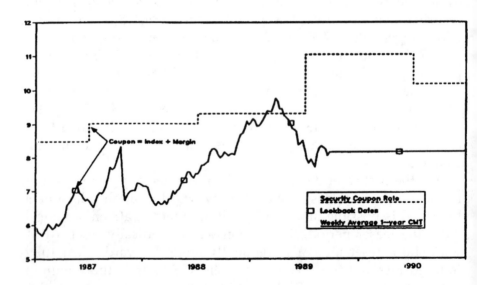

down by no more than 2 percentage points on each anniversary date, regardless of the amount of change in the index value. COFI ARMs, however, usually do not have periodic coupon caps.

Periodic coupon cap mechanics can easily be illustrated. Consider a one-year CMT ARM with an index value of 8%, a net margin of 200 basis points, and a 2% per annum interest rate cap. The current ARM rate is equal to the index plus margin, or 10%. Assume that one year later the one-year CMT has risen from 8% to 10.5%. The index plus margin (the fully-indexed rate) is 12.5%. Since there is a 2% periodic interest rate cap, the ARM loan may not increase higher than 12% (10% plus 2%). The limit on periodic adjustments in rate can also act as a floor to limit downward periodic movements in the mortgage rate. As in the previous example, it is important to note that interest rate caps are expressed in absolute percentage points, not as a percentage of the index rate.

Instead of coupon caps, some ARMs restrict periodic adjustment by limiting changes in the borrower's monthly payments. Annual payment caps—usually 7.5% for COFI ARMs—are expressed as a percentage of the payment. If a rise in interest rates would cause the monthly payment to increase by more than the payment cap allows, the borrower's monthly payment would be adjusted upward only to the capped level. If total cash flows are not sufficient to meet interest payments, negative amortization results—the unpaid interest is deferred and added to the outstanding balance of the loan.

Negative amortization can occur because the interest rate adjusts fully while the payment level does not. Most often negative amortization results from a monthly coupon adjustment and an annual payment change. The maximum amount of negative amortization is usually limited to a certain specified percentage of the original loan balance; when that level—typically 12.5% of the original balance—is reached, the monthly payment is increased without regard for any payment caps to a level sufficient to amortize the current balance over the remaining term. In addition, there is often a requirement that the mortgage be recast—principal and interest schedule recomputed—at specific time intervals (e.g., every five years) to fully amortize the unpaid principal balance.

Indices, caps, margins, teasers, and resets create a heterogeneous market. Each of these features can complicate ARM analysis. Some investors have been uncomfortable with the lagging, uncertain nature of COFI. All things considered, however, many ARMs often show similar coupon trends. Exhibit 8 presents historical ARM coupon patterns for two generic securities—a FNMA COFI ARM and a conventional one-year CMT ARM. Through different sources, both coupon streams imperfectly match market interest rate movements. Generic COFI ARMs reset monthly without regard to periodic coupon caps, but the index responds sluggishly to market interest rate movements. The one-year CMT is essentially a market interest rate, but generic CMT ARMs reset annually with 2% interest rate caps.

Exhibit 8: ARM Coupons—11th District COF Index vs. 1-Year CMT

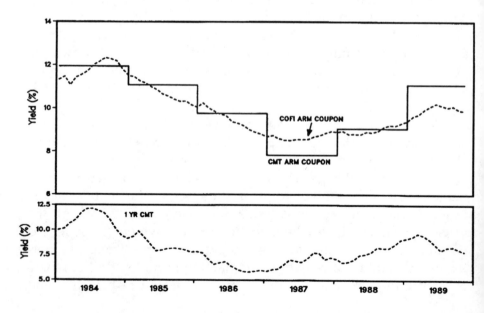

ARM Security Types

Each of the three major agencies (GNMA, FNMA, and FHLMC) has programs under which ARM securities trade in reasonable volume. In addition, privately issued ARM securities are becoming more common. At the present time, however, only one type of ARM trades on a generic basis.

FNMA COFI TBAs (to be announced) comprise the only generic ARM market. To qualify, a fully-indexed FNMA COFI ARM must fulfill certain good delivery requirements. Some of the crucial pool characteristics are:

- lifetime cap of at least 13%

- security margin of 1.25%

- monthly accrual rate reset

All other securities trade on a pool-specific basis.

GNMA securitizes FHA-insured ARM loans on single-family homes. The U.S. government's full faith and credit guarantees timely payment of principal and interest. GNMA ARMs are indexed to the one-year CMT and have a 1% annual and a 5% lifetime cap. Coupons reset annually, except for the first reset, which can be as much as 15 months from the date of origination. There are four possible adjustment dates under the GNMA program: the first day of January, April, July, or October.

Conventional ARM loans, those lacking FHA insurance, are securitized by FNMA and FHLMC. A diverse group of collateral is used for a wide range of programs, covering all major loan types. The agencies have issued similar securities, but have tended to concentrate on different indices. For ARMs without payment caps, FNMA and FHLMC both guarantee timely payment of interest at the ARM coupon rate. FHLMC, unlike FNMA and GNMA, guarantees ultimate, rather than timely, collection of principal.

Most FNMA ARMs are indexed to COFI and have an interest accrual rate that resets monthly at 125 basis points over COFI, with a two or three month lookback. FHLMC dominates the CMT ARM sector with pools having 2% periodic interest rate caps and carrying security margins usually within the range of 150 to 250 basis points.

FNMA and FHLMC have recently initiated new ARM programs intended to increase the liquidity of specific issues. FNMA Megapools and FHLMC Giants are created by grouping individual pools with similar characteristics. With an average original balance of $38.7 million, FNMA Megapools tend to be about five times larger than individual pools. The FHLMC WAC program is composed of large individual pools backed by heterogeneous loans.

Securities in these programs are not only more liquid, they have greater collateral diversification than their constituent pools. There are two additional benefits to the larger size and greater diversification. First, prepayments tend to be less erratic. Second, reset risk is reduced for some loan types. Reset risk results when a coupon adjusts infrequently off a volatile index.

The megapool concept, by combining loans or pools with different reset dates, mitigates reset risk—only a fraction of the collateral resets on any given date. Average time to reset is shorter than that of the underlying pools so that the security behaves more like a floater. In Exhibit 9, reset risk is illustrated for a one-year FNMA CMT ARM. Transient fluctuations in the index on the annual reset date can determine coupon payments for the entire year. Coupons on the Megapool, however, are continually rolling over to reflect changing market interest rates. These attractive features have made the Megapool/Giant concept very popular. Currently about 21% of FNMA/FHLMC CMT collateral has been placed in these securities.

Private label ARMs are similar to FNMA/FHLMC ARMs.[1] These securities are backed by whole loans that do not conform to agency pooling requirements, usually because they exceed FNMA/FHLMC size limits. Mortgage loan characteristics span the same spectrum as agency ARMs. Collateral quality and various

---

[1] For further information see Chapter 6.

Exhibit 9: 1-Year Treasury-Indexed ARM Coupon Rates (45-Day Lookback)

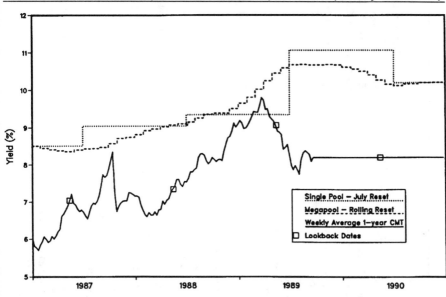

credit enhancements such as pool insurance or senior/subordinated structure, rather than agency guarantees, typically provide credit support in sufficient quantity to warrant a AA rating. Pools are usually large and composed of mortgages with a variety of gross margins and reset dates. Like Megapools, Giants and WAC pools, coupon resets roll over gradually, rather than on one specific date.

Over the 1986-88 period, the private label sector of the ARM market rapidly expanded. More recently, however, new risk-based capital guidelines have been introduced for thrifts and banks. Regulatory changes have increased the effective costs of some credit supports, especially the senior/subordinated structure. A moderation of market growth has resulted. Nonetheless, the considerable incentives to securitize these loans may generate a substantial flow of new issuance when interest rates and ARM originations are high.

Exhibit 10: ARM Securities

	GNMA	FNMA/FHLMC	PRIVATE LABEL
INDEX	1-Year Constant Maturity Treasury	1-Year, 3-Year, 5-Year Constant Maturity Treasury 6-Month Treasury Bill FHLB 11th District Cost of Funds National Median Cost of Funds	1-Year, 3-Year- 5-Year, 10-Year Constant Maturity Treasury 3-Month, 6-Month Treasury Bill FHLB 11th District Cost of Funds National Median Cost of Funds
RESET INTERVAL	Annual	1-Year Tsy: Annual 3-Year Tsy: Annual 5-Year Tsy: Annual 6-Month Tsy: Semiannual 11th District: Monthly, Semiannual National Median: Monthly	Similar to FNMA/FHLMC programs
PERIODIC CAP (Rate cap unless indicated)	1%	1-Year Tsy: 1% or 2% 3-Year Tsy: 2% 5-Year Tsy: 7 1/2% payment 6-Month Tsy: 1/2% 11th District: 7 1/2% payment National Median: 7 1/2% payment	Similar to FNMA/FHLMC programs
LIFE-OF-LOAN CAP (Over initial rate unless indicated)	5% rate cap	1-Year Tsy: Varies with loan 3-Year Tsy: 5% rate cap 5-Year Tsy: 5% rate cap 6-Month Tsy: 4% rate cap 11th District: 5% rate cap National Median: 3% rate cap over index + margin at time of loan closing	Similar to FNMA/FHLMC programs
NEGATIVE AMORTIZATION	None	1-Year Tsy: None 3-Year Tsy: None 5-Year Tsy: Loan recast every 5 years to fully amortize ARM during remaining term 6-Month Tsy: None	Similar to FNMA/FHLMC programs

Exhibit 10: ARM Securities (continued)

	GNMA	FNMA/FHLMC	PRIVATE LABEL
NEGATIVE AMORTIZATION (continued)	None	11th District: Loan recast every 5 years to fully amortize ARM during remaining term National Median: Loan recast every 5 years to fully amortize ARM during remaing term	Similar to FNMA/FHLMC programs
GROSS MARGIN	200 basis points	1-Year Tsy: 200-400 3-Year Tsy: 150-350 5-Year Tsy: 100-350 6-Month Tsy: 200-400 11th District 200-400 National Median: 200-400	175-325 basis points
SECURITY SPREAD	150 basis points	1-Year Tsy: 125-350 3-Year Tsy: 75-250 5-Year Tsy: 25-275 6-Month Tsy: 100-300 11th District: 100-300 National Median: 125-200	100-250 basis points
ISSUANCE VOLUME THROUGH 1989	$5.5 billion	1-Year Tsy: $32.6 billion 3-Year Tsy: $ 1.5 billion 5-Year Tsy: $ 0.8 billion 6-Month Tsy: $ 3.0 billion 11th District $41.8 billion National Median: $ 3.0 billion	1-Year Tsy: $7.2 billion 3-Year Tsy: $0.2 billion 5-Year Tsy: $0.1 billion 10-Year Tsy: $1.0 billion 6-Month Tsy: $0.5 billion 3-Month Tsy: $0.3 billion 11th District: $9.9 billion National Median: $0.2 billion
UNDERLYING COLLATERAL	FHA insured single family	Conventional single-family and multi-family	Conventional single-family and multi-family

ARMs comprise a heterogeneous secondary market. Exhibit 10 summarizes the major ARM types by issuer and loan characteristics.

THEORETICAL VALUATION

The yield on floating-rate assets cannot be known in advance because interest payments are based on unknown future market interest rate levels. The mortgage rate of the ARM will fluctuate with changes in the level of the underlying index subject to the limiting effects of the caps. As with fixed-rate mortgages, the cash flows from an ARM consist of coupon income, scheduled principal amortization, and prepayments. All these components are interrelated and dependent on market interest rates.

The yield of an ARM can be estimated by projecting a likely future path of interest rates and the associated cash flows— coupon, amortization, and prepayments. This single scenario yield would provide valuable information, but it does not tell the whole story. Each ARM contains a basket of options—such as caps and prepayments—and the bundle differs from security to security. Scenario analysis alone cannot be used to accurately value options. Moreover, subtle variations in ARM features and their interactions can confound market intuition. For example, how much more or less valuable is a CMT ARM with a 13% lifetime cap, 1% periodic caps, and 2.75% gross margin than a similar ARM with a 12.50% cap, 2% periodic caps, and 3% gross margin?

Investors occasionally take positions based upon an opinion of future interest rate levels. Absent a specific viewpoint, accurate relative value recommendations require that option valuation techniques be employed for ARM analysis. The options based approach does more than just estimate a fair price. It quantifies the sensitivity of price to changes in market interest rates, shows the tradeoffs between caps and margins, and provides insight as to funding ARMs to reduce gap ratios and hedge interest rate risk.

The main factors affecting the theoretical option valuation of ARMs are as follows:

- Index type and relationship of the index to other capital market rates

- Initial interest rate level and yield curve shape

- Gross and net (security) margin

- Reset frequency

- Periodic rate/payment caps/floors

- Lifetime caps/floors

- Expected interest rate volatility

- Prepayment rate assumptions

- Discount rate at which to calculate the present value of future cash flows

First Boston computes the expected value of an ARM over thousands of potential interest rate scenarios. Future interest rates are generated at random according to the implied market volatility and the interest rate expectations embodied in the current Treasury yield curve. On each future date, ARM cash flows are determined by the security characteristics, the interest rate environment, and index and prepayment forecasts. The discount rate used to value cash flows is the constant (option-adjusted) spread over Treasury yield curve that would compensate an investor for holding the ARM. The average of all present values is the theoretical, or expected, price of the ARM. If the ARM price is already known, the process is reversed. Different option-adjusted spreads are entered into the model until one is found that makes the average present value equal to the price.

Index and prepayment forecasts are among the most important facets of ARM valuation. A major change in these forecasting models would significantly alter an ARM's theoretical value. The First Boston ARM prepayment and COFI forecasting models are described in the following sections.

First Boston's ARM and option pricing methods can be used to quantify the impact of various features on ARM value—initial coupon, coupon caps, volatility, security margin, reset frequency, etc. Conceptually, these factors alter the relative importance among the security's option, floating-rate and fixed-rate features. ARM value and interest rate sensitivity (effective duration) reflect the balance of many influences.

Interest rate sensitivity derives from changes in the spread between a bond's coupon level and market interest rates. Therefore, the price of a pure floater will not display any interest rate sensitivity. Prices of fixed-rate bonds and options, interpreted as leveraged bond positions, can be very sensitive to interest rate movements. The exact mix of fixed-rate and option characteristics is required to determine ARM value and effective duration.

Coupon caps are short interest rate put options sold by the investors, which decrease ARM value. The greater the worth of the cap, the lower the value of the ARM. Higher absolute cap levels or market expectations of falling Treasury yields reduce cap values. Interest rate volatility tends to raise the value of caps because it increases the likelihood of, and extent to which, the cap will limit coupon growth. Coupon floors, long interest rate calls that benefit investors, are subject to the same forces as coupon caps. When binding, caps and floors can be thought of as introducing fixed-rate characteristics into ARM securities.

Security performance, which is determined by the interaction of many ARM features, is not exactly equal to the sum of its parts. For example, the impact of volatility on the value of an ARM depends on the index level. If 25% interest rate volatility is assumed for the one-year CMT with an expected yield of 10.00% one year hence, then the index will be between 7.50% and 12.50% in roughly 68% of the cases. If instead the expectation is 5.00%, than the equivalent probability band is 3.75% to 6.25%. The wider band generated by the higher interest rate level implies a greater likelihood that caps will become binding. Therefore, increased volatility or a higher initial index will decrease theoretical ARM value.

A volatility assumption is necessary to calculate an option-adjusted spread. This refers to the yield volatility of short-term Treasury securities, which is approximately equal to that of the one-year CMT index. COFI volatility, however, is much lower. Nonetheless, because option-adjusted spread is derived from the Treasury yield curve, a Treasury volatility must still be used. The COFI forecasting model internally translates the Treasury volatility to a COFI volatility.

In spite of the interdependency of ARM features, the qualitative impact of varying important parameters can be examined. Exhibits 11 and 12 present the results of this exercise for a FHLMC CMT and a FNMA COFI ARM, respectively. Differences in these securities—coupon caps for CMTs and a sluggish index for COFIs—are reflected in the contents of these exhibits.

The initial rate affects the value of the ARM in two ways. First, the pricing of the ARM will be a function of the initial ARM rate relative to current interest rate levels. Second, the lifetime cap of the ARM is often based off the initial rate. A low initial rate could cause the ARM to be capped out with only a modest rise in index value.

As anticipated, teasers decrease ARM value. Moreover, a greater impact is felt by CMTs—the teaser period is longer and annual coupon resets are restricted by 200 basis points periodic coupon caps. An upward sloping yield curve, by emphasizing rising interest rate scenarios, magnifies the expected cost to investors of this feature.

A teaser is an initial, below market coupon rate. Until the first reset date, the coupon is fixed, and the security can be viewed as a fixed-rate mortgage. Just as with any interval between coupon adjustments, the further off the reset, the longer the coupon is fixed at its current level. In effect, long reset intervals increase the mortgage's fixed-rate component and extend its duration. For a CMT

Exhibit 11: Theoretical Prices and Durations of CMT ARMs*

	Initial Coupon	Lifetime Cap	Price	Time to Reset	Effective Duration	Volatility
Lifetime	9.78	None	101-31	12	1.16	15%
Cap	9.78	15%	101-21	12	1.36	15%
Effect	9.78	13%	101-06	12	1.64	15%
Teaser	9.78	15%	101-21	12	1.36	15%
Effect	7.78	13%	98-24	12	2.18	15%
Time to	9.78	15%	101-21	12	1.36	15%
Reset	9.78	15%	101-26	6	0.81	15%
Effect	9.78	15%	100-28	3	0.49	15%
Volatility	7.78	13%	95-21	12	2.69	30%
Effect	7.78	13%	98-24	12	2.18	15%
	9.78	15%	99-09	12	2.13	30%
	9.78	15%	101-21	12	1.36	15%

* CMT	=	7.78%
Net Margin	=	2.00%
Servicing	=	0.75%
OAS	=	110

ARM, if the teaser is more than 200 basis points below the fully-indexed rate, the coupon will not achieve its fully-indexed rate until the second coupon reset. A small change in market interest rates will not affect the mortgage coupon for two reset intervals, thus lengthening the security's duration.

Most COFI ARMs reset monthly without rate caps and are therefore fully indexed immediately after the teaser period. Consequently, security value and duration will not drift along a coupon reset cycle. Due to its sluggish nature, the index is much less volatile than market interest rates. As a result, small interest rate changes will not significantly affect near-term coupon flows and

Exhibit 12: Theoretical Prices and Durations of COFI ARMs*

	Initial Coupon	Lifetime Cap	Price	Effective Duration
Lifetime	9.845	None	101-27	1.30
Cap	9.845	15%	101-23	1.36
Effect	9.845	13%	101-17	1.49
Teaser	9.845	13%	101-19	1.53
Effect	7.845	13%	100-25	1.58

* COFI	=	8.595%	Volatility		
Net Margin	=	1.250%	Treasury	=	15%
Servicing	=	0.750%	COFI	=	3.49%
OAS	=	85			

duration will consequently be longer. Moreover the decrease in index volatility reduces the implicit cost of lifetime coupon caps.

Many other factors can affect ARM value. Relative value analysis and proper duration calculations can be very complicated. The preceding discussion was meant to be informative rather than comprehensive. Actual transactions should be carefully approached on a case by case basis.

FORECASTING THE 11TH DISTRICT COST OF FUNDS INDEX[2]

The performance of COFI ARMs is highly dependent upon the value of the 11th District Cost of Funds index. Both coupon and principal cash flows are primarily determined by index movements. An increase in COFI directly raises the coupon rate. Moreover, the higher the index relative to other mortgage market rates, the greater the incentive for homeowners to refinance their mortgages. In order to accurately value COFI ARMs and properly

---

[2] Much of the information discussed in this section is contained in *Forecasting the 11th District Cost of Funds Index*, Fixed Income Research, The First Boston Corporation, November 1988 and "Hazards in Forecasting the 11th District Cost of Funds Index," *Mortgage-Backed Securities Letter*, October 23, 1989.

hedge portfolios containing these instruments, it is necessary to understand how COFI responds to movements in market interest rates.

COFI and market interest rates have a very complicated relationship. The index reflects the average interest rate across a variety of new and existing liabilities—savings deposits, advances from the Federal Home Loan Bank, reverse repurchase agreements, and other borrowings. Savings deposits are divided by size, term, the availability of checking privileges, and interest rate characteristics. Advances and other borrowings also vary by maturity, with advances frequently used to fund long-term mortgage loans and other borrowings weighted towards medium-term notes and mortgage-backed bonds. As shown in Exhibit 13, savings deposits are the largest liability type, accounting for 72.3% of index as of September 30, 1989.

Only a small proportion of thrift liabilities rolls over in any one month. Existing liabilities pay contracted interest rates, which reflect previous, not current, market conditions. As a result, COFI

Exhibit 13: Components of 11th District Cost of Funds Balances as of September 30, 1989

Savings Balances	
Passbook Accounts	4.2%
Transaction Accounts	3.8
Money Market Deposit Accounts (MMDAs)	6.5
Fixed Maturity, Fixed Rate Liabilities (Original Maturity):	
6 months or less	19.9
6 months to 1 year	17.4
1 year to 3 years	12.6
More than 3 years	6.7
Fixed Maturity, Variable Rate Liabilities All Maturities:	1.2
Total Savings Balances	72.3%
Federal Home Loan Bank Advances	10.3
Reverse Repurchase Agreements	6.8
Other Borrowing	10.8
Total Funds	100.0%

changes slowly in response to market interest rate movements. The issue, then, is how to forecast the cost and timing of new liabilities. A respectable forecast one month in advance can be achieved by taking the latest published value of COFI plus a small adjustment for recent yield curve shifts. Models such as these will become less accurate as the forecasting horizon moves farther out, because each month's value depends on knowing the previous month's value. Most COFI forecasting models we are aware of are based on a variation of this "lagged dependent variable" process.

First Boston has a unique approach to forecasting COFI. A structural econometric model has been developed to explicitly account for changes in both the composition and cost of thrift liabilities. The model is intended to provide forecasts over entire interest rate scenarios. Based upon the selected scenario, balance sheet evolution is projected. Each month maturing liabilities roll off at historical costs and new funds are booked at current costs. Liability proportions and their individual costs are then combined to derive the path of COFI over time. Exhibit 14 presents the COFI

Exhibit 14: Projected COFI
Stable LIBOR Scenario
December 20, 1989 Levels

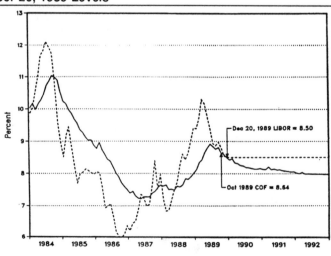

forecast based upon constant interest rates as of December 20, 1989. COFI was projected to decrease about 65 basis points from its October 1989 level.

Exhibit 15 shows that the First Boston approach is very accurate in explaining the historical values of COFI. Disaggregated liability projections enhance forecast precision in two ways. First, thrifts adapt their liability mix to market conditions. This substitution alters funding costs when there is a yield differential between long- and short-term costs. Second, liability costs differ in their level and interest rate sensitivity.

Deposits with different maturities can be viewed as alternative investments. When interest rates are high, thrifts are reluctant to supply long-term CDs. Long-term yield spreads to market rates tighten, yields on short fixed-term deposits appear more attractive,

Exhibit 15: Historical Forecasting Accuracy for COFI

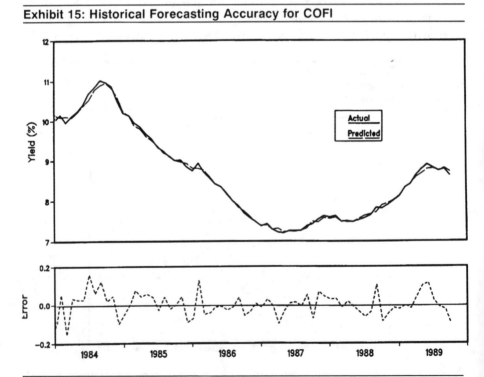

Exhibit 16: Deposit Mix Varies with Interest Rates

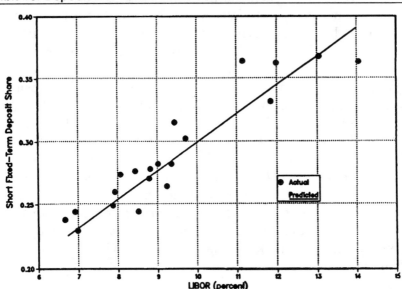

and liabilities shift to the short end. When interest rates are low, investors are hesitant to commit capital long term. During periods of moderate interest rates thrifts are not deterred by high rates, depositors find rate levels and market stability attractive, and the long-term deposit share tends to increase. Exhibit 16 describes the empirical relationship between short-term deposits and market interest rates.

Adjustments in the thrift liability mix affect COFI because each liability cost has a unique level and response to interest rate movements. Some liabilities are relatively simple to forecast. Passbook, transaction and money market deposit accounts show little interest rate sensitivity. Advances and reverse repurchase agreements are spread off general market rates. CD rates, however, which account for over 50% of the index, have traditionally been difficult to predict.

CD rates generally reflect market levels, but only slowly respond to interest rate movements. Moreover, deposit rates in-

crease more slowly when market interest rates rise than they decline when market yields fall. A national market for jumbo CDs
tends to moderate this asymmetry. Nonetheless, thrifts usually experience some disintermediation when interest rates rapidly increase and retail CD rates fail to keep pace.

First Boston forecasts CD rates by maturity and deposit size.
Projections are based on a long-term correspondence to market
rates and an asymmetric, sluggish response to market movements.
Model performance for three-month retail CD rates is described in
Exhibit 17. Shown is the scenario forecast that would have been
rendered on June 1984 if future interest rates, but nothing else,
were known. In particular, consideration is not given to the de-
regulation occurring early in the period or the recent industry-
wide reorganization. In spite of the decade's massive upheaval,
the model closely tracks actual CD rates without resorting to
"technical" considerations.

Exhibit 17: Thrift CD Rates Can be Modeled with Market Interest Rates
Scenario as of June 1984
Small Three-Month CDs

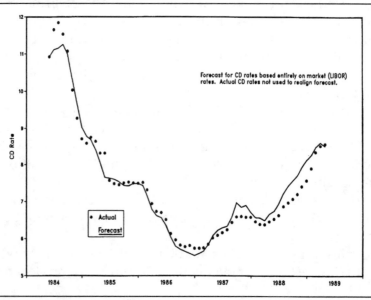

Some analysts manually "adjust" COFI forecasts for technical considerations. Although these occasionally provide some insight into recent market developments, manual adjustments do not belong in a long-term forecasting model. Unanticipated market changes, by their very nature, are impossible to predict. Moreover, without strong data in support, an impact for previous structural change should not be assumed—it is the easy way out, it is often spurious, and it difficult to quantify.

Many analysts argue that resolution of the thrift crisis will put downward pressure on COFI. Although a very real possibility, its potential magnitude may be exaggerated. Many thrift costs—such as MMDAs, reverse repurchase agreements, advances, retail deposits—are unlikely to significantly decline. Jumbo CDs, which might benefit from decreased competition, comprise about 25% of the index. Therefore, a 40 basis point narrowing of spreads would only lower the index by 10 basis points. Moreover, even if jumbos fetch 200 basis points more than other liabilities, a dramatic drop in the jumbo liability share to 15% would lower the index by only 20 basis points. Together, these two factors result in a 30 basis point decline in the index.

THE FBC PREPAYMENT MODEL FOR ADJUSTABLE-RATE MORTGAGES[3]

Until recently, investors have lacked a consistent set of prepayment assumptions for adjustable-rate mortgages. In large part this state of affairs is attributable to the dearth of historical information on ARM prepayments. With the growth of the market over the past few years, however, the availability of data has increased. Between 1988 and 1989 the amount of information available for analysis has virtually doubled. There are more data on existing pools and prepayments have been observed across a range of in-

---

[3] The information in this section appears in *Prepayment Models for Fixed and Adjustable-Rate Mortgages*, Fixed Income Research, The First Boston Corporation, reprinted November 1989.

terest rate levels. The First Boston model now conforms to a grow-ing historical experience as well as the economic fundamentals of mortgagor prepayment. The degree of precision, however, will be less than with fixed-rate prepayment models.

Prepayments derive from mortgage contractual provisions. Mortgage rates are tied to market interest rates, but a variety of loan characteristics—index, teaser rates, coupon caps, long reset periods—prevent ARM coupon rates from precisely tracking yield curve movements. These features determine the pattern of ARM prepayments.

Exhibit 18 compares long-term prepayment patterns for adjust-able- and fixed-rate mortgages. ARM prepayments tend to be faster and more stable than fixed-rate prepayments. Financial in-centives and demographic differences both contribute to these characteristics.

Prepayment incentives vary among ARMs, reflecting the secu-rity's particular mix of floating- versus fixed-rate characteristics.

**Exhibit 18: Prepayment Sensitivity
ARMs and Fixed-Rate Mortgages**

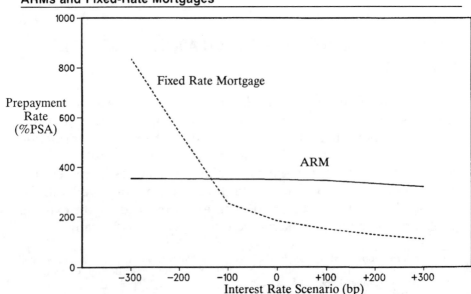

The greater the fixed-rate component, the more prepayments will mirror those on similar fixed-rate mortgages. Specifically, this means that refinancings will significantly increase with falling interest rates. To the extent the loan resembles a floater, however, refinancings will play a smaller role. For a perfect mortgage floater that always reflects market interest rates, there is no economic incentive to refinance. For these loans, prepayments display little interest rate sensitivity and primarily reflect household mobility.

From the homeowner's viewpoint, ARMs are riskier than fixed-rate mortgages. A rise in interest rates might increase the loan rate and monthly payment. ARMs, however, are often originated at a below market teaser rate and thus have a short-run cost advantage over their fixed-rate counterparts. A homeowner who anticipates moving within a few years is exposed to little risk, but still benefits from the initial teaser rate. ARMs naturally attract mobile mortgagors, which tends to elevate the base level of prepayments.

ARM prepayments have much greater short- than long-term variability. In the short run, prepayments resemble fixed-rate behavior because coupons take time to adjust to interest rate shifts. Differences between premiums and discounts, however, are not quite as great as with fixed-rate mortgages. Unless the coupon hits a lifetime cap or floor, financial incentives to refinance are moderated by the coupon's eventual adjustment to market rates. Moreover, upon completion of the coupon adjustment, prepayment rates will return to their long-term levels.

Exhibit 19 illustrates the prepayment adjustment process for a FHLMC CMT ARM with an annual 200 basis point coupon cap. Prepayment patterns for three interest rate scenarios are presented—constant rates, and up and down 300 basis points. On the first reset date, coupons adjust 200 basis points. On the second reset one year later, all coupon levels are equal. Prepayment rate differences, reflecting scheduled coupon trends, continually diminish in size. After two years all three prepayment patterns converge, but not to a constant level. Month-to-month fluctuations are the result of several factors.

Exhibit 19: Long-Run Prepayment Stability
FHLMC CMT

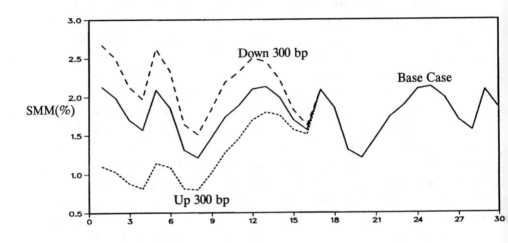

Factors Influencing ARM Prepayments

The three basic ARM types—GNMA pools backed by FHA loans and conventional CMT and COFI securities—vary in their prepayment experience. As in the fixed-rate sector, conventional mortgages generally have higher prepayments than FHA-insured loans, although this relationship does not strictly hold in the case of premiums because of other structural elements. Important differences exist across ARM types but, common to all, are the basic fundamentals of mortgagor prepayment behavior.

ARM prepayments, like those on fixed-rate loans, are greatly affected by refinancing incentives, collateral age, and season. ARM aging and seasonal prepayment patterns closely resemble those of their fixed-rate counterparts. The aging profile is similar to the PSA Standard Prepayment Model. Moreover, the seasonal prepayment cycle reflects general housing market activity, the holiday calendar, and the academic schedule. It is indistinguishable from similar fixed-rate mortgages with prepayments tending to rise in the spring and summer and decline in the autumn and winter.

The incentive to refinance a mortgage depends upon both its monthly payment and expected mortgage rate. The greater the monthly payment or expected mortgage rate relative to the financing alternatives, the more likely a homeowner is to prepay. Housing affordability is in large part determined by the monthly mortgage payment. An increase makes loan service more difficult, and can affect homeowner prepayment decisions.

With standard fixed-rate mortgages neither coupon nor payment levels change over the life of the loan. Therefore, refinancing incentives can essentially be described by the relative coupon—the difference between the loan's mortgage rate and the current secondary mortgage market rate (current coupon). Incentives are much more complicated for ARMs because both coupons and payments change with interest rates. Moreover, for some ARMs payment and coupon levels adjust on different dates. In application, most ARMs fall into one of two categories—CMT and COFI indexed ARMs.

Prepayments on CMT ARMs

Most Treasury-based ARMs are indexed to the one-year CMT. On conventional ARMs annual resets are most common, and coupon changes are usually limited to a maximum of 200 basis points per year. Coupons and payments adjust on the same date so that the expected mortgage rate, relative to the alternatives, fully describes the incentive to refinance.

In order to accurately capture the incentives to refinance a CMT ARM we compute the effective relative coupon, an extension of the fixed-rate relative coupon concept. The effective relative coupon, a value which is computed rather than observed directly, is equal to the effective mortgage coupon minus the effective current coupon. For a fixed-rate loan effective relative coupon is equal to relative coupon.

Effective mortgage coupon is equal to the anticipated average mortgage rate over an intermediate horizon, considering the gross margin, reset frequency and cap structure. A greater than average gross margin will permanently raise the effective mortgage coupon, whereas a high current rate will eventually vanish if the gross margin is low.

Effective current coupon takes into account refinancing opportunities in both fixed- and adjustable-rate markets. The CMT rate is tied to the short end of the Treasury yield curve while the fixed-rate current coupon is spread off the intermediate part of the curve. When the yield curve is inverted, homeowners are attracted to the fixed-rate market, and long-term prepayment rates rise. Exhibit 20 displays the effect of yield curve shape on long-term prepayment forecasts for GNMA CMT ARMs.

One additional factor, not relevant to fixed-rate mortgages, is the reset cycle. Mortgagors are usually notified one to three months before coupon resets, which alter the mortgagors' monthly interest expense, and lead to a new evaluation of the financing alternatives. Historical prepayment data show a strong tendency

Exhibit 20: Effects of Yield Curve Shape
Seasoned Fully-Indexed GNMA CMTs

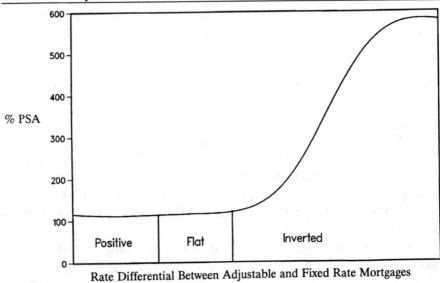

Rate Differential Between Adjustable and Fixed Rate Mortgages

Exhibit 21: Reset Cycle Effects for One-Year CMT ARMs

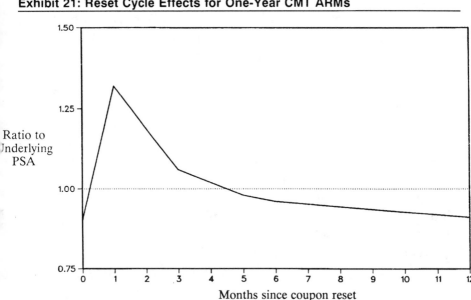

Ratio to Underlying PSA

Months since coupon reset

for prepayments to increase immediately following a coupon reset, and to decline gradually thereafter. For many ARMs, the reset cycle effect is substantial. The one-year reset cycle is shown in Exhibit 21.

Prepayments on COFI ARMs

The basic conclusions about CMT ARM prepayments apply to COFI ARMs as well. Long-term prepayment rates are faster and more stable than similar fixed-rate loans. Moreover, prepayments follow the same aging and seasonal patterns. Differences in index performance and security structure, however, alter how the incentive to refinance is quantified.

COFI ARMs usually have monthly coupon resets without periodic caps. Although the spread between the coupon and index is, for the most part, constant, a mortgagor might prepay for two reasons. First, monthly mortgage payments reset yearly and are limited to 7.5% annual changes. In a falling rate environment home-owners can substantially reduce their monthly payment by taking out a new loan. Second, the index responds sluggishly to interest rate movements. It can deviate from its long-term level for long periods of time.

Short-term prepayment decisions take both monthly payment and mortgage rate into account. The mortgage rate as of the last payment reset date is a good empirical proxy for these considerations. Intuitively, it can be viewed as a combination of the effective coupon and reset cycle for CMT ARMs. Effective relative coupon can be approximated by subtracting the fixed-rate current coupon. Prepayments are not very sensitive to changes in COFI because coupons reset monthly. Exhibit 22 illustrates the accuracy of the First Boston COFI ARM prepayment model.

Over the long term, monthly payments will conform to coupon rates. Therefore, the spread between COFI and other mortgage market alternatives will determine prepayment rates. A COFI pro-

Exhibit 22: Model Performance
Seasoned FNMA COFI ARMs

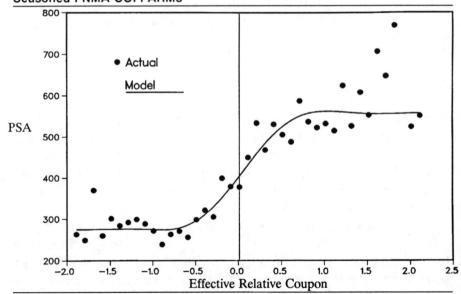

jection is thus a crucial input into any prepayment forecast. Unfortunately, the relationship between COFI and market interest rates is very complicated. At First Boston, a unique method has been developed to forecast COFI. A complete description of our COFI forecasting model is contained in the previous section of this chapter.

Just as with CMT ARMs, yield curve shape will affect long-term prepayment rates. For example, a yield curve inversion will significantly lower the fixed-rate current coupon. COFI, because thrift liabilities span a range of maturities, can be viewed as a weighted average of the yield curve. Therefore, the decline in long maturity liability costs will be partially offset by an increase in short maturity liability costs. The incentive to refinance into a fixed-rate mortgage is thus increased.

Prepayment Forecasts

CMT ARMs' short-term prepayments, adjusting for age and season, usually approximate their long-term levels. A COFI projection is required for long-term prepayment forecasts on COFI ARMs. Nonetheless, because ARM coupons adjust to their fully-indexed rate, general prepayment expectations can be described.

In the current interest rate environment, fully-indexed COFI ARMs are expected to prepay in the range of 300-400% PSA, fully-indexed conventional CMTs at 350-400% PSA, and fully-indexed GNMAs at 110-125% PSA. For most forecast horizons, these are approximate PSAs and should be used only as a guide. ARMs are complex instruments and even minor differences in parameters (caps margins, reset months, etc.) can have large effects on prepayments.

RELATIVE VALUE IN THE ARM MARKET

Option-adjusted spread (OAS) is an important indicator of ARM value. It is the only tool that fully accounts for the many option

Exhibit 23: Price History of FNMA COFI ARMs

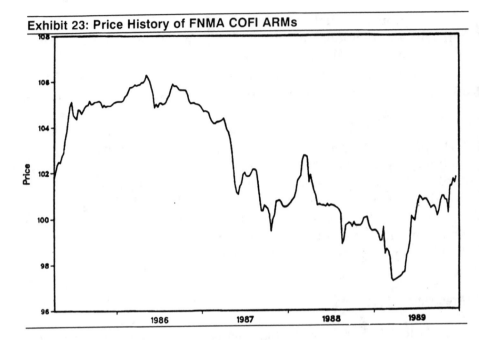

features embedded in an ARM, and it is used to make trading judgments. Nonetheless, numerous other factors, such as accounting rules, regulatory changes, and market technicals, also effect ARM value. Moreover, many investors use other analytical methods designed to address their particular objectives and constraints. Understanding how the major investment groups perceive relative value is important for interpreting general market trends. Regardless of the orientation, examination of option-adjusted spreads is the best place to start an investment analysis.[4]

Current relative value, as expressed by OAS, static yield, and technical considerations, is often a primary motivation of money managers, mutual funds, bank trust accounts, and others. One strategy employed by some of these "total return" investors is to shift their resources between sectors in search of attractive values. Security performance is often analyzed using scenarios with horizons shorter than maturity. When FNMA COFI ARMs cheapened

---

[4] OAS technology is discussed in Chapter 27.

during the winter of 1989, as suggested by Exhibit 23, total return investors entered the market.

Total return investors often analyze securities based upon a one-year investment horizon. Scenario total returns are calculated taking coupon and principal payments and price changes into account. Cash flows are generated based upon security contractual features, such as margins and caps, using First Boston analytical models. Year-end prices are derived by holding OAS constant. Exhibit 24 contains one-year holding period returns for a FNMA six-month Treasury-bill ARM, and a comparison with the two-year Treasury. In each scenario the ARM outperforms the Treasury. A large base case yield spread compensates for Treasury price appreciation when interest rates decline. Moreover, in rising rate scenarios Treasury prices show substantial declines, whereas ARM prices are bolstered by upward coupon adjustments.

Funded investors, such as banks and thrifts, which have been the major ARM purchasers, prefer to perform a funding analysis. For each in a series of interest rate scenarios, asset yield is compared to funding cost. Interest rate swaps can be used to tailor investment performance to particular institutional preferences. Due to the stability of ARM prepayments, optimal notional swap amounts will show little interest rate sensitivity. Swap mismatches, which have occurred with fixed-rate mortgage funding strategies, are thus less troublesome. As usual, diversification is recommended to limit pool specific prepayment risk.

A sample funding analysis is presented in Exhibit 25. The purchase of a FNMA CMT is funded using six-month LIBOR, resetting every six months. Unhedged results are provided in the upper panel. The average year end coupon/LIBOR spread is about 140 basis points, but it falls below 80 in the up 200 basis point scenario. Hedging this investment with an interest rate swap, as described in the lower panel, improves the rising rate scenarios, but at a cost of lowering the spreads in the falling rate environments.

Funded investors generally must base yield calculations on accounting income as determined by the Financial Accounting

---

Exhibit 24: Total Return Analysis

EXAMPLE: FNMA Pool #66417, @102-00
9.961% Coupon, 12.879% Cap/ 50 bp Periodic Cap
26-week moving average of 6-month T-bill (discount)
3 months to Weighted Average Reset
Annual Reset
WAM = 28.5 years
Index = 7.61

1-YEAR HOLDING PERIOD RETURNS

Interest Rate Scenario	Average First Year Coupon	Ending Coupon	Ending Price	Appproximate Cash Flow SMM	Total Return
-200 bp	9.92%	9.49%	104-00	2.50%	10.42%
-100	9.94	9.52	102-29	2.50	9.74
0	10.12	10.11	101-30	2.25	9.36
+100	10.34	10.80	100-28	2.25	8.85
+200	10.38	10.88	99-11	2.00	7.84

COMPARATIVE TOTAL RETURNS

Interest Rate Scenario	FNMA #66415	2-Year Treasury	Difference
-200 bp	10.42%	9.93%	+0.49%
-100	9.74	8.98	+0.76
0	9.36	8.05	+1.31
+100	8.85	7.13	+1.72
+200	7.84	6.22	+1.62

Exhibit 25: Funding Analysis

EXAMPLE: FNMA Pool #70016, @102-08
9.389% Coupon, 13.469% Cap/ 200 bp Periodic Cap
1-year CMT + 200
4 months to Weighted Average Reset
Annual Reset
WAM = 28.3 years

UNHEDGED FUNDING ANALYSIS

Interest Rate Scenario	Average First Year Coupon	Average Funding Cost*	Spread	Ending Coupon	Ending 6-mo. LIBOR	Spread
-200 bp	8.55%	7.65%	90 bp	8.11%	6.25%	186 bp
-100	9.08	8.19	89	8.90	7.25	165
0	9.60	8.73	87	9.68	8.25	143
+100	10.12	9.27	85	10.45	9.25	120
+200	10.51	9.81	70	11.04	10.25	79

HEDGED FUNDING STRATEGY
TWO-YEAR INTEREST RATE SWAP

Pay Fixed @ 8.21%
Receive Floating @ 6-month LIBOR
Notional Amount @ 25% Original Balance

Interest Rate Scenario	Ending Coupon	Ending 6-mo LIBOR	Hedge Income**	Spread
-200 bp	8.11%	6.25%	-.59%	+127 bp
-100	8.90	7.25	-.31	+134
0	9.68	8.25	+.01	+144
+100	10.45	9.25	+.31	+151
+200	11.04	10.25	+.61	+140

* Funding costs at LIBOR plus capital reserve expense.
** Year-end balance estimated using the First Boston ARM prepayment model.

Standards Board's statement number 91 (FAS 91). It is a complicated rule for which precise interpretation requires professional advice. On a conceptual level, however, the rule requires investors to book income each period so that a level yield is recognized over the life of the asset in an unchanged scenario. Application of this principle is not always simple.

Many other characteristics, such as first year yield, are examined by some investors. The great variety of investment considerations indicates that opportunities frequently arise for alert participants in the ARM market. In order to profit from these opportunities, which often requires quick decisions, advance preparation is extremely valuable. Investors will be well served by an understanding of the products, markets, and determinants of relative value.

CHAPTER 9

MULTIFAMILY PROJECT SECURITIES

Ed Daingerfield
Mortgage Trading
Smith Barney, Harris Upham & Co., Inc.

The multifamily project market offers attractive opportunities for fixed-income investors. Project securities are fully guaranteed by the United States Government or one of its Agencies, and they trade at substantial discounts to other mortgage-backed pass-through securities. This combination of impeccable credit backing and high yield means that projects can provide the greatest risk-adjusted return in the spectrum of fixed-income assets. In addition, the call protection provided by projects makes many of these securities the most convex assets in the MBS universe. Many investors are unfamiliar with the specific details of project securities, and so do not take advantage of the value this sector of the market offers. This chapter provides an introduction to projects, and highlights the most relevant features of the project market.

GENERAL BACKGROUND: TWO PRIMARY STRUCTURES OF PROJECT SECURITIES

Projects are mortgages on multifamily homes that are insured by the Federal Housing Administration (FHA) under various federal programs of the National Housing Act of 1934, as amended. For over fifty-five years, one of the primary goals the government has set for the FHA is to enhance the nation's supply of multifamily housing. Several FHA programs have evolved to ensure the construction financing and permanent mortgage financing on multifamily residences (including rental units, condominiums, and cooperatives), on nursing homes, residential facilities for the elderly and on health care units, as well as to rehabililtate or refinance mortgages on these types of properties.

Projects most commonly trade in two forms: either as FHA-insured pass-through securities or as GNMAs. Regardless of form, all projects are government-guaranteed by the U.S. Department of Housing and Urban Development (HUD) through the FHA insurance fund. Projects may be originated only by mortgage lenders in good standing with the FHA and HUD, and all projects are first created as *FHA-insured whole loans*. However, FHA-insured whole loans may be purchased only by FHA-approved lenders, and so the secondary market for projects in whole loan form is relatively small. More common are *FHA pass-throughs*, in which a newly originated, FHA-insured project loan is used to collateralize a pass-through security issued by an approved mortgage banker. *GNMA project pass-through securities* are created when a mortgage banker originates an FHA-insured project but then selects the additional guarantee and standardization provided by GNMA securities. This is analogous to the single-family market, where the FHA or VA insures mortgages that are then issued as GNMA pass-throughs. The credit backing of all FHA and GNMA projects derives from the FHA insurance fund, and so projects issued in both GNMA and FHA form enjoy the full faith and credit backing of the U.S. Government.

There are several important differences between projects issued in FHA-insured form and projects issued as GNMA securities, and as a result, GNMA project securities command a price premium over FHA projects. In the event of default, GNMA project pass-through securities incorporate the same standardized procedures as single-family GNMA pass-throughs: full and timely reimbursement of principal and interest is guaranteed in the event of default, and claims are paid out in cash, generally within thirty days. In contrast, procedures are not standardized with FHA project securities: investors may have to rely on specific information written into the servicing agreement to determine the exact default proceedings. Although FHA projects do guarantee full payment of principal and interest, the FHA takes a 1% administrative fee when a project defaults, and so the investor receives only ninety-nine cents on the dollar. Also, the FHA does not guarantee timely payment of principal and interest. Investors may have to wait several months in the event an FHA-insured project defaults, although interest does continue to accrue during this time (with the exception of a one-month grace period). Finally, although all projects issued in GNMA form pay cash in the event of default, claims on some FHA project defaults are paid in cash, while others are paid in FHA debentures, which are Federal Agency debt issues of the FHA. Many FHA projects are designated either "cash pay" or "debenture pay" at origination, whereas others are designated cash or debenture pay at the time of default at the option of either the mortgagee or of HUD. FHA projects designated "cash pay" will always pay default claims in cash; those designated "debenture pay" may pay default claims either in FHA debentures with a twenty-year maturity, or in cash, at the option of HUD.

PREPAYMENTS

Most project pools consist of one large mortgage loan, unlike single-family pools, which are backed by numerous smaller mortgages. Consequently, projects do not trade to estimates of prepayment speeds like single-family mortgage-backed securities. Rather, prepayments on projects are driven by the definite incentives most mortgagors have to prepay their mortgages. The likelihood that a project will prepay is based largely on the economics of the underlying building and the characteristics of the mortgagor, as well as on the specific prepayment restrictions and penalties of each project.

Prepayments Unlikely on Nonprofit Projects

A key determinant of prepayment likelihood in projects is whether the borrower is a profit-motivated private enterprise or a not-for-profit group. As a general rule, profit-motivated developers prepay project mortgages as early as is economically feasible, while nonprofit developers rarely prepay. Most nonprofit groups that operate projects are state or local housing authorities, church, or community groups. As nonprofit entities, these groups are not concerned with prepaying a mortgage to access built-up equity, or with refinancing to generate increased tax benefits. Also, since such groups are not likely to default, or to convert a rental project to a cooperative or sell out to another developer for a profit, prepayments on not-for-profit projects are rare. These projects provide reliable call protection, and since their cash flows are consistent, most nonprofit projects trade to their final maturity rather than to any assumed prepayment date.

Prepayments Unlikely on Projects with Section 8

One feature of projects that provides call protection to investors exists when a project has a Section 8 rent subsidy contract between the project owner and HUD. Under a Section 8 Housing Assistance Payment (HAP) contract, HUD agrees to pay the difference between what a tenant can afford to pay for rent (based on tenant income) and the prevailing market rate for a similar apartment in the same area. Typically, tenants pay 30% of their monthly income for rent, and Section 8 subsidies cover the balance. To be eligible for Section 8 payments, tenants must be very low-income families whose incomes do not exceed 50% of the median income for the area; over 3.5 million families are currently served by some form of Section 8 subsidy. Subsidy payments are made directly to the owner of the project, which assures a reliable cash flow from the project, and makes prepayments from default less likely. Section 8 subsidy payments also provide additional call protection, since the project owner may not prepay the mortgage while the HAP contract is in force (most HAP contracts are for twenty years and are renewable). Section 8 contracts cannot be transferred or terminated, and remain with the project under a change of ownership. Section 8 HAP contracts may cover fewer than 100% of the rental apartments in a given project; obviously, projects with higher percentages of Section 8 provide the greatest call protection.

Prepayments from Refinancing

Private sector, profit-motivated borrowers may refinance projects if interest rates decline, but they also have incentives to refinance loans at current or even somewhat higher rates. For existing properties that have increased in value, selling the property or refinancing at a higher loan-to-value ratio enables developers to take equity out of a project. The economics of a profit-motivated developer's business often dictates that private sector project borrowers refinance to capitalize available equity. Refinancing a for-profit project may also be driven by a need for the mortagor to raise money to refurbish or rehabilitate a property without putting up scarce equity. Also, if a project does not continue to serve the same use, it must be prepaid. Thus, before a mortgagor on a rental project could convert the property to a cooperative or condominium, the mortgage must be prepaid.

As for-profit projects age, the probabilities increase that private developers will prepay the mortgage to rehabilitate the project or to take out equity. The likelihood and timing of prepayments on profit-motivated projects depends on several factors, including the loan-to-value ratio of the project, the type and location of the project, and the type of borrower. Borrowers are more likely to prepay projects with lower loan-to-value ratios, since this permits them to access a substantial amount of equity quickly. Also, projects built for moderate-income rather than low-income tenants are generally more likely to refinance, since they typically have more amenities (balconies, pools, etc.), are generally in better neighborhoods, and so are more likely to increase in value or be converted to condominiums. Moderate-income projects also tend to prepay faster because developers often need to refinance so they can access equity to refurbish and maintain the project to protect their investment. Projects in high-growth areas and other favorable locations more frequently increase in value, and so tend to prepay faster.

Tax considerations also provide some motivation for many private investors and limited partnerships to refinance projects. The Tax Reform Act of 1986 curtailed accelerated depreciation, which had provided significant incentives to refinance older projects. Projects originated since 1986 must be depreciated over 27.5 years, using a straight line method. However, tax factors remain a consideration in refinancing decisions. The tax shelter provided by mortgage interest payments, coupled with the tax advantages that remain under the current depreciation rules, begin to abate in years ten to twelve, as the project mortgage amortizes. This makes it advantageous for partnerships and individuals to refinance project mortgages.

CLC/PLCs

Under multifamily insurance programs, the government insures the construction financing of projects as well as the permanent mortgage on the completed structures, unlike single-family mortgage pass-throughs, in which the government only insures mortgages on completed homes. Investors purchase new projects by committing to fund construction costs on a monthly basis until the project is built. When construction is completed, the investor's cumulative monthly construction financing payments are rolled into a permanent mortgage on the building. The construction financing portion of a project trades in the secondary market as an insured *Construction Loan Certificate (CLC)*, in either FHA-insured or GNMA form.

CLCs operate as follows: each month during a predetermined construction period (typically eighteen to twenty-four months), the contractor completes a specified portion of the construction and then submits a bill for the work to the local FHA office. The FHA then sends an inspector to the job site, and if the work meets specifications, the FHA issues an insured CLC for that month's work. The investor funds the work by fulfilling a commitment to purchase each monthly CLC. When the project is completed, the investor exchanges all the monthly CLCs for an insured *Permanent Loan Certificate (PLC)*.

The PLC is an insured pass-through security backed by the final mortgage on the completed property. As such, PLCs typically have a thirty-five to forty-year maturity, depending on the type of project. There are vastly more PLCs than CLCs in the market, owing to the long economic lives of project structures, and while CLCs are generally held by one investor over a relatively short construction period, PLCs trade frequently in the secondary market. Determining value in PLCs is a function of many factors, such as coupon, seasoning, and call protection.

PREPAYMENTS, CALL PROTECTION, LOCKOUTS

FHA/HUD does not directly prohibit profit-motivated developers from prepaying or refinancing project mortgages, and prepayments on nonprofit projects are also permitted as long as the mortgagor first secures HUD's approval. There are some exceptions to this rule, since projects built under several programs may not be prepaid. For example, projects with Section 8 carry significant prepayment restrictions (see above).

Most project pass-throughs are whole pools backed by one building, and so a full prepayment effectively ends the investment. As a result, most project investors write prepayment restrictions and penalties into the loan contract with the mortgagor. HUD has approved three basic types of prepayment restrictions and penalties (see HUD mortgagee letter 87-9): (1) prepayment lockout restrictions that extend to a maximum of ten years plus the stated construction period; (2) prepayment penalties of 1% or less, ten years after the stated construction period; and (3) some combination of prepayment lockout and penalties with a lockout less than ten years and a premium no more than 1% ten years after the stated construction period. At present, the two most common forms of call protection are ten-year lockouts, and five-year lockouts with prepayments then permitted in year six at 105% of par, declining to 101% in year ten.

COINSURANCE

In 1983, HUD/FHA introduced a coinsurance program under which private lenders could share the risk of a multifamily project with HUD. Under this coinsurance program, mortgage bankers did the due diligence and underwriting for project loans. At that time, the feeling was that the government could minimize risk to the FHA insurance fund by enabling private sector lenders to risk their own capital on a project in return for a potential greater reward. Unfortunately, the program ran into problems. By the late 1980s, it became clear that underwriting standards on several projects had received a lower priority than mortgage lenders' desire for the lucrative fee income generated by originating new projects. In addition, several cases of outright fraud were well publicized; in 1990 HUD canceled the old coinsurance program. A significant number of coinsured GNMA project securities remain in circulation, and trade regularly in the secondary market. Since these outstanding projects are in GNMA form, investors are shielded from credit risk by the U.S. Government guarantee of GNMA. Recently,

HUD has proposed a new delegated processing program that requires that ultimate due diligence and underwriting responsibilities reside jointly with two HUD-approved mortgage bankers and with the FHA. Under this delegated processing program, the first mortgage banker prepares all the required economic and underwriting analysis and all HUD documentation. The second mortgage banker must then review all the information before certifying to HUD that the project qualifies for FHA insurance.

SPECIFIC PROJECT PROGRAMS

The FHA has established numerous multifamily insurance programs since its creation under the National Housing Act of 1934. Each program serves a specific purpose, and is referred to by the section of the housing act under which it was created. Specific characteristics vary from program to program, since the types of projects, their purposes, allowable mortgage limits, prepayment features, and other criteria often differ. As discussed above, regardless of which program a project is insured under, securities backed by insured mortgages may exist in either GNMA form or as FHA pass-throughs. The following is a brief discussion of several of the most common multifamily insurance programs. Exhibit 1 provides a quick reference on these programs; Exhibit 2 illustrates the relative size of each program within the project market,.

Multifamily Housing

Section 221(d)4: Rental Housing for Low- to Moderate-Income Families: The 221(d)4 program is the largest Project program, with $24.6 billion in cumulative insurance issued on 7,560 projects, and $20.3 billion insurance remaining in force since the program began in 1959.[1] This program insures mortgages made by private

---

[1] All data concerning the programs discussed in this section are from the U.S. Department of Housing and Urban Development, as of December 31, 1990.

lenders to finance construction or substantial rehabilitation of multifamily rental or cooperative housing for low- to moderate-income or displaced families. Projects insured under Section 221(d)4 must have five or more units, and may consist of detached, semidetached, row, walk-up, or elevator structures.

Section 221(d)4 projects may be owned by either nonprofit or profit-motivated developers, and these projects may be insured for up to 90% of their FHA-determined replacement cost. Although 100% of the funds invested in project securities is insured, the mortgagor only borrows 90% or less of replacement cost; the balance represents owner equity. The majority of loans insured under Section 221(d)4, and most new production, is unsubsidized, market-rate projects. That is, project owners set the rental rates (subject to HUD approval), and there are no income restrictions on tenants. Nonmarket-rate projects may also be insured under Section 221(d)4, and Section 8-subsidized projects are financed through the 221(d)4 program; only these Section 8 projects have restrictions on monthly rents and tenant income.

The maximum term of mortgages insured under Section 221(d)4 is either forty years or 75% of the FHA-estimated remaining economic life of the project, whichever is less. The majority of these projects carries forty-year terms. FHA/HUD does not restrict prepayments on Section 221(d)4 mortgages, although prepayment lockouts and penalties are usually negotiated between the mortgagee and mortgagor. HUD may allow mortgagors to prepay up to 15% of a mortgage per year, unless documents that record the transaction specify in the lockout that the bonds are noncallable in whole or in part for a specified period of time. However, even if documents do not prohibit prepayments, the 15% prepayment option is not exercised often, since U.S. Government backing makes project financing much less expensive for developers than private financing alternatives.

Section 221(d)3: Rental and Cooperative Housing for Low- to Moderate-Income Families: The 221(d)3 program has two components. The first was an older, below-market interest rate program

(BMIR) that provided financing to sponsors of lower-income housing projects. The claim rate on BMIRs has been high, and so the BMIR program was closed in 1972 (of the $2.87 billion BMIRs originally insured, only $1.3 billion remain outstanding).

More important is the second component of Section 221(d)3, the market rate program; the market rate program is similar to the 221(d)4 program. The market rate 221(d)3 program remains in force, with $3.2 billion in cumulative insurance issued on 2,058 projects and $2.7 billion insurance in force since the program began in 1954. The primary difference between the 221(d)3 and the 221(d)4 program is that Section 221(d)3 provides developers with more leverage, since HUD may insure up to 100% of a project's FHA-determined replacement cost under this program, versus only 90% under Section 221(d)4. The majority of market rate projects insured under Section 221(d)3 has Section 8 rental subsidies, and, unlike projects insured under Section 221(d)4, 221(d)3 projects can include cooperatives. Finally, during the first twenty years of a mortgage insured under Section 221(d)3, borrowers must obtain HUD's permission before making any prepayments on the mortgage. Aside from these differences, the 221(d)3 market rate program closely resembles the 221(d)4 program. The program may be used for new construction or substantial rehabilitation of various types of buildings.

7.43 Putable Projects: Older FHA Projects Insured Under Sections 221(d)3 and 221(d)4: FHA projects insured under Section 221(d)3 and 221(d)4 before 1984 included a twenty-year put feature. This put option gives the FHA pass-through holder the right to assign, or put, the mortgage to HUD for a one-year period twenty years after the original mortgage was endorsed by HUD/FHA. When investors put the securities, they receive FHA series MM debentures with a ten-year maturity; these debentures are obligations of the FHA, and as such are unconditionally guaranteed by the U.S. Government as to payment of interest and principal. The debentures' face value will equal the unpaid principal balance of the mortgage plus accrued interest. The servicers of most project loan pools automatically exercise this put option and then liquidate the debentures for investors, unless bond holders who represent a controlling interest in the pool object. The investors then receive the proceeds as a cash distribution from the project pool.

Before December 1983, many FHA projects were auctioned by GNMA. The majority of these projects was purchased by servicers as 7.50% loans, and issued as FHA pass through securities with 7.43% coupons. They are commonly referred to as 7.43s, since the issuers often retained seven basis points of servicing. The vast majority of 7.43s was auctioned between 1979 and 1983; consequently, most 7.43s are putable between 1999 and 2003, and trade at a spread over the ten-year Treasury. Most of the projects underlying 7.43s carry Section 8 contracts (see above), which provide the investor with a defined cash flow and also limit prepayments. This cash flow certainty coupled with the ten-year put feature make putable 7.43s very convex securities.

The exact value of the FHA debentures definitely affects the value of the put option. To compensate for the additional market risk and record-keeping associated with debentures, investors have typically valued FHA debentures at ninety-six to ninety-eight cents on the dollar. However, the Federal budget law for fiscal 1991 changed the put process on 7.43s in order to reduce the budget deficit. At present, investors in 7.43s putable 1995 or earlier can elect to receive cash in lieu of debentures when the bonds are put, and investors who valued the put option assuming they would receive debentures worth ninety-six can now receive cash, or par. As a result, the put option is now worth more than most investors assumed at purchase. Further, the shift from debenture pay to cash pay shaved the Federal budget deficit substantially, and many observers think it likely that future budget laws will extend the change from debenture pay to cash pay to reduce future budget deficits. Thus, a case can be made that the put option on 7.43s is worth more than a ninety-six to ninety-eight assumption implies.

Finally, investors should note that not all 7.43s are putable; 7.43s issued under some project programs are not putable. Most of these nonputable 7.43s also carry Section 8 contracts, and so provide defined cash flows to maturity. Nonputable 7.43s trade in the secondary market at a spread over long bonds, as opposed to the putable projects, which trade off the ten-year Treasury.

Section 223(f): Purchase or Refinancing of Existing Multifamily Projects: The 223(f) program was created to insure the purchase or refinancing of existing rental apartment projects, to refinance existing cooperatives, or to purchase and convert existing rental projects to cooperative housing. Section 223(f) was added to the National Housing Act by the Housing and Community Development Act in 1974, in order to help preserve an adequate supply of affordable housing. Rental projects insured under Section 221(d)4, as well as housing projects issued under any other section of the National Housing Act, can be refinanced by using Section 223(f). Since 1974, 1,636 projects have been originated under Section 223(f), representing $8.4 billion of insurance written, with $6.1 billion remaining in force.

Section 223(f) is a market-rate, unsubsidized program created primarily to improve the financing flexibility for profit-motivated project developers by making it easier for owners to refinance, convert a project to a co-op, and buy or sell an existing building. To qualify for insurance under Section 223(f), a project must be at least three years old, must contain five or more units, and must have sufficient occupancy to pay operating expenses, annual debt service, and maintain a reserve fund for replacement requirements. A mortgage insured under Section 223(f) cannot exceed 85% of the HUD/FHA estimated value of the project, although this requirement can be raised to 90% for cooperatives and those projects located in Target Preservation Areas as designated by HUD.

The maximum term for mortgages insured under Section 223(f) is either thirty-five years or 75% of the FHA-estimated remaining economic life of the project, whichever is less. Most 223(f) projects carry thirty-five-year terms. As with other programs, HUD/FHA permits prepayments on mortgages insured under Section 223(f), although prepayment lockouts and penalties are usually negotiated between the mortgagee and mortgagor.

Section 207: Section 207 was enacted in 1934 as the first program used by the FHA to finance construction or rehabilitation of multifamily housing projects. Section 207 projects are primarily moderate-income projects sponsored by for-profit developers. The 207 program is rarely used today, as multifamily projects are now originated under Sections 221(d)3 and 221(d)4. However, seasoned Section 207 projects continue to trade in the secondary market. Total cumulative insurance issued under Section 207 was $4 billion, with $1 billion insurance remaining in force.

Section 213: The Section 213 program was enacted in 1950 to provide mortgage insurance on cooperative projects. Section 213 insurance can be used for new construction, rehabilitation, acquisition, conversion, or repair of existing housing in several types of cooperative projects that consist of five or more units. The program is available both for nonprofit cooperative corporations as well as for profit-motivated developers who build or rehabilitate a project and sell it to a cooperative corporation. Total cumulative insurance written under Section 213 is $1.6 billion on 2,043 projects, with $878 million insurance remaining in force.

Section 220: The Section 220 program was created to insure mortgages and home improvement loans on multifamily projects in urban renewal areas. Before 1980, Section 220 insurance was available in urban renewal areas in which federally assisted slum clearance and urban redevelopment projects were being undertaken. In 1980, the Housing and Community Development Act expanded the scope of the Section 220 program to include those areas in which housing, development, and public service activities will be carried out by local neighborhood improvement, conservation, or preservation groups. The main focus of Section 220 is to insure mortgages on new or rehabilitated multifamily structures located within designated urban renewal areas. Over 540 projects have been insured under Section 220, which represents $3.1 billion in total cumulative insurance with $1.8 billion remaining in force.

Health Care and Housing for the Elderly

Section 231: Rental Housing for the Elderly or Handicapped: In 1959, Congress enacted Section 231 of the National Housing Act to provide insurance for the construction or rehabilitation of rental housing for the elderly. Section 231 was expanded to include housing for the handicapped in 1964. Residents of projects for the elderly must be at least sixty-two years old, whereas residents in projects for the handicapped must be people with a long-term physical impairment that substantially impedes an independent living arrangement, but who could live independently in suitable housing.

Projects must have eight or more units to qualify for insurance under Section 231, and the maximum term for mortgages insured under Section 231 is forty years or 75% of the project's estimated economic life. In addition, HUD may insure up to 100% of the estimated replacement cost for projects originated by nonprofit and public borrowers, but only up to 90% of replacement cost for profit-motivated mortgagors. Total cumulative insurance issued under Section 231 is $1.1 billion, with $847 million insurance remaining in force.

Section 232: Nursing Homes, Intermediate Care Facilities, and Board and Care Homes: Under Section 232, HUD insures mortgages to finance new construction or rehabilitation of Nursing Homes for patients who require skilled nursing care and related medical services, as well as Intermediate Care Facilities and Board and Care Homes, for patients who need minimum but continuous care provided by licensed or trained people. Section 232 insures

mortgages on any of these facilities; also, nursing homes, intermediate care, and board and care homes may be combined within the
same facility and insured under Section 232. Board and care
homes must have a minimum of five one-bedroom or efficiency
units, whereas nursing homes and intermediate care facilities must
have twenty or more patients who are unable to live independently but are not in need of acute care. Mortgage insurance
under Section 232 may also cover the purchase of major equipment needed to operate the facility. Also, Section 232 may be used
to purchase, rehabilitate, and/or refinance existing health care
projects already insured by HUD.

Legislation establishing this program was enacted in 1959. Borrowers may include private nonprofit associations or corporations,
or for-profit investors or developers. To qualify for insurance under Section 232, sponsors must first qualify for licensing in the
State of the facility, and must comply with all relevant State regulations. Total cumulative insurance issued under Section 232 is
$3.6 billion on 1,723 projects; total insurance remaining in force is
$2.6 billion.

**Section 236: Interest Rate Subsidies for Low- to Moderate-In-
come Families and Elderly Individuals:** Section 236 was added to
the National Housing Act in 1968, but was suspended during the
subsidized housing moratorium of 1973, and has never been re-
vived. The 236 program combined governmental mortgage insurance on projects, with subsidized payments to reduce the project
owners' monthly debt service payments. These reduced interest
payments, in turn, are passed on to tenants of the project in the
form of lower rents. To qualify for rental assistance under Section
236, tenants' annual income must be less than 80% of the median
income of the area. The program serves both elderly individuals
and low-income families.

The maximum mortgage amount for limited-dividend sponsors
is 90% of replacement cost; for nonprofit sponsors, the maximum
mortgage amount can be 100%. In certain defined high-cost areas,
maximums may be increased up to an additional 75%. The maxi-

mum term under this program is forty years, and prepayments are prohibited for at least twenty years without prior approval from HUD. Total cumulative insurance issued under Section 236 was $7.5 billion on over 4,000 projects; $6.1 billion insurance remains in force.

Section 242: Mortgage Insurance for Hospitals: In 1968, Congress enacted Section 242 of the National Housing Act to provide insurance for the construction or rehabilitation of hospitals. Major equipment used in the hospital may also be included in an insured mortgage under Section 242. Hospitals built or rehabilitated under Section 242 must have appropriate licenses and meet the regulatory requirements of the State in which they are located, and must be approved by the U.S. Department of Health and Human Services. A Section 242 mortgage may not exceed 90% of the FHA-estimated replacement cost, and the maximum term for these mortgages is twenty-five years.

Borrowers under Section 242 may be either profit-motivated or not-for-profit hospitals. HUD permits full or partial prepayments on profit-motivated Section 242 projects, subject to prepayment restrictions and penalties negotiated between the mortgagor and mortgagee, but prepayments by nonprofit mortgagors are permitted only with the written consent of HUD. Total cumulative insurance issued under Section 242 is $6.9 billion on 280 projects, with $5.1 billion insurance remaining in force.

Exhibit 1 shows the relative size of the various programs that constitute the project securities market. The Appendix to this chapter provides a quick reference on projects.

Exhibit 1: Relative Size of the Various Programs that Constitute the $58 Billion Project Securities Outstanding as of 12/31/90 (HUD Data)

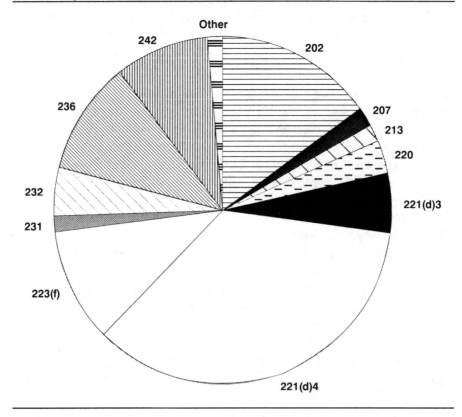

APPENDIX

QUICK REFERENCE ON PROJECTS

SECTION 202

Type of Program: Direct loans for housing the elderly or handicapped

Type of Borrower: Private, nonprofit sponsors (including nonprofit cooperatives)

Maximum Loan Amount: The lesser of: 95% of anticipated net project income or 100% of the project's development costs

Maximum Term: Fifty years by Statute, but HUD has limited loans to forty years

Date Program Enacted: 1959 (amended 1974)

Additional Features: Older loans fixed rate; newer loans adjust annually at a HUD-determined margin over Treasuries. All projects under Section 202 have 100% Section 8 HAP contracts (see Section 8, p. 4)

Program Status: Active

Insurance in Force: $8.7 billion

SECTION 207

Type of Program: Construction or rehabilitation of rental housing

Type of Borrower: Primarily profit-motivated sponsors

Date Program Enacted: 1934

Prepayment Restrictions: Negotiable

Program Status: Authorized but not used; multifamily rental projects now issued under Sections 221(d)3 and (4)

Insurance in Force: $1 billion

SECTION 213

Type of Program: New construction, rehabilitation, acquisition, conversion or repair of cooperative housing projects

Type of Borrower: Profit-motivated co-op sponsors as well as nonprofit corporations or trusts

Date Program Enacted: 1950

Prepayment Restrictions: Negotiable

Program Status: Authorized but not used; cooperative projects now issued under Sections 221(d)3 and 221(d) 4

Insurance in Force: $878 million

SECTION 220

Type of Program: New construction or rehabilitation of projects in designated Urban Renewal Areas
Type of Borrower: Profit-motivated and nonprofit sponsors
Date Program Enacted: 1949 (expanded 1980)
Prepayment Restrictions: Negotiable
Program Status: Active but infrequently used; Urban Renewal projects are being eliminated
Insurance in Force: $1.8 billion

SECTIONS 221(D)3 and 221(d)4

Type of Programs: Construction or rehabilitation of multifamily rental or cooperative housing for low- or moderate-income tenants
Type of Borrower: For-profit corporations or partnerships (developers, builders, investors); also nonprofit public or community groups
Maximum Loan Amount: 221(d)4: 90% of FHA-estimated replacement cost (maximum can be higher only with explicit FHA approval) 221(d)3: 100% of FHA-estimated replacement cost
Maximum Term: Forty years from origination
Date Programs Enacted: 221(d)3: 1954; 221(d)4: 1959
Additional Features: FHA pass-throughs auctioned before 1/1/84 have an option that permits investor to put the mortgage to HUD in its twentieth year
Prepayment Restrictions: Negotiable between mortgagor and mortgagee unless project has a Section 8 HAP contract
Program Status: Active
Insurance in Force: 221(d)4: $20.3 billion; 221(d)3 Market Rate Only: $3.2 billion

SECTION 223(f)

Type of Program: Purchase or refinancing of existing multifamily projects
Type of Borrower: Primarily profit-motivated sponsors
Maximum Loan Amount: 85% of HUD estimated value (may be raised to 90% with HUD approval)
Maximum Term: Thirty-five years from origination
Date Program Enacted: 1974
Prepayment Restrictions: Negotiable
Program Status: Active
Insurance in Force: $6.1 billion

SECTION 231

Type of Program: Rental housing for the elderly or handicapped
Type of Borrower: Profit-motivated and nonprofit sponsors
Maximum Loan Amount: 90% (for-profit project) or 100% (nonprofit project)

of the FHA-estimated replacement cost
Maximum Term: Forty years, or 75% of the project's estimated economic life
Date Program Enacted: 1959
Prepayment Restrictions: Negotiable
Program Status: Active
Insurance in Force: $847 million

SECTION 232

Type of Program: Construction or rehabilitation of nursing homes, intermediate care facilities, and board and care homes
Type of Borrower: Profit-motivated and nonprofit sponsors
Maximum Loan Amount: 90% of FHA-estimated value of property (includes the value of equipment used to operate the facility)
Maximum Term: Forty years from origination
Date Program Enacted: 1959
Prepayment Restrictions: Negotiable
Program Status: Active
Insurance in Force: $2.6 billion

SECTION 236

Type of Program: Interest rate subsidies for low- to moderate-income families and elderly individuals
Type of Borrower: Profit-motivated and nonprofit sponsors
Maximum Loan Amount: 90% of FHA-estimated replacement cost (100% or higher permissible for nonprofit sponsors)
Date Program Enacted: 1968
Prepayment Restrictions: Negotiable
Program Status: Inactive
Insurance in Force: $6.1 billion

SECTION 242

Type of Program: Construction or rehabilitation of public or private hospitals (includes major movable equipment)
Type of Borrower: Profit-motivated or nonprofit sponsors
Maximum Loan Amount: 90% of FHA-estimated replacement cost
Maximum Term: Twenty-five years from origination
Date Program Enacted: 1968
Prepayment Restrictions: Negotiable; nonprofit sponsors may make prepayments only with HUD's written consent
Program Status: Active
Insurance in Force: $5.1 billion

SECTION III

PREPAYMENT FORECASTING

CHAPTER 10

MODELING AND PROJECTING MBS PREPAYMENTS

Charles N. Schorin, PhD
Vice President
Kidder, Peabody & Co., Inc.

INTRODUCTION

Prepayments are fundamental to mortgage-backed securities (MBS). Were it not for the right of mortgagors to prepay their mortgages without penalty, a mortgage security would be similar to an ordinary bond; but from the right of mortgagors to prepay, the risk characteristics of mortgage-backed securities are derived, and they differ dramatically from those of ordinary bonds. As important as prepayments are to the risk and return pattern of mortgage pass-throughs, they are especially crucial to the performance of derivative mortgage products, such as interest-only/principal-

This model was developed when the author was at Drexel Burnham Lambert, and the chapter was written when the author was at Smith Barney.

only strips (IOs/POs) and real estate mortgage investment conduits (REMICs), particularly the companion bonds and residual pieces.

With prepayments playing such an important role in the performance of mortgage-backed securities, it is imperative that market participants have a means of estimating prepayments. Ideally, these prepayment estimates will be derived from a formal mathematical model that has been estimated statistically over historical data. A model of this type can be used to evaluate prepayments on mortgage pass-throughs, and therefore to price both pass-throughs and more complicated derivative mortgage instruments and structured products.

The alternative to employing a formally estimated statistical or econometric model is to use some sort of arbitrary assumptions or "rules of thumb" to evaluate prepayments of mortgage securities. One such arbitrary assumption is to use the PSA "model." Although the PSA curve approaches the general notion that prepayments on mortgages initially are slow and then increase gradually as the mortgages season, the relationship between the actual pattern of prepayment rates and the PSA curve is extremely tenuous. A graph of projected prepayments for FNMA 9 1/2s and the PSA curve is displayed in Exhibit 1. The prepayment projections for the FNMA 9 1/2s were generated from the Smith Barney Prepayment Model. (The wiggles in the prepayment rate path of the FNMA 9 1/2s represent changes in prepayment rates owing purely to seasonal factors.)

It is clear from Exhibit 1 that both the level and shape of actual prepayments differ from those depicted by the PSA curve. Even if different multiples of the PSA curve were to be used, the shape of the prepayment path still would differ from the PSA curve. In addition, if interest rates were to fall so that the FNMA 9 1/2 were to become a premium security, then the seasoning of the FNMA 9 1/2s would be even faster than displayed in Exhibit 1, yet the PSA curve would be unresponsive to this change in interest rates. This point will be revisited in the section of this chapter on seasoning patterns.

Exhibit 1   FNMA 91/2 CPR Path and 100% PSA Curve

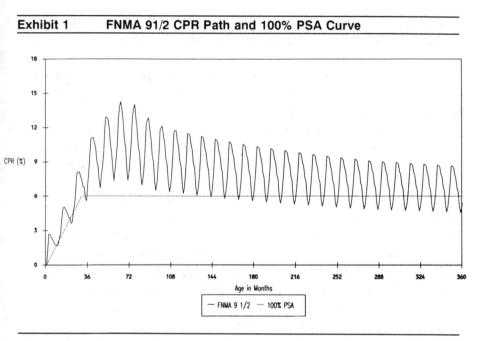

Another pitfall of not using an econometric prepayment model comes when one attempts to evaluate prepayment rates under various interest rate scenarios. A "quick and dirty" method of estimating prepayments used by many market participants is to begin with dealer prepayment estimates for a particular coupon displayed by financial information vendors such as Telerate or Bloomberg, and for, say, a 200-basis-point interest rate decline, use the stable rate prepayment estimate for the coupon that is 200 basis points higher than that of the coupon of interest.

The problem with this method is that if the higher coupon security is a premium, then it most likely has a shorter remaining maturity than the coupon of interest, and already has undergone a refinancing phase. Because of this, it is likely to prepay at a slower rate than would a new security faced with a sudden interest rate decline for the first time. Aside from the conceptual incorrectness of this approach, the practical result of using this method is that theoretical MBS prices derived using these prepayments display only very slight degrees of negative convexity. This not only is counter-intuitive, but counter to what was observed in the market in the 1980s.

Analyzing and projecting prepayment behavior for the variety of available mortgage pass-throughs requires not *a* prepayment model, but rather a *group* of models. Separate models must be used to evaluate prepayments on GNMA thirty- and fifteen-year, FHLMC thirty- and fifteen-year, FNMA thirty- and fifteen-year, and private pass-through thirty- and fifteen-year mortgage securities. This is necessitated by differences in the features of the underlying mortgages, the demographic characteristics of the respective borrowers, and the monthly reporting cycles of the agencies. Adjustable-rate mortgages present an additional level of complexity owing to a variety of possible indices, reset periods, caps and floors, and teaser rates. This chapter, however, will focus on prepayment behavior of fixed-rate mortgage-backed securities. The next chapter will focus on the prepayment behavior of adjustable-rate mortgage-backed securities.

The first section of this chapter discusses the primary determinants of prepayments. An example is included to demonstrate how a model's explicit incorporation of the seasonal aspect of prepayments crucially affects one's understanding of a security's rate of return. This is followed by a discussion of the modeling techniques used to construct the prepayment model employed by Drexel Burnham Lambert. Results of the model are presented, along with a discussion of both in-sample and out-of-sample accuracy. The chapter concludes with prepayment projections for some selected securities under various interest rate assumptions.

Current market conditions make this an opportune time to emphasize the importance of understanding prepayments in evaluating mortgage-backed securities and to underscore the importance of projecting prepayments from a formal model that incorporates all of the determinants of prepayment behavior. This chapter provides this emphasis. Several aspects of the present environment give this chapter particular currency:

- The proliferation of mortgage pricing models based on option-adjusted spread (OAS) technology, the results of which are heavily driven by prepayment projections.

- The emergence and growth of a market in derivative mortgage products containing planned amortization classes (PACs) and targeted amortization classes (TACs), for which the timing of the prepayment pattern affects the likelihood that prepayments will violate their respective collars, and companion tranches, the cash flows of which are heavily dependent on the prepayment pattern.

- The general thrust toward regulatory conformity among all varieties of financial institutions, and expanding and evolving regulatory involvement in issues relating to mortgage securities, such as risk-based capital rules for commercial banks and thrifts, proposed guidelines regarding permissible investments by financial institutions in derivative mortgage instruments, and the move toward mark-to-market accounting for debt instruments held as assets by financial institutions.

- Continuing liquidations by the Resolution Trust Corporation of mortgage securities held in the portfolios of capital-impaired thrift institutions.

- The tremendous growth in issuance of private label MBS, and the commencement of the RTC's REMIC program.

- The changing profile of the mortgage-backed securities investor, namely the increasing involvement of commercial banks and insurance companies and the diminished participation of thrift institutions.

- Uncertainty among market participants about the direction of interest rates in general, resulting from the demonstrated inability of the government to cope with the federal budget deficit.

Nontheoretical and nonstatistically estimated "models" provide little substance to support prepayment projections, and are particularly vulnerable to changing market conditions. Likewise, simple, but unfortunately simplistic, ad hoc assumptions and "rules of thumb," such as "thirty months to season" and "200 basis points interest rate differential" provide little guidance in analyzing prepayments. If these are used as the basis of a prepayment "model," then one uses the resultant projections at one's peril.

DETERMINANTS OF PREPAYMENTS

Mortgage-backed securities can be thought of as composite securities. The holder of the mortgage security essentially has a long position in a noncallable bond and a short position in a call option. The call option derives from the right of mortgagors to prepay their mortgages without penalty. The primary determinants of mortgage prepayments are refinancing and homeowner mobility. Owing to the fixed costs involved in originating a mortgage, the likelihood of either refinancing or mobility is related to the age of the mortgage. Mobility also is related to the month of the year, as the timing of the school year, homebuilding, and weather make relocation more likely in the late spring and summer and less likely in the late autumn and winter. This model incorporates the separate effects of refinancing, mortgage age, and month of the year. Each of these is discussed in turn.

Refinancing

Just as the holder of a mortgage security can be thought of as holding a composite security, a mortgagor can be thought of as holding a composite asset. This composite asset consists of a long position in the mortgaged property and a short position in an annuity. The short annuity position is the stream of mortgage payments that the mortgagor must make. The present discounted value of this composite asset, net of the prepayment option on the mortgage, can be written as:

$$V_t = H_t - \sum_{i=t}^{360} \frac{m_0}{(1 + r_0)^i}$$

where V_t is the value of the asset at time t, H_t is the value of the property at time t, m_0 is the monthly mortgage payment, r_0 is the mortgage interest rate, and $(1 + r_0)$ is the discount factor. Elementary calculus shows that when interest rates fall, the value of the annuity increases, but since the mortgagor has a short position in the annuity, the value of the composite asset falls (all else equal).[1]

The mortgagor's prepayment option provides the right to cancel the short position in the annuity by purchasing the annuity at par. Since the drop in interest rates increased the value of the annuity above par, purchasing it (prepaying the mortgage) at par is advantageous, as long as any associated transactions costs (the refinancing costs) do not exceed the benefit of the higher annuity value. After refinancing at the new interest rate, the new annuity value (on the right-hand side of the composite asset value equation) is par, and the value of the composite asset is greater than before the refinancing, because the annuity position has a smaller negative value (a short position of smaller value).

Two issues are involved in the refinancing decision. The first was alluded to above, namely the point at which the benefits of purchasing the annuity at par outweigh the costs. This will vary for different individuals, depending on the age of the mortgage, different refinancing costs at different lending institutions, and the expense of time and effort to obtain information from various institutions. The second is the interest rate differential between the originally contracted mortgage rate and the prevailing mortgage

---

[1] In this case, "all else equal" means that the property value does not change for a marginal change in interest rates.

market rate. A commonly used "rule of thumb" is that refinancing becomes profitable at an interest rate differential of about 200 basis points. In a theoretical context, however, in which a mortgage prepayment is viewed as equivalent to purchasing an annuity to close out a short position, it is inappropriate to consider the differential in absolute basis point terms. It is more meaningful to consider the *relative* difference between the prevailing market interest rate and the rate at which the mortgage was contracted. This is because the magnitude of the increase in the value of the annuity brought about by a fall in interest rates depends on the initial rate at which the annuity was sold (i.e., the rate at which the mortgage was contracted), which defines the par value of the annuity. For this reason, the prepayment model developed here uses the percentage interest rate, rather than absolute basis point, differential as the explanatory variable capturing the refinancing incentive.[2]

A scatter diagram of GNMA monthly prepayment rates plotted against percentage interest rate differentials is shown in Exhibit 2.[3] The interest rate differential, or spread, is taken to be the number

---

[2] As an extreme example, consider the difference in annuity values for a 360-month 20% annuity in an 18% interest rate environment, as opposed to a 360-month 4% annuity in a 2% environment. In the former case, a $1 par value annuity would be worth $1.11, whereas in the latter case it would be worth $1.29, even though in both cases the drop in interest rates was 200 basis points. Since both annuities can be purchased at par ($1), there is a greater incentive to purchase the annuity in the latter situation, where the 200-basis-point interest rate decline amounts to a 50% reduction in rates, than to purchase the annuity in the former situation, where the 200-basis-point drop amounts to a decline of only 10%.

[3] Prepayment rates may be expressed in terms of either SMM, CPR, or PSA. SMM stands for "single monthly mortality," and represents the percentage of a security's outstanding balance that prepaid in a given month. CPR is the "conditional (or constant) prepayment rate," and is the annualization of the monthly prepayment rate, or SMM. PSA refers to the Public Securities Association standard prepayment benchmark, which depicts prepayments as increasing at the annual rate of 0.2% per month for the first 30 months of a mortgage, and then remaining constant at the annual rate of 6% thereafter. Prepayment rates are then stated as percentages of the PSA benchmark. There are straightforward arithmetic conversions between prepayments expressed in terms of SMM, CPR, and PSA (although the conversion from SMM and CPR to PSA for an average prepayment rate over a period of time that includes part of the first thirty months of a mortgage is less straightforward). It generally is preferable to work with data in the form of SMM (the raw data used in estimating the prepayment model were in this form), and then convert to CPR or PSA as necessary for the purpose at hand.

of basis points between the weighted average coupon (WAC) and the effective mortgage rate prevailing in the market at the time of the observation,[4] divided by the WAC (with the entire expression multiplied by 100 so that the values read as percents). Note that there is relatively little dispersion in the points for negative spreads and for positive spreads less than 10%. Positive spreads that are less than 10% provide little or no incentive to refinance. Negative spreads not only provide no incentive to refinance, but they actually deter mobility, because those who prepay would be burdened with higher mortgage payments. Nonetheless, there always will be some mobility due to changed circumstances of homeowners, so that at least at the aggregate or generic level, there always will be some prepayments, even when the interest rate differential is negative. For spreads between 10% and 30%, however, there is considerable dispersion in the SMMs realized for given interest rate spreads. This dispersion relates to the "path dependency" of prepayment rates and the "refinanced out" phenomenon.

The issue of path dependency is that prepayment rates depend not only on the relative interest rate differential between the WAC and the prevailing mortgage rate at a point in time, but also on the path mortgage rates have taken to arrive at this point. As an example, consider a mortgage security with a WAC of 12%, when the prevailing mortgage market rate is 9%. This 300-basis-point differential results in a relative spread of 25% (12% – 9% / 12%). Whether the SMM at the 25% spread in Exhibit 2 is likely to be among the higher observations, such as above the level labeled A, or among the lower, such as level B, depends on the path taken by interest rates since the security was issued. If the mortgage rate was 12% at issuance and then rose or stayed fairly constant for a period of time before suddenly dropping to 9%, then prepayments

---

[4] The effective mortgage rate is constructed as a weighted average of various lags in the mortgage market interest rate. This lag structure was estimated statistically and accounts for the lag between the realization of mortgage rates and household behavior, as well as the lag between the collection of prepayments by mortgage servicers and the reporting of these prepayments on agency factor tapes.

Exhibit 2   SMM and Mutliplicative Interest Rate Differential

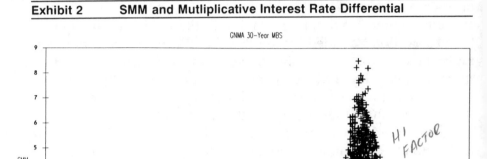

would likely be considerably higher than if rates went from 12% at issuance, to, say, 8%, then 7%, and slowly rose to 9%. The reason that SMMs would be so different in the two scenarios is that in the former scenario, mortgagors had not previously had an attractive opportunity to refinance their mortgages before the present environment of 9% rates. It is likely that there would be a burst of refinancing as mortgagors act to lock in the lower rate. In the latter scenario, however, mortgagors had considerable opportunity, often at rates even more attractive than available at present, to refinance previously. It is likely that many mortgagors would already have taken advantage of these opportunities in the latter scenario, so that by the time the current 9% mortgage rate environment arrived, those remaining in the mortgage pool are less sensitive to refinancing opportunities. The SMM that actually is realized for the given WAC of 12% and mortgage rate of 9% thus depends on the path taken by the mortgage rate to arrive at its prevailing rate.

The discussion of path dependency suggests that as a mortgage security continues to experience refinancings on its underlying mortgages, those mortgagors remaining in the security's pool are increasingly less sensitive to refinancing opportunities. Eventually, the security is said to be "refinanced out" or "burned out," as those mortgagors remaining in the pool have only a slight responsiveness to interest rates. An example of this process is given by the GNMA 15s issued in 1981. When only twenty-two months old, the SMM for this class of GNMAs peaked at 4.93%. Now, however, this class is so refinanced out that its SMM in February 1989 was only 1.49%, despite an interest rate spread of over 30%, and its SMM in May 1990 was only 1.08%, despite an interest rate spread of 34%. The refinanced out process is reflected in Exhibit 3 with the prepayment projections from the Smith Barney Prepayment Model for the FNMA 12.

Exhibit 3   FNMA 12 SMM Path

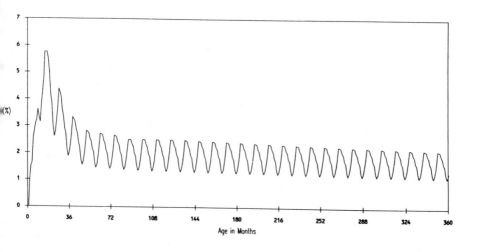

The refinanced out effect is noticeable especially for premium securities (and securities that had been premiums), but even current coupons and discounts experience a bit of a slowdown in prepayments once they reach the stage of being fully "seasoned." Of course, if the securities are current coupons or discounts and have never been premiums, then the slowdown in their prepayments cannot properly be termed a "refinanced out" effect, and perhaps "burned out" is a more appropriate term. Nonetheless, current coupons and discounts do eventually experience a distinct slowdown in prepayments, though one that is less pronounced than for premiums. This aspect of prepayment behavior will be revisited in the discussion of the seasoning process of mortgages in the next section.

One of the primary challenges confronting prepayment model builders is the manner in which to incorporate the path dependency and refinanced out concepts into the model. Put differently, with the wide range of historical SMMs in response to a given interest rate spread (as in Exhibit 2), the task is to construct a model that incorporates the elements necessary to determine accurately the magnitude of the SMM for given market conditions.

Research conducted by the author has revealed that the most important element allowing analysts to determine prepayments for a given interest rate spread is the security's factor (or the generic security's aggregate factor). The factor is the percentage of the original amount of a security (or generic class) that remains outstanding. Other methods of capturing path dependence were considered, such as constructing a "refinanced variable" that reflects the relationship between the path of prepayments and the time that the respective generic security had been a premium.[5] These other measures and methods all were inferior to using the aggregate factor.[6] The aggregate factor allows the incorporation of

---

[5] Several different definitions of premium were employed, but none proved adequate for this purpose.

[6] A particular security's factor may decline because of scheduled principal payments, prepayments or both. That the aggregate factor best captures path dependency is an empirical, rather than theoretical, determination.

the path dependency and refinanced out concepts. It also is critical in quantifying the responsiveness of prepayments to given interest rate differentials.

Consider again the scatter diagram in Exhibit 2. At interest rate differentials greater than about 10%, there appears to be an amorphous cloud of SMM observations, with several seemingly equally likely to be realized for a given spread. Through the modeling process, however, it was determined that underlying this seemingly shapeless cloud of points is a family of well defined curves, each of which is determined by a range of factors. Curves defined by high factors are toward the top of the cloud of points (running through points above level A), and factors decline as one moves vertically down through the cloud of points. An example of a well defined curve for a factor group is given in Exhibit 4 for the 0.8-to-0.9 factor group. Securities that have experienced very little principal paydown, say, with factors of 0.90, are likely to be very responsive to a refinancing opportunity.[7] For a given interest rate spread, their SMMs are likely to be toward the top of the cloud of points in Exhibit 2. As the factor declines with both scheduled and unscheduled principal payments, the remaining mortgagors are less responsive to a given interest rate spread (or they would have refinanced already). Their prepayment rates are likely to lie on curves below those defined by higher factors, and they are likely to prepay at lower rates for a given interest rate spread than similar securities with higher factors. Thus, as factors decline, prepayments slow, incorporating the path dependency effect. As factors decline further, prepayments decline further, reflecting the refinanced out effect for premiums (and the prepayment slowdown effect to a lesser extent for current coupons and discounts).

---

[7] The exception is that *extremely* new securities, with factors very close to 1, are not very responsive to a given refinancing opportunity because of the costs involved in refinancing, coming on top of the expenses recently incurred to close the present mortgage. The age of the underlying mortgages also is included in the model, but for expository convenience, it is held constant for the present discussion. The issue of age and seasoning is discussed below.

Exhibit 4	SMM and Multiplicative Interest Rate Differential

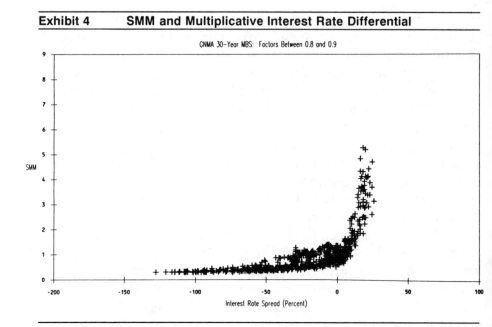

Seasoning

Mortgage-backed securities display a distinct seasoning, or aging, process. Prepayment rates tend to increase slowly for a period of time, before increasing more rapidly, reaching a peak (at which point they are said to be "fully seasoned"), and then slowing down. The PSA curve tried to capture this notion by its assumption that prepayments would increase at the annual rate of 0.2% per month over the first 30 months of a mortgage's life, then remain at the annual rate of 6% until maturity. While this does convey the concept that prepayments start off at low levels and gradually increase until the security is "seasoned," the PSA curve fails to capture adequately the seasoning process for most mortgage-backed securities. The same reason that the PSA curve is woefully inadequate in its characterization of prepayments in general is the reason why it is an inaccurate representation of the seasoning process in particular: it fails to capture the effect of interest rates.

It must be noted that part of the seasoning process is independent of interest rates. Home buyers clearly are unwilling to relocate shortly after purchasing a new home. Some will encounter unforeseen circumstances that will require them to sell their home and move, but these occurrences are likely to be fairly rare for the first several months of the mortgage, due both to the costs involved in moving and to the small likelihood that familial or occupational circumstances would have changed very much since purchasing the home. Over time, however, as these circumstances do change, homeowners are more likely to relocate. After a certain period of time, the proportion of those relocating, as a share of those remaining in the mortgage security's pool, tends to drop off slightly. With the exception of this slight decline in prepayment rates, this was the general notion that the PSA curve tried to capture. However, because part of the seasoning process depends quite heavily on interest rates, by not incorporating their effects, the PSA curve fails egregiously in its attempt to depict prepayments.

The period of time that it takes prepayments on mortgage securities to reach their peak depends quite substantially on interest rates: premiums season much faster than currents, and currents season much faster than discounts. This is referred to here as "behavioral seasoning," to contrast it to various "definitional seasoning" notions, be they twenty-four, thirty, thirty-six, or however many months. Exhibits 5, 6, and 7 demonstrate this point. Each displays the seasoning pattern for a FNMA security superimposed on graphs of the PSA curve and a multiple of the PSA curve. The FNMA in Exhibit 5 is a discount security, whereas in Exhibit 6 it is a current coupon, and in Exhibit 7 it is a premium. All of these securities are assumed to be newly issued in a 10.25% mortgage rate environment.[8]

Although it is unlikely that a mortgage security with a gross coupon of 8.80% or 12.70% would be issued when the prevailing

---

[8] The path for the later years of the mortgage is an extrapolation from the model, as there are few observed data for these years.

Exhibit 5   FNMA 8 CPR Path and PSA Curves

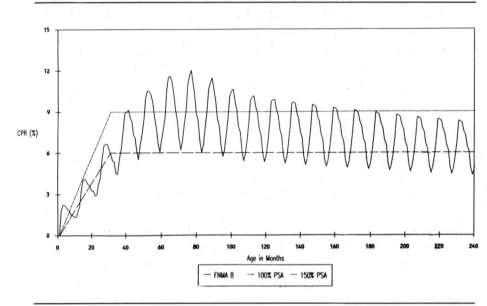

Exhibit 6   FNMA 91/2 CPR Path and PSA Curves

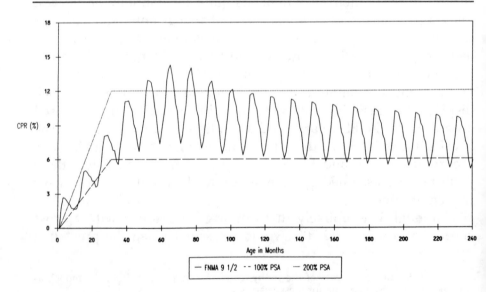

Exhibit 7   FNMA 12 CPR Path and PSA Curves

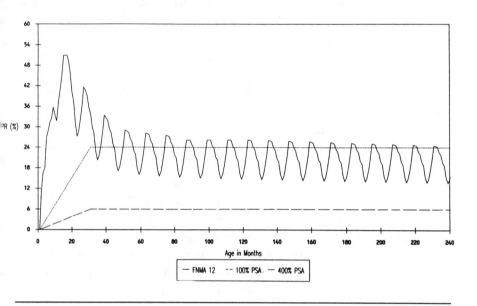

market rate is 10.25%, these diagrams are included for two reasons: first, by showing the projected path of prepayments of these
securities away from par, the effect of interest rates on the seasoning process is made clear; and second, these diagrams approximate the prepayment rate paths that would be projected if interest
rates were to shift instantaneously and remain at levels considerably different from the rates prevailing at the time the mortgages
were originated. One of the most common applications of prepayment models is to examine prepayment projections under scenarios of instantaneous interest rate shifts. This type of analysis is
requested both to satisfy regulatory guidelines (for example, under
Thrift Bulletin 13, thrifts must evaluate their portfolios under scenarios of instantaneous interest rate shifts of 100, 200, 300, and 400
basis points in both directions, as well as stable interest rates), and
to evaluate derivative structures to determine the interest rate scenarios under which PAC and TAC bands would be violated. Pass-
through investors also analyze securities under instantaneous

interest rate shifts, however unlikely the actual occurrence of some of these scenarios. The examination of projected prepayments under some admittedly implausible interest rate scenarios is a stress test designed to gauge the likely outer bounds of a security's prepayment speed, as well as the sensitivity of prepayments to different interest rate scenarios.

It is clear from Exhibits 5, 6, and 7 that the speed of seasoning differs drastically for these securities. Whereas the FNMA 8 in Exhibit 5 prepays roughly at the pace of the PSA curve over the first 30 months, its CPR peaks at a level that is twice that of the PSA curve, before returning to it.[9] The FNMA 8, however, is not fully seasoned until about month seventy-six. Discount securities have a negative interest rate differential, which acts to deter mobility and extend the seasoning process. The current coupon FNMA 9 1/2 basically stays between the 100 PSA and 200 PSA curves through month 50, but then extends above it to a level of almost 250 PSA, before gradually slowing down but remaining above the 100 PSA curve (except for the winter trough in prepayments). Not only are the levels after month thirty considerably different for the FNMA 9 1/2 and the PSA curve, but the shapes of the paths also are vastly different. Note also that the FNMA 9 1/2 is not fully seasoned until about month sixty-four. Turning last to the FNMA 12, we see that the seasoning is much faster, and the CPR levels much higher, than the PSA curve. The FNMA 12 is fully seasoned at only 15 months, at which point its prepayment rate is roughly 1,700 PSA.

These graphs indicate that the seasoning process is about four times longer for a current coupon FNMA than for a premium, and about five times longer for a discount FNMA than for a premium (the actual multiples depend on the specific gross coupons of the securities being compared, as well as the prevailing mortgage market interest rate). Similar graphs for the GNMA 8, 9 1/2, and

---

[9] Note also that when the FNMA path returns to roughly the level of the PSA curve, the FNMA CPR pattern is above the PSA curve in the spring and summer months, and below the PSA curve in the late autumn and winter. This is especially important for IOs and POs.

12% coupons are shown in Exhibits 8, 9, and 10. These graphs indicate that GNMAs take even longer to season than FNMAs. For example, the GNMA 8 is not seasoned until about month 124, whereas the GNMA 9 1/2 is seasoned at month 100, and the GNMA 12, at month 28. Even though the shapes of the GNMA curves differ somewhat from those for the FNMA securities, the basic principle that it takes longer to season for the discount than for the current coupon, and for the current coupon than for the premium, is the same. More generally, the graphs indicate that any concept of "seasoning" that fails to consider the interest rate differential between the MBS and the prevailing mortgage market rate is sorely lacking, to the point of being meaningless and potentially harmful.

Exhibit 8   GNMA 8 CPR Path and PSA Curves

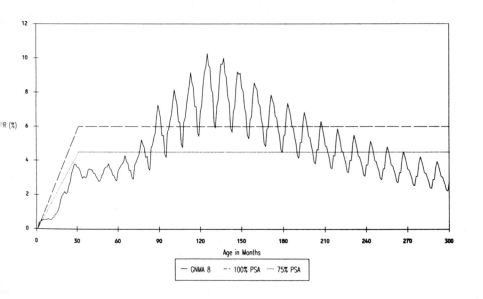

Exhibit 9   GNMA 91/2 CPR Path and PSA Curves

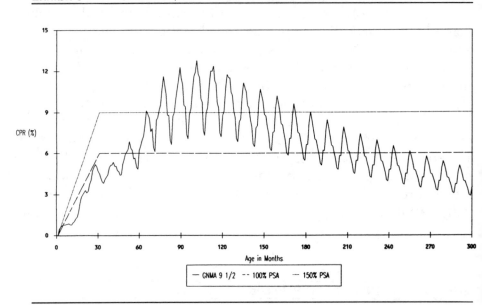

Exhibit 10   GNMA 12 CPR Path and PSA Curves

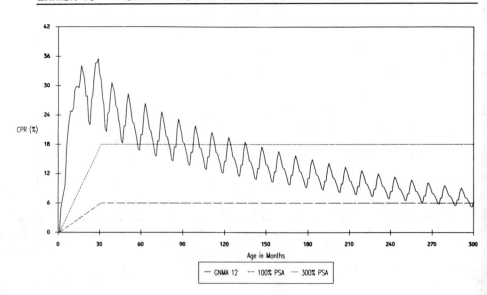

Seasonality or Month of Year

Prepayment rates display a definite seasonal pattern, reflecting activity in the primary housing market. Just as housing activity picks up in the spring and gradually reaches a peak in the late summer, before slackening in the fall and reaching a trough in winter, prepayment rates rise through the spring from their February or March trough, usually peaking in August, and then declining in the winter.[10] This pattern reflects the timing of home building, the school year, and weather, all of which influence household mobility.

Monthly seasonal factors for thirty-year GNMAs are displayed in Exhibit 11.[11] Although the magnitudes of the factors may vary slightly for other MBS programs, the patterns of the monthly movements are similar to that of the GNMAs.[12] These factors were obtained from the econometric estimation of the prepayment models. Note that the GNMA seasonal factors follow the pattern described above, with the slowest prepayment month being March (reflecting February behavior at the household level), and the fastest prepayment month being August (reflecting July behavior at the household level). This pattern is reflected in the "wiggles" in the prepayment rate graphs used throughout this chapter.

---

[10] The convention here is to date observations by the month that they are reported on the agency factor tapes. The prepayment rates reported on the factor tapes for any month for FNMA and GNMA reflect actual *household behavior* primarily in the prior month. Therefore, GNMA's March trough in prepayments means that *households* generally prepay at their lowest rate in February (all else equal). For the FHLMC Guarantor and Gold programs, prepayments reported in any month reflect household activity from the middle of the second month prior to the reporting month through the middle of the month prior to the reporting month. Therefore, FHLMC's reported prepayments for March, for example, actually occurred between the middle of January and the middle of February.

[11] The specification of the prepayment equation requires various mathematical transformations, detailed in a later section of this chapter, to solve for the predicted SMM. Therefore, the monthly factors in Exhibit 11 are approximations derived from the projections of the model, rather than specific coefficients in the prepayment equation.

[12] FNMA securities display a seasonal pattern similar to GNMAs, while FHLMCs tend to lag the FNMA pattern by one month owing to their different reporting periods, as discussed in an earlier footnote.

Exhibit 11   GNMA Prepayment Model: Monthly Seasonal Factors

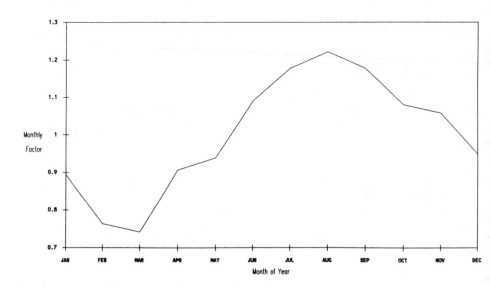

It is important to point out that the seasonal prepayment pattern described here refers to the marginal influence of each respective month of the year, *all else equal.* The term "all else equal" is
crucial to understanding the seasonal prepayment pattern. In the
estimation of the prepayment model, coefficients for the months of
the year relate to influences that vary systematically with the
months of the year and are not captured by the other explanatory
variables. Mathematically, the monthly coefficients (like all regression coefficients) are partial derivatives: that is, they attempt to
measure the effect of a change in the explanatory variable on the
dependent variable, holding everything else constant. If, however,
"everything else" (particularly interest rates) is not "constant,"
then realized prepayment rates will not necessarily display the
pattern shown in Exhibit 11. This situation occurred in 1989, when
mortgage commitment rates climbed to 11.22% in March. These
relatively high rates just before the spring put a damper on home-

owner mobility and severely muted prepayment activity over the late spring and summer of 1989. A late spring-summer bond rally, however, translated into lower mortgage rates by late summer, with mortgage commitment rates falling to 9.68% in August. Rather than agency factor tapes in autumn reporting seasonal decreases in prepayment activity, the autumn prepayment reports indicated an increase in homeowner mobility and prepayment activity that was prompted by the decline in mortgage interest rates over the summer. Thus, while there is a tendency for prepayments to follow the seasonal pattern depicted in Exhibit 11, the extent to which this pattern is realized depends heavily on the level of mortgage interest rates.

The seasonal pattern of prepayments crucially affects the timing of the cash flows generated by mortgage securities, so that models that imply different seasonal patterns of prepayments are likely to project different rates of return on securities. The issue to examine is why various models would imply different seasonal prepayment patterns. As an example, one firm's report on their prepayment model purports a seasonal pattern of prepayments considerably different from the prepayment model discussed here. The proponents of this other model argue that the peak month of prepayments for GNMAs occurs in November, with December prepayment rates similar to those of July and greater than those of June. This suggests that household mobility reaches a peak in *October*, with November activity similar to June and greater than May. This result is completely counterintuitive, and goes against a body of research on household mobility.

Their result, however, may be explained by their reliance on an arbitrary weighting scheme to give greater weight to more recent observations and less weight to data further back in time. This gives considerable weight to data from 1986 (since their model was estimated in the first half of 1988), data that have been colored by a one-time-only phenomenon caused by administrative factors, *not* by anything having to do with actual seasonal behavior. In particular, that year saw the FHA reach its statutory credit ceiling on the issuance of mortgage insurance prior to the close of

the 1986 fiscal year on September 30, 1986. Few, if any, FHA mortgages were issued in August and September of that year. When
the 1987 fiscal year began on October 1, 1986, there was a rash of
prepayments. As the pent-up prepayment behavior at the household level occurred in October, this showed up as a surge in prepayment rates in November, followed by atypically high
prepayments in December. In fact, for many securities for 1986,
November actually *was* the peak prepayment month, and December was uncommonly strong. However, this presumably was a
one-time event that will not occur systematically in the future.
Therefore, this event should not so strongly influence projections
for future prepayment rates. Were it not for their arbitrary weighting of observations, other data reflecting more normal seasonal
patterns would have overwhelmed the data from 1986, and their
seasonal factors would have been both more intuitive and closer
to those of the model presented here.

   Returning to our model, the important effect that incorporating
the monthly seasonal effects has on prepayment projections is apparent from Exhibit 12. Two prepayment rate paths for the thirty-
year FNMA 9 1/2 are displayed in Exhibit 12. Both of the paths
were generated from the Smith Barney Prepayment Model; however, the dashed line incorporates the monthly seasonal effects
and the solid line uses for each month the average of the monthly
seasonal coefficients. In effect, seasonality has been "turned off"
for the solid line. Not surprisingly, the failure to capture the seasonal component of prepayments (solid line) causes projected prepayment rates to be substantially overstated in the late autumn
and winter, and substantially understated in the late spring and
summer. The following example demonstrates that this difference
is not strictly academic, but rather has profound importance for
investing.

   Consider a FNMA 10 Principal-Only Strip (PO) with a WAC of
10.75%, a WART of 320 months, and a price of 56:00. The returns
for POs are very sensitive to prepayment levels. We would like to
calculate the projected rate of return on this PO for a four-month
holding period of May through August under a stable interest rate

Exhibit 12   Influence of Seasonality on Prepayment Rates

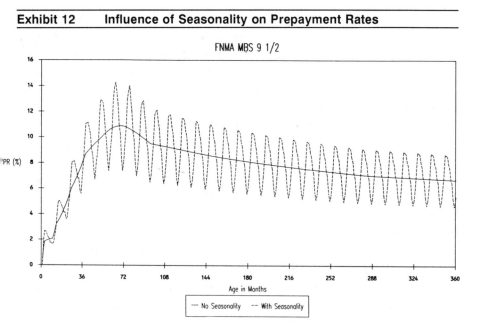

FNMA MBS 9 1/2

scenario. If we *ignore* the effects of seasonality by using for each month the average of the monthly seasonal coefficients (similar to the solid line in Exhibit 12), an annualized rate of return of 10.44% is obtained. However, if we include the effects of seasonality in the analysis (similar to the dashed line in Exhibit 12), the annualized rate of return over this 4-month period is 11.86%, a difference of 142 basis points. A difference of this magnitude could certainly have a marked impact on investment decisions and on performance.

Other Candidate Variables

Other variables were considered in constructing the prepayment model. One of these variables was volatility. The argument for including it in the model is a direct application of option pricing theory. Greater volatility increases the likelihood that an option will be "in the money," and so increases its price.[13] To the extent that a mortgage contains an embedded option, greater volatility increases the value of that option, making the holder of the option (the mortgagor) less likely to part with it (exercising the option or prepaying the mortgage). One might thus expect mortgage prepayments to be negatively related to volatility.

The argument against including it, however, is that volatility already is implicitly included in the mortgage rate via the MBS-to-Treasury yield spread. The secondary market MBS-to-Treasury yield spread is used (along with the ten-year Treasury rate and a servicing fee) in the prepayment model to generate primary market mortgage rates off of which the prepayment model projects prepayment rates. Even if the Treasury rate does not move, an increase in volatility widens the MBS-to-Treasury yield spread by lowering the price of the mortgage security relative to the Treasury (the greater volatility increases the value of the embedded call option so the MBS buyer will pay less to be short this option) and increasing its yield; the wider yield spread increases the proxied primary market mortgage rate. This increase in the mortgage rate would narrow the difference between the WAC on a mortgage security and the mortgage rate available in the market. Reducing this interest rate differential would tend to lower prepayments. This is the same result that was intuited above in the discussion of the effects of volatility on option values and prepayment rates. Therefore, it was not necessary, indeed it would have been redundant, to enter volatility separately into the estimating equation.[14]

The emergence and growth of adjustable-rate mortgages (ARMs) suggests that their presence as an alternative to fixed-rate

---

[13] The effect of volatility on option value is discussed in John C. Cox and Mark Rubinstein, *Options Markets* (Englewood Cliffs, NJ: Prentice-Hall, Inc., 1985), Robert A. Jarrow and Andrew Rudd, *Option Pricing* (Homewood, IL: Dow Jones-Irwin, 1983), and Fischer Black and Myron Scholes, "The Pricing of Options and Corporate Liabilities," *Journal of Political Economy*, May-June 1973.

[14] At the risk of redundancy (and to satisfy curiosity), volatility was tested as a separate explanatory variable in the estimating equations. As the MBS-to-Treasury yield spread relationship suggested, no independent significant effect of volatility on prepayment rates was found.

mortgages may have an impact on the prepayment rates of fixed-rate mortgage-backed securities. On the one hand, the opportunity to refinance out of fixed-rate mortgages into ARMs with low "teaser" rates may increase prepayment rates on fixed-rate MBSs, although regulatory disfavor owing to the experience of thrift institutions combined with an environment of a relatively flat yield curve to make heavily teased ARMs less readily available to mortgagors. On the other hand, to the extent that there is a self-selection process at work, whereby those homeowners who are likely to prepay relatively quickly choose adjustable-rate mortgages, fixed-rate mortgage pools will prepay at slower rates than would have been the case had the ARM mortgagors chosen fixed-rate mortgages instead. Unfortunately, since ARMs have become a significant component of the market only relatively recently, it is not yet possible to document conclusively their influence on fixed-rate mortgage prepayments.

Effort was made to examine the effect of ARMs on fixed-rate prepayments. Ideally, one would use as an explanatory variable the share of total mortgage originations that were adjustable-rate in each month of fixed-rate mortgage origination. This would get at the self-selection mechanism described above. Alternatively, one would use the ARMs share of mortgage originations in the month of prepayment to get at the availability to fixed-rate mortgagors of ARMs at attractive terms (although this presents the problem of how to project prepayments when future values of the ARMs proportion of originations are unknown). Unfortunately, there are reliable data on ARM originations only as far back as 1984, so that using a variable for ARMs would require ignoring all fixed-rate data prior to 1984. This would mean throwing out a substantial amount of data, especially for GNMAs.

A way around the issue of lack of ARMs data is to use the steepness of the yield curve as a proxy for the availability and likely importance of ARM originations. This variable may be thought to be important because fixed-rate mortgages generally are priced relative to the ten-year portion of the yield curve, whereas ARMs are priced off of the two-year sector of the curve.

Unfortunately, the yield curve variable did not turn in results that were statistically significant. The importance of ARMs is an issue that will be reexamined in future estimations of the model.

In addition to the question of ARMs, introducing any one of several macroeconomic variables into the model was considered. The following variables were tested: industrial production, mortgage originations, three-month change in interest rates (as a predictor of the future direction of rates), mortgage commitments, housing starts, sales of existing homes, and unemployment rate. The only macro variable that consistently was statistically significant and of appropriate sign was sales of existing homes, but this really introduces no information that is not already incorporated within prepayment data. That macroeconomic variables do not add significantly to prepayment equations suggests that either virtually all relevant macro information is incorporated within the prevailing mortgage market interest rate in the expression for the interest rate differential, or the prepayment data do not embody enough cycles of the economy and housing market to determine statistically a relationship between macroeconomic variables and prepayment behavior.

There is a practical problem with including macroeconomic variables in a prepayment model of this kind. This is that the projection of prepayments would then heavily depend on the ability to project the macro variables. In pricing mortgages, a prepayment model is invoked by an OAS model as it moves through thirty years of randomly generated interest rate paths. To include a macro variable in the model would require making 360 macroeconomic forecasts contingent on the interest rate path.[15] Although a very tight relationship has been established between relative interest rates and prepayment rates, there is not enough information to establish a similarly tight long-range relationship between other macro variables and prepayment rates.

---

[15] For fifteen-year MBSs, the pricing model moves through fifteen years of randomly generated interest rate paths, which would require 180 macroeconomic forecasts if a macro variable were to be included.

THE PREPAYMENT MODEL

Each MBS program's prepayment equations are of similar functional form. The explanatory variables in the model capture the determinants of prepayments discussed in the previous section of this chapter. The explanatory variables are the percentage interest rate differential, the age of the underlying mortgages, and monthly dummy variables.[16] For each MBS program, the data were grouped by aggregate factor, and equations were estimated by factor groups to capture the path dependency of prepayments on interest rates.

Mortgage Securities Data

The mortgage data consist of securities at the generic year class level. A generic year class security groups together all of a respective program's securities of a given coupon from a given year class.[17] For each coupon of each generic year class, weighted average age, mortgage rate, aggregate factor, original balance, outstanding balance, prepayments, etc. are computed. For example, all GNMA thirty-year single-family securities bearing coupons of 9% that were issued in 1986 would comprise a single generic year class security. The GNMA data begin in 1973 and extend through late 1989.[18] Data for conventionals begin with the introduction of these programs and extend through late 1989. There is an observation for each aggregate coupon class for each month that securities of each respective class have been outstanding. This produces a pooled time series–cross-section data set.

---

[16] Some equations also include the aggregate factor as an explanatory variable.

[17] Generic GNMAs are aggregated by issue year classes, whereas generic conventionals are aggregated by WAM year classes.

[18] The model equations should be reestimated periodically as more observations are realized.

Econometric/Statistical Issues[19]

One of the econometric issues concerned the pooled time series–cross-section nature of the data. The question concerned the extent to which it is possible to exploit time series characteristics of the data. This is possible only if the data are stationary; if the data are nonstationary, then making statistical inferences based on estimation is improper, since nonstationarity violates a fundamental assumption of regression, namely that observations are independently drawn from a stable population.

The exception to this is that statistical inference is proper when the individual variables are nonstationary, but a linear combination of the variables is stationary. In this case, the variables can be thought of as being jointly stationary, and are said to be cointegrated.[20] If the data are cointegrated and then are differenced to obtain what are *believed* to be stationary data, the data would, in fact, have been *over*-differenced. Intuitively, this can be thought of as squeezing so much informational content out of the data that none remains. The procedure is to test the data for stationarity, and if it is determined that they are nonstationary, to test for cointegration. If the data are shown to be cointegrated, they are employed as is; however, if the data prove to be nonstationary and not cointegrated, they first are filtered to obtain stationary time series.

A second econometric issue concerned seasonality. The seasonal pattern followed by prepayment rates was discussed in a previous section: low in the winter, rising in the spring, rising further in the summer until peaking in August (or perhaps Septem-

---

[19] The following two sections discuss specific statistical aspects of the model's construction and estimation. Readers who are less mathematically inclined may skip ahead to the *Results* section without loss of intuitive understanding of the model.

[20] Cointegration is a relatively new topic in statistics. For background, see C.W.J. Granger, "Some Properties of Time Series Data and Their Use in Econometric Model Specification," *Journal of Econometrics*, 1981, and "Developments in the Study of Co-Integrated Economic Variables," *Oxford Bulletin of Economics and Statistics*, 1986, and Robert F. Engle and C.W.J. Granger, "Co-Integration and Error Correction: Representation, Estimation and Testing," *Econometrica*, March 1987, and the references cited therein.

ber), then declining as autumn proceeds and winter commences. The question was whether to work with seasonally adjusted or unadjusted data. The prevailing econometric wisdom is to use seasonally unadjusted data, and to account for seasonal effects by including dummy variables in the estimating equation. This is the procedure followed here. The problem with using seasonally adjusted data is that the seasonal adjustment process itself may introduce its own spurious "seasonal" pattern, as was shown to be the case in other contexts.[21]

Estimation

The econometric estimation of the prepayment equations was performed by fitting to the data a curve that is derived from the algebraic manipulation of the expression for a particular statistical distribution's cumulative distribution function. The properties of this distribution allow the expression for the cumulative probability to be written in closed-form, thus facilitating algebraic manipulation. In the current application, the probability is interpreted to be the probability that a mortgagor will prepay a mortgage, which is represented by the SMM. The use of this class of models stands on the solid theoretical foundation of the economics of consumer choice, and has a long history in the econometric applications of consumer choice and labor market theory.[22]

The use of this econometric technique guarantees that fitted values and projections of the prepayment rate will lie between 0% and 100%. The blind application of standard regression to this problem cannot guarantee that the estimated SMMs will lie in the 0% to 100% interval, even though all of the observed values of the

---

[21] See C.W.J. Granger and Paul Newbold, *Forecasting Economic Time Series* (New York: Academic Press, 1977), and A.C. Harvey, *The Econometric Analysis of Time Series* (Oxford: Philip Allan), 1981.

[22] Typical applications of this technique involve consumer decision-making, such as "to buy" or "not to buy," and labor market decisions (say, for marginal workers), such as "to enter the labor market" or "not to enter the labor market." These basically are yes/no decisions, similar to the choice of whether "to prepay" or "not to prepay."

dependent variable lie in this range. The dependent variable in this model is the natural logarithm of the ratio of the probability of prepayment to the probability of nonprepayment. In lieu of the true population probabilities, the sample proportions, given by the observed SMMs, are used. The explanatory variables, discussed above, are the age of the underlying mortgages, the percentage interest rate spread, and monthly dummy variables to reflect activity in the primary housing market.[23] Without question, the most important explanatory variable in terms of statistical significance is the interest rate differential.

Attempting to estimate this type of model by ordinary least squares (OLS) will result in heteroskedastic errors. Corrections for this are made by weighting each observation of all variables by an expression that is a function of the SMM and the outstanding balance at that point in time. Estimation of the equation using the variables weighted in this manner is a generalized least squares (GLS) technique. Tests for heteroskedasticity were conducted using the Goldfeld-Quandt procedure. After applying the correction for heteroskedasticity and estimating by GLS, all equations in the model passed the Goldfeld-Quandt test, indicating that they are free of heteroskedasticity, as required for efficient estimation of model parameters.

The estimation of the model equations produces fitted values of the ratio of the probability of prepayment to the probability of nonprepayment, weighted by the GLS corrections for heteroskedasticity. But what is desired is the estimate of the *unweighted* SMM, not that of the weighted ratio. Extracting the predicted SMMs requires first unweighting the fitted ratio. However, one *cannot* simply rearrange terms of the unweighted ratio to obtain the optimally predicted SMM; if this were done, we would obtain the optimal *median* predictions, whereas what is desired are the optimal *mean* predictions. The reason is that the fitted ratios are distributed approximately lognormally, so a transformation is required to derive the optimal mean estimates of the embedded

---

[23] In some equations, the aggregate factor also is an independent variable.

SMMs. The transformation involves a function of the residual variance of the estimate of the respective observation.[24] Applying this transformation, the optimal mean estimates of the SMMs can be recovered.

Scatter plots of the actual and estimated SMMs showed each equation to fit very well; however, an objective numerical measure of the goodness-of-fit is desired. Even though a goodness-of-fit statistic is not an absolute measure of the "correctness" of the model, it is, nevertheless, one more diagnostic statistic worth examining. Unfortunately, the usual measure of fit, the R^2 adjusted for degrees of freedom, is invalid in the presence of GLS corrections. However, one can construct a goodness-of-fit statistic appropriate for GLS estimation.[25] This statistic represents the proportion of the weighted variation in the SMMs explained by the regression equation. Since the equations are reestimated as more observations are realized, there is no one value that can be reported for the goodness-of-fit statistic. However, using the appropriately defined fit statistic, the GNMA model equations generally explain about 92% of the variability in prepayment rates. For the conventionals models, this amount is about 90% of the variability.

An example of the FNMA model's in-sample fit is given in Exhibit 13 for the generic FNMA 10s with WAM year of 2008, and in Exhibit 14 for the generic FNMA 12s with WAM year of 2009. Even though for the FNMA 10s the model underestimated the magnitude of the initial surge in prepayments in 1986, it tracked all of the other observations extremely closely, including the second surge in prepayments in 1987. The in-sample tracking for other coupons, across the programs, is very good as well.

---

[24] The precise form of the transformation can be found in N.A.J. Hastings and J.B. Peacock, *Statistical Distributions* (New York: Halsted Press, 1974).

[25] G.S. Maddala, *Limited-Dependent and Qualitative Variables in Econometrics*, (Cambridge: Cambridge University Press, 1983), and George S. Judge, et al, *The Theory and Practice of Econometrics*, Second Edition (New York: John Wiley & Sons, 1985).

Exhibit 13   FNMA 10% Coupon, 2008 WAM Year

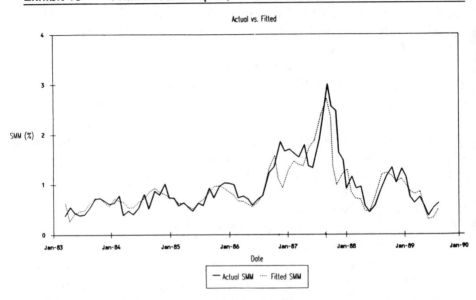

Exhibit 14   FNMA 12% Coupon, 2009 WAM Year

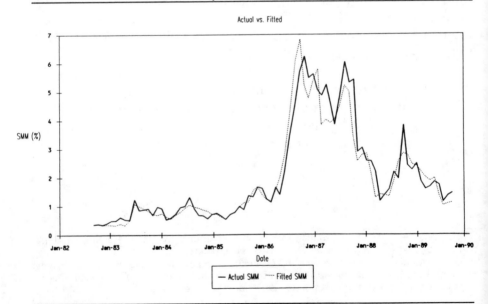

RESULTS

Model Testing

This section reports on the out-of-sample accuracy of the prepayment model. Given that we have reported an R^2, or goodness-of-fit statistic, of over 90%, and presented graphs demonstrating the in-sample tracking of the model, it would be superfluous to dwell on the closeness of fitted and actual values *within* the sample. The real test of a forecast model is how well it performs *outside* of the sample.

GNMA prepayment rates for the first half of 1990, as well as those projected by the GNMA prepayment model for these months, are displayed in Exhibit 15. These observations were not included in the sample set over which the model was estimated. The observations in Exhibit 15 are at the generic issue year level. A generic issue year security is the dollar-weighted average of all GNMA securities of a given coupon issued in a given year.

Several generic year classes are represented in Exhibit 15, with a few year classes for each coupon level between 8% and 12%. The list in Exhibit 15 by no means incorporates the entire universe of GNMA year classes, but rather is intended to summarize broadly the model's performance over several coupon and issue year classes.[26]

The results in Exhibit 15 support the contention that the prepayment model does very well at projecting out-of-sample SMMs. While not every projection was within, say, five-hundredths of a percentage point, it also is the case that overall the projections are very accurate.

It is apparent from Exhibit 15 that month-to-month variation in SMMs can be considerable. There are a few instances in which the observed prepayment rates were higher (or the same) in February than in January, even though the model projected that they would be lower in February. This happens. The prepayment equations

---

[26] An exhaustive list of coupons and year classes would cover five pages just for GNMA thirty-year single-family securities.

Exhibit 15: GNMA SMM Prepayment Projections——First Half 1990

Coupon	Year Class	January Actual	January Project	February Actual	February Project	March Actual	March Project	April Actual	April Project	May Actual	May Project	June Actual	June Project
8%	1976	0.53	0.55	0.49	0.47	0.44	0.44	0.54	0.52	0.58	0.52	0.57	0.62
	1986	0.16	0.24	0.22	0.23	0.22	0.25	0.22	0.24	0.23	0.24	0.28	0.27
	1987	0.29	0.28	0.26	0.27	0.23	0.28	0.31	0.26	0.33	0.25	0.32	0.29
8 1/2 %	1986	0.32	0.28	0.26	0.27	0.28	0.28	0.37	0.29	0.33	0.30	0.37	0.33
	1987	0.36	0.31	0.37	0.30	0.31	0.31	0.40	0.32	0.43	0.32	0.46	0.35
	1989	0.04	0.05	0.07	0.05	0.06	0.05	0.08	0.05	0.07	0.06	0.12	0.07
9%	1979	0.58	0.80	0.56	0.63	0.50	0.59	0.59	0.72	0.60	0.75	0.70	0.86
	1986	0.41	0.39	0.43	0.36	0.35	0.37	0.47	0.40	0.48	0.41	0.52	0.44
	1987	0.37	0.36	0.39	0.34	0.35	0.36	0.45	0.37	0.47	0.38	0.49	0.41
	1988	0.29	0.29	0.31	0.28	0.24	0.29	0.37	0.31	0.36	0.32	0.41	0.37
	1989	0.04	0.06	0.06	0.05	0.05	0.05	0.10	0.06	0.08	0.06	0.12	0.07
9 1/2%	1979	0.65	0.81	0.56	0.62	0.49	0.59	0.62	0.77	0.66	0.80	0.68	0.92
	1986	0.53	0.52	0.51	0.47	0.47	0.45	0.61	0.56	0.62	0.56	0.66	0.59
	1987	0.44	0.43	0.46	0.41	0.39	0.42	0.50	0.43	0.54	0.44	0.62	0.49
	1988	0.26	0.33	0.32	0.32	0.28	0.33	0.41	0.33	0.40	0.35	0.42	0.41
	1989	0.13	0.08	0.14	0.08	0.16	0.07	0.21	0.08	0.21	0.08	0.25	0.13
10%	1985	0.48	0.67	0.77	0.58	0.56	0.53	0.57	0.67	0.70	0.68	0.57	0.74
	1986	0.69	0.69	0.72	0.61	0.57	0.55	0.76	0.68	0.73	0.69	0.76	0.75
	1987	0.51	0.62	0.57	0.64	0.46	0.62	0.58	0.56	0.65	0.54	0.66	0.59
	1988	0.41	0.56	0.40	0.62	0.36	0.59	0.52	0.47	0.54	0.43	0.56	0.50
	1989	0.21	0.15	0.21	0.17	0.23	0.17	0.30	0.19	0.29	0.19	0.35	0.24
10 1/2%	1985	0.96	1.27	0.96	1.08	0.88	0.98	0.95	1.07	0.85	0.97	0.88	1.02
	1987	0.90	1.08	0.79	1.05	0.69	0.97	0.94	0.97	0.80	0.85	0.78	0.83
	1989	0.56	0.58	0.68	0.61	0.47	0.64	0.45	0.60	0.43	0.55	0.47	0.59
11%	1983	1.34	1.60	1.18	1.39	1.07	1.28	1.19	1.37	1.15	1.26	1.10	1.44
	1988	1.23	1.68	1.72	1.56	1.30	1.38	1.70	1.48	1.34	1.29	0.96	1.25
11 1/2%	1983	1.69	1.59	1.58	1.45	1.32	1.37	1.55	1.52	1.33	1.40	1.33	1.68
	1985	2.08	1.99	2.00	1.76	1.67	1.64	1.89	1.79	1.50	1.65	1.71	1.94
12%	1984	1.90	1.93	1.76	1.76	1.34	1.67	1.68	1.87	1.69	1.73	1.56	2.08
	1985	1.97	2.07	1.89	1.89	1.61	1.79	1.87	2.00	1.74	1.85	1.55	2.23

are statistical relationships subject to random deviations about them. The econometric model summarizes statistically the behavior within the sample, but both within the sample and outside of it there may be individual observations that deviate from this pattern.

An example of the randomness of monthly observations is given by the GNMA 12s of the 1984 issue year. The actual prepayment rate for this generic year class in January 1990 was 1.90%, which by being only 0.03 less than projected by the prepayment model resulted in an error of just 2% (0.03/1.90 = 0.02). In February, GNMA 12s of 1984 prepaid at 1.76%, exactly as projected by the model. In March, however, the model misestimated the extent of the decline in the prepayment rate. Rather than declining by a more moderate amount, actual prepayments fell by 0.42 (or 24%), and so the model erred in its prediction by 0.33 (or 25%). (In the same month, however, the model predicted prepayments on GNMA 11 1/2s from the 1983 and 1985 year classes to within 0.05 [or 4%] of their actual values.) The model was much more accurate for the GNMA 12s in April, whereas in May, the model projection was just 0.04 above the actual prepayment rate, for an error of only 2%.

Prepayment Projections

This section presents prepayment projections for three GNMA coupons under the following interest rate scenarios: rates fall by 100 basis points over 12 months, rates remain stable, and rates rise by 100 basis points over 12 months. The rate movements are conjectured to occur evenly over the twelve months, after which rates are taken to be stable at their new levels. The initial effective mortgage market rate is 10.25%.

The securities are the GNMA 8, with a WART of 323 months; the GNMA 9 1/2, with a WART of 352; and the GNMA 11 1/2, with a WART of 303. For their respective coupons, these three classes represent the liquid, actively traded securities.

The projections are graphed in Exhibits 16, 17, and 18, for the GNMA 8, 9 1/2, and 11 1/2, respectively.[27] Each graph has three lines, with each line depicting the SMM path for a scenario. The horizontal axis measures time, with the actual curve beginning at the appropriate average age of the underlying mortgages. The first point in each graph represents the July 1990 projection.

A few aspects of Exhibits 16, 17, and 18 are worth mentioning. Note the differences for each of the securities in their paths to the steady state under the three alternate scenarios. The refinanced

Exhibit 16   GNMA 8 SMM Paths Under Alternate Interest Rate Scenarios

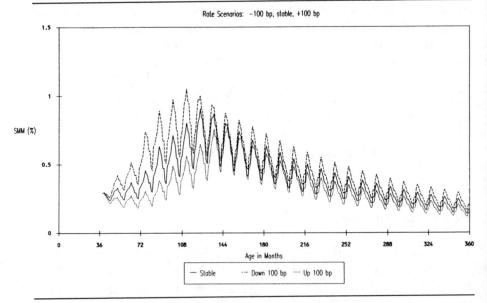

Rate Scenarios: −100 bp, stable, +100 bp

— Stable   ·− Down 100 bp   −· Up 100 bp

---

[27] A single long-term number is often reported for a security's prepayment projection. Smith Barney calculates this number in the following manner: (1) The prepayment model generates prepayment projections for a given interest rate scenario for each month until maturity of the security, as in any one of the curves in Exhibits 16, 17, and 18; (2) then, given these projections and their resultant cash flows and the security price, the yield on the security is calculated; and (3) given the calculated yield, the *one* PSA is found that, *if* it were to occur each month until maturity, would result in the same yield as given by the sequence of monthly projected prepayments. This is the long-term PSA that is reported. The long-term SMM is calculated separately, but in a manner similar to the long-term PSA.

Exhibit 17   **GNMA 91/2 SMM Paths Under Alternate Interest Rate Scenerios**

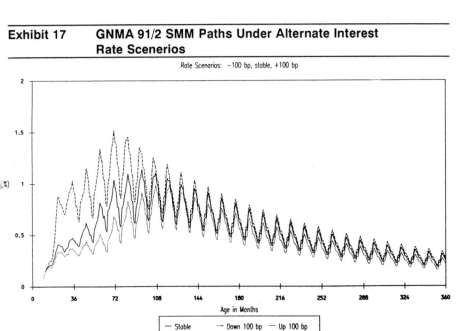

Rate Scenarios: −100 bp, stable, +100 bp

— Stable   -- Down 100 bp   -- Up 100 bp

Exhibit 18   **GNMA 11 1/2 SMM Paths Under Alternate Interest Rate Scenarios**

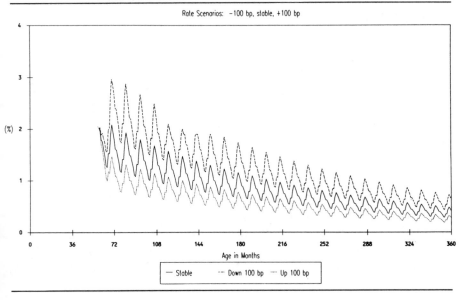

Rate Scenarios: −100 bp, stable, +100 bp

— Stable   -- Down 100 bp   -- Up 100 bp

out, or prepayment slowdown, effects are particularly pronounced for the falling interest rate environment. When rates fall 100 basis points (the top line in each of Exhibits 16, 17, and 18), the GNMA 8s are less "out of the money" and show a bit of a pickup in prepayments relative to the stable and rising rate scenarios. Although the projected prepayments on the GNMA 8s do not represent refinancing, the lower interest rates in the falling rate scenario make homeowner mobility less burdensome and so increase projected prepayments. The GNMA 9 1/2s become slight premiums when interest rates fall, and their SMM path in this case shows a considerable difference relative to the paths under stable and rising rates, which are remarkably similar to each other. The GNMA 11 1/2s, which already are premiums and already are refinanced out, become further "in the money" if rates fall 100 basis points, and they prepay relatively quickly before experiencing further prepayment slowdown. Exhibits 16, 17, and 18 display the fundamental aspects of the model: refinancing incentive, age of the underlying mortgages, month of the year, seasoning pattern, path dependency, and prepayment slowdown.

CONCLUSION

The importance of prepayments in evaluating mortgage-backed securities cannot be overemphasized. It is the right of mortgagors to exercise their mortgages' embedded call options by prepaying their mortgages that makes MBS valuation different from that for an ordinary noncallable bond. As important as accurate analysis of prepayments is for standard fixed-rate pass-through securities, it is even more crucial for derivative mortgage securities and structured products.

The primary determinants of prepayment behavior are the refinancing incentive and household mobility, both of which are affected by the age of the underlying mortgages. Prepayments also display a distinct seasonal pattern reflecting underlying activity in the primary housing market. All of these influences—refinancing, age, month of the year—are incorporated into the prepayment model.

The model also incorporates the concept of "path dependency," which is that prepayments depend not only on the interest rate differential at a point in time, but also on the path that the differential has taken to arrive at that point. The factor of a security (or aggregate factor of a generic security) is the best indicator of the sensitivity to refinancing incentives of the remaining loans in a given pool.

The model was estimated by adapting a class of models used in the economics and econometrics of consumer choice and labor market decisions. These models have been used in other applications to model binary decisions of the yes/no variety. It is a natural extension to apply this class of models to the decision of "to prepay" or "not to prepay."

Several results emerge from the model. One is that it is not possible to make a blanket definition of a "seasoned" security as one that has attained a certain age. The seasoning process differs for current coupons, discounts, and premiums, both as to the month in which prepayment rates peak and then begin to slow down, and the shape of the path followed by prepayment rates. It also is not possible to make a blanket statement that refinancing becomes advantageous at a certain absolute basis point differential between the coupon on the security and the mortgage rate prevailing in the market. What determines refinancing is the relative interest rate differential. This differential, in fact, is the most important determinant of mortgage prepayments, in terms of statistical significance.

Another result from the model is that the month of the year is extremely important in making prepayment projections, and, therefore, in using those projections to compute rates of return. Also important to the projections is the recognition and incorporation of the prepaid out, or refinanced out, phenomenon. This enables the accurate modeling of the timing of cash flows, which is extremely important for structured transactions.

The nature of the prepayment slowdown effect was apparent in the presentation of the paths of prepayment rates projected for GNMA securities. These were included to show how the model would behave under certain scenarios. These paths displayed different seasoning and slowdown patterns, not just for the different securities, but also for the same security under alternate scenarios.

Rather than stressing how the model fits the data within the sample, the chapter presented out-of-sample results for several coupons and year classes for the first half of 1990. The model performed very well in predicting the SMMs out-of-sample.

CHAPTER 11

PREPAYMENT AND VALUATION MODELING FOR ADJUSTABLE-RATE MBS

Scott F. Richard, PhD
Vice President
Mortgage Securities Research Department
Goldman, Sachs & Co.

Lynn M. Edens
Vice President
Mortgage Securities Research Department
Goldman, Sachs & Co.

In this chapter, we discuss two models used for analyzing the prepayment behavior of adjustable-rate mortgages (ARMs). We construct separate models for conventional one-year constant

The authors express their thanks to Ashwin Belur, Andrew Bird, Aaron Gurwitz, Kevin Ingram, Guy Muzio, Scott Pinkus, and Tim Sears for useful discussions and suggestions. They are also grateful for the assistance of Ashwin Belur in assembling the data. Dr. Richard is now a portfolio manager at Miller, Anderson & Sherrerd.

maturity Treasury (CMT) index ARMs and for Eleventh District Cost of Funds Index ARMs, based on 4,366 pools and 982 pools, respectively. We will first discuss our one-year CMT ARMs model, and then our COFI ARMs model.

CONVENTIONAL ONE-YEAR CMT ARms MODEL

Our prepayment model of conventional one-year CMT ARMs is based on four interactive effects: the age or seasoning of the mortgage pool, the interest rate incentives, the periodic cap size, and seasonality or month of the year. We will consider each of these effects in turn.

Aging or Seasoning

It is well known that prepayment rates on fixed-rate mortgage (FRM) pools increase for a period of time after issuance, simply because the mortgages are aging or seasoning and not necessarily because of the movement of interest rates. A familiar, if not altogether accurate, portrayal of the seasoning process is the standard Public Securities Association (PSA) function in which prepayment rates increase from a 0% per annum conditional prepayment rate (CPR) at issue to 6% CPR after thirty months, and then remain level.[1]

The seasoning process for ARMs differs from that of FRMs in several important ways. As in the case of FRMs, prepayments rates on ARMs increase after issue and then reach a plateau. The time needed to reach the plateau differs among programs, but is always shorter than the fixed-rate counterpart. After a period at

---

[1] For a more accurate description of the seasoning process for FRMs, see Chapter 10, and Scott F. Richard and Richard Roll, "Prepayments on Fixed Rate Mortgage-Backed Securities," *Journal of Portfolio Management* (Spring 1989), pp. 73-82. In the latter study, it is shown that the time to fully season a FRM pool depends on the extent to which the pool's weighted average coupon is a discount or premium. For example, a current coupon conventional mortgage pool takes about 40 months to fully season, while a 200 basis points premium seasons in about 20 months.

this plateau (and unlike the rate for FRM pools), the prepayment rate on ARM pools then declines to a new plateau.

Exhibit 1 shows our model's projections for seasonally adjusted prepayment rates on conventional one-year CMT ARMs. The ARMs season in about twenty-six months, reach a plateau at 15.6% CPR for approximately twenty months, and then gradually decline to a second plateau at 12.3% CPR after another thirty months have passed. As indicated, this example is based on an ARM with an initial, or "teaser," weighted average coupon (WAC)

Exhibit 1: Seasonally Adjusted Prepayment Rates for One-Year CMT ARMs

CPR (%)

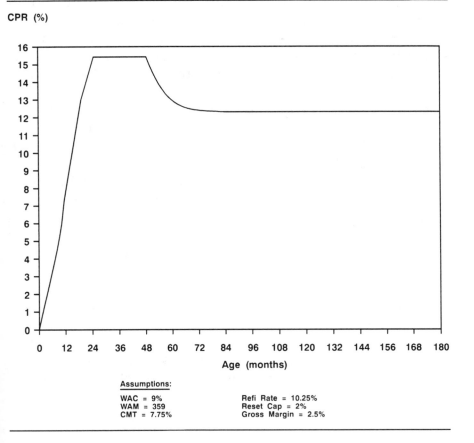

Age (months)

Assumptions:

WAC = 9%	Refi Rate = 10.25%
WAM = 359	Reset Cap = 2%
CMT = 7.75%	Gross Margin = 2.5%

of 9%, 11 months to reset, a weighted average maturity (WAM) of 359 months, 2% annual reset caps, and 250 basis points of gross margin. The prepayment projection is based on a constant one-year CMT rate of 7.75% and a fixed mortgage refinancing rate of 10.25% for new conventional mortgages.

The unusual seasoning process for ARMs probably results from the self-selection of ARM mortgagors. We reason that two types of homeowners prefer ARMs: those with short time horizons and those who prefer a floating-rate liability to a fixed-rate liability. Mortgagors with short horizons are attracted to ARMs because of their lower initial coupon. Other homeowners may prefer an ARM to a FRM because they see the floating-rate liability as a better hedge or offset to their floating-rate assets. The presence of short-horizon mortgagors causes the rapid seasoning of an ARM pool; the subsequent deseasoning of the pool simply reflects the exit of the short-horizon homeowners. Those mortgagors who remain after forty-five months are either those who prefer a floating-rate liability or those who have revised their plans for a rapid turnover of the property, and, lacking an incentive to refinance, choose to hold their loan. We present further evidence regarding the self-selection of ARM mortgagors in our discussion of the periodic cap effect later in this chapter.

The deseasoning of ARMs prepayment rates should not be confused with the "burnout" of premium FRM pools, which refers to the behavior of prepayment rates on FRM pools after a sustained market rally. Typically, if mortgage rates fall 200 basis points or more from their current levels, there will be a surge of prepayments caused by refinancing among mortgagors who now have 200 basis points (or more) premium mortgages. Premium burnout occurs after the interest rate-sensitive mortgagors exit the pool, leaving only mortgagors who are less inclined to refinance. This causes the pool's prepayment rates to slow or "burn out," even though interest rates have not increased. In contrast, the evidence indicates that ARM pool deseasoning is not due to a decline in interest rates, and is not limited to ARMs that have become premiums.[2]

Two notes of caution about the ARM's seasoning process are warranted. First, the deseasoning of prepayments occurs mainly during 1988, 1989, and 1990. Prepayment rates on fixed-rate mortgage-backed securities (MBSs) have slowed during 1989 and 1990. In estimating our ARMs models, we attempted to control for this secular slowdown[3]. Even with this correction, the deseasoning effect in ARMs persists strongly. (The results shown in all exhibits include this correction). Second, we have relatively little information (only 370 observations) on ARMs prepayments for pools with WAMs under 240 months. Hence we must extrapolate the evidence from the first ten years of a pool's life to forecast its behavior during its last twenty years.

Interest Rate Incentives

An adjustable-rate mortgagor may choose to prepay his mortgage either in the course of selling his home or in order to refinance. The incentive to prepay an ARM—either to move or to refinance—depends, of course, on the interest rates being charged in the marketplace for alternative home financing. Basically, the homeowner can substitute either into another ARM or into a FRM. The rate being charged for substitute ARMs is reflected in the current one-year CMT index, and the rate for a substitute FRM is given by the current conventional FRM interest rate. The incentives to prepay or hold an adjustable-rate mortgage will also be influenced by the size of the annual reset caps and the lifetime cap.

We use two related measures of the homeowner's incentive to prepay as inputs to our model: the current refinancing spread and the anticipatory refinancing spread. The current refinancing spread is the difference between the homeowner's current WAC

---

[2] We tested both of these hypotheses and could find no evidence to support either one.
[3] We used annual multiplicative dummy variables to correct for idiosyncratic annual variations in prepayment rates.

and the FRM rate. This obviously is intended to capture the home-owner's incentive in the current month. The homeowner's coupon rate on a CMT ARM resets annually, however, and a rational mortgagor will anticipate these resets. To capture the effect of the reset, we also calculate the average gross coupon for the next year using the current CMT rate as the anticipated CMT rate at the next reset.[4]

The anticipatory spread is the difference between this average coupon and the current FRM rate, which is the rationally antici-pated FRM rate at reset. We find that both measures are statisti-cally significant explanatory variables at very high degrees of confidence. Furthermore, we find that the size of these effects var-ies depending on the sign of the differences. That is, as Exhibit 2 illustrates, if the current ARM WAC is 100 basis points above the FRM rate, the increase in prepayments is much greater than the decrease implied by an ARM WAC 100 basis points below the FRM rate.

Exhibit 2 shows our model's projections for prepayment rates on conventional one-year CMT ARMs in various interest rate envi-ronments. The ARMs modeled are the same as those used in Ex-hibit 1, and, as a point of reference, the center line (CMT = 7.75%) in Exhibit 2 duplicates Exhibit 1. The lower line (CMT = 6.75%) shows what the model projects would happen to this pool's pre-payment rates if the yield curve steepened. Specifically, if the CMT rate were to decline to 6.75% in equal monthly reductions over the next year but the FRM rate were to remain at 10.25%, the homeowner's incentive to refinance into a fixed-rate mortgage clearly would be greatly diminished: the plateau prepayment rate would fall from 15.6% CPR to 12.1% CPR.

---

[4] We arrived at a one-year horizon through experimentation. We also tried the yield to other horizons—namely, to maturity, ten years, five years, two years, and six months. The explanatory power of the model peaked with the horizon at one year. While a one-year horizon is short, it does not necessarily mean that adjustable-rate mortgagors are myopic. Many homeowners in ARMs pools have short horizons because of planned moves. Others may be uncomfortable trying to forecast interest rates beyond one year.

Exhibit 2: Effect of Yield Curve Steepening on One-Year CMT ARMs Prepayment Rates (Seasonally Adjusted)

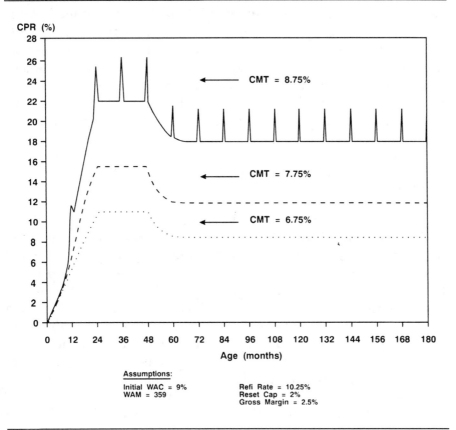

Assumptions:

Initial WAC = 9%   Refi Rate = 10.25%
WAM = 359   Reset Cap = 2%
                         Gross Margin = 2.5%

An unusual and unique aspect of our model—namely a reset month effect—becomes apparent if the yield curve flattens, as shown by the upper line in Exhibit 2 (CMT = 8.75%). Specifically, if the one-year CMT rate increases to 8.75% over the next year in equal monthly increments but the FRM rate remains fixed at 10.25%, the homeowner's coupon rate after resetting will be 11.25%. This would be higher than the fixed rate of 10.25%, and the homeowner's incentive to enter into an FRM (either as a refinancing or in conjunction with a move) would be enhanced: The plateau prepayment rate would rise to 22.3% from 15.6%, while in the reset month the rate would peak at over 26% CPR. There are two reasons for the prepayment spike in the reset month. When the ARM is to reset as a premium for the first time, mortgagors have an increased economic incentive to refinance. In future reset months, the prepayment spike is probably a notification effect. Prior to reset, each mortgagor is notified that the rate for the next year is to be increased. At the margin, this is likely to induce some of the mortgagors to notice that the FRM rate is lower and to refinance.[5]

Periodic Cap Size

For at least two reasons, the observed prepayment rate on an ARM pool should depend on the size of the periodic cap and lifetime cap. First, periodic caps and lifetime caps are options, and, all other things being equal, their value increases as these cap levels tighten. Prepaying the mortgage destroys the value of the cap options. Hence, a tighter periodic cap or a lower lifetime cap should induce slower prepayment rates. Second, homeowners with longer horizons can be expected to self-select tighter caps (at the cost of higher points, initial rate, or margin) because they will be more likely to exercise the option during their longer intended ownership period. For both of these reasons, we expect ARM prepayment rates to decline with tighter periodic caps or lower lifetime caps.

We capture these effects in our model in two different ways. First, both types of caps will keep a homeowner's WAC lower in a rising rate environment, thus slowing prepayment rates through the interest rate incentives discussed above. Second, an additional effect should be evident either because of a self-selection bias or

---

[5] The reset month effect for premium ARMs is statistically highly significant and of approximately equal magnitude for the first four annual resets. Our estimate of the fifth year reset effect is similar in magnitude to our estimates for the first four years, but we do not have enough data to conclude that it is statistically significant.

because a tighter cap is a more valuable option, even if rates are currently steady.

This second effect is apparent in the data for the periodic cap, but not for the lifetime cap. The history of interest rates in the 1980s makes it difficult to measure the effect of lifetime caps, because we have very few observations of ARM prepayments when the lifetime cap is binding or even near binding. (Our prepayment data for conventional CMT ARMs do not begin until January 1985.) Exhibit 3 shows the effect of different annual periodic caps.

Exhibit 3: Effect of Reset Caps on Prepayment Rates for Conventional One-Year CTM ARMs (Seasonally Adjusted)

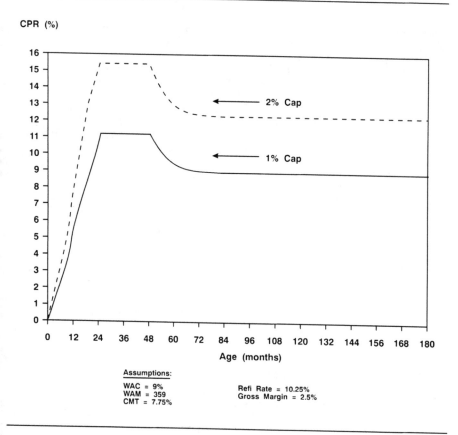

CPR (%)

Age (months)

Assumptions:
WAC = 9%
WAM = 359
CMT = 7.75%

Refi Rate = 10.25%
Gross Margin = 2.5%

The upper line (2% cap) is the same prepayment projection as shown in Exhibit 1 for the identical ARM. The lower line in Exhibit 3 (1% cap) shows our model's forecast in the same interest rate environment for an ARM pool with identical characteristics, except for the lower annual periodic cap. The difference is considerable, with the 1% cap ARM reaching a plateau prepayment rate of only 11.8% CPR, whereas the 2% cap ARM peaks at 15.6% CPR.

Exhibit 4: Seasonal Pattern of Prepayment Rates for One-Year CMT ARMs

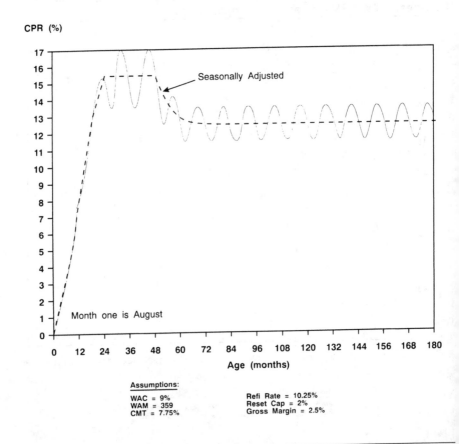

Seasonal Effect

It is well known that FRM prepayment rates exhibit a strong seasonal pattern caused by the seasonality of housing sales. Specifically, FRM prepayments peak in August and trough in February throughout the country, mainly because of the school year and holiday calendar. It is reassuring to find that prepayment rates on ARMs have a similar seasonal pattern. This is apparent in Exhibit 4, where we have superimposed the seasonal variation on the seasonally adjusted prepayment rates shown in Exhibit 1.

COFI ARMs

Our model of monthly reset FNMA COFI ARMs is similar to our CMT ARMs model, but modified to recognize important differences in the programs. The COFI ARMs model is also based on four interactive effects, but it omits the periodic cap effect, and it adds a geographic effect to reflect the high concentration of COFI mortgagors in California. Because the COFI ARM model is similar to the CMT ARM model, we will discuss the seasoning and interest rate incentives only briefly before introducing the new geographic effect.

Seasoning and Interest Rate Incentives

As in the case of CMT ARMs, prepayment rates on COFI ARMs have a seasoning process (see Exhibit 5). The pool will season to its plateau of 21.6% CPR after 18 months, remain at the plateau until the WAM decreases to 300 months, and then deseason to a 16.5% CPR prepayment rate. The upper line in Exhibit 5 (COFI = 8.09%) shows our model's projected prepayment rates for a COFI ARM pool with a WAM of 354 months, a margin of 2.25%, conventional FRM rates at 10.25%, 100% of the loans backed by property in California, and COFI fixed at 8.09%.

Exhibit 5: Effect of COFI Change on COFI ARMs Prepayment Rates

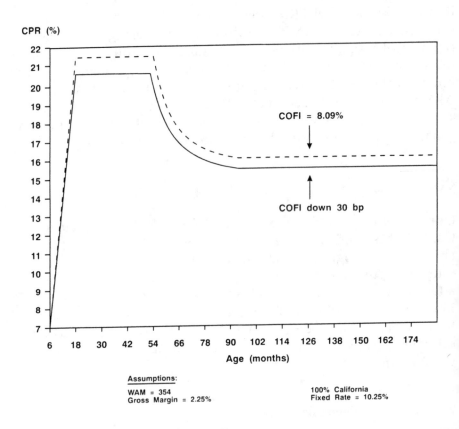

Assumptions:

WAM = 354
Gross Margin = 2.25%

100% California
Fixed Rate = 10.25%

The prepayment rates on COFI ARMs are also sensitive to the shape of the yield curve. The lower line in Exhibit 5 (COFI down twenty basis points) shows our model's projections if COFI declines twenty basis points over the next year in equal monthly reductions. The decrease in COFI relative to fixed rates makes holding a COFI ARM marginally more attractive to a mortgagor, resulting in a slowing of prepayment rates to 20.6% at the plateau.

We omit the periodic cap effect for COFI ARMs because they have no monthly rate caps, and all have identical 7.5% annual payment reset caps. Hence, there is no diversity in the data to allow an estimate of a periodic cap effect. Similarly, we could not measure the effect of lifetime rate caps.

Geographic Effect

In constructing a COFI ARM prepayment model, we must recognize the great concentration of COFI mortgagors in California. We cannot meaningfully speak of a "generic" COFI ARM, independent of the location of the properties mortgaged, because on average, the prepayment rates in California have been much higher than the rates in the rest of the nation. Hence, we introduce as an additional explanatory variable the fraction of the pool value at origination in California.

Exhibit 6 portrays the dramatic effect of loan concentration in California. Referring to the ARM pool described above, we reproduce the upper line in Exhibit 5 as the upper line in Exhibit 6 (100% CA) for ease of reference. The lower line in Exhibit 6 (0% CA) shows an otherwise identical pool, except that none of the loans are in California. Plateau prepayment rates drop from 21.6% to 13.9%, reflecting the activity in California housing relative to other areas with COFI ARMs. At the lower plateau level, COFI ARM prepayment rates are only a little lower than prepayment rates on similar CMT ARMs.

For at least two reasons, however, we must be cautious in using the California concentration ratio as an explanatory variable. First, California's housing turnover may not continue at the same relatively rapid rate as it did during the past six years. Second, the California concentration ratio will change as time passes for all pools except those that are either 0% or 100% California loans at inception. This is because on average, California mortgagors will prepay at a higher rate than other COFI borrowers, thus reducing the percentage of California loans remaining in the pool.

Exhibit 6: Effect of Pool Geography on COFI ARMs Prepayment Rates (Seasonally Adjusted)

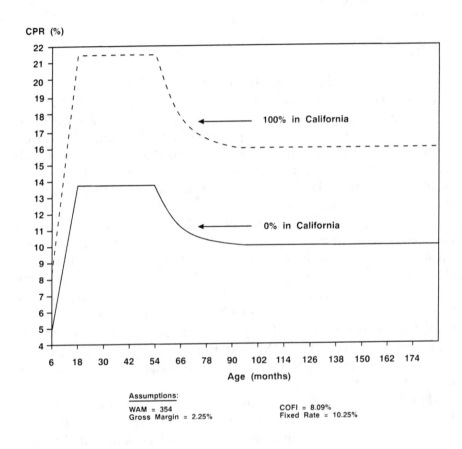

Assumptions:

WAM = 354
Gross Margin = 2.25%

COFI = 8.09%
Fixed Rate = 10.25%

VALUATION OF ARMs

Our new ARM prepayment models have important implications for valuation. In this section, we examine the change in value caused by varying some of the most important inputs to our ARM prepayment models. To do this, we employ a simulation model for valuation and use an option-adjusted spread (OAS) as our benchmark of relative value.[6] In addition to analyzing the sensitivity of our valuation results to the inputs of the prepayment models, we also note where the market's current pricing of various ARM features appears inconsistent with the projections of our new prepayment model.

The Performance of Seasoned ARMs

As we discussed earlier, ARMs have a complex seasoning process, showing rapid increases in prepayment rates for the first eighteen to twenty-six months, a plateau period, and finally falling prepayment rates that eventually stabilize at lower levels. In fact, if we define the term "fully seasoned" as the age at which ARMs' prepayment rates are no longer affected in any way by further aging, then ARMs can take as long as seven years to fully season—much longer than the period required for most fixed-rate mortgage securities. As a result, aging continues to affect our assessment of ARM prepayments and value beyond the standard thirty-month seasoning process assumed by the PSA prepayment function, and beyond the point where further aging would influence our estimates of prepayments on fixed rate securities.

Exhibit 7 shows the impact of aging on the value of a representative 9.5% one-year CMT ARM. In the analysis presented, we hold constant all the contractual features of the ARM except for the age of the mortgages underlying the security. The first two years of seasoning lower the value of the instrument, since it is priced at a premium and this period of aging brings more rapid prepayment rates. However, the value of the ARM begins to increase as the security ages beyond twenty-five months—about the point where the ARMs reach their peak prepayment rates resulting from seasoning. The increases in value that accompany further

---

[6] Our model uses the Black-Derman-Toy model for interest rates. (See Fischer Black, Emanuel Derman, and William Toy, *A One-Factor Model of Interest Rates and Its Application to Treasury Bond Options*, Goldman, Sachs & Co., June 1988.) The analysis in this chapter assumes an interest rate volatility of 12%.

Exhibit 7: Impact of Seasoning on Treasury ARM Value* (August 22, 1990)

Weighted Average Maturity	Price at 80 bp OAS	Market Price	Difference
359	$102.62	$102.25	$0.37
347	$102.26	$102.22	$0.04
335	$102.13	$102.13	$0.00
323	$102.21	$102.06	$0.15
311	$102.34	$102.03	$0.30
299	$102.39	$102.00	$0.39

* Treasury ARM features: 9.5% coupon, 2% margin, 2% per payment caps, 13% life cap, 75 bp servicing, six months to reset, 74-day delay, remaining term as shown.

aging reflect the slower prepayments we expect on more-seasoned ARM securities. Only after the ARM ages beyond seventy-six months does further aging cease to influence our prepayment estimates. At that point, changes in the value of the security with further aging are solely a function of the decrease in the time to maturity of the instrument.

Exhibit 8 presents a similar analysis for a monthly COFI ARM. Again, because the ARM shown is currently priced at a premium, the value of the security increases with age after about twenty-five months, since greater age is accompanied by slower prepayment

Exhibit 8: Impact of Seasoning on COFI ARM Value* (August 22, 1990)

Weighted Average Maturity	Price at 79 bp OAS	Market Price	Difference
359	$100.93	$100.75	$0.18
347	$100.78	$100.75	$0.03
335	$100.75	$100.75	$0.00
323	$100.78	$100.75	$0.03
311	$100.82	$100.75	$0.07
299	$100.86	$100.75	$0.11

* COFI ARM features: 9.35% coupon, 2% margin, 7.5% per payment caps, 13% life cap, 100 bp servicing, one month to reset, 54-day delay, remaining term as shown.

projections. The magnitude of the prepayment slowdown that occurs later in the seasoning process is greater for the COFI ARM shown here than for the Treasury ARM shown in Exhibit 7. However, the COFI ARM currently trades much closer to parity than does the Treasury ARM. As a result, the impact of seasoning on the value of the security is currently less dramatic for the COFI ARM than it is for the Treasury ARM. Naturally, ARMs trading at greater premiums than those analyzed here would show greater benefit from the prepayment slowdown associated with the later stages of the ARM aging process, while the value of ARMs trading at discounts would be adversely affected.

Because the market's experience with more-seasoned ARM securities has been limited and the impact of aging on prepayments has not been well understood, pricing of ARMs in the secondary market does not currently reflect the actual seasoning process of ARMs. In fact, there appears to be little or no differential pricing of ARMs related to the seasoning process beyond the first two years or so of an ARM pool's life. As a result, many of the more-seasoned ARM pools currently offer attractive values relative to newer ARM securities with comparable features. This conclusion applies not only to monthly reset COFI ARMs, where a thriving TBA market trades without regard to the age of the loans underlying the securities, but also to Treasury-indexed ARMs, which typically trade on a pool-specific basis.

Relative Value of CMT ARMs with Different Periodic Caps

As we discussed in the previous section, mortgagors prefer adjustable-rate mortgages with tighter periodic caps, all other things being equal. Hence, CMT ARMs with 1% periodic caps prepay more slowly than otherwise similar ARMs with 2% periodic caps. This slower prepayment behavior raises the value of 1% capped ARMs relative to 2% capped ARMs while the securities are trading at premiums, and lowers the relative value of 1% capped ARMs when the securities are trading at discounts. This slower prepayment behavior also influences our valuation of other features of the ARMs. In particular, by lengthening an ARM's maturity, a slower prepayment rate also increases the value of the periodic and lifetime interest rate caps that the ARM investor is short. This can partially offset the benefits offered by slower prepayments on ARMs that are trading above parity but have relatively low coupons.

Exhibit 9 illustrates the differences in value between 1 and 2% cap ARMs. To isolate the differences in value attributable to the two caps—separate from the value of the differential prepayments—we performed the following experiment: we valued otherwise identical ARMs with both 1 and 2% caps, assuming that the 1% ARM borrowers did not anticipate the value of the 1% cap in future interest rate environments and therefore prepaid exactly as 2% cap ARM borrowers with similar current mortgage rates. The differences in value attributable only to the contractual differences of the ARM securities (i.e., the different periodic caps) ranged from $0.63 to $1.25, depending on the current coupon of the ARM security.[7] That is, if both the 1 and the 2% cap ARM borrowers paying identical current mortgages rates were assumed to have identical incentives to refinance, the 2% cap ARMs would be worth $0.63 to $1.25 more to the investor than otherwise identical ARMs with 1% caps.

As we noted, however, 1% cap Treasury ARMs also prepay differently from 2% cap Treasury ARMs, because borrowers prefer the tighter caps. This difference further influences the relative value of the ARMs. In fact, if we analyze the 1% capped Treasury ARMs using prepayment projections that fully reflect the value of this cap to borrowers, the difference in value between the 1% capped ARMs and otherwise comparable 2% capped ARMs ranges from –$0.18 to +$1.03. These figures are less than the value of the cap differences calculated previously, and reflect the value

---

[7] To determine these differences in value, we analyzed 1% cap ARMs at the OASs at which otherwise similar 2% capped Treasury ARMs were trading at the time of the study.

Exhibit 9: Relative Value of Treasury ARMs With Different Periodic Caps

Security Description*	Pricing OAS	Price Using 2% Cap Prepayment Model		Diff. Cap Models	Using 2% Cap Ppay With 2%	Using 1% Cap Ppay Model	Model Difference
		2% Per. Caps	1% Per. Caps		2% Per. Caps	1% Per. Caps	
8.5% Coupon	96	$101.25	$100.00	$1.25	$101.25	$100.22	$1.03
9.5% Coupon	89	$102.25	$101.75	$0.50	$102.25	$102.08	$0.17
10.5% Coupon	84	$102.94	$102.31	$0.63	$102.94	$103.11	($0.18)

OAS at Current Market Prices

Security Description*	2% Per. Cap Market Price	OAS	Duration	1% Per. Cap Market Price	OAS	Duration
8.5% Coupon	$101.25	96	1.83	$100.31	94	2.91
9.5% Coupon	$102.25	89	1.45	$102.03	90	2.12
10.5% Coupon	$102.94	84	1.38	$102.78	91	1.68

* All securities shown are one-year CMT ARMs with 2% margin, 13% life cap, 75 bp servicing, six months to reset, 74-day delay, and 359-month remaining term.

relative to Premium

Beware of Time

of slower prepayments to the investor who owns 1% cap Treasury ARMs. The appreciation in value that occurs with slower prepayments diminishes as the coupon on the 1% cap ARM decreases. This occurs not only because the price approaches parity but also because the option value of the periodic caps on these instruments increases by a greater amount.

The lower portion of Exhibit 9 presents these 1 and 2% capped Treasury ARMs valued at their current market prices. As shown, the value of the slower prepayments experienced by 1% capped Treasury ARMs appears fully realized in the market, and these ARMs currently trade at OASs that are similar to those of 2% capped ARMs.

Valuing High Premium ARMs

Investors have historically been reluctant to pay high premiums for ARMs with relatively high coupons because they had little information about how ARMs with coupons greater than the prevailing fixed rate were likely to prepay. During the past two years we have been able to observe the prepayment behavior of these high premium pools, thus increasing the reliability of our forecasts.

Our analysis, presented in Exhibit 10, reveals that high premium pools offer values roughly comparable to those associated with ARMs trading at lower prices. The table shows one-year CMT ARMs of various coupons and ages analyzed at their current market prices. In general, although seasoned securities appear

Exhibit 10: Current Market Analysis of High Premium Treasury ARMs

| | 359 WAM | | 323 WAM | | 299 WAM | |
Coupon	Price	OAS	Price	OAS	Price	OAS
9.5%	$102.25	89	$102.00	86	$101.97	91
10.0%	$102.69	84	$102.44	85	$102.38	91
10.5%	$102.94	84	$102.22	86	$102.19	91
11.0%	$103.16	84	$102.66	84	$102.59	91

somewhat cheaper than newer versions of the same coupon, relative value between coupons is reasonably consistent. In fact, each of these securities would reset to the same coupon (9.90%) in six months if interest rates remained constant over that time. Therefore, the anticipatory refinancing spread, which includes the effect of the coupon reset in six months, is nearly equal across all of the securities analyzed. As a result, our prepayment projections for these ARMs are similar as well.

Geographic Influences on Value

The relatively limited number of ARM pools makes it difficult to do a comprehensive study on the effect of regional influences on prepayments. However, the concentration of California loans in monthly COFI pools does allow us to estimate the effect of a geographic concentration in that state, as we discussed in the previous section. We find that the impact of a concentration of loans in California is similar for both ARMs and fixed-rate MBSs.[8]

It is reasonable to assume that this similarity extends to other states as well. For instance, ARMs from states with markedly slower fixed-rate prepayments than the national average—New York or Massachusetts, for example—are likely to experience slower-than-average ARM prepayments as well. It may be difficult to verify this with the usual statistical confidence because of the limited number of ARM securities available to study. Nevertheless, investors may wish to incorporate an estimate of the impact of a particularly concentrated geographic distribution of loans into their valuation of Treasury ARMs and other ARMs where geographic influences are not specifically incorporated into our prepayment model. This modification may be particularly important for investors valuing ARM servicing portfolios. As we indicated earlier, however, regional prepayment effects are subject to change over time, and must be estimated and applied with care.

---

[8] For a brief discussion of the impact of loan concentrations on prepayments of fixed rate MBSs, see Goldman Sachs' weekly *Mortgage Market Comment* for March 9, 1990.

CONCLUDING REMARKS

Our latest prepayment models for conventional ARMs have several unique features. Foremost among them is the aging process, in which ARM pools first season to a plateau rate and then deseason to a second, lower plateau. The deseasoning of ARM pools has important implications for valuation, since premium ARMs become more valuable and discounts less valuable at lower prepayment rates. The market has yet to factor the value of slower prepayments on more seasoned premium ARMs into the pricing of those issues. As a result, these older ARMs often appear cheap on an option-adjusted basis.

The influence of annual reset caps on one-year CMT ARMs prepayment rates is our second interesting result. These caps help determine prepayment rates in two ways: first, if interest rates rise, they limit the adjustment of the mortgagor's coupon rate, thus slowing prepayments. Second, even in a stable interest rate environment, the greater option value of a tighter periodic cap discourages prepayments. Investors who own 1% cap ARMs will find slower prepayments attractive, since most issues currently trade at premiums. The benefit of slower amortization of the premium paid outweighs the cost of the small increase in periodic and lifetime cap values that results from slower prepayments.

A third unique feature is the reset month prepayment spike for premium CMT ARMs. Investors should be aware of this result so they do not confuse this transient effect (the roll month spike) with an increase in prepayment rates.

Finally, COFI ARMs buyers must account for the concentration of loans in California—as well as seasoning, interest rates, and seasonality—in projecting pool prepayment rates. This is due, of course, to the historically faster housing turnover in the California real estate market. Other regional biases in prepayment rates probably also exist for ARMs. Rather than rely on the limited ARM data available, investors may wish to study the regional pattern of FRM prepayment rates to determine the likely geographic biases of ARM prepayments.

SECTION IV

COLLATERALIZED MORTGAGE OBLIGATIONS AND STRIPPED MBS

CHAPTER 12

INTRODUCTION TO COLLATERALIZED MORTGAGE OBLIGATIONS

Gregory J. Parseghian
Managing Director
The First Boston Corporation

Collateralized mortgage obligations (CMOs) are a dynamic innovation in the mortgage securities market. Since their introduction in June 1983, CMOs have grown into a $400 billion market. CMOs generally retain many of the yield and credit quality advantages of pass-throughs, while eliminating some of the administrative burdens imposed by the traditional mortgage-backed security. Each group of bonds issued in a CMO deal is referred to as a tranche. The shorter final maturity, enhanced call protection, and semiannual payments found on many CMO tranches make them suitable for some investors who cannot incorporate pass-throughs into their portfolios or strategies. As a result, the profile of participants in the CMO market differs from that of pass-through owners. The wide range of risk and return characteristics found within the universe of CMO securities gives them the potential to meet the needs of a broader investor group than can the more homogeneous pass-through market.

The purpose of this chapter is to provide an overview of CMOs: their basic characteristics, the types of CMO tranches, and the techniques for evaluating them. In later chapters, more detail will be provided on each type of tranche. In Chapter 27, the application of option-adjusted spread technology to the valuation of CMOs will be explained.

THE CMO PRODUCT

CMOs are bonds that are collateralized by whole loan mortgages, mortgage pass-through securities, or stripped mortgage-backed securities. In addition to the security afforded by the fully dedicated collateral, some CMO issues also possess minimum reinvestment rate and minimum sinking fund guarantees. The cash flows generated by the assets in the collateral pool are used first to pay interest and then pay principal to the CMO bondholders.

A key difference between traditional pass-throughs and CMOs is the mechanics of the principal payment process. In a pass-through, each investor receives a pro rata distribution of any principal and interest payments (net of servicing) made by the homeowner. Because mortgages are self-amortizing assets, a pass-through holder receives some return of principal each month. Complete return of principal and the final maturity of the pass-through, however, do not occur until the final mortgage in the pool is paid in full. This results in a large difference between average life and final maturity, as well as a great deal of uncertainty with regard to the timing of principal return.

The CMO substitutes a principal paydown priority schedule among tranches for the pro rata process found in pass-throughs. In the early CMO structures, principal payments were made in a sequential basis, with all distributed principal going to one tranche until it was retired. The next tranche in the schedule then would become the exclusive recipient of principal payments. This pattern would be repeated until the final CMO tranche. Innovations in the CMO structure designed to create extremely stable average life tranches (see the section on PAC bonds) and to create floating-rate tranches (see the section on FRCMOs) have resulted in principal payments to multiple tranches simultaneously. The common denominator between the sequential pay CMOs and those where multiple tranches receive principal payments simultaneously is that the guidelines governing principal return are stipulated in the prospectus of the deal. Further, it is possible to calculate the precise impact of shifting collateral prepayment rates on each CMO tranche.

The effect of the CMO innovation is to use cash flows of long-maturity, monthly pay collateral to create securities with short-, intermediate-, and long-final maturities and expected average lives. On the offering date of the first FHLMC(A) deal, for example, the final maturities of the tranches ranged from five to twenty-five years, and the expected average lives of the bonds ranged from three to twenty-one years. The shorter classes clearly held more appeal than the underlying collateral for investors seeking low exposure to interest rate risk. Since the shorter tranches had to be retired before longer tranches received principal payments, the longer tranches had a form of call protection. This feature appealed to investors who required less call and reinvestment risk than pass-through securities or whole loans carry.

CMOs are an important innovation because they broaden the range of investment objectives that can be achieved by using mortgage securities. Prior to the introduction of FHLMC CMO in June 1983, the mortgage securities market was dominated by fifteen- and thirty-year final maturity pass-throughs. The inherent problem was that this structure did not meet the needs of the entire universe of fixed-income investors. Hence, some market participants effectively were excluded from the major segment of the mortgage securities market. The shorter average life CMO tranches frequently meet the requirements of investors requiring lower duration and faster return of principal. The longer CMO classes offer a greater degree of protection against call and reinvestment risk. PAC tranches offer greater cash flow stability at the expense of a small yield give-up. The conclusion is that a greater array of investors is able to participate in the mortgage market because of the introduction of CMOs. This is extremely important, because investors have limited choices among high-quality, fixed-income securities with higher yields than Treasuries.

THE BASIC CMO STRUCTURE

Exhibit 1 illustrates the structure of a typical CMO issue and demonstrates how cash flows get from the collateral to the bondholders. Interest is paid to each of the three tranches of bondholders. Cash flow generated by the collateral, in excess of that required to pay interest to all bondholders, is paid exclusively to the first tranche bondholders. In this example, it is assumed that monthly cash flows generated by the collateral are reinvested until the semiannual bond payment date. The inclusion of this reinvestment income means that the amount available for the semiannual distribution to bondholders exceeds the sum of the six monthly cash flows from the collateral. Exhibit 2 illustrates the effect on cash flows after the first class is retired; it shows that the second tranche then becomes the exclusive recipient of principal payments.

EVOLUTION OF THE CMO

Early Developments

A review of the history of CMO development demonstrates the innovations that have made CMOs an increasingly popular financing alternative and investment vehicle. From the viewpoint of an issuer, one objective is to tailor the cash flows due bondholders to

Exhibit 1: Cash-Flow Diagram for a CMO at Origination of the CMO

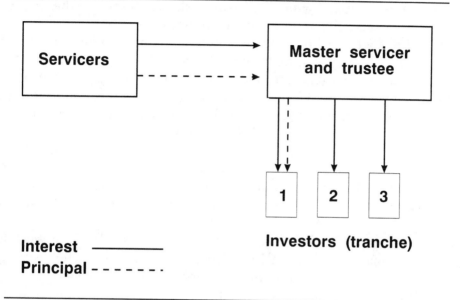

Interest ————

Principal - - - - - - ·

Investors (tranche)

Exhibit 2: Cash-Flow Diagram of a CMO after the First Tranche Is Retired

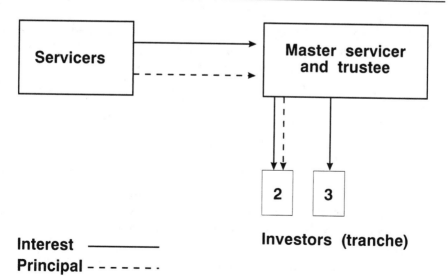

Interest ————

Principal - - - - - - ·

Investors (tranche)

closely resemble those produced by the mortgages. Deviations from this standard generally result in less proceeds at the time of the bond sale relative to the value of the collateral.

CMOs were further enhanced to better suit the requirements of investors. Methods of using whole loan collateral, graduated payment mortgages (GPMs), and conventional mortgages improved the yields that could be passed through to investors. The introduction of the accrual bond provided a uniquely call-protected mortgage security and enabled larger offerings of three-year and five-year final maturity tranches. The concentration on meeting the liquid asset requirements of thrifts and the needs of insurance companies to fund guaranteed investment contracts (GICs) and other intermediate liabilities had further effects on the CMO structure.

The original FHLMC CMO deal, comanaged by First Boston and Salomon Brothers in June 1983, was a three-tranche offering with a guaranteed minimum sinking fund. The collateral was level-pay whole loans, the credit of which was guaranteed by FHLMC. FHLMC's guaranteed sinking fund was structured to approximate a 100% FHA prepayment rate on the underlying collateral.

Pulte Homes, through its subsidiary Guaranteed Mortgage Corporation, issued the first private CMO in July 1983. ("Private" refers to the absence of any government agency acting as guarantor for the bonds; the security is publicly traded.) The collateral for the Pulte A deal, the first offering from the Pulte Guaranteed Mortgage Corporation I shelf, was GNMA level-pay (SFs) and GPMs. In order to overcome the potential problem of insufficient cash flow generation in the early years by the GPMs to service the bonds, Pulte set aside capital with a trustee to cover the greatest possible shortfall due to negative amortization. This fund, referred to as the debt-service reserve fund, is an innovation that enabled inclusion of GPM mortgages in the collateral pool.

Subsequent Pulte and American Southwest CMOs began to employ techniques that eliminated the need for the debt-service reserve fund. There were two innovations that enabled this to occur. The primary idea was the creation of the accrual bond, a bond that receives neither principal nor interest payments until all previous tranches are fully retired. The accrual bonds are designed to have negative amortization and hence absorb that created by the GPM collateral. Other means of absorbing negative amortization include coupon income from premium mortgages and unscheduled principal return from discount mortgages.

CMOs with semiannual payments to bondholders have a potential problem making coupon payments if large monthly flows of principal from the collateral must be reinvested in a low interest rate environment. The rating agencies stipulated that a reserve fund be set aside for this risk or that excess mortgages be put up to collateralize the bonds. The "calamity clause," introduced by Pulte Homes, eliminated the need for these measures by stipulating that prepayments beyond a specified rate could be passed through monthly to bondholders.

The next significant step in CMOs involved the collateral included in private deals. Most of the early private CMO deals used only GNMA, FNMA, and FHLMC guaranteed pass-throughs. Subsequent deals, however, included conventional mortgages insured by private entities such as MGIC, General Electric, and Aetna. CitiMac's CMO offering went several steps further. First, the credit guarantee on the conventional whole loans was provided by Citicorp and CitiMac, the issuer of the CMO. Second, CitiMac guaranteed a minimum sinking fund that approximates an SMM (Single Monthly Mortality), as opposed to an FHA prepayment rate on the collateral.

SPECIAL FEATURES IN EARLY DEALS

The preceding section dealt with CMOs assumed to have the simplest possible structure. There are a large number of special features on various CMOs, however, that must be detailed in order to evaluate accurately the universe of CMO securities.

Guaranteed Minimum Sinking Fund

The speed at which principal is retired on CMO bonds is highly dependent on the cash flow generated by the underlying collateral. Future cash flows from coupon income and amortization of the collateral are known. The rate of prepayments that will be received, however, cannot be predicted with certainty. Hence, the best cash flow that can be guaranteed to be generated by the mortgages is that assuming a zero percent prepayment rate on the collateral.

Some issuers, such as FHLMC and CitiMac, guarantee a minimum repayment schedule on the CMOs that exceeds that guaranteed to be generated by the collateral. If cash flow received from the underlying collateral is insufficient to meet the sinking fund requirement, then the issuer is obligated to advance an amount sufficient to cover the shortfall. The amount guaranteed to be retired each semiannual period is expressed in the prospectus as a percentage of the remaining principal balance of the CMO. The sinking fund schedule generally reflects an approximation of a selected FHA or SMM prepayment rate on the underlying collateral. In subsequent periods, issuers generally can recover advances made to the extent that cash flow generated by the collateral exceeds the minimum amount guaranteed to the bondholders.

Exhibit 3 demonstrates the mechanics of the guaranteed minimum sinking fund feature. In period 1, the sinking fund guarantee is assumed to require a principal payment of at least $1,000. The collateral, however, generated cash flow sufficient for only $500 of principal payments, meaning that the issuer had to advance the other $500. In period 2, the collateral produced enough to cover the guarantee, but no excess. In period 3, another $100 had to be advanced by the issuer, bringing the total advanced to $600. The collateral generated a $200 excess in period 4. Since advances must be repaid with excess before excess can be applied to retire more bond principal, the entire $200 was retained by the issuer and used to reduce the $600 in advances outstanding to $400. In period 5, the first $400 of excess cash flow generated by the collateral is

Exhibit 3: Guaranteed Minimum Sinking Fund

Period	[1] Principal Guaranteed to Bondholders	[2] Cash Flow Generated by Collateral in Excess of that Needed for Interest	[3] [2] - [1] Excess (+) or Shortfall (-)	[4] Advance Required by Issuer	[5] Return of Advances	[6] [3] - [5] Excess Paid to Bondholders
1	$1,000	$ 500	$ -500	$500	0	N/A
2	900	900	0	0	0	0
3	800	700	-100	100	0	N/A
4	700	900	200	0	200	0
5	600	2,000	1,400	0	400	1,000

used to return the remaining advance outstanding. The remaining $1,000 of the $1,400 excess may then be used to retire more CMO principal. An additional wrinkle found on some CMOs is that the advance account accrues interest. For purposes of this example, we assumed no such accrual.

The effect of the minimum guaranteed sinking fund is to place a floor on the minimum pace of bond retirement above what can be guaranteed solely by cash flows from the collateral. This feature is particularly valuable in a rising interest rate environment, when prepayments tend to decline. A bond with no sinking fund guarantee may experience a greater lengthening of its expected average life than will a bond with a minimum guaranteed sinking fund. This sinking fund guarantee limits cash flow and average life uncertainty, and adds value to a CMO.

Guaranteed Minimum Reinvestment Rate

In CMOs that make semiannual payments to bondholders, the monthly cash flows generated by the collateral must be reinvested until the payment date to bondholders. The rate earned on the cash flows reinvested can have a material effect on the amount available to pay bondholders and on the average life of the CMO tranches. A guaranteed minimum reinvestment rate requires the guarantor (generally a triple-A bank or agency) to supplement the reinvestment income if it does not meet the minimum rate. The effect is to quicken the pace of bond retirement relative to what would be retired if there were no guarantee in periods of very low short-term interest rates.

Credit Guarantee on Mortgages

The issuer of a CMO may establish a reserve fund to absorb some or all of the losses upon defaults of the whole loans or pass-throughs in the collateral pool. Generally, this type of guarantee exists only in CMOs such as CitiMac's that are backed by whole loans. In contrast, most bonds issued by home builders need no supplemental credit guarantees, since the mortgages are insured by GNMA, FNMA, or FHLMC.

Removal of Excess Cash Flow by Issuer

The issuer of a CMO is always required to pay interest on CMO bonds. In addition, the issuer must pay down enough CMO principal so that the outstanding CMO bonds remain fully collateralized. If cash available on a payment date to bondholders exceeds the sum of required principal and interest payments, then this amount is termed the excess. This excess also is referred to as the CMO residual.

There is wide variation among CMO deals on the method by which to calculate and distribute this excess. Some deals allow the issuer to retain the entire excess, while others stipulate that the entire amount be distributed to bondholders. Many CMO indentures contain a formula dividing the excess between CMO bondholders and the issuer.

It is clear that distribution of the excess to the bondholder shortens the expected average life of the CMO. Investors should not be alarmed, however, if the indenture provides that the issuer retains part or all of the excess. The yield table for each deal, which generally lists yields, timing of principal payments, final maturity, duration, and average life under a range of collateral prepayment rates, fully reflects the provisions relating to the handling of the excess. Hence, it is critical to scan the yield table in order to gain an understanding of how the various features of a particular CMO work together to influence cash flows.

Special Reserve Fund for Negative Amortization Collateral

Some CMO offerings contain special reserve funds to supplement, if necessary, the cash flows from the portion of collateral that experiences negative amortization, such as would occur with GPMs. This feature is generally termed the "debt-service reserve fund." The effect of this feature is to bias upward the speed at which bonds are retired.

Prepayment Reserve Fund

In a CMO that makes semiannual payments to bondholders, the issuer must pay coupon income on the entire principal balance outstanding at the beginning of the six-month period. This can pose difficulty if the reinvestment rate available on monthly principal return from the collateral is less than the coupon rate on the bonds. Some CMOs overcome this hurdle with a calamity clause that allows the issuer to make monthly principal payments to the bondholder.

CMOs without a calamity clause frequently have a prepayment reserve fund. This fund, which represents capital set aside by the issuer at the outset of the deal, is used to supplement the reinvestment income on monthly principal received from the collateral.

This supplement may be required to make interest and principal payments to bondholders.

While it is easy at first glance to categorize the preceding special features as good and bad, these labels do not necessarily lead to an accurate assessment of the relative value of the particular CMO. For example, excess income removal provisions frequently appear in combination with special reserve funds for negative amortization securities. Under close scrutiny, it becomes apparent that the approximate net effect of the provisions is to cancel out and generate cash flows to bondholders similar to those in more simply structured CMO offerings. The critical yardstick is the yield table, which enables the investor to scrutinize the cash flow characteristics of the bonds under a range of prepayment assumptions on the collateral.

IMPORTANCE OF THE ISSUER

All CMO offerings to date are backed by collateral that is held in trust exclusively for the benefit of bondholders. This means that bondholders retain possession of the collateral in the event of default of the CMO issuer. The credit quality of the CMO issuer is important only to the extent that promises made to bondholders cannot be satisfied by the collateral. Examples of this include guaranteed minimum sinking funds, guaranteed minimum reinvestment rates, and credit guarantees on the underlying collateral. A generalization that can be made is that CMOs issued by home builders tend to be structured to meet obligations to bondholders exclusively with cash flow from the collateral. In contrast, FHLMC, CitiMac, and other financial institutions that have issued CMOs more frequently have provisions that may result in bondholder reliance on the issuer to supplement cash flows generated by the collateral.

LATER DEVELOPMENTS IN CMO EVOLUTION

All of the early CMO deals featured solely fixed-rate bonds with a sequential pay principal retirement format. The primary economic rationale for CMO issuance was the creation of securities with the yield advantage and credit quality of mortgages, and a range of expected final maturities and average lives broader than that available in the pass-through market.

Later developments in CMO structure featured the introduction of floating-rate CMOs (FRCMOs) and planned amortization classes (PACs). FRCMOs created the first significant availability of London InterBank Offered Rate (LIBOR)-based assets with quality similar to agencies in the mortgage market. Deals featuring PAC and PAC support bonds disproportionately allocate average life variability among tranches. PAC classes generally carry lower yield and lesser average life variability than the collateral, whereas support bonds most frequently have wider yield spreads to Treasuries but greater average life variability compared to the collateral.

The recent innovations in CMOs have brought about an alphabet soup of PACs, TACs, jump Zs, and PAC support bonds. Whereas the original intent of the CMO process was to segment the average lives of mortgage-backed assets, many of the more recent developments were made to stratify the degree of cash flow variability with respect to changes in prepayments on the underlying collateral. Portfolio managers now may tailor portfolios to reflect not only desired duration but also required convexity and exposure to prepayment trends.

As investment banks became the dominant issuer of CMOs, a market developed for the placement and trading of CMO residuals. Residuals are the cash flows generated by the collateral in excess of those required to pay bondholders and fees associated with the deal. A residual investor also assumes responsibility for absorbing any tax liability or credit caused by the difference between the taxable income generated by the collateral, and the interest paid and expenses associated with the trust.

SPECIAL TYPES OF CMO TRANCHES

Accrual Bonds[1]

Many CMO issues include one or more tranches that are accrual bonds. An accrual bond does not receive any cash payments of principal *or interest* until all tranches preceding it are retired. In effect, an accrual bond is a deferred-interest obligation, resembling a zero coupon bond, prior to the time that the preceding tranches are retired. The accrual bond, also termed the Z-bond, then receives cash payments representing interest and principal on the accrued amount outstanding. This amount is the original principal balance plus the compounded accrued interest. Accrual bonds are purchased most frequently by investors who require the greatest degree of protection against reinvestment and call risk, or who seek the greater price leverage afforded by these classes.

Exhibit 4 demonstrates the effect of an accrual bond in a CMO structure. Interest accrues on, but is not paid to, the accrual bond (the fourth tranche in this example) until the first three tranches are fully retired. The sequential payment of principal concept is not affected by the existence of an accrual bond. Since interest payments on this tranche are deferred, however, the payment of principal on the prior classes is accelerated by the amount of interest deferred on the accrual bond. Exhibit 5 shows that the second tranche in the sequence becomes the sole recipient of principal after the first tranche is retired. One should note that an accrual bond need not be the last class, and that some deals have more than one accrual bond tranche.

---

[1] Accrual bonds are discussed further in Chapter 19.

Exhibit 4: Cash-Flow Diagram for a CMO with an Accural Tranche

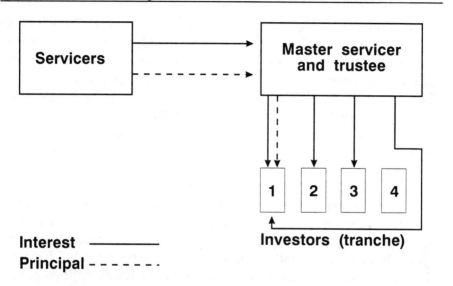

Interest ————
Principal – – – – – –

Investors (tranche)

Exhibit 5: Cash-Flow Diagram for a CMO after the First Tranche Is Retired

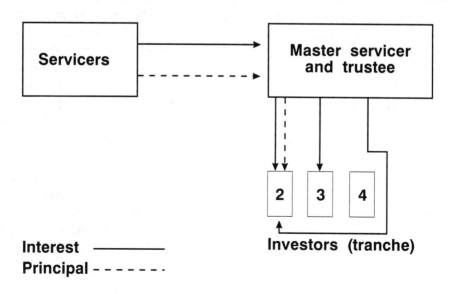

Interest ————
Principal – – – – – –

Investors (tranche)

CMO Residuals[2]

CMO residuals represent the "equity" interest in a CMO transaction. In general, the residual holder will receive the difference between the cash flows derived from the collateral and those applied to make payments to the bondholders and to pay trust expenses. Exhibit 6 graphically depicts the residual on a fixed-rate CMO with four tranches backed by 9.5% collateral.

The cash flows to the residual owner depend critically on the prepayment rate of the underlying collateral. When CMOs contain floating-rate tranches, the level of LIBOR also plays a key role in the cash flows to the residual holder. The value of a residual is based on the expected cash flows over a range of possible interest rate scenarios, as well as consideration of factors such as liability for expenses and income tax consequences. Market participants typically project the pattern of yields or returns provided by a particular residual in order to determine its suitability to their investment needs and analyze both pretax and after-tax yields.

Exhibit 7 displays the expected yield on the residual of Morgan Stanley Trust Series 30, a bearish residual initially priced to yield 13.00%. Bearish residuals increase in yield as interest rates rise, and decrease as rates decline. This kind of residual typically stems from a CMO structure where the mortgage collateral only backs fixed-coupon CMO tranches. The major factor influencing the yield and performance of the residual is the rate at which the collateral prepays. As depicted in the exhibit, the yield of the residual declines as interest rates fall and prepayments rise. Yield drops because the more rapid prepayments are applied to the shorter, lower coupon tranches, reducing the coupon spread between the CMO and the collateral, and shortening the period over which the holder receives the residual cash flows. Conversely, in a rising rate environment, the yield of the residual rises, benefiting from a wider average coupon spread between the CMO bonds and the collateral and longer average life of the residual cash flows.

---

[2] For a more detailed discussion of CMO residuals, see Chapter 22.

Exhibit 6: CMO Residual

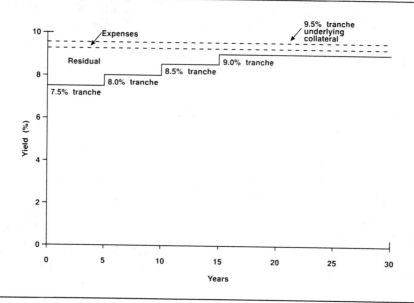

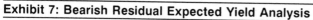

Exhibit 7: Bearish Residual Expected Yield Analysis

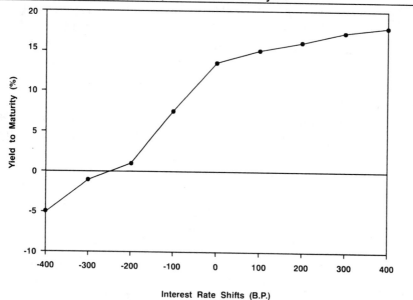

Other types of residuals include humped and stable residuals, whose names also are derived from their patterns of expected yields as interest rates change. These projections require assumptions on future LIBOR rates as well as the prepayment projections on the underlying collateral.

Controlled Amortization Bonds: The PAC Structure[3]

A PAC bond has two important features that distinguish it from a conventional CMO class. First, a PAC amortizes with a sinking fund that is predetermined as long as the prepayments on the underlying collateral remain within a broad range of speeds. Second, a PAC can make principal payments at the same time as some or all of the other CMO classes. Thus, unlike traditional CMO tranches, the PAC is not a "serial pay" bond. It will receive its scheduled payments regardless of the status of its companion classes.

The most attractive feature of a PAC class to the CMO investor is its enhanced degree of cash flow certainty. Except in extreme prepayment scenarios, the PAC bond can be expected to pay down principal according to its specified sinking fund. In a typical PAC backed by current coupon FNMAs, the investor can expect to receive the scheduled cash flow unless the prepayment speed on the underlying collateral slows to less than 50% PSA or increases beyond 350% PSA.

Due to the enhanced degree of cash flow certainty, PAC bonds represent a significant value to the CMO buyer, and especially to buyers who have avoided the mortgage market because of cash flow uncertainty. Each PAC should be evaluated independently with respect to this specific cash flow characteristic, but it is clear they should trade at a premium to comparable average life traditional CMO. PACs generally trade ten basis points to forty basis

---

[3] See Chapter 14 for a further discussion of this structure.

points richer than comparable traditional CMO tranches of similar collateral and average life characteristics.

The cash flow certainty of the PAC bond is facilitated by reallocating cash flow uncertainty to other tranches of the CMO, often referred to as the non-PAC tranches. The extent to which these other tranches are affected depends on the structure of the specific PAC. Investors considering the non-PAC tranches of a PAC CMO series should consult CMO yield tables and evaluate total return risk before making an investment decision. Total return and average life variability of non-PAC tranches is generally greater than traditional tranches in a CMO that contains no PACs.

PAC Bond Impact. Assume that by the terms of the bond indenture, PAC investors are scheduled to receive $1 million per quarter beginning in two years and continuing for ten years thereafter. This $1 million comes from the cash flow on the underlying collateral, and the PAC class *receives priority* over all other tranches in receipt of principal. For example, if the collateral pays as expected at 175% PSA and generates $2 million in principal in a given quarter, $1 million goes to the PAC bond and the other $1 million goes to the CMO tranche that is currently receiving principal.

If, however, prepayment rates on the underlying collateral slow, and only $1.5 million of principal is generated, the PAC still receives its scheduled $1 million, but the current CMO tranche receives only $500,000. Thus, the other CMO tranches provide a buffer for the PAC bond. If prepayments slow dramatically, and only $750,000 of principal is generated, then the PAC bond receives the entire amount and no principal is passed through to the other tranches. In addition, the PAC has first call in future quarters on the $250,000 to which it was entitled but failed to receive; that is, the PAC has a cumulative right to its scheduled principal.

If prepayments on the underlying collateral increase, then the PAC continues to receive its scheduled $1 million, and all other principal received goes to pay down the current CMO tranche. As in the slow prepayment scenario, the other tranches absorb the cash flow uncertainty. In cases of extremely fast prepayments, the other CMO tranches would be retired early. It is possible that the PAC (no longer cushioned) would then be forced to receive larger than scheduled principal payments, resulting in early retirement of the PAC.

Effect of PAC on Other Tranches. The following example compares average life and total return sensitivity of a CMO with a PAC tranche to a traditionally structured CMO with no PACs, under various interest rate scenarios. The M.D.C. Mortgage Funding Corporation, Series M (MDC-M) CMO serves as the example of a structure containing a PAC bond. For purposes of analyzing the effect of a PAC bond within a CMO, a hypothetical MDC-M CMO with similar characteristics was structured without a PAC tranche. This hypothetical CMO will be referred to as "Ex-PAC."

The MDC-M CMO is comprised of five tranches, totaling $200.1 million at issue, backed by new FNMA 9.5s. The fourth tranche is a $60.6 million PAC, and provides for a minimum mandatory sinking fund over ten years beginning in 1988. The scheduled payments to the PAC tranches are provided below in Exhibit 8.

Exhibit 8: MDC-M CMO Scheduled PAC Tranche Payments

Period	Quarterly Sinking-Fund Payment
10/1/88-7/1/91	$1,675,000
10/1/91-7/1/95	1,750,000
10/1/95-1/1/96	1,500,000
4/1/96-7/1/96	1,250,000
10/1/96-7/1/97	1,000,000
10/1/97-7/1/98	750,000

The Ex-PAC CMO is comprised of four tranches, also assumed to be backed by FNMA 9.5s. The first three tranches have the same average lives as those in the MDC-M CMO at the pricing speed of 175% PSA. The fourth tranche of the Ex-PAC CMO is an accrual bond with an average life marginally longer than the accrual tranches of the MDC-M CMO.

The PAC tranche receives priority on prepayments to meet the sinking fund schedule. In periods of slow prepayment rates, prepayments on the underlying collateral would first be allocated to the PAC tranche, thus lengthening the average life of companion tranches.

In periods of fast prepayment rates, the PAC receives only the stipulated principal amounts set forth in the sinking fund schedule. Under such a scenario, average lives of the surrounding tranches would shorten as excess principal flows are redirected around the PAC tranche.

Average Life Analysis. Exhibit 9 illustrates that the average life variability of the second and accrual tranches is significantly

---

Exhibit 9: Average Life Variability

MDC Mortgage Funding Corporation Series M CMO
(MDC-M)

	Estimated Average Lives per Tranche				
Interst-Rate Change	First Tranche	Second Tranche	Third Tranche	Accural Tranche	PAC Tranche
+200 bp	3.2 yrs	8.5 yrs	13.3 yrs	21.8 yrs	6.4 yrs
+100	2.9	7.3	12.5	21.1	6.4
+ 50	2.8	6.9	12.3	20.0	6.4
Unchanged	2.4	5.6	10.9	19.7	6.4
- 50	1.9	4.1	8.3	17.5	6.4
-100	1.5	3.0	5.4	14.7	6.4
-200	1.0	2.0	3.0	4.4	6.0

Hypothetical MDC Series M CMO Without PAC Tranche
(Ex-PAC)

	Estimated Average Lives per Tranche			
Interst-Rate Change	First Tranche	Second Tranche	Third Tranche	Accural Tranche
+200 bp	2.9 yrs	6.9 yrs	12.8 yrs	22.3 yrs
+100	2.7	6.4	12.1	21.7
+ 50	2.7	6.3	11.9	21.5
Unchanged	2.4	5.6	10.9	20.4
- 50	2.1	4.6	9.1	18.1
-100	1.7	3.7	7.2	14.9
-200	1.2	2.5	4.5	9.5

greater within the PAC structure than under the CMO that contains no PACs. To a lesser extent, the third tranche suffers more variability under the PAC structure, whereas the first tranche exhibits little difference between the two structures.

The second tranche under the PAC structure has a potential for lengthening to an 8.5-year average life versus 6.9 years for the second tranche in the hypothetical CMO with no PACs, assuming a +200 basis points interest rate rise. This may be attributable to the similar average life assumptions at pricing of the second tranche (5.6 years) and the PAC tranche (6.4 years). The PAC tranche average life target under the pricing speed takes preference over any other tranche. Thus, slower prepayments render it difficult to realize both average life estimates, and the non-PAC tranche suffers accordingly.

Evaluating the second tranche at slower prepayment rates underscores its average life sensitivity in rising interest rate environments. The potential risk of diverting second tranche principal cash flows to the PAC tranche becomes more pronounced. This represents a very small potential change in average life variability for the early tranche; Exhibit 9 demonstrates, however, that it can have a more significant effect on the second tranche. In the MDC-M CMO, the PAC tranche's sinking fund does not commence for two years, allowing the first tranche a significant period during which it alone amortizes. Its average life variability is less than that of the second tranche.

In bull market scenarios, the MDC-M accrual tranche runs the risk of a dramatic shortening in average life versus the accrual tranche under a non-PAC structure. Under a yield curve shift of 200 basis points' decline, the MDC-M fourth tranche would have an expected average life of 4.4 years, as opposed to 9.5 years for the Ex-PAC. In the bear market scenarios, the average life variability is similar. The PAC tranche with its sinking fund may only receive a set amount of principal prepayment regardless of the speed at which the underlying collateral pays off. The excess prepayments are allocated to the earliest tranches, thereby shortening all tranches in falling rate environments.

Exhibit 10: Average Life Range (MDC-M vs. MDC-M Ex-PAC)

Interst-Rate Change	Average Lives per Tranche (+/-200 bp)				
	First Tranche	Second Tranche	Third Tranche	Accural Tranche	PAC Tranche
Initial pricing assumption	2.4 yrs	5.6 yrs	10.9 yrs	19.7 yrs.	6.4 yrs
MDC-M	1.0-3.2	2.0-8.5	3.0-13.3	4.4-21.8	6.0-6.4
MDC-M Ex-PAC	1.2-2.9	2.5-6.9	4.5-12.8	9.5-22.3	—

The actual PAC tranche in the MDC-M CMO has an average life range of 6.0 to 6.4 years across all interest rate environments examined. Clearly, companion tranches bear the burden of ensuring the average life or cash flow certainty of the PAC tranche. Exhibit 10 summarizes estimated average life ranges for the PAC and Ex-PAC CMOs.

Non-PAC tranches within a PAC-structured CMO trade at significantly wider yield spreads to Treasuries than standard structure CMOs. The cash flow uncertainty that is reallocated to these non-PAC tranches suggests that they should be priced at higher yields than otherwise comparable tranches in CMOs that contain no PACs.

As expected, PAC tranches with enhanced cash flow certainty trade considerably richer than similar average life "plain vanilla" tranches. To analyze whether or not the yield sacrifice for less negative convexity is warranted, total return scenario analysis must be employed.

Projected Total Returns. Comparative total return analysis indicates that the existence of a PAC tranche serves to transfer incremental negative convexity to the second and third tranches (Exhibits 11 and 12).

Exhibit 11 graphs the returns for second tranches under both the PAC and plain vanilla structures and the actual PAC tranche. The negative convexity of the second tranches under both structures (MDC-M2 and Ex-PAC) is obvious. The dotted line repre-

Exhibit 11: Total Return Curve Second and PAC Tranche Comparison (1-Year Holding Period)

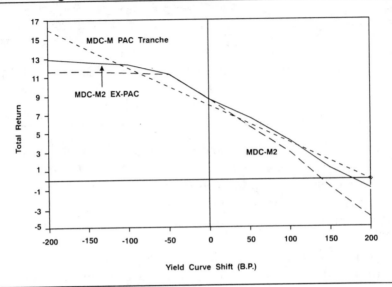

Exhibit 12: Total Return Comparison Third Tranche Comparison (1-Year Holding Period)

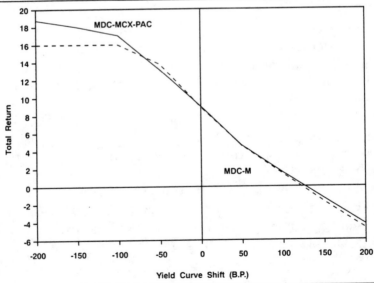

sents the expected returns of the PAC tranche itself, and exhibits very slight positive convexity.

In comparing the MDC-M2 tranche under the Ex-PAC structure with the PAC bond itself, the PAC bond may be expected to outperform in a volatile interest rate environment. Upward or downward yield curve shifts of more than 100 basis points point to the superior return characteristics of the PAC bond. For yield changes in either direction of 100 basis points or less, the traditional second tranche outperforms.

The effects of shifting cash flow uncertainty under the PAC CMO to the second tranche were illustrated by Exhibit 9. The negative convexity of returns for the MDC-M2 tranche is more pronounced than that of the second tranche in the non-PAC CMO structure (MDC-M2 Ex-PAC). The MDC-M2 will underperform under virtually any rate scenario, and only equal the return of its non-PAC counterpart in an unchanged to minus fifty basis point rate environment.

The results of the scenario analysis indicate that the PAC tranche outperforms only in the most volatile rate environments. This is clearly due to the superior convexity evidenced by a PAC tranche. Superior performance occurs in the extreme bull market case where the PAC returns 15.69% versus 12.71% for the hypothetical non-PAC second tranche. In the extreme bear market scenario, the PAC outperforms by only 1.20% in terms of total return.

In the simulation of total returns, the PAC tranche was priced twenty basis points richer than a similar average life tranche in a plain vanilla structure. In cases where the sacrifice in yield for more favorable convexity characteristics exceeds twenty basis points, the total return profile of PAC bonds may not be as attractive.

Thus, a PAC tranche exhibits favorable convexity characteristics in comparison to a similar average life CMO tranche under a standard structure. However, in an environment of small net interest rate changes, the standard structure CMO outperforms.

Exhibits 13 and 14 illustrate that the expected returns of first and accrual tranches are roughly equivalent under both the PAC

Exhibit 13: Total Return Comparison First Tranche Comparison (1-Year Holding Period)

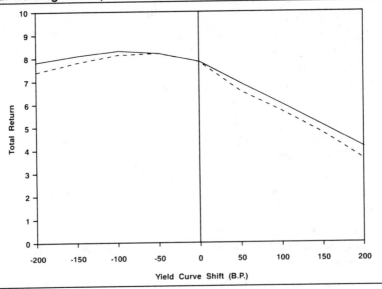

Exhibit 14: Total Return Comparison Accrual Tranche Comparison (1-Year Holding Period)

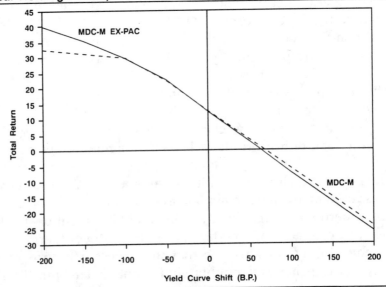

and Ex-PAC structures, although the Ex-PAC accrual tranche marginally outperforms under almost every interest rate scenario.

Accrual tranche performance differs primarily in the case of an extreme bull market. The Ex-PAC accrual tranche does not shorten in duration to the extent of its PAC counterpart. Thus, the accrual tranche under the traditional structure outperforms the PAC accrual tranche in a 200 basis points scenario by 40.4% to 32.6% in total return.

It appears that the first and accrual tranches in a PAC structure are less susceptible to the unfavorable effects of cash flow uncertainty. The sinking fund of the PAC class does not begin for two years. During these two years, the first tranche may amortize substantially. The accrual tranche does not receive principal on a current basis until such time as the PAC and other tranches mature. Principal cash flows to the outer tranches, first and accrual, do not coincide with the operation of the sinking fund to the degree that the intermediate tranches (second and third) do. Hence, the first and accrual tranches bear less of the burden in ensuring the cash flow certainty of the PAC tranche.

The investment conclusions are twofold:

1. Nonaccrual CMO tranches under an Ex-PAC structure outperform similar average life tranches of a CMO with a built-in PAC tranche in virtually all interest rate environments. Correspondingly, intermediate tranches (second and third) in a PAC structure bear the primary burden of ensuring the cash flow certainty of the PAC tranche.

2. An actual PAC tranche will equal or fall short of total return generated by a similar average life Ex-PAC tranche, given small net changes in interest rates; only in a volatile environment, 100 basis points or more, will a PAC tranche outperform.

Floating-Rate CMOs[4]

Another significant innovation in the CMO market is the floating-rate tranche, which was introduced in the fall of 1986 and has become an integral part of the CMO sector. Although floating-rate CMO volume has been low lately due to relatively high short-term rates, floaters have broadened the CMO market by attracting a large number of traditional investors in the non-mortgage-related floating-rate securities. CMO floaters generally offer higher yields than comparable floating-rate notes and fixed-rate securities, without sacrificing credit quality.

As the volume of these securities has increased, so too has the complexity of analyzing each deal from an investor's point of view. The CMO floaters that have been issued have contained various quoted margins or spreads, coupon cap schedules, payment delays, gross-up provisions, and other features. The following discussion explores the various features of floating-rate CMOs and their impact on returns to investors.

Quoted Margin or Spread. The majority of CMO floaters issued have used the LIBOR as the index. The term of the index has varied: one-, three-, and six-month LIBORs have been used. There is nothing to preclude the use of other indexes in the future, should investor interest exist.

The coupons on CMO floaters are reset at a fixed spread over the index rate. This spread is referred to as the quoted margin (or spread), and is usually expressed in basis points. The quoted spreads of CMO floaters have ranged from twenty-five to seventy basis points. The actual spread an investor will receive may differ from the quoted spread, depending on the features of the issue.

The size of the quoted spread is based on several factors. The average life of the floating-rate tranche is one determinant of quoted spread. The longer the average life is, the greater the quoted spread will be. This is due to the ordinarily upward-slop-

---

[4] For more information on floating-rate tranches, see Chapter 13.

ing shape of the yield curve and investors' concerns over maturity extension and rate caps.

Maximum coupons, or caps, also affect the amount of quoted spread. CMO floaters issued to date have contained two types of caps: stepped caps and lifetime caps. Stepped caps are limits that are set initially (i.e., at 8 to 9%), increasing by a small increment each year (i.e., to 11 to 12%) after four to five years. This type of cap has been used in floaters with two- to three-year average lives. A lifetime cap is a coupon limit in effect over the bond's entire life. Lifetime caps have ranged from 11 to 13%, and are generally present in floaters with longer average lives.

Factors that determine the level of coupon caps are the weighted average coupon rate of the fixed-rate classes in the CMO, and the par amount and weighted average pass-through rate of the collateral (as more fully discussed later). Once an approximate cap schedule is determined, issuers set the quoted spread at an amount that is attractive to investors. Investors are compensated with higher quoted spreads for the risk of the coupon being capped out. In general, the amount of quoted spread has an inverse relationship to the level of the cap. Thus, a low cap would be indicative of a high quoted spread, and vice versa.

Another determinant of quoted spread is the type of collateral. As is the case with fixed-rate CMOs, floaters backed by FNMAs and FHLMCs yield more than floaters backed by GNMAs because of the preceived higher, government-guaranteed credit quality of GNMAs. To date, FNMA- and FHLMC-backed floaters have had mean quoted spreads of forty-seven and forty-eight basis points, respectively, versus a mean on GNMA-backed floaters of thirty-five basis points.

The amount of quoted spread is not necessarily the actual or effective spread that an investor will receive from a CMO floater. Coupon caps, coupon refix and payment frequencies, payment delays, and gross-up provisions may all have an effect on quoted spread that reduces the realized spread to the investor.

Maximum Coupons or Caps. All CMO floaters are backed by fixed-rate mortgages or mortgage-backed securities. Therefore, to

ensure that the cash flow will always be sufficient to pay the coupon interest, there are caps on the floating interest rates. Most caps
are set at a rate above the pass-through rate of the underlying collateral. This does not mean, however, that if the coupon rate of the
floater reached the cap, the cash flows from the collateral would
not be sufficient to pay the bonds. Issuers have combined floating-
rate tranches with fixed-rate tranches in CMOs and used over-collateralization to compensate for the notional shortfall. By
combining floating- and fixed-rate tranches in a CMO, issuers
limit the amount of coupon interest that would have to be paid
under rising interest rate scenarios. The effect of the floating-rate
tranche reaching its maximum coupon under such a scenario is
offset somewhat by the lower fixed coupons of the other classes.
As long as the weighted average coupon on the bonds (assuming
the floating tranche is at its maximum cap rate) is less than the
weighted average pass-through rate on the collateral, the cash
flows from the collateral will be sufficient to pay the required
bond cash flows. For example, ML Trust V is a two-tranche CMO
with a $375 million floating-rate first tranche and a $375 million
6% fixed-coupon second tranche. The floater has a coupon of
three-month LIBOR plus 0.5%, subject to a cap of 13%. The CMO
is backed by $750 million par amount of 9.5% FHLMC certificates.
Under a scenario in which the coupon of the first class reaches the
cap, the weighted average coupon of the CMO would be 9.5%
[(375/750 × 13%) + (375/750 × 6%)]. Thus, the 9.5% FHLMC collateral could support the bonds in the event the floating-rate coupon
reached the cap.

   Another method of ensuring the supportability of the floating-
rate CMOs in a rising interest rate environment is over-collateralization. Over-collateralization entails backing either a CMO floater
with fixed-rate mortgage or mortgage-backed securities with a
higher principal amount than the principal amount of the bonds.
The FBC Mortgage Securities Trust VII Series A CMO, for example, is a $240 million par amount single-tranche floating-rate CMO
with a coupon of three-month LIBOR plus 0.5%, subject to a lifetime cap of 11.5%. It is backed by $260 million par amount of

FHLMC certificates with a weighted average pass-through rate of 10.51%. Under a scenario in which the floating-rate coupon has reached the cap, the CMO would pay interest of 11.5% on a quarterly basis. The collateral pays a weighted average coupon of 10.51% on a monthly basis. In order to make the two rates comparable, it is necessary to express the monthly weighted average coupon of the collateral as a quarterly rate. The resulting quarterly rate is 10.60% $\{4 \times [(1 + 10.51\%/12)^3 - 1]\}$. Applying this rate to the $260 million par amount of the collateral gives approximately the same coupon income as the amount needed to pay interest on $240 million of bonds when they have a coupon of 11.5% ($260 million × 10.60% = $240 million × 11.50%).

Coupon Refix and Payment Frequency. The coupon refix frequency of a CMO floater refers to the periodic reset of a floater's coupon to current market levels. CMO floating-rate coupons refix on monthly, quarterly, and semiannual bases. All else being equal, a shorter refix period reduces the likelihood that a coupon will vary from market levels. The benefit of a shorter refix period is not without a cost, however; the spreads between one-month LIBOR and three-month LIBOR and one-month LIBOR and six-month LIBOR have averaged approximately five and fifteen basis points, respectively, in recent years. Thus, an investor who bought a quarterly pay, monthly reset floater would earn less coupon income than one who bought a quarterly pay, quarterly reset floater, assuming that all else is constant.

The effect of a shorter refix period should not be analyzed without taking coupon payment frequency into account. CMO floaters offer monthly, quarterly, and semiannual payments. For the same nominal coupon rate, more frequent coupon payments will result in a higher effective yield, due to the reinvestment of cash flows.

The periodicity of the coupon refix and the reset index do not necessarily have to match. The period of the reset index can exceed the period of the coupon refix, and vice versa (although the latter case is rare). In a positively sloped yield curve environment,

Exhibit 15: Hypothetical LIBOR Scenarios

	LIBOR		
Scenario	One-Month	Three-Month	Six-Month
1	6.05%	6.10%	6.20%
2	6.55	6.60	6.70
3	7.05	7.10	7.20

a refix period shorter than the index period provides two benefits: compounding of interest and the use of a higher index.

An example will help to illustrate the effects of coupon refix and payment frequency. For simplicity, assume the three hypothetical LIBOR scenarios shown in Exhibit 15. For each scenario, we have assumed that the spread among one-, three-, and six-month LIBOR conform to recent experience.

Exhibit 16 shows the effective spread over three-month LIBOR for four CMO floating-rate tranches when the nominal coupons are expressed on the consistent quarterly pay basis. FBC Mortgage Securities Trust VII Series B is a typical quarterly pay, quarterly refix tranche with a coupon of three-month LIBOR plus 0.4%. Its quoted spread and effective spread are the same. The GMAC Class B-1 floater is a monthly pay, monthly reset tranche with a coupon of one-month LIBOR plus 0.25%. When viewed on a quarterly pay basis, the effective spread of the GMAC-B1s is less than the quoted spread because the advantage of monthly compounding (three to four basis points) is offset by the negative spread between one-month and three-month LIBOR (five basis points). The Oxford A-1s have a monthly pay, monthly reset coupon of three-month LIBOR plus 0.5%. Since the coupon resets off three-month LIBOR, the effective spread is not negatively affected by the one-month to three-month LIBOR spread. The effect of monthly compounding adds four to five basis points to the quoted spread. The FBC Mortgage Securities Trust IX Series A floater is the only semiannual pay, semiannual reset floater issued to date. When viewed on a quarterly basis, its effective spread is greater than its quoted spread because the positive spread between three-

Exhibit 16: Impact of Coupon Refix and Coupon Payment Frequency

Issuer and Series	Coupon Refix Frequency	Coupon Payment Frequency	Nominal Coupon	Nominal Coupons under 3 LIBOR Scenarios	Nominal Coupons as Quarterly Rate	Effective Spread over 3-Month LIBOR
FBC Mortgage Securities Trust VII Series B	Q	Q	3-month LIBOR + .4%	6.50%	6.50%	.40%
				7.00	7.00	.40
				7.50	7.50	.40
GMAC Mortgage Securities Series B, Class B-1	M	N	1-month LIBOR + .25%	6.30	6.33	.23
				6.80	6.84	.24
				7.30	7.34	.24
Oxford CMO Trust 1 Series A, Class A-1	M	M	3-month LIBOR + .5%	6.60	6.64	.54
				7.10	7.14	.54
				7.60	7.65	.55
FBC Mortgage Securities IX Series A	S	S	6-month LIBOR + .7%	6.90	6.84	.74
				7.40	7.33	.73
				7.90	7.82	.72

month and six-month LIBOR (ten basis points) is more than enough to offset the negative impact of semiannual versus quarterly compounding (six to eight basis points).

This example does not attempt to show what would happen in a changing interest rate environment. In an increasing rate environment, the short refix period floaters could offer higher effective spreads, depending on the magnitude of interest rate changes. The analysis above could be performed in conjunction with an investor's interest rate forecast to determine more accurately the effects of coupon refix and payment frequency.

Coupon Payment Delays. A coupon payment delay on a bond refers to a situation in which the end of a coupon period does not correspond to the coupon payment date. A payment delay reduces effective yield because interest does not accrue between the end of the coupon period and the payment date. Payment delays on CMO floaters have ranged from thirty to fifty days, with most issues having no delay. At current rates, the delay may cost an investor up to eight basis points in yield. Exhibit 17 compares the effective spread over LIBOR of three CMO floating-rate tranches with payment delays of zero, thirty, and fifty days, using the LIBOR scenarios in Exhibit 16. The example shows that a thirty-day delay reduces the quoted spread by four to five basis points, and a fifty-day delay reduces the quoted spread by six to eight basis points.

Gross-Up Provisions. Another factor that affects returns from a CMO floater is the "gross-up" provision. These provisions relate to the payment day convention of a CMO floater. In general, the payment day convention of a CMO floater is not the same as that of LIBOR. LIBOR is quoted on an actual/360-day year basis, whereas CMOs typically pay interest on 30/360-day basis. In order to eliminate this discrepancy, some CMO floaters pay interest on an actual/360-day year payment basis. Others "gross up" LIBOR to the equivalent rate on a 30/360-day year payment basis. Example coupon calculations for three CMO floating-rate tranches will help to illustrate this point. Exhibit 18 shows hypothetical coupon calculations for American Pioneer CMO Trust 1-A, Ryland

Exhibit 17: Impact of Payment Delay

Issuer and Series	Tranche	Nominal Coupon	Nominal Coupons under 3 LIBOR Scenarios	Coupon Payment Delay	Effective Coupon after Impact of Delay	Effective Spread over LIBOR Index
TMAC CMO Trust 1986-2	2-A	3-month LIBOR + .5%	6.60%	0 days	6.60%	.50%
			7.10		7.10	.50
			7.60		7.60	.50
Dean Witter CMO Trust 1	A	3-month LIBOR + .5%	6.60	30	6.56	.46
			7.10		7.06	.46
			7.60		7.55	.45
CMO Trust 13	A	1-month LIBOR + .5%	6.55	50	6.49	.44
			7.05		6.98	.43
			7.55		7.47	.42

Exhibit 18: Hypothetical Floating-Rate Coupon Computations

Issuer and Series	Tranche	3-Month LIBOR	Gross-Up Factor	Quoted Spread	Floating-Rate Coupon*	Payment Basis	Interest Period 3/1/87- 6/1/87	Interst per $1,000 Bond	Effective Spread over 3-Mo LIBOR 30/360	Actual/360
American Pioneer CMO Trust 1	1-A	6.25%	365/360	40%	6.74%	30/360	90 days	$16.842	.49%	.34%
Ryland Acceptance Corp. Series 23	23-A	6.25	N/A	40	6.65	Actual/ 360	92	16.994	.55	.40
N.W. Acceptance Corp. Series A	A-1	6.25	N/A	50	6.75	30/360	90	16.875	.50	.35

* Computed as follows: LIBOR × gross-up factor + quoted spread

Acceptance Corp. Four 23-A, and N.W. Acceptance Corp. A-1 CMOs; three-month LIBOR remains constant at 6.25% and the three bonds have the same payment period. The American Pioneer tranche pays interest on a 30/360-day basis but contains a gross-up provision. The Ryland Acceptance tranche pays interest on an actual/360-day basis. The N.W. Acceptance tranche pays interest on a 30/360-day basis with no gross-up provision. The results of the hypothetical computation show that the American Pioneer and N.W. Acceptance tranches have roughly equivalent effective coupons, and the Ryland Acceptance floating-rate tranche has an effective coupon greater than that of the N.W. Acceptance floating-rate tranche by five basis points. A comparison of the three floating-rate tranches without performing this analysis would lead one to believe that the coupon of the N.W. Acceptance tranche exceeded that of the other two by ten basis points.

Methodology for Comparing Returns of CMO Floaters. Using the methods discussed above, it is possible to express the quoted spreads of CMO floaters on a consistent quarterly pay basis. The spreads so derived incorporate the effects of differing coupon refix and payment frequencies, coupon payment delays, and gross-up provisions. Expressing the spreads on a consistent basis will help to identify relative value among floating-rate CMO tranches.

EVALUATING CMOs

The objective of most mortgage security analysis is to gain insight and create expectations of the cash flow pattern in various market environments. A three-step process can be employed in applying this type of analysis to CMO securities. The first phase involves examination of the pass-throughs or whole loans that collateralize the offering. The second step is to review the process by which principal and interest received from the collateral flows through to the bondholders of various tranches. The third phase of the analysis involves a determination of the impact of other special features on the expected cash flows to bondholders. Taken together, the three steps in the analysis process seek to make a determination of the likely pace of cash flows to CMO bondholders under various market environments.

Generally, greater uncertainty surrounding the timing of cash flows is perceived to represent the risk in a mortgage security. The end result is to evaluate the sufficiency of the yield to compensate the investor for the risks undertaken.

The Underlying Collateral

The following factors should be considered:

1. Average coupon and maturity

2. Range of coupons and maturities

3. Cash flow pattern of mortgages

    a. Level pay

    b. Graduated payment

    c. Other

4. Geographic distribution

5. Due-on-sale provisions

6. Prepayment history if seasoned

7. Amount of collateral relative to amount of bonds

The average and range of coupons and maturities, in combination with the geographic distribution, due-on-sale provisions, and prepayment history, are needed to forecast prepayments on the underlying collateral. It is necessary to forecast prepayments under various scenarios because of the impact they have on the amount of cash flow generated by the collateral.

Structure and Seasoning of a CMO

The amount of collateral backing the deal relative to the amount of CMO bonds outstanding is very significant. If a deal becomes over-collateralized, meaning that the amount of collateral exceeds that necessary to make payments to bondholders under any market scenario, the remaining bonds will be paid relatively quickly. If, however, the issuer is empowered to retain excess cash flow generated by the collateral, the bonds would not enjoy as much benefit of expected shortening of average life produced by over-collateralization. A build-up in the amount of collateral relative to the quantity of bonds can be caused by a number of factors. If the reinvestment rate or prepayment rate experience is more favorable than the extremely conservative assumptions employed when constructing the asset pool, then over-collateralization is likely to occur. Another assumption frequently employed is that if premium bonds (above the need to pay interest to CMO bondholders) are used to retire additional bonds, then the remaining principal amount of collateral will be greater than the remaining principal amount of bonds.

The sequential pay feature on CMOs makes the seasoning process even more significant for CMOs than for pass-throughs. As a first tranche is retired, for example, the holders of the second tranche move from no receipt of principal to an environment of rapid principal paydowns. Amortization and prepayments on the underlying collateral and retirements of CMO bond principal have an effect on both the long and short CMO tranches. Faster-than-anticipated retirement of the first tranche of bonds may shorten the final maturity and expected average life of not only the second tranche but also the longer tranches in the CMO offering. The yield tables, generally revised on the dates of prepayments to bondholders, reflect the effects of principal retirement and passage of time. Since actual prepayment speeds and expected amortization rates of the underlying collateral change over time, it is critical to use updated yield tables.

Sensitivity to Prepayment Changes

The major risk inherent in a mortgage security is the uncertainty of timing of cash flows. The primary source of uncertainty in a CMO is the prepayment rate on the underlying collateral. In order to determine the likely price sensitivity of a particular CMO to changing prepayments, one must consider several factors.

1. *Yield Effect.* If the price of a CMO bond differs from par, then the rate of prepayments has an effect on yield. For CMOs trading at a discount, a higher prepayment rate connotes faster retirement of principal and higher yield. A CMO trading at a premium to par suffers a decline in yield if prepayments rise on the underlying collateral.

2. *Average Life Effect.* Changes in the prepayment rate on the collateral generally affect the average life and final maturity of a CMO bond. The extent to which this occurs depends on the structure of the CMO offering.

3. *Yield-Spread Effect.* Most CMO bonds are quoted in terms of yield spread to the Treasury curve. Changes in the prepayment rate have a dual effect on this relationship. First, the CMO's yield may change if the price differs from par. Second, if the Treasury yield curve has a positive or negative slope, the reference yield on the Treasury curve may change from that originally assumed. A third factor must be considered for in-depth analysis. If prepayment rates rise and a CMO with an original average life assumption of seven years moves to an average life assumption of four years, then the required spread to the Treasury curve may change. Assuming that yield spreads should tighten as the expected average life shortens, this would exert upward pressure on a CMO's price.

4. *Special Features.* A change in prepayments may trigger a minimum guaranteed sinking fund. To the extent that this fund mitigates the effect of slower prepayments on cash

flow to bondholders, it reduces the bond's sensitivity to changes in prepayment rates.

The net effect of the factors listed above determines the impact of changing prepayment rates on the price and return of CMOs. An investor must be aware of CMO yield, yield spread to Treasuries, and the comparison point on the Treasury yield curve in order to evaluate sensitivity to prepayments. The universe of CMO tranches has vastly differing sensitivities to prepayment rates on underlying collateral. To the extent that this sensitivity causes risk, the investor must be compensated in the form of yield.

The Coupon Rate and Relationship of CMO Price to Par

These factors will determine the current yield and likely impact of increased prepayments on yields and returns. All else being equal, a CMO trading at par should have a greater yield spread to Treasuries than a CMO trading at a discount. As in all other fixed-income sectors, the incremental call risk in a current coupon relative to a discount coupon requires incremental yield spread to represent fair value. It should be recognized, however, that the speed of retirements will be more dependent on the interest rates of the collateral pool than on the price of the CMO bonds.

CHAPTER 13

FLOATING-RATE COLLATERALIZED MORTGAGE OBLIGATIONS

Lakhbir S. Hayre, DPhil
Director of Mortgage Research
Financial Strategies Group
Prudential Securities Inc.

THE FLOATING RATE CMO MARKET

The Market So Far

The first floating-rate collateralized mortgage obligation (FRCMO) was issued on September 22, 1986. This issue, SLB CMO Trust D, was a four-class CMO with the first class having a coupon that was to be reset quarterly at 37.5 basis points above three-month LIBOR. The FRCMO was an immediate success, with close to $20

The author would like to thank the following individuals for their assistance: Vito Lodato, Gladys Cardona and Lisa Pendergast.

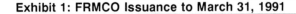

Exhibit 1: FRMCO Issuance to March 31, 1991

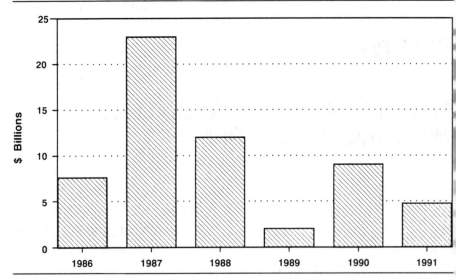

billion in FRCMO bonds issued in the six months after its introduction. Since then, floaters have been a staple of the CMO market, with the amount of FRCMOs dependent to a large extent on
the spread between Treasury rates and LIBOR. Exhibit 1 shows
issuance of FRCMOs since their introduction in 1986.

The market has stabilized and matured considerably since the
first FRCMO issue, much of this being spurred by the need to
make FRCMOs comparable to traditional floating-rate notes
(FRNs) in the international markets.

Indices and Margins. Most FRCMOs have used LIBOR as the index, primarily because it is the rate used as a base by major international investors in floating-rate instruments; there have,
however, been FRCMOs that have used other indices, such as the
Eleventh District Cost-of-Funds Index (EDCOFI) and the prime
rate. The margin over LIBOR was 37.5 basis points in the first FR-
CMO issue, but this subsequently increased. This was partly due
to an increased supply of FRCMOs, and partly due to investors
realizing the impact of payment delays, coupon caps, prepayment

uncertainty, and the use of a 360-day year compared with the 365-day year used for FRNs (discussed in detail later). Margins over LIBOR have generally been between fifty and eighty basis points, depending on the maturity of the floater and the coupon cap.

Payment Delays. The delay in interest payments, a common fixture of fixed-rate CMOs, has been generally eliminated from floating CMO classes, again to make them more comparable to FRNs. There is no delay in the bond payments. Until the advent of FRCMOs, most CMOs, which at the time were generally quarterly pay, had a one-month delay, primarily to collect three mortgage payments before the first quarterly bond payment. Such delays are not a major concern to CMO investors, because delays are taken into account when yields are calculated. However, traditional investors in floating-rate instruments are not accustomed to delays. As a result, delays were eliminated from most FRCMOs to make them more comparable to other floating-rate instruments. The elimination of the payment delay may force the issuer to advance money to make the first bond payment. To reduce the size of any such cash advance, a number of FRCMOs have been issued with the floating class having no delay and the fixed-rate classes having a one-month delay (the payment dates are the same for all classes, so in effect the floating class has a long first coupon).

Coupon Caps. The caps on floater coupons, a structural necessity, have been simplified. The first few FRCMOs had a series of ascending caps that leveled off after a few years. The first FRCMO, for example, had a cap of 9% in the first year, 10% in the second, 11% in the third, 11.5% in the fourth, and 12% from the fifth year onward. However, after the initial few issues, most FRCMOs, like capped FRNs, had a single lifetime cap.

Maturity and Paydown Structure. Early FRCMOs were structured with the first tranche as the floating-rate class and all the subsequent tranches as fixed rate. Structural diversity has grown since these early issues, and many FRCMOs have had several floating classes of varying maturities. The need to support floating-rate bonds with fixed-rate collateral has led to the development of a distinctive type of CMO bond: *inverse floaters*, whose coupons move in the reverse direction to LIBOR. These are discussed in more detail in the next section.

Structuring Considerations

To date, FRCMOs have been collateralized by fixed-rate mortgage securities. In order for a CMO to receive a AAA rating, the collateral cash flows, supplemented if necessary by a Letter of Credit (LOC) from a AAA-rated institution that guarantees to make up any cash flow shortfalls, must be able to support the debt service to the bonds under any level of interest or prepayment rates. Since the coupon index (generally LIBOR) could theoretically increase without limit, a LOC without a cap on the coupon would be prohibitively expensive. This in effect makes a cap on the coupon a structural necessity.

To avoid the necessity of a LOC, issuers have devised bonds that often pay down simultaneously with the floating-class bond, with the weighted-average coupon (WAC) of the simultaneous bonds being such that the debt service to the bonds can be supported by the collateral cash flows, whatever the interest and prepayment levels. One such type of bond is a low-coupon, deep-discount class. However, the most common complement to FRCMOs are inverse floaters.

Inverse Floaters. Introduced in October 1986, an inverse floater moves in the reverse direction to LIBOR, with the size of the move being chosen so as to balance the change in the floater coupon. The coupon on the inverse floater is changed according to a specified formula. An example is provided by the $1 billion FHLMC Series 128 issue, underwritten by Prudential Securities, Incorporated (PSI) in January 1990 and collateralized by FHLMC 9% pass-

Exhibit 2: FRCMO and Inverse Floater Classes in FHLMC 128

Deal ID	: FHL0128	Deal Date	: 01/03/90
Series	: 128	Delivery Date	: 01/30/90
Underwriter	: PB	Dated Date	: 01/15/90
Issuer	: FEDERAL HOME LOAN MORTGAGE CORPORATION		
Collateral	: 100% FH (Real)	Deal Type	: CMO
NWAC (Orig)	: 9.000 (9.000)	Pricing Speed:	: PSA 165.00
GWAC (Orig)	: 9.749	Rating	: AAA S&P
WAM (Orig)	: 29.197 (29.830)	Coupon Range	: 9.000-9.000
Size	: 1,000,000,000		
Trustee	: FEDERAL RESERVE BANK OF NEW YORK	Modeled	: Y

Class	Coupon	Mat	Amt 000	Avg. Life	Sprd.	Price	Yield		Description
...	...	...	...	...	...	...	...	...	.....
128K	9.025	4/20	64,000	13.7	65	100-00	9.200	FLT	LIBOR - 1M+65, Cap 11.25
128L	8.900	4/20	16,000	13.7	53	79-12	12.310	IFL	12.310 IFL 42.4 - (4.0 × LIBOR - 1M)
...	...	...	...	...	...	...	...	...	.....

throughs. The floater is class K, and the inverse floater is class L (see Exhibit 2).

The floater class size is $64 million and the inverse floater class size is $16 million; the two pay down simultaneously, with the floater receiving $4 of principal for every $1 of principal received by the inverse floater. The floater coupon is reset monthly at sixty-five basis points over one-month LIBOR, subject to a cap of 11.25%, while the coupon on the inverse floater is calculated using the formula

$$Coupon = 42.4 - 4 \times LIBOR \qquad (1)$$

with a floor of 0%. All inverse floaters issued so far have coupons calculated according to a formula very similar to the one above. The multiplier, 4, of the LIBOR rate in the formula can be termed the "leverage" of the inverse floater. This number is largely dictated by the size of the inverse floater class relative to the size of the floater class; if the floater class is four times as big as the inverse floater class, then the inverse floater coupon must move four basis points in order to balance the effect of a one-basis-point move in the floater coupon. Note that in this example, the weighted average coupon on the floater and the inverse floater is always equal to 9%, the coupon on the collateral.

In some cases, the inverse floater does not balance the floater exactly; some variation is allowed while ensuring that the WAC is less than the collateral coupon.

INVESTMENT CHARACTERISTICS

Investing in Floating-Rate Instruments

Institutional investors who participate in the floating-rate market are motivated by one or more of the following factors:

- Floaters have low price volatility compared to fixed-rate bonds. Essentially, they behave like money market instruments and are priced close to par. Floaters have lower interest rate risk than fixed-rate debt, and thus are considered defensive instruments.

- Floaters allow better asset/liability matching for institutions with liabilities that have low interest rate volatilities and for institutions, such as banks and thrifts, with floating-rate liabilities.

- Floaters are viewed by certain investors as passive substitutes for shorter-term money market holdings. Investors save on the cost of constantly rolling over short-term investments as they mature, and floating-rate instruments generally provide slightly higher coupons. Most floaters are based on LIBOR, which is usually the highest short-term rate available. Floaters have consistently outperformed money market instruments in the past, although of course there is no guarantee that they will do so in the future.

- Some participants, such as banks, finance these securities at floating rates and attempt to lock in the margin, that is, the spread between their borrowing rate and the coupon rate on the floaters. Other types of arbitrage with varying degrees of risk are also possible. For example, an institution could borrow at one-month LIBOR and invest in a six-month LIBOR floater, earning a margin equal to the spread between the one-month and six-month LIBORs. The risk here is that one-month LIBOR might exceed the six-month rate over any coupon period.

Floating-rate CMOs were introduced to widen the appeal of CMOs to international investors who traditionally have been major buyers of FRNs. Therefore, they were intentionally structured to have many similarities to traditional FRNs. In many ways, FRC-MOs combine MBS features, such as uncertain maturity, high credit quality, and collateralization, with the properties of FRNs, such as the periodic resetting of the coupon based on LIBOR. However, certain differences remain.

Collateralization. Whereas traditional FRNs are direct obligations of the issuer, CMOs are often issued through a special-purpose entity, which is legally distinct from the sponsor or the issuer.[1] The entity issuing the CMO usually has no assets or income other than the collateral supporting the CMO issue.

The CMO is fully collateralized, in the sense that the incoming cash flows from the collateral (combined, in a few cases, with a LOC from a AAA-rated entity) are sufficient to pay the CMO bonds under any interest rate or prepayment levels. Even in cases in which an FRN is collateralized—for example, collateralized

---

[1] REMICs issued by FNMA and FHLMC are direct obligations, of course, of the issuer.

Eurodollar thrift FRNs—FRCMO is characteristically different. The thrift FRN:

- remains, in general, a direct obligation of the issuer—the collateral coming into play only when the issuer is unable to meet the interest and principal payments.

- has a maturity that is fixed at issuance and is not dependent on the behavior of the underlying collateral. The collateral itself can be of various types, including mortgages, MBSs, U.S. Treasury obligations, and money market instruments. Since cash flows are not matched to the cash flow on the FRN, significant over-collateralization is required to justify high credit quality.

Rating. The credit quality of FRNs spans the spectrum of FRN issuers, from sovereigns to BBB-rated issuing organizations. FRCMOs, on the other hand, typically have low default risk and are rated AAA in almost all cases. The rating agencies impose very strict conditions before they will issue a AAA rating on a CMO: it has to be fully collateralized (if necessary, with a LOC from a AAA-rated institution), as discussed previously; if the collateral is not agency (GNMA, FHLMC, and FNMA) pass-throughs, which have U.S. Government or quasi-government guarantees against default, then it must be insured by a AAA-rated guaranteeing company, and the collateral must be held in trust by a third-party custodial bank. These considerations indicate that a CMO bond has virtually no chance of defaulting. Even if the issuer were to become bankrupt, the bondholders are not likely to be affected.[2]

---

[2] This actually happened with a CMO issuer—the Epic Acceptance Corporation. Epic went bankrupt after issuing a CMO in March 1985, but the fully collateralized structure of the CMO, combined with the fact that the collateral was held in trust by a third-party bank, ensured that the bondholders were not affected.

Uncertainty in Maturity. Traditional FRNs have fixed and known maturities (except for perpetual floaters). Even when the maturity is modified by call and put features, the investor can usually make reasonable assumptions as to the probable redemption date. In any case, when the note is redeemed, it is paid in full. The FR-CMO, on the other hand, has uncertain cash flows, and principal repayment occurs in variable amounts in every payment period. The payments are largely, but not totally, interest-rate sensitive. To the extent that the redeemed mortgages are refinanced at fixed rates, the prepayments can be sensitive to long-term rates rather than to LIBOR or other short-term rates. However, unless the cap is reached on the coupon, cash flow uncertainty is not typically a major concern for floating-rate investors, since interim cash flows can be reinvested in new floaters.

Caps. While the majority of traditional FRNs is issued without limits on coupon rates, one key characteristic of the FRCMO, as mentioned previously, is the cap. The higher spread of LIBOR of FRCMOs, as compared with transitional FRNs, is in some respects compensation for the presence of the cap. However, the spread is somewhat higher than for high-quality, capped FRNs, as discussed further later in this section. As discussed later in this section, the FRCMO generally offers higher returns on a cap-adjusted basis than most FRNs.

Sensitivity Under Interest Rate Changes

A key characteristic of MBSs is that their future cash flows are dependent, through prepayments, on future interest rates. This makes prepayment assumptions and projections critical in evaluating the investment characteristics of MBSs. FRCMOs reduce the importance of prepayments, since, like other floating-rate instruments, their durations are low and relatively unaffected by the level of prepayments. The floating coupon also means that rein-

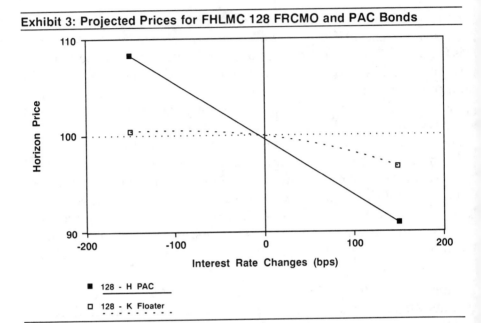

Exhibit 3: Projected Prices for FHLMC 128 FRCMO and PAC Bonds

vestment risk is not a major consideration; the coupon on the floater will generally move in line with reinvestment rates.

As stated previously, floating-rate instruments are defensive in nature. As rates increase, the coupon on the floater increases, and, unless the coupon is close to a cap, the floater will be priced at or close to par. By contrast, a fixed-rate instrument will gain in price if rates fall (although there is some price compression for MBSs because of increasing prepayments) and decrease in price if rates rise, thus providing both greater upside and greater downside potential.

This is illustrated in Exhibit 3, which shows projected prices, assuming OASs stay unchanged, under parallel interest rate shifts for the FHLMC 128 floater and for tranche H of this CMO, a PAC bond with a similar average life to the floating class.

Like typical fixed-coupon bonds, the PAC will perform well if rates decline and perform poorly if rates increase. The floating-rate bond's return follows that market, in that the coupon rises if rates go up and decreases if rates go down, and hence the price stays close to par. However, note that as rates rise, the 11.25% coupon begins to have an effect and lowers the price.

Comparing FRCMOs and FRNs: The Discount Margin

The yield calculation and quoting conventions of the FRCMO are those of the domestic MBS markets. FRNs, on the other hand, are generally evaluated by calculating a margin over the reference index (LIBOR). The most common valuation technique in the international FRN market is the *discount margin* over the index, and this has become a common means of comparing FRCMOs with other floating-rate instruments. The marketing and subsequent popularity of FRCMOs in Europe focused attention on a number of differences between the conventions for MBSs and those used to calculate the discount margin. These differences include the following.

Compounding Frequency. The yields of MBSs, like those of Treasury or corporate securities, are quoted on a bond-equivalent basis, which assumes semiannual compounding of interest. The discount margin is based on the actual frequency of payments.

Number of Days of Interest. FRCMO bonds, like all MBSs, pay interest on a 30/360 basis. In other words, a year is assumed to have 360 days and each month is assumed to have 30 days. On the other hand, the discount margin, while assuming a 360-day year for purposes of coupon calculation, pays interest for the actual number of days. For example, in a monthly pay case, if the coupon is 7% and a given month has thirty-one days, then the FRCMO will pay interest equal to

$$Balance \times 7\% \times (1/12), \tag{2}$$

whereas the FRN will pay interest equal to

$$Balance \times 7\% \times (31/360) \tag{3}$$

Exhibit 4: Discount Margins for FHLMC 128K FRCMO and for a FRN

	Index Value	Coupon	Approximate Adjustments Monthly-Pay	Day Count	Discount Margin 1-Month LIBOR (bps)
FHLMC 128K 1m L +65	6.1875	6.8375	N/A	-10bps	56
FRN 6m L +20	6.50	6.70	-9.5bps	N/A	30

Note: Both securities assumed to be priced at par. Analysis based on LIBOR at close of April 23, 1991. Cash flows for FHLMC 128K derived using Prudential Securities prepayment model prjections.

---

so that over a whole year, other things being equal, the FRN will pay 365/360 (or 366/360 in a leap year) times as much interest as the FRCMO.

The appendix to this chapter gives a formula that defines the discount margin.[3] Although this appears complicated, it bears a strong resemblance to the formula defining cash flow yield. In fact, as shown in the appendix, a simple yet accurate approximation for the discount margin can be derived in terms of the cash flow yield.

Exhibit 4 shows a comparison, by means of the discount margin, of two floaters: the FHLMC 128K FRCMO, which pays and adjusts monthly at sixty-five basis points over one-month LIBOR subject to a cap of 11.25%, and a hypothetical semiannual pay capless AAA-rated FRN that adjusts semiannually at twenty basis points over six-month LIBOR.

Exhibit 4 also shows the approximate value of two adjustments made in the calculation of the discount margin. The first adjustment is made to obtain a common coupon frequency, which is assumed to be monthly in this example. This adjustment is made to the semiannual par FRN, and lowers its coupon by about 9.5 basis

---

[3] This definition assumes a money market actual/360 calendar basis. The discount margin can also be calculated using a 30/360 bond-equivalent basis; see the PSA's Uniform Practices Manual.

points. The second adjustment is for the day count convention; the FRCMO pays on a 30/360 basis, whereas the FRN pays on an actual/360 basis. Adjusting the FRCMO for an actual/360 basis lowers its effective coupon by about 10 basis points.

Based on the discount margins, the FRCMO appears to offer better value. However, the discount margin suffers from two serious flaws as a comparative valuation measure. First, it essentially ignores coupon caps, so that the negative affect of the FRCMO's cap is not reflected in the discount margin. Second, it ignores the information provided by the LIBOR and swap curves, that is, it does not calibrate the analysis to the LIBOR "term structure." Below, we describe how option-adjusted spread analysis can be used to incorporate the effects of coupon caps and of the LIBOR term structure into a sound comparative valuation of floaters and other instruments.

Option-Adjusted Analysis

This section describes how option-adjusted spread (OAS) analysis[4] can be used to evaluate the cost of the coupon cap for a FRCMO. Such an evaluation factors in all relevant variables, such as interest rate volatility, the paydown structure of the CMO, the prepayment characteristics and potential of the collateral, and so on. While the concept of a "cap-adjusted" discount margin, which uses similar methodology, was developed earlier by the author, the advantage of option-adjusted analysis is that as well as evaluating the cost of the cap, it also allows FRCMOs to be compared with floating-rate instruments based on different indices, and in fact with fixed-rate securities as well.[5]

The methodology involves the usual steps in OAS analysis: a large number of random paths of interest rates are generated, and

---

[4] For a general description of option-adjusted analysis, see Chapter 27.
[5] Option-adjusted analysis is also essential for obtaining accurate salvage values in horizon analysis of FRCMOs, with the horizon price being calculated so as to a given specified OAS.

cash flows for the collateral and CMO bonds are obtained for each path and discounted to the present by the short-term Treasury rates on the path plus a spread. The spread that makes the average of the present values over all paths equal to the market price of a bond is defined to be the bond's OAS. Since the discount rates are calibrated so that all on-the-run Treasuries have a zero OAS, the OAS can be interpreted as the incremental return over the riskless rate (which is defined as the return obtained from investing in on-the-run Treasuries).

In addition to calibrating the discount-rate paths to the Treasury curve, the LIBOR paths can be calibrated to the LIBOR/Treasury swap curve, so that an investor is indifferent between the floating and fixed sides of the swap. As with the discount-rate calibration, this introduces implied trends into the paths of LIBOR rates.

Exhibit 5 gives OASs for the FHLMC 128K FRCMO.

Exhibit 5: Option-Adjusted Spreads for FHLMC 128K FRCMO

	Index Value	Coupon	OAS Volatility			
			0%	10%	15%	20%
FHLMC 128K	6.1875	6.8375	108	71	36	9

Note: The FRCMO is assumed to be priced at par. Analysis based on prices and yields at close of April 23, 1991. Cash flows for FHLMC 128K derived using PSI prepayment model projections.

The OAS is expressed on a bond-equivalent (BE) basis; that is, assuming semiannual compounding and a 30/360-day count basis. It is also in essence a spread over Treasuries rather than LIBOR. The monthly pay FRCMO gains both from the conversion to a semiannual pay basis, and from the current differential of about twenty basis points between one-month LIBOR and short-term Treasury rates. This explains why the zero-volatility OAS, at 108 basis points, is higher than the nominal margin of 65 basis points over LIBOR.

The differences between the OASs at 0% and higher volatilities measure the effects of coupon caps and prepayment variations. Recall that the OAS of a security can be interpreted as its excess return over the risk-free rate, which is defined as the return obtained by investing in on-the-run U.S. Treasuries. Hence, after adjustments for features such as payment frequencies, day count conventions, and coupon caps, and assuming a Treasury bill rate volatility of 15% per annum, the FRCMO is projected to provide an average return thirty-six basis points higher than the risk-free rate. This allows us to compare the FRCMO and other securities on a sound apples-to-apples basis.

Cost of the Cap for Generic FRCMOs. The exact analysis of a FRCMO, such as the one in Exhibit 5, will involve modeling the particular CMO structure. However, a quick approximate estimate of the cost of the cap on a FRCMO can be obtained by means of a table such as the one shown in Exhibit 6. The cost is defined to be the difference in OASs (in basis points) between the FRCMO and a hypothetical uncapped but otherwise identical FRCMO.

Exhibit 6 shows the cost of the cap for generic FRCMOs of several different average lives, for caps from 11% to 14%, and volatilities of 10%, 15%, and 20%, and an initial value for one-month LIBOR of 6.5%. A traditional, clean, five-tranche sequential-pay structure is assumed, with the amounts chosen so that the first four classes, which are floating-rate, have average lives of approximately two, five, seven, and ten years. Results are shown for two types of collateral: FNMA 9s, a slight discount coupon, and GNMA 11s, a low premium coupon. The margins over LIBOR are representative for the given average lives; for margins different from those shown, interpolation can be used. For example, if the actual margin for a two-year FRCMO is sixty basis points (instead of the fifty basis points used in Exhibit 4), and the cap is 13%, then since we are ten basis points closer to the cap, we can assume a cap of 12.90%. We can then determine the cap cost by interpolating between the 12% and 13% caps. Interpolation can also be used for different initial values of LIBOR. For example, an initial LIBOR

Exhibit 6: OAS Cost of the Cap for Generic FRCMOs

FNMA 9 Collateral			Cost (in bps) of a Coupon Cap of			
	FRCMO Average Life	Spd Over LIBOR (bps)	11%	12%	13%	14%
Volatility						
10%	2	50	12	4	1	0
	5	65	27	11	4	1
	7	80	39	19	9	4
	10	100	49	26	14	8
15%	2	50	31	16	8	3
	5	65	62	38	23	14
	7	80	79	51	33	22
	10	100	93	62	42	28
20%	2	50	56	35	22	14
	5	65	102	72	51	36
	7	80	122	89	65	47
	10	100	135	100	74	55

GNMA 11 Collateral

	FRCMO Average Life	Spd Over LIBOR (bps)	11%	12%	13%	14%
Volatility						
10%	2	50	17	6	2	0
	5	65	36	18	8	4
	7	80	46	24	13	7
	10	100	56	31	17	10
15%	2	50	46	26	15	8
	5	65	81	53	34	22
	7	80	92	62	41	28
	10	100	102	70	47	32
20%	2	50	82	56	38	26
	5	65	128	93	68	50
	7	80	137	101	75	55
	10	100	144	108	81	60

A sequential-pay five class CMO structure is assumed, with the floating-rate class successively assumed to be the first, second, third and fourth tranche of the CMO. The cost of the cap is defined to be the difference in OASs at a 0% and at the stated volatility.

The stated volatility is that of short-term Treasury rates. Mortgage rates are assumed to be 60% as volatile as short-term rates. LIBOR is assumed to move in parallel with short-term Treasury rates, with the initial value of LIBOR being 6.5%.

rate of 8.5% and a cap of 13% is comparable to an initial value of 9% and a cap of 13.5%.

Exhibit 6 provides insight into the interaction of market volatility, collateral characteristics, and bond maturity on the value of the cap. Some observations:

- Increased market volatility increases the likelihood of hitting the cap, hence the greater the cost of a specified cap for a particular average-life FRCMO.

- The longer the average life, the more the time available for the cap to be hit, hence the greater the cap cost.

- In general, all other things being equal, the caps on FRCMOs collateralized by premium coupons cost more than on those collateralized by current coupons. This can be explained by the fact that if interest rates increase (and the coupon cap is reached), the prepayments on the premium coupons will slow down much more than on current coupons or discounts, and this will accentuate the effect of the coupon cap.

Exhibit 6 can be used to assess the effects of different collateral, LIBOR spreads, and life caps. For example, for FNMA 9 collateral, at a 15% short-term rate volatility, a five-year average life FRCMO with a 13% cap has about the same cap cost as a seven-year average life FRCMO with a 14% cap. Alternatively, we can say that, generally speaking, if FRCMOs with WALs of five and seven years have the same cap, then the margin on the seven-year FRCMO should be about ten basis points higher. An important caveat, of course, is that this generic analysis does not consider possible structural differences (and resulting average-life sensitivity to prepayments) between different FRCMOs.

THE RESIDUAL OF A FRCMO

The residual cash flows from a CMO with floating-rate classes are more complex than those from a fixed-rate CMO. Typically, the major component of CMO residual cash flows is the spread between the coupons on the collateral and those on the bonds. For a CMO with all fixed-coupon classes, this spread does not change as interest rates change. Hence, if interest rates increase, prepayments will decline, leaving collateral principal outstanding for a longer period of time. This leads to larger residual cash flows and higher returns for the residual holders. Similarly, if interest rates decline, prepayments will speed up, leaving principal outstanding for a shorter period of time; this leads to smaller residual cash flows and lower returns for the residual holders.

However, for a CMO with floating classes, the average spread between the collateral and the bond coupons will decrease as interest rates increase and increase as interest rates decrease, thus balancing to some extent the effects of changes in prepayments. The exact effects on the residual cash flows of the interaction between changes in the floating coupons and changes in prepayment rates will depend on the particular CMO issue. Important factors include:

1. The size of the floating classes relative to the total CMO size—the larger the floating amounts, the greater the effects of the coupon changes.

2. The relative positions of the floating class or classes, since shorter-maturity classes are the most important for the residual.

3. The types of other classes in the issue—a floater combined with an inverse floater behaves basically like a fixed-rate class, whereas deep-discount bonds contribute to a large average spread between the collateral and bond coupons, and reduce the relative importance of the spread between the collateral and the floating-class coupons.

However, the most important factor is generally the collateral, and, in particular, its prepayment volatility if interest rates change. Three cases may be distinguished.

Current-Coupon Collateral. There may be a minor slowdown in prepayments if rates rise, and an increase in prepayments if rates decline more than 100 or so basis points. This type of FRCMO residual generally has little upside potential. If rates increase, the larger floating coupons will lead to lower returns, and if rates fall, there may be an increase in return for small drops. For larger declines (100 basis points or more), increasing prepayments will tend to overwhelm the benefits of smaller floater coupons. This type of FRCMO residual has been referred to as a "humped" or "peaked" residual.

Low-Premium Collateral. Collateral with underlying mortgage coupons between 200 to 300 basis points above current mortgage rates have the greatest prepayment volatility and produce the most interesting FRCMO residuals. The collateral may already be experiencing fairly high levels of prepayments. If rates increase, there may be a dramatic slowdown in prepayments that will balance the effect of the increases in the floater coupons. If rates decline, there may be an initial increase in prepayments, but this increase will level off as rates fall further. Hence, the returns on the residual may decline initially but then start increasing as rates fall further. Therefore, the residual is fairly stable across a range of interest rate moves, and has been referred to as a "stable" residual.

High-Premium Collateral. Prepayments will not change greatly for interest rate moves of up to 100 to 200 basis points. The return on the residual will rise if interest rates decline, since prepayments will already have peaked, and the return will drop if interest rates go up, due to the decreasing spread between the collateral and bond coupons. The residual's behavior is thus the reverse of a standard fixed-rate CMO residual, and it may be termed a "bull residual." To date, no FRCMO has been issued with this type of collateral.

An important caveat is that the preceding discussion assumes that LIBOR and mortgage rates move in parallel. There is no certainty, of course, that they will actually do so. A steepening of the yield curve, with short-term rates declining and long rates stable, will tend to benefit investors in FRCMO residuals. On the other hand, an increase in LIBOR without a corresponding increase in mortgage rates may adversely affect an FRCMO residual.

SUMMARY

FRCMOs are a major innovation in the CMO markets. They are designed to appeal to traditional investors in floating-rate instruments, particularly in the international FRN market.[6] They have proven to be immensely popular and have considerably broadened the market for CMOs. The major reason for their success is that they combine very high credit quality (as indicated in this chapter, there is little chance of a CMO bond defaulting, and their AAA rating arguably means more than a similar rating on a corporate bond or a traditional FRN) with the defensive attributes of floating-rate instruments: low price volatility and little reinvestment rate risk. At the same time, they provide yields that are higher than those of other comparable floating-rate instruments or money market securities.

The discount margin, typically used to compare FRNs, is inadequate as a valuation measure for capped floaters. This chapter has discussed how OASs can be a useful technique for valuing capped floating-rate instruments. It can be used to obtain the cost of a cap of a FRCMO bond or a capped FRN. It also allows comparative evaluation of capped floating-rate instruments with different caps, reset margins, maturities, and other features. It can

---

[6] Incidentally, one effect of FRCMOs has been to increase the margins over LIBOR offered on FRNs.

thus serve the same purpose for comparing FRCMOs as the effective margin does for ARMs.

In summary, it seems clear that FRCMOs will remain a major segment of the secondary mortgage markets. Their defensive nature, high credit quality, and high yields relative to comparable floater or money market instruments are likely to keep them popular with institutional investors.

APPENDIX: AN APPROXIMATION FOR THE DISCOUNT MARGIN

The discount margin, (equation), is defined as the solution of the equation[7]

$$P + I = \sum_{i=1}^{N} \frac{CF_i}{(1 + (L_1 + d)t_1)(1 + (L_2 + d)t_2). \, . \, .(1 + L_i + d)t_i)} \, .$$

P = Price.
I = Accrued interest.
L_i = Assumed value of the LIBOR index in period i.
CF_i = Cash flow in period i.
N = Number of periods.
t_j = Actual number of days in the jth period divided by 360.

Assume that $L_i \equiv L$, i.e., LIBOR is assumed to be constant for the life of the security.[8] In practice, L is usually taken to be the current value of LIBOR.

Let f = payment frequency per year (e.g., $f = 4$ if the bond is quarterly pay).

Now, $t_j = \frac{365.25}{360 \times f} + e_j = t + e_j$, say, for $j \geq 2$,

---

[7] This is the traditional definition, based on money market (actual/360) conventions. The PSA's *Uniform Practices Manual* also gives a second definition which used a bond-equivalent (30/360) basis.

[8] Note that for the first period, the number of days is measured from the settlement date to the first payment date.

where t = the average number of days in a payment period, divided by 360

and e_j = the difference between t and t_j.

For $j = 1$, $t_j = \theta t + e_j$, where θ is the length of the period from settlement to the first coupon expressed as a proportion of t.

The error term e_j is, first, very small in all cases (for example, for quarterly pay bonds, $t = 91.3125/360$, while t_j varies between $90/360$ and $92/360$) and, second, consecutive e_j's tend to cancel each other, so that over one year, the sum of the e_j's is essentially zero. (It would be exactly zero if leapyears are forgotten and a figure of 365 days is used instead of 365.25.)

Substituting $t_j = t + e_j$ ($t_j = \theta + e_j$ for $j = 1$) into equation (1) and using a Taylor series expansion shows that to a very close approximation, the discount margin is the solution of

$$P + I = \sum_{i=1}^{N} \frac{CF_i}{1 + (L + d)t)^{i + \theta - 1}}. \tag{2}$$

The cash flow yield, on a compounding frequency basis of f, is the solution of

$$P + I = \sum_{i=1}^{N} \frac{CF_i}{(1 + \frac{y}{f})^{i + \theta - 1}} \tag{3}$$

For positive cash flows, equation (2) [or equation (3)] has a unique solution. Hence

$$(L + d)t = \frac{y}{f}.$$

or

$$d = y \times \frac{360}{365.25} - L.$$

If y is the yield on a bond-equivalent (semi-annual compounding basis), then

$$y = f(1 + \frac{y_s}{2})^{2/f} - f.$$

Therefore, the discount margin is approximately given by

$$d = (f(1 + \frac{y_s}{2})^{2/f} - f) \times \frac{360}{365.25} - L.$$

This approximation is very accurate, the error being less than 0.2 basis points in most cases. If the periods of the bond's cash flows do not include a leap year, then 365.25 should be replaced by 365.

CHAPTER 14

INTRODUCTION TO CMO PAC BONDS

William J. Curtin
Senior Vice President
Lehman Brothers Inc.

Paul T. Van Valkenburg
Principal
Mortgage Industry Advisory Corp.

For years, some investors reluctantly decided to forgo the investment opportunities available in mortgage-backed securities because of their unwillingness to accept the uncertainty inherent in the cash flows. Collateralized mortgage obligations (CMOs), with their sequential prioritization of cash flows, were created primarily to address this concern. Although extremely successful, the initial CMO structures did not restrict the cash flow uncertainty to a degree sufficient for some investors.

Planned amortization class (PAC) bonds were the next step in satisfying those investors' needs. PAC bonds significantly increase the certainty and stability of the cash flows, while retaining much of the higher yields that mortgage-backed securities provide. These structures protect investors from having their bonds called when interest rates fall, and also from extending when interest rates rise. As a result, PAC bonds typically have small negative convexities or sometimes even positive convexities. The combination of cash flow stability, high credit quality, small negative convexities, and high yields make PAC bonds an attractive investment vehicle in the fixed-income markets.

In this chapter we will describe the features of PAC bonds and their characteristics that affect their rate-of-return profile. In Chapter 19, PAC accrual bonds are discussed. In Chapter 25, PAC bonds in which the collateral is a principal-only MBS are covered.

PAC BOND FEATURES

PAC bonds have several unique features not found in other mortgage-backed securities. Each PAC tranche has a specific principal payment schedule that is met as long as prepayment rates stay within a specified range. This certainty of cash flow is extremely valuable to many types of investors.

The scheduled principal payments of PAC bonds are protected from varying prepayments *by prioritizing the principal payments from the underlying collateral.* The PAC tranche is senior in order of receipt of principal, while the companion tranches (i.e., non-PAC or support tranches) are subordinate. In effect, the companion bonds serve to protect or cushion the PAC bond(s). As a result, the impact of varying prepayment levels on the cash flows of companion bonds is exaggerated. If prepayments increase, the companion bonds receive all the additional principal to ensure that there is not an overpayment of principal on the PAC. When prepayments are slow, principal is redirected from the companion tranches to the PAC in order to meet its specified principal payment schedule. In this sense, PAC bonds may be thought of as somewhat analogous to corporate sinking fund bonds. Many PAC classes also accrue all prior principal shortfalls to the PAC schedule, ensuring that all of these shortfalls are eventually recaptured when the principal is available.

THE PREPAYMENT COLLAR

As the prepayments on the underlying collateral reach and sustain certain levels (either high or low), the scheduled principal cash flow of the PAC can be disrupted. Prepayment collars are the highest and lowest possible prepayment rates that could be sustained until maturity of the PAC and not cause such a disruption. This does not imply, however, that if prepayments fall outside the collar the PAC's principal schedule is automatically broken. Neither does it imply that if the PAC schedule is broken, this is a permanent condition. The implications of prepayments falling outside the collar are discussed in more detail in the following section.

The PAC bond's prepayment collar is an important feature in assessing its relative value. It is the prepayment collar that determines the degree of call protection and extension risk for a PAC. Some PAC bonds have very weak collars (little call protection), whereas others are protected to the point where the principal payment needed to satisfy the schedule is guaranteed for all intents and purposes. Thus, in order to compare PAC bonds against each other or versus other fixed-income securities, it is important to understand the role of the prepayment collar.

The PAC collar is created by initially generating the principal cash flows from the collateral at different constant prepayment speeds. The principal cash flows of DBL Q are displayed when the collateral prepays at 75 and 350% PSA in Exhibit 1. The dashed line represents the principal cash flows when the collateral prepays at 350% PSA, and the solid line represents the principal cash flows when the collateral prepays at 75% PSA. Notice that at the lower PSA rates the principal payments are very stable. In the early years, more of the principal cash flow comes from prepayments, and in the later years the scheduled principal payments

---

Exhibit 1: Available Cash Flows for a PAC Bond (DBL Q)

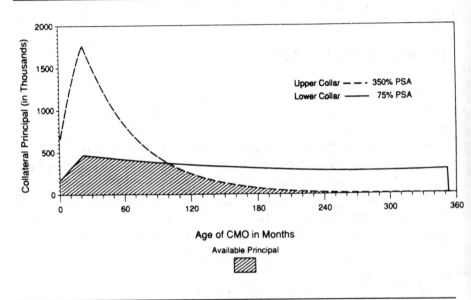

rise as prepayment dollars decline. In the faster prepayment rate case, high prepayments in the early years lead to large principal payments that decline sharply as fewer and fewer mortgages are outstanding. The striped region under the two lines represents the principal cash flow that is available at both of these prepayment rates. In addition, the striped region also represents principal cash flow that is available at every PSA rate between 75 and 350%.

   PAC bonds are created out of the cash flows that satisfy both the upper and lower limits of the prepayment collar. There is nothing magical about the choice of collars. Issuers simply select a prepayment range that investors feel comfortably protects them against prepayment variability. Often, a PAC is split into a series of sequential PACs in order to create bonds with varying average life and duration characteristics. The DBL Q deal is an example of a REMIC with sequential PACs. The terms, average lives, and actual prepayment collars of the various PAC classes of DBL Q are displayed in Exhibit 2, and their scheduled cash flows are shown

Exhibit 2: Description of DBL Q Tranches

Tranche	Coupon (%)	Original Amount ($M)	Average Life At Pricing (years)	Tranche Type	Original PSA Collar*
Q-1	7.75	7,000.0	1.1	PAC	75-1370
Q-2	8.45	17,000.0	3.4	PAC	75-635
Q-3	8.95	7,000.0	5.8	PAC	75-545
Q-4	9.00	7,000.0	7.3	PAC	75-350
Q-5	Floater	54,670.0	10.5	Floater	NA
Q-6	0.00	22,330.0	10.5	Non-PAC	NA
Q-7		287.0		Residual	NA

PSA rate assumed at initial pricing: 175% PSA.

* The initial collars for every PAC bond were listed as 75% PSA to 350% PSA. In reality, the actual collars for the Q-1, Q-2 and Q-3 PACs were wider.

in Exhibit 3. The scheduled principal cash flows of each of these PAC bonds are met if the collateral prepays at any PSA rate be-

Exhibit 3: Scheduled Cash Flows for a Multi-PAC Bond CMO (DBL Q)

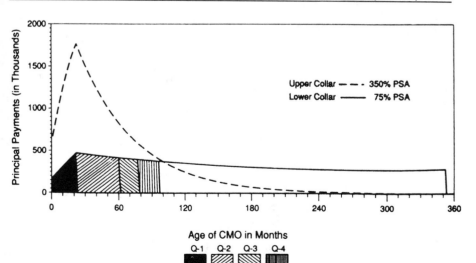

Exhibit 4: Scheduled Cash Flows for a PAC Bond (DBL Q-4)

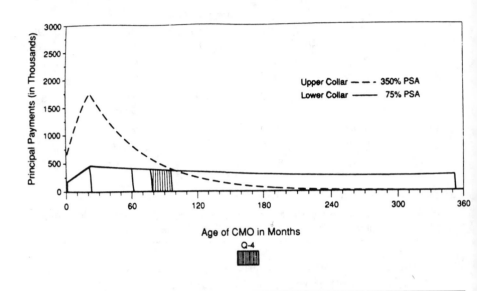

Exhibit 5: Scheduled Cash Flows for a PAC Bond (DBL Q-2)

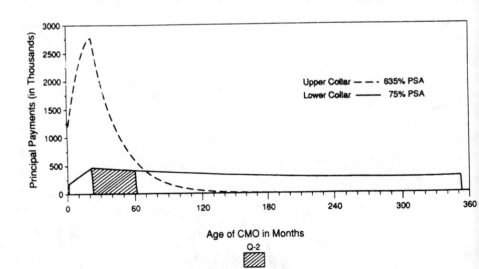

tween 75 and 350%. This splitting of the PAC actually results in the shorter-term PACs having wider collars. In fact, only the DBL Q-4s have collars of 75 and 350% PSA (see Exhibit 4). The Q-1s, Q-2s and Q-3s each have a higher upper collar. The DBL Q-2s, for example, have an upper collar of 635% PSA (see Exhibit 5).

BREAKING THE PAC COLLAR

A very important issue for investors is what happens to the PAC when prepayment rates do fall outside the collar. It is important to emphasize that, generally, the cash flows of a PAC bond are severely affected only if prepayments are outside the collar for a sustained period of time. Breaking the lower collar for a few months could result in a cash flow different than that expected; but if subsequent prepayments are within the collar, the PAC should return to its original principal schedule. Likewise, the upper collar must usually be exceeded for a sustained period of time in order to disrupt the PAC schedule.

There are a number of features that aid the PAC if prepayment rates fall below the lower collar. The first is that the claim of the PAC is senior to all other classes in its right to principal payments. Second, most (but not all) PACs have a "cumulative shortfall feature," that is, their seniority extends not only to the scheduled principal for each period but to any missed prior payments. Finally, the lower collar declines when prepayment rates are below the lower collar. The phenomenon of the collar shifting over time is discussed in detail in the next section.

An example of how the principal cash flows of a PAC are disrupted if prepayment rates are consistently below the lower collar is provided in Exhibit 6. The principal cash flow schedule of the DBL N-2 PAC tranche with a lower collar of 125% PSA and an upper collar of 400% PSA is plotted. The original average life and collar of this tranche along with the average lives of the other tranches in the deal are presented in Exhibit 7. The current average life of the DBL N-2 is 5.03 years. The dashed line in Exhibit 6

Exhibit 6: Continually Breaking the Lower PAC Collar (DBL N-2 Principal Cash Flows at Constant 100% PSA).

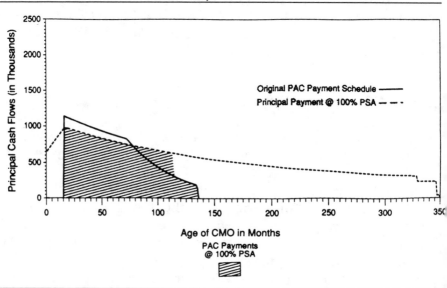

depicts the principal cash flows of the REMIC were the collateral consistently to prepay below the collar at 100% PSA. At this lower prepayment rate, the principal cash flows on the collateral backing the REMIC are less than the PAC's scheduled principal payments for several years. The shortfalls are then recouped in the later

Exhibit 7: Description of DBL N Tranches

Tranche	Coupon (%)	Original Amount ($M)	Average Life at Pricing (years)	Tranche Type	Original PSA Collar
N-1	8.50	80,000.0	2.4	Non-PAC	NA
N-2	8.60	83,000.0	5.8	PAC	125-400
N-3	9.55	32,000.0	10.8	Non-PAC	NA
N-4	10.00	5,000.0	18.4	Non-PAC	NA
N-5		500.0		Residual	NA

PSA rate assumed at initial pricing: 250% PSA.

months, when the principal cash flows of the collateral exceed the PAC schedule. The resulting principal cash flows for the N-2 bonds are indicated by the shaded area. It should be noted that this particular tranche contains a cumulative shortfall feature: if it did not, the principal cash flows would follow only their initially scheduled pattern whenever possible, and shortfalls would be made up after the last scheduled principal payment. When prepayments are below the lower collar, early cash flows are delayed to later months, which often causes the average life of the PAC to lengthen. In the case of the DBL N-2s, if the collateral prepays at 100% PSA, the average life rises to 5.41 years.

The effects on the PAC of prepayments above the upper collar depend on how high and how long they are above the collar. Prepayment levels in excess of the upper collar early in the PAC's life do not disrupt early cash flows, but immediately affect projected cash flows. Only when the companion bonds are paid down does the PAC begin to be affected. The smaller the companion bonds, the less cushion they can provide the PACs in future periods. If prepayments are above the upper collar for only a brief period of time and then slow to within the PAC range, the PAC schedule may not be disrupted at all.

When prepayment rates are consistently above the upper collar but are not extremely fast, the PAC schedule is not disturbed until the later months of its life. The impact of a consistent prepayment rate of 475% PSA on the DBL N-2s is shown in Exhibit 8. The PAC schedule is broken in the later months and the principal payments are extended beyond the PACs scheduled maturity. The companion bonds cushion the PAC bond from initially greater dollars of principal spun off at the higher prepayment rate. Thus, later principal payments are smaller than, and extend beyond, the original maturity. In this case, the current average life of the PAC lengthens to 5.24 years.

An example of the cash flow pattern when prepayment rates are considerably above the upper collar, in this case 600% PSA, is shown in Exhibit 9. When the prepayment rate is consistently high, the companion bonds retire early, before the PAC is paid

Exhibit 8: Continually Breaking the Upper PAC Collar (DBL N-2 Principal Cash Flows at Constant 475% PSA).

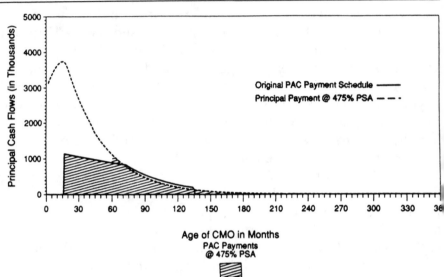

Exhibit 9: Continually Breaking the Upper PAC Collar (DBL N-2 Principal Cash Flows at Constant 600% PSA)

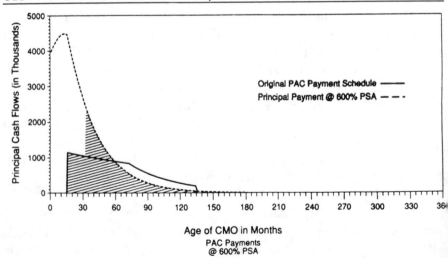

down. The PAC's buffer against excess principal disappears. As a result, the total amount of principal outstanding equals the total amount left to retire the PAC, and each dollar of principal must be paid directly to that bondholder. In the example in Exhibit 9, the majority of the principal cash flows for the PAC occur prior to when they were scheduled, causing its average life to shorten to 4.24 years.

HOW THE COLLAR CHANGES OVER TIME

As mentioned, the prepayment collar is not fixed and actually changes over time. As a result, PAC bonds with the same initial collar and similar structures actually can, over time, provide varying degrees of prepayment protection. The change in the PAC collar is dependent on the specific prepayments experienced by the REMIC and the structure of the REMIC.

The reason the collar changes is that, when prepayment rates vary from the upper or lower prepayment boundary (they have to vary from at least one of them), the amount of dollars outstanding is different than that originally projected at the respective boundary. If the prepayment rate is below the upper boundary, for example, more dollars are outstanding than would have been the case if prepayments had equaled the upper collar. Since more dollars are outstanding, the prepayment level can be slightly higher than the original upper collar before the PAC's scheduled cash flows are disrupted. This process occurs month to month, and, therefore, the collar typically shifts on a monthly basis.

The further the actual prepayment experience is from the current collar, the more the collar changes. The upper and lower collars have opposite responses to actual prepayment behavior. The upper collar increases whenever the actual prepayments are below the current upper collar, and falls when the prepayments are above the upper collar. The lower collar, on the other hand, rises whenever the actual prepayments are above the current lower collar, and declines when they are lower than that collar. The differing types of collar changes are outlined below.

Actual PSAs below the Lower Collar

An example of what happens to the DBL S-2 PAC collar when prepayments are always below the lower collar is provided in Exhibit 10 (the terms of the DBL S deal are provided in Exhibit 11). When prepayments are below the lower collar, more dollars are outstanding than were expected at either of the original prepayment speeds. In projecting cash flows from this new, greater basis, one finds that, for the lower collar, a lower prepayment rate is sufficient to meet all the future scheduled payments. Thus, the lower prepayment boundary declines. Conversely, the upper collar rises. The lower actual prepayment rate has left more dollars in the companion tranches than originally projected at the upper-collar PSA rate. Thus the companion bonds can provide greater cush-

Exhibit 10: PAC Collars Responding to Actual Prepayments (Prepayments Below the Lower Collar)

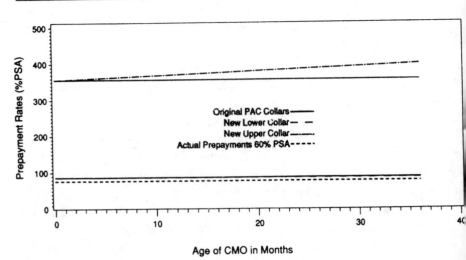

Age of CMO in Months

Exhibit 11: Description of DBL S Tranches

Tranche	Coupon ($)	Original Amount ($M)	Average Life at Pricing (years)	Tranche Type	Original PSA Collar
S-1	8.50	96,500.0	2.4	Non-PAC	NA
S-2	9.00	75,000.0	7.8	PAC	70-355
S-3	9.00	68,500.0	10.5	Non-PAC	NA
S-4	9.50	10,000.0	20.3	Non-PAC	NA
S-5		625.0		Residual	NA

PSA rate assumed at initial pricing: 175% PSA.

ioning and the entire PAC schedule still can be satisfied at a higher prepayment rate. If prepayments are below the lower collar before the PAC begins its scheduled principal payments, the collar widens at no expense to the PAC holder. A constant prepayment rate of 60% PSA for thirty-six months results in the S-2 having a new collar of 69 and 400% PSA, as opposed to the original collar of 70 and 355% (see Exhibit 12).

Exhibit 12: Simulated DBL S-2 PAC Collar Behavior

Simulated Prepayment Behavior for 36 Months	Original Collar	Projected Collar After 36 Months
60% PSA	70-355	69-400
400% PSA	70-355	125-345
100% PSA	70-355	71-390
325% PSA	70-355	100-370

Actual PSAs above the Upper Collar

The story is much different when the actual prepayments are always above the upper collar (Exhibit 13). In this case, the collar narrows as the upper collar declines and the lower collar increases. The higher prepayment rates result in there being a smaller amount of dollars outstanding than there would have been had the prepayments been at or below the upper collar. With

---

Exhibit 13: PAC Collars Responding to Actual Prepayments (Prepayments Above the Upper Collar)

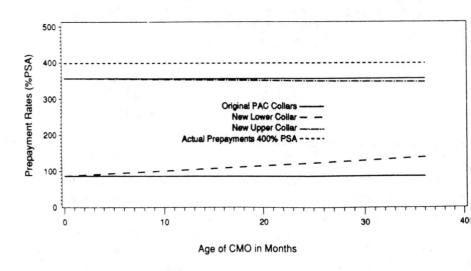

Age of CMO in Months

---

fewer dollars outstanding, the companion bonds do not protect the PAC bonds as well as originally expected. As a result, the future prepayments have to be lower than the original upper collar to ensure that the PAC's principal schedule is not disrupted. In addition, the lower amount of principal outstanding means that the lower collar no longer produces enough principal to meet the PAC schedule. Therefore, a higher bottom collar is required in order to produce sufficient cash flows. If the collateral backing DBL S were to prepay at 400% PSA for thirty-six months, for example, the new collar narrows to 125 and 345% PSA.

Actual PSAs in the Middle of the Collar

When prepayment rates are within the current collar, the collar tends to widen (Exhibit 14). In this case, there are more dollars outstanding than were originally expected at the upper collar, but

---

Exhibit 14: PAC Collars Responding to Actual Prepayments (Prepayments Within the Collar Range, in the Middle and Near the Lower Collar)

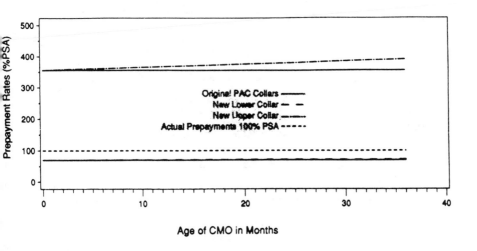

Age of CMO in Months

---

fewer dollars than projected at the original lower collar. With more dollars outstanding than projected at the original upper collar, the companion bonds provide more cushioning than originally expected in the falling interest rate environment, causing the upper collar to increase. Prepayments above the lower collar cause an increase in this boundary, however. With fewer dollars outstanding than expected at the lower collar, prepayments must be faster in order to meet the PAC's principal schedule. In general, the collar widens because the upper collar increases at a quicker rate than does the lower collar. If the collateral of DBL S prepays at 100% PSA for the next thirty-six months, for example, the lower collar rises slightly to 71% PSA, whereas the upper collar jumps to 390% PSA. An exception to this tendency is when prepayment rates are consistently near the upper collar. Here, the collar tightens because the upper collar increases at a slower rate than does the lower collar (see Exhibit 15). If the collateral were to prepay at

---

**Exhibit 15: PAC Collars Responding to Actual Prepayments
(Prepayments Within the Collar Range and Near the Upper Collar)**

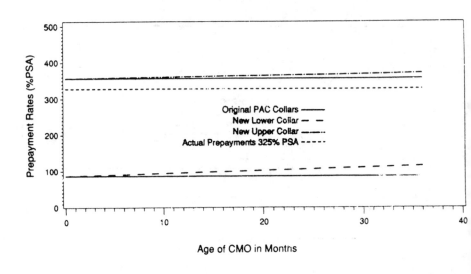

Age of CMO in Months

325% PSA for the next thirty-six months, the lower collar rises to 100% PSA, and the upper collar increases to only 370% PSA.

Under unusual prepayment behavior, prepayment rates can be fully within the *initial* prepayment collars, and the PAC schedule still may not be met. A PAC bond with an initial collar of 50 to 300% PSA, for example, will have its schedule disrupted if prepayments are 300% PSA for the first year and 50% PSA each month thereafter. While the prepayment rate is 300%, the lower collar increases modestly each month. After one year, the lower collar is slightly higher than 50% PSA, and therefore a constant prepayment of 50% PSA is no longer adequate to meet fully the PAC schedule. The shortfalls, however, last only a few months at most, and this scenario does not significantly alter the cash flow for the PAC bondholder.

A METHOD FOR COMPARING THE STRENGTH OF DIFFERENT PAC COLLARS

In order to assess the prepayment risk in a PAC bond properly, investors should know what the current collar is, how the collar could change in the future, and the likelihood of the collar being violated. Each PAC collar is dependent on the amount of prepayment risk in the underlying collateral, and how that risk is reallocated through the structure of the CMO. Investors comparing the specific prepayment risk of different PAC tranches should assess the bonds' anticipated behavior under identical interest rate scenarios. Examining PACs under different interest rate scenarios may, for example, show that one PAC will likely violate its schedule if interest rates rise 300 basis points, and another's schedule is not violated until interest rates increase 400 basis points.

It is often difficult to find two different CMOs with identical collateral and average lives. The typical case is where two PAC bonds have different collateral attributes and different collars. How can investors assess which bond has the stronger collar in such cases? Investors should translate the PSA collars into interest rate collars by using a prepayment model. An investor can then determine how much interest rates must move before the PAC collars are broken.

TOTAL RETURN PAC BONDS, FRAMEWORK TO COMPARE TREASURIES AND HIGH-GRADE CORPORATES

PAC bonds exist with different prepayment collars, different collateral types and collateral coupons, different bond coupons and average lives, and often complex interdependencies of tranches. With so much complexity, how can investors determine relative value among PAC tranches or between PAC tranches and other securities? A total rate-of-return methodology provides a way to observe how the various features of the PAC influence its performance under changing interest rate scenarios. Investors who simply examine the yield spreads over a given average life are exposing themselves to the risks of the collateral without a thorough understanding of the specific risk to the tranche. Using a total rate-of-return valuation methodology more accurately describes the current risk/return profile of each security, and incorporates all the subtle CMO structural dependencies.

SUMMARY

PAC bonds open up a new frontier for fixed-income investors. Investors can take advantage of both the high yields of mortgage products and the lack of event risk, while owning a security that has a significant amount of call protection. PACs compare favorably with corporates and Treasuries of similar duration, and also can be created to meet specific asset/liability needs.

The scheduled principal payments of a PAC are protected within a range of prepayment rates. This range is called the prepayment collar. The amount of call protection and extension risk reduction is determined by the strength (or width) of the prepayment collar, the collateral, and the structure of the CMO. To compare the strength of one PAC's collar to another, investors should determine how much interest rates have to change in order for the prepayment rates of the underlying collateral to fall outside the prepayment collar.

A prepayment collar is not static, but rather changes over time. The direction and magnitude of the change in the collar depends on the actual prepayment rates of the collateral underlying the CMO. The change in the collar typically is not dramatic, but may be significant enough to affect the value of the PAC. It is important to note that if the collar is broken temporarily, the PAC bond may not be severely affected, and may be totally unaffected. When prepayments are above the upper collar, for example, the PAC principal payment schedule is not immediately affected, and may never be if future prepayments quickly fall back to within the collar. Prepayments below the lower collar do cause immediate disruptions in the cash flow, but the shortfalls are redeemed in sub-sequent months if prepayments rise.

PACs have a distinctive risk/return profile. This often means that various bonds that might appear similar at first blush, in reality have varying sensitivities to changes in economic conditions. Therefore, these securities should trade at different prices and different spreads. This presents investment opportunities to those who understand the value of the different features. A proper understanding of the mechanics of these structures will enable investors to take advantage of these opportunities in this important and growing sector of the fixed-income market.

CHAPTER 15

INTRODUCTION TO CMO TAC BONDS

William J. Curtin
Senior Vice President
Lehman Brothers Inc.

Paul T. Van Valkenburg
Principal
Mortgage Industry Advisory Corp.

TAC (Targeted Amortization Class) bonds are a modification of the PAC bond concept. TACs are designed to provide call protection, but there is a strong likelihood that their average life will extend. The TAC, like a PAC, has a priority in receiving principal payments. The TAC principal schedule is not protected for a wide range of prepayments, however. If prepayments remain at the pricing speed for the life of the TAC, the TAC principal payments will be received exactly as originally specified in the prospectus. The performance of the TAC in other prepayment scenarios can be broken into three categories: prepayments below the TAC PSA rate, prepayments above the TAC PSA rate, and very fast prepay-

ments. The purpose of this chapter is to discuss the TAC performance in these three prepayment scenarios.

TAC CASH FLOWS WHEN PREPAYMENTS ARE BELOW THE TAC PSA RATE

The average life of the TAC lengthens when prepayment rates are
consistently below the TAC PSA rate. The principal shortfalls that
occur in the early months of the TAC are eventually redeemed in
the latter months or even beyond the expected maturity date. The
Drexel Burnham Lambert Trust T-3 TAC shown in Exhibit 1 has a
TAC PSA rate of 125%. The initial average life of the TAC is
eleven years (see Exhibit 2 for the terms of the DBL T tranches). At
100% PSA, the principal cash flow from the collateral is insufficient in the early months of the TAC and more than adequate in
the latter months. When the principal received is sufficient to meet
the TAC schedule, the principal shortfalls of the early months are
paid before the other non-TAC classes receive principal. Once the
shortfalls are paid, the TAC resumes its original schedule. If the
DBL T collateral prepays at a constant prepayment rate of 100%
PSA, the average life of the T-3 tranche extends to 12.88 years.

TAC CASH FLOWS AT PREPAYMENTS ABOVE THE TAC PSA RATE

The average life of the TAC also lengthens when actual prepayments fall within a range of rates above the TAC PSA rate, as
shown in Exhibit 3. In this case, the TAC schedule may not be
broken initially. The companion bonds that had been absorbing
the excess are retired before the TAC is paid down, however.
Therefore, the TAC receives all of the principal cash flow from the
remaining collateral. This cash flow is not enough to cover the
TAC's principal payment schedule, and thus cash flows are received beyond the original maturity date of the TAC. If the collat-

Exhibit 1: DBL T-3 TAC Bond (Prepayments Below the TAC PSA Rate; Average Life Extends)

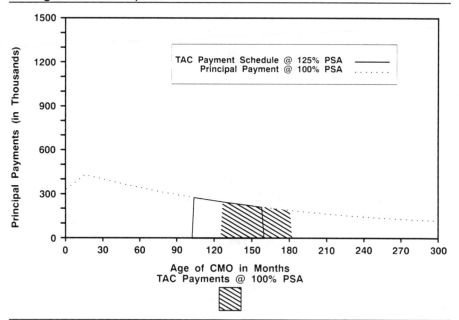

Age of CMO in Months
TAC Payments @ 100% PSA

Exhibit 2: Description of DBL T Tranches

Tranche	Coupon (%)	Original Amount ($M)	Average Life at Pricing (years)	Tranche Type
T-1	8.45	39,700.0	3.4	TAC*
T-2	8.45	7,500.0	8.0	TAC*
T-3	8.45	15,000.0	11.0	TAC*
T-4	8.45	6,600.0	14.7	TAC*
T-5	0.00	15,000.0	13.8	Companion
T-6	6.00	4,200.0	23.3	Companion
T-7		220.0		Residual

PSA rate assumed at initial pricing: 125% PSA.
* TAC PSA rate is 125% PSA.

Exhibit 3: DBL T-3 TAC Bond (Prepayments Above the TAC PSA Rate; Average Life Extends)

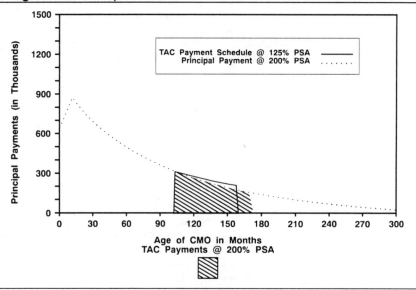

Exhibit 4: DBL T-3 TAC Bond (Prepayments Far Above the TAC PSA Rate; Average Life Shortens as All Other Classes Are Retired)

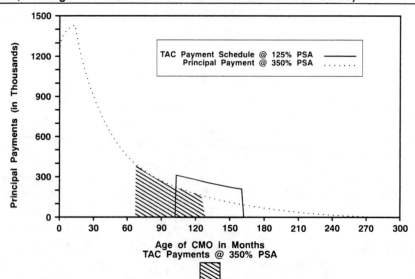

eral consistently prepays at 200% PSA, for example, the average life of the DBL T-3 lengthens to 11.22 years.

TAC CASH FLOWS AT VERY FAST PREPAYMENTS

If prepayment rates are very fast over a long period of time, all the other non-TAC classes are retired and the TAC bond is the only outstanding bond. The TAC bond then receives all the remaining principal payments, which results in higher payments in the early months than originally scheduled. If the increase in payments is early and significant enough, the average life of the TAC bond will shorten (see Exhibit 4). The DBL T-3s, for example, shorten to 7.9 years if the collateral consistently prepays at 350 percent PSA. The PSA rates at which the TAC's average life begins to shorten depend on the collateral and the TAC structure. For an investor to compare call protection of a TAC to other TACs and other callable securities, the investor should find the first constant PSA rate that causes the average life of the TAC bond to shorten (all prepayment rates above this also cause the TAC to shorten), and then estimate the interest rate movement necessary to cause prepayment rates to increase to this level. The magnitude of this interest rate movement indicates the amount of call protection of the specific TAC bond.

The TAC PSA rate, like the PAC collar, changes each month that prepayments are not equal to the current TAC PSA rate. In fact, the TAC can actually develop a narrow collar. When prepayment rates are below the TAC PSA rate, more dollars are outstanding than were expected. At this point, a constant PSA rate that is slightly slower or faster than the original TAC PSA rate now generates sufficient principal to meet the scheduled principal payments of the TAC. The TAC will not suffer any additional principal shortfall, and develops a weak prepayment collar.

SUMMARY

TAC bonds are a variation of the PAC bond concept. Instead of a prepayment range, however, there is one prepayment rate at which the principal cash flows are satisfied. The TAC has priority to the principal cash flow of the collateral over the other tranches in the CMO, providing the TAC with some degree of call protection, although not nearly as much as with the PAC.

CHAPTER 16

NOT ALL TACs ARE CREATED EQUAL: GENERIC TACs VERSUS TAC POs

Sean C. Gallop
Vice President
J.P. Morgan Securities Inc.

Targeted Amortization Class (TAC) bonds were introduced in 1986 in an effort to offer investors a protected class with wider spreads than Planned Amortization Class (PAC) bonds. At that time, investors were concerned about the shortening of average lives due to the rapid prepayments that were occurring as interest rates declined. Many investors were willing to forego the protection against extension risk afforded by PAC bonds in order to receive a higher yield. As a result, the typical TAC class was constructed so that its average life was stable in a falling interest rate environment, but could extend if prepayments were to decline.

Currently, TAC classes trade at spreads through plain vanilla tranches, but wider than PAC classes of the same average life. In today's market, a three-year support TAC trades at a static spread of approximately 125 basis points off the three-year Treasury note compared to 77 basis points for a comparable average life PAC. Comparable average life companion tranches trade near 165 basis points off the three-year note.

In 1988, CMOs backed by principal only strips (POs) were first introduced to the market. The usual variety of bonds were created using POs—vanillas, PACs, TACs, support classes, etc. The classes formed from such collateral paid only principal. While structurally equivalent to generic TACs, the price/yield performance of TAC POs is quite different. In this chapter, we examine why TAC POs differ from regular TACs and argue that TAC PO investors should demand wide spreads over generic TACs to compensate them for the negative performance characteristics of TAC POs.

ANTICIPATED PERFORMANCE OF GENERIC TACs

Like PACs, TACs amortize according to a sinking-fund schedule. Unlike PACs, however, the TAC's scheduled cash flows are guaranteed if and only if actual prepayments occur precisely at the targeted prepayment level (i.e., the TAC speed). When the outstanding balance of the TAC differs from that implied by the TAC schedule, the outstanding balance of the TAC will amortize more quickly or more slowly in such a way that the scheduled amortization is resumed as quickly as possible. However, deviation from the TAC speed will quickly result in a mismatch between actual and scheduled balances. It is for this reason that the schedule associated with a TAC is said to be *targeted* rather than *planned*.

Typically, investors look at the performance of the TAC at constant prepayment levels both above and below the TAC speed. When prepayments are faster than the TAC speed, the TAC's sinking fund is met and excess cash flow is distributed to the support bonds. This reduces the outstanding balance of the collateral relative to the TAC schedule and requires sustained collateral prepayment above the TAC speed if the scheduled amortization is to be met. Thus, we say that the TAC speed migrates upward in pre-payment scenarios above the TAC speed.

On the other hand, when actual prepayment falls below the TAC speed, the TAC sinking fund is not met and the unpaid balance is added to the following period's expected payment. Unless actual prepayment rises to levels above the TAC speed, the TAC's average life will extend and for discount TACs, the yield will fall. In this way, TACs are protected against shortening but are vulnerable to performance-degrading extension. Again, the speed below which the TAC is vulnerable to extension migrates upward.

Exhibit 1 outlines prepayment scenarios for a TAC from a CMO deal backed by FNMA 9.5% collateral issued in late 1990. The solid line for each scenario represents the TAC's targeted outstanding balances at each time period from issuance until maturity. The dashed line represents actual outstanding balances under each scenario.

Exhibit 1

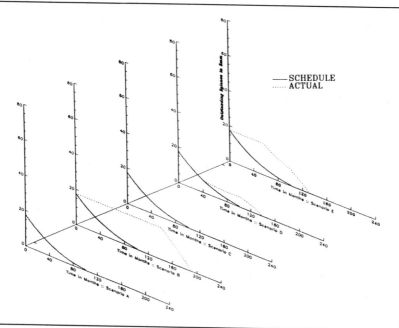

Scenarios A, B, and C illustrate the commonly requested "base," "slow," and "fast" prepayment scenarios. When, for example, actual prepayment coincides with the TAC speed of 138% PSA, as in scenario A, the sinking fund and actual principal payments coincide. When actual prepayment falls consistently below the TAC speed to 100% PSA, as in scenario B, however, amortization is delayed and the TAC's average life extends. This scenario particularly hurts discount TACs on account of the delayed return of principal. Scenario C depicts consistently high prepayment above the TAC speed at 165% PSA. Here, the actual principal payments provide ample cash flow to meet the schedule and the average life of the TAC is maintained as excess cash flow passes on to the support tranches whose combined maturity is greater than that of the TAC bond.

Constant prepayment scenarios understate the primary weakness of a TAC: its inability to maintain the prepayment protection implied by the TAC schedule against even moderate deviations from the TAC speed. In real life, seasonal variation alone assures that variable prepayment scenarios such as D and E are less the exception than the norm. It is these scenarios which most clearly illustrate the weakness of targeted payment securities against prepayment volatility. It should be noted that scenarios D and E represent a moderate, one-time prepayment change. They are, therefore, less strenuous than a more realistic scenario in which prepayment levels oscillate on a seasonal rather than a one-time basis.

In scenario D, a moderately high initial amortization level (165%) is followed by sustained prepayment at the TAC speed (138% PSA) from month 40 onwards. Initially, the TAC schedule is maintained. Once prepayments return to the TAC schedule, however, there is insufficient cash flow to meet the TAC's targeted balance. The initially high prepayments have reduced the outstanding collateral balance to such an extent that, by month 40, a prepayment level well in excess of the TAC speed is required to meet the targeted amortization. In this way, we see that the effective TAC speed has migrated upwards.

Scenario E, however, illustrates the reverse scenario in that pre-payment is moderately low (100% PSA) for the first 40 months and returns to the TAC speed (138% PSA) thereafter. The TAC receives virtually no cash flow during the first 40 months. While more cash flow is available thereafter, insufficient cash flows are received to return the TAC to its scheduled amortization (note that two lines do not converge in this scenario). Level II PACs, like the TAC, have not received their scheduled principal payments. Given that these PACs are senior to the TAC, the TAC will not begin to return to its schedule until such time that the more senior tranches have resumed their respective scheduled amortization. To return the TAC to its schedule amortization, therefore, future prepay-ment levels significantly in excess of the TAC speed are required. Thus, we can see that the TAC speed has again migrated up-wards, and the prepayment protection offered by the TAC sched-ule has been impaired.

OAS ANALYSIS

Option-adjusted analysis reveals some of the deficiencies of the TAC bond relative to PACs since OAS evaluates a security's cash flows through numerous interest/prepayment rate scenarios. Op-tion-adjusted analysis attempts to value the option component of a security by computing the average discounted value of a security's cash flow over a large universe of arbitrage-free interest rate paths. Unlike the often-quoted static spreads, Option-Adjusted Spread (OAS) represents an effective spread in basis points over the entire yield curve taking into account the relationship between interest rates and prepayments. Given that the mortgage investor has shorted the prepayment option to the homeowner, one would expect the OAS to be less than the static spread. For more stable, less negatively convex bonds such as Level I PACs, we would ex-pect the margin between OAS and static spread to be no wider than 5-15 basis points depending on pricing. The formidable protection provided by the PAC schedule is sufficient to maintain scheduled amortization for all but a small subset of scenarios.

Exhibit 2 shows that at a comparable option adjusted spread of 58 basis points, a three-year generic TAC would have to trade at a spread of 176 basis points compared to a spread of 75 basis points for a comparable duration generic PAC. This additional spread is meant to compensate the TAC investor for the additional negative convexity. It should be noted that for an investor who believes volatility will be lower or more importantly that prepayment sensitivity will be less than that assumed in the OAS analysis, the TAC bond could still represent value regardless of the tighter spread level. The option-adjusted analysis enables an investor to put all market assumptions (i.e., long and short volatility, prepayment functions, seasoning factors, etc.) into a single framework.

Exhibit 2

	SPREAD	OAS	DUR	CONV
Generic TAC	176/3 yr	58	3.19	-143
Generic PAC	75/3 yr	58	3.38	13

TAC POs

We now turn our attention to the PO sector of the TAC market. As Exhibit 3 illustrates, at a spread of 300 basis points off the three-year Treasury note, TAC POs appear extremely cheap.

Exhibit 3

	SPREAD	OAS	DUR	CONV
Generic TAC	130/3 yr	23	3.13	-154
TAC PO	300/3 yr	-172	8.92	-475

Enthusiasm is dampened, however, when one compares the margin of the TAC PO's OAS to its static spread. This margin indicates the severity with which the option component inherent to mortgages will work against the investor over the investment horizon. The more negatively convex the bond, the wider this margin will be. With generic TACs, we saw that this margin was approximately 120 basis points. As we can see in Exhibit 3, the margin for TAC POs is 500 basis points! In fact, for the TAC PO to trade at a comparable OAS to the more liquid generic TAC in Exhibit 3, the TAC PO's static spread would have to widen to 624 basis points. TAC PO investors, therefore, may expect a wide divergence between expected and actual performance unless, of course, they carefully hedge their exposure. Clearly, the OAS of -172 indicates that 300 basis points is insufficient compensation given the TAC PO's considerable negative convexity. Once again, this assumes that the investor accepts the volatility, prepayment, and seasoning assumptions implicit in the analysis.

Why are TAC POs so much more negatively convex than generic TACs? The TAC schedule for generic TACs helps maintain cash flow stability particularly against high prepayment scenarios and improves OAS performance by limiting the volatility of return against variable prepayment scenarios. For TAC POs, however, the schedule works *against* the investor for two reasons.

First, the schedule prevents performance-enhancing acceleration of principal in that excess cash flows available under high prepayment scenarios are passed on to the support tranches. This has the additional effect of reducing the outstanding collateral balance at a faster rate relative to the TAC balance than that implied by the TAC schedule. As we have seen earlier in this chapter, this asset-liability mismatch increases the likelihood of further performance-reducing delays in the return of principal by increasing the effective TAC speed. Since the TAC schedule is protected at a single speed, there is no protection against extension. Deviations below the TAC speed likewise increase the duration and decrease yield. The TAC schedule, therefore, prevents yield-enhancing shortening and does little to prevent adverse extension. While the name TAC PO sounds like a protected class that the investor should pay up for, in reality, it enjoys little benefit from this protection. In short, TAC POs suffer all the downside associated with POs while enjoying few if any of the benefits.

Secondly, the TAC schedule is typically generated at a prepayment speed significantly below the pricing speed. TAC schedules for three recently issued TAC POs were generated at an average of 13% slower than their respective deal pricing speeds. This causes two problems. First, investors who assume that all cash flows generated at the pricing speed are available to the TAC PO are mistaken. In fact, the cash flow attributable to the TAC PO will be significantly smaller. Furthermore, if one assumes that prepayments will occur over the short run near the deal speed, the outstanding collateral balance will decline more quickly than implied by the TAC schedule. This means that successively higher prepayments will be required to maintain the TAC schedule. Thus, by setting the TAC speed well below the deal speed, the likelihood that the effective TAC speed will migrate upwards increases and performance correspondingly decreases.

Exhibit 4 illustrates the drain on the TAC PO's total return performance caused by its negative convexity. Provided that the yield curve remains constant throughout the one year investment period, the TAC PO, on account of its wider static spread, will outperform a comparable duration Treasury strip. As volatility increases, however, the TAC PO significantly underperforms that same strip. Exhibit 4 confirms the high negative convexity levels suggested by the option-adjusted analysis.

It should be noted that the analysis in Exhibit 4 overestimates the TAC PO's performance for the following reasons. First, the analysis assumes that the rates are shocked instantaneously and remain constant thereafter. This underestimates the volatility generally associated with large moves in the yield curve and thereby undervalues the prepayment option. Furthermore, even if interest rates were to remain relatively constant, we would still expect seasonal prepayment variation. Therefore, prepayment volatility, which is not entirely captured by interest rate change, will further impair the TAC PO's performance.

Exhibit 4

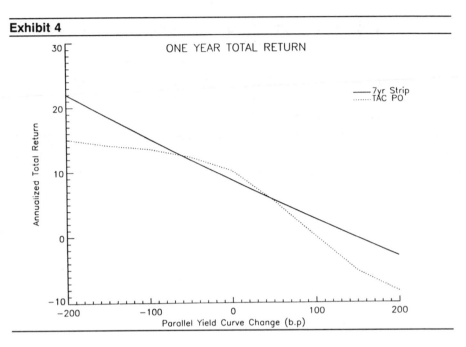

ONE YEAR TOTAL RETURN

— 7yr Strip
········ TAC PO

Annualized Total Return vs *Parallel Yield Curve Change (b.p)*

CONCLUSION

TAC PO investors should raise their acceptance criteria when approaching these securities. Unlike criteria targeted for less exotic tranches, standard, stable rate analysis will not capture the option component of these securities and will significantly overestimate performance. Investors should run TAC POs against a battery of variable rate scenarios which simulate such factors as seasonality, prepayment seasoning, and sudden and ongoing change in interest rates. Such testing was the impetus for the creation of OAS, and, if available, option-adjusted analysis will be helpful in discerning value in this sector.

While the margin between the expected and actual performance will remain large, the static spread will hopefully be wide enough to maintain a minimum performance level. Furthermore, given the sensitivity of these instruments to prepayment volatility, their ongoing complexity, and their limited liquidity, additional compensation should be demanded. TAC PO value, therefore, is represented by a static spread sufficiently high to compensate the TAC PO investor for these factors.

TAC POs are structurally "problematic bonds" in that for all but a small set of statistically unlikely scenarios, the static spread will not be earned. Contributors to this profile include a TAC schedule which prevents shortening, PO collateral which increases downside yield volatility, and a TAC speed which is selected below the deal speed. The single upside of a TAC PO is its *generous* initial spread, and wary investors should demand a great deal of it.

CHAPTER 17

THE EFFECT OF PAC BOND FEATURES ON PERFORMANCE

Linda Lowell
Vice President, Head
Mortgage Investment Strategies
Smith Barney, Harris Upham & Co., Inc.

Planned amortization classes or PAC bonds represent one of the largest sectors of the CMO market. Among the factors expanding the market for these bonds were widespread defections from the corporate market by investors who were attracted by the high yields and triple-A credit quality and discouraged in their natural habitat first by limited supply and tight spreads, and later by event risk.

With the increased size of the market and an expanding investor base came greater standardization of certain PAC features and improved liquidity. While typical PAC buyers still tend to be life insurance companies and commercial banks, the PAC market appeals as well to investors with active bond management strategies. These investors may have, for instance, opinions about the direction of mortgage-Treasury spreads or mortgage-corporate spreads, they may wish to execute barbell or other strategies designed to take advantage of expectations regarding the shape or direction of the yield curve, or they may be seeking value advantages, either between the PAC and other CMO sectors, or within the PAC sector, among PACs with different features.

The main attraction of PAC bonds[1] lies in the fact that they provide a defined schedule of principal payments (or, similarly, target balances), which is guaranteed so long as prepayment rates remain within a specified range. (Hence the name, planned amortization.) Holders are insulated to a significant degree from the uncertainty regarding the cash flows of most MBSs which arises from the right of mortgage borrowers to prepay their loans at any time. The fact that the prepayment process is interest rate-sensitive—that the tendency of homeowners to move or refinance is inversely related to the direction of interest rates[2]—has a material impact on the average life, duration, and performance of mortgage securities. MBSs shorten in rising markets and extend in declining markets. To compensate investors for taking this risk, passthroughs and other MBSs are priced at higher yields than other, noncallable bonds of similar credit quality (such as agency debt). PAC bonds partake of the incremental yield available in the MBS market while at the same time providing more certain cash flows. In addition to providing guaranteed payments within a range of prepayment behavior, PAC bonds can be further refined to concentrate payments over a shorter period of time or "window." PACs with narrow windows are perceived to be better substitutes for corporate and Treasury bonds with bullet principal payments, and therefore often trade at higher levels than PACs with wider windows.

This chapter is intended to serve both classes of investors—the buy and hold PAC buyer, who wants to partake of the high yields in the mortgage market but whose liabilities or actuarial require-

---

[1] See Chapter 14 for a discussion of PACs.
[2] See Chapter 10 for a discussion of prepayments.

ments necessitate more stable cash flows than either pass-throughs or standard CMOs can provide, and the active portfolio manager. The chapter examines the different features of PAC bonds, the nature of the supply and demand for bonds bearing such features, and the incremental spread or penalty accorded by the market to different PAC characteristics. In addition, where it is possible to isolate a specific characteristic, an attempt is made to model and examine its impact on the average life and yield behavior of the bond, as well as on its theoretical or option-adjusted value. It is hoped that, in addition to providing a rational framework for evaluating buy-and-hold PAC strategies, this discussion will alert active investors to instances of overlooked value.

THE TERM STRUCTURE OF CMO YIELDS

The yields investors require for occupying different average life sectors of the PAC market are determined by the same factors that influence other fixed-income investors: portfolio objectives and constraints, the current and anticipated shape of the yield curve, expectations regarding the underlying monetary and economic determinants of interest rates, and so forth. In addition, PAC buyers require additional yield as they extend the maturity of their investments to compensate them for the increased risk that the prepayment collars may be broken, as well as the greater average life volatility of the later tranches in a transaction when the prepayment collars are broken. An indication of the average life volatility of PAC tranches of different nominal average lives is provided by Exhibit 1. The graph depicts the average lives of a series of PACs from a single CMO issue[3] at two prepayment speeds extreme enough to break both the upper and lower collars of all the PAC bonds. The range between the average lives at the extremes gradu-

---

[3] This example assumes a structure in which PACs have priority to excess principal payments in the order of their scheduled maturities after the companions have been retired.

Exhibit 1: Extension and Shortening of PAC Bond Average Lives as Prepayments Vary between 0% PSA and 600% PSA

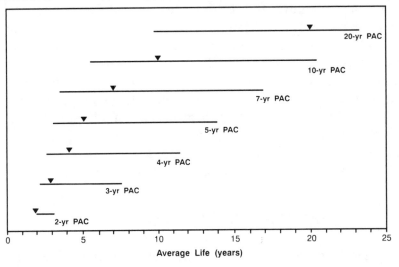

▼ Average life at issue.
PAC Bonds backed by FNMA 9s with prepayment collars of 85-300% PSA.

ally widens for longer expected average lives to its widest point among the intermediate-term PACs.

As a result of investors' demand for greater compensation for holding longer-term PACs, the generic CMO yield curves are more steeply sloped than the Treasury yield curve. Generic yields for current coupon PACs backed by current coupon conventional collateral and for on-the-run Treasuries are depicted in Exhibit 2. Although a satisfying discussion of the issue is beyond the scope of this chapter, it should be noted that CMO spreads are also influenced by the same factors that affect pass-through spreads— volatility of market yields, prepayment expectations, supply of new product, and so forth. Normally CMO spreads track pass-through spreads, with the relationship enforced by the existence of CMO arbitrage opportunities. When pass-throughs cheapen relative to CMOs, new transactions are marketed, increasing the supply of CMOs and ultimately allowing CMOs to cheapen relative to pass-throughs, thereby reducing the arbitrage opportunity.

Exhibit 2: Treasury and PAC Yield Curves

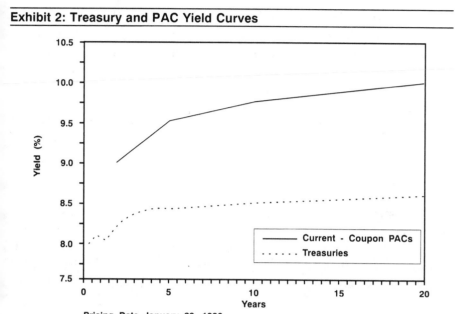

Pricing Date January 29, 1990

Other features of the structure, such as the collateral coupon, the PAC's coupon, the collars, and the window result in additional adjustments to the required yields. In addition, the cash flow performance of the bond outside the collars is affected by other characteristics, such as whether its schedule is supported by accrual from a longer-term Z-bond later in the structure, and its priority for receiving excess cash flow. These characteristics determine how volatile its average life and returns are outside the collars, and so also affect the marketability of a PAC bond.

COLLARS AND COLLATERAL

The strength of the collars—whether they will be broken by actual prepayment experience—should be investors' primary concern. The strength is only nominally indicated in the differential between the top and bottom collar speeds. This range must be related to the specific collateral to gauge the strength of the protection provided. The type of collateral—the agency, the differential between current mortgage rates and the mortgage rates on the underlying loans, seasoning of the loans, and the degree to which the pools have prepaid in the past—determines how quickly or slowly the collateral will prepay in different interest rate scenarios. The collars simply define a range of prepayment speeds for which the PAC payments will not vary. When prepayments fall outside the collars, payments to the PAC holders may be either delayed or accelerated (the collars could be broken temporarily without affecting the payment schedule). A given set of PAC collars will provide stronger or weaker protection, depending on the collateral. For example, a top collar of 300% PSA provides greater call protection should interest rates decline if the collateral is a current coupon than if it is a premium coupon. Similarly, a bottom collar of 100% PSA provides better protection from extension if the collateral is a conventional pass-through than if it is a GNMA.

All else being equal, PAC bonds backed by premium coupon collateral do exhibit greater average life variability than PACs backed by current coupon collateral. This is illustrated by the comparison in Exhibit 3, which displays the average lives at different prepayment speeds of two series of PACs, one backed by FNMA 9s (9.77% weighted average coupon [WAC], 349-month weighted average remaining term [WART]) and scheduled at 85 to 300% PSA, the other backed by FNMA 10 1/2s (11.13% WAC and 347-month WART) and scheduled at 95 to 350% PSA.[4] (Similar comparisons could be made in the case of discount and current coupon collateral, but are omitted from this discussion for the sake of brevity.)

Investors recognize the stability lent by discount collateral and will pay ten to twenty basis points over yields commanded by structures backed by current coupon collateral. Premium-collateral-backed PACs also require wider spreads than commanded by

---

[4] These examples were created in January 1990, when 9% coupon pass-throughs were priced below but closest to par, and permitted the creation of tranches with coupons at current market yields across the PAC CMO yield curve.

Exhibit 3: Impact of Collateral Coupon on the Average Life Variability of PAC Bonds

Average Life (years)

Payment Speed (% PSA)	FNMA 9% Collateral (85-300% PSA Collars)							FNMA 10.5% Collateral (95-350% PSA Collars)						
	2-yr.	3-yr.	4-yr.	5-yr.	7-yr.	10-yr.	20-yr.	2-yr.	3-yr.	4-yr.	5-yr.	7-yr.	10-yr.	20-yr.
0	3.20	7.70	11.44	13.74	16.97	20.50	22.75	3.63	8.81	12.78	15.06	18.11	21.01	22.61
50	2.23	3.61	5.25	6.67	9.37	13.49	19.24	2.27	3.79	5.60	7.16	10.06	13.82	19.07
85	2.14	3.05	4.16	5.16	7.13	11.22	19.23	2.16	3.15	4.37	5.45	7.57	11.33	19.07
95	2.14	3.05	4.16	5.16	7.13	11.22	19.23	2.14	3.05	4.16	5.16	7.13	11.22	19.07
300	2.14	3.05	4.16	5.16	7.13	11.22	19.23	2.14	3.05	4.16	5.16	7.13	11.22	19.07
350	2.14	3.05	4.16	4.99	6.29	9.69	17.06	2.14	2.05	4.16	5.16	7.13	11.22	19.07
400	2.14	3.05	3.93	4.40	5.51	8.48	15.09	2.14	3.05	4.16	4.88	6.28	9.81	19.03
450	2.14	2.98	3.52	3.93	4.90	7.52	13.43	2.14	3.04	3.83	4.33	5.56	8.67	15.17
600	2.10	2.38	2.67	2.97	3.67	5.54	9.86	2.14	2.51	2.86	3.22	4.10	6.32	11.11

Exhibit 4: Principal Cash Flows at 300% and 85% PSA - FNMA 9% Collateral

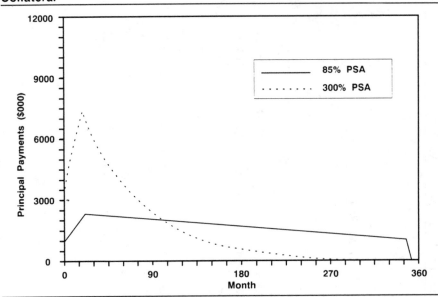

Exhibit 5: Effective Top PAC Prepayment Collars - FNMA 9% Collateral

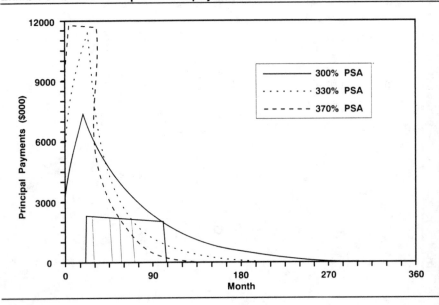

current-coupon-backed PACs. A general rule of thumb adds five basis points to the spread for every point the bond is priced above par.

INTERACTION OF COLLARS AND COLLATERAL

Before further examining the contribution of the collar to the PAC's value, it is useful to review the mechanics of defining a collar and creating a payment schedule. Visualizing the cash flows is also helpful in seeking to understand the behavior of the structure in different scenarios. The PAC schedule is defined by projecting the paydowns from the given collateral at a high and a low constant prepayment speed. Those payment amounts that can be satisfied by both sets of projected principal payments (that is, the smaller of the two amounts generated for each date) make up the schedule. This is depicted graphically in Exhibit 4 by the shaded region. The example depicted was structured from $500 million FNMA 9s with a 9.77% WAC and a 349-month WART[5] on the underlying mortgages, assuming collars of 85 to 300% PSA and a two-year lockout (the period before the first scheduled principal payment).

The faster speed results in a cash flow pattern with the bulk of the principal thrown off during the first five to seven years of the issue's life. The slower speed produces a more level set of smaller cash flows extending to the final maturity of the collateral. The intersection of these two sets of payments forms the schedule. In the example, the bottom collar determines the payment amounts during the first 100 or so months of the schedule, and the top collar the amounts in the remaining months.

The graph of *any speed between* those of the top and bottom collars also would contain the area of the schedule below it. The graph of any speed *faster* than the top collar would bunch more principal in the first years and truncate the tail of the schedule in

---

[5] The scheduled amortization for the collateral is determined by the WAC and WART.

front of the point where the top and bottom collars intersect. Similarly, the graph of any speeds *slower* than the bottom collar would reduce the size of paydowns in the front years. At very slow speeds, most of the principal payments are pushed into the back years.

Once the scheduled principal payments are defined at given collars, the PAC schedule may be further divided into classes with different average lives. The example in Exhibit 5 is split into seven tranches. Some of the earlier bonds in the structure have higher *effective top* collars. An effective collar is the highest (or lowest) constant prepayment speed that would satisfy the entire tranche's payments. For instance, many speeds faster than 300% PSA will contain the first tranche in this example. The fastest speed containing all of the first tranche is that bond's effective upper collar. Effective top collars are shown in Exhibit 5 for the third and fourth tranches. These effective collars are approximately 370 and 330% PSA, respectively. It should be apparent as well that earlier tranches have still higher effective collars.

Likewise, the lower collars used to structure the PACs in Exhibits 4 and 5 do not fully indicate the degree of extension protection the longer average life bonds, tranches 6 and 7, actually possess. Speeds below 85% PSA throw off principal too slowly to satisfy the scheduled payments in the early PAC tranches, but they provide more cash than needed to meet payments after about month 100, where the upper collar binds the schedule. For example, the effective bottom collar on tranche 7 is 55% PSA. Since tranche 6 begins to pay at the point where the top and bottom collars intersect, its effective collar is the same as the structuring collar.

When PACs first became popular, a wide variety of collar ranges and levels were used to generate the schedules, and even as late as the first quarter of 1989, it was not uncommon still to see some variety in collars on new CMO issues backed by similar collateral. However, the smorgasbord of prepayment collars largely has given way to increasing standardization of the speeds at which PAC schedules are created. This standardization is in part the result of demand for liquidity on the part of the growing PAC clientele. It also may have been aided by the fairly homogenous choice of collateral for new issues in 1989. Owing to the shape of the yield curve and other factors,[6] the nature of the available arbitrage resulted in the vast majority of transactions being done in current coupon conventionals.

The standard speeds used to create PAC schedules represent the aggregate opinion of what constitutes a "good" collar. The market's acceptance of these levels is based in part on very recent historical experience. In 1989, typical collar speeds for current coupon conventionals were 75 or 85% PSA at the lower band and 300% PSA at the upper band. In 1990, the higher band tended to creep below 300% PSA for this collateral as the market consensus recognized slower actual prepayment experience. Investors should not extrapolate future prepayments from recent experience. Investors should translate the PSA collars into interest rate collars by using an econometric prepayment model to determine how much interest rates must shift to break the collars. Once the collar speeds are explicitly linked to interest rate shifts, investors can determine if the collar does deliver "good" protection over the scenarios appropriate to the investor's outlook and portfolio.

New issue PACs may be marketed either at the collars used to create the schedule or at their effective collars, although since 1990 the trend has been to advertise effective collars. Unless the effective collar is known, the extent of the PAC's protection against shifts in interest rates cannot be determined. Investors, therefore, should insist on this information, as well as analysis of the bond's performance outside the effective collars. By the same token, investors cannot assume that a new issue, short-term average life

---

[6] Such as different degrees of demand from investors occupying different maturity sectors as a consequence of their liabilities and other portfolio constraints, a reluctance to buy bonds above par, the limited market for excess interest in the form of residuals or IOs, and so forth.

PAC with a very high effective collar is better than a PAC from a series with a single collar indicated.[7]

With greater standardization of structuring speeds, the PAC market has developed a two-tiered structure, with standard PACs in the first tier and PACs with weaker collars in the second, trading fifteen to twenty-five basis points cheaper than "good" PACs. In mid-1989, issuers began to issue both types of PACs from the same transaction by layering a second set of PACs with narrower collars over the first. These two-layered PACs are, in essence, companion bonds with schedules. They are discussed at length in Chapter 20.

PAC COLLAR DRIFT

Many investors do not understand that the PAC collars are not fixed for the life of the tranche, but instead change over time with the actual prepayment experience of the collateral. This is evident from the number of investors who seek to evaluate trades in the secondary PAC market by looking at the collars advertised at issue (which could be either structuring or effective collars). Instead, off-the-run PACs should be evaluated by looking at the current effective collars. In most cases, they can be determined by the security dealers or third-party data services that have modeled the structure and know the current bond and collateral balances.

The effective collars simply express the highest (or lowest) constant prepayment speeds at which the given collateral can continue to meet the scheduled prepayments. Unless the collateral prepays at precisely the collar speed (and then it can match only one, the upper or the lower collar speed), it will have a different

---

[7] If effective collars are indicated, it is usually easy enough to deduce the schedule speeds if information on all the tranches is available. Early PACs in the series will have the same bottom collar—the structuring collar—and varying effective top collars. One or more intermediate PACs will have the structuring collars. Later PACs will show the structuring collar as their top collar and varying effective collars for the bottom. Doing so permits first cut comparisons with PACs offered with their structuring collars stated.

balance than was projected when the schedule was defined. Likewise, the amount of companions (and proportion of companions to PACs) will be different. Prepayment rates below the top collar cause the collar to shift upward over time (as there is a greater amount outstanding than anticipated), while the collar is lowered if prepayments are higher. Likewise, prepayments above the bottom collar cause it to rise, while prepayment rates below the bottom collar cause it to shift down. Prepayment rates somewhere between the top and bottom collars—historically, the common occurrence—cause the effective collars to drift up and to widen as the top collar changes more quickly than the bottom collar, unless prepayments are very near the top collar.[8]

Prepayment experience has been moderate to slow for most pass-throughs used in outstanding PAC structures. As a result, upper bands have generally drifted up, improving the call protection on the remaining PACs. On the other hand, lower bands have been eroded by prepayments at levels above typical good bottom collars.

Investors seeking to identify value correctly must incorporate collar drift in their analysis. For example, many premium-backed PACs may be undervalued, as their prepayments typically have been well within the collars. As discussed, bonds backed by premium collateral trade at wider spreads, owing to their higher perceived call risk. This same risk, however, can be reduced by the upward drift of the collars. At the same time, the greater likelihood that the lower band can be violated is actually a plus for bonds with above market coupons.

PAC BOND COUPON

Breaking a PAC's schedule and causing it to be partially called or extended are not necessarily negative events for the bond's economic performance. The bond's coupon relative to market yields

---

[8] These mechanics are discussed at greater length in Chapter 14.

(or the bond's price relative to parity[9]) determines the effect pre-payments outside the collar have on the realized yield or total re-turn. A PAC with a discount coupon may benefit if the upper collar is broken, returning principal at par earlier than anticipated at pricing. Similarly, the extension caused by breaking the lower collar adversely affects the performance of a discount coupon PAC. In the case of a premium coupon PAC, it benefits perform-ance when the bottom collar is broken, since the principal remains outstanding longer than anticipated, earning additional coupon in-terest. And of course, the higher the coupon, the worse the effect of breaking the top collar. Although considerable PAC demand is driven by investors who are maturity-matching liabilities, PAC pricing should reflect these effects to some degree.

In general, market spreads reflect the coupon effect in bonds with average lives of five or more years, with longer lives requir-ing larger adjustments. Investors are more discriminating in the current coupon collateral sector of the market, where the bulk of the new bonds are now produced and where the greatest volume of secondary market trading takes place. Spreads for ten-year PACs historically have been twenty basis points wider for low coupon premiums. In the twenty-year sector, deep discounts have traded thirty basis points tighter, and lower coupon premiums about fifteen basis points wider.

WINDOWS

A PAC "window" is the interval over which scheduled principal payments are made to the bond holder. As long as prepayment speeds remain at a constant speed within the upper and lower protection bands, or PAC collars, the dates of the first and last principal payments (and equivalently, the length of the repayment

---

[9] The delay in passing payments through to investors from the mortgage borrowers lowers the yield slightly for any given price because the cash flows are pushed out into the future. Different prepayment speeds do not change the yield if a bond is purchased at the parity price (slightly below 100), which adjusts par for the payment delay.

period) are certain. PAC buyers in general prefer tighter windows. To some extent, this preference reflects the practicalities of managing their portfolios. The match between a single liability and a single asset is easier to conceptualize when payments are concentrated over a short period. They also are easier to convert to floating rate assets with swaps. A shorter window also means fewer and larger repayments. Most investors, however, have liabilities spread over time, which suggests the preference may be more psychological than financial, reflecting, for example, the fact that many PAC buyers are traditionally corporate investors. Tighter windows producing a more bullet-like paydown are, conceptually at least, better substitutes for corporates.

Generally, the longer the average life of the bond, the more value the market assigns to tight windows, although investors are most discriminating in the five-, seven-, and ten-year sectors of the market. Buyers of shorter-term PACs are less concerned with the length of the window, while the desire for tight windows in the twenty-year sector is very difficult to satisfy, owing to the "tailish" nature of the cash flows in the later years of the transaction. That is, the principal payments scheduled for the later years are relatively small. This is easily confirmed by glancing at Exhibit 4. Carving the "tail" into shorter windows would result in more classes with odd, less marketable average lives.

A "good" window in the five-year sector is two years long; an "OK" window is three to four years. Among seven-year PACs, three-year windows are preferred; among ten-years, four to five years is desirable. The value of good windows varies with supply and generally improves with longer-term average lives. A very good window on a ten-year PAC, for example, might be worth five to ten basis points in spread.

It may be that some investors appear to prefer tight windows because they expect superior performance. For example, they may believe a tighter window has less average life variability when prepayments are outside the PAC collars. This hunch is disproved by experimenting with different window lengths in otherwise identical PACs (same collateral, same average lives). Exhibit 6

Exhibit 6: Impact of Window Size on the Average Life Variability of PAC
Bonds

| | Average Life (years) | | | | | |
| | 5-Year PAC | | | 10-Year PAC | | |
Payment Speed (% PSA)	0.5 yr. Window	2.2 yr. Window	4.4 yr. Window	3.2 yr. Window	5.0 yr. Window	7.3 yr. Window
0	13.78	13.69	13.38	20.68	20.61	20.50
50	6.68	6.67	6.65	13.70	13.62	13.49
75	5.49	5.48	5.48	11.42	11.47	11.50
100	5.16	5.16	5.16	11.22	11.22	11.22
300	5.16	5.16	5.16	11.22	11.22	11.22
350	5.01	4.96	4.87	9.68	9.69	9.69
400	4.40	4.41	4.41	8.47	8.48	8.48
450	3.93	3.94	3.96	7.51	7.51	7.52
600	2.97	2.98	3.00	5.53	5.53	5.54

Note: All structures are backed by $500MM FNMA 9s, 9.77 WAC, 349 WAM and
have 85% to 300% PSA collars.

shows two such experiments manipulating the windows of the
five- and ten-year PACs in a structure containing a complete series
of PACs with average lives from two to twenty years, backed by
$500 million FNMA 9s (9.77% WAC, 349-month WART) and pro-
tected between 85 and 300% PSA. Even at fairly extreme prepayment speeds (0 and 600% PSA, for instance), there is little
difference in the average lives of otherwise comparable PACs with
different windows. *In general, as a result of their slightly wider
spreads, PACs with average or wide windows should outperform those
with tight windows.* This result suggests that investors who do not
require a bullet-like repayment of their investment, but rather can
accommodate greater payment dispersion, should not discriminate
between window sizes. Investors who can adapt to a longer paydown period by such means as modifying their cash management
procedures, adopting more sophisticated techniques for modeling
and managing their asset-liability positions or other procedural

changes, would also be able to take advantage of the relative cheapness of wide windows.

Tighter windows may affect performance when the PAC is a current pay bond. In this case, a shorter window reduces the likelihood that prepayments can accelerate or decelerate to levels outside the bands before it is fully retired according to schedule. Tight windows also enable a bond to roll down the yield curve move effectively, an issue for holders of short- and, in some environments, intermediate-term PACs.

LOCKOUT

A lockout is properly a feature of the companion rather than the PAC bonds in a CMO structure. A portion of the PAC schedule is paid to companion bond holders; PAC bonds are "locked out" of the structure for the period over which those principal payments are diverted to the companion classes. Lockouts typically occur over the first twelve to twenty-four months of the issue's life. The desired effect of the lockout is to stabilize the early companion class. This is achieved by acquiring for the companions the principal cash flows that in effect have the highest effective collars (that is, they will be realized across a very wide range of prepays). Depending on the amount of seasoning in the underlying collateral, a certain amount of principal will be generated at zero prepayment rates. These cash flows, which have a high degree of certainty, are used during the lockout to pay the companions. Some market participants, however, speak of the lockout as a PAC bond characteristic or feature; they may be viewing the lockout as a device for narrowing the PAC window. Others may perceive the lockout as somehow detrimental to the PACs in the structure, perhaps assuming that the PACs are somehow hurt to the extent the companions are helped.

Whether any of these assumptions are valid should be apparent from the example in Exhibit 7. The table contrasts the volatilities of three-, seven-, and ten-year average life bonds from a

Exhibit 7: Impact of Lockout Feature on the Average Life Variability of PAC Bonds

Payment (Speed (% PSA)	Average Life (years)					
	No Lockout			2-Year Lockout		
	3-yr.	7-yr.	10-yr.	3-yr.	7-yr.	10-yr.
0	11.14	18.98	21.96	7.46	16.57	20.72
50	4.41	10.22	14.36	3.60	9.23	13.75
85	3.05	7.10	11.22	3.05	7.10	11.22
300	3.05	7.10	11.22	3.05	7.10	11.22
355	3.01	6.26	9.70	3.05	6.34	9.68
400	2.84	5.49	8.49	3.02	5.58	8.47
450	2.66	4.89	7.53	2.89	4.96	7.51
600	2.17	3.66	5.55	2.37	3.71	5.53

Note: Both structures are backed by $500MM FNMA 9s, 9.77 WAC, 349 WAM and have 85% to 300% PSA collars.

structure without any lockout with those from one with a two-year lockout. Both structures are backed by the same collateral, FNMA 9s, with a 9.77% WAC and 349-month WART, and use the maximum PAC schedule consistent with collars of 85 to 300% PSA, and, as appropriate, a lockout. The sizes of the bonds compared have been adjusted to match their average lives within two decimal places. (The twenty-year bonds are not included in the comparison because their average lives were too different after matching the earlier bonds.)

   The lockout, according to the exhibit, benefits the PAC bonds by reducing both call and extension risk. Earlier bonds benefit more than later bonds, with the ten-year classes displaying only marginal reductions in average life volatility. Two effects are at work here. First, the lockout reduces the size of the schedule by removing all payments in the first two years. This results automatically in a smaller amount of PAC bonds relative to the companions; conversely, more companions protect the remaining PAC schedule. Since they contain those cash flows from the collateral with the lowest degree of call risk, the companions are much less vulnerable to call risk, and even at very high prepayment speeds a larger proportion of companion bonds remain outstanding to shelter the PAC bonds than would otherwise have been the case. At the same time, these principal amounts are no longer bound to a schedule, meaning that later scheduled payments have a better likelihood of being paid on schedule in event of speeds below the bottom collar.

IS THERE A Z IN THE DEAL?

A Z- or accrual bond ("Z" standing for zero coupon) is a type of CMO bond structure that pays no interest until it begins to pay principal. Until that time, the interest payments are accrued at the coupon rate and added to the principal amount outstanding. A Z-bond is most typically included in a CMO structure as the last bond class to be retired. Of course, the underlying collateral continues to pay coupon interest; the portion that would have gone to the Z-bond holders, had it been structured as a coupon-paying bond, is used instead to retire the earlier classes. In effect, then, the presence of a Z-bond permits CMO structurers to increase the size of the earlier classes, since the "accrual" amounts are additional to the projected principal payments from the collateral. More pertinently, the "accrual" helps to stabilize the earlier bonds, since a portion of the cash flow used to retire them is not directly determined by the level of prepayments.

The interaction of Z-bonds with earlier classes is discussed in detail in Chapter 19. Readers who are unfamiliar with the Z-bond structure or interested in more complex manifestations of the Z-structure, should refer to that chapter. The objective of this discussion is to examine the value, if any, that a long-term Z-bond contributes to PACs. A related issue also is explored, namely the possibility that accrual from the Z-bond is used to stabilize earlier companion bonds and not the PAC bonds. Such a mechanism might not be explicitly disclosed when the bonds from the structure are traded, and may only be indicated in the prospectus.

Two CMO structures were modeled to examine more closely the impact of a Z-bond on their performance and relative value, again backed by the same FNMA 9% collateral, and containing the maximum principal amount of PACs given collars of 85 to 300% PSA and the relevant accrual mechanism. The schedule has been divided into a series of bonds with nominal average lives of two, three, four, five, seven, ten, and twenty years, the average lives of all but the twenty-year matching to within two decimal places (as in the lockout example, because the schedules differ significantly in amount, the twenty-year bonds are not comparable).

Both structures contain twenty-year Z-bonds. The first passes accrual to PAC and earlier companion bonds alike, the second to earlier companions only. The average lives of the two PAC series at various prepayment rates are displayed in Exhibit 8.

Investors should note the difference in average life performance between the PACs supported by a Z-bond and the PACs whose companions alone are supported by the Z-bond. The *Z-bond stabilizes the PAC bonds when prepayments break the lower collar.* This makes sense—accrual cash flow is generated as long as the Z-bond is outstanding. On the other hand, *PAC bonds shorten more sharply* in the structure with the Z-bond when the upper collar is broken, because a smaller proportion of companion bonds is outstanding at any time to cushion PACs from high rates of prepayments. In fact, the faster the prepayments, the smaller the principal balance of the Z-bond when it begins to absorb excess cash, and the quicker it can be extinguished. This example should warn investors not to assume, however, that because a Z-bond is present in the structure, that the PACs will have less extension risk. There is no rule in the marketplace requiring issuers to pay accrual to PAC bonds. In some market environments, diverting accrual to the companions can make them more marketable, and a CMO arbitrage more viable. If this is the case, then issuers will structure their CMOs accordingly. The moral of the story: ask for the priorities in detail and read the prospectus.

Readers also may have noticed that the average life profile of the PACs that receive no accrual in this example is identical to

Exhibit 8: Impact of Z-Bond Accrual on the Average Life Variability of PAC Bonds

Prepayment Speed (% PSA)	Average Life (years)													
	Accrual to PACs and Companions							Accrual to Companions Only						
	2-yr.	3-yr.	4-yr.	5-yr.	7-yr.	10-yr.		2-yr.	3-yr.	4-yr.	5-yr.	7-yr.	10-yr.
0	2.74	6.03	9.05	11.04	14.01	17.11		3.20	7.70	11.44	13.74	16.97	20.50
50	2.21	3.53	5.07	6.40	8.85	12.24		2.23	3.61	5.25	6.67	9.37	13.49
85	2.13	3.05	4.16	5.16	7.13	11.23		2.13	3.05	4.16	5.16	7.13	11.22
300	2.13	3.05	4.16	5.16	7.13	11.23		2.13	3.05	4.16	5.16	7.13	11.22
350	2.13	3.00	4.13	4.76	6.19	9.68		2.13	3.05	4.16	4.99	6.29	9.69
400	2.13	2.82	3.68	4.19	5.93	8.47		2.13	3.05	3.93	4.40	5.51	8.48
450	2.13	2.21	3.30	3.74	4.83	7.51		2.13	2.95	3.52	3.93	4.90	7.52
600	1.97	1.82	2.52	2.84	3.62	5.53		2.10	2.38	2.67	2.97	3.67	5.54

Note: Both structures are backed by $500MM FNMA 9s, 9.77 WAC, 349 WAM and have 85% to 300% PSA collars.

that of the PACs backed by the same collateral in a structure with no Z-bond. (See Exhibit 3.) In other words, for PAC buyers, diverting accrual to the companions is the same as not including a Z-bond in the structure at all. This makes sense—the same aggregate amount of companion bonds is available to support the PAC bonds, with the only difference being that the weight of companion principal payments is shifted forward in time since the payments to the non-Z companions consist in part of interest accrued by the Z-bond.

EFFECT OF JUMP-Zs AND VADMs ON PAC BONDS

During 1990, structurers began to create a special bond class from the accrual thrown off by a Z-bond. Variously called thrift liquidity bonds, VADMs (Very Accurately Determined Maturity), or SMAT (Stated Maturity), these bonds first appealed to savings and loan institutions who are required by regulation to maintain a portion of their assets in very high-quality, short-term investments, and who, accordingly, are willing to pay a premium for instruments that qualify *and* offer yields more attractive than those of, for example, government issues. These bonds appeal to investors such as commercial banks who are sensitive to the extension risk associated with rising yield environments, so that VADMs with final maturities greater than two years have been issued in growing amounts. The size of a VADM class is determined by the amount of accrual (or accrual and principal) thrown off at a zero prepayment rate up to the desired final maturity; obviously, faster prepayments will shorten the maturity, but no event can lengthen it. The presence of a VADM has the same effect on the PAC performance as diverting the accrual to the companion classes has in the preceding example.

In a handful of issues, structurers have designed the companion Z-bonds to convert to a "payer" early, changing their priority among companions for principal from last to current. There are a variety of ways to make a Z "jump"; the chief ones are described in Chapter 19. Once the Z-bond converts to the current pay bond and begins to pay coupon interest, its support is no longer available to the PAC classes. The effect on PAC performance is generally the same as in the basic example above. However, the degree to which the PACs lose extension protection is moderated by the amount of time it takes to trigger the conversion, and by whether the jump is a temporary response to some condition (such as a specified prepayment threshold) or permanent (a "sticky" Z).

PRIORITY TO RECEIVE EXCESS CASH FLOWS

The PAC schedule is protected by the existence of companion classes. The mechanism is simple—in any period the companions absorb all principal in excess of the scheduled payments, and any current-paying PACs have first claim on all principal received. This protection ceases when all the companion classes have been fully retired, an event that occurs if the collateral consistently pays at speeds above the top collar. Once the companions are retired, any principal is distributed to the outstanding PACs, according to priorities defined for the particular CMO issue. Frequently, these priorities pay excess principal to the outstanding PACs in order of final maturity, but this is not always the case. A wholesale examination of CMO prospectuses will unearth numerous examples of structures that pay excess in the reverse of maturity order or otherwise insulate some classes at the expense of others. The impact of such schemes has, as would be expected, a significant affect on the average life volatility of the various PACs.

A simple example contrasting two priority schemes is shown in Exhibit 9. This exhibit compares the average lives of two sets of PACs at various prepayment speeds—one receiving excess principal in the maturity order, the other in the reverse maturity order. As the exhibit indicates, reversing the order in which PACs are subjected to prepayments above the top collar drastically alters the

Exhibit 9: Impact of Excess Payment Order on the Average Life Variability of PAC Bonds

Average Life (years)

Speed (% PSA)	Excess in Order of Maturity							Excess in Reverse Maturity Order						
	2-yr.	3-yr.	4-yr.	5-yr.	7-yr.	10-yr.	20-yr.	2-yr.	3-yr.	4-yr.	5-yr.	7-yr.	10-yr.	20-yr.
0	3.20	7.70	11.44	13.74	16.97	20.50	22.75	3.20	7.70	11.44	13.74	16.97	20.50	22.75
50	2.73	3.61	5.75	6.67	9.37	13.49	19.24	2.73	3.61	5.75	6.67	9.37	13.49	19.24
85	2.14	3.05	4.16	5.16	7.13	11.22	19.23	2.14	3.05	4.16	5.16	7.13	11.22	19.23
300	2.14	3.05	4.16	5.16	7.13	11.22	19.23	2.14	3.05	4.16	5.16	7.13	11.22	19.23
350	2.14	3.05	4.16	4.99	6.29	9.69	17.06	2.14	2.05	4.16	5.16	7.14	11.95	5.42
400	2.14	3.05	3.93	4.40	5.51	8.48	15.09	2.14	3.05	4.16	5.16	7.17	9.65	4.07
450	2.14	2.95	3.52	3.93	4.90	7.52	13.43	2.14	3.04	4.16	5.16	7.26	7.56	3.35
600	2.10	2.38	2.67	2.97	3.67	5.54	9.86	2.14	2.51	4.16	5.16	7.24	3.09	2.27

Note: Both structures are backed by $500 MM FNMA 9s, 9.77 WAC, 349 WAM and have 85% to 300% PSA collars.

average life performance of the PACs, if prepayments are outside of the collars. As would be expected, shorter PACs benefit at the expense of the longer. When the excess is paid in reverse, the short- and intermediate-term PACs are more significantly stable; when prepayments increase, longer PACs, with ten- and twenty-year average lives, shorten up much more significantly.

THE OPTION COSTS OF PAC FEATURES

Most participants in the PAC market evaluate individual bonds by examining their average life and yield over various constant prepayment scenarios outside the collars, a technique similar to the one used in this chapter to analyze the various PAC features. The procedure has recognized disadvantages, some of which can be reduced to the complaint that they use a constant prepayment assumption. Using such tools, investors can devise investment criteria for PACs such as "I will buy ten-year PACs with four-year windows at 120 off if they don't shorten to less than eight years average life given an instantaneous 200 basis point drop in yields." Implicitly, they are using these tools to measure and value the prepayment options embedded in their PAC bonds. However savvy and tough-minded the criteria sound, they are at bottom purely subjective guesses about how much the random exercise of those options will impair or help investment results.

It is possible to measure the impact of prepayment risk on the yields earned by PACs by employing the option pricing models already extensively used to evaluate pass-throughs. These models generate spreads, durations (price sensitivity), and convexities (the sensitivity of duration to yield changes) that are explicitly adjusted to account for expected prepayments on a large sample of possible interest rate paths over the life of the PAC. In particular, these models derive the cost of the prepayment options in the PAC, and determine the reduction in total spread caused by interest rate volatility.[10] The model, in simple terms, summarizes hundreds more scenarios than investors can digest looking at price/yield tables. The scenarios, moreover, are more realistic in that they permit interest rates to move randomly at each point along the path.

Option-adjusted spreads (OAS) vary with market conditions. For this reason, a discussion of current OASs is inappropriate here. However, the option costs derived from the analysis are not very sensitive to current market yield levels (although they will vary somewhat with changes in the level of implied volatility), and can be discussed here without becoming hopelessly stale with the next rally or correction in fixed-income markets.

As expected, PACs demonstrate very low option costs. *Option costs in the current-coupon-backed structures discussed in this chapter generally ranged from zero to twenty basis points for bonds with three- to twenty-year average lives.* By comparison, the collateral (FNMA 9s) had thirty-five basis points of option cost. The PAC bonds backed by premium collateral (FNMA 10 1/2s) had demonstrably higher option costs, ranging from three to over forty basis points. The collateral had an option cost of sixty-eight basis points.

The general pattern revealed by the option-pricing model is illustrated in Exhibit 10. The option costs are calculated for the series, described in earlier sections, of two-, three-, four-, five-, seven-, and twenty-year average life PACs backed by FNMA 9s. (See Exhibit 3 for the average life profile of these bonds.) The patterns displayed by option costs for premium-backed PACs are shown in Exhibit 11. The option costs for these series are analyzed

---

[10] The model employed in this discussion, like many other OAS models, uses Monte Carlo simulation and an econometric prepayment model. A minimum of 200 paths was generated in the analysis. The total spread computed is a total spread to the entire Treasury yield curve (precisely, the forward rates implied by current Treasury yields), as opposed to a single benchmark. It roughly approximates the spread to a particular Treasury quoted in the market, but differs more or less depending on the slope of the yield curve. The total spread is the spread over Treasuries the security would earn given its current market price if there were zero volatility. The option-adjusted spread (OAS) is the average spread earned across a large sample of interest rate scenarios given the market price. The option cost is measured as the difference between total and option-adjusted spread, and captures the reduction in total spread caused by interest rate volatility.

Exhibit 10: Sensitivity of Option Costs in PACs to Interest Rate Shifts (Current-Coupon Conventional Collateral)

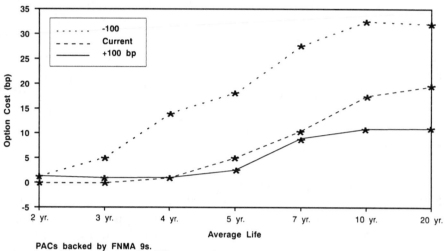

PACs backed by FNMA 9s.
Instantaneous interest-rate shifts assumed.

Exhibit 11: Sensitivity of Option Costs in PACs to Interest Rate Shifts (Premium-Coupon Conventional Collateral)

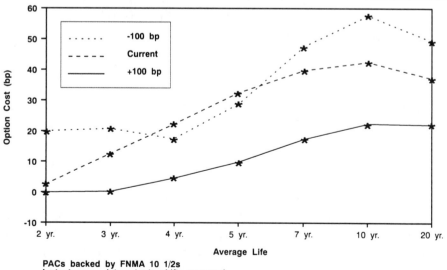

PACs backed by FNMA 10 1/2s
Instantaneous interest-rate shifts assumed.

in three scenarios: assuming the interest rate environment (of January 23, 1990) remains constant and assuming instantaneous parallel shifts in interest rates of up and down 100 basis points. Assuming a constant option-adjusted spread, the shifts in the up and down cases are typically large enough to give the tranches, which currently are priced close to par, a discount or premium price. In this way it is possible to draw some conclusions about the sensitivity of the structure to interest rate shocks. Ranging from three to over thirty basis points, the option costs demonstrated by the current-coupon-backed PACs in the bullish scenario are consistent, as well, with the general magnitude of option costs observed in premium-coupon-backed PACs.

As expected, the option costs rise with the average life of the PAC. This result is expected if only because the probability an option will be exercised is greater the later its expiration date. Comparing the current and bearish cases, the increase in extension risk as interest rates rise results in a slightly higher option cost for two- and three-year PACs. Of greater interest is the fact that, going from the ten-year PAC to the twenty-year, option costs either decline or increase at a slower rate in every interest rate case. This result holds for the option costs in a similar set of PACs depicted in Exhibit 11, backed in this instance by premium coupon collateral (the average life profile is in Exhibit 3). *The fact that option costs tend to peak with ten-year PACs rather than twenty-year PACs* should take some market participants by surprise, and suggest to others that the ten basis points (on average) of incremental spread required by twenty-year PAC buyers represents extra value, especially when it is considered that the twenty-year sector usually is the highest yielding among the on-the-run Treasuries. The result is intuitively appealing as well. The twenty-year PAC consists of the tail of the PAC schedule, and the low, widely dispersed payment amounts lend stability. Moreover, the prepayment model used to project prepayments over various interest rate paths correctly reflects the tendency of mortgage pools to "burnout" following sustained periods of fast prepayment rates. As a result, prepayments tend to slow down in the later years of the pool's life. In addition, as long as the PACs have sequential priority to excess cash flow, the last PAC in the series is protected by the earlier PACs.

When the effect of a lockout was examined using average life profiles (Exhibit 7), the benefits to the PACs were more pronounced the earlier the bond came in the series. By explicitly valuing the option costs for the same example, a similar effect is observed, as is shown in Exhibit 12. However, the seven- and ten-year tranches receive no benefit from the lockout on an option-cost basis, whereas their average lives are observed to lengthen less sharply in extremely slow prepayment rate environments. The exhibit also indicates a benefit to the twenty-year PAC, except when interest rates drop and the collateral becomes a premium security and subject to faster prepayments. The twenty-year PACs were not compared in Exhibit 6 since, given a different amount in the schedules, it was not possible to match the average lives of all four bonds (the twenty-year in the lockout structure had an average life

Exhibit 12: Sensitivity of Option Costs in PACs to Interest Rate Shifts In Structures With and Without a Lockout

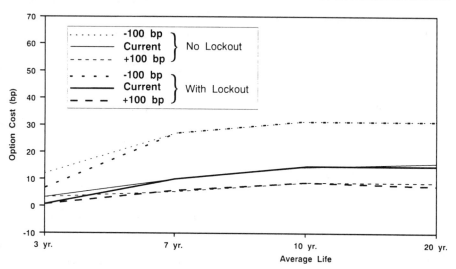

PACs backed by current-coupon conventional collateral.
Instantaneous interest-rate shifts assumed.

close to sixteen years). This difference also may account for the lower option cost imputed to the twenty-year in the lockout structure.

The impact of various window lengths on five- and ten-year PACs also was examined, with no increase or diminution of option costs observed, except for the five-year bonds in the bullish case. Even then, only slight differences, at best three basis points, were manifested. This underscores the conclusion, stated earlier, that windows are less relevant from a value viewpoint.

Some security analysts and investors resist this result. They believe, for instance, that a tight window lowers the likelihood of breaking the collars during the paydown period. Therefore, they reason, the prepayment options that they effectively hold should be less costly. The time value of the options, however, includes the period prior to the first payment, because the protection implicit in the collars can be damaged or enhanced by prepayment experience in earlier months or years of the structure's life. Several full interest rate and housing industry *cycles* can occur before a single principal payment is made to a five- or seven-year PAC, with periods of slower prepayments tending to improve a PAC's call protection and faster prepayments tending to erode it. If prepayments violate the lower collar when earlier PACs are paying, both the call and extension protection of the later PACs can actually improve! When many such possibilities are simulated, the net effect should be small or negligible.[11]

The option costs for two series of PACs in Z-bond structures, one funded by the Z-bond and one not, are displayed in Exhibit 13. The fact that the Z-bond helps to reduce the extension risk in the PACs but exposes them to additional call risk is illustrated. The PACs paid down with accrual tend to have higher option costs, except in the bearish case, where prepayments are less likely to retire the Z-bond before the PACs have been paid. (The rela-

---

[11] The first PAC, then, should benefit the most from a tight window. A two- or three-year PAC, however, already tends to have a short window and very low option costs, for reasons previously explained.

Exhibit 13: Sensitivity of Option Costs in PACs to Interest Rate Shifts When Z-Bond Funds Companions Only & When Z-Bond Funds PACs and Companions

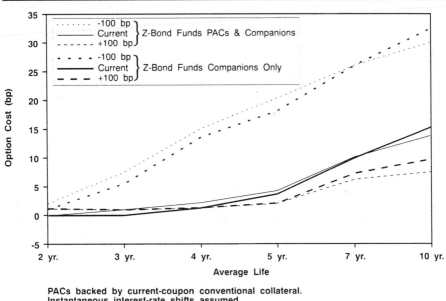

PACs backed by current-coupon conventional collateral.
Instantaneous interest-rate shifts assumed.

tionship appears to weaken for twenty-year bonds, but this most likely reflects the fact that the twenty-year bonds have very different average lives as a result of matching the earlier bonds. The twenty-year PAC paid by accrual actually has an average life of over twenty-six years.)

Reversing the priorities when the top collar is broken, so that the last PAC in the schedule is the first to receive excess principal after the companions are retired, has a very large effect on the option costs in the seven-, ten-, and twenty-year PACs. This effect is apparent in Exhibit 14. The higher the priority, the greater the call risk and the higher the option costs. The impact is, as expected, accentuated as declining yields elevate the risk of prepayment. By contrast, shifting the call risk to the later tranches strips most of the already low option costs from the earlier tranches.

Exhibit 14: Sensitivity of Option Costs in PACs to Interest Rate Shifts When Excess Cash Is Paid to PACs in Sequential and Reverse Orders

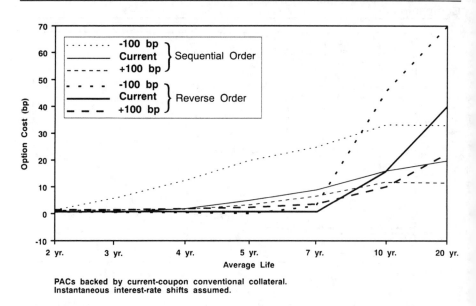

PACs backed by current-coupon conventional collateral.
Instantaneous interest-rate shifts assumed.

CONCLUSION

The scheduled payments of PACs, protected over a wide range of possible prepayment speeds, appeal primarily to insurance companies and other buy-and-hold investors who are matching specific liabilities. The liquidity, yields, and wide diversity of features in the market also attract growing numbers of active bond managers. Misconceptions about the value of certain PAC features have created a number of opportunities for investors in both groups. Most notably, many premium-coupon-backed PACs may be undervalued when their current effective collars are taken into account; the length of the PAC window does not contribute to economic value; lockouts benefit short-term average life PACs as well as companions; and Z-bonds can protect earlier PAC bonds from extension risk.

The considerable standardization of the PAC market achieved since 1988 should not distract investors from the need to carefully examine the performance of every bond outside the stated collars. Investors who fail to stress-test PAC investments may overlook the fact that effective collars are significantly different from those stated at issue. Any kink or deviation from sequential order in the prioritization of excess cash flow to the PACs after companion classes are retired must be detected, as it could drastically affect the performance of the longer-term PACs. Although the impact on value is less dramatic, investors should also determine whether a long-term Z-bond pays companions or PACs in the structure.

PACs are normally evaluated by examining the yields and average lives of PAC investments over a variety of prepayment scenarios. Such analyses must be carried a step further and linked to possible interest rate scenarios. The soundest way to do this is to employ a prepayment model that explicitly recognizes the determinants of prepayment behavior. Such an analysis can be supplemented and its insights extended by employing option-based pricing methods. The results of explicitly measuring the option costs associated with a variety of PAC features have been summarized in this chapter, and confirm the general results derived from a price-yield-average-life evaluation of the same series of PAC bonds. In some instances, the option-pricing approach differentiated more strongly between the contribution or subtraction to value made by different PAC features. For example, it was observed that option costs decline or are little higher for twenty-year PACs than those for ten-year PACs, whereas the required spreads for twenty-year PACs are substantially higher than those of ten-years. This finding suggests valuable opportunities in the twenty-year sector.

CHAPTER 18

PAC IOs

Bella Borg*
Associate Director
Financial Analytics & Structured Transactions Group
Bear, Stearns & Co., Inc.

David Martin
Associate
Financial Analytics & Structured Transactions Group
Bear, Stearns & Co., Inc.

Michael Naughton
Managing Director
Financial Analytics & Structured Transactions Group
Bear, Stearns & Co., Inc.

Sarah Wolf
Associate Director
Financial Analytics & Structured Transactions Group
Bear, Stearns & Co., Inc.

---

* Bella Borg is currently employed by Merrill Lynch.

A PAC IO is a planned amortization class of a CMO/REMIC that receives interest stripped off of one or more PAC tranches within a CMO. It is distinguished by its small amount of principal (minimum of $10,000) and high coupon (maximum of 1199%). The principal portion of the PAC IO pays simultaneously with the underlying PAC tranche(s). Since the cash flow of the PAC IO stems primarily from interest, its performance characteristics are similar to a PAC at prepayment speeds within the PAC band and an IO outside the PAC band. The appendix to this chapter shows how to calculate the coupon of a PAC IO given the principal face of the PAC IO and the principal face given the coupon of the PAC IO.

Exhibit 1 contains the yield, average life, and duration profile of a 5-year PAC IO and a 5-year PAC from FNMA 9165. The PAC IO is a 100 basis point strip off of the 5-year and 6-year PACs. The PAC IO is offered at 130 basis points over the 5-year Treasury while the PAC is priced at 80 basis points over the 5-year Treasury. The PAC band is 80% to 240% PSA.

The "IO-like" yield sensitivities of the PAC IO are illustrated in Exhibit 1. At constant prepayment speeds below the lower end of the PAC band, such as 50% PSA, the yield of the PAC IO exceeds the yield of the PAC bond by 600 basis points, whereas at faster speeds such as 400% PSA, the PAC IO considerably underper-

Exhibit 1: Yield, Average Life and Cash Flow Duration

			FNMA 9165 I3: 5-Year PAC IO				
PSA	50%	75%	100%	**150%**	200%	300%	400%
Yield	14.617	10.258	9.200	**9.200**	9.200	6.793	-2.820
Avg. Life	7.42	6.11	5.87	**5.87**	5.87	5.41	4.21
Duration	2.93	2.69	2.65	**2.65**	2.65	2.54	2.28
			FNMA 9165 Y4: 5-Year PAC				
PSA	50%	75%	100%	**150%**	200%	300%	400%
Yield	8.521	8.671	8.706	**8.706**	8.706	8.751	9.015
Avg Life	6.77	5.57	5.35	**5.35**	5.35	5.06	3.97
Duration	5.06	4.34	4.21	**4.21**	4.21	4.04	3.27

forms. *The only prepayment scenario in which the yield of a PAC IO is negatively impacted is a sustained increase in prepayments.*

PERFORMANCE OF PAC IOs UNDER DYNAMIC PREPAYMENT SCENARIOS

Valuing a PAC IO under static prepayments does not reveal its inherent value: the performance of a PAC IO is dependent upon the shifting nature of PAC bands in dynamic prepayment scenarios. If prepayments are slower than the upper end of the PAC band, the effective upper band of the PAC will shift upwards, giving the PAC IO more call protection at faster prepayment speeds. This occurs because there are more support tranches outstanding to support the PACs if prepayments increase. On the other hand, if prepayments are faster than the lower end of the PAC band, the effective lower end of the PAC band will shift upwards. This is because there are fewer support tranches outstanding to support the PACs if prepayments slow down.

The performance of the 5-year PAC IO of FNMA 9165 is illustrated in the example in Exhibit 2. We assume that prepayments speed up to 400% PSA for 12 through 38 months, and then slow down to 150% PSA for the remaining life of the PAC IO. It is only after 38 months of fast prepayments that the yield of the PAC IO declines below its initial offering level of 9.20%. Thus variability of prepayments such as slower prepayment speeds or a combination of faster and then slower prepayment speeds may increase the yield of a PAC IO.

Exhibit 2: Performance of FNMA 9165 5-Year PAC IO
400% PSA for 12 through 38 Months, 150% PSA Thereafter

	Base	12 Mos	24 Mos	36 Mos	38 Mos
Yield	9.200	9.200	9.200	9.708	9.007
Avg. Life	5.87	5.87	5.87	5.99	5.84
Duration	2.65	2.65	2.65	2.67	2.64

In this type of prepayment scenario, as prepayments speed up, the tranches that support the PACs pay down more quickly; eventually there is not enough underlying collateral to meet the PAC schedules at slower speeds that were initially within the PAC band. At these slower speeds the average lives and durations of the PACs will extend. The extension risk of the PAC is a benefit to the PAC IO. As the average life of the PAC extends, the PAC IO remains outstanding longer causing its yield to increase.

The amount of call protection that a PAC IO provides depends on the average life sector it is stripped from. In general, the 2-year and 3-year PACs have the widest effective PAC bands, so a PAC IO stripped off these PACs will have more call protection. However, a shorter maturity PAC IO will not experience any significant lengthening in average life or duration if prepayments slow down. A PAC IO stripped off the intermediate maturity PACs has the narrowest effective PAC band and, therefore, the least call protection, but has the most potential for average life and duration extension, and a corresponding increase in yield if prepayments slow down.

Finally, a PAC IO stripped off of 20-year PACs will have a similar effective band as intermediate PAC IOs: however, it will exhibit more stable yields at prepayment rates above the effective PAC band because the 20-year PACs are usually the last bonds in the CMO to pay down. In the example shown in Exhibit 3, at static prepayments speeds, the 20-year PAC IO of FNMA 9159 will extend only 0.27 years if prepayments on the underlying collateral slow down to 50% PSA. At faster prepayments of 400% PSA, the

Exhibit 3: Yield, Average Life and Cash Flow Duration

FNMA 9159 I3: 20-Year PAC IO							
PSA	50%	75%	100%	**150%**	200%	300%	400%
Yield	10.180	9.870	9.870	**9.870**	9.870	8.828	6.272
Avg. Life	20.18	19.91	19.91	**19.91**	19.91	17.87	14.45
Duration	8.47	8.36	8.36	**8.36**	8.36	7.92	7.11

	Base	12 Mos	36 Mos	48 Mos	60 Mos	72 Mos	85 Mos
Yield	9.870	9.870	10.302	10.725	10.482	10.207	9.845
Avg. Life	19.91	19.91	20.68	22.19	21.62	21.03	20.32
Duration	8.36	8.36	8.54	8.82	8.69	8.56	8.41

Exhibit 4: Performance of FNMA 9159 20-Year PAC IO 400% PSA for 12 through 84 Months, 165% PSA Thereafter

average life of the 20-year PAC IO shortens 5.5 years, and its yield only falls 3.598%.

The high degree of yield protection of the 20-year PAC IO is illustrated in Exhibit 4 using a similar stress test that was used on the 5-year PAC IO. Since the underlying collateral is FNMA 9s, prepayments are assumed to speed up to 400% PSA for months 12 through 85, and then to slow down to 165% PSA for the remaining life of the PAC IO. For example, if prepayments speed up to 400% PSA for 48 months and then slow down to 165% PSA for the remaining life of the PAC IO, the average life of the PAC IO will extend to 22.19 years with its duration extending to 8.82 years. It is only after 85 months of fast prepayments that the yield of the PAC IO declined below its initial offering level of 9.87% or 145 basis points over the 30-year Treasury.

COMPARISON OF PAC IOs TO PACs

Since January of 1991, spreads of PAC IOs have tightened 50 to 75 basis points and, at the time of this writing, trade at spreads 40 to 60 basis points wider than similar average life PAC bonds. In addition, they have significantly shorter OAS (or effective) durations and higher OAS than their underlying PACs. Factoring in the newness of the market and the higher prepayment risk associated with derivative IOs, spreads of PAC IOs should continue to tighten and eventually trade somewhere around 25 basis points wider than PACs or even tighter.

Exhibit 5: FNMA 9165: PACs vs. PAC IOs

		PAC Tranches			PAC IO Tranches		
Maturity	Offering Spread 6/18/91	Avg. Life	OAS	OAS Duration	Avg. Life	OAS	OAS Duration
2 yr	55/2 yr	2.21	61	1.87	2.12	142	0.72
3 yr	75/3 yr	3.43	61	2.94	3.43	168	0.79
4 yr	75/4 yr	4.43	62	3.69	4.43	188	0.67
5 yr	75/5 yr	5.43	72	4.45	5.43	190	0.73
6 yr	80/6 yr	6.43	71	5.06	6.43	184	0.99
7 yr	80/7 yr	7.27	78	5.29	7.27	185	1.39
8 yr	87/7 yr	7.94	82	5.61	7.94	189	1.80
10 yr	90/10 yr	9.44	86	6.31	9.44	200	2.98
10 yr	100/10 yr	11.44	82	7.45	11.44	191	4.54

In Exhibit 5, the PAC tranches of FNMA 9165 are listed at their current offering levels with their corresponding OAS and OAS durations. *One hundred basis points of interest is stripped off each PAC and priced as a PAC IO at the same yield as the underlying PACs.* Although the PAC IO has the same average life as its PAC, the PAC IO has a significantly shorter OAS duration, and the OAS of every PAC IO is approximately 2 to 3 times the magnitude of the OAS of the underlying PAC.

Furthermore, PAC IOs are excellent investment alternatives to PACs because they offer higher expected returns. Exhibit 6 shows the OAS and expected one-year returns of 3-year, 5-year, 10-year and 20-year PAC IOs to the underlying PACs from which they are stripped. All the PAC IOs have higher OAS, shorter OAS durations and offer higher returns in unchanged and rising rate scenarios than the underlying PACs. If rates fall, the PAC IOs are expected to underperform because of their lower OAS durations and the faster prepayments associated with lower interest rates.

The 3-year PAC IO of FNMA 9159 is stripped off the 2-year through 5-year PACs and has an average life of 3.26 years and is offered 50 basis points wider than 3-year PACs. It is a zero OAS duration security priced at 280 basis points over 3-month Treasury bills.

In the 10-year sector, FNMA 9186 I1 is a 10-year PAC IO that receives 75 basis points of interest from the 10.5-year average life PAC and 100 basis points from the 12-year average life PAC. The PAC band for the 10-year PACs is 90% to 250% PSA. The PAC IO has an average life of 11.51 years, an OAS of 240 basis points and an OAS duration of 3.73. As long as prepayments are within the PAC band or below, the PAC IO will maintain a stable return profile and will outperform the 10-year PAC in all rising rate scenarios but will underperform in the down 100 basis point rate scenario because of its shorter OAS duration. If rates fall 200 basis points, however, the projected prepayment speed is 382% PSA, which is clearly higher than the upper end of the PAC band, and the 10-year PAC IO will underperform.

Twenty-year PAC IOs are the cheapest sector within the PAC IO market, trading approximately 35-40 basis points wider than 20-year PAC and 25 basis points wider than 20-year PAC Zs. The

Exhibit 6: PACs vs. PAC IOs

Issue	Offering 6/28/91	OAS	OAS Dur	-200	-100	Flat	+100	+200	Wtd Avg Return
				1-Year Holding Period Returns Up and Down 200 Basis Points					
FNMA 9159 I1 3yr PAC IO	125/3yr	222	-0.27	-0.51	9.07	9.16	9.15	10.22	8.45
FNMA 9159 Y3 3yr PAC	75/3yr	72	2.94	12.10	10.82	8.88	6.88	4.73	8.67
FNMA 9165 I3 5yr PAC IO	130/5yr	235	0.93	1.27	11.32	10.46	9.40	8.69	9.45
FNMA 9165 Y4 5yr PAC	80/5yr	74	4.38	16.02	13.02	9.50	5.87	2.18	9.21
FNMA 9186 I1 10yr PAC IO	140/10yr	240	3.73	11.87	15.43	11.02	7.24	4.02	10.48
FNMA 9186 Y7 10yr PAC	95/10yr	71	7.14	21.88	15.52	9.20	2.83	-3.53	8.84
FNMA 9186 I2 20yr PAC IO	145/30yr	224	9.61	32.09	22.34	10.20	1.87	-4.98	11.30
FNMA 9186 Z3 20yr PAC	120/30yr	101	16.77	42.74	25.37	9.85	-6.16	-21.53	9.02

20-year PAC IO of FNMA 9186 is stripped off the 10-year and 20-year PAC Zs. Although the PAC Zs will not receive any interest for approximately 15 years, the PAC IO receives interest immediately. This is reflected in the shorter duration of the PAC IO relative to the 20-year PAC Z. Although the PAC IO underperforms the PAC Z in falling rate scenarios, the PAC IO outperforms by more than 800 and 1600 basis points in up 100 and 200 basis point scenarios and offers a 228 basis point return advantage on a weighted average basis.

STRUCTURE

One important aspect to consider is how the PAC IO is structured. For example, a 5-year PAC IO can be created by stripping interest off the underlying 5-year PAC or via a barbell, that is, stripping interest off the 2-year and 20-year PACs of a CMO. Both PAC IOs will have very different expected return profiles. For example, the 5-year PAC IO of FNMA 9165 is stripped off the 5-year and 6-year PACs so its return profile is solely determined by the 5-year and 6-year PACs. For the barbell PAC IO, if prepayments speed up, the 2-year PAC will pay down along with the 2-year segment of the barbell PAC IO, leaving the barbell PAC IO with the 20-year segment, thereby increasing the duration of the barbell PAC IO. A 20-year PAC IO has limited extension ability but at the same time can sustain faster prepayments for a longer period of time.

Exhibit 7 illustrates the 5-year PAC IO of FNMA 9165 in comparison to the barbell PAC IO. Both PAC IOs are offered at 130

Exhibit 7: Comparison of 5-Year PAC IOs: FNMA 9165 I3 vs. Barbell PAC IO

Issue	Avg Life	OAS	OAS Dur	1-Year Expected Returns Up and Down 200 Basis Points					Wtd Avg Return
				-200	-100	Flat	+100	+200	
FNMA 9165 I3	5.87	241	0.93	1.564	11.424	10.550	9.446	8.685	9.535
Barbell PAC IO	5.92	172	4.21	15.573	13.764	9.175	5.793	3.076	9.340

basis points over the 5-year Treasury. Although both PAC IOs have similar average lives, their OAS durations are substantially different. The duration of the 5-year PAC IO is slightly higher than the OAS duration of the 1-year Treasury bill; it is effectively offered at 287 basis points over the 1-year Treasury BEY. In contrast, the barbell PAC IO has an OAS duration of 4.21, similar to the duration of the 5-year Treasury.

The higher total returns of the barbell PAC IO versus the 5-year PAC IO in falling rates reflect the barbell PAC IO's longer duration and that the 20-year segment of the barbell PAC IO can sustain faster prepayments. In rising rates, the 5-year PAC IO can extend more than the barbell PAC IO, resulting in higher total returns for the 5-year PAC IO. On a probability weighted average basis, the 5-year PAC IO outperforms the barbell PAC IO by 20 basis points. The 5-year PAC IO of FNMA 9165 offers a 69 basis point pick-up in OAS, substantially shorter OAS duration, and higher weighted average expected returns than the barbell PAC IO.

OTHER TYPES OF PAC IOs

Limited PAC IO

A limited PAC IO is an interest strip off a limited PAC class. Since the limited PAC has a narrower PAC band, at slower speeds the average life of the limited PAC IO will extend more than a regular PAC IO; however, at faster speeds its average life will contract more than a regular PAC IO. Limited PAC IOs stripped off shorter maturity tranches such as 3-year limited PACs have greater potential for average life extension and yield appreciation than longer maturity tranches.

Partial Accrual IO

A partial accrual IO is a PAC IO stripped off a PAC Z tranche. For example, if the coupon of the PAC IO is 1000% and the underlying PAC Z accrues at 6.5%, then the PAC IO will pay 993.5% interest and accrue at 6.5%. When the PAC Z becomes a coupon payer, the PAC IO will pay 1000% interest.

Exhibit 8 shows how the interest and principal cash flows are calculated. Starting with a principal balance of 100,000 on 7/91, the interest on the partial accrual IO is 83,333.33, the principal accrual is 541.66 and the total cash flow to the investor is the interest less the principal accrual.

Exhibit 8: Calculation of Cash Flows for Partial Accrual IO

Date	Balance	Interest Owed $\dfrac{1000}{1200} \times$ Balance	Principal Accrual $\dfrac{6.5}{1200} \times$ Balance	Total Cash Flow Interest Owed − Principal Accrual
7/91	100,000.00	83,333.33	541.66	82,791.67
8/91	100,541.66	83,784.72	544.60	83,240.12
9/91	101,086.26	84,238.55	547.55	83,691.00

Appendix

I. Given the principal face amount of the PAC IO, the maximum amount of interest available to the PAC IO is calculated as follows:

$$\text{PAC IO Interest} = \left[\frac{\left[\left(\frac{\text{Total PAC}}{\text{Principal}} + \frac{\text{PAC IO}}{\text{Principal}}\right) \times \frac{\text{Collateral}}{\text{Coupon}/100}\right] - \frac{\text{Total PAC}}{\text{Interest}}}{\text{PAC IO Principal}} \right]$$

Example: FNMA 9165 I1 is a 2.7-year average life PAC IO stripped off the 2-year, 3-year and 4-year PACs.

Tranche	Principal Amount	x	PAC Coupon	=	Interest
Y1	108,019,500		.075		8,101,462.50
Y2	57,946,500		.08		4,635,720.00
Y3	63,318,000		.082		5,192,076.00
	229,284,000				17,929,258.50

Thus, the interest available to the FNMA 9165 I1 class is:

$$\left[\frac{[(229,284,000 + 156,000) \times .085] - 17,929,258.50}{156,000} \right] = \begin{array}{l} 10.08424 \text{ or} \\ 1008.424\% \end{array}$$

II. Given the coupon of the PAC IO, the principal face amount of the PAC IO that will pay concurrently with each PAC (rounded to two decimal places) is calculated as follows:

$$\text{PAC IO Principal} = \frac{\left(\begin{array}{l} \text{Collateral} \\ \text{Coupon} \end{array} - \begin{array}{l} \text{PAC} \\ \text{Coupon} \end{array} \right) \times \begin{array}{l} \text{PAC} \\ \text{Principal} \end{array}}{(\text{PAC IO Coupon} - \text{Collateral Coupon})}$$

Example: Using FNMA 9165 I1 as an example and assuming the PAC IO coupon is 1008.424, then the principal face amount to pay with each PAC is:

PAC Tranche	PAC Amount	PAC Coupon	PAC IO Amount
Y1	108,019,500	7.5	108,027.71
Y2	57,946,500	8.0	28,975.45
Y3	63,318,000	8.2	18,996.84
	229,284,000		156,000.00

CHAPTER 19

Z-BONDS

Linda Lowell
Vice President, Head
Mortgage Investment Strategies
Smith Barney, Harris Upham & Co., Inc.

Bruce Mahood
Senior Portfolio Strategist
Merrill Lynch Capital Markets

Traditional accrual CMO bonds are long-term bonds structured so that they pay no coupon interest until they begin to pay principal. Instead, the principal balance of an accrual bond is increased by the stated coupon amount on each payment date. Once the earlier classes in the CMO structure have been retired, the accrual bond stops accruing and pays principal and interest as a standard CMO bond. Accrual bonds are commonly called Z-bonds because they are zero-coupon bonds during their accrual phase. Bonds created in this way provide investors with long durations, very attractive yields, and protection from reinvestment risk throughout the accrual period. The cash flow pattern produced is suited to matching long-term liabilities, and, as a result, the bonds are sought after by pension fund managers, life insurance companies and other investors seeking to lengthen the duration of their portfolios and reduce reinvestment risk.

Z-bonds have been a staple product of the CMO market since its earliest days. The bulk of the Z-bonds currently outstanding are from traditional, sequential pay CMOs, but the generic structure has adapted well to the PAC-based CMOs favored by the market since the late 1980s, and the inclusion of an accrual bond in the last class continues to be common practice. At the same time, the Z-bond was the focus of innovation in the CMO market, as issuers created a significant amount of intermediate average life Z-bonds, a growing number of bonds of various average lives that accrue and pay according to a PAC schedule, and bonds that use various conditions or events to turn the accrual mechanism on or off. These innovations have expanded the traditional market for Z buyers by improving the stability of Z-bonds' cash flows, issuing Z-bonds in a wider range of average lives, or by creating bonds that perform well in rallies and preserve their high yields in declines.

The chapter discusses this important sector of the derivative mortgage securities market. We begin with an examination of the mechanics of the traditional Z-bond as well as Z-bonds issued with PACs, and focus on the behavior of these structures in different prepayment scenarios. We also consider the effect Z-bonds have on the other bonds in a CMO, and the relationship between the basic characteristics of the Z-bond and its market properties and economic performance. A discussion then follows of the characteristics of more complex Z-bond structures, such as serial Z-bonds, Z-PACs, and Jump-Zs.

THE BASIC ACCRUAL STRUCTURE

Most Z-bonds have been issued from traditional, sequential pay CMO structures. Typically, they were the last in a four-class bond issue, and had nominal average lives of twenty years. The principal and interest cash flows for a traditional, sequential pay CMO containing a Z are diagrammed in Exhibit 1. As the graph indicates, the first class pays principal and interest until it is retired, at which time the second class begins to pay down. The coupon-paying bonds, Classes A, B, and C, receive payments of interest at their stated coupon rates on their original principal balances. The Z-bond, Class Z, however, receives no payments of interest until the preceding classes are fully retired. Instead, its principal balance increases at a compound rate, in effect guaranteeing the bondholder a reinvestment rate equal to the coupon rate during the accrual period, and insulating the investment from reinvestment risk as long as the earlier classes remain outstanding. The principal balance can triple or quadruple in amount over the accrual period projected at issue. This is graphically depicted in Exhibit 2, which indicates the growth of the principal balance of the Z-bond in Exhibit 1 over its expected life at an assumed constant prepayment speed of 165% PSA. The principal balance of the tranche at issue is $25 million, and grows to a maximum level of $79.5 million by about the 150th month. From that point, coinciding with the last payment to the preceding tranche, the balance begins to decline as scheduled amortization and prepayments from the collateral are paid to the bondholders.

If actual prepayments occur at a faster rate than 165% PSA, the principal balance of the Z-class at the end of the accrual period will be smaller than the $79.5 million shown in the diagram. Since the earlier tranches pay down sooner, the Z-bonds accrue over a shorter period of time, and the total amount of accrued interest is less. Conversely, slower prepayments allow the Z-bond to accrue for a longer period, resulting in a larger principal balance at the time when the Z-bond begins to generate cash for the bondholders. Principal balances at the end of the accrual period are shown

Exhibit 1: Total Principal and Interest Payments of a Traditional Sequential Pay CMO with a Z-Bond

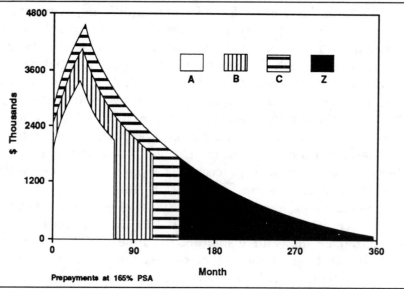

Prepayments at 165% PSA

Exhibit 2: Principal Balance of a Z-Bond Over Time - $25 Million Beginning Balance

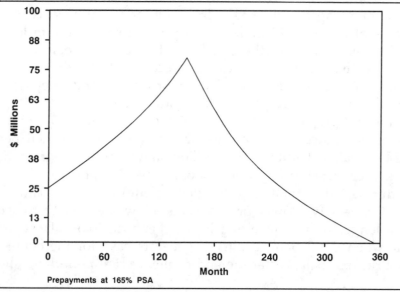

Prepayments at 165% PSA

Exhibit 3: Effect of Prepayment Speed on the Length of the Accrual Period and the Principal Balance at the End of the Accrual Period of a $25 Million, Twenty-Year Average Life Z-Bond Class*

Payment Speed (% PSA)	Principal Balance Outstanding ($MM)	Months From Issue
75	115.4	194
100	102.1	180
125	91.8	166
165	79.5	150
200	71.4	135
250	63.4	119
300	57.2	106
350	52.9	96
425	46.6	80
600	41.1	64

* Total issue $300 million sequential-pay CMO backed by FNMA 9 1/2s.

for various constant prepayment speeds in Exhibit 3. At the pricing speed of 165% PSA, the balance in this example reaches an amount more than three times the size of the original face amount at issue. At a faster speed of 350% PSA, the original face amount doubles, and at a slower speed, 100% PSA, it quadruples. Likewise, faster prepayments accelerate the receipt of the first payment of principal and interest. In the example, the first payment jumps from halfway into the twelfth year at 165% PSA to the beginning of the ninth year at 350% PSA. If prepayments slow to a constant rate of 100% PSA, the first payment to the Z-bond is not made until the beginning of the sixteenth year after issue.

The effect of faster or slower prepayments on the average life and yield of this same example is shown in Exhibit 4, under the heading "Z-Bond in a Traditional Sequential Pay CMO." The average life of the Z-bond at the pricing assumption of 165% PSA is about 18.5 years; traditional Zs typically have average lives at pricing of 18 to 22 years (and expected accrual periods of 8 to 10

Exhibit 4: Yield and Average Life at Various Prepayment Speeds of Comparable CMO Twenty-Year Average Life Bonds in Structures with and without Z-Bonds (Pricing Assumption: 165% PSA)

	Coupon-Paying Bond in a Traditional Sequential Pay CMO		Z-Bond in a Traditional Sequential Pay CMO		Z-Bond in a PAC Structure	
Payment Speed (% PSA)	Yield* (%)	Average Life (Years	Yield** (%)	Average Life (Years)	Yield*** (%)	Average Life (Years)
75	9.97	25.01	9.82	22.91	10.17	22.91
100	9.98	23.25	9.83	21.71	10.20	21.71
125	9.94	21.40	9.83	20.47	10.24	20.47
165	10.00	18.55	9.85	18.55	10.30	18.55
200	10.02	16.41	9.86	17.02	10.35	17.02
250	10.05	13.88	9.89	15.02	10.44	15.02
300	10.08	11.92	9.91	13.37	10.52	13.54
350	10.11	10.38	9.93	11.96	10.69	12.48
425	10.15	8.66	9.98	9.80	11.18	8.38
600	10.27	6.18	10.06	7.61	13.02	3.05

*   Price: 96:28
**   Price: 96.29
*** Price: 90:10

years). If prepayments occur at a constant rate of 100% PSA, the bond lengthens modestly, to an average life of about twenty-two years. Like other last tranches, the Z has more room to shorten. In this example, the Z shortens to an average life of about twelve years at 350% PSA, and down to about 7.5 years at 600% PSA.[1]

---

[1] Average life calculations are intended to measure the weighted average time until receipt of principal payments. Some measures of expected life may include the accrued interest as a cash flow. These increases in the principal balance can enter the calculation as negative weights applied to the elapsed time to early payment dates, and the actual principal payments as positive weights applied to the elapsed time to later payment dates. By placing negative weights on small numbers and positive weights on large numbers, the results can be larger than the remaining term of the underlying collateral (for example, a number of years greater than thirty). To avoid this unrealistic result, the convention in the CMO market is to exclude from the calculation all increases in the factor or balance, with the understanding that this method can substantially understate the true interest rate sensitivity of a security.

The yield received on a Z-bond is less sensitive to differences in prepayment speeds the closer to par it is priced. At deeper discounts, Z-bonds, like other discount mortgage-backed securities, will benefit as their average lives shorten, since principal is returned at par earlier than assumed at pricing. The deeper the discount, the sharper the boost in yield at faster prepayment speeds. Conversely, the yield declines as a function of a slowdown in prepayments and the original discount. Traditional twenty-year average life Zs have been issued at original prices as low as thirty, but prices above eighty-five currently are more common. In general, issuers can lower the coupon, achieving a more attractive price, by using discount collateral or by stripping interest into another class (either another regular bond or the residual).

HOW THE Z INTERACTS WITH OTHER BONDS IN THE STRUCTURE

The interaction of the Z-bond with earlier bonds in the CMO structure is a key determinant both of its own behavior and that of the other bonds. By including an accrual bond in the CMO structure, issuers accomplish two purposes: (1) a higher proportion of the total issue can consist of tranches with earlier final maturities than if there were no Z-bond in the structure, and (2) the earlier classes have more stable cash flows and average lives across a range of prepayment rates than in a comparable structure without a Z-bond. Furthermore, since the timing of cash flows from the Z-bond depends on when the earlier tranches are retired, the Z-bond itself also is more stable.

An accrual bond supports a larger proportion of early classes because the coupon interest that would have been paid on the outstanding balance of the Z-bond is added to the principal payments from the collateral and used to retire the earlier classes. At the same time, the principal amount of Z-bonds is increased by the dollar amount of interest diverted. Although at first glance this may look like sleight of hand, the accrual procedure maintains a

Exhibit 5: How a Z-Bond Accrues and Pays: A Simplified Example

Collateral:	$100 10% loan amortizing in 10 annual payments	CMO:	Class A $50 paying 10% coupon Class Z $50 Z with 10% coupon

	Collateral			Class A			Class Z		
	Payments			Payments			Payments		
Payment	Interest ($)	Principal ($)	Balance ($)	Interest ($)	Principal ($)	Balance ($)	Interest ($)	Principal* ($)	Balance ($)
0	0.00	0.00	100.00	0.00	0.00	50.00	0.00	0.00	50.00
1	10.00	10.00	90.00	5.00	15.00	35.00	0.00	(5.00)	55.00
2	9.00	10.00	80.00	3.50	15.50	19.50	0.00	(5.00)	60.50
3	8.00	10.00	70.00	1.95	16.05	3.45	0.00	(6.05)	66.55
4	7.00	10.00	60.00	0.34	3.45	0.00	6.66	6.65**	60.00***
5	6.00	10.00	50.00	0.00			6.00	10.00	50.00
6	5.00	10.00	40.00	0.00			5.00	10.00	40.00
7	4.00	10.00	30.00	0.00			4.00	10.00	30.00
8	3.00	10.00	20.00	0.00			3.00	10.00	20.00
9	2.00	10.00	10.00	0.00			2.00	10.00	10.00
10	1.00	10.00	0.00	0.00			1.00	10.00	0.00

* Amounts in parentheses are not cash flows but upward adjustments of principal balance.

** $6.65 = Principal Remaining after Class A Retired

*** $60 = Previous Balance - Principal Paid = $66.55 - $6.65

simple algebraic relationship in which the sum of the principal balances of the outstanding bonds always equals the outstanding principal balance of the collateral. The simple numerical example in Exhibit 5 illustrates this relationship. In the example, the collateral pays a 10% coupon and a $100 principal balance in ten equal payments. Both Class A and Class Z have stated coupons of 10%, so that the sum of the interest paid to Class A and either accrued or paid to Class Z is always equal to the interest paid by the collateral. (In an actual CMO, there can be a differential between interest on the collateral and the interest paid to the bondholders, which is then payable to the residual holders.) Notice that Class A is paid down more quickly than it would be if the Z were a coupon-paying bond.

The accrual structure permits issuers to create larger classes with short- and intermediate-term average lives. The effect of an accrual bond on the size of the earlier classes is graphically illustrated in Exhibit 6, a diagram of the principal payments only from the CMO in Exhibit 1. The discontinuity between the size of principal payments to the Z and those to the earlier tranches reflects the fact that the Z-bond's pro rata share of coupon interest is treated as principal in order to pay down larger earlier tranches (if the last payment to the fourth would be much smaller). This strategy was particularly attractive to issuers when the CMO arbitrage depended primarily on the shape of the yield curve, and larger profits could be made the larger the amount of bonds that could be priced off the front end of the yield curve. In periods when the yield curve flattened or inverted, this strategy helped issuers minimize the proportion of longer-duration bonds in the issue. This works because interest payments from the collateral, which would have been paid to holders of the last tranche, are used to support the first tranche. Just how much of an effect an accrual class can have on the allocation of principal to the earlier classes is shown in Exhibit 7. The exhibit compares two four-tranche sequential pay CMOs backed by the same collateral, one with a Z and one without. The four tranches in each issue have the same average lives, roughly three, seven, ten, and twenty years. (The fourth tranches

Exhibit 6: Total Principal Payments of a Traditional Sequential-Pay CMO with a Z-Bond

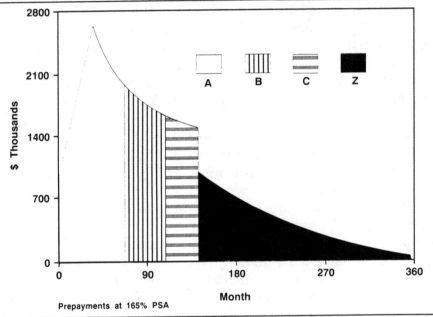

Prepayments at 165% PSA

from these examples, all nominally twenty-year bonds, are included as well in Exhibit 4.) The two structures differ in the way the collateral's principal is distributed among the classes. For example, in the Z-bond structure, a $25 million Z-bond class supports a $136 million three-year first tranche. The structure without a Z-bond has $120 million three-year bonds in the first class and $79 million twenty-year bonds in the fourth tranche.

The accrual mechanism imparts greater stability to all the bonds in a typical structure. This is readily apparent in Exhibit 8. Each column compares the average life at different prepayment speeds of the different tranches from the sample structures. In each case, the average lives of the tranches are less variable across all scenarios for the structure containing a Z-bond than in the structure without.

Exhibit 7: Comparison of Various CMO Structures Created With and Without Z-Bonds

	Traditional CMO Without Z		Traditional CMO With Z		PAC CMO with Z	
	Original Balance	Average Life	Original Balance	Average Life	Original Balance	Average Life
Class A	$120,000,000	3.0 Years	$136,000,000	3.0 Years	$ 80,000,000	2.8 Years
Class B	66,200,000	7.4	84,000,000	7.4	70,000,000	7.0
Class C	34,500,000	10.9	55,000,000	10.9	125,000,000	7.3
Class D	79,300,000	18.6				
Class Z			25,000,000	18.6	25,000,000	18.6
Total	$300,000,000		$300,000,000		$300,000,000	

Collateral: FNMA 9 1/2s
Structured at 165% PSA

Exhibit 8
Effect of a Z-Bond on the Average Life Variability of the Various Classes in a Traditional, Sequential-Pay CMO

	Average Life in Years							
	3-Year Tranche		7-Year Tranche		10-Year Tranche		20-Year Tranche	
Prepayment Speed	No Z-Bond	With Z-Bond	No Z-Bond	With Z-Bond	No Z-Bond	With Z-Bond	Coupon Bond	Z-Bond
75% PSA	5.2	4.7	13.2	11.1	18.4	14.9	25.0	22.9
165% PSA	3.0	3.0	7.4	7.4	10.9	10.9	18.6	18.6
425% PSA	1.6	1.7	3.4	3.8	4.8	5.9	8.7	10.3

Collateral: FNMA 9.5s

CMOs WITH PACs AND A Z-BOND

The Z-bond has a similar effect on earlier bonds in a typical PAC^2 structure. For a given collateral and pricing assumption, accrual from the Z can be used to support a larger amount of PAC and companion bonds in the earlier tranches. The principal and interest payments for a structure containing three- and seven-year PACs, a seven-year companion, and a twenty-year Z are shown in Exhibit 9. The yield and average life at various prepayment levels of the Z-bond from this structure are included in Exhibit 4, and the size and average life of the various classes are shown in Exhibit 7. (In fact, the average life of the Z-bond is 18.6 years, matching, for the sake of discussion, the average lives of the Z and regular coupon-paying tranches in the other examples.) Funding the earlier classes from the Z-bond's accrual generally creates a much larger portion of available principal, for a given pricing speed, from which to carve PACs, allowing issuers to increase the size of the PAC classes.

Since companion bonds absorb the prepayment volatility from which the PACs are shielded, the proportion of PACs to companions is an important parameter in determining the degree to which the average lives of the companions will vary over various prepayment scenarios. The presence of a Z-bond increases the total amount of principal available at the pricing speed to pay both the PACs and the companions. This means that, all other factors being equal, more PACs may be issued with less negative effect on the stability of the companion bonds. In turn, the length of the accrual period is more stable. Nonetheless, the Z-bonds created to support PAC tranches are necessarily more volatile than Z-bonds in the traditional CMO issues. The truth of this can be seen by comparing the average life at various prepayment speeds of a Z from a PAC structure to those of a Z from a traditional CMO, as was shown in Exhibit 4. As is the case with the fourth tranches in the sample traditional deals, this Z also has an average life of 18.6

---

[2] Readers interested in a detailed discussion of PACs should refer to Chapter 14.

Exhibit 9: Total Principal and Interest Payments of a CMO with PACs and a Z-Bond

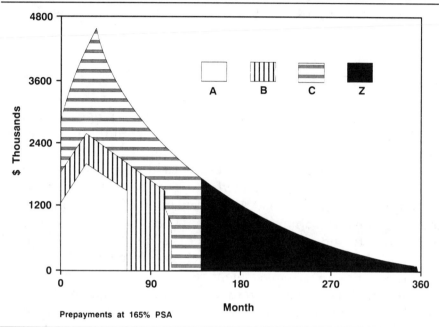

Prepayments at 165% PSA

years at 165% PSA. As the exhibit indicates, the average life of the Z from a PAC structure would extend more significantly as well, since slow prepayment rates will delay the retirement of the companion bonds, further extending the accrual period for the Zs. (This effect is obscured by over-simplification of the example.)

If the companion tranche(s) in front of a Z are TACs, the Z may be more volatile than if structured with standard companions. When the priorities enforcing the structure require that principal in excess of the TAC (and PAC) payments be paid to the Z, then the Z may begin to receive payments before the companion TAC is retired. This kind of structure produces a Z that is much more volatile in bull markets than a traditional or companion Z-bond. Prepayment speeds fast enough to shorten a traditional twenty-year Z to a ten-year can shorten this bond to a one-year. When they carry a low coupon, these bonds are priced to produce generous returns from accelerating prepayments. Indeed, this is one way to create the bullish Z-bond the market has dubbed a "Jump-Z." The Jump-Z is discussed in greater detail later in this chapter.

PERFORMANCE OF Z-BONDS

The variability in the yield of a Z-bond over a range of prepayment rates gives at best an imperfect indication of the Z's expected price, and hence, economic performance in different interest rate scenarios. A major drawback of using yield as a measure of a Z-bond's, or for that matter, any mortgage-backed security's expected performance is that the calculation of yield-to-maturity presumes that the amount and timing of cash flows are known with certainty and are reinvested over the life of the investment at a rate equal to the yield. In actuality, mortgage-backed securities are more exposed to reinvestment risk than other common fixed-income investments. Pass-throughs pay both principal and interest monthly, while CMOs may pay monthly, quarterly, or semiannually. More importantly, prepayments of principal normally accelerate when market rates decline, just as the yields available on reinvestment opportunities are declining. The opposite occurs as market yields rise; prepayments decline, slowing the receipt of principal just as more attractive reinvestment opportunities appear. Z-bonds are protected somewhat from reinvestment risk, since the reinvestment rate is locked in over the accrual period. They are not fully protected, however. The accrual period is of uncertain length, and when it ends the bonds begin to pay exactly like a coupon-paying CMO bond. For these reasons, yield does not capture the difference in the Z-bond's performance relative to a security with lower reinvestment risk, such as a Treasury bond that pays only coupons until maturity, or one with a fixed accrual period, such as a Treasury zero.

Prepayment risk also exposes investors to call and extension risk, and these have additional consequences for market value. For mortgage-backed securities purchased at prices above par, the early return of principal at par is a negative event, since less interest is earned over the investment horizon. Reflecting the market's perception of these risks, the prices of premium coupon CMOs, including Z-bonds, rise more slowly the steeper the decline in interest rates. Investors also are exposed to possible declines in market value when the bond's average life extends and it shifts outward on a positively sloped yield curve. When a bond lengthens in an upwardly sloping yield curve environment, the discount rate applied to the expected cash flow rises, resulting in a lower market value.

Another characteristic that yield calculations cannot reflect is the call provisions established for CMOs. These are more important in the case of older, non-REMIC CMOs. These bonds, mostly issued before 1987, used call provisions to insulate the transaction from a more onerous sale tax treatment. Newer issues tend to have more favorable clean-up call provisions, designed to pay off the bonds when the remaining balance falls below a certain low level. The market considers as fairly favorable terms that permit the bonds to be called at par, ten or fifteen years after issue, when the outstanding balance of the tranche has declined by 10 to 20% of its original amount. These also are the most common. Less favorable terms stipulate a higher remaining balance, a shorter period, or both. A handful of Z-bonds currently outstanding could have been called as early as 1990, and a significant number become callable after 1994. Investors are advised to carefully examine the call provisions of Z-bonds before trading them.

As with any other fixed-income security, investors should look beyond the yield and average life tables when analyzing prospective investments in Z-bonds. Total rate-of-return analyses are preferred because they incorporate all the components of economic return in the period measured: the change in market value, the change in the principal balance (and hence the degree to which the prepayments shield the initial investment from a price decline or prevent it from benefitting from an increase), the coupon income or accrual, and reinvestment income. Such analyses can be constructed to incorporate the expected prepayment behavior of the collateral, the structural characteristics of the Z, and the impact of the risks, outlined above, on the terminal price of the investment at the end of a reasonable horizon.

MORE FUN WITH ACCRUAL BONDS

Some of the CMOs issued since the beginning of 1989 make more creative use of the basic accrual mechanism. The variations on the accrual theme include Z-PACs and structures containing an inter- mediate- as well as long-term Z-bond or a series of Z-bonds of various average lives. Other structures turn the accrual mecha- nism on and off depending on the amount of excess principal available after scheduled payments are met. As complex and ex- otic as these structures may appear at first glance, the same basic principles at work in traditional Z-bonds continue to apply. And in most cases, any additional complexity is accompanied by con- siderable additional value for investors with particular objectives and investment criteria.

Z-PACs

Z-PACs combine the cash flow characteristics of a standard Z- bond with the greater certainty of a PAC regarding the amount and timing of actual payments. When prepayments occur within the range defined by the PAC collars, the Z-PAC will accrue to a scheduled principal balance over a fixed period and make sched- uled payments thereafter. As with more familiar, coupon-paying PACs, any excess cash flow is absorbed by companions as long as they are outstanding. Similarly, the coupon interest earned on the Z-PACs' outstanding balance during the accrual period is used to support earlier classes in the structure, and the balance of the Z- PAC is increased by an equal amount. For prepayment levels within the PAC collars, the structure eliminates reinvestment risk over a defined accrual period, and then provides predictable payments until maturity. This structure is particularly well suited to matching liabilities. The fact that Z-PACs are issued in a range of average lives (typically five, seven, ten, or twenty years) increases their applicability. Furthermore, the call and extension protection provided by the planned payment schedule means that the duration of the investment is less likely to increase as interest rates rise (or decrease as interest rates decline) than is the duration of a standard or companion Z. That is to say, the Z-PACs are less negatively convex than standard or companion Zs. For this reason, active portfolio managers should consider using the Z-PAC to lengthen the duration of their portfolios in anticipation of market upswings.

STRUCTURES WITH MORE THAN ONE Z-BOND

Although the practice of issuing two or more Zs from a single structure is not new, more of these structures have been created since 1989 than previously. Considerable variety is possible in structuring deals with multiple classes of Z-bonds, but the two most common strategies have been to issue a sequential series of Zs with a range of average lives (five, seven, ten, and twenty years, or seven, ten, fifteen, and twenty years, for example), or a pair of Z-bonds having intermediate- and long-term average lives (five- and twenty-year bonds or ten- and twenty-year bonds are common examples). In the case of an intermediate- and long-term average life pair, the bonds do not necessarily pay in sequence, but more typically pay down before and after intervening coupon-paying classes. Both strategies have been employed in traditional CMOs as well as in structures containing PAC bonds.

In general, multiple accrual classes in a CMO interact with the rest of the structure in the same way a single traditional Z-bond does, supporting the repayment of earlier classes, which themselves may either pay current coupon interest or accrue it. In a series of Zs, the longer Zs lend stability to the shorter Zs, just as they would to coupon-paying bonds with earlier final maturities.

Exhibit 10: Total Principal and Interest Payments of a Sequential-Pay CMO with a Series of Z-Bonds

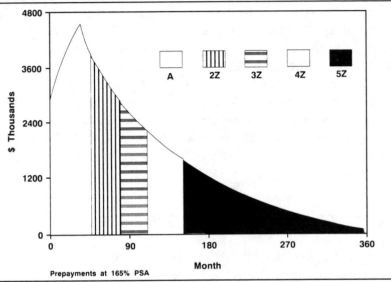

Prepayments at 165% PSA

Accrual from the later Zs can be used to retire earlier Zs when they become current paying bonds, just as if they were coupon-paying bonds.

The cash flows from a sequential-pay CMO containing a series of five-, seven-, ten-, and twenty-year Zs preceded by a two-year coupon-paying tranche are shown in Exhibit 10. This example was constructed using the same collateral and pricing speed as in the previous examples containing a single Z. The last tranche, 5Z, is the same size as in the previous example as well, and for this reason has the same average life at various prepayment speeds. For the sake of discussion, the first tranche is also the same size as the first tranche in the traditional CMO with a Z-bond, $136 million. As indicated in Exhibit 11, the large amount of accrual bonds in the structure has the effect of shortening the average life of this bond from three years at 165% PSA in the single Z example, to two years in this. (Readers will note that this example is not necessarily realistic. Structurers would be concerned to issue larger amounts of short-term average life bonds that can be sold at lower

Exhibit 11: Average Lives at Various Prepayment Speeds of the Bonds in a Sequential-Pay CMO with a Series of Z-Bonds

	Average Life (years)				
	A	2Z	3Z	4Z	5Z
75% PSA	2.5	6.6	10.1	14.0	22.9
165% PSA	2.0	5.0	7.6	10.5	18.6
425% PSA	1.4	3.1	4.5	6.0	10.3

yields for greater arbitrage profits, manipulating the coupon and offer price, and so forth.) Exhibit 11 lists the average lives of the first five classes at various prepayment speeds. In general, intermediate-term Zs demonstrate considerable stability. This is more evident when the seven- and ten-year Zs are compared to the seven- and ten-year coupon-paying bonds from earlier examples in Exhibit 8. The ten-year is supported by a twenty-year Z, and is noticeably less variable than one in a CMO without a Z. As would be expected, given the larger amount of accrual being passed to successively shorter bonds in the current example, the five-year Z-bond is considerably more stable than a comparable five-year standard payer supported by a single Z. The general result is that the shorter Zs in a series of Zs are "cleaner," that is, they have progressively less average life variability than otherwise comparable coupon-paying bonds. Intermediate-term average life Zs interspersed among coupon-paying classes in a structure supported by a twenty-year Z (the other common strategy) will benefit similarly. They will be more stable than otherwise, and the degree of stability will depend on the size of the Z-bond supporting them.

The consequences of multiple-Z strategies are that they produce bonds possessing relatively stable cash flow patterns—not as stable as PACs with decent collars, but more stable than traditional sequential-pay bonds. These stable bonds also possess the partial shield against reinvestment risk that is a chief attraction of traditional Z-bonds, and they make it available in any array of expected lives, broadening the appeal of Z-bonds to investors with intermediate- rather than long-term horizons.

Tricky Zs

More innovative approaches to Z-bonds have begun to make their appearance in the late 1980s. The common theme of these "trick" Zs involves turning the accrual mechanism on or off under certain conditions. One such condition might be a date; for example, the rule of allocating cash flows between classes might be "accrue until such and such a date" instead of the traditional "accrue until A, B, and C tranches are retired." Or, the decision to accrue the Z-bond might depend on the amount of principal available to make payments to the nonaccrual bonds currently paying. The use of such rules results in bonds with performance characteristics that can be very different from the Z-bonds discussed above.

CMO issuers have tinkered with the accrual mechanism of Z-bonds to create CMO classes that alternate between paying interest and accruing interest. These special-purpose classes are structured with a set of rules that turn their accrual mechanism on or off according to certain cash flow conditions. These accrual rules are often designed to help preceding classes meet their cash flow schedules and/or expected maturity dates. Beginning in 1988, issuers included these variable-accrual bonds in CMO structures to help earlier classes meet the five-year maturity requirement for inclusion in thrift liquidity portfolios. These benevolent Zs pay as follows: when cash flows from the mortgage collateral are insufficiently large enough to retire the liquidity bonds according to schedule, their accrual mechanisms are turned on and corresponding coupon from the collateral is applied to the earlier classes; when cash flows are sufficient to retire the liquidity bonds on schedule, their accrual mechanisms are turned off and the bonds act like standard coupon payers. Incorporating a conditional accrual rule into a bond class is an effective way to reduce extension risk on earlier classes. Of course, the extension risk is not eliminated but is instead largely transferred to the benevolent Z and other, later bond classes.

Another wrinkle is to permanently transform Z-bonds into coupon-paying bonds when certain cash flow levels are met. An example of this Z-bond structure was issued as the last of nine classes in FNMA 89-15. This bond was not marketed with any distinguishing label. The other bonds in the structure were a series of PACs and TACs followed by a companion dubbed an "S" bond. The Z-bond pays as follows: any excess above the scheduled PAC and TAC payments is distributed to the Z-bond as an interest payment; if the amount is less than the amount that was accrued, the shortfall is accrued; if the amount is greater, the excess is distributed as principal; beginning in the month following the first payment of a complete interest payment, the so-called Z-class distributes interest each month. One month of exceptional prepayment experience can trigger the conversion to coupon bond. Thereafter, the average life will be shorter than it would otherwise have been, owing to the fact that a portion of its cash flows is dispersed over what would have been the accrual period. Any protection against reinvestment risk offered by this "chameleon" bond is ephemeral at best. Once converted, the bond behaves like any other companion bond.

Even Z-PACs have been subjected to genetic alteration. The first Z-PAC issued, the fifth tranche in Ryland Acceptance Corporation Four, Series 88, accrues only until the date of its first scheduled payment or until non-PAC classes in the deal have been retired. Until that date, the Z-PAC is the first PAC in line for excess cash flows should the companions be paid down, and after that date it is last in line. This means it has greater call risk during the accrual period. As a result, its average life is only stable at or below the pricing speed (90% PSA for this deal backed by GNMA 8s). The resultant average life volatility is more typical of a reverse TAC, which does not extend but has considerable call risk.

Jump-Zs

Another Z-bond innovation, the notorious Jump-Z, made its debut in the CMO market during the summer of 1989. Generically, the Jump-Z is a bullish companion Z-bond that is designed to convert to a current payer and to receive excess principal when prepayments accelerate. Under bullish scenarios, this bond "jumps" ahead of other bond classes in the order of priority for receiving principal payments. Once triggered, a Jump-Z typically receives all excess principal (above scheduled PAC payments) until it is retired. Conceivably, holders of the Jump-Z could receive these payments early in the accrual period. This acceleration of principal can shorten the bond's average life significantly—a Z-bond issued with a twenty-year average life might shorten to less than one year. Since these bonds typically have low coupons and are issued at significant discounts to par (in the eighties), Jump-Z holders can realize high returns in a rally. In general, a Jump-Z priced at a deeper discount will trade at a tighter spread, because investors assign more value to the jump feature. Investors often purchase Jump-Zs to offset the negative convexity of mortgage securities and to enhance the performance of their MBS portfolios in bullish scenarios.

Tranche Y of FNMA 90-106 provides a good example of the bullish price performance of Jump-Zs. This bond accrues interest at 10% and is the longest class in the CMO, with an average life at issuance of 20.4 years. Priced approximately 140 basis points over thirty-year Treasuries, this bond trades at a significant discount to par (around ninety, to yield about 9.9% at pricing). The price and average life characteristics of this Jump-Z change dramatically, however, should prepayments rise above 150% PSA. At a prepayment speed of 155% PSA, for example, the Jump-Z converts to a current pay bond and receives all excess principal above the PAC schedule. Accelerating the return of principal shortens the bond's average life to 1.3 years. In its new form, this short bond will trade like a one-year clean payer, priced around par, to yield about seventy-five basis points over the one-year Treasuries. In other words, this Jump-Z should appreciate nearly ten points in price when its jump conditions are met. (It is worth noting that this bond jumped on July 25, 1991 after prepayments accelerated during the spring and summer months.)

Jump-Z bonds have been issued with an extremely diverse set of jump rules. Although apparently lacking uniformity or standardization, these rules have the common objective of increasing the bonds' performance in bullish economic environments. Jumps are typically activated by an event associated with a market rally: rising prepayment rates, declining interest rates, or increased cash flow. At the time of this writing, most Jump-Zs have been structured with prepayment triggers—the bonds shorten when prepayment rates on the underlying mortgage collateral rise above a CMO's pricing speed or some other predefined prepayment level. Generally, prepayments above the pricing speed will shorten the average life of the Jump-Z considerably. In structures containing TAC bonds, Jump-Zs are often designed to shorten when prepayments exceed the speed that defines the TAC schedule. In addition to prepayment triggers, CMO issuers have also structured Jump-Zs with interest rate triggers that are activated when Treasury yields fall below some threshold level. Interest rate triggers eliminate the need for investors accurately to forecast prepayment rates, and ensures that Jump-Z holders will benefit even in a market rally that is not accompanied by rising prepayments. FNMA 1990-37-Y, for example, jumps when the yield on ten-year Treasury bonds declines below 8.15% or prepayments exceed 196% PSA. In general, the closer the jump trigger is to actual prepayment speeds or current interest rates, the more valuable the Jump-Z.

Jump-Z bonds can be classified as "cumulative" or "noncumulative," as well as "sticky" or "nonsticky." A cumulative trigger is activated when since-issuance prepayment rates, or other cumulative measures of prepayment experience, exceed some threshold value. In contrast, a noncumulative trigger only requires prepayments to satisfy the jump condition during a single period. Holders generally prefer noncumulative triggers, since a single month of abnormally high prepayments will force early retirement of their discount security. The adjectives "stick" and "nonstick" indicate whether a Jump-Z bond will revert back to its original priority in the CMO structure if jump conditions are no longer met.

Once triggered, a sticky-Z will continue to receive principal payments, even if prepayments subsequently decline below the threshold value. On the other hand, a nonstick-Z can revert back to an accrual bond once its jump rules are no longer satisfied. Holders generally assign the greatest value to Jump-Zs with noncumulative sticky triggers, because a single increase in monthly prepayment rates can force early retirement of the entire bond class. For Jump-Zs backed by unseasoned mortgage collateral, a tiny increase in prepayments can often trigger a jump—a small increase in CPR can translate into a large PSA spike when prepayments are benchmarked off the early part of the PSA ramp.

The other common approach for creating a Jump-Z bond—preceding it with a TAC and other companion bonds in a PAC structure—was described earlier. The Jump-Z acts like a traditional companion bond and absorbs volatility from both PACs and TACs. Preceded by a TAC, the Jump-Z receives principal when principal payments from the underlying collateral and Z-accrual exceed the amount required to meet the PAC and TAC schedules. The degree to which the bond's average life will shorten depends on its jump rules and the overall deal structure. Jump rules control whether the bond jumps in front of the TAC class when payments break the TAC schedule (sticky-Z) or receives only excess payments above the PAC and TAC schedules (nonsticky-Z). All else being equal, the average life of a sticky-Z is likely to shorten more than a comparable nonsticky-Z. Preceded by PACs, TACs, and other support bonds, these Jump-Zs have a negligible amount of extension risk since they are typically structured as the last companion class in the CMO. In addition to their jump rules, the average life variability of Jump-Zs is also affected by the features of their preceding PAC bonds. For example, PAC lockouts, typically one to two years in length, can accentuate the shortening of Jump-Z average lives. Since no scheduled principal payments are made during a lockout, there is a much larger amount of cash flow available to pay down a Jump-Z in the event it is triggered.

This simple form of Jump-Z (simple to visualize and analyze) does not involve any modification of the standard accrual mechanism—the Z's share of interest is added to principal payments used to pay down earlier bonds according to the schedules and order of priorities established for the deal. Many of the Jump-Zs issued during 1990 and 1991, however, have modified accrual mechanisms that impose conditions under which accrual is turned on or off. These rules can control how coupon interest is paid both before and after the bonds have jumped. Perhaps the most common example of accrual manipulation occurs with Jump-Zs that pay only a portion of their coupon interest and accrue the shortfall. The exact amount of interest that a Jump-Z will pay, after being triggered, often depends on the number and size of the companion classes that the bond jumped over. For example, when preceded by both Level I and II PACs, the amount of coupon interest paid to a Jump-Z bond will depend on whether it jumps over the secondary PACs. If the Jump-Z remains subordinate to the Level II PACs, then part of the Jump-Z's coupon interest can be used to support the second-tier PACs.

Clearly, Jump-Zs can be structured to have exceptional value in a rally or even with a transient pop in prepayment experience. The amount of these bonds available to trade, however, is small. Not all CMO issuers employ the structure, as it detracts from the marketability of other bonds in the transaction, particularly the companion bonds, both because the structure is difficult to model and analyze in its entirety and because it can modify the average life variability of other bonds in the structure. Supply is further constrained by the tendency of some issuers to retain the Jump-Z for their own accounts.

The market quickly recognized that a Jump-Z could affect the average life profile of accompanying companion bonds. It responded with surprise, however, during autumn 1990, when many participants realized that the PACs are affected as well. Interdependencies between Jump-Zs and companions are the easiest to understand. When Jump-Zs are triggered, they receive cash flows that would otherwise be allocated to other companion classes, causing those companions to extend. In these instances, the earlier companion classes usually experience the most severe average life extensions. FHLMC 1014 illustrates this effect very well. When prepayment rates rise from 185% PSA to 190% PSA, for example, its Jump-Z is triggered, and the average life of its three-year support TAC lengthens from 3.8 to 19.9 years. Jump-Zs affect companion bonds to a much greater extent than PACs.

The impact of Jump-Zs on PAC bonds depends on whether or not the accrual is used to construct the PAC schedule.[3] In fact, most CMOs containing both PACs and Jump-Zs do not use Z-accrual to support their PAC schedules. If accrual from the Z does not support the PAC schedule, then a jump will not further affect the stability of the PAC classes, but will cause remaining companion bonds to extend. Since the jump will not change the overall proportion of companions to PAC bonds, the PAC bands will remain constant. In the rarer event that Z-accrual is used to support the PAC schedule, then the jump affects the PAC bands. The effect is most noticeable with a sticky-Z in a scenario where prepayment speeds accelerate enough to trigger the Jump-Z before slowing to the bottom collar speed used to structure the bonds. (Remember that the bottom collar defines the PAC schedule for short maturity PACs.) Without accrual from the Jump-Z, the underlying mortgage collateral will not generate enough principal at the lower PAC band to meet the PAC schedule. In order to satisfy the PAC schedule, the collateral must throw off principal at a faster rate each month to replace the missing accrual. In other words, the jump forced the bottom PAC band to rise. A nonstick-Z has a similar but less dramatic effect. Each jump or conversion to payer lowers the Jump-Z's principal amount outstanding, likewise reducing the amount of accrual that otherwise could be passed to the PAC bonds. In either case, the jump erodes the PACs' extension protection, especially that of the longer classes. The effect may not be significantly negative. In the unlikely event that prepayments trigger a jump and then fall to the lower PAC collar to remain there over the entire life of the CMO, a ten-year PAC may lengthen only one-half year in average life.

---

[3] See Chapter 14 for a more complete discussion of this topic.

The moral of the Jump-Z story is that wise CMO investors read prospectuses before purchasing bonds. The Jump-Z serves as a warning to investors that not all TACs, or for that matter, PACs, Zs, and other supposedly generic CMO structures are created alike. Examples of structures that merely superficially satisfy the common definitions are only too common.

CONCLUSION

Z-bonds offer investors some of the longest durations and highest yields available in the derivative MBS market, as well as a cash flow pattern well suited to matching long-term liabilities. They also are one of the most liquid varieties of CMO bonds traded in the secondary market. The favorable economics of issuing these bonds will help ensure that a steady supply continues to be produced. Recent innovations have introduced accrual bonds with new and valuable characteristics, including greater stability or accelerated return of principal in rallies, and have widened the availability of intermediate-term Zs. Given the large number of Z-bonds outstanding, and the wide familiarity they already enjoy, this trend should continue, creating bonds that meet distinct investor requirements.

CHAPTER 20

COMPANIONS WITH SCHEDULES

Linda Lowell
Vice President, Head
Mortgage Investment Securities
Smith Barney, Harris Upham & Co., Inc.

INTRODUCTION

Collateralized mortgage obligations (CMOs) were first devised to meet two general objectives. The first was to make a better match between a wide range of investors' maturity requirements and the expected cash flows from a pool of mortgages. The second was to redistribute prepayment risk to different classes at levels that many more investors would accept. The initial solution to the problem simply split the returning principal among a series of sequential pay bonds. Subsequently, this structure has evolved into an array of reduced-risk CMO bond structures, the most heavily issued of which is the planned amortization class (PAC). PACs provide investors with payments scheduled as to payment date

461

and amount, occurring within a defined paydown period (window), and protected over a range of likely prepayment scenarios.

Companion bonds are the natural by-product of creating PAC bonds.[1] In order to protect the schedules of PAC bonds in a CMO issue, a sufficient amount of bond classes must be created to absorb excess principal paydowns and to provide a buffer from which scheduled payments can be made when prepayments are slow. Because companion classes accept additional prepayment volatility, their payments are necessarily more uncertain than either PACs or traditional CMO bonds. As a result, the actual yields or economic returns realized from an investment in companion bonds can vary widely from those projected at the time of investment. Investors recognize this risk and demand yields that compensate them accordingly.

Issuers and underwriters also have developed a variety of devices that serve either to reduce the risk of a portion of the companion classes or to create more volatile instruments that reward holders when interest rates (and presumably prepayment rates) move strongly in a particular direction. Lockouts[2] are among the first group, while Super POs, Jump-Zs and interest-only strips are typical of the second. Another strategy employed to good effect, especially since the end of the second quarter of 1989, is to create companions with floating and inverse floating rate coupons. Assuming these assets are funded by short-term liabilities, total interest rate risk is minimized and the holder is accordingly less concerned with average life volatility. One of the oldest and most extensively employed strategies, however, is to give schedules to a portion of the companion classes and to provide those schedules

---

[1] Other structural devices intended to reduce or transform prepayment risk for some classes in a CMO issue also create support classes. The discussion here should not be presumed to apply to them. Unless clearly indicated, the term "companion" when used in this chapter means PAC companion.

[2] A lockout shifts to a companion bond principal payments that otherwise might be used in a PAC schedule. The effect of a lockout is to push forward the beginning of the first PAC window to a specified date and to stabilize the companion. Lockouts are normally applied to the first PAC for a period of two or three years, lending stability to the earliest companion class.

with more limited prepayment protection. This family of reduced-risk companions is the subject of this chapter.

Companions having schedules partake either of the properties of targeted amortization classes (TACs), so that they are protected against call or extension risk (a reverse TAC) but not both, or of PAC bonds, so that they have call and extension protection over a range of prepayment scenarios (a "Level II" PAC). The largest class of these bonds, companion TACs, has been issued since 1988, and is now one of the most liquid of generic CMO classes. Reverse TACs were introduced more in the middle of 1988, but have been marketed explicitly as reverse TACs only since the beginning of 1989. The concept of Level II PACs is not new, but it really took hold during the third quarter of 1989.

The following discussion explains how these bonds are structured, and how their structures affect their performance in different prepayment scenarios. The effect of adding a TAC, reverse TAC, or Level II PAC on the behavior of the remaining companion bonds is also explored. Finally, some consideration is given to the spread and relative value relationships that exist between them.

COMPANION BASICS

Companion classes are created from the principal payments remaining after the PAC schedules are defined. In general, companion classes have second claim on excess principal after the PAC schedules, and pay sequentially until all the companions are retired. At the pricing prepayment assumption, companion classes pay simultaneously with the PACs. At very slow constant prepayment rates, they must wait to receive principal until the PACs have been retired. At very high speeds, they pay simultaneously with the short-term average life PACs and are quickly retired, after which the PACs themselves must absorb excess paydowns and are retired ahead of schedule.

A simplified example of a PAC/standard companion structure is depicted in Exhibit 1. The large unshaded area paying from the

Exhibit 1: PAC with Standard Companion Bonds, 165% PSA

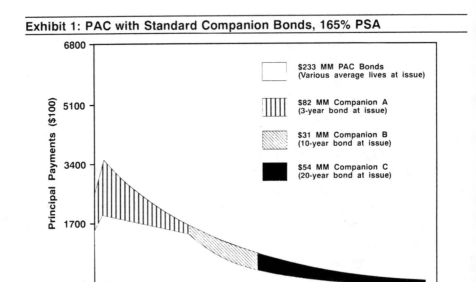

first to about the 300th month contains *all* the scheduled payments that would be available to construct PAC bonds assuming collars of 85% and 300% PSA, and FNMA 9% collateral with a WAC of 9.76% and a WAM of 339 months.[3] Normally, structurers would divide this PAC region into a number of PACs with varying average lives. The actual number of PACs created would depend on the demand for particular maturities and windows (the time elapsed between first and last principal payments to the PAC bondholders). For ease of exposition, the PAC region in this and subsequent examples is not divided. The companion bonds are not influenced by the partitioning of a single PAC region into individual bond classes; they are affected, instead, by the size of the entire region in relation to the total size of the companion classes. (In general, the larger the PAC class, given a fixed amount of collateral, the more volatile the companion class is.) The principal pay-

---

[3] This is the largest PAC region that could be accommodated by this collateral for the collars given.

ments left over after the PAC region is defined constitute the companion classes. In Exhibit 1, these are depicted by the shaded areas. At a pricing prepayment assumption of 165% PSA, the companions pay sequentially over the entire remaining life of the collateral. In this example the companion paydowns at 165% PSA have been divided into three classes with average lives of 3.1, 11.5, and 20.3 years (nominally a series of 3-, 10- and 20-year bonds).

The impact of actual prepayment experience on the size and timing of principal payments to the companion classes is graphically depicted in Exhibits 2 and 3. When prepayments occur at a constant speed of 300% PSA (the upper PAC collar), as shown in Exhibit 2, the PAC schedule is not disturbed, but the companions shorten dramatically and are all fully retired by the eighth year. By contrast, when prepayments slow to 85% PSA (the lower PAC collar), the first companion does not begin to pay until about the eighth year, as Exhibit 3 indicates. The resultant average life volatility is very significant. Bonds with average lives at pricing of 3, 10, and 20 years shorten to 1.0, 2.5, and 5.8 years, respectively, at 300% PSA, and at 85% PSA, the bonds have average lives of 15.0, 21.1 and 25.6 years, respectively.

The average life variability of a companion bond is generally a function of the size of the PAC region relative to the entire issue, the size of the companion relative to the remaining companions, and its average life at the pricing prepayment assumption. A detailed examination of how these characteristics interact to produce the actual behavior of companion bonds in different prepayment scenarios is beyond the scope of this chapter. Still, it is worth outlining the basic relationships between companion structure and behavior because they apply as well to the more complex, schedule-based techniques which are the subject of this chapter.

The order in which a companion is scheduled to receive excess cash flows also can profoundly affect its average life behavior. It is normally assumed that companions will receive payments in the order of their average lives at issue throughout the term of the transaction (indeed, that assumption is made throughout this dis-

Exhibit 2: PAC with Standard Companion Bonds, 300% PSA

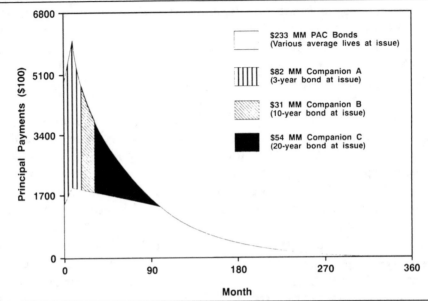

Exhibit 3: PAC with Standard Companion Bonds, 85% PSA

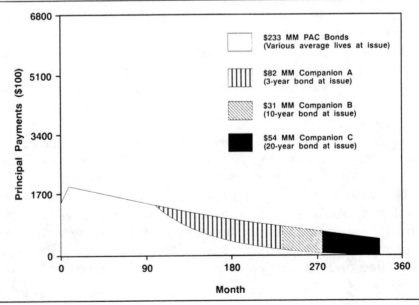

cussion). This assumption, however, is altered frequently, generating results that are entirely specific to the transaction in question. Rather than assume that a certain order of priorities is standard, investors must assure themselves that they understand the priorities and other rules on which the structure is based, as well as the conditions under which they may be switched on or off.

There are basically three different ways to vary the relative size of the companions. Lockouts, already mentioned above, are typically employed to improve the stability of payments to the earliest companion class in the issue. Moreover, with two or three years of schedulable paydowns added to its size, the first companion can provide a larger buffer against call and extension for subsequent companions. A similar technique is to pay the later years or "tail" of the PAC schedule to the companions projected to be paying at the same time. Intermediate or long-term companions can benefit from this technique. The third, tightening the collars, can increase the size of the companions.

Raising the bottom collar increases the principal available for companion classes in the early years (generally the first quarter to first third of the remaining term of the collateral) and lowering the top collar increases principal in later years.

It also should be apparent that the smaller the scheduled PAC payments, the more principal will be available to make payments to companions at any given prepayment speed. This means that extension risk is reduced; call risk is also reduced. The smaller the PAC region, the larger the projected paydowns to the companion in any one period and the smaller the excess principal as a proportion of the projected companion principal payment will be. In other words, excess principal has a proportionally smaller impact on the dollar weights used to compute the companion's average life.

For similar algebraic reasons, changing the proportion of PACs, while holding the average lives about the same, has a bigger impact on the volatility of companions constructed from cash flows at the tail, because smaller dollar weights are applied to later dates. The absolute magnitude of the average life at issue of a companion also determines how much it can lengthen or shorten. This is also very intuitive: the longer the average life at issue, the less room to lengthen and the more room to shorten. Similarly, short-term bonds have less room to shorten, more to lengthen.

The shortening of a CMO bond's average life in a bull market, or, conversely, its lengthening in a bear market generally are negative events from the investor's point of view. Two effects are of particular concern. For one, the additional cash flow accelerates or decelerates at the wrong time. As a consequence of the interest rate sensitivity of the prepayment process, reinvestment opportunities are most likely to have declining yields when prepayments are increasing, and rising yields when prepayments are drying up. Second, as average life varies, so to does the bond's duration or price sensitivity. In a bull market, the bond's price appreciates more slowly as market yields decline, generating a lower economic return than a bond of like but stable average life. In a bull market, the companion's value depreciates more quickly as yields rise.[4]

Since companion bonds absorb additional volatility from the protected bonds, changes in expected average life resulting from changes in prepayment experience in the collateral are of heightened concern to investors who hold them. As crucial as an accurate model of the prepayment process is for anticipating the performance of other mortgage-related products in various interest rate scenarios, it is even more valuable in the evaluation of companion bonds. Without appropriate prepayment projections, such as can be derived from an econometric prepayment model, it is not possible to link changes in interest rate levels to meaningful estimates of the yield or total rate of return of a companion.

---

[4] Structurers can improve the appeal of volatile securities to some investors by manipulating the coupon so that they are priced as deep discounts to benefit from fast prepayment speeds or as high premiums to benefit from slow prepayments.

COMPANION TACs

Since their introduction in the third quarter of 1988, companion TAC bonds have proven to be a highly marketable innovation. Indeed, since the first TACs were issued, the market has evolved away from TAC-only structures to prefer companion TACs. Clean TAC bonds (from structures without PACs) now are offered less frequently.

A TAC schedule is created by projecting the principal cash flows for the collateral at a single constant prepayment speed. This speed is typically the prepayment speed at which the bonds are priced. In the case of a clean TAC, the projected principal payments define the schedule. In the case of the companion TAC, projected principal remaining after scheduled PAC payments are made defines the schedule. The TACs have first priority after the PACs to principal payments, and their schedules are protected from call risk by the existence of other companion classes that absorb any principal paydowns that exceed both the scheduled PAC and TAC payments in any period. The larger these "support" classes are in relation to the companion TAC, the greater the protection provided to the TAC schedule.

Compared to a clean TAC with similar (in the example they are the same) average life and underlying collateral, the companion TAC necessarily receives less protection, because a larger proportion of the total collateral has already been allocated to high priority PAC bonds, and a much smaller proportion of principal remains to be allocated to lower priority support tranches. For this discussion, a simplified example of a companion TAC was created from the three-year companion in Exhibit 1. This was done simply by defining a schedule as the principal payments to the three-year companion assuming a constant prepayment speed of 165% PSA. Since it is identical at 165% PSA to the PAC/standard companion example, readers should refer to the cash flow diagram in Exhibit 1 to understand this structure. The impact of faster prepayments on this PAC/TAC structure is shown in Exhibit 4. At 300% PSA, the higher priority given the TAC schedule forces the ten- and

Exhibit 4: PAC with Standard Companion TAC, 300% PSA

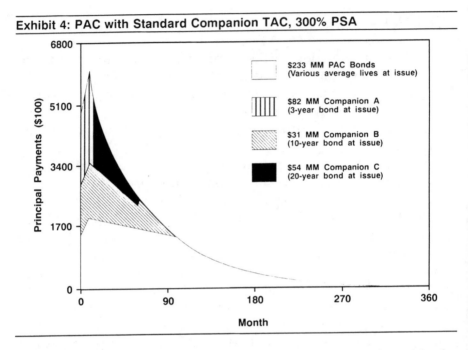

twenty-year companions to pay down simultaneously with the TAC (instead of sequentially as in the first example). Readers will note that the shape of the companion TAC at 300% PSA is almost, but not entirely identical to its shape at 165%, indicating that the schedule is still well protected at this speed. The size and timing of later payments has been altered slightly at the higher prepayment speed for reasons discussed below.

Companion TACs generally have the same properties as clean TACs: they provide a degree of call protection and little extension protection. Many structures actually will first extend, when prepayments slightly exceed the TAC speed, before shortening at higher speeds. The important difference is that companion TACs have significantly less call protection since they must absorb excess principal once the remaining unscheduled companions are retired. This can be seen by examining Exhibit 5, in which the average lives of various three-year CMO bonds at various prepayment speeds are compared. For comparison, a clean TAC with a

Exhibit 5: Average Lives at Various Prepayment Speeds of Different Three-Year PAC Companion Structures (Pricing Assumption 165% PSA)

Prepayment	Average Life (Years)			
Speed (% PSA)	Clean TAC	PAC Companion	Companion TAC	Level II PAC
0	16.7	24.7	24.7	23.3
50	8.0	19.9	19.9	16.8
85	6.0	14.9	14.9	9.5
90	5.2	13.7	13.7	3.1
125	4.0	7.2	7.2	3.1
165	**3.1**	**3.1**	**3.1**	**3.1**
225	3.1	1.6	3.1	3.1
275	3.1	1.2	3.1	2.7
300	3.1	1.0	3.2	2.5
475	3.1	0.6	1.6	1.5
600	3.1	0.5	1.2	1.1

3.1-year average life has been constructed from the same collateral used to create the PAC/standard companion and PAC/TAC examples. The clean TAC has unnaturally exceptional call protection (it is protected by $360 million of companion bonds, which comprise the remainder of the structure). The smaller size of the clean TAC also results in its having a lower average life at very low prepayment speeds than the companion TAC does (the clean TAC is small enough for even small paydowns at low speeds to reduce its principal balance significantly in the early years).

The more important comparison, since so few clean TACs are issued at present, is with the three-year companion from Exhibit 1. The companion TAC clearly provides meaningful call protection, requiring speeds in excess of 600% PSA before it shortens as much as the standard companion does at 300% PSA. The two bonds extend identically. This happens because they both have the same priority after the PACs to receive principal paydowns and no companions in front of them (the TAC would have priority over an earlier companion, which would protect it to a degree from extending, whereas the standard companion would wait until earlier companions were retired, which would cause it to extend). Notice that at 300% PSA, the companion TAC's average life is about a month longer than at the pricing speed (rounding exaggerates the difference—at several more places of significance the difference is really about 0.08 year). This phenomenon occurs at relatively high speeds, as principal payments become more bunched in the early months and trail off more sharply in later months. Exhibit 4, as mentioned above, gives some indication of what is happening at this speed to the principal cash flows thrown off by the collateral. The paydowns become more "tailish" toward the end of the companion's schedule, forcing it to wait as excess payments are, going into the tail, not large enough to meet the schedule.

The other great difference between PAC/TAC structures and both clean TAC and PAC/standard companion structures is how much more volatile the unscheduled companions can be. The

---

Exhibit 6: Average Lives at Various Prepayment Speeds of Twenty-Year Companions from Different CMO Structures (Pricing Assumption 165% PSA)

Prepayment Speed (% PSA)	Average Life (years)		
	PAC Structure	PAC/TAC Structure	Layered PAC Structure
0	27.7	27.7	27.8
50	26.8	26.8	27.0
90	25.3	25.3	25.6
125	23.3	23.4	23.3
165	**20.3**	**20.3**	**18.2**
190	18.0	18.0	12.5
225	13.6	13.1	5.1
250	10.4	9.2	3.8
275	7.4	5.7	3.1
300	4.8	2.6	2.6
475	2.0	1.0	1.3
600	1.5	0.7	1.0

presence of additional risk-reduced structures forces the remaining companions to absorb more prepayment volatility. This is demonstrated in Exhibit 6, where various twenty-year companion structures are compared. At prepayment speeds above 225% PSA, the companion in the PAC/TAC structure begins to shorten much more quickly than the standard companion.

REVERSE TACs

Payment rules and priorities also can be devised that protect a companion bond from extension risk while leaving it more exposed to call risk. These structures fittingly are termed "reverse TACs." Significant amounts of reverse TACs have been issued since the beginning of 1989, stimulated in part by the bearish sentiment prevalent during much of the first half of the year. These structures typically are created as twenty-year companion classes. Their long lives make them natural candidates for this treatment, as they have not, in any case, more than six or maybe eight years to extend. Additionally, these structures are priced at significant discounts from par in order to benefit from increases in prepayments.

An example of a reverse TAC was created for this discussion by defining a payment schedule for the fourth tranche of the PAC/companion structure depicted in Exhibits 1, 2, and 3. A cash flow diagram for prepayments at 85% PSA is included in Exhibit 7. (At 165% PSA and faster speeds, the PAC/reverse TAC structure, as will be explained below, pays exactly like the PAC/standard companion, which is depicted at 165% PSA in Exhibit 1 and 300% PSA in Exhibit 3.) The schedule was run at 165% PSA, the pricing speed in all of these examples, and has priority after the scheduled PAC payments are made. The reverse TAC receives excess cash flow only after the three- and ten-year companions are retired. These arrangements preserve the schedule at prepayment speeds slower than those used to generate the schedule, but not at

Exhibit 7: PAC with Reverse TAC Bond, 85% PSA

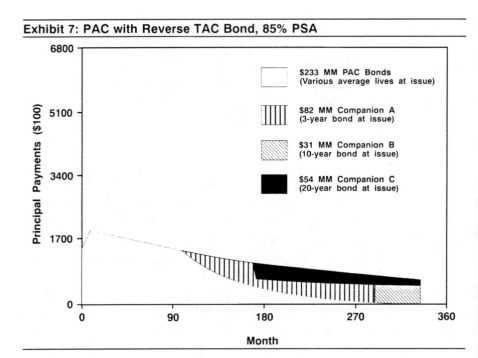

faster speeds. The reverse TAC does not begin to extend until prepayments fall below a constant rate of about 70% PSA.

The average life volatility of the reverse TAC is compared to that of other twenty-year companion structures in Exhibit 8. The reverse TAC in the example has an average life of 20.3 years; in the worst case, that of no prepayments, the bond's average life only extends to 24.5 years. By comparison, the last tranche of the simple structure extends to 27.7 years. The cash flow diagrams in Exhibits 3 and 7 make it clear why this is so. In the simple PAC/companion structure (Exhibit 3), at a speed equal to the upper collar, the companions pay down sequentially after the PAC bonds are retired. In the structure with the reverse TAC (Exhibit 7), the three- and ten-year companions extend to permit the scheduled reverse TAC payments to be met. At 85% PSA, the lower PAC collar, the short- and intermediate-term companions pay simultaneously with the reverse TAC. At slower prepayment

Exhibit 8: Average Lives at Various Prepayment Speeds of Twenty-Year PAC Structures (Pricing Assumption 165% PSA)

Prepayment Speed (% PSA)	Average Life (years)		
	PAC Companion	Reverse TAC	Level II PAC
0	27.7	24.5	24.6
50	26.8	20.7	20.3
85	25.6	20.3	18.1
125	23.3	20.3	18.1
165	**20.3**	**20.3**	**18.1**
190	18.0	18.0	18.1
225	13.6	13.6	18.1
250	10.4	10.4	14.7
275	7.4	7.4	
300	4.8	4.8	5.8
350	3.3	3.3	3.7
475	2.0	2.0	2.2
600	1.5	1.5	1.6

speeds, the average lives of both companions exceed that of the reverse TAC.

The reverse TAC imparts considerably more volatility to the other companions when prepayments slow, but it does not cause them to be more volatile in faster prepayment scenarios. This effect can also be seen by comparing the average lives of three-year companions from both structures listed in Exhibit 9. This is a natural consequence of the one-sided protection afforded by targeted amortization structures.

Schedules can also be applied to intermediate-term companion bonds to protect their average lives from extending in slow prepayment scenarios. At the same time, the structure is "protected" from call risk in moderately fast prepayment scenarios by taking advantage of the natural tendency of TACs to extend slightly as prepayments exceed the pricing speed. The resulting average life profile can be reasonably stable across a significant range of prepayment speeds (for example, extending no more than two or

Exhibit 9: Average Lives at Various Prepayment Speeds of Three-Year Companions from Different CMO PAC Structures (Pricing Assumption 165% PSA)

Prepayment Speed (% PSA)	Average Life (years)		
	PAC Structure	PAC/ Reverse TAC Structure	Layered PAC Structure
0	24.7	26.3	26.1
50	19.9	22.7	22.7
85	14.9	16.5	18.3
90	13.7	15.0	17.4
100	11.5	12.4	14.5
125	7.2	7.2	8.7
165	3.1	3.1	3.1
225	1.6	1.6	1.5
275	1.2	1.2	1.1
300	1.0	1.0	1.0
475	0.6	0.9	0.6
600	0.5	0.6	0.5

three years across a range from 50% or 75% PSA to 225% or 250% PSA, assuming a schedule run at 165% PSA). In effect, an intermediate-term companion TAC can be constructed to provide PAC-like stability. A number of such bonds have indeed been issued, some of them with monikers indicating that the payments are stabilized or controlled.

LAYERED PACs

The value of companion classes also can be enhanced by establishing secondary PAC schedules for a portion of the principal remaining after the primary PAC payments are met. A cash flow diagram for an example of a two-tiered PAC structure, run at a pricing speed of 165% PSA, is shown in Exhibit 10. This example uses the same collateral as the previous examples. The same collars—85% to 300% PSA—were used to create the same amount of

Exhibit 10: Layered PAC Structure, 165% PSA

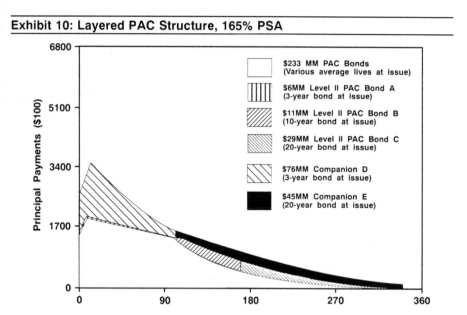

primary or Level I PACs—$233.0 million of a total original balance of $400 million CMO bonds. Collars for the second tier of PACs were set at 90% to 225% PSA. The second tier PAC region was further divided into a series of nominally ten- and twenty-year bonds, the companions into three- and twenty-year bonds. (In order to match the 3.1 year average lives in the previous examples, it was necessary to accept long-term bonds in the layered PAC example with average lives closer to 18 than to 20 years. This does not vitiate the comparison.) The Level II PACs appear in the figure as a narrow band between the PAC region and the companions: at 165% PSA they pay down simultaneously with the primary PACs in the deal. The size of the second tier of PACs is a function of the collars—the tighter the protection band the larger the amount of PACs that can be created. In this example, protecting the Level II schedule up to 225% PSA limits the amount of three-year Level II PACs that can be created to $5.6 million. In total, the second layer of PACs only amount to about 11% of the transaction (58.25% of the transaction is standard, Level I PACs).

The Level II PAC schedule remains intact until prepayment speeds break the primary PAC collars. For example, Exhibit 11 shows the principal payments at 300% PSA. At this speed, the primary PAC schedule is not violated, but payments to the Level II PACs are significantly accelerated, shortening to average lives of 2.5, 3.9, and 5.8 years, respectively. Similarly, when prepayments slow to a constant speed of 85% PSA, primary PAC payments are made on schedule, but the payments to Level II PACs are delayed. At 85% PSA, as shown in Exhibit 12, the companion PACs have average lives of 9.5, 11.3, and 18.1 years, respectively. As would be expected, the longer Level II PACs are more volatile on the upside, when prepayments accelerate, and the shorter PACs are more volatile on the downside, when prepayments decelerate. The three- and twenty-year bonds receive no principal until the Level

Exhibit 11: Layered PAC Structure, 300% PSA

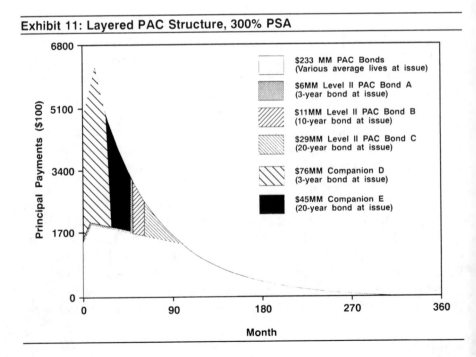

Exhibit 12: Layered PAC Structure, 85% PSA

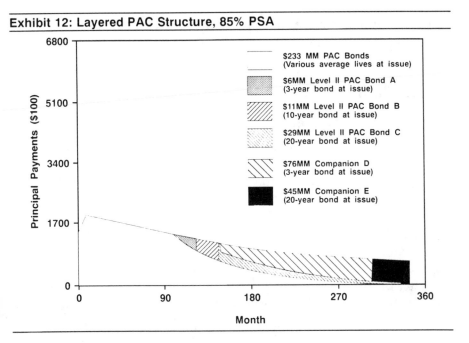

Legend:
- $233 MM PAC Bonds (Various average lives at issue)
- $6MM Level II PAC Bond A (3-year bond at issue)
- $11MM Level II PAC Bond B (10-year bond at issue)
- $29MM Level II PAC Bond C (20-year bond at issue)
- $76MM Companion D (3-year bond at issue)
- $45MM Companion E (20-year bond at issue)

Y-axis: Principal Payments ($100), values 0, 1700, 3400, 5100, 6800
X-axis: Month, values 0, 90, 180, 270, 360

II PACs are paid, extending their average lives to 18.3 years and 25.8 years, respectively.

The average life volatility of Level II PACs is compared to that of companion TACs and three-year standard companions in Exhibit 8. Although not as well protected as primary PACs, Level II PACs do provide modest call protection and decent extension protection. Moreover, these examples demonstrate that they can shorten and extend less vigorously than their TAC and reverse TAC counterparts when prepayments move outside the appropriate protective boundary. The companions of layered PACs are somewhat more volatile over moderate prepayment shifts. As the comparison in Exhibit 6 with a twenty-year standard PAC companion and a reverse TAC suggests, the twenty-year layered PAC companion shortens faster between 165% and about 250% PSA than either of its counterparts. Similarly, Exhibit 9 indicates that the three-year layered PAC companion lengthens more abruptly than its counterparts at prepayment speeds between 165% and 50% PSA.[5]

CONCLUSION

The average life volatilities of the three-year companion structures discussed in this chapter are summarized in Exhibit 13, as are those of the twenty-year companions in Exhibit 14. The graphs make plain the differences in call and extension protection that can be provided by furnishing companion classes with TAC or PAC schedules. The Level II PACs have stable average life patterns between the upper and lower collar speeds. (A Level I PAC would have a similar pattern, only it would be stable over a wider range, say 75% to 300% PSA, and owing to the presence of the companions, would shorten or lengthen more moderately outside that range.) By comparison, the standard companions demonstrate steep and continuous changes in average life over the same ranges for which the Level II PACs are protected. The TACs, as would be expected, provide call protection, but no extension protection, while the reverse TACs are stable at slower speeds, but shorten abruptly when prepayments occur at faster constant rates than the prepayment assumption.

On the whole, market yields for generic companion structures reflect the relative volatility of these bonds: Level II PACs trade tighter than companion TACs, and companion TACs trade tighter than plain companions. Typical yield curves for Treasuries and companions are displayed in Exhibit 15.

Readers will note that the companion yield curves are upwardly sloping; investors receive additional compensation for assuming additional risk. In general, Level II PACs trade fifteen to twenty-five basis points behind Level I PACs with comparable av-

---

[5] Readers are reminded that all these examples are highly simplified and furnish a basic understanding of how the structures behave. Actual CMO issues frequently are more complex, containing other structures or variations on those discussed in this chapter. Additional complexity could result in behavior valuably different from that of these examples.

Exhibit 13: Different Three-Year CMO Companion Structures (Average Lives over a Range of Constant Prepayment Speeds)

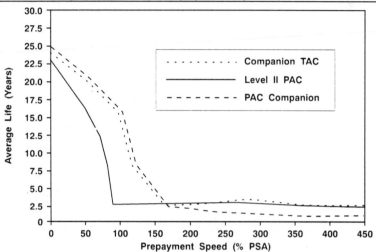

Note: The average lives of the Companion TAC and PAC Companion are the same between 0% and 165% PSA; the lines have been separated for readability.

Exhibit 14: Different Twenty-Year CMO Companion Structures (Average Lives over a Range of Constant Prepayment Speeds)

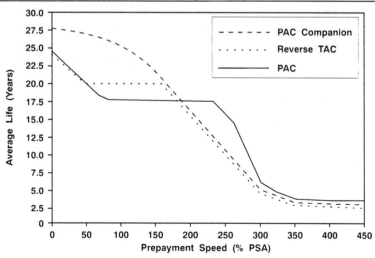

Note: The average lives of the PAC Companion and Reverse TAC are the same at prepayment speeds above 165% PSAs. The lines are separated for readability.

Exhibit 15: Treasury and CMO Yield Curves

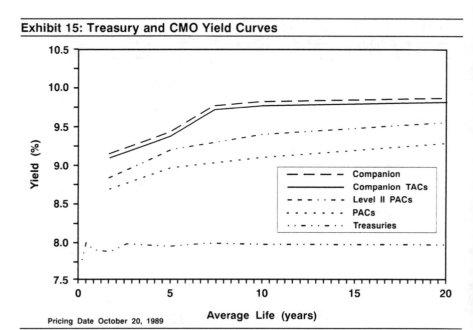

Pricing Date October 20, 1989   Average Life (years)

erage lives, with the actual spread depending on several factors, the most prominent of which is the relative quality of the collars. Buyers of Level II PACs are, in effect, buying more than an average life profile—they are buying the liquidity and familiarity PACs now enjoy with a wide diversity of investors. Despite their notable stability, companion TACs and reverse TACs trade from twenty-five to fifty basis points wider than primary PACs, and only about five basis points tighter than standard companions. Whether enough additional risk is present in the TACs over the PACs to warrant this difference in spreads is a matter for investors to evaluate. For those who can meet their objectives by purchasing the TACs, the spread between the two should represent an exceptional investment opportunity.

CHAPTER 21

INVERSE FLOATING-RATE CMOs

Bella Borg*
Associate Director
Financial Analytics & Structured Transactions Group
Bear, Stearns & Co., Inc.

Brian Lancaster
Vice President
Financial Analytics & Structured Transactions Group
Bear, Stearns & Co., Inc.

Jane Tang
Senior Analyst
Financial Analytics & Structured Transactions Group
Bear, Stearns & Co., Inc.

* Bella Borg is currently employed by Merrill Lynch.

INVERSE FLOATER FUNDAMENTALS

Inverse floaters continue to be a focal point in CMO issuance. The analysis presented in this chapter shows the fundamentals of how inverse floaters are created and how, by themselves or in synthetic combinations with floating-rate CMOs or IOs, they can enhance portfolio yields.[1]

An inverse floater is a floating-rate security whose coupon varies inversely with a selected index at specified intervals. Indices most commonly used are one-month LIBOR, the 11th District Cost of Funds Index (COFI), and a Treasury index, such as the one-year Constant Maturity Treasury (CMT) or ten-year CMT. For example, the coupon of a LIBOR-based inverse would reset upward as LIBOR decreases, and downward as LIBOR increases.

Inverse floater coupons reset according to a formula, such as:

$$\text{Coupon} = 13.36618 - 0.7117 \times \text{1-month LIBOR}$$
$$\text{for LIBOR less than } 10.3499\%, \text{ otherwise } 6\%$$

Exhibit 1 translates various LIBOR rates into corresponding coupons based on this formula.

The coupon of the inverse floater may reset by more or less than the change in the index. The coupon of a LIBOR-based inverse is scaled by a factor, for example, 0.50 or 6.0; that is, a 100-basis point decrease in LIBOR would increase the coupon by 50 basis points or 600 basis points. In the above formula, 0.7117 is the scaling factor, and is commonly referred to as the *coupon leverage*.

Inverse floaters have coupon caps and floors. The addition of these features may limit downside risk should the underlying index move adversely, or limit upside potential should the index move favorably. For example, the coupon of the inverse floater shown above has a floor of 6%, that is, it will never fall below 6%

---

[1] Yields are only one measure of value, and not necessarily indicative of total returns. Yet yields are commonly used to illustrate the characteristics of securities. The more theoretically correct measure of value but less widely used standard is the option-adjusted spread (OAS).

Exhibit 1: Coupon Rates for Various LIBOR Rates for an Inverse Floater

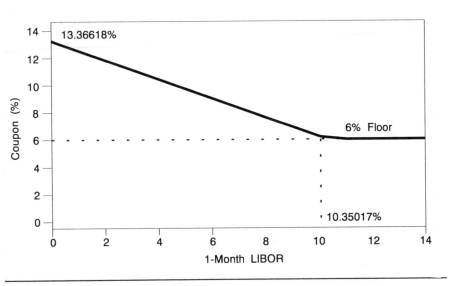

---

no matter how high LIBOR rises. This inverse floater also has a coupon cap of 13.36618%.

The Impact of Interest and Prepayment Rate Changes on Yield

Inverse floaters are created by splitting a fixed-rate bond into two floating-rate parts, a floating-rate bond and its mirror complement, the inverse floater.[2] The stripping of a floating-rate bond out of the fixed-rate bond implies that the inverse floater buyer has bought, in effect, a "prepackaged leveraged position" in the underlying fixed-rate bond, funding in the short-term market at whatever index the inverse is based, and a cap on funding costs. The purchaser of the inverse floater receives the interest differential between the coupon of the underlying fixed-rate bond and the coupon on the floater tranche. The value of such a position, or

---

[2] See the Appendix for mechanics of how this is done.

price of the inverse, will be determined primarily by the value of the underlying fixed-rate bond, such as a companion, PAC, balloon, or VADM and any embedded caps. Thus, it is conceivable that the price of an inverse could decline even if the index on which it is based falls. This would happen if the value of the underlying fixed-rate bond or caps fall.

Because the investor, in effect, has purchased a long position in the underlying fixed-rate bond, the yield of the entire investment position will be affected if prepayment speeds change. The yield of inverse floaters that have greater leverage or are backed by more volatile classes of bonds, such as companions, will be affected more by changing prepayments. Whether the value of the inverse floater is positively or negatively affected will depend on whether the inverse was purchased at a discount or premium. If purchased at a discount, a pick-up in speeds would increase the yield of the inverse floater. If purchased at a premium, the yield could be reduced.

Yield matrices are helpful in understanding the performance of an inverse floater because they capture the impact of various changes in short-term funding costs and prepayment speeds on the yield of the leveraged position. For example, as LIBOR falls the yield of the inverse floater will increase. They do, however, assume that the value of the fixed-rate bond underlying the inverse remains constant.

Low, Medium, and High Leverage Inverse Floaters

The companion inverse floater is characterized by the level of its coupon leverage. Low leverage inverse floaters have a coupon leverage ranging between 0.5:1 to 2:1. Medium leverage bonds are greater than or equal to 2:1 and less than or equal to 4.5:1. High leverage inverses are greater than 4.5:1. A lower leverage inverse floater provides more downside protection than the higher leverage variety. In contrast, the high leverage inverses outperform in falling rate scenarios while underperforming in rising rate environments.

One characteristic common to nearly all *companion* inverse floaters is the shortening in average lives and modified durations that occurs when prepayments increase. Companion inverse floaters typically support PAC tranches in a deal. Thus, when rates fall, it is possible that prepayments could increase, causing a dramatic shortening in the average life of the security just when it is least desired, since the coupon of the inverse would have increased significantly. Similarly, when rates rise and the coupon declines, the average life of the companion inverse will increase if prepayments slow, again when it is least desired. Therefore, the average life variability of a companion inverse whether high, low, or medium leveraged, is the key to value along with the coupon and type of collateral underlying the REMIC. In general, the less negatively convex the collateral, the better the inverse floater. Thus, inverse floaters backed by fifteen-year securities, balloon securities, or lower coupon, thirty-year fixed-rate mortgage securities will tend to have better average life stability and convexity characteristics, all other things being equal.

Exhibit 2 shows the performance of several types of inverse floaters if one-month LIBOR is 5.5%.

Exhibit 2: Types of Inverse Floaters and Their Performance at 5.5% One-Month LIBOR*

Type of Inverse Floater	Example	Coupon Leverage	Price	Yield	Base PSA	Avg. Life
Low Leverage Companion Inverse	FNMA 9198 S2	0.75:1	100:00	11.48%	165	24.10
Medium Leverage Companion Inverse	FNMA 90138 S	3.80:1	97:24	23.49%	180	11.19
High Leverage Companion Inverse	FNMA 9093 Q1	6.33:1	106:06	29.00%	180	7.49
Plain Vanilla Low Leverage Inverse	MLT-11 Q1	1.80:1	88:16	14.97%	155	8.50
PAC Inverse	FNMA 91141 S1	0.71:1	98:03	10.00%	165	7.94
VADM Inverse	FHLMC 1121 S1	3.50:1	105:11	16.50%	165	7.05
IO Inverse	FNMA 9181 S	229:1	3085:01	28.00%	250	6.00
COFI Inverse	FNMA 9130 S3	5.00:1	87:10	15.00%	165	17.00
TTIB Inverse	FNMA 91132 S2	6.78:1	92:09	11.00%	165	20.37
Balloon Inverse	FNMA 9191 S	3.40:1	110:16	14.37%	250	4.49

* All prices and yields are as of 9/19/91.

Exhibit 3: Graphical Presentation of Low, Medium, and High Leverage Inverse Floaters versus CMO Floater*

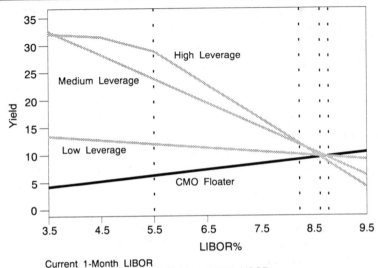

Current 1-Month LIBOR
Low Leverage Breakeven Yield at 8.25% LIBOR
High Leverage Breakeven Yield at 8.61% LIBOR
Medium Leverage Breakeven Yield at 8.75% LIBOR

*   All prices and yields are as of 9/19/91.

Exhibit 3 shows graphically, and Exhibit 4 in table form, the yield, average life, and cash flow duration sensitivities of LIBOR-based companion inverse floaters with coupon leverages of 0.75:1, 3.8:1, and 6.3:1 versus FNMA 9152 F2, a LIBOR-based companion floater that resets at 95 basis points over one-month LIBOR subject to an 11% cap priced at 100:0. The lower leverage inverse floater has a coupon floor of 8.3125%.

Clearly, the low leverage inverse has a less volatile yield profile than the higher leverage inverses, and has a yield floor of 8.484% if LIBOR rises more than 400 basis points. The inverse floaters will outperform the CMO floater unless LIBOR rises more than 275, 325, and 311 basis points, for the low, medium, and high leverage inverses, respectively.

Exhibit 4: Low, Medium, and High Leverage Inverse Floaters*

Yields and Cash Flow Durations of Low Leverage Inverse (FNMA 9198 S2) at 100.0
(165% PSA, 5.5% LIBOR) Coupon Reset Formula: 15.3628 - .75 × 1 mo LIBOR

PSA		75%	100%	125%	145%	165%	225%	300%
1-Month LIBOR	**Avg Life**	**28.51**	**27.83**	**26.80**	**25.65**	**24.10**	**4.19**	**2.34**
3.50	Yield	13.026	13.026	13.026	13.026	13.025	12.951	12.874
	Duration	7.29	7.27	7.24	7.19	7.11	3.06	1.92
4.50	Yield	12.254	12.254	12.254	12.254	12.253	12.200	12.145
	Duration	7.70	7.68	7.64	7.58	7.49	3.11	1.94
5.50	Yield	11.483	11.483	11.483	11.483	11.483	11.450	11.417
	Duration	8.16	8.13	8.08	8.01	7.90	3.16	1.96
6.50	Yield	10.713	10.713	10.713	10.713	10.713	10.702	10.691
	Duration	8.66	8.62	8.56	8.48	8.36	3.21	1.98
7.50	Yield	9.944	9.944	9.944	9.944	9.944	9.955	9.966
	Duration	9.22	9.17	9.10	9.00	8.85	3.27	2.00
8.50	Yield	9.175	9.175	9.175	9.175	9.176	9.209	9.242
	Duration	9.84	9.78	9.69	9.58	9.40	3.32	2.02
9.50	Yield	8.484	8.484	8.484	8.485	8.485	8.538	8.591
	Duration	10.46	10.40	10.29	10.15	9.94	3.37	2.04

Yields and Cash Flow Durations of Medium Leverage Inverse (FNMA 90138 S) at 97:24
(180% PSA, 5.5% LIBOR) Coupon Reset Formula: 42.56 - 3.8 × 1 mo LIBOR

PSA		75%	100%	125%	150%	180%	250%	350%
1-Month LIBOR	**Avg Life**	**23.33**	**21.12**	**17.46**	**13.63**	**11.19**	**4.28**	**1.46**
3.50	Yield	31.672	31.675	31.727	31.834	31.927	32.221	32.876
	Duration	2.97	2.96	2.71	2.31	2.05	1.51	0.96
4.50	Yield	27.414	27.418	27.474	27.590	27.687	28.031	28.797
	Duration	3.45	3.43	3.11	2.62	2.31	1.64	1.00
5.50	Yield	23.201	23.207	23.266	23.388	23.486	23.880	24.762
	Duration	4.08	4.04	3.64	3.02	2.65	1.80	105
6.50	Yield	19.034	19.042	19.103	19.266	19.322	19.769	20.772
	Duration	4.95	4.87	4.34	3.56	3.11	1.98	1.10
7.50	Yield	14.915	14.926	14.987	15.106	15.197	15.694	16.827
	Duration	6.21	6.06	5.33	4.30	3.74	2.21	1.15
8.50	Yield	10.847	10.861	10.919	11.029	11.114	11.655	12.927
	Duration	8.14	7.84	6.79	5.40	4.65	2.51	1.21
9.50	Yield	6.835	6.852	6.852	6.999	7.078	7.649	9.073
	Duration	11.26	10.65	10.65	7.11	6.04	2.89	1.28

Exhibit 4: Low, Medium, and High Leverage Inverse Floaters (Continued)

Yields and Cash Flow Durations of High Leverage Inverse (FNMA 9093 Q1) at 106:06
(180% PSA, 5.5% LIBOR) Coupon Reset Formula: 64.5925 – 6.33 × 1 mo LIBOR

PSA		75%	100%	125%	150%	180%	250%	350%
1-Month LIBOR	Avg Life	21.51	19.45	17.05	13.94	7.49	1.37	0.69
3.50	Yield	43.036	43.035	43.032	43.008	42.212	38.148	32.646
	Duration	2.15	2.15	2.15	2.13	1.73	0.87	0.52
4.50	Yield	36.315	36.313	36.307	36.277	35.556	0.92	0.54
	Duration	2.57	2.57	2.56	2.53	1.99	25.381	20.696
5.50	Yield	29.697	29.693	29.683	29.645	29.002	25.381	20.696
	Duration	3.16	3.15	3.13	3.07	2.34	0.98	0.57
6.50	Yield	23.179	23.171	23.156	23.109	22.547	19.157	14.872
	Duration	4.05	4.02	3.98	3.84	2.81	1.05	0.59
7.50	Yield	16.754	16.742	16.720	16.665	16.187	13.040	9.148
	Duration	5.50	5.43	5.30	5.01	3.47	1.13	0.62
8.50	Yield	10.415	10.397	10.369	10.309	9.917	7.029	3.523
	Duration	8.14	7.89	7.53	6.87	4.43	1.21	0.65
9.50	Yield	4.150	4.129	4.098	4.039	3.734	1.124	-2.004
	Duration	13.52	12.69	11.62	10.03	5.92	1.30	0.68

* All prices and yields are as of 9/19/91.

Two-Tiered Index Bonds (TTIB)

A recent innovation in the CMO market is the creation of an inverse floater whose coupon is fixed within a specified range of one-month LIBOR and floats when LIBOR is above the upper end of that range. The term "two-tiered" refers to the fixed-rate first tier of the inverse floater, that is, the coupon is fixed when LIBOR is between 0% and a certain upper end "strike" level (see Exhibit 5), and the floating-rate second tier where the coupon resets according to a formula when LIBOR is above the strike level.

For example, the inverse floater, FNMA 91132 S2 has a 9.5% LIBOR strike, that is the coupon of the inverse is fixed at 9.806% as long as LIBOR is between 0% and 9.5% and will float to the formula:

Exhibit 5: FNMA 91-132 S2 TTIB Inverse Offered at 11.0% Yield at 5.5% One-Month LIBOR and 165% PSA

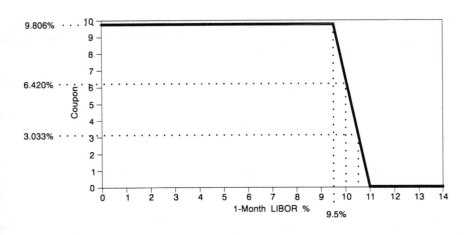

Coupon = 74.17 – 6.775 × one-month LIBOR
when LIBOR is greater than 9.5%, otherwise 9.806%

Exhibit 5 shows how the coupon of the inverse resets at varying levels of one-month LIBOR. As long as one-month LIBOR is between 0% and 9.5%, the coupon of the inverse is 9.806%. If one-month LIBOR is 10%, the coupon resets to 6.42%. At 10.5%, the coupon continues to adjust downwards to 3.033%. At 10.95%, the coupon of the inverse resets to zero. Thus, the inverse floater is long one unit of a fixed-rate bond with a 9.806% coupon, short, or "in effect has sold," 6.775 units of a 9.5% one-month LIBOR cap, and is long or "has purchased" 6.775 units of a 10.95% one-month LIBOR cap.

A TTIB allows the investor to avoid the inconvenience and cost of hedging an inverse floater. It is designed for the investor who believes that LIBOR will remain at current levels or even increase substantially. For example, the TTIB, FNMA 91-132 S2, in September 1991 was offered at a price of 92:09 to yield 11.00% at 165% PSA, 550 basis points over current one-month LIBOR. This yield

Exhibit 6: Yields and Cash Flow Durations of TTIB (FNMA 91-132 S2) at 92:09 (165% PSA, 5.5% LIBOR)

Coupon Reset Formula: 74.17 – 6.775 × 1 mo LIBOR when LIBOR > 9.5% otherwise 9.806%

	PSA	50%	75%	100%	125%	145%	165%	225%
1-Month LIBOR	**Avg Life**	**28.25**	**27.42**	**26.18**	**24.46**	**22.67**	**20.37**	**4.84**
4.50	Yield	10.913	10.918	10.927	10.943	10.963	11.000	**12.856**
	Duration	8.58	8.54	8.46	8.33	8.16	7.87	**2.69**
5.50	Yield	10.913	10.918	10.927	10.943	10.963	**11.000**	12.856
	Duration	8.58	8.54	8.46	8.33	8.16	**7.87**	2.69
6.50	Yield	10.913	10.918	10.927	10.943	**10.963**	11.000	12.856
	Duration	8.58	8.54	8.46	8.33	**8.16**	7.87	2.69
7.50	Yield	10.913	10.918	10.927	**10.943**	10.963	11.000	12.856
	Duration	8.58	8.54	8.46	**8.33**	8.16	7.87	2.69
9.50	Yield	10.913	10.918	**10.927**	10.943	10.963	11.000	12.856
	Duration	8.58	8.54	**8.46**	8.33	8.16	7.87	2.69
10.00	Yield	7.175	**7.182**	7.194	7.214	7.240	7.283	9.086
	Duration	12.02	**11.90**	11.70	11.38	10.99	10.40	3.03
10.50	Yield	**3.513**	3.522	3.536	3.560	3.588	3.634	5.323
	Duration	**18.11**	17.77	17.24	16.46	15.58	14.37	3.50

would be maintained even if one-month LIBOR rises 400 basis points. The investor is, however, giving up all potential increases in coupon should rates fall. For example, if one-month LIBOR falls 100 basis points to 4.5% and prepayments stay at 165% PSA, the inverse still yields 11.00%. The yield of a TTIB priced at a discount will rise if prepayments increase. In the case of FNMA 91-132 S2, which was priced at 92:09, the yield would rise to 12.856% if prepayments speed up to 225% PSA (see Exhibit 6).

IO Inverse Floaters

An IO inverse is created by either combining an inverse floater tranche with the IO-ette of the CMO into one bond, or by stripping an inverse floater into an IO-ette and PO components. As rates rise, the higher yield of the IO due to slower prepayments will offset the decline in the coupon of the inverse. As rates fall, the increased coupon of the inverse will offset the decline in the yield of the IO arising from faster prepayments.

For example, the IO inverse of FNMA 9181, an IO stripped from a plain vanilla inverse floater (see Exhibit 7), was offered in September 1991 at a 28% yield at 250% PSA. If LIBOR rises 200 basis points to 7.5% and prepayments slow down to 175% PSA, its yield will decline to 16.316%. By comparison, under the same scenario, the yield of FNMA Trust 80 IO (similar WAC and WAM collateral) will increase to 15.331%—267 basis points less. Conversely, if LIBOR falls 100 basis points to 4.5% and prepayments speed up to 350% PSA, the yield of the inverse will increase to 29.621%, while the yield of the IO drops to 1.444%—28.177% less yield! Other scenarios are shown in Exhibit 8.

Exhibit 7: Structure of FNMA 9181

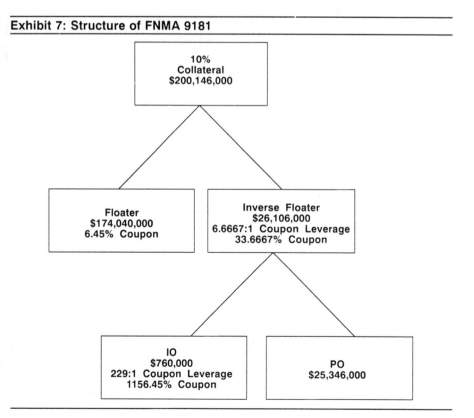

Exhibit 8: Yields and Cash Flow Durations of IO Inverse (FNMA 9181 S) at 3085:01 (250% PSA, 5.5% LIBOR)

			Coupon Reset Formula: 2530.45 – 229 × 1 mo LIBOR					
	PSA	*100%*	*150%*	*175%*	*200%*	*250%*	*350%*	*450%*
1-Month LIBOR	**Avg Life**	**11.40**	**8.94**	**8.01**	**7.23**	**6.00**	**4.41**	**3.44**
3.50	Yield	54.880	51.611	49.960	48.297	44.935	38.063	30.977
	Duration	1.46	1.47	1.47	1.47	1.48	1.49	1.50
4.50	Yield	46.200	42.978	41.351	39.712	36.398	29.621	22.630
	Duration	1.71	1.72	1.72	1.73	1.73	1.74	1.75
5.50	Yield	37.666	34.490	32.885	31.269	28.000	21.313	14.412
	Duration	2.05	2.06	2.06	2.07	2.07	2.08	2.09
6.50	Yield	29.267	26.134	24.551	22.956	19.730	13.128	6.311
	Duration	2.54	2.54	2.55	2.55	2.56	2.57	2.57
7.50	Yield	20.968	17.878	16.316	14.743	11.559	5.041	-1.697
	Duration	3.27	3.28	3.28	3.28	3.29	3.03	3.30
8.50	Yield	12.675	9.633	8.095	6.544	3.407	-3.023	-9.676
	Duration	4.49	4.50	4.50	4.50	4.50	4.51	4.51
9.50	Yield	4.062	1.086	-0.420	-1.938	-5.012	-11.319	-17.854
	Duration	6.76	6.76	6.77	6.77	6.77	6.78	6.77
Trust 80 IO	Yield	18.660	15.331	13.646	11.947	8.507	1.444	-5.885
Strip at 39:12	Duration	3.57	3.61	3.63	3.64	3.68	3.76	3.84

PAC Inverse Floaters

The PAC inverse allows the investor to capitalize on the best features of an inverse floater while benefiting from the average life stability of a PAC bond. At any level of LIBOR, the inverse maintains a stable yield within the PAC band and an identical average life profile under all prepayment scenarios. For example, the S1 tranche of FNMA 91-141, a low leverage seven-year PAC inverse with a coupon resetting monthly to the formula 13.36618 – 0.7117 × one-month LIBOR, was offered to yield 10%, 178 basis points higher than the seven-year PAC from the same CMO. It maintains the identical average life profile as the seven-year PAC at all prepayments speeds while offering a 10% yield at 5.5% LIBOR within its band of 90% to 250% (see Exhibit 9). Outside the band, the

Exhibit 9: Yields and Cash Flow Durations of PAC Inverse (FNMA 91-141 S1) at 98:03 (165% PSA, 5.5% LIBOR)

	Coupon Reset Formula: 13.36618 - 0.7117 x 1 mo LIBOR							
	PSA	50%	75%	90%	150%	200%	250%	300%
1-Month LIBOR	Avg Life	10.20	8.66	7.94	7.94	7.94	7.94	7.11
3.50	Yield	11.436	11.467	11.486	11.486	11.486	11.486	11.512
	Duration	5.81	5.29	5.02	5.02	5.02	5.02	4.68
4.50	Yield	10.691	10.723	10.742	10.742	10.742	10.742	10.769
	Duration	6.01	5.45	5.16	5.16	5.16	5.16	4.80
5.50	Yield	9.947	9.980	10.000	10.000	10.000	10.000	10.028
	Duration	6.21	5.61	5.30	5.30	5.30	5.30	4.92
6.50	Yield	9.206	9.240	9.260	9.260	9.260	9.260	9.289
	Duration	6.42	5.78	5.45	5.45	5.45	5.45	5.05
7.50	Yield	8.466	8.501	8.522	8.522	8.522	8.522	8.522
	Duration	6.64	5.96	5.61	5.61	5.61	5.61	5.18
8.50	Yield	7.728	7.764	7.785	7.785	7.785	7.785	7.816
	Duration	6.88	6.14	5.77	5.77	5.77	5.77	5.31
9.50	Yield	6.992	7.029	7.051	7.051	7.051	7.051	7.082
	Duration	7.12	6.33	5.94	5.94	5.94	5.94	5.45
FNMA 91141 Y4 7-year PAC	Average Life	10.20	8.66	7.94	7.94	7.94	7.94	7.11
	Yield	8.207	8.215	8.220	8.220	8.220	8.220	8.227
	Duration	6.70	6.00	5.64	5.64	5.64	5.64	5.21

yields of both the inverse and the PAC change by only a few basis points.

Based on market conditions as of September 19, 1991, the PAC inverse also compares favorably on an option-adjusted basis. The OAS of the PAC inverse is eight basis points greater than that of the seven-year PAC at 12% yield volatility, and five basis points higher at 9% volatility (see Exhibit 10). In addition, its convexity cost[3] is four basis points, fifteen basis points less than that of the seven-year PAC.

---

[3] Convexity cost is measured as the difference in OAS at 0% and 12% yield volatility.

Exhibit 10: Option-Adjusted Analysis of PAC Inverse (FNMA 91-141 S1) at 98:03 and Seven-Year PAC (FNMA 91-141 Y4) at 98:31

Security Type	Price	Yield (%)	PSA (%)	Avg Life (yrs.)	OAS at 9% Vol.	OAS at 12% Vol.	Convexity Cost	OAS Duration	Convexity
FNMA 91141 S1 PAC Inverse	98:03	10.000	187	7.94 yrs	81 bps	75 bps	4 bps	8.21	-0.109
FNMA 91141 Y4 PAC	98:31	8.220	187	7.94 yrs	76 bps	67 bps	19 bps	5.17	-0.180
Difference		1.780		0	+5 bps	+8 bps	-15 bps	+3.04	+0.071

VADM Inverse Floaters

A VADM inverse will maintain its average life and expected maturity at prepayment speeds between 0% and at least the pricing PSA.[4] For example, FHLMC 1121 S1, a VADM inverse, is guaranteed to have an average life between 7.05 years at 165% PSA and 7.11 years at 0% PSA. It will contract only 0.88 years to 6.17 years at 300% PSA (see Exhibit 11). The slight extension in average life from 165% PSA to 0% PSA occurs because this particular inverse contains interest stripped from the three-year vanilla class, thereby adding IO-like characteristics to the inverse.

This VADM inverse is positively convex, has virtually no extension risk, and contracts minimally. As shown in Exhibit 12, as volatility rises from 12% to 15%, the OAS of the VADM inverse increases by 27 basis points to 251 basis points, and its convexity cost[5] improves by 27 basis points.

---

[4] A VADM tranche is created from the accrued interest on Z bond(s) within a CMO structure. As the Z accrues interest, the Z accrual is used to pay the principal of the VADM. Therefore, at slower prepayment speeds including 0% PSA, the VADM will maintain its average life and expected maturity, thereby protecting the VADM against any extension in average life.

[5] A negative cost of convexity implies that the security is positively convex, that is, as volatility increases the OAS of the security increases.

Exhibit 11: Yields and Cash Flow Durations of VADM Inverse (FHLMC 1121 S1) at 105:11 (165% PSA, 5.5% LIBOR)

Coupon Reset Formula: 34.90992 – 3.5 × 1 mo LIBOR

PSA		75%	100%	125%	145%	165%	225%	300%
1-Month LIBOR	Avg Life	7.08	7.08	7.07	7.07	7.05	6.76	6.17
3.50	Yield	24.549	24.288	24.077	23.937	23.817	23.539	23.290
	Duration	2.78	2.79	2.80	2.80	2.81	2.80	2.75
4.50	Yield	20.902	20.626	20.407	20.264	20.143	19.867	19.625
	Duration	3.08	3.09	3.10	3.11	3.12	3.11	3.03
5.50	Yield	17.286	16.994	16.768	16.622	16.500	16.228	15.994
	Duration	3.44	3.46	3.47	3.49	3.49	3.48	3.37
6.50	Yield	13.701	13.392	13.159	13.011	12.889	12.623	12.399
	Duration	3.87	3.89	3.92	3.93	3.94	3.91	3.76
7.50	Yield	10.146	9.820	9.581	9.431	9.310	9.051	8.839
	Duration	4.40	4.42	4.45	4.48	4.49	4.44	4.22
8.50	Yield	6.621	6.278	6.032	5.883	5.762	5.513	5.315
	Duration	5.03	5.08	5.11	5.14	5.16	5.07	4.78
9.50	Yield	3.126	2.766	2.515	2.365	2.247	2.010	1.827
	Duration	5.83	5.88	5.94	5.97	6.00	5.86	5.45

Exhibit 12: Relation Between Volatility, OAS, and Convexity Cost for a VADM Inverse (FHLMC 1121 S1) at 105:11

Volatility	OAS	Convexity Cost
9%	194 bps	-19 bps
12%	224 bps	-49 bps
15%	251 bps	-76 bps

COFI Inverse Floaters

COFI inverses have increased in popularity because of the drop in the COF index in 1991 and expectations of further declines because of its lagging nature. Between January and September of 1991, one-month LIBOR fell 188 basis points to 5.50%, while COFI declined 97 basis points to 6.998%. COFI has continued to decline because of the fall in short-term rates, the elimination of failing thrifts from the index, and the increased weighting of short-term deposits in the composition of the index. It is expected to decline further even if short-term rates rise as more "higher cost" thrifts are removed from the index. As of August 1991, eight institutions representing 7%[6] of the total liabilities of the 11th District member institutions were placed under the conservatorship of the RTC, and as yet have not been eliminated from the COF index.

Investors are taking advantage of the anticipated fall in COFI and its inherent lag by buying COFI-based inverse floaters. FNMA 9130 S3, a COFI-based inverse, has a 5:1 coupon leverage and as of September 1991 was offered at a 15% yield at a 6.998% COFI rate and 165% PSA. The Bear Stearns' model projects that COFI will fall fifty-six basis points to 6.44% over the next twelve months if short-term rates remain unchanged. At this level, the yield of this inverse would increase to 18.205%. COFI inverses also offer limited downside risk. Over the last five and one-half years, COFI has never risen above 8.964%. At this level the inverse yield falls to 3.756%. Exhibit 13 shows the yield and duration sensitivities for this inverse floater under instantaneous shifts in COFI.

Low leverage COFI inverses are attractive alternatives to COFI floaters offering higher yields under nearly all rate scenarios. For example, FNMA 91-141 S4, a 1.0725:1 coupon leverage inverse with a 6.855% coupon floor, resets monthly to the formula 17.6869 (1.0725 × COFI), and as of September 1991 was offered at a 10.55% yield at 6.998% COFI and 165% PSA. Assuming COFI behaves according to Bear Stearns' projection, the inverse floater will yield 11.164%, 371 basis points greater than the yield of FNMA 91-141 F4, a COFI floater from the same CMO. This floater resets at ninety basis points over COFI, subject to an 11% coupon cap, and was offered in September 1991 at 99:20.

Exhibit 14 shows that the yield of the low leverage COFI inverse will dramatically outperform that of the COFI floater unless short-term rates rise by more than 280 basis points. If short-term rates increase 300 basis points, the yield of the inverse will under-

---

[6] FHLB San Francisco—Percentage of liabilities calculated as of 12/31/90.

Exhibit 13: Yields and Cash Flow Durations of COFI Inverse FNMA 9130 S3 at 87:10 (165% PSA, 6.998% COFI)

					Coupon Reset Formula: 47.5 - 5 x COFI			
	PSA	75%	100%	125%	145%	165%	225%	300%
COFI	Avg Life	26.22	24.89	23.11	21.29	17.00	3.19	1.69
5.00%	Yield	26.713	26.716	26.722	26.733	26.985	29.773	33.366
	Duration	3.55	3.55	3.54	3.54	3.28	1.85	1.17
6.00%	Yield	20.629	20.636	20.648	20.668	20.936	23.929	27.607
	Duration	4.62	4.61	4.60	4.57	4.13	2.04	1.25
7.00%	Yield	14.661	14.674	14.697	14.729	14.999	18.196	21.951
	Duration	6.47	6.43	6.36	6.27	5.47	2.27	1.33
8.00%	Yield	8.843	8.865	8.900	8.945	9.193	12.576	16.399
	Duration	10.06	9.90	9.65	9.34	7.81	2.53	1.42
9.00%	Yield	3.232	3.259	3.302	3.354	3.556	7.070	10.950
	Duration	18.06	17.40	16.46	15.44	12.32	2.83	1.52
10.00%	Yield	0.521	0.549	0.591	0.643	0.814	4.359	8.264
	Duration	25.66	24.34	22.57	20.74	16.17	3.00	1.58
11.00%	Yield	0.521	0.549	0.591	0.643	0.814	4.359	8.264
	Duration	25.66	24.34	22.57	20.74	16.17	3.00	1.58

Exhibit 14: Comparison of Low Leverage COFI Inverse vs. COFI Floater Under Changing Rate Scenarios According to Bear Stearns' Model

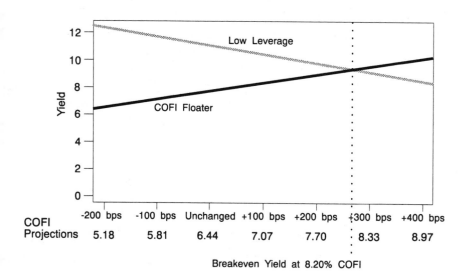

| COFI Projections | -200 bps 5.18 | -100 bps 5.81 | Unchanged 6.44 | +100 bps 7.07 | +200 bps 7.70 | +300 bps 8.33 | +400 bps 8.97 |

Breakeven Yield at 8.20% COFI

perform by only 21 basis points, and by 152 basis points if short-term rates rise 400 basis points.

Balloon Inverse Floaters

A balloon inverse refers to an inverse floater tranche in a CMO backed by five- or seven-year balloon collateral.[7] The most common type of balloon inverse is a plain vanilla inverse. The shortage of regular COFI ARM securities, increased demand for short and more stable average life floaters by ARM funds, and regulations restricting thrift mortgage investments have boosted demand for synthetic CMO COFI floaters and inverses. Balloon collateral allows for the creation of floaters and inverses with short and more stable average lives, typically four and five years, and short stated final maturities between five and seven years. In the first nine months of 1991, $2.5 billion of CMOs backed by balloon mortgage securities were issued. All but one issue ($225 million) contained inverse floaters.

Exhibit 15 shows the yield and cash flow duration sensitivities for the vanilla balloon inverse of FNMA 9191, which is backed by seven-year, 8.5% balloons. This inverse has a coupon leverage of 3.4:1, and resets monthly to the formula: 36.04 − 3.4 × one-month LIBOR. As of September 1991, it was offered at a price of 110:16 to yield 14.372% at a 5.5% one-month LIBOR and 250% PSA. The underlying collateral has been prepaying at 311%, 261%, and 289% PSA over the last one, three, and twelve months. Even at 500% PSA, the yield of the inverse is about 800 basis points over LIBOR.

Because of their short stated final maturities, balloon inverses may also be combined with LIBOR caps to hedge some of their risk in a rising rate environment. For example, three-year, nonamortizing, one-month LIBOR caps with a 6% LIBOR strike may be

---

[7] A balloon mortgage security is a mortgage in which periodic installments of principal and interest (usually based on a thirty-year amortization schedule) are paid to the investor until a prespecified balloon date. On the balloon date, usually five or seven years after origination, the outstanding principal balance is paid in one lump sum.

Exhibit 15: Yields and Cash Flow Durations of Balloon Inverse (FNMA 9191 S) at 110:16 (250% PSA, 5.5% LIBOR)

		Coupon Reset Formula: 36.04 – 3.4 × 1 mo LIBOR						
	PSA	100%	125%	160%	250%	325%	400%	500%
1-Month LIBOR	Avg Life	5.53	5.34	5.08	4.49	4.06	3.68	3.26
3.50	Yield	21.530	21.437	21.305	20.956	20.655	20.345	19.920
	Duration	2.84	2.77	2.68	2.48	2.32	2.18	2.02
4.50	Yield	18.198	18.110	17.985	17.652	17.363	17.065	16.656
	Duration	3.08	3.01	2.91	2.67	2.50	2.34	2.15
5.50	Yield	14.889	14.806	14.688	14.372	14.096	13.811	13.417
	Duration	3.36	3.27	3.16	2.89	2.69	2.51	2.30
6.50	Yield	11.604	11.526	11.415	11.116	10.854	10.581	10.203
	Duration	3.68	3.58	3.45	3.14	2.91	2.70	2.46
7.50	Yield	8.343	8.270	8.166	7.884	7.636	7.377	7.016
	Duration	4.04	3.93	3.78	3.42	3.16	2.92	2.65
8.50	Yield	5.105	5.038	4.940	4.677	4.443	4.198	3.853
	Duration	4.46	4.33	4.154	3.74	3.43	3.16	2.85
9.50	Yield	1.892	1.830	1.740	1.494	1.275	1.043	0.716
	Duration	4.94	4.79	4.58	4.10	3.75	3.44	3.08

combined[8] with the inverse above. In September 1991, these caps could be purchased for an up-front cost of 460 basis points to reduce the initial yield of the inverse by 477 basis points from 14.372% to 9.601% at 250% PSA. However, if one-month LIBOR rises 300 basis points to 8.5%, the yield of the combination falls to 8.422%, 348 basis points above the inverse floater unhedged. If one-month LIBOR falls 100 basis points to 4.5% and prepayments speed up to 325%, the yield of the inverse unhedged rises to 17.36%, 543 basis points higher than the combination (see Exhibit 16).

---

[8] To hedge the total proceeds of a $10 million investment, $37.570 million of caps would be purchased ($10 million of principal × 3.4 coupon leverage × 110:16 dollar price).

Exhibit 16: Balloon Inverse FNMA 9191 S

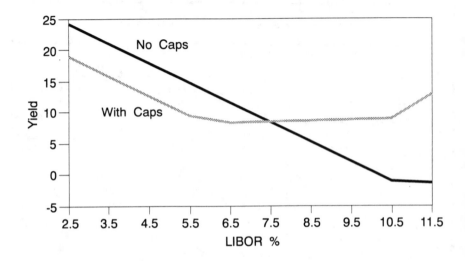

CREATING SYNTHETIC SECURITIES

Inverse floaters can be combined with other derivative mortgage-backed securities, such as floating-rate CMOs and IOs, to create synthetic securities with stable cash flow yields and OASs in excess of those obtainable from traditional mortgage-backed securities. Three particularly attractive synthetics result from the combination of (1) a COFI inverse with a COFI floater, (2) a companion LIBOR inverse with an IO strip, or (3) a LIBOR inverse with a LIBOR floater.

Synthetic Idea #1

By adding a small percentage of COFI inverses to their portfolios, traditional COFI floater investors can boost their yields significantly in a declining rate environment with only a minimal reduction in yield if rates rise. For example, as shown in Exhibits 17 and 18, by combining 25% of a COFI companion inverse, such as FNMA 9154 S2, with 75% of the COFI floater, FNMA 9154 F2, the investor can pick-up 233 basis points if short-term rates remain unchanged based on Bear Stearns' COFI projections. If rates fall 100 to 200 basis points, respectively, the yield of the combination will outperform that of the COFI floater by 388 to 537 basis points. If short-term rates rise 300 basis points, this synthetic will result in only a 31 basis point give-up in yield. The COFI inverse and the synthetic combination will break even in yield if short-term rates rise 265 basis points.

The FNMA 9154 S2 inverse has a coupon resetting to the formula 38.82 − 3.88 × COFI, and as of September 1991 was offered at 86:00 to yield 14.25% at 6.998% COFI and 165% PSA. The FNMA 9154 F2 floater resets at 100 basis points over COFI, subject to an 11% coupon cap, and was offered at 100:08 to yield 8.04% at the same COFI prepayment speed.

Exhibit 17: Synthetic Combination vs. COFI Floater and Inverse

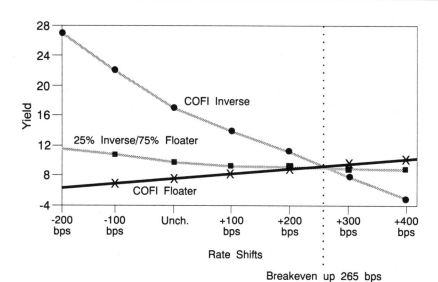

Exhibit 18: Yields and Cash Flow Durations of Synthetic Combination: 75% COFI Floater (FNMA 9154 F2) at 100:08 and 25% Inverse Floater (FNMA 9154 S2) at 86:00 Using Bear Stearns' COFI Projection Model

	PSA	75%	100%	125%	145%	165%	225%	300%
Short Term Rates	Avg Life	26.28	24.87	22.95	20.95	17.03	4.21	1.98
-200 bps	Yield	10.199	10.204	10.211	10.222	10.271	10.845	**11.588**
	Duration	8.94	8.82	8.62	8.35	7.31	2.98	**1.69**
-100 bps	Yield	9.967	9.972	9.980	9.992	10.042	**10.637**	11.407
	Duration	9.10	8.98	8.76	8.48	7.41	**3.00**	1.70
Unch.	Yield	9.735	9.740	9.749	9.761	**9.813**	10.429	11.226
	Duration	9.27	9.14	8.91	8.62	**7.52**	3.01	1.70
+100 bps	Yield	9.503	9.508	9.517	**9.530**	9.583	10.220	11.045
	Duration	9.44	9.30	9.07	**8.76**	7.63	3.03	1.70
+200 bps	Yield	9.271	9.276	**9.286**	9.299	9.354	10.012	10.864
	Duration	9.62	9.47	**9.23**	8.90	7.74	3.04	1.71
+300 bps	Yield	9.038	**9.044**	9.054	9.068	9.124	9.803	10.683
	Duration	9.81	**9.65**	9.39	9.05	7.86	3.06	1.71
+400 bps	Yield	**8.805**	8.811	8.822	8.836	8.894	9.594	10.501
	Duration	**10.00**	9.83	9.56	9.21	7.98	3.07	1.72

Synthetic Idea #2

By combining 30% of a typical companion medium leverage in-verse floater, such as FHLMC 1055 S2, with 70% of Trust 6 IO Strips, a highly liquid, benchmark IO, an investor can create a syn-thetic asset in the current economic environment with a cash flow duration of 4.47 years yielding 14.301%, more than double that of the 5-year Treasury (7.059%). FHLMC 1055 S2 is a companion me-dium leverage inverse with a 3.5:1 coupon leverage resetting to the formula 35.072 − 3.5 × 1-month LIBOR backed by 9% collateral as is the Trust 6 IO. It was offered at 81:20 to yield 20.5% at 5.5% one-month LIBOR and 165% PSA. Exhibit 19 shows yields and cash flow durations for various scenarios. Although history is not a guarantee of future performance, the fastest prepayment speed experienced by Trust 6 IOs was 224% PSA when one-month LIBOR was 6% in July 1991. Assuming a 224% PSA and a 6% one-

Exhibit 19: Yields and Cash Flow Durations of Synthetic Combination: 70% IO (Trust 6 IO) at 40:16 and 30% Inverse (FHLMC 1055 S2) at 81:20

1-month LIBOR	PSA	75%	100%	125%	145%	165%	225%	300%
3.50	Yield	20.787	19.947	19.140	18.506	17.850	14.827	**8.829**
	Duration	3.842	3.892	3.935	3.953	3.939	3.429	**2.601**
4.50	Yield	19.136	18.257	17.418	16.762	16.095	**13.259**	7.689
	Duration	4.071	4.130	4.181	4.204	4.189	**3.615**	2.715
5.50	Yield	17.448	16.527	15.651	14.975	**14.301**	11.682	6.579
	Duration	4.324	4.396	4.459	4.488	**4.471**	3.818	2.837
6.50	Yield	15.714	14.743	13.830	**13.134**	12.458	10.091	5.500
	Duration	4.607	4.697	4.778	**4.813**	4.795	4.042	2.968
7.50	Yield	13.917	12.891	**11.938**	11.226	10.555	8.484	4.453
	Duration	4.925	5.039	**5.142**	5.190	5.170	4.290	3.107
8.50	Yield	12.036	**10.948**	9.954	9.231	8.577	6.853	3.438
	Duration	5.287	**5.437**	5.572	5.637	5.613	4.565	3.256
9.50	Yield	**10.041**	8.881	7.849	7.124	6.502	5.191	2.455
	Duration	**5.705**	5.908	6.092	6.179	6.147	4.871	3.415

month LIBOR, the 30% inverse/70% IO synthetic combination would yield approximately 10.837% or 534 basis points above one-month LIBOR.

The performance of the synthetic will be influenced by the slope of the yield curve, performing best when the yield curve is steep and unchanging, and poorly if it is inverted and changing. This is because prepayment speeds are strongly influenced by the intermediate part of the curve, and the coupon of the inverse is driven by the short end. When the yield curve is steep, the IO will tend to prepay slowly, and the coupon of the inverse floater will tend to be high. When the yield curve inverts, the speed of the IO will tend to increase and the coupon of the inverse decline.

Since Trust 6 was issued, the worst LIBOR/prepayment combination occurred in late 1988, when the yield curve was inverted. The prepayment speed of the Trust 6 IOs hovered around 150% PSA for several months while one-month LIBOR was in the 9.5% area. At these levels, this synthetic would have yielded about 6.974%, 253 basis points below LIBOR. The lower right corner of

Exhibit 19 reflects scenarios in which the yield curve is sharply inverted. For example, if one-month LIBOR rose 300 basis points to 8.5% and prepayments sped up to 300% PSA, the yield of this synthetic would fall to 3.438%.

Synthetic Idea #3

Applying the same strategy as outlined in synthetic idea #1, investors can boost the yields on their LIBOR-based portfolios by adding a small percentage of LIBOR inverses. For example, by combining 20% of the inverse, FHLMC 1055 S2, with 80% of the floater, FNMA 9152 F2, investors can achieve 275 basis points higher yield over the LIBOR floater alone at a one-month LIBOR rate of 5.50% (see Exhibit 20).

Exhibit 20: Yields and Cash Flow Durations of Synthetic Combination: 80% Floater (FNMA 9152 F2) at 100:00 and 20% Inverse (FHLMC 1055 S2) at 81:20

	PSA	75%	100%	125%	145%	165%	225%	300%
1-Month LIBOR	Avg Life	**26.08**	24.61	**22.66**	**20.74**	**18.36**	**9.21**	**3.26**
3.50	Yield	9.327	9.328	9.332	9.341	9.368	9.500	**9.930**
	Duration	9.527	9.368	9.117	8.809	8.320	5.369	**2.647**
4.50	Yield	9.282	9.284	9.290	9.302	9.329	**9.500**	10.027
	Duration	9.577	9.416	9.161	8.850	8.850	**5.363**	2.648
5.50	Yield	9.237	9.241	9.249	9.262	**9.290**	9.501	10.123
	Duration	9.628	9.465	9.206	8.890	**8.389**	5.357	2.650
6.50	Yield	9.191	9.197	9.208	**9.223**	9.251	9.502	10.218
	Duration	9.678	9.514	9.252	**8.931**	8.424	5.351	2.651
7.50	Yield	9.146	9.154	**9.167**	9.184	9.213	9.502	10.313
	Duration	9.730	9.563	**9.297**	8.972	8.459	5.345	2.653
8.50	Yield	9.102	**9.111**	9.126	9.145	9.174	9.503	10.408
	Duration	9.781	**9.612**	9.343	9.014	8.494	5.339	2.653
9.50	Yield	**9.057**	9.068	9.389	9.106	9.136	9.503	10.502
	Duration	**9.833**	9.662	9.085	9.055	8.529	5.334	2.656

FHLMC 1055 S2 is a companion medium leverage inverse with a 3.5:1 coupon leverage resetting to the formula 35.072 – 3.5 × one-month LIBOR backed by 9% collateral, as is the floater. As of September 1991 it was offered at 81:20 to yield 20.5% at 5.5% one-month LIBOR and 165% PSA. FNMA 9152 F2 is a companion floater that resets to one-month LIBOR plus 95 basis points, subject to an 11% coupon cap, and was offered at 100:00 to yield 6.539% at the same one-month LIBOR and prepayment speed. If one-month LIBOR falls 100 basis points to 4.5%, this combination offers a 380-basis point pick-up versus the floater alone. If one-month LIBOR rises 100 to 200 basis points, the investor still picks up 166 and 58 basis points versus the floater.

Exhibit 21 shows the yield of various combinations of the inverse and floater versus the floater alone. The break-even yield between all synthetic combinations of the inverse and floater is 9.15% that occurs at 8.05% one-month LIBOR.

Exhibit 21: Synthetic Combinations vs. LIBOR Floater

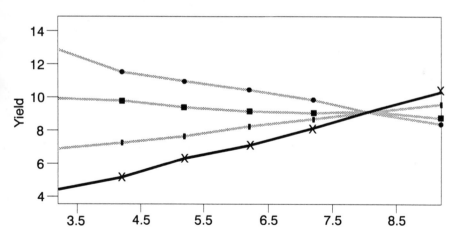

Breakeven Yield at 8.05% 1-Month LIBOR

VALUATION OF INVERSE FLOATERS

Yield to Forward LIBOR and OAS

Inverse floaters offer value when using either a yield to forward LIBOR or an OAS methodology. As shown in Exhibit 22, the yield to forward LIBOR is the yield to maturity of each inverse floater assuming that one-month LIBOR resets to the monthly forward rates implied by the LIBOR curve.

Exhibit 22: Valuation of Inverse Floaters Using Forward LIBOR and OAS Methodology

Type of Inverse Floater	Example	Price	Base PSA	Offering Yield	Yield to Fwd LIBOR	OAS at 9% Vol.	OAS at 12% Vol.	OAS Dur.	Conve xity Cost	Spread To A/L TSY
Low Leverage Companion Inverse	FNMA 9198 S2 (0.75:1)	100:00	165	11.48%	9.37%	148	128	6.12	28	144/30 yr
Medium Leverage Companion Inverse	FNMA 90138 S (3.8:1)	97:24	180	23.49%	14.26%	540	498	12.86	177	633/30 yr
High Leverage Companion Inverse	FNMA 9093 Q1 (6.33:1)	106:06	180	29.00%	16.41%	554	457	10.47	332	848/30 yr
Low Leverage Plain Vanilla Inverse	MLT-11 Q1 (1.8:1)	88:16	155	14.97%	10.51%	294	260	14.68	33	290/10 yr
PAC Inverse	FNMA 91141 S1 (0.71:1)	98:03	165	10.00%	8.27%	81	75	8.21	4	86/7 yr
VADM Inverse	FHLMC 9121 S1 (3.50:1)	105:11	165	16.50%	8.84%	200	225	14.02	-62	142/7 yr
IO Inverse	FNMA 9181 S (229:1)	3085:01	250	28.00%	12.22%	439	330	4.94	363	430/30 yr
TTIB Inverse	FNMA 91132 S2 (6.775:1)	92:09	165	11.00%	10.91%	72	5	13.18	296	299/30 yr
Balloon Inverse	FNMA 9191 S (3.4:1)	110:16	250	14.37%	8.57%	136	138	12.55	7	148/5 yr

The LIBOR curve is the "market's expectation" of future levels of LIBOR. The first three years of the LIBOR curve are derived from the Eurodollar futures market. Beyond three years, rates are generated from a combination of the first three years of Eurodollar futures and the Treasury swap curve. Monthly implied LIBOR forward rates are calculated from this curve. As of September 19, 1991, one-month LIBOR was 5.5%, 6.071% twelve months forward, 7.379% twenty-four months forward, and 8.337% sixty months forward. These implied forward rates are used in calculating OAS for LIBOR-based floaters and inverse floaters (see Exhibit 23).

Although the implied LIBOR forward curve is steep, the inverse yields are still higher than the yields of comparable fixed-rate tranches. For example, in September 1991, MLT 11 Q1, an inverse floater from a vanilla structure, offered a yield of 14.97% assuming LIBOR remains constant at 5.50%, and 10.508% when using the implied forward rates, a 290-basis point spread over the ten-year Treasury. This compares favorable to ten-year fixed-rate

---

Exhibit 23: Implied Monthly Forward LIBOR Rates, as of September 19, 1991

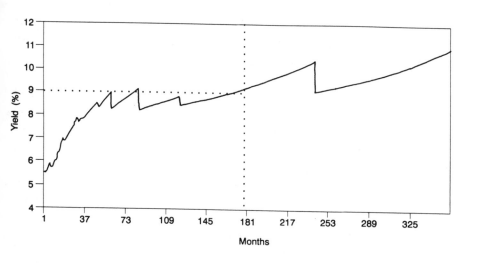

vanilla tranches that are offered at about 115 basis points over the ten-year Treasury.

Inverse floaters in general perform well when a yield to forward LIBOR is calculated, because market expectations of LIBOR, as represented by forward LIBOR rates, remain at fairly low levels. In September 1991, as indicated in Exhibit 23, forward LIBOR rates rarely rise above 9% for the first 15 years, about 350 basis points above LIBOR. This is best illustrated by the high leverage inverse FNMA 9093 Q1, which offers the highest yield to forward LIBOR (16.41%) and one of the highest OASs (457 basis points). As shown in Exhibit 3, the high leverage inverse offers the highest yield of any of the companion inverses shown as long as one-month LIBOR remains below 8.61%. LIBOR forward rates rise above 10% only after twenty years, when the present value of the future cash flows is low.

Conversely, FNMA 91141 S1, a low leverage PAC inverse, offers the lowest yield to forward LIBOR, 8.27%. Its yield is reduced because of its low leverage and tighter offering yield. In addition, the PAC inverse is priced off the shorter end of the curve, which is also the steepest. Therefore, future cash flows will be discounted by higher forward rates, resulting in a lower yield to forward LIBOR.

The yield to forward LIBOR of the TTIB, FNMA 91132, is 10.91%, only nine basis points below its offering yield, the narrowest differential of any inverse in Exhibit 22. This is because the TTIB has a 9.5% LIBOR strike, that is, its coupon will not fall below 9.806% unless LIBOR rises above 9.5%. As shown in Exhibit 24, the monthly forwards rarely rise above 9.5%. However, the TTIB also has the lowest OAS, five basis points, at a 12% yield volatility. Adding volatility "shocks" the implied forward curve, causing the monthly forward rates to rise above 9.5% more frequently, thereby reducing the OAS of the security. The sensitivity of the security to higher levels of volatility is manifested by its high degree of negative convexity. This security is attractive to investors who believe that LIBOR will be stable and volatility will remain unchanged or decline.

Exhibit 24: Implied Monthly Forward LIBOR Rates, as of September 19, 1991

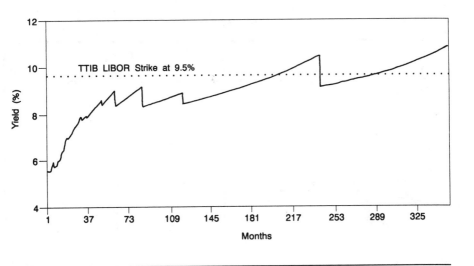

Price Sensitivity of Inverse Floaters

To date, inverse floaters have dramatically outperformed similar average life Treasuries (see Exhibit 26). With short-term rates at historically low levels, some investors are concerned about the potential price depreciation of an inverse should short-term rates rise. However, as stated earlier in this chapter, the price of the inverse will be primarily determined by the value of the underlying fixed-rate bond. Exhibit 25 shows the decline in price that an inverse floater can sustain over a one-year horizon before the total return of the inverse falls below the total return of a similar average life Treasury. The analysis assumes a 5.50% reinvestment rate, if rates remain unchanged, and 6.50% if rates rise 100 basis points.

In an unchanged or rising rate environment, the highest leverage inverses can sustain the greatest price declines. This is because high current coupons generate a large cash cushion that absorbs greater price erosion. For example, assuming rates remain unchanged, the price of FNMA 9093 Q1, a 6.3:1 coupon leverage in-

Exhibit 25: Dollar Price Point Drop to Treasury Total Rate of Return

Security	Beginning Price	Unchanged		+100 bps	
		Total Rate of Return	Price Decline	Total Rate of Return	Price Decline
5-Year Treasury		8.11%		4.89%	
FNMA 9191 S (Balloon Inverse)	110:16		8:04		8:22
7-Year Treasury		8.05%		3.78%	
FNMA 91141 S1 (PAC Inverse)	98:03		0:25		5:10
FHLMC 1121 S1 (VADM Inverse)	104:26		10:11		11:30
10-Year Treasury		7.97%		2.06%	
MLT-11 Q1 (Plain Vanilla Low Leverage)	88:15		5:03		8:30
30-Year Treasury		8.02%		-2.02%	
FNMA 9198 S2 (Low Leverage)	100:00		3:07		12:27
FNMA 90138 S (Medium Leverage)	97:24		15:22		22:24
FNMA 9093 Q1 (High Leverage)	106:06		22:25		27:01
FNMA 9130 Se (COFI Inverse)	87:10		13:08		17:12
FNMA 91132 S2 (TTIB)	88:24		2:16		11:31

verse, would have to fall 22:25 points before its return equaled the 8.02% return of the long bond. If rates rise 100 basis points, the inverse could sustain a 27:01 point decline. The price of MLT 11 Q1, a plain vanilla low leverage inverse, would have to fall by 5:03 points for its total return to break even with the return of the ten-year Treasury of 7.97%, assuming interest rates remain unchanged. If rates rise 100 basis points, the decline in price can widen to 8:30 points.

Actual Performance of Inverse Floaters: A Total Rate of Return Analysis

In the first half of 1991, inverse floaters have produced some of the highest total rates of return available in the fixed-income markets (see Exhibit 26). For example, the COFI inverse floater gener-

Exhibit 26: Actual Returns of Inverse Floaters vs. Similar Average Life Treasuries for the Period March 18, 1991 Through September 18, 1991

		3/18/91 Beginning Price	9/18/91 Ending Price	Holding Period Return*	Annualized Return
10-Year Treasury	USTN 7.75% of 2/15/2001	97:11	100:22	7.44%	14.88%
30-Year Treasury	USTB 7.875% of 2/15/2021	94:31	98:26	8.21%	16.43%
Low Leverage	MLT 11 Q1 (1.8:1)	80:00	88:16	17.03%	34.05%
Med. Leverage	FNMA 90138 S (3.8:1)	92:16	97:24	16.09%	32.19%
High Leverage	FNMA 9093 (6.3:1)	103:29+	106:06	14.63%	29.26%
COFI Inverse	FNMA 9130 S3 (5:1)	75:29	87:10	25.01%	50.01%

* A reinvestment rate of 6.34%, the yield of the 1-year Treasury bill on March 18, was assumed.

ated an actual rate of return of 25.01%, more than three times the return realized by the thirty-year Treasury. On an annualized basis, the COFI inverse produced the stellar return of 50.01%! In fact, the lowest actual return was 14.63%, produced by the high leverage premium priced inverse, almost twice that of the long bond. The outstanding performance of the COFI inverse can be explained by the eighty-five-basis point drop in COFI, its high 5:1 coupon leverage, and the almost twenty-five-point discount purchase price on March 18. The performance of the high leverage inverse was impeded by lack of price appreciation stemming form its premium pricing on March 18, 1991.

APPENDIX

In this Appendix we explain the formulas for calculating (1) coupon leverage, (2) principal amounts, (3) initial coupons, and (4) floors and caps of floaters and inverse floaters.

Two approaches are used to allocate the principal face to the floater and inverse floater tranches. The first allocates principal based on the maximum coupon leverage available; the second uses a specified coupon leverage that is less than the maximum. Two examples are presented below to illustrate the effects on the principal split between the floater and inverse floater and their coupons when using either approach.

Example 1: Using the Maximum Coupon Leverage

Total Principal of Floater and Inverse Floater:	$10,000,000
Underlying Collateral Coupon:	9.0%
Current LIBOR:	5.5%
Floater Cap:	11.0%
Floater Margin (Spread over LIBOR):	80 basis points
Coupon Leverage	Maximum

1. Floater Coupon = Current LIBOR + Floater Margin

   Floater Coupon = 5.5 + 0.80 = 6.30%

2. Maximum Coupon Leverage = $\dfrac{\text{Collateral Coupon}}{\text{Floater Cap} - \text{Collateral Coupon}}$

   Maximum Coupon Leverage = $\dfrac{9}{11.0 - 9.0}$ = 4.5

3. Floater Principal = $\dfrac{\text{Coupon Leverage} \times \text{Total Principal}}{(1 + \text{Coupon Leverage})}$

   Floater Principal = $\dfrac{4.5 \times 10,000,000}{(1 + 4.5)}$ = $8,181,818.18

4. Inverse Principal = Total Principal – Floater Principal

   Inverse Principal = \$10,000,000 – \$8,181,818.18 = \$1,818,181.82

5. Inverse Coupon

The total amount of interest paid to the floater and inverse floater in any time period must be less than or equal to the total interest available from the underlying collateral coupon.

$$\left[\begin{matrix} \text{Floater} \\ \text{Coupon} \end{matrix} \times \begin{matrix} \text{Floater} \\ \text{Principal} \end{matrix}\right] + \left[\begin{matrix} \text{Inverse} \\ \text{Coupon} \end{matrix} \times \begin{matrix} \text{Inverse} \\ \text{Principal} \end{matrix}\right] \leq \left[\begin{matrix} \text{Collateral} \\ \text{Coupon} \end{matrix} \times \begin{matrix} \text{Total} \\ \text{Principal} \end{matrix}\right]$$

In this example, a total of \$900,000 of interest will be split between the two tranches (9.0/100 × \$10,000,000).

If the floater coupon is 6.3% and \$515,454.54 of interest is allocated to the floater tranche (6.3/100 × 8,181,818.18), then the remaining \$384,545.46 of interest (\$900,000 – \$515,454.54) is allocated to the inverse floater. The initial inverse floater coupon is calculated by dividing this amount by the inverse principal expressed as a percent, (\$384,545.46/1,818,181.82) × 100 which is 21.15.

From the above formula,

$$\begin{matrix} \text{Initial Inverse} \\ \text{Coupon} \end{matrix} \leq \frac{\left[\begin{matrix} \text{Collateral} \\ \text{Coupon} \end{matrix} \times \begin{matrix} \text{Total} \\ \text{Principal} \end{matrix}\right] - \left[\begin{matrix} \text{Floater} \\ \text{Coupon} \end{matrix} \times \begin{matrix} \text{Floater} \\ \text{Principal} \end{matrix}\right]}{\text{Inverse Principal}}$$

$$\begin{matrix} \text{Initial Inverse} \\ \text{Coupon} \end{matrix} = \frac{\left[9.0 \times 10,000,000\right] - \left[6.2 \times 8,181,818.18\right]}{1,818,181.82} = 21.15\%$$

The inverse coupon is always expressed as a function of the inverse cap and leverage (see derivation of the inverse cap below).

Inverse Coupon = Inverse Cap – (Coupon Leverage × Current LIBOR)

6. Inverse Floor

The floor refers to the minimum coupon that the inverse floater can reset to. It is computed by assuming that the floater coupon has reached its life cap.

$$\left[\begin{array}{c} \text{Collateral} \\ \text{Coupon} \end{array} \times \begin{array}{c} \text{Total} \\ \text{Principal} \end{array} \right] - \left[\begin{array}{c} \text{Floater} \\ \text{Cap} \end{array} \times \begin{array}{c} \text{Floater} \\ \text{Principal} \end{array} \right] \geq \left[\begin{array}{c} \text{Inverse} \\ \text{Floor} \end{array} \times \begin{array}{c} \text{Inverse} \\ \text{Principal} \end{array} \right]$$

In this example, if the floater coupon is equal to its life cap of 11%, then all of the $900,000 interest available (11/100 × 8,181,818.18) is allocated to the floater and no interest is allocated to the inverse floater. The floor is calculated by dividing this amount by the inverse principal, (0/1,818.181.82) which is zero.

From the above formula,

$$\text{Inverse Floor} \leq \frac{\left[\begin{array}{c} \text{Collateral} \\ \text{Coupon} \end{array} \times \begin{array}{c} \text{Total} \\ \text{Principal} \end{array} \right] - \left[\begin{array}{c} \text{Floater} \\ \text{Coupon} \end{array} \times \begin{array}{c} \text{Floater} \\ \text{Principal} \end{array} \right]}{\text{Inverse Floater Principal}}$$

$$\text{Inverse Floor} = \frac{\left[9.0 \times 10,000,000 \right] - \left[11.0 \times 8,181,818.18 \right]}{1,818,181.82} = 0\%$$

Note that if the coupon leverage is at its maximum, then the floor will always be equal to zero.

7. Inverse Cap

The inverse cap is the maximum coupon that the inverse floater can reset to. It is computed by assuming that LIBOR is equal to zero. When LIBOR is zero, the floater coupon is equal to its margin.

$$\left[\begin{array}{c} \text{Collateral} \\ \text{Coupon} \end{array} \times \begin{array}{c} \text{Total} \\ \text{Principal} \end{array} \right] - \left[\begin{array}{c} \text{Floater} \\ \text{Coupon} \end{array} \times \begin{array}{c} \text{Floater} \\ \text{Principal} \end{array} \right] \geq \left[\begin{array}{c} \text{Inverse} \\ \text{Cap} \end{array} \times \begin{array}{c} \text{Inverse} \\ \text{Principal} \end{array} \right]$$

In this example, the floater coupon is equal to 0.80% when LIBOR is zero. The interest allocated to the floater is $65,454.55 (.80/100 × 8,181,818.18) and the remaining $834,545.45 of interest ($900,000 − $65,454.55) is allocated to the inverse floater. The inverse cap is calculated by dividing this amount by the inverse principal expressed as a percent, ($834,545.45/$1,818,181.82) × 100 which is 45.90%.

From the above formula,

$$\text{Inverse Cap} \leq \frac{\left[\begin{array}{c}\text{Collateral} \\ \text{Coupon}\end{array} \times \begin{array}{c}\text{Total} \\ \text{Principal}\end{array}\right] - \left[\begin{array}{c}\text{Floater} \\ \text{Coupon}\end{array} \times \begin{array}{c}\text{Floater} \\ \text{Principal}\end{array}\right]}{\text{Inverse Principal}}$$

$$\text{Inverse Cap} = \frac{\left[9.0 \times 10,000,000\right] - \left[0.80 \times 8,181,818.18\right]}{1,818,181.82} = 45.90\%$$

Example 2: Using a Specific Coupon Leverage

Total Principal of Floater and Inverse Floater:	$10,000,000
Underlying Collateral Coupon:	9.0%
Current LIBOR:	5.5%
Floater Cap:	11.0%
Floater Margin :	80 basis points
Coupon Leverage	3.0

1. Floater Coupon = $5.5 + 0.80) = 6.30%

3. Floater Principal = $\dfrac{3 \times 10,000,000}{(1 + 3)}$ = $7,500,000

4. Inverse Principal = $10,000,000 − $7,500,000 = $2,500,000

5. Inverse Coupon = 33.60 − (3 × 5.5) = 17.10%

6. Inverse Floor = $\dfrac{(9 \times 10,000,000) - (11 \times 7,500,000)}{2,500,000}$ = 3.00%

7. Inverse Cap = $\dfrac{(9 \times 10,000,000) - (0.8 \times 7,500,000)}{2,500,000}$ = 33.60%

CHAPTER 22

UNDERSTANDING INVERSE FLOATER PRICING

Michael L. Winchell
Senior Managing Director
Risk Management Group
Bear, Stearns & Co., Inc.

Michael Levine
Vice President
Mortgage Trading
Bear, Stearns & Co., Inc.

THE COMMON MISTAKE

Many investors mistakenly expect the price of an inverse floater to increase with a decline in short-term rates. In fact, the major impact on the price of inverse floaters comes from changes in long-term rates, since so many inverse floaters are created out of long average life, fixed-rate cash flows.

Inverse floaters are characterized by a coupon rate designed to reset inversely with changes in an index, most often that of a short-term rate such as LIBOR. Some inverse floaters have coupon rates that change four, five, or six times as much as the change in the rate index, a multiplicative effect often described as the coupon leverage of the inverse floater. For an inverse floater with high coupon leverage, any drop in the short-term rates causes a large increase in its coupon rate, and thus a sharp increase in the income to the investor in the payment period. It is not surprising, therefore, that many investors expect a drop in short-term rates to cause a price increase in the inverse floater.

However, the expectation that changes in short-term rates have a great impact on the price of inverse floaters does not recognize the direct relation between inverse floaters and the fixed-rate bonds from which they are derived.

Inverse floaters are almost always carved out of an underlying fixed-rate tranche, in conjunction with the creation of a floating-rate tranche. It may be difficult to "see" the fixed-rate tranche behind a floater and its inverse, but it is there nonetheless.

Since the floater and its inverse constitute the entire underlying fixed-rate bond when combined, there must be a "conservation" of market value. A simple observation is that the typical floater remains priced near par given changes in both short- and long-term yields. Its market value remains more or less constant. Thus, any change in the market value of an inverse floater must be primarily the result of a change in the value of the underlying fixed-rate bond, and any change in the market price of the underlying fixed-rate bond must cause a change in the value of the inverse floater. To determine the correct price of an inverse floater, or its price change, the investor should determine the price or price change of the underlying fixed-rate bond, or that of a similar bond in the marketplace.

VIEWING THE INVERSE FLOATER AS A LEVERAGED PURCHASE OF THE FIXED-RATE BOND

Many investors misprice inverse floaters in the secondary market because they fail to recognize the similarity between the cash flows of an inverse floater and the cash flows generated by financing, at a floating rate, a fixed-rate bond similar to the underlying fixed-rate bond. The cash flows of an inverse floater resemble the cash flows available if the investor had purchased the underlying fixed-rate bond from which the inverse was derived, and then financed most of the purchase at the short-term rate used as the index for the floater and the inverse.

If an investor were willing to buy a fixed-rate bond and finance it at short-term rates, then the inverse floater represents a similar opportunity to earn a net interest margin in a steep yield curve environment.

Purchasing an inverse floater may offer a few advantages over purchasing a fixed-rate tranche that is financed at short-term rates. The inverse floater contains an embedded, amortizing, and prepay-sensitive cap on the funding costs, the result of which is that the net interest will never be negative. In addition, funding for the life of the fixed-rate bonds is made secure through the issuance of a floater tranche, perhaps at a lower cost than would be available to the investor otherwise, without concern for any future margin calls. Finally, traditional interest rate cap and funding agreements are subject to the risk of counterparty nonperformance. The REMIC/CMO trust eliminates performance risk. Thus, the investor who desires to earn the net interest margin of long-term assets funded at short-term rates can do this economically through the purchase of an inverse floater, and in a more secure fashion.

THE PARALLEL BETWEEN INVERSE FLOATER RESIDUALS AND INVERSE FLOATER TRANCHES

To see how the inverse floater relates to its underlying fixed-rate bond, consider the many early CMO deals in which only a floater tranche was issued. Pools of fixed-rate mortgage collateral were placed in trust. A single floating-rate tranche was issued by the trust, and the proceeds from the sale of the floater were used to pay for the collateral. From the trust's perspective, a floating-rate liability was issued to *finance* the purchase of fixed-rate mortgage assets, and the liability will amortize with the fixed-rate assets.

In these simple deals, the inverse floater cash flows remain as the *residual* of the CMO deal. The residual holder is entitled to the *net interest margin* between the coupon rate of the collateral, and the coupon rate on the floater. In other words, the inverse floater residual receives any interest left over after having paid the financing cost (*given by the floater coupon rate*) of the fixed-rate pools held by the trust. And as the principal of the assets is paid down, an equal amount of the liabilities is paid down.

Thus, the value of the residual represents the difference in value between the assets, fixed-rate mortgage pools, and the liability, a floating-rate tranche. The fact that inverse floater *tranches* are carved from fixed-rate companion bonds or PAC bonds or plain vanilla bonds does not change the fundamental relation between the inverse and its "collateral."

Inverse floater tranches, just like inverse floating-rate residuals, offer the investor the opportunity to buy both sides of a "balance sheet." On the asset side, the inverse floater represents the underlying fixed-rate bonds. On the liability side, the inverse floater represents a short-term financing arrangement for the assets.

HOW RISKY IS THE INTEREST RATE MISMATCH BUILT INTO AN INVERSE FLOATER?

The allure of inverse floaters is the ability to profit from a steep yield curve through leverage and a significant interest margin. The greater the leverage available to the investor, the higher the potential return on capital, and, accordingly, the greater the risk. Thus, the purchase of an inverse floater in many ways resembles the leveraged funding of long-term mortgage assets at short-term rates that had been the bread-and-butter trade of the thrift industry a decade ago.

What differentiates the inverse floater from the strategy formerly employed by many thrifts is that the inverse floater buyer obtains an amortizing and prepay-sensitive cap on the financing rate (*through the cap on the floater*), and locks in access to funding over the term of the underlying fixed-rate bond, and need not reserve capital for potential margin calls. Neither of these two benefits were readily available to thrifts then, nor are these safety features readily available in the mortgage market today, outside of the inverse floater.

An interest rate cap is an option that pays the investor if the reference rate rises above a strike rate. Without a cap, the investor funding a long average life, fixed-rate asset at short-term rates can be faced with *negative* net interest margin, or in other words, interest expense greater than interest income. Inverse floaters have embedded interest rate caps. Coupon rates can never go below 0%, and some are structured with caps that limit coupon declines at relatively high coupon levels.

This is not to say that the buyer of fixed-rate bonds cannot also buy a cap to provide insurance for a financing arrangement. But consider that, if available, the purchase of an amortizing and prepay-sensitive interest rate cap entails counterparty risk. And the financing arrangement itself presents the potential for losses due to counterparty nonperformance. For instance, if the market value of fixed-rate bonds increases during the term of a repurchase agreement, the investor is exposed to the financier's failure to deliver the assets at the expiration of the agreement. Consequently, inverse floaters provide some advantage over a simple strategy of short-funding long-term fixed-rate assets.

A SIMPLE METHOD TO VALUE INVERSE FLOATERS

A simple technique to arrive at fair value is to ascertain the value on two pieces of the puzzle, and arrive at the third by addition or subtraction.

To value the inverse floater tranche, one need only calculate the total market value of the underlying fixed-rate bond from which it is derived, and then subtract the total market value of the floater that accords the inverse both its cap and its leverage.

Assuming a floater always remains priced at par, all of the change in value of an inverse floater tranche must be the result of a change in the value of the underlying fixed-rate bonds.

Therefore, if $50 million in inverse floaters are derived from $100 million in underlying fixed-rate bonds, and if the floater remains priced at par, the price change of the inverse floaters will be *twice* the price change of the underlying fixed-rate bonds. If only $20 million in inverse floaters are derived from $100 million in the underlying fixed-rate bonds, then given no change in the floater price, the inverse will change in price *five* times more than the underlying fixed-rate tranche.

Floaters, however, do not always remain at par, because the value of embedded interest rate caps often changes. The spread over LIBOR offered by the floater may at times be more than enough compensation for the short cap position, and at other other times, not enough. However, we can still rely on this relatively simple approach to the valuation of inverse floaters because we can continue to use the market price of the floater as a starting point, even if that price isn't par.

HOW THE LEVEL OF THE SHORT-TERM RATE AFFECTS THE VALUE OF INVERSE FLOATERS THROUGH THE CAP

In a steep yield curve environment, a reasonably creditworthy buyer of a five-year Treasury note could probably finance 98% to 99% of the proceeds at a monthly or overnight rate well below the yield of the five-year note. The steeper the curve, the higher the spread and the greater the income.

We would not, however, expect the price of the five-year note to change with the level of overnight repo rates, even though the net interest margin between the assets and the funding costs increases. We expect the price of the five-year note to change only when five-year yields change.

So too is it with inverse floaters. We should expect a change in the price of an inverse floater when market conditions (*yields and prepayment assumptions, for example*) cause a change in price of the underlying bond and similar bonds.

Where the level of short-term rates correctly enters into the valuation process for inverse floaters is through the evaluation of the cap on financing provided by the cap on the floater. This embedded interest rate cap has a value that is commonly determined by reference to the implied forward rate curve, and, since the interest rate cap agreement is an option agreement, by the volatility of short-term rates.

Fixed-income analysts often refer to the *implied forward rate curve* when inverse floaters are analyzed to describe how the coupon rate of the security is expected to change through time. In essence, the market's expectation of future short-term rates are defined by the shape of the yield curve. To explain a steep yield curve, for instance, it must be the case that investors are willing to accept the low yields of short-term securities today because they expect rates to rise in the future.

The implied forward curve is derived in such a way as to make the continuous rollover of an investment at the short-term rate for five years, for example, equivalent to the realized compound yield (total return) of a five-year note. The most common implied forward rate curve used by the market is a Eurobond curve. Some of the curve is derived directly from the Eurodollar futures market, the rest from the swap curve, or swap spreads and the Treasury curve extrapolated for thirty years.

To properly value the cap embedded in the inverse floater properly, one needs the implied forward rate curve and an estimate regarding rate volatility to value the cap. One could use these parameters within an option pricing method such as the option-adjusted spread (OAS) model. However, this supposes we "know" what the right OAS for an inverse floater is.

As an alternative to an OAS model, the investor can approximate the market value of the cap by pricing nonprepay-sensitive, amortizing, over-the-counter caps. To do this, the investor could choose upper and lower bounds for the range of expected prepayments and specify a number of other prepayment estimates. The investor would price different amortizing cap agreements, each based on the outstanding balance of the floater at various prepayment assumptions, but all having a strike rate given by the cap on the floater. The investor would then calculate an average price for the embedded mortgage security interest rate cap, given a weight for each of the prices of the over-the-counter cap agreements.

Note that we use the amortization of the floater to determine the total market value of the cap agreements outstanding. This is because the floater, as the financing arrangement, defines the number of caps available.

WHAT DOES A YIELD SENSITIVITY MATRIX REVEAL?

Yield, as an internal rate of return, assumes the investors put up a certain amount of cash today to receive cash flows in the future. Yield measures the rate of return on a fully paid investment over the life of the security, ignoring reinvested cash flows.

The typical yield sensitivity matrix of an inverse floating-rate tranche or of an inverse floating-rate residual essentially reveals the rate of return generated by fixed-rate bonds that have been financed by the issuance of floating-rate debt. As in any financing of fixed-income assets, the total return depends on the ultimate net interest margin. As in any mortgage financing, the total return can be affected by the rate of prepayment.

The cash flows of a financed purchase of fixed-rate bonds could be expressed as a rate of return on capital assuming various levels of financing rates. We could examine the "yield" of any fixed-rate bond in this fashion.

An Example Comparing an Inverse Floater to the Financing of the Underlying Fixed-Rate Bond

Below we show the similarity between a yield sensitivity matrix for a LIBOR inverse floater tranche carved from a REMIC PAC tranche to the return on equity of the same PAC tranche financed at LIBOR.

Consider the PAC tranche shown in Exhibit 1, similar to many available in the mortgage market priced at 100.10604 to yield 8.09%. The tranche is backed by new FNMA 9.00% MBS pass-throughs.

Exhibit 1: Fixed-Rate PAC Tranche

Coupon Rate	7.9750%
Maturity Date	06-25-21
Projected Average Life	7.95 years
Prepay Assumption	165% PSA
PAC Range	90% to 250% PSA
Face Amount	42,108,000
Price	100.10604

PSA	50%	165%	300%
Average Life	10.21	7.95	7.12
Yield	8.09%	8.09%	8.09%

Before we calculate the returns of a leveraged purchase of the PAC tranche, examine the alternative. Instead of issuing the PAC tranche above, a floating-rate tranche and an inverse floating-rate tranche could have been issued using LIBOR as the index rate to reset the coupon on each. The cash flows that would otherwise be paid to the PAC tranche are instead divided between the floater and the inverse floater.

The first step in the process is to carve out a floater tranche. Suppose we want to issue a floating-rate tranche priced at par. Market conditions require that a monthly floater, having this type of amortization schedule and average life, pay forty basis points over one-month LIBOR, and be subject to a coupon rate cap no lower than 10.75%. If we want to issue the maximum amount of floater bonds to achieve the greatest leverage, we will allocate the principal between the floater and the inverse in such a way as to exhaust all available interest from the underlying fixed-rate cash flows at the level of LIBOR at which the floater caps out. This results in a floater tranche face amount of $31,238,260.

The inverse floater is allocated the remaining principal, and both tranches return principal pro rata. The face amount of the inverse floater is $10,869,740.

Assume the level of one-month LIBOR equals 5.6375% on the pricing date. The descriptions of the two tranches that could have been issued, along with the familiar yield sensitivity tables, are shown in Exhibits 2 and 3. The floating-rate tranche now provides built-in financing at forty basis points over LIBOR, capped at 10.750%, with matched amortization and no counterparty credit risk. We can think of the forty-basis-point spread over LIBOR as the market's current evaluation of the embedded interest rate cap.

The inverse floating-rate tranche benefits from the leverage provided by the floater tranche. That is, the investor is able to capture the net interest margin of approximately $42 million in fixed-rate PAC bonds financed at LIBOR +40 basis points, with a cap at a cost of $10,914,390.

The structure shown in Exhibit 3 represents the opportunity to buy a leveraged position in the underlying fixed-rate PAC tranche

Exhibit 2: LIBOR Floating Rate PAC Tranche

Initial Coupon Rate	6.0875%
Coupon Rate Cap	10.750%
Maturity Date	06-25-21
Projected Average Life	7.95 years
Prepay Assumption	165% PSA
PAC Range	90% to 250% PSA
Face Amount	31,238,260
Price	100.0000

PSA	50%	165%	300%	
Average Life	10.21	7.95	7.12	LIBOR
Yield	5.79%	5.79%	5.79%	5.3125
Yield	8.84%	8.84%	8.83%	8.3125
Yield	10.93%	10.92%	10.92%	11.3125
Yield	10.93%	10.92%	10.92%	14.3125

Exhibit 3: LIBOR Inverse Floating-Rate Tranche

Initial Coupon Rate	7.9750%
Coupon Rate Cap	29.750%
Maturity Date	06-25-21
Projected Average Life	7.95 years
Prepay Assumption	165% PSA
PAC Range	90% to 250% PSA
Face Amount	10,869,740
Price	100.410773
Total Capital Invested	$10,914,390

PSA	50%	165%	300%	
Average Life	10.21	7.95	7.12	LIBOR
Yield	14.82%	14.81%	14.81%	5.3125
Yield	5.96%	5.96%	5.97%	8.3125
Yield	0.07%	0.09%	0.10%	11.3125
Yield	0.07%	0.09%	0.10%	14.3125

through the inverse floater. The investor could execute a similar strategy by financing the PAC tranche directly. What differs is the financing rate, the presence of a prepay-sensitive interest rate cap, and the absence of counterparty credit risk and margin calls.

Exhibits 4, 5, and 6 display the return on capital of financing the underlying PAC tranche given similar leverage—that is, similar capital invested. In the first example (see Exhibit 4), no cap is purchased, as is evident from the negative returns given high LIBOR levels. In the second example (see Exhibit 5), a cap is purchased that amortizes coincident with the outstanding balance of the PAC tranche at the pricing prepayment assumption of 165% PSA. The third example, shown in Exhibit 6, reveals the returns if a cap is purchased to provide protection on a balance equivalent to 50% PSA. Just as is the case for an inverse floater, the rate of return is a function of the level of LIBOR (*assumed to be constant at the indicated rate over the life of the financing arrangement*) and the prepayments that occur.

In the three financing arrangements presented in Exhibits 4, 5, and 6, the market value of the PAC tranche is assumed constant over the term to maturity. Accordingly, there would be no margin calls that would require additional capital.

Exhibit 4: Short-Term Financing of a Fixed-Rate PAC Tranche, No Interest Rate Cap Agreement

---

Interest Rate Cap Strike	None
Interest Rate Cap Cost	None
Financing Rate	LIBOR Flat
Total Capital Invested	$10,914,390
Initial Amount Financed	$31,238,261

PSA	50%	165%	300%	LIBOR
R.O.E.	16.04%	16.03%	16.02%	5.3125
R.O.E.	7.14%	7.14%	7.15%	8.3125
R.O.E.	−1.53%	−1.50%	−1.49%	11.3125
R.O.E.	−9.93%	−9.89%	−9.87%	14.3125

Exhibit 5: Short-Term Financing of a Fixed-Rate PAC Tranche, Interest Rate Cap Agreement Matched at 165% PSA

Interest Rate Cap Strike	10.750%
Interest Rate Cap Cost	$440,675
Financing Rate	LIBOR Flat
Total Capital Invested	$11,355,065
Initial Amount Financed	$31,238,261

PSA	50%	165%	300%	LIBOR
R.O.E.	15.22%	15.11%	15.04%	5.3125
R.O.E.	6.58%	6.47%	6.42%	8.3125
R.O.E.	-0.67%	-0.40%	-0.26%	11.3125
R.O.E.	-2.78%	-0.40%	0.69%	14.3125

The embedded cap of the inverse floater distinguishes the two strategies most. The investor in an inverse floater pays for the cap in the spread over LIBOR paid on the floater. This may be more or less than the direct cost of an interest rate cap agreement, and, in addition, the investor must weigh the risk of counterparty performance. Consider too, that many floaters and inverse floaters are carved out of fixed-rate REMIC tranches having average lives of

Exhibit 6: Short-Term Financing of a Fixed-Rate PAC Tranche, Interest Rate Cap Agreement Matched at 50% PSA

Interest Rate Cap Strike	10.750%
Interest Rate Cap Cost	$718,480
Financing Rate	LIBOR Flat
Total Capital Invested	$11,632,870
Initial Amount Financed	$31,238,261

PSA	50%	165%	300%	LIBOR
R.O.E.	14.73%	14.55%	14.46%	5.3125
R.O.E.	6.24%	6.07%	5.97%	8.3125
R.O.E.	-0.55%	-0.26%	-0.11%	11.3125
R.O.E.	-0.55%	1.86%	2.93%	14.3125

fifteen years or longer. Although an amortizing, prepay-sensitive cap of such a long term might be available in the market, many investors are unwilling to accept potential performance risk for such a long time span.

SUMMARY

Investors need to compare the relative cost of financing a fixed-rate tranche directly to the implied financing rate of the inverse floater, taking into consideration the relative value of the interest rate cap embedded in the inverse floater, the secure nature of the funding agreement, and the absence of margin calls.

Investors must recognize that the value of inverse floaters depends both on the value of the underlying fixed-rate cash flows and on the value of the floater that provides the inverse with its leverage and its cap. Short-term rates will only impact the value of an inverse floater to the extent they affect the floater and its cap, or the underlying fixed-rate cash flows. Otherwise, the value of an inverse floater and its price movements can be compared to that of the underlying fixed-rate tranche.

CHAPTER 23

CMO RESIDUALS

Adrian Katz
Director
Prudential Securities Inc.

Vincent Pica
Managing Director
Prudential Securities Inc.

Rick Villaume
Vice President
Prudential Securities Inc.

In 1991, the CMO/REMIC new issuance market experienced a record year, with over $240 billion in volume. Each deal included a residual.

Residuals can be extremely complex instruments. A thorough comprehension of the cash flow dynamics allows the investor to use a residual either for the purpose of hedging or to build a stable portfolio of securities. Whatever the application, there is no doubt that a complete understanding of residuals is a definite advantage to the investor.

In this chapter, we intend to address the following issues—where do residuals come from? what types of residuals are available? and what affects their value? In addition, we will discuss hedging considerations, risk-based capital requirements, accounting issues, and phantom-income and phantom-loss implications.

WHAT IS A RESIDUAL?

The word "residual" aptly describes the investment as it is comprised of the remaining cash flows from the underlying mortgages after all other cash flows are securitized into either a bond or a pass-through security. In essence, a residual's cash flow is comprised of the difference between the cash flows of the collateralizing assets and the collateralized obligations. For certain residuals, reinvestment income and servicing fees are also components of the cash flows. Residuals can take the form of scheduled principal and interest-bearing securities or of cash flows with neither a defined coupon nor any principal. The amount of cash flow can vary tremendously, from very small to even being the largest component of an issue. The legal characteristics of the offering can be as simple as a government agency security with a REMIC (Real Estate Mortgage Investment Conduit) tax election, or as complex as an Owner Trust equity private placement. Residual cash flow features can span the entire performance spectrum; they can be either bullish or bearish in nature or can act as either a long or short straddle. The multitude of available performance characteristics is a function of client-requested design, economic realities (i.e., the shape of the yield curve), and changes in the tax, accounting, and regulatory environment.

History of the Residual Market

The first CMO was issued in 1983 by FHLMC as a debt obligation collateralized by a designated pool of FHLMC mortgage pass-through certificates. The collateral remained an asset on FHLMC's balance sheet, while the fully cash flow-supported bond obligations remained a liability. A necessary outgrowth of this structure was the equity component (otherwise known as the residual). The tax treatment of residuals as equity implied that, in a rather illiquid manner, the only method for investing in residuals was through the creation or purchase of an issuing vehicle. For tax benefits, many of the earlier issuers were builder conduits, with only a few precocious investors creating arbitrage subsidiaries. These conduits or subsidiaries required up-front capital investments for such expenses as legal, accounting, and SEC filing fees. Since residuals were integral components of the issues, the awkward and expensive legal treatment significantly impaired the early growth of CMO issuance and residual liquidity.

In 1985, Wall Street, in conjunction with legal counsel, created a "better mousetrap" with the introduction of the Owner Trust residual structure. This structure allowed for the sale of equity partnerships in a residual. The immediate effect was the proliferation of Wall Street subsidiaries establishing registration shelves with the SEC to become CMO issuers. The innovation permitted the investor in a residual to be decoupled from the bond-issuance business. Further, the residual could now be purchased in percentages deemed small enough to eliminate accounting concerns over on-balance-sheet recognition. Typically, the ownership percentage was understood to be less than 50%, in order to maintain the off-balance-sheet treatment. The residual investor base was now expanded to include investors with no special knowledge of bond origination and investors who required the off-balance-sheet treatment.

Probably the most significant development in the cash flow engineering of residuals occurred in 1986 with the introduction of the floating-rate bond class. Up until 1986, the residual cash flows were comprised of either fixed-coupon spread or principal (invariably in the form of overcollateralization). The residual's investment dynamics therefore were either bullish or bearish, with the dominant influence being the prepayment rate on the underlying mortgages securing the deal. The introduction of the floating-rate class and the natural leftover effect of inverse floating-rate cash flows allowed the residual characteristics to vary with more subtlety. It was now possible to design a residual with characteristics previously external to the mortgage product securing the issue, such as the inclusion of LIBOR as an index for some of a issue's coupons. Furthermore, the effects of prepayments (usually influenced by long rates) now could be combined with the effects of coupon adjustments (usually influenced by short rates).

The enactment of the REMIC tax law in 1986 significantly improved the previously clumsy legal structures by removing many of the potential economic disadvantages associated with prior regulations. Essentially, REMIC allowed for the creation of fast-pay/slow-pay, multiclass pass-throughs whose mortgage cash flows would be passed through to investors with no equity retained by the issuer. Thus, in most cases, the transaction would be accounted for by the issuer as a sale of assets for tax purposes, and taxed at the investor level. For financial accounting purposes, the issuer can treat the transaction as either a sale of assets or as a financing. In sum, REMICs reduce inefficiencies, increase flexibility, and enable more issuers to enjoy the economic benefits of off-balance-sheet, multiclass mortgage financing.

Under REMIC, residuals can be structured so that they are sold as rated, SEC-registered bonds with no restrictions on transferability, financial statement consolidation concerns, or contingent liability for expenses. There would be numerous enhancements to and simplifications of the REMIC laws through subsequent Technical

Corrections Bills, providing further flexibility to issuers and investors. The more flexible and efficient treatment of residuals under REMIC helped to increase the investor base significantly—and in turn helped to create a more liquid and more active residual market. The tax implications associated with residuals are discussed later in this chapter.

In 1986, another significant cash flow engineering development occurred with the introduction of PAC (Planned Amortization Class) bonds. This method of cash flow separation allowed for classes to be designed with more or less prepayment stability, and this flexibility implied the ability to design long-straddle or short-straddle investments. Not only could residuals now be influenced by long and short interest rates, but also could react with substantial variation with respect to anticipated changes in interest rate volatility.

The inversion of the Treasury yield curve in 1988 and the economic reality that accompanied it provided the stimuli for more stable performing residuals. As floating-rate classes became too expensive to include in issues, residuals were less able to offer inverse-floater characteristics. Even bearish, fixed-coupon spread was not easily created, as a flat yield curve suggested that all classes of deals include the same coupon, which was typically the same as the underlying collateral coupon. By 1989, this trend had in fact stimulated the formation of residuals with insignificant cash flow value, sometimes called *de minimus* residuals.

Residual Investment Characteristics

By now we have indicated that a kaleidoscope of residuals exists. Here, the various types of residuals currently available are categorized and explained. Specific hedging techniques as they apply to different residual types are explained in the next section.

Bear Residuals. The first residuals consisted primarily of coupon spread, that is, the differential between the higher coupon on the

underlying mortgage collateral and the lower coupon on the outstanding obligation. For example, if mortgages with a net coupon
of 10% secured a single-class obligation with a coupon of 9%, the
cash flow difference available to be passed through to the residual
would be 1%. Since the balance on which the amount of interest
due varies with prepayments, some discussion of the prepayments
is appropriate.[1]

Home owners are less inclined to prepay their mortgages if the
prevailing interest rate environment is higher than the rate on
their obligation. Conversely, in a lower-rate environment, a home
owner is more likely to prepay a mortgage in order to refinance at
a lower cost. This suggests that in a higher-rate environment the
effect of slower prepayments would cause more cash to be paid to
the residual holder, since the coupon is based on a higher outstanding principal balance. Conversely, when rates are falling, the
probability is that the outstanding principal balance will decline
more rapidly due to an increase in prepayments, hence generating
less coupon payments and inherently less cash flow to the residual
investor.

Investments that perform well in rising-rate environments are
considered to be bearish. The degree of bearishness is determined
by the coupon on the underlying collateral relative to current market rates and the structure. The most bearish investments typically
are those with anticipated short durations. Short-duration investments have the potential to extend the most, ultimately creating
higher returns as more cash flow is returned to the investor over a
longer period of time. Coupon cash flows from companion
classes, volatile bonds themselves, tend to increase the bearish
behavior of a residual. Conversely, coupon cash flows from PAC
classes naturally tend to stabilize the performance. In addition, re-

---

[1] For a discussion of prepayments, see Chapter 10. Also see Lakhbir Hayre, Kenneth
Lauterbach, and Cyrus Mohebbi, "Mortgage Pass-Through Securities," in Frank J.
Fabozzi (ed.) *Advances and Innovations in the Bond and Mortgage Markets* (Chicago, IL:
Probus Publishing, 1989), and Lakhbir Hayre and Cyrus Mohebbi, *Prepayment Behavior
of 15-Year Pass-Through Securities,* (New York, N.Y.: Financial Strategies Group,
Prudential Securities Incorporated, May 1989).

Exhibit 1: Typical Bearish Residual Return Profile

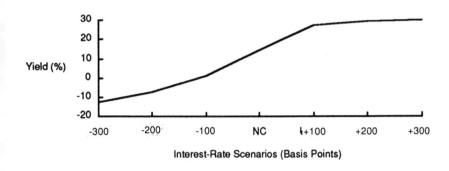

Yield (%)

Interest-Rate Scenarios (Basis Points)

siduals from higher-coupon underlying cash flows tend to be more volatile as a function of more volatile prepayment behavior. This in turn causes the bearish residuals from such collateral to be even more accentuated. Bearish residuals can act as excellent hedging tools for a fixed-income portfolio, or for a balance sheet whose combined assets have a longer duration than its liabilities (see Exhibit 1).

Bull Residuals. Since interest spread is what leads to the creation of bearish residuals, it is not surprising that a residual comprised only of principal cash flows is considered to be bullish. As the principal of a mortgage is returned in full (at par), the issue most affecting a bullish residual consisting only of principal is the timing of the return of the principal. Therefore, higher prepayment rates, which are experienced in declining interest rate environments, positively influence the performance of bullish residuals. Conversely, an increase in rates causes underperformance (see Exhibit 2). Residual "principal" can be created by overcollateraliza-

Exhibit 2: Typical Bullish Residual Return Profile

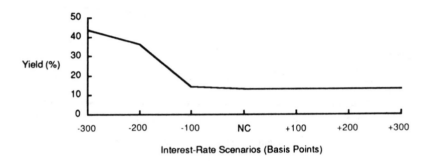

tion over time. This "principal" is typically returned once the bonds have matured.

Bullish investments can be more or less leveraged based on the structure from which they are carved and the coupon on the underlying collateral. Generally speaking, longer-duration principal cash flows are more volatile, as they are purchased at a greater discount price to par, and thus have the greatest upside potential when they are returned at par sooner than anticipated. Further, principal cash flows that are derived from companion bonds within structures containing PAC bonds tend to be more bullish. This effect can be attributed to the added volatility implicit in these structures, which increases the possibility of tremendous upswings in value in the event of increased prepayments. By contrast, PAC principal cash flows stabilize the residual fluctuations. The uses of bullish residuals in fixed-income portfolio management range from lengthening the effective duration of a portfolio that is inadequately positioned for a rally, to providing a hedge to a mortgage servicer.[2]

Humped Residuals (Short Straddles). Residuals derived from structures that contain floating-rate classes may vary significantly due to such factors as the coupon on the underlying collateral, the size of the floating-rate component as a percentage of the deal, the position of the floater in the deal, the floating-rate index, and the absolute level of the floating-rate cap relative to the current coupon. In most cases, there is a common cash flow characteristic, which is evident when scenario analysis reveals that the residual tends to underperform when interest rates vary from the initial environment. This behavior is a function of the combined effect of changes in prepayments and the coupon adjustments.

In a rising interest rate environment, the amount of interest rate spread declines while, at the same time, prepayments decline. Therefore, the remaining spread is outstanding for a longer period of time. These influences may be offsetting. As rates rise sufficiently for the floating-rate class(es) to approach its (their) coupon cap, the residual cash flow typically is curtailed, and hence the residual's performance is undermined. When interest rates decline, the coupon spread increases and prepayments accelerate; thus the amount of time during which the spread is outstanding is abbreviated. If rates decline sufficiently for prepayments to be almost instantaneous, the residual cash flow becomes insignificant, and the residual will underperform. These so-called "humped" residuals (so named because of their return profiles in declining and rising rate scenarios; see Exhibit 3) are therefore not well suited for an investor anticipating a volatile environment. In contrast, investors who foresee a market stall will be well rewarded by the higher base-case yields associated with humped residuals.

---

[2] For details on hedging mortgage servicing, see Adrian Katz, Vincent Pica, and Michael Sternberg, *Strategies for Mortgage Bankers in a Bullish Environment*, Financial Strategies Group, Prudential Securities Incorporated, May 29, 1989 and Adrian Katz, Vincent Pica, and Michael Sternberg, *Strategies for Traders and Investors in a Bullish Environment*, Financial Strategies Group, Prudential Securities Incorporated, June 14, 1989.

Exhibit 3: Typical Humped Residual Return Profile

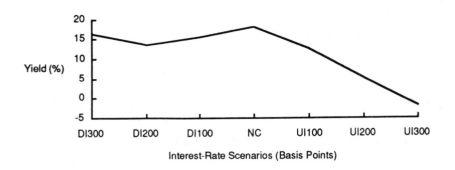

A further subtlety relating to the shape of the yield curve should be noted here. Yield-curve movements seldom occur in parallel, and the implications of a steepening or inverting yield curve for these humped residuals are critical. First, keep in mind that floating-rate coupons are indexed off a short interest rate, and that prepayments typically are triggered by changes in long interest rates. In an environment in which long rates are increasing and short rates are declining, humped residuals experience an increase in available coupon spread and a longer time period over which the spread is received. Hence, the steepening is doubly beneficial.

However, the opposite holds true when the yield curve is inverted, and, in fact, the effect is doubly disadvantageous. Any serious attempt to hedge this type of short-straddle residual should not only address the question of volatility but also the potential fluctuations in the shape of the yield curve. Due to these implied vulnerabilities and the range of cash flow fluctuations, these residuals are the most volatile generically. (The coupling of very high base-case yields and sharp declines in value outside the base case should come as no surprise to the reader.) The majority of residuals being offered by the thrift industry through liquidations fall into the humped residual category.

Smile Bonds (Long Straddles). Mortgage securities, by their nature, are "buy/writes" consisting of a long-bond component (scheduled payments by the home owner) and a short-call component (the prepayment option held by the home owner). Therefore, with mortgage securities as the collateral for CMO structures with multiple classes and a residual, it is fairly difficult to design a long-straddle residual, and very few exist. Residuals with superior performance in highly volatile environments invariably consist of short-duration interest spread and long-duration principal. The compromise for the smile bond residual investor is that the anticipated yield for the base-case scenario (no interest rate change) tends to be below Treasuries.[3] See Exhibit 4 for a typical smile bond return profile.

Stable Residuals. There is no rule that requires residuals to be complex or volatile. Indeed, when a residual consists of PAC cash flows, the residual is more stable than the underlying collateral, and actually could be designated the most stable class in the entire issue (see Exhibit 5). In many structures, the residual is a class carved from a regular PAC component, and may even pay in parallel with such a PAC. Not surprisingly, stable residual investments of this type offer purchasing opportunities to a very broad spectrum of investors.

De Minimus **Residuals.** As shown later in this chapter, the residual class of a REMIC bears the tax liability of the entire REMIC. Noneconomic, or *de minimus* residuals, receive little or no cash

---

[3] For details on smile bonds, see Howard Chin, Alan Galishoff, and Vincent Pica, *Structured Portfolio Trades: Unruliness Begets Opportunity*, Financial Strategies Group, Prudential Securities Incorporated, October 25, 1989.

Exhibit 4: Typical Smile Bond Return Profile

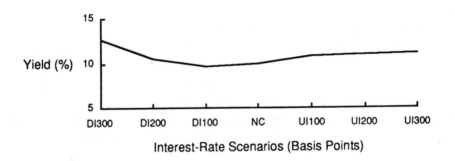

Interest-Rate Scenarios (Basis Points)

Exhibit 5: Typical Stable Residual Return Profile

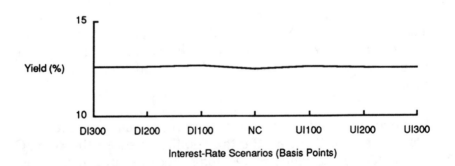

Interest-Rate Scenarios (Basis Points)

flow. Given minimal (or no) economic value, these instruments then become a tax strategy unto themselves. An investor can use these instruments to create or modify an existing tax strategy.

This type of residual is typically sold with a zero or "negative" price (i.e., the investor receives cash at settlement). The investor then reinvests this money in securities that, on an after-tax basis, generate enough cash to pay the tax liabilities of the REMIC (recalling that all taxable income from a *de minimus* residual is nonshelterable). After the "income period" of the REMIC, the investor can then use the losses created by the REMIC to offset other sources of income. In short, the investor is "buying" these tax losses in the future.

THOUGHTS ON HEDGING RESIDUALS

As could be inferred from our above comments, residuals can be divided into two basic groups—those that allow the investor to take a position on the direction of future interest rates, and those that allow the investor to take a position on interest rate volatility. Bearish and bullish residuals essentially take a position on the direction of rates. Humped (short-straddle) residuals appeal to investors who expect interest rates to remain generally the same (i.e., low volatility). Long straddles and stable residuals typically appeal to investors who expect at least some degree of interest rate volatility. Hedging against adverse interest rate moves is fairly straightforward—take the opposite position for the amount of expected risk (i.e., the chance of rates reversing). Hedging residuals based on a volatility position is more complex.[4]

---

[4] The analyses for all securities/hedges discussed in this section were generated using the Prudential Securities Structured Portfolio/Synthetic Security (SP/SS) System. All results were stated on a pre-tax basis. SP/SS total returns are the "all-in" percent return on an investment, assuming complete reinvestment of all interim cash flows at the assumed reinvestment rate. In all cases, the analysis was done based on immediate parallel shifts of the yield curve by the appropriate amount.

Bearish Residuals

As mentioned in the previous section, bearish residuals tend to perform better in rising rate environments. The obvious hedge for this type of residual is a bullish security with similar underlying prepayment characteristics. For those wishing to add to their residual portfolio, bullish residuals of similar collateral are an obvious hedge. For the investor concerned about using additional residuals to hedge a current position, leveraged PO classes provide good protection. With the large variety of PAC structures being created, there are numerous opportunities to obtain Companion or Targeted Amortization Class (TAC) POs that are custom-designed to provide the necessary cash flow "kick" in declining interest rate environments without the tax implications of some bullish residuals. The investor who purchases a bearish residual as an investment rather than as a hedging instrument has implicitly taken a position on the direction of future rates. Duration-matched hedges in this scenario do not make economic sense. Instead, the investor should use expectation-weighted matching; for example, if the investor believes that there is a 20% chance of rates reversing and the total exposure is $10 million, then approximately $2 million in bullish securities should be added to the portfolio (all other things, such as leverage and yield sensitivity, being equal). See Exhibit 6 for a return profile of this hedge.

Bullish Residuals

Since bullish residuals tend to perform better in declining rate environments, the obvious hedge is a bearish security using similar underlying collateral. A typical nonresidual hedge for this type of residual is a TAC IO, generally purchased at a very low yield, that has some call protection but little, if any, extension protection. The lengthening of the TAC IO's duration in rising rate environments provides for a yield pick-up, making the TAC IO a good hedge for bullish residuals. See Exhibit 7 for a return profile of this hedge. The purchase of a bullish residual for investment purposes indi-

Exhibit 6: Performance Characteristics of a Bearish Residual and a Super PO Hedge

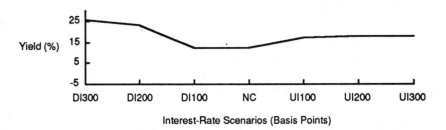

Exhibit 7: Performance Characteristics of a Bullish Residual and an IO Hedge

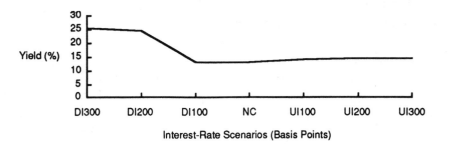

cates that the investor has an opinion on the direction of future interest rates. Again, investors must consider the probability of interest rates reversing direction before any hedging program is established.

Humped Residuals (Short Straddles)

Humped residuals are volatility plays—the investor believes that there will be little or no interest rate change and no prepayment change from current levels. These residuals are effectively short positions on both short-term and long-term rates. Decreases in short-term rates (and the floating-rate coupons based on these rates) typically are offset by increases in prepayments (assuming parallel shifts in the yield curve). Decreases in prepayment speeds are usually offset by increases in short-term rates (again, using parallel shifts for example purposes). When factors such as non-parallel shifts and inversions in the yield curve are added to the equation, you have an instrument that is a challenge to hedge.

At any point in time, the holder of a humped residual is at the no-interest-rate-change point in Exhibit 8. The curve may slope differently in different rate environments (and may even turn bullish or bearish), but generally has the characteristic hump shape. While the investor may believe that interest rates will remain close to where they are now (i.e., low/no volatility), he probably has an opinion as to the most likely direction of future rates.

If short-term rates rise and the corresponding decrease in coupon spread causes a less negative effect than changes in prepayments (in parallel shifts, one would expect a benefit), then there is little benefit in hedging against prepayment risk since the additional cost of hedging would result in little or no gain. Conversely, if the holder expects long-term rates to decrease (prepayments to increase) and the residual is more sensitive to increases in prepayments than decreases in short-term rates, then there is little benefit in hedging short-term-rate risk. In brief, the investor must consider the following three questions:

Exhibit 8: Performance Characteristics of a Humped Residual

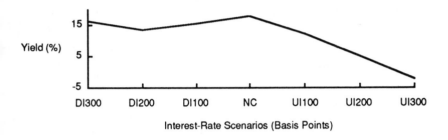

- Which rate, long or short, is expected to move the most (or cause the most harm)?

- In which direction is the rate expected to move?

- How long is this rate change expected to affect the residual?

When these questions are answered, a hedging program that fits the investor's expectations can be established.

Working Through an Example

To answer the questions above, assume that short rates will rise, while long rates will remain more or less stable. In addition, assume that the change will last for two months (similar to year-end changes in LIBOR). The dollar amount of the floating-rate classes in the underlying CMO is the amount of short-term rate exposure that must be hedged; for example, a $300 million CMO with $150 million in floating-rate class(es) has $150 million in short-term rate exposure. To hedge the entire amount of exposure, LIBOR caps must be purchased, with an expiration date approximating the expected time period to be hedged. As the floating-rate classes prepay, the hedge needs to be rolled off on a 1:1 basis, e.g., if, in month one, $5 million in the floating-rate classes pays off, then $5 million of the hedge needs to be rolled off. Ideally, the gain (loss) on the hedge should approximate the loss (gain) in cash flows on the residual. See Exhibit 9 for a return profile of this 1:1 hedge.

This strategy of matching hedging to expected changes in interest rates requires constant monitoring of the residual and hedge instruments. A month-by-month adjustment in hedge positions must be undertaken, as well as a constant review of short-term and long-term interest rate expectations.

Exhibit 9: Performance Characteristics of a Humped Residual with a One-Year LIBOR Cap Hedge

---

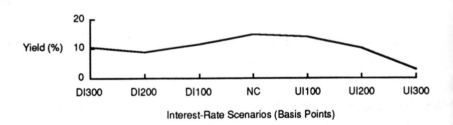

This example illustrates the hedging of short-term expected cash flows. For longer-term hedging, the investor should use something closer to duration matching. Smile bonds or stable residuals with durations similar to that of the humped residual can be used.

Stable Residuals and Smile Bonds (Long-Straddles)

Stable residuals and smile bonds are also volatility plays—they presume that there will be high levels of interest rate volatility, but that its direction will not be easy to discern. These residuals, by their nature, tend to sell at lower yields than other types. Since stable/long-straddle residuals have flat (stable) to smile-shaped (long-straddle) return profiles, hedging them against interest rate movement is not beneficial; they are a hedge themselves. The primary use of these residuals is to pick up yield outside the base case, which makes them a good match for humped residuals. For both bearish and bullish residuals, stable residuals and smile bonds provide some protection by lessening declines in adverse rate environments.

RISK-BASED CAPITAL CONSIDERATIONS

Banks

Residuals fall within the 100% risk weight basket for banks under their risk-based capital standards. In meeting its risk-based capital requirements, a bank must hold capital equal to 8% times 100% of the residual value. Relative to other securities, this is five times the amount required for an equivalent amount of FNMA and FHLMC pass-throughs (20% risk weight), and the same as for an equivalent amount of IO/PO strips (100% risk weight).

Thrifts

Residuals fall within the 100% risk weight basket for thrifts under their risk-based capital standards. Thrifts must hold 8%[5] of 100% of the residual value in capital. The Office of Thrift Supervision has indicated that residuals may be moved to a lower risk weight category when an interest rate risk component of capital is introduced. Thus, the interest rate risk calculation will be used to determine the capital required based on the interest rate-related volatility separately from capital required for credit risk. Residuals that reduce the overall volatility of a thrift's market value of portfolio equity (the present value of all asset cash flows less the present value of all liability cash flows plus the present value of all off-balance-sheet cash inflows less outflows) could potentially lower the capital required for interest rate risk. If the reduction of capital for interest rate risk exceeded the marginal capital required for residual credit risk, the overall risk-based capital required could be reduced.

Both banks and thrifts can benefit by maximizing the return on capital generated by the assets they hold. In purchasing assets, they should consider the spread-to-funding generated given the capital allocation. This will continue to be a consideration particularly for capital-constrained institutions in light of their other existing investment criteria.

GAAP AND TAX ACCOUNTING FOR RESIDUALS

GAAP income for REMIC residuals may be calculated according to the Statement of Financial Accounting Standards No. 91 (SFAS 91) method.

The Emerging Issued Task Force (EITF) of the Financial Accounting Standards Board (FASB) discussed a method of accounting for nonequity CMO investments on December 14, 1989. It was

---

[5] This requirement is being phased in. The actual requirement is 6.4% until 12/30/90; 7.2% from 12/31/92; and 8% after 12/31/92.

determined during these discussions that CMOs that were carried as long-term investments would be considered to be nonequity if the investor had little or no control of the cash distribution for the CMO structure. Securitized residuals (i.e., bond form) are considered to fall into this category.

SFAS 91 details the appropriate method for income recognition. Specifically, SFAS 91 states that income should be calculated by applying the "interest method," using a yield that is recalculated for every period in which the remaining projected cash distributions will differ from those previously projected. This will occur whenever the prepayment assumptions for future cash flows are changed or the current distribution differs from that last projected. The original yield is calculated by using the purchase price and the residual cash flow at the pricing speed. When a distribution occurs that is other than that projected, a new yield is calculated by using the actual distributions to date, the new projected distributions, and the original purchase price. The yield is then used to compute a new carrying value of the residual by discounting the new set of future cash flows at this rate to the current accounting date. When the carrying value of the residual is changed, a corresponding adjustment should be made to income from that period. If this new yield is less than zero, the investment is subject to an *impairment test*.

If the residual is an equity interest in an Owner Trust, the appropriate accounting method is determined by the percentage owned. Ownership of greater than 50% of the residual may require full consolidation of assets and liabilities, with adjustments made for minority residual interests. Investors with ownership of less than 50% but greater than 20% may be able to use the equity method, or SFAS 91. With the equity method, an investor reports the pro-rata share of GAAP earnings, reported by the issuer, corresponding to the percentage owned. Investors with ownership of less than 20% in an Owner Trust may not use the equity method. The EITF is considering a proposal that would recommend the use of the SFAS 91 method for all residuals that are considered to be nonequity CMO investments. This would include all securitized residuals and equity interests of less than 50% in Owner trusts.

Taxable income on residuals is computed under a different method than SFAS 91. Taxable income is computed by taking the excess collateral and reinvestment income over the REMIC regular interest deductions, expenses, and ongoing fees. If the regular interest expense relative to the outstanding bond principal amount increases over time, there will be less relative expense at the beginning, with greater relative expense toward the end. This increase will occur if shorter-maturity regular interests have lower yields than longer-maturity ones. This is typically the case in a normal yield-curve environment. This results in phantom income followed by phantom losses. The excess taxable income over economic income is referred to as phantom income. The sum of all phantom income and phantom losses will equal zero, and the total taxable income will be equal to the total GAAP income over the life of the residual.

Phantom Income and Phantom Losses of Residuals

What is phantom income? Simply stated, phantom income is created when taxable income exceeds economic income (GAAP income). How is this phantom income created? From the standpoint of the Trust that owns the collateral supporting a REMIC transaction, the collateral is an asset and the payments received are income. Conversely, the bonds outstanding are liabilities and the payments due to the bondholders are expenses. In a positive yield-curve environment, phantom income is created when these deductible weight-average expenses are deferred through the tranching of the collateral into bonds with different yields and maturities. The creation of phantom income is increased if the collateral going into the Trust is "bought-in" below par. The IRS treats this market discount as if it were an Original-Issue Discount, and thus it must be accreted into income. In addition, certain types of bonds, such as Z bonds, also increase phantom income due to the accrual feature. Usually, however, the majority of phantom income/loss is created through timing and yield mismatches between the assets and the liabilities of the Trust. In the later years, when earlier tranches have been retired, the relationship between the assets and the liabilities flip-flops such that phantom losses are created when economic income exceeds taxable income. (For many investors, phantom losses are desirable since they shelter cash flow that otherwise would be taxed.) These phantom amounts always net out to zero at maturity, or, in other words, taxes are due only on the *true* economic income of the residual over the entire life of the residual.

Of additional interest, and of perhaps dominating import given the volatility extant in the fixed-income marketplace, the actual accounting for phantom income and phantom losses is dominated by *prepayments*. Specifically, if the entire issue pays down because of prepayments accelerating through the pricing speed (thus retiring early tranches very quickly and long tranches commensurately early), the amount of phantom income/phantom losses will be dramatically lower than projected at pricing. This is due to the foreshortening of the timing disparities between the assets (the collateral) and the liabilities (the bonds). In the case of a powerful rally after pricing, the difference between the *projected* phantom income and the *actual* phantom income can be dramatically in favor of the residual holder. In contrast, if there is a dramatic market decline, this will cause the timing disparities between the assets and the liabilities to be outstanding longer. This results in actual phantom income exceeding the pricing projections. It is a function of the nature of mortgages, however, that this is not a symmetrical relationship. Mortgage collateral that is going into a REMIC issue generally has a weighted-average maturity that is not *dramatically* shorter than its original maturity. Thus, it cannot get that much longer. This is why not as much additional phantom income is created in a market decline as is destroyed in a rally. In short, a mortgage can get prepaid tomorrow, but there isn't any chance that homeowners will pay one more month than they are required to!

Excess Inclusions/Unrelated Business Taxable Income

While not by any means an exhaustive discussion of the causes of phantom income, the above text does present an accurate picture of the major components of phantom income. Of more interest to sophisticated investors would be the economic effect of phantom income on the yield of a residual held in portfolio. The economic effect is the reduction of the effective after-tax yield during the early years of the CMO, caused by the present value of the taxes being paid on phantom income exceeding the present value of the tax savings due to phantom losses.

With very limited but important exceptions, all residual income, including phantom income, is always subject to tax, because such income is treated as an excess-inclusion item. The "excess-inclusion amount" is the amount of interest income generated by the residual that is greater than 120% of the *Federal Long-Term Rate*.[6] If the residual is held by a tax-exempt entity such as a pension plan or any entity that is only taxed on its Unrelated Business Taxable Income (UBTI), phantom income will be treated as UBTI.

As far as exceptions go, there are few, and what follows is a general, not detailed, description of them.

1. If a residual does not have significant value, all income from a residual is treated as excess inclusion. Significant value generally is regarded as being at least 2% of the value of the REMIC. Thus, ultrasmall residuals are always part of the excess-inclusion base.

2. Thrift institutions are exempt from the rule that prohibits excess inclusions from being offset by unrelated losses. In addition, qualified subsidiaries[7] of the thrift can be consolidated for tax purposes with respect to offsetting losses of

---

[6] By statute, the Federal Long-Term Rate is defined as the average of the current yields on U.S. Treasury obligations that have a remaining term to maturity of greater than nine years. The IRS computes this figure and publishes it monthly.

[7] A qualified subsidiary is one whose stock and substantially all of its indebtedness is owned by the thrift. The qualified subsidiary also must be operated and organized for the express and exclusive purpose of operating one or more REMICs.

the thrift against excess inclusions realized by the qualified subsidiary.

3. Real Estate Investment Trusts (REITs) and Registered Investment Companies (RICs) can offset excess-inclusion income with a dividends-paid deduction. The excess-inclusion taxation issue is passed along to the shareholders.

SUMMARY

At this time, there exists an incredible variety of residuals; it is hoped the above abbreviated history of their issuance will help the investor understand the breadth of choices available and the inherent complexities. Of course, we anticipate that the future of the residual market is likely to be an improvement on the past with respect to flexibility, creativity, and liquidity.

CHAPTER 24

CMO CONSTRUCTS

Mary A. Maier, PhD
Research Associate
Gifford Fong Associates

In today's market collateralized mortgage obligations (CMOs) stand out as one of the most unique fixed income securities. Their diverse features enjoy great marketing appeal while creating unique problems for those interested in modeling. The objective this chapter is to offer a set of simple attributes which uniquely describe CMO constructs. This should enable one to categorize (the first step to modeling) most CMO tranches in today's market. Even if one is not interested in modeling CMOs, the attributes discussed in what follows will hopefully give an overview of CMOs enabling comparison of tranche types and offering greater insight into tranche behavior in various prepayment environments.

INTRODUCTION

CMOs are very simple, in principal. A companion fixed-income security worth discussing for comparison purposes is a STRIP. This variant of traditional bonds is accomplished by creating two bonds from one. The original bond's cash flows are distributed to two component bonds: interest going to one bond holder while principal goes to the other. Each component is referred to as a STRIP (Separate Trading of Registered Interest and Principal of Securities) and is a bond in its own right.

Bond variants created in this way lend themselves to *life cycle* vernacular (often used in the description of random processes). In this terminology *sibling* will be taken to be synonymous with the component bonds on the liability side of the deal while *parent* is synonymous with the underlying collateral on the liability side. When the parent bond is a MBS the principal may, and generally does, pay down faster than is scheduled. It only takes a moment to realize the performance attributes (price, duration, convexity etc.) for these STRIP siblings differ vastly from each other under various interest rate scenarios. In fact the STRIP's behavior differs from the parent's behavior as well.

STRIPs, as one example of bond variants, divide a bond's cash flows into nontrivial component bonds. The time to maturity of the siblings is identical to the time to maturity of the parent. CMOs, like STRIPS, create component bonds by dividing the cash flows of the underlying collateral. An additional feature is that the sibling bonds generally have dissimilar maturities and their maturities are dissimilar from the parent bond as well.

A CMO is also a variant on a traditional bond. Both the asset and liability sides of a CMO consist of bonds. As the acronym implies, the underlying collateral of a CMO consists of mortgage-backed securities (MBSs). To help distinguish between bonds on the asset and liability side, the component bonds forming the liability side of the CMO are referred to as *tranches*. Derived from "trench" this would imply CMOs carve (trench) out cash flows from the underlying collateral and channel them to component trenches. The French version of *tranche* may have been used for aesthetic purposes. Tranches have their own coupon, maturity and face values. The word "tranche" is used when referring to a specific component bond while "CMO" is used when referring to the deal as a whole, with all of its tranches and underlying collateral. Monthly incoming cash flows of the MBSs are divided (and subsequently paid out to the tranches) by a method of allocation peculiar to each CMO. The method is designed by the CMO issuer and specified in the prospectus. Details of the principal allocation are often referred to as the *deal structuring* or *deal description*. Originally, the pay down of tranches was simply sequential. However, today's CMOs are rich in variation from this simple theme and offer a variety of investment strategies.

There is very little else which will be said with respect to the underlying collateral. It may (or may not) be a government issue (GNMA, FNMA or FHLMC). It may have a fixed or variable rate coupon. The details as to pool number, maturity, coupon, face value, etc. are made available by the CMO issuer.

Most of the remaining discussion will be on tranche characteristics and contingencies. Some time will be spent on specific examples of tranche payment prioritization. There are many variations of this theme in today's CMO market. First, however, elementary tranche characteristics need to be listed. Since a tranche is simply a bond, its relevant characteristics are coupon, maturity and face value.

Coupon is more easily addressed than maturity. The coupon rate of a tranche is specified in the CMO prospectus. If the coupon rate is zero, the tranche is generally sold at a discount. Nontrivial rates may be fixed or variable (variable includes floating, ascending, graduated etc.)

The face value of a tranche is specified in the prospectus as well. It remains constant until the tranche begins to pay down, unless the tranche is an accrual bond. A tranche is said to be an *accrual tranche* if it does not receive interest until some specified date. Considering the life cycle of a tranche, the *birth date* of an interest bearing tranche might then be defined as the first date of principal payment. Interest not paid to the owner is added to the tranche principal value until the birth date. After the birth date an accrual tranche is paid interest on the remaining principal until death (remaining principal is exactly zero). Of course, what makes CMOs interesting is the nature of a tranche's birth. A regular accrual bond, in our vernacular, is *born* at some pre-defined deterministic date. Hence its remaining balance at any point in time is deterministic. An accrual tranche, by comparison, has a stochastic birth date. For most accruals, this date is contingent upon the stochastic variable of interest rates. The interest rate is one of the factors driving prepayments of the underlying collateral. A tranche's birth date is also contingent upon the specifics of the CMO's deal structuring. In fact the birth date of almost all component tranches in a CMO is a stochastic variable.

Tranche cash flows are made monthly, quarterly or semi-annually as specified in the prospectus. For this discussion all tranches within a CMO will have the same period of payment, monthly.

Tranche maturities are contingent upon the deal structure of a CMO. Tranche worst case maturities are published in the prospectus. Virtually all CMO deal structuring is concerned with specifying how the incoming principal from the underlying collateral is divided among the tranches. Thus, one assumes the incoming interest from the underlying MBS collateral will adequately cover the interest due the tranches. The only exception to ignoring interest in the deal structuring discussion is for CMOs containing accrual tranches.

The balance of this chapter describes variations on tranche characteristics and contingencies. No mention is made of tranche valuation, duration, yield etc. These performance attributes will be briefly mentioned in a later section. For what follows, the reader may assume tranche valuation to be computed using discounted cash flows. As seen in the next few sections, determining a tranches expected cash flows can be quite a challenge.

COLLATERAL SCHEDULED AND UNSCHEDULED PRINCIPAL PAYMENTS

Once a prepayment function is chosen (and possibly an interest rate environment depending upon the prepayment model chosen) the monthly scheduled principal payments from the underlying collateral are easily computed using standard amortization formulations. There are a number of models which forecast prepayments—the unscheduled principal cash flows. One of the simpler models is the Public Securities Association, PSA, model of prepayments. In this model prepayments begin at zero for a MBS with age zero months and increases linearly to 6% at 30 months. Prepayments remain constant at 6% until the MBS age is 360 months. MBS prepayments are indicated by quoting a multiplier, or speed, of this function. Thus 200% PSA means prepayments reach 12% at 30 months and remain constant after that. When using the PSA model one always quotes a speed to indicate a level of prepayments. Exhibit 1 shows stylized graphs of the collateral principal payments (graphs on left) for a generic MBS which would be paid monthly at various PSA speeds (corresponding functions shown at right). The exact functions are not plotted since the desired qualitative information is conveyed in a sketch. This type of sketch, principal versus time to pay down of the collateral, will be used repeatedly in the following discussion. Using the portfolio view of a CMO, the collateral cash flow coming into the issuer on a monthly basis must equate to the sum of the payouts made to the tranches. Because of this equality, the collateral and tranche principal cash flows are normally sketched on the same graph.

Since virtually all CMOs are structured using the PSA model, a comment is in order regarding the choice of this model. A computational advantage (and a theoretical disadvantage) of this model is its lack of dependence on the current level of interest rates. *It is simply a model of convenience for deal structuring.* Its use in no way implies future prepayments will in fact mimic the model's output. In fact, any prepayment model may be used when one finally does valuation modeling.

Exhibit 1: Principal Payments vs. Time MBS Age (Months) for Varying PSA Speeds

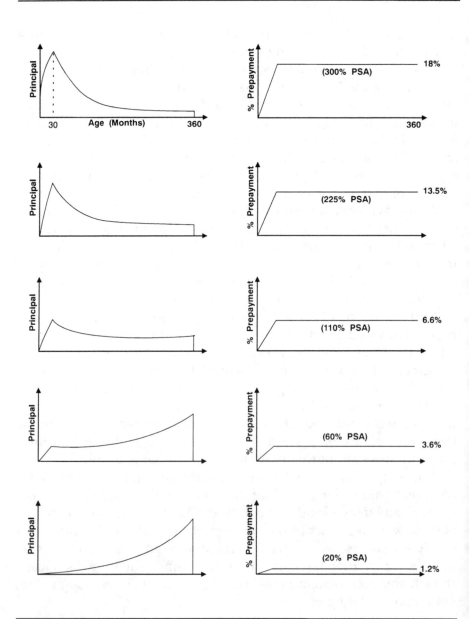

THE FIRST CMOS

CMO tranches were originally developed to create bonds with less prepayment risk than the underlying MBS collateral. Exhibit 2a shows incoming principal from collateral payments in a 120% PSA prepayment environment. The four sections indicate how the incoming collateral principal payments are paid out to the tranche holders. For this simple example, suppose the issuer purchased $400 million GNMA 12% to collateralize the CMO. Exhibit 3 presents the tranche characteristics.

A stylized deal structure for this CMO is found as follows:

Stylized deal structure for tranches described in Exhibit 3
Pay the incoming collateral's principal to:

1. T_1 until completely paid down.

2. T_2 until completely paid down.

3. T_3 until completely paid down.

4. T_4 until completely paid down.

Shown in Exhibits 2b, 2c, 2d and 2e are the interest and principal payments made to the four tranches T_1, T_2, T_3, T_4.

Though tranches are simply another type of bond, there are inherent differences from most traditional fixed-income securities. Traditional bonds have deterministic birth and death dates (using the *life cycle* vernacular of birth instead of first and last principal payment). In that sense the birth and death of CMO tranches are contingent upon the *health* of their nearest neighbors. Therefore, computing a tranche's performance attribute (such as yield or duration) must be done in context of the CMO's *complete* deal structure.

One can see from this simple example how tranches are created with less risk than the underlying collateral. It should be obvious that a CMO does not eliminate a MBS's prepayment risk, it simply redistributes it. For example, T_1 will obviously have shorter duration than the underlying collateral while T_4 will have a longer

Exhibit 2: Construction of Cash Flows in a Four Tranche CMO

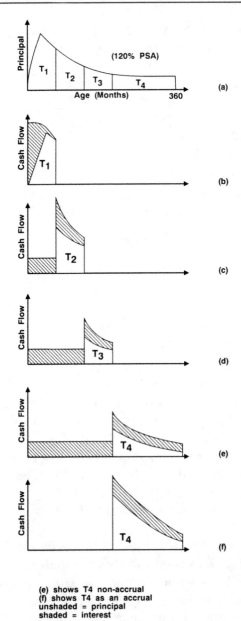

(e) shows T4 non-accrual
(f) shows T4 as an accrual
unshaded = principal
shaded = interest

Exhibit 3: Four Tranche CMO

Tranche Name	Original Principal Amount (in millions)	Coupon
T₁	$ 90	9.0%
T₂	$110	9.25%
T₃	$105	10.0%
T₄	$ 95	10.0%

duration. Redistribution of risk will be discussed further in other sections.

EFFECT OF PREPAYMENTS ON TRANCHE PAY DOWN

In the discussion that follows WAL is used as a measure of tranche performance. Exhibits 4a, 4b and 4c show how changing interest rate environments (assuming rates and prepayments are inversely related) affect payments made to the tranches. In the previous section's example the tranche paid first is affected far less than the tranche paid last. Specifically, T_4 has a larger reduction in WAL than T_1 in the rising prepayment environments of 120% to 200% PSA.

One may think of the relationship as follows. Some of the changes in prepayments of the underlying MBSs are simply responses to changing interest rate environments. The embedded option driven by these prepayments adds risk to the MBS relative to a comparable fixed-income security with no embedded option. In our simple input-output view of CMOs, whatever comes in to the issuer (for example, principal from the collateral) must be exactly what goes out to the tranches (in sum). This applies to risk as well. If the underlying collateral's measure of risk is, say 400 basis points due to the embedded option, that is what must be passed along to the tranches (in sum). In our example, T_1 obviously has less than its prorata share of risk. To maintain a balance, some other tranche must have more than its prorata share of risk. The

Exhibit 4: Impact of Prepayments on Four Tranche Sequential Pay Down CMO

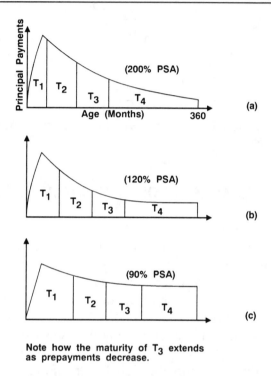

Note how the maturity of T_3 extends as prepayments decrease.

notion of redistribution of risk will be mentioned again in a later section.

ACCRUAL TRANCHES

In the early CMOs if an accrual tranche was in the structure it was the last of four sequentially paid tranches T_A, T_B, T_C, and T_Z to receive cash flows. T_Z, the accrual, began paying down upon the death of its immediate predecessor, T_C. Today an accrual tranche may appear anywhere in the deal structure of a CMO that may have many more than four tranches. Also the contingency of its birth may be extremely complicated. For example instead of birth after the death of a single tranche it (the accrual tranche's pay down) may be born after the death of a set of tranches. Or pay down may begin when some neighboring tranche is paid down to some specified non-zero amount. In this case the birth of an accrual tranche might be said to depend upon the *health* of its neighboring tranches.

As a simple example, consider the hypothetical CMO of Exhibit 3. Modify this to make T_4 an accrual tranche. The deal structure might read something as follows:

Deal structure exhibiting accrual tranche
Pay the incoming collateral's principal to:

1. T_1 until completely paid down.
   Pay what remains of the incoming collateral plus any interest due but not paid to the accrual tranche T_4 to:

2. T_2 until completely paid down.

3. T_3 until completely paid down.

4. T_4 until completely paid down.

Distributing T_4's accrued interest as principal starting with T_2 above is just for sake of example. The deal could just as easily have been structured by applying it first to T_1 of step 1. It depends on what types of tranches the issuer wants to create. Exhibits 2b, 2c and 2d still approximate the behavior of tranches T_1, T_2 and T_3. Exhibit 2f shows how T_4 behaves as an accrual tranche. Note that it receives no interest until its *birth*.

At first glance it may seem that our definition of deal structure is in need of modification. Recall that *deal structure* was said to be a CMO's prioritization of *principal* pay down to the tranches, no mention is made of interest. In the above example the deal structure is specifying how accrued interest is being distributed. However the interest due the accrual (and not paid) is transformed into principal. Simply semantics. The deal structure is still specifying how principal is being distributed. The distinction over principal versus interest may seem pedantic. However categorization and subsequent modeling of CMOs can only be accomplished after a consistent definition of *deal structure* has been made.

FLOATING-RATE TRANCHES

Two types of variable coupon tranches are floaters and inverse floaters. The wording here gets a little confusing as both types are often referred to "floaters". In this section italics will be used in reference to specific instances of floaters, such as *floater, inverse floater* and *super floaters*. Any floating-rate tranche is periodically reset to an index (typically LIBOR). The general coupon formulation, C_{fl}, for a *floater* is:

$$C_{fl} = Sp + m \times Index$$

with imposed bound $C_{floor} \leq C_{fl} \leq C_{ceiling}$

where Sp = spread or margin.
An example of a *floater's* formulation is:

$$C_{fl} = 0 + 1.0 \times Index$$

with imposed bound $0.55 \leq C_{fl} \leq 11.0$

for an initial value of, say, index = 9.0%.

Initially, *floaters* used only slope values of m = 1.0. Then *super floaters* were defined as floating-rate tranches with m > 1.0. Obviously there is a risk taken on by the issuer in the form of a rise in the Index. To offset this risk, a CMO with *floaters* will usually contain *inverse floaters*. These tranches have rates that move in the opposite direction of the *floater*. Continuing with the above example, an *inverse floater's* generic formulation might look like:

$$C_{infl} = Sp + m \times Index$$

with imposed bound $C_{floor} \leq C_{infl} \leq C_{ceiling}$

where a complementary numerical example might be given as:

$$C_{infl} = 66.1827 - 6.3333 \times \text{Index}$$

with imposed bound $0.0 \leq C_{infl} \leq 66.1827$.

Floaters may appear anywhere in the deal structure. CMOs may also have floating-rate accrual tranches. The specifics of the floating formulation Sp, m, Index and the period of reset are given in the prospectus.

COMPANION TRANCHES

A variation on the sequential pay down of CMO tranches is that of concurrently paying tranches. Concurrent pay down is exemplified by the following hypothetical CMO. The collateral's original principal is $300 million with T_a, T_b, T_c and T_d having original principals of $100, $100, $25 and $75 (all in millions), respectively. The deal structure found in the prospectus might read something as follows:

Deal structure exhibiting companion tranche
Pay the incoming collateral's principal to:

1. T_a until completely paid down.

2. T_b and T_c prorata until both tranches are completely paid down.

3. T_d until completely paid down.

T_b and T_c are called companion tranches since they pay down simultaneously. It is not necessary that companion tranches pay down prorata as in this example. Any fractional allocation may be specified. Exhibits 5a, 5b and 5c give a rough sketch of how prepayments affect this hypothetical CMO. Since the companion tranches pay down prorata there is simply an identical lengthening of maturities for this example.

Exhibit 5: Four Tranche CMO with Companions

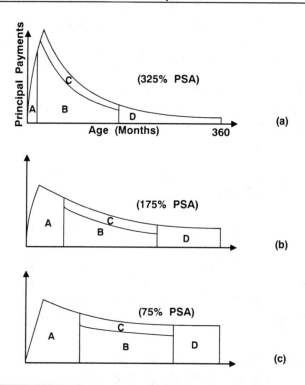

CMO CONSTRUCT/QUALITY/RESIDUAL TRANCHES

Exhibit 6 is a schematic of the asset-liability balance of CMOs at any arbitrary but fixed point in time. From a modeling point of view, a CMO is simply a portfolio with tranches for liabilities and MBS's for assets. The profit to the issuer is a monthly servicing charge, S. If the issuer rating is AAA rated, we have:

$$P+I+S = \sum_i (P_i + I_i)$$

where P and P_i are monthly principal payments to collateral and the i-th tranche, respectively. Notice that the portfolio perspective generates useful formulations for performance attributes as well.

Exhibit 6: Portfolio View of CMOs

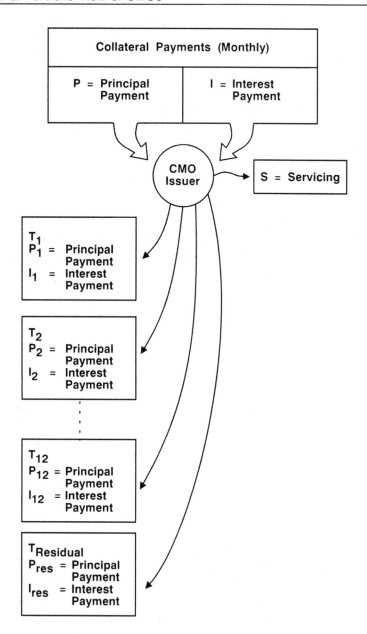

The value, V, of the bonds would follow $V = \sum_i w_i V_i$ where w_i = the weight of the ith tranche in the portfolio and V, V_i are the valuations of the collateral and i^{th} tranche, respectively. The portfolio perspective forces the "sum of the parts to equal the whole" and shows analytically how the valuation, in this example, is distributed to the tranches. This point is being emphasized to ward off any misconception about a CMO's risk level. It is sometimes thought that CMOs may be constructed in which all component tranches have lower risk of prepayments than the underlying collateral. This is simply not true. The risk may be redistributed so that some tranches receive less risk but in that case there must be some other tranche which receives more.

If the issuer is of a lower quality rating, AAA status can be obtained by overcollateralizing the CMO. For example, if the collateral principal is P = \$400.5 million, the tranches might then sum to $\sum P_i$ = \$400 million. It didn't take long in the evolution of CMOs before that extra \$0.5 million was bundled into yet another tranche, called the *residual* tranche. If the CMO has a residual tranche, we have:

$$P+I+S = \sum(P_i+I_i) + P_{res} + I_{res}$$

The residual tranche of a CMO is entitled to a portion of the surplus funds (if any) after all nonresidual tranches receive their principal and interest payments and the service fee to the issuer has been paid.

RESIDUALS

Originally if a CMO had a residual tranche, it had only one, it bore no coupon and was last in priority for principal payment. Exhibit 7a sketches the pay down of a hypothetical CMO with a residual tranche. Zero coupon and last to be paid made the residual tranche in this deal structure extremely risky.

Exhibit 7: CMO with Residual Tranche

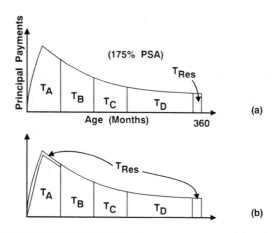

The generic description of residuals has changed considerably. In the present market, CMOs may have more than one residual tranche, it may bear interest and it may appear anywhere in the deal structure. But one attribute remains the same. A residual is entitled to a portion of the surplus cash flow (if any) after non-residual tranche principal and interest payments have been made.

Exhibit 7b shows a typical embedding of a residual tranche in a hypothetical five tranche CMO. It has concurrent pay down with the first tranche, T_A, for part of its life to help reduce risk relative to the generic residual class described above. It stops paying down in that priority level upon the death of T_A. It then appears last in priority for pay down. Suppose for this example the collateral totals $400.5 million with tranche original principals of $100 million for T_A, T_B, T_C and T_D while T_{res} has $0.5 million. The deal structure might be written as:

Deal structure exhibiting residual tranche
Pay the incoming collateral's principal to:

1. 0.35/400.5 to T_{res} and 100/400.5 to T_A until T_A is completely paid down.

2. T_B until completely paid down.

3. T_C until completely paid down.

4. T_D until completely paid down.

5. T_{res} until completely paid down.

These simple examples are presented to show the timing of residual payments. In this example the residual tranche has a small pay down early in the deal (step 1). It appears again at the very end of the deal for the final pay down. Its location in the pay down prioritization and its small size target it as a high-risk tranche. Most residuals are used to buffer potential risk created by floaters and accruals in CMOs.

SCHEDULED CLASSES

The tranches of CMOs may have scheduled principal repayment, somewhat in the spirit of traditional sinking fund securities. Scheduled principal repayment reduces the risk induced by collateral prepayment of principal. The increased risk protection may be against a range of prepayment values or against a single value. A planned amortization class (PAC) is a scheduled tranche protected against a range of prepayment values while a targeted amortization class (TAC) protects against a single value.

The Behavior of PACs

As seen in the previous examples, even tranches paid first take on some prepayment risk. Scheduled tranches in a CMO were introduced to further control prepayment risk. As the name implies these tranches guarantee principal pay down by specific schedules. The guarantee holds except in extreme (to be defined later) prepayment rate environments. PACs (planned amortization classes) are virtually risk free for an entire range of PSA prepayments. The shaded area in Exhibit 8a represents the minimum amount of principal the issuer would receive from the collateral so long as prepayments never fell below 75% nor rose above 300%. This shaded region is used to construct a schedule of principal payments for a PAC. In this example four tranches are formed where the first tranche to pay down is a PAC. Exhibit 8c shows the principal pay down to the tranches in a *normal* prepayment rate environment of 150% PSA. The deal structure found in the prospectus might read as follows:

Deal structure exhibiting a PAC and support tranche
Pay the incoming collateral's principal to:

1. T_A up to the amount shown in the shaded region of Exhibit 8c.

2. T_B, T_C and T_D sequentially until all are paid down.

3. T_A until completely paid down.

Scheduled tranches appear at least twice in a CMO deal. Here T_A occurs in step 1 as a scheduled tranche and step 3 as an un-scheduled tranche. T_A will probably not live long enough to pay down by step 3. However, there could be extreme prepayment rate environments where T_A is still alive after the deaths of T_B, T_C and T_D. In this case T_A would proceed to pay down as an un-scheduled tranche as in step 3.

T_A is risk free with respect to prepayments in the PSA prepay-ment range [75,300] of speeds[1]. A decrease in risk for T_A must be offset by an increase in risk in the remaining support tranches. T_B absorbs the least while T_D absorbs the most of this extra risk. Nor-mally the schedule for a PAC specifies the planned remaining principal balance at each payment date, not the planned principal payment at each date (there is a difference). In today's CMO mar-ket, one may find accrual, residual and floating-rate PACs.

---

[1] Since a PAC has a protection interval, the mathematical notation for interval is used when denoting the actual range. The convention used in this chapter is that the endpoint values (for example in [75,300] 75 and 300 are the endpoints) refer to the PSA speeds used in schedule construction.

Exhibit 8: Constructing a PAC

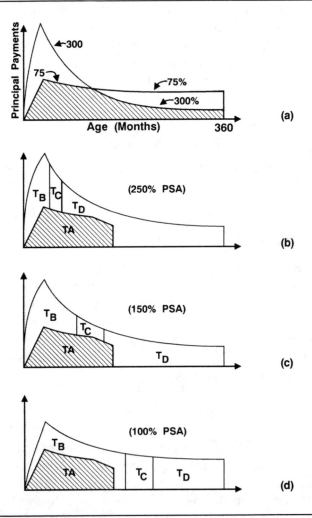

Exhibits 8b and 8d show the impact of *reasonable* prepayment changes on this four tranche CMO. Notice that the PACs pay down is unaffected by the change in prepayments from 100% to 250% PSA, while T_B, T_C and T_D all shorten. Since T_A is absorbing none of the prepayment risk in this range, we expect T_B to take on more of the excess risk and T_D most of the excess risk. Excess in this context is taken to mean the risk T_A avoids relative to an identically structured deal where T_A is non-scheduled, just like the other three tranches.

PAC Schedule Construction

Though PAC schedules are specified in the CMO prospectus, the mechanics of schedule construction are informative. The following outlines the procedure used to compute the tabulated values for a simple hypothetical PAC.

Consider a sequentially paid four tranche CMO with $400 million in underlying collateral. The four tranches T_1, T_2, T_3 and T_4 have original balances $125, $40, $75 and $160 (all in millions), respectively. T_1 is a PAC with protection range [75,275] PSA. The deal structure reads as:

Deal structure exhibiting PAC tranche
Pay the incoming collateral's principal to:

1. T_1 until its remaining balance is as scheduled (method of construction described below).

2. T_2, T_3 and T_4 sequentially until completely paid down.

3. T_1 until completely paid down.

The following method is used to construct the PACs schedule. Compute the collateral's expected cash flows at 75% PSA and 275% PSA (the PAC protection range endpoints) and call the series $CF_{75}(n)$ and $CF_{275}(n)$, respectively. The index n (n = 1, 2, 3.... 360) indicates the payment period. Cash flows are generated using standard amortization formulations with prepayments. Then define an interim cash flow series, $CF'(n)$ as:

$$CF'(n) = \min\{ CF_{75}(n), CF_{275}(n) \}$$

By construction, this cash flow bounds our PAC protection region. However, the resulting cash flows probably no longer sum to $400 million, so a scaler multiplier needs to be applied. Let:

$$B' = \sum_n CF'(n)$$

and define the cash flow series of interest as:

$$CF(n) = 400,000,000 \times CF'(n)/B'$$

This last operation simply assures us our collateral cash flow sums to the original balance of $400 million. Using this cash flow, we log the payments to tranches T_1 through T_4 based on the deal structure described in steps 1 to 3 above. We simply ignore the phrase in step 1 about T_1's schedule and pay it as a non-scheduled tranche. When all cash flows have been recorded, extract the cash flows for T_1. Those make up the PAC schedule.

Most PAC schedules specify the remaining principal balance of the payment period instead of principal to be paid per period. In the example above if prepayments exceed 275% PSA, the excess is directed sequentially to T_2, T_3 and T_4. It is possible that prepayments would be so high that T_4 would completely pay down while T_1 is still alive. In that situation, T_1 begins to pay down as a non-scheduled tranche. If prepayments are less than 75% PSA, the PAC will simply have a higher outstanding balance on the payment periods than is scheduled.

The Behavior of TACs

PACs have what is referred to as two-sided protection against adverse interest rate environments. Consider an interest rate environment producing a prepayment speed in the center of the PAC speed interval. The holder of that PAC is protected against both rising and falling prepayments, so long as prepayments stay within the protection range. TACs offer one-sided protection, the TAC owner is only protected against a rise in prepayments.

Exhibit 9b shows collateral principal pay down for a PSA speed of 175%. The four sections indicate the deal structure of a hypothetical CMO in a *normal* prepayment rate environment of 175% PSA. The TAC schedule is generated by using the expected collateral principal payments shown in Exhibit 9b. The deal may be structured as:

Deal structure exhibiting TAC tranche
Pay the incoming collateral's principal to:

1. T_A up to the amount shown in the shaded region of Exhibit 9b.

2. T_B, T_C and T_D sequentially until all are paid down.

3. T_A until completely paid down.

T_A has one-sided protection—against a rise in prepayments. It is guaranteed scheduled principal payments except in *extreme* conditions. Exhibit 9d indicates what extreme means for a speed of 600% PSA. The dashed line between Exhibit 9b and 9c shows how even the TAC will extend if prepayments go low enough. The dashed outline of Exhibit 9c is meant to indicate the scheduled pay down of T_A. Notice that T_D pays down before T_A in this environment. The value of 600% PSA was simply chosen as a likely speed where T_D would pay down before T_A. For an arbitrary TAC within a CMO, the actual speed where this schedule collapse occurs depends on how the deal is structured.

Just as with PACs, a TAC schedule normally specifies the targeted remaining principal balance at each date, not the targeted principal payment at each date. There are CMOs in today's market with accrual, residual and floating-rate TACs.

Exhibit 9: TAC Behavior

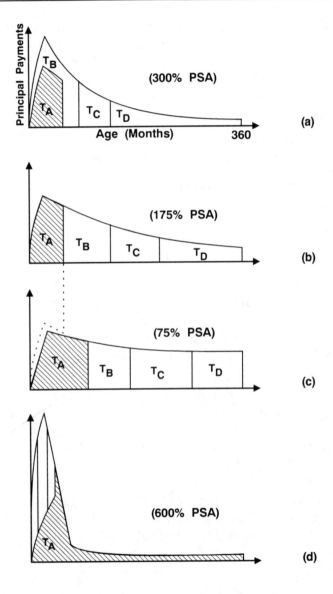

The deal is structured by diagram (b).

TAC Schedule Construction

TAC schedule construction is identical to PAC construction, only easier. Suppose in the PAC schedule construction discussion above that T_1 was actually a TAC with a target of 300% PSA. In this case, we simply generate one cash flow, $CF_{300}(n)$, at 300% PSA. There is no need to scale the cash flow series. Apply this collateral cash flow to the deal structure described in that example and the cash flow to T_1 defines the TAC schedule.

The schedule construction emphasizes the remark that TACs have only a one-sided prepayment protection against a rise in prepayments while a PAC has two-sided protection.

Comparing Scheduled Tranches

The above simple examples show that scheduled tranches have reduced exposure to prepayment risk. The direction of protection has only two categories, upside in a TAC versus two-sided in a PAC. However, the magnitude of protection is not so easily described. For example, consider a PAC whose protection interval is quoted to be [75,200]. As was mentioned earlier, if there is not enough principal to pay the PAC schedule, it simply receives less of a payment with virtually no penalties. The first PSA value where the schedule cannot be met will be lower than 75% PSA, the left hand endpoint of this PAC's protection interval. Exactly how much lower is contingent upon how the deal is structured. Specifically, PACs from two distinct CMOs even with the same quoted PAC range may behave quite differently outside of that protection range. A similar argument holds for TACs.

MULTIPLE SCHEDULED TRANCHES: 1

One method of creating CMOs with more than one PAC tranche is as follows (TACs follow the same method). The following hypothetical CMO has multiple PACs but all of them have the same protection interval.

Exhibit 10: Multiple PAC Construction

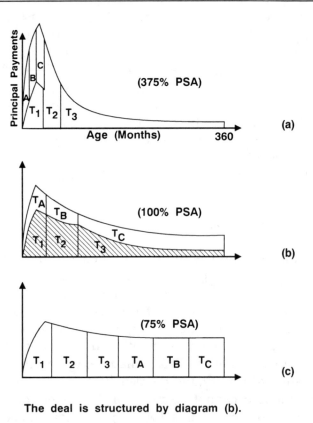

(a)

(b)

(c)

The deal is structured by diagram (b).

Exhibit 10b shows a CMO pay down with a PAC protection range carved out at [75,300]. T_1, T_2, and T_3 are all PACs with this same protection range. T_A, T_B and T_C are their support nonscheduled tranches. Exhibits 10a and 10c show what may happen in extreme conditions. The prospectus might read as follows:

Deal structure exhibiting multiple PACs with support tranches
Pay the incoming collateral's principal to:

1. T_1 up to the amount indicated by the shaded region of Exhibit 10b.

2. T_2 up to the amount indicated by the shaded region of Exhibit 10b.

3. T_3 up to the amount indicated by the shaded region of Exhibit 10b.

4. T_A, T_B and T_C sequentially until all are paid down.

5. T_1, T_2 and T_3 until completely paid down.

Though Exhibit 10 is meant to exemplify the methodology of multiple PAC constructs, one may also observe the affect of extreme prepayment environments on the PACs pay down. The PAC T_1 is affected the least while the support tranche, T_C, bears most of the prepayment risk.

MULTIPLE SCHEDULED TRANCHES: 2

An alternate method of creating CMOs with more than one PAC tranche is as follows. The following hypothetical CMO has two PACs with different protection intervals.

Exhibit 11a shows a CMO pay down with a PAC protection range carved out as [75,250]. From that a subregion is formed with protection interval [5,300] (Exhibit 11b). The final deal is structured schematically in Exhibit 11c. Tranches T_1 and T_2 are PACs while T_3 is a support tranche. The embedded tranche, T_1, has the maximum protection range and is referred to as a super PAC while the PAC from which it was carved, T_2, is called a subordinate PAC. The prospectus might read as follows:

Deal structure exhibiting super PAC tranche
Pay the incoming collateral principal to:

1. T_1 up to the amount indicated by the shaded region of Exhibit 11c.

2. T_2 up to the amount indicated by the shaded region of Exhibit 11c.

Exhibit 11: Super PAC Construction

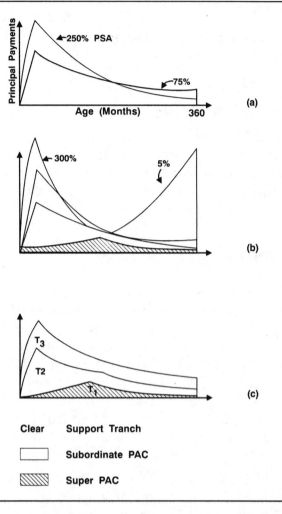

Clear	Support Tranch
☐	Subordinate PAC
▨	Super PAC

3. T₃ up to the amount indicated by the shaded region of Exhibit 11c.

4. T₁, T₂ and T₃ sequentially until all are paid down.

Super PACs were designed to carry even less risk than a traditional PAC. This is accomplished by using an extremely wide PAC range for the super PAC and then embedding it within another PAC. The important feature of this last item is not the fact that the support tranche is a PAC, the important feature is that there is a support tranche and generally a large one as measured by its outstanding balance relative to the entire deal. The greater the weight of the support tranche, the greater the protection. In this simple example prepayments would have to go much lower than 5% PSA before T_1 was affected since T_3 and T_2 serve as support tranches. The same holds true for extremely high prepayment environments, T_1 is virtually unaffected.

SUMMARY

There are many tranche types in today's CMO market which have not been mentioned in this chapter (one example is a toggle-Z tranche). However, this brief introduction to CMO constructs will hopefully enable the reader to easily assimilate the mechanics of new tranche types. As was stated in the introduction, one of the objectives of this chapter was to develop a set of criteria by which CMO tranches may be categorized. The following list of obvious items is suggested:

    i) coupon (zero, fixed or variable)

    ii) weight of the tranche

    iii) accrual vs non-accrual

    iv) scheduled vs non-scheduled

    v) residual

    vi) contingencies of interest and principal payments

Obviously all the items are necessary to uniquely describe a tranche, but are they sufficient? For example an accrual tranche in this chapter is described as a bond whose accrual period is *one* interval in time with initial point defined as a date contingent

upon the behavior of some neighboring tranche. If we simply substitute "set of intervals" for "interval" in our definition of accrual,
then we immediately have a "new" accrual tranche, the toggle-Z.
To just finish off this example, the toggle-Z is a tranche whose
accrual period is one or more finite intervals in time with endpoints contingent upon events as specified in the prospectus. The
reader may note that the details of item (vi) for actual CMOs can
be quite complex. Contingency conditions may be based on interest or prepayment rate environments or on the health of a
tranche's neighbors or on a variety of other (normally stochastic)
variables. It would seem that the rather simple list of items (i)
through (vi) enables one to uniquely describe most tranches in today's CMO market.

COMMENTS ON MODELING

Only a few things on CMO tranche valuation will be mentioned.
The valuation formulation for a fixed-income security with uncertain cash flows is computed as the expectation of the appropriate
stochastic cash flow formulation. The cash flows of a CMOs underlying collateral (those of the MBS) fall into this uncertainty
category.
    Consider for a moment the task of valuing a MBS, formidable
in and of itself. Modeling MBS's prepayments as a function of the
stochastic variable of interest rates is an active area of research in
the financial community. Assume, for the moment, a prepayment
model has been chosen. It would depend on interest rates (one,
two or multifactor model) as well as other factors. As a first cut,
assume no other factor dependence. That is, consider a prepayment model whose only stochastic dependence is on interest rates.
In this case the valuation as the expectation of future cash flows is
the expectation of a Markov process. The expectation, an integral
equation, may be solved by the Monte Carlo technique. As a further specialization one might use a single factor lognormal interest
rate model. The valuation solution could then be reduced to the

well known binomial method. Even if a more theoretically sound interest rate model is used, the assumptions imposed on the prepayment function (no path dependence) result in a valuation process which is Markov (a stochastic process exhibiting no path dependence). The advantage of this assumption is the one-to-one correspondence between the expectation of a Markov process and the solution of an equivalent PDE (partial differential equation). If each method (Monte Carlo and PDE solver) is implemented correctly and the same set of assumptions used both will generate the same valuation numbers. Of course, higher dimensional interest rate models will require longer computation times. Which method should be used, Monte Carlo or PDE solver? A rough rule of thumb is that valuation is more efficiently computed as the solution of the equivalent PDE for systems with less than five state variables. For more state variables, the Monte Carlo method should be used.

Now consider the case where a more sophisticated model of prepayments is used. In addition to dependence on interest rates, consider a model which also depends on the current remaining balance of the MBS (burnout factor). The valuation formulation is now path dependent due to the inclusion of the burnout factor. We can no longer assume the existence of an equivalent PDE for our expectation operator of valuation. For a limited number of non-Markov processes, of which the MBS valuation is one, it is still possible to equate the expectation operator to an equivalent PDE. A simplistic view is that the path dependence is "handled" by making the path dependent variable (in this case the remaining balance) an additional state variable. A single factor interest rate model would not generate a valuation PDE of dimension two, a two factor model equates to a three dimensional model, and so on.

Roughly, *if* an equivalent PDE can be obtained, each path dependent variable will add an additional dimension to the basic list of state variables. Something like a jump-Z tranche would add two or three state space variables depending upon how many principal pay down contingencies are specified in the prospectus. It also automatically inherits two or three additional state space variables for the interest rate model and prepayment function. Simple arithmetic dictates the Monte Carlo method as more efficient than PDE solution for the valuation of CMO tranches.

CHAPTER 25

STRIPPED MORTGAGE-BACKED SECURITIES

Lakhbir S. Hayre, DPhil
Director of Mortgage Research
Financial Strategies Group
Prudential Securities Inc.

Errol Mustafa, PhD
Vice President
Financial Strategies Group
Prudential Securities Inc.

As the mortgage pass-through market has matured, a number of derivative mortgage products have been introduced to appeal to

The authors would like to thank Patricia Brehm, who played a major role in the development and writing of this chapter; Massoud Heidari, Gary Isaacs, and Vincent Pica for their valuable comments; Vito Lodato for his help with the graphics and data analysis; and Gladys Cardona, Lisa Pendergast, and Laura Campbell for assistance in the preparation of this chapter.

different investors of the fixed-income market. In 1983, the Federal Home Loan Mortgage Corporation (FHLMC) launched the Collateralized Mortgage Obligation (CMO) structure that enabled issuers to tailor-make mortgage securities according to investor coupon, maturity, and prepayment risk specifications. In July 1986, the Federal National Mortgage Association (FNMA) introduced a new addition to the mortgage security product line—Stripped Mortgage-Backed Securities (SMBSs). By redistributing portions of the interest and/or principal cash flows from a pool of mortgage loans to two or more SMBSs, FNMA developed a new class of mortgage securities that enabled investors to take strong market positions on expected movements in prepayment and interest rates.

SMBSs are highly sensitive to changes in prevailing interest and prepayment rates and tend to display asymmetric returns. SMBS certificates that are allocated large proportions or all of the underlying principal cash flows tend to display very attractive *bullish* return profiles. As market rates drop and prepayments on the underlying collateral increase, the return of these SMBSs will be greatly enhanced, since principal cash flows will be returned earlier than expected. Conversely, SMBSs that are entitled to a large percentage or all of the interest cash flows have very appealing *bearish* return characteristics, since greater amounts of interest cash flows are generated when prepayments of principal decrease (typically when market rates increase).

This chapter is divided into three sections. The first section provides an overview of the SMBS market and discusses the various types of SMBSs. The second section examines the investment characteristics of SMBSs. A review of the fundamentals of mortgage cash flows is first presented, followed by an investigation of the price, OAS, total rate of return, performance, effective duration, and convexity characteristics of SMBSs. The third section describes various SMBS applications and the use of SMBSs in portfolio hedging strategies.

OVERVIEW OF THE STRIPPED MORTGAGE-BACKED SECURITIES (SMBS) MARKET

Size of the SMBS Market

The SMBS market has grown substantially since the introduction of the first SMBS in July 1986 (see Exhibit 1). In total, an estimated $34.8 billion SMBSs in 134 issues have come to market and, as of July 1, 1990, approximately $28.2 billion SMBSs were outstanding. FNMA has been the predominant issuer of SMBSs. The remainder of new SMBSs have been issued by private concerns and, more recently, FHLMC.

Exhibit 1: Issuance of SMBSs (July 1986 through June 1990)

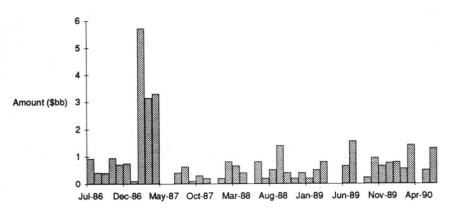

Types of SMBSs

Strip securities exist in various forms. The first and earliest type of mortgage strip securities is called *synthetic-coupon pass-through securities*. Synthetic-coupon pass-throughs receive fixed proportions of the principal and interest cash flow from a pool of underlying mortgage loans. Synthetic-coupon pass-throughs were introduced by FNMA in mid-1986 through its "Alphabet" Strip Program. *IOs and POs*, the second and most common type of strip security, were introduced by FNMA in January 1987. IOs and POs receive, respectively, only the interest or only the principal cash flow from the underlying mortgage collateral. More recently, a third type of strip security, the *CMO strip*, has become popular among issuers and investors. As implied by their name, CMO strips are tranches within a CMO issue that receive only principal cash flows or have synthetically high coupon rates.

Development of the SMBS Market

The First Mortgage Strips—FNMA SMBS "Alphabet" Strip Securities. FNMA pioneered the first stripped mortgage security in July 1986 through its newly created SMBS Program. For each issue of SMBS Series A through L, FNMA pooled existing FHA/VA and GPM mortgage loans that had been held in its portfolio and issued two SMBS pass-through certificates representing ownership interests in proportions of the interest and principal cash flows from the underlying mortgage loan pool. Alphabet strips were subsequently called synthetic discount- and premium-coupon securities since the coupon rate of the alphabet strip was quoted as a percentage of the total principal balance of the issue.[1] In total,

---

[1] For example, a strip that receives 75% interest and 50% principal of the cash flow from a FNMA 10% would be a synthetic 15% coupon security, since the 7.50% coupon is expressed as 100% of principal (i.e., 7.50% coupon/50% principal = 15.00% coupon/100% principal). By the same logic, a strip security from a FNMA 10% that receives 50% interest and 1% principal would be a 5,000% coupon security.

twelve alphabet strip deals were issued by FNMA in 1986, totaling $2.9 billion.

The FNMA SMBS Trust Program and IOs and POs. The successive and current FNMA strip program, the SMBS Trust Program begun in 1987, provides a vehicle through which deal managers (e.g., investment banks) can swap FNMA pass-throughs for FNMA SMBS Trust certificates. In the swapping process, eligible FNMA pass-through securities submitted by the deal manager are consolidated by FNMA into one FNMA Megapool Trust. In return, FNMA distributes to the deal manager two similarly denominated SMBS certificates evidencing ownership in the requested proportions of that FNMA Megapool Trust's principal and interest cash flows.[2]

To date, the majority of FNMA SMBS Trusts have contained IO and PO securities. IOs and POs represent the most leveraged means of capturing the asymmetric performance characteristics of the two cash flow components of mortgage securities. Recently, however, the SMBS market has witnessed a resurgence in synthetic-coupon security issuance (see FNMA Trust 66, 68, and 72). Although IOs and POs can be combined in different ratios to create synthetic-coupon securities, some investors have shown a preference for one-certificate synthetic securities due to their bookkeeping ease.

To promote liquidity in the SMBS Market, all FNMA SMBS certificates (except FNMA SMBS Series L) have a unique conversion feature that enables like-denominations of both classes of a FNMA SMBS issue or Trust to be exchanged on the book-entry system of the Federal Reserve Banks for like-denominations of FNMA MBS certificates or Megapool certificates. The Federal Reserve generally charges an administration fee for this service. Any

---

[2] FNMA tightly restricts the type of collateral that can be placed in Trust. For example, all mortgage securities must have the same prefix (be of the same loan type) and be within certain WAC and WAM ranges to correspond with preliminary pricing. Moreover, the minimum initial principal balance of each SMBS Trust must be $200 million.

converted FNMA MBS certificate or Megapool certificate is subsequently *not* exchangeable for SMBS certificates. Because of the potential for profitable arbitrages, the aggregate price of the two classes of any same FNMA issue or Trust tends to be slightly higher than the price of a comparable-coupon and remaining-term FNMA pass-through certificate.

All FNMA SMBS pass-throughs (alphabets and Trusts) have the same payment structure, payment delays, and FNMA guarantee as regular FNMA pass-throughs. Payment histories and other relevant information can be obtained by referencing the pool number of the Megapool Trust. As of July 1, 1990, eighty-two FNMA SMBS Trust deals have come to market, totaling approximately $23.1 billion.

Private Issuance. Investment firms began to issue private-label SMBSs in late 1986. To date, it is estimated that twenty-six private-label SMBS issues totaling approximately $6.5 billion have been brought to market. Many of these private-label SMBSs were issued through REMIC structures. Since one class of a REMIC issue must be designated the residual interest, the super-premium coupon class of many of these private-label SMBSs is often the residual interest of the REMIC deal. Unlike investing in FNMA SMBSs, investors who purchase these residual securities are responsible for the tax consequences of the entire REMIC issue.

Recent Developments in the SMBS Market

A number of recent developments have occurred in the SMBS market that should further enhance its depth and efficiency. Among them are:

PO-Collateralized CMOs. Profitable arbitrage opportunities have led to the recent introduction of CMO securities collateralized by POs. PO-collateralized CMOs allocate the cash flow from underlying PO securities between several CMO tranches with different maturities and payment patterns. The potential for profitable arbitrages with PO securities has enhanced the efficiency of the SMBS market by effectively placing a floor on the price potential of POs and a price ceiling on corresponding IOs in a given market environment. To date, forty-six PO-collateralized CMOs totaling approximately $12 billion have been issued by FNMA and private issuers.

CMO Strip Securities. Strip securities are increasingly included in CMO issues as regular-interest (nonresidual) CMO tranches. CMO strip securities that pay only principal or large proportions of interest cash flows (relative to principal cash flows) over the underlying mortgage collateral's life are termed PO securities and "high-interest" securities,[3] respectively, and tend to have performance characteristics similar to FNMA SMBSs. Other types of CMO strip securities receive initial and ongoing collateral principal or interest cash flows after other classes in the CMO issue are retired or have been paid. These types of strip CMO securities are structured as PO or "high-interest" PACs, TACs or Super-POs, and perform differently from FNMA SMBSs.

FHLMC Stripped Giant Program. FHLMC has recently become a participant in the SMBS market. In October 1989, FHLMC announced its Stripped Giant Mortgage Participation Certificate Program. As of July 1, 1990, FHLMC had issued fourteen FHLMC Giant PO and IO PCs totaling approximately $2.3 billion.

FHLMC's Stripped Giant Program is similar to FNMA's swap SMBS Trust Program. Deal managers submit FHLMC PCs to FHLMC; FHLMC, in turn, aggregates these PCs into Giant pools and issues Strip Giant PCs representing desired proportions of principal and interest to the deal manager. All FHLMC Strip PCs

---

[3] Since regular interests of a CMO issue currently must have a notional principal balance to qualify for REMIC tax status, true IO CMO securities do not exist. Typically, 99.5% of the initial value of a high-interest security is comprised of interest cash flows and .5% is comprised of principal.

have the same payment structure, payment delays, and payment guarantee as regular FHLMC PCs. Like FNMA Smbss, FHLMC Giant Strip IOs and POs have a conversion feature that allows them to be exchanged for similarly denominated FHLMC PCs. Characteristics of each FHLMC Giant Strip issue can be referenced by their pool number. Thirty-year and fifteen-year FHLMC IO securities are identified by the FHLMC prefix 90 and 92, respectively, while thirty-year and fifteen-year PO or synthetic securities have 80 and 82 prefixes, respectively.

GNMA Collateral for FNMA SMBSs. FNMA recently began to issue SMBSs collateralized by GNMA pass-through certificates. Since the beginning of 1990, FNMA has issued five trusts (FNMA SMBS Trusts 70, 71, 73, 74, and 78) that have had underlying GNMA collateral. The increased availability of GNMA SMBSs should broaden further the investor base of SMBSs, enhance the liquidity of the SMBS market, and increase the number of hedging alternatives available to GNMA investors.

Buyers of SMBSs

The asymmetric returns of SMBSs appeal to a broad variety of investors. SMBSs can be used effectively to hedge interest rate and prepayment exposure of other types of mortgage securities, such as CMO residuals and premium-coupon mortgage pass-through securities. SMBSs also can be combined with other fixed-income securities such as U.S. Treasuries and mortgage securities to enhance the total return of the portfolio in varying interest rate scenarios. Insurance companies and pension funds with conservative duration-matching needs frequently use SMBSs as a method of tailoring their investment portfolio to meet the duration of liabilities, and thus minimize interest rate risk.

SMBSs are used by various types of investors to accomplish their investment objectives. Insurance companies, pension funds, money managers, and other total rate-of-return accounts use

SMBSs to improve the return of their fixed-income portfolios. PO securities, which tend to have long durations, enable pension funds to manage more effectively the duration of their portfolios. Thrift institutions and mortgage bankers often use PO securities to hedge their servicing portfolios or use IO securities as a substitute for servicing income.[4]

INVESTMENT CHARACTERISTICS

SMBSs enable investors to capture the performance characteristics of the principal or interest components of the cash flows of mortgage pass-through securities. These individual components display contrasting responses to changes in market rates and prepayment rates. Principal-only (PO) SMBSs are bullish instruments, outperforming mortgage pass-throughs in declining interest rate environments. Interest-only (IO) SMBSs are bearish investments that can be used as a hedge against rising interest rates.

Variation of Interest and Principal Components with Prepayments

The cash flows that an MBS investor receives each month consist of principal and interest payments from a large group of homeowners. The proportion of principal and interest in the total payment varies, depending on the prepayment level of the mortgage pool. Exhibit 2 illustrates these cash flows for a $1 million thirty-year FNMA 9.5% pass-through security at various PSA prepayment speeds.

The top portion of Exhibit 2 shows the interest component and the lower portion shows the principal component of the monthly cash flows. Since the interest is proportional to the outstanding

---

[4] According to the applicable risk-based capital guidelines, strip securities that are backed by agency (FNMA, FHLMC and GNMA) pass-through securities (agency-issue or private-label issue) are in the 100% risk-based category for thrift institutions and commercial banks.

Exhibit 2: Interest and Principal for a FNMA 9.5% Pass-Through at Various Prepayment Speeds

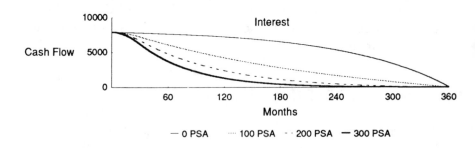

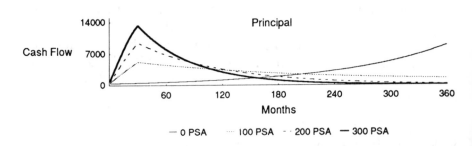

balance, the top part of Exhibit 2 also can be viewed as showing the decline in the mortgage balance at the various prepayment speeds.

At a zero prepayment level, the interest and principal cash flows in Exhibit 2 compose a normal amortization schedule. In the earlier months of the security's life, the cash flows primarily contain interest payments. This occurs because interest payments are calculated based on the outstanding principal balance remaining on the mortgage loans at the beginning of each month. As the mortgage loans amortize, the cash flows increasingly reflect the payment of principal. Towards the end of the security's life, principal payments make up the the bulk of the cash flows.

Prepayments of principal significantly alter the principal and interest cash flows received by the mortgage pass-through investor. Homeowners who prepay all or part of their mortgage loans return more principal to the investor in the earlier years of the mortgage security. All else being equal, an increase in prepayments has two effects:

1. The time remaining until return of principal is reduced, as shown in Exhibit 2. At 100% PSA, the average life of the principal cash flows is 12.4 years, whereas at faster speeds of 200% PSA and 300% PSA, principal is returned in average time periods of 8.2 years and 6 years, respectively.

2. The total amount of interest cash flows is reduced, which also is illustrated in Exhibit 2. This occurs because interest payments are calculated based on the amount of principal outstanding at the beginning of each month, and higher prepayment levels reduce the amount of principal outstanding.

Effect of Prepayment Changes on Value

A mortgage pass-through represents the combined value of the interest and principal cash flows. The effects of prepayments on the present value of each of these components tend to offset each other. Increases in prepayments reduce the time remaining until repayment of principal. The sooner the principal is repaid, the higher the present value of the principal. Conversely, since increasing levels of prepayments reduce interest cash flows, the value of the interest decreases.

Thus, the interest and principal cash flows individually are much more sensitive to prepayment changes than the combined mortgage pass-through. This is illustrated in Exhibit 3, which shows the present values of the principal and interest components of a FNMA 9.5% pass-through at various prepayment levels.

Exhibit 3: Present Values of Principal and Interest Components of Cash Flows at Various Prepayment Speeds

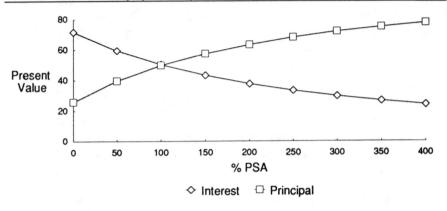

Note: A constant bond-equivalent discount rate of 10% was used to obtain the present values.

The greater sensitivity of IOs and POs to prepayment changes is further illustrated in Exhibit 4, which shows the realized yields to maturity (or internal rates of return) for the FNMA Trust 63 IO and PO and for the underlying collateral for given purchase prices.

The IO and PO reflect sharply contrasting responses to prepayment changes; the IO's yield falls sharply as prepayments increase, while the PO's yield falls sharply as prepayments decrease. The yield of the underlying collateral is, on the other hand, relatively stable, since it is priced close to par.

Price Performance of SMBSs

The discussion above indicates that prepayment speeds are by far the most important determinant of the value of an SMBS. Since the price response of an SMBS to interest rate changes is determined, to a large extent, by how the collateral's prepayment speed is affected by the interest rate changes, we will start with a discussion of mortgage prepayment behavior.

Exhibit 4: Realized Yields to Maturity for FNMA Trust 63 IO and PO and Collateral at Various Prepayment Speeds

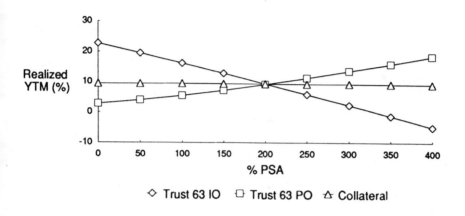

◇ Trust 63 IO   □ Trust 63 PO   △ Collateral

The Prepayment S-Curve. The prepayment speed of an MBS is a function of the security's characteristics (such as coupon and age), interest rates, and other economic and demographic variables. While detailed prepayment projections generally require an econometric model, the investor can obtain some insight into the likely behavior of an SMBS by examining the spread between the collateral's gross coupon and current mortgage rates.

This spread is generally the most important variable in determining prepayment speeds. With respect to this spread, prepayment speeds have an "S" shape; speeds are fairly flat for discount coupons (when the spread is negative and prepayments are caused mainly by housing turnover), start increasing when the spread becomes positive, surge rapidly until the spread is several hundred basis points, and then level off when the security is a high premium. At this point, there is already substantial economic incentive for mortgage holders to refinance, and further increases in the spread lead to only marginal increases in refinancing activity. This S-curve is illustrated in Exhibit 5, which shows projected prepayments for the FNMA 9.5% collateral of FNMA Trust 63 for

---

Exhibit 5: Projected Prepayments for FNMA 9.5s

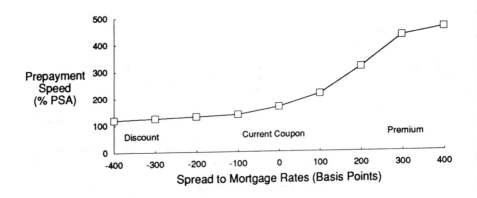

---

specified changes in mortgage rates. In the remainder of this section, we make repeated references to Exhibit 5, as the performance of an SMBS can be explained to a large extent by the position of its collateral on the prepayment S-curve.[5]

---

[5] However, the investor should note that not all aspects of prepayment behavior are explained by the spread between the coupon and the mortgage rate. The projected prepayments shown in Exhibit 5 are long-term averages. Month-to-month prepayment rates vary (for example, due to seasonality) even if mortgage rates do not change.

If a substantial and sustained decline in mortgage rates occurs, then mortgage holders exposed to refinancing incentives for the first time initially exhibit a sharp increase in prepayments. This gradually decreases as the homeowners most anxious and able to refinance do so. This non-interest rate-related decline in the prepayment speeds of premium coupons usually is referred to as "burnout." The projected speeds shown in the declining-rate scenarios are the averages of the high early speeds and lower later speeds.

For seasoned coupons that have experienced a heavy refinancing period, burnout implies that prepayments may be less responsive to declines in interest rates. This applies to the majority of premium coupons currently outstanding.

The age effect on prepayments is well known. Prepayment speeds are low for new mortgages and increase gradually until the mortgages are two to three years old, after which the age is less important. This means that, other things being equal, an IO is worth more if it is collateralized by new FNMA 9s, for example, than by seasoned FNMA 9s.

Exhibit 6: Projected Prices for FNMA Trust 63 IO and PO

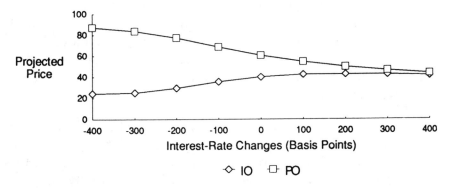

Projected Price Behavior. Exhibit 6 gives projected price paths for the FNMA Trust 63 IO and PO for parallel interest rate shifts.[6] The FNMA 9.5% collateral used in FNMA Trust 63 has a gross coupon (or WAC) of 10.28%, which was close to current mortgage rates at the time of writing. Thus, the collateral is essentially a current coupon, and the projected price behavior of the SMBSs as interest rates change can be explained largely by the prepayment S-curve in Exhibit 5.

- As rates drop from current levels, the FNMA 9.5% collateral begins to experience sharp increases in prepayments. Compounded by lower discount rates, this causes substantial price appreciation for the PO. For the IO, how-

---

[6] The prices are calculated to give an option-adjusted spread (OAS) of 100 basis points in all cases. A discussion of OAS analysis is given in the next section. Note that if it is also priced at an OAS of 100 basis points, the collateral price is just the sum of the IO and PO prices.

ever, the higher prepayments outweigh the lower discount rates, and the net result is a price decline.

*   If rates drop by several hundred basis points, the FNMA
    9.5% becomes a high-premium coupon, and prepayments
    plateau. The rates of price appreciation of the PO and
    price depreciation of the IO both decrease. Eventually the
    IO's price starts to increase, as the effect of lower dis-
    count rates start to outweigh the effect of marginal in-
    creases in prepayments.

*   If rates rise, the slower prepayments and higher discount
    rates combine to cause a steep drop in the price of the
    PO. The IO is aided initially by the slower prepayments,
    giving the IO negative duration, but eventually prepay-
    ments plateau on the lower side of the prepayment S-
    curve, and the IO's price begins to decrease.

Effective Duration and Convexity. Exhibit 6 indicates that for current or low-premium collateral, POs tend to have large, positive
effective durations, whereas IOs have large, negative effective durations.[7] For high-premium or deep-discount collateral whose prepayments are fairly insensitive to small interest rate changes, both
POs and IOs are similar to fixed cash flow securities and have
positive durations. This is illustrated in Exhibit 7, which shows the
effective durations of the Trust 63 IO and PO obtained using the
projected price paths in Exhibit 6.

The effective durations in Exhibit 7 reflect the price paths in
Exhibit 6:

*   For the PO, as rates decline, the effective duration in-
    itially increases, reflecting its rapid price appreciation as
    prepayments surge. Note that this is in complete contrast
    to traditional measures such as Macaulay or modified du-

---

[7] Effective duration is a measure of the proportional price change if interest rates
change by a small amount.

Exhibit 7: Effective Durations of FNMA Trust 63 IO and PO

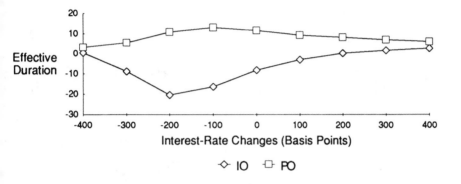

ration, which, reflecting the shortening maturity of the PO, would actually decrease. As rates continue to drop, the PO's effective duration levels off and then decreases, reflecting both a leveling off of prepayments and the fact that, to calculate the effective duration, we are dividing by an increasing price. If rates increase, the PO's duration decreases but remains positive.

- For the IO, the effective duration is initially negative and decreases rapidly as rates drop, before eventually increasing and becoming positive after prepayments plateau. If rates increase, the duration increases and eventually becomes positive.

Convexity measures the rate of change of duration and is useful in indicating whether the trend in price change is likely to accelerate or decelerate. It is calculated by comparing the price change if interest rates decrease with the price change if rates in-

---

Exhibit 8: Convexities of FNMA Trust 63 IO and PO

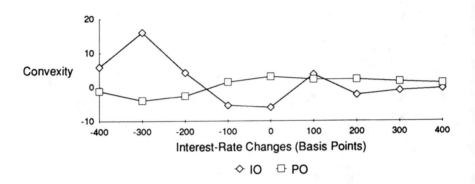

---

crease.[8] Exhibit 8 shows the convexities obtained using the pro-jected prices in Exhibit 6.

Comparing Exhibit 8 with Exhibits 6 and 7 shows that the con-vexity indicates how the duration is changing. When the duration is increasing (as in the case of the PO when rates begin to decline from the initial value), the convexity is positive, and when the du-ration is decreasing, the convexity is negative. For example, the IO's convexity is initially negative but begins to increase after rates fall by more than 100 basis points; although the duration is still negative at 200 basis points, the positive convexity indicates that the duration is increasing. The peak in the convexity of the IO at a change of 300 basis points indicates that the *rate* of increase in its duration is greatest at this point, as shown in Exhibit 7; the slope of the IO's duration curve is higher from 200 to 300 than from 300 to 400.

---

[8] Convexity is calculated by comparing the price changes if rates move up or down by small amounts.

In summary, the prepayment S-curve implies that for SMBSs collateralized by:

- *Current or discount pass-throughs* (including the majority of SMBSs issued to date): the PO has substantial upside potential and little downside risk, while the converse is true for IOs;

- *Low premiums*: there is somewhat comparable upside potential and downside risk;

- *High premiums*: the PO has little upside potential and significant downside risk, whereas the reverse is true for IOs.

Since most SMBSs issued to date are collateralized by current or discount coupons, this asymmetry in potential performance explains why IOs tend to be priced at much higher yields than POs.

Pricing of SMBSs and Option-Adjusted Spreads

The strong dependence of SMBS cash flows on future prepayment rates, combined with the typically asymmetric response of prepayments to interest rate changes, make traditional measures of return such as yield to maturity of limited usefulness in analyzing or pricing SMBSs. The most common method of pricing SMBSs is with OASs. OAS analysis uses probabilistic methods to evaluate the security over the full range of interest rate paths that may occur over its term. The impact of prepayment variations on the security's cash flows is factored into the analysis. The OAS is the resulting average spread over Treasuries provided by the security.[9] It gives a long-term average value of the security assuming a market-neutral viewpoint on interest rates.

---

[9] For more detailed descriptions of the OAS and how it is calculated, see Chapter 27.

Exhibit 9: OAS Analysis of SMBSs

OAS Analysis of SMBSs

						OAS @ Vol.		Opt.
		Price	YTM	WAL	SPD/Tsy.	0%	15%	Cost
FNMA Trust 63	PO	54-16	9.18	8.4	8	8	100	–92
FN Coll.	IO	41-22	12.04	8.4	294	300	100	200
WAM 25-08 Years Proj. PSA: 147%	PT	96-06	10.38	8.4	128	130	100	30
CMO Trust 25PO	PO	63-11	10.72	5.3	163	167	100	67
GN 12.5% Coll.	IO	43-24	10.11	5.3	102	105	100	5
WAM 23-04 Years Proj. PSA: 264%	PT	107-03	10.48	5.3	139	142	100	42

Note: PT stands for pass-through, projected prepayment speeds are obtained from the Prudential-Bache Prepayment Model; and the option cost is the difference in OASs at short-rate volatilities of 9% and 15% per annum. Analysis based on yield curve from close on May 20, 1990.

Exhibit 9 shows the use of OAS analysis for FNMA Trust 63 and the private-issue CMO Trust 25, and the underlying pass-through collateral. In each case, the price is chosen to give an OAS of 100 basis points at a 15% annual volatility of short-term interest rates. Also shown are the yields to maturity and standard spreads over the WAL Treasury at these prices, using a projected prepayment speed.

The OAS at a 0% volatility when mortgage rates stay at current levels, is typically close to the standard Treasury spread. The difference between the OASs at 0% and 15% volatilities, which we label the *option cost*, is a measure of the impact of prepayment variations on a security for the given level of interest rate volatility. The option cost, to a large extent, does not depend on the pricing level or the absolute level of prepayment projections (although it does depend on the slope, or response, of prepayment projections to interest rate changes). Hence, the option cost is a measure of the intrinsic effect of likely interest rate changes on an SMBS.

Before discussing the option costs in Exhibit 9, note that, in general, interest rate and prepayment variations have two effects on an MBS:

1. For any callable security, being called in a low interest rate environment typically has an adverse effect, since a dollar of principal of the security in general would be worth more than the price at which it is being returned. (An exception is a mortgage prepayment resulting from housing turnover, when the call could be uneconomic from the call-holder's point of view.) To put it another way, the principal that is being returned typically has to be reinvested at yields lower than that provided by the existing security.

2. For MBSs priced at a discount or a premium, changes in prepayments result in the discount or premium being received sooner or later than anticipated. This may mitigate or reinforce the call effect discussed in (1).

In general, the first effect is much more important than the second; however, for certain deep-discount securities, such as POs, the second effect may at times outweigh the first. The net result of the two effects depends on the position of the collateral on the prepayment curve shown in Exhibit 5.

- The majority of actively traded SMBSs are collateralized by *current* or *discount* coupons. FNMA Trust 63, shown in Exhibit 9, illustrates the characteristics typical of these SMBSs. For discount or current-coupon collateral, prepayments are unlikely to fall significantly, but could increase dramatically if there is a substantial decrease in interest rates. This asymmetry means that the PO is, on average, likely to gain significantly from variations in prepayment speeds. The option cost for the PO is usually negative, i.e., the PO *gains* from interest rate volatility, indicating that the benefits of faster return of principal outweigh the generic negative effects of being called in low interest rate environments. On the other hand, the underlying collateral tends to have a positive (but usually small in the case of discount collateral) option cost; the negative effects of being called when rates are low outweigh the benefits of faster return of principal. Finally, the IO typically has a large positive option cost; the asymmetric nature of likely prepayment changes, discussed above, means that the IO gains little if interest rates increase (since prepayments will not decrease significantly), while a substantial decline in rates is likely to lead to a surge in prepayments and a drop in interest cash flows.

- A less typical example of an SMBS is provided by the private issue CMO Trust 25, collateralized by seasoned GNMA 12.5s. For *premium* collateral, there is, generally speaking, potential for both increases and decreases in prepayments, and the net effect of prepayment variations will depend on the particular coupon and prevailing mortgage rates. Seasoned premiums, for example, will not have potential for substantial increases in speeds, and hence, the CMO Trust 25 PO has a positive option cost. The collateral has a positive option cost for the same reasons. The IO has an option cost close to zero, indicating that the call effects and prepayment variations more or less cancel each other.

The importance of likely variations in prepayments makes the standard yield to maturity of very little relevance in pricing SMBSs, and therefore, they tend to be priced (as in Exhibit 9) on an OAS basis. Thus, while all the SMBSs in Exhibit 9 are priced at the same OAS, the yields to maturity differ widely. For example, the Trust 63 PO has a yield to maturity of only 9.18% compared with a yield to maturity of 12.04% for the Trust 63 IO.

Holding-Period Analysis

The OAS provides a measure of the long-term average value of a security, assuming a market-neutral viewpoint about interest rates. An alternative, complementary method is to analyze the security across a range of specified interest rate environments and for a given holding period. This provides an investment profile of the security and allows an assessment of the likely return from the security over a given horizon and for a specific market outlook. This is particularly useful for SMBSs, since their returns are especially dependent on interest rate behavior.

For shorter holding periods, the horizon salvage price is often the key determinant of the total holding period return. As discussed above, OAS analysis is generally the preferred method for calculating projected SMBS prices. A common approach is to calculate the current OAS and assume that it remains constant in order to obtain horizon prices. However, the SMBS market is not always efficiently priced due to technical factors. Thus, assuming that OASs stay constant may result in transferring current mispricings into the calculation of horizon salvage prices.

A number of historical studies have indicated a high degree of correlation between OASs and subsequent six-month or twelve-month holding period returns.[10] This may occur because pricing disparities often correct themselves over a six- or twelve-month period. Thus, securities with higher than average OASs at the beginning of a period often may experience more price appreciation than similar securities with lower OASs. To reflect this empirical behavior in the total-return calculation, the horizon price can be obtained using an OAS that reflects a current average OAS for similar securities rather than the security's current OAS. This is the approach used here.

Exhibit 10 gives a one-year horizon analysis for the FNMA Trust 63 PO and a similar-duration Treasury STRIP. The current

---

[10] One such study is described in Chapter 27.

Exhibit 10: One-Year Horizon Analysis for the Trust 63 PO and a Treasury STRIP

				Interest-Rate Move (Bps.)				
		-300	*-200*	*-100*	*0*	*100*	*200*	*300*
	Proj. PSA	441	310	185	150	132	126	120
Trust 63 PO	YTM	29.55	18.96	11.08	9.27	8.42	8.13	7.88
Price: 54-09	Hor. Price	79-30	71-29	62-23	55-27	50-28	47-05	44-05
	Total Return	50.40	38.45	21.40	10.10	1.77	-4.48	-9.69
Tsy. STRIP	YTM	9.14	9.14	9.14	9.14	9.14	9.14	9.14
of 5/15/01	Hor. Price	54.48	49.43	44.86	40.74	37.01	33.64	30.59
Price: 40.581	Total Return	41.96	30.47	19.57	9.24	-0.56	-9.86	-18.68
PO Advantage (Bps.)		844	798	183	86	233	538	899

Note: A parallel shift in interest rates is assumed to occur gradually over one year. The PO prices are calculated assuming an OAS of 100 basis points and a short-rate volatility of 15%. The initial reinvestment rate is assumed to be 8.5%.

Analysis based on prices and yield curve at close on April 23, 1990.

OAS of the PO is 110 basis points; the horizon prices are obtained assuming an OAS of 100 basis points.[11]

As Exhibit 10 makes clear, both the PO and the Treasury STRIP are powerful bullish instruments. However, while at current rate levels the returns from the two instruments are not too different, the PO performs much better in both rising and declining interest rate environments. If rates increase, both securities perform very poorly, but the PO does slightly better because the return of principal mitigates the effect of price declines, and also allows some advantage to be taken of higher reinvestment rates.

If rates decline, both the Treasury STRIP and the PO experience rapid price appreciation. However, the increase in prepay-

---

[11] Using the same OAS to obtain the horizon price in all scenarios may be questionable, but is done for simplicity. If the OAS is a risk premium over the risk-free rate, investors may well demand a different risk premium when the risk-free rate is 6% than when it is 12%.

ments and the resulting return of principal at par for the PO give it significantly superior returns.

It should be noted that for a one-year holding period, the PO's horizon return varies more than the yield to maturity as interest rates change, reflecting the changes in the horizon price. For longer holding periods, the importance of the salvage price decreases and the horizon returns will be more in line with the yields to maturity in Exhibit 10.

Probability-Weighted Total Returns. A horizon analysis such as the one in Exhibit 10 provides a useful investment profile of the security for short-term investors. However, most investors would not consider the different interest-rate changes to be equally probable. A synthesis of the scenario returns that incorporates some assessment of the likelihoods of the different interest rate moves can provide a useful complement to the analysis in Exhibit 10. An example is given in Exhibit 11, which shows probability-weighted

Exhibit 11: Probability-Weighted One-Year Total Returns (%)

	Interest-Rate Move (Bps.)						
	-300	-200	-100	0	100	200	300
Trust 63 PO	50.40	38.45	21.40	10.10	1.77	-4.48	-9.69
Tsy. STRIP 5/01	41.93	30.47	19.57	9.24	-0.56	-9.86	-18.68

Probability Weights (%)							
Bearish	0.4	3.6	12.3	21.6	23.8	18.8	19.6
Neutral	2.5	11.3	22.9	26.2	19.8	10.9	6.5
Bullish	11.0	24.2	28.9	20.9	10.2	3.6	1.2

Probability-Weighted Returns (%)	Scenario		
	Bearish	Neutral	Bullish
Trust 63 PO	4.08	12.38	23.05
Tsy. STR	0.02	8.99	18.94

Note: The probability weights are calculated assuming a lognormal distribution with a volatility of 15%. For the bearish scenario, the median of the distribution at the horizon is assumed to be 100 basis points higher than the initial mortgage rate; for the neutral scenario, it is equal to the initial mortgage rate; for the bullish scenario, it is 100 basis points lower.

total returns for the two securities in Exhibit 10 under three interest rate outlooks: neutral (rates equally likely to increase or decrease), bullish (rates expected to decrease by 100 basis points over the next year), and bearish (rates expected to increase by 100 basis points over the next year). In each case, the probability weights are obtained by assuming that relative interest rate changes have a "bell-shaped" probability distribution around the expected trend.

On a probability-weighted basis, the Trust 63 PO is much more attractive than the Treasury STRIP for all three market outlooks. The PO's performance is particularly worth noting in the neutral scenario, when the positive convexity in the projected return pattern makes the probability-weighted return higher than the base case (no change) projected return.

Summary of Performance Characteristics

The previous discussion has indicated the unusual investment characteristics of SMBSs. IOs have large negative durations, something that is almost unique among MBSs, while POs are bullish instruments comparable to long zero-coupon securities. These properties are a consequence of the powerful effect of changes in prepayments on IOs and POs, which can overwhelm the usual effects of changing interest rates.

IOs tend to be priced at wide spreads to Treasuries. However, they typically are adversely affected by changes in interest rates and resulting changes in prepayments because of the asymmetric response of prepayments to interest rate changes. Hence, as independent investments, they are most suitable for bearish investors or investors who expect interest rate volatility to be low. Primarily, however, IOs should be looked upon as attractive hedging vehicles; their negative durations can help reduce the interest rate risk of a typical fixed-income portfolio. This is discussed further in the next section.

In contrast, POs are priced at low spreads to Treasuries due to the typically favorable effect of prepayment variations on POs. Hence they are not suitable for investors who expect low interest rate volatility or who are bearish. POs should be considered by bullish investors who want to increase the durations of their portfolios, since POs compare very favorably in this respect with long Treasury or corporate zero-coupon bonds. POs also can be used as hedges for negative duration instruments such as servicing portfolios, as discussed in the next section.

HEDGING APPLICATIONS

Hedging Prepayment Risk and Interest Rate Risk

The much higher price sensitivity and yield sensitivity of IOs and POs to changes in interest rates and prepayments compared with nonstripped mortgage pass-throughs have been discussed in the preceding section. It is natural, therefore, to consider whether a portfolio of several mortgage pass-through securities can be hedged adequately for short-term holding periods against changes in prepayments or interest rates with a small but highly price-sensitive position in either IOs or POs. Before discussing details of how such a hedge works in practice, it is important to consider the relationship between prepayment risk and interest rate risk.

Prepayment risk for a security is defined as the price sensitivity of the security to changes in the rate at which unscheduled principal is prepaid. All other factors that may affect price, in particular interest rate movements, are held constant in order to isolate prepayment risk. The much greater price sensitivities of IOs and POs to changes in prepayments compared with mortgage pass-throughs were discussed in the previous section and illustrated in Exhibit 3.

A second component of price sensitivity, referred to as interest rate risk, arises from changes in interest rates over a given holding period. Shifts in prevailing interest rates have a direct impact on the present values of a security's cash flows, and, hence, its price. In addition, changes in interest rates affect projected prepayment rates, which, in turn, have a bearing on the security price. Thus, shifts in interest rates affect price both directly and indirectly (via changes in prepayments).

Mechanics of a Hedge

In the previous section, two risks that are relevant to hedging MBSs—changes in interest rates and prepayments—were described. In this section, the issue of quantifying the degree of hedging is addressed.

In hedging a portfolio of securities against a particular risk, the investor must be willing to sacrifice some portion of his potential profit (in favorable market environments) in order to reduce the variation in portfolio performance across a wide range of market environments. The investor also must consider how long the portfolio will be held before either closing out or rehedging the position. This holding period could vary from one day for an interest rate-sensitive portfolio in a volatile market, to perhaps a month or two in a more stable environment. For short holding periods, the market value of the hedge position at the end of the period is the measure of portfolio performance used in this section. An investor who wishes to evaluate a hedge on this basis must then decide:

1. The range of interest rate (or prepayment) changes to hedge against. For example, for a one-month holding period, the investor may wish to hedge the market value of the portfolio only against gradual interest rate moves of between +200 basis points and -200 basis points in the yield on six-month Treasuries.[12] In general, a greater variance in market value is implied by a wider range of interest-rate or prepayment changes.

---

[12] Assuming a normal distribution for relative interest rate changes, an initial interest rate of 8% and a volatility of 15%, there is a probability of approximately two-thirds that interest rates will change by no more than thirty-five basis points over the course of a month. Although unlikely, interest rate moves of up to 200 basis points within a short period have occurred in recent years, e.g., following October 19, 1987.

2. The spread in market value of the portfolio that is considered to be acceptable. The extreme case is to hedge so that there is no change in market value across the range chosen in (1). In practice, a small variation of a few percent in market value may be acceptable.

The calculation of the market value of a hedged portfolio is done using an "average" OAS for each security in the portfolio, as described in the previous section. Two specific examples that illustrate the unique hedging characteristics of SMBSs are discussed later in this section.

Hedging Characteristics of IOs and POs

One reason for the attractiveness of IOs and POs as instruments for hedging MBS portfolios is that they have much higher (absolute) effective durations than mortgage pass-throughs (see Exhibit 7, for example). This implies a much greater price sensitivity to changes in interest rates. An investor who wishes to reduce the price sensitivity of a portfolio to changes in interest rates can achieve this by establishing a small position in the appropriate SMBS. (The market value of the SMBS need only be a small fraction of the market value of the portfolio.) The large negative durations of IOs make these securities appropriate for hedging portfolios with an overall positive duration; POs may be used for hedging portfolios with an overall negative duration. In each case, the hedged portfolio exhibits a lower (absolute) effective duration than the unhedged portfolio. Exhibit 12 illustrates the effect of an IO and a PO on reducing the effective duration of two MBS portfolios.

The first portfolio matches the large negative duration of the Trust 63 IO with the positive duration of a GNMA 8% pass-through. A combination of approximately $49 million market value of the IO with $51 million market value of the GNMA pass-through has an overall effective duration of close to zero, and should show little price sensitivity to small changes in interest

---

Exhibit 12: Matching Effective Duration with SMBSs

Portfolio 1*: GNMA 8 and FNMA Trust 63 IO

IO Market Value ($mm)	0	10	20	30	40	49	80	100
GNMA 8 Market Value ($mm)	100	90	80	70	60	51	20	0
Effective Duration of Portfolio	6.0	4.8	3.5	2.3	1.1	0.0	-3.8	-6.3

Portfolio 2*: FNMA 10 Servicing Portfolio and FNMA Trust 63 PO

PO Market Value ($mm)	0	10	20	30	40	51	80	100
Servicing Portfolio Market Value ($mm)	100	90	80	70	60	49	20	0
Effective Duration of Portfolio	-12.1	-9.7	-7.4	-5.0	-2.7	-0.1	6.8	11.5

* Total market value of portfolio is $100 mm.

Note: The servicing portfolio of FNMA 10% pass-through collateral receives a gross coupon of 75 basis points.

---

rates. The second portfolio combines the Trust 63 PO with a servicing portfolio of FNMA 10% pass-throughs as collateral (from which the servicer receives a gross coupon of seventy-five basis points). The servicing portfolio exhibits the features of an IO, e.g., large negative effective duration for low-premium collateral, and as such is a bearish security. The combination of $49 million market value of the servicing portfolio with $51 million of the PO has an overall effective duration of close to zero. For both portfolios in Exhibit 12 variations in the mixture of the appropriate SMBS results in a synthetic security that exhibits either bullish, bearish, or neutral price characteristics (as measured by overall effective duration).

Additional points in favor of using SMBSs for hedging include:

- The market for SMBSs is becoming increasingly liquid as more investors take advantage of the characteristics offered by these securities. Increased liquidity facilitates the use of SMBSs for particular hedging purposes, since the appropriate SMBS or combination of SMBSs is more easily assembled in a liquid market. In a less liquid market, the limited availability of certain SMBSs would restrict

Exhibit 13: Market Value of FNMA Trust 63 IO/GNMA 8 Synthetic Security

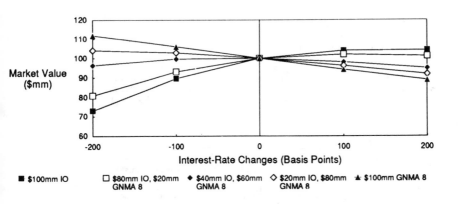

the type of portfolio that can be hedged. One particular concern in an illiquid environment would be a mismatch between some of the factors affecting prepayment characteristics of the portfolio under consideration and those of the available SMBSs.[13]

- Prepayment risk for mortgage pass-throughs is best hedged with mortgage instruments such as SMBSs, since Treasuries, by their very nature, have no prepayment sensitivity.

Hedging Portfolio Market Value

Exhibits 13 and 14 illustrate the sensitivity of the market value of the Trust 63 IO/GNMA 8 synthetic security and the Trust 63

---

[13] One such factor is the geographic origin of the mortgages underlying the security.

Exhibit 14: Market Value of FNMA Trust 63 PO/FNMA 10 Servicing Portfolio Synthetic Security

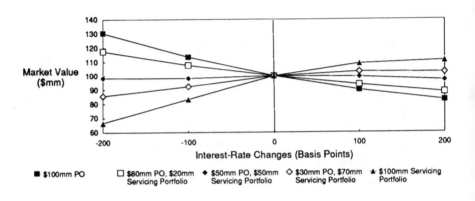

PO/FNMA Servicing Portfolio synthetic security to sudden parallel shifts in the yield curve. The holding period is one month in each case, and the initial market value of each portfolio is $100 million.

The total market value of each portfolio is shown for various interest rate scenarios and for different proportions of the hedging security (SMBS). The least variation in total market value, i.e., the flattest profile, for interest rate shifts of -200 basis points to +200 basis points is obtained when approximately $40 million of the GNMA/IO combination is invested in the Trust 63 IO, and $50 million of the FNMA Servicing Portfolio/PO combination is invested in the Trust 63 PO. These amounts result in a low or zero overall effective duration for each of these portfolios in the NC case (see Exhibit 12). This is hardly surprising, since a portfolio with a zero effective duration (and small convexity) in the NC base case should have a flat-market value profile for small (i.e., local) changes in interest rates.

Summary

POs and IOs offer the investor the opportunity to hedge a portfolio of MBSs against interest rate and prepayment risks for short-term holding periods. In addition, an investor can choose to adjust the proportion of the SMBS hedge in the portfolio according to his perception of market direction. The resulting customized portfolio would then offer optimal performance in a market environment that adheres to investor expectations.

SECTION V

VALUATION TECHNIQUES

CHAPTER 26

A COMPARISON OF METHODS FOR ANALYZING MORTGAGE-BACKED SECURITIES

Andrew S. Davidson
Managing Director
Mortgage-Backed Securities Research
Merrill Lynch Capital Markets

Michael D. Herskovitz
Director
Mortgage-Backed Securities Research
Merrill Lynch Capital Markets

Investors that own or contemplate owning mortgage-backed securities (MBSs) need a method for valuing them. The central issue in

The authors thank H. Halperin, K. Rogers, J. Van Lang, B. Starr, and N. Perrotis for their
assistance. In addition, the authors acknowledge the contributions of R. Kulason and L.
Murakami.

all MBS valuation methods is the treatment of prepayment uncertainty. The homeowners' right to prepay their loans introduces a significant degree of uncertainty to the cash flows, and consequently the value, of MBSs.

The relationship between interest rates and MBS prepayment rates directly influences MBS pricing. In a bond market rally prepayment rates rise, reducing the price gains of mortgage-backed securities. In a bear market, however, prepayment rates slow, resulting in increased price losses. This price movement pattern is commonly referred to as "negative convexity".

The dependence of prepayment rates on interest rates affects not only MBS returns but also their interest rate risk. A traditional measure of the price sensitivity of fixed income securities, modified duration, gives the percent change in price caused by a 100 basis point shift in the yield curve. Modified duration is a reasonable price sensitivity measure for securities with constant cash flows. It is often inadequate for MBSs, however, because prepayment rates, and consequently cash flows, vary as interest rates change.

The inadequacy of traditional fixed-income analytical tools for valuing MBSs has led to the development of alternative methods. This chapter reviews four approaches to quantifying MBS return and risk characteristics. The methods discussed are: (1) static cash flow yield (SCFY) analysis, (2) total rate of return scenario analysis (SA), (3) option-adjusted spread (OAS) Monte Carlo models, and (4) the refinancing threshold pricing (RTP) model. The first three methods constitute the currently accepted set of valuation techniques. The final method, refinancing threshold pricing, is an approach pioneered at Merrill Lynch.

Multiple approaches to valuing MBSs exist because no single methodology has been shown to explain completely the price performance of these securities. Each of the methods listed has its strengths and weaknesses. SCFY analysis is the simplest approach; however, it ignores a number of factors critical to the valuation of MBSs by assuming constant future interest rates. SA improves on the SCFY methodology by projecting MBS performance in a limited set of interest rate scenarios. OAS Monte Carlo models extend SA by simulating MBS performance over numerous interest rate paths. Critical to the SA and OAS approaches is the manner in which the future interest rate paths are selected and the specification of the relationship between interest rates and MBS prepayment rates. RTP is a binomial option-pricing-based methodology that differs fundamentally from the SA and OAS approaches. RTP directly models the refinancing decision of the individual mortgagor instead of attempting to specify aggregate MBS prepayment rates as a function of interest rates.

The chapter is divided into five sections. One section is devoted to each of the valuation methodologies, and a final section outlines our conclusions and recommendations. Each methodology section contains a description of the technique, the value and risk measures provided, the sensitivity of the results to input parameters, and a summary of the advantages and disadvantages of the approach. Throughout the chapter thirty-year GNMA single family (SF) 8.0%, 9.5%, and 11.0% pass-throughs are used as examples to allow the comparison of results across methodologies. At the time the analyses were conducted, the GNMA 9.5% pass-through was the current coupon. The GNMA 8% and 11% pass-throughs were selected to represent the characteristics of discount and premium MBS, respectively.

STATIC CASH FLOW YIELD

The static cash flow yield (SCFY) is the discount rate that equates the value of future MBS cash flows with their market price. The future cash flows are projected based on the prepayment rate that is anticipated if interest rates remain stable for the life of the security.

SCFY is the basic measure of value in the mortgage market. Its primary advantage is its simplicity; the only required assumption is a prepayment projection. After a prepayment rate has been specified, cash flows can be generated and a yield calculated based on the security's market price. The tradeoff for simplicity is that SCFY analysis ignores a number of factors critical to the valuation of MBSs, including the shape of the yield curve, the distribution and volatility of future interest rates, and the relationship between interest rates and MBS prepayment rates.

Required Assumptions

The only assumption required to compute the SCFY of MBSs is the projected prepayment rate assuming static interest rates. Typically, prepayment projections are made based on the results of a statistical analysis of historical prepayment data, and are generally quoted as conditional prepayment rates (CPR) or percentages of the Public Securities Association (PSA) prepayment model. Investors should be aware that prepayment forecasts based on statistical models imply a confidence interval, which in turn implies a range of possible values for MBS.

Exhibit 1 illustrates the average prepayment forecast and the forecast range for seasoned GNMA pass-throughs made available by thirteen firms through Telerate on March 15, 1988. Using the width of the range as a proxy for forecast uncertainty, it is clear that the level of uncertainty is significant for all coupons and is greatest for premium MBS.

Value Measures

Given a prepayment forecast for an MBS and its market price, its cash flow yield is uniquely determined. *The spread between the MBS static cash flow yield and either its average life or duration-matched Treasury issue has traditionally been used as a measure of value in the mortgage market.*

One way to interpret MBS static cash flow yield spreads to Treasuries is in a historical context. Based on current yield spreads, an evaluation can be made as to whether the mortgage market is historically rich or cheap relative to Treasuries. Further,

Exhibit 1: Average Prepayment Forecast and Forecast Range for Seasoned GNMA Pass-Throughs

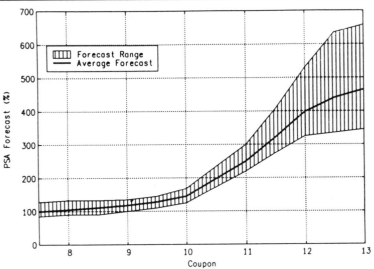

spread differentials between discounts, currents, and premiums can be compared to determine intra-MBS market relative sector values.

Exhibit 2 shows GNMA MBS yield spreads to the ten-year Treasury bond as a function of the distance of the MBS coupon from the current coupon for selected historical dates.

Premium MBS spreads decline relative to the current coupon spread because the shorter durations of these securities cause them to trade off of the short end of the yield curve. In order to adjust for the distortion introduced by mismatched durations, Exhibit 3 displays MBS spreads to duration-matched Treasury issues.

Exhibits 2 and 3 demonstrate that MBS spread levels have varied significantly over time. Spread level variation can be related to changes in interest rates and corresponding changes in the option value of mortgage securities. In general, increases in interest rate volatility will raise the value of the short option positions embedded in MBSs, which in turn reduces the prices (widens the spreads) of the securities. Conversely, lower volatility reduces the

Exhibit 2: GNMA Yield Spreads to the Ten-Year Treasury Bond for Selected Historical Dates

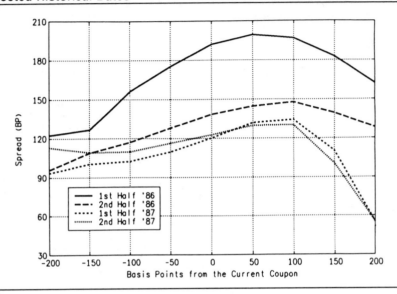

Exhibit 3: GNMA Yield Spreads to Duration-Matched Treasury Issues for Selected Historical Dates

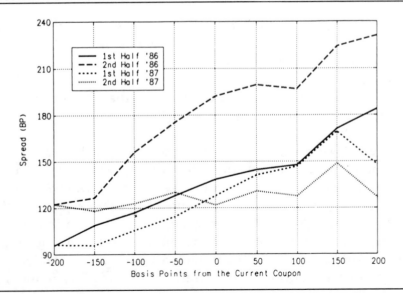

value of the short option components, thereby increasing the prices (reducing the spreads) of MBSs.

The relationship between spreads and volatility is demonstrated in Exhibit 4, which shows a high degree of correlation between the yield volatility of the ten-year Treasury and the spread between the current coupon GNMA and the ten-year Treasury between January 1985 and January 1988. This is strong evidence that the market uses its assessment of interest rate volatility in pricing MBSs.

In addition to interest rate volatility, SCFY spreads are also affected by the state of the housing market. A robust housing market will generally increase MBS supply, leading to wider MBS yield spreads.

Consequently, an evaluation of MBSs based on SCFY spreads to Treasuries should incorporate current interest rate volatility levels and housing market conditions, and investors' beliefs about the future directions of these factors.

Exhibit 4: Yield Volatility of the Ten-Year Treasury Bond and the Spread Between the Current Coupon GNMA and the Ten-Year Treasury Bond

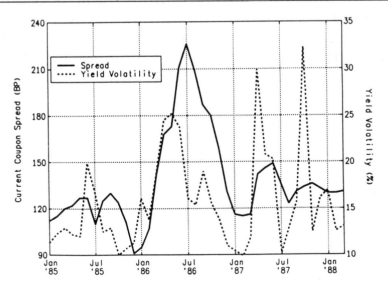

Interest Rate Risk Measures

The weighted average life (WAL) of a MBS is the average time to receipt of the principal of the security. It is used as a measure of the effective maturity of MBS in the place of stated maturity. Stated maturity is a poor measure of effective maturity for MBSs because most principal is amortized or prepaid well before this date. Although an exact relationship between MBS WAL and MBS price sensitivity to interest rates does not exist, it is generally true that the longer the WAL, the greater the interest rate sensitivity. Consequently, WAL can be employed as an indicator of the price risk of MBSs.

Another risk measure that can be obtained from SCFY analysis is Macaulay duration. The Macaulay duration of a security is the present value weighted average time to receipt of its cash flows. For true fixed-income instruments this measure can be shown to be equivalent to the price elasticity of the security with respect to interest rates. However, for MBSs, where cash flows are dependent on interest rates, Macaulay duration is often a poor measure of price sensitivity.

In the sections of this chapter dealing with option-adjusted spread Monte Carlo models and the refinancing threshold pricing model, MBS WALs and Macaulay durations will be compared to effective durations estimated by models that account for the dependence of MBS cash flows on interest rates.

Parameter Sensitivity

Changing the prepayment assumption can materially alter the yield, weighted average life, and duration of MBSs. Exhibit 5 demonstrates this sensitivity, displaying static cash flow yields, weighted average lives, and Macaulay durations for GNMA 8.0%, 9.5%, and 11.0% pass-throughs at constant prices at three different prepayment rates: the minimum, average, and maximum forecasts depicted in Exhibit 1.

Exhibit 5: Effect of Prepayment Rate Specification on SCFY Risk and Return Measures

		SCFY (%)			WAL (YRS)			Macaulay Duration		
GNMA	Price	MIN	AVG	MAX	MIN	AVG	MAX	MIN	AVG	MAX
8.0%	90-20	9.59	9.64	9.79	12.9	12.2	10.6	6.6	6.4	5.8
9.5%	99-10	9.74	9.75	9.75	12.8	10.9	9.2	6.5	5.9	5.3
11.0%	107-00	9.36	9.17	8.97	6.2	5.4	4.7	4.1	3.7	3.4

As prepayment rates increase, the yield on the discount increases and the yield on the premium decreases. The yield on the current coupon is insensitive to the projected prepayment rate, since it is priced close to par. Weighted average lives and durations for all the pass-throughs decrease with increasing prepayment rates. Because MBS duration depends on the projected prepayment rate, the calculated yield spread to duration-matched Treasuries also depends on this assumption. This is true even for the current coupon, for which the SCFY is nearly independent of the assumed prepayment rate.

Summary

The major attractions of the SCFY methodology are its simplicity and its acceptance by the market as the standard measure of MBS value. The only assumption required is a prepayment projection. After specifying a prepayment rate and generating cash flows, a yield can be calculated based on the security's market price. The tradeoff for simplicity is that by assuming constant future interest rates, the approach ignores a number of factors critical to the valuation of MBSs, including the shape of the yield curve, the distribution and volatility of future interest rates, and the relationship between interest rates and MBS prepayment rates. Consequently, investors who rely on this methodology must subjectively decide how much spread is required to compensate them for the uncertainty introduced by these factors.

Despite these problems, a historical analysis of SCFY spreads is a useful adjunct to the other valuation methodologies presented in this chapter. In particular, the SCFY approach is most useful for the high premium and deep discount MBSs having cash flows with little sensitivity to interest rates.

SCENARIO ANALYSIS

Scenario analysis (SA) can be used to supplement SCFY analysis by examining the dynamic nature of MBSs. It consists of calculating MBS holding period returns for a variety of possible future interest rate scenarios. For each scenario, cash flows are generated based on coupon, scheduled principal amortization, and prepayments. Cash flows that occur prior to the horizon are reinvested to the end of the holding period. At the horizon, the value of the remaining principal balance is calculated. The rate of growth necessary to equate the initial investment with the sum of the reinvested cash flows and the value of the remaining principal balance at the horizon is the total return for the scenario. The total scenario return is then converted to an annualized rate of return based on the length of the holding period.

Scenario analysis differs from the other approaches presented because it requires the use of a separate valuation model in order to arrive at the security's horizon price. Consequently, it can be employed in conjunction with OAS models or the RTP model to assess the implications of these pricing models for the dynamic performance of MBS in a holding period return context.

A simple but useful alternative horizon pricing model values the MBSs based on SCFY spreads and projected horizon prepayment rates. The scenario horizon prepayment rate determines MBS WAL at the horizon. A MBS is then priced at a spread to its WAL-matched Treasury issue. Scenario spreads are determined by the SCFY spreads at which the same relative coupon MBS are currently trading. This approach has the advantage of investigating the implications of existing spread relationships on holding period returns. It determines the scenario holding period returns of MBSs assuming current spread relationships are maintained. Using this pricing methodology, SA can be used in conjunction with a historical analysis of SCFY spreads to make assessments of MBS relative sector values. For example, if the expected returns of discount MBSs are inordinately large relative to premium MBSs using this approach, an argument can be made that discount MBS spreads are too large relative to premium MBS spreads. Consequently, discount MBSs would be the better value.

Required Assumptions

Holding Period. The length of the holding period affects the shape of the total rate of return profile. Assuming monotonic parallel yield curve shifts, the effect of the reinvestment rate for interim cash flows will tend to offset the effect of the change in the value of the remaining principal balance at the end of the holding period. Higher interest rates imply greater reinvestment income but lower horizon prices for the remaining principal balance. For short holding periods, the price change of the security will dominate the reinvestment effect; the total scenario rate of return will decrease as interest rates increase. For sufficiently long holding periods, the reinvestment effect will dominate the impact of the horizon price, and total scenario rate of return will increase as interest rates rise.

When employing SA, the conventional practice is to evaluate MBSs based on a one-year holding period. Most investors have an opportunity to rebalance their portfolios at least this often. Further, a one-year holding period limits the effect of the reinvestment rate assumption. A short holding period, however, increases the importance of the horizon pricing model.

Prepayment Rate Function. The specification of the relationship between scenario interest rates and prepayment rates is critical. This relationship defines the embedded option in MBSs, and is what differentiates MBSs from true fixed-income securities. As noted in the SCFY analysis section, the uncertainty of prepayment forecasts for MBSs assuming static interest rates is substantial. The level of difficulty associated with forecasting prepayment rates assuming nonconstant paths of future interest rates is much greater, implying even wider confidence intervals for such projections. Consequently, it is important that investors assess the sensitivity of SA risk and return measures to the prepayment rate function specification.

Interest Rate Distribution and Volatility. The type of interest rate probability distribution and volatility level determine the weights that are assigned to each scenario. This is important when calculating the expected return and the variance of returns across all scenarios. The most popular distributions are the bell-shaped normal and the right-skewed log-normal. Normal implies equal probability of equal absolute changes, while log-normal implies equal probability of equal percentage changes. At low levels of volatility the two assumptions give similar results.

Instead of selecting a probability distribution and a volatility assumption, an investor can subjectively assign probabilities to each of the scenarios. This is feasible only if a small number of scenarios are run.

Generally, the lower the volatility assumption, or for subjective probability distributions, the more heavily weighted the scenarios near the central scenario, the higher the expected return and the lower the variance of returns. The increase in expected return results from the negative convexity of MBSs.

Central Scenario. The interest rate scenarios must be centered on a base case. Two conventional central scenarios are the unchanged market and the implied forward rate scenarios. In the unchanged market scenario, interest rates remain unchanged over the holding period. For the implied forward scenario, interest rates follow paths described by the implied forward rates. Generally, the other scenarios selected assume parallel yield curve shifts about the central scenario. It is also possible to specify scenarios in which yield curve rotations occur. However, the added complexity of specifying such scenarios and assigning probabilities limits their usefulness.

The implied forward scenario is generally considered to be the more theoretically sound central scenario. It also has the advantage of simplifying comparisons between different duration securities; for example, the expected returns on all Treasury bonds are equal under this scenario, independent of maturity.

Horizon Pricing Model. The horizon pricing model is another critical aspect of scenario analysis. It determines the value of the remaining principal balance of MBSs at the horizon. The shorter the horizon, the greater the impact of horizon prices on holding period returns will be.

Number of Scenarios Simulated. The number of scenarios simulated can also affect calculated expected returns and variances of returns. Generally, for MBS pass-throughs these values converge to their asymptotic values when scenarios are run at 50 basis point intervals between −400 and +400 basis point shifts in the yield curve, assuming a one-year horizon.

Reinvestment Rate. The impact of the reinvestment rate is proportional to the length of the holding period. For short holding periods its effect is negligible. Since the standard approach is to assume a one-year holding period, the reinvestment rate assumption is relatively unimportant. If analyses are conducted employing longer holding periods, the sensitivity of the results to this assumption increases.

Value Measures

The expected return is the weighted average of the total rates of return of all the scenarios, where each scenario is weighted by its probability. The scenario weights depend on the assumed level of interest rate volatility and the probability distribution employed.

A more complete value measure is a graph of total returns versus interest rate scenarios (it could also be deemed a risk measure because the dispersion of the returns is evident). This approach has the advantage of visually displaying the dynamic performance characteristics of MBSs. However, comparisons between securities can be difficult, since it is unlikely that one security will completely dominate another.

Interest Rate Risk Measures

One of the most widely used statistical measures of dispersion is variance. The square root of variance is called standard deviation. This measure is particularly useful when dealing with normally distributed data. In this case, approximately 68% of the observations can be expected to lie within one standard deviation of the mean, and 95% within two standard deviations. The greater the variance and standard deviation, the wider the dispersion of scenario returns, and consequently the riskier the security.

Parameter Sensitivity

Exhibit 6 demonstrates the effect of the length of the holding period on the total return profile of a GNMA 9.5% pass-through. As the length of the holding period increases, the profile rotates counter-clockwise due to the increasing effect of the reinvestment rate and the reduced impact of the horizon price on scenario returns.

Due to their shorter durations, the corresponding return profiles for premium MBSs would be flatter for the one-year holding period and rotate further counter-clockwise as the length of the holding period increased. Discount MBSs would display the opposite behavior.

Exhibit 7 shows the effect of the specification of the prepayment rate function on the total return profile of a GNMA 11% pass-through. The underlying prepayment model was shifted up

Exhibit 6: Effect of Holding Period on the Total Return Profile of a GNMA 9.5% Pass-Through

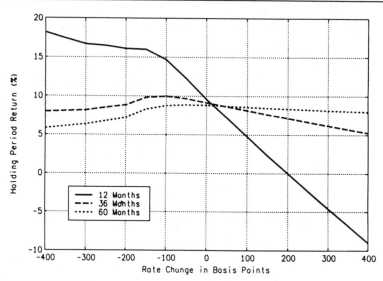

Exhibit 7: Effect of Prepayment Rate Specification on the Total Return Profile of a GNMA 11.0% Pass-Through

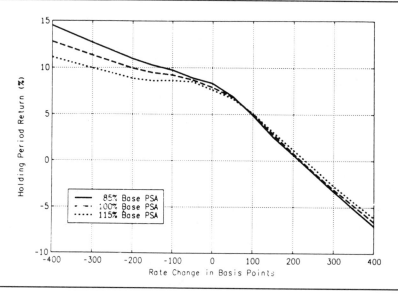

and down 15%. A faster prepayment rate specification results in reduced holding period returns in falling interest rate scenarios and increased returns in rising interest rate scenarios, due to the reduction in the duration of MBS cash flows. Current and discount MBSs would behave similarly.

Exhibit 8 displays the effect of interest rate volatility on the expected returns and the standard deviations of returns of GNMA 8%, 9.5%, and 11% pass-throughs, assuming future changes in interest rates are log-normally distributed. The base volatility level was shifted up and down 40%. Increased interest rate volatility results in reduced expected returns and increased standard deviations of returns. The normal distribution would result in slightly higher expected returns, due to its symmetry.

Exhibit 8: Effect of Interest Rate Volatility on SA Risk and Return Measures

	Expected Return (%)			Standard Deviation of Returns (%)		
GNMA	LOW	MID	HIGH	LOW	MID	HIGH
8.0%	8.16	8.01	7.85	3.97	6.30	8.29
9.5%	8.32	7.95	7.47	3.55	5.39	6.88
11.0%	7.43	6.81	6.22	1.75	3.10	4.25

The expected return of the GNMA 8.0% pass-through displays little sensitivity to interest rate volatility because its embedded prepayment option is far out of the money. The interest rate volatility assumption is more important for current coupon and premium MBS.

Exhibit 9 demonstrates the effect of the central scenario yield curve on the expected returns and the standard deviations of returns for GNMA 8%, 9.5%, and 11% pass-throughs. The implied forward scenario shifts the return profiles downward relative to the unchanged market scenario, and consequently results in lower expected returns. This effect is due to the rising implied forward rates embedded in an upward-sloping yield curve. An inverted yield curve would cause the opposite effect. Although the choice

Exhibit 9: Effect of Central Yield Curve Scenario on SA Risk and Return Measures

	Expected Return (%)		Standard Deviation of Returns (%)	
GNMA	Implied Forward	Unchanged Market	Implied Forward	Unchanged Market
8.0%	8.01	9.07	6.30	6.41
9.5%	7.95	9.00	5.39	5.50
11.0%	6.81	7.74	3.10	3.15

of the central scenario yield curve has a large effect on the absolute levels of MBS expected returns, it has little impact on their relative levels.

Summary

The SA approach extends the SCFY methodology by examining the dynamic nature of MBSs. It can be used in conjunction with other MBS pricing models to assess their implications for the dynamic performance of MBSs in a holding period return context. If the SCFY spread-based pricing approach described in this section is employed, SA investigates the impact of existing spread relationships on MBS holding period returns. This approach can be very useful when used in conjunction with a historical analysis of SCFY spreads. Relative value between MBS market sectors can be evaluated by reviewing existing spread levels in a historical context, and by assessing their impact on MBS expected returns and variances of returns. MBS value relative to other fixed income markets can be evaluated in a similar fashion through a comparison of these values to those calculated for the alternative markets. Further, the historical analysis of SCFY spreads can be used to assess likely future spread movements. This information can in turn be used when evaluating the spread sensitivity of SA results.

Ideally, an investor would like to select the security with the highest expected return and the lowest variance of returns. Usually this is not possible, since it would probably indicate that the security was mispriced. Under normal circumstances, an investor must accept additional risk in order to obtain a higher expected return. SA has the advantage of delineating the available sets of MBS risk/return profiles for specific holding periods.

An additional advantage of SA is that the limited number of scenarios allows the investor to review the assumptions and results of each scenario. A relatively small set of scenarios, however, may not adequately model the effect on value of the complete distribution of future interest rate paths.

OPTION-ADJUSTED SPREADS

In an attempt to improve on the static cash flow yield and scenario analysis measures of MBS value, mortgage market participants have begun to rely on option-adjusted spread (OAS) simulation models. The OAS simulation approach generates numerous interest rate paths that then determine future MBS cash flows. These cash flows are discounted by the simulated interest rates plus the option-adjusted spread. The model solves for the spread that equates the market price to the average simulated price. The simulation approach provides a method for estimating MBS yields and spreads to the Treasury yield curve that are adjusted for the embedded options in these securities. In addition, these models can provide estimates of MBS option cost and effective MBS duration and convexity.[1]

Required Assumptions

Prepayment Rate Function. One of the two critical assumptions in the OAS simulation methodology is the link between interest rates and prepayment rates. If the relationship between interest rates, time, and MBS prepayments is misspecified, the calculated value

---

[1] Michael D. Herskovitz, "Option-Adjusted Spread Analysis for Mortgage-Backed Securities," Chap. 21 in Frank J. Fabozzi (ed.), *The Handbook of Fixed-Income Options*, (Chicago, IL: Probus Publishing, 1989).

and risk measures will be biased. The sensitivity of OAS model results to different prepayment function specifications is explored in the parameter sensitivity section.

Interest Rate Diffusion Process. The second critical assumption in the OAS simulation approach is the specification of the interest rate diffusion process. Most models assume that interest rates evolve as a log-normal random walk with a drift that centers the distribution on the implied forward rates. If the yield curve is upward sloping, the implied forward rates will indicate an upward bias to short-term interest rates. This may not reflect investors' rate expectations. However, the use of implied forward rates with the typical positively sloped yield curve builds in the requirement that longer-duration securities must yield more than shorter-duration securities in order to be fairly priced. This is necessary to price noncallable bonds correctly, and is consistent with option pricing theory.

Most models diffuse a single short-term rate. In these models the current MBS coupon, which drives the prepayment function, is assumed to shift deterministically based on the change in the short-term rate. Other models seek to introduce a greater amount of realism into the interest rate process by diffusing both a short- and long-term rate. In this approach the short- and long-term rate changes are less than perfectly correlated, thereby allowing for the possibility of yield curve inversions. The long-term rate is used to drive the prepayment function, while MBS cash flows are discounted back along the short-term rate paths.

Interest Rate Volatility. In addition to specifying an interest rate process, an assumption about interest rate volatility must be made. Higher volatility assumptions increase the dispersion of the simulated interest rate paths. Since MBSs are effectively short a call option, increasing interest rate volatility will increase calculated option cost and decrease option-adjusted spread. The sensitivity of these results to this parameter is discussed in the sensitivity section.

Number of Scenarios Simulated. The reliance of the OAS approach on a set of randomly generated interest rate paths introduces additional uncertainty into the results of these models. The magnitude of the additional uncertainty is inversely proportional to the number of interest rate paths simulated. Consequently, there is a tradeoff between computational efficiency and the confidence intervals of the results.

Averaging Methodology. OAS values are also sensitive to the method used to aggregate the information from the individual interest rate paths. For example, the cash flows for the paths could be averaged first, and then the OAS calculated as the spread that equates this average cash flow vector with the market price of the security. Alternatively, OAS could be defined as the spread that equates the mean of the individual prices for each of the simulated interest rate paths to the market price. Each of these methods will produce different OAS values.

The Merrill Lynch OAS model employs the latter averaging methodology. Under this approach, OAS values can be interpreted as the expected yield spreads of MBSs to Treasuries over the full range of probable interest rate scenarios. The alternative methodology does not fully account for the relationship between scenario interest rates, prepayment rates, and MBS value.

Value Measures

Option-Adjusted Spread. Option-adjusted spread is the primary value measure produced by OAS models. Most models define OAS as the spread that equates the average simulated price to the market price. Implicit in this methodology is the assumption that the fair option-adjusted yield curve for mortgages is a fixed spread over the Treasury yield curve.

When the interest rate diffusion process is centered on the implied forward rates, the OAS has embedded in it the requirement that different duration securities must have different yields in order to be fairly priced. Consequently, OAS values for different duration MBS should be directly comparable.

Option Cost. Spread to Treasury alone may not be a good indicator of MBS relative value. In order to compare various MBSs, the yield spreads should be benchmarked to an appropriate level, namely, the static cash flow yield. The static cash flow yield spread minus the OAS equals the implied option cost.

Interest Rate Risk Measures

Effective Duration and Convexity. By shifting the simulated interest rate paths up and down slightly and holding the OAS fixed, estimates of MBS price sensitivity can be calculated. The average percentage price change can be used to calculate a security's OAS effective duration. OAS effective convexity can be computed by observing the rate of change of the OAS effective duration. These price sensitivity measures can be useful for hedging, since they incorporate the effect of the prepayment option. However, OAS effective durations are measures of price sensitivity, and not of maturity.

OAS Macaulay Duration. A measure of MBS maturity that is adjusted for the prepayment option is the OAS Macaulay duration. This duration measure represents the present value weighted average time to receipt of MBS cash flow averaged across all simulation trials. Exhibit 10 shows the SCFY WAL, SCFY Macaulay

Exhibit 10: A Comparison of SCFY and OAS Risk Measures

GNMA	SCFY WAL (YRS)	SCFY Macaulay Duration	OAS Macaulay Duration	OAS Effective Duration
8.0%	11.5	6.1	5.5	5.8
9.5%	10.5	5.6	4.8	4.1
11.0%	5.8	3.9	3.9	2.3

duration, OAS Macaulay duration, and OAS effective duration of GNMA 8%, 9.5%, and 11% pass-throughs.

The OAS Macaulay durations of the GNMA 8.0% and 9.5% pass-throughs are shorter than their SCFY Macaulay durations. This result is consistent with expectations. Using the simulation approach, discount and current coupon securities are likely to experience an increase in prepayments relative to the static forecast, as prepayments are near their minimum based on the assumed prepayment model. The OAS effective durations of all the pass-throughs are below their SCFY Macaulay durations, reflecting the negative convexity of MBS. On a relative basis, the OAS effective duration of the GNMA 11.0% pass-through is depressed the most below its SCFY Macaulay duration, while the OAS effective duration of the GNMA 8.0% pass-through is depressed the least.

Parameter Sensitivity

Exhibit 11 demonstrates the effect of the specification of the prepayment rate function on the OAS, option cost, OAS Macaulay duration, and OAS effective duration of GNMA 8%, 9.5%, and 11% pass-throughs. The underlying prepayment model was shifted up and down 15%. A faster prepayment rate specification results in a reduction in both the OAS Macaulay and OAS effective durations of MBSs. A faster prepayment rate specification will generally also increase the OAS of discount MBS and reduce the OAS of premium MBSs.

Exhibit 11: Effect of Prepayment Rate Specification on OAS Risk and Return Measures

GNMA	OAS (BP)			Option Cost (BP)			OAS Macaualy Duration			OAS Effective Duration		
	Low	Mid	High	Low	Mid	High	Low	Mid	High	Low	Mid	High
8.0%	66	79	108	48	35	6	5.8	5.5	5.2	6.0	5.8	5.7
9.5%	51	60	56	67	58	62	5.1	4.8	4.6	4.3	4.1	3.9
11.0%	16	4	-13	102	114	131	4.3	3.9	3.6	2.9	2.3	1.9

Exhibit 12: Effect of Interest Rate Volatility on OAS Risk and Return Measures

---

	OAS (BP)			Option Cost (BP)			OAS Macaualy Duration			OAS Effective Duration		
GNMA	Low	Mid	High	Low	Mid	High	Low	Mid	High	Low	Mid	High
8.0%	104	79	74	10	24	40	5.8	5.5	5.0	6.2	5.8	5.3
9.5%	102	60	24	16	58	94	5.1	4.8	4.4	4.5	4.1	3.7
11.0%	56	4	-41	62	114	160	3.9	3.9	3.7	2.2	2.3	2.5

Exhibit 12 displays the effect of interest rate volatility on the OAS, option cost, OAS Macaulay duration, and OAS effective duration of GNMA 8%, 9.5%, and 11% pass-throughs. The base volatility level was shifted up and down 40%. Increased interest rate volatility results in higher option costs and lower OAS. The OAS effective duration of premium MBSs and discount MBSs is increased and decreased respectively as volatility increases.

Summary

The OAS methodology has a number of advantages over both the SCFY and SA approaches. The large number of simulated future interest rate paths may better model the complete distribution of future rate paths, and improve the statistical significance of the risk and return measures. Further, the risk measures account for the dependence of MBS prepayments on interest rates. If the interest rate diffusion process and the relationship between interest rates and prepayment rates are correctly specified, these price sensitivity measures should be more useful for hedging than their SCFY counterparts.

The major drawback to the OAS approach is that it is basically a black box into which an investor puts assumptions and out of which comes risk and return measures. The prepayment functions and term structure models embedded in OAS models are generally proprietary, precluding the possibility of an investor inspecting these key aspects of the model. Even if the model specifications are available, it may be difficult to evaluate them.

This makes it imperative that the investor who employs these models determine their sensitivity to the required assumptions.

Because of the sensitivity of OAS results to model specification and assumptions, these values are difficult to compare on an absolute basis between models. OAS results are best employed as indicators of relative value between similar securities run under identical assumptions using a consistent methodology.

REFINANCING THRESHOLD PRICING MODEL

The refinancing threshold pricing (RTP) model is a binomial option-pricing-based methodology that differs fundamentally from the SA and OAS approaches. RTP directly models the refinancing decision of the individual mortgagor instead of attempting to specify aggregate MBS prepayment rates as a function of interest rates. This approach is based on three main concepts:

- An options approach is effective in modeling mortgage prepayments, as the mortgagor's ability to prepay the mortgage constitutes an option.

- The costs a mortgagor incurs when refinancing are not paid to the holder of the MBS.

- Mortgagors have different interest rate levels, or thresholds, at which they prepay their mortgages. That is, different homeowners face different levels of refinancing costs.

The concept of heterogeneous mortgagors provides a fundamental and innovative insight into analyzing MBS value and serves as the starting point for the refinancing threshold pricing model. The RTP models the underlying economics of MBSs by focusing on the refinancing decision of the individual mortgagor. These individual refinancing decisions are observed as prepayments. Models that estimate prepayments based on interest rate levels, however, reverse this process. They examine the effect rather than the cause. The RTP provides the potential for robust results and additional insights into MBS valuation because RTP models the underlying process.

The process of valuing a mortgage pool begins with modeling a single mortgage loan. The RTP values individual mortgagor cash flows, given their refinancing costs. This procedure, however, is not repeated for each mortgage in the pool. Instead, the pool is divided into groups of borrowers who share similar refinancing costs. Using market data, the RTP endogenously determines both the costs that mortgagors face, as well as the proportion of the pool in each refinancing cost class. This division into mortgage groups is termed pool composition.[2]

Required Assumptions

Interest Rate Diffusion Process. The first assumption required is the specification of the interest rate diffusion process. A term structure model generates a binomial interest rate tree. The rates at the successive branches of the tree, as well as probabilities of interest rates increasing and decreasing, are selected in a manner that is consistent with the observed prices on the current Treasury securities.

The interest rate tree is used by a binomial option pricing model to value each of the endogenously determined refinancing classes in MBSs. When the present value of the mortgagor's cash flows exceeds the remaining principal plus refinancing costs, the mortgage is assumed to be refinanced, and the market value of the mortgage is set equal to the principal amount of the mortgage. Refinancing is not economic when the remaining principal plus refinancing costs is greater than the present value of the cash flows to be paid by the mortgagor.

---

[2] For a more detailed discussion of the RTP approach, refer to *The Refinancing Threshold Pricing Model: An Economic Approach to Valuing MBS,* Merrill Lynch Mortgage-Backed Securities Research, November 1987.

Interest Rate Volatility. In addition to specifying an interest rate process, an assumption about interest volatility is required. Higher assumed interest rate volatility generally results in a reduction in MBS price due to the increase in the value of the embedded short option position.

Pool Composition. The third required assumption is the pool composition and the associated thresholds. Mortgages in a pool are divided into three classes, according to interest rate sensitivity: very sensitive, moderately sensitive, and not interest rate-sensitive. The degree of interest rate sensitivity depends on the mortgagors' refinancing costs. Mortgagors considered very interest rate-sensitive face low refinancing costs, while mortgagors with less interest rate sensitivity have correspondingly higher refinancing costs. While the pool could be divided into any number of classes, three captures the major implications of heterogeneous borrowers for descriptive purposes.

The model assumes that nonrefinancing prepayments occur at a constant rate over the life of the mortgage pool, and are proportionally drawn from the three refinancing cost classes. At origination, the distribution of mortgagors in refinancing cost classes is assumed to be identical across all pools. This does not imply that each seasoned pool contains an equal number of high, medium, and low interest rate-sensitive borrowers, but rather, the proportion of highly interest rate sensitive individuals in a GNMA 8% pool at origination equals the proportion of highly interest rate-sensitive individuals in a GNMA 10% pool at origination. Over time, the proportions will shift as mortgagors refinance or move. Consequently, one would expect seasoned GNMA 14s to have very few highly and moderately interest-sensitive borrowers remaining in the pool, while seasoned GNMA 7s may have proportions that have not changed much since origination.

After assuming an initial pool distribution, pool composition and refinancing cost levels at origination are determined by recursively comparing market prices with model results until the difference between the two is minimized. These implied pool compositions generally remain stable over time and are consistent with prepayment expectations. Once the value of each of the refinancing classes has been determined, a weighted average is calculated based on the pool composition to determine MBS value.

Value Measures

Price. The RTP directly computes the theoretical price of MBSs. Comparisons between theoretical values and actual market prices may help investors determine MBS relative value.

Implied Spread and Implied Volatility. The term structure model within the RTP model creates a binomial tree of future Treasury rates based on the prices of the current Treasury securities. The RTP model discounts MBS cash flows back through this binomial lattice at the Treasury rate plus some constant spread. This spread reflects the yield premium of MBSs after accounting for the prepayment option held by the mortgagor. The implied spread and volatility are calculated by varying the respective parameter, holding the other constant, and finding the level at which the model price equals the market price. In general, the larger the implied volatility and spread, the cheaper the security.

Interest Rate Risk Measures

By shifting the yield curve up and down slightly, estimates of MBS price sensitivity can be calculated in a manner analogous to that described in the OAS section. In addition, the price sensitivity of MBSs to changes in interest rate volatility can be computed. Exhibit 13 shows the SCFY WAL, SCFY Macaulay duration, RTP effective duration, RTP effective convexity, and RTP dP/dVol[3] of GNMA 8%, 9.5%, and 11% pass-throughs.

---

[3] dP/dVol is defined as the price change of MBSs resulting from a 1% reduction in interest rate volatility.

Exhibit 13: A Comparison of SCFY and RTP Risk Measures

GNMA	SCFY WAL (YRS)	SCFY Macaulay Duration	RTP Effective Duration	RTP Effective Convexity	RTP dP/dVol
8.0%	11.5	6.1	6.0	0.37	-0.02
9.5%	10.2	5.6	5.1	-0.94	0.16
11.0%	5.8	3.9	2.8	-2.48	0.62

Consistent with expectations, the RTP effective durations of the pass-throughs are all below their SCFY Macaulay durations, due to the negative convexity of MBSs. The convexities of the current coupon and premium pass-throughs are negative, whereas that of the discount is slightly positive. The dP/dVol estimates are consistent with the convexity estimates; the more negatively convex a security, the faster its price increases as volatility falls.

Parameter Sensitivity

Exhibit 14 demonstrates the effect of the refinancing cost specification on the RTP price, RTP effective duration, and RTP convexity of GNMA 8%, 9.5%, and 11% pass-throughs. Refinancing costs were shifted up and down 25%. Higher refinancing costs reduce the value of the short option position embedded in MBSs, which results in higher model prices. Higher refinancing costs also extend the duration of MBSs due to the reduction in the incentive for mortgagors to prepay their loans.

Exhibit 14: Effect of Refinancing Cost Specification on RTP Risk and Return Measures

GNMA	RTP Price			RTP Effective Duration			RTP Effective Convexity		
	Low	Mid	High	Low	Mid	High	Low	Mid	High
8.0%	90-22	90-26	90-27	5.9	6.0	6.1	0.34	0.37	0.38
9.5%	99-00	99-10	99-15	4.8	5.1	5.4	-0.70	-0.94	-0.22
11.0%	105-12	106-29	107-27	0.9	2.8	3.2	-1.57	-2.48	-0.86

Exhibit 15: Effect of Interest Rate Volatility on RTP Risk and Return Measures

	RTP Price			RTP Effective Duration			RTP Effective Convexity		
GNMA	Low	Mid	High	Low	Mid	High	Low	Mid	High
8.0%	90-22	90-26	90-27	6.1	6.0	5.6	0.53	0.37	-0.01
9.5%	99-15	99-10	98-18	5.4	5.1	4.5	-0.89	-0.94	-0.66
11.0%	107-31	106-29	105-09	3.9	2.8	2.0	-0.89	-2.48	0.57

Exhibit 15 displays the effect of interest rate volatility on the RTP price, RTP effective duration, and RTP effective convexity of GNMA 8%, 9.5%, and 11% pass-throughs. The base volatility level was shifted up and down 40%. Increased interest rate volatility generally results in lower prices and shorter effective durations. The largest effects occur for the current coupon and premium pass-throughs. Discount pass-throughs are less affected by interest rate volatility because their embedded prepayment options are far out of the money.

Summary

As with the OAS approach, the RTP model provides risk and return measures that account for the dependence of MBS prepayments on interest rates. The major attraction of the RTP methodology is its independence from an exogenous prepayment function. By directly modeling the refinancing decision of mortgagors, the method provides the potential for more robust results.

Despite its conceptual relevance, RTP is still essentially a black box into which the investor puts assumptions and out of which comes risk and return measures. The endogenously determined pool compositions are available for inspection, as are the parameters defining the interest rate process. However, it may be difficult for the typical investor to assess the reasonableness of these values. As with the OAS approach, this makes it imperative that the investor assess the sensitivity of RTP results to the required assumptions.

CONCLUSIONS

Multiple approaches to valuing MBSs exist because no single methodology has been shown to explain completely the price performance of these securities. All of the valuation methods discussed in this chapter are useful. However, it is critical that the results of each methodology be assessed in terms of their sensitivity to the specification of, and assumptions required for, each model. Investors should examine not only point estimates of MBS risk and return, but also the confidence intervals associated with these point estimates.

SCFY analysis was the simplest approach reviewed. Although it ignores a number of factors critical to the valuation of MBSs, historical analysis of SCFY spreads is a useful check on the results of other methodologies, and can provide a historical perspective on the MBS market.

SA is a valuable extension of the SCFY approach, examining the dynamic nature of MBSs in a holding period return context. If the spread-based horizon pricing model described in the SA section is used, SA investigates the implications of existing spread relationships for holding period returns. Used in conjunction with a historical analysis of SCFY spreads, this can be an important tool in assessing the relative attractiveness of different MBS coupons.

OAS Monte Carlo models extend SA by simulating MBS performance over a large number of interest rate paths. If the interest rate diffusion process and the relationship between interest rates and prepayment rates are correctly specified, this class of model has the potential to provide MBS risk and return measures superior to those available from SCFY analysis.

The RTP model is a binomial option-pricing-based methodology that differs fundamentally from the OAS approach. RTP directly models the refinancing decision of the individual mortgagor instead of attempting to specify aggregate MBS prepayment rates as a function of interest rates. As with the OAS approach, RTP provides risk and return measures that account for the dependence of MBS prepayments on interest rates. A major attraction of the RTP methodology is that it does not depend on the specification of an exogenous prepayment function. By directly modeling the refinancing decision of mortgagors, RTP provides the potential for more robust results.

The major drawback of both the OAS and RTP approaches is that they are essentially black boxes into which an investor puts assumptions and out of which comes risk and return measures. Even if model specifications are available for inspection, it may be difficult to evaluate them. Consequently, it is imperative that investors determine the sensitivity of the results of these models to the assumptions employed. OAS and RTP results should not be used in isolation, but only in conjunction with the results of SCFY analysis and SA. The simpler approaches can be used as checks on the reasonableness of the results of the more sophisticated models.

CHAPTER 27

OPTION-ADJUSTED SPREAD ANALYSIS OF MORTGAGE-BACKED SECURITIES

Lakhbir S. Hayre, DPhil
Director of Mortgage Research
Financial Strategies Group
Prudential Securities Inc.

Kenneth Lauterbach
Vice President
Financial Strategies Group
Prudential Securities Inc.

INTRODUCTION

The proper valuation of debt securities is generally recognized as one of the central problems in quantitative financial analysis. It is

The authors would like to thank David Audley, Robert Samuel, Cyrus Mohebbi, and Vincent Pica for their assistance and helpful comments; and Gladys Cardona, Lisa Pendergast, Joseph Reel and Efren Alba for the preparation and editing of the manuscript.

particularly important for securities with interest rate-dependent cash flows, such as floating-rate instruments, callable corporate bonds, and mortgage-backed securities (MBSs). The dramatic growth over the last few years in the size and diversity of the bond market and an increase in volatility and competitiveness has forced portfolio managers to focus more closely on the investment characteristics of such securities and to estimate their relative value within the spectrum of fixed-income securities.

This chapter describes a general valuation methodology that can be used to compare debt securities with widely differing cash flow patterns. It differs from traditional bond valuation in two major ways. First, instead of using constant discount rates to calculate the present values of cash flows, it uses discount rates derived from the term structure of interest rates. Second, instead of assuming that interest rates remain at their current levels over the life of the security, the methodology evaluates a security based on the full range of interest rate environments that could occur over the life of the security.

Interest rate movements are described by means of a probabilistic model. There are several different mathematical means for describing and evaluating the effects of interest rate changes; the approach used here is a statistical, or "Monte Carlo" simulation by means of computer-generated random numbers.[1] Monte Carlo simulation is used to generate a large number of random paths for interest rates in a way that is consistent both with the term structure of interest rates and historical interest rate behavior. Security cash flows are then obtained along each path. A value of the security for each interest rate path is obtained by calculating the present value of its cash flows using discount rates based on that path. The distribution of these security values gives a risk/reward profile for the security.

---

[1] The other main approaches are continuous time diffusion processes, which lead to differential equations, and binomial lattices. Our model uses statistical simulation since this seems to provide the most flexibility in dealing with complex securities such as MBSs, whose cash flows may depend on both the current and past values of several correlated interest rates.

A key output in the analysis is a spread, usually referred to as the "option-adjusted" spread (OAS), which represents an incremental return or risk premium over Treasury securities. On-the-run (OTR) Treasuries are assumed to provide a "risk-free" rate of return, and the valuation model is calibrated so that all on-the-run Treasuries have an OAS of zero. For other securities the OAS is the implied risk premium, or extra return relative to on-the-run Treasuries. The OAS hence provides a generally applicable return measure that has been adjusted for interest rate volatility and for the effects of embedded options, and thus allows the relative comparison of widely differing securities.

The methodology was initially developed for evaluating the impact of the embedded options in MBSs and callable corporate bonds, and hence is often referred to as OAS analysis. It can be applied to any security, however, regardless of cash flow structure or uncertainty.

In the chapter we give a basic overview of OAS analysis. The concept of an incremental return over the Treasury curve and the modeling of interest rate variation are discussed first. Calibration of the interest rate distribution against the Treasury curve is also described. Then we apply the methodology to mortgage pass-through securities and collateralized mortgage obligation (CMO) bonds; the OASs provide an indication of the relative prepayment risks of different MBSs. Analysis of average lives on the individual, randomly generated interest paths can be used to assess the effect of prepayment uncertainty on investment life. Finally, a historical study is described showing how OAS-based trading strategies can provide significant pick-ups in returns.

VALUATION OF A STREAM OF CASH FLOWS

The standard method for valuing a security is to find the present value of its expected future cash flows using a chosen discount rate. The discount rate that equates the present value of the security to its market price is the yield-to-maturity (YTM). A security's extra return relative to Treasuries is obtained by comparing the security's YTM to the yield of a Treasury with a similar maturity. The difference in yields is the security's spread over the "comparable" Treasury. Interest rate volatility is generally ignored in traditional analysis; securities are evaluated based on current interest rate levels, or in some cases by assuming a specified change in rates.

There are several problems in using traditional analysis to evaluate a security:

- In calculating the YTM, the same discount rate is used to calculate the present values of cash flows received at different points in time. This ignores the term structure of interest rates (exemplified, say, by the Treasury yield curve), which implies that the market assigns different discount rates to cash flows of differing maturities. In essence, the YTM is an averaged discount rate that does not fully use the information provided by the term structure about the market values of cash flows of different maturities.

- The choice of a "comparable" benchmark Treasury against which the security's yield is compared can be arbitrary and even misleading. For example, a zero-coupon ten-year bond and a coupon-paying ten-year bullet bond both would be compared to the ten-year Treasury, although the cash flow patterns of the two securities are very different. This problem is especially acute for securities with interest rate-contingent cash flows, such as MBSs and callable corporate bonds, whose maturity may depend on the future course of interest rates.

- The effect of interest rate volatility on securities with interest rate-contingent cash flows can obviously be critical, but is typically ignored in standard fixed-income analysis. This is a particularly relevant now since much of the recent growth in the fixed-income sector has been securities with contingent cash flows.

The valuation methodology described in this chapter, and generally described as OAS analysis, attempts to deal with the drawbacks of traditional analysis described above. It differs from traditional fixed-income analysis in two fundamental ways:

- OAS introduces interest rate volatility. Instead of assuming that interest rates remain at their current levels over the life of the security, OAS analysis evaluates securities under the more realistic assumption that interest rates are likely to vary in an unpredictable manner over the life of the security.

- In OAS analysis, each cash flow from the security is individually compared to a corresponding Treasury cash flow, and the security's higher return is in essence expressed as an incremental spread over the whole Treasury curve; the OAS measures the extra return the security provides relative to an investment in on-the-run Treasuries (which is assumed to provide the risk-free rate of return).

CALCULATION OF IMPLIED RISK PREMIUM OR OAS

Most investors are familiar with the concept of present value. If $R(1)$, $R(2)$, . . . is a set of discount rates for time periods 1, 2, . . . then the present value of $1 to be received at time t is

$$1/[(1 + R (1)) (1 + R (2)) \ldots (1 + R (t))]$$

Suppose that $R(1)$, $R(2)$, . . . represent a "risk-free" rate (for example, a Treasury bill rate). In practice, investors can, by incurring some extra degree of risk, obtain higher returns. If the appropriate discount rate for a particular investment or security is the riskless rate plus a risk premium s, then the present value of $1 to be received from this security at time t is:

$$1/[(1 + R(1) + s)(1 + R(2) + s) \ldots (1 + R(t) + s)]$$

This gives the discount function applicable to a cash flow received from the security at time t, and we will label it $DISCF(t,s)$. If the security pays cash flows $CF(1), CF(2), \ldots$ at time periods 1,2, $\ldots$ then the value of the security is obtained by present valuing all the cash flows using the appropriate discount factors:

$$PV(s) = CF(1) \times DISCF(1, s) + CF(2) \times DISCF(2, s) + \ldots$$

This can be thought of as the value of the security corresponding to a particular set (or path) $R(1), R(2), \ldots$ of riskless rates, and a specified risk premium s over the riskless rate. In practice, of course, when trying to value a security we do not know the path that interest rates will take over the term of the security. One approach in dealing with this uncertainty is to use statistical methods to generate a large number of possible interest rate paths that can occur over the term of the security and calculate $PV(s)$, the value of the security, for each path. The average of the security values so obtained can be thought of as the true or "fair" value of the security:

Value of Security = average of PV(s) over all interest-rate paths
$$= AVGPV(s) \tag{1}$$

This gives the fair value of a security for a given risk premium or spread s over the riskless rate.

Definition of the OAS

Equation (1) gives the fair value of a security assuming that its fair risk premium is s. Typically, however, we are more likely to know the market price of a security, and the question that the OAS answers is: what risk premium or incremental spread over the riskless rate does this security provide? The answer is obtained by finding the value of s that makes the average present value of the security, calculated as described above, equal to the market price of the security:

$$Price = AVGPV\,(s) \qquad (2)$$

The solution of this equation gives the security's implied spread or risk premium over the riskless rate, and is what is typically termed the OAS. By definition, it follows that for any security providing the risk-free rate of return, the solution of equation (2) is zero.

Calibration Against Treasury Curve

The risk-free rate has been defined here as the return received by investing in OTR Treasuries. Hence, assuming that they are efficiently priced, each OTR should have a risk premium or OAS of zero. That is, the valuation model should be calibrated so that for each OTR,

$$Market\ Price = AVGPV\,(0) \qquad (3)$$

where AVGPV(s) is as defined in equation (1). In practical terms, this involves making appropriate statistical adjustments to the sample of possible interest rate paths used in calculating the OAS; the result, roughly speaking, is that the average or mean interest rate path will correspond to the usual implied short-term Treasury forward rates. The next section provides more discussion on this.[2]

---

[2] For some technical details, see the Appendix to Lakhbir S. Hayre and Kenneth Lauterbach, "Stochastic Valuation of Debt Securities," in Frank J. Fabozzi (ed.), *Managing Institutional Assets* (Chicago, IL: Probus Publishing, 1990).

MODELING INTEREST RATE AND CASH FLOW UNCERTAINTY

The previous section gave a general description of the calculation of the OAS. Exhibit 1 gives a schematic representation of this process. Below we discuss some of the details of these steps as implemented in the model used to analyze mortgage securities.

Exhibit 1: Option-Adjusted Valuation of a Security

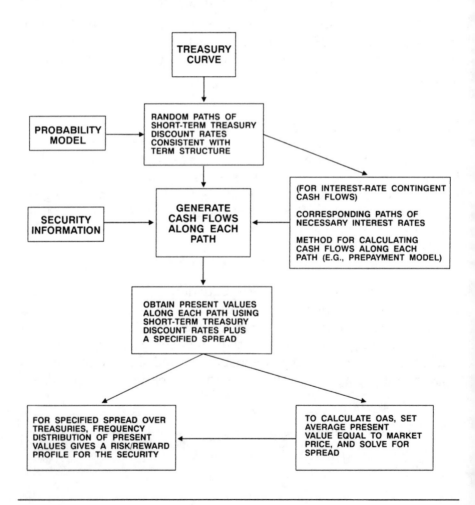

Modeling Interest Rate Fluctuations

As is fairly common in modeling interest rate movements, we assume that percentage changes in interest rates have a bell-shaped or "normal" frequency curve.[3] Computer-generated random numbers are used to obtain paths of interest rates, with the random numbers scaled so that the volatility displayed by the simulated interest rate movements matches observed market volatilities. The number of possible interest rate paths that could occur over the term of the security is theoretically infinite. Hence, a sufficient number of paths are chosen randomly so as to obtain an adequate statistical representation of the whole universe of possible paths.

Fluctuations in short-term Treasury discount rates should be modeled in a manner that is consistent with the term structure. In this chapter, consistency has been defined to mean that all on-the-run Treasuries have a zero incremental spread or risk premium over the risk-free rate (i.e., the OTRs constitute the set of risk-free securities). In other words, referring to equation (3) above, the average present value of an on-the-run Treasury obtained by discounting its cash flows by the short-term rates and then averaging across interest rate paths, is equal to the market price of the security. This is acheived by appropriate trends or "drift" terms into the lognormal process used to generate interest rate paths.

The rationale for calibrating interest rate movements against the Treasury curve is illustrated in Exhibits 2 and 3, which show frequency distributions of the present values of the cash flows from two-year, ten-year, and thirty-year Treasuries. These present values are obtained by discounting each Treasury's cash flows by the short-term rates along each path; thus, each randomly generated path gives a present value for the security. The frequency distributions in Exhibits 2 and 3 are the outcomes of 2,000 random interest rate paths.

---

[3] The interest rate is said to be "lognormal." A "mean reversion" process is applied to stop the rates from going to abnormally high or low levels. The Appendix to *Hayre and Lauterbach, op. cit.*, gives a more detailed description of the interest rate generation process.

Exhibit 2: Distribution of Present Values of Treasury Cash Flows with No Drifts in Short-Term Rates

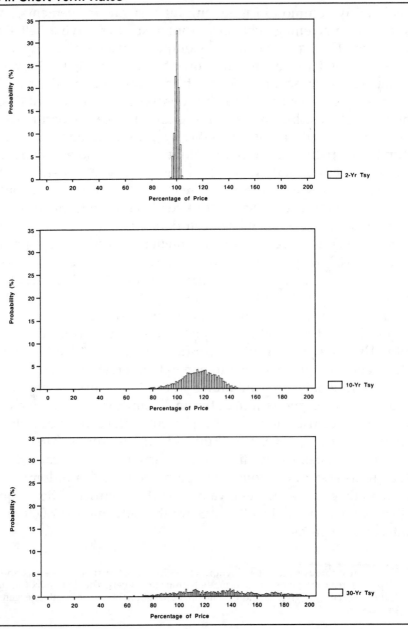

The distributions in Exhibit 2 are obtained assuming no trend in short-term Treasury rates. Since the yield curve was upward sloping at the time of this analysis, the longer Treasuries have higher coupons (or YTMs), and the centers of their distributions are higher (i.e., the average or expected present values are greater). On the other hand, the dispersion of present values is also greater for longer maturities. The market pricing of these Treasuries (all three being priced close to par) in some sense reflects the market's balancing of the greater average present values of the longer Treasuries with their greater variability in values, as well as possibly reflecting other factors such as expectations of interest rate changes, liquidity, supply and demand, etc.

Exhibit 3 shows the distributions of present values after trends or "drifts" have been introduced into the paths of short-term rates.[4] These drifts are chosen so that all on-the-run Treasuries, including the ones shown in Exhibit 2, have the average of their present values equal to their current market prices. The drifts "normalize" the analysis with the on-the-run Treasuries as a baseline. All on-the-run Treasuries have an OAS of zero; thus, it is assumed that the on-the-run Treasuries are priced efficiently and reflect accurately the values that the market assigns to riskless cash flows of differing maturities. Other securities are then valued relative to on-the-run Treasuries; the on-the-runs, which perhaps are the most liquid and desirable (for a given price) of securities, are used as the benchmark for the relative valuation of securities.[5]

---

[4] To avoid the connotation that interest rates are expected to trend upward or downward, the drifts can be viewed simply as discounting adjustments made to bring the prices from the model into line with market prices.

[5] In principle, the probability distribution can be calibrated against any reference group of securities. For example, if attention is restricted to a particular sector of the corporate market, a set of benchmark bonds in this sector can be chosen as the reference set. However, for a general valuation method, the on-the-run Treasuries seem to be the most logical reference set. This process of calibration is sometimes referred to as ensuring that the model is "arbitrage-free," since the objective is to ensure that, theoretically, the securities in the reference group are fairly priced relative to each other, that is, the model does not indicate arbitrage opportunities between these securities.

Exhibit 3: Distribution of Present Values of Treasury Cash Flows with Implied Drifts in Short-Term Rates

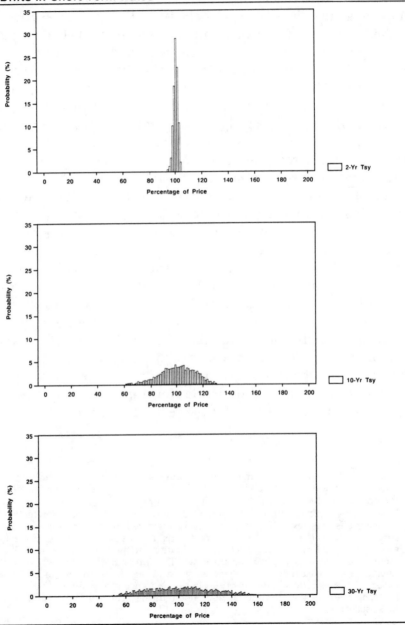

Cash Flows on Interest Rate Paths

For straight securities, such as noncallable Treasuries, agencies, or corporates, the cash flows are the same on all interest rate paths. For interest rate-contingent cash flows, such as MBSs, a method for generating cash flows (e.g., a prepayment model) as a function of the interest rate path is needed.

Present Values on Interest Rate Paths

For a chosen spread, the cash flows on each interest rate path are discounted to the present by the short-term discount rates along the path plus the spread. If this spread is considered a "fair" risk premium over Treasuries for the security, then the present value on a path can be considered to be the fair or theoretical price for the security, *given this particular realization of interest rates*. Some interest rate paths will affect positively the value of the security, while other interest rate paths will affect adversely the present value of the security. The average of these present values can be considered the fair price corresponding to this particular spread over Treasuries.

As an illustration, Exhibit 4 shows the distribution of present values for an agency security for an incremental spread of fifty basis points; in other words, for each interest rate path, the cash flows from the agency are discounted by the short-term rates on the path plus fifty basis points. A short-term rate volatility of 15% per year is assumed. The agency is the FNMA 9.35% debenture maturing on February 12, 1996. It is noncallable, and hence its cash flows are fixed. Thus, variation in present values is caused by variation in the short-term Treasury discount rates. Since the coupon on the agency is fixed, low interest rate paths lead to high present values for the security, while high interest rate paths lead to low present values.

Also shown in Exhibit 4 is the average of the present values. For a spread of fifty basis points, the average is 100.54; this is the

---

Exhibit 4: Distribution of Present Values for the FNMA 9.35% Debenture of February 12, 1996

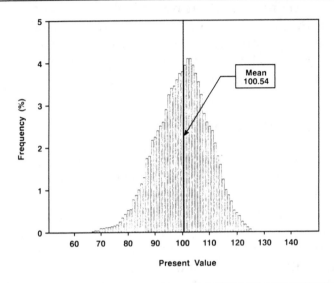

"fair" price if fifty basis points is considered to be a fair spread over Treasuries for this agency debenture.

The actual price of the FNMA debenture is 101.1875. Calculation of the OAS requires finding the spread that makes the average present value equal to this price.[6] An iterative solution method gives the OAS as being equal to thirty-eight basis points; in other words, if a spread of thirty-eight basis points is added to the short-term Treasury discount rates, the average of the resulting present values for the agency's cash flows is equal to 101.1875, the current price of the security.

---

[6] The spread is calculated by a process of iteration. An initial guess for the spread is chosen, then the average present value is calculated for this spread and compared with the specified price. The spread is then adjusted up or down repeatedly until the average present value is equal to the specified price.

COMPARISON OF THE OAS AND TRADITIONAL YIELD SPREADS

To summarize, it can be seen that the OAS differs from the traditional spread over Treasuries in two ways:

- The traditional spread is a spread off a single point on the current Treasury curve. The OAS can be viewed as an average spread over the whole Treasury curve.[7]

- Interest rate volatility is factored into the calculation by allowing random fluctuations in discount rates, and, for interest rate-contingent cash flows, calculating the security cash flows separately for each interest rate path. This explains the term *option-adjusted* spread, since by considering the likely cash flows over the spectrum of possible interest rate paths, we are averaging out, or adjusting for, the effects of embedded options on security cash flows.

The differences between the OAS and the traditional yield spread is illustrated in Exhibit 5 in the simplified case of zero interest rate volatility. The discount rates used are the implied short-term rates obtained from the current Treasury curve, plus a spread. The OAS is the spread that makes the present value equal to the market price of the security. The discount rates are hence different for different periods. In traditional analysis, a constant discount rate is used to calculate the present value of the cash flows, with the YTM being the constant discount rate that equates the present value to the market price.

In financial terms, the OAS can be interpreted as the average extra return that is received for investing in a particular security instead of investing in the "safe" alternative of OTR Treasuries. To those who would ask, "which OTR?," the theoretically correct reply is that it does not matter, since the model has been calibrated

---

[7] Although mechanically it is calculated as a spread over short-term Treasury discount rates, these rates are derived using the current Treasury curve, allowing the OAS to be interpreted as a spread over the whole curve.

Exhibit 5: Traditional Yield Spread and OAS in the Zero-Volatility Case

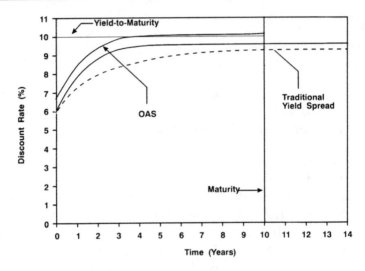

* Refers to implied short-term forward rates.

so that all OTRs have a zero OAS, making us indifferent as to which OTR we invest in. In fact, however, there is a very strong connection between the OAS and the traditional Treasury yield spread. For securities with fixed (non-interest rate-dependent) cash flows, the OAS is typically very close to the traditional Treasury yield spread. For securities with interest rate-dependent cash flows, the effect of using a large sample of possible interest rate paths and calculating a projected set of security cash flows for each path is to capture the impact of changing interest rates on the security. The resulting spread over Treasuries has hence been adjusted for the effects of embedded options, and thus the name OAS.

The OAS, in short, represents a generalization of the traditional Treasury spread, and can be used to compare securities with or without embedded options.

OPTION-ADJUSTED ANALYSIS OF PASS-THROUGHS

Mortgage pass-throughs, like all fixed-rate securities (we only consider fixed-coupon pass-throughs in this section), are subject to interest rate risk; the value of their coupon payments changes inversely to interest rates. In addition, pass-throughs are subject to prepayment risk, a form of call risk; mortgage holders generally have the right to prepay at any time all or part of their mortgages. Prepayment levels are heavily dependent on interest rates, thus leading to complex interdependent changes in the value of a pass-through as interest rates change.

Exhibit 6 shows OASs for several GNMA coupons.

Exhibit 6 shows that the GNMA 11 has a regular spread of 116 basis points, compared with a spread of 96 basis points for the GNMA 8, suggesting that the GNMA 11 provides a higher return over comparable-maturity Treasuries. However, once interest rates and prepayment volatility are considered, the GNMA 11 looks less attractive; the GNMA 11 has an OAS of seventy-one basis points, compared with eighty-six basis points for the GNMA 8. This results from the negative convexity of the GNMA 11. A drop in interest rates tends to lead to an increase in the prepayment rate of

Exhibit 6: Yield Spreads and OASs for GNMAs

Coupon	Price*	Rem. Term	Proj. PSA**	Yield	Avg. Life	Spread•	OAS••	Option Cost
GNMA 8	94-22	26-09	99	9.02	10.4	96	86	15
GNMA 9	99-30	29-05	113	9.12	11.0	106	76	35
GNMA 10	104-08	29-03	180	9.23	8.1	123	77	55
GNMA 11	107-28	25-02	255	8.95	5.5	116	71	47
GNMA 12	111-26	24-02	309	8.47	4.6	82	51	27

* Prices and prepayment projections as of April 2, 1991.
** Projected prepayment rate is expressed as a percentage of the benchmark Public Association (PSA) curve.
• Spread is the difference between the yield of the GNMA and the Treasury curve yield at the average life.
•• OAS is calculated using a short-rate volatility of 15%.

the premium GNMA 11, thus reducing the benefits of the higher coupon compared to lower discount rates, as well as returning the premium faster. On the other hand, if interest rates rise, the decline in the GNMA 11 prepayments is beneficial because the premium is returned at a slower rate; however, it also means that the negative effect of the higher discount rates is increased, due to the higher outstanding principal balances.

In contrast, the GNMA 8 has low prepayment volatility. Interest rates would have to drop several hundred basis points before prepayments increase significantly. Hence, once interest rate volatility is considered, the GNMA 8 offers better value than the GNMA 11. From Exhibit 6, it is clear that low-premium coupons, which not coincidently are the ones with the highest prepayment volatility and negative convexity, tend to be most affected by interest rate volatility.

Sensitivity of OASs to Changes in Volatility

Interest rate volatility changes also have the greatest effect on low-premium coupons. Exhibit 7 shows the OASs of the GNMA coupons in Exhibit 6 at annual interest rate volatilities of 0, 10, 15, and 20%.

The OASs of all coupons are reduced by heightened interest rate volatility, with the low-premium coupon most affected. In an options theory context, this can be explained by viewing an MBS as a noncallable bond minus a call option; the higher the volatility,

Exhibit 7: Sensitivity of GNMA OASs to Volatility Changes

	OAS at Volatility of			
	0%	10%	15%	20%
GNMA 8	101	93	86	80
GNMA 9	111	91	76	65
GNMA 10	132	99	77	62
GNMA 11	118	89	71	58
GNMA 12	78	65	51	41

the greater the value of the call option, and hence the lower the value of the MBS.

The difference between the OASs at zero volatility and at specified higher levels gives an indication of the impact of interest rate volatility on various coupons, and may be termed an "option cost." The option cost is relatively low for discounts, increases to a maximum for low premiums, and then starts decreasing for the high premiums, which, like discounts, have low prepayment volatility.

The negative impact of interest rate volatility even on discount coupons that benefit from increased prepayments can be explained by considering the effect of higher prepayments if interest rates drop. If there is a substantial drop in interest rates, the discount coupons gain from a faster return of principal, but this leaves a lower outstanding balance with which to benefit from the differences between the coupons and prevailing short-term rates.

As Exhibit 7 indicates, interest rate volatility is a critical parameter in OASs. It is useful to look at the OASs at several volatility levels to obtain a clearer understanding of the option-adjusted value of the MBS (see Exhibit 7). Not only do the OASs change as volatility changes, but also, to a lesser extent, even the relative values of different coupons can change. For example, from Exhibit 7, at an assumed volatility of 10% per year, the GNMA 10 has an OAS of ninety-nine basis points, which is greater than the OAS of ninety-three basis points for the GNMA 8; however, at a volatility of 15%, the GNMA 9 has an OAS of eighty-six basis points compared with an OAS of seventy-seven basis points for the GNMA 10, indicating that the GNMA 8 is a better value at the higher volatility level.

Distribution of Present Values

Each computer-generated random path of interest rates represents a possible realization of the future. The present value of a security's cash flows on this path represents the outcome of investing in the security for this particular realization of interest rates. The dispersion and range of present values obtained from a large number of randomly generated interest rate paths provides valuable insight into the risks and rewards of investing in the security.

Exhibit 8 shows the distribution of present values obtained from 2,000 simulations for a GNMA 7, GNMA 11, and GNMA 15. The present values were calculated using the OASs in the discounting; for ease of comparison, the present values are stated as a percentage of the current market price, so that the average for each distribution is 100%.

The distribution of the GNMA 7, a deep-discount coupon, is only slightly skewed. Because of its substantial call protection (mortgage rates would have to drop to about 5% before it experiences very high prepayments), the properties of the GNMA 7 are somewhat comparable to those of the ten-year Treasury shown in Exhibit 4.

The GNMA 11 is a low-premium coupon with very high prepayment volatility at current mortgage rate levels. This is reflected in the distribution of present values. The distribution is heavily skewed to the left. The chances of large upside gains are limited by prepayment risk; if interest rates decline, increasing prepayments cancel part of the gain in value from the lower rates. On the other hand, the distribution of present values is concentrated in a relatively narrow range; the fast principal paydown means that the GNMA 11 is basically a short-term security.

In terms of relative risk, as measured by the dispersion of present values, it is interesting to note that the GNMA 11 has a narrower range of present values than the ten-year Treasury. Thus, despite the fact that the GNMA 11 is a thirty-year security and is subject to prepayment variability, it is possible to say that it has less investment uncertainty than the ten-year Treasury (assuming liquidity and credit quality are roughly comparable).

This emphasizes the points made in the previous section about the causes of uncertainty in the value of a security. For high-quality, liquid securities, there are generally two main reasons for this uncertainty: the value of the security's coupon payments relative

Exhibit 8: Distribution of Present Values for a GNMA 7, GNMA 11, and GNMA 15

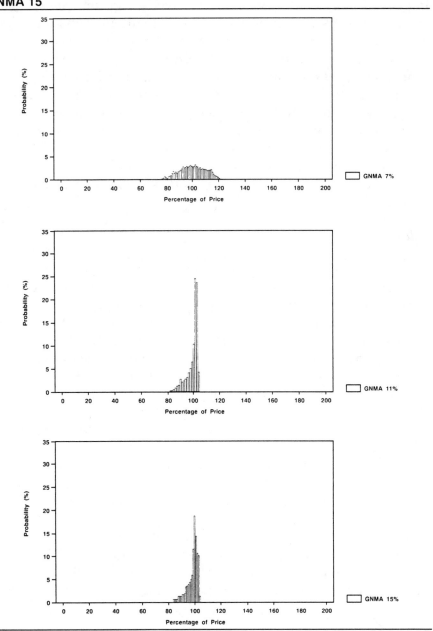

to prevailing rates in the future, and, for callable securities, the impact of the call features. The ten-year Treasury suffers only from the first risk, whereas the GNMA 11 suffers from both. However, the first risk has more impact on the ten-year Treasury than on the GNMA 11 because the GNMA's principal is reduced over time, making its coupon payments relatively less important.

Finally, for the GNMA 15, the distribution of present values is less skewed. The GNMA 15 is a very high-premium security and its prepayment levels will not change significantly unless there is a substantial increase in prepayments. Thus, like the GNMA 7, the GNMA 15 has only limited prepayment volatility, and its investment profile is similar to that of a shorter-maturity Treasury.

CMO BONDS

A CMO segments mortgage cash flows in order to create a number of bonds of varying maturities. A basic or prototype CMO contains three to five sequential-pay bonds, with one often structured as an accrual class or "Z-bond." Although the last few years have seen the creation of a vast diversity of CMO structures, including floating-rate classes, bonds with more or less guaranteed paydown schedules ("PAC" bonds) and simultaneous-pay bonds, for illustrative simplicity our attention is restricted to the basic CMO structure described above. In practice, the OAS of a specific CMO bond requires using the exact paydown structure of that CMO issue.

As an example, a generic four-class "ABCZ" CMO (i.e., four sequential-pay classes with a Z-bond as the final class) is used. All principal paydowns from the collateral are paid to Class A until it is retired, then to Class B, and so on. The collateral is GNMA 9 pass-throughs. The par amounts of the bonds in each class are chosen so that the four classes have average lives of approximately two, five, seven, and twenty years, respectively. The bonds are assumed to be monthly pay, with a thirty-day delay.

Exhibit 9: OASs for a GNMA 9 CMO*

							OAS at Volatility of		
Class	Par Amt.($)	Price**	Cpn.	Avg. Life (Yrs.)	B-E Yield	Trsy. Spread	10%	15%	20%
A	35.1	99.7522	8.0	2	8.03	100	84	73	59
B	19.0	98.3658	8.5	5	8.97	115	108	94	79
C	18.0	98.9966	9.0	7	9.28	125	103	103	91
D	27.9	92.0439	9.0	16	9.81	150	117	117	111

* The GNMA 9 is assumed to have a remaining term of 28-05 years; the CMO is priced
  assuming a projected prepayment speed of 110% PSA.
** All prices shown in decimal form. Analysis is based on prices and yield curve at close of
  April 22, 1991.

Exhibit 9 gives traditional and OAA for the four-class ABCZ CMO described above.

Interest rate volatility has a greater effect on the value of the CMO bonds then on the GNMA 9. This is because a given change in the prepayment rate on the GNMA 9 has a proportionately greater effect on the CMO bond that is paying down at the time. For example, Class A comprises about one-third of the total issue; hence a 1% prepayment on the GNMA 9 means approximately a 3% prepayment for Class A. This makes the OASs of the CMO bonds more sensitive to changes in interest rate volatility, and, hence, prepayment rate volatility, than the OAS of the GNMA 9.[8]

In terms of investment characteristics, Class C is the bond most comparable to the underlying GNMA 9. In general, however, because of differing maturities, a direct comparison of CMOs and pass-throughs may not always be relevant. For example, investors in the short-maturity Class A bonds would have different maturity needs than investors in the GNMA 9 pass-through, suggesting that the A bond should be compared to short-maturity corporate bonds or Treasuries rather than the GNMA.

---

[8] In this sense, the CMO bonds can be said to have greater prepayment uncertainty than the GNMA 9. However, in terms of cash-flow uncertainty, the CMO bonds have less prepayment uncertainty than the GNMA 9, since for a particular bond, the cash flows are concentrated in a smaller time period than the thirty-year GNMA. A distinction thus has to be made between the effects of prepayment uncertainty on value and on cash-flow timing.

HISTORICAL PERFORMANCE OF OAS-BASED TRADING STRATEGIES

Although stochastic security analysis is theoretically more sound and more consistent than traditional analysis, does it really help the portfolio manager to increase portfolio returns? Historical analysis for MBS trading versus Treasury trading indicates that the use of OASs can significantly improve the returns from such trades. These results are consistent with other studies of the historical performance of OAS-based trading strategies.[9]

The actual return from any fixed-income security over a holding period depends to a large extent on interest rate changes. To reduce this rate-change dependence, GNMA pass-throughs were matched with similar-duration Treasuries. Starting in September 1985, it was assumed that each GNMA was purchased at the beginning of each month, and a similar-duration Treasury was sold short to finance the purchase. Each trade was unwound six months later.

OASs have varied widely over the last few years, as shown in Exhibit 10.

To a striking degree, the return of a GNMA relative to a similar-duration Treasury over six-month holding periods is related closely to the OAS of the GNMA at the beginning of the six-month period. This is illustrated in Exhibit 11, which shows the OASs and six-month returns relative to similar-duration Treasuries for a GNMA 11.

Exhibit 12 gives details of OASs and subsequent six-month return performances for all major GNMA coupons.

Analysis for three-month and twelve-month periods gives results very similar to those in Exhibit 12. These results suggest that high OASs are excellent indicators of value for MBSs.

---

[9] For example, see David P. Jacob and Alden L. Toevs, "New Valuation and Price Sensitivity Models for Mortgage-Backed Securities," *Housing Finance Review*, Volume 7, No. 1 (Spring 1988).

Exhibit 10: OASs for Selected GNMAs: 1985 to Present

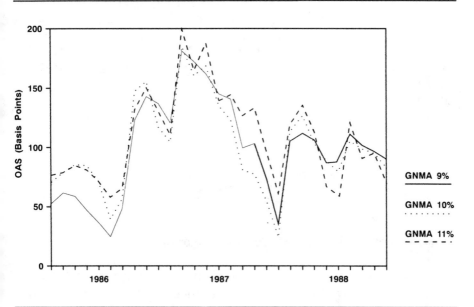

Exhibit 11: OASs and Six-Month Returns over Treasuries for a GNMA 11

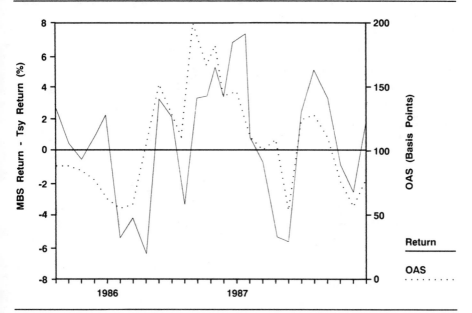

Exhibit 12: OASs and GNMA Returns over Treasuries

OAS*	Frequency of MBS Outperforming Similar-Duration Treasury Over Next Six Months (%)	Average Difference Between GNMA and Similar-Duration Treasury Returns**
Less than 50	13	-5.98
50 to 100	32	-0.82
100 to 150	76	2.86
Greater than 150	100	6.24

Note: Period covered is from mid-1985 to the present.
  * OASs are calculated assuming a volatility of 15%.
 ** Constant reinvestment rate of 6.5% is assumed.

Relative Predictive Power of OASs and Regular Spreads

The results above show that OASs possess excellent predictive power concerning likely MBS performance. Do the simpler regular yield spreads over comparable Treasuries possess the same predictive powers? Our analysis suggests that although regular spreads have reasonably good predictive powers, they are significantly inferior to those of OASs.

We first compared correlations. The correlation between the regular spread and the subsequent six-month return of the GNMA over a comparable-duration Treasury was 53% for the sample period mid-1985 to mid-1988. The corresponding correlation using the OAS was 68%, a marked improvement in statistical terms.

As another comparison test, we considered two alternative strategies:

A: At the beginning of each month, purchase the GNMA with the highest regular spread, and finance the purchase by shorting a comparable-duration Treasury. Unwind the trade six months later.

B: Same as A, except that the GNMA pass-throughs are chosen based on the highest OAS.

Exhibit 13: Performance of OAS and Spread-Based Trading Strategies		
	Strategy A (Spread)	Strategy B (OAS)
Frequency of Positive Returns	62%	81%
Average Return	0.84	2.58

Exhibit 13 shows the results of the two strategies over the sample period.

In only 8% of the cases did the spread-based strategy lead to a higher return than the OAS-based strategy. These results indicate that the portfolio manager obtains a distinct improvement in results by switching from a spread-based to an OAS-based trading strategy.

SUMMARY

The bond markets have undergone a major transformation in the last decade. Volatility has increased dramatically, increasing both the risks and rewards for bond investors. This has been accompanied by a tremendous expansion in the size and diversity of the market. Large sectors of the market now consist of securities, such as floating-rate instruments, MBSs, and callable corporates, which often have complex, interest rate-dependent cash flows. These factors have combined to make it more difficult for the professional portfolio manager to identify value in the bond markets and assess the risk of a particular security.

Traditional bond valuation methods can be inadequate and even misleading, especially when dealing with interest rate-contingent cash flows. This chapter has described OAS analysis, a bond valuation methodology that attempts to improve on traditional methods. It uses the term structure of interest rates in calculating the present values of cash flows, and it introduces interest rate volatility into the analysis. All securities are valued relative to a base reference group, which in this chapter has been on-the-run

Treasuries. This allows a consistent and theoretically sound comparison of different securities, including those with interest rate-contingent cash flows. Historical analysis indicates that these new valuation methods can help the portfolio manager to improve returns significantly.

It is important, however, to note the assumptions and limitations of these new valuation methods. The probabilistic model used to describe interest rate movements is consistent with historical interest rate behavior; however, there is no guarantee that future interest rate movements will follow historical behavior. The techniques used to obtain cash flows for a given interest rate realization (namely, the prepayment model for MBSs) are again based on historical data. The risk premium over the risk-free rate (the OAS) has been assumed to be an additive constant; there is no particular reason to assume this except for simplicity and the fact that it is consistent with the traditional method of stating a fixed-income security's return as yield spread over a comparable Treasury. Finally, differences in credit quality and liquidity between securities have not been addressed.

Despite these caveats, it is clear that stochastic valuation methods are a powerful tool for the bond portfolio manager. They allow for a sound analysis and comparison of securities with widely differing cash-flow patterns. The proper use of stochastic valuation methods can aid the portfolio manager in improving returns while keeping risk within tolerable limits.

CHAPTER 28

ANALYZING THE PATH DEPENDENCE OF MBSs

Andrew S. Davidson
Managing Director
Mortgage-Backed Securities Research
Merrill Lynch Capital Markets

Michael D. Herskovitz
Director
Mortgage-Backed Securities Research
Merrill Lynch Capital Markets

INTRODUCTION

Analytical tools, which once required the expertise of so-called rocket scientists, have become part of the mainstream of fixed-income analysis. Investors have moved well beyond the early duration measures and now routinely evaluate convexity, option-adjusted spread, and expected returns.

Without question, existing analytics provide a good summary of relative value and performance. Often, however, these more sophisticated methods gloss over important information regarding the value and risk of the securities.

In this chapter we focus on the path-dependence risks of fixed-income securities, with special emphasis on mortgage-backed securities (MBSs). In other words, we will show why the MBS investor should not only be concerned about the scenario where interest rates are expected to fall 100 basis points over one year, but also about the path that interest rates take to reach that point.

This chapter begins with a discussion of how prepayments and security structure affect the path-dependence risks of MBSs. We discuss currently used analytical models and present a new method for examining MBS risk and return. The chapter concludes with applications of the new technology to individual security analysis.

Extension of the analytic techniques from single securities to entire portfolios offers new perspectives for portfolio risk and return analysis.

PREPAYMENTS

The standard analysis of MBS prepayments examines the relationship between prepayment rates and interest rate levels. This simple, yet useful approach helps when examining the average life variability of MBSs and CMOs. A more thorough analysis of MBS prepayments must reflect the relationship between a path of interest rates and prepayment rates.

Interest Rate Levels

Numerous factors affect prepayment rates. They include refinancing incentive, age of the loan, time of year, and housing economics. The refinancing incentive, however, dominates the other factors. Differences or ratios between the borrower's coupon and

---

Exhibit 1: Effect of Prepayments on Average Life
This exhibit compares average life for the PAC classes of a CMO (FHLMC 65) and its underlying collateral (FHLMC 30-year PC 10%). The PAC classes maintain average life stability until rates decline more than 100 basis points.

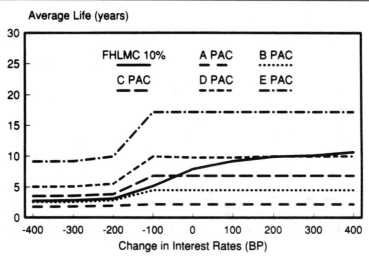

Average Life (years)

the yield of a current coupon thirty-year mortgage, serve as proxies for the incentive.

In order to measure the impact of prepayments on relative value, market participants make use of scenario prepayment rate forecasts. These forecasts contain the long-term prepayment rate, measured in terms of the Public Securities Association (PSA) model. On their own, the scenario prepayment rates are somewhat theoretical measures of MBS cash flow sensitivity. In order to obtain a more concrete grasp on the prepayment issue, weighted average lives (WALs) can be calculated for each of the scenarios. Exhibits 1 and 2 contain the WALs for a FHLMC thirty-year PC 10% and for selected classes of a CMO (FHLMC 65) collateralized by FHLMC 10s.

The PAC classes retain cash flow stability until interest rates decline more than 100 basis points, at which time PAC bands are broken and the bonds shorten. In order to maintain the general stability of the PAC classes, the prepayment risk must be trans-

---

Exhibit 2: Effect of Prepayments on Average Life
This exhibit compares the average lives of the non-PAC classes of the CMO (FHLMC 65) with the underlying collateral. The non-PAC classes contain considerably more average life risk than the collateral.

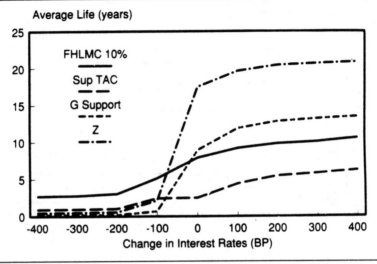

---

ferred to other bonds. Exhibit 2 contains the average life profiles for the non-PAC classes.

Relative to the underlying collateral, the average lives of the non-PAC issues exhibit considerably more sensitivity to changing interest rates. Average life sensitivity comes as no surprise to investors, who have come to rely on analytical methods to determine the relative value of the more risky securities.

Path Dependence of Prepayment Rates

The relationship between interest rate levels and prepayment rates described in the previous section provides a useful, yet incomplete view of MBS prepayment risk. Focusing on interest rate levels involves two simplifying assumptions. The first assumption is that interest rates shift once and then remain constant until the matur-

Exhibit 3: Interest Rate Paths
To examine the role of path dependence two sample interest rate paths have been constructed. After month 48 these paths converge and both move down 200 basis points.

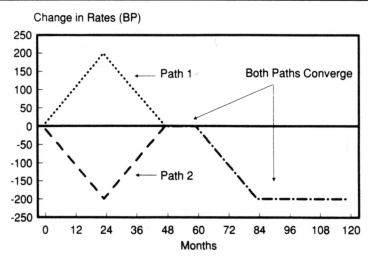

ity of the bond. The second is somewhat more subtle, and revolves around an understanding of the mortgage pool.

Mortgage pools contain a cohort of borrowers who share at least one thing in common—they obtained loans of roughly the same coupon at roughly the same time. Other than that, the borrowers may be quite different in their demographics, economic acumen, and financial resources. Consequently, borrowers differ in their willingness or ability to prepay their loans under favorable circumstances. As a result, when interest rates fall, those borrowers most likely to prepay exit the pool first, skewing the pool to contain borrowers with less propensity to prepay. The relationship between future prepayment rates and past interest rates has been commonly termed path dependence. To illustrate the concept in further detail, two sample interest rate paths have been set up in Exhibit 3, with corresponding prepayment rates for a seasoned 10% FHLMC thirty-year PC in Exhibit 4. The prepayment rates derive from the Merrill Lynch Prepayment Model.

Exhibit 4: Prepayment Rate Path
The comparison of the CPR paths shows the effect of path dependence. Although the interest rate paths converge after month 48, prepayment rates diverge as interest rates decline.

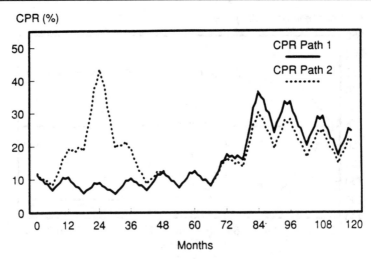

For Path 1, interest rates rise then fall over the first forty-eight months, whereas for Path 2 rates fall then rise over a similar period. After the fourth year the rate paths follow a similar course, remaining constant for a time, then falling 200 basis points. Corresponding prepayment rates for the two paths can be seen in Exhibit 4.

For the first four years, the path of prepayment rates follows a predictable course. Prepayments decline as interest rates rise (Path 1) and rise as interest rates fall (Path 2). During the next interest rate decline, prepayments for the two paths differ. From month seventy-two and onward prepayment rates for Path 1 exceed those of Path 2. As rates fall the second time, the most interest rate-sensitive borrowers have already exited from the pool that followed Path 2, leading to a group of less interest rate-sensitive borrowers. It is this relationship between past interest rates and future prepayment rates that characterizes path dependence.

Burnout

Along both prepayment paths in Exhibit 4, a decline in prepayment rates occurs after month eighty-four even though interest rates remain constant. The term "burnout" connotes this occurrence of lower prepayment rates over time despite a constant refinancing incentive. Path dependence and burnout effects have a rather subtle, yet important, difference on prepayment behavior. Burnout describes the path of prepayments holding interest rates constant, while path dependence relates to the impact of the path of previous interest rates on future payments.

Within the Merrill Lynch Prepayment Model the controls for path dependence and burnout depend on the pool factor. The level of paydown serves as a proxy for both the quantity of interest rate-sensitive borrowers and the degree of financial incentive for remaining borrowers to refinance. This relationship between factor and refinancing incentive can be seen in Exhibit 5.

Exhibit 5: MBS Prepayment Rate Burnout
Holding refinancing incentive constant, prepayment rates on MBSs have been observed to decline as the pools pay down. This effect, known as burnout, has been modeled as a relationship between the relative coupon and pool factors.

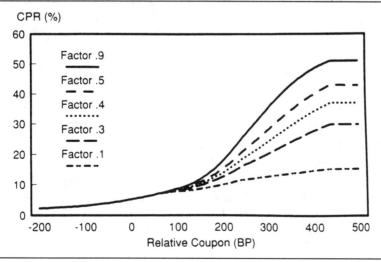

In Exhibit 5, prepayment rates are shown based on the relative coupon and factor. The relative coupon equals the weighted average coupon (WAC) minus the current coupon yield. Negative levels indicate discounts, whereas positive values represent premiums.[1] The exhibit indicates that even as the incentive to refinance remains constant, prepayments will decline as the pool pays down. At very low factors the relationship between prepayments and relative coupon appears almost flat.

Path Dependence and Security Structure

Complications abound when the assessment of path dependence from MBSs to CMOs is extended. Not only does the path of interest rates affect the prepayment behavior of the MBS pool, but the path also leads to changes in the underlying deal structure. As a result, measurements of risk, such as average life and duration, may show dramatic movements.

To illustrate this relationship between path dependence and CMOs, three sample interest rate paths have been constructed. These paths, illustrated in Exhibit 6, converge at the same terminal point, yet diverge during the first 48 months.

At month forty-eight, the expected average lives and modified durations have been determined for the various classes of FHLMC 65, a CMO collateralized by FHLMC 10% thirty-year PCs. The result can be seen in Exhibit 7.

Average lives and durations are rather similar across Paths 1 and 2. However, the support TAC and support bonds show some lengthening in Path 1 relative to Path 2. This can be attributed to the slower prepayments due to the intervening higher rates—more principal remains at the end of four years.

The results for Path 3 show some surprises. As interest rates fall over the first two years, the support class pays off entirely. After rates begin to rise again, the support TAC and Z classes

---

[1] Within the Merrill Lynch Prepayment models, the relative coupon is measured by examining the ratio between WAC and current coupon yield.

Exhibit 6: Sample Interest Rate Paths
To illustrate the relationship between path dependence and CMOs three sample rate paths have been considered. These paths share the same initial and terminal levels but have different interim rate shifts.

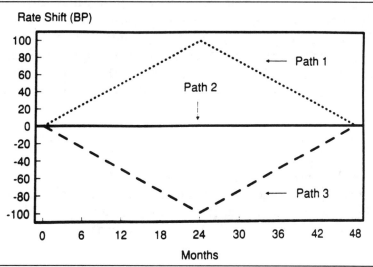

Exhibit 7
At month 48 the average lives and duration depend on the path of interest rates. Both measures show particular sensitivity to cases when rates fall, then rise (Path 3).

FHLMC 65	AVERAGE LIFE			MODIFIED DURATION		
CLASS	PATH 1	PATH 2	PATH 3	PATH 1	PATH 2	PATH 3
B PAC	1.16	1.16	1.20	0.94	0.94	0.97
C PAC	2.86	2.86	3.15	2.32	2.32	2.54
D PAC	5.86	5.86	6.30	4.21	4.21	4.46
E PAC	13.26	13.26	13.26	7.09	7.09	7.29
F Sup TAC	2.56	1.66	14.44	2.01	1.34	7.09
G Support	6.27	5.07	*	4.39	3.72	*
Z	14.11	13.62	22.95	11.08	10.34	8.28

* Bond Pays Off

show considerable lengthening, as these bonds now provide the buffer to keep the PAC classes on their schedules.

Standard scenario analysis, which is discussed in the next section, uses only a single path for each end-point, and thus would not fully capture the risk of these securities. Although these paths have the same end-point, the market value of the security at the horizon depends on the path that led to that point. By examining these types of scenarios (where several paths lead to the same end-point), complex securities can be evaluated more completely.

SCENARIO ANALYSIS

The interrelationship between MBS value and prepayments necessitates the application of analytical methods that account for prepayment risk when measuring value. One approach creates interest rate scenarios and measures total returns.

Scenario Analysis Methodology

Measuring performance based on changes in the yield curve provides a straightforward method to access nearly all fixed-income and derivative securities. For securities whose cash flows depend on the level of interest rates, the scenario approach can give a reasonable approximation of the relationship between the embedded options and relative value.

True to its name, scenario analysis involves the calculation of holding returns over various interest rate scenarios. In most cases, the holding period will be set to one year and the interest rate shifts will assume parallel shifts in the yield curve. Most adaptations of the method, however, allow for nonparallel curve shifts.

MBS cash flows for each scenario depend on coupon income, scheduled principal amortization, and prepayments. Cash flows occurring prior to the horizon will be reinvested until the end of the holding period. The value of the cash on hand at the horizon, which equals the reinvested cash flows plus the market value of the remaining principal, will be compared to the initial price of the security. The rate of growth necessary to equate the amount of cash at the horizon with the current market value equals the holding period return.

Weighting scenarios by probabilities leads to the estimation of an expected holding period return. The probabilities will be contingent on a volatility estimate and some determination of the probability function for interest rate changes. Most models assume a log-normal distribution for interest rates. In addition, the weights should be based either on returns quoted on an annualized yield basis or on the terminal cash values. The probability weighted return should then be placed on a bond equivalent basis.

Two crucial model assumptions have a significant impact on the results. The first involves the choice of an appropriate base case curve. The standard Merrill Lynch approach uses the implied forward spot curve as the base case. Scenario shifts will reflect changes in the implied forward curve. Use of the forward curve has significant technical appeal over assuming a base case curve equal to current rates. This latter method leads to material biases—in an upward sloping yield curve environment it will result in artificially high returns for long duration securities and suggest the potential for simple arbitrage by trading in current coupon Treasuries.

Applying Scenario Analysis

By allowing the cash flows to vary based on the differing prepayment rates for each scenario, the method helps to reflect the embedded option component. In addition, option-adjusted models can be used in order to determine the horizon principal value. From an investor's perspective, a comparison of return profiles should indicate quickly if a particular security makes sense for a portfolio.

Assuming a one-year holding period, scenario returns have been determined for a FHLMC 10% thirty-year security and for

Exhibit 8: One-Year Holding Returns for PAC Classes and Collateral
Relative to the collateral, the PAC classes of FHLMC 65 do not experience as much negative convexity.

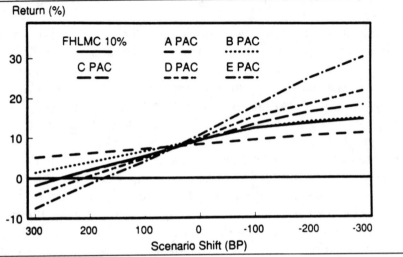

classes of the previously analyzed FHLMC 65 CMO. Results for the PAC classes can be seen in Exhibit 8.

The PAC class performance shows more convexity than the collateral. As rates decline, however, the PAC returns begin to flatten. Overall, performance depends strongly on duration; the larger duration means a steeper performance curve. Holding period returns for the non-PAC classes can be seen in Exhibit 9.

The return profiles reflect the reallocation of prepayment risk to the various tranches. The PAC bonds, for instance, provide linear returns, whereas the support tranches have considerably different profiles. The Z class exhibits high positive convexity, but the support G class contains a good degree of negative convexity.

A major strength of scenario analysis is that it can capture security performance based on a relatively small set of paths. On the other hand, the method fails in cases when security performance depends critically on the path of rates from the starting point to the horizon.

Exhibit 9: One-Year Holding Return for Non-PAC Classes and Collateral
In order to create more convexity for the PAC classes, the support classes contain a good deal of negative convexity. The Z class exhibits the highest degree of leverage, yet performance peaks as the price rises to par.

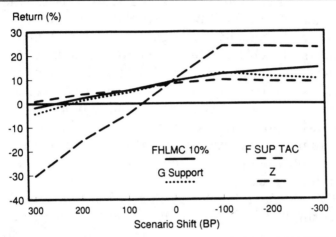

OAS ANALYSIS

In order correctly to price the level of embedded risk, several types of analytical models have been developed. For MBS option-adjusted spread (OAS) and pricing analysis one can employ two general modeling frameworks: Monte Carlo Simulation (a common method used by dealers and investors) and binomial option pricing methods.

OAS Methodology

OAS models are a method to calculate the price of embedded option risk. This risk stems from the level and shape of the yield curve as well as the path of interest rates. In order to capture the risk related to changing interest rates, OAS models generally employ either a Monte Carlo interest rate simulation process or a binomial lattice of rates. The Merrill Lynch MBS OAS model applies the interest rate simulations, whereas the Refinancing Threshold

Pricing (RTP) model applies the binomial lattice approach.[2] While both approaches can be used to analyze standard pass-through MBSs, only the Monte Carlo OAS model can be applied to CMOs.[3] The following discussion and analysis will focus on the Monte Carlo OAS model. (For brevity this will be called the OAS model.)

By relying on the ability of digital computers to generate random numbers, the OAS model can perform simulations of future interest rates. The OAS model simulates two Treasury rates simultaneously: a short Treasury rate and a long Treasury rate. In the simulation process, which assumes a monthly time step, both rates diffuse according to a mean reverting log-normal process.

Month-to-month interest rate changes depend on the assumed level of volatility and correlation between the two rates. Each simulation trial typically includes two paths of rates covering 360 months. By construction, average rates across time equal the forward rates implied by the current Treasury yield curve. Testing and adjustment procedures enhance the likelihood that the simulated rates accurately price the current coupon Treasury securities.

The simulated long rates drive the prepayment function, which, in turn, determines the appropriate MBS cash flows. These cash flows will be discounted by the simulated short rates. For each simulation trial the summation of the discounted cash flows represents the current present value of the MBS.

In order to solve for the option-adjusted spread, the present values are averaged after simulating a large number of trials. When discounting at a flat spread to Treasuries, this average present value will usually exceed the current market value of the MBS. The OAS model solves for the spread, which must be added to the simulated Treasury rates so that the average of the present values equals the current market price. OAS levels will then be

---

[2] For more information on the valuation models refer to *The Refinancing Threshold Pricing Model* and *Analyzing MBS: A Comparison of Methods*, Merrill Lynch Mortgage-Backed Securities Research, November 1987 and April 1988, respectively.

[3] In general, binomial models cannot evaluate path-dependent securities. The Merrill Lynch RTP model has been specially designed to evaluate the prepayment related path-dependence effects, but the method cannot be adopted to security structure related path-dependence effects.

converted from monthly equivalent to a bond equivalent yield basis.

OAS and the Pricing of MBS Risk

OAS measures the expected spread over Treasuries earned while holding the MBS to final maturity. The method implicitly assumes that, after adjusting for the option component, MBSs trade at a constant spread regardless of the level or shape of the yield curve or the duration of the instrument. The result represents the probabilistic weighted result over a sufficiently large number of simulation trials.

Comparing the OAS with the spread calculated based on either a simple prepayment rate forecast or by running the model assuming zero volatility provides a benchmark of the embedded option cost. Securities such as IOs will typically have large option costs, reflecting the substantial difference between the cash flow spread and OAS. Positively convex MBSs, such as POs, may actually have negative option cost, reflecting the potential gains from additional volatility.

The large number of simulated Treasury rates cover numerous instances of changes in the level and shape of the yield curve. In addition, the effects of path dependence and burnout will be reflected in the prepayment rates. The behavior of the MBSs in these cases will be boiled down by the OAS procedure into one number, the spread. By concentrating solely on the spread, a significant amount of valuable information will be overlooked.

EVALUATING PATH-DEPENDENCE RISK

Option-adjusted spread is the standard measure of value in the MBS market. Scenario analysis is the standard measure of performance. The OAS bucket approach, introduced below, combines these two approaches and produces measures of value and performance that account for the path dependence of MBS.

Hidden Information in the OAS Model

When calculating option-adjusted spread, the security's performance is calculated over hundreds, and at times thousands of individual interest paths. When the OAS results are presented, these
paths are all lumped together and a single OAS is reported. Far
more performance data than are presented in the typical scenario
analysis are hidden in that OAS number. The trick is extracting
that information.

Whereas standard OAS analysis discards valuable performance
data, standard scenario analysis does not go far enough in analyzing a security's performance. Typically, scenario analysis consists
of a small set of parallel yield curve movements occurring immediately or ramping over time. The performance of the security is
calculated for each path. This method gives some sense of performance, but cannot capture the essence of more complex securities. For prepayment-sensitive securities, the path that rates take
can have a significant impact on the value of a security.

The new method produces an analysis of the performance data
from the individual paths in the OAS analysis. No one could be
expected to sift through all the paths generated by an OAS analysis to understand security performance. It would take days just to
analyze one bond. However, it is possible to summarize the performance of the bond in a reasonably sized matrix by grouping
similar paths together into buckets.

Buckets can be selected in any number of ways. We chose to
concentrate on a set of buckets that reflects the approach usually
taken to perform scenario analysis, and then expanded that approach to include enough information to analyze the path dependence aspect of MBSs.

OAS Windows and Buckets

The theory of buckets is really just an expansion of the theory of
OASs. As mentioned above, the first step in calculating an OAS is
to simulate many possible interest rate paths. The second step is to

calculate the cash flows of the security for each path. For MBSs, that means forecasting the prepayment rate for each month along the path based on the simulated rates. Next, the present value of the cash flows is calculated for each path. The simulated interest rates for each path plus a spread are used to discount the cash flows of that path. All of these present values are then averaged together to produce a single price. The spread in the discounting equation is adjusted until the average price from the model equals the price in the market. That spread is the OAS.

Suppose we interrupt that process in the middle, after calculating the present value but before averaging to produce a single price. For each path we have a price. This price is the value of the security if that path occurs. These prices are the crucial pieces of information that will let us extract performance data from the OAS analysis.

A simple example seems in order. Suppose you calculated the OAS of a par Treasury bond. By definition, the OAS would be zero and the average of the prices from all the paths would equal par. Imagine that you examined one path in which rates remained below current market levels. The present value of the bond's cash flows for that path would be above par, because you would be discounting the cash flows of a bond at discount rates below the coupon on the bond. Conversely, a path in which rates were generally well above the coupon would produce a price below par.

Of course, looking through all those paths to find the right ones would be very inefficient. Instead, why not group similar paths into buckets? The price calculated for each path in the bucket could be averaged to produce a bucket price. Each bucket answers the question: What is the value of this bond assuming that interest rates pass through the windows that define this bucket? Imagine taking a graph of all the interest rate paths and drawing a series of windows at a specific horizon date. The window that the interest rate path passes through determines which bucket it lands in. It does not matter where the path goes before or after passing through the window.

Exhibit 10: Formation of 4-Year Buckets
The paths that pass through the window at year 4 form the -100 basis point bucket. The exhibit contains a sample of the long-term Treasury rates simulated by the Monte Carlo process. The highlighted rate paths represent the 100 basis point bucket at month 48.

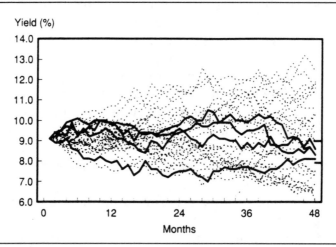

Some buckets would represent rising rates and some would represent falling rates. The difference in price from rising rate and falling rate buckets would be a measure of the riskiness of the bond. Bonds with little sensitivity to interest rates would show little variation in value from bucket to bucket. More volatile securities would show greater dispersion.

To add some visual representation to the bucket concept, consider the rate paths illustrated in Exhibit 10.

Exhibit 10 contains a sampling of long-term Treasury rates computed by the Monte Carlo simulation process. The highlighted rate paths represent the bucket containing the rate paths that fall by 100 basis points at month forty-eight.

This method also provides a means of comparing bonds. For each path we can calculate the cash flows and the discounted value for two different bonds. We can compare these prices directly, or compare the results in the buckets. For example, Exhibit 11 shows a comparison of two Treasuries. The definition of the

---

Exhibit 11: Present Value Comparison of Treasuries
The 10-year Treasury exhibits greater price volatility than the 5-year Treasury. Prices represent average present values of bonds based on rate buckets at year 4.

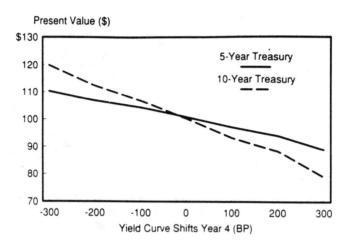

---

buckets is very simple. Each bucket is defined by where the short-term rate is at the end of four years, broken into 100-basis-point increments. (See Exhibit 10.)

Exhibit 11 shows that the longer maturity bond exhibits more volatility than the shorter maturity bond. That is, its value goes up more when rates fall, and goes down more when rates rise.

Using Buckets To Analyze Path Dependence

Analysis of path dependence is just a small step. If the buckets separate into different paths that reach the same point, then the bucket analysis will show the impact of the different paths.

The highlighted paths from Exhibit 10 can be split further into their path-dependent components. Some of these paths rose before falling back to the near unchanged level, and some of those paths fell first. By splitting that bucket into several buckets it is possible to analyze the impact of path dependence. These buckets are

---

Exhibit 12: MBS and Treasury Present Value Comparison
The exhibit compares performance of an MBS and a Treasury. Using OAS buckets formed by windows at year 4 demonstrates the negative convexity of the MBS. As rates fall the MBS underperforms the Treasury.

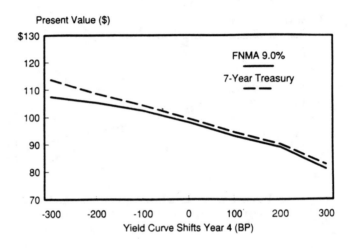

---

formed by using a set of windows, say, a window at year two and a window at year four. The path must pass through both windows to fall into that bucket.

For a bond without much path dependence, the impact of rates rising and then returning to current levels should be roughly equal and opposite to the effect of rates falling and then rising to current levels. For path-dependent bonds, the two paths are not likely to offset each other.

The next example shows the performance of an MBS relative to a Treasury and demonstrates the impact of path dependence. Exhibit 12 shows the relative performance of the two instruments based on buckets formed at the end of year four. The MBS has similar performance to the Treasury in rising rate environments, but underperforms the Treasury as rates fall.

The path dependence of the MBS can be seen by looking more closely at the down 100 basis point scenario. Exhibit 13 shows the relative performance of the MBS versus the Treasury for scenarios

---

Exhibit 13: MBS and Treasury Relative Performance Comparison
The down 100 basis point bucket at year 4 can be split into buckets that reflect path dependence. Paths that are lower than average at year 2 produce lower returns for the MBS. The nonpath-dependent Treasury has a symmetric relative performance profile.

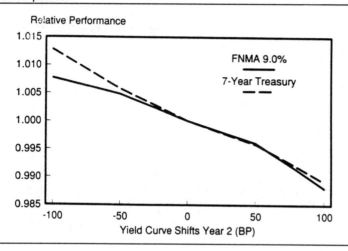

that ended up in the down 100 bucket at year four, but took different paths to get there. The graph clearly shows that if rates fall below the standard path that ends at down 100 basis points after year four, the MBS substantially underperforms the Treasury.

Defining the Buckets

Typically, the bucket method involves establishing a standard matrix of buckets for all the bonds under evaluation. After choosing some arbitrary horizon, the simulated paths can be placed into various buckets. These buckets reflect the level of rates, relative to the implied forward rates.

Between the present time and the horizon, another point will be chosen. Rates will be sampled at this point and partitioned relative to a straight line interpolation between current rates and the horizon. In other words, the base case would assume that rates move linearly between the present time and the horizon. An ex-

---

Exhibit 14: Percentage Of Simulations Falling Into Buckets
This exhibit shows the likelihood of paths falling into any one bucket. The 24-month shifts are defined relative to straight-line interpolation to the 48-month shift.

RATE SHIFTS (BP) AT 24-MONTH HORIZON	RATE SHIFTS AT 48-MONTH HORIZON (BP)							
	<-200	-200	-100	0	+100	+200	>+200	TOTAL
<-100	0.0	0.7	0.8	1.0	0.7	1.1	0.8	5.1
-100	0.4	0.9	2.7	2.2	1.7	1.9	1.0	10.8
-50	0.4	2.6	4.8	4.4	2.5	1.9	1.2	17.8
0	0.7	3.4	5.6	6.5	5.8	3.4	1.6	27.0
+50	0.5	1.9	5.0	4.8	4.2	1.3	1.4	19.1
+100	0.4	1.5	2.1	3.1	2.8	1.2	0.7	11.8
>+100	0.2	1.0	1.1	1.9	1.9	1.5	0.8	8.4
Total	2.6	12.0	22.1	23.9	19.6	12.3	7.5	

---

ample of this partitioning can be seen by the frequency distribution in Exhibit 14 for the simulated long Treasury rates.

Based on the frequencies in Exhibit 14, cases in which rates fell 100 basis points by the end of year four and fell fifty basis points at year two constituted 4.8% of all OAS simulation trials. Examining the totals indicates that the no-change scenarios constitute the bulk of the frequencies; at the end of year four 23.9% of the simulation trials exhibited no change relative to the implied forward rates. Higher frequencies for rising rate scenarios can be related to the log-normal assumptions built into the model.

Standard Deviation Analysis

In addition to looking at the detailed performance for each scenario, the standard deviation of performance for paths that have a common end-point can provide a measure of path dependence.

Exhibit 15: Standard Deviation of Absolute Prices at 48-Month Horizon
IOs and POs exhibit different degrees of path dependence. IOs have less path-dependence risk, which increases as rates fall. The path-dependence risk of POs falls as rates rise.

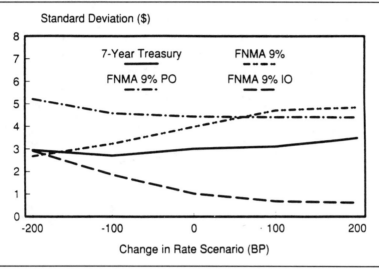

Standard Deviation ($)

Change in Rate Scenario (BP)

Exhibit 15 compares the standard deviations of absolute prices across the scenarios at year four for several securities.

Even though the cash flows of the Treasury are not path dependent, the performance of the bond is still path dependent because of the impact of using different discount rates for each bucket. As expected, the MBS exhibits greater path-dependence risk than the Treasury, with greater path dependence as rates fall.

In the rising rate scenarios the IO exhibits very little path-dependence risk. This indicates that the present value of the IO is fairly stable for all paths in which rates eventually rise. On the other hand, in falling rate scenarios the value of the IO is very dependent on the path of rates. The IO will tend to have a substantially higher present value if rates remain constant or rise slightly before falling than if rates fall immediately and then remain low. It is not surprising that POs produce the opposite profile, with the greatest path-dependence risk in the rising rate cases.

Exhibit 16: Applying Path Dependence to Total Return
The typical horizon analysis has been extended to consider interim yield shifts.
The graph shows three general parallel shifts of a Treasury rate. Around each
parallel shifts are three paths.

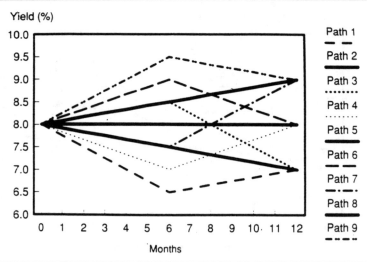

Extending Total Return Analysis

The OAS bucket approach leads to insights regarding present value based on the path-dependence characteristics of MBS. This path-dependence aspect lends itself well to total return analysis. In particular, the notion of parallel shifts can be extended to consider interim yield shifts. For example, Exhibit 16 contains sample paths of the single Treasury rate.

The exhibit contains three parallel shifts (Paths 2, 5, and 8), representing a base case and two parallel shifts of 100 basis points. Around each parallel shift are three paths, and one represents a linear change between the initial point and the horizon (Path 8, for example). Two other paths contain interim shifts of plus and minus 100 basis points at six months (Paths 7 and 9, for example). Tying this path-dependent approach with total return analysis can provide insights into both security and portfolio performance.

CMOs

The strength of the method can be seen clearly in evaluating CMOs. One of the challenges of investing in MBSs is understanding the risk characteristics of new securities. This method allows the investor quickly to understand how risk is apportioned among the various bonds.

The first way to examine CMO structure would be to calculate the standard deviation of prices, as in Exhibit 15. This approach has been performed on a particular CMO, FNMA 88-30 (collateralized by FNMA 9.5% thirty-year MBS), and the results can be seen in Exhibit 17.

The standard deviation in Exhibit 17 measures the dispersion of present values in each bucket. Looking across the zero-change bucket, the standard deviations increase according to the sequence of the tranches. In the down 100 bucket, the D PAC exhibits the highest level of price risk. As rates rise, the support and Z classes

Exhibit 17: Standard Deviation of Absolute Prices Using 48-Month Buckets
This table examines the price variance of FN88-30. The standard deviation of price measures the dispersion of present values in each bucket. Higher standard deviations indicate more price volatility.

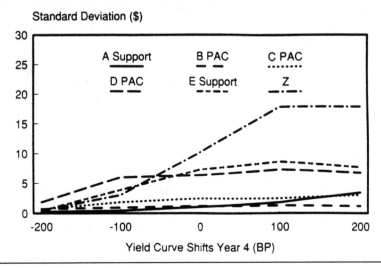

Exhibit 18: Average Present Values Given Buckets at 24 Months and No Change at 48 Months
The exhibit contains data based on the relative position of rates at two time periods. Support and Z classes exhibit more exposure to path dependence.

PRESENT VALUES BASED ON YIELD BUCKETS AT MONTH 24

FN 88 30

CLASS	-200	-100	0	+100	+200	AVERAGE
A Support	101-25	101-23	101-13	100-21	98-21	101-02
B PAC	103-10	102-25	101-25	100-27	99-19	101-22
C PAC	105-07	103-17	102-17	100-23	97-29	102-00
D PAC	105-19	101-28	99-23	97-13	94-15	98-27
E Support	102-27	100-11	96-19	94-05	89-16	96-20
Z	101-17	101-21	98-17	93-08	85-10	96-30

---

absorb most of the risk. In addition to the level of standard deviation, the slope of the profile indicates how price sensitivity changes across rate buckets. The PAC classes generally show flatter profiles.

The analysis can be taken a step further in order to look at the sensitivity of the deal structure to path-dependence risk. In this case, the forty-eight-month bucket in which rates are unchanged has been selected. This bucket will be further partitioned according to the relative position of rates at month twenty-four. Prices for each of the twenty-four-month windows can be seen in Exhibit 18.

In the exhibit, the average represents the mean present value across all the rate windows at month twenty-four, assuming no change at month forty-eight. The 200 column in Exhibit 18 would correspond to cases where rates fell 200 basis points at the end of year two, and by the end of year four had closed at no change. In other words, rates initially fell then rose. The +200 column would have a similar interpretation—rates initially rose then fell. Comparing prices across the rows, relative to the averages, provides some insight regarding the exposure of the class. The degree to which prices change and deviate from the average reflect the sensitivity of the bond to the path of interest rates.

The data in Exhibit 18 lead to several observations concerning the structure of the CMO. The Z and E support classes show the most sensitivity to path-dependence risk, based on the range of prices across the rows. When rates fall then rise (represented by the 200 and 100 columns), the PAC classes exhibit considerably better performance than the support classes, as call protection helps preserve value. In situations where rates rise then fall (the +100 and +200 columns), once again PAC bonds outperform the support classes.

YIELD CURVE TWISTS

In the preceding analysis, total return analytics have been extended from simple parallel yield curve shifts to a synthesis of path-dependence risk and yield curve shifts. The simplifying assumption of parallel shifts masks sensitivity to changes in the shape of the curve. Unlike a bullet bond, the amortizing nature of the MBS leads the present value of its cash flows to be strongly related to the shape of the curve.

Analyzing the Shape of the Curve

Over the past few years attention has been refocused on the shape of the Treasury curve and the valuation of fixed-income securities. This attention stems from the impact on value related to the previous curve inversion and subsequent return to a positive shape. By adjusting portfolio holdings to accommodate the shape of the curve, portfolio managers have been in a better position to control the risk and return portfolio profile of their positions.

The shape of the curve influences value for several reasons. At one level of analysis, prices will change for securities priced based on a spread to a point on the curve. On a more fundamental level, value reflects the discounted sum of future expected cash flows. Two valuation methods may be used to discount cash flows. The first method discounts flows at the yield to maturity of the security, whereas the second method discounts each cash flow by its associated theoretical zero coupon rate. The first method ignores the shape of the yield curve and assumes that each cash flow will be reinvested at the current yield to maturity. On the other hand, discounting by the theoretical zero coupon rates reflects the shape of the yield curve and provides a useful method to gauge the relationship between the change in the shape of the curve and value.

On a more subtle level, the changing shape of the curve has an additional impact on MBS value. Traditionally, the valuation models assume that current expectations for future yield curves can be found in the implied forward rates. Models, such as the OAS, use the implied ten-year forward Treasury rates to drive the prepayment functions. Changes in the shape of the curve lead to new forward rates, and, consequently, change MBS cash flow expectations.

The valuation methods previously described can be used to estimate the impact of twisting the yield curve. To illustrate this concept of yield curve twists, examine the yield curves in Exhibit 19.

Although yield curve twists can be implemented in countless ways, the rotations in Exhibit 19 represent changes to the curve based on short rates. The impact of the twist scenarios in Exhibit 19 can be seen in both a total return and OAS context.

Total Returns and Yield Curve Twists

The flexible nature of the total return model allows for combinations of parallel shifts, interest rate paths, and yield curve twists. Previously, the parallel shifts and path-dependence aspects have been examined. To carry the analysis further, the impact of yield curve twists has been applied to a CMO and to its underlying collateral.

Using a one-year holding period, total returns for the scenarios used in Exhibit 19 have been calculated. In addition to the two twists and the base case, two additional parallel-shift scenarios have been added. These parallel shifts help to compare the impact

Exhibit 19: Yield Curve Twist Scenario
Two twist scenarios have been created. The scenarios encompass a curve steepening and flattening through shifting the 2-year and 10-year Treasury yield spread by 100 basis points.

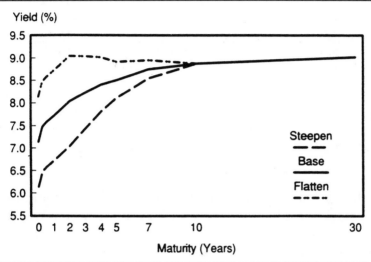

of parallel versus nonparallel shifts. Results can be seen in Exhibit 20.

As the two-year Treasury to ten-year Treasury curve steepens and flattens by 100 basis points, the shorter duration CMO classes as well as the underlying collateral and five-year Treasury experience changes in one-year total return. Relative to the parallel yield curve shifts, the twisting scenarios have less of an impact on total return.

OAS and Yield Curve Twists

The influence of changing the shape of the curve can also be measured using the OAS model. Using the process of constant OAS pricing based on instantaneous yield curve shifts, the impact of yield curve twists (measured by relative price changes) can be seen in Exhibit 21. The steepening and flattening cases correspond

Exhibit 20: One-Year Total Rate of Return
The data in the exhibit compare parallel yield curve shifts with yield curve twists. The securities show more sensitivity to parallel shifts, although changing the shape of the curve has a noticeable impact on short CMO classes.

SECURITY	PARALLEL -100	STEEPEN -100	BASE	FLATTEN +100	PARALLEL +100
FN88 30 A Support	10.96%	11.27%	9.88%	8.54%	6.76%
FN88 30 B PAC	9.93	9.93	9.12	8.32	8.32
FN88 30 C PAC	14.32	12.31	10.13	9.37	7.49
FN88 30 D PAC	18.89	12.76	12.76	12.76	7.09
FN88 30 E Support	17.84	11.86	11.83	11.83	6.41
FN88 30 Z	21.16	12.33	12.33	12.33	-2.25
FNMA 30-Year 9.5%	13.31	9.91	9.52	9.13	5.96
5-Year Treasury	11.95	10.56	8.75	6.97	5.63

to shifting the short end of the yield curve while holding the long end constant. Keeping the long end constant dampens the effect of changing prepayments.

Results based on the constant OAS method indicate that CMO sensitivity to curve movements varies based on the direction of the shift. Support classes as well as short PACs exhibit more sensitivity to the shape of the curve. The interaction between the refinancing relationship and yield curve shows up in the non-symmetrical relationship between returns from rising and falling yield curves.

Exhibit 21: Price Sensitivity to Yield Curve Twists and Shifts
The exhibit contains the relative price change assuming immediate curve shifts and constant OAS pricing.

SECURITY	PARALLEL -100	STEEPEN -100	FLATTEN +100	PARALLEL +100
FN88 30 A Support	1.33%	1.33%	-1.15%	-3.82%
FN88 30 B PAC	1.48	1.48	-1.54	-1.74
FN88 30 C PAC	3.22	1.47	-1.90	-4.53
FN88 30 D PAC	6.40	0.32	-0.54	-6.83
FN88 30 E Support	3.33	1.18	-1.58	-5.91

Yield Curve Twists and OAS Buckets

The OAS bucket approach can be extended to an analysis of sensitivity to yield curve shape. The OAS model simulates two interest rates—short and long Treasury yields. The differences between the two yields relative to the current spread can be used to represent changes in the slope of the curve.

Combining the twist sensitivity with the buckets, present values can be aggregated according to the difference between the long and short rates relative to the forward rate expectation. In order to control for the prepayment effects, the twist buckets were selected based on no change in the simulated long Treasury rate. Based on a sampling at thirty-six months, average present values for the twist buckets can be seen in Exhibit 22.

The base case represents no change from the current shape. All the securities exhibit a higher present value as the yield curve steepens (going from flatter 120 to steeper 30), reflecting the benefits of discounting cash flows at lower rates. On a relative basis, the IOs have the largest price gain as the curve steepens, while the seven-year Treasury has the smallest relative price change. This performance conforms to the cash flow pattern of the securities. The cash flow pattern of an IO shows more sensitivity to the short end of the yield curve then noncallable bullet bonds.

Exhibit 22: Yield Curve Twists and Present Values
The bucket approach has been extended to examine yield curve shape. Buckets were selected based on changes in the spread between long and short rates at month 36. Prices were averaged across the present values falling into the bucket. As the yield curve steepens, present values increase.

CHANGE IN YIELD CURVE SLOPE AT 36-MONTHS

SECURITY	FLATTER 120 BP	FLATTER 60 BP	BASE CASE	STEEPER 30 BP
7-Year Treasury	104-04	102-17	104-25	105-19
GNMA 9% MBS	96-18	98-09	100-17	102-15
GNMA 9% PO	44-10	44-30	45-30	47-00
GNMA 9% IO	52-08	53-11	54-19	55-15

CONCLUSION

The cash flows to mortgage-backed securities are path dependent. This path dependence arises from prepayment characteristics and security structure. Heterogenous borrowers within a pool of mortgages lead to prepayment patterns where future prepayments are affected by past levels of interest rates. Complex security structures that allow for apportioning of prepayment risk also have path-dependent features.

Traditional analytical techniques are insufficient to analyze properly the risk of path-dependent securities. The standard scenario analysis approach ignores path dependence. OAS models mask the role of path dependence. A synthesis of the two methods leads to a new risk and return technique. The OAS bucket approach provides a rigorous method for analyzing the performance of path-dependent securities. Corresponding enhancements to incorporate path dependence into scenario analysis allow for better evaluation of complex securities.

Yield curve twists can also have a significant impact on security value. Changes in the shape of the yield curve affect both the discount rates used to value a security and the forecasted prepayment rates, which influence the security's cash flows.

The approach to evaluation of yield curve twists and shifts in a path-dependent framework presented in this chapter is a significant step forward in the evolution of fixed-income valuation tools.

CHAPTER 29

CONSISTENT, FAIR AND ROBUST METHODS OF VALUING MORTGAGE SECURITIES

R. Blaine Roberts, PhD
Senior Managing Director
Financial Analytics and Structured Transactions Group
Bear, Stearns & Co., Inc.

David Sykes, PhD
Managing Director
Financial Analytics and Structured Transactions Group
Bear, Stearns & Co., Inc.

Michael L. Winchell
Senior Managing Director
Risk Management Group
Bear, Stearns & Co., Inc.

Over the past decade, mortgage market participants have spent vast sums of money to develop the financial engineering technology in place today. This technology enabled arbitrageurs to slice and dice the cash flows of mortgage pass-throughs in very complex ways, and to allocate across derivative securities, in various degrees, the imbedded call option we know as prepayment. This made the task of assessing the fair value of a mortgage security all the more difficult; determining the fair value of simple pass-throughs alone was difficult enough in 1986. As a result, mortgage investors also have spent heavily to build mortgage pricing models.

In spite of these efforts, many portfolio managers and traders argue that the pricing of mortgage securities remains more art than science, more dependent on market savvy and experience than on prepayment algorithms and contingent cash flow models. To some degree, they are correct. Though state-of-the-art bond valuation models claim to price correctly all securities with contingent cash flows, the results generated by such models do not always mesh with our intuitions about relative value and expected price performance, and for good reason.

Indeed, mortgage valuation models have become more robust. State-contingent cash flow models are crucial to the valuation of securities with cash flows that are dependent on the level of interest rates. The most common of these models is the one-factor stochastic model known as the option-adjusted spread (OAS) model. But as demonstrated below, the relative value of a mortgage security also depends on the impact of nondeterministic factors on cash flows. When factors outside the realm of the model affect the present value of a security, a premium must be earned by the investor. In the context of the one-factor model, nondeterministic prepayment uncertainty must be compensated by additional option-adjusted spread. Only by recognizing the impact of nondeterministic cash flows on value can portfolio managers determine when one mortgage security is cheap relative to another mortgage security. But such fair value determination need not remain an art.

In this chapter we present a definition of fixed-income securities that results in logical benchmarks to test all bond valuation models, and that provides clear insight into the fair value of a mortgage pass-through or derivative, or any other fixed-income security. We present the OAS model as an example of a technique that is quite necessary in the valuation of mortgage securities, but also discuss the limitations of the model when applied to mortgage securities. We demonstrate that under standard, simplifying assumptions, securities having cash flows that are *solely* determined by the level of interest rates should have a zero OAS. We then investigate the impact of the nondeterministic factors on mortgage cash flows. This analysis dispels an erroneous notion that all mortgage securities should earn the same option-adjusted spread.

We believe that the OAS model satisfies the minimum requirements for a bond valuation model. It could be better. We can take point with its assumptions. But we cannot replace it with something that does not satisfy simple benchmarks. OAS cannot be expected to price securities completely when some returns of cash flows are not determined by the rate process on which the model is based. But it doesn't mean we are rudderless, or that the OAS framework is useless.

BENCHMARKS FOR VALUATION MODELS

Without any reliance on a specific stochastic process or any form of expectations hypothesis, preferred habitat theory, or the like, much can be derived from the assumptions of no risk-free arbitrage and no transaction costs. The arbitrage-free pricing principle states that the market will value securities so that whenever a portfolio can be created that matches exactly in every scenario the future values of a given bond, then that portfolio will cost exactly the same as the bond itself. Risk-free arbitrage should not be possible by borrowing or lending at the riskless rate. Investors should not be able to combine fairly priced derivatives in such a way as to generate arbitrage profits; that is, the value of the whole must equal the sum of the parts.

We hold that the arbitrage-free pricing principle provides the minimal requirements for all bond valuation models. These are consistency, fairness, and robustness. A model that adheres to arbitrage-free valuation will price securities fairly. A model that produces values reflective of market conditions is consistent. A model that prices securities fairly and consistently in all states of the world is robust.

The assumption of no risk-free arbitrage also leads to the simple axiom that a pure floater is always worth par. That is a powerful axiom. It allows us to draw a direct relation between the value of a certain cash flow, the default-free payment of principal, and the value of an instrument with completely uncertain but deterministic cash flows, the interest payments of a pure floater, and permits the analysis of some financial components, typically but not always embedded within bonds, having option characteristics. As a result, we can establish benchmarks to test the consistency, fairness, and robustness of bond valuation models.

The Zero-Coupon Yield Curve, the Term Structure

Traditionally, the valuation of fixed-income securities begins with a benchmark of certainty, Treasury securities that have no default risk and no cash flow uncertainty. Assuming no transaction costs and the existence of Treasury securities for every future period in which other securities are to be valued, one can derive the *theoretical* Treasury zero-coupon yield curve, which, if there is no arbitrage, must equal the *actual* Treasury zero yield curve.

Given a default-free term structure, then all bonds with fixed cash flows can be priced easily. This applies whether the world is one of certainty or uncertainty; bonds with *certain cash flows* can be valued given only the no-default yield curve. It is only for securities with *uncertain cash flows* that more is required. Bonds with uncertain cash flows have embedded optional components that need to be priced. However, we need not rely on stochastic models to determine relative value relations among such components, only logic. And any stochastic model we use to determine absolute prices should generate results that are consistent with such logic.

This is not to say that the yield curve is not affected by the degree of uncertainty or randomness of future rates; it is. But the yield curve embodies the valuation of this volatility for bonds with certain cash flows. Thus, *given a yield curve*, a change in volatility will not change the value of fixed cash flow securities. It is another issue as to whether and how a change in volatility affects the yield curve.

The Riskless Short-Term Lending Rate

Determining relative value among alternative investments can be much more difficult when the properties of the instruments vary markedly. How much return should be given up for call protection? How much should we discount a floater when it reaches its cap? Specifically, what is the price of risk? To know this, we must first define a riskless security.

In the context of fixed-income securities, the riskless security is one that returns all principal on demand and without risk of default, and that pays the prevailing riskless rate on the outstanding balance as long as the debt is outstanding. The riskless security has no default risk and no liquidity risk. Because it has no interest rate risk, it is a *pure floater*. If the investor's opportunity cost of lending is always equal to the risk-free rate, and borrowing and lending can be done without transaction costs, then liquidity is not a concern; the term to maturity of any pure floater free of default risk is irrelevant. By simple extension, the timing or amount of principal redemption is not relevant either.

Options on the Riskless Rate

Ignoring credit and liquidity risk, one way to determine the relative value of any financial instrument is to describe, as much as possible, all bond cash flows as a function of the riskless rate. If we can arbitrarily nominate cash flows as principal and interest, then the definition of interest can be expanded to include a payment made on a collection of options written with respect to the level of the riskless rate. Interest rate swaps are explicitly viewed in this manner when the payer of fixed, and also the receiver of floating, is described as being long an interest rate cap and short an interest rate floor, and when those instruments are seen to be, in turn, a collection of individual options on the riskless rate in each payment period.

Options are agreements that specify a payment under certain market conditions (states of the world). An option on the riskless rate would specify a payment, at expiration, given a level of the riskless rate.

Using this perspective, the interest cash flows of a wide variety of fixed-income securities can be described in a manner that highlights the differences and similarities among the instruments using a common yardstick. If two securities represent a collection of identical options, then they should be valued identically.

Describing a Fixed-Rate Note

As an example, consider a simple, three-year U.S. government fixed-rate note paying 10% interest. For ease of presentation, suppose interest is paid annually. We can decompose each interest payment into three separate options on the riskless rate, or the stream of interest payments as a combination of cap and floor agreements. The noteholder is entitled to receive, in every period in which principal is outstanding: (1) the riskless rate, and (2) the difference of 10% minus the riskless rate whenever the riskless rate is *less than* 10%. But the noteholder also gives up (3) the difference of the riskless rate and 10% whenever the riskless rate *exceeds*

10%. While this may seem to be a complex way to describe a 10% interest payment, the approach offers insight into the valuation of fixed-income securities, a way to link the pricing of caps, floors, swaps, floaters, inverse floaters, and fixed-rate securities.

In fact, we present below a set of derivative securities and financial instruments for analysis, all created from the fixed-rate three-year note. To determine whether a contingent cash flow model consistently values the properties of these securities, it is essential to determine which properties or elements are common among the set of securities. The logical relations that describe the common elements of the three-year note and its derivatives form a benchmark against which any bond valuation model should be measured.

Using Options to Define Debt

Defining debt instruments in terms of options on the riskless rate leads to better assessment of relative value of financial instruments and the ability to use one security to hedge another.

A set of financial instruments can be defined as follows:

r is the riskless rate

c is a strike rate for the option on the riskless rate

$F(c)$ is the value of an interest rate floor that receives $c - r$ if $c > r$

$C(c)$ is the value of an interest rate cap that receives $r - c$ if $r > c$

$C(0)$ is the value of an interest rate cap that receives r for all levels of r

P is the value of the lump sum principal paid at maturity

B is the value of a fixed-rate note with coupon c

α is the decimal share of the principal payment for a floater security

FL is the value of a floater with a cap c/α, derived from B

INV is the value of an inverse floater that is a companion to FL

S is the value of an interest rate swap paying r and receiving fixed-rate c

IO is the value of a fixed-rate interest-only strip

The three-year fixed-rate note pays a fixed-rate c regardless of the level of r. If there is no arbitrage, then

$$B = P + C(0) + F(c) - C(c)$$

From this we can derive a floater from the fixed-rate note. Interest will be paid equal to the riskless rate multiplied by the outstanding amount of principal allocated to the floater, subject to a cap. Principal is paid when the three-year note matures. If the floater can claim all the available interest in a given period, the cap strike rate is a function of the principal allocated to the floater:

$$FL = \alpha P + \alpha C(0) - \alpha C(c/\alpha)$$

The inverse floater receives all excess interest, and gets its share of principal paid at maturity as well. The inverse floater is long the interest rate cap that the floater is short:

$$INV = [1 - \alpha]P + [1 - \alpha]C(0) + F(c) - C(c) + \alpha C(c/\alpha)$$

An interest rate swap agreement, in which the investor receives a fixed-rate of c and pays the floating rate, for a period of three years, can also be described:

$$S = F(c) - C(c)$$

Defining Relative Performance and Hedging

Under the assumption of no arbitrage, the value of a pure floater is always par because the security always earns the riskless rate r for every level of r. In other words, the value of a *pure floater* is constant for any change in r. For this to be the case, it must be that if the value of the principal zero changes, the value of $C(0)$ always changes, in an equal but offsetting amount.

$$pure\ FL = P + C(0) \equiv 1$$

$$\Delta \ pure \ FL = \Delta \ P + \Delta \ C(0) = 0$$

$$\Delta \ P = - \ \Delta \ C(0)$$

As the pure floater is always par, the value of the fixed-rate note is:

$$B = 1 + F(c) - C(c)$$

Thus, if the fixed-rate note is also at par, then:

$$F(c) = C(c), \ S = 0, \ \text{and} \ C(0) = IO(c)$$

Given that the financial instruments are related as previously defined, and given that the value of a pure floater is constant, we can state that the change in value of these instruments is a function of the change in the value of the options, as follows:

$$\Delta \ B \ = \ \Delta \ F(c) - \Delta \ C(c)$$

$$\Delta \ S \ = \ \Delta \ F(c) - \Delta \ C(c)$$

$$\Delta \ FL \ = \ - \ \Delta \ aC(c/\alpha)$$

$$\Delta \ INV \ = \ \Delta \ F(c) - \Delta \ C(c) + \Delta \ \alpha C(c/\alpha)$$

$$\Delta \ INV \ = \ \Delta \ [1 - \alpha]P + \Delta \ \alpha F(c/\alpha)$$

$$\Delta \ IO \ = \ - \ \Delta \ P + \Delta \ S$$

Most of these price performance statements are commonly accepted. For example, swap market participants have always shown that the change in the value of the swap equals the change in the value of the fixed-rate note. The change in price of a floater should be a direct result of the change in the value of the cap. The change in the value of the inverse is equal to the change in the value of the fixed-rate note plus the change in the cap value. The change in the value of an IO is equal to the negative of the change in the value of the PO plus the change in the value of the swap struck at c. The value of the zero strike cap and the value of an IO of the par bond are always equal.

Not defined directly is the value of any cap or floor other than C(0). While we can define one cap or floor in terms of another, such as:

$$\Delta\ \alpha F(c/\alpha)\ =\ \Delta\ [1 - \alpha]C(0) + \Delta\ F(c) - \Delta\ C(c) + \Delta\ \alpha C(c/\alpha\ )$$

it is difficult to define any cap or floor without reference to other caps and floors.

Using the Methodology to Sharpen Intuition

We can use this approach to answer some intriguing relative value questions:

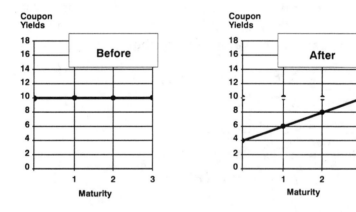

What would happen to the value of a three-year 10% interest rate cap agreement after the yield curve steepens?

The intuitive response is that the 10% cap would have less value if the one-year rate were 6%. However, recall that the value of the fixed-rate note is given by the equation: *fixed-rate note* = P + C(0) + F(c) – C(c). The pure floater is worth par. The fixed-rate note is still worth par. That means the value of [F(c) – C(c)] is unchanged, and any change in F(c) will be equal to the change in C(c). There is not enough information to prove C(c) went up or down, but if C(0) is worth more, it would seem to follow that C(c) is also worth more.

What would happen to the value of a three-year 10% interest rate floor agreement after the yield curve steepens? The intuitive response is that the 10% floor is worth more. From the foregoing analysis of C(c) in the second case, any change in the value of C(c) must be matched by the change in F(c). If the value of the floor is higher when short rates decline, so too is the value of the cap. At this point, it seems our intuition about the cap was wrong and our intuition about the floor was right. It is certain, however, that either both the floor and cap are worth more or they are both worth less.

What would happen to the value of the inverse floater after the yield curve steepens? Suppose that the floater is structured to receive 80% of the principal (α = 0.8) so that the inverse floater has a 4:1 leverage ratio; that is, the inverse floater's coupon rate increases 4% for every 1% decrease in the riskless rate. With short-term rates dropping to 6% from 10%, the floater coupon would decline to 6% from 10%, and the inverse floater coupon would jump to 26% from 10%.

Intuition says that the inverse floater is worth more now. However, remember that the change in the value of the floater must be the negative of the change in the value of the cap, $\alpha C(c/\alpha)$. Intuition also says the cap with a 12.5% strike is worth less. If the value of the cap is less, then the floater is worth more.

But if the floater is worth more and the fixed-rate note is still par, then the inverse is worth less! Because $\Delta\ INV = \Delta\ F(c) - \Delta\ C(c) + \Delta\ \alpha C(c/\alpha)$ and $\Delta\ B = \Delta\ F(c) - \Delta\ C(c) = 0$, if not for $\alpha C(c/\alpha)$, the value of the inverse would be unchanged. Here too we seem to have conflicting intuitions.

The Monotonicity Postulate

To resolve the apparent conflict regarding relative value, it is necessary to postulate a relation among caps of various strikes, and likewise floors.

Without resorting to any form of expectations hypothesis and without specifying a particular, parametric stochastic process, we can go further in pricing options by the monotonicity postulate.

Proposition: If any particular interest rate cap increases in value, then all caps with the same notional amortization structure and a higher strike cannot decrease in value. If any interest rate floor increases in value, then all floors with the same notional amortization structure and a lower strike cannot decrease in value.

$\Delta\ C(c) > 0$ implies $\Delta\ C(c') \geq 0$ for all $c' > c$

$\Delta\ F(c) > 0$ implies $\Delta\ F(c') \geq 0$ for all $c' < c$

Because $C(c')$ is a subset of $C(c)$ if $c' > c$, and $F(c')$ is a subset of $F(c)$ for $c' < c$, it follows that $C(c) \geq C(c')$, and $F(c) \geq F(c')$ in the foregoing statements, but it is not necessarily the case that $\Delta\ C(c) > \Delta\ C(c')$ for $c' > c$.

What would be the change in the value of the interest rate cap agreements $C(0)$, $C(c)$, and $C(c/\alpha)$?

After short rates drop, the yield on the three-year zero-coupon principal would be greater than 10%, approximately 10.28%, because it must be created by being long a three-year 10% fixed-rate note and short the "more expensive" earlier maturing zero-coupon payments. After the decline in short rates, P would be worth 0.58% less. If we hold that a pure floater equals $P + C(0)$ and is always equal to par, if P is worth less, then $C(0)$ is worth 0.58% more.

Given the postulate of monotonicity, if the value of $C(0)$ increases, so too must the values of $C(c)$ and $C(c/\alpha)$ increase, even though by reference to the short-term rate alone, they are more "out-of-the-money." We also know that the change in the value of the inverse floater is positive, and equal to $\Delta\ \alpha C(c/\alpha)$.

Generalization and Extension

It is a straightforward extension to define the fixed-rate note and components to be collections of period-specific cash flows and to value each period independently. Thus, for example, $C(c)$ becomes $C(c,t)$, which is an interest rate option that receives any positive value of $c - r$ for period t only. Then, the value of an interest rate cap agreement with maturity T is the sum of the values of the period-specific options.

This extension allows one to derive relations between securities with different maturities. For example, securities or agreements with maturities of T and $T + 1$ differ in value only by the single-period values of period T.

The approach is not limited to securities that pay a certain amount of principal on a single and certain maturity date. The analysis can easily be extended such that P is the value of the principal paid as $a(r,t)$, where $a(r,t)$ is an amortization function that depends on r, the riskless rate, and time, t. $A(t)$ is the sum of all prior amounts amortized. Usually $A(T) = 1$; the security is fully amortized by the maturity date T.

$F(c)$ and $C(c)$ now receive interest based on $[1-A(t)]$, the unamortized amount. This is a relatively generalized formulation where $a(r,t)$ could be determined by a set schedule such as the scheduled principal payment of a fixed-rate, level pay mortgage, or by the exercise of a call option by the issuer.

All the relations derived in the previous section for the fixed-rate note and its derivatives still hold. In particular, we still have:

$$B = P + C(0) + F(c) - C(c)$$

and

$$P + C(0) \equiv 1$$

What is lost is that P can no longer be priced solely by referencing the no-default Treasury yield curve for fixed cash flow securities if $a(r,t)$ depends on the stochastic riskless rate at future times. Thus, one needs a reference market or benchmark set of securities as a replacement, or needs to use a specific stochastic process, or both.

Incorporating Observable Futures, Forwards, and Options Markets

The value of a callable bond, B_c, can be related to that of a noncall-able bond, B, and the value of a call option, $OC_t(k)$, exercisable at t at a strike price of k:

$$B_c = B - OC(k_t)$$

$$B_c = P + C(0) + F(c) - C(c) - OC_t(k)$$

If k is par, because $P + C(0)$ is par, the value of the call option at expiration is:

$$OC_t(k) = max \ [F_t(c) - C_t(c), \ 0]$$

Prior to time t, the call option will have a value greater than or equal to the value of a noncallable forward swap commencing at t because the range of values of the swap $F_t(c) - C_t(c)$ is a subset of the range of values of $OC_t(k)$. The value of the option at expiration is equal to all of the possible positive values of the swap and greater than all of the negative values of the swap.

As above, we may go further in bounding the price response of a callable bond without reference to term structure theories or any specific random process by appealing to a more general monoton-icity postulate. In line with the postulate stated above, it would be natural to assume that if a current swap increases in value, $\Delta \ F(c) - \Delta \ C(c) > 0$, forward swaps at the same strike would not decrease in value, $\Delta \ F_t(c) - \Delta \ C_t(c) \geq 0$; and further, that the value of the call option would not decrease in value, $\Delta \ OC_t(k) \geq 0$. This produces relations among noncallable bonds, current swaps, forward swaps, call options, and, thus, callable bonds.

THE NECESSITY OF VALUING SECURITIES UNDER CONDITIONS OF UNCERTAINTY

The simplest valuation model for fixed-income securities, includ-ing mortgages, is one where the world never changes. In this world, all bonds have the same coupon rates and all would be priced at par. This is far from observed markets.

In the mid-1970s, yield was introduced on Wall Street for bond valuation. A simple yield model is one where the world has changed, but it is presumed that it will never change again. The current yield curve is flat, but there exist other bonds with coupons different from the current yield curve. All bonds are priced to have the same yield as the current yield curve. This simple model for valuation must be rejected.

The next level of sophistication still assumes a world of certainty. In this model, the world may have changed in the past and will change in the future, but that change is certain and determinant from the yield curve. Bonds have different coupons and are priced so that the yield of each cash flow equals the yield of the corresponding Treasury zero security. Options trade at their intrinsic value at expiration appropriately discounted back to the present. Options out-of-the-money have no value; there is no time premium. This model is also inconsistent with observed markets.

A bond-pricing model commonly in use today is the spread-to-the-average-life model. In this framework, the world is uncertain and changing, but uncertainty is not modeled explicitly. Securities trade to a constant spread to the riskless Treasury of the same average life, or in a somewhat more sophisticated variation (but still in the same category), at a constant spread to the Treasury with the same duration.

This model must also be rejected on the basis of fairness. Consider the previous example where the yield curve changes from flat at 10% to upwardly sloping, with a 6% one-year, 8% two-year, and 10% three-year. Fairness requires that the three-year zero-coupon bond's spread to the three-year coupon bond increase from zero to twenty-eight basis points, even though both the three-year zero and the three-year coupon bond have the same average life.

Using duration-matched spreads makes little difference. In the case of the flat yield curve, the durations, as conventionally measured, of the coupon bond and the zero are 2.49 and 2.73, respectively. Once the short-term rates drop, the duration of the coupon bond is unchanged, and the duration of the zero declines to just 2.72. On a duration-matched basis, the error in fair pricing is virtually the same as it would be using the average life.

Thus, the principles of consistency, robustness, and fairness require the broad use of a model that explicitly takes into account the stochastic nature of financial markets. Not to do so invites substantial mispricing and consequent losses when arbitrageurs enter the market. Yield models are not robust. *There is no correct yield for an option.*

THE OPTION-ADJUSTED SPREAD MODEL

Logic alone will not provide us with fair, *absolute* prices for each of the above financial instruments. For that we need a model that explicitly values interest rate uncertainty.

Models will differ in the underlying assumptions and approaches. What is most important is that the model meet the minimal requirements of fairness and consistency, and the usefulness of the benchmarks in assessing a particular model should be apparent.

The OAS model, as presented here, is a robust, fair, and consistent bond valuation model that satisfies all of the benchmarks for valuation models set forth above. Default-free bonds with cash flows that are entirely determined by r, the risk-free interest rate, will be fairly priced at a zero OAS. So too will the components and derivatives be fairly priced at a zero OAS. This is demonstrated below. However, the OAS model values only interest rate uncertainty. When other factors affect the cash flows of a security, these conclusions do not hold.

Over the last decade, the inherent value associated with interest rate uncertainty or volatility has received increasing recognition from the fixed-income markets. This is reflected in the explosive growth of option or option-like instruments whose future cash flows are a function of interest rates, either directly (e.g., caps, floors) or indirectly (option on a fixed-rate bond). Moreover, it is increasingly recognized that all fixed-income products display varying degrees of option-like properties such as convexity, and to this extent their value is affected by interest rate uncertainty.

One-Factor Model

This has caused sophisticated market participants to move away from naive static valuation techniques that ignore volatility and the shape of the yield curve, toward more sophisticated term structure-based stochastic models that are capable of quantifying the value of volatility. One of the more straightforward stochastic, term structure models is the one-factor model of the riskless rate, r. This framework is the foundation for a variety of pricing models, ranging from the mortgage-backed securities' OAS model, to models for pricing American options on fixed-rate bonds, interest rate swaps, and the like.

The one-factor approach models uncertainty as follows. Assume the shape of the term structure depends only on r, the riskless rate. While we know the level of the riskless rate today, we do not know its level at any future time period, $r(t)$. However, suppose that proportional changes in r from one period to the next are normally distributed with a known mean value and standard deviation. The standard deviation (volatility) represents uncertain percentage changes in $r(t)$, which for convenience we assume is constant in each time period, and the mean (drift) represents certain expected percentage changes that may vary across time periods.[1]

---

[1] While the OAS technique can seem very complex, at its core is a simple assumption. The methodology is based on the assumption that there is a known volatility of the riskless rate and there is embedded in the pricing of, for example, Treasury securities, the market's valuation of that volatility. The value of volatility, plus the market's implied expectation of future levels of the riskless rate, combine to specify the mean of the distribution of possible changes in riskless rates.

We can always take point with an assumption, argue that the model could be better, or that it doesn't accurately reflect reality. What is necessary is that if we reject one model in favor of another, that the chosen model still meet very basic criteria, that it satisfy the benchmarks we have outlined in this presentation.

This single-factor process becomes a valuation model when the arbitrage-free pricing principle is invoked as the economic rationale behind the pricing process. In other words, we can derive the market's assessment of the value of uncertainty from two components: an observation of the current term structure and an assumption about the volatility of the riskless rate through time.

Implied Forward Rates

Coupled with the arbitrage-free pricing principle, the one-factor model has its simplest incarnation in a world of certainty (no volatility), where it takes the form of the familiar implied forward rate, naive expectations hypothesis. Under certainty, arbitrage considerations imply that the rate of return to holding a default-free bond of any maturity M until it matures must equal the rate of return on cash invested over the same time period earning only the riskless rate. Otherwise, we could earn arbitrage profits by borrowing funds at the riskless rate and investing in the bond, or by short selling the bond and investing the proceeds at the riskless rate, depending on the relation between the bond yield and the riskless rate.

To illustrate, consider the flat term structure shown in Exhibit 1, where the yields on all zero-coupon bonds of various maturity equal 10%. For convenience, lending at the riskless rate is described as an investment in successive one-period bonds, with the term of a riskless period defined to be one year.

Exhibit 1: Value of Three Successive Zero-Coupon Bonds, Constant Discount Rate

Bond Maturity	Bond Yield	Bond Price	Value of a Series of One Period Bonds
1	10.00%	90.9090 =	$\dfrac{100}{(1 + 0.10)}$
2	10.00%	82.6446 =	$\dfrac{100}{(1 + 0.10) \times (1 + 0.10)}$

If volatility is known to be zero, then by definition the future values of r are known with certainty. The arbitrage-free condition implies that the path of r must be a constant at 10%. If the riskless rate were higher at 12%, one could reap an arbitrage profit by selling a two-year bond at 82.6446 against a sequence of one-year bonds (lending at the riskless rate) at a total cost of 81.1688, for an arbitrage profit of 1.4758. Conversely, if the riskless rate were lower at 8%, one could earn profits without risk by selling the sequence of one-year bonds (borrowing at the riskless rate) worth 84.1751 and investing in the two-year bond at a price of 82.6446, for a gain of 1.5305. No arbitrage would be available if the one-period rate were 10% in each period, exactly as expected. Exhibit 2 illustrates this.

Exhibit 2: Value of a Two-Period Zero-Coupon Bond, Rate Varies Over Time

Rate Path	Period 1	Period 2	Value of Two Year	Value of a Series of One Period Bonds
Higher	10.00%	12.00%	81.1688 =	$\dfrac{100}{(1 + 0.10) \times (1 + 0.12)}$
Flat	10.00%	10.00%	82.6446 =	$\dfrac{100}{(1 + 0.10) \times (1 + 0.10)}$

Using the arbitrage-free pricing principle, *a given term structure, and the assumption of no volatility*, we can derive the market's expectations of the riskless rate in the future, or, as it is generally known, the *implied forward rate*.

Adding Uncertainty to the Framework

The basic tenet under certainty is that in each time period, the rate of return on every default-free bond must equal the prevailing riskless rate. Extending this to valuation in an uncertain world, it is generally referred to as the local expectations hypothesis, which

entails pricing on the basis of expected values: the *expected* rate of
return on every default-free bond must equal the riskless rate. The
approach is as follows. Assume the observed term structure prices
reflect the market's risk attitude and valuation of rate uncertainty.
Then "tune" the drift term in the riskless rate process so that the
model generates expected prices for the term structure bonds that
match the observed market prices of those bonds. Thus, the arbitrage-free pricing principle and the assumption that risk assessment is embodied in the term structure allows us to value on the
simple basis of *expected* values without assuming that the market
is necessarily risk-neutral. That is, this approach does not imply
that the market actually expects all default-free bonds to earn the
riskless rate; rather, by incorporating the value of uncertainty into
the model's drift term, this approach enables us to price *as if* this
were the case. Thus, in addition to market expectations about the
future values of the short rate, the drift term captures the market
price of risk. Moreover, under uncertainty it is generally not possible to determine what portion of the drift term represents risk
valuation versus expectations; furthermore, it is not generally necessary.

In practice, there are two methods commonly used to generate
the potential future values of r. The rates can be regarded as either
a binomial branching lattice or as a set of independent paths. Both
methods will effectively replicate the same underlying stochastic
model of the term structure. The decision to use a particular
model is driven by the relation of a particular security's cash flows
to interest rates; it does not pertain per se to the fundamental issues of how best to model the term structure under uncertainty.

Given the set of financial instruments presented earlier, and
the relations among them that form the benchmarks for valuation
models, the following examples demonstrate the fairness, consistency, and robustness of the OAS framework for securities having
cash flows entirely determined by the prevailing level of the riskless rate.

For convenience, we will use a simple binomial lattice to demonstrate the consistency and fairness of the OAS model. We as-

sume that in any given future period, the prevailing riskless rate can be either higher or lower than it was in the prior period, with equal likelihood.[2] Given a "flat" term structure under 15% volatility, the potential paths of r are shown in Exhibit 3.

Exhibit 3: Potential Levels of Riskless Rate Assuming 15% Volatility

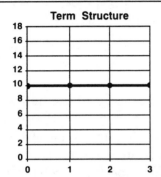

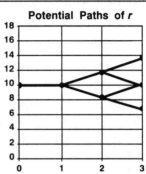

Rate Path	Period 1	Period 2	Period 3
1	10.00%	11.51%	13.28%
2	10.00%	11.51%	9.84%
3	10.00%	8.53%	9.84%
4	10.00%	8.53%	7.29%

Benchmarking the OAS Model

To benchmark the OAS model, we price the components of a bond and its derivatives using the simple lattice presented above. To do this, we present the cash flows of each instrument given each potential level of r, and subsequently calculate the expected present value of those cash flows using the prevailing rate.

---

[2] The interest rates shown in the exhibit are generated by the formula

$$r_1 = 10\% \times e^{\mu \pm 0.15}, \text{ and } r_2 = r_1 e^{\mu \pm 0.15}$$

They are rounded for presentation purposes. The rate process is "tuned" to the term structure presented in Exhibit 3 by solving for a μ in each time period so that the term structure bonds are correctly priced.

Exhibit 4: Expected Present Value of a 10% Fixed-Rate Bond

Path	Rate	Cash Flow	Rate	Cash Flow	Rate	Cash Flow		Present Value
1	10.00%	10.00	11.51%	10.00	13.28%	110.00	=	96.4066
2	10.00%	10.00	11.51%	10.00	9.84%	110.00	=	98.8874
3	10.00%	10.00	8.53%	10.00	9.84%	110.00	=	101.3561
4	10.00%	10.00	8.53%	10.00	7.29%	110.00	=	103.3499

Expected Present Value of 10% Fixed-Rate Bond   =   100.0000

Exhibit 4 shows the expected present value of the default-free, three-year fixed-rate bond paying interest annually at a 10% coupon rate, and all principal at maturity. The face value of the bond will be 100. While the cash flows are certain each period, the value of the cash flows is not. However, the expected present value of the bond is par; it is the average of the bond values given the four possible paths of the riskless rate over time.

To see how the present value of the security is determined for any specific rate path, recall that each cash flow is discounted using the rates prevailing from its payment date back to today along the path. The present value of the fixed-rate bond's cash flows for Path 1 are shown in Exhibit 5.

Exhibit 5: Present Value of a Fixed-Rate Bond's Cash Flows Given a Rate Path

Period	Cash Flow	Present Value		
1	10.00	9.0909	=	$\dfrac{10}{(1 + 0.10)}$
2	10.00	8.1525	=	$\dfrac{10}{(1 + 0.10) \times (1 + 0.1151)}$
3	110.00	79.1633	=	$\dfrac{110}{(1 + 0.10) \times (1 + 0.1151) \times (1 + 0.1328)}$

Total Present Value   79.1633   96.4066

Exhibits 6 and 7 show the expected value of a 10% interest rate cap agreement and the expected value of a 10% interest rate floor agreement, respectively. Recall that the cap returns a cash flow only when the riskless rate exceeds 10%; the floor only returns a cash flow when the riskless rate is below 10%.

Exhibit 6: Expected Present Value of a 10% Interest Rate Cap Agreement

Path	Rate	Cash Flow	Rate	Cash Flow	Rate	Cash Flow		Present Value
1	10.00%	0.00	11.51%	1.51	13.28%	3.28	=	3.5934
2	10.00%	0.00	11.51%	1.51	9.84%	0.00	=	1.2327
3	10.00%	0.00	8.53%	0.00	9.84%	0.00	=	0.0000
4	10.00%	0.00	8.53%	0.00	7.29%	0.00	=	0.0000

Expected Present Value of 10% Interest Rate Cap Agreement = 1.2065

Exhibit 7: Expected Present Value of a 10% Interest Rate Floor Agreement

Path	Rate	Cash Flow	Rate	Cash Flow	Rate	Cash Flow		Present Value
1	10.00%	0.00	11.51%	0.00	13.28%	0.00	=	0.0000
2	10.00%	0.00	11.51%	0.00	9.84%	0.16	=	0.1201
3	10.00%	0.00	8.53%	1.47	9.84%	0.16	=	1.3561
4	10.00%	0.00	8.53%	1.47	7.29%	2.71	=	3.3499

Expected Present Value of 10% Interest Rate Floor Agreement = 1.2065

As specified by the benchmarks, the cap and floor should have equal value when the fixed-rate bond is valued at par.

Exhibit 8 demonstrates that the value of a pure floater is par, as it should be. Exhibits 9 and 10 show the expected value of the floater's two components.

Two derivatives of the fixed-rate bond are the floater and the inverse floater, created by dynamically allocating the interest cash flow of the fixed-rate bond given levels of r, and assigning a portion of the principal to each derivative. Given 80 floater bonds derived from 100 of the fixed-rate bonds, and 20 inverse floater

---

Exhibit 8: Expected Present Value of a Pure Floater

Path	Rate	Cash Flow	Rate	Cash Flow	Rate	Cash Flow		Present Value
1	10.00%	10.00	11.51%	11.51	13.28%	113.28	=	100.0000
2	10.00%	10.00	11.51%	11.51	9.84%	109.84	=	100.0000
3	10.00%	10.00	8.53%	8.53	9.84%	109.84	=	100.0000
4	10.00%	10.00	8.53%	8.53	7.29%	107.29	=	100.0000
		Expected Present Value of Pure Floater					=	100.0000

Exhibit 9: Expected Present Value of the Principal Payment

Path	Rate	Cash Flow	Rate	Cash Flow	Rate	Cash Flow		Present Value
1	10.00%	0.00	11.51%	0.00	13.28%	100.00	=	71.9667
2	10.00%	0.00	11.51%	0.00	9.84%	100.00	=	74.2219
3	10.00%	0.00	8.53%	0.00	9.84%	100.00	=	76.2624
4	10.00%	0.00	8.53%	0.00	7.29%	100.00	=	78.0749
		Expected Present Value of Principal Paid at Maturity					=	75.1315

Exhibit 10: Expected Present Value of Pure Floater Interest, a 0% Cap Agreement

Path	Rate	Cash Flow	Rate	Cash Flow	Rate	Cash Flow		Present Value
1	10.00%	10.00	11.51%	11.51	13.28%	13.28	=	28.0333
2	10.00%	10.00	11.51%	11.51	9.84%	9.84	=	25.7781
3	10.00%	10.00	8.53%	8.53	9.84%	9.84	=	23.7376
4	10.00%	10.00	8.53%	8.53	7.29%	7.29	=	21.9251
		Expected Present Value of Principal Paid at Maturity					=	24.8685

bonds, the cash flows and expected present values would be as shown in Exhibits 11 and 12.

Exhibit 11: Expected Present Value of a Floater Having a 12.50% Interest Cap—80.00 Face Amount

Path	Rate	Cash Flow	Rate	Cash Flow	Rate	Cash Flow		Present Value
1	10.00%	8.00	11.51%	9.21	13.28%	90.00	=	79.5508
2	10.00%	8.00	11.51%	9.21	9.84%	87.87	=	80.0000
3	10.00%	8.00	8.53%	6.82	9.84%	87.87	=	80.0000
4	10.00%	8.00	8.53%	6.82	7.29%	85.83	=	80.0000

Expected Present Value of Floater Having a 12.50% Rate Cap = 79.8877

Exhibit 12: Expected Present Value of an Inverse Floater—20.00 Face Amount

Path	Rate	Cash Flow	Rate	Cash Flow	Rate	Cash Flow		Present Value
1	10.00%	2.00	11.51%	0.79	13.28%	20.00	=	16.8558
2	10.00%	2.00	11.51%	0.79	9.84%	22.13	=	18.8874
3	10.00%	2.00	8.53%	3.18	9.84%	22.13	=	21.3561
4	10.00%	2.00	8.53%	3.18	7.29%	24.17	=	23.3499

Expected Present Value of an Inverse Floater = 20.1123

Note that the floater and inverse floater present values add up to the collateral, and that the difference between the two securities' value and par (20 and 80, respectively), is given by the value of the 12.50% cap. The floater is short the cap, the inverse floater is long the cap. The value of the cap is presented in Exhibit 13.

Exhibit 14 shows the impact of a call option on the value of a fixed-rate bond. In this example, the issuer has the right to exercise a call option, and is assumed to do so when it is economical. The entire bond is callable.

Exhibit 13: Expected Present Value of a 12.50% Interest Rate Cap Agreement, 80.00 Notional Amount

Path	Rate	Cash Flow	Rate	Cash Flow	Rate	Cash Flow		Present Value
1	10.00%	0.00	11.51%	0.00	13.28%	0.62	=	0.4492
2	10.00%	0.00	11.51%	0.00	9.84%	0.00	=	0.0000
3	10.00%	0.00	8.53%	0.00	9.84%	0.00	=	0.0000
4	10.00%	0.00	8.53%	0.00	7.29%	0.00	=	0.0000

Expected Present Value of 10% Interest Rate Cap Agreement   =   0.1123

Exhibit 14: Expected Present Value of a Callable, 10% Fixed-Rate Bond

Path	Rate	Cash Flow	Rate	Cash Flow	Rate	Cash Flow		Present Value
1	10.00%	10.00	11.51%	10.00	13.28%	110.00	=	96.4066
2	10.00%	10.00	11.51%	10.00	9.84%	110.00	=	98.8874
3	10.00%	10.00	8.53%	110.00	9.84%	0.00	=	101.2327
4	10.00%	10.00	8.53%	110.00	7.29%	0.00	=	101.2327

Expected Present Value of a Callable, 10% Fixed-Rate Bond   =   99.4399

Exhibit 15 shows the cash flows and expected present value of an amortizing, partially callable, 10% fixed-rate bond. Similar indexed sinking fund bonds have been issued in the fixed-income market. Among the various financial instruments presented, this bond is the one most like a mortgage security. The difference is that the call feature of these bonds, unlike the typical mortgage security, is *completely* determined by the interest rate process. There are no prepayments due to death or divorce, no lock-in effect, and no "burnout." Interest and principal components of the total cash flow are separately presented.

Note that this 10% fixed-rate coupon bond has a price that is at a discount to par, and at a discount to the noncallable 10% fixed-

Exhibit 15: Expected Present Value of an Amortizing, Partially Callable, 10% Fixed-Rate Bond

Path	Rate	Int.	Prin.	Rate	Int.	Prin.	Rate	Int.	Prin.		Present Value
1	10.00%	10.00	10.00	11.51%	9.00	1.80	13.28%	8.82	88.20	=	96.8085
2	10.00%	10.00	10.00	11.51%	9.00	1.80	9.84%	8.82	88.20	=	98.9965
3	10.00%	10.00	10.00	8.53%	9.00	89.10	9.84%	0.09	0.90	=	101.1106
4	10.00%	10.00	10.00	8.53%	9.00	89.10	7.29%	0.09	0.90	=	101.1285

	Expected Present Value of an Amortizing, Partially Callable Bond								=	99.5110

rate bond. Like a completely callable bond, this discount reflects the value of the call(s) implicit in the amortization scheme. Like a mortgage, this bond's paydown schedule varies inversely with the level of interest rates. Because the bond will pay down more rapidly as interest rates fall, the investor's ability to participate in any market rally is reduced. This compresses the value of the bond, as illustrated by the compressed price appreciation associated with paths three and four, relative to the performance of a noncallable bond. Note as well the higher present value of the amortizing bond in paths one and two relative to the noncallable bond. (See Exhibit 4.) This is the result of the early redemption of principal in an environment in which prevailing rates exceed the coupon rate.

Valuing to a Zero Option-Adjusted Spread

The above values were all discounted across the rate paths at the riskless rates themselves, with no spread (OAS) added or subtracted. That is, all the above securities were priced to a zero OAS. The reason goes back to the basic arbitrage arguments underlying the option pricing methodology. In particular, if a security's cash flows and/or amortization are a certain function of interest rates, then at the start of any single time period it is possible to create a portfolio of term structure bonds that, at the end of the time period, will have the same future value as this security for every possible value of the short-term rate. Thus the security must cost the same at the start of the time period as the portfolio of Treasuries. Since any portfolio of Treasuries has a zero OAS, it follows that the security itself must have a zero OAS. Intuitively, the idea is that as long as we can exactly recreate the performance of an arbitrary security with a portfolio of Treasuries, then the value of the portfolio and the security must be the same at the start of the hedging period.

This can be shown to be the case for all of the financial instruments presented so far. Any one of them can be recreated by a portfolio of the zero-coupon Treasury securities given by the term structure.

For example, consider the case of the three-period interest rate cap agreement struck at 10%. While on the surface this may appear to be a difficult candidate to replicate with a Treasury portfolio, it is actually quite natural. In fact, it is perfectly analogous to the original Black-Scholes arbitrage-free pricing methodology, wherein a portfolio containing the underlying stock and short-term debt is constructed to replicate the performance of a call option on the stock.

To the extent that short-term rates over time are tied to the term structure, the cap is in effect an option on the term structure. Thus we should be able to replicate the performance of the cap by analogously constructing a portfolio containing an appropriate combination of an underlying term structure bond and short-term debt.

In the case of the simple example presented above, it is not difficult to calculate that the 10% cap can be replicated in the first period by lending 99.20177 for one period and shorting 107.6621 of the two-period bond. If we calculate the price of this portfolio we get:

	Face Amount	Price		Cost
One-Period Bond	99.20177	0.909090	=	90.183426
Two-Period Bond	-107.66207	0.826446	=	-88.976887

				1.206539

The cost of this portfolio is exactly the same as the cap valued above at zero OAS. Clearly, any valuation of the cap to a nonzero spread would create an arbitrage between the cap and the market for term structure bonds. At the end of the first period, the value of the short-term rate for the second period becomes known. At this time, the hedge is rebalanced so as to hedge out the risk for the second period, and so on for the remainder of the future periods.

RELATIVE VALUATION WHEN CASH FLOWS ARE NOT DETERMINISTIC

Callable Bonds When Option Exercise Is Inefficient

In the case of mortgage-backed securities, the exercise of borrower call options is *not* solely a deterministic function of interest rates, but rather a function of various demographic factors and borrowers' financial status. Such conditions can constrain an otherwise economic exercise of the call option, or induce a noneconomic exercise of the option. Furthermore, in the case of conventional mortgages, lenders can exercise put options that generally can be construed as optimal from a financial standpoint, but are restricted to circumstances when the home is sold.

These factors introduce elements that are not determined by the prevailing rate of interest. Even so, the relations that we have derived above for deterministic bonds, their components and derivatives, must also hold for mortgage-backed securities and their components and derivatives. These include floaters, inverse floaters, PAC, companion, interest- and principal-only securities, and the like.

When the one-factor pricing model is applied to the valuation of mortgage product, principal prepayments are made a function of the stochastic rate process. In other words, principal prepayments are treated as completely deterministic with respect to interest rates. As a result, a future prepayment is *known*, within the context of the model, given the prevailing rate of interest. The effects on prepayments of other factors, such as economic growth, housing inflation, month of the year, and age of the loan as a proxy for demographic influences, are typically assumed to be certain and fixed in the model.

We would not expect a model that uses the prevailing interest rate as the only random variable to provide a meaningful fair value for IBM stock. Nor should we expect such a model accurately to value death, divorce, and the "lock-in" effect. Of course, mortgage market participants recognize the limitations of prepayment algorithms; historical experience of specific pools and trusts consistently reveals such limitations.

Confronted with the positive OAS on GNMA pass-through securities, which are free of default risk, the spread must be compensation for prepayment uncertainty. While some analysts point out that an OAS could also be compensation for the increased operational costs of investing in a monthly pay security, and for a lack of liquidity, the impact of these factors in today's mortgage market must be minimal.

Why Different Mortgage Products Should Have Different Option-Adjusted Spreads

When evaluating the vast array of mortgage products, an implicit assumption often used in the marketplace is that fairly priced mortgage securities would have the *same* OAS. This, in general, is not correct.

When a security's return is affected by nondeterministic cash flows, its fair price, in the context of the OAS model, must be such that the investor is compensated for that uncertainty. It follows, then, that the more deterministic are the cash flows of a particular mortgage security, the lower the option-adjusted spread. Thus, wide range, narrow window PAC bonds should have relatively low option-adjusted spreads, and companion/support tranches should have relatively high option-adjusted spreads. To the degree that the value of a bond's cash flows is unaffected by nondeterministic aspect of prepayments, so too should the bond have a lower option-adjusted spread. Thus, high cap floaters should have low spreads, and inverse floaters should have high spreads.

Put another way, just as fairly valued securities with embedded options can have different yields, so too can fairly valued mortgage securities have different option-adjusted spreads.

A Pure Floater with Nondeterministic Amortization

Consider a simple example. Suppose that we created two REMIC tranches using a fixed-rate GNMA pass-through security as the underlying collateral. The two tranches are a floater and an inverse floater, both indexed to the one-month Treasury bill rate. The floater is structured with a very high cap, perhaps as high as 50%. Such a floater might be considered a close approximation to a default-free mortgage floater, a *pure* floater. Just as we argued that the *maturity* of a pure floater is irrelevant, that it would always be worth par, so too might we argue that the *amortization* of a pure floater is irrelevant. We do not need to model prepayments or consider in any way how much principal will be outstanding in any period. As long as the security pays the prevailing rate of interest, it will be worth par. It will also have, in the standard OAS framework, a zero option-adjusted spread.

Fairness requires that the value of the floater and the inverse floater add up to the value of the GNMA collateral. Thus, if the collateral is priced in the market to yield a positive OAS, then the dollar value of that discount giving rise the positive OAS of the collateral must be completely embodied in the inverse floater. It can be shown that the OAS on the inverse is approximately equal to the OAS on the collateral multiplied by the ratio of the market value of the collateral to the value of the inverse floater at a zero OAS. As a rough approximation, the relative OAS of the inverse will be equal to the leverage ratio times the collateral OAS.

**Explicitly Valuing Prepayment Uncertainty—Pricing to an Option and Pre-
payment-Uncertainty Adjusted Spread**

In the preceding pages we found that logic alone can be used to
provide approximate relative values for interest rate uncertainty,
but cannot provide fair, absolute prices without modeling that uncertainty. The same is true for prepayment uncertainty. The statistical error of empirically based prepayment models *can* be
explicitly incorporated into the OAS framework. To satisfy the
benchmarks for stochastic models, this random error must be
"tuned" to a set of securities in a way similar to that in which the
random interest rate process is "tuned" to the Treasury curve.

This will result in the market's implied price of prepayment
uncertainty over time. Then, as this prepayment uncertainty is allocated disproportionately to derivatives, they will be priced to
meet the benchmarks of fairness, consistency, and robustness.

We propose such a model be termed an Option and Prepayment Uncertainty Adjusted Spread (OPAS) model. Within this
framework, fairly priced mortgage securities will have the same
OPAS, but in general, different OAS values, just as fairly priced
deterministic securities can have the same OAS, but different
yields.

CHAPTER 30

DURATION AND CONVEXITY DRIFT OF CMOs

David P. Jacob
Managing Director
J. P. Morgan Securities Inc.

Sean Gallop
Vice President
J. P. Morgan Securities Inc.

Duration and convexity are the standard measures of the price sensitivity of fixed-income instruments. They are used to compare the relative risk of bonds and portfolios, and help investors look for relative value by enabling them to classify bonds with similar risk profiles. Total rate of return managers often use duration to position their portfolios relative to the major bond indices, and asset/liability managers use these measures to control risk by matching the duration and convexity characteristics of their assets to those of their liabilities.

Duration and convexity are, of course, only summary measures of a security's sensitivity to instantaneous changes in interest rates. They do not provide insight into how a bond's characteristics will change over time. It is important, however, for both the asset/liability manager and the total rate of return manager to know in advance how a security's characteristics can evolve.

For example, an insurance company might use duration and convexity to set up a portfolio of mortgage-backed securities or corporate bonds to back its GIC portfolio. The insurer would like to remain matched so as to minimize the need to rebalance, which would result in increased transaction costs and potential negative impact on surplus. However, simply being matched at the onset does not insure that the book remains matched. In fact, unless the manager perfectly matches the cash flows of the assets and liabilities at the beginning for all future interest rate environments, the duration of the assets and liabilities will inevitably drift apart. The question is how much and how quickly will this drift or mismatch arise. Knowing this beforehand is important for proper management. As we will see, for CMOs, the evolution of the characteristics are sometimes not so obvious.

Alternatively, consider the case of the total rate of return manager who matches the duration, and, perhaps, the convexity of his portfolio with that of some index, and attempts to outperform the index by loading up with bonds that appear to offer substantial up-front yield. If, at the end of the performance measurement period, the price sensitivity characteristics of these bonds have changed substantially (for example, their duration has increased and they are more negatively convex) the market will likely price these bonds at wider spreads, and thus hurt the performance of these securities. For Treasury securities and noncallable corporates this is not a problem, since the duration of bonds with periodic, noninterest-sensitive cash flows, for the most part decline in a well defined and predictable manner as time passes. As a result, experienced portfolio managers either intuitively know or can readily calculate how the duration and convexity of these types of bonds change as time passes.

Unlike Treasuries, however, mortgage-backed securities (MBSs) and their derivatives can exhibit very different, and at first, often nonintuitive price sensitivity characteristics at the performance horizon. Moreover, for many MBSs, the horizon characteristics will be a function of not just the ending interest rate environment, but of what occurs during the holding period as well. For the asset/liability manager, this could necessitate unexpected portfolio rebalancing, and for the total rate of return manager, inferior performance under certain scenarios. For MBSs, the degree to which price sensitivity characteristics improve or deteriorate over time is determined by such factors as prepayment assumptions, yield curve shapes and levels, and liquidity, and for CMOs, structural considerations.

The major conclusion reached in this chapter is that using current price sensitivity characteristics such as duration and convexity as a basis for estimating performance or anticipating the cash flow characteristics of MBSs can be misleading. Investors must assess the current performance characteristics as well as how these characteristics change over time. They should not rely on their intuition derived from traditional bonds. We believe that by using an analytic framework that anticipates a security's horizon characteristics, the investor can more readily distinguish between bonds that appear to offer good value from ones that actually do.

REVIEW OF DURATION AND CONVEXITY FOR TREASURIES

Before discussing the unusual evolution of the duration and convexity of CMO bonds, we first quickly review this evolution for an ordinary Treasury note.

Consider the 7.75 of 2/15/01 which, on 4/3/91, was offered at 98-2 to yield 8.036%. Its modified duration was computed to be 6.701 years. One year forward, assuming the same yield, its duration is 6.232 years. In fact, for a 100-basis point shift up or down in the horizon yield, the duration will vary by no more than 0.12 years. Similar stability would be computed for the convexity.

Thus, an asset/liability manager can readily tell how this bond's price sensitivity characteristics change, and therefore anticipate the potential drift between the duration of this bond and that of a liability payment due 6.7 years. Similarly, a manager interested in computing horizon returns can do so easily because he knows that the bond at the horizon will be one year shorter in maturity and roughly half a year shorter in duration. Thus, the horizon price can be computed using an appropriate yield.

EVOLUTION OF DURATION AND CONVEXITY FOR CMOs

Consider instead the bonds shown in Exhibit 1, which were selected from a recently issued CMO. In this FNMA deal the collateral was 9.5%, and the pricing speed was 165 PSA. Exhibit 1 contains the usual information supplied to the portfolio manager by a dealer, or which might have been obtained from an information service.

Exhibit 1: Three-Year PAC Bonds

| | | | | | Avg. Life @ PSA | | |
	Spread	First Pay	Last Pay	PAC Band	105	125	165
PAC	66bp/3yr	7/15/92	6/15/93	90-380	2.8	2.8	2.8
PAC	120bp/3yr	4/15/91	9/15/04	140-250	7.6	4.6	3.1

Both bonds are planned amortization classes (PAC bonds) with average lives (at the pricing speed of 165) of approximately three years. As a result, they are priced at spreads off the three-year Treasury. The first bond is a standard three-year PAC bond, whereas the second is a level 2 PAC, since its average life is protected for a tighter range of PSA and its principal amortization is junior to that of the first bond. The second column shows the spread off the three-year Treasury. The next two columns show the first and last principal payment dates. The following column shows the PSA bands for which the average life is constant. The primary PAC is protected from 90 PSA to 380 PSA, whereas the level 2 PAC is only protected from 140 PSA to 250 PSA. Since the collateral to date has been prepaying at 125 PSA, we show the average life at some speeds below the original pricing speed of 165 PSA. The last three columns in Exhibit 1 show that even at the slower speeds, the average lives remain the same for the first bond. This is because 105 PSA and 125 PSA are still within its PAC band. However, the average life of the second bond, at 125 PSA, extends to 4.6 years and, at 105 PSA, it extends to 7.6 years. Since these slower speeds are outside the lower band, the extension in average life is expected.

Most managers stop at this point and try to decide whether or not the extra fifty-four basis points provided by the level 2 PAC is sufficient to compensate them for the potential adverse average life variability (i.e., negative convexity). We will return to this point later. At this juncture we would like to analyze what happens to the average life, and the average life sensitivity as time passes.

Exhibit 2 describes how this evolution takes place for the simplest scenario. The exhibit shows the expected average life and sensitivity for each bond at pricing as well as one year forward

Exhibit 2: Evolution of Average Life and Average Life Sensitivity

	3-Year PAC		
	PSA		
	105	*125*	*165*
Current	2.8	2.8	2.8
1 Year Forward	1.8	1.8	1.8
2 Years Forward	0.8	0.8	0.8

	Level 2 PAC		
	PSA		
	105	*125*	*165*
Current	7.6	4.6	3.1
1 Year Forward	8.9	5.2	3.1
2 Years Forward	9.5	5.7	3.3

and two years forward. The first row repeats the numbers from Exhibit 1. For example, at pricing the 3-year PAC has a 2.8 year average life at each of the three PSA speeds listed. In the second row we show the average life and how it varies at the end of the first year, assuming that for the first year the collateral paid at 125 PSA and thereafter at 105, 125, or 165 PSA. For the 3-year PAC, we see that after one year has passed the average life has shrunk by 1 year from 2.8 years to 1.8 years. This is as expected, since, as indicated in Exhibit 1, principal does not begin paying until 7/15/92. Moreover, even if from the end of the first year forward the speed changes up to 165 PSA or down to 105 PSA, the expected average life would still be 1.8 years.

However, the level 2 PAC paints a different picture. As before, the second row shows the average life and how it varies one year out, assuming that during the first year the collateral pays at a 125 PSA. The surprising result is that not only does the average life increase from 4.6 years to 5.2 years, but the sensitivity increases as well. Now, the average life can increase by 3.7 years if speeds decrease to 105 PSA, and can decrease by 2.1 years if speeds increase to 165 PSA. The third row shows the situation two years out assuming 125 PSA for the first two years. The average life and average life sensitivity continue to increase. Since higher prepayment speeds are usually associated with lower interest rates, this security has not only increased in duration as time has passed, it has also become more negatively convex!

Exhibit 3 shows how the average life evolves for each of the bonds for their entire lives for level 105, 125, and 165 PSA scenarios. For example, from the graph in the foreground one can see how the average life under a 105 PSA scenario first increases and then decreases for the level 2 PAC, whereas for the primary PAC, the decline is linear.

Before we examine why such behavior occurs, we note that this example demonstrates how unexpectedly average life can change given a very simple tranche from a very simple deal under a very simple scenario. One can expect even more dramatic effects as the complexity of the deal and realism of the analysis increase.

Exhibit 3: Change in Average Life as Time Passes—Three-Year PACS

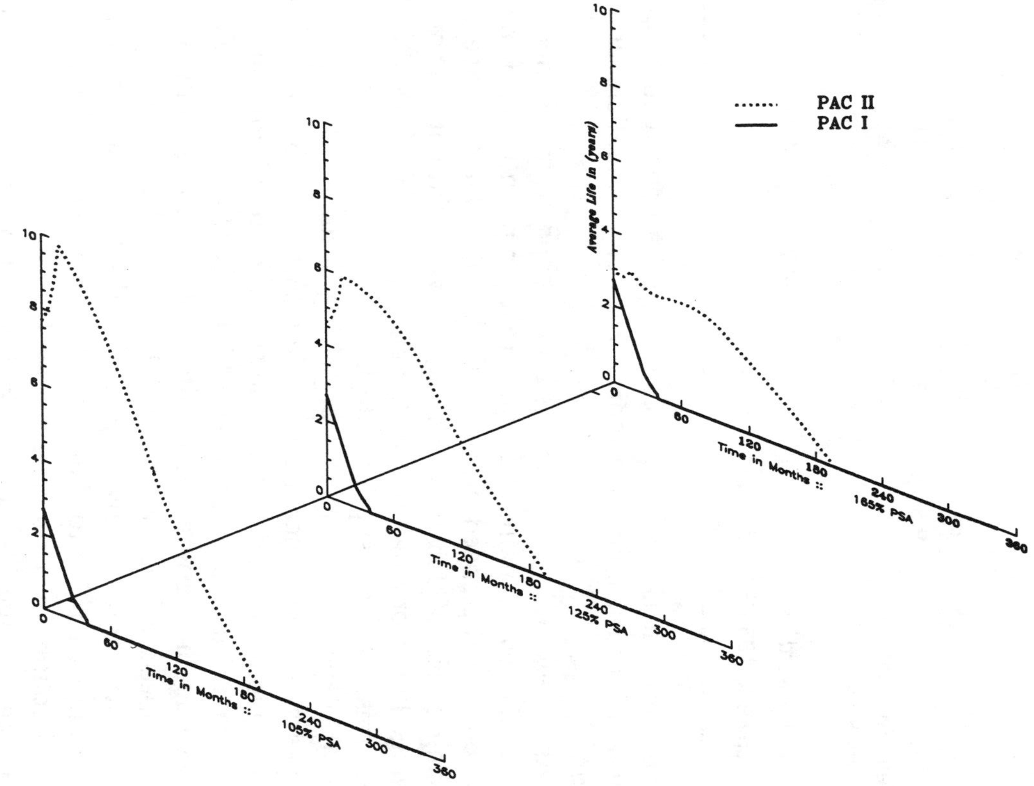

| Exhibit 4: Evolution of Average Life | | | | |

PSA

	90	125	155	165	200
Current	9.5	4.9	3.0	3.5	2.5
1 Year Forward	8.8	4.2	2.3	2.8	1.8
5 Years Forward	8.4	4.1	2.2	4.0	2.2
5 Years Forward (with spike to 165 PSA for 1 month)	12.6	8.2	4.7	4.0	2.2

For example, it is entirely possible to find a bond, which for two different scenarios, has two radically different durations and convexities.

As an example, consider a support bond from another recent deal. This deal contains a Z bond[1] that jumps in front of the support bond if the speed on the FNMA 9.0% collateral exceeds the pricing speed of 155 PSA. The first row of Exhibit 4 shows the average life at pricing for speeds ranging from 90 PSA to 200 PSA. Since this bond is a support and is thus junior to the PACs in the deal, its expected average life at pricing declines from 9.5 years to 3.0 years as speeds increase from 90 PSA to 155 PSA. At 165 PSA, its average life extends a bit because the Z bond jumps in front of it. As prepayments occur at still higher speeds such as 200 PSA, the average life resumes its decline. This is because ultimately the higher speed offsets the fact that the Z bond gets paid first. The other rows show, at several points in the future, the average life assuming that prior to that time the speed was 125 PSA. In the second column of Exhibit 4, we see that if the speed stays at 125 PSA, the average life declines at the end of the first year to 4.2 years, and to 4.1 years by the end of 5 years. The next to the last column shows that if the speed stays at 125 PSA for five years and

---

[1] A Z bond is one that accrues rather than pays its interest until other bonds in the deal have been retired. A jump-Z is one that, based on some event, stops accruing and begins paying interest and principal.

then jumps to and remains at 165 PSA, the average life declines only from 4.9 years to 4.0 years. This is because the Z bond's balance accretes for the first five years, so that when it does jump it has a greater impact than if it had jumped immediately. As a result, the effect of the jump offsets the higher speeds.

Now suppose, instead of these relatively simple scenarios shown in the first three rows of Exhibit 4, the speed starts at 125 PSA, remains there for five years, then jumps for one month to 165 PSA, and finally returns to either 90, 125, 155, 165, or 200 PSA. The expected average life at that point becomes 12.6, 8.2, 4.7, 3.8, or 2.1 years, respectively. It is incredible that this one-month jump could cause this bond's horizon average life and average life sensitivity to be so radically different from that at the beginning or from that five years out, where there was no one-month spike to 165 PSA. Most analyses ignore the horizon characteristics, particularly for complicated scenarios. All the investor is likely to have seen would be the initial average life table and/or price/yield table, neither of which inform him of the possibility of this behavior, let alone explaining why it could happen.

IMPLICATIONS FOR PERFORMANCE AND RISK MANAGEMENT

Given that the price sensitivity of a bond affects the spread at which it trades, one can imagine that the implications for performance and risk management can be substantial. Price sensitivity characteristics of a bond affect the spread at which it trades. Typically, for the same average life, spreads widen as negative convexity increases. Also, everything else equal, the greater the average life, the wider the spread. Exhibit 5 shows recent generic CMO spreads for PAC bonds, TAC bonds, Vanilla bonds, and level 2 PACs at increasing average lives, and the Treasury yield curve as of mid-May 1991. One can see that, in general, the bonds that are the shortest and have the most protection, such as the two-year PACs, trade at the tightest spreads, and the longer, more nega-

---

Exhibit 5: Generic CMO Spreads

	2yr	3yr	4yr	5yr	7yr	10yr	20yr
PAC	59	66	76	84	87	93	105
TAC	95	104	108	110	113	116	130
Vanilla	98	106	111	114	116	120	134
Level 2 PAC	110	120	124	130	134	139	143
Treasury Yields	6.84	7.15	7.36	7.75	7.98	8.11	8.20

---

tively convex bonds, such as the twenty-year level 2 PACs trade at the widest spreads.

Consider again the first example, in which we compare a three-year PAC with a three-year level 2 PAC. In Exhibit 6 we show some of the pricing information on these bonds. Investors must decide between the prepayment protection of the level 1 tranche and the extra yield of the level 2. From an OAS standpoint, in this case, the primary PAC looks like the slightly better value. However, since there are many assumptions that go into an OAS evaluation, and OAS does not give a complete picture of prospective performance, most managers will want to perform a total return analysis. While this deal was priced at 165 PSA, we feel that a 125 PSA makes more sense given the consistently slow prepayment history to date.

Exhibit 6: Yield/Average Life at PSA 3-Year PAC Bonds

			Yield/Average Life @ PSA					
	Price	Coupon	105	125	165	OAS	Dur.	Conv.
3yr Primary PAC	103-14	9.375	7.82/2.8	7.82/2.8	7.82/2.8	62	2.5	7
3yr Level 2 PAC	102-12	9.500	9.14/7.6	8.69/4.6	8.35/3.1	52	2.7	-69

In order to compute the expected total return for a year, we need to compute the terminal prices, but, as we have seen, yield spreads, which determine prices, are a function of the average life and sensitivity of the security.

Consider first the regular three-year PAC. At the end of 1-year, we found in Exhibit 2 that this bond's average life moved from 2.8 years to 1.8 years. The difference between the two-year and three-year Treasury is negative thirty-one basis points, and the difference between the two-year and three-year PACs is negative seven basis points. No adjustment is made for change in quality, since the bond remains well protected at the horizon. In total, the horizon yield of 7.44% is thirty-eight basis points tighter than the starting yield of 7.82%. This results in an ending price of 102-21, which translates into a total return of 8.54%.

Now consider the level 2 PAC. At the end of the first year, its average life has risen from 4.6 years to 5.2 years, assuming a 125 PSA. The difference between the four-year and the five-year Treasury is thirty-nine basis points (*this bond has rolled up the yield curve*), and the difference between four-year and five-year level 2 PACs is six basis points.

As we noted previously in Exhibit 2, not only has this bond got longer, but its quality has deteriorated, since its average life is more adversely sensitive (i.e., it extends when speeds slow down/rates rise, and contracts when speeds increase/rates fall). As a result we will penalize this bond by an additional four basis points.* Thus, the horizon yield is forty-nine basis points greater than at the original yield. The computed terminal price is 101-00, which produces a total return of 7.44%. These results are summarized in Exhibit 7.

Exhibit 7: Performance Results

	Initial Price	Yield @ 125 PSA	Spread Adjustment Treasury	CMO	Quality	Total	Horizon Price	1 Year Total Return
3yr Primary PAC	103-14	7.82	-31	-7	0	-38	102-21	8.54
3yr Level 2 PAC	102-12	8.69	+39	+6	+4	+49	101-00	7.44

---

* For the purposes of this chapter, we arbitrarily used a penalty of four basis points. To be more precise, one needs to look more closely at break-even returns at the market assessment of the value of the additional negative convexity.

The total return of the primary PAC (8.54%) is considerably higher than its yield of 7.82% at a 125 PSA. On the other hand, the level 2 PAC's total return of 7.44% is not only lower than its expected yield of 8.69%, but it is also lower than the expected yield of the primary PAC.

In Exhibit 8 we show the one-year returns for the two bonds for the base case, assuming shifts of 100 basis points up and down, where, as before, we have made adjustments to the horizon spread where appropriate. The level 2 PAC underperforms the primary PAC in all three scenarios. Since the level 2 PAC was initially more negatively convex than the primary PAC, it is not surprising that its relative performance suffers as rates move up or down. This is particularly true in the +100 basis points scenario, because the average life of the level 2 PAC extends considerably. What is unusual in this example is that even in the no-change-in-rates scenario, the level 2 PAC performs so poorly. This occurs because again the bond's performance characteristics have weakened over the holding period.

Exhibit 8: 1 Year Total Returns

| | Shift in Rates, Basis Points | | |
	-100	0	+100
Primary PAC	10.07	8.54	7.03
Level 2 PAC	9.07	7.44	3.07
PSA	165	125	105

Of course, one could debate the various spread adjustments used in this example, but the notion that the terminal characteristics of a bond are important in analyzing performance is indisputable. While we chose a straightforward PAC structure to demonstrate the effect on performance, this impact will be still greater for more complicated bonds under more realistic scenarios.

Although the initial OAS differential provides a hint of the prospective performance profile, it is not sufficient to quantify the scenario analysis. Some analysts perform what is known as constant OAS total returns. In this framework the ending price in each scenario is computed by adding the initial OAS to the horizon yield curve in each scenario, and then computing the expected discounted value of projected cash flows. This analysis skirts the issue of the security's ending characteristics, because the methodology directly incorporates the terminal sensitivity of the cash flow. We believe that this type of analysis is a good start, and is far better than computing returns based on constant yield spread analysis. Nevertheless, it is still deficient, because the market tends to price instruments with different durations and convexities at different OAS levels. The difference is sometimes market-directional. For example, when the market is bullish, the demand for interest-only strips (IOs) from mortgage securities declines. While the decline may be justified, it is often dramatic and the OAS for IOs widen greatly during the initial stages of a bullish environment, as the durations become more negative.

Another reason why constant OAS total return is insufficient for the practitioner is because the analysis does not provide insight into the reasons for unusual performance patterns. In order for the investor to be able to distinguish between genuinely attractive opportunities and ones that only appear as such, he needs to know what causes the behavior and how to anticipate it.

The starting point for analyzing these bonds, as with any, should be a thorough understanding of the cash flows. Exhibit 9 shows the monthly principal payments for the primary PAC and the level 2 PAC that were discussed in the first example. The three diagrams show the monthly principal payments for level 105 PSA, 125 PSA, and 165 PSA scenarios. In each diagram the horizontal axis represents time in months, and the vertical axis represents the principal payment in millions of dollars. The dark set of flows are from the primary PAC. The combination of the separate diagrams when read laterally shows that the "shape" of the PAC cash flow is invariant to changes in prepayment.

The lightly shaded region shows the paydown of the level 2 PAC. Under each of the scenarios, we see a significant paydown in principal in the first year, and then it begins to tail off. In the 105 PSA scenario the principal paydown is initially high, then drops,

Exhibit 9

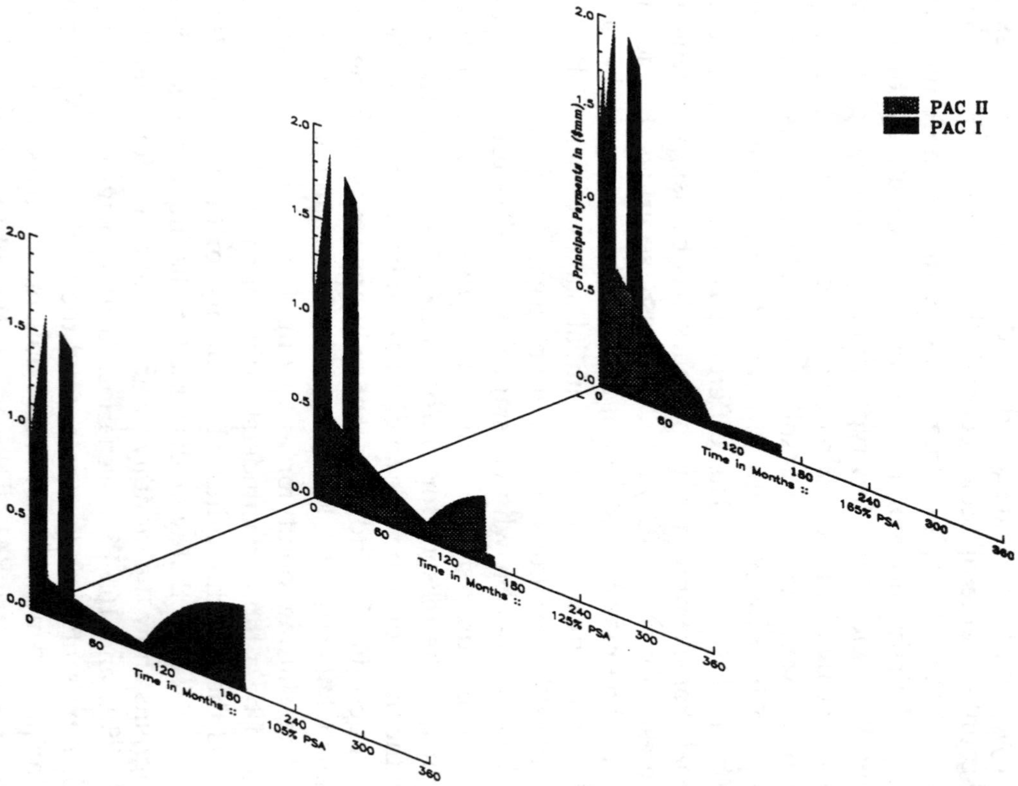

and finally begins to pick up toward the end of the bond's life. Looking at this picture, it is no wonder that the average life increases after the first year. The early payments—from a vantage point of time 0—reduce the expected average life. After they are paid down, however, the remaining average life is longer.

The extreme case of this would be a portfolio consisting of two zero coupon bonds of similar balances but different maturity. One zero matures in one year, and the other in ten years. The initial average life of this portfolio is 5.5 years. One year later, however, the average life of the portfolio has risen to nine years assuming that the investor does not reinvest the proceeds of his short zero. Indeed, it is true that the investor could rebalance his portfolio at the end of a year. Such a strategy, however, generates larger transaction costs and greater reinvestment risk.

The diagrams in Exhibit 9 make clear how it is possible that the average life increases. However, these diagrams only represent simple, level PSA scenarios. They do not show how average life sensitivity can vary. In order to do this, one needs to be able to project forward the cash flows for varying PSA scenarios. As we will show, this is crucial in the next example.

The cash flow patterns of the second example are more complicated because the jump Z leads to highly path-dependent cash flow patterns. As a result, it is very important to analyze the flows of all the bonds in such a deal under a variety of nonlevel PSA scenarios. Exhibit 10 shows the monthly principal cash flow at 90 PSA, 125 PSA, 155 PSA, and 165 PSA for the support bond and jump Z that were discussed in the second example. For the level 90 PSA scenario, a principal cash flow pattern similar to that of the level 2 PAC from the first example emerges. At 125 PSA, the principal cash flow compresses considerably. Mentally combining these two diagrams allows one to understand why, if the collateral paid at 125 PSA for five years and then paid at 90 PSA for the rest of its life, it extends from 4.9 years to 8.2 years (see Exhibit 4). Under the 90 PSA, 125 PSA, and 155 PSA scenarios, the Z bond does not begin paying for many years. However, recall that the Z bond jumps when prepayments rise above 155 PSA. As a result,

Exhibit 10

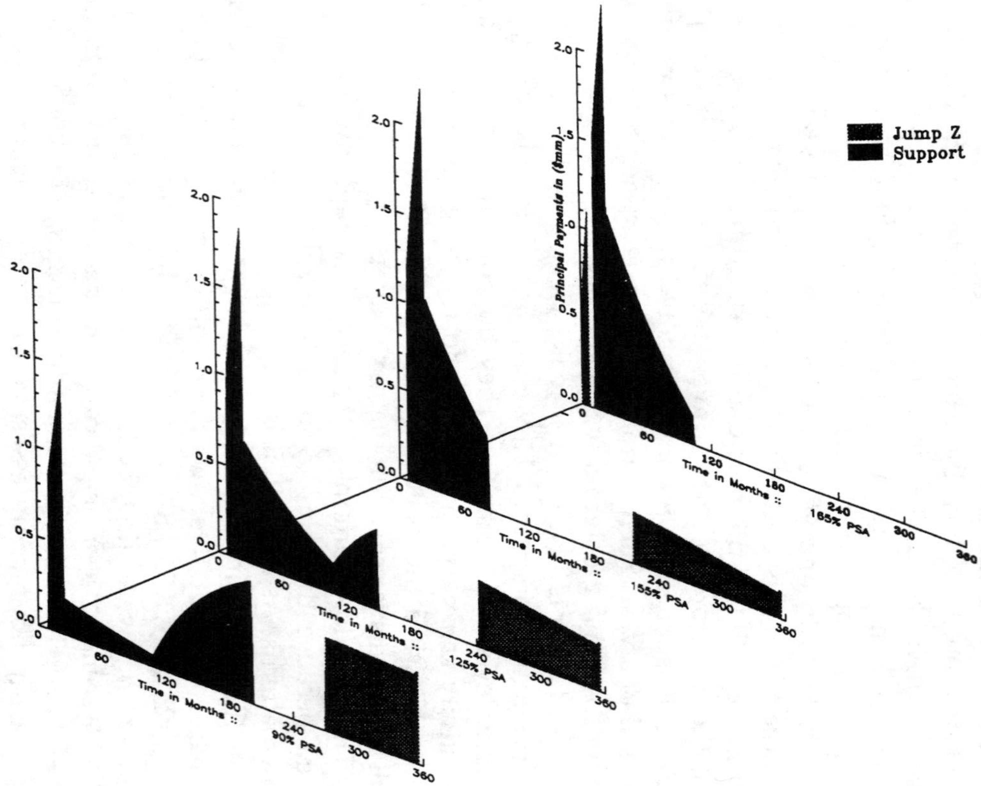

Exhibit 11

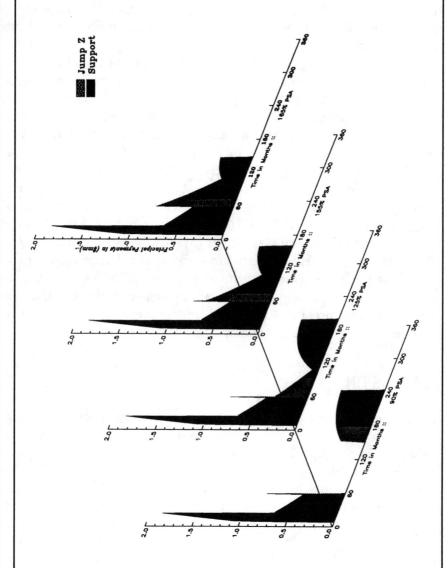

the jump Z bond moves in front of the support bond, thereby causing the extension one observes in the average life table of this deal at pricing.

This exhibit, however, tells only a small part of the story, since, with level scenarios, the Z bond either jumps in the beginning or not, and is therefore, not given the opportunity to have its balance increase via accretion. In order to assess the impact of this, consider Exhibit 11. In these diagrams we show the cash flow that corresponds to the scenarios in the last row of Exhibit 4. In that scenario, the collateral pays at 125 PSA for five years, then spurts to 165 PSA for one month (recall that this causes the Z bond to jump), and then pays at either 90 PSA, 125 PSA, 155 PSA, or 165 PSA. This one month of 165 PSA causes the principal cash flows of the support bond to split apart. In the 90 PSA scenario there is a 90-month hiatus during which the support bond receives no principal. It is for this reason that the average life after 5 years extends from 4.9 years at pricing to 12.6 years in this scenario. We feel that these diagrams are invaluable for understanding, and, therefore, anticipating the nature of the bonds under consideration.

CONCLUSION

CMO tranches have cash flow patterns which often do not resemble those of more intuitive fixed-income securities. Moreover, the cash flow is not static. It is interest-sensitive and path-dependent. Therefore, as time passes and interest rates and prepayment scenarios unfold, some bond classes undergo radical changes in their price sensitivity characteristics. Pricing at the horizon will reflect these altered sensitivities. For the total return account, this can have significant impact on performance. In order to discern value and anticipate the potential decline in quality, the manager should analyze the cash flow carefully. The asset/liability manager must assess the impact of a CMO's changing cash flow on the exposure of his book.

Clearly, some investor several years from now will be holding the bonds that are created today. Duration and convexity do not tell the whole story, since they are summary instantaneous measures. In order to understand how a bond's characteristics can change, investors need to analyze the performance of their securities and picture their cash flows.

CHAPTER 31

THE SEASONING OF PREPAYMENT SPEEDS AND ITS EFFECT ON THE AVERAGE LIVES AND VALUES OF MBS

David P. Jacob
Managing Director
J. P. Morgan Securities Inc.

Clark McGranery
Vice President
J. P. Morgan Securities Inc.

Sean Gallop
Vice President
J. P. Morgan Securities Inc.

Lynn Tong
Vice President
J. P. Morgan Securities Inc.

In this chapter we demonstrate how, in many cases, mortgage-backed securities (MBS) take far longer to season than suggested by the PSA curve and how, by using the PSA curve, as is, one can make serious errors in calculating value and performance characteristics of MBS and their derivative products. In this chapter the notion of fully seasoned at 30 months is challenged, and the impact on the valuation of MBS is discussed.

THE PSA CURVE

Speeds are quoted as percentages of the PSA curve. 100% PSA indicates that the annual prepayment rate begins at 0.2% of the principal balance in the first month and increases by 0.2% per month until the 30th month when the annual prepayment rate reaches 6%. At 100% PSA it is assumed that the annual prepayment rate is constant at 6% of the principal balance for the remaining term of the mortgages.

The standard yardstick against which prepayment speeds are measured is the PSA curve. Yields, average lives, durations, and PAC bands use the PSA standard. The PSA curve was devised by the industry trade group as a standard for comparing prepayments among mortgage securities. The linear increase in prepayment rates during the first 30 months of the PSA curve is meant to give recognition to the fact that prepayments on pools of mortgages are low when the mortgages are new, and that over time they increase gradually until they level off to some fairly constant rate dictated by demographic components such as propensity to move, retire, die, etc. This phenomenon is commonly known as *seasoning* or *aging of the pools*. The PSA curve is applied by the industry to all mortgages, 15-year, 30-year, GNMAs, FNMAs, FHLMCs, ARMs, CMO tranches, etc.

EVIDENCE FROM PREPAYMENT DATA

We first look at the prepayment data to establish the fact that seasoning can take far longer than 30 months. Consider, for example, GNMA 8.5. By the PSA standard, both GNMA 8.5 of 1986 (of which there were $3.3 billion issued and of which $3.0 billion are now outstanding) and GNMA 8.5 of 1976 (of which there were $2.2 billion issued and $800 million are now outstanding) should be fully seasoned. Therefore, they should be prepaying at the same prepayment rate. Yet in April 1990, the 12 month CPR for the 1976 issue year was 7%, whereas the 1986 issue year prepaid at a 3.6% rate.

We find a similar result for FHLMC 8.0, when we compare the 2008 WAM year to the 2016 WAM year. Once again the FHLMC 8.0 of 2008 are prepaying substantially faster than FHLMC 8.0 of 2016. This is despite the fact that the WAC in the 2016 WAM year is 75 basis points *higher* than that of the 2008 WAM year. Exhibit 1 shows the monthly CPR from May 1989 to April 1990.

Exhibit 1: CPRs from May 1989 to April 1990

	1990				1989								12
	Apr	Mar	Feb	Jan	Dec	Nov	Oct	Sep	Aug	July	June	May	Month
GNMA 8.5 1976	6.8	6.8	6.4	7.6	6.5	7.7	7.5	7.8	6.3	7.2	6.8	6.7	7.0
GNMA 8.5 1986	4.3	3.3	3.1	3.8	3.8	3.8	3.8	4.2	3.1	3.7	3.8	3.2	3.6

	1990				1989								12
	Apr	Mar	Feb	Jan	Dec	Nov	Oct	Sep	Aug	July	June	May	Month
FHLMC 8.0 2008	6.8	7.4	7.9	7.3	9.8	8.9	9.5	8.2	8.6	7.3	7.3	7.2	8.1
FHLMC 8.0 2016	5.6	5.2	5.5	5.8	6.6	6.4	8.5	7.6	6.3	6.7	6.2	6.4	6.5

It is clear from Exhibit 1 that despite the fact that the later issues are fully seasoned by the PSA standard, they are clearly prepaying at different rates. In order to figure out how long it could take to fully season, the data must be carefully chosen. First, one has to refer to earlier issue years in order to analyze a sufficient set of data to observe the convergence. Second, one has to choose issue years carefully so as not to draw erroneous conclusions from

Exhibit 2

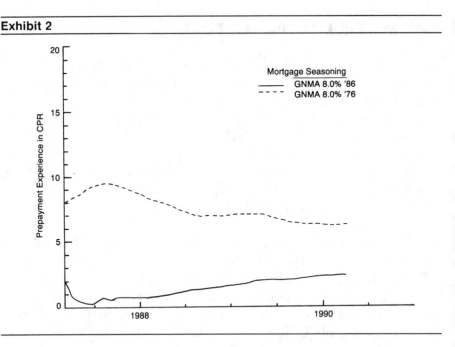

small samples. We show the results for GNMA 8, GNMA 9, and GNMA 11.

In Exhibit 2 we plot for each month beginning in January 1988 the 12 month CPR for GNMA 8 of 1986 and 1976. According to the PSA standard, somewhere in 1989 these two lines should have converged.

Instead we see that convergence did not yet take place well into 1990. In order to observe convergence, we have to choose earlier issue years. Exhibit 3 shows the results for GNMA 9 of 1975 and 1979. Here 12 month CPR is plotted from January 1981.

Convergence takes place somewhere in 1989, approximately 100 months out. Figure 4 shows the results for GNMA 11 of 1983 and 1980. In this case the situation is more complicated. Because mortgage rates dropped throughout the second half of the 1980s, prepayments picked up dramatically on the GNMA 11. The pick-up was first experienced by the 1980 issue year, and then by the 1983 issue year. After a while we observe that the 1983 issue year

Exhibit 3

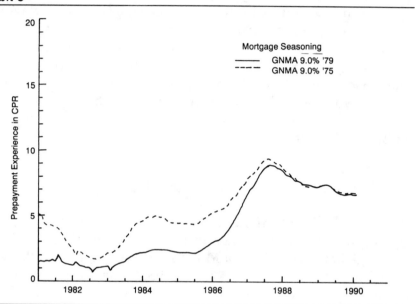

Exhibit 4

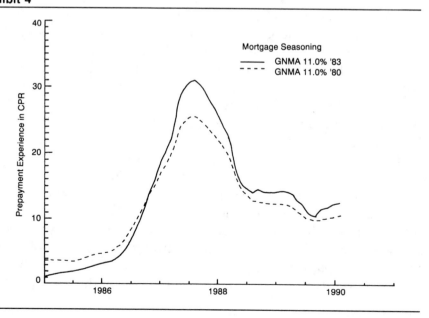

experienced higher prepayment rates that the 1980 issuer year due to the "burnout" effect in the earlier group. That is, prepayments can tail off once the hot money (quick to refinance) has left the group. Because of the burnout phenomenon, convergence of the later issue year to the prepayment pattern of the early issue year takes place from above. Nevertheless, in this case, again we see that the two groups did not yet converge. All three of these examples show clearly how different the prepayment seasoning pattern is from the PSA standard.

IMPACT ON VALUE AND PERFORMANCE

While there will be variance from these results, for different mortgage collateral, the difference from the 30 month standard is so dramatic that investors should consider the impact on the value and performance characteristics of MBS. Some analysts take comfort in using slower prepay assumptions to account for the longer seasoning. This, however, can lead to distortions, since value and performance are dependent on the *pattern* of cash flow and not simply the average life of the security.

Consider first the generic MBS market. For purposes of illustrating how much the value and performance characteristics can be affected by seasoning patterns, we limit the discussion to discounts, since the seasoning pattern for premiums is far more complicated as demonstrated by the GNMA 11. Suppose a GNMA 8.5 with a remaining term of 346 is priced at 91, and the yield is calculated to be 10.14% at a 95 PSA. Now, instead of assuming that it will be fully seasoned at 30 months, suppose it really will take 100 months to fully season. Using 95% of this adjusted PSA curve, the yield is computed to be 9.99%. The corresponding average lives would be 11.53 years and 13.11 years. Even though one could find a slower PSA which would give rise to the same yield as found by using an adjusted PSA curve, the security would be different since its cash flow pattern would be different. Exhibit 5a shows the cash flow pattern at 95 PSA. Exhibit 5b shows the cash flow pattern at

95 PSA where full seasoning occurs at month 100. Exhibit 5c
shows the cash flow pattern where we have lowered the PSA to 63
in order to get the yield implied by the adjusted PSA curve. It is
clear from these graphs that, although the final maturity is the
same under all three scenarios, the timing of the cash flows is significantly different, and therefore the performance profile would
be different even though the cash flows produce the same yield.

Exhibit 5

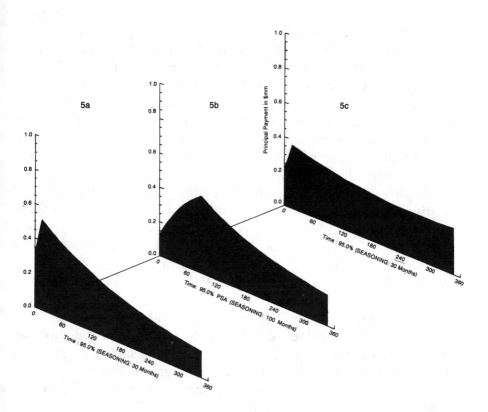

IMPACT ON DERIVATIVES AND OAS

The impact on pricing is more dramatic for derivative MBS product, and as a result, greater errors can be made by not analyzing the slowdown in aging. Consider a FNMA 9.5 interest only strip with a WAM of 350 and WAC of 10.10 priced at 47. At 150 PSA the yield would be 13.31%, whereas at 150 PSA, assuming 100 months to fully season, the yield would be 17.10%. We are not suggesting that all MBS will take 100 months to season, but rather demonstrating how sensitive their values can be to this assumption.

Option-adjusted spreads (OAS), durations, and convexities are also affected by this phenomenon. Option-adjusted models must use a prepayment function to describe how prepayments will evolve over time and as interest rates change. Some of the more sophisticated (not necessarily better) prepayment functions incorporate seasoning directly and fit the function to the data. Thus, they seek to avoid the problem by entirely ignoring the PSA standard seasoning. Most, if not all, of these models do not use the large set of data required to fully capture seasoning. Others use a very simple relative coupon prepayment function and rely on the PSA curve to adjust for seasoning.

To demonstrate the potential impact on OAS using a typical relative coupon prepayment function, consider again the FNMA interest only strip described above. At the assumed price, using the Treasury curve as of 4/23/90 and a volatility of 11%, one would find an OAS of 223 and an option-adjusted duration of negative 2 years using the standard PSA curve to incorporate seasoning in the prepayment function.

If instead one used a PSA curve adjusted to fully season at 100 months, the OAS would be 658 and the option-adjusted duration would actually be *positive* 1 year. Clearly, with such a disparity in the potential value and duration for this type of security, each investor must carefully resolve in his/her own analysis the appropriate prepayment seasoning pattern to be applied.

We next turn our attention to the CMO market. Exhibit 6 provides a summary of selected tranches from a FNMA deal issued in 1990 and backed by FNMA 9.5. The average life at different speeds for each tranche, assuming the standard PSA seasoning, and the corresponding values assuming 100 months to fully season is shown. In addition, option-adjusted spreads and durations are computed. The pricing speed was 180 PSA.

For the PAC bonds, the collar goes from 90 PSA to 300 PSA assuming the standard 30 month seasoning. However, if the collateral is not fully seasoned until 100 months, the bonds begin to lose their average life stability well within the bands. For example, tranche 2 is supposed to have an average life of 3.4 years. Under the longer seasoning assumption it has an average life of 4.5 years at 90 PSA.[1] Tranche 3 which is supposed to have a stable 4.6 year average life down to 90 PSA extends to a 5.9 year average life. It is for this reason investors should pay up (relative to the standard PAC bonds) for structures which provide protection at lower PSA levels.[2] Note that the longer PAC, tranche 6, was not affected at all within the bands. The reason for this is that due to the longer seasoning there is less cash flow in the beginning, whereas in the later months there will be more than ample flow to meet the PAC schedules, and thus the shorter PACs are more affected.

More dramatic distortions occur in tranches 7, 9, and 10. Tranche 7, under standard seasoning assumptions, has an average life of 3.4 years between 125 PSA to 250 PSA. (It is what is known as a level II PAC.) If the collateral does not fully season until month 100, tranche 7 has an expected 6.4 *year average life* at the pricing speed! At 125 PSA it extends to 9.4 year average life. Tranche 10, a support tranche, is designed to be a 3.5 year average life bond at the pricing speed. However, assuming a longer seasoning period, its expected average life at the pricing speed be-

---

[1] Lest we forget, new FNMA 9.5 prepaid at a 94 PSA in March of 1989.
[2] One such structure involves using only Z accretion to pay down the stabilized bonds. In this way even at 0 PSA the stabilized bonds' average lives do not extend dramatically. These bonds with short average lives have often been called liquidity bonds. An example of this is cited later in this text.

Exhibit 6: Average Life (Years)

DEAL 1

Type	Collar	PSA	Tranche	50	90	125	180	225	250	300	400	OAS b.p.	O.A. Dur
PAC	90-300	Standard	1	2.5	2.3	2.3	2.3	2.3	2.3	2.3	2.3	27	2.1
		Adjusted		2.9	2.7	2.6	2.5	2.4	2.4	2.3	2.3	21	2.2
PAC	90-300	Standard	2	4.2	3.4	3.4	3.4	3.4	3.4	3.4	3.4	41	3.0
		Adjusted		5.2	4.5	4.1	3.7	3.5	3.5	3.4	3.4	26	3.3
PAC	90-300	Standard	3	5.8	4.6	4.6	4.6	4.6	4.6	4.6	4.1	59	3.7
		Adjusted		7.0	5.9	5.3	4.7	4.6	4.6	4.6	4.6	45	4.1
PAC	90-300	Standard	4	7.5	5.8	5.8	5.8	5.8	5.8	5.8	5.8	73	4.5
		Adjusted		8.6	7.2	6.4	5.8	5.8	5.8	5.8	5.8	62	4.8
PAC	90-300	Standard	5	10.1	7.8	7.8	7.8	7.8	7.8	7.8	6.0	87	5.5
		Adjusted		11.0	9.1	8.0	7.8	7.8	7.8	7.8	7.8	87	5.7
PAC	90-300	Standard	6	17.1	17.1	17.1	17.1	17.1	17.1	17.1	13.3	94	8.4
		Adjusted		17.4	17.1	17.1	17.1	17.1	17.1	17.1	16.0	103	9.0
PAC	125-250	Standard	7	15.0	10.1	3.4	3.4	3.4	3.4	3.2	2.5	59	2.9
		Adjusted		15.7	12.1	9.4	6.4	4.9	4.4	3.7	3.4	9	4.5
PAC	125-250	Standard	8	19.2	17.9	17.8	17.8	17.8	17.8	5.8	3.4	107	6.8
		Adjusted		19.5	18.1	17.8	17.8	17.8	17.8	17.4	10.1	144	7.9
TAC		Standard	9	13.4	8.7	6.0	3.5	4.0	2.6	2.0	1.6	20	3.0
		Adjusted		10.1	12.9	10.4	7.2	5.5	4.9	4.1	3.3	31	4.3
Companion		Standard	10	20.8	17.6	13.1	3.5	1.4	1.2	1.0	.8	-13	3.3
		Adjusted		21.3	18.7	16.5	13.2	10.6	9.2	7.2	4.6	59	6.5
Z		Standard	11	25.9	24.2	22.5	19.1	9.7	2.7	2.0	1.5	36	8.5
		Adjusted		26.1	24.7	23.3	20.6	17.8	16.0	11.5	6.8	73	15.6

DEAL 2

Type	Collar	PSA	Tranche	50	90	125	180	225	250	300	400	OAS b.p.	O.A. Dur
Liquidity		Standard	1	2.6	2.6	2.6	2.6	2.6	2.6	2.6	2.6	45	2.3
		Adjusted		2.6	2.6	2.6	2.6	2.6	2.6	2.6	2.6	45	2.3
Stabilized		Standard	4	7.9	7.9	7.9	7.9	7.9	7.9	7.9	7.9	87	5.5
		Adjusted		7.9	7.9	7.9	7.9	7.9	7.9	7.9	7.9	87	5.5

comes *13.2 years*. Tranche 9 was designed to be a 3 year TAC, however, under the alternate assumption it looks more like the underlying collateral. Unfortunately, the investor paid up to get TAC performance.

Not all bonds look worse under the assumption of longer seasoning. The longer term level II PAC, tranche 8, performs better if seasoning takes longer. For example, under the standard 30 month seasoning the bond's average life shrinks from 17.8 years average life at the pricing speed to 5.8 at 300 PSA, and 3.4 at 400 PSA; whereas if we assume it takes 100 months to season, its average life is still over 17 years at 300 PSA and 10.1 years at 400 PSA. Similarly, the Z bond, tranche 11, has a better average life profile under the alternative assumption. The option-adjusted spreads confirm our conclusions drawn from the average life sensitivity analysis. Since tranches 2 and 3 no longer have the expected stability, their OAS drop from 41 to 26 and 59 to 45, respectively. This is because the investor has assumed some negative convexity without compensation. Tranche 6 actually improved slightly because of the better stability. The value of tranche 7 on an OAS basis drops significantly from 59 basis points to 9 basis points, whereas tranches 8, 10, and 11 improve in value due to their more stable average life patterns.

Another 1990 FNMA deal also backed by FNMA 9.5 included a liquidity bond. This bond had an average life at the pricing speed of 2.6 years. Regardless of which of the two seasoning patterns we use, its average life remained at 2.6 years, with its first cash flow occurring in 5 years with PSA between 0 and 500. As a result, the OAS and option-adjusted durations were identical under both seasoning patterns. The bond was offered in April 1990 at approximately 18 basis points through the 65 basis point spread of a comparable average life PAC. To some, this may seem to be a big give-up. However, option-adjusted analysis reveals that its spread was slightly above that of the OAS for comparable average life PACs assuming the standard PSA seasoning curve and substantially above the OAS for comparable PACs assuming the longer seasoning period. The fourth tranche in the deal which also used the Z accretion had a 7.9 year average life which was stable from 0 to 420 for both seasoning patterns. The tranche was offered at roughly 7 basis points through comparable average life PACs. On an OAS basis, this bond and the comparable PAC were nearly identical. Thus, in this deal, an investor seeking a bond with greater stability than PACs was not giving up any value, but simply fairly trading yield for convexity.

CONCLUSION

From the examples cited in this chapter, it should be clear that the value and performance characteristics of MBS is very dependent upon the seasoning pattern. We have seen that for discounts seasoning can take far longer than 30 months. One can conceivably argue that in today's housing market, seasoning may take longer than in the days when home prices were rapidly increasing. For premiums, convergence also can take a long time, but its pattern is very different from discounts. Because of burnout, the later issue year will converge to the earlier issue year from above. Over the life of an MBS, depending upon the coupon, it is likely it will at some point be a discount and some point a premium. While we have only examined the impact of a simple alteration of the seasoning pattern, it should be apparent that the values of MBS are sensitive to this parameter. As a result, quoting speeds, creating PACs, looking for stability within bonds based on the PSA curve can obscure some of the risks of MBS and their derivatives. Properly building this phenomenon into a prepayment function for OAS is complicated by the fact that one has to consider long periods of time to observe this phenomenon and fitting data to such a lengthy period could cause distortions in estimations in the other parameters. Investors must be careful to evaluate the impact of a *broad variety* of prepayment patterns in deciding the trade off between risk and value of MBS.

The data suggest that different collateral such as FNMAs and FHLMCs versus GNMAs or 30 year versus 15 year product, or

ARMs versus fixed rate all have different seasoning patterns. For example, conventionals will typically season more quickly than GNMAs but will still take far longer than the 30 month PSA standard. This would indicate that investors seeking to assess the relative value of PAC bonds backed by GNMA versus FNMA collateral should do more than adjust the pricing speed and PAC collars in their analysis.

CHAPTER 32

AN UNBIASED METHOD OF APPLYING HISTORICAL PREPAYMENT SPEEDS TO PROJECT FUTURE CASH FLOWS

Dan Spina
Associate Director
Financial Analytics and Structured Transactions Group
Bear, Stearns & Co., Inc.

David Sykes, PhD
Managing Director
Financial Analytics and Structured Transactions Group
Bear, Stearns & Co., Inc.

Hendrik Van Schieveen
Associate Director
Financial Analytics and Structured Transactions Group
Bear, Stearns & Co., Inc.

The authors would like to thank Frank Ramirez and Song Jo for providing the impetus for this study, and Blaine Roberts and Peter Cherasia for helpful comments and discussion.

There are several methods of applying historical prepayment numbers to project the future cash flows of mortgage products backed by a collection of mortgage pools such as an interest-only–principal-only (IO-PO) trust. The usual approaches of aggregating either the historical prepayments of the individual pools or their WACs/WAMs or both are shown to be biased estimates of future paydowns. However, given the mathematical form of the biases, a linear combination of the usual approaches can be devised that is not biased: this is our BLUE (best linear unbiased estimator) projection of future prepayments. The degree of bias depends on the degree of prepayment dispersion in conjunction with WAC/WAM dispersion. To measure this we introduce two indices, a prepayment dispersion index and a WAC/WAM dispersion index.

THE ALTERNATIVE METHODS

There are at least three possible methods to apply historical prepayment speeds to a collection of mortgage pools.

1. Calculate a single speed based on aggregate balances and apply this speed to amortize the entire trust as if it were a single mortgage with a maturity and coupon equal to the average WAC and WAM of the pools in the trust. Although this method of amortizing may be an acceptable approximation in simple cases, it will produce incorrect cash flows if there is dispersion in the WACs and WAMs of the underlying pools. Nevertheless, this method is often used in practice.

2. Incorporate all available pool information into the valuation process by using the aggregate prepayment speed to amortize each pool individually. The resulting cash flows are then totaled for stripping, slicing, or dicing, according to the issue's structure.

The use of a single aggregate speed suggests itself because of the relatively homogeneous character of the pools that comprise most trusts. To the extent that the pools are similar, prepayment dispersion across pools is largely noise. Hence, in the long run, each pool is expected to prepay at pretty much the same average speed. Thus the *aggregate* "model" for applying historical speeds to project future cash flows regards a weighted average speed at a given point in time as representative of the lifetime average speed expected of all the pools in the trust.

3. A further step in using pool level data involves not only amortizing each pool individually, but also applying prepayment speeds on a pool-by-pool basis. The intuition is that this *individual* method may be more appropriate when a trust is comprised of pools that are fundamentally different in respects that affect their prepayment speeds; that is, when there is some basis for expecting slow pools to continue to prepay relatively slowly, and similarly faster-paying pools to remain relatively faster.

The difference between methods (1) and (2) is one of amortization techniques. To calculate the cash flows that a given prepayment speed will produce, one has to amortize pools separately if there is WAC and/or WAM differences among the pools. However, when the prepayment speed being applied is regarded as a reasonably accurate approximation of prepayments to come, the imprecision arising from treating the pools as one large pool can often be regarded as negligible. A more interesting difference, and the one we focus on here, is in the individual method vis-à-vis the aggregate method of applying historical prepayment speeds to project future cash flows.

ANALYSIS OF THE INDIVIDUAL AND AGGREGATE METHODS

There are two levels of analysis. The first concerns the effect of the two approaches on the projected rate of paydown/amortization, independent of any statistical properties. The second level of analysis deals with the question of the statistical soundness of the alternative methods.

Implications for Relative Rate of Projected Paydown

The relative rate of amortization/paydown between the two approaches depends on the degree of prepayment dispersion across the pools in the trust, and on the amount of WAM/WAC dispersion. These two properties of a collection of mortgage pools can be quantified by a Prepayment Dispersion Index (PDI), and a WAM/WAC Dispersion Index (WDI). The PDI is on a scale of 0 to 1, with 0 indicating no dispersion and increasing values as prepayment dispersions increase. Most actual deals have PDI values under 0.60. The PDIs for a number of FNMA Strip Trusts are shown in column 6 of Exhibit 1. If a Trust consists of only a single pool, then of course the PDI is 0.0, as is the case for Trust 25 and 26.

The WDI is on a scale of -1 to +1, with negative values indicating the extent to which shorter WAMs are associated with faster speeds, and positive values indicating the extent to which shorter WAMs are associated with slower speeds. Intuitively, if a trust contains some relatively older shorter WAM pools, then one might expect these "burned-out" pools to be associated with relatively slower stable speeds. Hence the WDI would be positive. However, virtually all existing trusts are comprised of relatively new pools, where, because of the seasoning process, shorter WAMs tend to be associated with faster speeds. See column 7 of Exhibit 1 for the WDIs on FNMA Strips.

The influence of the WAC/WAM dispersion on cash flow projections depends on the prepayment dispersion. For example, in the extreme case where there is no prepayment dispersion, all pools are paying at the same speed, and, consequently, there

Exhibit 1: Percent Balance Reduction Using Different CPP Projections (One Year)

(1) FNSTRI	(2) AGG	(3) BLUE	(4) IND	(5) CDI	(6) PDI	(7) WDI
2	11.0624	10.7117	10.4468	.55278	.55163	-.00115
22	11.1922	10.9377	10.7360	.40900	.40884	-.00016
16	10.4328	10.2055	9.9958	.39545	.39579	.00033
13	15.0467	14.8060	14.6175	.38885	.38520	-.00365
17	10.6018	10.4342	10.2524	.31541	.31466	-.00076
10	11.3177	11.1339	10.9768	.30513	.30484	-.00029
21	8.8023	8.5976	8.4640	.31130	.31107	-.00023
11	9.4591	9.2942	9.1598	.27384	.27350	-.00034
15	14.1567	14.0013	13.8718	.26065	.25803	-.00263
24	7.6916	7.5399	7.4099	.26285	.26275	-.00010
19	9.1445	9.0023	8.8846	.23842	.23790	-.00052
1	8.2802	8.1421	8.0330	.22920	.22903	-.00017
23	8.2022	8.0744	7.9598	.22437	.22379	-.00057
20	9.7545	9.6564	9.6187	.12365	.12359	-.00006
14	8.9659	8.9360	8.9041	.05674	.05688	.00013
18	8.6625	8.6414	8.6179	.04115	.04095	-.00020
25	11.2493	11.2493	11.2493	.00000	.00000	.00000
26	8.6557	8.6557	8.6557	.00000	.00000	.00000

would be no effective difference between the aggregate and individual method. This is reflected in the construction of the PDI and WDI, in that a PDI of zero will result in a WDI of zero. More generally, the WDI will tend to be larger the greater the PDI.

Together, the PDI and WDI interact to determine the relative rate of paydown that will be projected under the individual versus the aggregate method. Specifically, the net of the two indices, the Collateral Dispersion Index (CDI = PDI − WDI), determines the difference that will occur in the projected balances under the two methods as follows:

$$\text{Bal}^{\text{IND}} (12) - \text{Bal}^{\text{AGG}} (12) = \text{Bal}^{\text{S}} (0) \times \text{CDI} / 100$$

where Bals (0) is the current aggregate balance before prepayments (i.e., the current *scheduled* balance), and Bal (12) refers to the balance projected twelve months forward. Thus the individual method is slower whenever the CDI is positive, and conversely the aggregate method will be slower whenever the CDI is negative.

Practically speaking, the individual method will always pay down more slowly than the aggregate method. This follows partly from the fact that most pools are deliberately constructed with relatively low WAC/WAM dispersions. Thus, in practice the PDI tends to overwhelm the WDI. Moreover, as previously discussed and as shown in Exhibit 1, the WDI is almost always negative, which reinforces a positive CDI.

The reverse result, where the aggregate method projects slower paydowns than the individual method, requires a relatively high positive WAC/WAM dispersion. For example, a two-pool example that produces this result is presented in Exhibit 2. The negative

---

Exhibit 2: High Positive WAC/WAM Dispersion

		Pool 1		Pool 2
WAC		10%		10%
WAM		30 years		6 years
CPP		10%		9.5%
	PDI		.0057	
	- WDI		-.1634	
	CDI		-.157	

CDI indicates that the aggregate method would project a larger balance one year from now than the individual method.

Exhibits 1 and 3 present the results of a dispersion analysis for a series of actual FNMA Strip Trusts. They are ranked in terms of greatest dispersion to lowest. Columns 2 and 4 of Exhibit 1 show the percent reduction in the balance projected by the aggregate and individual method, respectively. The aggregate method projects a greater balance reduction in all cases, with the difference in

Exhibit 3: Percent Balance Reduction Using Different CPP Projections

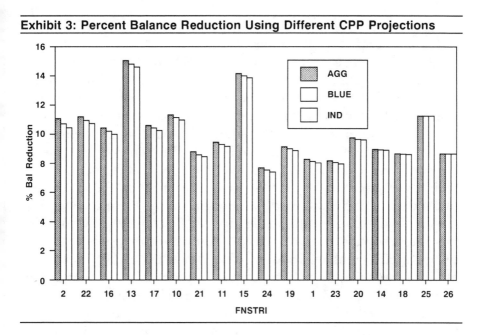

projected reductions being greater, the greater the CDI. This correlation of the size of the balance difference with the CDI is illustrated in Exhibit 3.

Thus, different methods of applying the same historical data can clearly affect value. This is especially true for securities like strips, whose values are quite sensitive to the rate of paydown.

Analyzing Statistical Properties and the BLUE Projection

To evaluate the relative merits of the different methods, we considered a simple statistical model with the prepayment rates normally distributed about a constant long-term speed. In this framework, both the individual and aggregate method of predicting prepayments are biased. To say a particular method is biased means that the balance (or prepayment) predicted by the method will be, on average, different than the actual value expected. This model thus provides a basis for determining which method "makes more sense"; the better method of the two is the one with the smaller bias.

As discussed earlier, the individual method seems intuitively more appealing if a trust can be identified as containing distinctly slow- and fast-paying pools, perhaps due to some fundamental characteristic such as geographic origin. This intuition is found to be valid within our statistical framework under the following condition: in addition to having significantly different average speeds, the pools in the trust also pay with relatively low variability about their average speeds. In this case, the bias of the individual method is distinctly smaller than the bias of the aggregate method.

The significance of the variability can be conveyed by considering the following case. A trust is comprised of pools that have distinctly different average speeds. However, certain pools that are on-average slow, sometimes pay faster than pools that are on-average fast; and, vice versa, some of the pools that are typically fast, occasionally have periods where paydowns are slower than the "slow" pools. Even though pools can be categorized as on-average distinctly slow, medium, fast, and so on, the variation from period to period "smears" the distinctive prepayment character of the individual pools. In this case, it is not intuitive that the historic prepayment speeds of the individual pools necessarily provide a better method of projecting future prepayments. This intuition is also borne out in our statistical framework: when pools have distinct average speeds but with high variability, then the bias of the individual and the aggregate are more or less equal.

In general, the bias of the individual method is primarily a function of the variability of the individual pools' prepayments: the more stable the pools' prepayments are, the smaller the bias in the individual method. The bias of the aggregate method depends primarily on the CDI: the greater the prepayment and WAM/WAC dispersion, the greater the bias of the aggregate method. Thus, a third case, where the pools in a trust all have close to the same average speed and thus a low CDI, would always favor the aggregate method.

Estimates of the biases for all of the trusts listed in Exhibit 1 were calculated. In all cases, the biases were in opposite directions and of more or less equal amounts, indicating no cases where the pools have both distinct average speeds and low variability about these averages. One implication of the size and direction of the two biases is that the individual method will always be more accurate during down trends in prepayment rates, whereas the aggregate method will always be more accurate during up trends.

Based on the above findings, we conclude that if one is to use a single static scenario cash flow projection to price a mortgage product, a hybrid of the aggregate and individual method that eliminates the bias should be used. We have devised such a prediction procedure, based on a linear combination of the balances that would be projected under the two methods, and with weights such that the predicted balance is unbiased. This procedure is our BLUE (Best Linear Unbiased Estimate) prepayment projection.

A comparison of the results of the BLUE projection can be seen in Exhibits 1 and 3. As designed, the BLUE estimator will project a balance twelve months forward about halfway between the projections of the aggregate and individual projections. Exhibit 4 illustrates the significance of the different methods in terms of yield. The BLUE yields tend to be closer to the aggregate speed, because although it is based on both methods, it is ultimately a single speed being projected over the life of the security. Thus, unlike the pure individual method where the "average" rate of paydown slows down as faster pools pay off, leaving only the slower pools, the BLUE paydown maintains a constant rate throughout the securities' projected life. This feature brings out the fact that the BLUE projection is a value based on a one-year time frame, using the most recent data available on a given trust. As the character of the trust changes over time, so will the BLUE projection.

Exhibit 4: Yield Impact of Different CPP Projections

(1) FNSTRI	(2) AGG	(3) BLUE	(4) IND	(5) CDI	(6) PDI	(7) WDI
2	12.595	13.002	15.043	.55278	.55163	-.00115
16	11.973	12.234	13.841	.39545	.39579	.00033
22	12.454	12.751	14.283	.40900	.40884	-.00016
17	11.799	11.992	13.366	.31541	.31466	-.00076
21	11.078	11.309	12.576	.31130	.31107	-.00023
10	12.309	12.523	13.700	.30513	.30484	-.00029
13	12.496	12.784	13.827	.38885	.38520	-.00365
11	11.708	11.896	12.991	.27384	.27350	-.00034
24	12.419	12.589	13.656	.26285	.26275	-.00010
19	13.483	13.646	14.604	.23842	.23790	-.00052
1	12.485	12.641	13.599	.22920	.22903	-.00017
23	12.978	13.123	13.895	.22437	.22379	-.00057
15	11.579	11.762	12.480	.26065	.25803	-.00263
20	12.878	12.991	13.385	.12352	.12346	-.00006
14	12.337	12.371	12.660	.05674	.05688	.00013
18	12.657	12.681	12.917	.04115	.04095	-.00020
25	13.237	13.250	13.250	.00000	.00000	.00000
12	11.331	11.343	11.343	.00000	.00000	.00000

SECTION VI

PORTFOLIO STRATEGIES

CHAPTER 33

SYNTHETIC MORTGAGE-BACKED SECURITIES

Anand K. Bhattacharya, PhD
Vice President
Financial Strategies Group
Prudential Securities Inc.

Howard W. Chin
Director
Financial Strategies Group
Prudential Securities Inc.

INTRODUCTION

With the growth in the market for mortgage-backed securities (MBSs) and the proliferation of various types of structures, the market has witnessed the creation of a virtual alphabet soup of different types of MBS structures—PACs, TACs, POs, PAC POs, TAC POs, super POs, IOs, PAC-IOs, IO-ettes, vanilla Z bonds, Z-PACs, companion Z bonds, jump-Z bonds, floaters, inverse floaters, and the like. These securities have appealing risk-return profiles and cash flow characteristics in certain states of nature. However, the state-dependent features of such securities can be exploited by combining them with other securities that have similar cash flow characteristics in alternative states of nature to obtain higher yielding synthetic securities. Additionally, the yield profile of such securities can be customized to be progressively bullish or bearish by changing the par amount of the combined securities. Moreover, by changing the amount of the combined securities, the interest rate sensitivity of the synthetic can either be magnified or dampened in order to attain a desired portfolio duration.

As an example, consider the case of stripped mortgage-backed securities (SMBSs), such as interest only (IO) and principal only (PO) securities. As prepayments on the underlying mortgage pass-through securities slow down due to an increase in interest rates, the underlying principal balance is outstanding for a longer period of time. Since IOs are associated with the interest from the principal balance, IOs will provide higher cash flows for a longer period of time as prepayments slow down. Due to this feature, IOs are bearish securities whose performance is enhanced in rising rate scenarios. On the other hand, POs are bullish securities as the value of such securities is enhanced due to an increase in prepayments caused by falling interest rates. Therefore, by combining IOs and POs, whose cash flows depend on the state of interest rates, and the associated prepayments, the resultant synthetic security can be tailored to be progressively bullish or bearish, while still maintaining yield in alternative states of nature. In addition to exploring further the case of synthetic MBSs constructed with IOs and POs, this chapter discusses other synthetic securities that can be constructed using various other types of structured MBSs.

SYNTHETIC COMBINATIONS USING SMBSs

With the introduction of SMBSs in 1986, investors were provided with securities that exhibited risk-return profiles quite distinct from the underlying collateral. The earliest form of SMBS issued by the Federal National Mortgage Association (FNMA) were synthetic coupon securities. These securities were commonly known in the industry as "alphabet strips" on account of the sequential usage of the alphabet in the trust (issuing entity) nomenclature. The creation of such securities involved the partial stripping of the underlying collateral to produce two classes of securities with synthetic coupons different from the pass-through rate of the underlying MBS. For example, a premium coupon could be structured to perform with slower prepayment characteristics, whereas a discount coupon could be structured with faster prepayment characteristics. In effect, such securities were created by altering the relationship between the underlying collateral coupon and its prepayment behavior. The recognition of the unique risk-return characteristics of such securities led to the creation of securities, which involved the complete separation of principal (including prepayments) and interest to create principal only (PO) and interest only (IO) securities.

Using SMBSs, investors can create customized securities designed for specific portfolio management objectives. Investors with firm convictions regarding interest rates and the associated prepayment behavior of mortgage collateral may choose to invest in the SMBS on a "stand alone basis." As a general rule, SMBSs exhibit a higher degree of price volatility than the underlying MBSs, suggesting that such securities are highly leveraged hedging vehicles. The value of such securities is determined by the prepayment behavior of the underlying collateral. Although the prepayment propensity of a pool of mortgages is determined by a variety of factors, such as demographics, seasonal influences, and the assumability of the underlying mortgages, the single largest determinant of prepayments is the influence of interest rates. As interest rates decrease, causing a resultant increase in prepayments, the holders of POs receive higher cash flows due to the faster paydown of principal. Due to the accelerated return of cash flows, the value of POs in bullish scenarios tends to increase. On the other hand, as prepayments slow down in higher interest rate environments, the cash flows due to the PO holders are "stretched" out over a longer period of time, resulting in lower values for the PO security. With respect to IOs, the interest rate-induced effect of changing prepayments is opposite to the associated effect on POs. Since interest lives off of principal, slower prepayments cause the cash flows due to the holders of IOs to increase. However, increases in prepayment speeds that lead to an erosion of principal result in reduced cash flows to the IO securities.

However, the prepayment-induced value effect on SMBSs is critically dependent on whether the collateral backing the structure is in the form of discount, current coupon, or premium mortgages. As interest rates decline, leading to an increase in collateral prepayment speeds, discount and current collateral POs will exhibit a greater increase in value than premium collateral POs. This contention is based on the thesis that the rate of change of prepayments will be greater for discount and current coupons than that for premium coupons, as the latter should already be at relatively high levels. As interest rates rise, leading to slower prepayments, discount coupon collateral speeds will not slow down significantly, as such collateral already should be prepaying at relatively low levels. However, prepayments on premium collateral will exhibit a sharp decline, resulting in a significant decline in the value of premium collateral POs as compared to POs collateralized by discount and current coupon collateral. On the other hand, a premium coupon IO strip may be a more useful hedging instrument than a discount coupon IO strip. As interest rates rise, leading to slower prepayments, the cash flows due to the premium IO holders will increase. Due to the fact that prepayments on premium coupon collateral are likely to be at high levels, premium IOs will not lose as much value as discount IOs, when interest rates fall.

Customized Risk-Return Profiles Using SMBSs

As an example of creating synthetic securities using SMBSs, consider the following situations that combine various amounts of discount, current, and premium coupons IOs and POs to create synthetic MBS. In Exhibit 1, the yield profiles of several bullish and bearish synthetic combinations created using FNMA SMBS Trust 85 IOs and POs, which are collateralized by FNMA 8s, are presented. As can be seen from the analysis, by increasing the par amount of the PO in the combination, the yield profile of the combination can be made successively bullish. By the same token, the yield profile of the synthetic can be made bearish by increasing the amount of the IO in the synthetic combination.

Similar synthetic combinations using higher coupon collateral are presented in Exhibits 2 and 3. A comparision of synthetic securities created using the various types of collateral indicates that bearish combinations using premium collateral outperform similar combinations using discount and current coupon collateral in rising rate scenarios. This suggests that premium IOs have the best hedge value. On the other hand, bullish combinations using discount collateral perform better than similar combinations using

Exhibit 1: Synthetic MBS Yields Using FNMA Trust 85 SMBS (Discount Coupon Collateral)

				Interest Rate Scenario			
	-300 bp	-200 bp	-100 bp	NC	+100 bp	+200 bp	+300 bp
Prepayment Speed (PSA)	451	231	163	140	131	126	122
Trust 85-PO	27.47%	13.76%	10.17%	9.05%	8.63%	8.40%	8.22%
Trust 85-IO	-13.03%	2.71%	7.32%	8.86%	9.45%	9.78%	10.05%
			Synthetic Combination				
1:1 Ratio	9.93%	9.23%	9.04%	8.98%	8.95%	8.94%	8.93%
2:1 Ratio	16.23%	10.90%	9.46%	9.00%	8.83%	8.74%	8.66%
1:2 Ratio	3.06%	7.35%	8.55%	8.94%	9.09%	9.18%	9.24%

FNMA Trust 85 is collateralized by FNMA 8.0s

Exhibit 2: Synthetic MBS Yields Using FNMA Trust 42 SMBS (Current Coupon Collateral)

	Interest Rate Scenario						
	-300 bp	-200 bp	-100 bp	NC	+100 bp	+200 bp	+300 bp
Prepayment Speed (PSA)	474	421	244	175	147	135	131
Trust 42-PO	22.91%	19.11%	10.87%	8.08%	7.03%	6.61%	6.47%
Trust 42-IO	-12.06%	6.49%	6.36%	11.14%	13.05%	13.86%	14.13%
			Synthetic Combination				
1:1 Ratio	8.76%	8.87%	9.13%	9.23%	9.26%	9.27%	9.28%
2:1 Ratio	14.02%	12.70%	9.79%	8.78%	8.39%	8.23%	8.18%
1:2 Ratio	2.79%	4.51%	8.36%	9.75%	10.29%	10.52%	10.60%

FNMA 42 is collateralized by FNMA 9.5s

current coupon and premium collateral POs. This is due to the fact that as interest rates decline, the rate of change of prepayments is highest for discount coupon collateral, as higher coupon collateral already exhibits faster prepayment speeds. Using the prepayment propensity of the underlying collateral and evaluating the nature of the type of mortgage pass-throughs collateralizing the SMBS structure, the expected yield profile of any synthetic security can be generated.

As a general rule, in order to create a $x\%$ synthetic rate from a SMBS with $y\%$ pass-through coupon, the $x\%$ synthetic is created by combining x units of the IO Class with y units of the PO class from the SMBS structure. For example, in order to create a 5% synthetic coupon from FNMA SMBS Trust 85, collateralized by FNMA 8s, the synthetic security would require five units of Trust 85 IOs and eight units of Trust 85 POs. Assuming the price of the IO was 40-18 and the price of the PO was 54-24, the effective price of the 5% synthetic would be given as:

[Synthetic Coupon/Collateral Coupon) × Price of IO]
= [5/8 × 40-18] + [54-24] = 80.10.

Exhibit 3: Synthetic MBS Yields Using FNMA Trust 50 SMBS (Premium Coupon Collateral)

	-300 bp	-200 bp	-100 bp	NC	+100 bp	+200 bp	+300 bp
			Interest Rate Scenario				
Prepayment Speed (PSA)	483	449	375	229	172	148	137
Trust 50-PO	15.95%	14.68%	12.04%	7.33%	5.71%	5.07%	4.79%
Trust 50-IO	- 5.38%	2.71%	2.95%	13.67%	17.07%	19.37%	20.13%
			Synthetic Combination				
1:1 Ratio	8.53%	8.66%	8.93%	9.43%	9.61%	9.68%	9.72%
2:1 Ratio	11.46%	11.04%	10.17%	8.59%	8.03%	7.80%	7.70%
1:2 Ratio	4.95%	5.74%	7.41%	10.49%	11.62%	12.08%	12.28%

FNMA 50 is collateralized by FNMA 10.5s

SMBS Synthetic Combinations Using Options

As noted above, the price performance, and hence the duration and convexity characteristics of SMBSs, are affected by the prepayment propensity of the underlying collateral. As a general rule, SMBSs collateralized by mortgage pass-through securities, such as deep discount collateral and super premium collateral exhibit interest rate sensitivity patterns similar to those of other fixed-rate securities. The main reason for this similarity with other fixed-rate instruments stems from the fact that deep discount and high premium collateral exhibit relatively minor changes in prepayments as interest rates change. However, for current or slight premium collateral, as interest rates fall, prepayments on the underlying collateral accelerate and cash flows to the IO holders are reduced. The amount of cash flow received by IO holders depends directly on the prepayment behavior of the underlying collateral. Since the cash flow pattern of the IO strip decreases (increases) as rates fall (rise), IOs have negative durations. This is in sharp contrast to most other fixed-income securities, which have positive durations.

With respect to convexity patterns, discount and slight premium coupon POs exhibit positive convexity. Prepayments for discount collateral and slight premium coupon collateral are likely to increase substantially as rates fall, but not decrease as dramatically when rates rise. Hence, PO prices are likely to rise at a faster rate in market rallies and decrease at a lower rate in market declines. It is for the same reason (i.e., the prepayment behavior of the underlying collateral) that IO prices are likely to fall at a higher rate as rates fall and increase at a lower rate as rates rise, indicating that IOs have negative convexity. However, for SMBSs collateralized by high premium mortgages that are already prepaying at high rates, the convexity patterns are reversed. Due to the high prepayment rate of the underlying collateral, the prices of premium IOs are likely to be relatively low, whereas those for premium POs are likely to be relatively high. At such levels, with prepayments expected not to change substantially, premium PO prices are likely not to rise much higher in the face of a market rally. However, there is a greater likelihood that PO prices could fall at a faster rate in the event of a market decline. In view of this consideration, such POs are likely to be negatively convex in price movement. At the same time, premium IO prices could rise much higher in the event interest rates rise, but would not fall much below existing low levels in the face of a market rally causing the price behavior to be positively convex.

Based on these results concerning the duration and convexity patterns of SMBSs, it is possible to characterize the SMBS position as an equivalent position in non-amortizing bonds and option positions. This description is similar to the analytical decomposition of MBSs as representing a long position in a bond and a short position in a series of call options, due to the homeowners' embedded option. By establishing such analytical analogs between SMBSs and equivalent positions in Treasury bonds and either OTC options or options on futures, arbitrage opportunities between the SMBS and Treasury/derivatives market can be exploited, or synthetic strategies that use SMBSs to replicate OTC/futures options positions can be created.

With respect to options, the following results have direct significance for the replication of SMBS positions using options and
non-amortizing bonds.

- A call option represents the option to buy a particular
  security at a predetermined price for a specified period of
  time. The addition of a call option to a debt portfolio
  adds convexity to the overall portfolio. The long call position increases the upside potential of the portfolio in a
  market rally, since the gains associated with the option
  position are limitless. At the same time, the returns in stable and rising rate scenarios are reduced by the cost of
  the convexity (i.e., the option premium).

- The addition of a short call option position to a debt portfolio reduces the convexity of the overall portfolio. This
  represents the option to sell a particular security at a predetermined price over a specified period of time. In return for this option, the call writer receives the option
  premium. A short call option benefits the call writer in
  stable or rising rate environments. The call writer's gain
  on the option is limited to the the premium received;
  however, the losses are virtually limitless. Hence, a short
  call position may be characterized as being negatively
  convex.

- A put option represents the right to sell a particular security at a predetermined price for a specified period of
  time in return for the payment of the option premium.
  Whereas losses in such a strategy are limited to the option premium, the profit opportunities are directly related
  to the reduction in the price of the underlying security.
  The investor's gain is the difference between the put
  strike price and the lower market price of the security.
  Therefore, the addition of long put options to a debt portfolio adds convexity to the overall position, as gains are

greater in a rising rate environment, whereas losses are limited in stable and falling rate scenarios.

- The seller of the put option receives the option premium and is obligated to buy the particular security at a predetermined price in the event the option is exercised. Since the gains are limited to the option premium received, whereas the losses with this strategy could be limitless, a short put position is associated with negative convexity.

Based on the duration and convexity patterns in SMBSs, the Treasury bond and option equivalent positions of such securities are presented in Exhibit 4. Note that a short position in a non-amortizing bond subtracts duration from the portfolio. Theoretically, while it is possible to create such synthetic positions, such combinations are likely to be fraught with mortgage to Treasury basis

Exhibit 4: Duration and Convexity Patterns of SMBSs

	Duration	Convexity
POs:		
Current Coupon & Slight Premium	Positive	Positive
High Premium	Positive	Negative
IOs:		
Current Coupon & Slight Premium	Negative	Negative
High Premium	Negative	Positive

SMBS Option Equivalent Positions

	Bond	Option
POs:		
Current Coupon & Slight Premium	Long	Long Call
High Premium	Long	Short Put
IOs:		
Current Coupon & Slight Premium	Short	Short Call
High Premium	Short	Short Put

risk and yield curve risk due to the fact the Treasury and mortgage markets are affected by different fundamental factors. In the event options on futures are used, there is the additional element of futures to cash basis risk. In view of this consideration, the ideal option analog in such instances is obviously options on MBSs. However, the use of such markets to create synthetic positions that replicate the return patterns of SMBSs is likely to be hampered by the reduced liquidity of OTC options markets and higher execution costs.

SYNTHETIC COMBINATIONS USING CMOs COLLATERALIZED BY POs

In recent years, as the ingenuity of financial engineering techniques has risen, SMBSs have been included in collateralized mortgage obligation structures either as collateral or as regular interest tranches. For example, POs have been included in CMO structures in which the underlying bullish features of such securities are either dampened or emphasized to satisfy various risk management and yield enhancement preferences of investors. A typical PO-backed structure may include PO planned amortization classes (PACs), Level II PO PACs, PO targeted amortization classes (TACs), and a Super PO. As with coupon-bearing PACs, PO PACs are designed to have a controlled paydown within stated prepayment speeds. Level II PO PACs provide more prepayment protection than the POs collateralizing the structure. However, the magnitude of this prepayment protection is less than that of higher order PO PACs, mainly due to the narrower PAC bands associated with lower order PO PACs. TAC POs are similar to coupon-bearing TACs in that the paydown of the bond is met as scheduled if the underlying collateral pays down at or faster than the pricing prepayment speed. Super POs are designed to leverage the cash flows in bullish scenarios. Depending on the structural characteristics of the PO derivative bonds in a CMO structure, it is possible to create bullish or bearish synthetics by combining such securities with other instruments.

Combining PO Derivatives with IO Strips

Since it is not possible to discuss every possible synthetic using PO derivative bonds, the discussion in this section is restricted to the analysis of synthetics using representative PO collateralized securities. In addition, a strategy using PAC POs, which allows investors to participate in a market rally by synthetically stripping the upper PAC collar, is also discussed in this section. Finally, the potential of using POs as well as structured POs, in which the bullish chararcteristics of the underlying collateral is either dampened or enhanced, with other fixed-income securities is also explored.

As an example of the creation of synthetic combinations using structured securities collateralized by POs, consider FNMA1990-130. This is a Real Estate Mortgage Investment Conduit (REMIC) structure collateralized by discount collateral (FNMA 8s) and is comprised of two, three, five, seven, ten, and thirty-year Level I PAC POs, several lower order PAC POs, a TAC PO, and a super PO class. Additionally, the interest stream of the underlying collateral was structured as FNMA Trust 85 IOs. The use of such derivative securities structured using the same underlying collateral insulates the synthetic combination from any "idiosyncratic" prepayment risk. The existence of this risk may affect the yield of the synthetic in that the change in prepayments concomitant with interest rate movements may not be proportional for the component securities. For example, in a combination of a PO with an IO, prepayments may remain either unchanged or may decrease as interest rates increase. In the event the combination has a bearish orientation, the synthetic yield may not increase, especially if the combination was structured to exploit the bearish characteristics of the IOs in the blend. It is for this reason that some market participants have labeled IOs as prepayment hedges rather than interest rate hedges, as the hedge value of the IO depends heavily on changes in prepayments.

In order to illustrate the effect of dampening and accentuating the prepayment propensity of the underlying collateral, the yield profiles of several synthetic combinations, using a long PAC PO (130K) that has a PAC band of 70 to 175 PSA, the TAC PO (130L), and the Super PO (130M) with the IOs from FNMA Trust 85 are presented in Exhibit 5. As noted above, the PAC POs are similar to sinking fund bonds, and have stated principal paydown schedules within the prepayment bands. Therefore, the yields of such securities do not change as long as the prepayment speed of the underlying collateral is within the ranges specified by the PAC collars. The TAC PO follows a predetermined paydown schedule, as long as the collateral speeds are within a range of prepayment bands. At very slow prepayment speeds, the TAC PO goes into

Exhibit 5: Synthetic MBS Yields Using PO Collateralized Securities and IOs

| | Interest Rate Scenario | | | | | | |
	-300 bp	-200 bp	-100 bp	NC	+100 bp	+200 bp	+300 bp
Prepayment Speed (PSA)	423	226	163	141	132	128	123
FNMA90-130K	113.41%	21.01%	9.49%	9.48%	9.48%	9.48%	9.48%
FNMA90-130L	16.40%	14.72%	14.34%	13.33%	11.24%	9.83%	8.56%
FNMA90-130M	n.a.	162.70%	31.80%	10.96%	8.19%	7.46%	6.82%
Trust 85-IO	-11.64%	2.47%	6.78%	8.26%	8.86%	9.13%	9.46%

Synthetic Combination

Combinations with Trust 85-IO

	-300 bp	-200 bp	-100 bp	NC	+100 bp	+200 bp	+300 bp
130K (PO PAC) (1:1 Ratio)	39.17%	12.05%	8.51%	9.01%	9.24%	9.34%	9.47%
130K (TAC PO) (1:1 Ratio)	3.62%	8.39%	10.28%	10.64%	10.04%	9.49%	8.98%
130M (Super PO) (1:1 Ratio)	155.35%	50.60%	17.59%	9.90%	8.42%	8.00%	7.65%

arrears for the shortfall, resulting in the extension of the maturity of the security. The Super PO class is an extremely bullish security and exhibits phenomenal returns in declining interest rate scenarios.

An analysis of Exhibit 5 shows that in bullish scenarios, the super PO combination performs best, followed by the combination with the PAC PO. This occurs mainly due to the extremely high yield of the levered PO, due in turn to faster prepayments. In extremely bullish scenarios, due to faster prepayments, the yield of the PAC PO synthetic combination is significantly higher, mainly because of the resultant higher cash flows caused by the PAC PO breaking out of the upper PAC bands. Since the yields of the TAC PO do not increase tremendously in bullish scenarios, the combined yield of the synthetic is significantly lower than those of the other combinations. This also occurs partly due to the negative yield associated with the IO as a result of faster prepayments. On the other hand, the PAC PO combination maintains its base case yield mainly on the strength of the yield protection provided by the PAC bands. The reduction in the yield of the super PO is significant in rising rate scenarios, essentially because of the countervailing effect of rising IO yields. Additionally, by changing the par amount of either the structured PO security or the IO, the yield of the synthetic combination can be designed to be either progressively bullish or bearish.

"Stripping" PAC Bands in PO PACs

In addition to providing opportunities to obtain attractive yields by combining PO-backed structured securities with IOs, some of these securities can also be combined with other POs to increase the bullish yield behavior of certain securities. An example of this strategy consists of synthetically "stripping" the upper PAC bands of a PO PAC and maintaining the PAC yield in bearish scenarios. Within the universe of zero coupon securities, PO PACs offer higher yields than equivalent duration Treasury strips. Within the

PAC bands, the yield and the average life of PAC POs remain constant due to the prepayment protection provided by the PAC bands. For prepayment speeds below the lower PAC collar, the PO PAC's yield is lower, as the cash flows are paid over a longer period of time. On the other hand, when prepayments exceed the upper PAC collar, the yield on the PO PAC increases due to the faster return of cash flows. This yield can be enhanced by neutralizing the upper PAC collar by including discount POs in a synthetic blend. In rising rate scenarios, the yield on the PAC PO is maintained due to the PAC feature of the bonds. At the same time, because of the discount nature of the PO coupon in the synthetic, the reduction in yield is not as significant. This is because of the fact that in rising rate scenarios, the slowdown of prepayments on discount collateral is not likely to be very substantial. On the other hand, as interest rates fall, the associated increase in prepayments should not have any impact on the yield of the PAC PO, as long as prepayment speeds are within the PAC bands. However, with the increase in prepayment speeds, the cash flows from the PO increase, leading to a higher overall blended yield.

As examples of this strategy, consider Class J of FNMA 1990-130, a ten-year PO PAC with a band of 85-175% PSA. As noted above, this deal, FNMA1990-130, collateralized by seasoned FNMA 8 POs, consists of Level I and II PO PACs, a TAC class, and a Super PO bond. The yield profiles of this PO PAC with

---

Exhibit 6: Synthetic MBS Yields Using PO PACs and Discount POs

| | Interest Rate Scenario | | | | | | |
	-300 bp	-200 bp	-100 bp	NC	+100 bp	+200 bp	+300 bp
FNMA90-130J	25.50%	9.28%	9.28%	9.28%	9.28%	9.28%	9.28%

	Synthetic Combination						
FNMA90-130J with Trust 12-PO							
1:1 Ratio	24.05%	11.03%	9.91%	9.52%	9.38%	9.27%	9.20%
2:1 Ratio	23.49%	11.84%	10.17%	9.61%	9.42%	9.27%	9.17%

varying par amounts of a discount PO, FNMA Trust 12, collateralized by FNMA 8.5s, are shown in Exhibit 6. As can be seen from
the analysis, in addition to enhanced yield in the base case, the
synthetic combination of the FNMA Trust 12 PO and FNMA1990-
130 Class J PO PAC allows investors to participate in a rally by
synthetically stripping the upper PAC collars of the bond. This occurs due to the yield enhancement provided by the discount PO in
falling rate scenarios. Additionally, the strategy does not substantially lose yield in rising rate scenarios because the slowdown in
prepayments for Trust 12 PO is not as severe, due to the discount
nature of the collateral. Inclusion of additional par amounts of the
discount PO in the combination enhances the synthetic yield in
falling rate scenarios without substantially losing yield in rising
rate environments.

Synthetic Combinations Using POs and other Fixed-Income Securities

Whereas the predominant use of POs in synthetic combinations
has been with other MBSs, such as IOs, that exhibit asymmetric
returns, the long duration feature of POs can be exploited to create
intermediate duration synthetics. For example, POs can be combined with short maturity Treasury instruments to form intermediate duration synthetic securities. In the same vein, POs may also
be combined with floating-rate instruments, such as European
FRNs, to offset the reduction in coupon cash flows as interest rates
decline. As noted above, the hedge value of SMBSs depends critically on the expected change in the prepayment behavior of the
underlying collateral as interest rates change. Nonetheless, the
success of such strategies may be hampered by any basis risk between the price movements of the short duration instrument and
the PO security. Additionally, to the extent the prepayment pattern of the underlying collateral does not increase with a decrease
in interest rates, the effectiveness of the PO as a hedge is also
likely to be hampered. Alternatively, POs may be used to hedge
the call risk of premium callable bonds. Assuming that the corporate bond was purchased at a premium, as interest rates decrease,

the call option of the bond becomes more valuable, and there is the risk that the bond may be redeemed by the issuer. In such circumstances, the holder of the bond stands to lose the premium paid for the bond. Under such conditions, POs may be used to hedge this call risk, as the cash flows of POs are likely to increase in bullish scenarios. However, the effectiveness of this cross-hedging strategy may be compromised by external factors that prevent the exercise of the call option on the corporate bond, as well as by any basis risk between corporate and mortgage price movements.

SYNTHETIC COMBINATIONS USING OTHER CMO SECURITIES

In addition to PO collateralized structures, IO strips have also been created in CMO structures. For example, an IO-ette involves stripping a certain portion of the interest stream associated with the underlying collateral to create a high-interest security with a relatively small amount of principal. The structure of an IO-ette (high coupon and low principal) is dictated mainly by the provisions of the REMIC election in a CMO structure, which prohibits the creation of true IO securities as regular interests. In order to meet the tests of this provision, CMO interest strips are usually created by associating a high coupon level with a low principal amount. PAC IOs and TAC IOs are created by stripping interest streams from blocks of coupon-bearing securities (PACs or TACs) that have coupons lower than the pass-through rate of the underlying collateral. Investors are attracted to such discount PACs and TACs for features such as the call protection provided by the prepayment bands, as well as the potential for price appreciation in a market rally. In the case of PAC IOs, the IO stream is stable within the PAC collars, and does not change within this prepayment band. On the other hand, TAC IOs exhibit a stable cash flow stream in prepayment scenarios within the TAC bands. At speeds faster than the upper TAC collar, the TAC IO will lose yield due to the erosion of principal. Conversely, at prepayment speeds slower than the lower TAC collar, the yield of the TAC IO will increase.

The simulataneous development of financial engineering techniques in creating various types of bearish securities, such as IO-ettes, PAC IOs, and TAC IOs, as well the creation of bullish instruments, such as Z bonds and inverse floaters, provide additional opportunities to create higher-yielding synthetic securities using such instruments. In the following sections, synthetic securities that combine PAC bonds with interest rate swaps to create synthetic CMO floaters; various types of Z bonds, ranging from vanilla Z bonds to jump-Z bonds, with IOs (and IO-ettes) combinations; and synthetics that blend inverse floater bonds with IOs are discussed.

Synthetic CMO and Asset-Backed Floaters

With the widespread use of financial engineering techniques in the capital markets, synthetic floaters that use CMO and other asset-backed securities (home equity loans, automobile loans, credit cards) can be created by simultaneously purchasing a fixed-rate asset and entering into an interest rate swap to pay fixed-rate and receive floating-rate cash flows. In the design of such asset swaps, it is important that the notional amount of the swap mirror the amortization pattern of the asset used in the strategy. With asset-backed securities, which have "bullet" structures and lockout features, this consideration can be included effortlessly in the asset swap design. However, for assets such as CMOs, it is also necessary to amortize the notional amount of the interest rate swap at the same rate as the asset balance.

Within the overall genre of structured MBSs, PAC bonds are ideal candidates for synthetic asset swaps, since the principal balance of a PAC tranche amortizes at a stated rate within the prepayment collars. Although other structured MBSs may also be used in the creation of synthetic floaters, the possibility of average life volatility associated with non-PAC bonds may result in the synthetic spread not being maintained over time. Since amortizing swaps can be replicated using a strip of swaps, the interest rate swap fixed rate is determined as a blended rate of individual "bullet" swap rates. This feature of amortizing swaps also permits flexibility of choice in that the investor may either enter into a series of swaps to match the amortization rate of assets, or enter into an amortizing swap at an annual blended rate. In a positively sloped yield curve environment, the use of amortizing swaps can usually be executed at spreads tighter than equivalent maturity "bullet" swaps, unless the CMO structure has "lockouts" that do not allow for the principal balance to amortize for a period of time. The longer the lockout period for principal amortization (i.e., the longer the PAC bond more closely mimics a "bullet" structure), the narrower will be the spread margin between amortizing and "bullet" swaps, unless the bond has wide principal windows, indicating that the amortization of the security takes place over a longer period of time.

For prepayment speeds within the PAC collars, the absolute amount of the asset coupon will be a declining amount due to the amortization of the principal. At higher interest rates (prepayments slower than the lower bound of the PAC collar), the asset coupon will be greater, due to amortization of the principal slower than the stated rate. At the same time, due to a wider spread between the floating-rate and fixed-rate swap cash flows, the synthetic coupon will be much higher. On the other hand, at lower interest rates (prepayments faster than the upper bound of the PAC collar), the asset coupon will be subject to shrinkage, due to a faster-than-expected paydown of principal. The erosion of the synthetic floating-rate asset coupon will further be determined by the extent of the narrowing of the spread between the swap floating and fixed cash flows. As indicated by this discussion, although PAC bond-based asset swaps can provide for a "predictable" synthetic floating rate coupon within a wide range of paydown scenarios, the prepayment risk of callable assets, such as mortgages, cannot be eliminated entirely. However, with the advent of swaptions, which provide for option-like features to be incorporated into swap contracts, an additional dimension of prepayment risk management can be included in the design of synthetic asset swaps.

Options on swaps, or swaptions, are relatively new developments in the swap market and can take several forms, but typically are options to pay or receive a predetermined fixed rate in exchange for LIBOR at some time in the future. As the market develops, it is likely that other floating-rate indices will be used in swaption contracts. Swaptions may also contain an option to cancel an existing swap. Note that the second structure is essentially the same as the first structure, since a swap can be cancelled by entering into a "reverse" swap. Such options can either be European (exercisable on only one date in the future), American (exercisable at any date in the future), or deferred American (exercisable at any date after an initial exercise "lockout" period).

As noted above, a floating-rate synthetic asset may be created by purchasing a fixed-rate asset and simultaneously entering into an interest rate swap to pay fixed-rate and receive floating cash flows. As an example, consider the case of an institution that owns fixed-rate assets with a coupon rate of 10%. In order to convert the assets to floating-rate instruments, the institution enters into an interest rate swap to pay fixed at 9.50% and receive floating at LIBOR for a period of five years. The net cash flows received by the institution are stated as follows:

Fixed Coupon of Asset + Floating Inflow of Swap – Fixed Outflow of Swap

Exhibit 7: Converting a Fixed-Rate Asset to a Synthetic Floating-Rate Asset

| | Interest Rate Scenario | | | | | | |
	-300 bp	-200 bp	-100 bp	NC	+100 bp	+200 bp	+300 bp
Fixed Coupon	10.00%	10.00%	10.00%	10.00%	10.00%	10.00%	10.00%
Swap Outflow (Fixed)	9.50%	9.50%	9.50%	9.50%	9.50%	9.50%	9.50%
Swap Inflow (LIBOR)	6.00%	7.00%	8.00%	9.00%	10.00%	11.00%	12.00%
Synthetic Coupon	12.50%	11.50%	10.50%	9.50%	8.50%	7.50%	6.50%

As indicated in Exhibit 7, regardless of the interest rate scenario, the fixed asset coupon is sufficient to pay the fixed cash flows of the swap. The interest rate swap dynamics of converting fixed-rate assets to floating-rate synthetic coupons and vice versa are essentially the same, except that the swap cash flows are reversed. However, most dealers will charge a higher spread (offer side) for fixed-rate paying swaps than for fixed-rate receiving swaps (bid side). This bid-ask differential, which is determined by variables such as dealer inventory, hedging expenses, and market demand and supply conditions, is used to compensate the dealer market-making function.

In designing asset-based swaps, it is also important to recognize timing differences in the asset and swap cash flows. This feature is especially important for assets that involve a delay feature in the "passing through" of coupon income to investors. For example, in a primary issue, credit card-backed, semiannual "bullet" security in which interest payments are received by investors with a fifteen-day delay, unless the swap cash flows are initiated with a forward settlement to incorporate the delay feature, the synthetic asset coupon cash flows will be mismatched, and may result in an erosion of the synthetic yield. Another relevant design point concerns accomodating the varying basis of the assets and the swap flows in the analysis. For example, corporate bonds and MBSs pay on a (30/360) days basis, whereas swaps usually pay fixed on an (actual/365) days or (30/360) days basis, and floating on an (actual/360) days basis. Therefore, unless the synthetic cash flow calculations are adjusted for the varying basis of the asset returns and the fixed and floating legs of the swap, the asset-based swap yield will be subject to error due to the basis mismatch.

The termination of asset-based swaps prior to the term of the swap involves the evaluation of risks involved in selling the asset and considerations involved in "unwinding" the interest rate swap. The simplest way to terminate an interest rate swap is to enter into an offsetting position. For illustrative purposes, consider the five-year swap used in the above example, paying fixed at a rate of 9.50% and receiving one-month LIBOR. After two years, the swap may be terminated by entering into a "reverse swap" by being a floating-rate payor and fixed-rate receiver. By matching the reset and settlement period of the reverse swap to that of the original swap, the floating-rate payment of the reverse swap is counterbalanced by the floating-rate inflow from the original swap. In falling (rising) interest rate scenarios, the new fixed rate on the reverse swap is likely to be lower (higher) than the fixed rate on the original swap. In such cases, there will be profit (loss) associated with the transaction if the fixed rate of the reverse swap is higher (lower) than the fixed rate on the original swap.

Instead of managing the cash flows of two swaps and the credit risk of two counterparties, the more common option is to terminate the swap for either a profit or loss in the secondary market. In the event current market swaps with a maturity equal to the remaining maturity of the swap to be terminated are being offered at a higher fixed rate, the swap could be sold for a fee. On the other hand, if current market swaps with a maturity similar to the swap to be liquidated are being originated at lower rates, then an exit fee may have to paid for terminating the swap. Formally, the termination value of a swap is determined as the present value of an annuity discounted for the remaining term to maturity at the current swap rate. The periodic value of the annuity payments are determined as the difference between the old fixed swap rate and the new fixed swap rate times the remaining notional amount of the orginal swap.

Mathematically, this is stated as:

$$\text{Termination Value of Swap} = \text{PV of Annuity} @ r_s, t$$

where annuity payments $= (r_s r_m) \times$ Notional Amount; $r_s =$ original swap fixed rate; $r_m =$ current swap fixed rate; and $t =$ time remaining to maturity of swap. In the event the original swap rate (r_s) is greater (lower) than the current swap rate rate (r_m), the term ($r_s r_m$) will be positive (negative), indicating that an exit fee will be paid (received) by the swap holder to terminate the swap.

Although it is difficult to exactly quantify the market risk inherent in the termination of asset-based swaps, several generalizations can be made. In rising rate scenarios, assuming unchanged credit spreads and liquidity premia, the value of the asset will decrease. However, in such cases, there will be profit associated with the termination of the swap due to higher fixed rates on new interest rate swaps. On the other hand, in falling rate scenarios, the increase in the value of the asset will be offset by losses incurred in the termination of the swap. In both cases, the net amount of the gain or loss will be determined by factors such as fundamental conditions in the relevant asset market, the spread between the original and new swap rates, and the notional amount of the swap in the transaction.

Synthetic MBSs Using Accrual Bonds with IO Strips

In CMO structures, accrual or Z bonds are structured such that the bond accrues interest at its stated coupon rate while earlier tranches receive periodic coupon and principal payments. The effect of this structural consideration is that the principal balance of the Z bond increases over time. Once all the earlier tranches have paid off, the Z bond begins to receive both interest income and principal. In slow prepayment scenarios, the Z bond has a stabilizing effect on the earlier tranches, because the accrual feature of the bond counters the reduction in the cash flows to the earlier tranches. With the development of the CMO market, several variations have been added to the plain vanilla (sequential pay) Z bond structure. In order to reduce the prepayment induced uncertainty associated with Z bonds, a variation that combines the accrual features along with the prepayment protection of PAC bands, labeled the Z-PAC, has been created to appeal to investors with liability defeasance objectives. Additionally, due to the existence of PAC collars, Z-PACs provide a higher degree of prepayment call protection than other types of accrual bonds.

In the earlier years of the development of the CMO market, prior to the advent of PAC bonds, most Z bonds received cash flows in a sequential fashion. However, recently, in certain structures, the priority of such flows has been made subordinate to that of PAC bonds, resulting in the Z bond bearing the "brunt" of reduced cash flows in slow prepayment scenarios, and getting paid down earlier than expected in fast prepayment scenarios. While such companion Z bonds still have a certain degree of call protection due to the longer maturity of the bond, other accrual bonds such as jump-Z bonds may "jump" ahead in principal payment priority over other companion bonds at the attainment of the "trigger" condition. The jump trigger is usually activated if the collateral prepayments are faster than the pricing speed of the CMO, although there have been deals in which the trigger can be activated upon the overall level of interest rates, as indicated by a market index, such as the ten-year Constant Maturity Treasury (CMT) index. In other instances, the overall level of interest rates may act as a secondary trigger condition.

As can been noted from the above discussion, Z bonds appeal to investors with either long-dated liabilities or bullish investors, due to the potential for high price appreciation during market rallies. However, by combining the Z bond with a bearish security, such as an IO (or IO-ette), a higher-yielding synthetic security can be designed that does not lose yield in bearish scenarios. As an example of this strategy, consider the following combination from Prudential-Bache CMO Trust 14, consisting of a Z bond (PB14G) and an IO-ette (PB14H), stripped off of the entire deal. The CMO structure, which is collateralized by GNMA 10s, consists of three, seven, and ten-year current pay bonds; two, seven, and ten-year Stated Maturity Bonds; the Z bond; and the IO-ette. The yield profile of the individual securities, along with the synthetic yield profile, and using various amounts of the securities, is shown in Exhibit 8. The IO-ette is noticeable by its low par amount, high coupon, and high price. As the analysis shows, the inclusion of the IO-ette in the combination enhances the yield of the Z bond in bearish scenarios. At the same time, by using prudent amounts of the IO-ette in the structure, the yield of the combination is maintained in bullish scenarios. Additionally, by increasing the amount

Exhibit 8: Synthetic MBSs Using Accrual Bonds and IO-ettes

			Interest Rate Scenario				
	-300 bp	*-200 bp*	*-100 bp*	*NC*	*+100 bp*	*+200 bp*	*+300 bp*
Prepayment Speed (PSA)	410	305	210	150	132	112	92
Z-Bond (PB14G)	10.93%	10.45%	10.06%	9.84%	9.78%	9.72%	9.66%
IO-ette (PB14H)	-5.24%	1.86%	8.07%	11.90%	13.03%	14.28%	15.53%

	Synthetic Combination Yield						
Par Amount							
11,000,000 (Z-Bond)+100,000 (IO-ette)							
	8.67%	9.25%	9.78%	10.14%	10.26%	10.40%	10.55%
11,000,000 (Z-Bond)+200,000 (IO-ette)							
	7.10%	8.39%	9.57%	10.37%	10.63%	10.93%	11.26%

	Duration	
	Macaulay Duration	*Effective Duration*
11,000,000 (Z-Bond)+100,000 (IO-ette)	12.38	6.08
11,000,000 (Z-Bond)+100,000 (IO-ette)	9.97	0.92

PB14G: Coupon 8.40%; Price at yield of 9.84% = 79-20
PB14H: Coupon 1204.65%; Price at yield of 11.90% = 5567-12+

of the IO-ette in the combination, the synthetic yield is further enhanced in the bearish scenarios, albeit at the expense of yield in bullish scenarios.

With respect to the inclusion of the IO-ette in the synthetic combination, another noteworthy point concerns the negative effective duration of the security. This measure of the bond's price sensitivity incorporates the effect of prepayment changes that may occur as a result of changes in interest rates. Macaulay duration and its related version, modified duration, do not adequately measure the price sensitivity of bonds with embedded options, as there is no allowance for the random nature of interest rates. Effective duration, on the other hand, computes the option-adjusted spread (OAS) of the security at a given price and yield curve. By holding OAS constant and shocking the yield curve, the price behavior of the security is determined. Since this duration figure is determined from realistic price movements that take into account the value of the embedded option, the effective duration is a better means of assessing the price sensitivity of the synthetic combination. As noted in Exhibit 8, the price sensitivity of the synthetic combination is overstated by relying on the Macaulay duration measure. On the other hand, the effective duration of the combination, which takes into account the negative duration of the IO-ette, is much shorter. This indicates that the combination will not be susceptible to a large price loss as rates increase. For example, in the synthetic combination that uses $11,000,000 principal amount of the Z bond and $200,000 par amount of the IO-ette, the Macaulay duration of the synthetic is 9.971 years. In this case, there is a tendency to compare the price and yield performance of the synthetic to that of a comparable duration-matched Treasury issue. In actuality, the synthetic closely emulates the price performance of a one-year, duration-matched security (effective duration = 0.925), and should be compared to the yield of the shorter-duration Treasury security in evaluating the yield pick-up. Herein also lies the advantage of including securities with negative effective durations, such as IO-ettes and IOs, in synthetic combination with positive-duration securities. In addition to stabilizing the yield profile of the combination, the inclusion of the IO-ette also dampens the interest rate sensitivity of the synthetic bond.

Synthetic Combinations with Different Accrual Bonds

The synthetic combination discussed above uses a current pay accrual bond with an IO-ette. However, the yield profile of the synthetic blend can be changed by including various types of accrual bonds in the combination. Similar to the case of CMOs collateralized by POs, in which the bullish characteristics of the underlying collateral can be dampened or magnified, similar modifications can be made to the accrual features of Z bonds. For example, the bullish characteristics of accrual bonds can be dampened by structuring the Z bond with PAC collars, in much the same way as is with PO and coupon-bearing PAC bonds. Alternatively, the bullish feature of accrual bonds can be magnified by structuring the Z bond with a "jump" feature with prepayment trigger.

In order to illustrate the synthetic yields of combinations that can be created using various types of accrual bonds and bearish securities, such as IOs, consider the example of FHLMC 1989-108, which is a deal collateralized by discount collateral (FHLMC 8.5). This CMO structure contains a variety of coupon-bearing PACs; short, intermediate, and long-dated Z-PACs; coupon and accrual companions; and a jump-Z bond. Synthetic combinations using Class 108G, the long-dated Z-PAC with PAC collars of 50-150 PSA; Class 108J, the long-dated companion Z; and Class 108K, the

Exhibit 9: Synthetic MBS Yields Using Various Accrual Bonds and IOs

	-300 bp	-200 bp	-100 bp	NC	+100 bp	+200 bp	+300 bp
			Interest Rate Scenario				
Prepayment Speed (PSA)	426	271	187	152	138	133	129
FHLMC90-108G (Z-PAC)	9.65%	9.38%	9.26%	9.25%	9.25%	9.25%	9.25%
FHLMC90-108J (Companion Z)	21.54%	14.60%	10.55%	10.31%	10.13%	10.08%	10.04%
FHLMC90-108K (Jump Z)	41.08%	28.65%	15.10%	9.25%	9.21%	9.19%	9.18%
Prepayment Speed (PSA)	493	420	278	193	157	142	138
Trust 2-IO	-11.23%	-5.62%	4.81%	10.79%	13.27%	14.29%	14.56%
			Synthetic Combination Yield				
Par Amount 1:1 FHLMC1990-108G Z-PAC + IO	8.64%	8.77%	9.06%	9.33%	9.48%	9.56%	9.57%
FHL90-108J (Companion Z + IO)	13.29%	11.47%	10.12%	10.34%	10.37%	10.41%	10.39%
FHL90-108K (Jump Z + IO)	8.19%	10.48%	11.84%	9.34%	9.44%	9.49%	9.50%

jump-Z with FNMA Trust 2 IOs, collateralized by FNMA 10s, are presented in Exhibit 9.

As the analysis shows, the yield of the Z-PAC is fairly stable within the PAC bands. However, for prepayment speeds outside the upper PAC band, the yield of the security increases substantially. On the other hand, the yield of the companion Z is higher in the base case and rising rate scenarios, and reflects the compensation for the support nature of the security. In sharp contrast, the yield of the jump-Z is much higher in bullish rate scenarios, mainly due to the jump feature of the bond, which alters the principal paydown schedule of the classes in the CMO structure by elevating the priority of this bond. With respect to the synthetic combinations, the inclusion of the IO enhances the yield of the Z-PAC marginally in stable and rising rate scenarios. However, in falling interest rate scenarios, where the IO loses yield due to increases in the prepayment speeds of the underlying collateral, the synthetic yield is much lower than the yield of the Z-PAC. On the other hand, the yields of the companion Z are higher for all interest rate scenarios, mainly due to the higher base case yield of the accrual bond, as well as the unrestrained change in cash flows as prepayments on the underlying collateral increase. The yield profile of the synthetic with the jump-Z falls in between the yield profile of the other synthetic combinations. As interest rates rise, leading to a slowdown of the prepayment speeds of the underlying collateral, the increased yield of the IO is restrained by the yield of the jump-Z bond. However, in falling interest rate scenarios, the increased yield of the jump Z is countered by the negative yields of the IO. This occurs due to the fact that as interest rates fall, prepayments on the underlying collateral increase, leading to reduced IO cash flows.

Combining Inverse Floaters with IO Strips

Inverse floaters are bullish, leveraged instruments whose coupon increases as the value of the index decreases. Although the most

Exhibit 10: Hedging IO Strips with Inverse Floaters							
	Interest Rate Scenario						
	-300 bp	*-200 bp*	*-100 bp*	*NC*	*+100 bp*	*+200 bp*	*+300 bp*
FNMA90-148J	37.81%	32.41%	25.24%	19.56%	14.33%	9.42%	4.62%
Trust 42-IO	-14.06%	-8.47%	4.91%	9.84%	11.82%	12.56%	12.90%
	Synthetic Combination Yield						
1:1 Ratio (FHLMC90-148J + 42-IO)	13.78%	14.29%	18.42%	16.79%	13.69%	10.19%	6.57%
2:1 Ratio FHLMC90-148J Coupon = 46.2 − (4.5 × 1 month LIBOR)	23.28%	21.47%	21.23%	17.95%	13.97%	9.85%	5.73%

commonly used index is one-month LIBOR, inverse floaters have also been structured using the 11th District Cost of Funds Index. Generally, the coupon on the inverse floater is determined as Cap − (Multiplier × Index). Inverse floaters are instruments designed for the bullish investor. If short-term rates rally, the holder of the inverse floater benefits from coupon appreciation, since the coupon adjustment is greater than the change in the index due to the leverage factor or mutiplier. Conversely, if long-term rates rally and the inverse floater is priced at a discount, an increase in prepayments combined with the discount pricing lead to significant yield pick-up. Due to the bullish orientation of inverse floaters, such instruments are ideally suited as hedges for IOs.

An example of this synthetic, which combines a bearish instrument such as an IO with an inverse floater, is presented in Exhibit 10. The analysis combines various amounts of FHLMC1990-148 Class J, a LIBOR-denominated inverse floater, with FNMA Trust 42 IOs, collateralized by FNMA 9.5s. The CMO deal consists of PACs, Z-PACs, companion bonds, LIBOR floater, and inverse floater, and is collateralized by FHLMC 9.0s. As the analysis shows, yields on the IO decrease more in falling rate scenarios than the increase in yield in rising rate environments, mainly due to the negative convexity of the IO. However, yields on the inverse floater increase at a faster rate in a falling rate environment than the decline of yields in a rising rate environment. Additionally, due to the leveraged effect of the coupon adjustment, an increase in the amount of the inverse floater in the combination has a magnifying effect on the synthetic yield in falling rate scenarios, without significantly affecting the combined yield in bearish scenarios.

HEDGING ARMs WITH IO STRIPS

Within the gamut of MBSs, adjustable-rate mortgages (ARMs) have always appealed to investors whose objective is to manage the spread between asset returns and liability costs. Although the traditional investors in such instruments have been financial institutions, the success of such instruments in providing a viable spread management vehicle has been noticed by investors such as mutual funds and investment advisory firms.

Although a complete discussion of ARMs is beyond the scope of this chapter, ARMs have certain distinguishing contractual characteristics. The most common indices for determining ARM coupons are the one-year CMT and the 11th District Cost of Funds Index (COFI), although indices such as the three-year and five-year CMT, the National Median Cost of Funds Index, and LIBOR have also been used. In order to prevent "borrower shock," which refers to the unconstrained upward adjustment of the ARM coupon in the face of rising interest rates, Treasury-based ARMs usually have a periodic and lifetime coupon reset caps, whereas COFI-based ARMs have a periodic payment cap and a lifetime interest rate cap. Additionally, due to marketing considerations, ARMs may be originated with an artificially low introductory rate, known as the "teaser" rate, for a short period of time, usually six months, after which the ARM becomes fully indexed.

From the viewpoint of the investor, the periodic and lifetime cap feature of the ARM is beneficial in falling interest rate regimes, as such caps also act as floors and prevent the full downward adjustment of coupon. However, the periodic cap feature

---

Exhibit 11: Yield Enhancement of ARMs with IO Strips

	-300 bp	-200 bp	-100 bp	NC	+100 bp	+200 bp	+300 bp
			Interest Rate Scenario				
1 Yr. CMT ARMs	5.29%	5.88%	6.58%	7.46%	8.49%	9.35%	10.15%
Trust 60-IO	-11.81%	-6.19%	5.67%	10.17%	12.02%	12.76%	13.10%
			Synthetic Combination Yield				
1:1 Ratio (ARM + Trust 60-IO)	0.74%	2.45%	6.27%	8.32%	9.44%	10.15%	10.78%
2:1 Ratio	2.68%	3.89%	6.39%	7.97%	9.04%	9.80%	10.50%
10:1 Ratio	4.70%	5.42%	6.53%	7.58%	8.62%	9.45%	10.22%

---

can also prevent the full upward adjustment of the coupon in bearish interest rate scenarios. Additionally, the ARM coupon is also constrained by the lifetime cap of the loan. In order to counter the possibility of reduced cash flows as interest rates rise, the ARM can be combined with prudent amounts of IOs in order to enhance the ARM yield. An example of this synthetic structure is presented in Exhibit 11, where the yield profiles of various combinations of a one-year CMT ARM with initial coupon of 7.50%, periodic cap of 2%, and lifetime cap of 13.50%, with varying par amounts of FNMA Trust 60, which is collateralized by FNMA 9.5s, are shown. As can be noted from the analysis, inclusion of the IO in the synthetic combination enhances the yield in the base case and rising rate scenarios. However, due to the reduction of the cash flows of the IO in bullish interest rate environments, any enhancement of the ARM yield due to the coupon floor is reduced. Additionally, in bearish rate scenarios, the yield enhancement of the ARM is an increasing function of the amount of IO used in the combination. By the same token, the elimination of the "floored" return of the ARM in bullish regimes is also directly affected by the amount of IO in the synthetic combination. Therefore, it is necessary to exercise prudence in the amount of IO to be included in the blended ARM, mainly due to the possibility of lower returns in bullish scenarios.

CONCLUDING COMMENTS

With the proliferation of financial engineering technology in structured finance, it is unlikely that the revolution occurring in the sculpting of cash flows to meet specific investors' demands is likely to stop. In certain instances, this has been manifested in the form of PAC bonds, which involved the use of such technology to eliminate certain types of risk, such as prepayment risk associated with the asset. In other instances, the prepayment propensity of the collateral has been exploited to create securities in order to meet higher-order risk preference criteria and specialized risk management needs. Although it can be argued that due to the relative youth of the MBS market, innovation is likely to slow down as the market matures, it is equally likely and plausible to project further innovation in structuring technology. This may occur in order to keep pace with consumer preferences in the primary market, where the raw material for securitization (i.e., mortgage loans) is originated, or in response to the dynamics of the regulatory, accounting, and tax environment. Given the innovation in structuring technology, any "idiosyncratic" prepayment risk, where despite similarities in contractual characteristics such as age and loan terms, the collateral exhibits different prepayment patterns, can either be eliminated or exploited in the synthetic structure. The former objective of eliminating this collateral-specific risk can be accomplished by including securities collateralized by the same pool of loans in the synthetic structure. The other objective, whereby this risk is exploited advantageously, can be achieved by selecting "slow pay" bearish securities and "fast pay" bullish securities. In any case, as newer securities are developed, some with asymmetric cash flow and return patterns, the combination of such securities with assets exhibiting opposite return profiles to create synthetic securities with desired risk and return patterns is likely to be an integral part of any asset management program.

CHAPTER 34

MORTGAGE POOL RISK AND RETURN: A SYSTEMATIC APPROACH

Peter Muller
Manager
Model Research Group
BARRA

INTRODUCTION

Traditional valuation of mortgages has centered on so-called "generics," aggregations of large numbers of mortgage pools by coupon and issue year. There are two main steps in pricing a generic mortgage. First, a model is needed to forecast the prepayment of generics under possible future evolutions of interest rates. Important factors in these prepayment models are coupon, age, season, and burnout.[1] Second, one needs to generate a "tree" of future interest rates and price the mortgage (using the prepayment

---

[1] See Chapter 10.

model) along each path of the tree. The result is a theoretical price of the mortgage today.

Because of a number of factors (uncertainty of cash flows, limited historical data, etc.), this is not a precise science. However, we are able to price generic mortgages slightly more accurately than high-quality optionable corporate bonds.[2] Exhibit 1 shows that market prices of mortgages can be fairly well approximated by a reasonable model.

When constructing portfolios, institutional investors typically think of mortgages in terms of generics. However, investors are not able to purchase generics; investors can only purchase individual mortgage *pools*. To our knowledge, little work has been done to measure how closely mortgage pools will track generics.[3] This chapter presents some preliminary research into this interesting area.

We discuss the following issues:

- What is the relationship between pool-specific prepayment and return?

- How can we measure pool-specific risk, or how closely the return to a mortgage pool will track a generic?

- What is the best way to track a generic?

- Can we find factors that forecast the differences in future prepayment of pools within a generic?

---

[2] The standard deviation of pricing errors across generic mortgages (using the BARRA mortgage model) is approximately $0.77 out of $100. For AAA-rated optionable bonds, this number is $0.86, while for nonoptionable AAA-rated corporates, the standard deviation of pricing errors is $0.69.

[3] For one example, see Alden L. Toevs and Mark R. Hancock, "Diversifying Prepayment Risk: Techniques to Stabilize Cash Flows and Returns from Mortgage Pass-Throughs," Chapter 39 in Frank J. Fabozzi (ed.), *The Handbook of Mortgage-Backed Securities: Revised Edition* (Chicago: Probus Publishing, 1988).

Exhibit 1: Market and Fitted Price for Seasoned GNMA 30-Year Generics—August 31, 1990

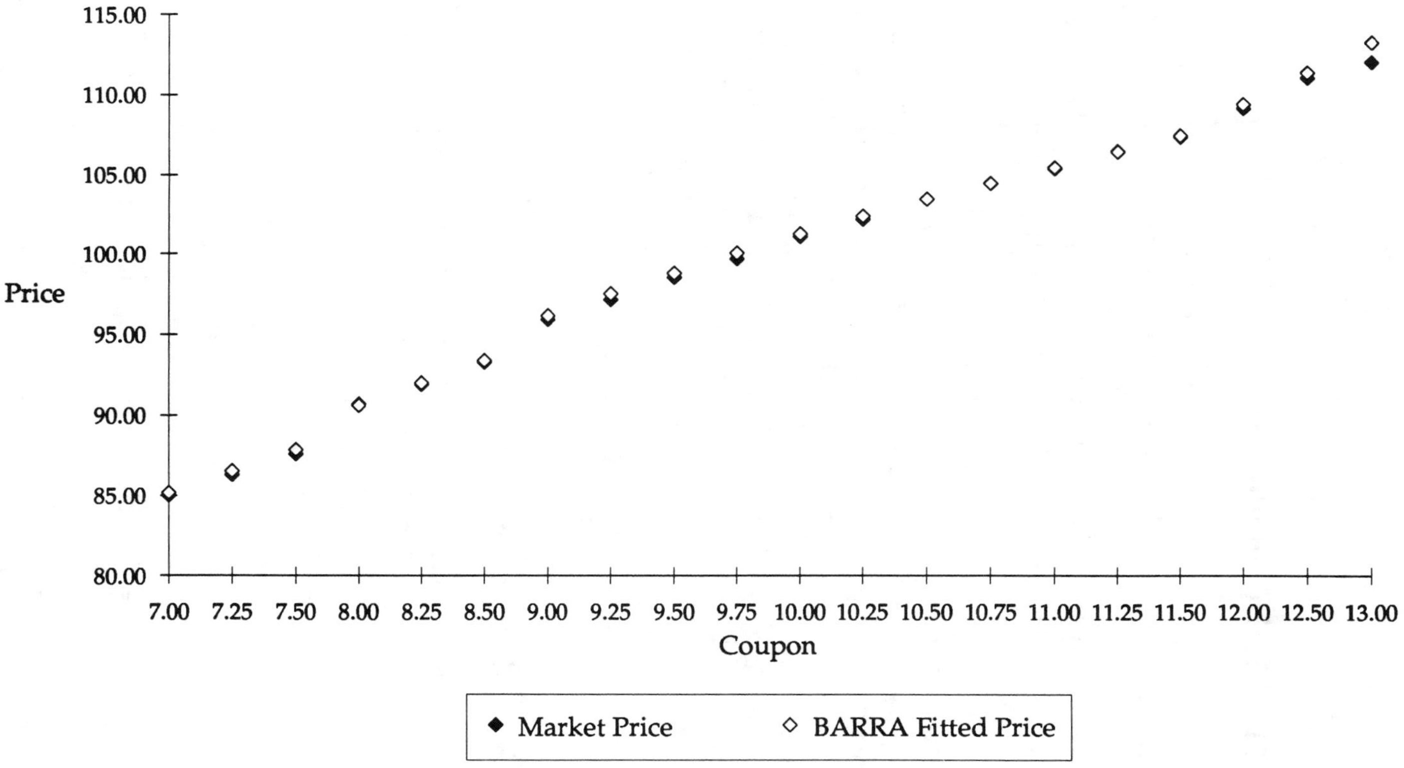

Price

115.00
110.00
105.00
100.00
95.00
90.00
85.00
80.00

7.00 7.25 7.50 8.00 8.25 8.50 9.00 9.25 9.50 9.75 10.00 10.25 10.50 10.75 11.00 11.25 11.50 12.00 12.50 13.00

Coupon

● Market Price   ◇ BARRA Fitted Price

POOL-SPECIFIC PREPAYMENT AND RETURN

We are interested in the difference between the return to our mortgage pool and the corresponding generic. We call this number the *active return* to our mortgage pool.

What happens if a mortgage pool prepays at a faster rate than others in its category? This is desirable if we hold a discount mortgage, since holders receive par instead of the below-par mortgage price. For premium mortgages the opposite is true; slower prepayment than average is desirable. Holders of par mortgages are essentially indifferent to differences between pool prepayment and generic prepayment, since principal can be reinvested at par.[4]

Exhibit 2 shows the active return corresponding to an absolute prepayment difference of 10% between a mortgage pool and the underlying generic as of August 31, 1990. For example, assume we own a seasoned 9% pool. Over the next year, the average (generic) prepayment of 9% pools is (say) 10% CPR. If our pool prepays at 20% CPR, we will receive an active return of plus forty-eight basis points due to the extra prepayment.

POOL-SPECIFIC RISK

We can now develop a formula that estimates how closely the return to a pool will track the return to a generic. First, we need to introduce some notation.

$P_G(t)$ = Price of generic at time t

$P_n(t)$ = Price of pool n at time t

C_G = Principal repayment of generic, scheduled and unscheduled (based on par = 100)

C_n = Principal repayment of pool n

---

[4] This ignores reinvestment costs. If transaction costs are taken into account, a holder of a par mortgage would slightly prefer less prepayment than for the generic.

Exhibit 2: How Does 10% Extra Prepayment Affect Return?

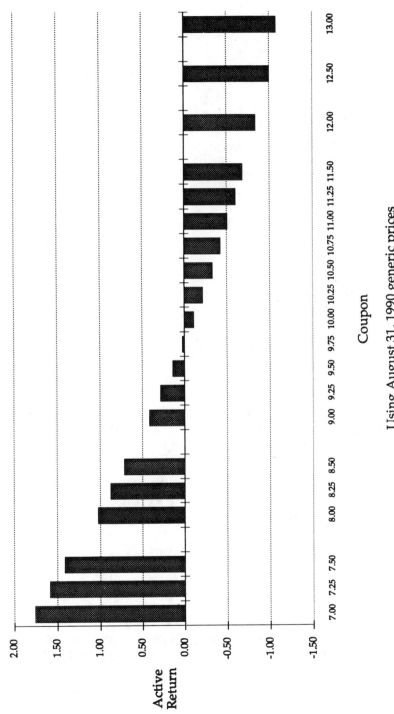

Using August 31, 1990 generic prices

I_G = Interest payment of generic (based on par = 100)

R_G = Return to generic

$R_{G,P}$ = Price return to generic

R_n = Return to pool n

$R_{n,A}$ = Active return to pool n

w_n = Amount outstanding of mortgage pool n

S_n = Unexpected pool prepayment

V_G = Measure of deviation of generic price from par

The repayment of the generic is the weighted average repayment of all pools comprising the generic.

$$C_G = \frac{\sum_n w_n \cdot C_n}{\sum_n w_n} \tag{1}$$

The unexpected pool prepayment, S_n, is the difference between the repayment of the pool and the repayment of the generic:

$$S_n = C_n - C_G. \tag{2}$$

By definition, the unexpected pool prepayment averages out to zero over all pools (if we weight the average by the amount outstanding for each pool):

$$\frac{\sum_n w_n \cdot S_n}{\sum_n w_n} = \frac{\sum_n w_n \cdot (C_n - C_G)}{\sum_n w_n} = C_G - C_G = 0 \tag{3}$$

We saw before that active return depends on how far away the generic is from par.[5] We measure this with the variable V_G.

---

[5] As is the usual convention, prices, interest payments, and principal payments are based on par being 100.

$$V_G = \frac{100 - P_G(t)}{P_G(t)} \tag{4}$$

The price return to a generic measures capital appreciation or depreciation (arising from interest rate or spread changes):

$$R_{G,P} = \frac{P_G(t + 1) - P_G(t)}{P_G(t)} \tag{5}$$

The total return to the generic has three components:

- Interest payments

- Principal repayments (scheduled and unscheduled)

- Price appreciation or depreciation

Interest payments are made on all mortgages. However, price changes only affect remaining principal, whereas repaid principal is valued at par. This gives rise to an expression for the return to a generic:

$$R_G = \frac{[I_G + C_G \cdot 100 + (1 - C_G) \cdot P_G(t + 1)] - P_G(t)}{P_G(t)} \tag{6}$$

Similarly, the return to mortgage pool n will be:

$$R_n = \frac{[I_G + C_n \cdot 100 + (1 - C_n) \cdot P_n(t + 1)] - P_n(t)}{P_n(t)} \tag{7}$$

We can combine equations (6) and (7) to get an expression for the active return to our mortgage pool. We make the not unreasonable assumption that the price of our pool (P_n) is the same as the price of the generic at both times t and $t + 1$.[6] Using this assumption, we get a formula for active return:

---

[6] This assumption is equivalent to saying that it is not possible accurately to forecast differential prepayment of mortgage pools within a generic (later results presented in this chapter notwithstanding), or that the expected value of S_n is zero.

$$R_{n,A} = R_n - R_G = \frac{S_n \cdot 100 - S_n \cdot P_G(t+1)}{P_G(t)} = S_n \cdot (V_G - R_{G,P}) \quad (8)$$

We're almost there! Active risk (or tracking variance) is the variability of active return:

$$VAR(R_{n,A}) = VAR\left\{ S_n \cdot (V_G - R_{G,P}) \right\}. \quad (9)$$

We can simplify this expression by making a few assumptions. First, we assume that the expected principal repayment of the mortgage pool is the same as the expected principal repayment of the generic. Second, we assume that this remains true even if we knew the price return to the generic in advance. This is the same as saying that knowing the future direction of interest rates does not help us select a specific mortgage pool within a generic.[7] Finally, we assume that the variability of prepayment within a generic is not correlated with the return to the generic.[8]

Mathematically, we are assuming:

a) $E[S_n] = 0$

b) $E[S_n \cdot R_G] = 0$

and c) $E[S_n^2 \cdot R_G] = 0$

This gives us the formula below:

$$VAR(R_{n,A}) \cong VAR(S_n) \cdot \left[(V_G)^2 + VAR(R_{G,P}) \right], \quad (10)$$

where $VAR(R_{n,A})$, or active risk (tracking variance), of a mortgage pool, is determined by $VAR(S_n)$, variability of pool prepayment, $VAR(R_{G,P})$, price risk of the generic, and V_G, a measure of the difference between generic price and par. Expressing tracking error as we do in equation (10) allows us to use separate models to estimate prepayment variability and volatility of return to the generic.

---

[7] Pools within a generic will have slightly different WACs or WAMs, which makes this assumption not entirely correct.

[8] This is perhaps our most tenuous assumption. It is only necessary to further simplify our formula for pool-specific risk.

Because V_G is smallest for mortgages closest to par, these pools are easiest to track. It turns out that prepayment variability, $VAR(S_n)$, is much higher for high-coupon pools than for low-coupon pools, so it is more difficult to track premium mortgages. This is true even though $VAR(R_{G,P})$ is lower for high-coupon pools.

Exhibit 3: How Closely Will a $2 Million Dollar Pool Track a Generic?

Coupon	Price	Standard Deviation of Generic Price Return (Last 24 Months)	Observed Std. Dev. of Prepayment (Last 12 Months)	Forecast Tracking Error of Pool (% Annual Std. Dev.)
7.5	87.59	7.91	3.42	0.55
8.0	90.69	7.23	3.59	0.45
8.5	93.31	6.75	4.11	0.40
9.0	95.97	6.26	4.58	0.35
9.5	98.59	5.68	4.68	0.27
10.0	101.13	5.04	5.14	0.27
10.5	103.47	4.14	7.81	0.42
11.0	105.38	3.52	7.79	0.48
11.5	107.38	3.15	8.12	0.61
12.0	109.19	2.93	9.61	0.86

August 31, 1990 data—Pool size between $2 and $2.25 million.

Exhibit 3 gives examples of predicted tracking error as of August 31, 1990 for mortgage pools with coupons between 7.5% and 12.0%. To estimate variability of prepayment, we used pools between $2 and $2.25 million.[9] We estimated the variability of price returns to each generic using twenty-four months of historical prices.[10] Exhibit 4 summarizes the numbers in Exhibit 3. This graph displays annual tracking error for $2 million pools of varying coupons.

---

[9] As will be shown later, variability of prepayment depends a great deal on pool size.
[10] Another way of estimating $VAR(R_{G,P})$ would be to use a generic prepayment model.

Exhibit 4: How Closely Will a $2 Million Pool Track a Generic?

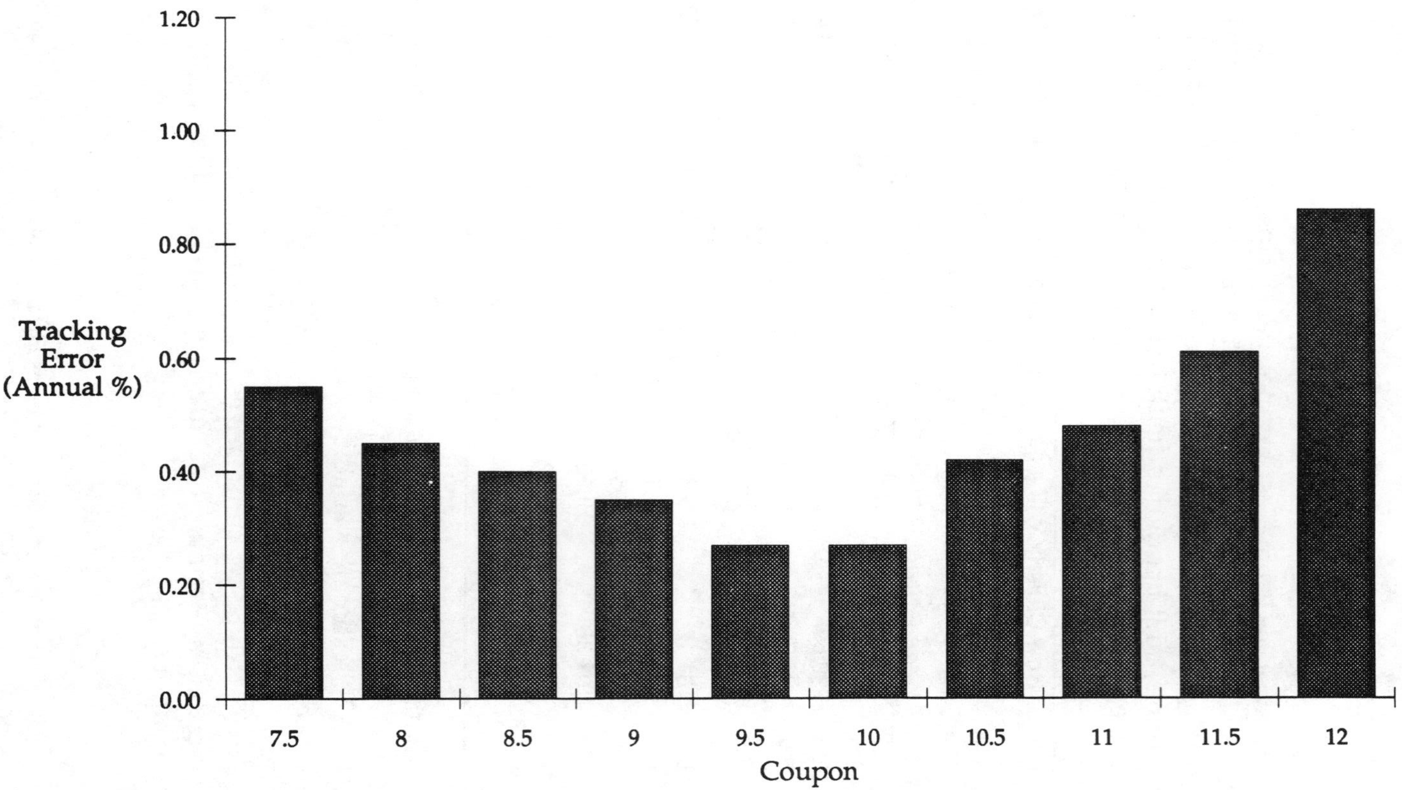

We can see from Exhibit 4 that a $2 million 9.5% mortgage pool trading roughly at par would be expected to track a 9.5% generic with an annualized standard deviation of return of 27 basis points. A 12% pool of similar size, however, would be expected to track a 12% generic with an annualized standard deviation of 86 basis points.

VARIABILITY OF PREPAYMENT

When we measured pool-specific risk in the previous section, we used a constant pool size of $2 million. We did this because variability of prepayment is strongly related to the size of a mortgage pool.

It should not be surprising that smaller pools tend to have more widely distributed CPR than larger pools. This is because the increased number of mortgages in larger pools already provides some diversification. Exhibit 5 shows the strong relationship between pool size and variability of prepayment. The observed standard deviation of prepayment for a $1 million pool is approximately 6%, whereas for a $5 million pool it is 4%. This suggests that the larger pool provides diversification, but not proportional to the increase in pool size. (If we randomly grouped together five $1 million pools, we would expect the standard deviation of CPR for the resulting aggregate to be $\frac{6}{\sqrt{5}} = 2.7\%$.)

Why do the larger pools provide less diversification than expected? There are two likely reasons. First, these pools may on average contain larger mortgages. As an extreme example, the standard deviation of prepayment of a $1 million pool consisting of twenty $50,000 mortgages should be similar to a $2 million pool consisting of ten $100,000 mortgages. More importantly, mortgages within pools tend to be for similar properties from the same location, which also has the effect of decreasing diversification.

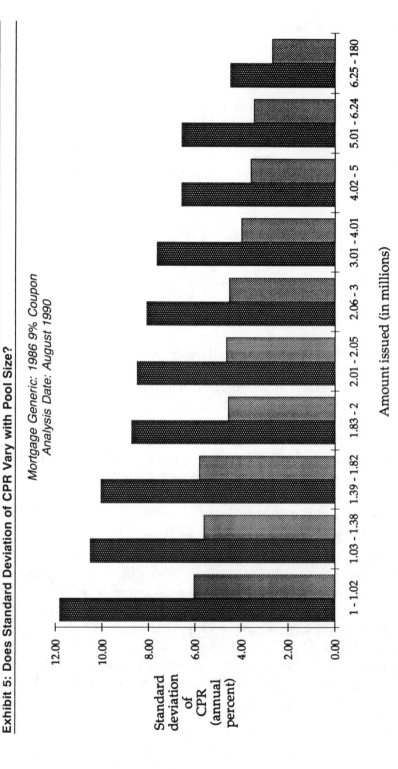

Exhibit 5: Does Standard Deviation of CPR Vary with Pool Size?

Mortgage Generic: 1986 9% Coupon
Analysis Date: August 1990

■ Standard deviation of CPR, last 3 months   ▨ Standard deviation of CPR, last 12 months

HOW TO TRACK A GENERIC

What if we had a fixed amount of money to invest in one generic and our only objective was to track the generic as closely as possible? Should we buy a lot of small pools or a few larger pools?

To answer this question, we did the following study. We divided 9% coupon 1986 mortgage pools into five bins, according to pool size. We then ran a Monte Carlo simulation, sampling $100 million of each bin. For each bin we calculated the standard deviation of the next 12 months' prepayments, over 734 simulations.[11] The results are shown in Exhibit 6. We found that investing $100 million in the smallest pools was the least risky, giving a standard deviation of 0.55% in CPR. The $100 million invested in the largest pools gave a standard deviation of 0.84% in CPR. We conclude that dollar for dollar, buying a lot of smaller pools is more diversifying than buying a few large pools.

Exhibit 6: Results of Monte Carlo Simulation ($100 Million Invested in Generic)

Quintile	Average Number of Pools	Mean CPR	Standard Deviation CPR
Smallest pools	105	4.9	0.55
Smaller	64	5.7	0.67
Average	47	5.2	0.63
Larger	27	5.8	0.72
Largest pools	10	5.5	0.84

Practical considerations, such as mortgage pool availability and transaction costs,[12] favor the purchase of larger pools. Investors wishing to track generics as closely as possible also need to take these considerations into account.

---

[11] The number 734 has no real significance other than that it was enough trials to ensure confidence in our results.

[12] Minimizing back-office hassles can also be a concern.

IS IT POSSIBLE TO FORECAST POOL-SPECIFIC PREPAYMENT?

The results presented so far in this chapter have focused on the variability of mortgage pool prepayment. We have shown what variables are important in forecasting how closely a mortgage pool will track a generic.

The final topic we address is whether or not it is possible to forecast pool-specific prepayment. For non-par mortgages, this is very valuable information.[13] If we own a premium mortgage, we want our pool to prepay slower than the generic. If we hold a discount mortgage, above-average prepayment is desirable.

The basic principle of forecasting is to use information at time t to forecast events occurring after time t. What information could we use to forecast future prepayment rates? Market knowledge suggests that pools originating in urban areas, especially on either coast, prepay much faster than similar pools originating in rural areas. City dwellers tend to move around more. Unfortunately, good data on mortgage pool location is not generally available.[14]

Another (related) piece of market knowledge is that "fast pools stay fast." Exhibit 7 shows an example for 8% mortgage pools issued in 1977. Notice that observed CPR from September 1989 to August 1990 is a decreasing function of the amount of each pool remaining as of September 1989. This implies that for these mortgages, faster pools did indeed stay fast. If we can extrapolate from this result, investors buying seasoned 8% pools should have a preference for pools with historically above-average prepayment rates.

We carried out a more systematic test of this phenomenon. Using all generics consisting of at least 1,000 pools as of September 1, 1989, we specified the following model:

---

[13] As already discussed, par mortgage holders are essentially indifferent to prepayment rates.

[14] As of this writing, most databases only contain information on the zip code of the agency pooling the mortgages. Many issuers pool mortgages from across the country.

Exhibit 7: Do Fast Pools Stay Fast? (Example: 8% Coupon, 1977)

Amount of Pool Remaining September 1, 1989	Number of Pools	Average Observed CPR September 1989- August 1990
25-35%	349	7.42
35-45%	943	7.11
45-55%	1,419	6.32
55-65%	711	6.15
65-75%	116	5.07

$$CPR_n(t - 12,t) = \mu_{CPR} + \hat{\beta} \cdot F_n(t - 12) , \qquad (11)$$

where $CPR_n(t\text{-}12,t)$ represents the realized CPR of pool n over the last twelve months, μ_{CPR} is the average CPR for the generic, and $F_n(t\text{-}12)$ is the percentage of pool n's principal remaining twelve months ago (this number is usually referred to as pool n's factor at time $t\text{-}12$).

The estimated coefficient $\hat{\beta}$ measures whether or not historically fast pools (as of September 1, 1989) continued above-average prepayment over the next year. A negative beta coefficient suggests that fast pools stay fast.

Results

We were surprised to find that beta came out negative for thirty-nine out of forty generics. Of these thirty-nine negative betas, thirty-seven were significant at the 95% level. Only for the highest coupon generic (1982 15% mortgages) did this relationship change. The full results are shown in Exhibit 8.[15]

---

[15] We achieved similar results (but not as strong) doing a similar test to try to predict pool-specific prepayment over the next three months. These are not shown here. An identical test run using August 1991 data produced 37 of 40 negative betas.

Exhibit 8: Relationship Between Historical Prepayment and Next 12 Month's CPR

Generic Coupon	Issue Year	Beta	T-stat
7.50	1977	-12.16	-13.66
7.50	1987	-11.92	-4.09
8.00	1976	-10.39	-10.23
8.00	1977	-8.19	-9.76
8.00	1978	-10.23	-7.43
8.00	1987	-14.28	-9.11
8.25	1978	-10.35	-5.73
8.50	1986	-9.21	-4.14
8.50	1987	-16.62	-12.10
9.00	1978	-9.24	-7.57
9.00	1979	-8.99	-8.66
9.00	1986	-13.16	-16.02
9.00	1987	-14.04	-10.67
9.00	1988	-20.13	-5.15
9.50	1979	-10.62	-10.16
9.50	1986	-11.16	-9.65
9.50	1987	-17.24	-12.83
9.50	1988	-19.33	-7.56
10.00	1986	-11.08	-8.86
10.00	1987	-15.98	-9.12
10.00	1988	-27.21	-14.02
10.50	1986	-3.69	-1.88
10.50	1987	-31.77	-13.54
10.50	1988	-62.02	-16.70
11.00	1980	-12.78	-8.29
11.00	1983	-9.13	-3.31
11.00	1985	-12.58	-9.88
11.00	1986	-7.85	-3.90
11.50	1983	-16.65	-10.12
11.50	1985	-9.19	-4.00
12.00	1983	-14.12	-4.35
12.00	1984	-22.58	-8.80
12.00	1985	-15.70	-7.47
12.50	1980	-16.22	-5.05
12.50	1983	-16.99	-3.82
12.50	1984	-13.76	-3.36
12.50	1985	-0.15	-0.04
13.00	1981	-15.59	-3.77
13.00	1984	-7.83	-1.54
15.00	1982	13.88	2.96
All Generics:		-12.53	-35.03

If we pool all of our observations together, our regression model estimates that for every 10% less outstanding (relative to initial amount issued), a mortgage pool will exhibit 1.25% higher prepayment over the next year.[16] For example, our model predicts that a pool with 70% of original amount outstanding will exhibit 2.5% higher prepayment over the next year than a pool (from the same generic, of course) with 90% of original amount outstanding.

SUMMARY

We have tried in this chapter to provide a more systematic approach to analyzing the specific risk of mortgage pools. We list below our main results:

1. A formula that measures pool-specific risk. Pool-specific risk depends on

   • variability of prepayment

   • difference between generic price and par

   • price risk (volatility) of the corresponding generic

2. High-coupon mortgages are more difficult to track.

3. If a fixed amount is to be invested in a single generic, buying a lot of smaller pools provides more diversification than buying a few larger pools.

4. Pools with above-average prepayment continue to prepay faster than average.

Many interesting avenues for future research remain.

---

[16] We controlled for different average CPRs across generics by subtracting out mean generic CPR before running the pooled regression.

CHAPTER 35

HEDGING INTEREST RATE RISKS WITH FUTURES, SWAPS, AND OPTIONS

Douglas T. Breeden, PhD
Research Professor of Finance
Fuqua School of Business
Duke University

Michael J. Giarla
Principal
Smith Breeden Associates, Inc.

This chapter presents a general approach to constructing hedges of interest rate risks for financial institutions such as savings and loans, commercial banks, and investment banks. The chapter is written at an introductory level that is intended for students, for financial officers, regulators, accountants, and members of boards of directors who have not had a large exposure to futures and options hedging. Yet, despite the relatively modest quantitative level of the chapter, almost all of the major concepts of hedging are illustrated in the context of realistic hedging problems. Both "macro" and "micro" hedges are examined. A large amount of data is provided, so that readers may also do their own analysis of mortgage hedges.

For financial intermediaries such as savings and loans and banks, hedging may be described as an attempt to protect the market values of their assets and liabilities from the effects of changes in interest rates. The basic concepts of hedging can be most effectively described by focusing on particular numerical examples. Therefore, the discussion of hedging found in this chapter will be structured around the experiences of three savings and loan associations—First Savings and Loan Association, Second Savings and Loan, and Third Savings and Loan Association.

The chapter is organized as follows. The first section presents background historical data on interest rates, mortgage prepayment rates, Treasury bond and Eurodollar futures prices, and mortgage prices. Interest rate futures markets are introduced, along with options on futures, interest rate caps and floors, and interest rate swaps. The second section presents the concepts of duration and price elasticity, and illustrates these concepts for bonds and mortgages with various coupon rates. The third section presents a calculation of a mark-to-market "liquidation value" for an entire firm, and illustrates historical changes in this value for a savings and loan (named First Savings here). This section also shows how systematically to examine interest rate risk for an institution for many potential changes in interest rates. How to construct an appropriately sized macro hedge for the institution with futures and/or interest rate swaps is shown in the fourth section, which also illustrates the risks involved in not changing the hedge position as time passes and as interest rates change. The fifth section shows how the hedge consisting of futures and swaps can be significantly improved with option positions. The sixth section presents micro hedging and correlation statistics for some actual hedges of mortgage securities (asset hedges). The section that follows presents liability hedging, and shows how to allocate futures contracts and their gains and losses to specific liabilities and to the appropriate accounting income statements. The final section concludes the chapter, and lists some of the relevant hedging issues that were not examined.

FUTURES, OPTIONS, AND SWAPS: HISTORICAL DATA

Interest Rates and Mortgage Prepayments

Since it is useful to refer to recent changes in interest rates, Exhibit 1 gives semiannually compounded yields to maturity on Treasury bills, notes, and bonds of various maturities for *January 31, 1979,* to December 31, 1990. In the late 1970s the United States' economy was facing its second major oil shock of the decade, a high rate of inflation, a low level of economic growth, and a declining dollar. On January 31, 1979, the three-month Treasury bill rate was 9.60% and the ten-year Treasury note rate was 9.12%. By September 31, 1979, the three-month and ten-year Treasury rates had risen to 10.16% and 9.21%, respectively.

In October 1979, the Federal Reserve changed its operating procedure from targeting the Federal funds rate to targeting a measure of the money supply. This change resulted in considerably more interest rate volatility, especially in short-term rates, during the next several years. By April 30, 1980, the three-month Treasury rate increased 482 basis points to 14.98%, and the ten-year Treasury rate increased 339 basis points to 12.60%. The slope of the yield curve also inverted substantially more from September 1979 to April 1980, going from a –95 basis point spread between 10-year and 3-month Treasury rates to a spread of –238 basis points.

In the second quarter of 1980, shortly after the establishment of credit controls by the Carter Administration, a brief, but sharp, two-quarter recession began, and interest rates, especially short-

Exhibit 1: Coupon Treasury Yield Curves: 1979-1990

	3 Mo	6 Mo	1 Yr	2 Yr	5 Yr	7 Yr	10 Yr	20 Yr	30 Yr	Slope 10-Yr minus 3-Mo
Jan 31 79	9.60	10.08	10.55	9.95	9.28	9.20	9.12	8.96	8.93	-0.48
Feb 29 79	9.61	9.93	10.12	9.60	8.94	8.93	8.92	8.84	8.80	-0.69
Mar 31 79	9.79	10.09	10.35	9.85	9.25	9.19	9.06	9.09	9.05	-0.73
Apr 30 79	9.77	10.05	10.14	9.68	9.18	9.10	9.08	9.01	8.98	-0.69
May 31 79	9.90	9.99	10.37	9.87	9.29	9.30	9.32	9.21	9.19	-0.58
Jun 30 79	9.89	10.03	9.87	9.53	9.01	9.00	9.04	9.05	9.06	-0.85
Jul 31 79	9.25	9.47	9.34	8.94	8.67	8.71	8.76	8.78	8.81	-0.49
Aug 31 79	9.48	9.82	9.68	9.26	8.86	8.96	8.97	8.91	8.95	-0.51
Sep 30 79	10.16	10.42	10.35	9.79	9.32	9.26	9.21	9.06	9.06	-0.95
Oct 31 79	10.44	10.79	10.78	10.05	9.46	9.45	9.42	9.29	9.23	-1.02
Nov 30 79	12.66	13.06	12.90	12.05	11.12	10.91	10.78	10.54	10.22	-1.88
Dec 31 79	11.95	12.32	11.98	11.35	10.45	10.44	10.36	10.08	10.06	-1.59
Jan 31 80	12.53	12.73	11.89	11.21	10.35	10.31	10.31	10.00	10.08	-2.22
Feb 29 80	12.54	12.79	12.32	11.73	11.09	11.15	11.11	11.11	11.08	-1.43
Mar 31 80	14.62	15.17	15.27	14.59	13.48	12.98	12.68	12.27	12.15	-1.94
Apr 30 80	14.98	15.98	15.68	14.57	13.25	12.58	12.60	12.40	12.27	-2.38
May 31 80	10.60	11.13	11.14	10.73	10.73	10.68	10.73	10.81	10.87	0.13
Jun 30 80	7.99	8.43	8.78	9.15	9.68	9.97	10.19	10.31	10.33	2.20
Jul 31 80	8.18	8.35	8.42	8.92	9.46	9.82	9.98	10.01	9.94	1.80
Aug 31 80	8.89	9.16	9.26	9.63	10.08	10.33	10.62	10.68	10.60	1.73
Sep 30 80	10.23	10.91	11.09	11.31	11.58	11.54	11.49	11.33	11.25	1.26
Oct 31 80	11.89	12.31	12.24	12.01	11.81	11.84	11.83	11.83	11.70	-0.06
Nov 30 80	13.29	13.83	13.67	13.08	12.55	12.44	12.38	12.30	12.20	-0.91
Dec 31 80	15.22	15.56	15.04	14.10	13.08	12.60	12.67	12.30	12.28	-2.55
Jan 31 81	15.02	14.96	13.97	13.01	12.57	12.47	12.43	11.96	11.94	-2.59
Feb 29 81	15.27	14.70	13.92	13.26	12.73	12.65	12.64	12.40	12.23	-2.63
Mar 31 81	15.11	15.23	14.74	14.07	13.89	13.53	13.41	13.15	12.95	-1.70
Apr 30 81	13.00	12.93	13.01	13.14	13.33	13.21	13.10	12.89	12.61	0.10
May 31 81	15.62	15.44	15.33	14.79	14.38	14.27	14.13	13.88	13.65	-1.49
Jun 30 81	15.54	14.94	14.46	14.15	13.74	13.49	13.29	13.10	13.10	-2.25
Jul 31 81	15.08	15.21	14.96	14.65	14.25	14.05	13.84	13.64	13.30	-1.24
Aug 31 81	15.60	16.17	16.10	15.77	15.27	14.97	14.72	14.26	13.93	-0.88
Sep 30 81	16.46	17.35	17.13	16.68	16.07	15.72	15.38	15.12	14.74	-1.08
Oct 31 81	15.15	16.25	16.64	16.69	16.18	16.04	15.76	15.58	15.20	0.61
Nov 30 81	13.32	14.01	14.32	14.50	14.21	14.72	14.64	14.69	14.34	1.32
Dec 31 81	10.94	11.79	12.13	12.64	12.96	13.47	13.27	13.58	13.03	2.33
Jan 31 82	11.54	12.88	13.31	13.60	13.89	14.12	13.93	14.05	13.61	2.39
Feb 29 82	13.11	13.78	14.05	14.17	14.09	14.24	14.19	14.17	13.88	1.08
Mar 31 82	13.04	14.12	14.29	14.41	14.11	14.07	13.99	14.05	13.80	0.95
Apr 30 82	13.90	14.27	14.29	14.45	14.30	14.36	14.17	13.86	13.66	0.27
May 31 82	12.96	13.59	13.71	13.95	13.74	13.84	13.81	13.55	13.35	0.85
Jun 30 82	11.97	12.52	12.93	13.57	13.78	13.81	13.69	13.63	13.38	1.72
Jul 31 82	13.32	14.07	14.32	14.55	14.51	14.52	14.32	14.06	13.84	1.00
Aug 31 82	10.12	11.51	12.07	13.15	13.55	13.72	13.63	13.61	13.40	3.51
Sep 30 82	8.66	10.20	11.10	11.94	12.72	12.86	12.77	12.55	12.47	4.11
Oct 31 82	7.79	9.22	10.24	11.23	11.68	11.66	11.93	11.58	11.74	4.14
Nov 30 82	8.15	8.84	9.19	9.83	10.53	10.61	11.05	10.75	10.97	2.90
Dec 31 82	8.51	9.00	9.31	9.92	10.47	10.77	10.69	10.98	10.94	2.18
Jan 31 83	8.13	8.40	8.66	9.46	10.21	10.27	10.31	10.65	10.64	2.18
Feb 29 83	8.36	8.68	8.92	9.59	10.44	10.67	10.75	11.08	11.18	2.39
Mar 31 83	8.15	8.38	8.61	9.40	9.92	10.14	10.24	10.62	10.68	2.09
Apr 30 83	8.95	9.20	9.31	9.86	10.42	10.51	10.59	10.82	10.85	1.64
May 31 83	8.30	8.52	8.70	9.28	9.91	10.07	10.18	10.47	10.50	1.88
Jun 30 83	8.91	9.23	9.46	10.09	10.49	10.77	10.79	11.10	11.13	1.88
Jul 31 83	9.04	9.38	9.60	10.23	10.80	10.85	10.89	11.15	11.13	1.85
Aug 31 83	9.58	10.07	10.49	11.02	11.68	11.73	11.80	11.98	11.91	2.22
Sep 30 83	9.56	10.10	10.47	11.10	11.71	11.88	11.92	12.03	11.96	2.36
Oct 31 83	9.00	9.36	9.77	10.48	11.15	11.34	11.39	11.60	11.46	2.39
Nov 30 83	8.81	9.28	9.74	10.58	11.35	11.58	11.71	11.92	11.80	2.90
Dec 31 83	9.17	9.56	9.91	10.61	11.40	11.51	11.58	11.77	11.64	2.41
Jan 31 84	9.20	9.50	9.80	10.56	11.33	11.47	11.65	11.80	11.76	2.45
Feb 29 84	9.46	9.88	10.16	10.97	11.70	11.86	12.02	12.17	12.14	2.56
Mar 31 84	10.12	10.52	10.78	11.55	12.27	12.38	12.50	12.53	12.51	2.38
Apr 30 84	10.07	10.56	11.05	11.85	12.52	12.66	12.80	12.86	12.85	2.73
May 31 84	10.10	11.27	12.09	12.92	13.70	13.80	13.91	13.78	13.81	3.81
Jun 30 84	10.28	11.40	12.23	13.15	13.71	13.75	13.82	13.73	13.62	3.54
Jul 31 84	10.68	11.28	11.75	12.57	12.83	12.88	12.93	12.97	12.86	2.25
Aug 31 84	11.01	11.44	11.84	12.50	12.80	12.82	12.85	12.67	12.49	1.84
Sep 30 84	10.58	11.08	11.32	12.00	12.46	12.47	12.49	12.34	12.26	1.91
Oct 31 84	9.34	9.84	10.21	11.05	11.49	11.59	11.68	11.65	11.53	2.34
Nov 30 84	8.71	9.16	9.55	10.43	11.14	11.55	11.57	11.68	11.56	2.86
Dec 31 84	8.04	8.49	9.18	9.93	11.10	11.45	11.50	11.67	11.57	3.46

Exhibit 1: Coupon Treasury Yield Curves: 1979-1990 (Continued)

	3 Mo	6 Mo	1 Yr	2 Yr	5 Yr	7 Yr	10 Yr	20 Yr	30 Yr	Slope 10-Yr minus 3-Mo
Jan 31 85	8.13	8.55	9.04	9.86	10.77	11.05	11.15	11.27	11.17	3.02
Feb 28 85	8.78	9.31	9.67	10.61	11.52	11.83	11.90	12.06	11.96	3.12
Mar 31 85	8.42	9.03	9.45	10.37	11.28	11.59	11.64	11.84	11.63	3.22
Apr 30 85	7.96	8.26	9.07	9.87	10.88	11.27	11.38	11.66	11.56	3.42
May 31 85	7.32	7.59	8.16	8.93	9.84	10.11	10.26	10.67	10.57	2.94
Jun 30 85	7.15	7.39	7.65	8.62	9.66	10.14	10.15	10.55	10.59	3.00
Jul 31 85	7.53	7.80	8.10	9.00	9.93	10.36	10.52	10.84	10.66	2.99
Aug 31 85	7.29	7.66	8.00	8.93	9.75	10.15	10.26	10.64	10.46	2.97
Sep 30 85	7.29	7.59	7.95	8.86	9.73	10.12	10.29	10.74	10.56	3.00
Oct 31 85	7.43	7.68	7.93	8.68	9.47	9.84	9.99	10.46	10.30	2.56
Nov 30 85	7.39	7.61	7.83	8.47	9.08	9.45	9.58	10.05	9.84	2.19
Dec 31 85	7.26	7.43	7.59	7.98	8.50	8.87	9.01	9.50	9.27	1.75
Jan 31 86	7.20	7.40	7.57	7.97	8.52	8.87	9.06	9.46	9.32	1.86
Feb 28 86	7.24	7.36	7.43	7.71	7.93	8.04	8.14	8.35	8.28	0.90
Mar 31 86	6.53	6.50	6.70	6.90	7.19	7.23	7.35	7.47	7.45	0.82
Apr 30 86	6.27	6.40	6.51	6.80	7.12	7.20	7.35	7.51	7.47	1.08
May 31 86	6.51	6.72	6.90	7.38	7.85	8.04	8.07	8.41	7.77	1.56
Jun 30 86	6.15	6.21	6.41	6.80	7.22	7.30	7.34	7.80	7.24	1.19
Jul 31 86	5.92	6.02	6.14	6.52	6.97	7.17	7.28	7.85	7.43	1.36
Aug 31 86	5.29	5.37	5.54	5.94	6.42	6.72	6.93	7.51	7.20	1.64
Sep 30 86	5.31	5.59	5.80	6.32	6.95	7.26	7.44	7.96	7.61	2.13
Oct 31 86	5.29	5.43	5.69	6.21	6.74	7.09	7.32	7.83	7.61	2.03
Nov 30 86	5.52	5.61	5.73	6.18	6.68	6.99	7.15	7.70	7.42	1.63
Dec 31 86	5.80	5.84	5.92	6.32	6.80	7.08	7.23	7.78	7.48	1.43
Jan 31 87	5.74	5.82	5.91	6.32	6.70	6.98	7.17	7.69	7.47	1.43
Feb 28 87	5.58	5.65	5.86	6.30	6.70	6.96	7.16	7.62	7.46	1.58
Mar 31 87	5.88	6.10	6.22	6.64	7.10	7.38	7.57	7.96	7.92	1.69
Apr 30 87	5.55	6.16	6.51	7.30	7.78	8.01	8.17	8.53	8.43	2.62
May 31 87	5.82	6.42	6.80	7.66	8.13	8.31	8.46	8.74	8.63	2.64
Jun 30 87	5.86	6.12	6.65	7.45	8.00	8.23	8.37	8.68	8.50	2.51
Jul 31 87	6.22	6.41	6.83	7.60	8.20	8.46	8.65	8.98	8.89	2.43
Aug 31 87	6.41	6.61	7.16	7.92	8.54	8.78	8.96	9.23	9.15	2.55
Sep 30 87	6.77	7.13	7.74	8.53	9.16	9.41	9.58	9.84	9.74	2.81
Oct 31 87	5.40	6.16	6.70	7.56	8.30	8.67	8.92	9.09	9.06	3.52
Nov 30 87	5.40	6.42	7.00	7.72	8.45	8.78	8.98	9.19	9.09	3.58
Dec 31 87	5.84	6.44	7.07	7.75	8.39	8.63	8.86	9.05	8.98	3.02
Jan 31 88	5.79	6.29	6.62	7.18	7.75	8.04	8.25	8.48	8.41	2.46
Feb 29 88	5.76	6.01	6.57	7.09	7.62	7.91	8.12	8.41	8.32	2.36
Mar 31 88	5.99	6.48	6.94	7.55	8.18	8.49	8.69	8.94	8.89	2.70
Apr 30 88	6.15	6.65	7.09	7.71	8.33	8.65	8.89	9.09	9.11	2.74
May 31 88	6.59	7.14	7.56	8.12	8.68	8.95	9.14	9.31	9.23	2.55
Jun 30 88	6.74	7.02	7.43	7.96	8.39	8.65	8.80	8.99	8.85	2.06
Jul 31 88	7.15	7.47	7.86	8.32	8.69	8.94	9.09	9.24	9.19	1.94
Aug 31 88	7.50	7.87	8.25	8.66	8.94	9.11	9.23	9.27	9.31	1.73
Sep 30 88	7.47	7.83	8.11	8.41	8.58	8.73	8.83	8.96	8.96	1.36
Oct 31 88	7.59	7.86	8.04	8.18	8.35	8.51	8.63	8.71	8.74	1.04
Nov 30 88	8.07	8.39	8.58	8.79	8.90	8.99	9.04	9.07	9.06	0.97
Dec 31 88	8.36	8.61	9.01	9.13	9.13	9.20	9.13	9.08	8.99	0.77
Jan 31 89	8.64	8.88	9.00	9.09	9.04	9.03	8.99	8.90	8.84	0.35
Feb 28 89	8.96	9.17	9.34	9.43	9.38	9.35	9.27	9.23	9.09	0.31
Mar 31 89	9.18	9.49	9.57	9.64	9.46	9.36	9.27	9.18	9.09	0.09
Apr 30 89	8.79	9.04	9.19	9.28	9.12	9.10	9.08	9.02	8.96	0.29
May 31 89	8.90	8.83	8.84	8.80	8.64	8.62	8.61	8.65	8.60	-0.29
Jun 30 89	8.24	8.13	8.09	8.03	8.00	8.08	8.08	8.13	8.03	-0.16
Jul 31 89	8.06	7.83	7.62	7.42	7.45	7.57	7.72	7.90	7.86	-0.34
Aug 31 89	8.15	8.20	8.27	8.37	8.26	8.28	8.25	8.32	8.19	0.10
Sep 30 89	8.15	8.29	8.45	8.44	8.33	8.35	8.28	8.36	8.23	0.13
Oct 31 89	8.03	7.99	7.89	7.86	7.84	7.90	7.90	8.00	7.90	-0.13
Nov 30 89	7.80	7.76	7.69	7.73	7.72	7.81	7.83	7.98	7.89	0.03
Dec 31 89	7.82	7.99	7.75	7.83	7.84	7.96	7.91	8.08	7.97	0.09
Jan 31 90	7.99	8.11	8.06	8.25	8.32	8.37	8.40	8.58	8.45	0.41
Feb 28 90	8.02	8.13	8.10	8.40	8.45	8.53	8.50	8.60	8.53	0.48
Mar 31 90	8.03	8.22	8.32	8.61	8.64	8.69	8.63	8.76	8.62	0.60
Apr 30 90	8.02	8.39	8.54	8.93	9.02	9.04	9.02	9.11	8.99	1.00
May 31 90	8.01	8.15	8.21	8.47	8.56	8.63	8.59	8.70	8.58	0.58
Jun 30 90	7.98	8.00	8.03	8.21	8.35	8.45	8.41	8.51	8.41	0.43
Jul 31 90	7.72	7.69	7.70	7.87	8.11	8.27	8.34	8.48	8.41	0.62
Aug 31 90	7.60	7.74	7.75	8.06	8.51	8.75	8.85	9.01	8.99	1.25
Sep 30 90	7.35	7.52	7.66	7.98	8.46	8.70	8.81	9.05	8.94	1.46
Oct 31 90	7.33	7.46	7.42	7.76	8.24	8.50	8.65	8.74	8.78	1.32
Nov 30 90	7.24	7.36	7.30	7.52	7.91	8.16	8.25	8.28	8.39	1.01
Dec 31 90	6.63	6.74	6.80	7.13	7.64	7.98	8.06	8.03	8.24	1.43

term rates, dropped dramatically. By August 31, 1980, after substantial easing by the Federal Reserve in the Spring and early Summer, the 3-month Treasury rate stood at 8.89% (down 609 basis points from April 1980) and the 10-year Treasury rate was 10.62% (down 198 basis points in the 4-month period). The yield curve went from being substantially inverted (–238 basis point spread) to significantly upward sloping (173 basis point spread).

Following the brief recession, interest rates again rose substantially and remained at very high levels throughout the remainder of 1980 and most of 1981. By June 30, 1981, 3-month Treasury rates reached 15.54% (up 665 basis points in 10 months), and 10-year rates stood at 13.29% (up 267 basis points). The yield curve had again inverted, with the slope changing by 398 basis points to – 225 basis points.

Interest rates fell somewhat during the subsequent recession, which lasted until late 1982, although both long-term and short-term Treasury rates remained at double-digit levels during most of the period. In early July 1982, amid the turmoil created by the impending Third World debt crisis, the shakiness of the United States' banking system (Penn Square Bank had just failed), and a still slumping domestic economy (the unemployment rate would soon reach 10%), Federal Reserve policy became more lenient and rates again fell rapidly. By the end of December 1982, 3-month Treasury rates had fallen to 8.51% (down 481 basis points), and 10-year rates fell to 10.69% (down 363 basis points from July 31 levels).

From late 1982 until early 1984 interest rates remained fairly stable, especially by comparison to the mid-1979 to mid-1982 period. On January 31, 1984, the three-month Treasury rate was 9.20%, and the ten-year Treasury was 11.65%. Four months later, in May of 1984, Continental Illinois' problems came to a head and interest rates on 3-month and 10-year Treasuries went to 10.10% (up 90 basis points) and 13.91% (up 226 basis points), respectively. From those levels, interest rates fell dramatically during the remainder of 1984, during 1985, and during the first eight months of

1986. At the end of August 1986, the 3-month rate was 5.29% (down 481 basis points from May 1984), and the 10-year rate was 6.93% (down 698 basis points). Both the level and the degree of upward slope of the term structure changed incredibly in that two-year period from May 1984 to August 1986. From August 1986 to September 1987, interest rates reversed their downward course and increased by 148 basis points on 3-month Treasury bills, and by 265 basis points on 10-year Treasury notes.

The stock market crash of October 1987 caused a general "flight to quality" reaction by investors and led the Federal Reserve to increase liquidity in the financial system. These actions resulted in an immediate decline in market yields on Treasury securities, as well as a significant steepening of the Treasury yield curve (from a 281 basis point difference between the 10-year and 3-month Treasury rates on September 30, 1987, to a difference of 352 basis points on October 31, 1987).

From October 1987 to April 1989, long-term Treasury rates were remarkably stable, while short-term Treasury rates steadily increased. During this period, the 3-month rate increased by 339 basis points (to 8.79%), whereas the 10-year rate increased by only 16 basis points (to 9.08%), resulting in a very flat term structure. Interest rates generally fell throughout the remainder of 1989, with this period being characterized by very flat and often inverted Treasury yield curves.

During late 1989 and 1990, amid recognition that the United States' economy was slowing and entering a recession, the Federal Reserve embarked on a policy of easier money and credit. As a result, interest rates generally declined, with short-term rates falling more than long-term rates, again resulting in a more steep yield curve. The general movements in the level of Treasury rates as well as changes in the slope of the term structure during the 1979–1990 period are more easily seen in the time series of three-month and ten-year Treasury rates found in Exhibit 2.

As interest rates decrease, prepayment rates on mortgages increase. Additionally, prepayment rates are positively related to the

Exhibit 2: 3-Month and 10-Year Treasury Rates: 1979 to 1990

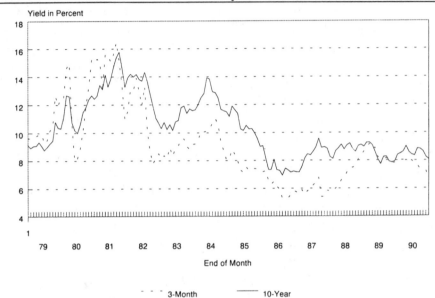

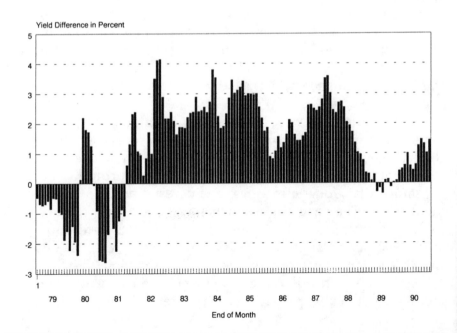

Exhibit 3: GNMAs: Annualized Percentage Paydowns from Prepayments

Month	GNMA Mortgage Coupon								30-Year Fixed Mortgage Rate %	Avg Refinancing Rate Prior Three Months
	8.00	9.00	10.00	11.00	12.00	13.00	14.00	15.00		
Jan 84	2.4	2.1	2.0	2.4	1.0	3.9	8.1	14.9	12.82	12.98
Feb 84	2.2	2.2	1.9	2.4	1.1	3.9	8.8	16.5	13.00	12.98
Mar 84	2.7	2.5	2.5	3.0	1.1	5.2	11.5	18.7	13.52	13.11
Apr 84	3.1	2.8	2.4	3.1	1.3	5.5	13.0	19.2	13.78	13.43
May 84	3.5	2.5	2.2	3.1	1.5	6.0	13.7	21.0	14.90	14.06
Jun 84	3.0	2.2	2.1	2.8	1.4	4.7	11.8	16.6	14.67	14.45
Jul 84	2.8	2.2	1.8	2.5	1.2	4.2	9.1	15.1	14.19	14.58
Aug 84	2.3	2.3	1.9	2.7	1.5	4.0	9.6	14.1	14.08	14.31
Sep 84	1.8	1.8	1.5	2.0	1.3	3.4	7.8	10.5	13.70	13.99
Oct 84	2.2	2.1	2.0	2.8	1.6	3.6	7.0	12.1	13.11	13.63
Nov 84	2.1	1.7	1.3	2.2	1.7	3.5	6.8	11.2	12.74	13.18
Dec 84	2.1	1.8	2.2	2.6	1.9	3.2	7.5	11.8	12.74	12.86
Jan 85	2.4	2.2	1.9	3.0	3.1	6.8	10.8	17.4	12.53	12.67
Feb 85	2.3	2.1	2.2	2.7	2.9	5.9	11.8	18.1	13.13	12.80
Mar 85	2.9	2.5	2.2	3.6	3.9	7.2	15.7	22.3	12.84	12.83
Apr 85	3.5	3.0	2.5	3.6	4.9	9.3	18.8	26.7	12.68	12.88
May 85	3.5	2.9	3.1	3.9	4.5	9.1	17.0	26.9	11.59	12.37
Jun 85	3.6	3.2	2.5	3.7	5.5	9.3	18.2	24.1	11.37	11.88
Jul 85	4.3	3.8	3.4	4.9	6.4	13.0	23.6	28.5	11.76	11.57
Aug 85	5.1	4.4	3.9	5.7	8.5	19.7	40.8	35.1	11.60	11.57
Sep 85	4.7	4.1	3.5	5.4	8.6	19.7	38.3	35.8	11.61	11.65
Oct 85	5.1	4.4	4.4	5.6	8.9	18.7	37.1	37.5	11.38	11.53
Nov 85	4.0	3.5	3.2	4.8	6.9	15.6	24.6	24.4	10.77	11.25
Dec 85	4.4	3.9	4.4	4.8	8.0	18.1	32.2	31.1	10.09	10.74
Jan 86	3.8	3.8	3.8	5.5	7.9	18.3	28.0	26.2	10.26	10.37
Feb 86	3.7	3.6	4.3	5.1	13.0	25.9	31.3	25.9	9.50	9.94
Mar 86	4.8	4.6	4.3	9.4	23.4	39.7	45.6	40.4	9.29	9.68
Apr 86	5.6	5.5	7.0	10.9	27.6	44.4	53.5	41.0	9.17	9.32
May 86	6.5	6.2	6.1	15.3	36.2	46.6	57.5	43.7	10.01	9.49
Jun 86	7.8	7.6	8.2	17.6	37.8	45.7	52.1	41.5	9.87	9.68
Jul 86	8.9	9.0	9.4	19.7	43.3	49.7	52.9	45.2	9.75	9.87
Aug 86	9.4	9.0	9.3	21.3	46.0	52.1	58.5	46.2	9.07	9.56
Sep 86	9.4	9.0	9.2	23.0	47.3	51.3	54.9	45.7	9.38	9.40
Oct 86	9.4	9.2	10.0	23.6	45.3	50.4	53.4	44.2	9.15	9.20
Nov 86	8.1	8.0	8.9	20.8	38.7	40.1	40.9	34.1	8.47	9.00
Dec 86	9.1	9.2	10.3	23.3	40.7	43.9	47.2	40.0	8.77	8.79
Jan 87	6.8	7.4	9.4	21.5	36.1	40.7	45.5	37.4	8.50	8.58
Feb 87	6.7	7.1	12.0	24.7	36.2	35.1	35.1	29.0	8.45	8.57
Mar 87	8.4	9.1	17.1	34.5	44.4	42.7	39.9	33.9	8.69	8.54
Apr 87	9.8	11.2	18.4	37.4	44.7	40.9	38.5	31.2	9.78	8.97
May 87	5.5	3.3	8.5	27.5	40.5	40.8	42.5	34.0	10.07	9.51
Jun 87	6.8	4.6	8.1	21.7	36.6	39.9	38.5	35.8	9.85	9.90

Exhibit 3: GNMAs: Annualized Percentage Paydowns from Prepayments (Continued)

Month	GNMA Mortgage Coupon								30-Year Fixed Mortgage Rate %	Avg Refinancing Rate Prior Three Months
	8.00	9.00	10.00	11.00	12.00	13.00	14.00	15.00		
Jul 87	4.8	3.3	6.6	17.7	30.8	36.9	39.7	35.6	9.85	9.92
Aug 87	3.7	3.0	5.5	13.4	24.6	29.9	30.7	29.1	10.04	9.91
Sep 87	4.9	3.6	5.4	11.8	23.1	29.4	27.2	29.1	10.70	10.19
Oct 87	3.4	2.8	4.6	10.6	19.6	24.5	23.7	24.6	10.36	10.36
Nov 87	2.8	2.3	3.8	8.7	15.8	20.1	22.0	19.9	10.12	10.39
Dec 87	6.3	3.2	4.4	9.5	18.2	24.0	23.2	23.9	10.11	10.19
Jan 88	2.3	2.1	3.4	7.7	15.1	18.6	16.2	16.5	9.50	9.91
Feb 88	2.6	2.3	4.0	8.2	16.5	19.6	21.7	18.8	9.43	9.68
Mar 88	4.2	3.8	5.4	13.0	23.6	25.1	25.8	23.4	9.76	9.56
Apr 88	3.7	3.9	5.7	16.3	26.2	27.7	26.8	21.4	9.94	9.70
May 88	4.1	4.4	6.4	17.2	28.3	28.2	27.4	23.8	10.20	9.96
Jun 88	5.8	5.1	7.2	16.3	27.4	29.1	28.0	24.6	9.83	9.99
Jul 88	4.1	4.5	6.5	13.6	22.3	24.9	22.4	21.3	10.15	10.06
Aug 88	4.5	4.7	7.0	15.4	25.5	27.0	26.9	26.9	10.24	10.07
Sep 88	5.2	4.6	5.3	12.8	20.1	21.8	20.6	20.6	9.91	10.10
Oct 88	3.8	4.3	6.8	11.9	19.0	19.7	18.5	18.9	9.62	10.10
Nov 88	3.9	3.9	5.9	11.0	17.9	20.0	20.5	19.6	10.05	9.92
Dec 88	4.8	4.5	4.5	12.5	18.7	20.1	17.8	19.6	10.48	9.86
Jan 89	3.2	3.9	6.0	9.7	16.1	16.4	17.0	16.7	10.25	10.26
Feb 89	2.9	3.2	4.8	8.4	14.8	17.3	16.2	16.7	10.57	10.43
Mar 89	4.4	4.4	4.5	10.1	16.9	19.4	17.9	18.4	10.81	10.54
Apr 89	3.5	4.4	6.1	9.3	15.2	18.6	22.2	22.6	10.58	10.65
May 89	4.0	4.7	7.8	10.3	16.1	20.4	25.6	22.0	10.09	10.49
Jun 89	4.8	4.8	5.0	11.1	15.9	18.7	25.6	23.0	9.70	10.12
Jul 89	4.1	5.0	8.5	11.7	15.6	16.7	21.7	21.3	9.33	9.70
Aug 89	6.9	6.0	8.9	15.3	20.4	19.6	24.8	23.2	9.90	9.64
Sep 89	4.7	5.6	6.0	15.1	20.3	19.7	17.9	19.3	9.88	9.70
Oct 89	4.7	5.3	5.3	16.4	24.0	22.1	22.7	22.4	9.47	9.75
Nov 89	4.8	5.2	7.4	14.9	20.2	20.5	17.6	18.0	9.42	9.59
Dec 89	6.4	6.6	8.2	12.1	20.3	16.3	17.6	18.2	9.45	9.44
Jan 90	5.7	6.3	6.8	11.7	19.4	16.2	NA	15.6	9.78	9.54
Feb 90	5.1	5.7	6.4	9.6	16.6	11.8	NA	13.4	9.89	9.70
Mar 90	6.4	6.7	7.6	11.3	19.6	15.7	NA	17.1	9.97	9.88
Apr 90	6.5	6.8	6.9	10.9	18.4	16.0	NA	15.1	10.33	10.06
May 90	6.8	7.7	8.4	11.1	17.0	17.6	NA	16.7	9.84	10.04
Jun 90	6.7	7.3	7.9	10.5	16.6	14.1	NA	16.2	9.67	9.94
Jul 90	6.9	7.7	8.6	10.2	16.2	15.0	NA	15.2	9.45	9.65
Aug 90	7.5	7.7	8.7	11.3	18.3	15.0	NA	18.0	9.80	9.64
Sep 90	6.4	6.6	6.6	9.1	14.8	10.6	NA	14.1	9.78	9.67
Oct 90	6.6	5.8	7.6	9.8	15.8	14.3	NA	16.3	9.76	9.77
Nov 90	5.7	5.7	6.0	8.5	13.0	12.8	NA	13.8	9.49	9.67
Dec 90	5.5	5.7	5.5	7.9	12.5	12.1	NA	13.8	9.27	9.50

Source: Salomon Brothers, "Mortgage Security Prepayment Rate Profile," Monthly.

strength of the economy, particularly to housing starts. Exhibit 3 shows how prepayment rates changed dramatically during the 1984–1990 period. As interest rates fell sharply from May 1984 to August 1986, prepayment rates on GNMA 13s changed from 6% to 52% annually. At the same time, prepayment rates on lower coupon GNMA 8s moved from 3.5% to 9.4%. Not surprisingly, people with lower rates on their fixed-rate mortgages are less inclined to pay them off early.

The top panel of Exhibit 4 displays the typical relationship between prepayments on fixed-rate mortgages and the average market refinancing rate on alternative mortgages. When refinancing rates are higher than a borrower's mortgage rate, he has little financial incentive to refinance. Not unexpectedly, the prepayment "curve" for GNMA 13% mortgage-backed securities (backed by mortgages with fixed interest rates of approximately 13.5%) is very flat for refinancing rates higher than 13%. Prepayments are at a fairly low level (4% to 5%), and do not change very much as mortgage rates rise further.

When refinancing rates fall, however, to levels 1% to 1.5% below the rate on borrowers' existing mortgages, a significant refinancing incentive exists, leading to dramatically higher levels of prepayments. Note the steep slope of the prepayment curve as refinancing rates fall to levels between 1.5% and 3.5% below borrowers' mortgage rates. At some point, at very low levels of market mortgage rates relative to the rate on borrowers' existing loans, prepayments increase much more slowly, usually peaking near the 50% (annualized) level.

The bottom panel of Exhibit 4 displays an interesting prepayment phenomenon most commonly referred to as "prepayment burnout" or "premium burnout." Since a pool of mortgages represents a heterogeneous mix of individual borrowers, not every borrower in the pool will have the same financial incentive to prepay at any given time. Some people may be less financially sophisticated than others. Some may view refinancing as a nuisance and assign it a higher cost than others (perhaps valuing their time

Exhibit 4: GNMA 13 Prepayment History

Prepayments are a Function
of Interest Rates

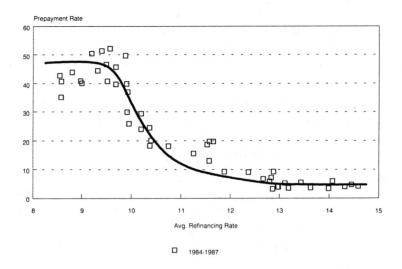

☐   1984-1987

An Example of Prepayment Burnout

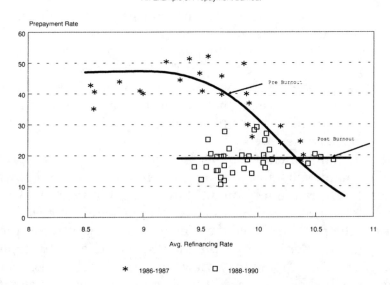

*   1986-1987   ☐   1988-1990

Note: Monthly observations. Data are not seasonally adjusted.

more than others). Some borrowers, whose property values or incomes have fallen, may find it difficult to qualify for a new loan. Borrowers whose loan size is small relative to their annual incomes may be less motivated to refinance than those whose monthly mortgage payments consume a higher percentage of their incomes.

Whatever the reason, it is clear that different borrowers face differing costs of refinancing. When a pool of mortgages encounters its first period of significant refinancing incentive (for GNMA 13s such a period existed in 1986 and 1987), prepayments usually reach a very high level as those borrowers who are more apt to prepay do so. After a period of time, the remaining borrowers represented in the pool are those who have (on average) a lower propensity to prepay. As a result, the pool is said to experience prepayment burnout as prepayment rates reach a much lower, stable level. The pool's prepayment rate is now much less sensitive to changes in refinancing rates than it was prior to the "burnout" period. Notice from the bottom panel of Exhibit 4 that during the 1988 to 1990 period GNMA 13 prepayment rates were very stable at around 20% (annualized), in spite of the fact that refinancing rates (between 9.5 and 10.5%) were significantly lower than the 13.5% coupon rates on the underlying mortgages. Note how much faster the GNMA 13s prepaid during the 1986 and 1987 period for similar levels of refinancing rates. Also note that during the 1986 to 1987 period, GNMA 13 prepayment rates were much more sensitive to changes in refinancing rates, increasing from 20% to 40% (annualized) as refinancing rates fell from 10.5% to 9.5%.

Interest rates, mortgage coupon rates, the health of the economy, the age of a mortgage (seasoning), the time of the year (seasonality), and past refinancing incentives (burnout) all play important roles in determining the level of prepayments on fixed-rate mortgages. Investors and mortgage lenders should understand the relationships between prepayments and these key variables in order to assess the potential risks and returns of their mortgage portfolios.

Futures Contracts and Prices[1]

Interest rate futures contracts are actively traded for four instruments: (1) twenty-year Treasury bonds, (2) ninety-one-day Eurodollar time deposits, (3) ninety-one-day Treasury bills, and (4) ten-year Treasury notes. By far the most liquid markets are the twenty-year Treasury bond ("T-bonds") and the ninety-one-day Eurodollar ("Euros") markets. End-of-month futures prices for T-bonds and Euros for the 1984–1990 period are given in Exhibit 5.

As an example of the terms of a futures contract, let us examine the T-bond contract in more detail. The twenty-year Treasury bond futures contract is an agreement between a buyer (the "long") and a seller (the "short") to trade a long-term Treasury bond at a future date (the "maturity date") at a price that is set today. Contracts are traded for only four maturity dates per year—March, June, September, and December. However, typically there are ten or eleven different contract maturities being traded at any point in time, covering quarterly futures maturities up to 2.5 to 2.75 years out from the present time.

For convenience in pricing and in computing yields, it is assumed that the bond delivered will have twenty years to maturity at delivery and have an 8% coupon rate. However, in actuality the seller has certain options on the time to maturity of the bond delivered, on its coupon rate, and on the date during the delivery month when delivery actually occurs. In particular, the seller may deliver any long-term U.S. government Treasury bond that is not callable for at least fifteen years from the futures maturity date. Of course, bonds that pay higher coupons are more valuable, so the futures invoice price is multiplied on delivery by an "adjustment factor" that reflects the coupon and maturity of the bonds actually delivered. The adjustment factor is the present value (per $1 par) of the bond's cash flows using a discount rate of 8%. In determin-

---

[1] This subsection contains basic institutional material on futures contracts. The next three subsections do the same for options on futures, interest rate swaps, and interest rate caps and floors, respectively. Readers familiar with these instruments should proceed to the next section.

Exhibit 5

20-Year Treasury Bond Futures Prices

End of	Near Ct Yield	Near	2nd	3rd	4th
Jan 84	11.84%	70.81	70.22	69.66	69.16
Feb 84	12.19%	68.84	68.22	67.72	67.25
Mar 84 •	12.69%	66.22	65.66	65.16	64.72
Apr 84	12.99%	64.69	64.13	63.69	63.31
May 84 •	13.97%	60.16	59.47	58.97	58.59
Jun 84 •	14.09%	59.63	59.00	58.56	58.22
Jul 84	13.03%	64.50	63.88	63.41	63.03
Aug 84	12.77%	65.81	65.16	64.63	64.19
Sep 84 •	12.49%	67.22	66.63	66.16	65.75
Oct 84	11.85%	70.78	70.03	69.44	68.91
Nov 84	11.70%	71.63	70.91	70.31	69.78
Dec 84 •	11.80%	71.06	70.34	69.72	69.19
Jan 85	11.44%	73.19	72.09	71.28	70.59
Feb 85	12.19%	68.88	67.88	67.09	66.47
Mar 85 •	12.03%	69.72	68.78	67.97	67.22
Apr 85	11.85%	70.75	69.72	68.81	68.00
May 85 •	10.78%	77.34	76.41	75.47	74.63
Jun 85 •	10.83%	77.06	76.06	75.09	74.16
Jul 85	11.12%	75.19	74.13	73.16	72.28
Aug 85 •	10.82%	77.13	76.03	75.00	74.06
Sep 85 •	11.08%	75.59	74.47	73.44	72.47
Oct 85	10.61%	78.53	77.19	76.03	74.97
Nov 85 •	10.16%	81.66	80.50	79.47	78.53
Dec 85 •	9.69%	85.22	84.25	83.38	82.63
Jan 86	9.64%	85.16	84.09	83.13	82.28
Feb 86	8.55%	94.81	94.00	93.31	92.72
Mar 86 •	7.77%	102.31	101.63	101.00	100.44
Apr 86	7.92%	100.75	100.00	99.19	98.41
May 86 •	8.65%	93.88	93.09	92.34	91.56
Jun 86 •	8.04%	99.56	98.75	97.97	97.19
Jul 86	8.22%	97.81	97.00	96.16	95.31
Aug 86 •	7.76%	102.41	101.72	100.81	99.91
Sep 86 •	8.36%	96.56	95.66	94.66	93.75
Oct 86	8.20%	98.09	97.19	96.19	95.22
Nov 86 •	8.03%	99.72	98.75	97.78	96.81
Dec 86 •	8.19%	98.19	97.19	96.19	95.19
Jan 87	8.03%	99.69	98.78	97.88	97.00
Feb 87	7.86%	101.44	100.44	99.50	98.59
Mar 87 •	8.16%	98.47	97.44	96.44	95.50
Apr 87	8.74%	93.06	92.09	91.22	90.41
May 87 •	8.85%	92.06	91.06	90.16	89.31
Jun 87 •	8.92%	91.50	90.56	89.69	88.84

91-Day Eurodollar Prices

End of	Near Ct Yield	Near	2nd	3rd	4th
Jan 84	10.04%	89.96	89.58	89.24	88.94
Feb 84	10.29%	89.71	89.19	88.81	88.50
Mar 84 •	11.28%	88.72	88.25	87.88	87.59
Apr 84	11.46%	88.54	87.96	87.51	87.13
May 84 •	11.97%	88.03	86.49	85.70	85.28
Jun 84 •	13.13%	86.87	86.05	85.61	85.30
Jul 84	12.03%	87.97	87.50	87.11	86.82
Aug 84	11.92%	88.08	87.62	87.27	86.99
Sep 84 •	11.56%	88.44	88.14	87.82	87.54
Oct 84	10.32%	89.68	89.28	88.87	88.49
Nov 84	9.46%	90.54	89.93	89.47	89.07
Dec 84 •	9.52%	90.48	89.88	89.38	88.95
Jan 85	8.93%	91.07	90.57	90.03	89.57
Feb 85	9.69%	90.31	89.45	88.86	88.44
Mar 85 •	9.77%	90.23	89.59	89.16	88.79
Apr 85	8.95%	91.05	90.29	89.75	89.31
May 85 •	7.76%	92.24	91.70	91.22	90.81
Jun 85 •	7.93%	92.07	91.58	91.15	90.79
Jul 85	8.36%	91.64	91.15	90.71	90.31
Aug 85 •	8.14%	91.86	91.52	91.12	90.72
Sep 85 •	8.23%	91.77	91.38	90.97	90.60
Oct 85	7.95%	92.05	91.83	91.46	91.09
Nov 85 •	8.03%	91.97	92.00	91.82	91.53
Dec 85 •	7.75%	92.25	92.13	91.92	91.66
Jan 86	7.88%	92.12	92.02	91.84	91.61
Feb 86	7.76%	92.24	92.39	92.36	92.19
Mar 86 •	6.97%	93.03	93.06	92.96	92.80
Apr 86	6.75%	93.25	93.26	93.13	92.90
May 86 •	7.07%	92.93	92.84	92.67	92.41
Jun 86 •	6.55%	93.45	93.35	93.14	92.84
Jul 86	6.43%	93.57	93.58	93.48	93.28
Aug 86 •	5.71%	94.29	94.36	94.27	94.08
Sep 86 •	5.99%	94.01	93.89	93.66	94.31
Oct 86	5.89%	94.11	94.10	93.91	93.61
Nov 86 •	6.03%	93.97	94.07	94.01	93.82
Dec 86 •	6.11%	93.89	93.86	93.76	93.57
Jan 87	6.31%	93.69	93.77	93.74	93.62
Feb 87	6.42%	93.58	93.67	93.66	93.57
Mar 87 •	6.65%	93.35	93.33	93.28	93.16
Apr 87	7.39%	92.61	92.31	92.12	91.95
May 87 •	7.26%	92.74	92.18	91.87	91.65
Jun 87 •	7.42%	92.58	92.31	92.09	91.89

Exhibit 5 (Continued)

20-Year Treasury Bond Futures Prices

End of	Near Ct Yield	Near	2nd	3rd	4th
Jul 87	9.15%	89.50	88.50	87.56	86.69
Aug 87	9.40%	87.50	86.53	85.63	84.78
Sep 87 *	10.16%	81.69	80.88	80.06	79.34
Oct 87	9.39%	87.56	86.59	85.78	85.06
Nov 87	9.38%	87.66	86.75	85.88	85.09
Dec 87 *	9.34%	87.97	86.94	86.06	85.25
Jan 88	8.65%	93.91	92.94	92.06	91.25
Feb 88	8.56%	94.66	93.63	92.66	91.78
Mar 88 *	9.09%	90.06	89.03	88.06	87.19
Apr 88	9.35%	87.91	86.94	86.06	85.28
May 88	9.61%	85.81	84.91	84.03	83.22
Jun 88 *	9.24%	88.75	87.88	87.06	86.28
Jul 88	9.62%	85.75	85.03	84.38	83.75
Aug 88	9.58%	86.06	85.50	84.94	84.38
Sep 88 *	9.24%	88.75	88.25	87.75	87.28
Oct 88	8.33%	91.41	90.84	90.31	89.84
Nov 88	9.26%	88.47	88.09	87.72	87.41
Dec 88 *	9.20%	89.13	88.81	88.56	88.34
Jan 89	9.00%	90.81	90.63	90.47	90.38
Feb 89	9.32%	88.09	88.19	88.19	88.19
Mar 89 *	9.29%	88.41	88.50	88.56	88.59
Apr 89	9.07%	90.19	90.09	90.00	89.94
May 89	8.74%	93.06	93.00	92.91	92.78
Jun 89 *	8.21%	97.94	97.78	97.56	97.34
Jul 89	8.03%	99.75	99.56	99.25	98.91
Aug 89	8.39%	96.25	96.22	96.03	95.78
Sep 89 *	8.43%	95.84	95.78	95.59	95.38
Oct 89	8.07%	99.34	99.31	99.09	98.84
Nov 89	8.05%	99.47	99.47	99.25	98.94
Dec 89 *	8.14%	98.66	98.53	98.31	98.03
Jan 90	8.61%	94.25	94.06	93.91	93.72
Feb 90	8.71%	93.31	93.19	93.03	92.84
Mar 90 *	8.88%	91.88	91.72	91.56	91.44
Apr 90	9.24%	88.81	88.63	88.47	88.31
May 90	8.76%	92.91	92.72	92.47	92.28
Jun 90 *	8.60%	94.34	94.03	93.78	93.53
Jul 90	8.56%	94.69	94.38	94.09	93.81
Aug 90	9.20%	89.16	88.81	88.44	88.06
Sep 90 *	9.17%	89.38	88.97	88.59	88.25
Oct 90	8.97%	91.09	90.69	90.25	89.84
Nov 90	8.54%	94.91	94.56	94.19	93.78
Dec 90 *	8.45%	95.72	95.28	94.84	94.13

91-Day Eurodollar Prices

End of	Near Ct Yield	Near	2nd	3rd	4th
Jul 87	7.29%	92.71	92.31	92.01	91.76
Aug 87	7.29%	92.71	92.07	91.73	91.46
Sep 87 *	8.60%	91.40	91.02	90.74	90.53
Oct 87	7.58%	92.42	92.22	91.74	91.38
Nov 87	7.68%	92.32	92.33	92.03	91.69
Dec 87 *	7.56%	92.44	92.20	91.86	91.52
Jan 88	7.04%	92.96	92.76	92.47	92.19
Feb 88	6.87%	93.13	93.00	92.75	92.47
Mar 88 *	7.28%	92.72	92.42	92.13	91.87
Apr 88	7.59%	92.41	92.03	91.76	91.56
May 88	7.77%	92.23	91.69	91.36	91.16
Jun 88 *	7.96%	92.04	91.70	91.52	91.36
Jul 88	8.49%	91.52	91.19	91.14	90.99
Aug 88	8.67%	91.33	90.81	90.86	90.69
Sep 88 *	8.78%	91.22	91.33	91.19	91.02
Oct 88	8.59%	91.41	91.58	91.51	91.37
Nov 88	9.15%	90.85	91.03	90.99	90.98
Dec 88 *	9.38%	90.62	90.56	90.53	90.35
Jan 89	9.54%	90.46	90.43	90.45	90.35
Feb 89	10.27%	89.73	89.47	89.51	89.64
Mar 89 *	10.71%	89.29	89.13	89.04	89.39
Apr 89	9.85%	90.15	90.25	90.21	90.40
May 89	9.46%	90.54	90.91	90.94	91.00
Jun 89 *	8.53%	91.47	91.66	91.79	91.69
Jul 89	8.21%	91.79	92.21	92.33	92.24
Aug 89	8.69%	91.11	91.30	91.50	91.44
Sep 89 *	8.95%	91.05	91.29	91.39	91.33
Oct 89	8.37%	91.63	92.02	92.00	91.88
Nov 89	8.37%	91.63	92.21	92.31	92.21
Dec 89 *	8.02%	91.98	92.16	92.15	91.92
Jan 90	8.35%	91.65	91.60	91.50	91.27
Feb 90	8.37%	91.63	91.59	91.49	91.30
Mar 90 *	8.69%	91.31	91.19	91.02	90.96
Apr 90	8.81%	91.19	90.92	90.71	90.61
May 90	8.40%	91.60	91.58	91.47	91.33
Jun 90 *	8.16%	91.84	91.82	91.79	91.64
Jul 90	7.89%	92.11	92.21	92.24	92.09
Aug 90	8.01%	91.99	92.08	92.01	91.86
Sep 90 *	8.06%	91.94	91.99	91.88	91.65
Oct 90	7.89%	92.11	92.32	92.26	92.08
Nov 90	8.22%	91.78	92.30	92.47	92.44
Dec 90 *	7.20%	92.80	92.89	92.78	92.47

* Old near contract expired. All contracts move one column left (nearer maturity).

ing which bond to deliver, the seller computes the price received (from the futures price and the adjustment factors) and the costs (from cash market prices) of all bonds eligible for delivery, and chooses the bond that is "cheapest to deliver"(i.e., the bond that maximizes profits for the seller). The advantage of this delivery procedure is that many bonds are eligible for delivery, which eliminates the possibility of someone buying all deliverable bonds and preventing delivery—a "short squeeze." Additionally, the seller may choose the day during the delivery month on which to make a delivery.

Most (about 97%) futures contracts do *not* result in delivery, since buyer and seller offset their positions by opposite trades (buyer sells and seller buys back) prior to the first day of the delivery month. However, the possibility of delivery makes the value of the futures contract reflect the provisions of delivery. Thus, since the seller has valuable options on the deliverable bond's coupon and maturity, as well as on the date of delivery, the price of a bond futures contract must be lower than a corresponding cash bond (without options). With these options and delivery risks, one might wonder whether or not the twenty-year Treasury bond futures contract's price moves closely with twenty-year bond prices. To check this, actual Treasury bond futures prices for the contract nearest maturity were used to find the yield on a twenty-year, 8% bond. The results are in the first column of Exhibit 5, corresponding to the prices in column 2. These yields were then regressed on the twenty-year cash bond yields in Exhibit 1 (for the 1984 to 1990 period), with the following statistical results:

Bond Futures Rate = 0.33% + 0.985 [20-year Treasury Coupon Rate]
$$(t=3.2) \ (t=141.5)$$

$R^2 = .996$ Correlation = .998

Standard Error of Residual = .10%.

Futures Yield minus 20-year Cash Yield:

Range: 2 basis points to 41 basis points

(Avg = 19 basis points)

Thus, despite the seller's options on delivery, the Treasury bond futures contract has a correlation of .998 with the 20-year Treasury rate. This is reassuring, and shows that little is lost in viewing a long or short position in T-bond futures as being synonymous with a long or short position in twenty-year Treasury bonds.

Futures contracts specify a standardized quantity to be delivered per contract. For example, twenty-year Treasury bond futures and ten-year Treasury note futures both have a standard delivery amount of $100,000 par. In contrast, the ninety-one-day Eurodollar contract and the ninety-one-day Treasury bill contract require delivery of $1 million par. The reason for this difference in par amounts is that the price volatilities of the ninety-one-day instruments are much smaller per dollar of par than those for the ten-year and twenty-year instruments (which have much longer durations). Futures contracts' quantities are set large enough so that typical daily gains and losses of a single contract are economically meaningful and of somewhat similar sizes in all markets. The typical daily gain or loss on one futures contract is usually $300 to $1,000, with good faith margin deposits required that are about four times the typical daily move ($1,200–$4,000).

Price quotes in Treasury bond and Treasury note futures are expressed as percents of par. Thus, given a standard quantity of $100,000 par, the T-bond futures price of 98.47% on March 31, 1987 (from Exhibit 5) represents a value of $98,470 for the T-bond contract. If one T-bond contract were sold short on March 31, 1987, at a 98.47% price, and bought back (offset) on May 31, 1987, at a price of 92.06% par, the gain would have been $6,410 ($98,470 $92,060). Of course, when rates fall, bond prices rise, and a short loses. To see this, note that one might have sold short the near T-bond contract on December 31, 1985, at 85.22% par and bought back on February 28, 1986, at 94.81% par, for a loss of $9,590 per contract. In T-bonds and T-notes, one price "point" is 1% of $100,000, or $1,000.

In ninety-one-day Eurodollars and ninety-one-day Treasury bill contracts, typical price quotes are not really prices, but indexes.

From Exhibit 5, the price index for the near Eurodollar futures contract was 89.96 on January 31, 1984. This means that each contract is for $1 million of 91-day Eurodollars at a contractual price that represents an annualized yield to maturity of 10.04% (–100 89.96), quarterly compounded. Thus, the increase in Eurodollar futures prices to an index of 92.71 on August 31, 1987, represents a fall in 91-day Eurodollar rates (91-day LIBOR) to 7.29% (–100 92.71). Every one point on the Eurodollar futures index represents a 1% increase in the annual interest rate on ninety-one-day Euros. Since that 1% higher rate is applied to a par amount of $1,000,000 for one quarter of a year to maturity, the change in value of a Eurodollar futures contract for a one-point move is: 0.01 × $1,000,000 × (1/4) = $2,500 per contract.

Exhibit 6 summarizes what the futures prices, contract values, and gains and losses are for interest rates from 4% to 20% for the major interest rate futures contracts—twenty-year T-bonds, ten-year T-notes, ninety-one-day T-bills and ninety-one-day Eurodollars. For hedgers in interest rate futures, this table provides critical information. For example, if interest rates are 8%, the typical dollar move in T-bond futures is $9,939 per contract for a 1% rate move, which is four times the $2,500 move in Eurodollars. However, with rates at 13%, the move in T-bonds drops to only $4,951 for a 1% rate change, which is only two times the $2,500 move in Eurodollars. In either case, note that $100,000 par in twenty-year bonds moves significantly more in value than does $1,000,000 par in ninety-one-day Eurodollars. Setting up or evaluating a hedge requires a thorough knowledge of these futures gains and losses that occur for various rate moves. In our hedging experience, a focus on the par amounts of these contracts, rather than on the dollar gains and losses for 1% rate moves, is probably the most consistent major error made by regulators and board members in critiquing hedging programs. The duration discussion of the next subsection will explain why the bond contract's movements get smaller as rates increase. Also, the third section of this chapter shows how to calculate correct sizes for futures hedge positions, using the "Average Move" data of Exhibit 6.

Exhibit 6: Interest Rate Futures Prices and Dollar Moves

20-Year Treasury Bond Futures

Interest Rate	Futures Price	Contract Value	Move If Rate Up	Average Move
4.00%	154.71	$154,711	$17,057	
5.00%	137.65	$137,654	$14,539	$15,798
6.00%	123.11	$123,115	$12,437	$13,488
7.00%	110.68	$110,678	$10,678	$11,557
8.00%	100.00	$100,000	$9,201	$9,939
9.00%	90.80	$90,799	$7,958	$8,580
10.00%	82.84	$82,841	$6,910	$7,434
11.00%	75.93	$75,931	$6,023	$6,467
12.00%	69.91	$69,907	$5,271	$5,647
13.00%	64.64	$64,636	$4,631	$4,951
14.00%	60.00	$60,005	$4,085	$4,358
15.00%	55.92	$55,920	$3,618	$3,852
16.00%	52.30	$52,302	$3,217	$3,417
17.00%	49.08	$49,085	$2,871	$3,044
18.00%	46.21	$46,213	$2,573	$2,722
19.00%	43.64	$43,640	$2,314	$2,444
20.00%	41.33	$41,326		

10-Year Treasury Note Futures

Interest Rate	Futures Price	Contract Value	Move If Rate Up	Average Move
4.00%	132.70	$132,703	$9,319	
5.00%	123.38	$123,384	$8,506	$8,913
6.00%	114.88	$114,877	$7,771	$8,139
7.00%	107.11	$107,106	$7,106	$7,439
8.00%	100.00	$100,000	$6,504	$6,805
9.00%	93.50	$93,496	$5,958	$6,231
10.00%	87.54	$87,538	$5,463	$5,711
11.00%	82.07	$82,074	$5,014	$5,239
12.00%	77.06	$77,060	$4,606	$4,810
13.00%	72.45	$72,454	$4,236	$4,421
14.00%	68.22	$68,218	$3,899	$4,067
15.00%	64.32	$64,319	$3,592	$3,745
16.00%	60.73	$60,727	$3,312	$3,452
17.00%	57.41	$57,415	$3,058	$3,185
18.00%	54.36	$54,357	$2,825	$2,942
19.00%	51.53	$51,532	$2,613	$2,719
20.00%	48.92	$48,919		

91-day Eurodollar Futures Contract and 91-day Treasury Bill Futures Contract

Interest Rate	Futures Price	Contract Value	Move If Rate Up	Average Move
4.00%	96.00	$990,000	$2,500	
5.00%	95.00	$987,500	$2,500	$2,500
6.00%	94.00	$985,000	$2,500	$2,500
7.00%	93.00	$982,500	$2,500	$2,500
8.00%	92.00	$980,000	$2,500	$2,500
9.00%	91.00	$977,500	$2,500	$2,500
10.00%	90.00	$975,000	$2,500	$2,500
11.00%	89.00	$972,500	$2,500	$2,500
12.00%	88.00	$970,000	$2,500	$2,500
13.00%	87.00	$967,500	$2,500	$2,500
14.00%	86.00	$965,000	$2,500	$2,500
15.00%	85.00	$962,500	$2,500	$2,500
16.00%	84.00	$960,000	$2,500	$2,500
17.00%	83.00	$957,000	$2,500	$2,500
18.00%	82.00	$955,000	$2,500	$2,500
19.00%	81.00	$952,500	$2,500	$2,500
20.00%	80.00	$950,000		

Call and Put Options on Futures

A *call option* is an option (your choice) to *buy* a fixed quantity of a certain "underlying asset" at a fixed exercise price, any time prior to the expiration date of the option. The most liquid interest rate options traded are options on twenty-year Treasury bond futures contracts and options on Eurodollar futures. For example, on December 28, 1990, for $1,422 (1 and 27/64%, according to the *Wall Street Journal*), one could purchase a call option on the March 1991, Treasury bond futures contract with an exercise price of 96% par (i.e., $96,000). (The standard quantity for the option is the same par amount as the T-bond futures contract—$100,000.) At the time, the March futures contract was selling for 95.25. Although this is an option to buy the March 1991 futures contract, the option expires the 15th of the month prior to the futures expiration (i.e., February 15, 1991).

Consider the possible values of that option on the last moment before it expires at noon, February 15, 1991. If the March futures price is 90 at that time, the option to buy at 96 is worthless—you would rather buy in the market for 90 than to exercise your option and buy in at 96. However, if the March futures contract is at 100, the option to buy at 96 is worth 4 points, or $4,000 (4% × $100,000). Better yet, if the March futures contract is at 110 on February 15, 1991, the option to buy at 96 is worth 14 points, or $14,000. Thus, the worst that the buyer of a call can do is to let the option expire worthless, losing the $1,422 paid for the option. Yet, the potential gains are essentially unlimited, depending only on how high the underlying asset's price might go.

One reason that this option is so cheap is that if the March futures contract stays at 95.25, then this option to buy at 96 becomes worthless. Thus, the March futures must move up 0.75 points before the option is worth anything at expiration. An option like this is said to be "out-of-the-money," in that the underlying asset's price must move favorably for it to be worth anything. An option to buy the March futures at an exercise price of 94 is "in-the-money," in that it is worth 1.25 points ($1,250) now if exercised. However, the market price of this 94 option is 2 and 34/64% ($2,531), so traders were paying an extra 1 and 18/64% for the prospect of a large increase in bond prices between December 28th and February 15th.

A *put option* is an option (your choice) to *sell* a fixed quantity of a certain "underlying asset" at a fixed exercise price, any time prior to the expiration date of the option. For example, on December 28, 1990, for $1,297 (1 + 19/64%), one could purchase a put option on March 1991, Treasury bond futures, with an exercise price of 94% par (i.e., $94,000). Other than being an option to sell, rather than to buy, the terms are identical to the corresponding call option. If one can sell for a higher price without the option, then the option is useless. Thus, at expiration (February 15, 1991), the put's value will be zero if the March T-bond futures is greater than 94. If the March futures is less than 94, then one should exercise the option to sell at 94, prior to its expiration.

Letting F be the futures price at expiration and letting X be the exercise price on the option, call and put payoffs may be described mathematically by:

Call Payoff At Expiration = maximum [0, F − X]

Put Payoff At Expiration = maximum [0, X − F]

Exhibit 7 illustrates in tabular form the payoffs on February 15, 1991, from (1) a long position in March futures, (2) a short position in March futures, (3) a call option on March futures with an exercise price of 96, and (4) a put option on March futures with an exercise price of 94. Entry prices for March futures positions are 95.25% par ($95,250), the call costs $1,422, and the put costs $1,297.

Exhibit 7 shows several things. First, market prices are such that there is no free lunch: all of these investments have their good and bad points. Second, both long and short futures positions have very symmetric payoffs, while options have very asymmetric payoffs. Both call and put options have the potential for very large gains, whereas their losses are limited. However, if market prices

Exhibit 7: Options and Futures Payoffs (% Par)

March 1991 Futures Price on Feb. 15, 1991		Profit on Long Future	Profit on Short Future	Profit on Call Option X = 96		Profit on Put Option X = 94	
% Par	Ct. Value			Gross	Net	Gross	Net
80%	$ 80,000	($15,250)	$15,250	$ 0	($ 1,422)	$14,000	$12,703
85%	$ 85,000	($10,250)	$10,250	$ 0	($ 1,422)	$ 9,000	$ 7,703
90%	$ 90,000	($ 5,250)	$ 5,250	$ 0	($ 1,422)	$ 4,000	$ 2,703
95%	$ 95,000	($ 250)	$ 250	$ 0	($ 1,422)	$ 0	($ 1,297)
100%	$100,000	$ 4,750	($ 4,750)	$ 4,000	$ 2,578	$ 0	($ 1,297)
105%	$105,000	$ 9,750	($ 9,750)	$ 9,000	$ 7,578	$ 0	($ 1,297)
110%	$110,000	$14,750	($14,750)	$14,000	$12,578	$ 0	($ 1,297)

do not move much, both the call and the put expire worthless, resulting in a net total loss of the price paid (while futures lose nothing). Finally, it bears emphasizing that there is no option aspect in a futures contract, in that losses are *not* limited in any useful way. Futures and options payoffs are very different.

Interest Rate Swaps

Consider a typical bank that receives short-term deposits (that roll over at market rates) and lends the funds to a corporation at a rate that is fixed for five years. The bank gets hurt if interest rates rise, and it has a negative gross spread if the cost of the deposits exceeds its lending rate. On the other hand, if rates fall, the bank's profit margin widens, assuming that the borrower cannot easily or cheaply prepay the loan. A typical interest rate swap is used by a financial institution or corporation to protect against such fluctuations in profitability due to interest rate movements.

With a typical interest rate swap, the bank pays another institution (the "counterparty") interest at a fixed rate semiannually on a stated principal balance (the "notional principal") throughout the term of the swap. In exchange, the counterparty pays the bank semiannually (simultaneously) interest on the same notional principal, but at a floating rate. The floating rate might be based on three-month or six-month LIBOR, Treasury bill rates, the prime rate or commercial paper rates. Of course, the floating rate index specified affects the fixed rate that the bank has to pay. For example, since LIBOR exceeds Treasury bill rates, one has to pay a higher fixed rate to receive LIBOR rather than a T-bill rate.

The fixed rate paid is usually quoted as the current Treasury rate for a maturity equal to the term of the swap, plus a swap spread that varies with the short-term rate chosen. For example, on a five-year LIBOR swap on December 31, 1990, the fixed rate paid was set at approximately seventy-nine basis points over the five-year Treasury rate of 7.64% (Exhibit 1), for a total of 8.43%. In exchange, the fixed-rate payer received six-month LIBOR, adjusted semiannually (nine times) during the five-year period. The initial six-month LIBOR of 7.63% is fixed for the floating-rate payer's first six months of the swap.

The hedging aspects of an interest rate swap are fairly easy to see. If rates jump up dramatically, the bank's cost of funds will jump, but will probably be approximately covered by increased interest received on the swap. On the other hand, if rates fall dramatically, the bank's cost of funds should fall similarly, but its swap income will also fall similarly. The hedge may well be imperfect: the bank's cost of funds may not move perfectly with LIBOR. For example, there may be lags in cost of funds changes. Still, over periods of a year or more, most of those adjustments are fully made, and the swap should reduce risk well, particularly with very large rate moves. Exhibits 8 and 9 show how this five-year swap can be used to effectively turn long-term loans into short-term loans, or, alternatively, turn short-term funding into long-term funding.

Consider the potential capital gains and losses on the swap after it has been initiated, but prior to its maturity. One pays a fixed rate for a fixed term, much like issuing (or shorting) a fixed-rate bond. One receives a fixed rate for the first six months, then the rate floats with market rates. Thus, the capital gains and losses on the swap are much like those of a short five-year bond position plus a long six-month fixed-rate CD. Just like a short Treasury bond futures position, the swap wins when rates increase more

---

Exhibit 8: Interest Rate Swaps Turn Long-Term Loans into Short-Term Loans

---

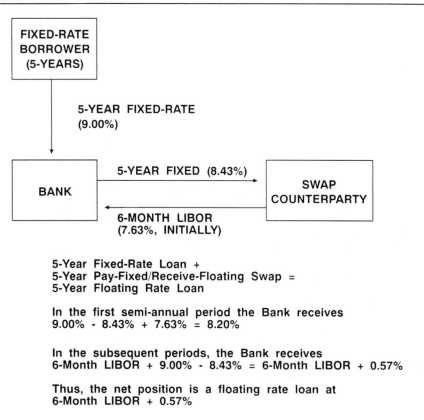

FIXED-RATE
BORROWER
(5-YEARS)

5-YEAR FIXED-RATE
(9.00%)

BANK

5-YEAR FIXED (8.43%)

6-MONTH LIBOR
(7.63%, INITIALLY)

SWAP
COUNTERPARTY

5-Year Fixed-Rate Loan +
5-Year Pay-Fixed/Receive-Floating Swap =
5-Year Floating Rate Loan

In the first semi-annual period the Bank receives
9.00% - 8.43% + 7.63% = 8.20%

In the subsequent periods, the Bank receives
6-Month LIBOR + 9.00% - 8.43% = 6-Month LIBOR + 0.57%

Thus, the net position is a floating rate loan at
6-Month LIBOR + 0.57%

---

than expected, and loses when rates fall short of expected. Thus, interest rate swaps are viewed in this chapter as alternatives to short futures hedge positions, with much of the interest rate risk analysis being virtually identical for the two. Credit risks, transaction costs, market liquidity, accounting treatment, and relative pricing usually determine whether an institution hedges more with swaps or futures at any point in time.

Aside from being an excellent risk reduction tool, interest rate swaps also allow an institution to borrow and lend at maturities where it has a comparative advantage, thereby maximizing eco-

---

Exhibit 9: Interest Rate Swaps Turn Short-Term Funding into Long-Term Funding

---

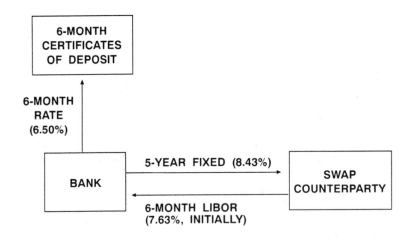

For the first 6 months, the Bank pays 6.50% - 7.63% + 8.43% = 7.30%.

In subsequent periods, the Bank pays CD rate - 6-Month LIBOR + 8.43%.

If the spread between 6-Month LIBOR and the 6-Month CD rate stays the same, the Bank pays 7.30% for five years.

If LIBOR rises relative to the CD rate, then the net cost will be less than 7.30%, and vice versa.

---

nomic profits. Exhibit 10 uses a simple example to illustrate this concept.

Suppose a bank manager, wishing to take a minimal amount of interest rate risk, has a choice of only six-month loans, three-year loans, six-month borrowings, and three-year borrowings. Note from Exhibit 10 that by funding each potential loan with borrowings with identical maturities (matched funding), the manager can earn a twenty-five basis point spread, and is indifferent between the six-month and the three-year pairs of assets and liabilities.

Exhibit 10

Bank manager is faced with the following choices of assets and liabilities:

Maturity	Asset Yield	Liability Yield	Spread
6 months	8.13%	7.88%	0.25%
3 years	8.79%	8.54%	0.25%

Assume manager can:

Roll 6-month asset at 6-month LIBOR for at least 3 years.
Roll 6-month liability at 6-month LIBOR minus 25 basis points for at least 3 years.

Market Interest Rates:

Maturity	Treasury Yield	LIBOR	Interest Rate Swap Spread
6 months	7.49%	8.13%	
1 years	7.48%	8.13%	
2 years	7.76%		0.51%
3 years	7.93%		0.61%

Which assets and liabilities should the manager choose?

If the manager chooses any pair of matched assets and liabilities, he will earn a spread of 25 basis points.

However, if he chooses the 3-year asset, the 6-month liability, and an interest rate swap (pay fixed for 3 years, receive 6-month LIBOR), he receives a wider spread:

Fixed Payments			_Floating Payments_	
Asset Yield:	8.79%		Liability Cost:	LIBOR - 0.25%
Swap Payment:	-8.54%		Swap Payment:	LIBOR
Fixed Net:	0.25%		Floating Net:	0.25%

Net Spread:
Fixed Net: 0.25%
Floating Net: 0.25%
                 0.50%

Swap (Risk Management) allowed the manager to borrow and invest at maturities where he had a comparative advantage (widest asset and tightest liability spread to the LIBOR curve), and earn a higher net spread.

NOTE: All rates shown have been converted to bond-equivalent, semi-annual compounded rates.

The bank, however, has a comparative advantage in long-term lending and short-term borrowing. For example, six-month liabilities are obtainable at twenty-five basis points under six-month LIBOR, whereas three-year liabilities cost an amount (8.54%) equal to the fixed interest rate on a three-year swap (7.93% plus the swap spread of 0.61%), roughly equivalent to a three-year LIBOR rate. The bank, therefore, can fund more cheaply to the LIBOR curve with its short-term borrowings.

On the asset side of the balance sheet, the bank can lend three-year money at an effective rate of LIBOR plus twenty-five basis points (8.79% vs. 8.54%), but can earn LIBOR only on its six-month loans. The bank's comparative advantage in long-term loans is demonstrated by this twenty-five basis point spread to LIBOR.

Exhibit 10 shows how by entering into an interest rate swap in which it pays a fixed rate for three years and receives six-month LIBOR, coupled with making three-year loans and funding these loans with six-month borrowings, the bank can earn a fifty basis point spread with minimal interest rate risk. The interest rate swap has not only corrected the maturity mismatch of the bank's assets and liabilities, it has also allowed the bank to borrow and invest at maturities where it has comparative advantages, thus enabling the bank to be a more profitable and effective financial intermediary.

Interest Rate Caps and Floors

Interest rate caps and floors are series of options on short-term interest rates where each successive option's time to maturity (known as the reset date) is greater by a fixed-length time interval (usually three months). The options in a specific cap or floor usually have identical strike rates. Caps and floors are traded for a large number of short-term interest rates, a similar set of interest rates for which interest rate swaps are available. Most often, however, caps and floors are based on one-, three-, or six-month LIBOR. The contract usually contains a specific notional amount (as does an interest rate swap), or (less often) a notional amount that varies with time.

Caps and floors protect the buyer from adverse movements in the underlying interest rate. Since a cap is a series of put options on a short-term interest rate, an increase in rates (with corresponding price decreases) makes the puts more valuable. Thus, caps protect the owner against rising rates, and floors, which are series of call options, benefit the owner when interest rates fall.

As with most options, the purchaser of a cap or floor usually pays the price (premium) for the contract at the time of purchase. In return for the premium the cap writer is obliged to pay the holder of the cap an amount equal to the greater of zero or the short-term spot rate in the market, minus the strike rate on the cap, times the notional amount of the cap at each reset date (maturity of each successive option in the cap). Similarly, the writer of a floor must pay its holder an amount equal to the greater of zero and the difference between the strike rate and the short-term spot rate on the floor's notional principal amount at each reset date.

Exhibit 11 displays how the payments work for a cap and a floor. For both contracts the strike rate is assumed to be 8%, and the index rate is three-month LIBOR. The cap and floor have a stated term of three years and thus contain eleven options, the first expiring in three months, the last in thirty-three months. Payments are made in arrears, meaning that a payment will be made three months following each reset date, bringing the last payment date to thirty-six months from inception of the contract. Most caps and floors are designed to pay in arrears. The purchaser of a cap or a floor must be careful to check on the characteristics of the option before purchase, since a lack of contract standardization exists.

Caps and floors are not traded on an exchange. On the contrary, the market for these options is an over-the-counter (OTC) market. The cap or floor holder is exposed to the credit risk of the option writer to the extent that he is owed payments on the option, or in the event that he wishes to sell the option. Thus, as with

Exhibit 11: Cap and Floor Cash Flows

Assumptions:
Short-term index rate: 3-month LIBOR
Strike Rate: 8.0%
Notional Principal: $10 million
Term: 3 Years
Frequency of Reset: 3 Months
Cap Price: 1.1% * Notional Amount
Floor Price: 2.05% * Notional Amount
Payments: In arrears

CAP CASH FLOWS
Cap Premium ($110,000) at Purchase

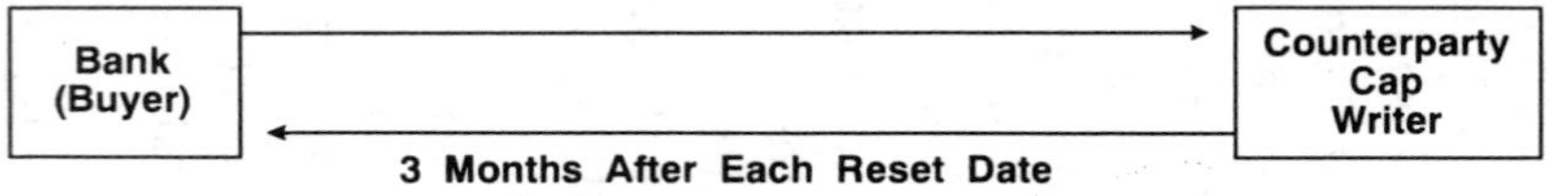

```
  Bank                                    Counterparty
 (Buyer)      ───────────────►               Cap
              ◄───────────────              Writer
```

3 Months After Each Reset Date

Maximum of zero and 3 months' interest on $10 million at rate of 3-month LIBOR at reset date minus 8%. If 3-month LIBOR at reset is less than 8%, payment is zero. If LIBOR is, say, 10%, payment is equal to 3 months' interest on $10 million at a rate of 2% (10% - 8%).

FLOOR CASH FLOWS
Floor Premium ($205,000) at Purchase

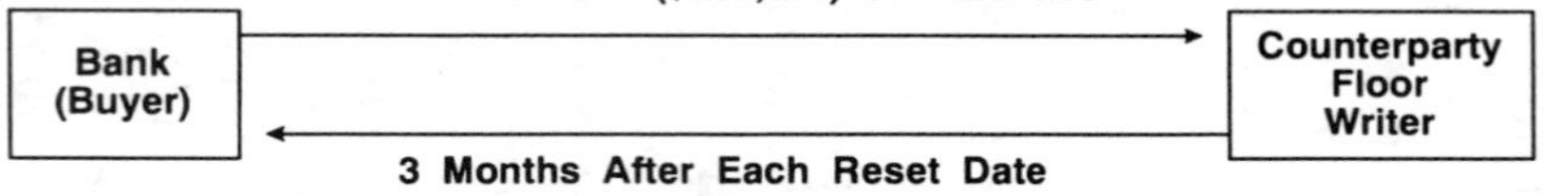

```
  Bank                                    Counterparty
 (Buyer)      ───────────────►              Floor
              ◄───────────────             Writer
```

3 Months After Each Reset Date

Maximum of zero and 3 months' interest on $10 million at rate of 8% minus 3-month LIBOR at reset date. If 3-month LIBOR at reset is greater than 8%, payment is zero. If LIBOR is, say, 6%, payment is equal to 3 months' interest on $10 million at a rate of 2% (8% - 6%).

Exhibit 12: Cap and Floor Prices, December 31, 1990

A. 3-month LIBOR Caps

	STRIKE RATE				
Maturity	8.00%	8.50%	9.00%	9.50%	10.00%
1 year	0.26	0.09	0.03	0.02	0.01
2 years	0.65	0.31	0.16	0.10	0.06
3 years	1.44	0.92	0.59	0.40	0.27
4 years	2.20	1.49	1.01	0.70	0.48
5 years	3.02	2.13	1.50	1.07	0.73

B. 3-Month LIBOR Floors

	STRIKE RATE				
Maturity	7.00%	7.50%	8.00%	8.50%	9.00%
1 year	0.08	0.35	0.59	0.89	1.22
2 years	0.13	0.40	0.90	1.53	2.30
3 years	0.22	0.63	1.27	2.10	3.12
4 years	0.38	0.88	1.69	2.70	3.94
5 years	0.51	1.12	2.04	3.21	4.65

NOTE: Prices are expressed as a percentage of an option's underlying notional amount.

3-Month LIBOR on 12/31/90 was 7.8125%.

interest rate swaps, counterparty credit risk is an important consideration when one is looking to purchase a cap or a floor.

Cap and floor prices (premiums) are quoted as a percentage of the contract's notional amount. Exhibit 12 displays quoted prices for (the purchase of) caps and floors on December 31, 1990. For example, at year-end 1990, a three-year, 8% cap with a notional principal amount of $10 million would cost $144,000 (1.44% of $10 million). Notice that cap and floor prices display the characteristics one would expect of options. For both caps and floors, prices increase as the time to maturity increases, holding the strike rate constant. For caps, which are puts, increasing the strike rate makes the security less valuable. For floors, which contain a series of calls, increasing the strike rate makes the security more valuable.

Compared to short-term exchange-traded options, caps and floors have several major advantages, but also possess some major disadvantages. Exchange-traded options on futures are much more liquid than caps and floors, and are thus more apt to be used, the more frequently one anticipates trading these options. In addition, the safety of the exchange provides comfort to the purchaser of options, in contrast to the buyer of a cap or floor who is subject to the credit risk of his counterparty for the remaining life (or holding period) of the option.

In spite of these disadvantages, caps and floors have become widely used hedges by financial institutions. The popularity of caps and floors largely stems from the fact that these contracts are a source of long-term options, and that the underlying LIBOR index is more highly correlated with the interest rates on financial institutions' assets and liabilities than Treasury rates. Since the options embedded in mortgages and other assets and liabilities of financial institutions are long-term in nature, a better hedge may often be obtained using caps and floors than by using short-term exchange-traded options on futures. These advantages, and the growing liquidity of the cap and floor market have made these options contracts a valuable and widely used risk management tool for financial institutions.

PRICE ELASTICITY, DURATION, AND CONVEXITY

To understand gains and losses on bonds that occur as interest rates move, it is important to understand the duration or *price elasticity* of an asset or liability. Quite simply, the price elasticity of an asset or liability is the percentage change in its market value that occurs for a 1% or 100 basis points move in interest rates. Thus, if a 10-year bond has a price elasticity of (minus) 6%, then its price will move up by about 6% if rates move down 100 basis points, and its price moves down by about 6% if rates increase 100 basis points. Obviously, a bond with a price elasticity of 6% is more sensitive to interest rates than a bond with an elasticity of 1%.

Exhibit 13: Example of Price Elasticity and Market Value Risk

	Par Amount	Price Elasticity	Market Value if: Rates Down 1%	Market Value if: Rates Up 1%
Assets:				
10-year fixed-rate bonds	$100 mln	.06	$106 mln	$94 mln
Liabilities:				
Money market deposit accounts	$ 95 mln	.00	$ 95 mln	$95 mln
Net Worth (market)	$ 5 mln		$ 11 mln	$-1 mln

The sensitivity of the market value of a *firm* to interest rates depends on the price elasticities of its assets and liabilities. Consider a simple example of a brand-new savings and loan that has $5 million in net worth, $95 million of money market deposit accounts (MMDAs) that reprice daily, and $100 million of ten-year fixed rate bonds. Since the liabilities reprice daily, their rates are always fair rates and their market values are always equal to their book or par amounts. Thus, the liabilities have a price elasticity of zero. Exhibit 13 gives the market values of this firm's assets and liabilities for the current case and for scenarios of 1% lower rates and of 1% higher rates. (Keep in mind that these are small moves relative to what has happened to market interest rates during the last decade.)

From Exhibit 13, one can see that a new and very solid firm with a true 5% capital/assets ratio goes to a minus $1 million true net value of its assets and liabilities with only a 1% move up in rates. Just that 1% rate move is sufficient to make the firm unable to pay off its depositors if it had to liquidate its assets. To prevent this possible failure, the firm might wish to hedge its interest rate risk with interest rate futures, swaps, or options.

This firm wins or loses (net) $6 million dollars for every 1% rate move. If one has to choose a simple single measure that indicates the net interest rate risk of the firm, this *value sensitivity to a 1% rate move* should be it. To compute the value sensitivity of the firm, one has to estimate the price elasticities of each of the firm's assets and liabilities, and then a computation similar to the one shown in Exhibit 13 can be made. Subsequent sections of this chapter will examine these types of risk in much more detail.

Duration, expressed in years, simply measures the weighted average time until cash flow payment for the financial instrument. *Modified duration* equals duration divided by one plus the interest rate. The reason that the duration computation is useful for interest rate risk management is that it can be shown mathematically and in practice that, for standard fixed-rate bonds (not mortgages), modified duration is equal to price elasticity, which is the best measure of interest rate risk.

Exhibit 14 gives an example of how to calculate duration for two bonds—a ten-year and a five-year bond, both with 12% coupons and par of $100. The current fair interest rate is assumed to be 12%. Note that the bond with the longer time to maturity has the larger duration and price elasticity, but not proportionally so. As can be seen, modified duration predicts the price elasticity very well for both bonds. The 5-year bond has a modified duration of 3.60 years, and the price elasticity (expressed as the average percentage price change for a 100 basis point increase and decrease in interest rates) is 3.61%. The 10-year bond's modified duration is 5.65 years, and the price elasticity is 5.66%.

Duration was derived by Macaulay long ago as an approximation to price elasticity, using an assumption that the cash flows of the investment are fixed and independent of interest rates. Unfortunately for this derivation, with fixed-rate mortgages the entire principal can typically be prepaid at any time, thereby changing the cash flows for the remaining twenty to thirty years of the mortgage. Thus, duration approximations to price sensitivity just do not work well for mortgages. The following actual data illustrate this point.

Exhibit 15 gives cash prices for GNMA-insured fixed-rate mortgages for each month-end during the 1984 to 1990 period for mortgage coupons from 8% to 15%. All of these price quotes are percents of par, so a price of seventy-five represents a mortgage

Exhibit 14: Duration, Modified Duration and Price Elasticity

Example: Rates start at 12% with bonds priced at par. Rates change to either 11% or 13%. At 11% the 10-year is worth $105.89 and the 5-year price is $103.70.
At 13% the price of the 10-year is $94.57 and the 5-year bond's price is $96.48.

Definitions:

Duration	= Weighted average of years when cash flows received, using PV fractions as weights.
Modified Duration	= Duration divided by 1 + R, where R is the current annual market interest rate.
Price Elasticity	= Percentage change in price expressed per 1% (100 bp) rate change.

10-Year Bond

Year	Discount Factor At: 11%	12%	13%	Cash Flow	Present Value at: 11%	12%	13%	PV/Total @12%	PV/Total x Years
1	0.901	0.893	0.885	12	$10.81	$10.71	$10.62	0.11	0.11
2	0.812	0.797	0.783	12	9.74	9.57	9.40	0.10	0.19
3	0.731	0.712	0.693	12	8.77	8.54	8.32	0.09	0.26
4	0.659	0.636	0.613	12	7.90	7.63	7.36	0.08	0.31
5	0.593	0.567	0.543	12	7.12	6.81	6.51	0.07	0.34
6	0.535	0.507	0.480	12	6.42	6.08	5.76	0.06	0.36
7	0.482	0.452	0.425	12	5.78	5.43	5.10	0.05	0.38
8	0.434	0.404	0.376	12	5.21	4.85	4.51	0.05	0.39
9	0.391	0.361	0.333	12	4.69	4.33	3.99	0.04	0.39
10	0.352	0.322	0.295	112	39.44	36.06	32.99	0.36	3.61
					$105.89	$100.00	$94.57	1.00	6.33

5-Year Bond

Year	Cash Flow	Present Value at: 11%	12%	13%	PV/Total @12%	PV/Total x Years
1	12	$10.81	$10.71	$10.62	0.11	0.11
2	12	9.74	9.57	9.40	0.10	0.19
3	12	8.77	8.54	8.32	0.09	0.26
4	12	7.90	7.63	7.36	0.08	0.31
5	112	66.47	63.55	60.79	0.64	3.18
		$103.70	$100.00	$96.48	1.00	4.04

	10-Year		5-Year	
Duration	=	6.33 Years	=	4.04 Years
Modified Duration	=	6.32/1.12 = 5.65 Years	=	4.04/1.12 = 3.60 Years
Price Elasticity	=	.5*[(105.89-100.0)+(100.0-94.57)]/100.0 = 5.66%	=	.5*[(103.70-100.0)+(100.0-96.46)]/100.0 = 3.61%

Notes:

For very small rate movements Price Elasticity converges to Modified Duration. This relationship can be proven by taking the derivative of the bond price with respect to the bond's yield and expressing the result as a percentage (in absolute value) of the bond's price.

For regular bonds, duration and price elasticity increase as rates fall and decrease as rates rise. For mortgages, the opposite is true, as mortgage prepayments increase as rates fall, thereby shortening durations. As discussed in the text, the above duration calculation should not be used for mortgages, as it ignores the prepayment option.

Exhibit 15: GNMA Cash Mortgage Prices

End of Month	Futures Prices (Near Contract)		Mortgage Coupon Rate								Approx. Par Mortgage	Bond Futures Yield
	T-Bond	Euro	8.0	9.0	10.0	11.0	12.0	13.0	14.0	15.0		
Jan 84	70.81	89.96	76.88	81.38	86.78	92.44	NA	102.63	106.50	108.75	12.50	11.84%
Feb 84	68.84	89.71	75.00	79.63	85.31	90.88	NA	102.63	106.06	108.13	12.75	12.19%
Mar 84	66.22	88.72	72.75	77.25	82.63	88.50	NA	99.13	106.13	107.63	13.25	12.69%
Apr 84	64.69	88.54	71.25	75.94	81.19	86.94	NA	97.94	102.50	105.38	13.50	12.99%
May 84	60.16	88.03	66.38	70.38	75.38	81.38	NA	92.19	97.38	101.38	14.50	13.97%
Jun 84	59.63	86.87	66.63	70.63	75.63	81.13	NA	92.31	98.06	101.75	14.50	14.09%
Jul 84	64.50	87.97	71.00	75.00	80.00	85.13	NA	96.00	101.47	104.41	13.75	13.03%
Aug 84	65.81	88.08	70.63	74.63	80.13	85.63	NA	96.38	101.50	104.44	13.75	12.77%
Sep 84	67.22	88.44	72.00	76.38	81.50	87.38	NA	98.00	102.13	105.50	13.50	12.49%
Oct 84	70.78	89.68	75.25	79.75	85.13	90.75	NA	100.25	104.00	106.50	13.00	11.85%
Nov 84	71.63	90.54	76.75	81.63	87.38	93.13	NA	101.63	104.88	107.88	12.50	11.70%
Dec 84	71.06	90.48	76.88	81.63	86.88	92.88	97.75	102.00	106.00	108.81	12.50	11.80%
Jan 85	73.19	91.07	78.25	82.88	88.38	94.38	98.75	102.88	106.63	109.13	12.25	11.44%
Feb 85	68.88	90.31	74.88	79.38	84.38	90.13	95.06	100.19	104.50	108.31	13.00	12.19%
Mar 85	69.72	90.23	76.44	80.69	85.94	91.56	96.53	101.53	106.53	109.13	12.50	12.03%
Apr 85	70.75	91.05	77.44	81.75	86.88	92.63	97.44	102.44	106.63	109.13	12.50	11.85%
May 85	77.34	92.24	83.06	87.63	93.00	98.00	101.88	105.50	108.75	110.69	11.50	10.78%
Jun 85	77.06	92.07	83.56	88.31	94.06	99.13	102.75	106.13	108.50	111.88	11.25	10.83%
Jul 85	75.19	91.64	82.19	86.63	92.00	97.00	101.69	105.75	109.13	112.25	11.50	11.12%
Aug 85	77.13	91.86	83.19	87.81	93.00	98.19	102.50	106.50	109.50	112.81	11.50	10.82%
Sep 85	75.59	91.77	83.63	88.06	93.19	97.88	102.56	106.56	109.50	111.50	11.50	11.09%
Oct 85	78.53	92.05	85.63	90.13	95.19	99.63	104.00	107.84	110.00	111.63	11.00	10.61%
Nov 85	81.66	91.97	87.78	92.31	97.38	101.94	106.19	108.56	110.31	112.00	10.50	10.16%
Dec 85	85.22	92.25	91.31	96.25	101.38	104.81	107.13	108.19	109.44	112.13	9.75	9.69%
Jan 86	85.16	92.12	90.25	95.00	100.28	104.19	106.84	108.56	110.25	113.13	10.00	9.64%
Feb 86	94.81	92.24	95.00	99.13	103.25	105.88	107.09	108.16	109.78	112.63	9.25	8.55%
Mar 86	102.31	93.03	95.81	100.19	104.38	106.75	107.88	108.19	110.25	114.00	9.00	7.77%
Apr 86	100.75	93.35	95.88	100.00	104.38	107.31	107.31	107.44	109.75	114.00	9.00	7.92%
May 86	93.88	92.93	91.25	95.44	101.38	104.94	105.63	106.50	109.38	114.38	9.75	8.65%
Jun 86	99.56	93.45	93.69	97.13	102.19	105.38	105.75	106.44	107.06	114.31	9.50	8.04%
Jul 86	97.81	93.57	95.25	97.88	103.44	106.44	106.94	107.44	110.00	112.00	9.25	8.22%
Aug 86	102.41	94.29	97.25	98.38	104.88	106.84	107.38	107.50	109.75	113.00	9.00	7.76%
Sep 86	96.56	94.01	95.38	98.63	104.25	107.13	107.81	108.38	109.06	113.88	9.25	8.36%
Oct 86	98.09	94.11	96.38	99.69	105.13	107.50	107.75	108.75	109.72	114.00	9.00	8.20%
Nov 86	99.72	93.97	98.56	102.06	106.88	107.59	107.69	108.53	109.66	114.00	8.50	8.03%
Dec 86	98.19	93.89	98.13	101.56	106.38	107.69	108.09	109.00	109.66	114.00	8.50	8.19%
Jan 87	99.69	93.69	99.13	102.88	106.94	107.69	108.13	109.31	110.56	114.00	8.25	8.03%
Feb 87	101.44	93.58	99.00	103.38	107.56	107.94	108.50	109.50	111.00	114.00	8.25	7.86%
Mar 87	98.47	93.35	97.19	102.09	106.63	107.81	108.94	110.00	112.25	115.00	8.50	8.18%
Apr 87	93.06	92.61	92.88	97.38	102.00	105.38	107.38	109.50	112.00	114.00	9.50	8.74%
May 87	92.06	92.74	92.06	96.00	100.38	104.44	107.44	109.75	112.00	114.00	10.00	8.86%
Jun 87	91.50	92.58	93.06	96.75	101.50	105.94	108.75	110.88	113.13	115.00	9.75	8.92%

Exhibit 15: GNMA Cash Mortgage Prices (Continued)

End of Month	Futures Prices (Near Contract)		Mortgage Coupon Rate								Approx. Par Mortgage	Bond Futures Yield
	T-Bond	Euro	8.0	9.0	10.0	11.0	12.0	13.0	14.0	15.0		
Jul 87	89.50	92.71	92.31	96.81	101.88	106.00	108.69	110.50	112.88	114.88	10.00	9.15%
Aug 87	87.50	92.71	90.88	96.19	100.03	105.13	108.56	110.75	112.56	114.75	10.00	9.40%
Sep 87	81.69	91.40	88.63	92.53	96.75	101.69	106.63	110.00	112.50	114.50	10.75	10.16%
Oct 87	87.56	92.42	90.41	94.72	99.19	103.31	106.94	109.56	111.94	114.56	10.25	9.39%
Nov 87	87.66	92.32	90.97	95.22	99.56	104.75	108.22	109.78	111.84	114.53	10.25	9.38%
Dec 87	87.97	92.44	91.44	95.56	100.06	104.38	107.81	109.75	111.75	114.31	10.00	9.34%
Jan 88	93.91	92.96	95.00	99.13	102.81	107.13	109.66	111.63	113.25	115.13	9.50	8.65%
Feb 88	94.66	93.13	95.13	99.38	103.44	107.31	109.69	111.94	113.50	115.25	9.50	8.56%
Mar 88	90.09	92.72	92.50	97.00	101.50	106.44	109.31	112.38	113.13	115.13	9.75	9.09%
Apr 88	87.91	92.41	91.81	96.38	100.69	105.28	108.84	111.31	113.31	113.13	10.00	9.35%
May 88	85.81	92.23	90.00	94.00	99.50	104.25	108.75	111.25	113.34	112.53	10.25	9.61%
Jun 88	88.75	92.04	92.59	96.84	101.09	106.06	109.59	112.09	113.72	114.06	9.75	9.24%
Jul 88	86.19	91.52	91.22	95.13	100.25	105.00	108.59	111.56	113.28	113.47	10.00	9.62%
Aug 88	86.06	91.33	90.66	94.44	99.75	104.03	107.75	110.69	113.22	113.16	10.25	9.58%
Sep 88	88.75	91.22	92.59	96.44	101.34	105.13	108.56	110.31	113.25	113.06	9.75	9.24%
Oct 88	91.41	91.41	94.72	98.28	102.81	105.81	109.22	110.81	113.28	112.66	9.50	8.93%
Nov 88	88.47	90.82	91.88	95.56	100.69	104.00	108.16	110.25	112.56	111.94	10.00	9.28%
Dec 88	89.13	90.62	91.13	94.44	99.38	102.88	107.03	109.28	111.81	111.19	10.25	9.20%
Jan 89	90.81	90.46	92.00	95.38	100.13	103.13	107.41	109.53	111.66	112.47	10.00	9.00%
Feb 89	88.09	89.73	90.38	93.88	98.56	101.94	106.53	108.97	111.28	112.09	10.50	9.32%
Mar 89	88.41	89.29	89.50	93.81	97.88	101.41	105.84	109.06	111.28	112.09	10.50	9.29%
Apr 89	90.19	90.15	90.19	94.63	98.75	102.03	107.28	110.72	113.47	113.47	10.50	9.07%
May 89	93.06	90.54	92.56	96.81	100.78	103.22	108.09	111.13	113.41	113.41	10.00	8.74%
Jun 89	97.94	91.47	94.81	98.44	102.38	104.53	109.00	111.59	113.66	113.66	9.50	8.21%
Jul 89	99.75	91.79	96.72	100.31	103.38	105.22	109.94	112.94	114.34	114.34	9.00	8.03%
Aug 89	96.25	91.11	93.75	98.13	101.19	104.22	108.91	112.47	113.81	113.81	9.75	8.39%
Sep 89	95.84	91.05	93.63	97.94	102.59	103.59	108.13	111.63	113.13	113.13	9.75	8.43%
Oct 89	99.34	91.63	95.66	99.75	103.13	104.50	108.53	111.84	113.44	113.44	9.25	8.07%
Nov 89	99.47	91.63	94.69	99.88	103.13	105.69	108.63	110.69	112.75	112.75	9.25	8.05%
Dec 89	98.66	91.98	95.63	99.56	103.00	105.88	109.00	110.88	112.75	115.44	9.25	8.14%
Jan 90	94.25	91.65	93.09	97.59	101.69	104.78	108.19	109.88	111.44	113.94	9.75	8.61%
Feb 90	93.31	91.63	93.38	97.38	101.69	104.41	108.03	109.75	111.69	114.53	9.75	8.71%
Mar 90	91.88	91.31	93.00	97.06	101.25	104.13	107.50	109.38	111.28	114.09	9.75	8.88%
Apr 90	88.81	91.19	90.44	94.81	99.53	103.13	107.19	109.53	111.09	113.56	10.25	9.24%
May 90	92.91	91.60	93.44	97.50	101.91	104.50	107.91	110.50	112.34	115.09	9.75	8.76%
Jun 90	94.34	91.84	94.44	98.47	102.69	105.22	108.06	110.44	112.47	115.25	9.25	8.60%
Jul 90	94.69	92.11	95.13	99.44	103.56	106.44	109.44	111.72	113.84	116.72	9.25	8.56%
Aug 90	89.16	91.99	92.69	97.06	101.88	105.53	109.25	111.69	113.41	116.06	9.75	9.20%
Sep 90	89.38	91.94	93.50	98.03	101.94	105.44	109.13	111.47	113.13	115.75	9.50	9.17%
Oct 90	91.09	92.34	94.06	98.34	102.06	105.53	109.66	111.63	113.38	116.13	9.50	8.97%
Nov 90	94.91	91.78	95.50	100.03	103.69	106.63	110.63	112.63	115.06	118.00	9.00	8.54%
Dec 90	95.72	92.80	96.34	100.63	102.38	106.78	111.19	113.81	115.81	118.78	8.75	8.45%

with a rate below current rates, selling at a 25% discount from par. Similarly, a price of 108 indicates a mortgage with a higher coupon than currently issued mortgages that are selling for an 8% premium. Typically, the higher the mortgage coupon, the more valuable the mortgage, since the mortgage payments are higher for higher coupons. Looking at the prices in Exhibit 15, it can be seen that mortgages increased in price from 1984 to 1986, as interest rates declined substantially. However, as interest rates increased during 1987, mortgage prices generally fell, at least for lower coupon mortgages. During the 1988 to 1990 period, mortgage prices were considerably less volatile than they were during the 1984 to 1987 time period. Most mortgages ended 1990 2% to 5% higher in price than they were at the end of 1987, with most of these gains being realized in the second half of 1990.

Standard calculations of duration for these mortgages, as in Exhibit 14, result in modified durations of five to six years. This implies that a 1% increase or decrease in interest rates should move mortgage prices by 5% to 6% in the opposite direction. For the 600 basis points decrease in rates from May 1984 to August 1986, standard duration methods predict mortgage price increases of 30% to 36%. In fact, GNMA 8s increased from 66.38 to 97.25, an increase of 46.5%, substantially more than predicted! GNMA 11s increased about as expected, from 81.38 to 106.84, or 31.3%. GNMA 13s increased significantly less than standard duration projects—going from 92.19 to 107.50, an increase of only 16.6%.

Exhibit 16 illustrates much more clearly what happens to price elasticities for mortgages and bonds as interest rates change. Exhibit 16 was constructed by choosing seven months of actual mortgage and bond prices from the complete set of data in Exhibit 15. The months chosen are months with twenty-year Treasury bond futures rates near 8, 9, 10, 11, 12, 13, and 14%. Thus, they span the entire range of interest rates covered during the 1984–1990 period. From these data, price elasticities are computed at each interest rate level for Treasury bond futures and for GNMA 9s, 11s, and 13s, respectively.

Exhibit 16: Price Elasticities for T-Bond Futures and GNMA Mortgages

Month End	Rate	Rate Change	Price	Elastic	Price	Elastic	Price	Elastic	Price	Elastic	Price	Elastic
		20-Year Treasury Bond Futures			**Prices and Elasticities for GNMAs**							
					GNMA 9s		**GNMA 11s**		**GNMA 13s**			
Nov 89	8.05%	0.83%	$99.47	-9.14%	$99.88	-3.40%	$105.69	-1.18%	$110.69	-1.43%		
Mar 90	8.88%	1.28%	$91.88	-8.69%	$97.06	-3.82%	$104.13	-1.64%	$109.38	-0.59%		
Mov 85	10.16%	0.96%	$81.66	-8.25%	$92.31	-6.41%	$101.94	-5.05%	$108.56	-2.70%		
Jul 85	11.12%	0.91%	$75.19	-7.99%	$86.63	-7.53%	$ 97.00	-6.16%	$105.75	-4.39%		
Mar 85	12.03%	0.96%	$69.72	-7.52%	$80.69	-6.13%	$ 91.56	-5.26%	$101.53	-3.68%		
Apr 84	12.99%	0.98%	$64.69	-7.15%	$75.94	-7.47%	$ 86.94	-6.53%	$ 97.94	-5.99%		
May 84	13.97%		$60.16		$70.38		$ 81.38		$ 92.19			

Several features of "the market's" price elasticities are evident from Exhibit 16.[2] First, Treasury bond futures elasticities are larger when rates are low than when rates are high. This means that Treasury bond futures prices rise at an increasing rate as rates decline. This phenomenon can also be seen from the dollar moves in Exhibit 6 for T-bond futures. Alternatively, as rates increase, T-bond prices fall by smaller and smaller amounts. The reason for this is explained by duration analysis. As rates increase, the present values of distant cash flows become smaller fractions of the bond's value, resulting in a smaller duration for the bond. As rates decrease, distant cash flows are a larger fraction of bond value, thereby increasing the bond's duration.

The change in duration as rates change is called "convexity." Changes of the type shown by T-bond futures are evidence of "positive convexity." All else held constant, positive convexity is a good thing if you are long the bond, and bad if you are short the bond. Note that as rates move, longs win increasingly large amounts as rates fall, and they lose smaller and smaller amounts as rates increase—a very nice situation indeed! Since the long's gains are the short's losses in futures markets, shorts see increasingly large losses as rates fall, and diminishing incremental profits as rates rise. Thus, the short effectively has negative convexity, or "concavity," which is bad.

Price elasticities on mortgages change much more than do those on T-bonds. When rates are low, mortgages have small price elasticities; when rates increase, price elasticities increase and mortgage prices fall by larger amounts. Thus, mortgages have adverse changes in elasticities for their owners (i.e., negative convexity). Mortgage holders can win only small amounts, but they can lose much larger amounts. This is surely one reason why mortgage rates appear high in relation to Treasury rates, since mortgage investors must be compensated to be induced to take on this negative convexity.

---

[2] All elasticities are expected to be negative, so those signs are ignored in the discussion.

Mortgages have negative convexity because of the prepayment option that borrowers possess. Since borrowers can always pay off their mortgages at 100% (par), mortgage prices cannot exceed par by much. (Since there are points and other costs involved in refinancing with another mortgage, mortgage prices can exceed par by 2% to 5%, and many borrowers will not prepay.) The likelihood of massive prepayments when rates fall sharply (verified in Exhibit 3) means that mortgage prices must increase at a slower and slower rate as interest rates decrease and send mortgage prices above par. In Exhibit 16, the GNMA 11s are the classic illustration of this prepayment option effect. When prices are below par, the GNMA 11s have a price elasticity of about 6%, but the elasticity drops to 1.6% at prices between 102 and 104, and drops further to 1.2% at prices above 104.

The GNMA 13s illustrate the same type of effect, but a closer look at Exhibit 15 reveals an unusual phenomenon. As T-bond rates increased from about 8% (in April 1986) to 9% (in June 1987), GNMA 13s actually increased in price (from $107.44 to $110.88). This presumably occurred as investors thought that the likely dramatic reduction in prepayments would offset the higher discount rate for the mortgages' cash flows. Thus, the price elasticity actually had the opposite sign of a standard elasticity at that time.

Many institutions buy GNMA mortgages and hedge them by shorting Treasury bond futures or by financing at long-term fixed rates. This hedging strategy typically reduces interest rate risk substantially. More precisely, the risk is changed from a prediction of where the level of interest rates is going to one of where mortgage rates are going relative to Treasury rates. This latter risk is the "basis risk" of a hedge of mortgages with Treasury bond futures. The basis is the difference between cash and futures prices. In this mortgage hedge, the relevant cash price is a mortgage price, whereas the futures hedge is in T-bonds. Thus, basis risk here is the risk that mortgage rates will increase relative to Treasury rates, thereby decreasing the market values of mortgages relative to Treasury bonds.

The year 1986 exhibited an amazing example of basis risk. Referring to Exhibit 15, put yourself in the position of an owner of GNMA 12s on December 31, 1985. Your hedge in Treasury bonds is a short position, since all data to that point showed that mortgage prices fall as interest rates increase. In the first 6 months of 1986, interest rates fall sharply, with T-bond futures prices increasing from 85.22 to 99.56, giving losses of more than $14,000 per contract shorted. That is not in itself a bad thing, as long as the other side of the hedge (the GNMA 12s) increases in value to compensate. Instead, the GNMA 12s actually decrease in value from 107.13 to 105.75. Both sides of the hedge have lost—an impossible situation! These losses showed up in investment banks' income statements during the second quarter of 1986, since they held many mortgages hedged with futures. (Similar losses would have appeared in savings and loans' income statements, if they had marked to market.)

In the second half of 1986, the poor hedge situation occurred again. Bond prices fell, so the short hedge profited. When the short hedge profits, one expects to see cash market losses, but the GNMA 12s increased in value. Thus, both sides of the hedge won in the latter half of 1986. The net result for the entire year of 1986 is that bond futures increased by thirteen points, whereas the GNMA 12s increased by about one point—just the usual positive correlation of bonds and mortgages! The risks shown by these unpredictable movements of mortgage prices relative to T-bond prices are extreme forms of basis risk. No hedge is perfect—there is always some basis risk left.

Exhibits 17 and 18 display this basis risk for current coupon mortgage securities for the 1984 to 1990 period. At each month-end the approximate yield on mortgages priced at par is compared to the yield on seven-year Treasury notes. The seven-year Treasury was chosen as the benchmark for comparison because it is the T-note whose price elasticity is most similar to that of current coupon mortgages. The difference between the yield on the mortgages and the yield on seven-year Treasury notes gives an estimate of the "basis"—the yield spread between mortgages and

Exhibit 17: Mortgage and Treasury Yields, 1984-1990

End of Month	FNMA Par Yield	7-Year Treasury Yield	FNMA Par Yield Minus 7-Year Treasury Yield
Jan-84	13.00	11.47	1.53
Feb-84	13.19	11.86	1.33
Mar-84	13.73	12.38	1.35
Apr-84	14.00	12.66	1.34
May-84	15.17	13.80	1.37
Jun-84	14.93	13.75	1.18
Jul-84	14.43	12.88	1.55
Aug-84	14.31	12.82	1.49
Sep-84	13.92	12.47	1.45
Oct-84	13.30	11.59	1.71
Nov-84	12.92	11.55	1.37
Dec-84	12.92	11.45	1.47
Jan-85	12.70	11.05	1.65
Feb-85	13.32	11.83	1.49
Mar-85	13.02	11.59	1.43
Apr-85	12.85	11.27	1.58
May-85	11.72	10.11	1.61
Jun-85	11.49	10.14	1.35
Jul-85	11.90	10.36	1.54
Aug-85	11.73	10.15	1.58
Sep-85	11.74	10.12	1.62
Oct-85	11.50	9.84	1.66
Nov-85	10.87	9.45	1.42
Dec-85	10.17	8.87	1.30
Jan-86	10.35	8.87	1.48
Feb-86	9.57	8.04	1.53
Mar-86	9.36	7.23	2.13
Apr-86	9.23	7.20	2.03
May-86	10.09	8.04	2.05
Jun-86	9.95	7.30	2.65
Jul-86	9.83	7.17	2.66 (H)
Aug-86	9.13	6.72	2.41
Sep-86	9.45	7.26	2.19
Oct-86	9.22	7.09	2.13
Nov-86	8.52	6.99	1.53
Dec-86	8.83	7.08	1.75
Jan-87	8.55	6.98	1.57
Feb-87	8.50	6.96	1.54
Mar-87	8.74	7.38	1.36
Apr-87	9.85	8.01	1.84
May-87	10.15	8.31	1.84
Jun-87	9.93	8.23	1.70
Jul-87	9.93	8.46	1.47
Aug-87	10.12	8.78	1.34
Sep-87	10.80	9.41	1.39
Oct-87	10.45	8.67	1.78
Nov-87	10.20	8.78	1.42
Dec-87	10.19	8.63	1.56
Jan-88	9.50	7.91	1.59
Feb-88	9.57	8.04	1.53
Mar-88	9.83	8.49	1.34
Apr-88	10.02	8.65	1.37
May-88	10.29	8.95	1.34
Jun-88	9.90	8.65	1.25
Jul-88	10.23	9.11	1.21
Aug-88	10.32	8.94	1.26
Sep-88	9.99	8.73	1.18
Oct-88	9.69	8.51	1.36
Nov-88	10.13	8.99	1.14
Dec-88	10.56	9.20	1.36
Jan-89	10.33	9.03	1.30
Feb-89	10.66	9.35	1.31
Mar-89	10.90	9.36	1.54
Apr-89	10.67	9.10	1.57
May-89	10.17	8.62	1.55
Jun-89	9.77	8.08	1.69
Jul-89	9.40	7.57	1.83
Aug-89	9.97	8.28	1.69
Sep-89	9.95	8.35	1.60
Oct-89	9.53	7.90	1.63
Nov-89	9.49	7.81	1.68
Dec-89	9.51	7.96	1.55
Jan-90	9.85	8.37	1.48
Feb-90	9.96	8.53	1.43
Mar-90	10.04	8.69	1.35
Apr-90	10.41	9.04	1.37
May-90	9.91	8.63	1.28
Jun-90	9.74	8.45	1.29
Jul-90	9.52	8.27	1.25
Aug-90	9.87	8.75	1.12
Sep-90	9.85	8.70	1.15
Oct-90	9.84	8.50	1.34
Nov-90	9.56	8.16	1.40
Dec-90	9.33	7.98	1.35 (L)

Standard Deviations: (in percent, monthly data)	FNMA Par Yield	7-Year Treasury Yield	FNMA Par Yield Minus 7-Yr Treasury
Levels	2.25	1.94	0.34
Changes	0.41	0.43	0.19

Correlations FNMA Par Yield vs. 7-Year Treasury Yield:	
Levels	0.965
Changes	0.899

Note: All rates are expressed as bond-equivalent yields.

Exhibit 18: Basis Risk Between Mortgages and Treasuries

FNMA PAR YIELD vs. 7-YR TREASURY YIELD

Monthly, 1984 to 1990

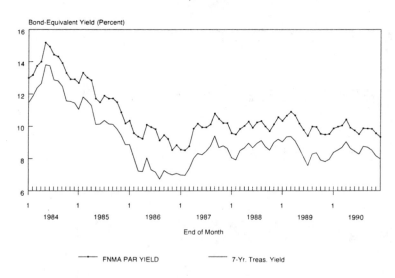

FNMA PAR YIELD MINUS 7-YR TREAS. YIELD

Monthly, 1984 to 1990

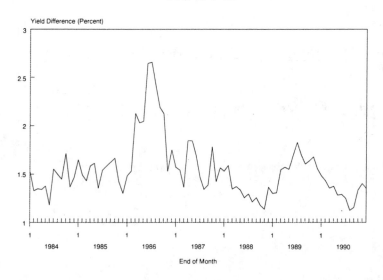

Treasury securities with similar risk characteristics. As Exhibits 17 and 18 show, the basis was always positive during the 1984 to 1990 period (meaning the mortgages yielded more than comparable Treasury securities), but this spread was hardly constant. At the beginning of 1984 the spread between mortgages and Treasuries was approximately 1.5%. This spread stayed fairly stable until early April 1986, when mortgage prepayments surged as long-term rates fell in tandem with oil price declines. The spread reached its widest level in July 1986 at 2.66%. This increase in the mortgage/Treasury basis largely explains why mortgage investors hedged with Treasury-based instruments lost money during most of 1986.

As discussed earlier, when the basis widens (an increase in the mortgage/Treasury yield spread), an investor who owns mortgages and hedges with Treasuries will experience either a loss or at least less profits than he expected. As described above, in 1986 many mortgage investors who hedged with Treasury securities suffered losses during the period due to widening yield spreads of mortgages relative to Treasuries.

Late in 1986, the spread began to decline, and it has continued to trend downward during the 1987 to 1990 period. This spread narrowing has been caused by *five* major factors:

1. Increased demand for mortgage-backed securities for use in collateralized mortgage obligations (CMOs);

2. A general increase in the number and characteristics of mortgage-backed securities' investors;

3. Increased investor sophistication and understanding of the prepayment behavior of mortgages;

4. Lower interest rate volatility, making the prepayment option less valuable to the borrower; and

5. Recently adopted risk-based capital requirements for financial institutions that established low capital requirements for mortgages relative to other asset types.

When the basis tightens, a hedger will usually experience larger than expected profits. This is especially true of those savvy investors who purchased mortgages in 1986, hedged the interest rate risk of these securities, and held onto their mortgages until at least late 1986 or early 1987.

Exhibits 17 and 18 also display the beneficial risk-reducing effects of hedging. Hedging reduced the risk to an investor in mortgages from the fluctuations in the nominal level of mortgage interest rates (high of 13.75%, low of 6.72%) to the fluctuations in the yield spread between mortgages and Treasuries (high of 2.68%, low of 1.12%). Note the high correlation between the yields of current coupon mortgages and seven-year Treasury notes during the 1984 to 1990 period (.985 for rate levels and .899 for monthly rate changes). These correlations indicate that such Treasury securities would have been an effective hedge of current coupon mortgages during this time period. Further evidence of hedge effectiveness is given by the fact that the standard deviations (the most common measure of financial risk) of monthly mortgage rate levels and changes (2.25% and 0.41%, respectively), representing unhedged mortgage portfolio risk, were significantly higher than the standard deviations of levels and changes in the mortgage/Treasury yield spread (0.34% and 0.19%, respectively), representing the risk of portfolios of current coupon mortgages hedged with seven-year Treasury notes.

Clearly, classic duration measures are very useful for standard bonds, but may be very misleading for mortgages. However, Wall Street now essentially defines the "effective duration" of a mortgage by its price elasticity. For the sake of simplicity of language, this chapter will use the terms "duration" and "elasticity" interchangeably to mean the percentage change in the market value of a financial instrument for a 100 basis point (1%) change in the level of interest rates. Thus, the description might be "duration," but the relevant calculation is "elasticity."

Given these elements of futures, options, swaps, caps, floors, mortgages, duration, convexity, and elasticity, we are now ready to examine the interest rate risk for a typical firm and to construct hedges for it.

LIQUIDATION VALUE AND INTEREST RATE RISK FOR A FIRM

Liquidation Value

The first step in evaluating the financial condition and interest rate risk of an institution involves calculating the market value of the firm's assets and liabilities. Since the main objective of a hedging program is to protect the firm against changes in its market value caused by changes in interest rates, the market value (not the book value) of the firm and its component parts must be calculated. The terms "market value" and "liquidation value" will be used interchangeably in the following discussion. The liquidation value may be thought of as being that amount of money which would be left over if the firm sold its assets and repurchased its liabilities at current market prices.

The condensed balance sheet of First Savings and Loan Association is found in Exhibit 19. On December 31, 1990, the date of the analysis, the institution had assets totalling $1.65 billion and a book net worth of $74.4 million (4.5% of assets). Exhibit 19 lists the book value, the average term to maturity or repricing, the actual interest rate, the current fair rate on those assets and liabilities, the price elasticity or modified duration, and the market value of each of the major balance sheet categories of the Association. The market value of each item is calculated by discounting its associated cash flows using the current market discount rate, as determined by the purchase price of like assets or the issue rate on new liabilities.

In the case of First Savings, since interest rates have fallen markedly during the nine months prior to the date of the analysis (December 31, 1990), many of the balance sheet items have market values that are significantly different from their stated book values. For example, the Association owns $1,189.6 million of fixed-

Exhibit 19: First Savings and Loan Association: Condensed Balance Sheet and Liquidation Value, December 31, 1990

	Book Value (Mil) (1)	Avg Term (Years) (2)	Avg Rate (%) (3)	Current Fair Rate (4)	Rate Change (5)	Elast or Mod. Duration (6)	Gain From Book (Mil) (7)	Market Value (Mil) (8)
Assets								
Liquidity Investments	179.3	0.1	6.85%	6.85%	0.00%	0.1%	0.0	179.3
Adjustable Rate Mortgages	224.2	0.5	10.44%	9.55%	0.89%	1.0%	2.0	226.2
Fixed Rate Mortgages	1,189.6	28.0	10.58%	10.08%	0.50%	3.8%	22.8	1,212.4
Commercial & Consumer Loans	55.6	0.7	11.94%	10.80%	1.14%	0.6%	0.4	56.0
Total Assets	1,648.7	20.3	10.20%	9.68%	0.52%	2.9%	25.2	1,673.9
Liabilities								
Money Market Accounts	132.2	0.0	6.62%	6.62%	0.00%	0.0%	0.0	132.2
FHLB Advances	192.1	4.8	9.06%	8.44%	-0.62%	4.4%	-5.2	197.3
Fixed Rate Deposits	1,250.0	0.8	8.52%	7.50%	-1.02%	0.8%	-9.6	1,259.6
Total Liabilities	1,574.3	1.2	8.43%	7.54%	-0.89%	1.1%	-14.8	1,589.1
Net Worth	74.4						10.4	84.8
Non-Balance Sheet Items:								
Interest Rate Swap	500.0	6.6	8.27%	7.74%	-0.53%	4.8%	-12.7	-12.7
Liquidation Value	74.4						-2.3	72.1

rate conventional mortgages. Since the average coupon rate on these mortgages is higher than the current market rate for conventional mortgages, the market value of these assets is greater than the stated book value. Exhibit 19 indicates that the market value of the firm's fixed-rate mortgages is $1,212.4 million, or $22.8 million greater than the stated book value ($1,189.6 million).

Similar market value gains (excesses over book value) are characteristic of most of the other asset categories, as well. For instance, the market value of the Association's commercial and consumer loan portfolio is $0.4 million in excess of its stated book value. An asset or liability's market value gain is approximately equal to the product of three items: (1) its price elasticity, (2) the rate change since purchase, and (3) the amount. For example, there are $55.6 million of consumer and commercial loans. Multiplying the favorable rate decline of 1.14% since origination by the elasticity of 0.6, gives a 0.68% capital gain on $55.6 million, for a gain of $0.4 million.

In spite of original terms to maturity of thirty years, the adjustable-rate mortgages show a much smaller gain (in both absolute and percentage terms) than the fixed-rate mortgages. This phenomenon is quite easy to explain. There is an average of 6 months to repricing, as indicated by an "average term" of 0.5 years. Since the adjustable-rate mortgages reprice quickly, the interest rate charged on these assets is brought back into line with the market only a short time after the level of market interest rates changes. Once interest rates change, these adjustable-rate assets earn either sub-market or higher-than-market rates for a much shorter period of time than do the Association's fixed-rate assets. The shorter the time period to repricing or maturity, the smaller (in percentage terms) is the effect of a given change in the level of interest rates on the market value of any financial asset or liability.

For example, since First Savings' short-term liquidity investments reprice (on average) every 30 days, the corresponding price elasticity or duration is small (0.1), indicating that a 100 basis point decrease in interest rates will result in only a 0.1% increase in the value of these assets. Conversely, the fixed-rate mortgages of the Association have a market value sensitivity to a 100 basis point interest rate change of approximately 3.8% (duration of 3.8 years). The average elasticity of the firm's assets, taken as a group, is approximately 2.9%. The elasticities of fixed-rate mortgages are significantly less than their stated terms to maturity because of the anticipated prepayments on these securities, as discussed in the previous section.

A brief look at the liability portion of the balance sheet indicates that the Association is paying above-market interest rates on its FHLB advances and fixed-rate deposits. Since the Association is paying a rate that is higher than the rate at which new liabilities could currently be issued (at par), First Savings has a market value loss on these liabilities. The rate on Money Market Deposit Accounts (MMDAs) adjusts almost instantaneously to changes in market interest rates. Since the speed of adjustment is so rapid on these instruments, changes in market interest rates have virtually no effect on the value of MMDAs. For this reason, MMDAs are shown in Exhibit 19 as having equivalent market and book values, and a duration of zero (negligible sensitivity to interest rate changes).

The Association's interest rate swaps are agreements by the firm to pay to counterparties an average fixed rate of 8.27%, semi-annually compounded, and to receive from the counterparty a floating rate (three-month LIBOR) every three months. The interest rate swap effectively "converts" $500 million of 3-month liabilities into $500 million of 6.6-year borrowings. The swaps were entered into during prior periods at then fair market rates for liabilities with corresponding maturities. Because market rates have generally fallen since the inception of these interest rate swaps, the Association will be paying a higher-than-market rate (unless interest rates rise) over the remaining life of the swaps. As shown in Exhibit 19, marking the swaps to market indicates a $12.7 million loss.

The liquidation value of the Association is now easily computed by adding the market value adjustments (from book value) of all financial assets and liabilities to the book net worth. As shown in Exhibit 19, First Savings' liquidation value stood at $72.1 million as of December 31, 1990, which is $2.3 million under its book value. It is this market or liquidation value that we wish to protect from changes in interest rates.

Of course, the liquidation value computation in Exhibit 19 can and should be done each month. As interest rates change and as the firm's composition of assets, liabilities, and swaps changes, the liquidation value of the firm will change. Like most financial institutions, the composition of First Savings' assets and liabilities does not change much from month to month. Therefore, before First Savings hedged with interest rate swaps, the dominant factor that changed the firm's liquidation value in the short run was the level of interest rates. Exhibit 20 shows the liquidation value of First Savings monthly from January 31, 1984, through December 31, 1990. The firm's value on January 31, 1984, was negative. When interest rates rose in early 1984, the firm sank rapidly. Then in late 1984 the firm began to recover as interest rates fell. As rates fell further in 1985 and in 1986, First Savings recovered and finally went into the black in liquidation value.

In early 1986, after again becoming solvent on a liquidation value basis, First Savings decided to hedge most of its interest rate risk. Notice, from Exhibit 20, how stable the firm's liquidation value became after April 1986. Exhibit 20 also displays how First Savings' liquidation value grew steadily during the 1986 to 1990 period in spite of significant fluctuations in market interest rates.

Interest Rate Risk

Now that the value of the firm and its component parts have been calculated, it is necessary to assess what the exact interest rate risks of the firm are at the date of the analysis, December 31, 1990. More specifically, how much money does the Association lose if rates increase by 1%, 2%, 3%, or 4%? How much does it win for decreases in rates that range from 1% to 4%? The discussion of

Exhibit 20: First Savings and Loan Association: Liquidation Value vs. Market Interest Rates, 1984-1990

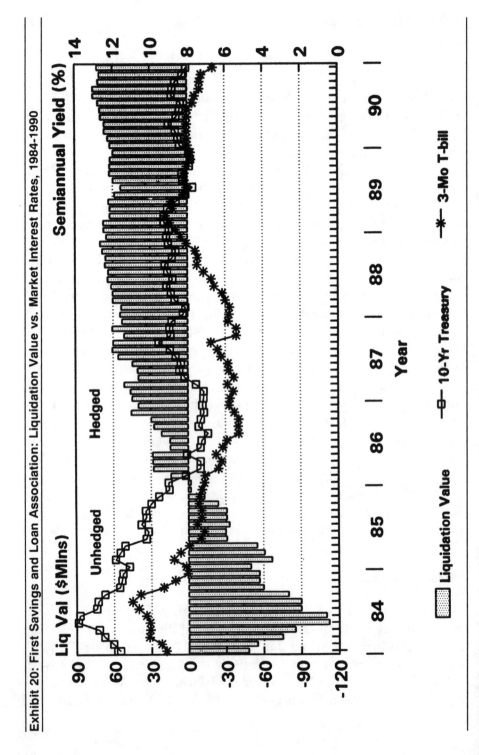

| Liquidation Value | 10-Yr Treasury | 3-Mo T-bill |

duration in the previous section briefly touched on this for the case of 1% moves up and down in rates.

Looking at the elasticity column in Exhibit 19 again, we can see that the average elasticity of First Savings' assets is 2.9%, yet the average elasticity of its liabilities is only 1.1% (not including its interest rate swaps). If the interest rate sensitivities of a firm's assets and liabilities are approximately equal, the firm is not subject to much risk from small parallel shifts in the term structure of interest rates. However, First Savings has a portfolio that is characteristic of many financial institutions—longer duration assets (mainly fixed-rate mortgages) funded primarily by shorter duration sources of funds (CDs). Therefore, if interest rates rose, First Savings' assets would decline in value by more than the gain on its liabilities.

In order to more easily demonstrate the fact that First Savings is exposed to changes in interest rates, it is useful to calculate the market values of the firm and its component parts under different interest rate scenarios. Exhibit 21 presents the estimated value of each asset and liability category for parallel shifts in the Treasury yield curve of between minus 4% and plus 4% (in increments of 100 basis points).

The line in Exhibit 21 labeled "Change in Economic Net Worth (Unhedged)" gives the net market value gain or loss that First Savings' balance sheet (not including its interest rate swaps) would incur from changes in interest rates ranging from 4% higher to 4% lower than base rates on December 31, 1990. This range of interest rates covers ten-year Treasury rates between 4.06% and 12.06%. The value of the firm's assets and liabilities would increase by $56.7 million (from $84.8 million to $141.5 million) if rates drop by 4%. If rates increase by 4%, the value of the firm's assets and liabilities drops by $165.3 million (from $84.8 million to minus $80.5 million). Without any hedging the economic value of the firm would go to zero with about a 2% increase in interest rates (to 10.06% on the ten-year T-note). For a 1% movement in interest rates in either direction, the unhedged First Savings would see its value change by approximately $31.2 million, or 42% of its book

Exhibit 21: First Savings and Loan Association: Analysis of Interest Rate Sensitivity, December 31, 1990

Market Values of Assets and Liabilities At Various Interest Rates

	-4.00%	-3.00%	-2.00%	-1.00%	-0.00%	1.00%	2.00%	3.00%	4.00%
Rate Change From Base:									
10-Year Interest Rate	4.06%	5.06%	6.06%	7.06%	8.06%	9.06%	10.06%	11.06%	12.06%
T-Bond Futures Price	146.75%	130.87%	117.32%	105.71%	95.72%	87.10%	79.63%	73.14%	67.47%
Assets									
Liquidity Investments	179.9	179.7	179.6	179.4	179.3	179.2	179.0	178.9	178.7
Adjustable Rate Mortgages	232.9	231.6	230.0	228.2	226.2	223.7	220.4	215.7	209.5
Fixed Rate Mortgages	1337.8	1317.9	1290.2	1256.4	1212.4	1163.3	1109.8	1054.2	997.9
Commercial & Consumer Loans	57.5	57.2	56.7	56.4	56.0	55.7	55.3	55.0	54.7
Total Assets	1808.1	1786.4	1756.5	1720.4	1673.9	1621.9	1564.5	1503.8	1440.8
Liabilities									
Money Market Accounts	132.2	132.2	132.2	132.2	132.2	132.2	132.2	132.2	132.2
FHLB Advances	235.4	225.1	215.4	206.1	197.3	188.9	181.0	173.4	166.2
Fixed Rate Deposits	1299.0	1288.9	1278.9	1269.2	1259.6	1250.2	1240.2	1231.8	1222.9
Total Liabilities	1666.6	1646.2	1626.5	1607.5	1589.1	1571.3	1553.4	1537.4	1521.3
Net Worth (Economic – Unhedged)	141.5	140.2	130.0	112.9	84.8	50.6	11.1	-33.6	-80.5
Change in Economic Net Worth (Unhedged)	56.7	55.4	45.2	28.1	----	-34.2	-73.7	-118.4	-165.3
Non-Balance Sheet Items:									
Interest Rate Swap	-125.9	-94.7	-65.6	-38.3	-12.7	11.2	33.6	54.7	74.4
Liquidation Value (Hedged)	15.6	45.5	64.4	74.6	72.1	61.8	44.7	21.1	-6.1
Change in Liquidation Value (Hedged)	-56.5	-26.6	-7.7	2.5	----	-10.3	-27.4	-51.0	-78.2

net worth. Clearly, this firm would have very significant interest rate risk relative to its net worth if it did not hedge.

First Savings' interest rate swaps reduce the firm's interest rate risk substantially, especially for small movements in interest rates. The bottom line in Exhibit 21 shows the changes in First Savings' liquidation value that would result from changes in market interest rates. Note the firm's value changes by an average of $6.4 million for a rate move of plus or minus 1%. This average change in value is only 20% of the change in value of the firm without its interest rate swaps. Thus, the interest rate swaps have reduced the interest rate risk of the firm's value (at the margin) by approximately 80%. Despite this achievement, the firm is still subject to some interest rate risk, as it loses value when rates rise and gains somewhat when rates fall. The firm's value falls substantially for large rate movements in either direction (reflecting the customer options inherent in its assets and liabilities), but the firm's value does not go negative unless rates rise almost 4% from current levels.

To identify very easily which assets and liabilities have the greatest dollar interest rate sensitivities for First Savings, the market values of each of the asset categories are graphed versus interest rate changes in Exhibit 22, and the liabilities and interest rate swaps are graphed in Exhibit 23. The liquidation value is plotted in Exhibit 24, as are the assets', the liabilities', and swaps' sensitivities. From Exhibit 22, it is seen that the fixed-rate mortgages have market values that are very interest rate-sensitive. The liquidity investments, adjustable-rate mortgages (ARMs), and First Savings' consumer and commercial loans have market values that are not very rate-sensitive. These numbers square with the duration and price elasticity analysis of the previous section. Similarly, the fixed-rate deposits, fixed-rate FHLB advances, and the fixed-rate interest rate swaps have somewhat rate-sensitive market values, whereas the MMDAs have values that are not sensitive to changes in interest rates.

The amount of rate sensitivity of the combined liabilities' and swaps' values is not as large as the assets' rate sensitivities, so the

Exhibit 22: First Savings and Loan Association: Interest Rate Sensitivities of Assets

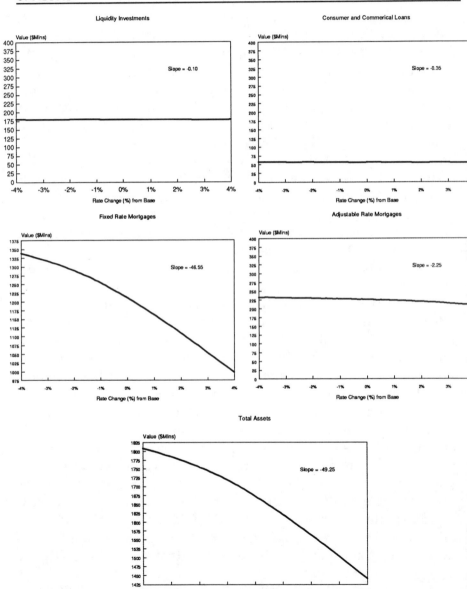

Note: Slopes are reported in millions of dollars and are evaluated at base rates.

Exhibit 23: First Savings and Loan Association: Interest Rate Sensitivities of Liabilities and Swaps

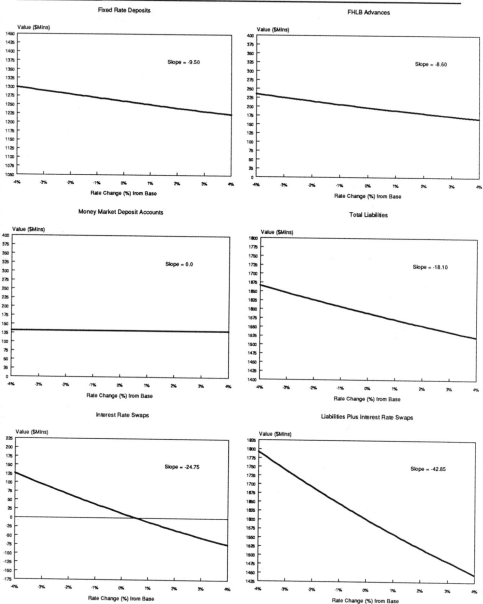

Note: Slopes reported are in millions of dollars and are evaluated at base rates.

Exhibit 24: First Savings and Loan Association: Current Portfolio (Aggregate) Liquidation Value

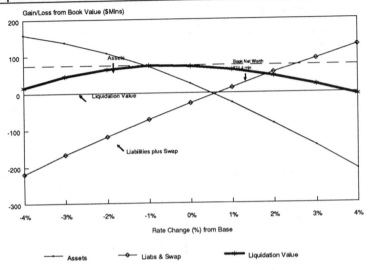

Exhibit 25: First Savings and Loan Association: Value Sensitivity to Rates, 1984–1990

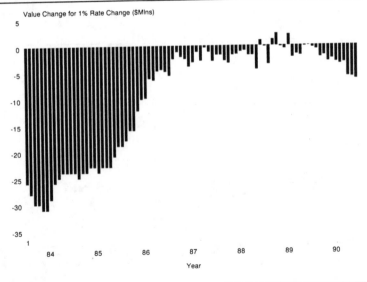

liquidation value has a rate sensitivity that is in the same direction as the assets (note Exhibit 24). For example, with a 4% rate increase the assets lose $233.1 million of market value, whereas the liabilities beneficially drop in value by $67.8 million and the interest rate swaps gain back 87.1 million. The net result is a decrease in liquidation value of $78.2 million (–233.1 + 67.8 + 87.1 = –78.2) from the base case. The graphs in Exhibits 22–24 apply to where First Savings stands on December 31, 1990. They are based on current (December 31, 1990) rates, current assets, liabilities, and swaps. They are the relevant graphs for current (December 1990) decision-making. However, they do not really give a historical perspective of the interest rate risk of the institution. Exhibit 20 shows the historical fluctuations in the liquidation value of the institution, prior to December 31, 1990. Exhibit 25 shows the interest rate sensitivity for 1% rate moves that First Savings has had monthly in the past seven years.

The firm's interest rate sensitivity gap has narrowed over the past seven years for three reasons. First, as rates fell, the mortgages held by First Savings prepaid more quickly, thereby shortening their durations and reducing their interest rate sensitivities. Second, beginning in early 1986, First Savings entered into a number of interest rate swaps. Third, the firm began to fund some of its assets with longer-term FHLB advances. This longer-term funding source more closely matched the interest rate risk of First Savings' mortgage assets than did its short-term deposit liabilities. This significantly closed the gap between the rate sensitivities of assets and liabilities. The interest rate swaps and FHLB advances help to protect the firm by having gains when rates are high, which is just when the assets are losing.

HEDGING WITH FUTURES AND SWAPS: CORRELATION STATISTICS

Referring again to Exhibit 21, First Savings and Loan currently (December 31, 1990) has a liquidation value of $72.1 million, which reflects gains and losses on assets, liabilities, and interest rate swaps. If rates increase by 1%, First Savings' liquidation value falls to $61.8 million. If rates decrease by 1%, the liquidation value increases to $74.6 million. Averaging the up ($2.5 million) and down ($10.3 million) movements in liquidation value, First Savings wins or loses about $6.4 million when interest rates move by 1%. The specific hedge employed should be designed to provide a gain when rates are up, which is when the firm needs the gain, because of its low "cash value." (The firm's net value excluding any hedges that are used is called its cash value.) The firm should expect to have a loss on the hedge when rates are down, since the firm is well-off then, with a high cash value. In the absence of any such hedging program, First Savings' long-run profit margin would be tenuous, at best.

Now that the direction and magnitude of the interest rate risk have been identified, the next step in the analysis is to select the instruments that will comprise the hedging position, and to determine the sizes of the hedging positions necessary to protect the institution from changes in interest rates. As discussed earlier in this chapter, the most liquid interest rate futures markets are those for twenty-year Treasury bonds (T-bonds) and those for ninety-one-day Eurodollar time deposits (Euros). Since these allow us to hedge long-term and short-term interest rate fluctuations separately, we will consider hedging only in T-bonds and Euros at the present time.

The direction and size of a futures hedge are both easy to compute and to understand. All financial officers, board members, and regulators should be able to do at least the following simple analysis and calculation. Short positions in these Treasury bond and Eurodollar futures contracts are the appropriate positions, because the hedge must be designed to benefit First Savings when the rest of its portfolio loses value (i.e., when interest rates increase). When interest rates increase, bond prices fall and the short wins. Conversely, the short futures position loses money when interest rates fall and the firm has economic gains. The number of contracts is chosen so as to equate the futures gains or losses with the "cash" losses or gains under the different interest rate scenarios. The total futures gain or loss is the product of the number of futures contracts held times the gain or loss per contract. Thus, to have futures gains and losses balance cash gains and losses for a 1% change in rates, one needs only solve the following equation:

$$
\begin{array}{c}
\text{Futures Gain} \\
\text{For 1\% Rate} \\
\text{Change}
\end{array}
=
\begin{array}{c}
\text{Number of} \\
\text{Contracts} \\
\text{Held Short}
\end{array}
\times
\begin{array}{c}
\text{Gain/Con-} \\
\text{tract of} \\
\text{Short For} \\
\text{1\% Rate} \\
\text{Change}
\end{array}
=
\begin{array}{c}
\text{- Change} \\
\text{in Present} \\
\text{Value of} \\
\text{Firm for} \\
\text{1\% Rate} \\
\text{Change}
\end{array}
$$

Solving:

$$
\begin{array}{c}
\text{Number of} \\
\text{Contracts} \\
\text{Held Short}
\end{array}
=
\frac{\text{- Change in PV of Firm For 1\% Rate Change}}{\text{Gain/Contract of Short For 1\% Rate Change}}
$$

To find the number of contracts to be held to give the correctly offsetting futures move, one must know how much is gained or lost in T-bonds and Euros if rates move by 1%. A table of these dollar moves at different rates is given in Exhibit 6, covering twenty-year Treasury bond futures, ten-year Treasury notes, ninety-one-day Treasury bills, and ninety-one-day Eurodollars. On December 31, 1990, the near Treasury bond futures price was 95.72, implying a yield near 8.45%. From Exhibit 6, at that rate level, a short T-bond futures contract wins about $8,620 if rates increase to 9.45%, and it loses about $9,980 if rates fall to 7.45%. The average dollar move for a T-bond contract is $9,300 for a 1% rate move. In contrast, a Eurodollar time deposit contract wins or loses only $2,500 for a 1% rate move. Thus, if short and long rates move in parallel by 1%, the T-bond contract will generate almost four times ($9,300/$2,500) as much dollar gain or loss as will the Euro contract, despite having a par amount that is only one-tenth the Euro's amount.

Given that the firm gains or loses on average about $6,400,000 for a 1% rate move, and given that one T-bond futures contract gains or loses about $9,300 at the same time, one can compute the approximate number of T-bond futures contracts that need to be held with the formula:

$$\begin{matrix} \text{Number of} \\ \text{Contracts} \\ \text{Held Short} \end{matrix} = \frac{-\$\ -6{,}400{,}000}{\$9{,}300} = 688 \text{ contracts short}$$

With this position, if rates move up 1%, the 688 T-bonds short will each gain $8,620, for a total of $5.9 million, which offsets a significant portion of the cash (nonfutures) loss that occurs. If rates fall, due to the "convexity" of T-bond prices, a slightly larger loss occurs: 688 × $9,980 = $6.9 million. If Euros were used in the hedge instead of T-bonds, the correct number of Euro futures contracts would be $6,400,000/$2,500 = 2,560 contracts short. The number of Euro contracts that must be held is almost four times the number of T-bond contracts, since each Euro moves only about one-quarter times as much as one T-bond (again assuming parallel shifts of short and long rates).

Banks and savings and loans must report their futures positions to their regulators. Note the difference in the par amounts reported with Eurodollar and Treasury bond hedges that have *the same average dollar moves*. With T-bonds, only 688 contracts are held short, each with a par amount of $100,000, for a total par amount of 688 × $100,000 = $68.8 million. This seems not to be an unreasonable futures position for a $1.8 billion institution, so it usually raises no regulatory concern. However, if the institution hedges with Eurodollars, the par amount is $1 million per contract times 2,560 contracts, for a total par shorted of $2.56 billion. Having a futures position with a par amount well over the amount of assets of the institution raises many red flags for bank examiners. Yet the position is correctly balanced, so it is appropriate. Of course, the difference is that the price elasticity (modified duration) of twenty-year T-bonds is about 10% (ten years), whereas the elasticity for ninety-one-day Eurodollars is only about one-fortieth that amount, at 0.25%. Thus, almost forty times the par in T-bonds must be held in Eurodollars for an equivalent hedge. To prevent poor analysis, the regulatory focus must be on dollar moves of the position for 1% rate moves, rather than on par amounts. Focus on par amounts has led and undoubtedly will continue to lead to many embarrassingly incorrect statements being made by examiners about hedging programs.

If the term structure always had parallel shifts, it would not matter whether the futures hedge was done with T-bonds or with Euros, as long as the correct number of contracts was held for the market used. However, as can be seen in Exhibit 1, the term structure does not always move in parallel ways. For example, comparing June 1985 rates to January 1986 rates, one sees that the 3-month T-bill rate increased by 5 basis points, whereas the 20-year rate decreased by 109 basis points. If First Savings' cash position moved mostly with short-term rates, and 688 T-bond futures contracts were shorted as a futures hedge, then the firm would not have gained on its cash position, but would have lost about $10,000 per contract on its futures (about $6.9 million in futures losses).

The risk that the cash position will move somewhat differently than the hedge position is the "basis risk" described in the second section. Exhibit 26 gives a good illustration of basis risk versus interest rate risk using the liquidation value history of First Savings. The top panel (also shown in Exhibit 20) shows the relationship between First Savings' liquidation value and market interest rates. Notice that there was a strong (negative) relationship between the firm's value and the level of interest rates until the firm began hedging in early 1986. Since the firm began hedging, there appears to be little relationship between changes in the firm's value and market interest rates.

The bottom panel displays the relationship between the firm's value and the interest spread between par coupon mortgages and comparable Treasury notes. In the early (unhedged) period there is little relationship between the mortgage/Treasury yield spread

Exhibit 26: First Savings and Loan Association: Liquidation Value vs. Short and Long Rates, and vs. Mortgage Spread

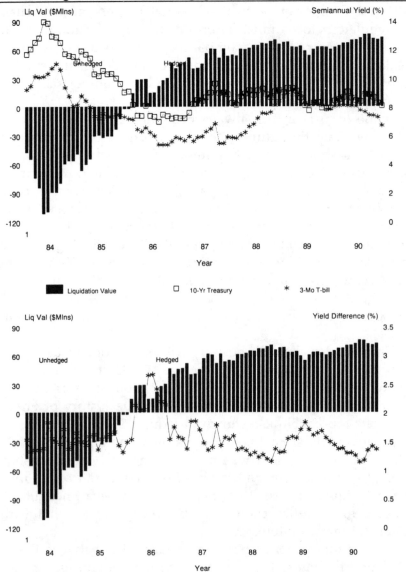

(the basis) and the firm's liquidation value. During the hedged period (after April 1986), the firm's value is significantly affected by changes in the basis. For example, when mortgage spreads to Treasury widened during mid-1986, the firm's value fell dramatically. As the basis narrowed in late 1986 and early 1987, the firm's value rose accordingly.

As these graphs clearly display, First Savings reduced its overall interest rate risk from that of its unhedged period (where month-to-month changes in the firm's value were largely determined by changes in the level of market interest rates) to that of the later "hedged" period (where changes in the firm's value were largely determined by changes in the yield spread between mortgages and Treasury securities). As Exhibits 17 and 18 have already shown, the basis risk is considerably smaller than the risk of going unhedged. By shorting contracts for the hedge that are most highly correlated with the cash position, this basis risk is minimized, but it is never eliminated. That is why hedging is correctly called "speculation in the basis." The good news is that the correlations between interest rate futures and cash market bond values are usually quite high, and the basis risk is considerably smaller than the risk of going unhedged.

Exhibits 27 and 28 present means, standard deviations, and correlations for GNMA mortgage prices for coupons from 8% to 15%, and for the near Treasury bond and Eurodollar futures contracts. The data used are those of Exhibit 15, which were obtained primarily from Salomon Brothers (to whom we are very grateful). Exhibit 27 calculates statistics for price levels and their correlations, whereas Exhibit 28 calculates statistics for monthly changes in those same price levels. Both sets of tables have value and present much the same story, but statisticians usually prefer to focus on Exhibit 28—the data on monthly price changes (as those monthly changes are more nearly serially uncorrelated). Since interest rates fell sharply during this period, particularly in late 1985 and early 1986, mortgage prices should and did behave differently later in the sample. For this reason, the data sample was divided into two major subperiods—the 1984–1985 subperiod (high rates),

Exhibit 27: Means, Standard Deviations, and Correlations Using Price Levels

A. Bond and Mortgage Prices: Means and Standard Deviations

Variable	Entire Period 1984–1990		First Subperiod 1984–1985		Second Subperiod 1986–1990		Third Subperiod 1986–1987		Fourth Subperiod 1988–1990	
	Mean	Std Dev'n	Mean	Std Dev'n	Mean	Std Dev'n	Mean	Std Dev'n	Mean	Std Dev'n
BondFut	87.41	10.80	71.32	6.23	93.01	4.71	94.47	5.88	92.23	3.73
Eurofut	91.63	1.46	90.23	1.60	92.12	1.03	93.06	0.73	91.62	0.79
GNMA 8	89.45	8.05	77.45	6.35	93.62	2.39	94.20	3.05	93.32	1.88
GNMA 9	93.63	7.92	81.92	6.51	97.71	2.36	98.15	2.91	97.47	1.96
GNMA 10	98.22	7.53	87.20	6.54	102.05	2.15	102.89	2.85	101.60	1.48
GNMA 11	101.98	6.50	92.56	6.09	105.25	1.55	105.92	1.58	104.90	1.40
GNMA 13	108.15	4.62	101.80	4.59	110.36	1.58	108.92	1.22	111.13	1.17
GNMA 14	110.57	3.70	105.67	3.57	112.27	1.66	110.78	1.46	113.07	1.12
GNMA 15	112.82	3.36	108.38	3.21	114.37	1.54	114.05	0.71	114.54	1.81

B. Correlation Matrix — Entire Period: 1984–1990

	BondFut	Eurofut	GNMA 8	GNMA 9	GNMA 10	GNMA 11	GNMA 13	GNMA 14	GNMA 15
BondFut	1.000	0.767	0.974	0.970	0.964	0.938	0.836	0.780	0.834
Eurofut	0.767	1.000	0.804	0.805	-0.824	0.842	0.680	0.608	0.763
GNMA 8	0.974	0.804	1.000	0.999	0.996	0.985	0.913	0.863	0.900
GNMA 9	0.970	0.805	0.999	1.000	0.996	0.992	0.921	0.872	0.910
GNMA 10	0.964	0.824	0.996	0.996	1.000	0.992	0.911	0.858	0.899
GNMA 11	0.938	0.842	0.985	0.987	0.992	1.000	0.932	0.884	0.922
GNMA 13	0.836	0.680	0.913	0.921	0.911	0.932	1.000	0.985	0.938
GNMA 14	0.780	0.608	0.863	0.872	0.858	0.884	0.985	1.000	0.922
GNMA 15	0.834	0.763	0.900	0.910	0.899	0.922	0.938	0.922	1.000

C. Correlation Matrix — First Subperiod: 1984–1985

	BondFut	Eurofut	GNMA 8	GNMA 9	GNMA 10	GNMA 11	GNMA 13	GNMA 14	GNMA 15
BondFut	1.000	0.935	0.992	0.993	0.993	0.992	0.960	0.911	0.920
Eurofut	0.935	1.000	0.941	0.943	0.945	0.958	0.956	0.928	0.951
GNMA 8	0.992	0.941	1.000	1.000	0.998	0.994	0.968	0.927	0.935
GNMA 9	0.993	0.943	1.000	1.000	0.999	0.996	0.970	0.929	0.937
GNMA 10	0.993	0.945	0.998	0.999	1.000	0.998	0.974	0.932	0.940
GNMA 11	0.992	0.958	0.994	0.996	0.998	1.000	0.981	0.944	0.952
GNMA 13	0.960	0.956	0.968	0.970	0.974	0.981	1.000	0.980	0.978
GNMA 14	0.911	0.928	0.927	0.929	0.932	0.944	0.980	1.000	0.986
GNMA 15	0.920	0.951	0.935	0.937	0.940	0.952	0.978	0.986	1.000

Exhibit 27: Means, Standard Deviations, and Correlations Using Price Levels (Continued)

D. Correlation Matrix — Second Subperiod: 1986–1990

	BondFut	Eurofut	GNMA 8	GNMA 9	GNMA 10	GNMA 11	GNMA 13	GNMA 14	GNMA 15
BondFut	1.000	0.510	0.873	0.850	0.833	0.625	-0.176	-0.258	0.119
Eurofut	0.510	1.000	0.616	0.590	0.689	0.829	-0.270	-0.377	0.265
GNMA 8	0.873	0.616	1.000	0.982	0.956	0.828	0.046	-0.067	0.318
GNMA 9	0.850	0.590	0.982	1.000	0.950	0.836	0.124	0.010	0.397
GNMA 10	0.833	0.689	0.956	0.950	1.000	0.874	-0.083	-0.195	0.247
GNMA 11	0.625	0.829	0.828	0.836	0.874	1.000	0.049	-0.060	0.433
GNMA 13	-0.176	-0.270	0.046	0.124	-0.083	0.049	1.000	0.953	0.557
GNMA 14	-0.258	-0.377	-0.067	0.010	-0.195	-0.060	0.953	1.000	0.508
GNMA 15	0.119	0.265	0.318	0.397	0.247	0.433	0.557	0.508	1.000

E. Correlation Matrix — Third Subperiod: 1986–1987

	BondFut	Eurofut	GNMA 8	GNMA 9	GNMA 10	GNMA 11	GNMA 13	GNMA 14	GNMA 15
BondFut	1.000	0.843	0.898	0.871	0.886	0.860	-0.532	-0.602	-0.287
Eurofut	0.843	1.000	0.832	0.765	0.832	0.839	-0.405	-0.568	-0.228
GNMA 8	0.898	0.832	1.000	0.984	0.981	0.931	-0.249	-0.423	-0.261
GNMA 9	0.871	0.765	0.984	1.000	0.984	0.929	-0.184	-0.350	-0.185
GNMA 10	0.886	0.832	0.981	0.984	1.000	0.959	-0.257	-0.423	-0.213
GNMA 11	0.860	0.839	0.931	0.929	0.959	1.000	-0.200	-0.366	-0.149
GNMA 13	-0.532	-0.405	-0.249	-0.184	-0.257	-0.200	1.000	0.899	0.537
GNMA 14	-0.602	-0.568	-0.423	-0.350	-0.423	-0.366	0.899	1.000	0.482
GNMA 15	-0.287	-0.228	-0.261	-0.185	-0.213	-0.149	0.537	0.482	1.000

F. Correlation Matrix — Fourth Subperiod: 1988–1990

	BondFut	Eurofut	GNMA 8	GNMA 9	GNMA 10	GNMA 11	GNMA 13	GNMA 14	GNMA 15
BondFut	1.000	0.255	0.830	0.823	0.733	0.366	0.399	0.348	0.348
Eurofut	0.255	1.000	0.604	0.640	0.664	0.899	0.669	0.539	0.664
GNMA 8	0.830	0.604	1.000	0.983	0.934	0.752	0.656	0.620	0.660
GNMA 9	0.823	0.640	0.983	1.000	0.940	0.781	0.689	0.636	0.712
GNMA 10	0.733	0.664	0.934	0.940	1.000	0.816	0.597	0.546	0.637
GNMA 11	0.366	0.899	0.752	0.781	0.816	1.000	0.719	0.659	0.728
GNMA 13	0.399	0.669	0.656	0.689	0.597	0.719	1.000	0.939	0.689
GNMA 14	0.348	0.539	0.620	0.636	0.546	0.659	0.939	1.000	0.656
GNMA 15	0.348	0.664	0.660	0.712	0.637	0.728	0.689	0.656	1.000

Exhibit 28: Means, Standard Deviations, and Correlations Using Price Changes

A. Bond and Mortgage Price Changes: Means and Standard Deviations

Variable	Entire Period 1984–1990		First Subperiod 1984–1985		Second Subperiod 1986–1990		Third Subperiod 1986–1987		Fourth Subperiod 1988–1990	
	Mean	Std Dev'n	Mean	Std Dev'n	Mean	Std Dev'n	Mean	Std Dev'n	Mean	Std Dev'n
BondFut	0.27	3.28	0.63	2.76	0.15	3.43	0.11	4.17	0.17	2.95
Eurofut	0.03	0.53	0.10	0.64	0.01	0.49	0.01	0.47	0.01	0.50
GNMA 8	0.21	2.12	0.63	2.40	0.07	1.99	0.01	2.08	0.11	1.95
GNMA 9	0.21	2.12	0.65	2.55	0.06	1.94	-0.03	2.08	0.11	1.86
GNMA 10	0.17	1.92	0.63	2.68	0.01	1.55	-0.05	1.79	0.05	1.40
GNMA 11	0.16	1.65	0.54	2.53	0.03	1.19	-0.02	1.26	0.05	1.15
GNMA 13	0.12	1.25	0.24	2.00	0.08	0.87	0.07	0.53	0.09	1.00
GNMA 14	0.10	1.24	0.13	1.78	0.09	1.00	0.10	0.93	0.09	1.04
GNMA 15	0.11	1.16	0.15	1.33	0.10	1.10	0.09	0.74	0.10	1.25

B. Correlation Matrix — Entire Period: 1984–1990

	BondFut	Eurofut	GNMA 8	GNMA 9	GNMA 10	GNMA 11	GNMA 13	GNMA 14	GNMA 15
BondFut	1.000	0.664	0.895	0.892	0.823	0.755	0.500	0.416	0.512
Eurofut	0.664	1.000	0.692	0.682	0.643	0.705	0.619	0.435	0.499
GNMA 8	0.895	0.692	1.000	0.985	0.927	0.880	0.676	0.579	0.595
GNMA 9	0.892	0.682	0.985	1.000	0.949	0.909	0.691	0.584	0.605
GNMA 10	0.823	0.643	0.927	0.949	1.000	0.938	0.689	0.571	0.556
GNMA 11	0.755	0.705	0.880	0.909	0.938	1.000	0.805	0.652	0.644
GNMA 13	0.500	0.619	0.676	0.691	0.689	0.805	1.000	0.828	0.760
GNMA 14	0.416	0.435	0.579	0.584	0.571	0.652	0.828	1.000	0.729
GNMA 15	0.512	0.499	0.595	0.605	0.556	0.644	0.760	0.729	1.000

C. Correlation Matrix — First Subperiod: 1984–1985

	BondFut	Eurofut	GNMA 8	GNMA 9	GNMA 10	GNMA 11	GNMA 13	GNMA 14	GNMA 15
BondFut	1.000	0.787	0.959	0.956	0.956	0.960	0.830	0.681	0.705
Eurofut	0.787	1.000	0.763	0.763	0.768	0.790	0.735	0.508	0.533
GNMA 8	0.959	0.763	1.000	0.997	0.992	0.981	0.876	0.755	0.768
GNMA 9	0.956	0.763	0.997	1.000	0.995	0.986	0.879	0.740	0.772
GNMA 10	0.956	0.768	0.992	0.995	1.000	0.992	0.882	0.734	0.765
GNMA 11	0.960	0.790	0.981	0.986	0.992	1.000	0.900	0.755	0.792
GNMA 13	0.830	0.735	0.876	0.879	0.882	0.900	1.000	0.843	0.852
GNMA 14	0.681	0.508	0.755	0.740	0.734	0.755	0.843	1.000	0.912
GNMA 15	0.705	0.533	0.768	0.772	0.765	0.792	0.852	0.912	1.000

Exhibit 28: Means, Standard Deviations, and Correlations Using Price Changes (Continued)

D. Correlation Matrix — Second Subperiod: 1986–1990

	BondFut	Eurofut	GNMA 8	GNMA 9	GNMA 10	GNMA 11	GNMA 13	GNMA 14	GNMA 15
BondFut	1.000	0.639	0.893	0.898	0.840	0.771	0.401	0.332	0.459
Eurofut	0.639	1.000	0.652	0.632	0.555	0.663	0.548	0.388	0.482
GNMA 8	0.893	0.652	1.000	0.979	0.907	0.858	0.559	0.477	0.514
GNMA 9	0.898	0.632	0.979	1.000	0.929	0.885	0.554	0.479	0.520
GNMA 10	0.840	0.555	0.907	0.929	1.000	0.880	0.447	0.412	0.429
GNMA 11	0.771	0.663	0.858	0.885	0.880	1.000	0.655	0.540	0.570
GNMA 13	0.401	0.548	0.559	0.554	0.447	0.655	1.000	0.826	0.751
GNMA 14	0.332	0.388	0.477	0.479	0.412	0.540	0.826	1.000	0.620
GNMA 15	0.459	0.482	0.514	0.520	0.429	0.570	0.751	0.620	1.000

E. Correlation Matrix — Third Subperiod: 1986–1987

	BondFut	Eurofut	GNMA 8	GNMA 9	GNMA 10	GNMA 11	GNMA 13	GNMA 14	GNMA 15
BondFut	1.000	0.732	0.861	0.869	0.799	0.672	-0.009	-0.164	0.151
Eurofut	0.732	1.000	0.599	0.640	0.698	0.698	0.076	-0.155	0.212
GNMA 8	0.861	0.599	1.000	0.979	0.922	0.785	0.189	-0.007	-0.051
GNMA 9	0.869	0.640	0.979	1.000	0.960	0.808	0.177	-0.000	0.051
GNMA 10	0.799	0.698	0.922	0.960	1.000	0.892	0.247	0.078	0.082
GNMA 11	0.672	0.698	0.785	0.808	0.892	1.000	0.437	0.124	0.121
GNMA 13	-0.009	0.076	0.189	0.177	0.247	0.437	1.000	0.545	0.109
GNMA 14	-0.164	-0.155	-0.007	-0.000	0.078	0.124	0.545	1.000	-0.205
GNMA 15	0.151	0.212	-0.051	0.051	0.082	0.121	0.109	-0.205	1.000

F. Correlation Matrix — Fourth Subperiod: 1988–1990

	BondFut	Eurofut	GNMA 8	GNMA 9	GNMA 10	GNMA 11	GNMA 13	GNMA 14	GNMA 15
BondFut	1.000	0.597	0.935	0.934	0.882	0.864	0.622	0.679	0.652
Eurofut	0.597	1.000	0.682	0.632	0.476	0.648	0.690	0.626	0.572
GNMA 8	0.935	0.682	1.000	0.980	0.902	0.903	0.703	0.725	0.727
GNMA 9	0.934	0.632	0.980	1.000	0.909	0.936	0.711	0.738	0.715
GNMA 10	0.882	0.476	0.902	0.909	1.000	0.875	0.566	0.624	0.606
GNMA 11	0.864	0.648	0.903	0.936	0.875	1.000	0.765	0.761	0.755
GNMA 13	0.622	0.690	0.703	0.711	0.566	0.765	1.000	0.920	0.860
GNMA 14	0.679	0.626	0.725	0.738	0.624	0.761	0.920	1.000	0.864
GNMA 15	0.652	0.572	0.727	0.715	0.606	0.755	0.860	0.864	1.000

and the 1986–1990 subperiod (low rates). The 1986–1990 subperiod is then divided into two other subperiods—1986–1987 and 1988–1990—in order to display the unusual behavior of mortgage prices during the 1986–1987 subperiod. All statistics are presented for the entire sample period, as well as for each of the subperiods.

Focusing on Exhibit 28, the standard deviations show that long-term T-bond futures prices were more volatile in 1986–1990 than in 1984–1985, but short-term rates were less volatile in 1986–1990 than earlier. Mortgage prices were less volatile in the 1986–1990 period, just as would be expected when rates are low and mortgage prices "cap out" above par, due to large prepayments. For example, the volatility of GNMA 11s dropped from 2.53% of par to 1.19% of par—the most dramatic change. In contrast, GNMA 8s never exceeded par, so their price volatility did not drop as much—from 2.40% to 1.99%.

Looking at the correlation matrices for the entire period in Exhibits 27 and 28, one sees that all of the mortgages have significant positive correlations with both T-bond futures and with Eurodollar futures. Using price levels, correlations with T-bonds ranged from .78 for GNMA 14s to .97 for GNMA 8s, and correlations with Eurodollars ranged from .61 for GNMA 14s to .84 for GNMA 11s.[3] For the entire sample period, correlations for monthly price changes are lower than for price levels, ranging from .42 to .90 with T-bonds, and ranging from .44 to .71 for Eurodollars. Again, these correlations are statistically significant, but their values clearly indicate the presence of basis risk. Higher-coupon securities have higher prepayments and lower price elasticities, so one expects them to be more highly correlated with short-term rates than with long-term rates. This occurs during most of the subperiods shown, as higher-coupon securities are more highly correlated with Eurodollar futures than with T-bond futures, whereas the reverse is true for low-coupon discount securities.

---

[3] The outstanding par amount of GNMA 14s is very small, so the price data for GNMA 14s are not nearly as high in quality as the data for the other coupons. This sampling error surely lowers the correlations of GNMA 14s with everything else.

As was discussed earlier in this chapter (Exhibit 15), 1986 was a very unusual year for mortgage price movements relative to Treasury bond prices. In the first half of the year, bond prices rose dramatically (from eighty-five to ninety-nine), whereas mortgages with coupons above 12% actually fell in price. In the second half of the year, this pattern reversed, as high-coupon mortgages increased in price and T-bond futures fell. These unprecedented moves clearly show a negative correlation of high-coupon mortgages with T-bonds during 1986. These negative correlations show up in the subperiod correlation matrices for the 1986–1987 subperiod, and show up as reduced correlations of high-coupon mortgages with T-bonds for the entire sample. In the first subperiod, when rates were high (1984–1985), all mortgage coupons examined had correlations with T-bonds in excess of .9, and coupons below 11 had correlations over .99. Even in the difficult 1986–1987 subperiod, correlations are quite good (lowest is .86) for mortgages with coupons up to 2% to 3% over the par coupons. But the correlations on super-high-coupon mortgages (with coupons more than 3% over par) were not reliable, and were often negative. Although researchers can understand why very high-coupon mortgages can have negative price elasticities, most would be uncomfortable long-hedging them, with the assumption of negative price elasticities. Suffice it to say that very high-coupon mortgages are difficult to hedge. However, that worry is mitigated by the fact that there is relatively little price volatility in them to hedge.

Let us use these correlation statistics to determine which contracts to short for First Savings' hedge. From the graphs of Exhibits 22–24, we see that the major liquidation value risk is generated by interest rate risk of the huge amount of fixed-rate mortgages that First holds. Thus, movements in liquidation value are likely to be quite closely related to mortgage rate movements. Assuming that these mortgage values are closely related to the GNMA 10 prices in Exhibit 28, the best hedge is found by looking at various futures' correlations with those GNMA 10 prices. Using price levels, the 3-month Eurodollar price has a correlation with GNMA

10s of .82, and the 20-year T-bond contract has a correlation with GNMA 10s of .96. Using price changes, the correlations of Euros and T-bonds with GNMA 10s are .64 and .82, respectively. Thus, if one had to choose one of those markets for the hedge, the twenty-year T-bond futures would be chosen for its highest correlation with the GNMA 10s.

If more futures markets and bond maturities were examined, one would see that GNMA 10s have the highest correlation with seven- to ten-year T-notes, for which the futures market is not as liquid as the futures market for T-bonds. However, since (with a smooth term structure) ten-year rates are much like a weighted average of three-month rates and twenty-year rates, the best correlation with First Savings' liquidation value is obtained with a mix of three-month Eurodollar futures and twenty-year T-bond futures, with most of the weight placed on the T-bonds. An attempt to find the exact composition of the best hedge is beyond the scope of this chapter; it would involve taking account of the changing durations of both the mortgages and the T-bonds as rates change. As shown earlier in this chapter, as rates fall, the durations of T-bonds lengthen, whereas the durations of GNMA 10s shorten due to higher prepayment rates on the underlying mortgages. Thus, the optimal hedge needs to be periodically rebalanced, as is illustrated in the next section.

Exhibit 29 displays the results of a hedge consisting of a short position of 1,280 91-day Eurodollar futures contracts and 344 20-year T-bond futures contracts. For a parallel rate increase of 1%, the portfolio will make about $6.2 million (1,280 × $2,500 + 344 × $8,620), which significantly reduces the cash losses and is similar to the sensitivities of the "all T-bonds" and "all Euros" positions calculated above. The graph displayed in Exhibit 29 contains three elements: (1) the December 31, 1990, liquidation value curve (hedged with swaps only) from Exhibit 24; (2) the futures gains and losses curve for this proposed position; and (3) the combined result of the liquidation value hedged with swaps and futures. Note the behavior of the three curves at the base level and plus or minus 1%. The liquidation value (without futures) falls rapidly as

Exhibit 29: First Savings and Loan Association: Liquidation Value Hedged with Swaps and Futures

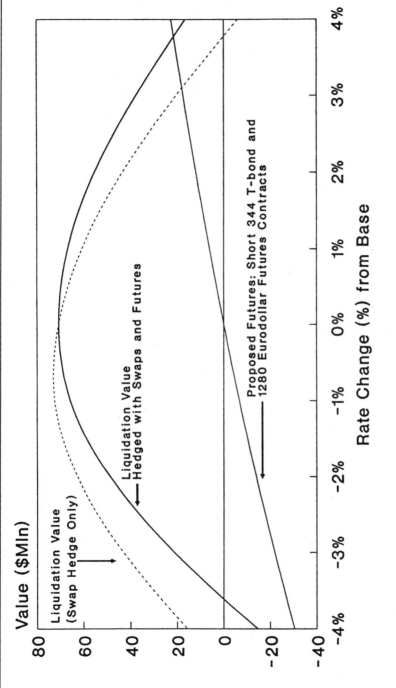

Value ($Mln)

Liquidation Value
(Swap Hedge Only)

Liquidation Value
Hedged with Swaps and Futures

Proposed Futures: Short 344 T-bond and
1280 Eurodollar Futures Contracts

Rate Change (%) from Base

----- Liq Val (Swaps Only) ——— Proposed Futures ——— Liq Val Hedged

Exhibit 29: First Savings and Loan Association: Liquidation Value Hedged with Swaps and Futures (Continued)

Millions

Rate Change from Base	-4%	-3%	-2%	-1%	0%	1%	2%	3%	4%
Liquidation Value Hedged with Swaps	15.6	45.5	64.4	74.6	72.1	61.8	44.7	21.1	-6.1
Gain/Loss on 344 Eurodollar Futures (Short)	-12.8	-9.6	-6.4	-3.2	0.0	3.2	6.4	9.6	12.8
Gain/Loss on 1280 T-Bond Futures (Short)	-17.5	-12.1	-7.4	-3.4	0.0	3.0	5.5	7.8	9.7
Total Gain/Loss on Futures	-30.3	-21.7	-13.8	-6.6	0.0	6.2	11.9	17.4	22.5
Liquidation Value Hedged with Swaps	15.6	45.5	64.4	74.6	72.1	61.8	44.7	21.1	-6.1
Liquidation Value Hedged with Swaps and Futures	-14.7	23.8	50.6	68.0	72.1	68.0	56.6	38.5	16.4

interest rates increase from base levels, and increases slightly as rates decrease. The futures hedge profits increase as rates decrease. The combined effect of futures gains and cash losses results in a fairly stable hedged value for the firm (between $68 and $72 million) for interest rate moves of 1% or less from base. Also note that the liquidation value falls by a small but equal amount for rate moves of plus or minus 1% from base. Thus, First Savings is in a position of neutrality with respect to the direction of interest rates, whereas before hedging with futures the firm clearly benefitted from (and was betting on) a decline in the level of market interest rates.

In studying Exhibit 29, one sees that although interest rate swaps and futures do a very good job of stabilizing the liquidation value of the firm for small rate moves, the precision of the hedge "falls off in the tails." That is, for large interest rate moves in either direction, the hedged liquidation value ultimately falls (and becomes negative for very low rates). The fact that the institution is significantly hurt by large interest rate moves in either direction is graphically displayed by the curved (concave or "negatively convex") shape of the hedged liquidation value line in Exhibit 29. When interest rates rise, the rate of prepayment on the Association's mortgages decreases, and the value of these mortgages falls faster than does the value of the institution's liabilities and the futures contracts and swaps employed as a hedge. At very low levels of interest rates the rate of prepayment on First Savings' mortgages increases dramatically, and the value of these mortgages rises at a slower rate than does the value of the liabilities and hedges. The Association's exposure to large interest rate moves can be hedged with options, which are examined in the next section.

HEDGING WITH OPTIONS

Most fixed-rate mortgage loans are written with options that are valuable to the borrower. Most commonly, the borrower has an option to prepay all or part of the mortgage at his discretion without penalty. When the mortgage was originally issued, the lender should have received compensation in the form of fees or a higher interest rate to offset the value of the option. Similarly, the owner of a fixed-rate mortgage-backed security is "short" a call option; that is, he has written a call option to the borrower on the present value of the mortgage payments.

The higher the level of prevailing mortgage rates relative to a borrower's mortgage rate, the lower is the value of his prepayment option, since he is less likely to refinance his mortgage. Conversely, the firm that owns a fixed-rate mortgage asset can expect that the level of prepayments (exercise of the options) on the security will increase as market rates decrease. Since the value of a prepayment option will increase as interest rate levels decrease, the Association will suffer a loss unless the change in the value of the prepayment option is hedged.

As interest rates change, the sensitivities of assets, liabilities, and hedging instruments may change by different amounts, leaving the firm in a situation of having to rebalance the hedge periodically. Consider Exhibit 29, which shows that the hedge is initially duration-matched, but as interest rate levels change, the hedge loses in both directions. When rates rise, the values of mortgages fall faster than the values of the institution's liabilities and hedges (the rate of prepayments decreases and the mortgages' durations lengthen). When rates fall, prepayments accelerate and the values of the mortgages rise at slower rates than do the values of both the liabilities and swap and futures hedges. This effect reflects changes in the value of the option component of the Association's fixed-rate mortgages. A hedge that initially matches the interest rate sensitivity of the assets with the sensitivity of the liabilities plus hedges (as was done with the futures hedge described above) will not necessarily be balanced after a change in interest rates has occurred.

One can choose to counteract this problem by rebalancing the hedge periodically. Rebalancing the hedge position entails costs (including transactions costs), which are akin to the cost of buying options and which increase with the volatility of interest rates and the frequency of rebalancing. With the development of, and liquidity present, in the markets for options such as LIBOR caps and floors, options on T-bond, and options on Eurodollar futures, it is feasible and often desirable to use these options markets to create more accurate hedge positions that protect the Association against changes in the value of the prepayment option. Since short-term rates sometimes move differently from long-term rates, options on long-term and short-term rates should play an important role in improving hedging precision.

Exhibit 30 (which has three graphs) displays First Savings' proposed options position (Exhibit 30b), which would complement its swaps and short futures position and complete its hedge. It is necessary to buy out-of-the-money puts (caps) and calls (floors) to create an options position with the (convex) shape exactly opposite to the (concave) shape of the graph of the liquidation value hedged only with swaps and futures (Exhibit 30a). Exhibit 30c graphs the new hedged value of the firm for different interest rate scenarios. Note that the inclusion of options in the hedge has eliminated the decline in Association value for large interest rate movements. In fact, the estimated hedged liquidation value for a 400 basis point increase in rates is $69.9 million. This compares to minus $6.1 million if unhedged, and to $16.4 million hedged with swaps and futures only.

As the previous section describing interest rate caps and floors indicated, these securities are a source of long-term options (unlike exchange-traded options on futures). As a result, caps and floors are often better hedges of the long-term options (prepayment options and rate caps) embedded in financial institutions' portfolios than are options on futures contracts. In practice, an institution's management may wish to design a hedge containing both short-term (more liquid) and long-term options, especially if hedge rebalancing occurs frequently. The costs of alternative options positions, in relation to their associated benefits, should always be carefully considered.

Exhibit 30a: First Savings and Loan Association: Liquidation Value Hedged with Swaps and Futures Only

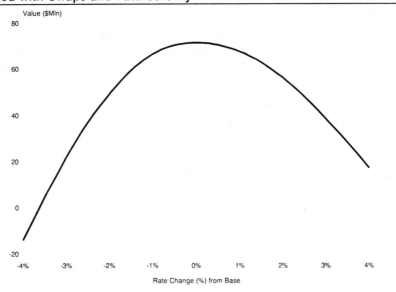

Exhibit 30b: First Savings and Loan Association: Proposed Options

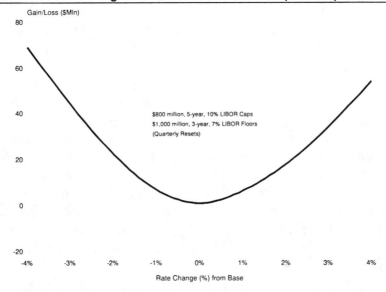

Exhibit 30c: First Savings and Loan Association: Effect of Proposed Hedge

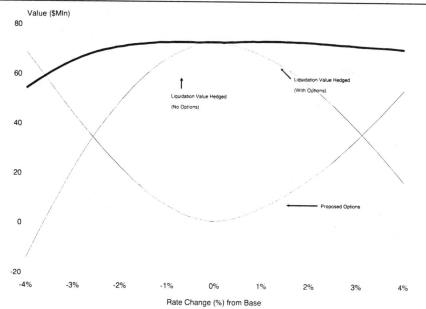

First Savings and Loan Association
Liquidation Value Hedged with Swaps, Futures and Options
($ Millions)

Rate Change from Base	-4%	-3%	-2%	-1%	0%	1%	2%	3%	4%
Liquidation Value Hedged with Swaps	15.6	45.5	64.4	74.6	72.1	61.8	44.7	21.1	-6.1
Total Gain/Loss on Futures	-30.3	-21.7	-13.8	-6.6	0.0	6.2	11.9	17.4	22.5
Liquidation Value Hedged with Swaps and Futures	-14.7	23.8	50.6	68.0	72.1	68.0	56.6	38.5	16.4
Gain/Loss on $800 Mln, 5-Yr, 10% LIBOR Caps	-5.8	-5.8	-5.3	-3.7	0.0	7.0	18.2	34.7	55.6
Gain/Loss on $1,000 Mln, 3-Yr, 7% LIBOR Floors	74.3	48.6	25.8	8.6	0.0	-1.9	-2.1	-2.2	-2.2
Total Gain/Loss on Caps and Floors	68.5	42.8	20.6	4.9	0.0	5.1	16.0	32.6	53.5
Liquidation Value Hedged with Swaps, Futures & Options	53.8	66.6	71.2	72.9	72.1	73.1	72.6	71.1	69.9

In summary, by using futures and options as hedging instruments, the net sensitivity of First Savings to changes in interest rates is reduced dramatically. In fact, even for extreme movements in rates (down 400 basis points and up 400 basis points), the resulting exposure represents less than 1% of assets and less than 25% of regulatory net worth. For 300 basis point moves the exposure is only 0.3% of assets and 8% of the institution's net worth. The hedge is well balanced throughout a wide range of interest rate moves as the result of using options contracts. Similar results can be attained by dynamically adjusting the futures hedge position, but the costs may be higher, and the firm would be exposed to changes in the volatilities of interest rates.

After a cursory examination of the graph found in Exhibit 30c, one may conclude that First Savings' options hedging strategy stochastically dominates the alternative strategy of not hedging with options. Since Exhibit 30 indicates that First Savings' liquidation value, after hedging with options, is everywhere (for all possible interest rate moves) greater than or equal to the firm's liquidation value without options, one could draw the conclusion that the options hedging strategy is superior in all instances. Certainly this conclusion must not be correct, since we have seen from an earlier section of this chapter that options do not provide the investor with a proverbial "free lunch."

The key to understanding this apparent paradox lies in the fact that the graph shown in Exhibit 30c demonstrates only the effect of *instantaneous* movements in interest rates on the liquidation value of First Savings. At the "split second" that the options are purchased, First Savings' liquidation value is the same (ignoring transactions costs) as it was before it purchased the options. Therefore, the liquidation value lines of Exhibit 30c are tangent to each other at "base" levels of interest rates. In reality, as time passes, these liquidation value curves drift upward and downward as the firm earns income.

Hedging strategies change not only a firm's liquidation value for sudden changes in interest rates, they also alter the rate at which the liquidation value "drifts" by changing a firm's income pattern over time, making it more stable. In this example, First Savings must begin to amortize the cost of the options ($1.9 million per year) immediately after their purchase. Obviously, if interest rates do not move very much, First Savings' options will expire worthless, and the firm would have been better off (in retrospect) by not hedging. If interest rates move substantially, causing large gains on the options, First Savings will have been better off by hedging with options. There also exist scenarios, for moderate movements in interest rates, where the firm would be neither better nor worse off by purchasing options than by not purchasing options.

First Savings' hedging strategy reduces risk in the sense that the firm's liquidation value and income are expected to be less volatile as a result. Of course, only one of the infinite number of possible interest rate scenarios will become reality, and First Savings may, in retrospect, have been better off if it had not purchased options in the first place. Since First Savings' management is risk-averse and does not have the ability to predict changes in interest rates, it chooses to hedge with options, thereby trading off the ability to earn slightly higher earnings (and liquidation value) during periods of less volatile interest rates for much improved earnings and value in the event of significant interest rate changes.

When thought about in this context, hedging with options may be considered akin to purchasing an insurance policy against adverse movements in interest rates. When purchasing insurance, the policyholder does not know what will eventually happen, but is concerned that under certain circumstances he will incur significant losses. The policyholder is willing to give up some current income (the policy premium) for the payoffs that he will receive if these adverse circumstances come to be realized. Just as the purchaser of insurance does not know if he will be better or worse off until the date his policy expires or pays off, the management of First Savings does not know if it would have been better off (by hedging with options) until its options have expired or have been exercised. However, the policyholder, the management, and the shareholders of First Savings are more comfortable knowing that the chances of large, and potentially catastrophic, losses have been eliminated.

MICRO HEDGING ASSETS: DYNAMIC HEDGING CORRELATIONS

With any well constructed hedge, it should always be possible to identify futures contracts with particular assets and liabilities. This view of hedging is termed "micro hedging," as opposed to a "macro hedging" perspective, which looks at the interest rate risks of the entire Association. Indeed, for regulatory and accounting purposes, the identification of futures contracts as micro hedges is necessary. After a little thought, it should be clear that the same steps that were described and followed for First Savings on a "macro" level can also be carried out for any subset of its assets or liabilities.

It should be pointed out that it is possible to micro hedge some assets and liabilities without hedging others, thereby making the firm actually *more* risky than without the hedge. By examining *all* assets and liabilities, the possibility of a risk-increasing set of micro hedges can be eliminated. Thus, the regulatory requirement that all hedges be identified as micro hedges is one that any good hedging program should be able to meet. However, it is not true that any hedging program that can be viewed as a set of micro hedges is "safe" or "appropriate" or even "risk-reducing." Complete asset and liability analysis, such as the one presented in the last two sections for First Savings, is necessary in order to obtain an assurance that the hedge is really risk-reducing.

The following example, that of Second Savings and Loan Association, focuses on the hedging of particular pieces of the institution's mortgage portfolio. In particular, Second Savings is hedging a $600 million portfolio of mortgages, consisting of $100 million par of each of GNMA 8s, 9s, 10s, 11s, 13s, and 15s. (Data on GNMA 12s and 14s were not available for the entire time period.) The statistical results achieved are certainly feasible, as the description of the procedure will demonstrate. The hedges are evaluated by marking to market the assets and hedges and accounting for the cash flow gains or losses in the interim. This is an "asset hedge," since futures contracts are allocated to particular assets. In the next section, a "liability hedge" is examined.

Second Savings starts with $100 million par of each of the six GNMA coupons. It is assumed that any paydowns that are received each month are reinvested in the same coupon (at whatever market prices are at the time), so as to keep the par amounts in all coupons at $100 million. Some additional financing may be required or paydowns of debt may occur in doing this, since, for example, par received at 100 and repurchased at 105 requires additional funds (borrowing). All financing is assumed to be done in the GNMA repo market at rates that are fifteen basis points below the near Eurodollar futures contract rate. Since the yield curve was upward sloping for a significant portion of the time period studied, this very likely overstates the cost of funds. Second Savings is assumed to have no offsetting liabilities or interest rate swaps for these mortgages, so the entire interest rate risk of the mortgages must be hedged.

In this analysis, it is assumed that only Treasury bond futures are used to hedge the mortgages. It is possible that better results could be obtained with a combination of T-bonds and Euros, but that is not done in this section. A *dynamic hedging* approach is employed, in that the hedge position for each mortgage coupon is adjusted at the end of each month, taking into account interest rates at that time. The level of interest rates affects the elasticities of the mortgages, as well as the dollar gains and losses on the T-bond futures. As rates fall, mortgage elasticities fall, while T-bond futures' elasticities increase. Thus, as rates fall, the optimal number of contracts for the hedge should also fall. By making these adjustments, better correlation statistics should be obtained than correlation statistics presented previously, which implicitly assumed constant hedge portfolios.

To make the present value hedging approach operational requires estimates of the elasticities of all of the various mortgage coupons at the end of each month. Gains and losses on T-bond futures are easy to compute, as was illustrated in Exhibit 6. The hedges are simulated with the same 1984–1990 data presented in Exhibit 15, as previously discussed. To avoid the benefits of hindsight, mortgage elasticities each month for each coupon are simply obtained from a table that was computed with January 31, 1984 mortgage prices. The hedges were initiated January 31, 1984, using data available at that time, and were followed until December 31, 1990.

More specifically, it was assumed that if bond rates fall 1%, then the prices of GNMA 10% mortgages will increase to where GNMA 11% mortgages currently are. Similarly, with a 1% rate decline, the GNMA 11% mortgage price is estimated to move to the current GNMA 12% price, and so on. Again, just January 31, 1984 prices were used in this way to estimate elasticities for various mortgages. The results of this approach are shown in Exhibit 31.

Exhibit 31: Assumed Mortgage Price Elasticities for Dynamic Trading

Initial Mortgage Price	Next Month's Estimated Price Elasticity
Less than $74.99	-.0600
$75.00 - 79.99	-.0585
80.00 - 84.99	-.0664
85.00 - 89.99	-.0651
90.00 - 94.99	-.0551
95.00 - 99.99	-.0522
100.00 - 104.99	-.0377
105.00 - 109.99	-.0211
110.00 - 114.99	-.0100
115.00 or more	.0000

NOTE: For prices between $75 and $109.99, estimated elasticities are those indicated by mortgage prices on January 31, 1984. Below $75, elasticities were assumed to be -.06. Between $110 and $114.99 elasticities were assumed to be -.01, and above $115, elasticities were assumed to equal 0.

Given these elasticities, the correct number of T-bond contracts to hedge a 1% decline in rates was computed, as was the number of T-bonds that would be ideal for a 1% increase in rates. The actual hedge position was chosen to be the average of the two hedge positions. With that hedge position, the futures gain or loss for the next month was then computed. For subsequent months, hedges were updated in the same way. The resulting dynamic hedge positions are given in the top portion of Exhibit 32 for every sixth month in the sample (although hedges were actually adjusted monthly).

Finally, to complete the analysis of performance of the hedge, prepayment data from Exhibit 3 were used to compute the gain or loss on prepayments. Also, the spread of the mortgage's coupon income over the Eurodollar-based financing cost was computed. The total of all of these gains and losses except the futures position was named the "Total Cash Gain" of the hedge. The bottom portion of Exhibit 32 gives the results of two sets of regressions of "Cash Gains" on "Futures Gains." The first set, labeled "Cumulative (Monthly)," displays the results of regressions of the "Cumulative Cash Gains" on the "Cumulative Futures Gains."[4] Plots of these cumulative data are in Exhibits 33 and 34. The second set of regressions in Exhibit 32, labeled "Monthly Changes," displays the results of regressions of monthly "Cash" gains and losses on monthly "Futures" gains and losses. Plots of these monthly changes are displayed in Exhibit 35. Let us now examine the results of these dynamic hedging strategies.

First, note that the hedge positions do make sense. As interest rates increased from 11.84% to 13.03% between January 1984 and July 1984, the aggregate hedge position increased from 5,026 T-bonds short to 5,943 T-bonds short. As rates increase, prepayments

---

[4] For each of the mortgage coupons studied, significant profits accumulated due to the spread between the mortgage's effective coupon rate and the associated funding cost. Since interest rates declined during the 1984–1990 period, regressions of "Cumulative Cash Gains" on "Cumulative Futures Gains" would largely attribute this "income effect" or trend to declining interest rates, biasing the slope coefficients higher (in absolute value). To eliminate this effect, the "Cumulative Cash Gains" were "detrended" by including a monthly coefficient (not shown) in the regressions.

Exhibit 32: Second Savings and Loan Association: Dynamic Hedge Adjustments and Correlations for Micro Hedges

Par Amount		Month-end Short Positions in Treasury Bond Futures On:													
	Jan 84	Jul 84	Jan 85	Jul 85	Jan 86	Jul 86	Jan 87	Jul 87	an 88	Jul 88	Jan 89	Jul 89	Jan 90	Jul 90	Dec 90
Coupon ($ min)															
T-Bond Price =	70.81	64.50	73.19	75.19	85.16	97.81	99.69	89.50	93.91	85.75	90.81	99.75	94.25	94.69	95.72
T-Bond Yield =	11.84%	13.03%	11.44%	11.12%	9.69%	8.22%	8.03%	9.15%	8.65%	9.62%	9.00%	8.03%	8.61%	8.56%	8.45%
Par Mortgage =	12.50%	13.75%	12.25%	11.50%	10.00%	9.25%	8.25%	10.00%	9.50%	10.00%	10.00%	9.00%	9.75%	9.25%	8.75%
8.00% $100.0	794	867	766	807	712	536	542	669	568	700	652	528	623	562	560
9.00% $100.0	882	905	851	900	664	551	476	624	593	651	601	463	581	588	495
10.00% $100.0	995	1013	960	878	597	493	327	556	520	576	534	478	512	518	504
11.00% $100.0	974	1141	941	823	621	335	329	382	358	396	550	321	528	351	347
13.00% $100.0	813	1050	772	500	429	338	334	212	198	222	385	183	365	196	196
15.00% $100.0	568	966	540	282	239	187	185	220	68	226	210	185	201	69	69
Totals $600.0	5026	5943	4829	4192	3262	2440	2193	2663	2306	2771	2932	2158	2810	2284	2170

Regression Results

Cash = a + b Futures

	Cumulative (Monthly)			Monthly Changes		
Coupon	Slope	t(b) (Abs)	Correlation	Slope	t(b) (Abs)	Correlation
8.00%	-.97	35.5	.990	-.90	21.3	.921
9.00%	-.94	34.9	.991	-.91	22.2	.927
10.00%	-.94	34.7	.991	-.86	18.2	.896
11.00%	-.93	29.0	.988	-.81	18.6	.900
13.00%	-.67	16.0	.977	-.60	9.5	.724
15.00%	-.59	9.7	.973	-.60	7.2	.624

Exhibit 33: Second Savings and Loan Association—Hedge Performance: Cumulative Cash, Futures, and Net Gains and Losses by Coupon

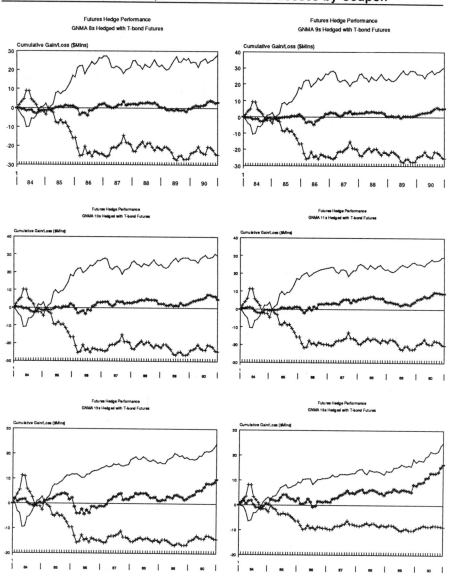

Exhibit 34: Second Savings and Loan Association—Scatterplots: Cumulative Cash and Futures Gains and Losses by Coupon

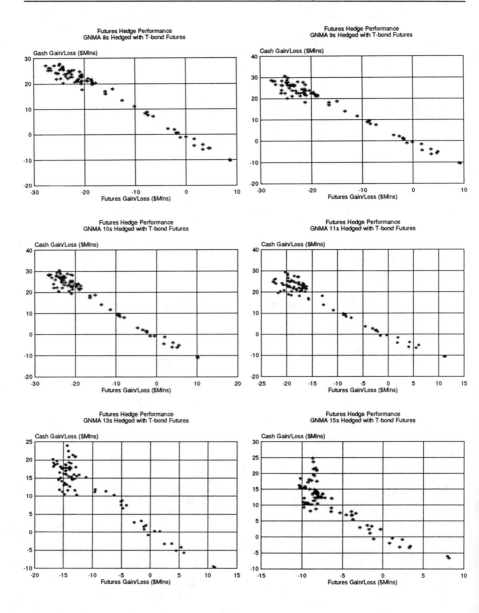

Exhibit 35: Second Savings and Loan Association—Scatterplots: Monthly Cash and Futures Gains and Losses by Coupon

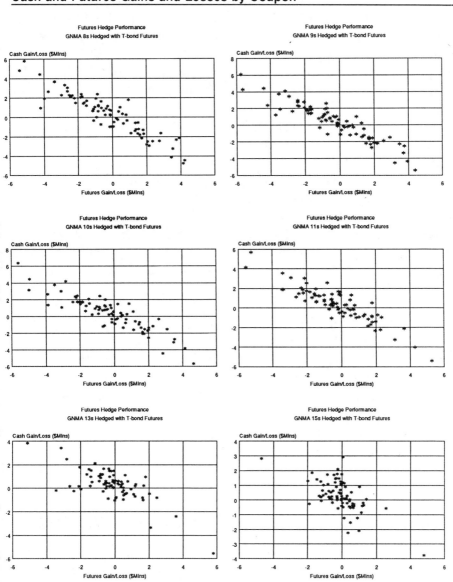

slow and effective durations of mortgages lengthen, while T-bond contracts move by smaller amounts. The combined effect predicts more contracts, which is verified here. Following July 1984 interest rates fell by 500 basis points to 8.03% in July 1989. As expected, the number of contracts fell dramatically from 5,943 to 2,158, as prepayments increased dramatically. Looking further at the portfolio detail, one sees that a coupon's hedge position does not fall rapidly until it exceeds par, which is due to the sharp drop in elasticities at that point in Exhibit 31. Again, this makes sense from the standpoint of option pricing and optimal exercises of call options by borrowers.

The statistical analysis of performance shows that quite high correlations are achieved by these positions, higher in all cases than those for the entire period in Exhibits 27 and 28, which correspond to static hedges. Using cumulative data, the lowest correlation found was .973 for GNMA 15s. This compares with a correlation of .834 (from Exhibit 27) for static hedges of GNMA 15s with T-bond futures. Using monthly changes, the lowest correlations were for GNMA 13s and GNMA 15s (.724 and .624, respectively). These "dynamic hedging" correlations compare favorably to the corresponding "static hedging" correlations found in Exhibit 28 (.500 for GNMA 13s and .512 for GNMA 15s). Coupons from 8% to 11% had correlations of cumulative futures gains with cash gains of (negative) .988 or higher, and correlations of monthly futures gains with cash gains of (negative) .896 or higher. Thus, the dynamic aspect of hedging certainly helps to form better hedges. Note that the unusual year 1986 is reflected in this performance. However, since 1986 was a year of low interest rates, the poor precision of hedges in 1986 was mitigated by the relatively small futures positions held during that time.

Ideally, for every dollar lost in futures, $1 is gained on the cash side. Thus, the ideal slope coefficient in the regression of futures on cash is 1.00. From Exhibit 32, all slope coefficients were lower (in absolute value) than 1.00, ranging from .97 for GNMA 8s to .59 for the difficult GNMA 15s, using cumulative data, and ranging from .91 for GNMA 9s to .60 for GNMA 13s and GNMA 15s, using monthly changes. Generally, the desired equal-but-opposite gains and losses were nearly achieved by the low-coupon mortgages, but were substantially off for the high-coupon ones.[5] Due to the one-month lag in portfolio adjustments and the general decline in rates, during the period, the slope coefficients are understandable. As rates fell sharply, futures positions were typically too large until the next adjustment at the end of the month. This resulted in futures losses that were too large relative to the cash gains. This effect was large enough to reduce the slope coefficients of cash gains regressed on futures gains below the ideal of 1.00 (absolute). This lag effect is more pronounced when the need for hedge adjustments is greater. This prediction squares with the larger slope errors in high-coupon mortgages that required the largest hedge adjustments.

Graphs that show how the aggregate cumulative cash gains offset the aggregate futures losses are displayed in Exhibit 33 and Exhibit 34. Exhibit 33 plots both cash and futures gains and losses against time. Exhibit 34 plots cash gains and losses against futures gains and losses. Exhibit 35 plots monthly cash gains and losses against monthly futures gains and losses. These graphs make it easier to visualize the very high (negative) correlation between the cash and the futures positions. As you can see, the futures are down when the cash is up, and vice versa. The net profit is much less volatile than either the cash, or the futures gains and losses.

The short hedge that Second Savings had in place was correctly viewed and accounted for as a set of micro hedges. At each point in time, the gains and losses on all Treasury bond contracts provided hedges against decreases in the market values of selected mortgage-backed securities that are identified by coupon.

---

[5] Note that a slope coefficient less than 1.00 (absolute) does not indicate that the strategy lost money over the 3.5-year period, since there was a constant term in the regression. In fact, all of these hedging strategies ended with cumulative hedged profits. During this period, mortgage spreads tightened relative to Treasury (see Exhibit 26), generating additional profits.

LIABILITIES HEDGING AND HEDGE ACCOUNTING

The case of Third Savings and Loan Association will serve as an introduction to "liabilities hedging" from the perspective of a financial institution. As before, there are both micro and macro issues that must be addressed by any prudent hedging program. Since the macro hedging issues have been adequately discussed in earlier sections of this chapter, this section will not dwell on the macro aspects of Third Savings' hedging program. The management of Third Savings has thoroughly evaluated the hedging program to insure that it is risk-reducing on both a micro and a macro level.

Exhibit 36 presents those items from Third Savings' balance sheet that are directly related to the Association's hedging program. The Association has ten-year, fixed-rate (nonamortizing) assets of $10 million that pay simple interest at a rate of 10.74% per annum on the last day of each year. These assets are funded by the liabilities shown in Exhibit 36. The liabilities consist of certificates of deposit (CDs) amounting to $10 million, which have maturities ranging from one to five years. For simplicity, it is assumed that these liabilities also pay simple interest on the last day of each year.

Exhibit 36 also presents those parts of the Treasury (zero and coupon) yield curves that are relevant to our discussion, as well as what are assumed to be the market (or fair) premia to Treasury for the assets and liabilities of the Association. The Treasury rates are expressed using annual compounding in order to facilitate the explanation of this hedging program.

The ten-year Treasury coupon rate shown in Exhibit 36 is 8.74%. Since the market premium to Treasury of assets similar to those of Third Savings is 200 basis points, the 10-year, $10 million of fixed-rate assets listed in Exhibit 36 (at 10.74%) should be priced (in the market) at par. Similarly, all of the liabilities listed in Exhibit 36 pay interest at rates that are exactly 100 basis points (the market premium to Treasury) over the corresponding Treasury coupon rates. Therefore, since all of the assets and liabilities are

Exhibit 36: Third Savings and Loan Association: Balance Sheet Subset

Assets			Liabilities		
Amount ($000)	Years to Maturity	Rate (Percent)	Amount ($000)	Years to Repricing	Rate (Percent)
$10,000	10	10.75	$ 6,000	1	8.00
			2,000	2	8.29
			750	3	8.62
			750	4	8.85
			500	5	9.07
$10,000			$10,000		

Assumed Premia To Treasury:	
Assets	200 basis points
Liabilities	100 basis points

Initial Treasury Yields:			
	Zero Coupon Treasury Rate (Percent)	One-Year Forward (Percent)	Coupon Treasury Rate (Percent
Year	(Annual Compounding)		
1	7.00	7.00	7.00
2	7.30	7.62	7.29
3	7.65	8.35	7.62
4	7.90	8.65	7.85
5	8.15	9.16	8.07
6	8.35	9.36	8.24
7	8.50	9.40	8.36
8	8.65	9.71	8.49
9	8.80	10.01	8.60
10	9.00	10.82	8.74

priced at par, the liquidation value of the portfolio shown in Exhibit 36 is equal to zero.

Exhibit 37 presents a traditional "interest rate sensitivity gap" analysis for the assets and liabilities of Third Savings. For ease of explanation, it is assumed that at the end of each year all maturing liabilities (net of the amount of maturing assets) are replaced by

Exhibit 37: Third Savings and Loan Association: Interest Sensitivity Gap Analysis

		Year of Maturity or Repricing									
		1	2	3	4	5	6	7	8	9	10
Interest-Earning Assets	($000)	0	0	0	0	0	0	0	0	0	10,000
Interest-Bearing Liabilities	($000)	6,000	2,000	750	750	500	0	0	0	0	0
Interest Sensitivity Gap (Incremental)	($000)	(6,000)	(2,000)	(750)	(750)	(500)	0	0	0	0	10,000
Interest Sensitivity Gap (Cumulative)	($000)	(6,000)	(8,000)	(8,750)	(9,500)	(10,000)	(10,000)	(10,000)	(10,000)	(10,000)	0
Interest Income	($000)	1,074	1,074	1,074	1,074	1,074	1,074	1,074	1,074	1,074	1,074
Interest Expense	($000)	822	858	925	956	1,010	1,036	1,040	1,071	1,101	1,182
Net Interest Margin	($000)	252	216	149	118	64	38	34	3	(27)	(108)
1 yr forward rates (liabs)		8.00	8.60	9.35	9.65	10.16	10.36	10.40	10.71	11.01	11.82
Average rate (assets)		10.74%	10.74%	10.74%	10.74%	10.74%	10.74%	10.74%	10.74%	10.74%	10.74%
Average rate (liabs)		8.22%	8.58%	9.25%	9.56%	10.10%	10.36%	10.40%	10.71%	11.01%	11.82%
Net Interest Margin		2.52%	2.16%	1.49%	1.18%	0.64%	0.38%	0.34%	0.03%	-0.27%	-1.08%

liabilities with maturities of exactly one year that bear a fair market interest rate (100 basis points over the prevailing one-year Treasury rate). In terms of the economics of the hedge today (and the interest rate risk implicit in an institution's current asset/liability mix), it does not matter which maturities are ultimately selected for the repricing liabilities. The date on which the current liabilities reprice, and the dollar amount of these liabilities (net of the dollar amount of maturing assets) are, however, quite relevant for evaluating the interest rate risk of the portfolio.

Note that in year one $6 million of CDs mature and must be rolled over for the remaining nine years in order to fund the longer-term assets. Similarly, in year two another $2 million of liabilities are scheduled to reprice. At this point there will be a cumulative interest sensitivity gap of $8 million ($6 million from year one plus $2 million from year two). As Exhibit 37 displays, the cumulative gap increases each year until the end of year five, when the Association has five years remaining on its fixed-rate assets. At this point, since none of the original liabilities remains, the cumulative gap has reached its maximum level ($10 million), and remains at this level until the end of year ten, when the assets themselves mature.

Exhibit 37 also displays the projected annual interest income, interest expense, and net interest margins implied by the Treasury yield curve shown in Exhibit 36. Since we are assuming that all maturing liabilities are "rolled over" (repriced) into one-year CDs, estimates of the interest rates that will be paid on these liabilities must be made. These expected future one-year "spot" rates of interest on the liabilities are derived using the one-year forward rates implied by the Treasury yield curve displayed in Exhibit 36. The following simple examples will explain the concept of a forward rate.

Assume that an investor can purchase a two-year zero coupon Treasury security that yields 7.30% per year (compounded annually). Alternatively, the investor may purchase a one-year zero coupon security yielding 7.00%, and in one year purchase another one-year Treasury security at the then prevailing one-year rate. In the absence of any strong investor preference for holding particular maturities, the two-year security may be considered to be essentially the same as the two consecutive one-year securities, the first yielding 7.00% and the second yielding the market's prediction of what the one-year Treasury rate will be one year from now. This market prediction, the forward rate, is that rate that will equate the yield on the two-year security with the combined yield of the two one-year securities.

Mathematically, the 7.30% rate must equal the geometric average of the 7.00% rate of the first year and the implied forward rate of the second one-year period. Therefore, the forward rate, F, may be calculated from the following equation:

$$(1.073)^2 = (1.070)^1 \times (1 + F)$$

where $F = .0760$ or 7.6%, as shown in Exhibit 36 in the column entitled *"One Year Forward Rate (%)."*

Similarly, the one-year Treasury rate nine years into the future, which is implied by the yield curve shown in Exhibit 36, is 10.82%.[6]

$$(1.090)^{10} = (1.088)^9 \times (1 + F)$$

where $F = .1082$ or 10.82%.

Exhibit 36 displays these forward rates for one-year Treasuries, and Exhibit 37 displays the projected liabilities costs at a spread of 100 basis points over the forward Treasury rates. For example, at the end of year one the Association will have $6 million of liabilities to roll forward for the remaining nine years (since the liabilities are used to fund ten-year assets). These liabilities are assumed to be rolled over at the end of each subsequent year at the then prevailing rate for similar liabilities. The projected one-year Treasury rate one year from the present is 7.60% (see above and Exhibit 36). The projected interest rate at which new one-year liabilities

---

[6] Note that the Treasury rates used in these examples are assumed to be for zeroes or strips.

could be issued (one year from the present) is 8.60% (100 basis points over the 7.60% Treasury rate).

The expected interest costs to the Association in year two are therefore equal to $858,000 (rounded to the nearest thousand), which is the sum of the following:

	Rate	Interest Expense
$6,000,000 (rollover for one year)	8.60%	$516,000
$2,000,000 (matures at end of yr 2)	8.29%	$165,800
$ 750,000 (matures at end of yr 3)	8.62%	$ 64,650
$ 750,000 (matures at end of yr 4)	8.85%	$ 66,375
$ 500,000 (matures at end of yr 5)	9.07%	$ 45,350
	Total:	$858,175

The annual interest income remains constant at $1.074 million (10.74% of $10 million) for ten years. As one might expect from the upward sloping structure of the initial Treasury yield curve, the forward rates implied by the yield curve display an increasing pattern. (The initial one-year Treasury rate is 7.00%, and the projected one-year Treasury rate at the end of year nine is 10.82%.) Therefore, the Association's net interest margin is projected to decrease each year until in years nine and ten it is actually negative.[7] However, the present value of these projected net interest margin cash flows totals $647,000, a significantly positive number. This present value number is positive in spite of the fact that the liquidation value (market value of the assets less the market value of the liabilities) is zero (see above discussion). The answer to this apparent paradox is that the $647,000 may be fair compensation for the risk inherent in the portfolio being held. (Remember that the market premium to Treasury on assets is 200 basis points, whereas the premium to Treasury on Third Savings' liabilities is only 100 basis points).

---

[7] Note that the profits or margin from previous years have not been reinvested in this example.

Exhibit 38: Third Savings and Loan Association: Changes in Future Interest Cost (Present Values)

Gains or Losses (Unhedged) for Changes in Interest Rates

Rate Change from Base (Percent)	Present Value Gain (Loss) (Unhedged) ($000)
-5	3,140
-4	2,374
-3	1,684
-2	1,063
-1	504
0	0
1	(454)
2	(863)
3	(1,232)
4	(1,564)
5	(1,864)

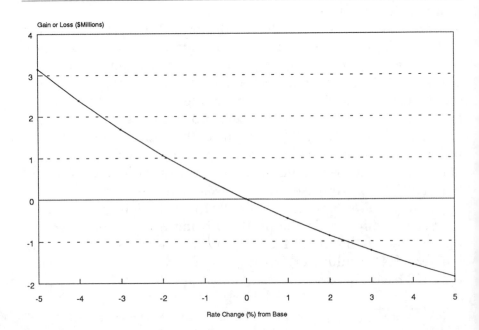

The goal of Third Savings and Loan Association's hedging program is to fix the interest rates that will be paid when the Association's fixed-rate liabilities (CDs) mature and are replaced at then prevailing rates. Since the Association's assets have a longer maturity than do the corresponding liabilities, the profit margin of the Association is subject to tremendous interest rate risk.

Exhibit 38 presents the gains or losses (in present value) to the Association implied by parallel shifts in the Treasury yield curve. For example, a 300 basis point increase in the level of interest rates implies increases in future borrowing costs for the Association in order to continue to fund the fixed-rate assets. The present value of the increased future borrowing costs due to a 300 basis point increase in rates is $1.232 million. Thus, the Association would be subject to an economic loss (unhedged) if interest rates rose 300 basis points. A decrease in the level of interest rates would result in a present value gain to the Association, since the expected future borrowing costs would decrease. For a decrease of 200 basis points, the present value gain to the Association would be $1.063 million.

Exhibit 39 displays the year-by-year results that the Association would realize if interest rates rose by 300 basis points at the beginning of year one. Note that the expected future borrowing costs, to be paid on the repricing liabilities, are now 300 basis points higher than the corresponding rates shown in Exhibit 37. For example, the expected one-year rate to be paid on the $6 million of liabilities that mature at the end of year one is now 11.60% (up from 8.60%). This increases the projected interest cost in year two by $180,000 (3% of $6 million), from $858,000 to $1,038,000.

The projected net interest margin in year two is $180,000 less than would have been expected if rates had not changed (down to $36,000 from $216,000—see Exhibit 39 "NIM [Base]," "NIM [after rates change]," and "Difference"). The present value of this decrease in net interest margin of $180,000 is a loss of $145,000 (shown in the row labeled "Present Value [Incremental]" in Exhibit 39). Similar losses are projected for the remaining years in which the liabilities are to be rolled forward. The loss for year

Exhibit 39: Third Savings and Loan Association: Net Interest Margin and Hedge Analysis (Rates Increase by 300 Basis Points)

		1	2	3	4	5	6	7	8	9	10
						Year of Maturity or Repricing					
Interest-Earning Assets	($000)	0	0	0	0	0	0	0	0	0	10,000
Interest-Bearing Liabilities	($000)	6,000	2,000	750	750	500	0	0	0	0	0
Interest Sensitivity Gap (Incremental)	($000)	(6,000)	(2,000)	(750)	(750)	(500)	0	0	0	0	10,000
Interest Sensitivity Gap (Cumulative)	($000)	(6,000)	(8,000)	(8,750)	(9,500)	(10,000)	(10,000)	(10,000)	(10,000)	(10,000)	0
Interest Income	($000)	1,074	1,074	1,074	1,074	1,074	1,074	1,074	1,074	1,074	1,074
Interest Expense	($000)	822	1,038	1,165	1,219	1,295	1,336	1,340	1,371	1,401	1,482
Net Interest Margin	($000)	252	36	(91)	(145)	(221)	(262)	(266)	(297)	(327)	(408)
1 yr forward rates (liabs)		11.00%	11.60%	12.35%	12.65%	13.16%	13.36%	13.40%	13.71%	14.01%	14.82%
Average rate (assets)		10.74%	10.74%	10.74%	10.74%	10.74%	10.74%	10.74%	10.74%	10.74%	10.74%
Average rate (liabs)		8.22%	10.38%	11.65%	12.19%	12.95%	13.36%	13.40%	13.71%	14.01%	14.82%
Net Interest Margin		2.52%	0.36%	-0.91%	-1.45%	-2.21%	-2.62%	-2.66%	-2.97%	-3.27%	-4.08%
NIM (Base)		252	216	149	118	64	38	34	3	(27)	(108)
NIM (After Rates Change)		252	36	(91)	(145)	(221)	(262)	(266)	(297)	(327)	(408)
Difference		0	(180)	(240)	(262)	(285)	(300)	(300)	(300)	(300)	(300)

Exhibit 39: Third Savings and Loan Association: Net Interest Margin and Hedge Analysis (Rates Increase by 300 Basis Points) (Continued)

Present Value (Incremental)	0	(145)	(172)	(167)	(161)	(149)	(132)	(116)	(101)	(88)
Present Value (Cumulative) (PV Gain or Loss)	(1,232)									
Theoretical Amount of Hedging Gain (Loss) ($000)	1,232									
Time Period (Years)	1	2	3	4	5	6	7	8	9	10
Portion of Hedging Gain (Loss) Invested (Borrowed) for period	0	145	172	167	161	149	132	116	101	88
Annualized Interest Rate	11.00%	11.30%	11.65%	11.90%	12.15%	12.35%	12.50%	12.65%	12.80%	13.00%
Terminal Amount (At end of Period)	0	180	240	262	285	300	300	300	300	300
NIM (Base)	252	216	149	118	64	38	34	3	(27)	(108)
NIM (After Rates Change--Unhedged)	252	36	(91)	(145)	(221)	(262)	(266)	(297)	(327)	(408)
Difference (Unhedged)	0	(180)	(240)	(262)	(285)	(300)	(300)	(300)	(300)	(300)
From Hedge (See "Terminal Amount")	0	180	240	262	285	300	300	300	300	300
NIM (Hedged)	252	216	149	118	64	38	34	3	(27)	(108)
Difference (Hedged)	0	0	0	0	0	0	0	0	0	0

three is $172,000 (the present value of a loss of $240,000 in three years), and the loss associated with year ten is $88,000 (the present value of a decrease in net interest margin of $300,000 in ten years). The economic loss to the Association due to a 300 basis point increase in interest rates is $1.232 million, which is the sum of the present values of the yearly increases in future interest costs to be paid on the rollover of liabilities shown in Exhibit 39 (see row labeled "Present Value [Cumulative]").

Now that the interest rate risk of this portion of the Association's portfolio has been estimated, an appropriate hedging position needs to be established. The following paragraphs illustrate the way the hedge should work.

We know that $6 million of CDs will mature at the end of year one, and are to be hedged against fluctuations in the interest rate that will be paid from the end of year one to the end of year two. If today the interest rate that is expected to be paid in year two rises by 300 basis points, the expected interest cost on the $6 million of rollovers increases by $180,000, as has been discussed earlier. In order to offset this higher anticipated interest cost, the hedge should provide profits today, which, when reinvested, compound to $180,000 by the end of year two. Similarly, if rates fall by 300 basis points, the hedge should provide offsetting losses (the Association would borrow additional funds) that compound to $180,000 by the end of year two.

Similar logic applies to each period (year) that contains repricing liabilities. Theoretically, if a perfect hedge were established, the hedge payoff to the Association, in the event of an immediate 300 basis point increase in rates, would be $1.232 million—exactly offsetting the present value of the increase in future borrowing cost anticipated from year one through year ten on the rollover of liabilities. Exhibit 39 displays how the Association could reinvest portions of the gains from the hedge in such a way that when the future net interest margin is combined with the future proceeds from the hedge reinvestment, the resulting "hedged net interest margin" is identical to the expected net interest margin, assuming rates had not changed.

If interest rates rose by 300 basis points and the hedge worked perfectly to produce gains of $1.232 million, the Association could immediately reinvest those funds in the amounts and maturities shown at the bottom of Exhibit 39. For example, the Association would invest $145,000 for two years at an annual rate of 11.30%. Note that 11.30% is 100 basis points over the new two-year Treasury zero coupon rate (10.30%). This is a conservative reinvestment rate since it is equal to the Association's new two-year cost of funds. At the end of year two this $145,000 would have grown to $180,000, which, when added to the net interest margin (unhedged) of $36,000, results in a hedged net interest margin of $216,000 (exactly equal to the NIM anticipated prior to the change in interest rates).

This procedure could be followed in order to offset the increase in the projected future borrowing cost from each subsequent period. In this way, by offsetting the deviations of the interest spread (margin) from what was originally planned, the Association would effectively "lock in" each year's interest cost. Of course, each year's interest cost could not be "locked in" with perfect certainty. There are always residual (basis) risks with any hedging program. In this example we have assumed parallel yield curve shifts as well as perfect correlation between the hedging instruments and the cash instruments. These assumptions were made for illustrative purposes only. However, the existence of some basis risk should not inhibit Third Savings from undertaking such a hedging program, since the residual risk is likely to be much less than the unhedged interest rate risk.

Exhibit 40 displays the same hedging logic for a rate decrease of 200 basis points. In this case, the future interest costs are less than planned, and the hedge produces losses. These losses are allocated in such a way (by borrowing different amounts for different numbers of years—$106,000 for two years, $132,000 for three years, etc.) that the effective net interest margin (hedged) is, once again, equal to the original planned net interest margin.

Since the Association's cost of funds is more closely tied to the CD rate than to Treasury rates, the CD or Eurodollar time deposit

Exhibit 40: Third Savings and Loan Association: Net Interest Margin and Hedge Analysis (Rates Decrease by 200 Basis Points)

						Year of Maturity or Repricing					
		1	2	3	4	5	6	7	8	9	10
Interest–Earning Assets	($000)	0	0	0	0	0	0	0	0	0	10,000
Interest–Bearing Liabilities	($000)	6,000	2,000	750	750	500	0	0	0	0	0
Interest Sensitivity Gap (Incremental)	($000)	(6,000)	(2,000)	(750)	(750)	(500)	0	0	0	0	10,000
Interest Sensitivity Gap (Cumulative)	($000)	(6,000)	(8,000)	(8,750)	(9,500)	(10,000)	(10,000)	(10,000)	(10,000)	(10,000)	0
Interest Income	($000)	1,074	1,074	1,074	1,074	1,074	1,074	1,074	1,074	1,074	1,074
Interest Expense	($000)	822	738	765	781	820	836	840	871	901	982
Net Interest Margin	($000)	252	336	309	293	254	238	234	203	173	92
1 yr forward rates (liabs)		6.00%	6.60%	7.35%	7.65%	8.16%	8.36%	8.40%	8.71%	9.01%	9.82%
Average rate (assets)		10.74%	10.74%	10.74%	10.74%	10.74%	10.74%	10.74%	10.74%	10.74%	10.74%
Average rate (liabs)		8.22%	7.38%	7.65%	7.81%	8.20%	8.36%	8.40%	8.71%	9.01%	9.82%
Net Interest Margin		2.52%	3.36%	3.09%	2.93%	2.54%	2.38%	2.34%	2.03%	1.73%	0.92%
NIM (Base)		252	216	149	118	64	38	34	3	-27	-108
NIM (After Rates Change)		252	336	309	293	254	238	234	203	173	92
Difference		0	120	160	175	190	200	200	200	200	200

Exhibit 40: Third Savings and Loan Association: Net Interest Margin and Hedge Analysis (Rates Decrease by 200 Basis Points) (Continued)

		1	2	3	4	5	6	7	8	9	10
Present Value (Incremental)		0	106	132	134	135	131	121	111	102	93
Present Value (Cumulative)		1,063									
(PV Gain or Loss)											
Theoretical Amount of Hedging Gain (Loss)	($000)	(1,063)									
Time Period (Years)		1	2	3	4	5	6	7	8	9	10
Portion of Hedging Gain (Loss) Invested (Borrowed) for period		0	-106	-132	-134	-135	-131	-121	-111	-102	-93
Annualized Interest Rate (Association Cost of Funds)		6.00%	6.30%	6.65%	6.90%	7.15%	7.35%	7.50%	7.65%	7.80%	8.00%
Terminal Amount (At end of Period)		0	-120	-160	-175	-190	-200	-200	-200	-200	-200
NIM (Base)		252	216	149	118	64	38	34	3	-27	-108
NIM (After Rates Change--Unhedged)		252	336	309	293	254	238	234	203	173	92
Difference (Unhedged)		0	120	160	175	190	200	200	200	200	200
From Hedge (See "Terminal Amount")		0	-120	-160	-175	-190	-200	-200	-200	-200	-200
NIM (Hedged)		252	216	149	118	64	38	34	3	-27	-108
Difference (Hedged)		0	0	0	0	0	0	0	0	0	0

futures markets should be used to hedge interest costs for as long as possible. The problem is that these futures markets extend out only six to eight quarters, so interest costs for only the first two to three years may be hedged with the CD or EURO futures markets.

The choice of which financial instruments to use to hedge the interest costs for the remaining years should be based on the correlation of the hedging instruments' movements with movements in the interest rate to be hedged. Exhibit 41 gives the means, standard deviations, and correlations of levels and changes in Treasury rates for a number of maturities ranging from three months to thirty years (for the time period *January 1979* to December 1990). For instance, the correlation between the 20-year Treasury bond rate and the 2-, 5-, 7-, and 10-year Treasury note rates are all very high (*.932, .983, .992 and .995, respectively*). Similarly, correlations of the changes in the 20-year Treasury bond rate and the changes in the 2-, 5-, 7-, and 10-year Treasury note rates also prove to be quite high (*.864, .928, .962 and .972, respectively*, for the *February 1979* to December 1990 time period). These figures indicate that T-bond futures may provide a good hedge of the future borrowing costs for years four through ten.

Treasury note futures may also be an effective hedging vehicle, and similar correlation analyses must be carried out in order to determine which futures contracts to use for the hedge. In choosing the most attractive contracts, the hedger should also assess such important factors as the liquidity of the futures markets being considered and the possible basis risk involved with each. For example, if Treasury bond or note futures were used to hedge the Association's future borrowing costs, the Association would still be subject to the risk that the spread between CD rates and Treasuries will be large after year three.

One way to avoid much of this CD–Treasury risk is to hedge with a LIBOR-based interest rate swap. In this case, the Association could enter into an interest rate swap in which it would receive LIBOR (reset often) and pay a fixed Treasury-based rate. To the extent that changes in the spread of LIBOR rates over Treasury rates correlate well with changes in the spread between Third Sav-

Exhibit 41: Means, Standard Deviations, and Correlations of Treasury Rate Levels and Changes (January 1979 to December 1990)

A. Treasury Rate Means and Standard Deviations

Variable	Rate Levels		Actual Changes		Absolute Values of Changes	
	Mean	Standard Deviation	Mean	Standard Deviation	Mean	Standard Deviation
3-Mo Tbill	9.08	2.73	-0.021	0.86	0.52	0.68
6-Mo Tbill	9.43	2.80	-0.023	0.89	0.56	0.69
1-Yr Treas	9.62	2.69	-0.026	0.86	0.57	0.64
2-Yr Treas	9.91	2.48	-0.020	0.75	0.52	0.54
5-Yr Treas	10.13	2.30	-0.011	0.63	0.46	0.42
7-Yr Treas	10.25	2.22	-0.009	0.56	0.43	0.36
10-Yr Treas	10.29	2.15	-0.007	0.52	0.41	0.33
20-Yr Treas	10.39	2.02	-0.007	0.49	0.38	0.31
30-Yr Treas	10.28	2.15	-0.005	0.46	0.36	0.30

B. Correlation Matrix: Rate Levels

Variable	3-Mo Tbill	6-Mo Tbill	1-Yr Treas	2-Yr Treas	5-Yr Treas	7-Yr Treas	10-Yr Treas	20-Yr Treas	30-Yr Treas
3-Mo Tbill	1.000	0.993	0.978	0.938	0.865	0.833	0.816	0.777	0.776
6-Mo Tbill	0.993	1.000	0.994	0.965	0.900	0.872	0.856	0.819	0.818
1-Yr Treas	0.978	0.994	1.000	0.984	0.932	0.908	0.894	0.859	0.859
2-Yr Treas	0.938	0.965	0.984	1.000	0.980	0.965	0.956	0.932	0.931
5-Yr Treas	0.865	0.900	0.932	0.980	1.000	0.997	0.994	0.983	0.982
7-Yr Treas	0.833	0.872	0.908	0.965	0.997	1.000	0.999	0.992	0.992
10-Yr Treas	0.816	0.856	0.894	0.956	0.994	0.999	1.000	0.995	0.996
20-Yr Treas	0.777	0.819	0.859	0.932	0.983	0.992	0.995	1.000	0.998
30-Yr Treas	0.776	0.818	0.859	0.931	0.982	0.992	0.996	0.998	1.000

C. Correlation Matrix: Rate Changes

Variable	3-Mo Tbill	6-Mo Tbill	1-Yr Treas	2-Yr Treas	5-Yr Treas	7-Yr Treas	10-Yr Treas	20-Yr Treas	30-Yr Treas
3-Mo Tbill	1.000	0.962	0.911	0.843	0.747	0.685	0.680	0.621	0.630
6-Mo Tbill	0.962	1.000	0.973	0.925	0.845	0.784	0.781	0.723	0.728
1-Yr Treas	0.911	0.973	1.000	0.976	0.918	0.863	0.858	0.801	0.800
2-Yr Treas	0.843	0.925	0.976	1.000	0.964	0.921	0.913	0.864	0.856
5-Yr Treas	0.747	0.845	0.918	0.964	1.000	0.979	0.970	0.928	0.919
7-Yr Treas	0.685	0.784	0.863	0.921	0.979	1.000	0.986	0.962	0.948
10-Yr Treas	0.680	0.781	0.858	0.913	0.970	0.986	1.000	0.972	0.968
20-Yr Treas	0.621	0.723	0.801	0.864	0.928	0.962	0.972	1.000	0.979
30-Yr Treas	0.630	0.728	0.800	0.856	0.919	0.948	0.968	0.979	1.000

ings' cost of funds and Treasuries, the interest rate swap will eliminate much of this CD–Treasury risk. (Interest rate swaps are discussed in more depth earlier in this chapter.) If Treasury-based futures are chosen as the hedging vehicle, the CD–Treasury risk is generally much smaller than the interest rate risk associated with an unhedged position.

Exhibit 42 displays a suggested futures position that could be used to hedge the interest rate risks discussed above. The allocation of the number of each type of contract necessary to hedge each year's borrowings is also listed in Exhibit 42. The hedge entails a short position of 44 Euro futures contracts and 46 T-bond futures contracts. The Euro futures are used to hedge the borrowing costs of the first three years, and the T-bond futures are used

Exhibit 42: Third Savings and Loan Association: Allocation of Futures Contracts to Future Periods (Years) of Borrowings

Year	Borrowings ($000)	PV of Changes in NIM ($000) for 100 Basis Point Rate Increase	Number of Contracts Euros	T-Bonds
1	0	0	0.0	0.0
2	6,000	-50	-20.0	0.0
3	8,000	-61	-24.0	0.0
4	8,750	-60	0.0	-8.0
5	9,500	-59	0.0	-7.9
6	10,000	-55	0.0	-7.4
7	10,000	-50	0.0	-6.7
8	10,000	-45	0.0	-6.0
9	10,000	-40	0.0	-5.3
10	10,000	-35	0.0	-4.7
		-454	-44.0	-46.0

Derivation:
Year three, Euros:
PV change in int. cost/$move per Euro ct = $60,000/$2,500 = 24.0 cts.
Year five, T-Bonds:
PV change in int. cost/$move per T-bond ct = $59,000/$7,450 = 7.9 cts.
(Consult Exhibit 6 for more detailed treatment of the dollar moves of futures contracts at different levels of interest rates).

to hedge the remaining exposure (years four through ten). In every case, the expected dollar change in the value of the futures contracts allocated to a particular period (year) is equal but opposite to the change in the present value of the future borrowing costs associated with the period's borrowings.

For example, the 24 Euro futures contracts used to hedge the third year's borrowing cost are expected to generate profits of $60,000 for a 100 basis point increase in interest rates ($2,500 per contract). The present value loss to the Association due to a 100 basis point increase in the borrowing costs associated with year 3 is $61,000. Thus, the hedge will theoretically provide profits that almost exactly offset the "cash" portfolio's losses. The same logic applies to the allocation of T-bond futures contracts to specific years' borrowings.

Exhibit 43 displays the accounting allocation of the gains or losses on the hedge to future periods. Since the hedge is designed to offset gains and losses expected to be incurred in future peri-

Exhibit 43: Third Savings and Loan Association: Accounting Allocation of Futures Gains and Losses to Future Periods (100 Basis Point Increase in Interest Rates)

Year	Number of Euros	Gain or Loss: Euros ($000)	Number of T-Bonds	Gain or Loss: T-Bonds ($000)	Gain or Loss: Total ($000)
1	0.0	0	0.0	0.0	0.0
2	-20.0	50	0.0	0.0	50.0
3	-24.0	60	0.0	0.0	60.0
4	0.0	0	-8.0	59.2	59.2
5	0.0	0	-7.9	58.5	58.5
6	0.0	0	-7.4	54.8	54.8
7	0.0	0	-6.7	49.6	49.6
8	0.0	0	-6.0	44.4	44.4
9	0.0	0	-5.3	39.3	39.3
10	0.0	0	-4.7	34.8	34.8
Totals:	-44.0	110	-46.0	340.6	450.6

Exhibit 44: Third Savings and Loan Association: Allocation of Futures Contracts to Specific Hedge Numbers

---

Hedge Number Definition

Hedge Number	Liabilities Amount ($000)	Years to Repricing	Rate (Percent)
1	6,000	1	8.00
2	2,000	2	8.29
3	750	3	8.62
4	750	4	8.85
5	500	5	9.07
	10,000		

PV of Change in Interest Cost for a 100 Basis Point Move (Increase) in Rates (by Hedge Number)

Year	Hedge Number 1	2	3	4	5	Total
1						
2	50.00	——	——	——	——	50.0
3	45.75	15.25	——	——	——	61.0
4	41.10	13.70	5.20	——	——	60.0
5	37.20	12.40	4.70	4.70	——	59.0
6	33.00	11.00	4.10	4.10	2.80	55.0
7	30.00	10.00	3.75	3.75	2.50	50.0
8	27.00	9.00	3.40	3.40	2.20	45.0
9	24.00	8.00	3.00	3.00	2.00	40.0
10	21.00	7.00	2.60	2.60	1.80	35.0

Sample Allocation (Hedge Number 1)

Year	EUROs/CDs	T-Bonds
1	0.0	0.0
2	-20.0	0.0
3	-18.3	0.0
4	0.0	-5.5
5	0.0	-5.0
6	0.0	-4.4
7	0.0	-4.0
8	0.0	-3.6
9	0.0	-3.2
10	0.0	-2.8
	-38.3	-28.5

Derivation:
Year three, Hedge #1, Euros:
PV change in int. cost/$move per Euro ct = $45,750/$2,500 = 18.3 cts.

Year five, Hedge #1, T-Bonds:
PV change in int. cost/$move per T-Bond ct = $37,200/$7,450 = 5.0 cts.

---

ods, much of the hedging gains and losses should be deferred for accounting purposes. The allocation of the hedging gains and losses to each future period is based on the prior allocation of specific numbers of futures contracts of each type to each period. For example, year 5 has 7.9 short T-bond futures contracts allocated to it. If long-term rates rise by 100 basis points and there is a decrease in the futures price of $7,406 per contract (see Exhibit 43), $58,500 of futures gains are allocated to year 5 (7.9 × $7,400).

The allocation of futures contracts can, and for regulatory and accounting purposes must, be made to specific hedge numbers. Exhibit 44 displays the allocation of futures contracts to specific hedge numbers. In this example, each of the five liabilities (which mature in different years) are assigned different hedge numbers (1 through 5). For example, the $6,000,000 liability that matures at the end of year one is assigned hedge number 1.

In order to determine the allocation of contracts to each hedge number, it is necessary to determine what proportion of each time period's projected borrowings is due to the projected borrowings associated with each hedge number. The allocation of contracts to hedge numbers is carried out according to the above proportions. For example, in year 5 there is a total of 7.9 T-bond contracts being used to hedge $9.5 million in borrowings, and $6.0 million of these borrowings are from hedge 1. It follows that hedge number 1 will have 5.0 (7.9 × $6.0/$9.5) T-bond futures contracts assigned to it for year 5.

Exhibit 45 displays the theoretical performance of the hedge under different parallel shifts in interest rates. As the final column in Exhibit 45 indicates, in theory, the hedge should work quite well, reducing the net hedged gain or loss to a mere 4.17% or less of the unhedged gain or loss, and 1.31% of total (book) liabilities even for extreme interest rate moves of 500 basis points in either direction. The graph in Exhibit 45 clearly shows how the hedging gains or losses offset the "cash" losses or gains due to changes in interest rates, thereby greatly reducing the volatility of the interest spread between the relevant assets and liabilities. (Refer to Exhibit 6 for dollar moves per futures contract.)

Exhibit 45: Third Savings and Loan Association: Changes in Future Interest Cost (Present Value)

Rate Change	Gain or Loss ($000)			Abs. Value of Net Gain or Loss as Percentage of:	
(%)	Cash	Futures	Net	Cash Gain/Loss	Tot. (Book) Liabs.
-5	3,140	(3,271)	(131)	4.17%	1.31%
-4	2,374	(2,437)	(53)	2.23%	0.53%
-3	1,684	(1,709)	(25)	1.49%	0.25%
-2	1,063	(1,069)	(6)	0.56%	0.06%
-1	504	(503)	1	0.20%	0.01%
0	0	0	0	0.00%	0.00%
1	(454)	451	(3)	0.66%	0.03%
2	(863)	858	(5)	0.58%	0.05%
3	(1,232)	1,227	(5)	0.41%	0.05%
4	(1,564)	1,564	0	0.00%	0.00%
5	(1,864)	1,874	10	0.54%	0.10%

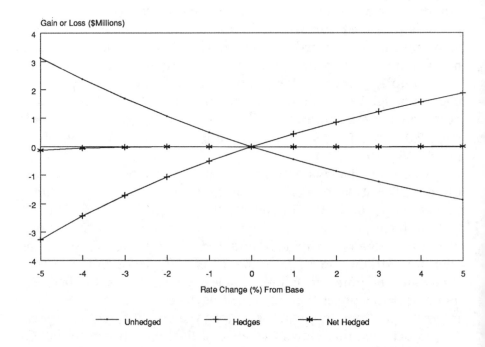

CONCLUSION

This chapter presented an integrated approach to the assessment and hedging of interest rate risk. The chapter started with the basics of futures, options, interest rate swaps, and mortgages, and proceeded to fairly complex hedging analysis. Issues of duration and price elasticities for mortgages were examined in detail, although more remains to be done. Changes in mortgage elasticities were documented using data from 1984 to 1990—a time of very volatile interest rates. The difficulties of hedging mortgages and the basis risks of hedging them with futures were dramatically illustrated.

Within the chapter are graphs that give a relatively complete elementary presentation of risk analysis and of the construction of futures and option hedges. The chapter can be read ignoring the statistics used to obtain this graphic presentation (particularly with the First Savings example). Still, we find that many investors, regulators, and portfolio managers are significantly beyond this elementary understanding, so the statistical data and results for dynamic hedging strategies are there for those readers.

The dynamic hedging strategies were shown to be very successful hedges, with a relatively simple and understandable approach to portfolio adjustment. Positions in Treasury bond futures were adjusted larger when rates increased, and made smaller when rates fell. This is necessary for hedging mortgages, since one is hedging the prepayment option—essentially by recreating that option with a dynamic trading strategy. It was shown that the cumulative gains and losses on cash positions in GNMA 8% mortgages through 15% mortgages had correlations in excess of .97 with the Treasury bond futures hedge gains and losses. For low-coupon securities, the correlations exceeded .99, despite a difficult hedging environment in 1986. Thus, despite the demonstrated basis risk, the hedges of mortgages are very effective over large interest rate swings. If one makes the case that the basis risk is so large as to vitiate the usefulness of futures, then one is simply not looking carefully at the data. The volatilities of the hedged positions are much, much smaller than the volatilities of unhedged positions.

A great amount of data on Treasury rates, futures prices, mortgages prices, and prepayments was presented, so that readers may pursue the many interesting questions that were not addressed in the chapter. Some of the significant issues not examined are: (1) optimal hedge portfolios of futures contracts, balancing both T-bonds and Eurodollar contracts with various maturities; (2) costs of option protection and the returns achieved with option-hedging strategies; (3) performance of interest rate swaps as hedges; and (4) optimal dynamic hedging strategies. Daily data and portfolio rebalancing would also be interesting, and would probably improve some of the hedge performance aspects, but at some transaction cost. These issues are beyond the scope of this chapter.

CHAPTER 36

OPTIONS ON MORTGAGE-BACKED SECURITIES

William A. Barr
Associate Director
Mortgage Department
Bear, Stearns & Co., Inc.

INTRODUCTION

Over-the-counter (OTC) options on mortgage-backed securities (MBSs) are a well developed, long established market. Sophisticated mortgage bankers use the market to hedge their pipeline, which is subject to fallout risk. Investors in MBSs enhance their returns by writing covered calls and puts on their mortgage portfolios. Market making in mortgage options is one of the services major dealers in MBSs offer their customers. With options on mortgages being a significant part of the general MBS market, understanding some of the unique features of this options market is important.

This chapter will discuss the conventions of the mortgage options market, the differences between Treasury options and mortgage options, the influence of prepayments on mortgage options, mortgage pipeline hedging, and split fee options. The chapter will conclude with two comments on mortgage options as a return enhancing tool for portfolio managers.

MARKET CONVENTIONS: OTC OPTIONS ON MORTGAGE-BACKED SECURITIES

Options require specification of five items: (1) the underlying security, (2) the strike price, (3) the expiration date, (4) whether the option is a put or call, and (5) whether the option is American or European. Below are the conventions the OTC mortgage options market uses to specify these items.

1. The underlying security is a TBA (the pools to be announced) MBS (GNMA, FNMA, FHLMC). The delivery month must also be specified for that security. The mortgage market prices forward delivery. If a mortgage option is exercised, the underlying mortgage must be delivered in the month specified by the option agreement. The option is valued using the price associated with the underlying security's delivery month.

2. The strike price is usually quoted as a price difference to the underlying price of the delivery month. For example, a dealer bidding at the money calls would set a strike price that is the bid price of the underlying security. A dealer offering a one point out of the money call would set a strike price one point above the security's offer price. Finally, a dealer bidding a one and one-half point out of the money put would set the strike one and one-half points down from the offer side of the market. Of course, a customer can ask a dealer to bid or offer an option with a specific strike.

3. Expiration dates for OTC mortgage options are also known as notification dates. Expiration/notification dates can be any business day prior to one week before delivery; the week before delivery allows time for inventory adjustments and allocations. Mortgage bankers seem to prefer expiration dates two weeks prior to the mortgage delivery date. The dealer community trades with expiration dates one week prior to mortgage delivery. If a customer does not specify the expiration date, then the option is priced to the same date as is the dealer convention, that is, one week prior to mortgage delivery.

4. The option must be a put or call.

5. The American or European designation of the option is not relevant. The dealer convention is that mortgage options are always European. The delivery of the underlying mortgage security and the delivery of the mortgage if the option is exercised are on the same date, and therefore there is virtually no carry component in the option value that could induce an early exercise.

DIFFERENCES BETWEEN TREASURY OPTIONS, OTC AND EXCHANGE-TRADED, AND OTC MORTGAGE OPTIONS

The primary difference between mortgage options and Treasury options is the underlying securities. To choose between one and the other is to take a position in the relative pricing of mortgages versus Treasuries. Also, depending on the maturity of the Treasury underlying the option, there could be yield curve risk as well. (Mortgage options versus options on a ten-year Treasury note would entail mortgage/Treasury pricing risk and little yield curve risk. Mortgage options versus options on a thirty-year Treasury bond or two-year Treasury note would include yield curve risk.) To choose between options on mortgages and options on Treasuries is therefore to make a market sector position decision.

INSTITUTIONAL DIFFERENCES BETWEEN EXCHANGE-TRADED TREASURY OPTIONS AND OTC MORTGAGE OPTIONS

The institutional distinction between the OTC mortgage options and OTC Treasury options markets is nominal. However, the institutional difference between the OTC options market and the exchange-traded options market is great. What are the differences between these two markets? Should positions ever be taken in exchange-traded Treasury options for institutional reasons when a position in mortgage options is preferred? The seven most important differences are as follows:

1. *Underlying security*: A Treasury futures contract is the underlying instrument for the exchange-traded option. A specific MBS is the underlying security of an OTC mortgage option. Since an exchange-traded option is in lieu of a mortgage option, there is relative price risk of the futures contract to the mortgage market. In particular, the price risk of a position in exchange-traded options incorporates cash/futures relative price risk, potential yield curve risk, and mortgage/Treasury relative price risk. There is no relative price risk associated with mortgage options, since the underlying security is a mortgage.

2. *Strikes*: There is only a set number of strikes to choose from in the exchange-traded options market. With OTC mortgage options, the customer can choose any strike. There is no restriction on the strike of an OTC mortgage option.

3. *Expiration dates*: There is only a set number of expiration dates to choose from in the exchange-traded options market. The expiration dates are one day a month, and the months with expirations dates are the current month and March, June, September, and December. With OTC mortgage options, the customer can choose any expiration date up to one week prior to the mortgage delivery date. There

is no restriction on the expiration date of an OTC mortgage option.

4. *Option liquidity*: With exchange-traded options the bid/ask spread is 3/64ths for front month expiration dates and 6/64ths to 10/64ths for back month expiration dates. Generally, $100 million par amount (thousand contracts) can trade at these prices. The bid/ask spread for mortgage options across the dealer market for front month expiration dates is 3/64th to 5/64ths (often, the option price market is locked, with the only distinction being the strike). For back month options the bid/ask spread is 4/64ths to 8/64ths. Exactly as with the exchange-traded options, $100 million par amount can trade at these prices. The option bid/ask spreads in both markets incorporate the price spread in the underlying security, and therefore are comparable. There is no liquidity lost in trading OTC mortgage options.

5. *Pricing information*: Pricing information is readily available from price vendors for exchange-traded options. This information can be supplied real-time. For OTC mortgage options, access to pricing information requires calling dealers for quotes. With a pricing service, price information is more readily available for exchange-traded options than for OTC mortgage options. Without a price service, there is no difference between OTC mortgage options and exchange traded options in the accessibility of price information.

6. *Commissions*: There are commissions associated with trading exchange-traded options. The prices quoted in the market are gross prices and not net commissions paid. In the OTC mortgage market, the prices quoted are net. There are no additional fees paid with an OTC mortgage option trade.

7. *Credit*: When buying options at an exchange, the contra-party credit exposure is with the exchange's clearing corporation. There is also credit exposure to the clearing member with whom the option position is held. The credit exposure

of an OTC mortgage option is with the dealer from whom the option is bought.

There is no reason to position exchange-traded Treasury options when the preferred trade position is mortgage options. The only significant institutional distinction between OTC mortgage options and exchange-traded options is with respect to credit exposure. If the OTC option is purchased from a well capitalized dealer, this distinction is nominal. The decision to position in OTC mortgage options versus exchange-traded options should be purely an economic one.

THE IMPACT OF PREPAYMENTS ON MORTGAGE OPTION PRICING

Mortgage option pricing is effected by the underlying mortgage's prepayment expectations. In particular, the faster the expected prepayment speeds of an option's underlying MBS, the lower the implied volatility used to value the option.

Prepayment of principal is a characteristic of MBSs. The prepayment of principal will shorten the life/maturity of a MBS. Modified duration is determined in part by the maturity of a security. With MBSs, it is estimated using the best guess of the mortgage's future prepayments.

When yields change, the change in a security's price is a function of the security's modified duration. The larger the modified duration, the greater a security's price change for a given change in yields. Price volatility is therefore a function of modified duration.

Prepayment speeds determine the maturity of a MBS, maturity determines the security's modified duration, and modified duration determines price volatility. Therefore, prepayments and the market's best estimates of future prepayment speeds influence the price volatility of a MBS. Since expected volatility is a fundamental part of option pricing and positioning, estimates of future mortgage prepayment speeds significantly influence option prices.

The likelihood of prepayment speeds being high or low is in part a function of alternative financing opportunities in the mortgage market. If an existing MBS has a high coupon relative to the current market mortgage origination rates (the price of the security would be above par), then the prepayment speed is expected to be high. If an exiting MBS has a low coupon relative to the current market mortgage origination rates (the price of the security would be below par), then the prepayment speed is expected to be low. Therefore, MBSs priced above par have shorter expected maturities, shorter modified durations, and lower price volatilities (given equal yield volatilities) than MBSs priced below par.

The impact of prepayment speeds on option pricing is significant. The higher the coupon of the MBS, the lower the option-implied price volatility. Exhibit 1 is a list of at-the-money options prices and implied price volatilities for GNMA securities expiring in May 1991. One can see how the implied volatilities fall as the coupons increase.

Also, for MBSs that are priced in the market near par and above, the strike price of an option will affect an option's implied price volatility. For these securities, out-of-the-money puts (and in-the-money calls) will have higher implied price volatilities than

Exhibit 1: At-the-Money Option Prices for GNMA Securities, Trade Date March 25, 1991

Coupon	May Price	Implied Volatility	Option Price	Expiration Date
8.00	94:03	5.78	0:24	5/07
8.50	96:25	5:48	0:23+	5/07
9.00	99:14	5.07	0:22	5/07
9.50	101:24	4.62	0:22	5/13
10.00	103:75	4.01	0:19+	5/13
10.50	105:15	3.20	0:15+	5/13
11.00	107:10	2.59	0:13	5/13

out-of-the-money calls (and in-the-money puts). Currently (April 11, 1991), the options market values strikes that are different from at the money with a change in implied price volatility of 0.3% per point. For options with strikes below at the money, implied volatility increases 0.3% per point compared with the at-the-money implied volatility. For options with strikes above at the money, implied volatility decreases 0.3% per point. (For example, if at-the-money options are valued at 5.0% implied price volatility, then two-point out-of-the-money puts would be valued at 5.6% implied price volatility. One-point out-of-the-money calls would be valued at 4.7% implied price volatility.)

The fact that the strike price influences the implied volatility of an option for current and premium priced MBSs is not surprising. Existing prepayment expectations are embedded in at-the-money options. For out-of-the-money options, not only are existing prepayment expectations accounted for in the option pricing, the change in prepayment expectations if the option moved closer to being at the money is also incorporated (i.e., the market price of the underlying security moved toward the strike price). If, for example, a MBS is priced at 99:00, and a call option on the MBS with a 102:00 strike is priced, then the implied volatility to price the option would incorporate both the prepayment expectations currently in the market with the 99:00 price and the expected prepayment speeds consistent with a 102:00 price level.

To summarize, prepayments influence option pricing in two ways. First, across MBSs, the higher the price of a MBS is, the faster its expected prepayment speed will be; the faster expected prepayment speeds are, the lower the implied price volatility used to value options on that MBS will be. Second, with a particular MBS, the higher (lower) the strike relative to at the money is, the lower (higher) the implied price volatility used to value the option will be. This option pricing adjustment is due to changes with expected prepayment speeds associated with the market moving to a price level that would make the strike at the money.

HEDGING THE OPTION EMBEDDED IN THE MORTGAGE PIPELINE

The management of mortgage pipeline risk is one of the primary determinants of a mortgage banker's profitability. The key to managing this risk efficiently and effectively is to understand that a major component of this risk is option risk. A mortgage banker who issues a commitment letter or who guarantees a firm rate when accepting a mortgage application has sold a put option to the potential borrower. After a commitment is made, the homeowner has the right but not the obligation to "take out the loan," that is, the option to sell or to put the mortgage loan to the mortgage banker. If rates fall or the home sale falls through, the homeowner may decide not to take out the mortgage. Thus, the mortgage pipeline manager has effectively sold a mortgage put option to the potential homeowner.

Managing the mortgage pipeline's implicit put option is critical to successful mortgage banking. In the following, pipeline risk is described and its put option component identified. Next, two ways to hedge the option embedded in mortgage origination are discussed. Finally, the way to choose between the two hedging methods is suggested.

Pipeline Risk-Price Risk and Fallout Risk

Price risk: Mortgage pipeline price risk arises from the difference between the terms of the borrower's mortgage loan and the terms available in the market where the loan is sold, that is, the price paid and the price received (sold) for the mortgage. The longer the period between the time a commitment is made to a borrower and the time the mortgage is sold in the market, the greater the price risk.

Mortgage bankers can deal with this risk by selling and delivering mortgage loans as soon as they are originated. Mortgages, though, are costly to sell in small lots; better execution is obtained if the mortgages are grouped and sold in fairly large amounts. To group the mortgages into large amounts, the mortgage banker has to hold mortgages in inventory, and waiting to accumulate large amounts of mortgages in inventory exposes the mortgage banker to changing interest rates. Selling mortgages for future delivery is a way to hedge inventory risk while accumulating large blocks. However, the availability of future inventory to be delivered against the forward sale must be known with certainty. Selling forward against mortgage commitments subject to fallout can leave the mortgage banker short if the mortgages do not close. How does the mortgage banker hedge commitments subject to fallout risk? Hedging the fallout risk is hedging the option component of mortgage origination.

Fallout risk: Fallout risk arises from the fact that the borrower can choose to close or not to close after the mortgage banker has made a mortgage loan commitment. Falling interest rates with cheaper alternative mortgage financing will cause closings on mortgage commitments to decrease. On the other hand, if mortgage rates rise, commitments with "locked-in rates" will have a high likelihood of closing, since alternative financing is more expensive. Rates up, the mortgage banker owns inventory; rates down, the mortgage banker is flat inventory. From the mortgage banker's viewpoint, he is in a lose/neutral situation. The fallout risk profile is exactly the same as the risk profile of a short put option.

Managing Fallout Risk: Two Alternatives

The solution to the fallout risk problem is to acquire a position that offsets the risk profile of commitments subject to fallout risk. There are two ways to acquire such a position: using OTC mortgage options or self-hedging.

Hedging with options: OTC mortgage put options generate the same but opposite risk profile of the commitment fallout risk.

Therefore, buying put options is one solution to the fallout risk problem. When interest rates go up, the owner of the put is short the MBS underlying the put. When interest rates go down, the put owner has no position in the put's underlying MBS. The mortgage banker has a win/neutral position that offsets the lose/neutral position of the fallout subject mortgage commitments.

What are the costs and benefits of owning put options? The cost is the price paid for the option—this fee is lost if the option is held to expiration. The benefit is that the price risk of the pipeline subject to fallout is known for certain and with at-the-money puts eliminated.

Self-hedging: How does a mortgage banker deal with the lose/neutral characteristics of the mortgage origination fallout risk without using options? If the mortgage banker does nothing and sells only forward pipeline that will certainly close, he then is faced with the lose/neutral position for interest rates going up or down. When interest rates go up, he will experience a loss as he becomes long inventory that was subject to fallout risk but is not yet sold. When interest rates come down, he loses nothing, since he never sold inventory forward that subsequently fell out. Alternatively, the mortgage banker could create a neutral/lose situation for interest rates up or down. He creates this scenario by selling all commitments forward, including commitments subject to fallout risk. If interest rates go up, he loses nothing, since the mortgages that are subject to fallout risk close and are delivered against the forward sells. On the other hand, if interest rates go down, then the mortgage banker experiences fallout, and ends up being short with the forward sells that were against the pipeline subject to fallout. The mortgage banker is betting on interest rates if he follows either course of action.

To self-hedge and not bet on interest rates, the mortgage banker can sell forward a "50%" hedge against the pipeline subject to fallout risk. The 50% hedge ensures that he is only exposed to half his fallout risk. If interest rates go up and all the pipeline subject to fallout close, the mortgage banker is long only half the inventory subject to fallout risk. If interest rates come down and none of the fallout pipeline closes, the mortgage banker is only short half the inventory subject to fallout risk. The mortgage banker loses in both scenarios, but the losses are less than if he either does nothing or if he sells all his commitments and is wrong.

What are the benefits and costs of self-hedging? The benefit is that there is no fee. Unlike a put option, where a fee is paid to own the right to sell mortgages, there is no fee paid for self-hedging. The cost of self-hedging is the unlimited loss potential that is embedded in the hedge position. If interest rates rise or fall dramatically (such as in April 1987 and October 1987), the losses from hedging only 50% of the pipeline subject to fallout can be substantial. Also, since the loses are potential at the time the self-hedge is implemented, the uncertainty associated with a self-hedging program is a source of anxiety, and this anxiety could also be considered a cost of self-hedging.

How to Choose between Hedging with Options and Self-Hedging

The mortgage banker must compare the costs and benefits of the two hedging methods in the context of his future outlook on interest rate changes.

- Hedging with Options

  Cost: The fee
  Benefit: No price risk and no anxiety.

- Self Hedging

  Cost: Unlimited price risk and the associated anxiety.
  Benefit: No fee

Hedging with at-the-money put options is the more cost-effective hedge if, by the option's expiration date, the market price of the MBS underlying the option is expected to move more than twice the option fee. Self-hedging is the more cost-effective hedging method if the market price of the MBS is expected to change less than twice the amount of the option fee. The mortgage banker must decide how much MBS prices will move over the term of the option, and compare that movement with the option price. The mortgage banker must also decide on the value of anxiety associated with the unlimited loss potential of self-hedging.

No matter which hedging method is chosen, there is a cost to hedging. The best result the mortgage banker can achieve is zero cost (which results from self-hedging with no subsequent price movement, and buying back the hedge at the original sell price). The cost of the implicit put that is a part of mortgage origination cannot be escaped. The mortgage banker can only minimize that cost by choosing the best hedging strategy.

SPLIT FEE OPTIONS

A split fee option is an option on an option. Split fee options are a commonly sold instrument in the OTC mortgage options market. The customers generally are mortgage bankers, who purchase them as an alternative to purchasing traditional OTC mortgage options when hedging their pipeline risk. Split fee options are also know as compound options, and calls on puts, or calls on calls.

This discussion will describe the characteristics of split fee options and give a framework for deciding whether or not to position them relative to traditional option positions.

Traditional options require five characteristics to be specified: a strike, an expiration date, an underlying security, whether the option is a put or call, and whether the option is American or European. With traditional options, the option owner will decide on the expiration date whether or not to exercise the option. There is only one decision for the option owner after the option is purchased.

Split fee options require the above five characteristics and two more, a second fee and a second fee expiration date (the window date). A fee is paid today for the split fee option. Then, on the window date the split fee option owner decides whether or not to pay the second fee. If the second fee is not paid, the option becomes void; if the second fee is paid, the option continues to be valid. Then the option owner must decide on the expiration date whether or not to exercise the option. With split fee options there are potentially two decisions to make after the option is purchased.

With traditional options, the purchaser will specify the option characteristics and then ask what is the fee or price for the option. With split fee options, the purchaser will specify the five items of a traditional option, and then will specify the fee that will be paid today for the split fee option, and the window date. The purchaser then asks what will be the second fee payable on the window date. The second fee is the decision variable with split fee options.

How is the second fee affected by the variables unique to split fee options and by implied volatility? The variables unique to split fee options are the window date and the amount that is set for the first fee (i.e., the fee paid today). The window date can be any day between today and the expiration date; the first fee can be any amount. How does changing the window date and first fee affect the second fee? Do different levels of implied volatility affect the sensitivities of the window date and first fee?

Exhibits 2, 3, and 4 compare a split fee pricing with a traditional option, and show the sensitivities of the second fee to the first fee, window date, and implied volatility. The price of a traditional option is also shown. The split fee option is on a GNMA 8.5 to be delivered if exercised on the regular PSA settlement date in June 1991. The date on which the split fee option is evaluated (trade date) is February 26, 1991. The strike price is at the money, which is 97:17. The expiration date is June 11, 1991. The split fee option is a put and is European. The window dates for the second fee are March 28, 1991, April 26, 1991, and May 28, 1991.

Exhibit 2 shows that the sum of the first and second fees is always greater than the fee of the traditional option. This relationship will hold for all window dates and for all combinations of

Exhibit 2: Fee Comparison: Split Fee Option to Corresponding Traditional Option

	Total Fee	First Fee	Second Fee
Traditional Option	1:04+	—	—
Split Fee Option Window			
3/28/91	1:09	0:16	0:25
4/26/91	1:17	0:16	1:01
5/28/91	1:29+	0:16	1:13+

Trade date: February 26, 1991
Strike and underlying price: 97:17
Implied volatility: 5.5%
Expiration date: June 11, 1991
European Put

first and second fees where the first fee is less than the fee of the corresponding traditional option.

Exhibit 3 shows the relationship of the first fee to the second fee for the split fee option with a March 28, 1991 window date.

Exhibit 3: Second Fee Sensitivities to Implied Volatilities and First Fee

	Implied Volatilities		
First Fee	4.5	5.5	6.5
0:04	1:12	1:26	2:08+
0:08	0:30+	1:10	1:22+
0:12	0:22	1:00	1:11
0:16	0:16	0:25	1:02+
0:20	0:10+	0:18+	0:27+
0:24	0:06	0:13+	0:21+

Trade date: February 26, 1991
Underlying security: GNMA 8.50 June
Strike and underlying price: 97:17
Expiration date: June 11, 1991
Window date: March 28, 1991
European Put

The first observation to be made from the exhibit is that the higher the first fee is, the lower the second fee will be. The second observation is that this relationship between fees is not linear. For a 32nd change ($312.50/million par amount) in the first fee, changes in the second fee vary depending on the initial level of the first fee. For a set change in the first fee, the smaller the initial level of the first fee, the larger is the change in the second fee. The third observation is that the higher the implied volatility, the higher is the second fee, and this relationship is linear.

Exhibit 4 shows the relationship of the second fee to the window date. The three window dates are March 28th, April 26th, and May 28th. The relationship between the window and the second fee is not linear. The days between March 28th and April 26th are cheaper in terms of the second fee than the days between April 26th and May 28th.

To summarize the sensitivities, the higher the implied volatility is, the higher the second fee will be. The lower the first fee, the higher the second fee, which will increase at a geometric rate. And finally, the farther into the future the window date is, the higher

Exhibit 4: Second Fee Sensitivities to the Window Date

	Window Date		
First Fee	3/28/91	4/26/91	5/28/91
0:04	1:26	2:18	3:11+
0:08	1:10	1:27	2:14+
0:12	1:00	1:12	1:27+
0:16	0:25	1:01	1:13+
0:20	0:18+	0:24	1:01
0:24	0:13+	0:16+	0:23

Trade date:	February 26, 1991
Underlying security:	GNMA 8.50 June
Strike and underlying price:	97:17
Expiration date:	June 11, 1991
Implied Volatility:	5.5%
European Put	

the second fee will be, which again will increase at a geometric rate.

Mortgage bankers use split fee options to attempt to reduce the fees they pay for their pipeline hedging. Instead of buying traditional options to cover their pipeline subject to fallout, the mortgage banker will purchase split fee options. The first fee of the split fee is less than the fee of the traditional option, and therefore initially the cost of hedging the pipeline is less than it would be using traditional options.

Now, if one of two events happen by the window date, the mortgage banker will be better off with owning split fees than if he bought traditional options. First, the mortgage banker will benefit from split fee options if, by the window date, the amount of pipeline subject to fallout is reduced from original estimates. By purchasing split fee options, the mortgage banker reduces the cost of his insurance by not paying traditional options fees for pipeline hedging he subsequently did not need. Second, if implied volatility falls, the cost of the identical option in the market could be cheaper than the second fee. The mortgage banker, instead of paying the second fee, could replace the split fee with the same option more cheaply from the market. If the implied volatility fell enough, the combination of the first fee and the price of replacing the option on the window date from the market could be less than the initial traditional option fee.

The cost of a split fee is the additional price that is paid over and above the price of the identical put that is a traditional option when combining the first and second fees. If the mortgage banker finally decides to exercise the second fee, he would have been better off purchasing the traditional option.

MORTGAGE OPTIONS TO ENHANCE PORTFOLIO RETURNS

Options as a return-enhancing device is a frequently discussed topic. Therefore, only two points will be mentioned concerning mortgage options for enhancing returns.

First, total return investors attempt to capture all the potential
value that can be generated from a collateral investment. With securities, returns are generated from coupon income, price appreciation, financing specials, and price volatility. To capture the
value derived from price volatility, the total return investor must
be involved with options. Investors can enhance returns by both
buying and selling options; choosing which to do and when is the
difficult part. When the investor does not think interest rates will
change significantly over a time period, selling options over the
same time period will increase returns by the amount of the option fee less any price movement. On the other hand, when the
investor expects interest rates to change significantly, options are a
way of creating leverage to benefit from the price move while limiting risk. Without participating in options, the total return investor is leaving a major contributor of value out of his collection of
investment tools.

Second, the mortgage options market is unique among short-
dated options markets. For other options markets, the net sum of
long and short option positions in the investor and dealer community is zero. For every option long in the investment community
there is an option short. With these options no net value is created
or lost in the investment community; only the price risk of the
underlying security has been redistributed.

Mortgage options are different. Homebuyers receive from
mortgage bankers puts as a part of the mortgage origination process. Mortgage bankers in turn buy puts from the dealer community to hedge the homeowner put position they are short. The
dealers either stay short options or purchase options from mortgage investors. Unlike in other security markets, the investor and
dealer community is net short options, with homebuyers net long
options. To induce the investment community to accept the net
short option position, homebuyers must pay a price for purchasing and taking away their options. By supplying a service to the
consuming public, returns to the investment community from being short options on mortgages are probably higher than being

short options on other securities, where the net investment community position is zero.

CONCLUSION

Over-the-counter mortgage options are an integral part of the market for MBSs. Mortgage bankers need to look at the mortgage options market to determine the value of the option embedded in their mortgage pipeline, and to hedge that pipeline. Investors in MBSs can use options to enhance the returns on their mortgage portfolios. Knowledge of the mortgage options market is important to achieve these goals.

CHAPTER 37

MORTGAGE-BACKED SECURITIES VOLATILITY RISK MANAGEMENT USING OVER-THE-COUNTER OPTIONS

William J. Curtin
Senior Vice President
Lehman Brothers

Nicholas C. Letica
Vice President
Bankers Trust Securities Corp.

Andrew Lawrence
Vice President
Greenwich Capital Markets, Inc.

INTRODUCTION

Managing interest rate volatility risk, although not entirely unknown to the general investment community, has been restricted largely to the ranks of option traders. As markets have become more volatile and securities increasingly leveraged and sophisticated, however, it has become incumbent upon fixed-income investors to have a good intuitive understanding of volatility and its effect on relative value in order to make appropriate portfolio allocation decisions. Securities that are embedded with either explicit or implicit options, such as mortgage pass-throughs, callable corporates, and derivative mortgage products (e.g., collateralized mortgage obligations [CMOs], stripped mortgage-backed securities [strips]), demand estimates of market volatility for accurate evaluation. A failure to estimate the effects of volatility on a portfolio of securities with embedded options can lead to underperformance relative to an index or other money managers.

The most natural tool for managing volatility risk (and also interest rate risk) is over-the-counter (OTC) options. Calls, puts, or combinations can be used to create customized hedging vehicles. The terms of OTC options are extremely flexible: strike prices and length of term can be adjusted to create a hedge at any specific market level (or cost) and horizon. Investors that are long or short mortgage-backed securities (MBSs), for example, can create hedges using MBS OTC options to protect the performance of their portfolios from swings in volatility and interest rates. In addition, OTC options can be used by investors to capitalize on expected changes in volatility or interest rates.

The purpose of this chapter is to familiarize investors with the effects of volatility on fixed-income securities and to present portfolio allocation strategies using MBS OTC options. The first section is an introduction to the behavior of volatility and the trading characteristics of fixed-income options. This section provides a review of basic concepts and an appropriate framework for our discussion of portfolio strategies. The second section illuminates a variety of effects changing volatility may have on the performance of various fixed-income securities, and also provides several suggestions for hedging these effects. While the specific examples given represent only a small portion of the variations in volatility risk, they are illustrative and provide insight into the many ways that options can be structured to satisfy a specific goal.

BEHAVIOR OF VOLATILITY AND TRADING CHARACTERISTICS OF FIXED-INCOME OPTIONS

Options Pricing: A Primer

Many fixed-income securities such as callable corporates and MBSs are a combination of two elements: a long position in a non-callable bond and an implicit or explicit long- or short-term options position. Therefore, to address the value of such a security properly, investors must address the option component. Volatility has a very strong influence on the option component, and thus becomes a very important parameter in the analysis of the composite security. Evaluating the impact of volatility on the option component (and therefore the security) is simply a matter of basic options theory. Although it is beyond the scope of this chapter to delineate a comprehensive options pricing theory, it is useful to review two of the essential parameters involved in the pricing of embedded options.

First, as volatility increases, the value of a given option rises. Investors that are long options have limited liability; the greatest loss they can incur is the option fee. Conversely, the upside potential is theoretically limitless. A long options position performs well when volatility rises, as the likelihood that the underlying security moves past the strike price increases. Thus, an investor is willing to pay more for an option where the underlying security is volatile, due to the possibility of unlimited profit without a similar increase in losses. The relationship between option value and volatility is displayed in Exhibit 1 for a call that is at the money (ATM), out of the money (OTM), and in the money (ITM). A short options position, on the other hand, performs poorly when volatility increases. Options sellers demand more of a premium when

---

Exhibit 1: Call Option Value versus Percent Price Volatility

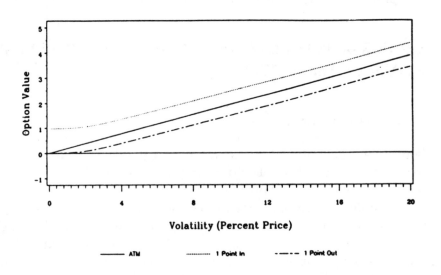

the underlying security is volatile, in order to compensate for the greater risk exposure. Option buyers (sellers) are volatility buyers (sellers), hoping that volatility will increase (decrease), resulting in increased (decreased) option value.

The second important rule to remember is that as the time to expiration declines, the value of a given option falls (time decay). The longer the time to expiration, the greater the likelihood that the underlying price will move past the strike price.

The effect of time to expiration on call value is shown in Exhibit 2. As the time to expiration lengthens, the influence of volatility on the value of an option increases exponentially. The impact of volatility at varying lengths of time to expiration is shown in Exhibit 3. Note that the slope of the line is steeper when there is a greater amount of time to expiration. As time passes, time decay and volatility compete with each other. Rising volatility acts to increase the option's value, whereas time decay serves to decrease it.

Exhibit 2: Call Option Value versus Underlying Security Price

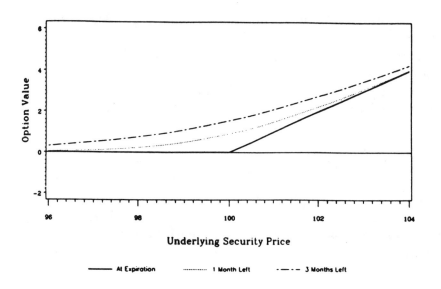

Exhibit 3: Call Option Value for Different Times to Expiration with Changing Volatility

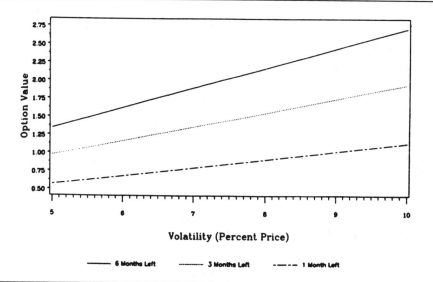

What Is Volatility?

Statistically, volatility is a measure of the dispersion or spread of observations around the mean of the set of observations. If volatility seems strangely like a standard deviation, then you remember your statistics. When someone speaks of volatility, all they really are talking about is a standard deviation.

For fixed-income securities, volatility is expressed in yield or price units, either on a percentage or on an absolute basis. Price volatilities can be computed for any security. Yield volatilities should be computed only for those securities with a consistent method for computing yield. Given the complexity of calculating a yield on a MBS and the variation of results, the predominant volatility measure in the MBS market is price volatility. The government bond market, where yields are easily calculated, favors yield volatility.

Types of Volatility

Empirical Volatility. Empirical volatility is the actual market volatility of a specific security that occurred historically. These numbers typically are calculated for varying time periods (10 days, 30 days, 360 days), and are ususally annualized (for this chapter, all volatilities are annualized).[1] Calculating an empirical volatility involves nothing more than calculating the standard deviation of a time series. Thus, an absolute volatility is the annualized standard deviation of daily price or yield changes, assuming a normal distribution. The distribution of daily yield changes of the thirty-year, constant maturity Treasury bond from 1982 to 1988 is displayed in Exhibit 4. This distribution is fairly normal, with a

---

[1] When annualizing a volatility, certain assumptions are inherent to the calculation. To convert from daily to yearly volatility, for example, the daily volatility is multiplied by the square root of the number of business days in the year, approximately 250. The various assumptions that are made when converting to an annual volatility, and the way to derive this number, are shown in Appendix B.

Exhibit 4: Thirty-Year, Constant Maturity Treasury, Distribution of One-Day Absolute Yield Changes (BP), 1/82–1/88

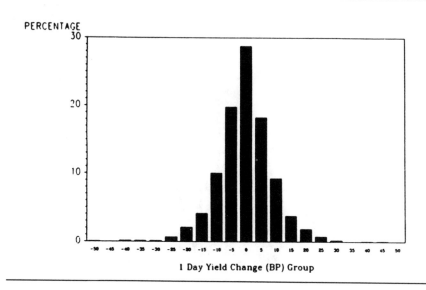

slight bias toward negative changes. This bias is primarily due to the bull market that dominated during this interval.

Percentage volatility is the annualized standard deviation of the daily change in the log of prices or yields, assuming a lognormal distribution of prices or yields. Exhibit 5 shows the distribution of the logs of daily yield changes of the thirty-year, constant maturity Treasury from the beginning of 1982 to the beginning of 1988. Similar to the daily absolute yield changes (Exhibit 4), the logs of the daily yield have a slight bias toward lower yields. The intuitive approach to calculating a percentage volatility is to find the standard deviation of daily *returns*, assuming a normal distribution. This approach is equivalent to the lognormal assumption, as long as the distribution can be characterized as being equally normal and lognormal, and the changes in prices are taken on a small interval (e.g., daily). A more complete explanation of the lognormal calculation can be found in Appendix A.

Exhibit 5: Thirty-Year, Constant Maturity Treasury, Distribution of One-Day Percentage Yield Changes (%), 1/82–1/88

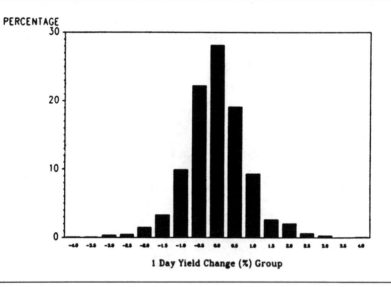

1 Day Yield Change (%) Group

As mentioned, empirical volatility can be measured over varying time periods. The most common interval on which the standard deviation is taken is thirty days. Other common intervals are 10 days and 360 days. The choice of an interval determines how quickly and to what degree an empirical volatility responds to deviations. As the time period shortens, volatility increasingly reflects current conditions, but is more unstable as each sample asserts greater influence in the deviation. Conversely, as the interval increases, more of a lag and a smoothing are introduced into the calculation. The effect of using different intervals when calculating volatility on the ten-year Treasury is displayed in Exhibit 6. The optimal sampling interval for analyzing empirical volatility depends on the application. When pricing an option on a MBS, for example, the interval used to calculate an empirical volatility should be chosen to match the length of the option contract. This provides the investor with an indication of how volatile the under-

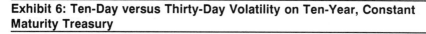

Exhibit 6: Ten-Day versus Thirty-Day Volatility on Ten-Year, Constant Maturity Treasury

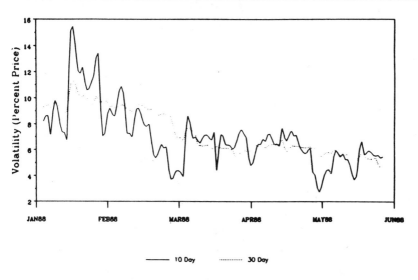

lying security has been recently, and how this relates to the volatility used to price the option.

As there is no industry standard for volatility units, converting between an absolute or percentage volatility either in price or yield units is a useful skill. The path to follow to convert from one unit to the next is shown in Exhibit 7. The modified duration of a security provides the link between price and yield volatilities. Modified duration is defined as the percentage change in price divided by the absolute change in yield.

Implied Volatility. Implied volatility is nothing more than the market's expectation of future volatility over a specified time period. Since an option's price is a function of the volatility employed, for an option where the price is known the volatility that is implied can be derived. Although it sounds straightforward, calculating an implied volatility is far more complicated than an empirical volatility, since expectations cannot be observed directly.

Exhibit 7: Converting Volatility Measures

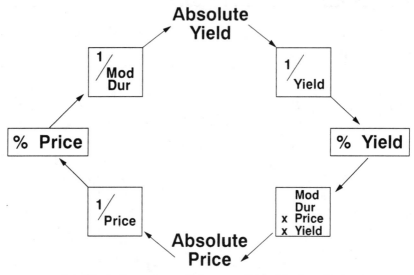

Modified Duration, Price and Yield Are Taken
from the Underlying Security

An option-pricing model along with a mathematical method to infer the volatility must be used. The result of this calculation is a percentage price volatility that can be converted to the various types of volatility measures discussed above (see Exhibit 7).

Owing to the existence and liquidity of fixed-income options, proxies for implied volatilities can be derived from Treasuries. The bond futures market on the Chicago Board of Trade (CBT) is one of the most liquid markets for fixed-income options, and provides the information necessary to calculate an implied volatility. The resulting implied volatility provides a good indication of the market's expected volatility for the Treasuries with maturities similar to that of the particular bond futures contract that is employed. The implied volatility on the twenty-year bond futures contract, for example, is a useful proxy for the market's expected volatility on long-term Treasury securities.

The Relationship Between Empirical and Implied Volatility

Comparing empirical and implied volatilities can be characterized as running forward but looking backwards. An implied volatility is the market's view of future volatility, whereas empirical volatility is a measure of what volatility has been. Exhibit 8 plots the empirical volatility on the thirty-year, constant maturity Treasury against implied volatility on the CBT bond futures contract for two recent years. Several characteristics of the relationship become clear from an examination of the graph. First, the two volatilities trend together. Second, implied volatility tends to be a smoothed function of empirical. Third, implied volatility, over time, generally is higher than empirical volatility.

The fixed-income market can be described as an unstable equilibrium that is put into disequilibrium by unforseen events. This description is consistent with the shapes of empirical volatility curves, where levels generally move in a saw-toothed, gradual fashion that is occasionally interrupted by large spiked move-

Exhibit 8: Actual Volatility (Thirty-Year, Constant Maturity) versus CBT Implied Volatility (Thirty-Day Actual Volatility; Daily Implied Volatility)

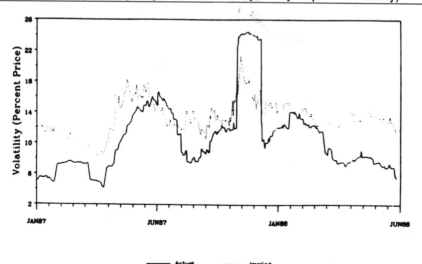

ments. Implied volatility seldom shows the kind of large deviations from the current mean that actual volatility exhibits. The effect of a single event does not usually have as great an influence on implied volatility as it does on empirical volatility, because the perspective is different. Implied volatility is a long-term estimate that is not likely to be drastically changed owing to a single event. The same reasoning also explains why implied volatility recovers more quickly from large deviations than does empirical. Implied volatility is an "instantaneous" measure of investor sentiment that does not have the lag effect inherent in a standard deviation of actual observations.

The Applications of Implied and Empirical Volatility

Implied and empirical volatility are the measures most commonly used to price explicit options or securities with embedded options. Properly evaluating any option requires the determination of a distribution of prices in the future. Given the current value of a security and its volatility, a price distribution can be constructed. The price for the option is then determined by taking a probability-weighted average of the results at each point in the distribution.

The pricing of most MBSs requires a model that evaluates the embedded option component. Constructing a distribution of MBS prices in the future is really a function of finding a distribution of interest rates. Since implied volatility represents the market's view of expected volatility, it is the most applicable volatility measure available. The implied volatility derived from the bond futures on the CBT can be used to generate a distribution of future interest rates.

Pricing an OTC option on a specific security also requires an estimate of volatility, but in this case it is of the underlying security. Estimating the volatility of a MBS for pricing an option typically involves a number of volatility considerations. To start, the recent empirical volatility of the security is considered. The empirical volatility for any fixed-income security depends on its maturity and/or coupon. For MBSs, empirical volatility tends to be higher for lower coupons. In addition to the empirical volatility for the security, option investors also evaluate current estimates of implied volatility. If implied volatility is rising, the volatility level at which an OTC option is priced would probably be increased by some proportional amount above the empirical volatility. If trying to determine a fair level of volatility for pricing options seems vague, it reflects the nature of the science. Although the implied and empirical volatility data are the most important determinants of a fair volatility level, intangibles such as supply and demand considerations and bid/ask spreads also influence the level of volatility employed.

Impact of Volatility on Fixed-Income Securities

Owing to the effect volatility has on securities with embedded options, investors should incorporate their opinion of the future direction of volatility when considering which fixed-income securities to purchase or sell. A matrix of interest rate direction and volatility direction is used in Exhibit 9 to identify some appropriate securities for various environments. The securities listed in each quadrant are appropriate given the respective expected volatility and interest rate environment. If interest rates and volatility are expected to rise, for example, long put options or long straddles provide good returns. In an environment of falling interest rates coupled with rising volatility, owning principal-only strips (POs) or long call options enhances returns. All of the securities above the horizontal axis are relatively better choices in rising volatility environments because they are either long options or (at the minimum) are not short options. POs, which benefit from prepayments, thrive in a falling rate environment. Government bonds, even those with call provisions, trade like noncallables. Treasuries are not explicitly long on option position, but when volatility is rising they are better to own than securities that have short option components. Conversely, positions that are short op-

---

Exhibit 9: Yield/Volatility Quadrant Analysis

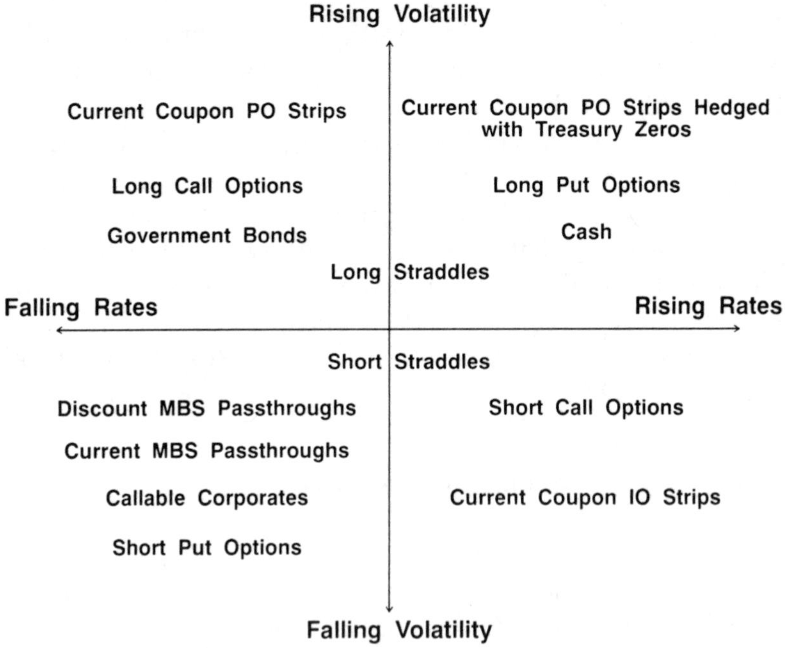

Rising Volatility

| Current Coupon PO Strips | Current Coupon PO Strips Hedged with Treasury Zeros |

Long Call Options   Long Put Options

Government Bonds   Cash

Long | Straddles

Falling Rates   Rising Rates
←——→

Short | Straddles

Discount MBS Passthroughs   Short Call Options

Current MBS Passthroughs

Callable Corporates   Current Coupon IO Strips

Short Put Options

Falling Volatility

---

tions and benefit from lower volatility lie below the horizontal axis. Callable corporates and MBS pass-throughs benefit as volatility declines, since the value of the embedded (short) option falls.

Changes in the level of implied volatility have traditionally had a strong influence on the value of MBSs relative to Treasuries. The effect of volatility on the spread of MBSs to Treasuries is well documented. When volatility increases, the embedded short options for MBSs tend to appreciate, causing the MBS to cheapen (and the spread to widen) relative to Treasuries. Thus, these securities typically underperform Treasuries in this environment. This relationship is illustrated in Exhibit 10, which examines the spread between the current coupon GNMA and the constant maturity, ten-year Treasury against the CBT implied volatility.

Exhibit 10: Implied Volatility versus GNMA to Treasury Yield Spread

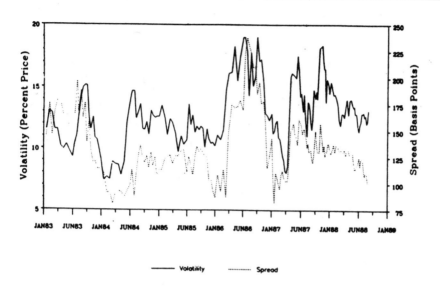

Volatility versus Spread: A Historical Example

MBS price performance in the spring of 1986 provides a convincing example of volatility's effect on MBSs. In February of 1986, percent price implied volatility on the CBT was approximately 10.7%. The spread between the current coupon GNMA and the ten-year Treasury was roughly ninety basis points. By June, volatility soared to 19%, and the spread reacted, widening to about 240 basis points. As volatility began falling in September, the spread began tightening. Volatility fell all the way to 8% in March of 1987, and the yield spread followed, falling to around 100 basis points.

Current coupon MBSs and slight premiums tend to show the greatest correlation to implied volatility. The embedded options for these securities are near or slightly in the money. When an option is trading near its strike price, its premium or time value is maximized because there is a high probability that the option can move into the money or out of the money.

THE USE OF MORTGAGE OPTIONS TO ENHANCE PERFORM-
ANCE AND MANAGE VOLATILITY RISK

In this section we discuss how OTC MBS options can be used to improve the performance of a portfolio of securities. Depending on how they are structured, OTC MBS options can enhance or protect the performance of a portfolio when volatility increases or decreases. To illustrate the usefulness and flexibility of OTC options, several portfolio strategy examples are provided. These examples have a broad application to a variety of investors, but should serve only as an indication of the many uses of OTC options. All of these examples share a similar methodology, which is described below.

The Methodology

For each of the portfolio strategy examples that follow, both the rate of return of the MBS and the rate of return of the OTC options must be calculated. In each case, there is an effort to use comparable volatilities for both the security and the option. For the first two portfolio examples, rates of return on the MBSs are calculated over different interest rate and volatility scenarios. To calculate the rate of returns, prices at the end of the horizon period are projected using a mortgage pricing model. The initial step in calculating the returns for a MBS is to compute an option-adjusted spread (OAS) using some estimate for volatility. This OAS is then held constant while volatility and interest rates are changed to calculate new rates of return. For the third portfolio example, price movements are calculated only under varying volatility scenarios (interest rates are held constant). To determine the rates of return of the OTC options, the terminal prices of the options are calculated under the corresponding volatility environment that is used when evaluating the underlying security.[2] The terminal price for the underlying security is used in valuing the option at the end of the horizon.

The analysis of option value in a portfolio must be performed with great care, as changes in volatility not only affect the explicit pricing of the option, but also the price of the underlying security. This, in turn, influences the value of the option. In general, the price of a MBS falls as volatility rises. The falling price of the MBS has a positive effect on a long position of puts and a negative influence on a long position of calls. If an investor is long puts in order to hedge against rising volatility, for example, an increase in volatility by itself makes the option more valuable. If a rise in volatility also causes the price of the MBS to fall, then the put further appreciates. With calls, volatility has the same effect on value as it does on the puts, but a falling MBS price causes a decline in the value of the call. This effect should be noted when considering option strategies that depend on volatility movement. In the cases described below, this kind of effect is pointed out where it becomes important.

Relative Behavior Under Changing Interest Rate and Volatility Environments: GNMA 8s, 10s, and a Principal-Only (PO) Strip

Before discussing any portfolio suggestions, it is helpful to illustrate how different securities respond to changes in volatility and interest rates. Terminal prices, terminal spreads, and rates of return for GNMA 10s under three volatility and interest rate scenarios for a three-month horizon are shown in Exhibit 11. The rates of return are for the three-month period, not annualized. The most significant impact on returns is the interest rate movement. The

---

[2] The volatility used in the mortgage pricing model is the CBT implied volatility, whereas the volatility used to price MBS options is an OTC volatility based on the underlying MBS. In the examples given, the range of volatilities for the MBS options were determined and then translated into a CBT volatility for use in valuing the underlying security through the mortgage pricing model. The CBT volatilities shown in the examples are rounded to the nearest whole percentage point.

Exhibit 11: GNMA 10 Three-Month Returns

	WAM	: 343 Months				
	OAS	: 56 bp with Initial Volatility of 12%				
	Starting Price	: 100:06				
	Horizon	: 3 Months				

		CBT Implied Percent Price Volatility				
		10%	*12%*	*14%*	*16%*	*18%*
	Return (%)	7.22	6.37	5.59	4.79	4.02
-100 bp	Price	105:05	104:09	103:15	102:20	101:27
	Spread* (bp)	130	149	166	185	203
	Return (%)	3.36	2.45	1.61	0.74	-0.08
Flat	Price	101:05	100:06	99:10	98:14	97:18
	Spread* (bp)	117	134	151	169	186
	Return (%)	-1.21	-2.05	-2.85	-3.67	-4.47
+100 bp	Price	96:13	95:17	94:22	93:27	93:00
	Spread* (bp)	105	122	139	156	173

*Yield of the security to the 10-year Treasury.

difference in the rates of return from a down-100-basis-point environment to an up-100-basis-point environment is approximately
800 basis points. Increasing volatility also affects returns. If volatility rises from 10% to 18%, for example, the rates of return fall by
an average of 330 basis pints over the three interest rate scenarios.
Note the yield spread of the MBS to the ten-year Treasury widens
as interest rates fall and also as volatility increases. Spreads widen
by as much as seventy-three basis points when volatility moves
from 10% to 18% (in the falling interest rate case).

The price of the GNMA 8s (see Exhibit 12) is not as sensitive to
varying levels of volatility. As explained previously, their embedded options are out of the money. Whereas the difference in the
rate of return for the 10s is an average of 330 basis points (over the
three interest rate scenarios) when the volatility assumption
changes from 10% to 18%, it is only 270 basis points for the 8s. The
larger negative returns for the 10s is a result of a greater price

Exhibit 12: GNMA 8 Three-Month Returns

	WAM	: 344 Months
	OAS	: 84 bp with Initial Volatility of 12%
	Starting Price	: 88:16
	Horizon	: 3 Months

		CBT Implied Percent Price Volatility				
		10%	12%	14%	16%	18%
	Return (%)	9.28	8.52	7.77	6.98	6.19
-100 bp	Price	94:28	94:06	93:16	92:24	92:01
	Spread* (bp)	118	130	143	157	170
	Return (%)	3.11	2.45	1.79	1.09	0.39
Flat	Price	89:07	88:20	88:00	87:12	86:23
	Spread* (bp)	114	126	138	150	164
	Return (%)	-2.92	-3.47	-4.02	-4.62	-5.23
+100 bp	Price	83:22	83:06	82:22	82:04	81:18
	Spread* (bp)	110	120	131	143	155

*Yield of the security to the 10-year Treasury.

drop as volatility increases. For a 2% change in volatility, the price movement for the GNMA 8s is about 10/32 less than that of the GNMA 10s. Similarly, for equivalent volatility movements, spreads widen by about six basis points less for the 8s than for the 10s. This serves to illustrate how sensitive the current coupon (the 10s) is to volatility changes.

Unlike pass-throughs, POs are securities that perform well in rising volatility environments. The impact of volatility on a PO strip backed by FNMA 9-1/2s, the FNMA Trust 4s, is illustrated in Exhibit 13. The performance of the Trust 4s improves as volatility increases. It is important to note that the POs are no more sensitive to volatility than the pass-throughs. The average difference in return between a volatility of 10% and that of 18% is 339 basis points over the three interest rate scenarios (as compared to 330 basis points for the GNMA 10s). The return for POs is extremely sensitive to interest rate movements, however, as their returns rise

Exhibit 13: FNMA Trust 4 PO Strip Three-Month Returns

	Collateral	: FNMA 9.5
	WAM	: 335 Months
	WAC	: 10.09%
	OAS	: 279 bp 12% Volatility
	Starting Price	: 52:02
	Horizon	: 3 Months

		CBT Implied Percent Price Volatility				
		10%	*12%*	*14%*	*16%*	*18%*
	Return (%)	15.54	16.51	17.31	18.06	18.57
-100 bp	Price	59:11	59:28	60:10	60:23	61:00
	Return (%)	1.69	2.78	3.82	4.68	5.36
Flat	Price	51:26	52:13	52:31	53:14	53:26
	Return (%)	-9.07	-8.15	-7.23	-6.37	-5.62
+100 bp	Price	45:31	46:15	46:31	47:14	47:27

by more than 1,300 basis points when interest rates fall by 100 basis points (as compared to 400–500 basis points for the GNMA 10s). When interest rates rise by 100 basis points, returns fall by approximately 1,100 basis points (as compared to about 445 basis points for the GNMA 10s).

Using Straddles to Enhance or Protect Performance

Straddles are a combination of a long position in calls and a long position in puts with the same strike price. Straddles are the purest way to buy volatility and not make a bet on the direction of interest rates. The downside risk of a straddle is limited to the amount paid for the options (the premium). If the price of the underlying securities moves more in either direction than the option premium, then the straddle produces a profit at expiration. Prior to expiration, the straddle may be sold at a profit if volatility increases enough and/or interest rates move sufficiently, as these occurrences cause the option to appreciate.

Straddles can be used by many different types of investors who feel that there will be a significant change in either volatility or interest rates in the near future. Investors who must maintain a specific proportion of assets in mortgages, such as mutual funds and thrifts, should find straddles particularly useful if they feel MBS spreads may widen. For example, many mutual funds that are designated as mortgage funds generally must maintain a fixed percentage of the portfolio in MBSs. This constraint can expose the fund to a tremendous amount of volatility risk. If volatility increases and causes the MBS to Treasury yield spread to widen, the fund most likely will underperform other fixed-income funds. The fund could buy POs to hedge against increasing volatility, but POs are extremely interest rate-sensitive instruments that could be very damaging to portfolio performance in rising interest rate environments. A better hedge against volatility risk is to buy a straddle using OTC options on MBSs.

To show how straddles can be used to protect returns from an increase in volatility, the returns for GNMA 10s are combined with the returns of a straddle position. The returns on a six-month at-the-money GNMA 10 straddle (long calls and long puts on GNMA 10s) with three months left to expiration are shown in Exhibit 14.[3]

The straddle is established with a ratio of 104 puts to every 1.0 call. The reason for this unbalanced ratio is to target the performance in the rising volatility, flat-rate environments. In these environments, the underlying security falls in price. This decline in the underlying security's price results in negative returns for the long calls (even though volatility increased). Long puts, however, benefit from the price drop as well as the volatility increase, and produce large positive returns. To take advantage of this pattern, the proportion of puts to calls is increased in order to weight the positive returns more than the negative returns (since the primary goal

---

[3] It is important to emphasize the effect of time to expiration on the value of options. Options react to volatility movement only when there is sufficient time remaining to expiration (see Exhibit 3). In order to use options to hedge volatility, the investor should buy options with expirations well beyond the horizon they are targeting.

Exhibit 14: GNMA 10 Six-Month Straddle Returns

	Mixture	: 1.4 Puts to 1.0 Calls
	Horizon	: 90 Days (90 Days to Expiration)
	Initial Volatility Level	: 6% Price
	Initial Strike Price	: At the money
	Straddle Cost	: 3:26

		Percent Price Volatility on GNMA 10				
		5%	6%	7%	8%	9%
	Return (%)	48.69	30.16	17.87	11.48	13.44
-100 bp	Price	5:21	4:31	4:16	4:08	4:10
	Return (%)	-34.10	-28.03	-14.75	4.43	26.72
Flat	Price	2:16	2:24	3:08	3:31	4:27
	Return (%)	16.89	48.20	78.85	108.69	139.67
+100 bp	Price	4:15	5:21	6:26	7:31	9:04

is to protect the portfolio against rising volatility). As a consequence, however, the returns for the straddles are not as attractive as an evenly balanced straddle in a falling interest rate environment. In this case the investor is holding more puts, which decline in value when prices move significantly higher. Under rising interest rates, the investor benefits from the large number of puts. Therefore, this strategy effectively hedges against rising volatility while leading to an unbalanced return pattern under rising and falling interest rate movements.

The six-month straddle shows positive returns with three months to expiration for all cases shown in Exhibit 14 except three, those in which interest rates are unchanged and volatility is flat, lower, and slightly higher. The negative returns for these three cases can be explained by considering the erosion of value due to the elapse of time, the lack of change in interest rates, and the lack of an increase in volatility. When volatility falls to 5% from its initial level of 6%, both volatility movement and time decay cause significant losses for the option position. In the case

Exhibit 15: Portfolio Returns of 1:1 GNMA 10s and Six-Month ATM Straddles with Three Months to Expiration

	Percent Price Volatility				
GNMA 10 Vol.	5%	6%	7%	8%	9%
CBT Implied Vol.	10%	12%	14%	16%	18%
-100 bp Return (%)	8.73	7.24	6.03	5.03	4.36
Flat Return (%)	1.98	1.33	1.01	0.88	0.90
+100 bp Return (%)	-0.54	1.33	1.01	0.88	0.90

when volatility rises to 7% from 6%, volatility helps the option position but not enough to overcome the time decay.

Combining the straddle with the GNMA 10 security enhances the performance of the 10s in the rising volatility and changing interest rate environments. The combined returns for a portfolio composed of equal face value of GNMA 10s and the straddles is displayed in Exhibit 15. Comparing the results of the GNMA 10 alone (Exhibit 11) with those of the GNMA 10 and straddle combination (Exhibit 15) shows how significantly this options strategy helps returns in all cases except for the three explained above (flat interest rate environment, volatility of 5%, 6%, or 7%). The performance benefit of the straddle combination can be as great as 700 basis points in the selected scenarios versus the unhedged position. The unhedged and hedged returns (from Exhibits 11 and 15) are compared to each other in Exhibits 16 and 17.

It is important to note that the ratios of the straddle to the underlying security can be modified to meet the concerns of the investor. If investors believe that there is a strong likelihood of volatility rising, then they may want to weight the straddle more heavily. The return of a portfolio with a two-to-one weighting of straddles to GNMA 10s is shown in Exhibit 18. The performance of this portfolio is better than the portfolio weighted one-to-one when interest rates shift significantly or volatility rises appreciably, but is worse in the flat, falling, or slightly rising volatility and unchanged interest rate environment.

Exhibit 16: Three-Month Returns for GNMA 10s Unhedged and Hedged with Straddles (Flat Interest Rates with Changing Volatility)

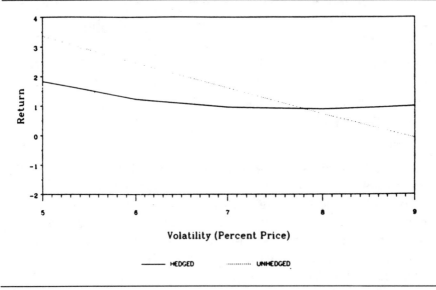

Exhibit 17: Three-Month Returns for GNMA 10s Unhedged and Hedged with Straddles (Rising and Falling Interest Rates, +100 BP and –100 BP)

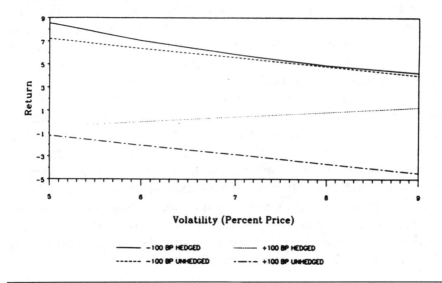

Exhibit 18: Portfolio Returns of 1:2 GNMA 10s and Six-Month ATM Straddles with Three Months to Expiration

		Percent Price Volatility			
GNMA 10 Vol.	5%	6%	7%	8%	9%
CBT Implied Vol.	10%	12%	14%	16%	18%
-100 bp Return (%)	10.15	8.05	6.45	5.26	4.68
Flat Return (%)	0.71	0.29	0.45	1.01	1.81
+100 bp Return (%)	0.07	1.51	2.94	4.28	5.73

One important feature of the options is that the quicker the change in volatility and/or interest rates, the greater the value of the option. Consider a one-month horizon for the GNMA 10s, with a three-month at-the-money straddle and two months remaining until expiration. The one-month returns, prices, and spreads for the GNMA 10s are shown in Exhibit 19 (note that interest rates change by only 50 basis points rather than the 100-ba-

Exhibit 19: GNMA 10 One-Month Returns

	WAM	: 343 Months
	OAS	: 56 bp with Initial Volatility of 12%
	Starting Price	: 106:06
	Horizon	: 1 Months

		CBT Implied Percent Price Volatility				
		10%	12%	14%	16%	18%
	Return (%)	3.84	2.94	2.11	1.26	0.44
-50 bp	Price	103:10	102:12	101:16	100:20	99:24
	Spread* (bp)	125	143	160	177	195
	Return (%)	1.77	0.85	0.01	-0.85	-1.68
Flat	Price	101:04	100:06	99:10	98:13	97:17
	Spread* (bp)	117	134	151	169	186
	Return (%)	-0.48	-1.36	-2.19	-3.04	-3.87
+50 bp	Price	98:26	97:28	97:00	96:04	95:08
	Spread* (bp)	110	128	145	162	180

*Yield of the security to the 10-year Treasury.

Exhibit 20: GNMA 10 Three-Month Straddle Returns

Mixture	: 1.4 Puts to 1.0 Calls
Horizon	: 30 Days (60 Days to Expiration)
Initial Volatility Level	: 6% Price
Initial Strike Price	: At the money
Straddle Cost	: 2:25

		Percent Price Volatility on GNMA 10				
		5%	6%	7%	8%	9%
	Return (%)	24.49	5.39	0.90	8.31	25.39
-50 bp	Price	3:15	2:30	2:26	3:00	3:16
	Return (%)	-27.64	-18.20	2.70	32.13	65.39
Flat	Price	2:00	2:09	2:27	3:22	4:19
	Return (%)	-12.58	28.32	63.60	104.94	146.29
+50 bp	Price	2:14	3:14	4:18	5:22	6:27

---

sis-point shift in the previous example, since the horizon is shortened).

The returns for the three-month ATM straddle with two months to expiration are shown in Exhibit 20. It displays a different pattern than the returns for the six-month straddle (Exhibit 14). The six-month straddle is evaluated at three months, or half the time to expiration. The three-month straddle is evaluated at one month, or one-third of the time to expiration. As a result of the greater percentage of time value remaining, the three-month straddle shows a greater response to either a change in volatility or a shift in interest rates. The returns in the flat-rate environment illustrate this result, as the return for the slightly rising volatility case, 7% from 6%, is 2.7% for the three-month straddle compared to 14.75% for the six-month straddle. The rising volatility movement overwhelms the time decay for the three-month straddle.

Exhibit 21: Portfolio Returns of 1:1 GNMA 10s and Three-Month ATM Straddles with Two Months to Expiration

		Percent Price Volatility				
GNMA 10 Vol.		5%	6%	7%	8%	9%
CBT Implied Vol.		10%	12%	14%	16%	18%
-50 bp	Return (%)	4.27	2.91	2.00	1.41	1.10
Flat	Return (%)	0.91	0.31	0.08	0.07	0.19
+50 bp	Return (%)	-0.79	-0.63	-0.34	-0.02	0.31

The returns of a portfolio with a one-to-one ratio of the GNMA 10 three-month, at-the-money straddle combined with a GNMA 10 are shown in Exhibit 21. Once again, the portfolio with options shows much improved returns in all but three scenarios. The performance is very impressive in the changing interest rate or rising volatility cases, owing to the strong returns of the straddle in these environments. The unhedged and hedged returns are illustrated in Exhibits 22 and 23. As with the six-month straddle, the ratio of

Exhibit 22: One-Month Returns for GNMA 10s Unhedged and Hedged with Straddles (Flat Interest Rates with Changing Volatility)

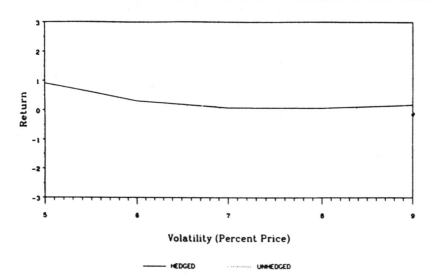

Exhibit 23: One-Month Returns for GNMA 10s Unhedged and Hedged with
Straddles (Rising and Falling Interest Rates, +50 BP and -50 BP)

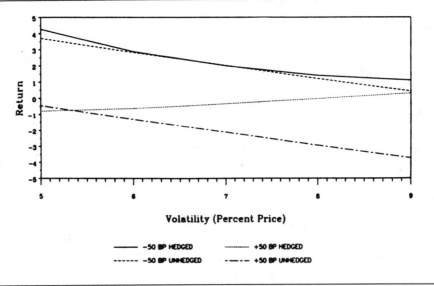

straddles to underlying security can be structured to suit the investor's needs.

The above analysis serves to illustrate how the use of straddles can be customized for specific goals. The same ratio of puts to calls (1.4 to 1.0) was used for both the three-month and the one-month horizon for comparative purposes, even though a smaller number of puts would hedge the one-month returns nearly as well in rising volatility cases, with a more balanced performance in the changing interest rate cases. Conversely, if an investor foresees a rise in volatility with an increase in interest rates, more puts should be purchased. Furthermore, the time period of the option can be shortened or lengthened to target a specific horizon.

Hedging POs or Interest-Only Strips (IOs) Against Volatility

Hedging IOs against volatility risk is similar to hedging a pass-through because they both perform poorly in rising volatility environments. The kind of analysis shown in the previous section applies to IOs as well as pass-throughs. Current coupon POs, as demonstrated above, may perform well with rising volatility but produce poor results when volatility falls. MBS options can be used to hedge POs in the falling volatility case. It is not clear what type of underlying security should be used for the options, however. The most common choice is the underlying collateral for the strip. Using the FNMA Trust 4 PO as an example, therefore, an investor would sell options on FNMA 9-1/2s (the collateral backing Trust 4). It is important to reiterate that investors that are short options are assuming more risk than those that are long options. The increased risk is due to the lack of downside protection beyond the strike price.

Once the choice has been made to sell options, the choice between whether to sell puts or calls depends on the investor's opinion of interest rate direction. Writing puts is for the strongly bullish investor who wants to hedge the PO against volatility risk while increasing the performance of the position in falling rate environments. Returns for a combination of Trust 4 POs and short puts are shown in Exhibit 24. Note the improvement in returns of Trust 4 alone (Exhibit 24 versus Exhibit 13). Short puts exacerbate the PO's poor performance in rising interest rate scenarios, however. When interest rates are unchanged and volatility falls, being short puts enhances the portfolio return. As volatility falls, the price of the FNMA 9-1/2 rises, which causes the price of the put to decline. The returns for the PO alone are higher than for the PO and short put combination when volatility rises. The returns of the

Exhibit 24: Portfolio Returns of 1:1 Trust 4 POs and Short Six-Month ATM Puts with Three Months to Expiration

		Percent Price Volatility				
FNMA 9.5 Vol.		*4%*	*5%*	*6%*	*7%*	*8%*
CBT Implied Vol.		*10%*	*12%*	*14%*	*16%*	*18%*
-100 bp	Return (%)	17.62	18.51	19.17	19.60	19.71
Flat	Return (%)	3.58	4.00	4.19	4.09	3.71
+100 bp	Return (%)	-11.95	-12.16	-12.44	-12.83	-13.27

Exhibit 25: Three-Month Returns for POs Unhedged and Hedged with Short Puts (Flat Interest Rates with Changing Volatility)

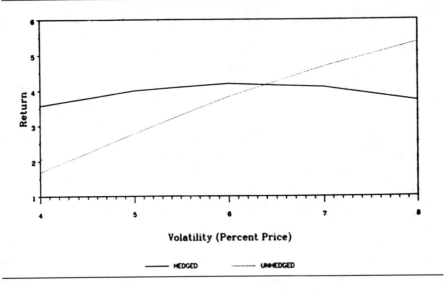

Volatility (Percent Price)

——— HEDGED   ·········· UNHEDGED

---

unchanged interest rate environment for the POs alone and for the POs hedged with short puts is shown in Exhibit 25.

Writing calls creates a partial hedge that protects against rising interest rates, but does not protect against falling volatility because of the rising price of the underlying security. The returns for a portfolio of a short six-month call position with three months to expiration and a Trust 4 PO are shown in Exhibit 26. Rising interest rates drive the calls down in value, creating a profit for the writer and hedging the POs (compare Exhibit 23 returns with

---

Exhibit 26: Portfolio Returns of 1:1 Trust 4 POs and Short Six-Month ATM Calls with Three Months to Expiration

		Percent Price Volatility				
FNMA 9.5 Vol.		*4%*	*5%*	*6%*	*7%*	*8%*
CBT Implied Vol.		*10%*	*12%*	*14%*	*16%*	*18%*
-100 bp	Return (%)	7.49	9.72	11.62	13.40	14.66
Flat	Return (%)	0.95	2.60	4.02	5.15	6.05
+100 bp	Return (%)	-6.50	-5.60	-4.77	-3.93	-3.20

those of Exhibit 13). Falling interest rates cause the calls to appreciate, however, and the short option position negates some of the upside potential of the POs. In the unchanged interest rate case, the price movement of the FNMA 9-1/2s is more important to the options value than falling volatility or less time to expiration. Thus, when volatility remains unchanged or falls, the price of the FNMA 9-1/2s rises enough to cause the call to appreciate. Since the investor is short the call, the combination underperforms the PO alone. Conversely, rising volatility causes the underlying security to fall in value, resulting in depreciation of the value of the option and a profit on the short position. Thus, the combination performs better than the PO alone.

Note that in these examples of selling volatility, the short option position is paired-off (covered) with half the amount of time left to expiration. Option writers often benefit from time decay, since the value of the option declines. The only advantage of a pair-off before expiration is to "lock in" a gain or limit a loss by "buying back" the option.

A more appropriate strategy for investors hedging POs that do not have a strong opinion on market direction is to write straddles. Straddle writing is a good way to take in fees, but exposes the seller to large losses if interest rates change dramatically. Returns for Trust 4 POs and a short ATM straddle are shown in Exhibit 27. With interest rates moving up or down, the portfolio underperforms the PO alone, as either the short call or short put moves deeply into the money. Conversely, stable and falling volatility cases in a flat interest rate environment result in large gains.

Exhibit 27: Portfolio Returns of 1:1 Trust 4 POs and Short Six-Month ATM Straddles with Three Months to Expiration

		Percent Price Volatility				
FNMA 9.5 Vol.		4%	5%	6%	7%	8%
CBT Implied Vol.		10%	12%	14%	16%	18%
-100 bp	Return (%)	9.71	11.84	13.57	15.02	15.85
Flat	Return (%)	2.81	3.79	4.38	4.57	4.42
+100 bp	Return (%)	-9.37	-9.58	-9.91	-10.29	-10.72

Writing straddles is a particularly useful strategy for money managers whose performance is based on yields. Fees that are received when writing options are a very good way to boost yields.

Hedging a Pass-Through Coupon Arbitrage

Coupon arbitrages are common trades for thrift and money managers. However, many investors are unaware that a coupon arbitrage is susceptible to volatility risk. As mentioned previously, current coupons are the MBSs most sensitive to changes in volatility. Discounts and premiums are less sensitive. The following example illustrates the volatility risk involved in a coupon swap.

An investor feels that FNMA 8s are rich to FNMA 10s, so the 8s are sold and the 10s purchased. In a stable or falling volatility environment, if the investor is correct and the market reacts to bring the securities back in line, then the coupon swap is profitable (in the absence of interest rate movements). If volatility should increase, however, the price spread between these two coupons may collapse, resulting in a loss on the swap. The rising volatility causes the 10s to fall in price faster than the 8s. The relative impact of the changing volatility on the prices of the FNMA 8s and 10s is shown in Exhibit 28. The price difference is found by subtracting the price at the base volatility (12%) from the price at a given volatility level. When implied volatility jumps from 12% to 14%, for example, the FNMA 10s drop 27/32, but the FNMA 8s only fall 17/32, resulting in a loss of 10/32 for the coupon spread.

The volatility risk inherent in a coupon swap can be hedged by buying options. Either puts or calls should be purchased if the investor has a strong opinion on the direction of interest rates. Otherwise, again, straddles are the best hedge. The price appreciation (from the base volatility of 5%) for a three-month ATM straddle with two months remaining to expiration is shown in Exhibit 29.

Combining straddles with the FNMA coupon swap involves a trade-off: there is a give-up in lower volatility scenarios for much improved performance in rising volatility environments. A portfo-

Exhibit 28: FNMA 8/10 Coupon Spread: Long 10s, Short 8s

Security	: FNMA 10
WAM	: 340 Months
WAC	: 10.62%
OAS	: 67 bp with Initial Volatility of 12%
Starting Price	: 99:23

	CBT Implied Percent Price Volatility				
	9%	12%	14%	16%	19%
Price	100:17	99:23	98:28	98:01	97:07
Price Difference	0:26	0:00	-0:27	-1:22	-2:16
Spread (bp)	108	126	145	163	183

Security	: FNMA 8
WAM	: 342 Months
WAC	: 8.89%
OAS	: 104 bp with Initial Volatility of 12%
Starting Price	: 88:31

	CBT Implied Percent Price Volatility				
	9%	12%	14%	16%	19%
Price	89:14	88:31	88:14	87:28	87:09
Price Difference	0:15	0:00	-0:17	-1:03	-1:22
Spread (bp)	125	135	148	160	174

	9%	12%	14%	16%	19%
Coupon Spread Price Appreciation	0:11	0:00	-0:10	-0:19	-0:26

Exhibit 29: FNMA 10 Three-Month Straddle

Horizon	: 30 Days (60 Days to Expiration)
Initial Volatility Level	: 5% Price
Initial Strike Price	: At the money
Straddle Cost	: 1:29

	CBT Implied Percent Price Volatility				
	4%	5%	6%	7%	8%
Straddle Price	1:18	1:19	1:31	2:16	3:03
Price Difference	-0:11	-0:10	0:02	0:19	1:06

Exhibit 30: Comparison of Price Appreciation of FNMA 8/10 Coupon Spread Alone to 3:2 FNMA 8/10 Coupon Spread and Long Straddles

	Percent Price Volatility				
FNMA 10 Vol.	*4%*	*5%*	*6%*	*7%*	*8%*
CBT Implied Vol.	*9%*	*12%*	*14%*	*16%*	*18%*
Spread Only	1:01	0:00	-0:30	-1:25	-2:14
Spreads and Straddles	0:11	-0:20	-0:26	-0:19	-0:02

lio of coupon swaps with straddles is compared to the coupon swaps alone (using a three-to-two ratio of swaps to straddles) in Exhibit 30. The price appreciation from an initial volatility level of 12% (5% on the option) is shown. In the falling and stable volatility environments, the portfolio with the straddles underperforms the spread alone by as much as 21/32. In rising volatility environments, however, the straddle portfolio improves the price performance by over two points in the highest volatility case shown.

Exhibit 31: Coupon Spread Unhedged and Hedged with Straddles, Portfolio Price Appreciation from Base Volatility of 5% (3:2 Coupon Spread to Straddles with the Hedge)

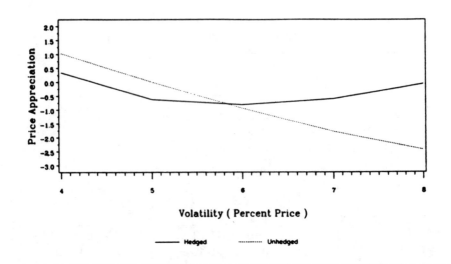

The price appreciation from the two cases is shown graphically in Exhibit 31. It is clear that as volatility rises from its initial level, the straddle hedges the collapse in the dollar spread.

CONCLUSION

This chapter provides an overview of volatility and how the volatility and interest rate risk of a security can be effectively hedged using OTC options. The volatility of a fixed-income security can be expressed in yield or price, as a percentage or as an absolute quantity. Either way, the volatility is merely the standard deviation of yields or prices. Volatility can be measured by two methods, empirical or implied. Empirical volatility is actual market volatility, calculated by finding the standard deviation of a price or yield history. Implied volatility can be found on any security for which options are traded. The implied volatility is found by doing a reverse options calculation: given the option price, the volatility that returns that price is found. As fixed-income markets have become more volatile, the importance of understanding the effect of volatility on the performance of a portfolio has become extremely important. A failure to anticipate the impact of volatility on a portfolio can lead to poor performance relative to other portfolio managers. The MBS sector in particular is one that is significantly influenced by volatility levels.

The relationship between interest rates and volatility levels on the prices of MBSs and derivative products can be demonstrated historically, and projected for the future by using option-pricing models that incorporate the influence of changing volatility. As volatility rises, MBSs tend to fall in price, causing spreads over the benchmark Treasuries to widen. This can lead to an underperformance of the mortgage sector relative to Treasuries. Conversely, falling volatility can strongly enhance the performance of the MBS sector.

Options on MBSs can be used to manage the inherent volatility risk of MBSs. OTC MBS options are not only useful in protecting a

MBS portfolio against volatility changes but also can be used to enhance performance. Buying straddles (purchasing a call and a put at the same strike price) is the most effective way to purchase volatility. The performance of a portfolio that is long straddles should be enhanced if volatility increases or interest rates change significantly. The options provide much flexibility and can be structured to meet the specific goals of the investor. Investors should become familiar with the various strategies that use MBS options in order to be able to use them when the investment environment is appropriate.

APPENDIX A: PERCENTAGE VOLATILITIES AND THE LOGNORMAL DISTRIBUTION

One could compute a percentage price volatility by finding the standard deviation of daily price returns, assuming a normal distribution, and then annualizing. Daily returns would be computed as follows:

$$R = (P_2/P_1) - 1, \tag{1}$$

where P_1 is the price on the first day and P_2 is the price on the next consecutive business day. A better way to compute the percentage volatility is to assume a lognormal assumption distribution of prices and find the standard deviation of the logs and the daily price quotients, that is, in (P_2/P_1). For the lognormal assumption to be accurate, the log of the daily price quotient and the daily return should be equal. This condition holds true if the price quotient is near 1, or:

$$\ln (P_2/P_1) = (P_2/P_1) - 1; \tag{2}$$

where $P_2/P_1 \approx 1$. For one-day price movements, this assumption is valid even on the most volatile days. For example, if a bond starts at par ($P_1 = 100$) and moves five points in one day ($P_2 = 95$), the price quotient $P_2/P_1 = 95/100 = 0.95$. The log of the price quotient

$\ln(0.95)$ is -0.051 whereas the return $R = 0.95 - 1$ is 0.05. Exhibit 5 shows the distribution of daily percentage changes of yields on the thirty-year constant maturity calculated by $\ln(P_2/P_1)$. The lognormal method is rendered computationally much quicker by taking advantage of the properties of logs $(\ln(P_2/P_1) = \ln P_2 - \ln P_1)$ and makes the price quotients equivalent to a continuously compounded return.

APPENDIX B: ANNUALIZING VOLATILITY

A standard deviation is based on the variance, a measure of the dispersion in squared units of the observations:

$$\text{Var}(X,Y) = \text{Var}(X) + (Y) + 2 \times \text{Cov}(XY),$$

where Var = variance and Cov = covariance. The standard deviation is the square root of the variance, which returns the measure to the original units of the observations. The daily variance is annualized by multiplying by the number of business days in the year, typically 250. Therefore, the standard deviation is annualized by multiplying by the square root of 250. For the conversion to be valid, we assume that there is no correlation between daily changes, that is, that the covariance is zero. Also, we assume no volatility on weekends or holidays. This assumption is reasonable because volatility over weekends or holidays does not appear to be greater than day-to-day volatility between weekdays.

CHAPTER 38

COLLATERALIZED BORROWING VIA DOLLAR ROLLS

Steven J. Carlson
Senior Vice President
Head of Whole Loan CMO Trading
Lehman Brothers Inc.

John F. Tierney
Senior Vice President
Mortgage Strategies Group
Lehman Brothers Inc.

The mortgage securities market offers investors a specialized form of reverse repurchase agreement known as a *dollar roll*. A dollar roll is a collateralized short-term financing, where the collateral is mortgage securities. These transactions provide security dealers with a liquid and flexible tool for managing temporary supply/de-

The authors would like to thank Chris Ames for his assistance in preparing this chapter.

mand imbalances in the market. An investor initiates a dollar roll by delivering securities to a dealer and agreeing to repurchase similar securities on a future date at a predetermined price. The investor assumes some delivery risk at the end of the roll period, for unlike a normal reverse repurchase agreement, the dealer is not obligated to return the identical securities to the investor. In return for this privilege, the dealer extends a favorable borrowing rate to the investor that may be anywhere from a few basis points to several points below current repo market rates.

This chapter first introduces collateralized borrowing via the dollar roll transaction. Second, it describes a methodology for calculating the cost of funds using an example of a typical transaction. Third, it describes the risks to the calculated cost of funds due to prepayments, the delivery option, and adverse selection. Fourth, it takes a snapshot view of the dollar roll market for 30-year agency securities using breakeven analysis. Finally, it displays dollar roll prices (drops) and their associated borrowing costs for GNMA securities for the 12-month period from August 1990 to July 1991, offering some insights into TBA (to be announced) GNMA trading.

DOLLAR ROLL DEFINED

A dollar roll can be thought of as a collateralized borrowing, where an institution pledges mortgage pass-throughs to a dealer to obtain cash. The dealer is said to "roll in" the securities. In contrast to standard reverse repurchase agreements, the dealer is not obliged to return securities that are identical to the originally pledged collateral. Instead the dealer is required to return collateral which is "substantially identical." In the case of mortgage pass-throughs, this means that the coupon and security type, i.e., issuing agency and mortgage collateral, must match. As long as certain criteria are met, dollar rolls may be accounted for as financing transactions (rather than sales/purchases) for financial accounting purposes. According to the American Institute of

Certified Public Accountants, the securities used in a dollar roll must meet the following conditions to satisfy the substantially identical standard.[1] The securities must:

1. Be collateralized by similar mortgages, e.g., 1- to 4-family residential mortgages;

2. Be issued by the same agency and be a part of the same program;

3. Have the same original stated maturity;

4. Have identical coupon rates;

5. Be priced to have similar market yields; and

6. Satisfy "good delivery" requirements, i.e., the aggregate principal amounts of the securities delivered and received back must be within 2.5% of the initial amount delivered.

The flexibility in returning collateral has value for a dealer because it provides a convenient avenue for covering a short position. That is, a trader may require a particular security for delivery this month, and by entering into a dollar roll agreement can effectively extend a delivery obligation to next month. If a dealer were required to return the identical security sold, as in the case of a standard repurchase agreement, the dealer would be unable to cover a short position. Dollar rolls offer dealers a convenient way to obtain promised mortgage securities, avoiding much of the cost of failing to make timely delivery. In theory, the dealer (the short coverer) will be willing to pay up to the cost of failure to deliver for the short-term opportunity to borrow or purchase securities required to meet a delivery commitment. For this reason most dol-

---

[1] For a detailed discussion of "substantially identical," see "Definition of the Term *Substantially the Same* for Holders of Debt Instruments, as Used in Certain Audit Guides and a Statement of Position," The American Institute of Certified Public Accountants, Statement of Position 90-3, February 13, 1990. Investors considering dollar rolls should discuss these issues with an accountant to ensure the transaction receives the desired accounting treatment.

lar rolls are transacted close to the monthly settlement date for mortgage-backed securities. Dollar rolls also allow dealers to even out the supply and demand for mortgage securities in the current settlement month and "back" months. Primary market mortgage originators frequently sell anticipated new mortgage security production in the forward market, for delivery 1 to 3 months (or more) in the future. This expected supply provides liquidity to the dollar roll market, by ensuring that dealers will have the securities required to close out dollar roll transactions.

In return for this service, dealers often offer dollar roll financing at extremely cheap rates and on flexible terms. Unlike most collateralized borrowings, there is no haircut, or requirement for over-collateralization. The investor gets 100% of the full market price, not a four to six point haircut as in a one- to three- month reverse repo. Dollar roll transactions are generally opened or closed as of the settlement date of each month, with the terms set some time prior to settlement. They typically cover the one-month period between consecutive settlement dates, but they may also extend over multiple months, for up to 11 months. The dollar roll market also allows investors to negotiate more flexible borrowing windows. Terms can be arranged for 34, 44, or 89 days (reverse repos tend to centralize around 30-, 60-, or 90-day intervals) thus enabling the investor to exploit short-term investment opportunities, such as certificates of deposit or banker's acceptances.

DOLLAR ROLL: COST OF FUNDS EVALUATION

In calculating the actual cost of funds obtained through a dollar roll there are several key considerations:

1. Price of securities sold versus price of securities repurchased. In a positive carry (or a positively sloped yield curve) environment, the repurchase price will be lower than the original purchase price. The drop (dollar roll price) is

the difference between the initial and ending prices plus the difference between the dealer's bid/ask prices.

2. Size of coupon payments.

3. Size of principal payments, both prepayments and scheduled amortization.

4. Collateral attributes of securities rolled in and securities rolled out.

5. Delivery tolerances. Both parties can over- or under-deliver. Most dollar roll agreements allow for the delivery of plus or minus 2.5% of the face amount.

6. Timing. The position of settlement dates within the months of the transaction impacts the accrued interest (paid to the seller at each end of the transaction). The days between settlements is the length of the borrowing period.

Each of these factors can influence the effective cost of funds implied by the dollar roll. For illustrative purposes, the calculations for a typical roll are described in the following section.

Dollar Roll Transaction Example

On July 9, 1991, a dealer and a mortgage security investor enter into a one-month dollar roll agreement as described in Exhibit 1. The dealer agrees to purchase $1,000,000 of recent production GNMA 10s at 104 and 5/32nds on July 22, 1991, and the investor agrees to repurchase $1,000,000 of face value GNMA 10s at 103 26/32nds on August 26, 1991. (The value of the drop is therefore 11/32nds of a point in price.) Good delivery is the delivery of anywhere from $975,000 to $1,025,000 of unpaid principal amount, since the investor and the dealer have the option of delivering plus or minus 2.5% of the original amount agreed upon. For the moment, let us assume that both parties deliver the notional quantity of securities, $1,000,000 of face value. On the first settlement

Exhibit 1: Sample Cost of Funds Calculation for Dollar Roll

Mortgage Security	GNMA	
Coupon	10.00%	
Servicing	0.50%	
Remaining Months to Maturity	342	
Prepayment Assumption (CPR)	7.80%	
Days of Accrual to 1st Settlement (7/22/91)	21	
Days of Accrual to 2nd Settlement (8/26/91)	25	
Days Between Settlement Dates	35	
Roll in Price	104-05	
Drop	11	
Roll Out Price	103-26	
Principal Payments:		
Scheduled Amortization	$468	
Prepayments	$6,745	
Cash Rolled In (Borrowed)	$1,047,396	(10%/12 × 21/30 × $1,000,000) + ($1,000,000 × $104 5/32 / 100)
Cash Rolled Out	$1,045,069	(10%/12 × 25/30 × $1,000,000) + ($1,000,000 × $103 26/32 / 100)
Price Spread (Dollar Roll)	$2,327	($1,047,396 − $1,045,069)
Interest Payment Foregone	−$8,333	(10%/12 × $1,000,000)
Principal Paydown Premium Gain:		
Due to Prepayment	$180	($6,745 × $4 5/32 / 100)
Due to Scheduled Amortization	$19	($468 × $4 5/32 / 100)
Total Financing Cost	−$5,707	($2,327 − $8,333 + $280 + $19)
Effective Annual Financing	5.60%	($5,707/$1,047,396 × 360/35)

date, July 22, the investor delivers the GNMA 10s and receives $1,047,396 in cash. Thirty-five days later, on August 26, the investor will purchase GNMA 10s from the dealer and pay $1,045,069. This amounts to a bonus to the investor of $2,327 resulting from the drop.

During the thirty-five days of the agreement, the dealer receives both coupon payments and principal payments from the security sold by the investor. As a result, the investor forgoes the coupon income due in August, equal to $8,333 (10%/12 × $1,000,000). The principal payments from the security will also be paid to the dealer. Because all payments of principal are made at par value, whoever owns a premium security loses the premium on the principal paid down (through normal amortization and prepayments). This month, it will be the dealer. The payment of principal to the dealer represents an opportunity gain to the investor equal to the premium times the August principal payment. Had this transaction been done with a pass-through security selling at a discount to its par value, principal payments to the dealer would be viewed as an opportunity loss from the investor's perspective.

The exact size of the investor's opportunity gain in this example depends on prepayments for July. Since these figures are not available until early August, a projection must be made. A good indicator of the next month's prepayments is the prior month's prepayment rate for comparable maturity securities. The last one-month annualized constant prepayment rate (CPR) for new production GNMA 10s with a weighted average maturity of 342 months is 7.8%. If we assume this annual constant prepayment rate, the investor's opportunity gain is $299 ($280 for prepayments + $19 for scheduled amortization). In this scenario, the investor effectively borrows $1,047,396 for 35 days at a cost of $5,707, giving an effective annual cost of 5.6%. This figure compares favorably with other cost of funds as of July 9, 1991, particularly the one-month GNMA repo rate of 5.95%.

RISKS

The cost calculation presented above is subject to risk arising from three sources. The first is prepayment uncertainty. If GNMAs trade close to par, then this risk is minimal; dollar rolls of coupons that trade away from par involve increased risk of prepayment. The second type of risk arises because the effective cost of funds can be influenced by the quantity of loans actually delivered. Since both parties have delivery tolerances, each has an option that is implicitly written by the other party. The third source of risk is the problem of adverse selection; investors are likely to be returned pools that exhibit less desirable characteristics. The impact of each of these risks is described below.

Prepayment Risk

In the cost of funds example, we assumed a CPR of 7.8%, but a faster prepayment rate reduces the effective borrowing cost. The investor gains because he avoids receiving the principal payments at par. If the security actually pays down at a 16% CPR, the effective cost of borrowing is reduced to 5.29%, a savings of 31 basis points over the expected borrowing cost of 5.60% (see Exhibit 2).

Exhibit 2 extends the example by presenting a sensitivity analysis of the effective cost of borrowing under various prepayment rate assumptions. Different prepayment rates can significantly change the effective cost of funds for GNMA 10s. This fact makes the dollar roll a useful tool for institutions that anticipate faster prepayments over a given period than the rest of the market participants do (the reverse is true for discounts). For dollar roll transactions with securities priced at or near par, prepayments become less important. Exhibit 2 also shows the effective cost of borrowing at various dollar roll prices. As the drop increases, the cost of funds decreases because the borrower repurchases the securities at a lower price.

Exhibit 2: Various Dollar Roll Cost of Funds
(Sensitivity Analysis is Based on Security Used in Exhibit 1)

Annual CPR	Dollar Roll Drop (1/32s)						
	7	8	9	10	11	12	13
0.00%	7.11%	6.80%	6.49%	6.19%	5.88%	5.57%	5.27%
4.00%	6.97%	6.66%	6.36%	6.05%	5.74%	5.43%	5.13%
8.00%	6.82%	6.52%	6.21%	5.90%	5.60%	5.29%	4.98%
12.00%	6.67%	6.37%	6.06%	5.75%	5.45%	5.14%	4.83%
16.00%	6.52%	6.21%	5.90%	5.60%	5.29%	4.98%	4.68%
20.00%	6.36%	6.05%	5.74%	5.43%	5.13%	4.82%	4.51%

Delivery Risk

The preceding example was based on the assumption that both parties to the dollar roll return exactly the notional amount of the transaction and deliver a substantially identical security that will bring the same price. In reality, both parties have delivery tolerances because they can under- or over-deliver by 2.5%. The delivery tolerance theoretically gives both parties put options: that is, the option but not the obligation to sell securities to each other. If the market price of the security to be rolled rises/falls between the contract date of the roll and the initial settlement, the investor will have an incentive to under/over deliver securities. For example, if the market price has risen before the roll is executed, the investor would deliver less securities at the lower roll price (i.e., would not exercise the put option on the balance of the acceptable amount of securities). Likewise, if at the end of the roll transaction, the market price of the underlying security is higher/lower than the repurchase price of the roll agreement, the dealer will have an incentive to under/over deliver securities. The effective cost of funds will be lower/higher than projected if the dealer under/over delivers relative to what the investor initially delivered. The investor's option has an exercise date as of the first settlement date and an "at-the-money" strike price equal to the roll-in price. The dealer's exercise date is the final settlement date, and the strike price is lower by the amount of the drop, or slightly "out-of-the-money".

In practice, neither party can fine tune deliveries to exploit fully the ex-post value to their delivery options. Fine tuning the delivery for either the dealer or investor becomes difficult when the delivery tolerance is only plus or minus 2.5%. These options exist in a notional sense, in most cases.[2]

Adverse Selection Risk

Because the dealer is not obliged to return the identical collateral, the dealer and the investor both have a clear incentive not to deliver collateral with attractive specified attributes, i.e., short WAM and fast prepay pools in the case of discounts or long WAM and slow prepay pools in the case of premiums. As a consequence, the parties would be ill-advised to roll in pools with above average attributes that could command a higher price. As a result, both parties usually transact the dollar roll with pools that are average or less attractive than the universe of deliverable securities. As long as both parties recognize this, there is little chance that one party or the other will be affected negatively.

Investors who wish to use high quality, specified securities for dollar rolls can stipulate that the securities returned must be of similar quality and/or that the drop be increased in recognition of the securities' more attractive attributes. As long as the lender and the borrower recognize that dollar rolls, like all TBA transactions, trade to the lowest common denominator, both parties will benefit from the transaction.

---

[2] This has been the case since April 11, 1987, when the PSA reduced delivery tolerance from ±5% to ±2.5%. The value of the delivery option is determined by the maturity of the roll agreement (the longer the roll maturity, the greater the dealer's delivery option) and by the price volatility of the coupon rolled (the greater the volatility, the greater the value of the dealer's option).

BREAKEVEN ANALYSIS

As has been demonstrated above, an assessment of the relative value of dollar rolls should include the alternative financing costs (that is, the one-month repo rate), the size of the drop, and the expected prepayment rate of the pass-through. These three factors are interrelated. For example, the size of the drop and the expected prepayment rate determines an implied repo rate for the dollar roll transactions. If the market rate is above this level, dollar rolls make sense, barring any outside considerations. Or combining a target short-term financing rate with the expected prepayment rate can help the borrower find a breakeven level for the drop. If the offered drop is larger than the breakeven level, again a dollar roll makes sense. Since the characteristics of the pass-throughs involved in a dollar roll are not fixed, breakeven analysis must be used judiciously. Prepayment sensitivity plays an important roll in the analysis. Dollar rolls on current coupons have little sensitivity to prepayments, while rolls on discounts and premiums are quite sensitive. A small increase in CPR on a premium security will drive the implied financing rate down, while the opposite will occur for a discount security. Because prepayment opportunity gain/loss is an important factor in dollar roll valuation, investors must keep prepayment sensitivity in mind when doing a breakeven analysis. An example of a breakeven/sensitivity analysis for actually traded pass-throughs appears in Exhibit 3.

To illustrate the use of the breakeven analysis, we offer the following example. Suppose an investor is evaluating a dollar roll on a GNMA 9. He receives a quote of 10/32nds for a one-month roll. Using the previous month's CPR, he calculates the implied financing rate to be 5.58%, 37 basis points below the current GNMA repo rate of 5.95%. On review of his breakeven levels, he sees that prepayments would have to rise to 47% CPR before the implied financing rate rose to 5.95%, and that the breakeven drop is 9/32nds. From this analysis, the investor knows that, financially, the trade is priced in his favor. He then considers the risk factors discussed earlier and makes his decision.

Exhibit 3: Dollar Roll Breakeven and Sensitivity Market Analysis for Selected 30-Year Coupons (July 9, 1991)
(Target Financing Rate is the GNMA Repo Rate)

Type	Coupon	Price	Drop (32nds)	1-mo. CPR	Age	Financing Rate	Breakeven Values (Target Fin. Rate: 5.95%) CPR	Drop (32nds)	Sensitivity Analysis Fin. Rate Decrease of 1/32 Drop (bp)	Fin. Rate Change of 1% CPR (bp)
GNMA	10.50%	106-09	9	20.15%	18	5.65	15.39%	8.0	29	-6
GNMA	10.00%	104-05	11	7.80%	18	5.60	NA	10.0	31	-4
GNMA	9.50%	101-24	10	2.90%	13	5.84	NA	9.5	31	-2
GNMA	9.00%	99-06	10	2.23%	11	5.58	47.23%	9.0	32	0
GNMA	8.50%	96-13	9	0.69%	13	5.59	11.40%	8.0	33	4
GNMA	8.00%	93-25	7	1.20%	13	5.98	0.60%	7.0	34	6
FNMA	10.50%	105-05	9	21.07%	20	5.84	19.07%	8.5	30	-6
FNMA	10.00%	103-17	10	9.44%	15	5.92	8.44%	10.0	31	-4
FNMA	9.50%	101-07	9	3.70%	10	6.17	19.50%	9.5	31	-1
FNMA	9.00%	98-23	9	1.85%	2	5.92	4.85%	9.0	32	1
FNMA	8.50%	96-07	9	1.60%	2	5.62	11.50%	8.0	33	3
FNMA	8.00%	93-28	9	4.85%	13	5.82	7.15%	7.5	34	6
GNMA	10.50%	105-12	9	14.64%	14	6.18	19.00%	10.0	30	-5
GNMA	10.00%	103-18	10	8.61%	14	5.97	9.01%	10.0	31	-4
GNMA	9.50%	101-16	9	3.60%	10	6.17	18.00%	9.5	32	-2
GNMA	9.00%	99-01	10	1.63%	8	5.59	39.00%	9.0	33	0
GNMA	8.50%	96-14	9	0.69%	11	5.59	11.60%	8.0	33	3

As mentioned, dollar roll deliveries are made on a TBA basis. As a general rule, a borrower will not use a security for a dollar roll that investors are willing to pay a premium for in the "specified pool" market. This is true because the borrower is likely to end the dollar roll with a security that trades in the TBA market (with a lower price). Against this background, the breakeven analysis should be based only on those securities likely to be traded in the TBA market.

To offer a longer term perspective, Exhibit 4 shows the one-month dollar roll prices (drops) along with the computed effective annual financing rates (using actual prepayments for TBA type loans), the one-month GNMA repo rate, and the benchmark GNMA coupon. This analysis of the bids on GNMA dollar rolls shows some interesting aspects of TBA trading activity, as well as highlighting some attractive financing opportunities that were available in 1990/91. The savings in finance costs can be seen by observing the difference between the dollar roll implied repo rate and the actual GNMA repo rate. Dollar rolls with coupons near current production tend to offer the lowest financing opportunities. This is mostly due to large forward sales of these coupons by mortgage originators wishing to hedge their origination pipelines. Heavy activity of this type tends to depress forward prices, thus increasing the drop. This translates into attractive financing opportunities for borrowers who hold pools with these coupons.

Dollar roll drops can vary significantly over the course of a year. In December 1990, drops were very low, resulting in implied repo rates well above the GNMA repo rate. In general, rolls collapse in December as year end balance sheet constraints and rising funding costs depress demand. Additionally, this period saw uncertainty about the U.S. recession, and the situation in the Persian Gulf further limited demand, and low production volume in new mortgage securities made dealers more reluctant than usual to sell securities short.

Exhibit 4: GNMA Dollar Roll Prices, Dollar Roll Implied Repo Rates, and GNMA Repo Rates for 12-Month Period (Aug-90 through July-91)

Coupon	Aug-90	Sep-90	Oct-90	Nov-90	Dec-90	Jan-91	Feb-91	Mar-91	Apr-91	May-91	Jun-91	Jul-91
1-mo GNMA Repo Rate	7.85%	7.95%	8.10%	7.75%	7.85%	7.30%	6.50%	6.35%	6.15%	5.85%	5.75%	5.95%
Benchmark GNMA	9.5%	9.5%	9.5%	9.5%	9.0%	9.0%	8.5%	9.0%	8.5%	8.5%	8.5%	9.0%

Roll Bids (Drops)

Coupon	Aug-90	Sep-90	Oct-90	Nov-90	Dec-90	Jan-91	Feb-91	Mar-91	Apr-91	May-91	Jun-91	Jul-91
10.5%	5	5	5	5	2	5	8	5	8	8	9	9
10.0%	5	5	5	5	2	5	9	7	7	8	10	11
9.5%	5	5	5	5	2	5	9	6	7	9	9	10
9.0%	4	4	4	4	2	6	9	7	7	10	9	10
8.5%	2	2	2	3	1	4	8	6	7	10	9	9
8.0%	2	2	2	3	1	3	6	5	5	5	8	7

Implied Repo Rate

Coupon	Aug-90	Sep-90	Oct-90	Nov-90	Dec-90	Jan-91	Feb-91	Mar-91	Apr-91	May-91	Jun-91	Jul-91
10.5%	7.41	7.83	9.87	7.93	8.30	7.36	7.22	7.01	6.02	6.18	4.89	5.69
10.0%	7.37	7.79	9.86	7.83	8.30	7.24	6.85	6.33	6.61	6.52	5.31	5.59
9.5%	7.21	**7.64**	**7.95**	7.59	8.23	7.06	6.71	6.54	6.45	6.08	5.64	5.81
9.0%	7.38	7.79	8.03	7.72	**8.01**	**6.42**	6.39	**5.87**	6.17	5.48	5.36	**5.56**
8.5%	7.95	8.39	8.47	7.86	8.21	6.90	**6.41**	5.99	**5.88**	**5.19**	**5.07**	5.61
8.0%	7.71	8.23	7.98	7.59	8.01	7.00	6.79	6.15	6.41	6.57	5.21	5.99

Bold face indicates the implied repo rate for the benchmark current coupon.

SUMMARY

Dollar rolls often offer an attractive means of borrowing at low cost primarily because they allow dealers to cover their short positions. We have focused our discussion of dollar rolls on GNMA fixed rate pass-throughs but it should be noted that there are also very active markets for dollar rolls in conventional fixed-rate and ARM pass-throughs, and that similar cost of funds savings can be found in these transactions. This chapter has demonstrated a methodology for calculating the effective cost of funds obtained through dollar rolls, and outlined the primary risks associated with the cost of funds calculation.

SECTION VII

ACCOUNTING, TAX AND OPERATIONAL CONSIDERATIONS

CHAPTER 39

FEDERAL INCOME TAX TREATMENT OF MORTGAGE-BACKED SECURITIES

James M. Peaslee
Partner
Cleary, Gottlieb, Steen & Hamilton

David Z. Nirenberg
Associate
Cleary, Gottlieb, Steen & Hamilton

INTRODUCTION

This chapter surveys the principal U.S. federal income tax rules governing mortgage-backed securities.[1] The law in this area was

---

[1] The discussion below is current through January 1, 1992, and is, of course, subject to change through subsequent judicial decisions, legislation or administrative actions. An expanded version of the following discussion is available in J. Peaslee and D. Nirenberg, *Federal Income Taxation of Mortgage-Backed Securities* (Chicago; Probus Publishing Company, 1989).

significantly revised by the Tax Reform Act of 1986 ("TRA 1986"). TRA 1986 gave birth to a new scheme for taxing pools of mortgages that qualify as real estate mortgage investment conduits ("REMICs") and the holders of REMIC securities. The legislation also changed the treatment of discount on non-REMIC mortgage-backed securities to take account of the unusual payment characteristics of those securities.

The mortgage-backed securities considered in this chapter are those which are supported exclusively (or almost so) by (i) payments made on a fixed pool of mortgages, or (ii) payments made on a fixed pool of mortgages together with earnings from the reinvestment of those payments over a limited period (generally, not more than six months).[2] Typically, these securities have two payment features that distinguish them from conventional publicly held debt obligations: their principal amount (if any) is payable in installments, and they are subject to mandatory calls to the extent the mortgages that fund them are prepaid. Certain mortgage-backed securities are further distinguishable from conventional, callable bonds by the fact that their value is attributable largely or entirely to rights to interest on mortgages or reinvestment earnings. These securities are issued at a very high premium over their principal amount (which may be zero). Because the unamortized premium is forfeited if the securities are prepaid, holders of such securities may experience a zero or negative rate of return, even in the absence of defaults.

In terms of tax attributes, mortgage-backed securities may differ from conventional, publicly offered debt instruments in two other respects. First, in the hands of institutional investors, certain types of mortgage-backed securities may qualify for certain tax benefits associated with investments in real property mortgages. Second, certain types of mortgage-backed securities are treated for tax purposes as ownership interests in the underlying mortgages

---

[2] Thus, debt obligations that are secured by mortgages, but have payment terms unrelated to those of the mortgage collateral, are not addressed.

rather than as equity or debt of the issuing entity. This "look-through" feature raises a host of tax issues.

The federal income tax questions peculiar to mortgage-backed securities relate to the features described above, the legal structures that are used in transforming pools of whole mortgages into non-REMIC mortgage-backed securities and the REMIC rules.

TYPES OF MORTGAGED-BACKED SECURITIES

The principal types of mortgage-backed securities that are currently available are pass-through certificates, pay-through bonds, equity interests in owner trusts that are issuers of pay-through bonds and REMIC interests. REMIC interests are either "regular interests" (which from a tax perspective resemble pay-through bonds) or "residual interests" (which from a tax perspective resemble equity interests in owner trusts). These securities have two common features: first, they can be used, alone or in combination, to repackage whole mortgages in a manner that increases their attractiveness as investments; and second, the issuers of the securities are not subject to tax on the income from the underlying mortgages as it passes through their hands to investors. If it were not possible to eliminate all material taxes on issuers of mortgage-backed securities—for example, if such securities were required to take the form of stock in a business corporation that was taxable at current corporate tax rates of up to 34% on the gross income from the mortgages it held without offsetting deductions for dividends paid on the securities—such securities would never have been issued.

The various types of mortgage-backed securities that are currently available address the problem of issuer level taxes in different ways. Pass-through certificates are generally issued by a "grantor trust" that is not considered to be a taxable entity; indeed, for almost all federal income tax purposes, the trust is simply ignored. Issuers of pay-through bonds (or the owners of such issuers) are generally subject to income tax on the taxable income from the mortgages supporting the bonds, but the burden of that tax is largely eliminated through interest deductions allowed with respect to the bonds. Pay-through bonds are often issued by owner trusts. An owner trust is classified for federal income tax purposes as either a grantor trust or a partnership, and in either case is not itself subject to tax. Instead, its taxable income is allocated among its equity owners. A REMIC is exempt from tax by statute (except for certain penalty taxes).

The section that follows further describes pass-through certificates, pay-through bonds, equity interests in owner trusts and REMIC interests. Although REMIC interests may take the form of pass-through certificates, pay-through bonds or equity interests in owner trusts, except when otherwise indicated, these terms will be used in this article to refer only to securities that are not subject to the REMIC rules.

Pass-through Certificates

In their most common form, pass-through certificates are issued by a trust that holds a fixed pool of mortgages.[3] The arrangement is brought into being by a sponsor, which transfers the mortgages to the trust against receipt of the certificates, and then sells all or a portion of the certificates to investors. The certificates evidence ownership by the holders of specified interests in the assets of the trust. Often, each certificate represents a *pro rata* interest in the mortgage pool. Thus, if 1,000 such certificates are issued, each would represents a right to 1/1,000th of each payment of principal and interest on each mortgage in the pool.[4] The mortgage payments passed through to certificate holders are reduced by fees for mortgage servicing, pool administration and any applicable guar-

---

[3] In some cases, the trust is replaced with a custodial arrangement, but in terms of tax analysis, the difference is mostly in the name.

[4] Pass-through certificates representing different proportionate interests in mortgage principal and interest are discussed below. *See also* footnote 27 below for a description of tax constraints imposed on the issuance by a single trust of multiple classes of pass-through certificates having different payment priorities.

antees or pool insurance. These fees are fixed in advance over the life of the pool so that certificate holders can be guaranteed a fixed "pass-through rate" of interest on the principal balance of the certificates, representing the earnings on the mortgages net of such fees.[5] The power of the trustee to reinvest mortgage payments received by the trust, or proceeds of the sale of mortgages held by the trust, is severely limited in order to avoid possible classification of the trust as an association taxable as a corporation[6] under the Treasury's entity classification regulations.[7] As a result, pay-

---

[5] However, when the pool includes mortgages with different interest rates and the fees are the same for all of the mortgages, the pass-through rate would be a weighted average of the interest rates (net of fees) on the mortgages. This structure is used more often in private transactions than in public offerings.

[6] If the trust were classified as an association taxable as a corporation, it is likely that the income realized by the trust with respect to the mortgages, net of fees paid by the trust, would be subject to the corporate income tax. The balance of such income remaining after payment of the corporate tax would be treated as taxable dividends when distributed to certificate holders.

[7] The classification for tax purposes of an unincorporated entity such as a trust is not controlled by what it is called, but depends instead on its functional characteristics and activities. Under Treasury Regulation § 301.7701-4, entities that qualify as trusts under state law are generally classified as trusts for tax purposes if they are passive and merely hold property to protect and conserve it; by contrast, they are generally classified as associations taxable as corporations if they engage in a profit-making business. In particular, a typical investment trust of the type that issues pass-through certificates would be classified as an association if there were any significant power to vary the investment of the trust beneficiaries (*e.g.*, by reinvesting mortgage payments in other mortgages). However, the Internal Revenue Service (the "Service") has ruled that the trustee of a trust holding mortgages that makes quarterly distributions to certificate holders can reinvest monthly mortgage payments in high quality obligations if the obligations mature prior to the next distribution date and are held to maturity. Revenue Ruling 75-192, 1975-1 C.B. 384. It is also permissible for the trustee to use the proceeds of a sale of pass-through certificates to acquire mortgages not specifically identified at the time of funding of the trust (Revenue Ruling 75-192, 1975-1 C.B. 384; Internal Revenue Service General Counsel's Memorandum 38456 (July 25, 1980)), for a trustee to accept an offer by a debtor to exchange old debt for new debt if the debtor is in default or if default will occur in the reasonably foreseeable future (Revenue Ruling 73-460, 1973-2 C.B. 424), for a trustee to accept new mortgages in exchange for defective mortgages in the mortgage pool that did not conform to representations and warranties made upon transfer of the mortgages in trust for some initial period following the date of the transfer (Revenue Ruling 71-399, 1971-2 C.B. 433 (substitution permitted for a period of two years)) or for a trustee to sell mortgages, provided the proceeds are not reinvested but are distributed to certificate holders (Revenue Ruling 78-149, 1978-1 C.B. 448). In addition, when a trustee receives upon the formation of a trust a contract to purchase bonds on a "when-issued" basis and there is a failure to deliver under the contract, the trustee may acquire similar replacement bonds within a short period (Revenue Ruling 86-92,

ments to certificate holders are usually made monthly, parallel with the receipt of mortgage payments by the trust.

A trust used in any commercially available pass-through arrangement will not have investment powers that risk classification of the trust as an association. Instead, such a trust will qualify as a trust for tax purposes and, in particular, will be a "grantor trust" taxable under section 671.[8] Consequently, for federal income tax purposes, the trust will effectively be ignored, and certificate holders will be recognized to be the owners of the mortgages held by the trust.

One consequence of disregarding the separate existence of a pass-through trust is that certificate holders who report income for tax purposes under a cash method of accounting (which would be true of virtually all holders who are individuals) must report income based on the timing of receipts of mortgage payments by the trust and not on the timing of distributions made to them by the trust.[9] The trustee is viewed as an agent collecting mortgage pay-

---

1986-2 C.B. 214). If certain requirements are met, a trust that is considered to have a business objective will be classified as a partnership and not as an association for federal income tax purposes. These requirements are not met in the case of virtually all trusts that issue pass-through certificates, although, as discussed below, they are met by most owner trusts that issue pay-through bonds. *Compare* footnote 30 below.

8   Except as otherwise noted, all section references herein are to the Internal Revenue Code of 1986 (the "Code"). For federal income tax purposes, a trust is usually recognized to be a taxpayer and is subject to tax, at the rates applicable to individuals, on that portion of its income that it does not distribute currently to beneficiaries. Income distributed to beneficiaries is taxable to them. Certain trusts, however, are ignored for most federal income tax purposes under the so-called grantor trust rules found in sections 671 through 679. These rules were devised in order to prevent the separate tax identity of a trust from being used to shift income to lower bracket taxpayers (*e.g.*, from wealthy parents to a family trust or to its beneficiaries) in cases where the grantor (the person creating the trust) retains an economic interest in, or significant rights of control over, the trust. The grantor trust rules provide that if the grantor of a trust retains specified interests in the trust, including a right to income, then he is treated for tax purposes as the owner of the assets of the trust in which he has such interests and is required to include income from those assets in his own tax return. To that extent, the trust is ignored for tax purposes. While the holder of a pass-through certificate issued by a trust holding mortgages is not, strictly speaking, the grantor of the trust, the grantor trust rules have been seized upon by the Internal Revenue Service as a basis for disregarding the issuing trust and treating certificate holders as tax owners of the mortgages, according to their interests.

9   Similarly, accrual method holders would report income as it accrues on the mortgages, as distinguished from the certificates, although the difference between the

ments on the certificate holders' behalf. While certificate holders are obliged to include in income the gross amount of interest on the mortgages, such certificate holders are allowed deductions for mortgage servicing and other expenses paid out of such interest, again on the theory that those amounts are paid on their behalf.[10]

Public rulings have been issued by the Internal Revenue Service that confirm the consequences described above in the case of pass-through certificates guaranteed by the Government National Mortgage Association ("GNMA"),[11] the Federal Home Loan Mortgage Corporation ("FHLMC"),[12] the Federal National Mortgage Association ("FNMA")[13] and certificates representing interests in pools of conventional mortgages that are supported by private mortgage insurance.[14]

Because the holders of pass-through certificates are treated as the owners of the assets of the issuing trust, to the extent those assets include mortgages on personal residences that are loans to individuals, the holders are subject to a special rule, described below, regarding the character of discount income that is realized as principal is paid.[15] For the same reason, institutional investors that derive tax advantages from the direct ownership of real property loans benefit equally from the ownership of pass-through certificates evidencing interests in those loans.[16] The existence of Federal Housing Administration insurance on, or a Veterans' Administra-

---

two should not be substantial.

[10] An individual certificate holder's deductions for servicing and other expenses may be limited, for regular tax purposes, under section 67, which provides that an individual is allowed certain miscellaneous itemized deductions (including deductions for investment expenses) only to the extent that the aggregate amount of such deductions exceeds 2% of the individual's adjusted gross income. No deduction is allowed for such servicing expenses for alternative minimum tax purposes.

[11] Revenue Ruling 70-544, 1970-2 C.B. 6, and Revenue Ruling 70-545, 1970-2 C.B. 7, both modified by Revenue Ruling 74-169, 1974-1 C.B. 147.

[12] Revenue Ruling 81-203, 1981-2 C.B. 137, Revenue Ruling 80-96, 1980-1 C.B. 317, Revenue Ruling 74-300, 1974-1 C.B. 169, Revenue Ruling 74-221, 1974-1 C.B. 365, Revenue Ruling 72-376, 1972-2 C.B. 647 and Revenue Ruling 71-399, 1971-2 C.B. 433.

[13] Revenue Ruling 84-10, 1984-1 C.B. 155.

[14] Revenue Ruling 77-349, 1977-2 C.B. 20.

[15] *See* footnote 51 below and accompanying text.

[16] *See* the discussion below of special rules for certain institutional investors.

tion guarantee of, the mortgages underlying pass-through certificates, or of a guarantee of the certificates by the United States or a U.S.-sponsored agency, is not considered to transform the certificates into government securities for these and most other tax purposes.[17]

Stripped Pass-through Certificates. Pass-through certificates may also be issued that represent, instead of a *pro rata* share of all payments on the underlying mortgages, a right to one fixed percentage of the principal payments on the mortgages and a different fixed percentage of the interest payments on the mortgages.[18] Such pass-through certificates are often referred to as "stripped" mortgage-backed securities or "stripped" pass-through certificates. They are generally sold when there is a divergence of views regarding prepayment rates. The principal component of a mortgage, viewed in isolation without interest, is more valuable the earlier it is repaid. On the other hand, interest ceases when princi-

---

[17] However, pass-through certificates guaranteed by the United States or a U.S.-sponsored agency are treated as "government securities" for the purposes of the diversification requirements for regulated investment companies found in section 851(b). The definition of that term, for purposes of section 851, is borrowed from the Investment Company Act of 1940. For a comprehensive analysis of the treatment of pass-through certificates in the hands of regulated investment companies, see Internal Revenue Service General Counsel's Memorandum 39626 (April 29, 1987). In addition, the Internal Revenue Service has ruled that pass-through certificates guaranteed by the Government National Mortgage Association are not to be treated as "mortgage notes (not including bonds) secured by real property" under the tax treaty in effect between the United States and the Netherlands Antilles, on the ground that, because the certificates are marketable, highly liquid investments and are issued in registered serial form, they more closely resemble "bonds." Revenue Ruling 79-251, 1979-2 C.B. 271. The treaty provides more favorable treatment for bonds than mortgage notes. This treaty was partially terminated by the United States effective January 1, 1988.

[18] In general, these percentages must be set at the time of issuance of the certificates and may not subsequently change. Otherwise, the trust issuing the certificates would be considered an association taxable as a corporation under the "Sears regulations" and would be subject to an entity level tax. *See* footnote 27 below. Most tax counsel believe that creating a class of pass-through certificates that provides for a floating pass-through rate of interest (*e.g.*, based on an index of market interest rates) could run afoul of the Sears regulations if the rate of interest on the underlying mortgages were fixed. However, if the underlying mortgages provide for interest at a floating rate, it may be permissible to allocate all interest up to a specified rate to one class of pass-through certificates and all remaining interest to another class without causing reclassification of the trust.

pal is repaid, so that the interest component of a mortgage, standing alone without principal, is more valuable the later the date on which principal is repaid. Thus, by varying the mix between principal and interest, the effect of prepayments on a class of pass-through certificates can be changed.

The earliest stripped pass-through certificates that were publicly available were structured to *reduce* the risk to investors of changes in prepayment speeds by transforming discount or premium mortgages into par securities. To illustrate this type of transaction, suppose that a thrift institution holds a pool of mortgages bearing interest at a rate of 10% (net of servicing) at a time when the current market rate of interest for pass-through certificates is 8%. If the thrift believes that investors will assume a higher prepayment rate and, thus, are willing to pay a smaller premium for a 100% interest in the mortgages than the thrift thinks is reasonable, the thrift could insulate investors from the risk of a reduction in yield resulting from prepayments by retaining a right to 1/5 of each interest payment on the mortgages and selling the pass-through certificates at par with an 8% pass-through rate.[19] Similarly, if the thrift holds discount mortgages and wishes to sell pass-through certificates at par based on those mortgages, it could accomplish its objective by allocating to the certificates all of the interest payments but only a fraction of the principal payments.[20]

More recently, stripped pass-through certificates have been created that are intended to *increase* the risk to *all* investors of vari-

---

[19] Alternatively, if the thrift could find a group of investors that have the same expectations that the thrift has regarding prepayment rates, it could sell to those investors the strip of interest payments. This could be done mechanically by transferring the mortgages to a trust in return for two classes of certificates that would be sold to the two investor groups. One class of certificates would be entitled to 100% of the principal payments and 80% of the interest payments on the mortgages; the other class would be entitled to 20% of the interest payments.

[20] Another example of a common pass-through arrangement that may be viewed as a sale of rights to different percentages of principal payments and interest payments is one in which the underlying mortgages have a range of stated interest rates and an "excess servicing" fee is charged to reduce the interest that is passed through on the higher coupon mortgages. Such arrangements are discussed further below.

ations in prepayment speeds by creating securities that have greater discounts and premiums than are inherent in the underlying mortgages. The most extreme case is one in which there is a complete separation in the ownership of rights to interest and principal. In a typical transaction, mortgages are transferred to a trust in exchange for two classes of certificates. One class (which may be referred to as "PO Strips") represents the right to receive 100% of each principal payment on the mortgages and the other class ("IO Strips") represents the right to receive 100% of each interest payment. PO Strips, which are similar to zero coupon bonds payable in installments, are issued at a substantial discount and are purchased by investors who, as compared to the market generally, expect a high rate of prepayments, or who wish to hedge against a risk of loss from declining interest rates. (Declining interest rates would generally increase prepayments and, thus, increase the value of PO strips.) IO Strips, which are issued with what amounts to an infinite premium, are purchased by investors who expect a low rate of prepayments, or who wish to hedge against a risk of loss from rising interest rates.

Senior/Subordinated Pass-through Certificates.   Pass-through certificates typically provide for some type of credit support that protects investors from defaults or delinquencies in payments on the underlying mortgages. Most often, the credit support takes the form of a guarantee, insurance policy or other agreement by the sponsor or a third party to replace defaulted or delinquent payments. However, in many private (non-agency) transactions, credit support has been provided by creating senior and subordinated classes of pass-through certificates. Mortgage defaults or delinquencies are charged first against distributions that otherwise would be made on the subordinated class until they are exhausted, thereby protecting the senior class. Additional credit support may be provided through a reserve fund that is funded either with cash provided by the sponsor or with monies diverted from the subordinated class during the early years of the pool. Under current law, it may be necessary to hold any such reserve fund outside the pass-through trust as security for a limited recourse guarantee of the mortgages, and to restrict the transfer of the subordinated certificates by the pool sponsor, in order to avoid classification of the trust as an association taxable as a corporation.[21]

Holders of senior or subordinated pass-through certificates are generally taxed as if the subordination feature did not exist. The subordination feature is analyzed as if the holders of the subordinated certificates wrote a guarantee of the underlying mortgages in favor of the holders of the senior certificates that was secured solely by the subordinated certificates.[22] Payments received by the

---

[21] The reinvestment of reserve fund assets by the trust could be viewed as a business activity that would be inconsistent with the required passivity of a grantor trust. *See* footnote 7 above. *See also* Internal Revenue Service General Counsel's Memorandum 39040 (September 30, 1983) that revoked Internal Revenue Service General Counsel's Memorandum 38311 (March 18, 1980) which had concluded that the limited reinvestment of certain reserve fund assets would not cause a trust to be an association taxable as a corporation. However, the revocation appears to have been based primarily on other grounds.

In addition, as further discussed in footnote 27 below, under the Treasury's trust classification regulations, a trust having more than one class of ownership interest is taxable as an association unless the multiple class nature of the trust is incidental to the purpose of facilitating direct investment in the assets of the trust. Treasury Regulation § 301.7701-4(c), Example (2), involves a trust holding mortgages that issues two classes of pass-through certificates. The classes are identical except that, in the event of a default on any of the mortgage loans, payments on one class are subordinated to payments on the other. The example states that the senior certificates were sold to investors and the subordinated certificates were retained by the pool sponsor. The example holds that the multiple class nature of the trust is incidental to the purpose of facilitating direct investment in the mortgages because the arrangement is substantially equivalent to a single class trust coupled with a guarantee secured solely by the pass-through certificates retained by the sponsor of the trust that is written by the sponsor in favor of the holders of the remaining certificates. Because the sponsor retained the subordinated certificates in the example, it has generally been assumed that a subordinated interest in a trust must be retained by the sponsor of the trust (or at least may not be freely traded) in order to fall within the example and avoid the risk of classification of the trust as an association taxable as a corporation. The Service recently issued a private letter ruling to this effect. As described below, the foregoing restrictions on maintaining a reserve fund in the trust and transferring subordinated interests would be avoided if the trust qualified as a REMIC and a REMIC election was made.

[22] This analysis is supported by Treasury Regulation § 301.7701-4(c), Example (2), discussed above in footnote 21.

senior certificate holders as a result of the subordination feature
are treated in the same manner as other payments under a guarantee, namely, as if they were the corresponding payments of principal or interest on the defaulted or delinquent mortgages. The
holder of the subordinated certificates is required to report income
as if such holder were entitled to receive such holder's full share
of the payments on the mortgages, even if some of those payments
are diverted to the holders of the senior certificates or are retained
in a reserve fund. The subordinated holder is treated as if such
holder had purchased the senior holders' share of the payments
on the mortgages that are delinquent or in default and generally is
allowed a bad debt deduction when the rights to those payments
become wholly or partially worthless.[23]

Pay-through Bonds

Unlike pass-through certificates, which represent an ownership interest in mortgages, a pay-through bond is a debt obligation of a
legal entity (typically an owner trust or a corporation) that is collateralized by mortgages. A holder is considered to own the bond,
but not an interest in the underlying mortgages, in the same way
that the holder of a public utility bond, for example, would be
considered the owner of the bond but not of the power-generating
station that secures the bond. Although the payment terms of a
pay-through bond and of the underlying mortgage collateral are
not identical, the relationship between them may be quite close. In
most cases, the mortgages and earnings from the reinvestment of
mortgage payments over a short period are expected to be the sole
funding source for payments on the bonds, and mortgage prepay-

---

[23] The deduction would be allowed under section 166. If the subordinated holder is not
a corporation, the deduction would be allowed only when the payment rights become
wholly worthless, and may be treated as a short-term capital loss, under the rules for
nonbusiness bad debts in section 166(d). If the holder is a thrift institution or a bank
that is not a "large bank," and accounts for bad debts under a reserve method, then
that method would be used to account for bad debts attributable to the subordinated
interest.

ments are "paid-through," in whole or in part, to bondholders in the form of mandatory calls on the bonds.

A collateralized mortgage obligation or "CMO" is a type of pay-through bond that is divided into classes typically having different maturities and payment priorities. Most often, CMOs are issued by an owner trust, or special purpose corporation, organized by a sponsor.[24] As explained below, an owner trust rather than a corporation is generally used when the sponsor wishes to sell the equity interest in the CMO issuer to other investors.

An owner trust is established pursuant to a trust agreement between the sponsor and an independent trustee, acting as owner trustee. The owner trustee is usually a commercial bank. In most transactions, the sponsor initially contributes a nominal amount of cash to the owner trustee against the receipt of certificates representing the equity or ownership interest in the owner trust. Upon issuance of the CMOs, the mortgage collateral is transferred to the owner trustee in exchange for the proceeds of the CMOs plus any additional cash equity contribution that may be made to the owner trust, either by the sponsor or by other investors in exchange for new certificates. The sponsor may retain its certificates or sell all or a portion of them to others. Pursuant to a bond indenture, the owner trustee pledges the mortgage collateral to another commercial bank acting as the bond trustee.[25] Over the life of the CMOs, the bond trustee collects payments on the collateral, reinvests those payments over a short period, makes payments on the CMOs, pays expenses and remits any excess to the owner trustee that distributes such excess to the owner trust equity owners. Equity interests in owner trusts are further discussed in the next section. If the issuer of CMOs is a corporation rather than an owner trust, the structure is substantially the same except that the

---

[24] The term "owner trust" is used to distinguish the trust from the indenture trust for the CMOs described below.

[25] The collateral backing CMOs often takes the form of pass-through certificates guaranteed by the United States or a U.S.-sponsored agency, although when the sponsor is a nongovernmental person, the CMOs themselves are not obligations of, or guaranteed by, the United States or such an agency.

corporation is substituted for the owner trust. Thus, the issuing corporation pledges the mortgage collateral to the bond trustee that remits any excess cash flow directly to the corporation. The corporation may in turn distribute the cash to its shareholders. The federal income tax treatment of the holders of CMOs is not affected by whether the issuer is an owner trust or a corporation.

CMOs are a more recent innovation than are pass-through certificates. CMOs are similar to pass-through certificates in that they are funded primarily out of payments received on a fixed pool of mortgages or interests in mortgages and, as a group, closely resemble those mortgages or interests in terms of the timing and amounts of payments.

Unlike pass-through certificates, CMOs are typically divided into classes that have different priorities as to the receipt of principal and, in some cases, interest. Often there are "fast-pay" and "slow-pay" classes. Thus, all principal payments (including prepayments) are made first to the class having the earliest stated maturity date until it is retired, and then to the class with the next earliest maturity date until it is retired, and so on. Alternatively, principal payments can be allocated among classes to ensure to the extent possible that certain designated classes receive principal payments according to a fixed schedule. Under that arrangement, the greater stability in the timing of payments on the designated classes is balanced by greater variability in the timing of payments on the remaining classes. Another common feature of CMOs is an "interest accrual" or "compound interest" class that receives no payments of interest or principal until all or certain prior classes have been fully retired. Until that time, the interest that accrues on such a class is added to its principal balance and a corresponding amount is paid as additional principal on prior classes.

Three other differences between CMOs and pass-through certificates are worth noting. First, CMOs may bear interest at a floating rate (a rate that varies directly or inversely with an index of market rates of interest, such as LIBOR), even though interest is paid on the mortgage collateral at a fixed rate. Second, CMOs generally provide for quarterly payments, with the issuer being responsible for reinvesting monthly receipts on the mortgages until the next CMO payment date. Finally, CMOs are usually callable at the option of the issuer when a more than *de minimis* amount of the CMOs remains outstanding, so that the issuer can potentially benefit from increases in the value of the collateral by selling the collateral and retiring the CMOs.[26]

Tax considerations dictated the original choice of pay-through bonds over pass-through certificates as the vehicle for creating mortgage-backed securities with different payment priorities or a floating interest rate not related to the mortgage collateral. If a non-REMIC pass-through trust issued multiple classes of pass-through certificates having these features, the pass-through trust would be classified as an association taxable as a corporation under the so-called Sears regulations and the certificates would be treated as stock.[27] As a result, the trust would be subject to corpo-

---

[26] The reinvestment of mortgage payments and call rights are needed in order to conclude that the CMOs will be recognized to be indebtedness of the issuer for federal income tax purposes. *See* footnote 28 below.

[27] With a limited exception, Treasury Regulation § 301.7701-4(c) classifies an investment trust as an association (or, in limited circumstances that would not apply to a typical mortgage pass-through trust, a partnership) if it has more than one class of ownership interest. These regulations were initially aimed in part at an issue of pass-through certificates sponsored by Sears Mortgage Securities Corporation which had a "fast-pay," "slow-pay" class structure similar to CMOs. For that reason, they are often referred to as the "Sears regulations." *See* Treasury Regulation § 301.7701-4(c), Example (1), which holds that a trust similar to the Sears trust will not be classified as a trust.

A trust that is used to create stripped pass-through certificates has more than one class of ownership interest. However, stripped pass-through certificates fall within an exception in the regulations that permits multiple classes of interest in a trust "if the trust is formed to facilitate direct investment in the assets of the trust and the existence of multiple classes of ownership interest is incidental to that purpose." Treasury Regulation § 301.7701-4(c), Example (4), holds that the exception would apply to a trust that has multiple classes of interest if those classes of interest are treated as stripped bonds or stripped coupons under section 1286. Section 1286 is discussed in the text below. Stripping transactions involve a separation in the ownership of identified principal or interest payments on an obligation. Dividing a fixed rate obligation into one ownership interest that bears interest at a floating rate and another that represents a right to interest at the fixed rate on the obligation minus what is paid on the first class is sufficiently removed from the mere separation in ownership of identified payments so that it is not clear that section 1286 (and hence Example (4) in the regulations) would apply. Example (2) in the regulations applies the exception for incidental multiple ownership classes to certain trusts that issue

rate income tax on the gross income from the mortgages the trust holds without being allowed a deduction for "dividends" paid to certificate holders. Although an issuer of pay-through bonds, or its owners, may be subject to corporate tax on the taxable income of the issuer, deductions are allowed, in determining such income, for interest on the bonds because they are recognized for tax purposes to be indebtedness of the issuer.

Another consequence of the status of pay-through bonds as debt obligations of the issuer rather than ownership interests in the underlying mortgages is that holders are taxed based on the payments they are entitled to receive on the bonds rather than on the payments received by the issuer on the underlying mortgages. For the same reason, pay-through bonds are not treated as obligations of individuals or real property mortgages for tax purposes. Because of the REMIC exclusitivity rules, discussed below, it is not anticipated that many non-REMIC CMOs will be issued on or after January 1, 1992, except perhaps for transactions in which principal on all classes of CMOs is repaid pro rata.

Equity Interests in Issuers of Pay-through Bonds

Typically, a portion of the cash received on the collateral for pay-through bonds (which portion may be small in proportion to the value of the collateral, but significant in absolute terms) is not needed to make payments on the bonds. This surplus cash may be attributable to the spread between the rates of interest on the mortgages and on one or more classes of the bonds, the excess of the reinvestment income actually realized over the amounts assumed in sizing the issue of bonds, profit resulting from the exercise of rights to call the bonds and any excess mortgages or reserves that are available to protect against mortgage defaults or delinquencies but are not in fact fully needed for those purposes.[28]

---

senior and subordinated classes of pass-through certificates. *See* footnote 21 above.

[28] One reason for ensuring that there is significant surplus cash flow attributable to the factors listed in the text is to avoid the possible recharacterization of the bonds for tax

If the issuer of the bonds is an owner trust, the rights to this surplus cash would be represented by the equity interest in the trust.
If the issuer is a corporation, those rights would be represented by
stock.

Owner trusts are often chosen over corporations as issuers of
CMOs because they permit effective consolidation of the issuer
with its owners for tax purposes, without the disadvantage of consolidation for financial accounting purposes, where equity ownership is divided in such a manner that no owner has as much as a

---

purposes as additional ownership interests in the issuer. Such a recharacterization
would result in the disallowance of deductions for interest on the bonds. See
Statement of Dennis E. Ross, acting Tax Legislative Counsel, Department of the
Treasury, before the Subcommittee on Taxation and Debt Management of the Senate
Finance Committee (relating to S.1959 and S.1978) (released January 31, 1986):

"although [the preferred] economic result might be accomplished by leaving the
issuer without significant capital and issuing obligations that, in the aggregate, exactly
mirrored the characteristics of the underlying mortgages, this would in turn threaten
the issuer's status for tax purposes as the owner of the mortgages and the issuer of
corporate debt. Thus, if the issuer had no significant equity and the CMOs were
designed to match exactly the cash flow from the underlying mortgages, the CMOs
could be deemed to constitute equity interests in the issuer or to represent instead
direct interests in the underlying mortgages. Either characterization could leave the
issuer with a tax liability on the mortgage income that would more than offset the
economic advantages of the multiple class structure."

The standards used by the accounting profession in determining whether the issuance
of pay-through bonds is a sale or a financing are similar to the tax standards, except
that greater weight is placed on the form of the bonds as debt. Pay-through bonds
and the related collateral are required to be recorded as liabilities on the issuer's
financial statements unless, among other things, "all but a nominal portion of the
future economic benefits inherent in the associated collateral have been irrevocably
passed to the investor," in which case the issuance of the bonds would essentially be
treated as a sale of that collateral. Financial Accounting Standards Board, FASB
Technical Bulletin No. 85-2—*Accounting for Collateralized Mortgage Obligations (CMOs)*
(March 18, 1985) at 2 (footnotes deleted). The Technical Bulletin states that the future
economic benefit inherent in the collateral associated with an issue of pay-through
bonds will be considered to be irrevocably passed to investor if "(1) Neither the issuer
nor its affiliates have the right or obligation to substitute collateral or obtain it by
calling the [pay-through bonds, with an exception for "clean up" calls]. (2) The
expected residual interest, if any, in the collateral is nominal." *Id.* (footnotes deleted).
Pay-through bonds that are not considered liabilities of the issuer under the Technical
Bulletin are unlikely to be considered debt obligations of the issuer for federal income
tax purposes. However, recognition of the pay-through bonds as debt obligations of
the issuer under the Technical Bulletin would not necessarily result in similar
treatment for federal income tax purposes.

50% interest.[29] Effective consolidation is achieved because owner trusts are classified for federal income tax purposes either as grantor trusts or partnerships.[30] In either case, an owner trust is not itself subject to tax; rather, the taxable income or loss of the owner trust (in general terms, the excess of the entire income from the mortgage collateral plus reinvestment income over the deductions allowed for interest paid on the bonds and expenses) is allocated to the equity holders in accordance with their respective interests.

---

[29] If an investor owned more than 50% of the equity interest in a CMO issuer, it may be required, under generally accepted accounting principles, to include the CMOs and the related collateral as debt and assets, respectively, in its consolidated financial statements. If the CMO issuer were a corporation, the issuer could file a consolidated federal income tax return with a shareholder only if the shareholder was a domestic corporation that owned at least 80% of the stock of the issuer, which is well above the threshold for financial statement consolidation. In the absence of tax consolidation, income of the issuer corporation could not be offset by shareholder losses, and earnings of the issuer would potentially be subject to a second layer of taxation when distributed to its shareholders (which might be reduced, but not eliminated, by the 70% or 80% dividends received deduction in the case of shareholders that are themselves corporations).

[30] The status of an owner trust will be determined under the Treasury's entity classification regulations (§§ 301.7701-1 through 301.7701-4). The regulations provide, in effect, that an owner trust will be classified as a trust if it does not have an objective to carry on a business for profit (and, in particular, if there is no power under the trust agreement to vary the investment of the owners). Whether an owner trust has such an objective will depend on the particular terms of the arrangement, but in many cases it will be difficult to establish with certainty that such an objective is not present. If an owner trust is not classified as a trust, then it will be classified as a partnership, and not as an association taxable as a corporation, if it lacks at least two of the following four corporate characteristics: continuity of life, centralized management, limited liability and free transferability of interests.

Owner trusts generally have the corporate characteristic of continuity of life since the bankruptcy, dissolution or withdrawal of equity investors will not cause the dissolution of the trust. On the other hand, under the typical owner trust agreement, (i) there is no centralized management because the equity investors have the power to direct the actions of the owner trustee, (ii) there is not limited liability because the equity investors are jointly and severally liable for the debts of the owner trust (other than the pay-through bonds), and (iii) there is no free transferability of interests because the ability of any equity investor to transfer an equity interest is subject to the consent of the other equity investors.

In order to ensure increased certainty of treatment for investors, some owner trusts are given powers that are incompatible with their classification as trusts. In addition, under the Sears regulations an owner trust that has more than one class of equity interest would not qualify as a grantor trust. In either case, such owner trusts would be classified as partnerships.

Because the taxable income of the equity owners is computed based on the net income from the collateral and bonds, it is possible that in any given period the taxable income allocated to an owner will differ significantly from the income such holder would have reported in that period if such holder were taxed based solely on cash distributions from the owner trust. Taxable income that exceeds an owner's income calculated based on cash distributions is often referred to as "phantom income." The possible sources of phantom income are discussed in detail later in this chapter.

REMICs

As the prior discussion indicates, a grantor trust cannot issue pass-through certificates that are divided into multiple classes with staggered maturities. Also, pay-through bonds cannot be created that provide for payments, in the aggregate, that precisely mirror the payments on a fixed pool of mortgage collateral. Thus, certain securities may be attractive economically but cannot be issued as either pass-through certificates or pay-through bonds, because they have a class structure inconsistent with the grantor trust rules and match the underlying mortgages too closely to be recognized for tax purposes as debt. Moreover, even if a security could be issued as a pay-through bond, compared with an ownership interest in mortgages, debt often has financial accounting disadvantages (the need to show the debt on someone's balance sheet) and tax disadvantages for certain institutional investors (the debt is not considered a real property loan). Finally, holders of equity interests in issuers of pay-through bonds may realize phantom income.

To address some of these concerns, TRA 1986 enacted the REMIC rules (sections 860A through 860G). These rules treat a pool of mortgages that meets certain requirements as a REMIC if an appropriate election is made and state how the REMIC and the holders of interests therein will be taxed.

The REMIC rules are applied to a pool of mortgages and related securities based on their functional characteristics, without regard to legal form. Thus, a REMIC may be a state law trust, corporation or partnership, or simply a segregated pool of mortgages that is not a separate legal entity. Similarly, REMIC interests may be evidenced by ownership certificates, debt instruments, stock, partnership interests or a contractual right to receive payments. The functional approach of the REMIC rules allows the state law legal form of a REMIC and the interests therein to be structured to best achieve financial accounting and other nontax objectives.

By statute, a REMIC is not subject to an entity level tax (except for certain penalty taxes).[31] Instead, the income from its assets is allocated among the holders of REMIC interests. All of the interests in a REMIC must be either "regular interests" or "residual interests," as those terms are defined in the REMIC rules. There is no required number of classes of regular interests. By contrast, a REMIC must have one (and only one) class of residual interests. In general, regular interests resemble conventional debt. There is no similar limitation on the economic characteristics of residual interests.

The income of a REMIC is allocated among the different classes of interests as follows: the income of holders of each class of regular interests is determined as if those interests were debt of the REMIC. The holders of the residual interest are allocated all income of the REMIC, determined as if it were a taxable entity but reduced by the interest deductions that would be allowed to the REMIC if the regular interests were debt.

The allocation of income among REMIC interests is similar to the allocation that would be made if the REMIC were an owner trust and the regular interests and residual interests were pay-through bonds and equity interests in the trust, respectively. How-

---

[31] Net income from a prohibited transaction is taxed at a rate of 100%. Prohibited transactions, as defined in Section 860F(a)(2), include, among other things, the disposition of a mortgage other than pursuant to certain specific exceptions and the receipt of income from a source other than qualified mortgages or permitted investments, as defined below. With limited exceptions, contributions to an existing REMIC are also subject to a 100% tax.

ever, there are important differences between REMICs and owner trusts. First, as previously noted, there is no requirement that a REMIC or REMIC interests take any particular legal form. Second, the characterization of regular interests as debt of a REMIC follows directly from the statute, and there is no requirement that a REMIC have any minimum equity value or that the payments on regular interests and the underlying mortgages be mismatched. In addition, for purposes of determining the taxation of the sponsor of a REMIC and the status of regular interests as real property loans in the hands of institutional holders, regular interests are treated as ownership interests in the underlying mortgages rather than as debt.

While the REMIC rules represent a significant step forward in the tax law governing mortgage-backed securities, they are not the answer to every prayer. The REMIC rules were created primarily to permit the issuance of multiple class pass-through certificates. Although they achieve that goal, they do little more. The REMIC rules do not, for example, offer much relief from the restrictions on management powers that apply to grantor trusts. The permitted activities of a REMIC are limited, in much the same manner as a grantor trust, to holding a fixed pool of mortgages and distributing payments currently to investors. Indeed, in some respects, a REMIC has even less freedom of action than a grantor trust. Another significant problem with the taxation of non-REMIC mortgage-backed securities—the phantom income that is recognized by issuers, or the owners of issuers, of certain pay-through bonds—is also not resolved by the REMIC rules. Indeed, they make it worse. When a REMIC issues multiple classes of regular interests with staggered maturities, phantom income is realized by residual interest holders in much the same manner as if they held equity interests in an owner trust and the regular interests were pay-through bonds. However, the REMIC residual holders must contend with certain anti-tax-avoidance rules that do not apply to owner trusts.

REMIC Qualification Tests. To qualify as a REMIC, an entity must elect to be a REMIC and must (1) meet a test relating to the interests in the entity (interests test), (2) meet a test relating to the assets of the entity (assets test), and (3) adopt arrangements designed to ensure that "disqualified organizations" will not hold residual interests.

As indicated above, the interests test requires all interests in a REMIC to be either regular interests or residual interests.

In general, a regular interest is an interest that is designated as a regular interest and provides for principal payments (or, if the interest is not in the form of debt, similar amounts) fixed as to amount, and interest (or similar amounts) on the outstanding principal amount at a fixed rate (or, to the extent permitted in regulations, a variable rate).[32] The Internal Revenue Service has announced that regulations will be issued allowing interest to be paid on regular interests at a variable rate that is based on an objective interest index or a weighted average of the rates of interest on the mortgages held by the REMIC.[33] However, the fixed or variable rate of interest may not be disproportionately high (i.e., an interest will not qualify as a regular interest if it is issued at a substantial premium, more than 25%, above its principal amount).[34]

Under legislation enacted in 1988, an interest may also qualify as a regular interest if it provides for a fixed principal amount (which may be zero) and interest that consists of interest on a specified portion of the interest on the mortgages held by the RE-

---

[32] The timing of principal payments may be contingent on mortgage prepayments or income from permitted investments (described below).

[33] Proposed Regulations interpreting § 860A-860G (and certain related code sections) (the "Proposed REMIC Regulations") were issued on September 27, 1991. *See* Proposed REMIC Regulations § 1.860G-1(a)(3); Notice 87-41, 1987-1 C.B. 500; Notice 87-67, 1987-2 C.B. 377. Each of the notices applies to REMIC regular interests issued on or after June 15, 1987. The Proposed REMIC Regulations permit regular interests that bear interest based on the highest, lowest or average of two or more objective interest rate indices.

[34] *See* Proposed REMIC Regulations § 1.860G-1(a)(5); H.R. Rep. No. 841, 99th Cong., 2d Sess. (September 18, 1986) (the "Conference Report") at II-229, and Joint Committee on Taxation, General Explanation of the Tax Reform Act of 1986 (JCS-10-87) May 4, 1987 (which, following convention, will be referred to as the "Blue Book") at 415.

MIC, and such portion does not vary during the life of the regular interest. There is no requirement that the interest on these types of regular interests not be "disproportionately high" compared with their principal amounts. The purpose of the expansion of the definition was to allow securities similar to IO Strips to be issued as regular interests.

An interest will not fail to be a regular interest because it is subordinated to other regular interests or the residual interest in the event of defaults or delinquencies on the underlying mortgages.[35]

A residual interest in a REMIC is any interest that is designated as a residual interest and is not a regular interest. As noted above, there is no requirement that a REMIC residual interest have any minimum value.[36]

There are no requirements as to the number of holders or concentration of ownership of either regular or residual interests.

The assets test requires that substantially all of the assets of a REMIC be "qualified mortgages" or "permitted investments."[37] A qualified mortgage is defined as any obligation (including any participation or certificate of beneficial ownership therein) that is principally secured by an interest in real property (whether residential or commercial), any REMIC regular interest or any "qualified replacement mortgage."[38] Thus, qualified mortgages include

---

[35] Proposed REMIC Regulations § 1.860G-1(a)(3)(iii). Also, a subordinated regular interest may be freely traded. Conference Report at II-228, footnote 7. Blue Book at 415, footnote 70. *Compare* footnote 21 above.

[36] *See* Proposed REMIC Regulations § 1.860G-1(c); Blue Book at 416.

[37] The phrase "substantially all" has been interpreted to allow a REMIC to hold only a *de minimis* amount of other assets. Proposed REMIC Regulations § 1.860D-1(b)(3); Conference Report at II-226. The asset test is applied at the close of the third calendar month beginning after the inception of the REMIC and continuously thereafter until the REMIC liquidates.

[38] The assets test, by permitting a REMIC regular interest to be a qualified mortgage, permits the creation of tiered REMICs which are used to create regular interests that have characteristics that may not be permitted to be created directly under the interests test, described above in the text.

In general, a "qualified replacement mortgage" is a mortgage or REMIC regular interest that is received by the REMIC in substitution for another mortgage or regular interest within three months of inception of the REMIC for any reason, or within two

IO and PO Strips and other pass-through certificates (including senior and subordinated pass-through certificates) to the extent the underlying mortgages are qualified mortgages.[39] Qualified mortgages also include loans principally secured by stock owned by a tenant-stockholder of a cooperative housing corporation, as well as loans secured by manufactured housing that meets certain minimum size requirements (including mobile homes but not recreational vehicles).[40] The only permitted investments are (i) "cash flow investments"—in general, short-term investments of the cash flow from qualified mortgages held pending distribution on the interests in the REMIC on the next distribution date; (ii) "qualified reserve funds"—in general, investments held in a reasonably required reserve fund to provide for full payment of the expenses of the REMIC, or payments due on the regular interests in the event of default on qualified mortgages or lower-than-expected earnings on cash flow investments;[41] and (iii) foreclosure property—in general, real property acquired by the REMIC in connection with the default of a qualified mortgage, provided the property is not held longer than a specified grace period.

Finally, a REMIC must adopt arrangements designed to ensure that residual interests are not transferred to a "disqualified organization." A disqualified organization is generally a governmental entity that would not be subject to tax on income from any residual interest that it held. The reason for limiting transfers to disqualified organizations is to prevent the avoidance of tax on such income. If, despite the arrangements adopted by a REMIC, a residual interest is transferred to a disqualified organization, a penalty

---

years if the replaced mortgage or regular interest is "defective."

[39] Conference Report at II-227, footnote 5; Blue Book at 413, footnote 67. Non-REMIC pay-through bonds would not be qualified mortgages. Proposed REMIC Regulations § 1.860G-1(a)(6); Blue Book at 413, footnote 67.

[40] Proposed REMIC Regulations § 1.860G-1(a)(5); Notice 87-41, 1987-1 C.B. 500.

[41] Section 860G(a)(7) requires that the amount of any reserve be promptly and appropriately reduced as payments on qualified mortgages are received. This requirement would not prevent the buildup of a reserve over time, so long as at all times the size of the reserve does not exceed the size required to provide adequate default protection or to pay expenses, as evidenced, for example, by rating agency requirements. See Proposed REMIC Regulations § 1.860G-2(g)(3)(ii).

tax is imposed on the transferor that is intended to compensate for the tax that would otherwise be imposed on the disqualified organization.

Exclusivity of REMIC Rules/Taxable Mortgage Pools. Beginning in 1992,[42] any entity (or any portion of an entity) that is not a REMIC or a thrift institution and otherwise meets the definition of a "taxable mortgage pool" will be classified as a corporation and will not be permitted to file a consolidated federal income tax return with any other corporation.[43] Thus, such an entity will be subject to an entity level tax.[44] Any entity (or any portion of an entity) will qualify as a taxable mortgage pool if (i) substantially all of its assets consist of debt obligations (or interests therein), more than 50% of which consist of real estate mortgages (or interests therein), (ii) the entity is the issuer of debt obligations with two or more maturities[45] and (iii) payments on the debt obligations issued by the entity bear a relationship to payments on the debt obligations (or interests therein) held by the entity. Thus, an

---

[42] More precisely, the rules for taxable mortgage pools described in the text will not apply to any entity in existence on December 31, 1991, unless there is a substantial transfer of cash or property to such entity (other than in payment of obligations held by such entity) after such date.

[43] For example, this rule would prevent a special purpose subsidiary that issues CMOs and meets the definition of a taxable mortgage pool from filing consolidated returns with its parent corporation even if the subsidiary would otherwise be permitted to file such consolidated returns.

[44] One exception to this rule is that a taxable mortgage pool that is a real estate investment trust or regulated investment company will continue to be allowed deductions for dividends distributed to its equity owners. However, the income of those owners would be subject to rules similar to the "excess inclusion" rules that apply to owners of REMIC residual interests. See footnotes 138 - 141 and accompanying text below. Also, dividends received by a corporation from a taxable mortgage pool (other than one electing to be taxed as a real estate investment trust or regulated investment company) would qualify for the 70% or 80% dividends received deduction under section 243. Those dividends would also appear to qualify under section 243(a)(3) for the 100% dividends received deduction for dividends received from a domestic corporation that is a member of the same affiliated group (in general terms, corporations connected through chains of 80% or greater stock ownership), but this is not certain.

[45] The Treasury has been granted authority to treat as debt obligations for these purposes equity interests of varying classes if those classes correspond to classes of debt with different maturities. Section 7701(i)(2)(D).

owner trust that issues sequential-pay CMOs after 1991 would be a taxable mortgage pool and could not generally avoid an entity level tax except by electing to be a REMIC.[46]

The general purpose of the taxable mortgage pool rules is to force REMIC elections, so that, among other consequences, the owners of the equity interests in the pool would become subject to the "excess inclusion" rules (discussed at footnote 139 below) that apply to REMIC residual interests.

TAXATION OF HOLDERS

This section addresses the taxation of mortgage-backed securities in the hands of investors. As the discussion above indicates, the mortgage-backed securities that are currently available are divided into two groups: those that are taxable as debt instruments, and REMIC residual interests and equity interests in owner trusts that are taxed based on an allocation of the taxable income of the REMIC or trust, respectively. The two groups of mortgage-backed securities are considered separately below, beginning with those that are taxable as debt instruments.

Mortgage-backed Securities Taxable as Debt Instruments

Mortgage-backed securities that are treated as debt instruments for tax purposes consist of (i) pass-through certificates, which are considered ownership interests in the underlying mortgages, (ii) CMOs and other pay-through bonds, which are debt obligations of the entity that issues them and (iii) REMIC regular interests, which the Code deems to be debt obligations of the issuing REMIC, regardless of their legal form. References in this section to

---

[46] Some non-REMIC CMOS, particularly those with respect to which at least one class of bonds bears interest at a floating rate, provide for all classes of bonds to be retired simultaneously. An issuer of such bonds would not be treated as a taxable mortgage pool.

mortgage-backed securities should be understood to be limited to one of these three types of securities.

In applying the tax rules for debt instruments to a pass-through certificate, it should be kept in mind that such a certificate is not generally considered a single security for tax purposes, but instead represents an ownership interest in each of the mortgages held by the issuing trust. Technically, the holder of a pass-through certificate should calculate income or loss with respect to each mortgage separately, by allocating among the mortgages, in proportion to their respective fair market values, the price paid for the certificate and the price received on resale. Such an allocation is rarely necessary in practice, however, because in most instances the tax results obtained by viewing the mortgages alternatively, in isolation or as a group, would be the same.[47] For convenience, and except when otherwise noted, the discussion below of the tax treatment of mortgage-backed securities will proceed as if the security in question were in all cases a debt obligation of one debtor (either an interest in a single mortgage or a single pay-through bond).

The mortgage-backed securities considered here are generally subject to the Code rules governing conventional debt instruments. Thus, for example, interest on such a security is taxable as ordinary income when such interest accrues, in the case of an accrual method taxpayer, or when it is received, in the case of a cash method taxpayer. Assuming the security is purchased at its principal amount, principal payments represent a nontaxable return of the investor's capital regardless of when principal is paid (discount and premium are discussed below). Upon sale of the security, gain or loss is recognized in an amount equal to the difference between the net proceeds of such sale and the seller's

---

[47] This statement assumes that all of the mortgages underlying a single pass-through certificate have identical terms. Although this is rarely true in fact, because all such mortgages are generally similar to one another, and information is not reported to investors on a mortgage-by-mortgage basis, an assumption of pool-wide uniformity of mortgages is usually made in practice. Cf. Internal Revenue Service Private Letter Ruling 8052046 (September 30, 1980).

"adjusted basis" in the security (generally, his cost for the security, with adjustments for principal payments and the amortization of discount or premium). Any such gain that is not characterized as interest income under the market discount rules, and any loss, is treated as capital gain or loss, respectively, if the security is held as a "capital asset," which would be the case unless the holder is a dealer in securities.[48] Capital gain is long term if the security has been held at the time of sale for more than one year. However, as a result of TRA 1986 and the Revenue Reconciliation Act of 1990, long-term capital gain is taxable at the same rate as ordinary income for most taxpayers other than certain individuals.[49] An amount paid as accrued interest upon the sale of a mortgage-backed security between interest payment dates is treated by the seller as an interest payment and may be used by the purchaser to offset the interest received on the next interest payment date. Two exceptions to the foregoing rules apply to REMIC regular interests, but they are likely to have little, if any, practical significance for most investors.[50]

---

[48] However, holders that are banks or thrift institutions always recognize ordinary income or loss from sales of debt obligations under section 582(c).

[49] It still may be necessary to know whether gain or loss is capital or ordinary because capital losses generally can be deducted only to the extent of capital gains.

[50] The exceptions are as follows: first, income from REMIC regular interest must always be reported under an accrual method even if the holder is otherwise a cash method taxpayer; second, gain recognized by an investor upon sale of a REMIC regular interest that otherwise would be capital gain will be treated as ordinary income to the extent such gain does not exceed the excess of (i) the income that would have been reported by the investor if the investor had reported income as it accrued based on a yield to the investor equal to 110% of the "applicable Federal rate" (generally, an average yield of U.S. Treasury obligations of different ranges of maturities published monthly by the Internal Revenue Service) in effect for the month in which the interest was acquired by the investor, over (ii) the ordinary income previously reported by the investor. These two exceptions should not have much practical significance. Section 448, enacted by TRA 1986, requires most investors other than individuals and small businesses (annual gross receipts of not more than $5 million) to report all income under an accrual method. Moreover, stated interest on many common mortgage-backed securities must be reported by all investors under an accrual method because such interest is treated as original issue discount (*see* discussion below at footnote 59 and accompanying text). As to the possible conversion of gain on sale from capital gain to ordinary income, for the moment the rate advantage of capital gain has been eliminated for most taxpayers.

The tax treatment of a mortgage-backed security is more complex if it was purchased at a price different from its principal amount, *i.e.*, at a discount (a price below such amount) or a premium (a price above such amount). If a mortgage-backed security is purchased at a discount, and the holder subsequently receives its full principal amount, the excess of the principal received over the cost of the security will represent additional income. A question then arises as to the proper timing of recognition of that income and as to its character as ordinary income or capital gain. Similar issues exist regarding the use of premium to offset income or increase loss. These questions are addressed hence.

Treatment of Discount and Premium.   The traditional approach to the tax treatment of a debt instrument deals separately with three sources of income—stated or coupon interest, original issue discount and market discount—and one item of expense, which is bond premium. Stated interest was discussed above; discount and premium are considered here.

In general, original issue discount is discount at which a debt obligation was originally sold to investors by the issuer or, in a public offering, by the underwriters, and market discount is discount that arises from decreases in the market value of a debt obligation following its issuance. The most important difference, in terms of tax consequences, between original issue discount and market discount is that, in general, original issue discount is includable in income by the holder of a discount obligation as the discount accrues, whereas market discount is taxable only when principal payments are received or the obligation is sold. The rule requiring the current inclusion in income of original issue discount has applied to corporate obligations since 1969, but was first extended to obligations of individuals by the Tax Reform Act of 1984 ("TRA 1984"), effective for obligations issued—which, in the case of mortgages, means closed—after March 1, 1984.

If a debt obligation has market discount, it must be determined whether the obligation was issued after July 18, 1984, the date of enactment of TRA 1984, or on or before that date. Gain from a sale to a new holder of a mortgage-backed security issued after July 18, 1984, is ordinary interest income to the extent of the market discount that accrued during the period the seller held the security rather than capital gain as was generally true under prior law. The manner in which market discount is allocated among principal payments will also differ depending on whether TRA 1984 applies.

The distinction between original issue discount and market discount is blurred by the "bond stripping" rules of section 1286. These rules apply when rights to principal and interest on a debt obligation are sold separately or in different proportions and play a significant role in the taxation of pass-through certificates. If rights to payments on a debt obligation qualify as "stripped bonds," all income from the holding of those rights (including income attributable to stated interest and all discount) is subject to taxation under the original issue discount rules.

A further distinction to keep in mind in determining the tax treatment of market or original issue discount is whether the debtor is an individual, a corporation or other legal entity. Gain realized upon the receipt of a payment of principal on an obligation of an individual (representing market discount, or original issue discount not previously included in income) is *always* ordinary income, whereas gain from the payment of principal on an obligation of a corporation or other legal entity may be capital gain if the obligation is held as a capital asset.[51] While this distinction has been important in the past, its significance has been

---

[51] This distinction is based on a technical quirk in the Code. In order for gain to be capital gain, it must result from a "sale or exchange" of a capital asset (*see* the definitions in section 1222). Under case law dating back to the early days of the tax law, gain from the extinguishment of a contractual claim, including gain realized upon retirement of a debt obligation, is not considered to result from a sale or exchange unless there is a Code provision that so states. Section 1271(a)(1) treats amounts received by the holder on retirement of a debt instrument as amounts received in exchange therefor, but this section does not apply to obligations of individuals (see section 1721(b)(1)). Since amounts received in retirement of an obligation of an individual are not received in a sale or exchange of the obligation, any resulting gain is ordinary income. However, if such an obligation is actually sold to a new holder, the sale or exchange requirement is satisfied and income from the sale can be capital gain.

eroded by recent legislation. TRA 1984 and TRA 1986 greatly narrowed the circumstances under which gain from a payment of principal will be capital gain in the case of an obligation of a legal entity, and the rate advantage for capital gain is available only to certain individual taxpayers.

Unlike discount, all premium on a given debt instrument is treated alike.[52] Premium on a debt instrument that is held for investment can be amortized as an offset to interest income if an election is made by the holder under section 171. Before TRA 1986, this election applied only to debt obligations of corporations or governments and, thus, was not available for obligations of individuals, such as residential mortgages, or obligations of owner trusts. However, TRA 1986 extended the election to obligations of all types of issuers, effective for obligations issued after September 27, 1985. TRA 1986 also requires the use of a constant yield method of amortization of premium that is similar to the method, described below, used in calculating accruals of original issue discount.

In order to understand fully the tax treatment of mortgage-backed securities, it continues to be necessary to distinguish between stated interest, original issue discount, market discount and premium and to take account of the rules applicable to each. Nonetheless, the law is clearly moving in the direction of taxing all income from the holding of mortgage-backed securities under the rules governing original issue discount. This trend is evidenced by a number of recent developments:

> First, with respect to many common types of mortgage-backed securities, stated interest is treated currently as original issue discount and, therefore, is directly subject to the original issue discount rules. In those instances where stated interest is not now treated as original issue discount,

---

[52] *But see* Internal Revenue Service Private Letter Ruling 8724035 (March 16, 1987), which distinguished between premium on a GNMA certificate that represented the value of the GNMA guarantee and premium that arises because of changes in interest rates. This distinction is of questionable merit, given that no separate allocation is made to the guarantee for other tax purposes.

the consequences for investors of characterizing such interest as original issue discount would be fairly minor.

Second, many of the pass-through certificates that are now being issued either are, or may be, subject to the bond stripping rules of section 1286. As noted above, the effect of those rules is to convert all discount and stated interest into original issue discount.

Third, TRA 1984 and TRA 1986 have reduced the importance of the distinctions between original issue discount and market discount, in terms of both the timing of income and the character of income as capital gain or ordinary income.

Fourth, TRA 1986 adopted a new method (referred to below as the "PAC method") for calculating accruals of original issue discount on mortgage-backed securities that takes account of expected prepayments and adjusts for differences between expected and actual prepayments. The legislative history of TRA 1986 generally contemplates that this method will be used in calculating accruals of market discount and premium amortization.

Finally, it has been argued that the Code should be amended to treat market discount in exactly the same manner as original issue discount, on the ground that the two are economically equivalent from the perspective of investors.[53] Given the congressional interest in revenue enhancement, it would not be surprising to see this argument prevail some time in the future.

In light of these factors, it would be reasonable, if perhaps somewhat premature, to view the rules governing original issue

---

[53] Such an amendment was included in H.R. 3545 (the House version of the Revenue Act of 1987 passed by the House on October 29, 1987), but was dropped in the House-Senate conference.

discount as the basic model for taxing all income from mortgage-backed securities (while recognizing, as the discussion below will indicate, that deviations from that model are required or permitted under current law). For that reason, the discussion below will first consider original issue discount, including the bond stripping rules, and then turn to market discount and premium.

The discussion of discount below assumes that the mortgage-backed securities in question have an original term to maturity of more than one year. A different tax regime, which is of little relevance to mortgage-backed securities, applies to discount on short-term obligations.[54]

Original issue discount. Original issue discount is defined as the excess of the "stated redemption price at maturity" of an obligation above its "issue price."[55] In the case of an obligation that

---

[54] In brief, the holder of a debt obligation that has an initial term of one year or less (a "short-term obligation") is not required to include the original issue discount, if any, relating to the obligation in income as it accrues unless such holder is an accrual basis taxpayer, a bank, a dealer holding the obligation in inventory or another class of holder specified in section 1281. Holders not described in section 1281 will include accrued original issue discount on a short-term obligation in income only when the obligation is sold or matures, but may be required under section 1282 to defer deductions for interest paid on any related borrowings under rules similar to those that apply to leveraged investments in long-term market discount obligations described later in this section.

[55] Section 1273(a). Under a *de minimis* rule, if the discount as so defined is less than 1/4 of 1% of the stated redemption price at maturity times the number of complete years to maturity, original issue discount is considered to be zero. Proposed regulations applying the original issue discount rules found in sections 1271 through 1275 were issued in 1986 (the "Proposed Regulations"). *See* 51 F.R. 12022 (April 8, 1986) with corrections at 51 F.R. 23431 (June 27, 1986). The Proposed Regulations state that, in the case of an obligation that provides for more than one payment includable in its stated redemption price at maturity (an "installment obligation"), the *de minimis* rule will be applied based on the weighted average maturity of the obligation, which will be calculated by dividing (i) the sum of the products of the amount of each payment includable in the obligation's stated redemption price at maturity and the number of full years (rounding down for partial years) from the issue date to the date on which each such payment is due by (ii) the sum of all such payments. *See* Proposed Regulations § 1.1273-1(a)(3)(ii). In the case of a debt obligation for which accruals of original issue discount are calculated under the PAC method, described below, taking account of a reasonable prepayment assumption, the same assumption should be applied in determining such weighted average maturity.

The Proposed Regulations provide a simpler, elective *de minimis* rule for installment

bears interest at a fixed rate payable at fixed intervals of not more than one year over the entire term of the obligation, the stated redemption price at maturity of the obligation is its principal amount. The issue price of an issue of publicly offered obligations is the initial offering price to the public (excluding bond houses and brokers) at which a substantial amount of the obligations is sold. Thus, neither the price at which the obligations are sold to the underwriters by the issuer, nor the price at which any particular obligation is sold to an investor, determines the issue price.

The definition of original issue discount applies quite differently in practice to pay-through bonds and REMIC regular interest, on the one hand, and pass-through certificates, on the other hand. Accordingly, these two categories of securities are discussed separately below. The bond stripping rules are described in the context of pass-through certificates.

1. *Pay-through bonds and REMIC regular interests*:   For convenience, the term "pay-through bond" will be used to refer to both pay-through bonds and REMIC regular interests.[56]

Pay-through bonds will often have original issue discount. It is not uncommon for them to be issued at a substantial discount below their principal amount, particularly when the mortgages themselves are purchased at a discount. In that event, the pay-through bonds will have original issue discount, even though the

---

obligations that call for principal payments to be made at a rate no faster than principal payments on a "self-amortizing installment obligation." A holder of such an obligation is permitted to compute the *de minimis* amount as the product of 1/6 of 1% of the stated redemption price at maturity and the number of full years (rounding down for a partial year) from the issue date to the final maturity date of the obligation. *See* Proposed Regulations § 1.1273-1(a)(3)(ii)(B). In general terms, a "self-amortizing installment obligation" is an installment obligation that calls for equal payments of principal and interest at fixed periodic intervals of one year or less with no additional payments at maturity. *See* Proposed Regulations § 1.1273-1(b)(2)(iii). Accordingly, the typical fixed rate residential mortgage would be a "self-amortizing installment obligation."

[56] In the case of an individual who holds a REMIC regular interest, Treasury Regulations may provide that in certain circumstances such holder's share of the REMIC's operating expenses must be included in that holder's gross income and allowed as a deduction, subject to the limitation of section 67. *See* below for a further discussion.

discount mirrors market discount on the underlying mortgages, because the pay-through bonds are new securities distinct from those mortgages.

In addition, a pay-through bond may be considered to have original issue discount if the rate at which interest is actually paid in each payment period (calculated by dividing the amount of the interest payment by the principal balance of the bond at the beginning of the period) is not the same for all periods and the change in the rate of interest payments is attributable to factors other than changes in an index of market interest rates.[57] In particular, interest on such a bond generally will be treated as original issue discount to the extent that it is paid at a rate exceeding the lowest rate at which interest is paid during any period over the entire life of the instrument.[58]

One common example of a pay-through bond that provides for interest payments at varying rates is an interest accrual bond (generally, a bond that bears interest over its entire life at a fixed rate but does not provide for any principal or interest payments until all bonds of the same series with earlier maturity dates have been retired). Because interest on an interest accrual bond is payable during the initial payment periods at a zero rate, all payments of interest on such a bond are treated as original issue discount. Thus, such a bond would have original issue discount equal to the sum of all interest payments thereon, even if it were issued with no discount below its principal amount. Although it is not entirely clear, stated interest also may for similar reasons be transformed into original issue discount in the case of any pay-through bond

---

[57] Floating rate debt instruments are discussed in the second following paragraph in the text. For an illustration, see Proposed Regulations § 1.1273-1(a)(3)(iii), Example 4.

[58] The reason for this result is as follows: original issue discount is defined as the excess of the stated redemption price at maturity of an obligation over its issue price. Section 1273(a)(2) defines the stated redemption price at maturity of an obligation to include all payments made on the obligation other than interest based on a fixed rate that is payable unconditionally at fixed periodic intervals of one year or less during the entire term of the obligation. Thus, to the extent that interest is paid in any particular period at a rate greater than the lowest rate at which interest is paid in any period over the entire life of the instrument, it is includable in the stated redemption price at maturity and, thus, in original issue discount.

that has a "payment-lag" feature (that is, provides for a lag between the end of the period over which interest accrues and the date on which such interest is paid) if the period between the issue date of the bond and the first payment date is longer than the interval between payment dates.[59]

In the case of a pay-through bond that provides for interest at a rate that floats based on changes in the value of an index of market interest rates (*e.g.*, LIBOR), the original issue discount rules should be applied by (i) assuming that interest will be payable in all accrual periods (as defined in footnote 67 below) at the rate or rates that would apply if the value of the index remained constant over the life of the instrument at its value on the issue date (this assumption eliminates the floating rate feature and, thus, permits the original issue discount and other tax rules to be applied as if

---

[59] For example, suppose that a pay-through bond provides for monthly payments of principal and interest on the twenty-fifth day of each month and that the interest that is paid on each payment date is the interest that accrued during the preceding calendar month (*e.g.*, the payment made on February 25 represents the interest that accrued during the month of January). The bond has a payment-lag feature because the period over which interest accrues ends 25 days before the interest is paid. It appears that all interest on the bond would be treated as original issue discount if the period between the issue date of the bond (that is, the settlement date for the initial sale of the bond by the issuer to the underwriter or other initial buyer) and the first payment date is longer than one month (which is the interval between payment dates). This result can be inferred from the Proposed Regulations. As discussed below in the text, holders of debt instruments having original issue discount are required to calculate income based on "accrual periods." In the case of a pay-through bond having a payment-lag feature, the Proposed Regulations define the accrual periods to be (i) the whole periods, beginning no earlier than the issue date of the bond, that correspond to the interval between payment dates and end on each payment date and (ii) a short initial period that begins on the issue date and ends on the day preceding the beginning of the first whole accrual period. (Thus, the pay-through bond described above would have whole accrual periods of one month ending on the 25th day of the month and one short accrual period beginning with the issue date and ending on the 25th day of the month.) If the period between the issue date and the first payment date is longer than the interval between payment dates, then no interest payment would be made at the end of the first accrual period. While the relationship between accrual periods and the definition of stated redemption price at maturity is not clear, it is possible that interest payments would be considered to be payable at fixed periodic intervals of one year or less during the entire term of an obligation (and hence would be excludable from the definition of stated redemption price at maturity) only if they are made at the end of each accrual period. (*See* footnote 58 above). Thus, if no interest is paid at the end of the first short accrual period, all stated interest may be included in the stated redemption price at maturity.

the loan provided for interest at a fixed rate or rates) and then (ii) for each accrual period, adjusting the interest income determined under the first step to reflect the difference between the assumed rate and the actual rate for such period.[60]

An investor that purchases a pay-through bond having original issue discount at a yield to maturity not less than the yield to maturity at which it was initially offered must include in income in each taxable year that such investor holds the bond the portion of the original issue discount that is considered to accrue in such year (regardless of whether such investor otherwise reports income under a cash or accrual method of tax accounting). As explained in more detail below, the portion of the original issue discount on a bond that is considered to accrue in any period generally equals the amount by which the value of the bond would increase during such period if it continued at all times to have a yield to maturity equal to its yield to maturity at the time of issuance calculated based on its issue price. This method of accruing original issue discount is known as the "constant yield" or "scientific" method.[61] It gives effect to the compounding of interest by including accrued but unpaid original issue discount in the base to

---

[60] For example, suppose that a pay-through bond with a principal amount of $1,000 pays interest quarterly at a rate equal to 100 basis points over the value of LIBOR at the beginning of the quarter. If the value of LIBOR was 8% on the issue date of the bond, then the bond would be taxed as if provided for fixed interest at a rate of 9%, except that the interest income for each quarter, as so determined, would be increased or decreased by the difference between the actual rate of interest paid at the end of the quarter and interest at the assumed 9% rate. The approach described in the text is based upon Proposed Regulations § 1.1275-5. That section applies only to "variable rate debt instruments" that are narrowly defined. A floating rate debt instrument that does not meet the definition (one example would be an instrument that pays interest that varies inversely with an index of market interest rates) is taxable under the contingent payment rules found in Proposed Regulations § 1.1275-4. (*See* footnote 85 below.) However, it is likely that future regulations will extend the principles of Proposed Regulations § 1.1275-5 to virtually all types of floating rate debt instruments, provided the floating rate is based on one or more indices of market interest rates and is the only contingent feature.

[61] The constant yield method was introduced into the tax law by the Tax Equity and Fiscal Responsibility Act of 1982 and first applied to corporate and governmental obligations issued after July 1, 1982. In the case of obligations issued on or prior to that date, original issue discount was accrued under a straight-line method, which allocated the same portion of the discount to each year.

which the yield to maturity of the bond is applied in calculating future accruals of such discount.

The yield to an investor of a debt obligation purchased at a discount is greater the shorter the life of the obligation. In the case of most pay-through bonds, it is highly probable that principal will be prepaid to some degree. The possibility of prepayments raises two related questions: first, whether original issue discount should be accrued based on a yield that is calculated assuming that prepayments will occur at some reasonable rate, and second, how income is to be adjusted to account for differences between the assumed prepayment rate (a zero rate or a reasonable estimate) and the actual prepayment rate. Prior to the enactment of TRA 1986, there were no certain answers to these questions.[62] Because of TRA 1986, it is now clear that, in the case of a pay-through bond issued after December 31, 1986, (i) the yield that is used in calculating accruals of original issue discount will be determined based on a reasonable assumption ("Prepayment Assumption") as to the rate at which the underlying mortgages will be prepaid, and, if earnings on temporary investments would affect the timing of payments of the bond, the rate of those earnings, (ii) income will be adjusted in each taxable year (whether or not principal payments are made on the bond in that year) to reflect the economic gain or loss for that year (calculated based on changes in present values assuming a constant yield) resulting from past and present differences between actual prepayment experience and the Prepayment Assumption, but assuming that future prepayments on remaining mortgages will conform to the Prepayment Assumption and (iii) in general, those adjustments will increase or decrease interest income and not be treated as capital gain or loss.[63] In general, the Prepayment Assumption with

---

[62] For a discussion of pre-TRA 1986 tax treatment of mortgage-backed securities, see James Peaslee, "Federal Income Tax Treatment of Mortgage-Backed Securities" in *The Handbook of Mortgage-Backed Securities*, Frank J. Fabozzi (ed.) (Chicago: Probus Publishing Company, 1985), 591-598.

[63] The new method is found in section 1272(a)(6), and applies, according to section 1272(a)(6)(C), to any regular interest in a REMIC, any qualified mortgage held by a REMIC and "any other debt instrument if payments under such debt instrument may

respect to any issue of bonds will correspond to the prepayment rate assumed in pricing the initial offering of the bonds and will be stated in the offering materials for the bonds.[64] Once determined, the Prepayment Assumption will not change to reflect changes in prepayment rates occurring after the issuance of the bonds. For convenience, the method for calculating accruals of original issue discount introduced by TRA 1986 will be referred to as the "prepayment-assumption-catch-up method," or "PAC method" for short.

The detailed workings of the PAC method can most readily be understood by first examining how it would apply to an obligation that provides for a single payment of principal. The extension of the method to obligations that provide for payments of principal in installments is straightforward, although the computations can rapidly become burdensome. For simplicity, we will begin by assuming that there are no anticipated or actual prepayments.

As an application of the PAC method assuming no prepayments, consider a pay-through bond having a principal amount of $1,000 that was issued at a price of $770.60 on April 1, 1987, bears interest at an annual rate of 8%, payable on April 1 and October 1, and matures on April 1, 1997. Principal is required to be paid prior to maturity out of principal prepayments on the mortgage

---

be accelerated by reason of prepayments of other obligations securing such debt instrument (or, to the extent provided in regulations, by reason of other events)." Thus, the method would apply to any pay-through bond issued after the effective date of the section, which is December 31, 1986.

[64] The method for determining the Prepayment Assumption will eventually be set forth in Treasury regulations (see section 1272(a)(6)(B)(iii)). However, the Conference Report at II-238-II-239 states that the conferees intended that the regulations will provide that the Prepayment Assumption for any pay-through bonds will be the assumption used in pricing the bonds, provided that assumption is not unreasonable based on comparable transactions, if any exist. In the case of publicly offered instruments, a prepayment assumption will be treated as unreasonable only in the presence of clear and convincing evidence. Unless regulations otherwise provide, the use of a mortgage prepayment assumption based on an industry standard (such as a percentage of "PSA") would be permitted. Typically, the prepayment assumption for a pool of mortgages would be expressed as an assumption that a specified percentage of the pool principal balance at the beginning of a period will be prepaid in that period. The specified percentage may change over the life of the mortgages in the pool (e.g., be lower in earlier periods).

collateral. The bond has original issue discount of $229.40. Suppose initially that the Prepayment Assumption is that no mortgage will be prepaid and that, under that assumption, the entire $1,000 will be paid at maturity. Given that assumption, the yield to maturity of the bond, based on semi-annual compounding, is 12%.[65]

A holder of the bond is required to include in gross income in each taxable year the sum of the "daily portions" of original issue discount for each day during the taxable year on which such holder holds the bond.[66] In the case of an investor who purchased the bond in the initial offering at the issue price, two steps are needed to determine the daily portions of original issue discount. First, a calculation is made of the portion of the original issue discount that is allocable to each "accrual period" during the term of the bond. For a bond that provides for payments at fixed intervals over its life except for a short initial or final period, the accrual periods are the periods that end on each payment date and begin on the day after the immediately preceding payment date (or, in the case of the first such period, begin on the issue date).[67] Second, the portion of the original issue discount attributed to each accrual period is allocated ratably to each day during the period to determine the daily portion of original issue discount for that day.

---

[65] In other words, the present value of all interest and principal payments on the bond, calculated using a discount rate for each semiannual period of 6%, equals the $770.60 purchase price.

[66] For this purpose, a holder is considered to hold the bond on the date of its purchase but not on the date on which it is sold to a new holder. Proposed Regulations § 1.1272-1(b).

[67] Section 1272(a)(5) defines the term accrual period as a six-month period (or shorter period from the issue date of the bond) which ends on a day in the calendar year corresponding to the maturity date of the bond or the date six months before such maturity date. This definition is subject to change through Treasury regulations and an elaborate set of rules for determining accrual periods (including the rule described in the text) is found in the Proposed Regulations at § 1.1272-1(d). In the case of a pay-through bond that provides for no payments for some period followed by payments at regular intervals (such as an interest accrual class of CMOs), the Proposed Regulations define the accrual periods in the same manner as described in the text, except that the dates in each calendar year corresponding to the payment dates would be substituted for actual payment dates with respect to the initial period during which no payments are made.

Under the PAC method, the amount of original issue discount on a bond that is attributed to each accrual period is the excess of (i) the sum of (A) the present value, as of the end of the accrual period, of all of the payments, if any, to be made on the bond in future periods and (B) the payments made on the bond during the accrual period that are includable in its stated redemption price at maturity, over (ii) the adjusted issue price of the bond at the beginning of such period. The present value of the future payments of the bond would be calculated for this purpose (i) assuming that the mortgages underlying the bond will be prepaid in future periods in accordance with the Prepayment Assumption (but taking account of the actual prepayments that have occurred to date) and (ii) using a discount rate equal to the original yield to maturity of the bond. The original yield to maturity is the discount rate, assuming compounding at the end of each accrual period, that will cause the present value of all future payments on the bond to equal its issue price on the issue date, calculated assuming that the bond will be prepaid in all periods in accordance with the Prepayment Assumption. The adjusted issue price of a bond at the beginning of an accrual period equals its issue price, increased by the aggregate amount of original issue discount on the bond attributed to all prior accrual periods, if any, and decreased by the amount of any payments made on the bond in prior periods that were includable in the stated redemption price at maturity of the bond. Thus, it represents the first purchaser's remaining capital investment in the bond adjusted for the amount of the original issue discount that has been earned and included in income for tax purposes but not yet paid.

Because the bond in the example above provides for payment on April 1 and October 1, the accrual periods for the bond are the six-month periods ending October 1 and April 1. The semiannual yield to maturity of the bond, based on compounding at the end of each accrual period and the Prepayment Assumption, is 6%.[68]

---

[68] Under Proposed Regulations § 1.1275-2(e)(1), all whole accrual periods determined for any debt instrument are considered to have the same length. If the first accrual is a

Thus, the original issue discount allocable to the first accrual period ending October 1, 1987 is $6.24. This represents the excess of (i) the sum of (A) the present value, as of October 1, 1987, of the future payments to be made on the bond, calculated using a discount rate equal to the initial yield to maturity of the bond and assuming, in accordance with the Prepayment Assumption, no future prepayments, or $776.84, and (B) the principal payments made on the bond in the accrual period, which are the only payments includable in its stated redemption price at maturity, or zero, over (ii) the adjusted issue price at the beginning of the accrual period, which for the first accrual period equals the issue price of $770.60. The corresponding amount for the second accrual period ending April 1, 1988 is $6.61 [($783.45 + $0) - $776.84]. If the initial holder of the bond reports income based on the calendar year, he would include in income for 1987 the sum of all daily portions for the first accrual period ending October 1, 1987 ($6.24) and the sum of the daily portions for the days in the second accrual period which are on or prior to December 31, 1987.[69] The second accrual period includes 180 days of which 90 are on or prior to December 31, 1987. Thus, the sum of the daily portions of original issue discount for the days in the second accrual period that are on or prior to December 31, 1987 is 90/180 times $6.61, or (rounding up) $3.31. The total amount of original issue discount includable in income by such holder in 1987 is therefore $9.55 ($6.24 plus $3.31).

---

short period, Proposed Regulations § 1.1272-1(f)(2) permits the yield to be calculated in accordance with an "exact" method or an "approximate" method. Under the exact method, the percentage yield for the short accrual period would be 100 x [(1 + Y/100)^F - 1], where Y is the yield for a full accrual period expressed as a percentage and F is the fraction of a full accrual period represented by the short accrual period. Thus, if the yield for a six-month accrual period was 6%, the yield for a short-period of three months would be 2.96%, which is computed using the formula and values of 6 and .5 for Y and F, respectively. Under the approximate method, the yield for a short accrual period would be Y x F.

[69] The example uses a 30-days-per-month/360-days-per-year convention. Proposed Regulations § 1.1275-2(e)(2) allows the use of any reasonable convention in counting the number of days in a short accrual period (whole accrual periods are treated in all events as having equal length).

It is sometimes necessary, with respect to a particular day that falls within an accrual period, to refer to the sum of the adjusted issue price at the beginning of that accrual period and the daily portions of original issue discount for all days in the accrual period that are on or before the day in question. That sum is referred to as the "revised issue price."[70] The revised issue price at the beginning of an accrual period is the same as the adjusted issue price at the beginning of that period. The revised issue prices for the bond in the example above are plotted as line A in Exhibit 1.

The example above involves an investor who purchased the bond in the initial offering at the issue price. The daily portions of original issue discount would be calculated in the same manner for a subsequent holder if such holder purchased the bond at a price not exceeding its revised issue price on the date of purchase. On the other hand, an investor who bought the bond at a price exceeding its revised issue price on the date of purchase (and, thus, at a yield lower than the bond's initial yield to maturity) would be allowed to offset that excess amount (which will be referred to as an "acquisition premium") against the daily portions of original issue discount calculated as described above.[71] In particular, each of those daily portions would be reduced by an amount equal to the product of such daily portion and a fixed fraction, the numerator of which is the acquisition premium and the denominator of which is the daily portions of original issue discount (determined without regard to any acquisition premium adjustment) for all days after the purchase date through the maturity date of the bond. Thus, if the acquisition premium for any bondholder represents 25% of the aggregate amount of original issue discount that remains to be accrued after the purchase date, the amount of original issue discount that would otherwise be required to be included in the holder's income for any day would be reduced by 25%.[72]

---

[70] Proposed Regulations § 1.1275-1(h).

[71] *See* section 1272(a)(7); Proposed Regulations § 1.1272-1(g).

[72] *See* Proposed Regulations § 1.1272-1(g)(1)(ii). The formula for accounting for acquisition premium described in the text would not always produce proper results

In the example above, it was assumed that the pay-through bond was not expected to be, and was not in fact, prepaid. However, the PAC method accommodates both expected and actual prepayments. Expected prepayments are taken into account by assuming that the mortgages underlying the bond will prepay according to the Prepayment Assumption, both initially in calculating the yield to maturity and over time in determining the present value of future payments. Actual prepayment experience is also important because it affects the amount and timing of the current payments and expected future payments that enter into the PAC formula.

To illustrate the consequences of different prepayment expectations, return to the bond in the example above. Suppose that the Prepayment Assumption is changed and that under the new assumption the entire $1,000 principal amount of the bond will be paid four years prior to maturity on April 1, 1993. Given that assumption, the yield of the bond would increase from 12% to 13.74%. Using that yield in the formula set forth above,[73] and assuming that prepayments occur in accordance with the Prepayment Assumption, the amounts of original issue discount allocable to the first two accrual periods would increase from $6.24 and $6.61, as calculated above, to $12.92 [($783.52 + $0) - $770.60] and $13.82 [($797.34 + $0) - $783.52], respectively. The revised issue prices of the bond based on the new Prepayment Assumption are shown as line B in Exhibit 1.

---

in a case where stated interest on a pay-through bond is included in its stated redemption price at maturity because the aggregate amount of daily portions to which the fraction described in the text would be applied would then vary depending on prepayments. The aggregate adjustment would vary correspondingly even though the acquisition premium is a fixed amount. Although there is no direct authority supporting such an approach, one simple solution that appears to be reasonable would be to exclude stated interest from original issue discount solely for purposes of accounting for acquisition premium.

[73] The Proposed Regulations at § 1.1272-1(f)(1) require yield, when expressed as a percentage, to be calculated with at least two-decimal-place accuracy. A greater number of significant digits was used in the example, with the results being rounded to the nearest cent.

Exhibit 1: Revised Issue Prices of Bond Under Different Prepayment Assumptions

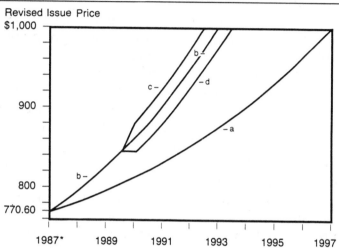

*The revised issue price plotted above each year is the revised issue price for April 1 of that year.

To illustrate the case where prepayments are received at a faster than expected pace, suppose that prepayments on the bond described in the immediately preceding paragraph conform to the Prepayment Assumption until October 1, 1990, but, because of greater-than-expected prepayments between October 2, 1990 and April 1, 1991, the bond is fully retired on April 1, 1991. In that event, the adjusted issue price on October 1, 1990 would equal $881.99, the present value at that time of all future payments on the bond, calculated assuming a $1,000 payment of principal on April 1, 1993. Under the PAC formula, the amount of original issue discount allocable to the accrual period ending April 1, 1991 would equal $118.01, which is the excess of the payments received during the accrual period that are includable in the stated redemption price at maturity, or $1,000, plus the present value of all future payments (zero, since the bond is fully retired at the end of the period) over $881.99. Thus, the original issue discount that otherwise would be included in income over two years and six months (October 1, 1990 through April 1, 1993) is allocated instead to the accrual period ending April 1, 1991 because of the earlier-than-expected prepayments.

The PAC method would also take account of changes in the timing of future payments. Return once more to the pay-through bond described in the second preceding paragraph. If prepayments follow the Prepayment Assumption until October 1, 1989, the adjusted issue price of the bond at that time would be $844.73, the present value of the future payments on the bond based on a $1,000 payment of principal on April 1, 1993. If mortgage prepayments continued to track the Prepayment Assumption throughout the next accrual period ending April 1, 1990, the amount of original issue discount allocated to that period would be $18.01. However, suppose instead that during that accrual period, mortgage prepayments are, alternatively, faster or slower than anticipated. As a result, it is determined (by applying the Prepayment Assumption to the mortgages held by the issuer at the end of the accrual period) that the $1,000 principal amount will be paid six months earlier, in the case of the faster prepayments, or six months later, in the case of the slower prepayments, than originally anticipated. Moving the expected retirement date forward (or back) increases (or decreases) the present value of the future payments on the bond as of April 1, 1990 from $862.74 to $881.99 (or $844.73), and thus increases (or decreases) the amount of original issue discount allocated under the PAC method to the accrual period ending April 1, 1990 to $37.26 (or 0), respectively.[74]

---

[74] If prepayments on mortgages backing a discount bond are slower than assumed, it may be possible for the PAC formula to produce an amount of original issue discount for an accrual period that is negative (although, because the Prepayment Assumption does not change to reflect actual experience, a negative amount is highly unlikely). The Conference Report states at II-239 that in such an event the amount of original issue discount allocable to the period would be treated as zero, and the computation of original issue discount for the next accrual period (and presumably for successive periods until the formula produced a positive amount of original issue discount) would be made by treating the first accrual period and the later ones as a single accrual period. If this approach were literally applied, it might not be possible to determine the income of one taxable year until several years later, because an accrual period could span a number of years, and any positive amount of original issue discount that eventually resulted under the formula would, under the normal discount rules, be allocated ratably over the entire period. Hopefully, the language in

The effect of the two six-month changes in expected retirement dates on the revised issue prices for the bond is shown graphically in Exhibit 1. Lines c and d show revised issue prices giving effect to the faster or slower prepayments, respectively, during the accrual period ending April 1, 1990 (assuming that there are no deviations from the Prepayment Assumption in subsequent periods). The effect of the difference in prepayments on the amount of original issue discount allocated to the accrual period ending April 1, 1990 is represented by the vertical distance between line b and line c or d, as the case may be, on that date.

The examples above involve a bond that provides for only a single payment of principal. In most cases, however, pay-through bonds provide for payments of principal in installments. The only difference that this change would cause in applying the PAC method is that the amount included in the formula for payments that are included in the stated redemption price at maturity would be positive for each accrual period during which some principal amount is paid.

2. *Pass-through certificates*: The degree to which the original issue discount rules will influence the taxation of a pass-through certificate depends primarily on whether the stripped-bond rules of section 1286 apply. If they do, then the original issue discount rules will play a central role. On the other hand, original issue discount

---

the Conference Report will be interpreted to mean only that no deduction for negative amounts of original issue discount will be allowed, and the adjusted issue price at the beginning of each accrual period (determined under normal rules) will be increased by any negative amounts of original issue discount for prior periods for which no deduction was allowed. It should be noted that the prohibition against negative amounts of original issue discount could potentially produce significantly different tax results for two bonds that are issued at the same discount below their principal amount and that are otherwise substantially identical except that the stated interest on one bond is treated as original issue discount (*e.g.*, because the bond has a lag feature), whereas the stated interest on the other bond is not treated as original issue discount. Clearly, it is much less likely that a given slowdown in prepayments would produce a net negative amount of original issue discount with respect to the first bond than the second. The difference between the two bonds would be eliminated if negative original issue discount could be offset against stated interest that is not treated as original issue discount, but, if the Conference Report is followed literally, such an offset will not be allowed.

is unlikely to be present in pass-through certificates that do not fall within that section, except in cases where interest on the underlying mortgages is scheduled to increase over time. The two types of pass-through certificates are considered below, beginning with those that are subject to the stripped-bond rules.

First we consider pass-through certificates that are subject to the stripped-bond rules. Section 1286, which was first enacted in 1982 as section 1232B, contains special rules governing the taxation of stripped bonds and stripped coupons. A stripped bond is defined as a bond issued with coupons (which, for this purpose, includes any rights to receive stated interest), where there is a separation in ownership between the bond and any coupons that have not yet come due. A stripped coupon is a coupon relating to a stripped bond. The tax treatment of stripped bonds and stripped coupons is generally the same, and the term stripped bond will be used in this discussion to refer to both.

Section 1286 transforms the discount at which a stripped bond is purchased (as well as any stated interest on the stripped bond) into original issue discount. More specifically, section 1286(a) provides that if a person purchases a stripped bond, then, for purposes of applying the original issue discount rules of the Code, the stripped bond will be treated, while held by that person, as a bond originally issued on the purchase date having original issue discount equal to the excess of the face amount of the stripped bond over its purchase price.[75] If a number of stripped bonds are pur-

---

[75] The stripped-bond rules also affect the computation of gain and loss by the seller by requiring that the seller allocate the adjusted basis in the obligation that is stripped between the stripped bonds that are sold and those that are retained in proportion to their respective fair market values. *See* section 1286(b). Thus, it is no longer possible, as it may have been before 1982, to allocate basis solely to rights to principal with no allocation being made to rights to interest payments regardless of their value. The basis allocated to the stripped bonds that are sold is compared with the proceeds of the sale to determine the seller's gain or loss from the sale. The seller is treated as having purchased the stripped bonds which he retains at a price equal to the basis allocated thereto. The difference between the purchase price and the face amount of the stripped bonds is treated as original issue discount under the rule of section 1286(a) described above in the text.

As a result of TRA 1986, another consequence of stripping a debt instrument having

chased together at one price, which is often the case, the purchase price is allocated among the stripped bonds in proportion to their respective fair market values.[76]

The classic example of a bond-stripping transaction is a sale by the owner of a whole bond of unmatured interest coupons to one investor and rights to principal to a second investor. (Alternatively, the seller could sell only the coupons or the rights to principal and retain the remaining interests in the bond.) IO and PO Strips represent the extension of this transaction pattern to mortgage-backed securities. Because of the extreme sensitivity of the yields of these types of securities to differences in rates of prepayments of the underlying mortgages, they may be thought to resemble equity securities, or possibly options or futures contracts, more than debt. Nonetheless, because the underlying mortgages are debt obligations, and the complete separation of rights to interest and principal on a debt obligation is the clearest possible example of bond stripping, there is little doubt that IO and PO Strips fall within the rules of section 1286.

The bond-stripping rules also extend to situations where there is some but not complete separation in the ownership of rights to principal and interest. One common example is the transaction described above (see footnotes 19 and 20 and accompanying text), in which a thrift institution holding discount or premium mortgages

---

market discount is that it causes the owner to recognize income equal to the accrued but not yet recognized portion of such discount. This rule applies only to debt instruments acquired after October 22, 1986 (the date of enactment of TRA 1986). It is possible but not certain that the rule is also limited to debt instruments issued after July 18, 1984 to which the TRA 1984 rules governing market discount apply. These rules are discussed below.

[76] Section 1286(a) does not indicate how the respective fair market values of stripped bonds purchased together should be determined where there is no market for the individual stripped bonds. Many tax advisers believe that an investor should assume that the fair market value of each such stripped bond equals the present value of the expected payments thereon computed using a discount rate equal to the yield to maturity to the investor of all stripped bonds purchased together (*i.e.*, computed with reference to the aggregate purchase price and to all payments due on the stripped bonds). Any method that attempted to take account of the different maturities of the separate stripped bonds in determining their fair market value would be very difficult to administer in practice. *See also* footnote 80 below for a discussion of the possible treatment of stripped bonds purchased together as a single installment obligation.

creates pass-through certificates that can be sold at par by retaining a share of interest payments (in the case of the premium mortgages) or a share of principal payments (in the case of the discount mortgages).[77]

Another example of a pass-through arrangement that may (perhaps inadvertently) be subject to the stripped-bond rules is one in which the underlying mortgages have a range of stated interest rates. In order to be able to quote to investors a single pass-through rate of interest that will apply over the life of the pool regardless of prepayment experience, it is common in these circumstances for the pool sponsor or the servicer to receive an "excess servicing fee." This fee is payable out of interest received on the higher coupon mortgages and equals the excess of the interest received on those mortgages over the interest that would have been received if those mortgages paid interest at the lowest rate of interest borne by any mortgage in the pool. Although this fee is labeled a servicing fee, it could also be characterized as an ownership interest in a fixed percentage of each interest payment on the higher coupon mortgages. Under that view, the certificate holders' interests in the higher coupon mortgages would be stripped bonds.

The consequences of recombining all of the stripped interests in a single debt instrument are not clear. It appears, however, that section 1286 would continue to apply to those interests in the hands of any person who had held any of them as a stripped bond, but would not apply to a new investor who purchases all of the stripped interests together.[78]

---

[77] Revenue Ruling 71-399, 1971-2 C.B. 433, analyzes the tax treatment of non-pro rata interests in interest and principal payments on mortgages in a pool, under the law in effect before enactment of the bond-stripping rules.

[78] Because section 1286 applies to any person who purchases a stripped bond, the status of an interest in a debt instrument as a stripped bond in the hands of any particular investor should be determined at the time that interest is acquired by that investor. See New York State Bar Association, Ad Hoc Committee on Original Issue Discount and Coupon Stripping, "Preliminary Report on Issues to be Addressed in Regulations and Corrective Legislation," reprinted in Tax Notes, March 5, 1984, at 993, 1022.

As indicated above, the interest income earned by the holder of a pass-through certificate that is composed of stripped bonds will consist entirely of original issue discount. This will be true regardless of whether the price paid by the holder equals, or is less or greater than, the principal payments on the underlying mortgages to which the holder is entitled, if any, and regardless of the date or origination of those mortgages.[79] Thus, the rules governing market discount and premium discussed herein will not apply. Under the original issue discount rules, the holder will report interest income in each taxable year based on the yield to maturity of the stripped bond to such holder. While not entirely clear under current law, such interest income should equal the interest income the holder would have reported if (i) he had purchased a single, hypothetical bond, having a single yield to maturity, which provided for payments corresponding to the payments on the underlying mortgages to which such holder is entitled and was issued, on the date on which the stripped bond was purchased by the holder, with an issue price equal to the price paid by such holder, and (ii) the PAC method applied to such hypothetical bond in his hands.[80] Under

---

[79] As stated above, the original issue discount rules of the Code were first extended to obligations of individuals by TRA 1984, effective for obligations issued after March 1, 1984 (*see* section 1272(a)(2)(D)). However, because section 1286 treats a stripped bond as being newly issued on each date on which it is purchased for purposes of applying the original issue discount rules of the Code (including section 1272), the date of origination of the whole debt obligation to which the stripped bond relates is not relevant in determining whether the original issue discount rules apply.

[80] There are two reasons why the result described in the text is uncertain under current law. First, it is not clear under current law that the PAC method applies to pass-through certificates. Except as provided in regulations, the PAC method applies only to REMIC regular interests, qualified mortgages held by a REMIC and "any other debt instrument if payments under such debt instrument may be accelerated by reason of prepayments of other obligations securing such debt instrument." A pass-through certificate does not literally meet this definition because the certificate itself is not a debt instrument and the underlying mortgages are not secured by other obligations. However, it is very likely that the PAC method will be extended to such certificates through Treasury regulations. Although the PAC method applies only to debt instruments issued after December 31, 1986, a stripped bond should be treated as being issued for this purpose at the time when it is purchased by each investor. The second source of uncertainty relates to the assumption that a pass-through certificate that is a stripped bond will be treated as a single hypothetical debt instrument with a single yield to maturity (rather than a collection of rights to individual payments, each of which might have its own yield to maturity based on its fair market value on

the PAC method, such holder's income would depend in part on the Prepayment Assumption applied to the underlying mortgages.[81] A number of issuers of pass-through certificates that are stripped bonds have stated that they will use the foregoing method (and a Prepayment Assumption that is consistent with the initial pricing of the certificates) to calculate income reported to investors and to the Internal Revenue Service.[82]

Special considerations apply in extending the PAC method to IO Strips (or more broadly, to any pass-through certificate that is composed of stripped bonds and is purchased at a price in excess

---

the date of purchase). Although this assumption may be thought to be contrary to the general principle that pass-through certificates are treated for federal income tax purposes as an ownership interest in each of the underlying mortgages and that each right to a separate payment on a debt obligation is a separate stripped bond, the result is supported by two arguments. First, Proposed Regulations § 1.1275-2(d) provides that all debt instruments that are issued in a single transaction and are not separately traded will be treated as a single debt instrument for purposes of applying the original issue discount rules. Stripped bonds are considered under section 1286 to be newly issued when purchased, and the rights to individual payments underlying a pass-through certificate are not separately assignable. Thus, the Proposed Regulations appear to have the effect of treating a pass-through certificate that is a stripped bond as a single debt instrument. Second, the PAC method relies on an assumption as to the rate of mortgage prepayments. Because such an assumption is likely to be plausible only for a pool of mortgages and not for individual mortgages, it would seem to be more consonant with the PAC method (if it is applied) to view a pass-through certificate as a single debt instrument, rather than a collection of individual payment rights.

[81] As discussed above, in the case of a pay-through bond, the Prepayment Assumption is generally the assumption used in pricing the initial offering of the bonds. Because each purchase of a stripped bond is treated as a new issuance of a debt instrument, it is possible (although not certain) that the Prepayment Assumption for any holder of a stripped bond would be determined based on conditions at the time he purchased the stripped bond. Redetermining the Prepayment Assumption at the time of each purchase might produce a more accurate measure of income, but it is not clear that the benefits would be substantial given the "catch-up" feature of the PAC method that takes account of differences between actual and assumed prepayment rates. Also, it is not clear how new Prepayment Assumptions would be determined. On the other hand, one reason for requiring the use of a single Prepayment Assumption in the case of a pay-through bond is to ensure consistency between the periodic amounts of original issue discount included in income by investors and deducted by the issuer. That reason does not apply to a stripped bond because there is no general correspondence between original issue discount income calculated under the stripped-bond rules and deductions allowed to the issuers of the bonds that have been stripped.

[82] Such reporting would generally be based on the income that would be reported by an investor that purchased his certificates in the initial offering at the initial offering price.

of the aggregate remaining amount of principal on the underlying mortgages to which the holder is entitled). As indicated above (footnote 74), if the PAC method produces a negative amount of original issue discount for any accrual period then, in general, that amount is not currently deductible but can only be used to offset positive amounts of original issue discount accruing in future periods on the bond. Because the PAC formula (before applying this limitation) could generate significant losses when applied to IO Strips in cases where prepayments are more rapid than anticipated, this limitation could prove to be quite important if it applied fully to IO Strips. However, the purpose of the limitation appears to be to prevent a loss deduction in circumstances where the loss is certain, or almost certain, to be reversed. In the normal case where original issue discount is represented by the excess of the principal amount of a debt instrument over its issue price, it is evident that the full amount of discount eventually will be paid, barring a default. By contrast, in the case of an IO Strip, losses resulting from rapid prepayments would not be certain (or almost certain) to be offset with future income, because the instrument has no principal component that will be paid in all events. Although the matter is uncertain under current law, hopefully, deductions will be allowed for negative amounts of original issue discount calculated with respect to a stripped bond under the PAC method, except to the extent that allowing those deductions would reduce the holder's adjusted basis for the stripped bond to below its remaining principal balance (if any).[83]

In the unlikely event that the PAC method is not extended to pass-through certificates that are composed of stripped bonds, then it is not entirely clear how income from those certificates would be calculated. The most likely approach would be to apply

---

[83] The other extreme would be to allow a deduction for negative original issue discount except to the extent that allowing such a deduction would reduce the holder's adjusted basis to below the *largest possible* sum of undiscounted payments which the holder may receive in future periods (*i.e.*, in the case of an IO Strip, the sum of the payments that would be received if no mortgages were prepaid). Such an approach would be difficult to reconcile with the principles of the PAC method in that it would disregard the Prepayment Assumption in estimating future prepayments.

a method that is similar to the PAC method except that the Prepayment Assumption used in calculating the yield to maturity and
present values would be an assumption that no future mortgage
prepayments will occur, and income or loss that results when a
mortgage is prepaid (calculated in a manner similar to the PAC
method by comparing the amount received, if any, as a result of
the prepayment with the present value of the payments that
would have been received if the mortgage loan had not been prepaid) would be income or loss from retirement of the mortgage
loan and not an adjustment to original issue discount. Any such
income or loss would be ordinary income or loss if the mortgage
loans are obligations of individuals, and generally would be capital gain or loss if they are obligations of corporations, partnerships
or other legal entities and the pass-through certificates are held as
capital assets.[84] Moreover, deductions for losses would not be
curbed by the PAC method limitation on deductions for negative
amounts of original issue discount. An alternative approach that
might be applied to IO Strips (or more generally to any certificates
purchased at a price in excess of the aggregate remaining amount
of principal on the underlying mortgages to which the holder is
entitled) would be to tax them under certain proposed rules governing contingent payment obligations.[85]

---

[84] Gain or loss from a prepayment would be capital gain or loss only if it resulted from
a "sale or exchange." As explained above, the retirement of an obligation of an
individual never results in a sale or exchange, but the retirement of an obligation of
any other type of issuer does result in a sale or exchange. Although the rule treating
retirements as a sale or exchange does not apply under section 1271(b)(2) to
obligations of partnerships or trusts issued before July 2, 1982, a stripped bond should
be considered for this purpose to be issued on the date of purchase by an investor.
There is some possibility that gain recognized from a prepayment that otherwise
would be capital gain would be treated as ordinary income under the
"intention-to-call" rule found in section 1271(a)(2).

[85] These rules are found in the Proposed Regulations at § 1.1275-4. Interest payments on
a debt instrument would not ordinarily be considered to be contingent merely
because those payments would be discontinued if the instrument was prepaid; the
cessation of interest payments would be the normal consequence of the return of the
investor's capital through a principal payment. However, where interest is separated
from the related principal, the argument for treating rights to interest as contingent
payments because of the possibility of prepayments is more compelling. In most
cases, the practical effect of applying the contingent payment rules in the Proposed
Regulations to a pass-through certificate would be as follows: The amount of original

Next consider pass-through certificates that are not stripped bonds. Original issue discount is not likely to be encountered in a pass-through certificate to which the stripped-bond rules do not apply unless, as discussed below, scheduled interest payments on the underlying mortgages increase over time. The exchange of such pass-through certificates for mortgages is not treated as a creation of a new debt security for tax purposes, so that the existence or lack of original issue discount is not affected by the price at which the certificates are originally sold. Rather, in testing for the presence of original issue discount, it is necessary to look to the terms of the original loan between the mortgagor and the mortgage originator, and mortgages are not typically originated at a discount.[86] In any event, the original issue discount rules of the

---

issue discount reported in any accrual period would equal the lesser of (i) the product of the adjusted issue price of the certificate at the beginning of the accrual period and the "applicable Federal rate" for the certificate determined at the time it was purchased by the investor and (ii) the amount of interest on the mortgages that is allocable to the certificate and accrues under the terms of the mortgages during the period, except that once the adjusted issue price has been reduced to an amount equal to the sum of the remaining principal payments to be made on the certificate, then all remaining rights to interest on the certificate would be includable in income as additional original issue discount as such interest accrues under the terms of the mortgages. Cash distributions generally would be treated as nontaxable returns of capital. However, a loss would be recognized when the last payment on the certificate is received equal to the excess, if any, of the holder's adjusted basis in the certificate over the amount of the payment. Such loss would be treated as a loss on retirement of the underlying mortgages. It is not clear whether any other loss deductions would be allowed. The applicable Federal rate is an average of current yields of U.S. Treasury securities for different ranges of maturities that is computed and published monthly by the Internal Revenue Service. For purposes of these rules, noncontingent interest (*i.e.*, interest on a mortgage for any period during which it is not subject to prepayment) would be treated as if it were additional principal. The contingent payment rules in the Proposed Regulations are significantly flawed in a number of respects (for a discussion, *see* New York State Bar Association, Tax Section, "Report of Ad Hoc Committee on Proposed Original Issue Discount Regulations," reprinted in *Tax Notes*, January 26, 1987, at 363, 388) (the "NYSBA 1987 Report"), and it is unlikely that they will survive as final regulations in their present form.

[86] While it is common for a mortgage lender to charge the borrower "points" in connection with the origination of a mortgage, such points are often paid out of the mortgagor's own funds and represent a prepayment of interest rather than original issue discount. *See* section 461(g) (special rule allows a cash basis mortgagor a deduction for prepaid interest paid in the form of points on a loan to finance a principal residence if the number of points does not exceed the number generally charged in the area in which the mortgage is originated). *See also* Proposed Regulations § 1.1273-2(f), which excludes points that are deductible under section

Code would not apply to whole or *pro rata* interests in mortgages which are obligations of individuals if those mortgages were originated before March 2, 1984.[87] TRA 1984 extended those rules to obligations of individuals for the first time, effective for obligations issued on or after that date. As noted above, a pass-through certificate would not fail to qualify as an interest in obligations of individuals because the mortgages or the certificates are guaranteed by the United States or a U.S.- sponsored agency.

In the case of a fixed rate residential mortgage originated after March 1, 1984, some portion of the stated interest payments will be included in original issue discount if the amount unconditionally payable as interest in each month, expressed as a percentage of the outstanding principal balance of the loan, increases over the term of the loan.[88] For example, such a mortgage will be consid-

---

461(g)(2) from original issue discount. However, the Internal Revenue Service has ruled that points paid in connection with a mortgage that is used to refinance an existing mortgage are not deductible under section 461(g), and consequently would be treated as discount. *See* Revenue Ruling 87-22, 1987-1 C.B. 146. *See also Huntsman v. Comm'r*, 905 F.2d 1182 (8th Cir. 1990). Moreover, even if points were viewed as discount, they may be less than a *de minimis* amount (*see* footnote 55 above), so that they would be disregarded in determining whether the mortgages are subject to the original issue discount rules of the Code. Under the special 1/6 of 1% *de minimis* rule for self-amortizing installment obligations, discount on a fixed rate residential mortgage would be considered *de minimis* if it were less than 5% of the stated redemption price at maturity in the case of a 30-year mortgage, and less than 2.5% in the case of a 15-year mortgage. Where a mortgage has a "buy-down" or other similar fund that is used to make interest payments on the mortgage in early years, a question may be raised as to whether the amount initially deposited in the fund should be included in the purchase price of the mortgage or should instead be excluded, thereby increasing the discount at which the mortgage is considered to have been issued. The answer depends on whether the fund is properly viewed as an asset of the mortgagor that is held as additional security for the loan, in which case the amount deposited in the fund would be included in the issue price of the mortgage, or instead as an asset of the lender. Under the terms of most buy-down arrangements, the mortgagor is liable for all payments on the mortgage, including those actually made out of the buy-down fund, and is credited with the balance in the fund in the event of prepayment or assumption. These features of the arrangement support the view that the fund is an asset of the mortgagor. For further discussion of points and buy-down funds, *see* NYSBA 1987 at 413-414.

[87] *See* section 1272(a)(2)(D).

[88] The reasoning supporting this conclusion is as follows: Original issue discount exists if the stated redemption price at maturity of an obligation exceeds its issue price. Thus, a mortgage that is purchased by the first buyer at its principal amount will have original issue discount if its stated redemption price at maturity is greater than its principal amount. This will be true only if the stated interest payments on the

ered to have original issue discount, even if it was originated at par, if it provides for negative amortization of principal or bears interest payable at fixed rates that are scheduled to increase over the life of the loan. The general effect of applying the original issue discount rules to loans with these features will be to require holders (i) of a negative amortization loan to include stated interest in income as it accrues, and (ii) of a loan that bears interest at increasing rates to take into income interest that accrues based on the yield to maturity of the loan (*i.e.*, a yield representing a blend of the stated interest rates).

In the case of an adjustable rate residential mortgage originated after March 1, 1984, the original issue discount rules generally should be applied by treating the mortgage as if it provided for fixed interest payments equal to the interest that would be paid if the value of the index were frozen at its value on the date of origination of the mortgage.[89] Under that approach, stated interest would be included in original issue discount only if the mortgage provides for a scheduled increase in interest payments not dependent on an increase in the index. Such an increase might occur, for example, because rates are adjusted to market levels following an initial incentive or "teaser" rate period.[90]

---

mortgage are included to some extent in the stated redemption price at maturity. The stated redemption price at maturity includes all payments made on an obligation with the sole exception of interest based on a fixed rate which is payable unconditionally at least annually during the entire term of the obligation. A negative amortization mortgage may bear interest at a fixed rate over its entire term, but interest is actually payable at a rate below the stated rate during the negative amortization period. During that period, the accrued and unpaid interest is added to principal. If a rate of interest payable was calculated for each month of the mortgage by dividing the interest payable during that month by the outstanding principal amount of the mortgage at the beginning of the month, and the lowest rate of interest payable as interest payable in any month was then determined, the amounts payable as interest in each month would be included in the stated redemption price at maturity to the extent they were payable at a rate greater than the lowest rate. Similarly, if a mortgage provided for payments of interest currently as the interest accrued but the stated rate of interest increased over the life of the loan, interest paid at a rate greater than the lowest rate would be included in the stated redemption price at maturity and hence would represent original issue discount.

[89] *See* the discussion at footnote 60 above and accompanying text.

[90] *See* NYSBA 1987 Report at 415-416, which proposes an expanded original issue discount *de minimis* rule that would have the effect of excluding most incentive rate

If a mortgage is considered to have been issued with original issue discount, an investor's interest therein would most likely be taxable under a method similar to the PAC method, except that the Prepayment Assumption used in calculating yield and present values would be an assumption that no prepayments will occur, and gain from a prepayment would be treated as gain from retirement of the mortgage loan and not as an adjustment to original issue discount.[91]

Market discount. Any discount at which an obligation is purchased below its principal amount (if the obligation has no original issue discount), or below its revised issued price (if the instrument does have original issue discount), is considered to be market discount. The treatment of market discount has been significantly altered by TRA 1984 and TRA 1986.

1. Overview: Prior to enactment of TRA 1984, market discount on a mortgage-backed security was generally allocated among all principal payments in proportion to their amounts regardless of when they were due. The discount was included in income as principal payments were received or when the security was sold. Thus, if an obligation having an outstanding principal amount of $1,000 was purchased by an investor for $750, the investor would report 25% of each principal payment as income when the payment was received while he held the obligation. Such income was ordinary income (although not interest income) if the obligation was the debt of an individual; otherwise, it was generally capital gain, assuming the obligation was held as a capital asset.[92] Given the same assumption, gain realized upon sale of the obligation was

---

mortgages from the original issue discount rules.

[91] While regulations could be adopted extending the PAC method to individual mortgage loans that are used to back pass-through certificates, such a development is less likely in the case of pass-through certificates that are not subject to the stripped-bond rules than in the case of certificates subject to those rules. In any event, if the stripped-bond rules do not apply, any such regulations would apply at the earliest only to mortgage loans that were originated after December 31, 1986.

[92] *See* footnote 51 and accompanying text.

always capital gain.[93] Such gain would reflect any market discount allocated to the principal of the obligation that remained unpaid at the time of the sale, since the seller's adjusted basis for purposes of computing gain would equal the portion of the initial purchase price, as reduced by the market discount, that was allocated to such unpaid principal.

TRA 1984 and TRA 1986 did not change the rule of prior law that permitted the reporting of market discount on an obligation to be deferred until the obligation is disposed of or principal thereon is paid. However, TRA 1986 introduced a rule for allocating discount among principal payments that can significantly increase the amount of market discount income that is recognized when a principal payment is made. In the case of an obligation that provides for partial principal payments in each accrual period, as is the case with many mortgage-backed securities, this change can have the effect of substantially eliminating the difference between original issue discount and market discount in terms of the timing of the inclusion of such discount in income.

As to the character of market discount income, as a result of TRA 1984, market discount income reported by the holder of an obligation is treated as ordinary interest income for most tax purposes to the extent of the portion of the discount that accrued while the holder held the obligation. TRA 1984 also provided rules to ensure that accrued market discount will not be exempted from tax under certain nonrecognition provisions in the Code. Finally, another TRA 1984 amendment defers deductions for all or a portion of the tax losses that might otherwise be generated by borrowing at market rates to finance low-coupon market discount obligations, claiming current deductions for interest expense on the borrowing and deferring the inclusion in income of the market discount until the obligation is disposed of or repaid. The new

---

[93] But *see* the discussion of special rules for certain institutional investors later in this chapter.

market discount rules do not apply to obligations that have an original term of one year of less.[94]

2. *Detailed discussion*: TRA 1984 added section 1276 to the Code, which applies to obligations issued after July 18, 1984, the date of enactment of the legislation. The section provides that gain from a sale or other disposition of an obligation acquired with market discount[95] will be treated as ordinary income (generally as interest income) to the extent the gain does not exceed the portion of the market discount that is considered to have accrued from the acquisition date to the time of the sale or other disposition. Subject to certain exceptions, such income is recognized notwithstanding other nonrecognition rules in the Code.[96] Thus, for example, a holder who makes a donative transfer of a market discount obliga-

---

[94] TRA 1984 also offers investors a new election, in section 1278(b), to treat market discount as original issue discount. Market discount obligations affected by the election are not subject to the income conversion and loss deferral rules described below. The election applies to all obligations acquired after the first day of the first taxable year to which the election applies, regardless of whether those obligations were issued before or after the date of enactment of TRA 1984, and continues in effect unless permission to terminate the election is obtained from the Internal Revenue Service. Barring unusual circumstances, such as an expiring net operating loss carryover, this election is unlikely to be made since it could result in the acceleration of income and in some cases greater conversion of capital gain into ordinary interest income.

[95] Market discount is defined in section 1278(a)(2) as the excess of the stated redemption price at maturity of an obligation over its basis immediately after the acquisition by the taxpayer. However, in the case of an obligation issued at a discount, the stated redemption price at maturity is replaced by the revised issue price. This rule has the effect of excluding unaccrued original issue discount from the definition of market discount. Also, under a *de minimis* rule, market discount is considered to be zero if it is less than 1/4 of 1% of the remaining stated redemption price at maturity multiplied by the number of complete years to maturity (after the taxpayer acquired the obligation). In the case of an obligation that provides for more than one payment that is includable in the stated redemption price at maturity, this *de minimis* rule would presumably be applied in the same manner as described in footnote 55 above.

[96] *See* section 1276(d). The exceptions allow, among other things, certain transfers of obligations to a parent corporation from an 80%-owned corporate subsidiary, by a partner to a partnership or to a partner from a partnership, or in connection with a corporate reorganization, without triggering recognition of accrued market discount income. As a result of TRA 1986, accrued market discount is recognized upon a transfer of market discount bonds to a corporation in a transaction that is otherwise tax-free under section 351. *See* footnote 201 below. Apparently, a similar rule would apply to a transfer to a REMIC. *See* footnote 204 below.

tion would recognize income up to the amount of accrued market discount even though gifts do not ordinarily trigger the recognition of gain. Similarly, the stripping of a market discount obligation is considered a disposition that triggers the recognition of accrued market discount.[97]

TRA 1986 introduced a new rule for determining the amount of market discount income that is recognized when a partial principal payment is made.[98] The rule, which is found in section 1276(a)(3), states that a partial principal payment on an obligation will be included in gross income as ordinary income to the extent of the accrued market discount on the obligation. In other words, the amount of market discount that must be included in income when a principal payment is received is not, as under prior law, the portion of the remaining market discount that is allocable economically to the principal that is paid (*e.g.*, half of such discount if half of the principal balance is paid), but is instead the lesser of the amount of the payment and the amount of market discount that has accrued (and not yet been included in income) on the obligation as a whole.[99] If an obligation provides for principal pay-

---

[97] *See* footnote 75 above.

[98] The rule applies to obligations to which section 1276 applies that were acquired by the holder after October 22, 1986 (the date of enactment of TRA 1986).

[99] In the case of an obligation having original issue discount as well as market discount, a principal payment would presumably not be treated as a payment of accrued market discount under the new rules to the extent it is considered a payment of accrued original issue discount. This point is not addressed in the statute or legislative history. The Proposed Regulations include a rule, at § 1.1272-1(e)(2)(ii), that treats payments of amounts includable in the stated redemption price at maturity of an installment obligation "first as a payment of original issue discount to the extent accrued as of the date of the payment and not allocated to prior payments, and second as a payment of principal." This rule predates TRA 1986 and its purpose is somewhat obscure. Nonetheless, it would provide an argument for treating payments of amounts includable in the stated redemption price at maturity first as payments of accrued original issue discount to the exclusion of market discount. Another open question is whether payments of coupon interest on an obligation that are includable in its stated redemption price at maturity will be treated to any extent as payments of accrued market discount. Section 1276(a)(3)(A) refers to a "partial principal payment" but the Conference Report at II-842 describes the rule as applying to amounts includable in the stated redemption price at maturity of a debt instrument. This distinction may not be very important if payments of amounts includable in the stated redemption price at maturity are treated first as a payment of accrued original issue discount (including as original issue discount the stated interest that is included

ments in each year at least equal to the market discount that accrues in that year, then the new rule would effectively require market discount to be included in income as it accrues.

Subject to the discussion in the next paragraph, market discount will be considered to accrue on an obligation under a straight-line method[100] unless the holder elects, on an obligation-by-obligation basis, to use a constant yield method.[101] If the election is made, accrued market discount for any period will equal the portion of such discount that would have been included in the holder's income during that period as accrued original issue discount under the rules described above if the obligation had been issued on the date on which it was purchased by the holder and the market discount had been original issue discount. Most sophisticated investors will make a constant yield election for all of their market discount bonds because the election will have the effect of slowing the rate at which market discount accrues.

TRA 1986 authorized the Treasury to issue regulations to determine the amount of accrued market discount with respect to an obligation on which principal is payable in installments. The legislative history[102] states that until these regulations are issued, holders of such obligations may elect to accrue market discount either in the same manner as original issue discount,[103] or (i) in the case

---

in the stated redemption price at maturity), with only the balance being available to be treated as a payment of accrued market discount.

[100] Under this method, accrued market discount is calculated by multiplying the market discount by a fraction, the numerator of which is the number of days the holder has held the obligation and the denominator of which is the total number of days after the holder acquired the obligation to and including the maturity date. See section 1276(b)(1).

[101] See section 1276(b)(2).

[102] See Conference Report at II-842. The methods for accruing market discount discussed in the legislative history technically would apply only to obligations acquired after October 22, 1986 that are subject to the new rule treating principal payments first as payments of accrued market discount. However, because the method of accruing market discount on obligations that provide for more than one principal payment was not clear under prior law, presumably the same methods could also be applied to obligations acquired on an earlier date.

[103] In other words, the amount of market discount that accrues during any period would be the product of (i) the total remaining market discount and (ii) a fraction, the numerator of which is the original issue discount for the period and the denominator

of debt obligations that have original issue discount, in proportion to the accrual of original issue discount, or (ii) for debt obligations that have no original issue discount, in proportion to payments of stated interest.[104] In the case of an obligation that would be subject to the PAC method for accruing original issue discount if the instrument had original issue discount (which would include any pay-through bond issued after December 31, 1986), the same prepayment assumption that would be used in accruing original issue discount will be used in accruing market discount, regardless of which of the foregoing methods is used.[105]

As already noted, section 1276 applies only to obligations issued after July 18, 1984. Thus, the section will apply to all pay-through bonds issued after that date. By contrast, it should apply to pass-through certificates issued after July 18, 1984 only to the extent they evidence interests in mortgages originated after that date. In other words, the pass-through certificates should not be viewed as new obligations, distinct from the underlying mortgages for this purpose.

TRA 1984 also added section 1277 to the Code, which requires the deferral of tax losses that would otherwise result from financing an investment in market discount obligations with debt that bears interest at a current market rate. Section 1277 applies to obli-

---

of which is the total remaining original issue discount at the beginning of the period.

[104] Thus, the amount of market discount in any period would be the product of (i) the total remaining amount of market discount and (ii) a fraction, the numerator of which is the amount of stated interest paid in the period and the denominator of which is the total amount of stated interest remaining to be paid on the debt instrument as of the beginning of the period. Presumably, if the instrument bears interest at a floating rate based on an index, a constant value for the index in the present period and future periods would be assumed. This method produces the same results as a "bond-years" method under which the portion of the market discount that is allocable to each principal payment is accrued ratably over the period from the date of acquisition of the obligation to the date on which such payment is due, and market discount is allocated among principal payments in proportion to the amount of the payments weighted by the length of those periods.

[105] For purposes of information reporting in the case of a class of regular interest (or CMO) issued with de minimis original issue discount, a REMIC (or CMO issuer) is permitted to elect to compete the market discount fraction based on the de minimis original issue discount. Treasury Regulations § 1.6049-7.

gations that are acquired after July 18, 1984 (regardless of when those obligations were issued).

Section 1277 allows a deduction in any taxable year for "net direct interest expense" with respect to a market discount obligation only to the extent such expense exceeds the market discount that accrues during the days in such year on which the taxpayer held the obligation. The rate of accrual of market discount is determined under the rules of section 1276 described above (including the election to use a constant yield method). Net direct interest expense is the excess of the interest paid or accrued during the taxable year on debt incurred (or continued) to purchase (or carry) the market discount obligation over the aggregate amount of interest on the obligation (including original issue discount) includable in gross income by the holder for the taxable year. The "incurred (or continued) to purchase (or carry)" standard used to link a borrowing with an investment in market discount obligations is amorphous and yet familiar, having been used for many years in determining whether investments in tax-exempt bonds are debt financed.[106] A special interest expense allocation rule applies to banks and thrifts.[107]

The deductions for net direct interest expense on a market discount obligation that are disallowed under section 1277 are allowed (i) when the market discount obligation is disposed of in a

---

[106] It is likely that the guidelines for determining whether a tax-exempt bond is debt financed, set forth in Revenue Procedure 72-18, 1972-1 C.B. 740, will also be followed in applying section 1277.

[107] In calculating net direct interest expense, a bank or thrift is required to allocate to each market discount obligation that it holds a portion of its interest expense on all outstanding borrowings, including deposits, determined by multiplying each expense by a fraction the numerator of which is the tax basis of all of its assets. While this rule will ensure an allocation by such an institution of some interest expense against any holdings of market discount obligations, the institution's average cost of funds may be significantly lower than the rate of interest payable on any specific borrowing that might otherwise be matched against the market discount obligations under a facts and circumstances test.

taxable transaction,[108] or (ii) if the taxpayer so elects,[109] to the extent necessary to offset any net interest income over interest expense on related borrowings recognized in subsequent years. While the character of the gain recognized upon the disposition of a market discount obligation issued prior to July 19, 1984 is not affected by section 1276, such gain is treated as ordinary income under section 1277(d) to the extent of the ordinary deduction for disallowed interest expense that is allowed with respect to the obligation in the year of its disposition. The purpose and effect of this rule is to ensure that the market discount income and deferred interest deduction offset each other in the holder's tax return in much the same manner as if the deferred interest expense had been capitalized and added to the tax basis of the market discount obligation.

The policy underlying section 1277 is that deductions for apparent losses resulting from a leveraged investment in a market discount obligation should be deferred, if and to the extent the losses are offset economically by the accrual of market discount, until the accrued market discount is included in income. Thus, if an investor borrows at 12% to finance the purchase of an 8% mortgage that has a yield, taking account of market discount, of 11%, the investor's economic loss is only 1%, the amount by which the rate of interest paid on the borrowing exceeds the yield on the mortgage. Income and expense would obviously be mismatched if a deduction were allowed for the apparent additional 3 percentage point loss before the corresponding amount of accrued market discount income is recognized.

In applying section 1277 to issuers of pay-through bonds or the holders of equity interests therein, it is not entirely clear whether

---

[108] If a market discount obligation is disposed of in a transaction in which gain or loss is not fully recognized, a deduction for the previously disallowed interest expense is allowed up to the amount of gain recognized in the transaction. The balance is preserved as a future deduction by the new holder of the obligation if his basis in the obligation is calculated by reference to its basis in the hands of the former holder, and otherwise will be available to the prior holder upon disposition of the property received in exchange for the market discount obligation.

[109] *See* section 1277(b)(1).

the deferral of interest expense would be calculated on an aggregate basis treating the mortgage collateral as a single debt instrument, or whether the issuer would be required instead to allocate interest expense among individual mortgages and to compare the net direct interest expense allocated to each mortgage with the market discount that accrues on that mortgage.[110] An aggregate approach would seem to address adequately the problem to which section 1277 is directed, and the alternative is quite complex. Nonetheless, there is a substantial argument that a mortgage-by-mortgage calculation is required under the Code.

Premium. In the case of a debt instrument acquired at a premium, section 171 allows the holder (unless the holder is a dealer in securities) to elect to amortize such premium over the life of the instrument. This section was significantly amended by TRA 1986, effective for debt instruments issued after September 27, 1985. Under section 171, as amended, if an election to amortize a premium is made, the premium must be amortized under a constant-yield method. Although the result is not certain, many tax advisors believe that, in amortizing premium under the amended section, prepayments should be accounted for under a method similar to the PAC method, at least in the case of a debt instrument issued after December 31, 1986 to which the PAC method would apply if it had been issued at a discount.[111]

---

[110] As further discussed below, market discount on the mortgages held by a REMIC is included in the REMIC's income, because it accrues as if it were original issue discount and neither section 1276 nor section 1277 applies. Similarly, neither section would apply if the mortgage collateral consisted entirely of mortgages to which the stripped-bonds rules applied because all of the market discount would be considered to be original issue discount under section 1286. *See* text accompanying footnotes 79 and 80.

[111] For a description of these instruments, *see* footnote 63 above. The discussion of bond premium in the legislative history of TRA 1986 is somewhat confusing. The Conference Report at II-842 states, in explaining the amendments to the sections of the Code dealing with market discount, that "until Treasury regulations are issued, in the case of a debt instrument on which principal is paid in more than one installment and that has no original issue discount, the amount of market discount that is considered to accrue in any accrual period will be, at the holder's election, either the amount that would accrue under a constant yield method or

In the case of a debt instrument issued on or before September 27, 1985, an investor may elect to amortize premium under section 171 only if the instrument was issued by a corporation or government.[112] If the election is made, bond premium would be amortized under the method of amortizing bond premium that the holder regularly employs, provided such method is reasonable, and otherwise under a straight-line method. In determining whether a premium may be amortized on a pass-through certificate evidencing an interest in residential mortgages, the date or origination of the mortgages would determine whether the new or the old version of section 171 would apply. Thus, an election could be made under section 171 to amortize the premium on a pass-through certificate backed by residential mortgages that are

---

the amount of discount that bears the same ratio to the total amount of remaining market discount that the amount of stated interest paid in the accrual period bears to the total amount of stated interest remaining to be paid on the debt instrument as of the beginning of the accrual period. "

The method described in the quotation is essentially a straight-line method. The Conference Report then continues:

"In the case of debt instruments that would be subject to the OID rules contained in new Code sec. 1272(a)(6) (without regard to whether the debt instrument has original issue discount), the same prepayment assumption that would be made in computing OID would be made in computing the accrual of market discount. In addition, the conferees intend that the same rules that apply to the accrual of market discount on debt instruments whose principal is paid in more than one installment, also is [sic] applied in amortizing amortizable bond premium (within the meaning of sec. 171)."

The last sentence quoted above refers to the rules for accruing market discount on debt instruments whose principal is paid in more than one installment and not to the rules for accruing original issue discount under section 1272(a)(6) (the PAC method). One possible implication of the reference is that, pending regulations, investors may amortize bond premium on substantially all mortgage-backed securities under a straight-line method. However, as this result is squarely contrary to the language of the section, it is uncertain whether investors may rely on the legislative history. On the other hand, because the prepayment assumption that would be used under the PAC method is also to be used in accruing market discount in the case of debt instruments to which the PAC method applies, the reliance on the market discount rules as a model in amortizing bond premiums should be read to authorize the use of a prepayment assumption in applying section 171 to such instruments.

[112] Non-governmental obligations that are merely guaranteed by the United States or a U.S.-sponsored agency would not be considered obligations of a government for this purpose.

obligations of individuals only to the extent the mortgages were originated after September 27, 1985.[113]

Premium on a debt instrument that is not amortized under section 171 is allocated among the principal payments to be made on the instrument and is allowed as a loss deduction when those payments are made. Such a loss would be an ordinary loss in the case of an obligation of an individual (or a partnership or trust if the obligation was issued prior to July 2, 1982) and otherwise would be a capital loss, provided the obligation is a capital asset.[114]

Equity Interests in Owner Trusts and REMIC Residual Interests

This section discusses the federal income tax treatment of equity interests in owner trusts and REMIC residual interests. The tax characteristics that are common to both types of securities are discussed first; special considerations applicable to owner trusts are discussed second; special considerations applicable to REMIC residual interests are discussed third; and so-called "phantom income" is discussed last. Except as otherwise indicated, in the balance of this section, the term "conduit issuer" means an owner trust or a REMIC, the term "equity interest" means an equity interest in a conduit issuer, and the terms "bond" and "CMO" include REMIC regular interests.

Common Tax Characteristics. As discussed above, conduit issuers are generally not subject to tax.[115] Instead, each holder of an equity interest is required to include in income that holder's share of the net income (or loss) of the related conduit issuer without regard to the distributions made by such issuer. In computing taxable income, the conduit issuer would have gross income consist-

---

[113] *See* Internal Revenue Service Private Letter Ruling 8724035 (March 16, 1987).

[114] Sections 1271(a) and (b). In the case of certain banks and thrifts, any loss attributable to bond premium would be an ordinary loss. *See* the discussion of special rules for certain institutional investors below.

[115] A REMIC is subject to certain penalty taxes. *See* footnote 31 above.

ing principally of interest and discount income from the mortgage collateral, from the reinvestment of mortgage payments and from any reserve funds, and would be allowed deductions for interest (including accruals of original issue discount) and retirement premiums with respect to the bonds and operating expenses of the issuer.[116] Deductions allowed in any period for bond interest and retirement premiums generally would equal the income that would be reported by original holders of the bonds if they bought the bonds on the issue date at the issue price (in the case of issues of bonds having more than one class, computed on a class-by-class basis), except that, in computing accruals of original issue discount, the 1/4 of 1% *de minimis* rule[117] would not apply.

Special Considerations Applicable to Owner Trusts.   As discussed above, an owner trust may be classified either as a grantor trust or as a partnership. A major difference between grantor trusts and partnerships is that a grantor trust is essentially ignored for federal income tax purposes, whereas a partnership is recognized as an entity for some tax purposes. Thus, if an owner trust is classified as a grantor trust, each holder of an equity interest therein would be treated as if he purchased and owned directly his share of the assets of the trust, subject to his share of the indebtedness of the trust. Accordingly, such holder would have an initial basis in his share of those assets equal to the cost to him of

---

[116] In the case of holders of equity interests that are individuals, the deductibility of the issuer's operating expenses may be limited for regular tax purposes under section 67 and disallowed entirely for alternative minimum tax purposes. *See* footnote 10 above. The general treatment by the issuer of underwriters' discount and other issuance expenses relating to an issue of bonds divided into classes is to (i) allocate those expenses among the classes in proportion to their issue prices, without regard to maturities, and (ii) deduct the expenses allocated to each class ratably over the life of that class. Revenue Ruling 70-359, 1970-2 C.B. 103. There appears to be no authority requiring amortization under a constant-yield method, although such a development would not be surprising. *See* NYSBA 1987 Report at 423. Also, it is not clear whether a prepayment assumption may be used in amortizing issuance expenses, although it would appear to be reasonable to use such an assumption. Any unamortized expenses relating to a class of bonds would be deducted when that class of bonds is retired. Special rules for the treatment of issuance expenses are discussed below.

[117] *See* section 163(e); Treasury Regulation § 1.163-7(b). The *de minimis* rule is described in footnote 55 above.

his equity interest plus his share of the revised issue price of the bonds at the time of purchase of the equity interests.[118] In addition, such holder's income would be computed under his own method of accounting and any elections that may be made, such as to amortize bond premium on the mortgage collateral, would be made separately by each holder.[119] If the holder sold his interest in the owner trust, he would be considered to have sold his interest in the underlying mortgages. Accordingly, if the holder was a thrift institution or bank, any resulting gain or loss would be ordinary income or loss. Distributions from a grantor trust are not taxable.

By contrast, if an owner trust is classified as a partnership, taxable income would be computed and, in general, elections would be made, at the partnership (or owner trust) level using the partnership's accounting method (which would almost always be an accrual method).[120] Each holder of an equity interest would report the share of the partnership's taxable income allocable to that holder in that holder's taxable year in which the taxable year of the partnership ends.[121] In most cases, the taxable year of the partnership would be the calendar year.[122] Each partner would be considered to own a partnership interest, which would have a basis in the hands of that partner equal to its original cost to the partner

---

[118] However, the revised issue price could be calculated without regard to the *de minimis* rule. *See* footnote 117 above.

[119] A holder would not be permitted to amortize underwriters' spread or other costs of issuing bonds unless he was a holder at the time those expenses were incurred. A subsequent holder would instead effectively include those expenses in his basis in the mortgages because that basis would include the revised issue price of the portion of the bonds that was used to pay issuance costs.

[120] Section 448 generally would require the partnership to use an accrual method if it has any partner that is a corporation not taxable under subchapter S.

[121] The partnership's taxable income would take account of the amortization of bond issuance expenses paid by the partnership. However, those expenses would not be considered to be paid by the partnership if the partnership is considered to have been formed, or terminated and reformed, after the issuance of the bonds. If there is only a single owner of an equity interest in the owner trust when the bonds are issued, and equity interests are sold to investors at a later date, a partnership would not be considered to be formed until there is more than one equity owner. Partnership terminations are discussed in the following paragraph in the text.

[122] *See* section 706(b).

(the cash purchase price or the basis of property exchanged for such interest in a tax-free exchange), increased by the share of partnership income and liabilities, and decreased by his share of losses and distributions, allowable to the partner. The amount of the partnership's liabilities in respect to the bonds would equal the bonds' aggregate revised issue price, as described above.

Unlike a grantor trust, a partnership is considered to have its own basis in its assets ("inside basis"). While initially the inside basis of an owner trust that is classified as a partnership would equal the sum of the holders' bases in their equity interests, a discrepancy could develop if equity interests are sold at a gain (or loss). This discrepancy could result in overtaxation (or undertaxation) of a subsequent holder. Such overtaxation (or undertaxation) would be mitigated or eliminated if the partnership makes an election under section 754 to adjust the basis of its assets for purposes of computing the taxable income of such successor partners,[123] or if the sale terminates the partnership under section 708. Under section 708, a partnership is considered to be terminated and re-formed if 50% or more of the total interest in partnership income and capital are sold or exchanged within a 12-month period.[124]

If an owner trust is classified as a partnership, then gain or loss from sale of an equity interest may be capital gain or loss, even though, in the case of a thrift institution or bank, a sale of a direct ownership interest in the mortgages held by the trust would be ordinary income or loss.[125] Such gain or loss would be computed by comparing the seller's basis in his partnership interest with the

---

[123] If a trust and the holders of the equity interest therein otherwise file tax returns on the basis that the trust is a grantor trust, a "protective" section 754 election can be made. The disclosure documents relating to the sale of an equity interest generally will indicate whether the trust intends to make an election under section 754.

[124] If a partnership terminates, it is considered to distribute its assets to its partners, including the purchasers who are considered to contribute those assets to a new partnership. Under the partnership tax rules, one effect of a termination is to bring the new partnership's inside basis in its assets into conformity with the partners' bases in their partnership interests.

[125] It is not clear whether the sale of a partnership interest in a partnership whose sole assets are debt instruments would be viewed as a sale of debt instruments for the purposes of section 582(c).

amount realized in the sale (which would include the seller's share of the trust's liabilities). Distributions of cash by a partnership to a partner are not taxable unless they exceed the partner's basis in the partnership interest, in which case the excess is treated as gain from sale of that interest. Because such basis could include the partner's share of the trust's liability for the bonds, such gain would be rare in the case of an owner trust.

A pension fund, charity or other tax-exempt investor that is subject to tax on its "unrelated business taxable income" under section 512 will be taxable on substantially all of its income from an equity interest in an owner trust, regardless of whether it is classified as a grantor trust or partnership.[126]

Special Considerations Applicable to REMICs.   The tax treatment of REMICs resembles a partnership more than a grantor trust. Thus, income or loss is computed at the level of the REMIC and is then allocated among the holders of residual interests as ordinary income or loss. In particular, taxable income or loss of the REMIC is computed as of the end of each calendar quarter and each holder of a residual interest is considered to earn, on each day the holder owns such interest, that day's ratable share of the REMIC's taxable income or loss for the quarter.[127] In computing taxable income, regular interests are treated as indebtedness of the REMIC, and all REMICs are required to use an accrual method of accounting.

In order to calculate the taxable income of a REMIC, it is necessary to determine the REMIC's basis in its assets. Generally speaking, a REMIC's aggregate basis in its assets at the time it is formed will equal the aggregate value at that time of all REMIC interests

---

[126] Such organizations are taxable on income that is "debt financed" within the meaning of section 514, and because substantially all of the cost of the assets of an owner trust would be financed with debt, substantially all of the income of an owner would be treated as debt-financed income.

[127] Limitations on the deductibility of losses are discussed in the text below.

(both regular interests and residual interests).[128] The most significant assets of a REMIC will be the qualified mortgages that it holds. Income from those mortgages will be determined under the rules discussed earlier, except that a REMIC will be required to include all discount in income as it accrues under the PAC method as if the mortgages had been issued on the date on which they are acquired by the REMIC with an issue price equal to their initial basis to the REMIC.[129]

No Code provision permits or requires adjustments to be made to a REMIC's basis in its assets to reflect subsequent purchases of residual interests at a price greater or less than the seller's adjusted basis. The legislative history of TRA 1986 indicates that it "may be appropriate" to make such adjustments, but leaves the issue unresolved.[130] Apparently, either Treasury regulations or further legislation will be needed to clarify whether (or how) any such adjustments will be made.

Special rules apply to the portion of the income from a residual interest that is characterized as an "excess inclusion." With limited exceptions, excess inclusions are always subject to tax, even in the hands of tax-exempt investors. The excess inclusion rules were adopted primarily to ensure taxation of "phantom income" and are discussed further in that context below. Income from residual

---

[128] Under section 860F(b)(2), a REMIC's initial aggregate basis in its assets equals the aggregate fair market value of those assets immediately after their transfer to the REMIC. It appears that such fair market value would be deemed to equal the sum of the issue prices of the regular interests and the residual interests. The "issue price" of an interest in a REMIC generally would equal its initial offering price to the public (excluding brokers and other middlemen) if the interest is publicly offered, the price paid by the first purchaser of the interest if the interest is sold privately and the interest's fair market value if the interest is retained by the sponsor of the REMIC. *See* section 860G(a)(10) (definition of issue price); Conference Report at II-231-II-232. Because the issue price of a REMIC interest is its cost to the investor (rather than the net proceeds to the issuer), issuance expenses would be included in the issue price and thus in the REMIC's basis in its assets. Apparently, no other deduction for issuance expenses would be allowed in calculating the taxable income of the REMIC.

[129] There is no similar rule that treats premium mortgages as if they are newly issued, allowing the REMIC to amortize such premium under section 171 even if the mortgages were originated before September 28, 1985. *See* the discussion earlier in this section.

[130] Conference Report at II-233, footnote 15.

interests that is not an excess inclusion should be exempt from tax in the hands of pension funds and other tax-exempt investors that are taxable only on unrelated business taxable income to the same extent as, for example, income from a partial ownership interest in mortgages (*i.e.*, the residual interest should not be considered debt financed income merely because the regular interests are considered debt obligations of the REMIC).

A REMIC will have a net loss for any calendar quarter in which its deductions exceed its gross income. Such a loss may not be carried over or back to other periods by the REMIC but is instead allocated among the current holders of the residual interest in the manner discussed above. However, the portion of such net loss that is allocable to a holder will not be deductible by such holder to the extent it exceeds such holder's adjusted basis in such interest at the end of such quarter (or at the time of disposition of such interest, if earlier), determined before taking account of such loss. Such adjusted basis would generally equal the cost of the interest to such holder, increased by any amount previously included in such holder's income with respect to such interest and decreased by any losses previously allowed to such holder as deductions and by any distributions such holder has previously received. Any loss that is not currently deductible by reason of the basis limitation may be used by such holder to offset his share of the REMIC's taxable income in later periods, but not otherwise.

Gain or loss from the sale of a residual interest will generally be capital gain or loss if the residual interest is held as a capital asset, except that if the holder is a bank or thrift institution, such gain or loss will always be ordinary.[131] In addition, under section 860F(d), and except as may be provided in Treasury regulations, to the extent that the seller of a REMIC residual interest reacquires such interest, or acquires any residual interest in another REMIC, an equity interest in an owner trust or other interest in a "taxable mortgage pool" (as defined on page 1061 above without regard to the January 1, 1992 effective date discussed therein) during the pe-

---

[131] *See* text accompanying footnote 147 below.

period beginning six months before and ending six months after the date of such sale, such sale will be treated as if it were a "wash sale" subject to section 1091.[132] Any loss realized in the "wash sale" would not be currently deductible, but, instead, would increase the seller's adjusted basis in the newly acquired interest.[133]

Phantom Income. The payments received on the mortgages held by a conduit issuer (net of administrative expenses) will be used for two purposes, to make payments on the bonds, and distributions to the equity owners. Thus, it would be possible to view those mortgages as consisting of two separate assets: the "bond related assets" consisting of the mortgage payments that will be used to make corresponding payments on the bonds,[134] and the "equity-related assets" consisting of the mortgage payments that will be used to make distributions on the equity interest.

As discussed above, the equity owners will be taxed based on the taxable income of the conduit issuer calculated by subtracting deductions allowed with respect to the bonds from the issuer's income from *all* of its assets. Thus, it would be possible to express the income reported in any taxable year by the equity owners as the sum of (i) the income of the conduit issuer attributable to the equity-related assets and (ii) a net amount of income or loss equal to the income of the conduit issuer attributable to the bond-related assets, less the deductions allowed with respect to the bonds. The net amount (positive or negative) described in clause (ii) in the

---

[132] Under section 1091 (without regard to section 860F(d)), loss arising from the sale of a security may be deferred if "substantially identical" securities are purchased within the period beginning 30 days before and ending 30 days after the date of sale.

[133] As discussed above, the taxable income allocable to the holder of a REMIC residual interest (and in certain circumstances the holder of an equity interest in an owner trust that is classified as a partnership) is not necessarily adjusted to reflect the holder's adjusted basis in the interest. Thus, the deferred loss would not necessarily be recovered over the life of the acquired interest but may be recognized only upon the disposition of that interest (subject to further application of the special wash sale rule if that interest is a REMIC residual interest).

[134] The conduit issuer may also have reinvestment earnings that are used to pay bonds and make equity distributions. The effect of reinvestment earnings on phantom income is considered below in footnote 136.

preceding sentence will be referred to herein as "bond-related income."

If the yield to maturity of the bond-related assets exceeds the initial weighted average yield to maturity of all of the bonds, then one component of bond-related income would be a net positive amount representing the economic profit resulting from the financing of the bond-related assets with the bonds. However, for reasons discussed below, bond-related income may also be increased in some periods by income that is not economic income because it necessarily will be matched by losses, reducing bond-related income, in other periods. Such noneconomic income or loss is sometimes labeled "phantom" income or loss. By definition, the phantom income and phantom losses recognized by an equity owner with respect to his equity interest in all taxable years (taking account of gain or loss from the disposition of such interest) must sum to zero.

In a typical offering of multiple class sequential pay bonds, some phantom income will be realized in the early years after the issuance of the bonds followed by a corresponding amount of phantom losses in subsequent years. The cause is a difference in the distribution over time of the yields that are used in calculating income and deductions.[135] In particular, deductions are calculated separately for each class of bonds, based on the yield to maturity of that class. Thus, the aggregate deductions allowed the conduit issuer in any year will be determined with reference to the weighted average yield of all classes of bonds outstanding in that year. With a rising yield curve, the yield to maturity is lower for earlier maturing classes of bonds than for later maturing classes. Thus, the weighted average yield to maturity of outstanding bonds increases over time as bonds are retired. By contrast, the

---

[135] For simplicity, it is assumed in the discussion below that income from the mortgages held by the conduit issuer is determined under a constant yield method similar to the PAC method, based on the yield to maturity of the mortgages calculated as if they were issued at the time they were purchased by the conduit issuer at a price equal to their cost to the conduit issuer. Similarly, it is assumed that deductions on the bonds are determined under the PAC method.

yield to maturity of the mortgages remains constant because they are not divided into sequential pay classes. The effect of using a fixed yield in calculating income and an escalating yield in calculating deductions is to skew deductions toward later years, producing the pattern of phantom income and losses described above.

The creation of phantom income may be illustrated with a simplified example. Consider a conduit issuer that purchases at par a $1,000 principal amount mortgage that bears interest at a rate of 10%, payable annually, and provides for two principal payments of $500, due one year and two years after the date of purchase, respectively. At the time of such purchase, the conduit issuer issues two bonds, each of which provides for a single principal payment of $500 at maturity. The first bond is issued at par, matures at the end of one year and earns interest at a rate of 8% payable at maturity. The second bond bears interest at a rate of 10% payable annually, matures at the end of two years, and is issued at a price of $491.44 to yield 11%. The conduit issuer will be required to make an equity investment of $8.56 to finance the purchase of the mortgage and will receive a cash distribution of $10 at the end of the first year and nothing thereafter, as shown in the following table.

| | Years from Bond Issuance | | |
	0	1	2
Mortgage Payments	($1,000.00)	$600	$550
Bond 1 Payments	500.00	(540)	-
Bond 2 Payments	491.44	(50)	(550)
Funds Available to Conduit Issuer	(8.56)	10	-

The taxable income of the conduit issuer, economic income and phantom income and loss for the two years that the bonds are outstanding are as follows:

	First Bond Year	Second Bond Year
Mortgage Income (10% of principal balance)	$100.00	$50.00
Deduction on Bond 1 (8% of principal balance)	(40.00)	-
Deduction on Bond 2 ($50 plus original issue discount of $4.06 in first year and $4.50 in second year)	(54.06)	(54.50)
Taxable Income (Loss) (mortgage income minus bond deductions)	5.94	(4.50)
Economic Income ($10 minus $8.66)	1.44	-
Phantom Income (Loss) (taxable income minus economic income)	4.50	(4.50)

Another way to describe the phantom income problem is that the owner of an equity interest is not permitted to amortize the cost of the interest directly against the cash distributions received—as would be permitted, for example, if the right to those distributions was treated for tax purposes as a debt obligation of the owner trust—but instead recovers the investment in the equity interest over a longer period. Thus, in the example above, although the equity interest in the conduit issuer becomes worthless following the distribution of the $10 payment at the end of the first year, the equity investor is permitted to treat as a return of capital in that year only $4.06 (the excess of the $10 distribution over taxable income of $5.94) rather than the full $8.56 cost of the equity interest.[136]

---

[136] A mismatch between the economic life of cash distributions and the period of cost recovery for tax purposes may also arise where the value of an equity interest is

1. Acceleration of net remaining phantom losses through sales of equity interests: When an equity interest is sold, the seller generally recognizes gain or loss equal to the difference between the amount realized in the sale and his adjusted basis in the interest. To the extent that the seller has recognized a net amount of phantom income, such adjusted basis would be increased without a corresponding increase in value. Accordingly, to that extent, the gain that otherwise would be realized from the sale would be decreased, or the loss would be increased. Consequently, the sale should in effect cause the acceleration of phantom losses that would otherwise be recognized over time. However, if the sale produces a loss, this result may not be achieved for two reasons. First, for most investors other than certain banks and thrifts, any loss realized on a sale of an equity interest will be a capital loss that, in general, can be offset only against capital gain.[137] Further, a loss recognized upon the sale of a REMIC residual interest may be deferred under the special REMIC "wash sale" rule discussed above.

2. Special rules for REMICs: In the case of a conduit issuer that is a REMIC, any phantom income is taxable to the holders of the residual interests. However, in contrast to the rules for equity interests in owner trusts, there is no tax requirement that a REMIC residual interest have any minimum economic value. Further, because phantom income is not economic income, a residual interest could produce substantial phantom income without having any eco-

---

attributable in part to a right to receive earnings of the conduit issuer from the reinvestment of mortgage payments. Although the right to receive distributions of such earnings may be viewed as an asset from the perspective of the equity investor, future reinvestment earnings would not be recognized to be a separate asset of the conduit issuer for tax purposes. Accordingly, the portion of the cost of the equity interest that is attributable to reinvestment earnings generally would be treated as an additional amount paid for the mortgages held by the conduit issuer and would be recovered over the life of the mortgages (rather than over the life of the reinvestment earnings stream).

[137] As noted above, a loss may be a capital loss even for banks and thrifts if the conduit issuer is an owner trust that is classified as a partnership. In the case of taxpayers other than corporations, capital losses may be used to offset up to $3,000 of ordinary income.

nomic value. Accordingly, absent special rules, the tax on phantom income associated with residual interests could be avoided easily by reducing the economic values of those interests and transferring them (and their related tax liability) to investors that are tax-exempt, or that are not currently paying federal income tax (for example, because they have net operating loss carryovers) whether or not they would ordinarily invest in mortgage securities. In order to frustrate such tax avoidance, a specified portion of the income from a residual interest, referred to as an "excess inclusion," is, with an exception discussed below for certain thrift institutions, subject to federal income taxation in all events. Thus, for example, an excess inclusion with respect to a residual interest (i) may not, except as described below, be offset by any unrelated losses or loss carryovers of an owner of such interest,[138] (ii) will be treated as unrelated business taxable income, and thus subject to tax if such owner is a pension fund or other organization that is subject to tax only on its unrelated business taxable income, and (iii) is not eligible for any reduction in the rate of withholding tax if such owner is a foreign investor, as further discussed later in this chapter.

In general terms, the excess inclusion with respect to a residual interest for a calendar quarter equals the excess of the income for that quarter from the holding of the residual interest over the income that would have accrued on that interest in that quarter if such interest had earned income at all times from its issuance through the end of such quarter at a constant, compounded rate equal to 120% of a long-term U.S. Treasury borrowing rate for the month in which the residual interest was issued.[139]

---

[138] This result is accomplished by providing in section 860E(a)(1) that the taxable income of the holder of a residual interest for any taxable year shall not be less than the excess inclusion for such year. Apparently, it would be possible to offset the resulting tax with any available credits, since they would not affect taxable income.

[139] More precisely, with respect to any holder of a REMIC residual interest, the excess inclusion for any calendar quarter is the excess, if any, of (i) the income of such holder for that calendar quarter from the residual interest, representing a share of the taxable income of the REMIC, over (ii) the sum of the "daily accruals" (as defined below) for all days during the calendar quarter on which the holder holds such residual interest. For this purpose, the daily accruals with respect to a residual interest are determined

As an exception to the general rule described above, the Treasury has authority to issue regulations to treat all income from the holding of REMIC residual interest as an excess inclusion, if the residual interest is considered not to have "significant value." However, no such regulations have been proposed. In addition, certain thrift institutions are now exempted from the rule (discussed above) that prevents excess inclusions from being offset with unrelated losses. However, the Treasury has authority to issue regulations (which may be retroactive) that would subject thrifts to that rule where necessary or appropriate to prevent the avoidance of tax. The legislative history of TRA 1986 indicates that none of the foregoing regulations will apply to a REMIC if the aggregate value of the residual interest equals at least 2% of the aggregate value of the residual interest and the regular interests. Under regulations recently proposed by the Internal Revenue Service, the excess inclusion rules will generally apply to a residual interest acquired by a thrift on or after September 27, 1991, unless (i) the aggregate issue price of the residual interest is at least equal to 2% of the aggregate issue price of all interests in the REMIC and (ii) the residual interest has at least a certain mini-

---

by allocating to each day in the calendar quarter its ratable portion of the product of the "adjusted issue price" (as defined below) of the residual interest at the beginning of the calendar quarter and 120% of the "Federal long-term rate" in effect at the time the residual interest was issued. For this purpose, the "adjusted issue price" of a residual interest at the beginning of any calendar quarter equals the issue price of the residual interest, increased by the amount of daily accruals for all prior quarters, and decreased (but not below zero) by the aggregate amount of payments made on the residual interest before the beginning of such quarter. The Federal long-term rate is an average of current yields on Treasury securities with a remaining term of greater than nine years, computed and published monthly by the Internal Revenue Service.

A (hopefully) unintended result of the definition of excess inclusion is that the amount of income that is treated as phantom income increases as the amount of economic income increases above 120% of the Federal long-term rate. For example, suppose that the Federal long-term rate is 10%, that the yield on a residual interest is 20%, and cash is distributed each year with respect to that interest equal to the economic income accruing in that year. Even if phantom income was virtually nonexistent (*e.g.*, because there was only one class of regular interests), income earned in excess of 12% of the adjusted issue price would be treated as an excess inclusion and, when distributed, would reduce the adjusted issue price for purposes of calculating excess inclusion in later periods.

mum economic life.[140] The Internal Revenue Service has also proposed a rule under which the transfer of certain residual interests would be ignored (leaving the associated tax liability with the transferor) unless no significant purpose of the transfer was to impede the assessment or collection of tax (for example, the transfer to a shell corporation of a residual interest when it is expected that the corporation will not have sufficient funds, from the residual interest or otherwise, to pay the associated tax liability).[141]

Special Rules For Certain Institutional Investors

Under section 7701(a)(19)(C), thrift institutions are required to hold a minimum percentage of their assets in certain investments, including residential real property loans, in order to qualify for special bad debt reserve deductions under section 593.[142] Similarly, a real estate investment trust ("REIT") will be eligible to deduct dividends paid to shareholders only if it holds a large percentage of its assets in the form of real property assets, including real property loans (*see* section 856(c)(3) and (5)). In general, pay-through bonds do not qualify as real property loans for these purposes, because they are not directly secured by real property (but only by other debt instruments that are so secured). Most pass-through certificates do so qualify to the extent the underlying mortgages are qualifying loans, because the holders of such certificates are treated for tax purposes as the owners of the underlying

---

[140] Proposed REMIC Regulations § 1.860E-1(a)(iii).

[141] Proposed REMIC Regulations § 1.860E-1(c).

[142] Prior to TRA 1986, a qualifying thrift was allowed to deduct up to 32% (40% reduced by 20% under section 291) of its taxable income as an addition to its bad debt reserves under section 593. While the maximum deduction for additions to bad debt reserves under the percentage of taxable income method was reduced under TRA 1986 to only 8% of taxable income, it may continue to be important for other reasons for a thrift to meet the asset test for qualification under section 593. For example, a thrift that fails to meet the requirement and that has more than $500 million in assets would not be permitted to use any reserve method for calculating bad debt deductions, would be required to recapture existing bad debt reserves under section 585(c), and would not be able to take advantage of the "thrift" exception" to the excess inclusion rules.

loans.[143] A REIT that owns an equity interest in an owner trust is considered to own real property assets to the extent the assets underlying the trust are qualifying assets; arguably, the same should be true for thrifts but the matter is not entirely certain.[144]

Both regular interests and residual interests in REMICs are qualifying assets for thrifts and REITs to the same extent that the assets of the REMIC are qualifying assets. However, if 95% or more of the assets of the REMIC are qualifying assets at all times during a calendar year, then the regular interests and the residual interests will be considered qualifying assets in their entirety for that year.[145]

---

[143] There is some uncertainty regarding whether IO Strips and other pass-through certificates that represent a right to a disproportionately high amount of interest qualify as interests in residential real property loans and real estate assets. IO Strips should qualify as real estate assets for REITS because IO Strips are "interests in" mortgages. The treatment of IO Strips as residential real property loans is less certain but most tax practitioners believe they should qualify. The uncertainty arises because of doubt as to whether an IO Strip can be considered a loan given that all or substantially all of the payments thereon are contingent on the absence of prepayments. *But cf.* Treasury Regulation § 301.7701-13(l)(2)(v) (unamortized premium is considered part of the acquisition cost of a mortgage loan for purposes of section 7701(a)(19)(C)).

[144] As noted above, an owner trust may be classified as a grantor trust or as a partnership. If an owner trust is classified as a grantor trust, thrift and REIT investors in the equity of the trust would be treated as if they owned the underlying mortgage loans directly. The same would be true for a REIT if the owner trust is classified as a partnership because under Treasury Regulation § 1.856-3(g), a REIT is considered to own directly its proportionate share of the assets of a partnership of which it is a partner. No similar regulation applies to thrifts. Thus, it is uncertain whether an investment by a thrift in an owner trust would be treated as an investment in the underlying assets if the trust is classified as a partnership.

Treasury Regulation § 1.856-3(g) would appear to permit a REIT to treat its share of the gross assets of an owner trust as real property assets and not limit such treatment to the fair market value of the equity interest held by the REIT.

[145] As noted above, the assets of a REMIC may include, in addition to qualified mortgages, cash flow investments, qualified reserve funds and foreclosure property. Under section 7701(a)(19)(C), in addition to residential real property loans, cash, time or demand deposits, obligations of the United States or instrumentalities of the United States and certain other assets are qualifying assets for thrifts. Proposed REMIC Regulations §§ 1.593-11(e)(2)(ii) and 1.856-3(b)(2)(ii)(B) provide that cash flow investments are treated as qualifying real property loans and real estate assets, respectively for thrifts and REITs. REMIC residual interests are treated as real property assets only to the extent of their fair market value. *Compare* footnote 144, above.

Qualified pension plans, charitable institutions and certain other entities that are otherwise exempt from federal income taxation are nonetheless subject to tax on their unrelated business taxable income ("UBTI"). Although UBTI generally does not include interest income or gain from the sale of investment property, such income is included in UBTI to the extent that it is derived from property that is debt-financed. Because an equity interest in an owner trust is generally viewed for tax purposes as an interest in the mortgage collateral that is financed with the related bonds, it appears that substantially all of the income on such an interest would be subject to tax in the hands of such investors even if the equity interest itself is not debt-financed. In the case of a REMIC residual interest, under section 860E, any amount that is an "excess inclusion" is deemed to be UBTI in the hands of a tax-exempt investor that is subject to tax on UBTI.[146]

The general rules of the Code relating to the accrual of discount and the amortization of premium on debt securities do not apply to life insurance companies. Under section 811(b), they are generally required to take discount into account under the method which they regularly employ in maintaining their books, if such method is reasonable and are effectively required to make an election under section 171 to amortize premium.

Under section 582(c), certain banks and thrift institutions are required to report gain or loss from the sale of an "evidence of indebtedness" as ordinary income or loss. In general, mortgage-backed securities are considered evidences of indebtedness whether in the form of pass-through certificates or pay-through bonds. Both regular and residual interests in REMICs are considered evidences of indebtedness for this purpose.[147]

---

[146] Income from a residual interest that is not an "excess inclusion," as well as income from pass-through certificates, pay-through bonds and REMIC regular interests, should not be considered UBTI, unless the security is itself debt-financed.

[147] Revenue rulings and Treasury regulations authorize mutual savings banks, building and loan associations and cooperative banks to amortize mortgage premiums and discounts on a composite basis (i.e., ratably over an assumed average life of the loans). Revenue Ruling 54-367, 1954-2 C.B. 109; Revenue Ruling 216, 1953-2 C.B. 38, and Treasury Regulation § 1.1016-9(c). It appears that the TRA 1984 and TRA 1986

Special Rules for Foreign Investors

A principal tax objective of non-U.S. investors purchasing mort-gage-backed securities issued in the United States is to avoid the U.S. 30% withholding tax on interest income. A second goal may be to hold such securities in bearer (as distinguished from regis-tered) form.[148] The first two parts of this section discuss the TE-FRA registration requirements that limit the issuance of debt instruments in bearer form and the withholding tax. The section concludes with a brief comment on the implications for mortgage-backed securities of the Foreign Investment in Real Property Tax Act of 1980.

TEFRA Registration Requirements.   With a view to increasing taxpayer compliance, the Tax Equity and Fiscal Responsibility Act of 1982 ("TEFRA") amended the Code to effectively prohibit, with limited exceptions, the issuance or holding of debt obligations in the United States in bearer form. More particularly, the TEFRA rules require all registration-required obligations (as defined below) to be in registered form. An obligation is in registered form for these purposes if (1) it is registered as to both principal and interest with the issuer or its agent, and can be transferred only by the surrender of the old obligation to the registrar and either its reissuance, or the issuance of a new obligation, to the new owner, or (2) principal and interest may be transferred only through a book entry system maintained by the issuer or its agent.[149] Any obligation that is not in registered form is considered to be in bearer form.[150]

---

amendments would supersede these earlier authorities to the extent they produce conflicting results.

[148] The TEFRA registration requirements are tax-related and distinct from any need to register securities with the Securities and Exchange Commission or state agencies under U.S. securities laws.

[149] Treasury Regulation § 5f.103-1(c)(1).

[150] Treasury Regulation § 5f.103-1(e). An obligation is considered to be in bearer form if it is currently in bearer form, or if there is a right to convert it into bearer form at any time during the remaining period that it is outstanding.

The issuance of a registration-required obligation in bearer form can result in severe issuer sanctions.[151] Any U.S. taxpayer that holds an obligation in bearer form in violation of the TEFRA rules is also subject to certain tax penalties.[152]

A registration-required obligation is defined in section 163(f)(2) as any obligation other than an obligation that (1) is issued by an individual, (2) is not of a type offered to the public,[153] or (3) has a maturity at issue of not more than one year. Thus, the TEFRA registration requirements do not apply directly to home mortgages and other consumer loans that are obligations of individuals. In fact, such obligations are almost never issued or held in registered form.[154]

In addition, for purposes of applying the issuer sanctions only, an obligation is not registration required if it is issued under the so-called Eurobond exception, which allows bearer paper to be of-

---

[151] The issuer of a registration-required obligation in bearer form is liable for an excise tax equal to the product of 1% of the principal amount of the obligation and the number of calendar years (or portions thereof) from its issue date to its maturity date (section 4701). Also, the issuer is not permitted to deduct interest paid on the obligation in computing taxable income or earnings and profits (sections 163(f) and 312(m)).

[152] In general, the holder of a registration-required obligation in bearer form is denied deductions for any loss from the obligation (section 165(j)), and any gain from the obligation that otherwise would be capital gain is converted into ordinary income (section 1287). The conversion of capital gain to ordinary income is of little significance to most taxpayers because there is a preferential rate for long-term capital gain only for certain individual investors. The holder sanctions apply to an obligation only if the issuer was not subject to the section 4701 excise tax (*see* footnote 151), and thus are generally a concern only for debt obligations that were issued under the Eurobond exception described later in the text. Furthermore, the holder sanctions do not apply if one of the four exceptions set forth in Treasury Regulation § 1.165-12(c) applies. These exceptions relate to obligations (1) held by certain financial institutions in connection with a trade or business, (2) held by certain financial institutions for their own investment account, (3) held through a financial institution which reports information with respect to the obligations to the Internal Revenue Service, or (4) that are promptly converted to registered form.

[153] An obligation is considered to be "of a type" offered to the public if similar obligations are in fact publicly offered or traded, whether or not the obligation itself is publicly offered or privately placed. *See* Treasury Regulation § 5f.103-1(b)(1) and (f), Example (3).

[154] Such obligations would also typically not be of a type offered to the public. *See* footnote 153. A note that can be assigned by the holder merely by endorsement, without notifying the issuer or its agent, is not in registered form. Most consumer loans, including residential mortgages, are assignable in this manner.

fered outside of the United States to non-U.S. investors.[155] In general, an obligation qualifies for the Eurobond exception if (1) the obligation is "targeted" to non-U.S. investors upon its original issuance,[156] (2) the obligation provides for interest to be payable only outside the United States, and (3) for any period during which the obligation is held in definitive bearer form, the obligation and each coupon contains a TEFRA legend.[157] However, U.S. government, or U.S. government-backed, securities can never be issued in bearer form.[158] For this purpose, a U.S. government security is any security issued or guaranteed by the United States or any U.S.-owned or -sponsored agency, including, for example, GNMA, FNMA and FHLMC. A security is U.S. government-backed if more than 50% of the income or collateral supporting it (whether as an asset underlying a pass-through certificate or as collateral for a debt obligation) consists of income, or principal, of a U.S. government security. Thus, any pass-through certificates guaranteed by the U.S. or a U.S.-sponsored agency, and pay-through bonds more than 50% collateralized by such certificates, may not be issued in bearer form.

---

[155] The Eurobond exception is set forth in section 163(f)(2)(B) and described in detail in Treasury Regulation § 1.163-5(c). Tax sanctions apply to certain U.S. taxpayers that hold in bearer form obligations issued under the Eurobond exception. *See* footnote 152.

[156] In the language of the statute, there must be "arrangements reasonably designed to ensure" that the obligation "will be sold (or resold) in connection with its original issuance only to a person who is not a United States person." *See* section 163(f)(2)(B)(i). To satisfy the arrangements test issuers of Eurobonds generally must satisfy detailed restrictions on offers, sales and deliveries of the securities during an initial "seasoning" period and obtain certification as to the non-U.S. status of investors. *See* Treasury Regulation § 1.163-5(c)(2)(i)(D).

[157] The TEFRA legend is a statement to the effect that any United States person who holds the obligation will be subject to the TEFRA holder sanctions. *See* Treasury Regulation § 1.163-5(c)(1)(ii)(B).

[158] Treasury Regulation § 1.163-5(c)(1) states that the Eurobond exception does not apply to U.S. government securities. While the existing regulations do not preclude use of the exception for privately issued securities that are backed by government or agencies securities, the Treasury has announced that regulations will be issued prohibiting the issuance, after September 7, 1984, of such securities in bearer form. *See* Treasury Department News Releases R-2835, September 10, 1984, and R-2847, September 14, 1984. The definition of U.S. government-backed securities given in the text is taken from these releases.

Although an obligation issued or backed by the U.S. government may not be held in bearer form, it can be held in targeted registered form if it was targeted to foreign investors upon its original issuance.[159] Targeted registered obligations are considered to be in registered form for purposes of the TEFRA requirements and accordingly may freely be resold to U.S. investors. As discussed below, the certification requirements that must be met by a foreign investor to receive interest on a registered obligation free of U.S. withholding tax under the portfolio interest exemption are more lenient for a targeted than a non-targeted obligation.

1. Mortgage-backed securities: The TEFRA rules apply in a straight-forward way to pay-through bonds and REMIC regular interests.[160] They are registration-required obligations and must be issued in registered form unless the Eurobond exception applies.[161] Although REMIC residual interests are probably not "obligations" for TEFRA purposes, as a practical matter they cannot be issued in bearer form without jeopardizing the issuer's status as a REMIC.[162]

The treatment of pass-through certificates under the TEFRA rules is more complex. As described earlier in this chapter, for substantive tax purposes, pass-through certificates are not recognized to be debt of the issuing trust; instead, they merely evidence ownership of trust assets by certificate holders. If this analysis

---

[159] The "targeting" requirements that must be met in order for an obligation to qualify to be held in targeted registered form are described in Treasury Regulation § 35a.9999-5(b), Q & A-13.

[160] Section 860B(a) treats a REMIC regular interest (if not otherwise a debt instrument) as a debt instrument "[i]n determining the tax under this chapter of any holder of a regular interest." While this language does not unequivocally state that a regular interest will be treated as an "obligation" for purposes of the TEFRA registration requirements, it would require great courage to put that proposition to the test.

[161] The statement in the text assumes that the pay-through bonds and regular interests in question are publicly offered (or obligations of a type that is publicly offered) and have an original term greater than one year.

[162] See the last paragraph under "REMIC Qualification Tests" above. A REMIC residual interest would not be treated as a single obligation under the regulations dealing with pass-through certificates described below in the text, because a REMIC is not a grantor trust.

were followed in applying the TEFRA rules, then pass-through certificates would not themselves be "obligations" that could be "registration-required." Further, registration of the certificates could not be mandated on the ground that they represent owner-ship interests in registration-required obligations if the underlying obligations are obligations of individuals or loans not of a type offered to the public. However, it would make little sense to ex-clude pass-through certificates from the reach of the TEFRA rules. They are generally liquid securities similar to traded debt instru-ments. In addition, if the status of a pass-through certificate under the TEFRA rules depended solely on the status of the underlying obligations, it would not be possible to issue bearer certificates un-der the Eurobond exception if the trust assets included any regis-tration-required obligations.

These unsettling results are avoided under regulations origi-nally issued in 1985 that effectively treat each "pass-through cer-tificate" (as defined in the regulations) itself as an "obligation" for TEFRA purposes.[163] Thus, the nature of the underlying obligations is irrelevant in applying the TEFRA rules to such certificates.[164] The certificates must be in registered form unless the Eurobond exception applies based on an offering of the certificates (as distin-guished from the obligations held by the trust) outside of the United States.[165]

---

[163] Treasury Regulation § 1.163-5T(d) (rules applying definition of registration-required obligation to pass-through certificates); Treasury Regulation § 35a.9999-5(e) (application of portfolio interest exemption, described in Part B, to pass-through certificates). These regulations were anticipated by the Joint Committee on Taxation, General Explanation of the Deficit Reduction Act of 1984 (JCT-41-84) 396, footnote 19 and accompanying text. Treasury Regulation § 1.163-5T(d) was accidentally repealed by T.D. 8110, 1987-1 C.B. 81, but was then retroactively reinstated by T.D. 8202, 1988-1 C.B. 78.

[164] In addition, if the assets of the trust include registration-required obligations in registered form, those obligations will not be considered to be improperly converted into bearer form because the trust issues bearer pass-through certificates under the Eurobond exception. Treasury Regulation § 1.163-5T(d)(2).

[165] This statement assumes, as would normally be the case, that the certificates, viewed as trust obligations, are registration-required because they are of a type offered to the public and have a maturity at issue of more than one year. For purposes of applying the section 4701 excise tax on issuers that violate the TEFRA registration requirements, the "issuer" of a pass-through certificate is considered to be the

The regulations define a "pass-through certificate" as a "pass-through or participation certificate evidencing an interest in a *pool* of mortgage loans" (emphasis added) to which the grantor trust rules apply, or a "similar evidence of interest in a similar pooled fund or pooled trust treated as a grantor trust."[166] An example in the regulations concludes that certificates of interest in a trust that holds 1000 residential mortgages that are obligations of unrelated individuals are "pass-through certificates."[167] Thus, the 1000 mortgages are considered a "pool."

The regulations also grant the Internal Revenue Service broad authority to characterize pass-through securities "in accordance with the substance of the arrangement which they represent" and to impose issuer sanctions accordingly.[168] The regulations indicate that this authority might be used to prevent a domestically offered bond from being issued indirectly in bearer form by issuing the bond in registered form to a trust that issues bearer pass-through securities.

Apart from the example of a trust holding 1000 residential mortgages, the regulations offer no guidance on the distinction between an interest in a "pool" of loans and pass-through securities that are subject to characterization "in accordance with the substance of the arrangement they represent." Nonetheless, applying the regulations to pass-through securities representing interests in residential mortgages should be straightforward. The regulations were apparently written with these securities in mind, and any group of home mortgages large enough to be grouped and used to support a pass-through security should qualify as a pool, even if the number of loans is significantly below 1000. On the other hand, suppose that a trust holds five commercial mortgage loans, each of which has a principal balance in excess of $5 million. It is much less obvious that those loans would be considered a pool.

---

recipient of the proceeds from issuance of the certificate. Treasury Regulation § 1.163-5T(d)(3).

[166] Treasury Regulation § 1.163-5T(d)(1).

[167] Treasury Regulation § 1.163-5T(d)(6).

[168] Treasury Regulation § 1.163-5T(d)(4).

Some guidance about the factors that may be relevant in determining whether a pool exists can be gleaned from an examination of typical residential mortgage pass-through securities, if they are taken as the clearest example of a pass-through certificate within the meaning of the regulations. Home mortgages have a number of characteristics that make them unattractive as direct investments. First, the creditworthiness of individual borrowers is unknown. Second, because of the possibility of prepayment, the cash flow from a single loan is unpredictable. Finally, any one loan is too small to make it divisible into units suitable for public trading. A pass-through arrangement addresses these problems by combining many home mortgages in a trust, adding insurance, a guarantee or other credit support, and creating trust interests in relatively small denominations. The aggregation of many mortgages evens out cash flows and credit risk from the perspective of any one investor; the credit support further simplifies the credit analysis; and the size of the pool enables the pass-through securities to trade actively in public markets. Thus, an analysis of these securities suggests that a group of loans held by a trust should be considered a pool (and interests in the trust should be treated as pass-through certificates within the meaning of the regulations) if individual interests in the trust are qualitatively different from the underlying loans by virtue of differences in predictability of payments, credit risk, and liquidity.

Withholding Tax. In general, a non-U.S. investor[169] that receives interest income from U.S. sources is subject to a 30% tax on the

---

[169] It is assumed in this part that the non-U.S. investor has no connection with the United States other than the holding of the mortgage-backed security under discussion, and in particular does not hold the security in connection with a U.S. trade or business conducted directly by the investor. For discussion of whether owner trusts are engaged in a trade or business, *see* footnote 178. It is generally assumed that the holders of pass-through certificates are not engaged in a trade or business because of the activities of the servicer of the underlying mortgages. The regulations applying the portfolio interest exemption to pass-through certificates (*see* text accompanying footnotes 183-184 below) would be nonsensical if this assumption were not true. Gain from the sale or exchange of a security is not subject to withholding tax because it is not the type of "fixed or determinable annual or periodical" income to which the tax

gross amount of such income,[170] unless the income is "portfolio interest" that benefits from the tax exemption described below, or the tax is reduced or eliminated under an income tax treaty between the U.S. and the country of residence of the investor. The tax is required to be collected and paid over to the Internal Revenue Service by any withholding agent in the chain of payment (generally, any person that pays the interest to a non-U.S. person), but is due whether or not it is collected by withholding.[171]

The source of interest income depends on the status of the borrower. Interest is generally U.S. source if the borrower is organized or resident in the U.S.[172] Thus, interest on pass-through certificates representing an ownership interest in home mortgages that are obligations of U.S. resident individuals, and interest on pay-through bonds issued by a U.S. corporation or owner trust,

---

applies. See Treasury Regulation § 1.1441-2(a)(3). However, as described in footnote 170, withholding tax that applies original issue discount is imposed at the time of a sale or exchange to the extent not previously imposed. Gain that is treated as interest for most tax purposes under the market discount rules introduced by TRA 1984 is not treated as interest for purposes of the withholding tax.

[170] The tax is imposed by sections 871 (individuals) and 881 (corporations). With an exception for obligations with an original term of 183 days or less, accrued original issue discount earned by a non-U.S. investor is generally subject to the tax in the same manner as other interest income. However, the tax is imposed on the original issue discount on an obligation only when (1) a payment on the obligation is made, in an amount not exceeding the lesser of (a) the total amount of tax on the accrued portion of such discount not previously taken into account and (b) the amount of the payment (net of any withholding tax imposed on the payment) or (2) the obligation is sold or exchanged, in an amount equal to the total amount of tax on the accrued portion of such discount not previously taken into account. For this purpose, accruals of original issue discount are calculated in the same manner as for domestic taxpayers with an exception for short-term obligations. See sections 871(a)(1)(C) and (g) and 881(a)(3). Until regulations are adopted, only the issuer of an obligation and its agents are required to withhold the tax on accrued original issue discount from the proceeds of a sale or exchange of the obligation under section 1441 or 1442 (described in footnote 171 and accompanying text). See Revenue Ruling 68-333, 1968-1 C.B. 390. Regulations imposing a broader withholding requirement have been proposed but not adopted (Proposed Treasury Regulation § 1.1441-3(c)(6)).

[171] The obligation of a withholding agent to withhold tax is imposed under section 1441 or 1442. A withholding agent may treat the payment as exempt from withholding, or may withhold at a reduced rate, in reliance on a treaty only if it receives an IRS Form 1001 from the foreign investor stating that the investor is eligible for the exception. Such a form is generally effective for three calendar years. See Treasury Regulation § 1.1441-6.

[172] See section 861(a)(1).

typically would be sourced in the United States.[173] Although there is no explicit source rule for REMIC interests, it is highly likely that income from both regular and residual interests would be sourced in the United States if the issuing REMIC is organized and operated in the U.S. and the underlying mortgages are obligations of U.S. borrowers. Apart from the source question, the withholding tax applies to REMIC regular interests in the same way that it applies to conventional debt obligations.

Income on a REMIC residual interest representing a share of the REMIC's taxable income is treated as interest for withholding tax purposes.[174] However, no exemption from such tax or reduction in rate applies to the portion of the income from a residual interest that is an excess inclusion.[175] The withholding tax is generally imposed on income from a residual interest when such income is paid or distributed (or when the interest is disposed of),[176] but such income may have to be taken into account earlier, under regulations, if the residual interest does not have significant value.[177]

---

[173] However, the source of interest paid by an owner trust that is classified as a grantor trust may depend on the residence or place of organization of the trust beneficiaries.

[174] Conference Report at II-237 - II-238; Blue Book at 425.

[175] See section 860G(b)(2).

[176] See section 860G(b). The Conference Report at II-236, footnote 18, and the Blue Book at 423, footnote 85, state that withholding upon disposition of residual interests is to be similar to withholding upon disposition of instruments having original issue discount. See footnote 170 above. Curiously, section 860G(b) applies by its terms only to holders of residual interests that are nonresident alien individuals or foreign corporations (and thus, for example, would not literally apply to a holder that is a foreign partnership). Compare section 1441.

[177] Section 860G(b), last sentence, states that regulations may accelerate the time when income is taken into account "where necessary or appropriate to prevent the avoidance of tax imposed by this chapter." The Conference Report at II-235 - II-236 and the Blue Book at 423 indicate that this standard may be met where a residual interest does not have significant value, and that a residual interest will be considered to have significant value if it meets the 2% test referred to in the text. Proposed REMIC Regulations § 1.860G-3(a) would disregard transfers of certain residual interests to foreigners (and thus the transferor would continue to be subject to tax on the income from the REMIC), where the transfer would be expected to result in the excess inclusions not being effectively taxed.

For withholding tax purposes, the holder of an equity interest in an owner trust, whether taxable as a grantor trust or as a partnership, is treated essentially as if he owned directly the underlying mortgages and other trust assets.[178] Thus, the 30% tax, to the extent it applies, is based on the gross amount of interest received by the trust (that is, without a deduction for interest payments made on the related bonds). For that reason, it is unlikely that a foreign investor would purchase an equity interest in such a trust unless the investor is certain that all interest received by the trust will be exempt from withholding tax, either as portfolio interest or under a tax treaty.[179]

Under sections 871(h) and 881(c), enacted by TRA 1984, interest on obligations issued after July 18, 1984 (the date of enactment of TRA 1984) is exempt from withholding tax if such interest qualifies as portfolio interest. With limited exceptions, most significantly for payments to certain related parties,[180] interest on an

---

[178] See Treasury Regulation § 1.1441-3(f). If the activities of an owner trust amounted to a trade or business, then a foreign holder of an equity interest would be considered to be engaged in that trade or business (see section 875) and would be taxed at the rates applicable to U.S. taxpayers on his share of the taxable income of the trust (see sections 871(b) and 882). It is very unlikely that a typical owner trust would be considered to be engaged in a trade or business. See Higgins v. Comm'r, 312 U.S. 212 (1940) (management of investments not a trade or business), recently reaffirmed in Comm'r v. Groetzinger, 480 U.S. 23, 107 S. Ct. 980 (1987); Continental Trading, Inc. v. Comm'r, 265 F.2d 40 (9th Cir. 1949) (foreign corporation that borrowed in connection with holding U.S. stocks and securities was not engaged in a U.S. trade or business). Consider also the possible application of section 864(b)(2) (statutory exception from the definition of trade or business for certain securities trading activities).

[179] Even if the investor is entitled to such an exemption, there would still be a withholding obligation if the investor failed to supply the withholding agent with any necessary certifications. See footnotes 171 and 181. If tax is required to be withheld from gross income allocable to a foreign investor's equity interest, distributions to that investor might not be sufficient to pay the tax. Because any shortfall might be collected from distributions to other equity owners, they would have a substantial interest in ensuring that there are adequate safeguards to prevent the tax from being withheld.

[180] Portfolio interest does not include (1) any interest paid by a corporation to a 10% shareholder (measured by voting power) or by a partnership to a 10% partner (measured by the higher of the capital or profits interest), or interest paid to a controlled foreign corporation related to the payor, or (2) except in the case of interest paid on an obligation of the United States, interest paid to a bank on an extension of credit pursuant to a loan agreement entered into in the ordinary course of its trade or business. See sections 871(h)(3) and 881(c)(3). For the application of the exception for 10% owners to pass-through certificates and to pay-through bonds and REMIC

obligation (including original issue discount) is portfolio interest if (1) the obligation is in bearer form, and was issued in compliance with the Eurobond exception to the TEFRA registration requirements described above, or (2) the obligation is in registered form, and the beneficial owner provides the withholding agent with a statement, signed under penalties of perjury, giving the owner's name and address and certifying that the owner is not a United States person.[181] In the case of an obligation issued in "targeted registered" form, a more lenient certification procedure applies if the obligation is held through an appropriate foreign financial institution. In such a case, the financial institution need only certify that the beneficial owner of the obligation is not a United States person, without disclosing the beneficial owner's identity.[182]

The portfolio interest exemption applies in different ways to pass-through certificates,[183] pay-through bonds and REMIC regular interests, equity interests in owner trusts and REMIC residual interests.

Prior to the issuance in 1985 of regulations applying the TEFRA registration requirements to pass-through certificates, it was unclear whether interest paid to non-U.S. investors on residential mortgage pass-through certificates could qualify as portfolio interest. Home mortgages are typically held in bearer form.[184] However, interest on a bearer obligation can qualify as portfolio

---

regular interests, see footnotes 185 and 187, respectively.

[181] Such statements are made on IRS Form W-8. See Treasury Regulation § 35a.9999-5(b), Q & A-9.

[182] The more lenient certification requirements are described in Treasury Regulation § 35a.9999-5(b), Q & A-14. Foreign financial institutions that are eligible to provide the more limited certifications include banks and other financial institutions that hold customers' securities in the ordinary course of their trade or business. The reduced certification requirements apply for any period during which an obligation originally issued in targeted registered form is held by a qualifying foreign financial institution, whether or not the obligation has been held continuously since issuance by such an institution.

[183] See the text at footnote 163.

[184] See footnote 154. Moreover, Treasury Regulation § 35a.9999-5, Q & A-8 adopted by T.D. 7967, 1984-2 C.B. 329, took the position that interest on an obligation in registered form could not qualify as portfolio interest unless the obligation was a registration-required obligation. This position was abandoned in an amended version of Q & A-8 adopted by T.D. 8111, 1987-1 C.B. 69.

interest only if the obligation was issued under the Eurobond exception, which would not be true for such mortgages. Thus, interest on residential mortgages, and apparently therefore interest on pass-through certificates representing ownership interests in those mortgages, could not have been portfolio interest.

The 1985 regulations solved this problem by treating pass-through certificates themselves as obligations for purposes of the TEFRA rules. Under the regulations, interest on a pass-through certificate can qualify as portfolio interest if (1) the certificate itself is in bearer form and was issued under the Eurobond exception, or (2) the certificate is in registered form and the appropriate investor certification is received, in each case without regard to the status of the underlying obligations.[185] However, a pass-through certificate continues to be treated as an ownership interest in trust assets for other tax purposes, including application of the effective date of the portfolio interest rules. Accordingly, interest on a pass-through certificate can be exempt from withholding tax as portfolio interest only to the extent that the mortgages backing the certificate were originated after July 18, 1984.[186]

Pay-through bonds and REMIC regular interests are considered debt instruments in their own right and thus can qualify for the portfolio interest exemption (assuming, in the case of pay-through bonds, an issue date after July 18, 1984) regardless of the date of origination of the underlying mortgages or mortgage-backed securities.[187]

---

[185] Treasury Regulation § 35a.9999-5(e). Because neither the issuing trust nor the obligors on the underlying residential mortgages would be corporations or partnerships, the exception to the portfolio interest exemption for 10% owners and related controlled foreign corporations (see footnote 180) would not pose a problem.

[186] Treasury Regulation § 35a.9999-5(e), Q & A-21, Q & A-22. Although in theory interest on a pass-through certificate should always be traced to each of the underlying mortgage loans to determine the percentage of the interest that is portfolio interest, hopefully, the Internal Revenue Service will permit simplifying assumptions to be made (such as an assumption that a fixed portion of the interest on a certificate is portfolio interest, equal to the portion by principal amount of all mortgages backing the certificate at the time of its issuance that were originated after July 18, 1984).

[187] For the treatment of REMIC regular interests, see section 860B(a); Treasury Regulation § 35a.9999-5(e), Q & A-21(ii). As described in footnote 180, the portfolio interest exemption does not apply to interest paid by a corporation or partnership to a 10%

Interest earned by an owner trust that is allocable to an equity interest held by a foreign investor should be eligible for the portfolio interest exemption to the same extent as if such interest were received directly by the foreign investor.[188] Thus, assuming that the investor provides appropriate certifications to the owner trustee or possibly other withholding agents, such interest should be tax free to the extent it is earned on mortgages or other obligations issued after July 18, 1984 (with the possible exception of interest on certain short-term obligations in bearer form).[189] Amounts

---

owner. Thus, the exemption would not apply to interest on a pay-through bond issued by a corporation or by an owner trust classified as a partnership if the payee is a 10% owner of the issuer. Further, if an owner trust is classified as a grantor trust, the exemption may not apply to interest paid by the trust to the extent allocable (as an expense) to any corporate or partnership beneficiary of the trust if the payee is a 10% owner of the beneficiary. It is not clear how the 10% owner limitation would be applied to a REMIC regular interest. It would seem to make sense to apply the rule based on the relationship between the holder of the regular interest and the obligors on the loans held by the REMIC, but the relationship with holders of residual interests may also be relevant. Because a REMIC is not treated as a corporation or partnership for tax purposes (section 860A(a)), the limitation should not be based on ownership of a 10% or greater interest in the REMIC.

[188] The portfolio interest exemption applies under sections 871(h) and 881(c) only to interest "received" by a foreign investor, and perhaps it could be argued that the exemption does not apply to interest paid to an owner trust in which an equity interest is owned by a foreign investor on the ground that the interest is not "received" by the investor. However, if the owner trust is classified as a grantor trust, payments received by the trust clearly would be considered to be received by its equity owners. If the trust is classified as a partnership, the argument would still fail. Sections 871(a) and 881(a), which impose the 30% tax, also apply to interest "received" by a foreign investor; thus, the portfolio interest exemption is coterminous with the tax. See also Revenue Ruling 81-244, 1981-2 C.B. 151 (holds that interest on bank deposits held by a trust is received by trust beneficiaries for purposes of applying the withholding tax exemption for bank deposits; the conduit theory of taxation of trusts referred to in the ruling applies equally to partnerships).

[189] Typically, the mortgage-backed securities owned by an owner trust and the equity interests in the trust are held in registered form. Thus, in determining whether interest earned on those securities is portfolio interest, problems raised by the existence of bearer obligations do not arise. However, an owner trust may also earn interest on short-term obligations that is not portfolio interest because the obligations are held in bearer form and were not issued under the Eurobond exception. (As indicated in the text following footnote 153, short-term obligations are not registration-required. Although the bearer or registered status of the obligations held by an owner trust would be irrelevant if the trust were classified as a grantor trust and the equity interests in the trust were treated as pass-through certificates within the meaning of the 1985 TEFRA regulations (see the text at footnote 163), neither result can be assumed.) Interest on short-term obligations may be exempt from withholding tax on other grounds. For example, there is an exemption for original issue discount

treated as interest that are paid to holders of REMIC residual interests are considered paid on the obligations held by the REMIC, not on or with respect to the residual interest itself.[190] Thus, such payments will qualify as portfolio interest to the extent the assets of the REMIC are interests in another REMIC or interests in a pass-through certificate, (in the case of a pass-through certificate, however, only to the extent that the underlying mortgages were originated after July 18, 1984). Because residential mortgages are typically issued in bearer form for tax purposes (see footnote 154, above) but are not issued pursuant to the Eurobond exception, payments made on a residual interest of a REMIC the assets of which are mortgage loans (as opposed to pass-through certificates, for example) will apparently not qualify for the portfolio interest exception. In no event, however, will that (or any other) exemption apply to income that is an excess inclusion.[191]

Section 2105(b)(3) effectively exempts debt obligations from the U.S. estate tax applicable to nonresident alien individuals if interest thereon would be eligible for the portfolio interest exemption if received by the decedent at the time of his death (without regard to any certification requirement). This exemption should apply to any mortgage-backed security to the extent income thereon is portfolio interest, although admittedly the question is a much closer one for equity interests in owner trusts that are classified as partnerships and REMIC residual interests than for pay-through bonds, REMIC regular interests[192] or interests in grantor trusts.

FIRPTA Rules. The Foreign Investment in Real Property Tax Act of 1980 ("FIRPTA") enacted section 897, which subjects non-U.S. investors to U.S. tax on gain from sales of certain U.S. real prop-

---

on obligations with an original maturity of 183 days or less (section 871(g)(1)(B)(i)) and for interest on bank deposits (sections 871(i)(2)(A) and 881(d)).

[190] Tr easury Regulation § 35a.9999-5(e), Q & A-21(ii).

[191] *See* section 860G(b)(2).

[192] Although the rule treating regular interests as debt instruments for purposes of taxing holders applies by its terms only for purposes of the income tax, it should be relevant in applying section 2105(b)(3) because the estate tax exemption under that section depends on how income from a security is taxed.

erty interests (including equity interests in "real property holding corporations"). Section 1445 imposes a related requirement to withhold tax from the proceeds of sales. The FIRPTA rules do not apply to interests in real property that are solely creditor interests with no participation in the income, revenues, or appreciation of the property.[193] Thus, a foreign investor holding a mortgage-backed security will not be affected by this legislation if the mortgages underlying the security lack such participation features.

TAXATION OF SPONSORS

Introduction

The discussion above concentrates on investors. This section looks at mortgage-backed securities from the perspective of a sponsor. With respect to any particular issue of mortgage-backed securities, the term sponsor will be used herein to refer broadly to any person who owned an interest in the underlying mortgages before those securities were created, and who also owns at some time some or all of those securities or some other interest in the issuer of those securities. The tax treatment of a sponsor may be affected by numerous factors. Therefore, the discussion is intended only as a general summary of the most likely tax results in a number of common situations.

The federal income tax consequences to a sponsor of the issuance and sale of mortgage-backed securities will depend primarily on whether the transaction is treated as a financing or sale, and, if it is a sale, what proportion of the property held by the sponsor is considered to be sold. Pledging an asset as security for a loan is not ordinarily considered a taxable disposition of the asset. On the other hand, if the asset (or an interest herein) is sold, the seller would recognize gain or loss equal to the difference between the amount realized in the sale and his adjusted basis in the property

---

[193] Treasury Regulation § 1.897-1(d).

sold. These fundamental tax principles produce different consequences for sponsors when applied to pass-through certificates,
pay-through bonds and REMIC interests.

Pass-through Certificates

If a sponsor transfers mortgages to a trust that is classified as a
grantor trust in exchange for pass-through certificates, the exchange of mortgages for certificates is not considered a taxable
disposition of the mortgages. However, when the sponsor sells
some or all of those certificates, he is treated as selling an interest
in the underlying mortgages and recognizes gain or loss equal to
the difference between the amount realized in the sale and the
portion of his adjusted basis in the mortgages that is allocated to
the certificates sold.[194] In addition, if the interest in the mortgages
retained by the sponsor represents rights to different percentages
of principal and interest, so that the bond-stripping rules apply,
then the sponsor may be required to recognize as ordinary income
all market discount and interest on the mortgages that has accrued
but not previously been included in income (including the portion
that is allocable to the interest in the mortgages that is retained).
However, the sponsor's adjusted basis in the mortgages and,
hence, the basis allocated among the certificates, would be increased by the amount so included in income. Under the bond-
stripping rules, the sponsor would be treated as if the sponsor had

---

[194] The sponsor would allocate the adjusted basis in the mortgages, in proportion to fair
market value, between the interest in the mortgages that is sold (represented by the
certificates that are sold) and *all* retained ownership interests in the mortgages
(represented by any certificates that are not sold, and any interest in the mortgages
not transferred to the trust, including any rights to mortgage payments that are
denominated as servicing fees but treated for tax purposes as a retained ownership
interest). *See* text accompanying footnote 77 above. If the sponsor retains a
subordinated class of certificates, then the basis allocation might be made by reducing
the proportionate value of the subordinated interest, for purposes of allocating basis,
to reflect the subordination feature. Alternatively, the sponsor might ignore the
subordination feature in valuing the certificates but treat some portion of the amount
realized in the sale as a premium paid for credit support. (Such a premium would be
ordinary income.)

purchased the retained interest in the mortgages at a price equal to the sponsor's adjusted basis in such retained interest, and the difference between that price and the gross amount of payments to be received in respect of the retained interest would be treated as original issue discount and taxed as it accrues.[195]

Pay-Through Bonds

Two steps may be involved in issuing pay-through bonds: (i) the issuance of bonds for cash and (ii) if the issuer is not the original owner, the transfer of all or a portion of the mortgage collateral by a sponsor to the issuer in exchange for cash and/or other consideration. The issuance of the bonds is not considered a sale of the collateral and is not otherwise a taxable event. The tax treatment of the transfer of the mortgages to the issuer is quite complex, and would depend on at least three factors, the first two of which are related: (i) whether for tax purposes the transfer is recognized to be a sale, or is instead viewed as an exchange of mortgages for an equity interest in the issuer,[196] (ii) the extent to which equity inter-

---

[195] For further discussion of the bond-stripping rules, see footnotes 75-80 above and accompanying text.

[196] A complete discussion of the circumstances under which a purported sale will be recharacterized for tax purposes as an equity contribution, or an equity contribution will be recharacterized as a sale, is beyond the scope of this chapter. However, the likelihood of recharacterization of a purported sale would clearly be high if the seller owns a substantial equity stake in the issuer and the stated consideration paid in the sale has a value less than the fair market value of the mortgages. A contribution of mortgages to an issuer that is a corporation solely in exchange for stock in a transaction subject to section 351 (see footnote 201) and a subsequent related distribution of cash may be integrated and treated as an exchange of the mortgages for stock and cash (and thus at least partially as a sale for purposes of gain recognition). An exchange of mortgages for an equity interest in an owner trust that is classified as a partnership, combined with a related distribution of cash by the owner trust, may be recharacterized as a sale under section 707(b) if the two events "when viewed together, are properly characterized as a sale of property." However, the likelihood of sale characterization under this section is reduced if, as would often be the case in connection with the transfer of mortgages to an owner trust, any cash that is distributed represents the proceeds of pay-through bonds and the portion of those proceeds that is distributed to any equity owner corresponds to the share of the equity interest that he owns. See Proposed Regulation § 1.707-5(b); H.R. Rep. 861, 98th Cong., 2d Sess. at 862; Joint Committee on Taxation, General Explanation of the Revenue Provisions of the Deficit Reduction Act of 1984 at 232. The discussion below

ests in the issuer are owned by the sponsor rather than unrelated investors, and (iii) whether the issuer is a corporation or an owner trust, and if the latter, whether it is classified as a grantor trust or partnership.

In very general terms, if the issuer is an owner trust that is classified as a grantor trust, then the sponsor would recognize gain or loss as a result of the transfer of mortgages to the issuer only if equity interests in the issuer are owned by persons other than the sponsor, and then only to the extent that the sponsor would recognize gain or loss if the sponsor transferred directly to those other persons an interest in the mortgages corresponding to the equity interest that they own. If the issuer is an owner trust that is classified as a partnership, gain from a sale of the mortgages to the owner trust would be recognized, but loss would not be recognized, at least if the sponsor owns more than 50% of the equity interests in the owner trust.[197] In general, no gain or loss would be recognized upon an exchange of mortgages for an equity interest.[198] If the issuer is a corporation, gain or loss from a sale of mortgages to the issuer by the sponsor would generally be recognized. However, if the sponsor is also a corporation and files a consolidated federal income tax return with the issuer, any such gain or loss would be deferred.[199] Moreover, even if the sponsor

---

of the tax consequences of sales, or exchanges of mortgages for equity interests assumes that it has first been determined that the transaction in question will be characterized for tax purposes as a sale or an exchange, respectively.

[197] If the sponsor is considered to own a greater than 50% interest in the capital or profits of the partnership owner trust, then loss would be disallowed under section 707(b). Certain attribution rules apply in determining whether the greater than 50% ownership test is met. If a sale of the mortgages to the owner trust occurs as part of a single transaction in which equity interests in the owner trust are sold to investors unrelated to the sponsor, then consideration should be given to the possible characterization of the transaction as a sale by the sponsor to those investors of a partial ownership interest in the mortgages corresponding to their equity interest in the owner trust, followed by the contribution by the sponsor and those investors of their respective interests in the mortgages to the owner trust in exchange for equity interests. Under that characterization, the sponsor would generally recognize gain or loss only with respect to the initial sale of a partial interest in the mortgages to those investors, which is the same result that would obtain if the owner trust were classified as a grantor trust.

[198] Section 721.

[199] Treasury Regulation § 1.1502-13. Any deferred gain or loss would be recognized by

and the issuer do not file a consolidated return, loss would be deferred if the sponsor owns more than 50% of the stock of the issuer.[200] If the mortgages are exchanged for stock (or stock and cash) upon formation of the issuer, loss would not be recognized in the exchange. Gain may be recognized, in an amount not exceeding the amount of cash received, but any such gain would be deferred to the same extent as gain from a sale.[201] The transferor may also recognize interest income up to the amount of accrued market discount on the mortgages not previously included in income.[202]

Regardless of whether the issuer is a corporation or owner trust or whether gain or loss was recognized upon transfer of the mortgages to the issuer, if the sponsor sells some or all of the equity interest in the issuer to unrelated investors, he will recognize gain or loss with respect to that sale equal to the difference between the amount realized and his adjusted basis in the portion of the equity interest that is sold.[203]

REMICs

A sponsor who transfers mortgages to a REMIC in exchange for regular or residual interests generally will not recognize gain or loss in the exchange.[204] However, the aggregate adjusted basis of

---

the sponsor as principal payments are received on the mortgages by the issuer, or when the issuer sells the mortgages outside of the group filing consolidated returns, or the sponsor or issuer leaves the group.

[200] Section 267(b)(3).

[201] Under section 351, gain or loss is not recognized upon a transfer of property to a corporation solely in exchange for stock if the transferors as a group control the corporation (generally, own at least 80% of its stock) immediately following the transfer. However, if a transferor receives cash or other property in addition to stock, then the transferor will recognize gain (but not loss) in the same manner as if the property had been sold, except that the recognized gain will be limited to the amount of cash or other property received.

[202] See footnote 96 above.

[203] Such a sale may also trigger the recognition of gains or losses from sales of mortgages to the issuer that were previously deferred, as described above.

[204] If the REMIC is a segregated pool of mortgages that is not a legal entity, the sponsor would be deemed to exchange the mortgages for the interests in the REMIC. Market

the property transferred (increased by properly allocable costs of acquiring the REMIC interests)[205] will be allocated among the REMIC interests received in proportion to their respective fair market values, and each time the sponsor sells an interest in the REMIC (whether a regular interest or a residual interest), he will recognize gain or loss equal to the excess of the amount realized over his adjusted basis in that interest.[206] The federal income tax consequences to the sponsor of a REMIC would be the same if, instead of transferring mortgages to the REMIC in exchange for interests therein, the sponsor contributed cash to the REMIC which used the cash to purchase the mortgages; the alternative transaction would be recharacterized for tax purposes as a purchase of the mortgages by the sponsor (if the mortgages were purchased by the REMIC from a person other than the sponsor), followed by their contribution to the REMIC.[207]

As the discussion above suggests, the major difference in tax consequences for a sponsor of pay-through bonds between making and not making a REMIC election relates to the portion of the sponsor's overall economic gain or loss (represented by the difference between the sum of the fair market values of the bonds and equity interest in the issuer and the sponsor's basis in the mortgages) that is recognized at the time of the bond offering and upon sale of equity interests in the issuer. Suppose first that no election is made, and the sponsor exchanges the mortgages for all of the equity interest in the issuer plus the net proceeds of the bonds and subsequently sells all or a portion of the equity interest. In that event, the sponsor would not recognize any portion of such

---

discount on any market discount bond that has accrued and not yet been included in income would be recognized upon transfer of the bond to a REMIC. The rule requiring recognition in section 1276(a)(1) applies "notwithstanding any other provision of this subtitle," and there is no explicit exception for transfers to REMICs. See footnotes 96 and 201 above.

[205] See Blue Book at 417.

[206] The amount realized will reflect the fair market value of the mortgages increased by any arbitrage profit realized in the transaction (i.e., the excess of the value of interests in the REMIC over the aggregate value of the mortgages and other assets transferred).

[207] Proposed REMIC Regulations § 1.860F-2; Blue Book at 417; Conference Report at II-230, footnote 8.

gain or loss at the time of the bond sale, but would recognize a portion of such gain or loss each time an equity interest is sold, corresponding to the portion of the equity interest that is sold. By contrast, where a REMIC election is made, the sponsor would recognize a portion of such gain or loss equal to the portion of *all* interests in the issuer (equity and bonds) that are sold, as those interests are sold. Thus, for example, if the bonds represent 95% of the value of all REMIC interests, 95% of such gain or loss would be recognized when the bonds are sold. The tax consequences for a sponsor of the creation and sale of pass-through certificates would be substantially the same whether or not a REMIC election is made.

REMIC securities are generally taxed as if they had been issued at their initial fair market values, and not at a price equal to the sponsor's initial basis in those interests. Under section 860F(b), while the sponsor holds any REMIC interest, the difference between the issue price of that interest and its initial basis in the hands of the sponsor is required to be included in income, if the issue price is higher, or is allowed as a deduction, if the issue price is lower, (i) in the case of a regular interest, as if that difference were original issue discount or bond premium, respectively, or (ii) in the case of a residual interest, ratably over the anticipated period during which the REMIC will be in existence.[208]

---

[208] *See* section 860F(b)(1); Proposed REMIC Regulations § 1.860F-2.

CHAPTER 40

ACCOUNTING FOR INVESTMENTS IN MORTGAGE-BACKED SECURITIES

James T. Parks, CPA
Vice President for Financial Standards and Corporate Taxes
Federal National Mortgage Association

A portfolio manager of mortgage-backed securities (MBS) must be aware of the extent to which accounting rules can affect reported returns. Although there are various methods of calculating MBS returns, including "total return," "quoted yield," and "cash yield," returns reflected in financial statements must conform with generally accepted accounting principles (GAAP). Because GAAP is usually the basis for defining the regulatory net worth of depository institutions, GAAP profitability can be critically important.

This chapter reviews the three different methods of accounting for investments in mortgage securities, illustrates the various methods of amortizing discount and premium through the use of examples, and discusses the accounting for CMO residual interests. Although the chapter's focus is on current GAAP, the Financial Accounting Standards Board has several projects underway that could result in revisions to the accounting methodologies discussed.

ACCOUNTING CLASSIFICATIONS AND METHODOLOGIES

There are three different methods of accounting for portfolios of MBS, or, for that matter, any other type of fixed-income security. The accounting classification assigned to individual securities determines the methodology that must be followed in reporting investment results in GAAP financial statements.

Held for Investment

Securities in this category are assumed to be held for the long term to earn an investment yield. The amortized cost method of accounting is used for all securities that meet the "held for investment" criteria, which generally require that the investor have the financial capability or *ability* to hold until maturity and the *intent* to hold for at least the foreseeable future. Because there is no current intent to sell those securities, their recorded value generally does not change with fluctuations in market value, other than to reflect the amortization of any related purchase discount or premium.

The income statement reflects the coupon rate of interest earned, adjusted for amortization of purchase discount or premium. Depository institutions and insurance companies typically account for the majority of their investment portfolios under the amortized cost method.

Held for Trading

This category is for securities that are being actively traded to earn short-term profits from market movements, and it requires use of the mark-to-market methodology. The income statement reflects the coupon rate of interest earned plus the unrealized gain or loss resulting from the net change in market value during the reporting period. Pension plans, mutual funds, brokers/dealers, and other firms that trade in securities use the mark-to-market method of accounting.

Held for Sale

In situations where investors either do not have the ability to hold securities to maturity, or otherwise intend to sell them, the securities must be included in the "held for sale" category. These securities are accounted for by the lower of cost or market (LOCOM) method. This approach is a combination of the first two methods in that the portfolio is written down to market when market is less than amortized cost. If market increases subsequently, the portfolio can be written back up, but no higher than amortized cost.

Discount or premium is amortized in the same fashion as it is under the cost method for as long as each security is owned. When securities are sold at a price higher than their amortized cost, unamortized discount is effectively recorded as part of the gain on sale.

Firms may not plan to have "held for sale" portfolios, but sometimes wind up with them anyway. For example, an institution may have to dispose of certain investments within a specified time period as a result of an order from its regulator (e.g., thrifts required to dispose of their junk bond holdings). In this situation, LOCOM accounting would be required, because the institution no longer has the ability to hold its investment to maturity.

Focus on the Cost Method

As demonstrated in the example in Exhibit 1, the same security can result in three different income results, depending on its categorization and the method of accounting followed. The cost

---

Exhibit 1: Differing Accounting Results

Assumptions

Principal	$100,000
Coupon Rate of Interest	10%
Purchase Price of Bond	$100,000

Recorded Values on Balance Sheet

	Market Interest Rate	Amortized Cost	Lower of Cost or Market	Mark-to-Market
At Purchase	10%	$100,000	$100,000	$100,000
End of Period 1 [1]	11%	$100,000	$ 98,000	$ 98,000
End of Period 2 [1]	9%	$100,000	$100,000	$102,000

Income Statement Effect [2]   *Income/(Loss)*

Period 1	0	($2,000)	($2,000)
Period 2	0	$2,000	$4,000

[1] Assumes no amortization of principal balance.
[2] Exclusive of coupon interest at 10% under all three methods.

---

method obviously has the least volatile effect on the income statement.

Although this chapter will focus on the amortized cost method of accounting, the discussion has relevance to all three categories of investments. For example, in order to apply the LOCOM method of accounting, amortized cost balance must be maintained along with market values. For the total return investor using mark-to-market accounting, the cost method can also be relevant as a benchmark of the base level of portfolio earnings.

By isolating the portion of total return related solely to coupon interest and discount/premium amortization, the investor can then determine the remaining amount of return that resulted from market movements.

FUNDAMENTALS OF CALCULATING ACCOUNTING RETURNS

Calculating the yield on a fixed-income security becomes complicated only when that security is purchased at a premium or discount. The following sections will explain the fundamentals of
how yields are calculated for MBS investments under GAAP.

Fixed-Maturity Securities

In the simple case of a fixed-maturity security that has no put or
call options, the GAAP return is a straightforward cash yield calculation. For example, assume a $100,000 face amount security
that pays 7% interest semiannually and all of the principal at the
end of ten years. If the investor paid 85 for that security, the
$15,000 of discount (15 percent) is amortized in such a way as to
report a level yield of 9.34%, which consists of 7% of coupon interest and 2.34% from discount amortization.

MBS and Call Options

Unlike fixed-maturity securities, however, MBS repay a portion of
the investor's principal each month. Based on the purchase price
and the monthly principal and interest cash flows, a cash yield is
also relatively easy to compute, assuming there are no prepayments of the underlying mortgages. It is this prepayment, or call
option, feature in every MBS that makes the calculation of the accounting return complicated. Although reasonable estimates can
be made of expected prepayment rates, actual prepayment experience usually will be different from the estimates, which can have a
substantial impact on both the effective maturity and the cash
yield of MBS investments.

Discount Amortization Under FASB 91

For most types of mortgage securities, *Statement of Financial Accounting Standards No. 91, "Accounting for Nonrefundable Fees and Costs Associated with Originating or Acquiring Loans and Initial Direct Costs of Leases"* (FASB 91) is the accounting "rule book" that is followed. FASB 91 allows two methods of factoring prepayment uncertainty into the amortization of discount and premium: the contractual method and the retrospective method.

Contractual Method: Under this methodology, discount and premium are amortized without anticipating any prepayments of the underlying loans. When prepayments occur, the unamortized discount or premium related to the portion of principal prepaid is recorded as interest income in addition to discount associated with the normal amortization of the loans (i.e., assuming no prepayments).

The mechanics of this methodology are illustrated in Exhibit 2. In this example, it is assumed that a standard pass-through MBS with a principal balance of $50 million and a 10% coupon was purchased at 90, resulting in $5 million of unamortized discount.

Assuming there are no prepayments of the underlying collateral, the investor would receive annual combined principal and interest cash flow of $5.304 million (column A). Based on this cash flow and the net investment price of $45 million, the internal rate of return (IRR) is 11.31% (column I). This is the same yield reported under GAAP, as long as there are no prepayments.

Exhibit 3, however, shows the effect of prepayments on the accounting yield. At the end of year one there is an assumed prepayment of 12% (column H) of the unpaid principal balance (after normal amortization) of the investment. Additional discount amortization of $589,000 ($680,000 in column C – $91,000 in column C of Exhibit 2) is recorded in year one as a result of the 12% prepayment. This, in turn, results in higher total interest income (column D), which drives the accounting yield up from 11.31% to 12.62% (column H).

Exhibit 2: Contractual Method: No Prepayments (Dollars in Thousands)

Assumptions:

Principal Balance:	$50,000	Weighted Average Maturity:		30 Yrs
Purchase Price (at 90):	$45,000	Principal + Interest (assuming no prepayments)		$5,304
MBS Coupon:	10%			

End of Year	Cash Flow	Coupon Interest	Discount Amort.	Total Interest Income	Ending Principal Balance	Unamort. Discount	Net Investment	Prepayment Rate	Net Yield
	(A)	(B)	(C)	(D)	(E)	(F)	(G)	(H)	(I)
Purchase	($45,000)				$50,000	($5,000)	$45,000		
1	5,304	$5,000	$91	$5,091	49,696	(4,909)	44,787	0%	11.31%
2	5,304	4,970	97	5,067	49,362	(4,812)	44,550	0%	11.31%
3	5,304	4,936	104	5,040	48,994	(4,708)	44,286	0%	11.31%
4	5,304	4,899	111	5,010	48,589	(4,597)	43,992	0%	11.31%
5	5,304	4,859	118	4,977	48,144	(4,479)	43,665	0%	11.31%
6	5,304	4,814	126	4,940	47,654	(4,353)	43,301	0%	11.31%
7	5,304	4,765	133	4,898	47,115	(4,220)	42,895	0%	11.31%
.			.						
.			.						
30			.						
			$5,000						

Notes:

A = Principal & Interest (P&I) + Prepayments $\quad E_t = E_{t-1} - (A_t - B_t)$

$B_t = E_{t-1} \times .10$ $\qquad\qquad\qquad\qquad\qquad F_t = F_{t-1} - C_t$

$C_t = D_t - B_t$ $\qquad\qquad\qquad\qquad\qquad\qquad G_t = E_t - F_t$

$D_t = G_{t-1} \times I_t$ $\qquad\qquad\qquad\qquad\qquad$ H = Prepayment rate

$\qquad\qquad\qquad\qquad\qquad\qquad\qquad\quad$ I = Level yield (IRR of cash flows in A.)

As indicated by Exhibit 3, the net yield reflected in GAAP financial reports (column I), under the contractual method, is highly sensitive to changes in prepayment rates (column H). When prepayments increase, the reported yield on discount securities also increases and when prepayments decline, so does the reported yield. If the prepayment rate returns to zero, as depicted in year six, the reported yield returns to 11.31%. If this investment had been purchased at a deeper discount (i.e., at a price less than 90), the volatility of reported yields, in response to changing prepayment rates, would be even greater.

Exhibit 3: Contractual Method: Varying Prepayments
(Dollars in Thousands)

Assumptions:

Principal Balance:	$50,000	Weighted Average Maturity:	30 Yrs
Purchase Price (at 90):	$45,000	Principal + Interest (assuming no prepayments)	$5,304
MBS Coupon:	10%		

End of Year	Cash Flow	Coupon Interest	Discount Amort.	Total Interest Income	Ending Principal Balance	Unamort. Discount	Net Investment	Prepayment Rate	Net Yield
	(A)	(B)	(C)	(D)	(E)	(F)	(G)	(H)	(I)
Purchase	($45,000)				$50,000	($5,000)	$45,000		
1	11,267	$5,000	$680	$5,680	43,733	(4,320)	39,413	12%	12.62%
2	9,880	4,373	594	4,967	38,226	(3,726)	34,500	12%	12.60%
3	9,799	3,823	627	4,450	32,250	(3,099)	29,151	15%	12.90%
4	6,690	3,225	376	3,601	28,785	(2,723)	26,062	10%	12.35%
5	6,850	2,879	415	3,294	24,814	(2,308)	22,506	13%	12.64%
6	2,734	2,481	65	2,546	24,561	(2,243)	22,318	0%	11.31%
7	4,191	2,456	199	2,655	22,826	(2,044)	20,782	6%	11.90%
.			.						
.									
30			$5,000						

Notes:

A = Principal & Interest (P&I) + Prepayments $E_t = E_{t-1} - (A_t - B_t)$

$B_t = E_{t-1} \times .10$ $F_t = F_{t-1} - C_t$

C_t = Normal discount amortization + amortization $G_t = E_t - F_t$
due to prepayments

Normal discount amortization = Amortization   H = Prepayment rate
assuming 0% prepayments

Amortization due to prepayments = Prepayment $I = D_t / G_{t-1}$
rate × (unamortized discount - normal
amortization)

$D_t = B_t + C_t$

The contractual method may not be desirable, or even appropriate, if MBS investments are purchased at a significant premium. In the early years of an MBS investment, prepayments are generally low, and, consequently, a smaller proportional amount of premium would be amortized as an offset to coupon interest under the contractual method. When prepayments accelerate in later years, the proportional amount of premium amortized will increase, and, as a result, significantly decrease the reported yield of a premium MBS investment. The higher yields reported in the early years could be viewed by auditors as an inappropriate over-statement of income in those periods. The contractual method may be particularly inappropriate for premium MBS, because high-cou-pon mortgages tend to prepay at a significantly faster rate than current coupon or discount securities.

Retrospective Method: Under FASB 91, if a security contains ". . . a large number of similar loans for which prepayments are prob-able and the timing and amount of prepayments can be reason-ably estimated, the enterprise may consider estimates of future principal prepayments in the calculation of the constant effective yield. . ." MBS backed by a large number of individual home mortgages generally meet the similar loan, predictable prepay-ment tests of FASB 91.

What this effectively means is that investors in most discount MBS can decide which of the two methods they will adopt for factoring prepayments into discount amortization. To illustrate how the retrospective method works, refer to Exhibit 4. In this ex-ample the assumptions are essentially the same as in Exhibits 2 and 3. At the date of purchase, however, an assumption is made about the expected prepayment rate. Based on an estimated an-nual constant prepayment rate (CPR) for the life of the investment, which is 12% in this example, the annual principal and interest cash flow (column A) is determined. Using this cash flow estimate and the purchase price of $45 million, an IRR of 12.54% is derived for the investment. The IRR is the "constant effective yield" re-ported for the investment (column I), which, in turn, is the basis for determining total interest income (column D) and amortizing discount (column C).

When actual prepayments deviate from the estimated rate, however, a "catch-up" adjustment is required under the retrospec-tive method to compensate retroactively for the change in re-ported yield. This occurs because use of the retrospective method under FASB 91 requires that:

Exhibit 4: Retrospective Method: Steady-Rate Prepayments (Dollars in Thousands)

Assumptions:

Principal Balance:	$50,000	Weighted Average Maturity:				30 Yrs
Purchase Price (at 90):	$45,000	Prepayment Speed				12% CPR
MBS Coupon:	10%					

End of Year	Cash Flow	Coupon Interest	Dis-count Amort.	Total Interest Income	Ending Principal Balance	Unamort. Discount	Net Invest-ment	Prepay-ment Rate	Net Yield
	(A)	(B)	(C)	(D)	(E)	(F)	(G)	(H)	(I)
Purchase	($45,000)				$50,000	($5,000)	$45,000		
1	11,267	$5,000	$643	$5,643	43,733	(4,357)	39,376	12%	12.54%
2	9,880	4,373	564	4,937	38,226	(3,793)	34,433	12%	12.54%
3	8,660	3,823	495	4,318	33,389	(3,298)	30,091	12%	12.54%
4	7,588	3,339	434	3,773	29,140	(2,864)	26,276	12%	12.54%
5	6,645	2,914	381	3,295	25,409	(2,483)	22,926	12%	12.54%
6	5,817	2,541	334	2,875	22,133	(2,149)	19,984	12%	12.54%
7	5,089	2,213	292	2,505	19,257	(1,857)	17,400	12%	12.54%
.			.						
.									
30			.						
			$5,000						

Notes:
See Exhibit 2 for formulas

If a difference arises between the prepayments antici-pated and actual prepayments received, the enter-prise shall recalculate the effective yield to reflect actual prepayments to date and anticipated future prepayments. The net investment in the loans shall be adjusted to the amount that would have existed had the new effective yield been applied since . . . acquisition. . .

To understand how this works, refer to Exhibit 5, which con-tains the same assumptions as Exhibit 4, with one exception. In year five the actual prepayment rate drops from 12% to 9%, and is expected to remain at that level for the remaining life of the in-vestment. Based on a recalculation of the investment IRR from the

**Exhibit 5: Retrospective Method: Varying Prepayments
(Dollars in Thousands)**

Assumptions:

Principal Balance:		$50,000	Weighted Average Maturity:		30 Years
Purchase Price (at 90):		$45,000	Prepayment Speed		Varying
MBS Coupon:		10%			

End of Year	Cash Flow	Coupon Interest	Discount Amort.	Total Interest Income	Ending Principal Balance	Unamort. Discount	Net Investment	Prepayment Rate	Net Yield
	(A)	(B)	(C)	(D)	(E)	(F)	(G)	(H)	(I)
Purchase	($45,000)				$50,000	($5,000)	$45,000		
1	11,267	$5,000	$643	$5,643	43,733	(4,357)	39,376	12%	12.54%
2	9,880	4,373	564	4,937	38,226	(3,793)	34,433	12%	12.54%
3	8,660	3,823	495	4,318	33,389	(3,298)	30,091	12%	12.54%
4	7,588	3,339	434	3,773	29,140	(2,864)	26,276	12%	12.54%
5	5,779	2,914	106	3,020	26,275	(2,758)	23,517	9%	11.49%
6	5,235	2,628	293	2,921	23,668	(2,465)	21,203	9%	12.42%
7	4,740	2,367	267	2,634	21,295	(2,198)	19,097	9%	12.42%
.			.						
.									
30			.						
			$5,000						

Notes:

See Exhibit 2 for all formulas, except for year 5 (explained below):

1. Calculate level yield over entire life using old (12%) and new (9%) prepayment rates.
2. Calculate discount amount that would have been recognized by end of catch-up year (year 5) assuming level yield in 1. above was used from year 1.
3. Compare amount in 2. with total discount amortized under existing method at end of year 4.
4. Difference between the two amounts is the catch-up adjustment, i.e., discount amortization amount for year 5.
5. $D_t = B_t + C_t$
6. $I_t = D_t / G_{t-1}$

date of acquisition, using actual principal and interest cash flows reflecting a 12% CPR in years one through four and an actual/estimated 9% CPR for years five through thirty (column A), the new IRR is 12.42%. Although this rate is reflected for subsequent years, the 12.54 yield reported in years one through four was too high. Under the retrospective method, there is a cumulative catch-up adjustment in the current year (e.g., year five) for over- (or under-) reporting in prior years.

The catch-up adjustment in year five, to compensate for over-recognition of income in prior years, drives the current reported yield down to 11.49%. Conversely, if an estimate of future prepayments is revised upward, a higher yield will result in the adjustment year as a result of a positive catch-up adjustment. Although this example illustrates just one adjustment during a year, catch-up adjustments are possible any time GAAP financial reports are prepared (e.g., quarterly or monthly). Whether these catch-up adjustments are actually recorded, however, will depend largely on their overall significance to the earnings of the investor in any particular reporting period. Consequently, the retrospective method under FASB 91 requires close monitoring of historical and estimated prepayment rates in order to lessen the possibility of a "surprise" catch-up adjustment of a significant amount.

ACCOUNTING FOR ADJUSTABLE-RATE SECURITIES

Adjustable- or variable-rate mortgage securities can pose a special problem in the calculation of discount. Because the coupon rate of interest is constantly changing, there is an additional variable to deal with in determining the constant effective yield that will be reported in GAAP financial statements.

The example in Exhibit 6 assumes that a $50 million investment is purchased at 90 and the coupon rate of interest at the date of purchase is 10%. For the sake of simplicity, a prepayment assumption of 0% is used. The reported constant effective yield (column I) and the discount amortization schedule (column C) are determined initially in the same way as in the fixed-rate examples discussed previously.

FASB 91 allows two methods for dealing with index adjustments. The first is simply to continue amortizing the discount using the same schedule determined at purchase with the original coupon rate of interest (e.g., 10 percent). Under this approach, the

---

Exhibit 6: Amortization of Adjustable-Rate MBSs: Yield Not Recalculated for Changes in Index (Dollars in Thousands)

Assumptions:

Principal Balance:	$50,000	Index + Margin (Coupon) -	
Purchase Price (at 90):	$45,000	Beginning Year 5:	12%
Index + Margin (Coupon) -		Prepayment Speed	0% CPR
Purchase:	10%		

End of Year	Cash Flow	Coupon Interest	Discount Amort.	Total Interest Income	Ending Principal Balance	Unamort. Discount	Net Invest- ment	Prepay- ment Rate	Net Yield
	(A)	(B)	(C)	(D)	(E)	(F)	(G)	(H)	(I)
Purchase	($45,000)				$50,000	($5,000)	$45,000		
1	5,304	$5,000	$91	$5,091	49,696	(4,909)	44,787	0%	11.31%
2	5,304	4,970	97	5,067	49,362	(4,812)	44,550	0%	11.31%
3	5,304	4,936	104	5,040	48,994	(4,708)	44,286	0%	11.31%
4	5,304	4,899	111	5,010	48,589	(4,597)	43,992	0%	11.31%
5	6,154	5,831	118	5,949	48,266	(4,479)	43,787	0%	13.52%
6	6,154	5,792	126	5,918	47,904	(4,353)	43,551	0%	13.52%
7	6,154	5,748	133	5,881	47,498	(4,220)	43,278	0%	13.50%
.			.						
.									
30			$5,000						

Notes:
See Exhibit 2 for discount amortization amounts (column C)

$I_t = D_t / G_{t-1}$

---

amortization schedule never changes (except for the impact of prepayments) regardless of subsequent changes in the coupon interest rate.

To illustrate this point, refer to the discount amortization schedule (column C) in Exhibit 6. When the rate changes from 10% to 12% in year five, discount amortization remains unchanged, as if the coupon were still fixed at 10% (i.e., the same as column C in Exhibit 2). Beginning in year five, however, the accounting yield increases to reflect the higher coupon rate of interest.

The other methodology, which is reflected in Exhibit 7, is to recalculate a new yield to maturity for the investment every time the coupon rate of interest changes. In the example it is assumed

Exhibit 7: Amortization of Adjustable-Rate MBSs: Yield Recalculated for Changes in Index (Dollars in Thousands)

Assumptions:

Principal Balance:	$50,000	Index + Margin (Coupon) -	
Purchase Price (at 90):	$45,000	Beginning Year 5:	12%
Index + Margin (Coupon) -		Prepayment Speed	0% CPR
Purchase:	10%		

End of Year	Cash Flow	Coupon Interest	Discount Amort.	Total Interest Income	Ending Principal Balance	Unamort. Discount	Net Invest- ment	Prepay- ment Rate	Net Yield
	(A)	(B)	(C)	(D)	(E)	(F)	(G)	(H)	(I)
Purchase	($45,000)				$50,000	($5,000)	$45,000		
1	5,304	$5,000	$91	$5,091	49,696	(4,909)	44,787	0%	11.31%
2	5,304	4,970	97	5,067	49,362	(4,812)	44,550	0%	11.31%
3	5,304	4,936	104	5,040	48,994	(4,708)	44,286	0%	11.31%
4	5,304	4,899	111	5,010	48,589	(4,597)	43,992	0%	11.31%
5	6,154	5,831	93	5,924	48,266	(4,504)	43,762	0%	13.46%
6	6,154	5,792	100	5,892	47,904	(4,404)	43,500	0%	13.46%
7	6,154	5,748	109	5,857	47,498	(4,295)	43,203	0%	13.46%
.		.							
.									
30		.							
		$5,000							

Notes:
In year 5, level yield is recalculated based on estimated future cash flows ($6,154 annually assuming no prepayments) and net investment at end of year 4 ($43,992).

that the rate increases from 10% to 12% at the beginning of year five. The calculation begins with the net investment at the end of year four of $43.992 million (column G). Next, an internal rate of return is calculated based on the remaining interest and principal cash flows to maturity assuming the new 12% coupon rate of interest (column A). In this example, the IRR is determined to be 13.46% (column I). Total interest income (column D) and discount amortization (column C) are calculated based on this new reported constant effective yield.

Interest income follows the new discount amortization schedule until the coupon rate changes again, when a new IRR/yield to maturity is determined in the same manner as described in the preceding paragraph. In this calculation it is important to note that the adjustment to unamortized discount is never retroactive, but rather a prospective adjustment of the rate of discount amortization in future periods.

The effect of prepayments on discount amortization, regardless of whether they are accounted for under the contractual or estimated method, can be determined independently of the effect of changes in the coupon rate of interest.

ACCOUNTING FOR DERIVATIVE SECURITIES

Derivative mortgage securities, as with regular MBSs, can have either discount or premium. In fact, some derivative securities are issued at prices significantly discounted from their par or stated values. Other derivatives, such as residual interests of multiclass securities, can have characteristics of both debt and equity investments. Depending on a security's characteristics, its accounting methodology is mandated by one of two accounting pronouncements: (1) FASB 91, discussed previously, or (2) EITF 89-4, which is a consensus opinion issued by the Emerging Issues Task Force on Issue No. 89-4, "Accounting for a Purchased Investment in a Collateralized Mortgage Obligation Instrument or in a Mortgage-Backed Interest-Only Certificate."

FASB 91 Applied to Certain CMO/REMIC Regular Interest Classes and Principal-Only Strips

As illustrated in Exhibits 3 through 5, either the contractual or retrospective method can be used to account for the effect of prepayments on returns reported under GAAP. Exhibit 8 illustrates how the retrospective method under FASB 91 is applied to a short-maturity tranche of a REMIC security. In this example, Tranche A, with a face amount of $40 million, was issued at a discount price of 98. A CPR of 10.5% for the underlying MBS collateral results in a reported yield for Tranche A of 10.19%, compared with the secu-

---

Exhibit 8: Amortization of Discount on REMIC Tranche: Retrospective Method (Dollars in Thousands)

Assumptions:	REMIC	Tranche A
Principal Balance:	$200,000	$40,000
Purchase Price (at 98):	–	$39,200
Coupon:	10.125%	8.00%
Pass-through:	9.5%	–
Weighted Average Maturity:	320 Months	23 Months
Prepayment Speed:	10.5% CPR	

End of Year	Cash Flow	Coupon Interest	Discount Amort.	Total Interest Income	Ending Principal Balance	Unamort. Discount	Net Invest- ment	Net Yield
	(A)	(B)	(C)	(D)	(E)	(F)	(G)	(H)
Settlement	($39,200)				$40,000	($800)	$39,200	
1	2,242	$267	$66	$333	38,025	(734)	37,291	10.19%
2	2,210	253	64	317	36,068	(670)	35,398	10.19%
3	2,179	240	60	300	34,129	(610)	33,519	10.19%
4	2,148	228	57	285	32,209	(553)	31,656	10.19%
5	2,118	215	54	269	30,306	(499)	29,807	10.19%
6	2,087	202	51	253	28,421	(448)	27,973	10.19%
7	2,056	189	48	237	26,554	(400)	26,154	10.19%
.			.					
.			.					
23			.					
			$800					

Notes:

Cash Flows are based on REMIC paydown schedule.

See Exhibit 2 for all formulas.

---

rity's fixed 8% coupon rate of interest. If the assumed prepayment speed is subsequently revised, a catch-up adjustment may become necessary.

The retrospective accounting methodology in FASB 91 generally is appropriate for most PACs (Planned Amortization Classes), TACs (Targeted Amortization Classes), and deep discount tranches of multiclass securities, as well as the principal only portion of MBS strip securities (POs). Accounting yields for POs, in particular, can be quite volatile with a relatively small change in prepayment speeds.

Exhibit 9 illustrates how the retrospective method under FASB 91 is applied to a PO. In this example, the underlying MBS collateral has a $50 million face value and a 9.5% coupon rate of interest. The issue price of the PO is 62 or $31 million, which results in unamortized discount of $19 million at issuance. Assuming a CPR of 10.5%, the accounting yield would be 7.14%. Because no coupon interest is received on this PO, the accounting yield is comprised solely of discount amortization.

If actual or expected prepayment rates differ from the assumed rate, the accounting yield can vary by a substantial amount. For

Exhibit 9: Amortization of Discount on Principal-Only (PO) Securities: Retrospective Method (Dollars in Thousands)

Assumptions:

Face Amount:	$50,000	MBS Coupon:	9.5%
PO Amount (at 62):	$31,000	Prepayment Speed:	10.5% CPR
IO Amount (at 38):	$19,000		

End of Year	Cash Flow	Coupon Interest	Discount Amort.	Ending Principal Balance	Unamort. Discount	Net Investment	PO Yield
	(A)	(B)	(C)	(D)	(E)	(F)	(G)
Settlement				$50,000	$19,000	$31,000	
1	$10,299	$4,750	$2,212	44,451	16,788	26,663	7.14%
2	9,183	4,223	1,974	39,491	14,814	24,677	7.14%
3	8,185	3,752	1,761	35,058	13,053	22,005	7.14%
4	7,293	3,330	1,571	31,095	11,482	19,613	7.14%
5	6,495	2,954	1,400	27,554	10,082	17,472	7.14%
6	5,781	2,618	1,247	24,391	8,835	15,556	7.14%
7	5,143	2,317	1,110	21,565	7,725	13,840	7.14%
.	.	.	.				
30							
	$89,089	$39,089	$19,000				

Notes:
Cash Flows in column A represent the total cash flows on the underlying securities.

PO yield of 7.14% is the IRR on the PO cash flows, i.e., outflow of $31,000 at settlement, and inflows equal to principal repayments (columns A - B) in years 1 to 30.

example, a CPR of 7.5% produces a yield of 5.52% and a CPR of 13.5% results in a yield of 8.85%.

EITF 89-4 Applied to Certain CMO/REMIC Classes and Interest-Only Certificates

In resolving the three issues under EITF No. 89-4, the EITF reached a consensus on Issue 2 that:

> . . . nonequity CMO instruments that have potential for loss of a significant portion of the original investment due to changes in (1) interest rates, (2) the prepayment rate of the assets of the CMO structure, or (3) earnings from the temporary reinvestment of cash collected by the CMO structure but not yet distributed to the holders of its obligations (reinvestment earnings) are *high risk* CMO instruments and should be accounted for as described in Issue 3 below (emphasis added). Nonequity CMO instruments include all CMO instruments issued in equity form that meet all six criteria listed in Issue 1.

The term "high risk" used in this definition is different from what it means in a normal investment context. For example, with a PO there is never any doubt that the full amount of the discount will be earned over the life of the investment (assuming there is no appreciable credit risk associated with the security). The key accounting and investment questions are how long will the security be outstanding, and what will be the resulting yield? The market value of a PO, however, can vary significantly during its life, as a result of changes in the level of interest rates and the rate of prepayments. Within the context of EITF 89-4, a PO is not defined as a "high risk" investment and, therefore, remains under the purview of FASB 91 for accounting purposes.

Limitations of FASB 91: Before discussing Issues 1 and 3 of EITF 89-4, it is important to understand first why the accounting methodologies in FASB 91 are not particularly well suited for high-risk CMOs and IOs. To illustrate the issue, refer to Exhibit 10, which is the IO that complements the PO in Exhibit 9. The cost of this IO investment is assumed to be 38% of the principal balance of the underlying MBS collateral, or $19 million.

Whereas column A reflects the total cash flow (i.e., principal and interest) expected for the underlying MBS collateral, column B reflects just the coupon interest that would be collected each year, assuming a 10.5% CPR for the related principal (the same prepay-

---

Exhibit 10: Amortization of Discount on Interest-Only (IO) Securities: Retrospective Method (Dollars in Thousands)

Assumptions:

Face Amount:			$50,000	MBS Coupon:			9.5%
PO Amount (at 62):			$31,000	Prepayment Speed:			10.5% CPR
IO Amount (at 38):			$19,000				

End of Year	Cash Flow	Coupon Interest	Ending Principal Balance	Premium Amort.	Net IO Income	Unamort. Premium	IO Yield
	(A)	(B)	(C)	(D)	(E)	(F)	(G)
Settlement			$50,000			$19,000	
1	$10,299	$4,750	44,451	$2,175	$2,575	16,825	13.55%
2	9,183	4,223	39,491	1,943	2,280	14,882	13.55%
3	8,185	3,752	35,057	1,735	2,017	13,147	13.55%
4	7,293	3,330	31,095	1,549	1,781	11,598	13.55%
5	6,495	2,954	27,554	1,383	1,571	10,215	13.55%
6	5,781	2,618	24,391	1,234	1,384	8,981	13.55%
7	5,143	2,317	21,565	1,100	1,217	7,881	13.55%
.	.	.		.	.		
.	.	.		.	.		
30							
	$89,089	$39,089		$19,000	$20,089		

Notes:

Cash Flows in column A represent the total cash flows on the underlying securities.

IO yield of 13.55% is the IRR on the IO cash flows, i.e., outflow of $19,000 at settlement, and inflows equal to coupon interest (column B) in years 1 to 30.

ment assumption used in Exhibit 9). Using this prepayment assumption, over the life of the IO investment, coupon interest would total $39.089 million. Column D reflects the amortization of the $19 million cost of the IO, resulting in net IO income in column E, totaling $20.089 million. Column F reflects the unamortized balance of the cost of the IO, which is the reported value of the investment for accounting purposes. Column D is amortized so that the net income reported in column E will result in a level yield relative to the unamortized premium balance shown in column F. Based on a 10.5% CPR, the accounting yield reported for the IO is 13.55%.

The calculations in Exhibit 10 are based on applying the retrospective method of FASB 91 to the underlying MBS collateral. If the contractual method under FASB 91 had been used for determining IO income, the coupon interest in column A would have been based on the unrealistic assumption of no prepayments. This would have resulted in estimated total coupon interest of approximately $102.521 million, and a yield of 23.87%, the maximum possible amount. In later years, as prepayments accelerate, there would be downward adjustments to IO income to reflect the fact that the future coupon interest related to those principal prepayments will never be received.

Even if the retrospective method under FASB 91 is used exclusively on IOs, however, there still would be problems. For example, assuming the retrospective method under FASB 91 was used to determine the initial IO yield of 13.55% (column G), a relatively small deviation form the 10.5% prepayment assumption would necessitate a significant catch-up adjustment to the unamortized balance of the investment under FASB 91. In essence, the difference between the cost of the IO investment ($19 million) and the interest income received (column B) is similar to the unamortized discount of a PO. A significant difference between IOs and POs, however, is that the unamortized discount of the POs is a fixed amount that will be recorded as interest income over a variable period of time. In the case of IOs, the amount of income that ultimately will be received can vary along with the effective time period over which it will be received.

Prospective Yield Method: Because the premium and discount amortization methodologies of FASB 91 did not produce meaningful results for IOs and certain types of CMO investments, a new methodology was devised. Issue 3 of EITF 89-4 prescribes the following method of accounting for IOs and "high-risk" CMO investments:

> At the date of purchase, an effective yield is calculated based on the purchase price and anticipated future cash flows. In the initial accounting period, interest income is accrued on the investment balance using that rate. Cash received on the investment is first applied to accrued interest with any excess reducing the recorded investment balance. At each reporting date, the effective yield is recalculated based on the amortized cost of the investment and the then-current estimate of future cash flows. This recalculated yield is then used to accrue interest income on the investment balance in the subsequent accounting period. This procedure continues until all cash flows from the investment have been received. The amortized balance of the investment at the end of each period will equal the present value of the estimated future cash flows discounted at the newly calculated effective yield. . . The estimated future cash flows at each reporting date should reflect the most current estimate of future prepayments.

An illustration of how the prospective yield method under EITF 89-4 is applied to an IO is depicted in Exhibit 11. This example uses the same facts and assumptions as those in Exhibit 10, except that the prepayment assumption is revised in year four. The calculation initially, and for the first three years in this example, is the same as using the retrospective method under FASB 91.

When the prepayment rate is increased to 12% in year four and succeeding years, however, the total amount of coupon interest (column B) expected to be received over the life of the investment declines to $36.672 million (compared with $39.089 million in Exhibit 10), resulting in a comparable reduction in total net IO income (column E) expected to be received.

Unlike FASB 91, the prospective yield method requires no retroactive adjustment to the 13.55% yield reported in previous periods. Based on the unamortized investment balance of $13.147 million (column F) at the end of year three and the new interest cash flow resulting from the revised prepayment rate (column B),

Exhibit 11: Amortization of Discount on Interest-Only (IO) Securities: Prospective Yield Method (Dollars in Thousands)

Assumptions:

Face Amount:	$50,000	MBS Coupon:	9.5%
PO Amount (at 62):	$31,000	Prepayment Speed (years 1-3):	10.5% CPR
IO Amount (at 38):	$19,000	Prepayment Speed (years 4-30):	12% CPR

End of Year	Cash Flow	Coupon Interest	Ending Principal Balance	Premium Amort.	Net IO Income	Unamort. Premium	IO Yield
	(A)	(B)	(C)	(D)	(E)	(F)	(G)
Settlement			$50,000			$19,000	
1	$10,299	$4,750	44,451	$2,175	$2,575	16,825	13.55%
2	9,183	4,223	39,491	1,943	2,280	14,882	13.55%
3	8,185	3,752	35,057	1,735	2,017	13,147	13.55%
4	7,814	3,330	30,574	1,742	1,588	11,405	12.08%
5	6,840	2,904	26,638	1,526	1,378	9,879	12.08%
6	5,984	2,531	23,185	1,337	1,194	8,542	12.08%
7	5,232	2,203	20,155	1,170	1,033	7,372	12.08%
.	.	.		.	.		
30							
	$86,672	$36,672		$19,000	$17,672		

Notes:

The IO yield is recalculated in year 4 as a result of changes in prepayment speeds.

The new level yield is calculated over the remaining life of the IO using future cash flows and the net investment at the end of year 3.

a "prospective" yield to maturity is calculated. In the example in Exhibit 11 that yield is 12.08%. In an actual situation, the reported yield is likely to be recalculated every reporting period to reflect actual prepayment experience and changes in the rate of prepayments expected in the future.

Residual Interests: Investing in residual interests of CMOs is similar to owning securities that have the characteristics of both debt and equity. They are like debt in that they may provide for periodic distributions of cash flow and are an expiring asset with a limited life; in addition, investors buy them for their expected yield. Residuals are like equity in that they have the most subordinated right to cash flows coming to a CMO from the underlying mortgage collateral, and in some cases take the form of common stock or partnership units.

Under Issue No. 1 of EITF 89-4, CMO instruments having the legal form of equity should be accounted for as nonequity (i.e., as debt), only when all of the following criteria are met:

1. The assets in the special-purpose entity were not transferred to it by the purchaser of the CMO instrument.

2. The assets of the special-purpose entity consist solely of a large number of similar high-credit-quality monetary assets (e.g., one or more high-credit-quality MBSs that provide an undivided interest in a large number of similar mortgage loans) for which prepayments are probable and the timing and amounts of prepayments can be reasonable estimated.

3. The special-purpose entity is self-liquidating.

4. Assets collateralizing the obligation of the special-purpose entity may not be exchanged, sold, or otherwise managed as a portfolio.

5. There is no more than a remote possibility that the purchaser would be required to contribute funds to the special-

purpose entity to pay administrative expenses or other costs.

6. No other obligee of the special-purpose entity has recourse to the purchaser of the investment.

The ability of a purchaser of a CMO instrument to call other CMO tranches of the special-purpose entity generally will not preclude treatment of the purchaser's investment as a nonequity instrument, provided all the above criteria are met. As a general rule, the residual interests of most CMOs would be considered nonequity (i.e., debt) instruments for accounting purposes.

Residual interests determined to be nonequity instruments are often accounted for by the prospective yield method because many have the potential for losing a significant portion of their original investment value as a result of changes in prepayments or interest rates.

CONCLUSION

It is important for investors to understand how yields on their mortgage securities investments will be reported in financial statements prepared under GAAP. As indicated in this chapter, the accounting policies can vary depending on the investor's financial capability and investment motives. Under the historical cost method, accounting yields can fluctuate significantly as a result of either the nature of individual securities or certain accounting choices available to the investor.

CHAPTER 41

COMPUTERIZED SUPPORT FOR MORTGAGE-BACKED SECURITIES INVESTING

Bruce E. Vollert
Vice President
Sungard Financial Systems

The continued evolution of the mortgage-backed securities (MBSs) and asset-backed securities (ABSs) marketplace has created opportunities for investors and challenges for the suppliers of computerized investment support systems. During the 1980s, the MBS/ABS market was characterized by numerous security product innovations, explosive trading volumes, and a complex array of new investment and financing strategies, all of which presented new critical information requirements for traders, portfolio managers, accountants, and back-office operations personnel. The suppliers of investment support systems, with few exceptions, are only now beginning to keep pace with the rate of change in this market and the accompanying demands of institutional investors.

This chapter examines the current state of computerized MBS/ABS support systems, and includes a review of numerous leading systems available on the market today. The opening discussion focuses on the four major functional areas of MBS/ABS automation, including trading support, back-office operations support, securities accounting, and portfolio management. This is followed by a review of the primary factors to consider when developing or selecting a system. The closing discussion examines newly developing technologies and takes a look at future MBS/ABS systems. This information should assist institutional investors searching to improve computerized MBS/ABS support systems, and is directed to insurance companies, mutual funds, investment advisors, commercial banks, thrifts, pension funds, and other major institutional investors. While many Wall Street investment banking firms have developed sophisticated mainframe-based MBS/ABS systems for in-house use, these systems are generally not available on a commercial basis; therefore, they will not be reviewed. Furthermore, the computerization needs of broker/dealers and issuers are beyond the scope of this chapter.

TRADING SUPPORT

Twenty-five years ago, institutional investors relied on broker information supplied over the telephone and paper-based research reports to make investment decisions. Today, vast amounts of up-to-the-minute market information are available electronically through a terminal at the investor's desk. With the interconnection of domestic and foreign financial markets, accessibility to current market information has become a vital aspect of investment management. Vendors such as Bloomberg, Reuters, Telerate, Quotron, and Knight Ridder have established high-speed communications systems that deliver a plethora of current securities pricing data, market indicators, and the latest newsbreaks. Most of these market information systems were initially designed for the broker/dealer community, and later were extended into the hands of investors demanding improved timeliness of market information.

Computerization of the trading support area is perhaps the most exciting of the MBS/ABS automation areas. Trading support systems deliver information that can be quickly converted into trading decisions and realized profits. These systems supply investment personnel with both the securities information and real-time analytical tools to evaluate trading strategies, identify potential mispricings within the market, and capitalize on market imperfections. Computerized market information services include both view-only sources and interactive systems that offer dynamic trade analytics.

The multitude of available quotation and electronic news services has led to the emergence of specialized vendors—such as Rich, Inc. and Micrognosis, Inc.—that consolidate many financial information sources for use on a single trader console. Rather than requiring one to contend with a complex array of video displays, keyboards, and communications equipment that result from multiple market information services, products from these vendors enable investors to have instant access from a single keyboard. These systems also offer direct links with personal computers, host computers, and external time-sharing systems. The largest market for these integrated trading workstations is in the broker/dealer community, where a single installation may involve more than 1,000 stations. For example, in March of 1986, Rich, Inc. announced the completion of the world's largest trading system at Merrill Lynch in New York. Over 1,200 trader stations were installed, covering equities, bonds, MBSs, and municipal markets. Many institutional investors with large investment departments and an abundance of market information services have also installed these integrated investment workstations.

Whereas these systems provide the communications and physical workstation equipment for investors, it is the market information and analytical trading software that is vital for decision making. Before selecting a software trading support system, investors should look for the capabilities described in the next sections.

Market Pricing

Since a unified MBS exchange does not exist, securities are traded over-the-counter in a market dominated by six primary dealers, which partially explains the lack of homogeneous pricing. The majority of pricing services provide so called "generic" MBS prices rather than quotes on specific pools. Generic prices represent aggregations of pools having identical issuer (such as the Government National Mortgage Association—GNMA) and coupon (such as 9%) into groups for market trading purposes, and, as such, generic prices do not represent specific securities. These prices are inferior to specific pool prices, as they do not incorporate important factors such as pool-specific prepayment experience, maturity date, duration, weighted average maturity (WAM), and weighted average coupon (WAC) for the underlying mortgages. With over 420,000 GNMA, FHLMC, and FNMA pools outstanding, it is easy to understand why the majority of actual trades is based on generic prices. Liquidity at the pool level is not sufficient to support continuous bid and ask pricing activity.

For designated pool trades, firm price quotes are available directly from the dealer. The bulk of the MBS market-pricing that vendors provide is generic pricing on completed transactions rather than current price quotations. Pricing systems that have a direct link to a dealer, such as the Bloomberg system with its link to Merrill Lynch, provide current quotes. The selected system should provide historical generic prices and yields to assist in evaluation of yield-spread relationships and historical price volatilities. For CMO issues, the system should provide a valuation capability that is based on a cash flow model that incorporates the complex payment hierarchy of multitranche CMOs, and a prepayment model applied to the underlying collateral. The cash flow model should apply prepayment estimates to the underlying collateral and incorporate the unique payment priorities and cash flow structure of other tranches in the CMO issue as specified in the prospectus.

On-Line Pool Information

Unlike generic trades, on-line MBS pool information is important in pool-specific purchases and sales. Investors should look for on-line systems that provide information such as original and remaining balance, the pooling agency, issuer, issue and maturity date, original and estimated remaining WAC and WAM, duration, average pool life, pool factor, and prepayment speeds. Additionally, investors should determine if the prepayment speed statistics offered match the investor's preference. Many systems offer prepayment statistics based on the Public Securities Association (PSA) prepayment model. The PSA model has become a standard in CMO and other MBS/ABS derivative pricing. Ideally, an on-line pool inquiry system should also provide pool factor history and a graphic display of the principal paydown experience over time.

Institutional investors that find on-line pool information services cost-prohibitive can opt for monthly subscription services that provide information in a microcomputer-readable format.

Yield/Price Calculations and Conversions

For trade analysis purposes, a trading support system should allow investors to manipulate a variety of fields interactively, such as price, yield, tax rates, reinvestment rates, prepayment rate assumptions, and settlement date, and then recalculate the other fields dynamically. The system should provide the corporate bond equivalent yield. Ideally, the system should also allow for specifying varying prepayment and reinvestment rates over the life of the security.

On-Line Position Reporting

Current trading position reports keep investors informed of unrealized MBS/ABS gains and losses based on current market prices.

Leading available systems report all trade commitments and settled positions on a trade date basis, and display amounts encumbered due to collateral pledging on reverse repurchase agreements, dollar rolls, other financings, hedge positions, or arbitrage transactions.

Horizon Return Analysis

Conducting a total return analysis over a predetermined horizon enables investors to evaluate MBS/ABS returns in relation to other investments. The horizon return analysis incorporates the investor's projected reinvestment rates over the period, estimated prepayment rates, and the security yield or price at the horizon date. This computation-intensive analysis is best served by a computer, and ideally should allow for comparative MBS/ABS horizon returns versus Treasuries, corporates, or other MBS/ABS pools.

More advanced analytical systems will allow for dynamic modeling in which prepayment rates and interest rates vary over the horizon period. The system should allow the investor to model nonparallel shifts in the future yield curve and model the impact on prepayment behavior. To model prepayment sensitivity properly, the system should allow for the input of prepayment estimates under multiple interest rate shifts (e.g., plus and minus 100, 200, 300 basis points). The resulting horizon period returns under each scenario would be evaluated independently and then may be probability-weighted for an overall expected horizon return and variance. The convexity statistic will provide insight into the behavior of prepayments under varying interest rate scenarios, and should be present. This type of analysis is of particular importance for CMO investments, where the complexity of a given deal structure can significantly alter the cash flow stream realized by the investor.

Break-Even Prepayment Rate Analysis

The break-even MBS/ABS prepayment rate is defined as the pre-pay rate required to duplicate the cash flows of the current coupon traded security (such as the GMNA, FHLMC, or FNMA coupon trading closest to 100 or par). This break-even rate provides useful insights when it is compared to actual and projected prepayment rates for a given mortgage security. The break-even analysis should allow users to enter a reinvestment rate scenario that corresponds to the investor's view of the future term structure of interest rates. A complete trading system should also offer comparisons among a variety of debt instruments.

Historical Yield Spread Analysis

For comparative purposes, investors require on-line access to historical price and yield information. The comparison of a generic mortgage security (or a specific pool) to U.S. Treasuries and other debt securities reveals relative values. An inclusive trading support system should provide current, high, low, and mean average yield basis point spreads over any investor-specified time period. Given the volatility in fixed-income markets, a graphic display of historical spreads is the most meaningful. Moreover, the system should flag securities that appear rich or cheap relative to historical spreads of comparable effective duration and convexity securities.

MBS Swap Analysis

A computerized swap analysis capability should be performed on-line from the investor's terminal. Based on current market prices, the analysis should include:

- Swap outcome under various reinvestment and prepayment rate assumptions.

- User-assigned federal, state, and local taxation rates.

- Before- and after-tax gains or losses and yield advantage on a yield-equivalent basis.

- Break-even reinvestment rate and horizon date.

- Duration and convexity comparisons and an indication of comparative historical price volatilities.

- Capability for multiple buy and sell candidates.

- Evaluation of gains at multiple horizon dates.

The swap evaluation should require minimum data entry requirements and should automatically extract pertinent security information, such as coupon rate and maturity date, from an on-line database.

Hedging Analysis

Computer support is required in order to assist investors in hedging against adverse market price swings. The analysis features should encompass hedging strategies using debt options, financial futures, interest rate swaps, CMO residuals and interest only (IO) stripped MBSs. The ideal system should provide an indication of the historical price correlation between differing instruments to disclose the effectiveness of a given cross hedge.

Dollar Roll Arbitrage Analysis

MBS dollar rolls frequently provide a lower-cost financing alternative to reverse repurchase agreements. Dollar rolls involve the sale of MBS pools in the current month and simultaneous purchase of "similar" pools in a forward month.

A computerized dollar roll analysis program allows for the designation of a short-term reinvestment instrument and calculates the net financing cost and arbitrage gain. The system should also permit users to enter alternative reinvestment rates, prepayment assumptions, and forward prices in evaluating the dollar roll.

OPERATIONS

The trading of MBSs has proven to be an arduous task for back-office operations personnel. Complications experienced in trade settlement, payment tracking, and securities clearance are unlike those for any other security in the market. This, combined with the generally slow pace at which technology has been adopted, and the astounding growth in trade volumes, has created immense market-wide operational difficulties. During heavy market trading in the latter part of 1986, as much as 40% of GNMA trades failed due to an inability to execute proper settlement. To give this some perspective, consider that annual trading volumes approached $1 trillion in 1986.

The high cost of MBS operations and "fails" has been felt by investors and brokerage houses alike. In 1986, the investment house of Morgan Stanley & Company sharply curtailed its MBS trading for two months as back-office operations, lacking adequate computer support, became swamped with high trading volumes.

Given today's advanced technology, the lack of sufficient market-wide automation has mystified many market participants. Out of concern, the Securities and Exchange Commission conducted an informal research study to determine why computerization has been so slow in coming. Until the advent of the Mortgage-Backed Securities Clearing Corporation (MBSCC), the GNMA market lacked a centralized depository and clearance system that would allow for the computerized book-entry form of settlement, as is available for other security types. Book-entry settlement effectively eliminates the need for physical delivery, thereby reducing fails and resulting financing costs. Physical certificates are safekept in the depository's nominee name in a centralized New York City vault, and trade settlements are accomplished through computerized record-keeping of ownership changes. Investors are no longer faced with the burden of scrambling physically to deliver securities or with the task of tracking safekeeping locations. On March 31, 1989, the Participants Trust Company (PTC) completed its purchase of the MBS depository from the MBSCC. PTC is a limited purpose trust company chartered by the State of New York and registered with the Securities and Exchange Commission as a clearing agency.

The PTC MBS depository solves many of the delivery and clearance problems associated with MBS trading, including a reduction in lost and stolen certificates. The PTC MBS depository will begin to yield large benefits as conversion to book-entry form expands among institutional investors.

The PTC MBS depository will not eliminate the need for institutions to comply with the Public Securities Association (PSA)[1] requirements for the receipt and delivery of MBS pools, which constitutes another major operational challenge.

Within forty-eight hours of settlement, the seller must communicate pools earmarked for delivery to the buyer, and combine the pools so as to comply with the PSA rules. These rules stipulate a maximum of three pools per $1 million traded, or a maximum of four pools per $1 million for coupons of 12% or more. Moreover, because the monthly reduction of principal reduces the outstanding balance of each pool to an odd dollar and cents amount, the task of matching buy and sell orders to the penny is near impossible. Consequently, the PSA rules call for the delivery of an outstanding principal amount that is within a 2.5% tolerance limit per $1 million and for the trade commitment value as a whole. These requirements are quite cumbersome, particularly for larger trades.

---

[1] The Public Securities Association is the national trade organization of banks and brokerage firms that underwrite, trade, and sell MBSs, municipal securities, money-market securities, and securities issued by the U.S. government and its agencies.

A $100 million 13% coupon trade could result in 400 individual pools and hours of effort grouping good delivery lots. A complete discussion of the rules governing MBS settlements can be found in PSA's document entitled "Uniform Practices for the Clearance and Settlement of Mortgage-Backed Securities."

Since pools designated for delivery are often communicated over the telephone and manually recorded, frequent errors are introduced. Moreover, as the settlement hour nears, institutions struggle to assemble pools for delivery on additional trades, and frequently buyers telephone back with pool cancellations and substitutions. Those securities not handled by the PTC MBS depository must be physically delivered by the 3 p.m. deadline (Eastern time).

If the committed pools do not change hands on settlement date, the transaction fails. Some institutions will accept a commitment for delivery beyond the settlement date, even though the trade has technically failed. This occurs because of the high cost of failed transactions to both investors and brokers.

Given the above and other factors, a computerized MBS operations support system ideally would provide the following automated features:

- Tracking of open trade commitments (pending settlements)

- Fail reporting and control

- Pledge status reporting

- Collateral monitoring

- Processing of pool delivery cancellations and substitutions

- Good delivery selection on sales (i.e., in compliance with the PSA rules)

- Auto-send of trade and settlement confirmations

- An automated interface to the PTC MBS depository, brokerage houses, and Fed Wire System

- Safekeeping location tracking

- To be announced (TBA) processing

Proper reporting of pending settlements and fails will require
that the system track both the contractual settlement date and the
actual delivery date. The process of entering pre- and post-settle-
ment date pool cancellations and substitutions should be accomplished with a minimum of effort and provide necessary audit
trails. This is an area few systems adequately address.

Increasingly, major New York brokerage systems are providing
computer-readable listings of pools earmarked for settlement. Investors should be equipped to receive this information via telecommunications directly into a computerized MBS system. Once
received, the system should automatically verify compliance with
PSA good delivery standards, and process the transactions.

Many investors also seek to computerize the automatic selection or allocation of pools for a sale in an optimal manner. A discussion of this process follows.

Optimal Pool Allocation

MBS allocation systems automatically select pools for delivery
from the investor's inventory of pools to fulfill a sale commitment
or dollar roll delivery. An optimal allocation program enables the
investor to specify selection parameters such as desired prepayment speed, WAC, WAM, duration, and maximum profitability. A
dealer also considers pair-off transaction advantages. The system
should select pools that meet these objectives and bundle them so
as to comply with the PSA good delivery standards (e.g., no more

than three pools per million or four pools per million for 12% plus coupons, and the 2.5% tolerance limit per million).

To optimize allocation fully, investors often seek to under- or over-deliver while remaining within the 2.5% rule to take advantage of price movements since initial trade commitment. If market prices rise following trade date, for instance, an optimal delivery would be 97.501% of the original trade amount (that is, under delivery yet within 2.5 percent). Alternately, if market prices drop following trade date, an optimal delivery would be 102.499% of the original trade. All this needs to be accomplished and communicated to the buyer within forty-eight hours of settlement date in accordance with the PSA rules. The PSA good delivery requirements can be waived given the mutual accord of both buyer and seller, as is the case with designated pool trades.

Following the investor's approval of the allocation, the computer system should automatically reduce the sale commitment, post the trade, produce and auto-send the trade ticket or confirmation, update the settlement inventory, and prepare data or reports to be transmitted to the custodian.

The operational problems in today's MBS market are analogous to those experienced by the New York Stock Exchange (NYSE) in the late 1960s, when the NYSE closed it doors early because of volume overloads. Technology in the form of more advanced computer software, hardware, and communications solved the NYSE problems, and will be the catalyst for the more efficient operation of the MBS market.

SECURITIES ACCOUNTING

Investment accounting requirements have increased in complexity with the advent of many new MBS types. Accounting standards for selected new derivative securities are still being developed. As the Financial Accounting Standards Board (FASB) and the American Institute of Certified Public Accountants (AICPA) finalize standards, software vendors take steps to incorporate proper accounting treatments.

In reviewing available computerized systems, investment accountants should require that systems address the full range of MBS types and perform interest accruals according to the Securities Industry Association standards. Required automated accounting reports would include security investment ledgers, historical transaction journals, and inventory position reports. Ideally, investment earnings reports should report accrued interest income and amortizations of premium or discount. A general ledger interface capability should be present to eliminate duplicate manual entries. Investors should confirm that retroactive adjusting entries to the general ledger will be produced automatically for fails, substitutions, cancellations, and other back-dated transactions. Sophisticated systems will support GAAP, tax, and regulatory reporting basis carrying values. This is important where institutions have made acquisitions under the purchase accounting method, involving a mark-to-market of the acquired institution's portfolio. Since many investment systems are limited to specific identification or specific lot accounting on sales, investors should verify, if appropriate, the availability of average cost, last-in-first-out (LIFO), or first-in-first-out (FIFO) methods. The reporting of realized gains and losses should be based on the selected inventory accounting method. A limited number of systems allow for an override capability in which, for example, investors applying the LIFO inventory method could override with the specific identification method on a given trade.

The actively traded portfolios of some institutions require mark-to-market accounting. This method varies substantially from the more common practice of adjusting the net carrying value of the investment position through an amortization of the premium or discount. Mark-to-market accounting involves a periodic market valuation of investments, and an adjustment to bring the carrying basis equivalent to current market. The unrealized gain or loss is recognized as income (or loss) in the current period. Mark-to-market accounting is found in an increasing number of commercially available systems.

MBS/ABS Payment Scheduling and Accounts Receivable Tracking

In the past, investors in the MBS/ABS market have been plagued by missing and past due monthly principal and interest payments. The lack of timely cash payments has diminished the realized cash flow yields on MBS investments, and has reduced total portfolio returns due to the high cost of tracking account receivables.

Failure to properly register the new MBS owner with the paying agent—either because of security fails or mail delays—causes the monthly checks to be forwarded to previous owners. Investors forego interest earnings on payments and are faced with verifying the correct payment, determining the registered owner, and submitting a claim letter. Computerization can greatly streamline this process. Through an interface to the Bond Buyer factor tape or other principal paydown factor service, a computer system can automatically calculate current entitlements for principal and interest on MBS/ABS and CMO positions. The factors represent the percentage of each pool's original face outstanding. The system should also store the factors for purposes of tracking historical receivables, and, at the same time, automatically create a transaction file for current month payments to eliminate the need for manual entry. A thorough system will track full or partially missing payments beyond a subsequent sale date, automatically produce claim letters, and chronologically classify aged receivables. A sophisticated system would continue to track payments on MBS pools pledged as collateral on reverse repurchase agreement financing, and would recognize that payments are not due on dollar-rolled MBSs. For a complete picture of receivables, the system should report historical transaction activity and position information online. Since investors also receive payments they are not entitled to, a comprehensive system would also track and report unclaimed payables.

Amortization of Securities Purchased at a Premium or Discount

The investor's monthly receipt of principal "passed through" from a pool's underlying conventional mortgages represents a reduction to both the current par and book value basis of an investment. Securities purchased at a premium price, or a price that exceeds the current par value, require an amortization of the premium ratably over the life of the security. Likewise, securities purchased at a discount price that is less than current par require amortization[2] of the discount amount. The amortized premium amount reduces current period interest income, and conversely, the discount amortization enhances current income.

Several complications exist for the amortization of premium or discount for MBSs. First, the monthly return of principal represents a portion of the original principal returned, and, hence, an equivalent proportional amount of the premium or discount amount remaining unamortized should be recognized. The monthly principal payment is treated similarly to a partial call for purposes of calculating current period amortizations. The unamortized premium or discount amount associated with the principal returned (sometimes referred to as a gain or loss) is recognized as an adjustment to interest income in the current period. A securities accounting system should automatically calculate these amounts, and, at the same time, calculate the additional amount of the outstanding or remaining unamortized premium or discount attributable to the current period. An advanced computer system would allow investors to select from a variety of amortization methodologies, including straight-line, constant- or level-yield,[3] or sum-of-the-years-digits.

The second complication for MBS amortizations relates to the determination of the security's life given fluctuating prepayment

---

[2] Discount amortization is sometimes referred to as accretion.

[3] This is also known as the scientific, or the effective interest rate method. This method adjusts the book value in order to maintain the original book-yield-to-maturity constant over the life of the security.

rates. It seems inappropriate to amortize MBS premiums over the contractual thirty-year life when 10% of the principal outstanding may be returned in a given month, as was the case for selected high-coupon GNMAs during the latter half of 1985. In practice, both the amortization periods selected and the methods used vary considerably. Prior to 1981, market yields were based on a twelve-year prepay assumption; consequently, many investors elected to calculate amortizations over a twelve-year life. As prepayments accelerated in the mid-1980s, investment accountants responded by applying shorter and shorter amortization periods.

In 1986, FASB introduced Financial Accounting Statement (FAS) 91, which applies to accounting for nonrefundable fees and costs associated with originating or acquiring loans, including debt instruments. This statement applies to all types of institutional lenders (or investors) and requires that MBS/ABS purchase premiums and discounts either be amortized under the constant-yield method over the contractual life of the security (30 years), or if prepayments can be reasonably estimated, investors may forecast prepayments for purposes of calculating the effective yield (or cash flow yield) to be applied in the constant-yield amortization method. FASB 91 further states that if estimated prepayments are used in the calculation, and differences arise between prepayments anticipated and those actually received, then the institution must recalculate the effective yield to reflect actual prepayments to date and estimated future prepayments. Moreover, the book value of the investment must be adjusted to reflect the current amortized book value that would have resulted had the new yield been applied in the constant yield amortization formula since purchase date. Needless to say, this additional layer of computational requirements compounds the complexities of the constant-yield amortization method and magnifies the need for adequate computer support.

PORTFOLIO MANAGEMENT

Portfolio management systems provide information that assists in making adjustments to the overall portfolio strategy, appraising risks, and in monitoring performance returns. In contrast to the automation of the trading support function, in which the focus is on specific trades, MBS portfolio management systems offer reporting at a macro level. Shifts in the portfolio composition are evaluated in the context of the resulting impact on taxation, asset/liability management, liquidity requirements, risk, returns, and regulatory and legal considerations.

Computer portfolio systems enable managers to be more responsive to changing market conditions by providing timely reporting. While the specific information requirements vary from one type of institution to the next, the following reporting areas should be present in a comprehensive system.

Portfolio Diversification and Quality Reporting

The need for assessing portfolio diversification and credit risk is commonly recognized where the portfolio composition includes a broad range of equity, fixed-income, and money market securities. The need for diversification reporting within a strictly mortgage-backed portfolio has increased in importance as a greater number and variety of both MBS issuers and products have emerged.

The structural and legal characteristics of new mortgage-derivative products carry with them risk elements not found in traditional agency-backed MBS issues. This is not to say that diversification reporting is inappropriate for portfolios composed strictly of GNMA, FHLMC, and FNMA pass-through securities. Differences in the principal and payment guarantees of these issues also warrant an assessment of portfolio diversification.

Whereas GNMA securities are backed by the full faith and credit of the U.S. Treasury, with a guarantee for the timely payment of both monthly principal and interest, FHLMC and FNMA are not explicitly backed by the U.S. Treasury. Most FHLMC securities not issued in its gold program differ further in that FHLMC guarantees the timely payment of interest and ultimate (but not timely) payment of principal (that is, within one year).

Certain risks exist even for GNMA securities. In the summer of 1987, GNMA took over nearly $900 million in troubled mobile home loan portfolios. Mounting loan defaults in the depressed U.S. oil patch forced GNMA to step in, purchase, and refinance the loans. Losses were realized by investors who had purchased high-coupon GNMA mobile home pools at a premium, as GNMA refinanced the loans and repaid investors at par, thereby acting within the state government guarantee. GNMA took the position that prepayment risk is inherent with any mortgage-backed investment. The financial losses realized by these investors caused them to reevaluate the government guarantees and reassess actual risk.

The need for a computerized monitoring system to assess exposure to issuer credit risk is greater with privately issued pass-throughs, where securities can be issued without guarantees by the issuing institution. A computerized diversification reporting system should allow for the classification of securities according to the inherent creditworthiness and report on the percentage- and dollar-risk exposure to given issuers.

The rating agencies for MBSs (such as Fitch Investors Service, Moody's Investor Service, and Standard and Poor's Corporation) issue ratings for both agency-backed and privately issued mortgage pass-throughs, mortgage pay-throughs, and mortgage-backed bonds. The ratings are quite valuable to portfolio managers when the structural, analytical, and legal issues are complex, as is the case with CMOs and other derivative mortgage-backed issues. A comprehensive portfolio management system must therefore track and report on quality ratings at both a summary and detail level. An ideal computerized system would also notify investors of any rating changes that occur, and update the system to reflect those changes.

Portfolio Horizon Return Analysis

Computer modeling of portfolio returns over a predetermined horizon period provides investors with a prehension of the impact of shifting interest rates and prepayment speeds on the portfolio returns. As with the horizon analysis for individual security trades, aggregate portfolio horizon return analysis would enable investors to project multiple reinvestment rate and prepay rate scenarios over the defined period. Period-end market values would be determined from the investor's estimate of future Treasury yield curves and MBS-to-Treasury spread relationships. Performing this analysis on the MBS/ABS portfolio as a whole requires significant number-crunching, and hence computer power.

Prepayment Modeling

Given the investor's expectation of future prepayment and reinvestment rates, the computer should calculate total portfolio yields and durations, and project future period cash flows. This modeling capability allows users to assess the impact of varying prepayment scenarios on portfolio yields, and provides cash flow information necessary for asset/liability modeling. An automated interface to the asset/liability management system minimizes redundant data entry.

Coupon Distribution Reporting

At a summary level, coupon distribution reporting gives an indication of potential price volatilities and coupon concentrations. Investors will find this information useful in assessing the potential impact of a falling rate environment.

Regulatory, Liquidity, and Legal Compliance Reporting

Whereas the requirements may vary by type of institutional investor, the computer system adopted should supply necessary regulatory and liquidity reports, and automatically monitor legal investment restrictions. Generalized report writers frequently enable the MBS system to address this need when specific regulatory reports are absent. Complex reports, however, such as the insurance industry's regulatory Schedule D report, require specifically designed programs and unique printing formats.

Performance Measurement Reporting

Computerization has furnished investors with the means to calculate and measure MBS portfolio returns against a MBS market index, other funds, or hypothetical baseline portfolios. To measure performance accurately, the system must offer a market-pricing capability and the ability to calculate the time-weighted return for the portfolio. The system's calculation for time-weighted returns should correspond to the Bank Administration Institute's (BAI) published formula or the Investment Counsel Association of America's (ICAA) proposed standard. Both of these methods calculate the portfolio manager's performance independent of cash flows that are beyond the control of the manager.

The measurement of a fixed-income portfolio's risk level with respect to changes in the level of interest rates normally can be measured using the duration model. The greater the portfolio duration the greater the price volatility, and hence risk, given changes in the general level of interest rates.

Two problems exist in applying the standard modified duration model to MBS risk measurement. First, because actual prepayment and cash flow experience varies considerably from market estimates, duration is at best a soft indicator of MBS market price volatility. Secondly, the phenomenon of negative convexity for high-coupon MBSs and many CMOs is a market price reaction contrary to that expected in the duration model. Higher-coupon premium bonds normally have a relatively lower duration and accompanying lower market risk. With high-coupon MBSs, however, a falling rate environment causes prepayment acceleration due to refinancings. Consequently, premiums must be amortized over a shorter life, and the principal reduction erodes current interest income. Market prices are reduced in order to compensate for the reduced earnings. An effective duration calculation that takes into account prepayment sensitivity to interest rate shifts and an accompanying effective convexity statistic will assist in more accurately measuring risk for MBSs and CMOs.

CONSIDERATIONS IN SELECTING OR DEVELOPING A MBS SYSTEM

Many of the leading investment systems on the market today were initially designed for semiannual paying corporates, Treasuries, and agency securities. Mortgage securities, with their characteristic monthly principal and interest payments, were in many instances retrofit into these previous database structures, with less than optimal results. Consequently, MBS investors frequently find existing systems inadequate. They are faced with the choice between purchasing a second system uniquely designed for mortgage securities, replacing the existing system with a comprehensive system, or simply limping along with the current system.

The factors to examine in the selection of a MBS system include the following:

Degree of Fit Between Requirements and System Capabilities:
Perhaps the most important criterion in selecting a MBS system is the degree to which user requirements are fulfilled by system capabilities. A personal discussion of needs with the vendor will help to explore the features in depth, but a demonstration is recommended to confirm capabilities.

Flexibility to Accommodate Change: Flexibility is of paramount importance in selecting a MBS system. The software selected must be designed to accommodate new security types, new accounting techniques, and new investment strategies; just as important, the vendor must have the staff expertise to anticipate, understand, and incorporate the changes. This criterion is best judged by examining the degree to which new market developments are in fact available in the product under evaluation, and evaluating the timeliness and completeness of such enhancements.

Degree of Technical Risk: Investors may wish to bring in data-processing personnel or seek the opinion of an outside consultant in determining the degree of technical risk with a given system. Many vendors on the market today tout benefits of new technologies that are unproven or inappropriate for the application. Fallout within the vendor client base is a red flag warning that technology claims are unsubstantiated.

Integration Between Trading, Operations, Accounting, and Portfolio Management Areas: A high degree of integration across trading support, back-office operations, securities accounting, and portfolio management support functions will help the institution immensely. Without integration, investors are faced with operating fragmented systems and performing unnecessary reconciliations between systems.

Financial Stability and Vendor Commitment: The software industry has relatively few barriers to entry, particularly in the PC workstation market. As a result, vendors rapidly enter new markets and frequently exit as quickly. Financial results over a historical period will reveal both financial stability and the degree of vendor commitment to the MBS systems area.

Expandability of the System: Potential buyers should assess the degree to which the system can accommodate increased volumes and an expanded number of users. The compatibility of hardware upgrades should also be clarified.

Reliability and Redundancy: Provisions for back-up redundancy during unexpected system down-time should be examined. Current users can provide references on the system's reliability. The opportunity cost of extended downtime could be severe during a market rally.

Support Adequacy and Timeliness of Implementation: Current system users can give references for these areas. Investors should also inquire about the support hours, support personnel qualifications, and longevity with the vendor.

Cost of Hardware, Software, Communications, Staffing, and Maintenance: The importance of this consideration is somewhat self-evident. Costs over a three- to five-year period should be evaluated, including the costs of system expansion to accommodate projected growth.

Development Considerations

The development of an in-house system represents a significant investment and a long-term commitment. Investors considering this avenue should carefully weigh the benefits to be realized from a tailored system versus the potential cost savings of an off-the-shelf product. The long-term cost of enhancing and maintaining the software should also be examined, and an assessment should be made of internal staff expertise. Relatively few programmers (albeit an increasing number) understand the intricacies of new derivative securities and the investment marketplace.

Institutions looking to develop in-house systems will naturally seek to develop a system that is flexible to accommodate long-term growth and one that closely represents actual needs when completed. A technique known as "prototyping" has been found to reduce the risk that systems may not turn out as expected. With prototyping, system developers and end users develop a pseudo-system jointly at the terminal, thereby making user input possible early in the development process.

A review of selected commercially available MBS/ABS systems follows.

BLOOMBERG FINANCIAL MARKETS

The Bloomberg system, previously Market Master, from Bloomberg Financial Markets, is a real-time trading support system offering current market pricing and analytical software support for investment traders. This system has received broad market acceptance since its introduction in March of 1983, reaching an installed base of 13,000 terminals in 1991. In addition to mortgage-backed and related derivative securities, the Bloomberg system addresses all fixed- and variable-rate debt instruments, equities, governments, corporates, agencies, money markets, futures, options, and municipal securities.

Bloomberg Limited Partners, headquartered in New York, employs a staff of over 650, with additional offices in London, Princeton, Singapore, Sydney, Tokyo, Toronto, and Washington. The Bloomberg system was used exclusively within the Merrill Lynch organization until September of 1984, when it became commercially available. Bloomberg Limited Partners is privately owned, with Merrill Lynch holding a non-increasing minority interest.

Bloomberg maintains a securities pricing database that is updated real-time by actual market-makers for over-the-counter securities, delayed exchange supplied ticker prices for listed securities, and foreign currency pricing from multiple top-tier interbank trading floors. The Bloomberg system also provides access to Bloomberg Business News, as well as feeds from the major newswires, and over 150 descriptive, research, and financial statistics on over 15,000 companies worldwide. Dealers worldwide display proprietary prices, offerings, and research to preferred customers via the Bloomberg system to facilitate securities sales and trading. Market indexes, economic time series, and market research reports are included, as well as pool-specific factors, prepayment statistics, and issuer information on MBSs.

The Bloomberg system accesses information on CMO issues and their unique cash flow structures via proprietary Bloomberg databases and models, and also through the CMO Passport system. The CMO Passport system is owned by Merrill Lynch with Bloomberg L. P. acting as distributor.

Bloomberg System Operation

The Bloomberg system is operated from a custom-designed keyboard and high-resolution, twelve-inch color monitor. The terminal(s) is connected through a dedicated lease line or via packet-switching networks to Bloomberg's remote host mainframe systems located in Princeton, New Jersey, London, England, and Tokyo, Japan. The system also interfaces with internal systems to facilitate portfolio maintenance, analytics, and pricing. The color-coded keyboard has been engineered specifically for the application, with function keys clearly labeled and programmed for particular operations.

In addition to the Bloomberg standard twelve-inch stand-alone color monitor, Bloomberg now offers The Bloomberg II, which allows access to two independent screens from a single keyboard, and The Bloomberg Traveler (formerly the Bloomberg Portable), a PC laptop version that accesses the system via remote dial-in telecommunications. The Bloomberg-supplied communications controller links the multiple Bloomberg terminals to the Bloomberg L. P. central data line and host mainframe systems. The Bloomberg delivers instantaneous or near-instantaneous response for all but the most complex analytical features.

Bloomberg MBS Trading Information

The Bloomberg system includes information on all MBSs (such as GNMA I and II, FHLMC, FNMA, and privately issued securities) CMOs, IOs, POs, GPMs, TPMs, and other mortgage-derivative products that have an active secondary market. New features and analytical screens have been added to keep pace with the burgeoning mortgage market. Mortgage securities information is accessed through a series of screens that display graphic or tabular formats of stored data such as pool, issuer, generic price, yield, and historical prepayment information. Spreads against a current Treasury are also available. Horizon return analysis is available for CMOs as well as MBSs. The unique payment characteristics of PAC CMOs, Z tranche positions and other derivatives are accessed and incorporated into the return analysis. Reverse video fields allow for dynamic entry of alternative prepayment projections, reinvestment rate assumptions, and future price estimates for a quick calculation of horizon period returns.

The dynamic nature of the Bloomberg system allows the investor to assess potential realized MBS yields under various prepayment scenarios. Yields for specific selected pools are shown with prepayments based on those actually experienced over the last three, six, and twelve months, and since issue date time intervals. The Quick Yield Analysis screen allows the investor to enter an annual PSA, CPR, or SMM prepayment rate assumption, or default to the dealer consensus or user-selected estimate. The sensitivity of yield or price to varying prepayment rates can be evaluated, as well as "effective values" indicating price sensitivity to changes in the general level of interest rates. Investors enter a relevant band of anticipated interest rate shifts (e.g., plus and minus fifty basis points), and Bloomberg models a resulting prepayment rate change under each scenario. Effective duration and convexity numbers are then calculated, providing insight into the security's price risk.

The characteristics of a specific pool can also be compared to the so-called "generic" security of equal coupon and type, with useful data such as WAC and WAM. A dollar roll analysis enables the investor to model varying forward prices, reinvestment rate assumptions, and prepayment predictions, with the net arbitrage gain and financing rate displayed for the investor. A MBS swap analysis capability also exists with a sophisticated analysis of the impact of parallel shifts in the yield curve as well as shifts in spread relationships and prepayment speeds at a selected swap horizon date. Swap evaluations can be performed between CMO tranches, or between a CMO and its collateral. Both sides of the swap can be compared on a single screen.

Bloomberg Portfolio System

The basic Bloomberg service also includes the Bloomberg Portfolio System. This system allows the investor to perform portfolio analysis using current market prices, prepayment statistics, etc. For MBSs, users manually enter pool number and original face information to access current paydown factors, expected principal and interest payments, historical prepayment statistics for each pool, and a calculated weighted average life based on a selected prepayment rate. CMOs can be entered by entering the CUSIP or by entering the ticker and tranche identifier (e.g., FNR 90-5 G). Pricing for CMOs on the Portfolio System and elsewhere on Bloomberg is available from the First Boston Corporation for an additional charge. Totals are provided for all dollar amounts, and multiple portfolios can be entered.

The mortgage Pool List allows the investor to enter the pool number and face amount of current MBS holdings and quickly retrieve factor and a calculated current face amount.

The Portfolio Details List screen provides historical prepayment statistics, yield, and current market price by pool. Average-life is calculated based on a selected prepayment rate.

The Bloomberg system offers considerable flexibility in defining prepayment models for MBS analysis. The selected model is automatically fed into all analytic screens (i.e., yields, effective duration, horizon analysis, etc.). Prepayment selections include historical pool-specific and historical generic speeds for one-month, three-month, six-month, one-year, and since-issue intervals. Users further specify prepayment model selections using CPR, PSA, or SMM. A custom personalized model can also be defined, or the investor may opt for a dealer estimate or the dealer consensus estimate.

Risk measurements displayed in the Bloomberg Portfolio System include effective duration and effective convexity, assuming fifty basis point shifts in interest rates.

CAPITAL MANAGEMENT SCIENCES

Founded in 1979, Capital Management Sciences (CMS) is a Los Angeles-based corporation providing PC-based, fixed-income portfolio software systems and consulting services to the investment management community. Software applications include fixed-income analytics, indexation, performance attribution, optimization, asset/liability dedication management, dynamic cash flow testing, and asset allocation. Over 250 institutional investors have selected the PC-based BondEdge system from CMS for sophisticated fixed-income analytics. In addition to its Los Angeles office, CMS maintains a regional office in New York for customer support and marketing.

The CMS BondEdge product operates on a single PC workstation or in a local area network environment. A distinguishing element of the BondEdge product and service is the combined offering of sophisticated analytical software and an extensive bond database that resides on the PC. The bond database includes information on over 20,000 investment-grade fixed-income securities (Treasuries, agencies, corporates, asset-backeds, and mortgages) including approximately 10,000 CMO tranches. Database information includes descriptive information (quality ratings, sectors, coupons and maturities), market pricing, call, put, and sinking fund data, an effective (option-adjusted) duration and convexity for each security, and incorporates the cash flow payment complexities of each CMO structure.

BondEdge Securities Level Features

BondEdge analytical capabilities are present for both individual securities and the overall portfolio level. The Securities Level provides simulation and review features for a single security, or multiple selected securities simultaneously. A *Securities Search* capability allows for instant retrieval of a security from the CMS database. A mortgage screen displays prepayment rates, average-life, and effective duration and convexity for MBSs, CMOs, and related derivatives. A feature referred to as *Bondscan* allows investors to narrow the universe of potential bond purchases and identify appropriate buy candidates given a screening criteria. The complete CMS database can be quickly scanned using multiple parameter data filters, including:

- Issuer

- Sector

- Quality

- Effective Duration

- Convexity

- Maturity

- Coupon

- Price

- Yield

- Option Provisions

- Amount Outstanding

Bondscan output can be sorted several different ways, and the report displayed or directed to the printer.

A *Securities Evaluation* module assists investors in assessing the fair market valuation of a security. Features here include a yield-curve analysis with which investors can report or graph historical Treasury yield curves versus duration. BondEdge allows for manual input or automated import of private placement securities information, including fields for scheduled principal payment amounts, and option provisions, including sinking fund, call, and put information. Private placement securities may be priced manually or with an option-adjusted spread to the Treasury curve. A CMS "theoretical pricer" prices the security by deriving an option-adjusted price according to its sector and quality classification, and then adjusting the price to reflect the dollar value of any embedded options. Yield, effective duration, and convexity are also calculated.

An option-adjusted spread analysis calculates and compares the option-adjusted value versus the duration matched Treasury. Here, the investor has the ability to alter price or yield dynamically. Sector spreads give insight to relative values across 32 sectors.

A BondEdge *Bondswap* capability offers multi-security swap analysis, incorporating and comparing yields, modified duration, effective duration, convexity, and horizon-period returns. The Securities Level *Calculator* allows detailed evaluation of securities under varying interest rate levels. The security Calculator automatically accesses the CMS mortgage prepayment model to generate the price, yield, duration, and convexity for the mortgage security under review. A mortgage screen indicates average-life, and both CPR and PSA prepayment rates. Users may also enter their own prepayment estimates. The second mortgage screen, accessed by simply paging down, simulates returns and dollar value under a range of interest rate shifts. Resulting effective duration and prepay rates are also displayed for each rate change. A tabular display of prepayment sensitivity to rate change is available during the mortgage analysis, as well as a graph of total return versus the simulated interest rate changes. The prepayment curve for a particular CMO tranche may also be displayed.

BondEdge Portfolio Level Features

The CMS BondEdge system offers a series of features designed for the overall portfolio analysis. A Portfolio Appraisal Report provides a detailed analysis of individual securities, and a Portfolio Summary Report provides a snapshot of portfolio totals, including analytical statistics. Accompanying distribution reports and graphs show the percentage of the portfolio by maturity date range, effective duration, coupon range, sector, quality rating, and option provisions, with all necessary data automatically drawn from the CMS bond database. Investment policy reporting allows for the comparison of actuals to investment authorization guidelines. The portfolio *Simulation* program allows investors to assess the overall portfolio impact of a proposed trade. Portfolio return simulations provide horizon-period return analysis given user-specified modeling of yield curve shifts (parallel or nonparallel), or yield-spread relationships. Portfolio total returns and cash flow reporting are also available.

A feature referred to as *Portfolio Scan* provides the same type of filtered search against the user portfolio(s) as the Bondscan provides for the CMS bond database.

Cash flows for individual securities and portfolios may be viewed on a static or a dynamic basis through basic BondEdge or the cash flow module. The cash flow simulations incorporate all kinds of security types, including CMOs, private placements, mortgages, and corporates. Entering a new PSA speed will recompute the average life, yield, and cash flow duration, and recast the cash flows that can be viewed in the security cash flow analysis and the cash flow module.

BondEdge CMO Database and Modeling

A unique feature of the BondEdge system is the accompanying PC-based bond database. As of this writing, this database includes some 10,000 individual CMO tranches representing approximately 1,300 CMO issues. The coverage includes CMO market issues with an original principal value of $100 million and greater. CMS gathers the CMO source data using prospectus data from FNMA, FHLMC, or the specific underwriter for other issues. This information includes the complexities of cash distribution for all tranches in the deal. CMO factors are updated monthly.

The CMS CMO database is accessible from the security and portfolio levels of CMS's BondEdge, Structured Products, and Asset/Liability systems. Direct portfolio access allows for the complete integration of CMOs in portfolios for simulation and reporting, including calculation of option-adjusted spreads.

CMO Prepayment Modeling: CMO collateral prepayment rates are calculated from the CMS MBS prepayment model which is a four-factor model incorporating: (1) differences between issuing agencies; (2) seasoning of the underlying collateral; (3) the so-called collateral "burnout effect" (i.e., where the refinancing prepayment sensitivity declines over successive interest rate drops); and (4) interest rate sensitivity (i.e., the relationship between pass-through coupons and market yields).

The four-factor model is applied to the underlying collateral in modeling CMO prepayments, convexity, option-adjusted spreads, and prices. The dealer consensus PSA rate is used for CMO average life and price/yield calculations.

The new CMS database and modeling capabilities released in the summer of 1990 include substantial enhancements over the prior versions. In addition to vanilla CMO bonds, the new release supports the majority of deal structures presently in the CMO marketplace, including:

- PACs, TACS, and Sequential pay tranches, including ordinary pay, accrual and zero coupons

- Explicit payment priorities as described in the prospectus

- Co-pay features

- IO and PO stripped CMOs

In the fall of 1991 CMS plans to release additional features for component tranches and floating and inverse floating rate tranches.

The CMO database in its entirety is redistributed to clients on diskettes monthly. Pricing is available on a daily basis via dial-in through a telecommunications network. The download procedure for the entire bond database takes approximately 12 to 15 minutes at 1,200 baud, and can be initiated in unattended mode with auto-dial and download. Users can optionally override price, yield, and collateral characteristics such as WAC, WAM, or PSA speed with BondEdge, recalculating duration, convexity, and average-life.

CMS BondEdge Reporting: All BondEdge reports are available in screen display or print version. A report writer provides access to approximately forty-five to fifty fields per security record, and enables the user to select a particular portfolio, fields, column sequences, and sorting. Distribution, Matrix and Policy reports may also be customized by the user.

CMS BondEdge is designed to allow for multiple import and export capabilities. Approximately 50% of the BondEdge users import portfolio holdings information directly from a securities accounting system. Exports are available for holdings, distributions, cash flow reports, etc., in ASCII format.

BondEdge is written in "C" language and operates on IBM or compatible 286, 386, or 486 PC equipment running DOS 3.3 or higher. A math compressor is required for 286 or 386 machines. A minimum of twenty megabytes of hard disk space is required for the basic system, and an additional eight megabytes for the CMO database. One high-density floppy drive (1.2 or 1.44 megabytes) is also required. A Hayes or compatible 1,200 baud or higher tele-communications modem is required for the Daily Pricing module. The local area network version requires Novell Netware, a minimum of two megabytes of RAM, and QEMM™ Version 5.11 Memory Manager.

PRINCETON FINANCIAL SYSTEMS, INC.

Princeton Financial Systems, Inc. (Princeton, New Jersey) has been in the business of developing, marketing, and supporting investment management systems since 1969. The company's initial investment software product, TALAS (Tax Lot Accounting System), is a mainframe-based system made available to clients on a remote processing basis. In 1989, Princeton Financial Systems, Inc. introduced PAM (Portfolio Accounting and Management), an investment management and securities accounting system operating in a PC local area network (LAN) environment. Designed specifically for insurance companies and investment management firms specializing in fixed-income management, PAM supports all types of fixed- and variable-rate debt securities, and offers considerable functionality for mortgage-backed and related derivative securities.

The PAM system is logically organized into major functional areas for portfolio management, trading, analysis, operations, and accounting, with each area sharing access to a common portfolio database.

PAM Portfolio Management Features

PAM provides real-time trade date position reporting and portfolio summary reporting, displaying market values, unrealized gains and losses, carrying value, maturity, duration, and quality rating. The system forecasts funds availability by manager, adjusted to reflect any recent transaction activity. Portfolio managers also have the ability to simulate the impact of a potential trade on the portfolio. Moreover, status reporting notifies the investor if the security is subject to call, corporate actions, etc.

A security swap analysis program evaluates potential swaps on a tax, GAAP, and statutory basis. Multiple securities are allowed on one or both sides of the swap under consideration.

The PAM system maintains multiple yields for each security holding. The prepayment assumptions used in calculating market yield are maintained independently from those used in calculating original purchase yield. This responds to a frequently expressed requirement by portfolio managers to review the "trading yield" rather than the "accounting yield."

A particular strength in the PAM system is the ability for users to define the complete cash flow characteristics for securities with nonstandard principal and/or interest payments. For example, PAM simply prompts the user for pertinent date and rate information for step-up bond purchases characterized by an initial zero coupon followed by one or more payment periods at an increased rate. The system then calculates a purchase cash flow yield, reflecting the deferred coupon payment schedule, and maintains a constant book-yield as required by constant-yield amortization. For CMO positions, nonstandard principal paydown schedules can be similarly defined, with the system calculating yield, duration, and convexity.

PAM Accounting Features

The PAM system conforms to the SIA standards for all accrual and yield calculations. PAM supports FAS 91 requirements by incorporating prepayment assumptions in the initial purchase yield calculation, and at the user's option, updating the prepayment, yield, and book value through an automated process. The FAS 91 processing includes a pro forma report indicating the book value impact prior to booking the resulting adjustment.

PAM maintains four independent accounting bases for GAAP, tax, statutory (insurance), and purchase GAAP reporting. The system automatically makes the proper entries to each basis for transactions such as intracompany trades and tax-free exchanges. For tax purposes, deferred gains and losses are supported for intracompany transactions. Complete reporting on all bases is provided to meet regulatory requirements, including Schedule D insurance schedules.

The system maintains a complete audit trail for all updates. Transactions are automatically reported in the proper accounting period, including prior-dated trades and corrections. Each portfolio can have separate accounting elections, chart of account structures, and closing schedules.

Journals of all transaction activity, as well as changes in valuations, are produced and summarized. An automated general ledger feed is available. In addition, reversal and reposting logic is present to record corrections or calculations in the proper period.

For analysis, the system calculates and reports yield, duration, and convexity for all fixed-income securities, including MBSs, ABSs, and CMOs. All of the cash flow yields within PAM for MBSs, ABSs, and CMOs incorporate standard CPR, PSA, and ABS prepayment models and conform to SIA and PSA standards. Time-weighted total returns are calculated using the PAM performance measurement subsystem, along with maturity, quality, and user-defined portfolio distributions.

PAM Operations Support Features

The PAM system includes specific features to assist in security settlement processing and the monitoring and reporting of pledged securities. An interface to the DTC-ID system automates the process of trade affirmation. PAM also offers interfaces to eight major custodian bank systems, allowing for settlement instructions to be transferred via telecommunications directly to the custodian. This facilitates early recognition of problem settlements and resolution with responsible parties.

A safekeeping and status-reporting subsystem is integrated with PAM. Settlement reporting is provided by location for operations control. Finally, status indicators flag items as subject to call option, pending settlement, available, or pledged, thereby aiding operations and trading personnel.

Block trading and order entry, as well as complete broker/dealer commitment and commission tracking, is also included.

PAM Technical Platform

The typical LAN hardware configuration for the PAM system includes multiple IBM or IBM-compatible 286/386-based PCs operating as front-end workstations and connected to a file server running Novell Netware or other network operating system.

Remote workstations are supported via dial-in or dedicated telephone lease-lines to the server. The product is written in ANSI-standard "C" language, with system-specific extensions facilitating platform portability.

PAM employs a relational database structure and an open system architecture. Access to all data is provided through third-party SQL-based front-end software products, such as LOTUS 1-2-3 (using DataLens), R & R, and Forest & Trees.

SECURITIES SOFTWARE & CONSULTING, INC.

In 1988, Securities Software and Consulting, Inc. (SS&C) developed the Complete Asset Management Reporting and Accounting System (CAMRA) for a large Midwest-based insurance company. Since this initial implementation, CAMRA has been installed at over thirty sites, including mid- to large-sized insurance companies, investment counsel firms, and other institutional investors. SS&C's headquarter offices are located in Bloomfield, Connecticut, with regional offices in St. Louis, Missouri, Chicago, Illinois, and Los Angeles, California.

Unlike many systems in this market that evolved from bond systems, the initial design for CAMRA incorporated requirements for MBSs. Today, CAMRA's support for mortgage-backed and related derivative instruments includes agency-backed MBS issues, CMOs, PAC CMOs, GPMs, CMO residuals, Z tranche positions, IOs, POs, IO-ettes, and privately issued ABSs.

Flexibility and platform portability were also clearly key objectives in CAMRA's initial design. The product is based on the "C" language and uses the Dataflex™ relational database management system from Data Access Corporation, Miami, Florida. The system's relational database system design provides considerable end-user flexibility. An ad hoc report writer and SQL database query capability provide flexible access to system data. In 1991, SS&C announced multicurrency processing and reporting enhancements for the CAMRA product. As advertised, the functionality for global securities goes well beyond tracking market value gain and loss versus foreign exchange gain and loss. CAMRA maintains multiple base currency values and supports FAS 52 reporting for transaction values. Multiple pricing interfaces are supported, as well as corporate action processing for foreign denominated issues. A global calendar is provided for monitoring dates by country, and forward pricing helps to support foreign exchange trading. Foreign currency cash balances are segregated in compliance with regulatory requirements.

CAMRA Portfolio Management Features

Portfolio Managers can turn to CAMRA for a real-time display of current inventory position and transactions. Standard management reports include current holdings, realized and unrealized gains and losses, and exposure reports. Short-term portfolio cash flow projection reports provide the manager with a view of pending settlements, anticipated maturities, and principal and interest for cash planning purposes. Longer-term cash flow projections incorporate put, call, and sinking fund options, and allow for modeling using alternative interest rate scenarios. For individual positions, including mortgage-backed, CAMRA allows the user to schedule and report principal and interest cash flows over the life of an investment. CAMRA also assists the investment manager in monitoring commitment takedown dates, and convertible and warrant expiration dates.

Investment analysis capabilities include conventional duration and convexity measures on an individual security basis, and portfolio weighted average calculations for yield, durations, coupons, maturities, and quality ratings. Securities market pricing and dividend information is gathered via dial-in, with automated interfaces to Interactive Data Corporation (IDC), Muller Data, and the Merrill Lynch pricing service. A pricing matrix module exists to assign a market price to private placements or thinly traded issues. A manual override is also present.

CAMRA Securities Accounting Features

The CAMRA product supports multiple amortization and accretion methods, including constant or level-yield. FAS 91 level-yield is supported for mortgage securities. CAMRA data entry captures PSA and CPR assumptions by issue to calculate cash flows and yields. A strength of CAMRA is the capability it provides for users to enter PAC CMO payment schedules or nonstandard principal and interest payment schedules.

Multiple-basis accounting capabilities exist, allowing for the maintenance of GAAP, tax, statutory, and management bases for each holding. Inter- and intracompany securities transfers are accounted for and a deferral of gain or loss applied. Automated features for processing MBS principal paydowns exist, with receivables tracking for past due payments. Sales may be processed using specific lot, FIFO, LIFO, average cost, or minimum/maximum gain selection, giving traders flexibility in managing recognized gains and losses. General ledger entries for security transactions are accumulated with chart of account numbers assigned, and a file is available for transmission or uploading to an institution's general ledger system. Multiple automated custodian interfaces are also made available.

Under the relational database design, CAMRA stores so-called security "attributes" in a subsidiary file. This file maintains floating-rate information, nonstandard payment schedules, put, call, and sinking fund schedules, PAC CMO schedules, and information on rights, warrants, and convertible options. CAMRA also provides portfolio managers with a tickler system for date-sensitive "attribute" information.

Front-Office Trading Support

In 1990, SS&C introduced FOTOS (Front-Office Trade Operations System), a multicurrency on-line trade-entry and order management system that operates in an integrated fashion with the CAMRA system. Similar to CAMRA, FOTOS is based on the "C" language and the Dataflex™ relational database management system. FOTOS captures and processes real-time trade information and automatically creates lot level accounting records for loading into the portfolio accounting system.

Once the trade is entered, SEC fees and taxes are calculated, broker commission reports are produced, and an ad hoc report writer provides access to trade information. Trade tickets are generated and cash balances are updated. Transactions are processed real-time, with the system employing user-friendly pop-up windows displaying valid field entries. Keystroking requirements are minimized through the "point and shoot" approach to data entry.

SS&C's systems operate on numerous operating platforms, including DOS-based local area networks (Novell, Banyan, Lan Manager, IBM PC LAN, 3COM), OS/2, UNIX (Pyramid, Sun, AT&T), XENIX, and VAX VMS.

CAMRA and FOTOS support simultaneous access by multiple users. Information can be maintained in a centralized file server or distributed database environment.

Individual PCs, intelligent workstations, or terminals are linked to the database server and can perform the majority of processing when configured in a distributed processing manner. Multiuser controls insure integrity of the data.

SHAW DATA SERVICES, INC.

Founded in 1976, Shaw Data Services, Inc. (New York) provides an on-line Portfolio Management Service and Research Service to over 300 institutional clients domestically and abroad, including major investment advisors, bank trust departments, and insurance companies. In aggregate, Shaw Data client's manage over 40,000 portfolios with a combined market value of over $400 billion. Clients access the system via dedicated telecommunications lines to the Shaw Data Center in Fairfield, New Jersey. Shaw Data maintains additional offices in Boston, London, and New York. In addition to GNMA, FHLMC, and FNMA MBSs, CMOs, IOs, POs and corporate ABSs, the Shaw Data Service supports common and preferred stock, convertibles, fixed- and variable-rate debt securities, futures, options, foreign-denominated securities, and zero coupons. Over 900 on-line displays and hardcopy reports can be accessed using the system.

Whereas the Shaw services are predominately on-line (i.e., to the remote host), Shaw also offers integrated PC workstation software referred to as GATEWAY. The GATEWAY system provides a communications link to the remote Shaw Data Center (or other timesharing system), and enables the investor to download portfolio data to a local PC for manipulation. The downloaded investment data file is formatted for import into popular electronic spreadsheets, PC database packages, and graphics software products.

Shaw has also introduced a PC-based Portfolio Management System named *Microshaw*. In contrast to the on-line system, this product is not as robust in its treatment of mortgage-related securities; therefore, the on-line service will be the focus of review in the following sections.

Shaw Data Accounting Features

For principal and interest tracking, the Shaw Data Portfolio Management Service provides on-line access to the Bond Buyer MBS pool database for principal paydown factor information. A Pass-Through Paydown Report schedules current month receivables for GNMA, FHLMC, and FNMA positions. Users have the ability to specify the report format on a portfolio-specific or composite basis, and may sort by pool number. A transaction update file is created during the report program execution, allowing users to review and update portfolio positions automatically. A payment exception report highlights potential data errors, such as missing pool factors. Shaw Data advertises Interactive Data Services, Inc. as its source for CMO and ABS paydown factors.

Shaw Data recommends on-line processing of principal and interest payments when processing less than 150 pools, and a batch processing method for posting larger files.

A Mortgage-Backed Securities Principal and Interest Report provides hardcopy output, including original face, current balance, current factor, and principal and interest payment information.

On-line displays support access to current and historical Bond Buyer pool information. This allows the investor to access information such as original issue date, issuer, state of issue, or other pool-specific information, as well as factor history. Information on new or missing pools can be entered directly by the user. This proves particularly useful for new issues not yet in the Bond Buyer database.

The Portfolio Management Service includes a broad array of accounting reports for fixed and variable rate investments, including MBSs. Selected reports are summarized below.

Amortization/Accretion Report: This report is clearly organized, with amortization/accretion information reported for the current month, total to date, remaining balance unamortized, and the current adjusted book value. Summary information is provided by security type. Straight-line, scientific, sum-of-the-years digits, and constant yield amortization methods are supported, and users may compute amortizations according to settlement or trade date.

Fixed-Income Summary: This is a one-page summary with the portfolio(s) classified by maturity, date range, sector, quality rating (Moody's or Standard & Poor's), and coupon range. Report values can be selected based on current market value, cost, or par. Portfolio statistics include averages for maturity, duration, market price, quality rating, coupon, and yield in an easy-to-read format.

Fixed-Income Holdings: This inventory report lists detailed holdings by security classification, with descriptive information on each investment, followed by annual income, duration, and yield information.

In selecting the standard Shaw reports, considerable flexibility exists in selecting reporting options.

Interest Accrual Report: This report indicates period-end accrual information by issuer. Recent payment information is included to assist in the reconciliation process.

Schedule of Investment Income: Projected coupon and dividend information is scheduled according to the user-defined reporting period. Features include the ability to segregate taxable versus nontaxable income into Federal and State categories.

For data entry purposes, users enter original face amount for all purchases and sales, with the system maintaining this information at the specific lot level. Current face may be entered or calculated. The pool factor database is accessed during trade processing for calculation of current face amount and cost/proceeds.

Shaw Data TBA Allocation Support

TBA processing is supported for MBSs where multiple pools are allocated for settlement delivery. An allocation Global Review feature provides an on-line status review for any TBA during the allocation process.

In order to indicate good delivery on the trade (i.e., per the PSA standards mentioned earlier in this chapter), the on-line review includes percentage variance allocated on the trade. Pool cancellations, substitutions, or the specification of a partial allocation can be accomplished easily through a Change TBA Allocation Screen. Once finalized, the user transmits the trade and a TBA confirmation is produced.

Shaw Data Portfolio Management Features

The Shaw Data System includes a rather extensive set of portfolio management reporting capabilities. Reports are available on a daily basis, with summary listings by issuer, security type, sector, maturity distribution, duration, or quality ratings.

Portfolio management information displays provide analysis on fixed-income investments held, with the computation of multiple yields, including current yield, purchase yield, yield-to-maturity, call or put date, yield-to-best, or yield-to-worst. Both Macaulay's and modified duration are calculated. Yield and duration calculations for MBSs and ABSs are based on the PSA cash flow model.

Extensive cross-referencing displays and reports are provided, fulfilling a key requirement for large institutional investment advisory firms. Investors can also compare current holdings to target asset allocations by client.

The Shaw Data System has been enhanced recently to include global portfolio features. Selected features here include market valuations in the portfolio base or local currency of issue, exposure reporting by currency or country of issue, on-line access to daily international securities prices and currency exchange rates, and the ability to evaluate and measure performance against international indices.

Performance measurement features, including time-weighted total returns, are provided with the standard Portfolio Management Service. The following add-on performance services are also available.

BAI Performance Service: The BAI Performance System is an additional optional service that conforms to the Bank Administration Institute's performance measurement calculation guidelines. This service establishes a database of up to fourteen years of monthly returns for the total portfolio and up to five user-defined segments (i.e., equity, fixed-income, etc.). Time-weighted performance can be viewed over a combination of any number of months compared to a selected benchmark. Most displays are flexible as to time period, indexes, and segments displayed.

Portfolio Attribution Service: The Portfolio Attribution Service maintains and processes portfolio performance and attribution data to produce time-weighted rates of return for the total portfolio and for each designated asset class.

SUNGARD FINANCIAL SYSTEMS INC.

Introduced in the fourth quarter of 1984, the SERIES 2 Investment Management System from Sungard Financial Systems Inc. offers securities accounting, portfolio management, operations, and trading support in one comprehensive system.

Sungard Financial Systems Inc. is a wholly owned subsidiary of Sungard Data Systems, Inc. (Wayne, Pennsylvania). Sungard Financial Systems Inc. serves a broad range of institutional investors that includes insurance companies, thrift institutions, commercial banks, broker/dealers, investment advisory firms, mutual funds, governments and governmental agencies, corporations, pensions, and endowments.

SERIES 2 addresses a broad spectrum of security types, including all fixed- and variable-rate debt instruments, common and preferred stock, governments, corporates, agencies, convertibles, money markets, municipals, options, futures, ABSs, and all mortgage securities, the latter of which include all agency-backed GNMA, FHLMC, and FNMA securities; CMOs; stripped MBSs (IO and PO); GPMs; ARMs; Z bond CMO tranches; CMO residuals, fifteen-year migits, dwarfs, and gnomes; mortgage-backed bonds; and privately issued pass-through securities. The system also provides complete handling of reverse-repurchase agreements, dollar rolls, security pledging, and all securitized liabilities. SERIES 2 also provides reporting for interest rate swaps and risk-controlled arbitrage positions.

SERIES 2 is highly regarded for its MBS features, and is the most widely used system within the nation's top 100 thrift institutions. At the time of this writing, some $80 billion in mortgage-backed and related derivative securities are accounted for and managed using the SERIES 2 Investment System.

The SERIES 2 system provides current on-line position and transaction reporting. Investors can turn to the terminal and select from nearly 150 standard reports. Users can also tailor reports using the SERIES 2 Report Writer or download information to LOTUS 1-2-3 or Symphony electronic spreadsheets. Portfolio information can also be downloaded into the PARADOX™, Oracle™, or dBASE™ database management systems.

SERIES 2 Accounting Features

SERIES 2 provides complete securities accounting for the full range of securities types, and was initially designed to incorporate MBS requirements. Interest accruals are calculated according to the SIA standards, with accurate adjustments for variable rate changes, partial sales, principal reductions, and other variations. Investment accountants can select from fifteen unique amortization methods. MBS amortizations can be calculated on a constant or level-yield basis to the contractual life, twelve-year life, or in accordance with FAS 91. Users can dynamically select levels of consolidation for multicompany, multiportfolio reporting, and report individually or in any combination. And for flexibility in asset segmentation, users may categorize asset classes for reporting with accounting attributes assigned by security class.

SERIES 2 supports generally accepted accounting principles, statutory, and tax basis accounting without the need for redundant data input or multiple sets of books. Specific lot values and amortization information are maintained for each basis. Reports are available on a trade or settlement date basis. For insurance companies, SERIES 2 directly produces camera-ready Schedule D regulatory reports. Reports can be printed locally or via diskette. Dial-in access to the National Association of Insurance Commissioners (NAIC) On-line Valuation Service is supported, and a convenient download and interface to the Freedom Group's annual statement package is available.

SERIES 2 supports FAS 91 reporting by allowing for the yield component of the constant yield amortization formula to be based on a prepayment rate assumption. Book value is periodically adjusted as prepayments vary from the original prepayment estimation. Cash flow yields are recalculated from original purchase to reflect actual cash flow payments to date and future estimated payments. A book value adjustment is then automatically calculated, equating amortized value to date to the value resulting from applying the revised cash flow yield in the constant yield amortization formula since original purchase. Users can enter the new estimated prepayment rate, or it can be automatically drawn from on-line historical CPRs or PSAs.

SERIES 2 schedules all current MBS and CMO principal and interest payments, and provides historical reporting for missing or past-due payments. Automatic access is provided to Sungard Financial Systems' On-line MBS Pool and CMO Databases. The MBS Pool Database contains the prior 13 months of paydown factors for over 420,000 MBS pools. The database also features CPR and PSA prepayment speed statistics for the one-, three-, six-, twelve-month, and since-issue periods.

Audit integrity is maintained throughout the system, and an auditor reporting module provides flexible transaction history reporting over any historical period. Inventory reports are produced by portfolio, security type, safekeeping location, and broker, or the user can tailor position reports according to desired sort and subtotal fields. Investment ledgers track all transactions for a given holding, and a general ledger interface produces detail and summary transaction files for automatic transmission and posting to an in-house general ledger system.

SERIES 2 Trading Support

SERIES 2 provides the investment staff with current-day, real-time position reporting. Trading position reports indicate market values, amounts pledged, and unrealized gains and losses. SERIES 2 also reports on pending sales and trade date commitments for a complete trading position. Position reports are displayed on-line at the investor's terminal, with complete information on all collateral pledgings. Traders can quickly determine if a given MBS position collateralizes a reverse repurchase agreement, and, if so, the date collateral will be available. Unencumbered collateral amounts available are also reported, facilitating new financings and collateral assignments for reverse repurchase agreements or dollar rolls.

An on-line query feature allows traders to access the Wismer MBS Pool Database and the CMO Database to review the one-, three-, six-, twelve-month, and since-issue date CPR and PSA prepayment rate statistics. WAC and revised WAM are also available. A cash flow yield report provides a MBS position listing with yields under user-specified or historically based CPR or PSA prepayment assumptions. Duration is calculated for fixed-income securities and MBSs, with an effective duration applying for MBSs where the user specifies prepayment rate sensitivity to shifts in interest rates. A convexity measure is also supported.

A Bond Swap program allows investors to evaluate fixed-income swap opportunities on-line under a variety of reinvestment rate scenarios. Yield pickup and after-tax dollar gains are indicated for up to five buy candidates.

The SERIES 2 front-end PC-Based Data Warehouse, operating on a single PC or PC network environment, and fully integrated with SERIES 2, is a fourth-generation language-based trading support system. Data Warehouse provides traders and portfolio managers with instant access to current portfolio information. An intelligent data extract automatically refreshes the PC portfolio database with trade information from the host master file, and allows the traders to perform interactive queries, graphics, and ad hoc reporting at the PC level.

SERIES 2 offers multiple automated market pricing sources used for market valuation. The securities market database includes current and historical market pricing, corporate actions, MBS and CMO factors, CPR and PSA prepayment statistics, and quality ratings. A matrix pricing and override pricing capability exists for private placements or thinly traded issues.

SERIES 2 Portfolio Management Reporting

SERIES 2 provides a wide variety of management reports designed to assist in overall portfolio strategy. Sample reporting areas include:

Portfolio Performance Reporting: Dollar- and time-weighted return figures and performance yields are calculated for each security type and the aggregate portfolio(s).

Maturity Distribution Reporting: Daily, monthly, and yearly distribution reports are available. Summary distributions provide average quality, coupon, yield, and other weighted average statistics by maturity range. Duration statistics provide insight into interest rate sensitivity and risk.

Broker/Dealer Activity Reporting: Assists management in monitoring trade activity levels with each broker/dealer.

Investment Risk Monitoring: Reports dollar or percentage investment risk exposure by issuer, broker, or security type. Exposure beyond established authorized guidelines is automatically flagged.

Portfolio Classification Reports: Include summary and detail reports by any of the following classifications: yield, coupon rate, maturity distribution, market value versus book value, SIC code, and quality rating. The portfolio classification reports provide current market values and a variety of weighted average statistics that are useful when contemplating major shifts in portfolio composition. A user parameter file provides considerable flexibility for the user in determining desired yield methods, classification ranges, and other reporting options.

   SERIES 2 provides an automated projection of future MBS cash flows based on user-defined or historical CPR or PSA prepayment assumptions. These future cash flow reports can be downloaded to Lotus 1-2-3 or Symphony electronic spreadsheets for convenient portability to an in-house asset/liability system.

SERIES 2 Operations Support

SERIES 2 tracks initial trade commitments and monitors pending purchase and sale transactions. The trade settlement process is streamlined through SERIES 2's direct access to the Sungard Financial Systems' On-line MBS Pool Database. Data entry requirements are minimized as SERIES 2 extracts needed information based on pool number. Presettlement date activities are eased with the SERIES 2 features for pool cancellations and substitutions on delivered pools.

The collateral tracking features within SERIES 2 are extensive for both reverse repurchase agreements and dollar rolls. Hundreds of collateral positions can be assigned to a given borrowing, and rollover features ease data entry requirements for reverse or dollar roll extensions. Collateral Monitoring Reports indicate whether collateral for repurchase agreements or reverse repurchase agreements is adequate, based on user-defined percentage requirements and a current market pricing evaluation. In addition, trade confirmations are automatically generated and can be electronically sent to contraparties. Safekeeping location reporting within SERIES 2 assists in locating securities for physical delivery and in reconciling with custodians.

A Variable Rate Notification Report keeps investors abreast of expected rate changes on variable rate securities. SERIES 2 also automatically produces and writes transactions reflecting scheduled rate changes to a file for portfolio posting. Multiple call and put dates on fixed-income securities are tracked and reported, including the ability to store, manipulate, and project calls and puts based on multiple redemption dates with associated prices and yields.

MBS Optimal Sales Allocation

The SERIES 2 MBS Sales Allocation Program is designed to identify and optimally select MBS pools from inventory to deliver against sale commitments or delivery for dollar roll sales. The program produces four reports and two transaction files. The Allocation Analysis Report indicates which securities are available for allocation, while the Allocation Good Delivery Millions Report and the Allocation As-Is Delivery Report indicate which securities would constitute an *optimal* sale allocation based on user constraints. The Allocation Broker Delivery Report provides the broker with delivery instructions.

SERIES 2 operates via remote processing to Wismer's Computer Center in California, or can be installed at the client site on IBM mainframe computer equipment or equipment from Prime Computer, Inc. Both alternatives support a multiple-user, multiterminal environment with concurrent reporting, updating, multiple-user passwords, and high-speed on-line response. Remote clients can operate on a dedicated computer or shared machine for greater cost efficiencies.

THE FUTURE OF MBS SYSTEMS

In the last decade we have witnessed an enormous surge in MBS trading volumes, and the introduction of a myriad of new derivative products. At the same time, technical developments in computer hardware, software, and communications have continued at an accelerated pace. These factors have placed pressure on the suppliers of MBS information systems to enhance and expand their increasingly complex computer software products. The conversion of agency-backed MBSs to computerized book-entry form with the PTC MBS depository constitutes a significant step in automating the MBS market—in particular, the clearance and settlement functions. This will contribute toward bringing the MBS market to the level of automation found with U.S. Treasury and listed securities.

With electronic trade clearance capabilities, security transaction fails will be largely eliminated and transaction costs consequently reduced. The market will in turn operate more efficiently, benefiting both investors and dealers. The PTC MBS depository will not, however, eliminate all of the operational peculiarities of this marketplace.

The continued trend toward securitization of our nation's nearly $2 trillion dollar commercial and residential mortgage loans, and the continued asset securitization of consumer loans, will create a secondary market of unparalleled proportions for ABSs. Financial engineering on the part of the investment banking community will bring about even greater diversity in the types of ABSs offered. This, combined with increases in trading volumes and in market participation, will create still greater demand for sophisticated computer support systems. Real-time systems for pricing and trade analytics will become the standard for all market participants, and a new generation of investment management software systems will be introduced that effectively eliminates the existing gap between market information systems and trading, operations, securities accounting, and portfolio management systems. Future systems will offer fully integrated solutions that address the need for up-to-the-second information on both the market and the investor's current portfolio position.

New technologies will dramatically alter the way users interface with MBS computer systems. Further advancements in voice-recognition systems will eliminate the need for manual data entry of trade information, and the developing electronic marketplace will expand its communications networks and transaction initiation capabilities to allow for terminal-based execution of trades. Where voice-recognition systems are inappropriate, touch screens or electronic data entry desk pads will help the investor execute trades automatically. Terminal-based trade execution systems will automatically feed back-office securities accounting and operations subsystems, and the trader's portfolio will be automatically updated to incorporate the executed trade.

Improved real-time links between market pricing and current portfolio information will allow traders to perform more advanced modeling and analytics, using live portfolio data. Future systems will continually search the marketplace for potential arbitrage and swap opportunities. As technologies of this nature develop further, securities market prices will more closely reflect equilibrium price levels as arbitrage opportunities are electronically identified and excess gains automatically removed from the marketplace. The current frequent mispricing of MBSs and ABSs, largely attributed to the difficulty in valuing the uncertainty of cash flows, will create opportunities for astute investors applying the most advanced software, hardware, and communications technology. Additionally, as further refinements are made in the area of fifth-generation programming languages that offer artificial intelligence, computer systems increasingly will make recommendations with respect to trading and portfolio strategies. Software industry leaders forecast that advanced artificial intelligence systems will become commercially available some time in the next ten years. Investors with the market knowledge to "teach" computers the logic of trading and portfolio strategies will stand to reap large rewards. These systems will be vastly superior to existing third- and fourth-generation systems, and will assist investors in defining optimal trading and hedging strategies, asset/liability strategies, and other important financial engineering advancements.

APPENDIX

Lakhbir S. Hayre, DPhil
Director of Mortgage Research
Financial Strategies Group
Prudential Securities Inc.

Cyrus Mohebbi, PhD
Vice President
Financial Strategies Group
Prudential Securities Inc.

MORTGAGE MATHEMATICS

Mortgage Cash Flow without Prepayments

Monthly Payment. For a level-payment mortgage, the constant monthly payment is

$$M_n = \frac{B_0 \left(\dfrac{G}{1200}\right)\left(1 + \dfrac{G}{1200}\right)^N}{\left[\left(1 + \dfrac{G}{1200}\right)^N - 1\right]}$$

where
- M_n = Monthly payment for month n;
- B_0 = Original balance;
- G = Gross coupon rate (%);
- N = Original term in months (e.g., 360).

Remaining Balance. The remaining balance after n months is

$$B_n = \frac{B_0\left[\left(1 + \frac{G}{1200}\right)^N - \left(1 + \frac{G}{1200}\right)^n\right]}{\left[\left(1 + \frac{G}{1200}\right)^N - 1\right]}$$

where B_n = Remaining balance at the end of month n.

Principal Payment. The amount of principal paid in month n is given by

$$P_n = \frac{B_0\left(\frac{G}{1200}\right)\left(1 + \frac{G}{1200}\right)^{n-1}}{\left[\left(1 + \frac{G}{1200}\right)^N - 1\right]}$$

where P_n = Principal paid in month n.

Interest Payment. The amount of interest paid in month n can be written as

$$I_n = \frac{B_0\left(\frac{G}{1200}\right)\left[\left(1 + \frac{G}{1200}\right)^N - \left(1 + \frac{G}{1200}\right)^{n-1}\right]}{\left[\left(1 + \frac{G}{1200}\right)^N - 1\right]} = B_{n-1}\left(\frac{G}{1200}\right)$$

where I_n = Interest paid in month n.
It should be noted that

$$G = S + C$$

where S = Service fee (%)
and C = Security coupon rate (%),

so $Servicing\ Amount = \left(\dfrac{S}{C + S}\right) I_n.$

Therefore, the cash flow to the security holder in month n is given by

$$CF_n = P_n + I_n - Servicing\ Amount = P_n + \left(\dfrac{C}{C + S}\right) I_n$$

Prepayment Measuring Conventions

For a given pool of mortgages, let

B_n = Remaining principal balance per dollar of mortgage at the end of month n if there are no prepayments.

C_n = Pool factor (i.e., actual remaining principal balance per dollar of mortgage) at the end of month n.

Let $Q_n = C_n/B_n$. If one thinks of the pool as consisting of a very large number of \$1 mortgages, each of which can terminate separately, then Q_n represents the percentages of mortgages still remaining at the end of month n. Then

Percentage of initial balance has been prepaid = $1 - Q_n.$

For month n, the single monthly mortality, or SMM, stated as a decimal, is given by

SMM = Proportion of \$1 mortgages outstanding at the beginning of the month that are prepaid during the month

$$\frac{Q_{n-1} - Q_n}{Q_{n-1}} = 1 - \frac{Q_n}{Q_{n-1}}$$

For the period from month m to month n, the constant SMM rate that is equivalent to the actual prepayments experienced is given by

$$(1 - SMM)^{n-m} = \frac{Q_n}{Q_m},$$

i.e.,

$$SMM = 1 - \left(\frac{Q_n}{Q_m}\right)^{\frac{1}{n-m}}$$

The conditional prepayment rate, or CPR (also expressed as a decimal), is the SMM expressed as an annual rate, and is given by

$$1 - CPR = (1 - SMM)^{12},$$

i.e.,

$$CPR = 1 - (1 - SMM)^{12}.$$

Inverting,

$$SMM = 1 - (1 - CPR)^{\frac{1}{12}}.$$

Percentage of PSA. If a mortgage prepays at a rate of 100% PSA, then the CPR for the month when the mortgage is n months old is

$$CPR = 6\% \times \frac{n}{30} \qquad \text{if } n \le 30$$

$$= 6\% \qquad \text{if } n > 30$$

$$= 6\% \times Min\left(1, \frac{n}{30}\right) \qquad \text{for any } n.$$

For a general prepayment rate of $x\%$ PSA, for age n,

$$CPR = 6\% \times \frac{x}{100} \times \frac{n}{30} \qquad \text{if } n \le 30$$

$$= 6\% \times \frac{x}{100} \qquad \text{if } n > 30$$

$$= 6\% \times \frac{x}{100} \times Min\left(1, \frac{n}{30}\right) \qquad \text{for any } n.$$

Conversely, if a mortgage of age n months prepays at a given CPR, the PSA rate for that month is given by

$$\% \ of \ PSA = CPR \times \frac{100}{6} \times \frac{30}{n} \qquad \text{if } n \leq 30$$

$$= CPR \times \frac{100}{6} \qquad \text{if } n > 30$$

$$= CPR \times \frac{100}{6} \times Max\left(1, \frac{30}{n}\right) \qquad \text{for any } n.$$

Mortgage Cash Flow with Prepayments

Let M_n, P_n, I_n, and B_n denote the actual monthly scheduled payment, scheduled principal, interest and remaining (end-of-month) balance for month n. Let SMM_n be the prepayment rate in month n, stated as a decimal, and let

$$Q_n = (1 - SMM_n)(1 - SMM_{n-1}) \ldots (1 - SMM_1).$$

The *total monthly payment* in month n is given by

$$\hat{M}_n = \frac{\hat{B}_{n-1}\left(\dfrac{G}{1200}\right)\left(1 + \dfrac{G}{1200}\right)^{N-n+1}}{\left[(1 + \dfrac{G}{1200})^{N-n+1} - 1\right]} = M_n Q_{n-1}.$$

The *scheduled principal* portion of this payment is given by

$$\hat{P}_n = \frac{\hat{B}_{n-1}\left(\dfrac{G}{1200}\right)}{\left[\left(1 + \dfrac{G}{1200}\right)^{N-n+1} - 1\right]} = P_n Q_{n-1}.$$

The *interest* portion is given by

$$\hat{I}_n = \hat{B}_{n-1} \left(\frac{G}{1200} \right) = I_n Q_{n-1}.$$

The *unscheduled principal payment* in month n is written as

$$PR_n = (\hat{B}_{n-1} - \hat{P}_n) \, SMM_n.$$

The *remaining balance* is given by

$$\hat{B}_n = \hat{B}_{n-1} - \hat{P}_n - PR_n = B_n Q_n.$$

The total cash flow to the investor is

$$\hat{CF}_n = \hat{P} + PR_n + \left(\frac{C}{C+S} \right) \hat{I}_n.$$

Average Life

Average life assigns weights to principal paydowns according to their arrival dates.

$$Average\ Life\ (in\ years) = \frac{1}{12} \sum_{t=1}^{N} \frac{(t + \alpha - 1)(Principal_t)}{\sum_{t=1}^{N} Principal_t}$$

where
t = *Time subscript, t = 1, ... N.*
Principal$_t$ = Principal arriving at time t.
N = Number of months until last principal cash flow comes in.
α = Days between settlement date and first cash flow date, divided by 30 (i.e., the fraction of a month between settlement date and first cash flow date).

Macaulay Duration

Duration assigns time weights to the present values of all cash flows.

$$\text{Macaulay Duration (in years)} = \frac{1}{12} \sum_{t=1}^{N} \frac{\dfrac{(t + \alpha - 1)\, C\,(t)}{(1 + r/1200)^{t + \alpha - 1}}}{\displaystyle\sum_{t=1}^{N} \frac{C\,(t)}{(1 + r/1200)^{t + \alpha - 1}}}$$

where
$C(t)$ = Cash flow at time t.
r = Cash flow yield of mortgage (%).

Cash Flow Yield

To obtain the cash flow yield, the present value of the security's cash flows on the settlement date is equated to its initial price P plus its accrued interest I.

$$P + I = \sum_{t=1}^{N} \frac{C\,(t)}{(1 + r/1200)^{t + \alpha - 1}}.$$

This equation is solved iteratively for r. The solution is called the *mortgage yield*.

Bond-Equivalent Yield

The interest on a mortgage security is compounded monthly, whereas the interest on bonds such as Treasuries and corporates is compounded semiannually. The compounding frequency is reflected in the yield of a security. Therefore, to make mortgage yields and bond yields comparable, the yield of a mortgage is normally converted to a bond-equivalent yield, i.e., a yield based on semiannual compounding of the mortgage's interest payments.

A yield based on monthly compounding can be converted to a bond-equivalent yield and vice versa as follows:

> r = Mortgage yield based on monthly compounding (%).
> y = Bond-equivalent yield (%).

$$y = 200 \left[\left(1 + \frac{r}{1200} \right)^6 - 1 \right],$$

$$r = 1200 \left[\left(1 + \frac{y}{200} \right)^{1/6} - 1 \right].$$

Total Return

$$y_h = \begin{array}{c} \text{Total return} \\ \text{over a holding period } h = \\ \text{(percent)} \end{array} \frac{\begin{array}{c} \text{Sales} \\ \text{proceeds} - \end{array} \begin{array}{c} \text{Total} \\ \text{price} + \\ \text{paid} \end{array} \begin{array}{c} \text{Total net cash flow} \\ \text{received during} + \\ \text{the holding period} \end{array} \begin{array}{c} \text{Total reinvestment} \\ \text{income during} \\ \text{the holding period} \end{array}}{\text{Total price paid}} \times 100 \, .$$

The bond-equivalent total return rate y_{BE} is given by

$$\left(1 + \frac{Y_h}{100}\right)^{12/h} = \left(1 + \frac{y_{BE}}{200}\right)^2 .$$

Modified Duration

Modified duration is given by

$$Modified\ Duration = \frac{Macaulay\ Duration}{1 + y/200}$$

where y = Bond-equivalent yield (%).

Index